Logic Programming

Logic Programming

Proceedings of the Eleventh International
Conference on Logic Programming

edited by Pascal Van Hentenryck

The MIT Press
Cambridge, Massachusetts
London, England

This book was printed and bound in the United States of America.

ISSN 1061-0464
ISBN 0-262-72022-1

Contents

Conference Chair

Maurizio Martelli — University of Genoa, Italy

Program Committee

Khayri Ali	SICS, Sweden
Maurice Bruynooghe	Catholic University of Leuven, Belgium
Philippe Codognet	INRIA-Rocquencourt, France
Yves Deville	University of Namur, Belgium
Hervé Gallaire	Rank Xerox Research Centre, France
Chris Hogger	Imperial College, England
Joxan Jaffar	IBM - T. J. Watson Research Center, USA
Giorgio Levi	University of Pisa, Italy
Jan Małuszyński	Linköping University, Sweden
Kim Marriott	Monash University, Australia
Maurizio Martelli	University of Genoa, Italy
Lee Naish	Melbourne University, Australia
Frank Pfenning	Carnegie Mellon University, USA
David Poole	University of British Columbia, Canada
Antonio Porto	Universidade Nova de Lisboa, Portugal
Raghu Ramakrishnan	University of Wisconsin - Madison, USA
Mario Rodriguez-Artalejo	Universidad Complutense de Madrid, Spain
Gert Smolka	DFKI, Germany
V. S. Subrahmanian	University of Maryland, USA
Peter Szeredi	IQSOFT (SZKI Intelligent Software Ltd.), Hungary
Evan Tick	University of Oregon, USA
Kazunori Ueda	Waseda University, Japan
Pascal Van Hentenryck	Brown University, USA
Peter Van Roy	Digital PRL, France
Andrei Voronkov	Uppsala University, Sweden
Mark Wallace	ECRC, Germany
Rong Yang	University of Bristol, England

The Association for Logic Programming

The Association for Logic Programming (ALP) was founded in 1986. In addition to this conference (ICLP '94) the ALP has sponsored International Conferences and Symposia in Melbourne (1987), Seattle (1988), Lisbon (1989), Cleveland (1989), Jerusalem (1990), Austin (1990), Paris (1991), San Diego (1991), Washington, D.C. (1992), Budapest (1993), and Vancouver (1993). The proceedings of all these meetings are published by The MIT Press.

The Association sponsors workshops, contributes support to other meetings related to logic programming, and provides limited support for attendance at its sponsored conferences and workshops by participants in financial need. Members receive the Association's newsletter quarterly and can subscribe to the *Journal of Logic Programming* at a reduced rate.

The affairs of the Association are overseen by the Executive Council. Current members are Krzysztof Apt, Saumya Debray, Manuel Hermenegildo, Giorgio Levi, Dale Miller, Leon Sterling, Pascal Van Hentenryck, Association President David Scott Warren, and Past-President Hervé Gallaire. Past members of the Council are Maurice Bruynooghe, Koichi Furukawa, Jean-Louis Lassez, John Lloyd, Ehud Shapiro, and David H. D. Warren. The current officers of the Association are: Robert Kowalski, Secretary; Fariba Sadri, Treasurer; Leon Sterling, Conference Coordinator and Conference Budget Auditor; and Andrew Davison, Newsletter Editor. Further information about the Association may be obtained from:

Valerie Anderson
ALP Administrative Secretary
Department of Computing
Imperial College
180 Queen's Gate,
London SW7 2BZ, UK

Tel: +44 71 589 5111 ext. 5011
Fax: +44 71 589 1552
E-mail: alp@doc.ic.ac.uk

Series Foreword

The logic programming approach to computing investigates the use of logic as a programming language and explores computational models based on controlled deduction.

The field of logic programming has seen a tremendous growth in the last several years, both in depth and in scope. This growth is reflected in the number of articles, journals, theses, books, workshops, and conferences devoted to the subject. The MIT Press Series in Logic Programming was created to accomodate this development and to nurture it. It is dedicated to the publication of high-quality textbooks, monographs, collections, and proceedings in logic programming.

Ehud Shapiro
The Weizmann Institute of Science
Rehovot, Israel

Preface

Logic programming originates from the discovery that a subset of predicate logic could be given a procedural interpretation which was first embodied in the programming language Prolog. The unique features of logic programming make it appealing for numerous applications in artificial intelligence, computer-aided design and verification, databases, and operations research as well as to explore parallel and concurrent computing. The last two decades have witnessed substantial developments in this field from its foundations to implementation, applications, and the exploration of new language designs.

ICLP '94 was the eleventh international conference on logic programming and one of the two major annual international conferences reporting recent research results in logic programming. The technical program for the conference included tutorials, invited lectures, and presentations of refereed papers and posters. This volume contains the papers presented at the conference, the abstracts of the tutorials, and some of the invited talks. The conference was sponsored by the Association of Logic Programming, the Prolog Vendors Group, and CNR (Consiglio Nazionale delle Ricerche).

The papers were selected out of 142 submissions received in response to the call for papers. Each paper was sent to 5 reviewers (in general three from the program committee and two outside). Almost all papers were reviewed by at least four reviewers and the average number of reviewers was above 4.77. The review process was followed by a 15-day email discussion period to resolve as many technical disagreements as possible before the meeting. The program committee met at Brown University to select the 43 papers included in this volume.

In addition to the contributed papers, ICLP '94 featured superb invited talks and tutorials. Zohar Manna, Alan Mackworth, Simon Peyton Jones, and Jeannette Wing were kind enough to accept our invitation to give invited talks. Sverker Janson, Antonis C. Kakas and Paolo Mancarella, Kung-Kiu Lau and Geraint Wiggins, and Paola Mello agreed to give tutorials on the implementation of Andorra-based languages, abduction and abductive logic programming, synthesis of logic programs, and modularity in logic programming.

Finally, to foster the link between academia and industry, ICLP '94 featured an industrial section to demonstrate industrial applications of logic programming. Barry Crabtree and Brian Tester (British Telecom), Mehmet Dincbas (Cosytec), Hans Nilsson (Ellemtel R\&D Inc), and Leon Sterling (Case Western) all accepted our invitation to talk about practical uses of logic programming technology.

Being program chair of ICLP is an unusual experience, because one needs to rely on so many people to manage the complexity of the task. I would like to spend the rest of this preface to express my gratitude to some of them, apologizing in advance for any omission; first to the authors of the papers (accepted or rejected) who sent their work to ICLP '94; there were too many high-quality papers and choosing among them was a difficult task; to the program committee members of ICLP '94 who worked very hard to produce high-quality reviews in the imposed deadlines, allowing the discussion period to be productive; they are the best set of people to have on your side when running such a meeting; to all other reviewers who also worked hard to ensure a fair selection of the papers; to Susan Platt who helped me beyond the call of duty before, during, and after the meeting; I am glad she joined the department last year; to Mike Benjamin and Viswanath Ramachandran who helped prepare and run the meeting; to Maurice Bruynooghe, Manuel Hermenegildo, and D. H. D Warren for wise advice and suggestions; to Maurizio Martelli, the conference chair, and his organizing committee with whom it was a real pleasure to work; to Lee Naish for taking care of the poster sessions efficiently; to Catuscia Palamidessi for organizing the workshops in a perfect way; to Yves Deville for his numerous invaluable suggestions and his help in preparing and concluding the meeting; to Beth LaFortune Gies and Bob Prior from The MIT Press who made the editing process so smooth that I almost forgot about them; and finally, to close the loop, to Alain Colmerauer and Robert Kowalski for inventing Prolog and logic programming; Prolog is the best language to write the software needed to automate the organization of the program for such a conference.

Pascal Van Hentenryck
Brown University

Referees

Salvador Abreu
Sibel Adali
Luigia Aiello
Messora Alessandro
José Júlio Alferes
Khayri Ali
Magnus Andersson
Jean-Marc Andreoli
Roberto Bagnara
Jose Balcazar
Roberto Barbuti
Jonas Barklund
Tony Beaumont
Frédéric Benhamou
Henri Beringer
Frank de Boer
Peter A. Bigot
Philippe Blache
Roland N. Bol
Piero Bonatti
Annalisa Bossi
Dmitri Boulanger
Antony Bowers
Johan Boye
Per Brand
Pascal Brisset
K. Broda
Antonio Brogi
Derek Brough
Maurice Bruynooghe
Khaled Bsaies
Hans-Jurgen Burckert
J. Caelen
Björn Carlson
Mats Carlsson
Jacques Chemla
M. Cialdea
Andrzej Ciepielewski
Ralph Clarke Haygood
Christian Codognet
John Conery

Marc-Michel Corsini
Isabel Cruz
José Cunha
Carlos Damasio
Björn Danielsson
Philip Dart
Andrew Davison
Mark Dawson
Danny De Schreye
Saumya Debray
Stefaan Decorte
Lars Degerstedt
Pierangelo Dell'Acqua
Giorgio Delzanno
Bart Demoen
Robert Demolombe
Marc Denecker
Yves Deville
Gill Dobbie
Wlodzimierz Drabent
Mireille Ducassé
Bruno Dumant
Phan Minh Dung
Norbert Eisinger
N. Elshiewy
François Fages
Moreno Falaschi
E. Fernandez Areizaga
Torkel Franzen
Laurent Fribourg
Thom Frühwirth
Ivan Futo
Maurizio Gabbrielli
John Gallagher
Hervé Gallaire
D. Galmiche
P. Garcia Calves
A. Gavilanes-Franco
Michael Gelfond
Carmen Gervet
Roberto Giacobazzi

Ana Gil-Luezas
Laura Giordano
Sergio Greco
Giovanna Guerrini
F. Guerts
Alessio Guglielmi
Michael Hanus
James Harland
Nevin Heintze
Fergus Henderson
Martin Henz
Alex Herold
Keiji Hirata
Chris Hogger
Kenji Horiuchi
Teresa Hortala-Gonzalez
Jean-Marie Jacquet
Joxan Jaffar
Gerda Janssens
Peter Kacsuk
Antonis C. Kakas
Tadashi Kanamori
Roland Karlsson
Tadashi Kawamura
David Kemp
Michael Kifer
Andy King
Helène Kirchner
Jan Komorowski
Kouichi Kumon
Gaby Kuper
T. K. Lakshman
Evelina Lamma
Kung-Kiu Lau
Baudouin Le Charlier
Javier Leach Albert
Alexandre Lefebvre
Giorgio Levi
Pierre Lim
Remi Lissajoux
John Lloyd

Rusty Lusk
Michael Maher
Jan Małuszyński
Margarida Mamede
Paolo Mancarella
André Mariën
Kim Marriott
Alberto Martelli
Bern Martens
S. Martini
Bart Massey
Mihhail Matskin
Michel Mehl
Micha Meier
Paola Mello
Richard Meyer
Spiro Michaylov
A. Miguel Dias
Rob Miller
Håkan Millroth
P. Moeller
Luís Moniz Pereira
Ugo Montanari
Johan Montelius
Remco Moolenaar
Shyam Mudambi
Anne Mulkers
Lee Naish
Joachim Niehren
Susana Nieva
Ulf Nilsson
Jacques Noye
Hans Olsen
F. Orejas
Manuel Ortega
Catuscia Palamidessi
Doug Palmer
Remo Pareschi
D. S. Parker
Frank Pfenning
Andreas Podelski
David Poole
Antonio Porto
Steven Prestwich
Maurizio Proietti
Zhenyu Qian
Raghu Ramakrishnan

Uday Reddy
Mark Reynolds
Gilles Richard
Olivier Ridoux
Mario Rodriguez-
Artalejo
Francesca Rossi
Michel Rueher
José J. Ruz
F. Saenz
Yehoshua Sagiv
Dan Sahlin
Patrick Saint-Dizier
Vítor Santos Costa
Vijay Saraswat
Taisuke Sato
Andrea Schaerf
Joachim Schimpf
Kees Schuerman
H. Schuetz
Jeffrey Schultz
Marek Sergot
Murray Shanahan
Kish Shen
Thomas Sjöland
Gert Smolka
Thierry Sola
Zoltan Somogyi
Harald Sondergaard
Liz Sonenberg
Divesh Srivastava
Leon Sterling
Peter Stuckey
V. S. Subrahmanian
S. Sudarshan
R. Sundararajan
Sripada Suryanarayana
Janson Sverker
Terrance Swift
Peter Szeredi
Jiro Tanaka
Sten-Åke Tärnlund
Frank Teusink
Evan Tick
Francesca Toni
Franco Turini
Hudson Turner

Naoshi Uchihira
Kazunori Ueda
Peter Van Roy
Andrei Voronkov
Marc Wallace
David H. D. Warren
David S. Warren
Geraint Wiggins
Will Winsborough
Jorg Wurtz
Rong Yang
Roland Yap
Haruo Yokota
Neng-Fa Zhou
Justin Zobel

Invited Talks

Lazy Functional State Threads: an abstract

John Launchbury and Simon Peyton Jones
University of Glasgow
G12 8QQ, Scotland

Abstract

Some algorithms make critical internal use of updatable state, even though their external specification is purely functional. Based on earlier work on monads, we present a way of securely encapsulating stateful computations that manipulate multiple, named, mutable objects, in the context of a nonstrict, purely-functional language.

The security of the encapsulation is assured by the type system, using parametricity. Intriguingly, this parametricity requires the provision of a (single) constant with a rank-2 polymorphic type.

A full version of this paper appears in the Proceedings of the ACM Conference on Programming Languages Design and Implementation (PLDI), Orlando, June 1994.

1 Overview

Purely functional programming languages allow many algorithms to be expressed very concisely, but there are a few algorithms in which in-place updatable state seems to play a crucial role. For these algorithms, purely-functional languages, which lack updatable state, appear to be inherently inefficient (Ponder, McGeer & Ng [1988]).

Take, for example, algorithms based on the use of incrementally-modified hash tables, where lookups are interleaved with the insertion of new items. Similarly, the union/find algorithm relies for its efficiency on the set representations being simplified each time the structure is examined. Likewise, many graph algorithms require a dynamically changing structure in which sharing is explicit, so that changes are visible non-locally.

There is, furthermore, one absolutely unavoidable use of state in every functional program: input/output. The plain fact of the matter is that the whole purpose of running a program, functional or otherwise, is to make some side effect on the world — an update-in-place, if you please. In many programs these I/O effects are rather complex, involving interleaved reads from and writes to the world state.

We use the term "stateful" to describe computations or algorithms in which the programmer really does want to manipulate (updatable) state. What has been lacking until now is a clean way of describing such algorithms in a functional language — especially a non-strict one — without throwing away the main virtues of functional languages: independence of order of evaluation (the Church-Rosser property), referential transparency, non-strict semantics, and so on.

In this paper we describe a way to express stateful algorithms in non-strict, purely-functional languages. The approach is a development of our earlier work on monadic I/O and state encapsulation (Launchbury [1993]; Peyton Jones & Wadler [1993]), but with an important technical innovation: we use parametric polymorphism to achieve safe encapsulation of state. It turns out that this allows mutable objects to be named without losing safety, and it also allows input/output to be smoothly integrated with other state mainpulation.

The other important feature of this paper is that it describes a complete system, and one that is implemented in the Glasgow Haskell compiler and freely available. The system has the following properties:

- Complete referential transparency is maintained. At first it is not clear what this statement means: how can a stateful computation be said to be referentially transparent? To be more precise, a stateful computation is a *state transformer*, that is, a function from an initial state to a final state. It is like a "script", detailing the actions to be performed on its input state. Like any other function, it is quite possible to apply a single stateful computation to more than one input state.

  So, a state transformer is a pure function. But, because we guarantee that the state is used in a single-threaded way, the final state can be constructed by modifying the input state *in-place*. This efficient implementation respects the purely-functional semantics of the state-transformer function, so all the usual techniques for reasoning about functional programs continue to work. Similarly, stateful programs can be exposed to the full range of program transformations applied by a compiler, with no special cases or side conditions.

- The programmer has complete control over where in-place updates are used and where they are not. For example, there is no complex analysis to determine when an array is used in a single-threaded way. Since the viability of the entire program may be predicated on the use of in-place updates, the programmer must be confident in, and be able to reason about, the outcome.

- Mutable objects can be *named*. This ability sounds innocuous enough, but once an object can be named its use cannot be controlled as readily. Yet naming is important. For example, it gives us the ability to manipulate multiple mutable objects simultaneously.

- Input/output takes its place as a specialised form of stateful computation. Indeed, the type of I/O-performing computations is an instance of the (more polymorphic) type of stateful computations. Along with I/O comes the ability to call imperative procedures written in other languages.

- It is possible to *encapsulate* stateful computations so that they appear to the rest of the program as pure (stateless) functions which are *guaranteed* by the type system to have no interactions whatever with other computations, whether stateful or otherwise (except via the values of arguments and results, of course).

  Complete safety is maintained by this encapsulation. A program may contain an arbitrary number of stateful sub-computations, each simultaneously active, without concern that a mutable object from one might be mutated by another.

- Stateful computations can even be performed *lazily* without losing safety. For example, suppose that stateful depth-first search of a graph returns a list of vertices in depth-first order. If the consumer of this list only evaluates the first few elements of the list, then only enough of the stateful computation is executed to produce those elements.

The full paper can be obtained by anonymous FTP from

```
ftp.dcs.glasgow.ac.uk
pub/glasgow-fp/tech-reports/FP-94-05:state.ps.Z
```

References

J Launchbury [June 1993], "Lazy imperative programming," in *Proc ACM Sigplan Workshop on State in Programming Languages, Copenhagen (available as YALEU/DCS/RR-968, Yale University)*, pp46–56.

SL Peyton Jones & PL Wadler [Jan 1993], "Imperative functional programming," in *20th ACM Symposium on Principles of Programming Languages, Charleston*, ACM, 71–84.

CG Ponder, PC McGeer & A P-C Ng [June 1988], "Are applicative languages inefficient?," *SIGPLAN Notices* 23, 135–139.

Advanced Tutorials

Implementation of Andorra-based Languages

Sverker Janson
Swedish Institute of Computer Science
Box 1263, S-164 28 KISTA, Sweden
sverker@sics.se

Abstract

The (basic) Andorra model was conceived by D.H.D. Warren in 1987 as an and/or-parallel execution model for Prolog. The basic idea is that goals with at most one matching clause can be reduced concurrently, yielding a potential for dependent and-parallel execution. When no such goal exists, a don't know nondeterministic step is performed with respect to some goal, e.g., the leftmost one. To execute full Prolog, it is also necessary to serialise the program where a conflict with sequential behaviour might arise.

It was soon realised, by Haridi, Brand, Bahgat, Gregory, and Saraswat, that the underlying principle, of delaying don't know nondeterministic execution steps, not only would serve to extract implicit and-parallelism from Prolog programs, but also as a predictable and useful principle for introducing don't know nondeterminism into concurrent (constraint) logic programming languages, and this in a way that enables new programming techniques for search problems.

This tutorial gives an overview of Andorra-based languages and their implementation, emphasising common aspects and current trends.

Some examples of languages in this family follow.

- Pandora is a combination of the Andorra model and Parlog. Concurrent execution also includes reduction of Parlog goals. A don't know nondeterministic step is performed when execution deadlocks [1].

- NUA-Prolog is a realisation of the Andorra model in Parallel NU-Prolog, which does not guarantee behaviour consistent with sequential Prolog [4].

- Andorra-I Prolog is an extension of Prolog based on an and/or-parallel implementation of the Andorra model, which guarantees behaviour consistent with sequential Prolog [2].

- AKL (Agents Kernel Language) is a deep-guard concurrent constraint programming language that supports both Prolog-style programming and committed choice programming [3]. Its control of don't know nondeterminism has been generalised to the notion of stability, which also deals with nondeterminism encapsulated in guards and aggregates (such as bagof) in a concurrent setting.

- Oz is a deep-guard higher-order concurrent constraint programming language [5]. A recent extension offers don't know nondeterminism controlled by stability, exploiting the higher-order facility to achieve programmable control of search.

References

[1] Reem Bahgat and Steve Gregory. Pandora: Non-deterministic parallel logic programming. In *Logic Programming: Proceedings of the Sixth International Conference*. MIT Press, 1989.

[2] Vitor Santos Costa, David H. D. Warren, and Rong Yang. The Andorra-I engine. In *Logic Programming: Proceedings of the Eighth International Conference*. MIT Press, 1991.

[3] Sverker Janson and Seif Haridi. Programming paradigms of the Andorra Kernel Language. In *Logic Programming: Proceedings of the 1991 International Symposium*, pages 167–186. MIT Press, 1991.

[4] Doug Palmer and Lee Naish. NUA-Prolog: An extension to the WAM for parallel Andorra. In *Logic Programming: Proceedings of the Eighth International Conference*. MIT Press, 1991.

[5] Gert Smolka, Martin Henz, and Jörg Würtz. Object-oriented concurrent constraint programming in Oz. Research Report RR-93-16, Deutsches Forschungszentrum für Künstliche Intelligenz, April 1993.

A Tutorial on Synthesis of Logic Programs from Specifications

Kung-Kiu Lau
Department of Computer Science, University of Manchester
Oxford Road, Manchester M13 9PL, United Kingdom
kung-kiu@cs.man.ac.uk

Geraint Wiggins
Department of Artificial Intelligence, University of Edinburgh
80 South Bridge, Edinburgh EH1 1HN, Scotland
geraint@aisb.ed.ac.uk

Abstract

1 Introduction

Program synthesis is concerned with deriving programs from their specifications. Such specifications (and corresponding derivations) may be *formal* or *informal*. Formal methods have an advantage over informal ones, in that they have the desirable[1] property of being able to formally prove the correctness of the derived programs.

Logic programming provides a uniquely uniform framework for specifications, programs and program synthesis. It is small wonder that in the early days of logic programming, program synthesis was one of the first topics that received attention. Most notable among this early work is that of Clark [2], Hansson [4], Hogger [6], and Tärnlund [5]. Although Hansson and Tärnlund and their colleagues at Uppsala implemented a derivation editor, the early work was not particularly geared towards automated synthesis. For some reason, work on logic program synthesis dwindled considerably in the Eighties. However, at the beginning of the Nineties, interest was rekindled, this time with a firm emphasis on automated or semi-automated synthesis. Now there is an annual international workshop on logic program synthesis and transformation.[2]

The tutorial is organised as follows. We shall first define the basic concepts. Then we shall describe a taxonomy of logic program synthesis methods. For the main approaches in the taxonomy, we shall give examples, with a view to illustrating the approaches as well as comparing them.

---

[1] Crucial, in the case of safety-critical applications.

[2] The relationship between synthesis and transformation is an intimate and intricate one. In this tutorial, we shall concentrate on synthesis, but we shall also see its relationship with transformation.

2   A Taxonomy

The first attempt at a taxonomy of logic program synthesis methods can be found in Deville and Lau [3]. This classifies methods as follows:

- Formal methods:

    - Constructive synthesis.

        The specification of a program P is a conjecture that for all inputs to P there exists an output that satisfies the input-output relation that P computes. A constructive proof of this conjecture is carried out, and then P is extracted from the proof.

    - Deductive synthesis.

        The specification is a set of if-and-only-if sentences (together with relevant axioms) defining the predicates of P. The clauses for P are deduced directly from the specification, for example by rewriting the sentences in the specification using unfold-fold transformation.

        An important sub-class of deductive synthesis is sometimes called *transformational synthesis*. Here the definitions are program clauses, and are transformed into equivalent clauses by unfold-fold transformations, or other transformations such as partial deduction.

    - Inductive synthesis.

        The specification is incomplete. Inductive synthesis derives P as a generalisation or completion of the specification. This whole area is now known as Inductive Logic Programming.

- Informal methods:

    These include methods such as general divide-and-conquer, stepwise refinement, schema-based program construction, and so on.

Owing to lack of space, we shall concentrate on formal methods, in particular constructive and deductive synthesis. Inductive synthesis, or Inductive Logic Programming, is now a research area in its own right, and is therefore best left outside the scope of this tutorial.

3   A Survey

Deville and Lau [3] also contains a brief survey of logic program synthesis methods. In this tutorial, we shall follow their style, and for each approach, we shall explain it with an example:

- For constructive synthesis, we shall base our description on the work by Bundy and Wiggins [1].

- For deductive synthesis, we follow that of Lau and Ornaghi [8]. For transformational synthesis by fold-unfold, we will describe the work of Sato and Tamaki [11]. For transformational synthesis by partial deduction, we will describe the work of Komorowski [7].

  Transformational synthesis exemplifies the intricate relationship between synthesis and transformation. Here we shall discuss this relationship, and explain the precise distinction and similarities between the two.

- For inductive synthesis, we can only briefly mention the work by Shapiro [10], and refer the readers to a comprehensive survey by Muggleton and De Raedt [9].

For each approach, we shall also survey other existing work and relate it to the chosen central example.

Furthermore, we shall also discuss the inter-relationships between the three approaches. In particular, constructive and deductive synthesis have been shown to be closely related to each other.

4 Conclusion

Logic program synthesis can be seen as a an important first step towards a logic-based approach to formal software development in any paradigm. The state-of-the-art already suggests that such a claim is not entirely groundless, although much work has yet to be done for the claim to be taken seriously. Nevertheless, we are confident that in due course logic programming will be leading the attack on the 'software crisis' that so far remains unresolved. We hope this tutorial will be a small contribution towards this cause.

References

[1] A. Bundy, A. Smaill, and G. Wiggins. The synthesis of logic programs from inductive proofs. In J.W. Lloyd, editor, *Proc. ESPRIT Symposium on Computational Logic*, pages 135–149. Springer-Verlag, 1990.

[2] K.L. Clark. The synthesis and verification of logic programs. Technical Report DOC 81/36, Imperial College, London, September 1981.

[3] Y. Deville and K.K. Lau. Logic program synthesis. *J. Logic Programming*. To appear in Special Issue on "Ten Years of Logic Programming".

[4] Å. Hansson. *A Formal Development of Programs*. PhD thesis, Dept of Information Processing and Computer Science, The Royal Institute of Technology and The University of Stockholm, 1980.

[5] Å. Hansson and S.-Å. Tärnlund. A natural programming calculus. In *Proc. IJCAI-79*, pages 348–355, 1979.

[6] C.J. Hogger. Derivation of logic programs. *J. ACM*, 28(2):372–392, April 1981.

[7] J.H. Komorowski. Synthesis of Programs in the Framework of Partial Deduction. Report Ser. A, No 81, Dept of Computer Science, Abo Akademi, 1989.

[8] K.K. Lau and M. Ornaghi. An incompleteness result for deductive synthesis of logic programs. In D.S. Warren, editor, *Proc.* 10th *International Conference on Logic Programming*, pages 456–477. MIT Press, 1993.

[9] S. Muggleton and L. De Raedt. Inductive logic programming. *J. Logic Programming*. To appear in Special Issue on "Ten Years of Logic Programming".

[10] E.Y. Shapiro. *Algorithmic Program Debugging*. MIT Press, 1983.

[11] T. Sato and H. Tamaki. Transformational Logic Program Synthesis. In *Proc. International Conference on Fifth Generation Computer Systems*, pages 195–201, 1984.

Modularity in Logic Programming

Evelina Lamma, Paola Mello
DEIS - University of Bologna
Viale Risorgimento, 2
I-40136 Bologna, Italy
evelina,paola@deis33.cineca.it

Abstract

The study of modularity in logic programming has gathered the interest of a growing number of researchers over the past decade and it has been the source of a still open debate. The need for a modular extension to logic programming has been always widely agreed upon. It was in fact acknowledged that relations provide a too fine-grained unit of abstraction for the design of large programs, and that having flat composition of clauses as the only mechanism at disposal leaves the programmer with rather poor tools for structuring programs.

There are several desirable properties that we should expect from a modular system. The system should in fact support the re-usability and ease maintenance of programs, allow for abstraction, parametrization and information hiding, and support rich calculus of transformation and compilation. At the same time, we should also expect that these features do not undermine the declarativity of logic programming as it stands, and therefore that the logical foundations on which the extension relies be as firm and well-established as those of the underlying language.

An important issue that should be addressed in the design of a modular language is related to the ability of the underlying abstraction mechanisms to provide an effective support for both the programming disciplines which are usually qualified as *programming-in-the-large* and *programming-in-the-small*. The interest in the aforementioned two dimensions of programming inspired the two orthogonal lines of research the study of modularity has evolved along.

Various proposals have focused primarily on the issue of programming-in-the-large, inspired by the work of Richard O'Keefe. The idea is to view programs as independent sub-programs, or fragments, to be composed to form larger programs. This idea is formalised by interpreting logic programs as elements of an algebra and by modelling their composition in terms of the operators of the algebra (e.g., union, deletion, closure and combination of the above). The distinguishing property of this approach is that the modular

---

This tutorial is derived from a joint work with Michele Bugliesi reported in the paper with title: Modularity in Logic Programming, to be published in *Journal of Logic Programming*, Special Issue on Ten Years of Logic Programming.

extension of logic programming takes place without any need to extend the language of Horn clauses.

Information hiding and encapsulation can also be accounted for in this framework quite elegantly. Algebraic program composition can be made more selective so as to distinguish, within a module, predicates to be imported from other modules and/or predicates to be exported to other modules.

Another approach to modularity originated with the work of Dale Miller and is inspired by the observation that logical systems richer than Horn clauses could be employed to provide a natural support for modular programming.

In particular, the idea is to model the operators for building and composing modules directly in terms of the logical connectives of a language defined as an extension of Horn Clause Logic, and based on the use of implication goals in the body of clauses. When D is a set of universally quantified clauses, the implication goal $D \supset G$, in a program $\mathcal{P}$, can be interpreted operationally as a request to load the clauses in D before attempting G, and then discard them after the derivation for G succeeds or fails.

This dynamic form of composition supports naturally a modular approach to writing code. Modules can be introduced as named collections of clauses and programs can be structured as collections of modules each one dedicated to answer a specific class of queries. Cross-referencing between modules and module-composition can then be accounted for relying on the workings of implication goals. If, in module M, the answer to a goal G requires that the clauses of module M_1 be loaded, then we will simply enforce the evaluation of G in the composition of M and M_1 by means of the implication goal $M_1 \supset G$.

A notion of *parametric* module can also be accounted for in this framework. The fact that we allow implication goals of the form $\exists x (D(x) \supset G(x))$ suggests that the clauses defining a module can contain free variables. Thus, modules can be referred to by names which have an arity and take arguments just as predicate names. The arguments for a module name designate the parameters of that module. Different instances will be then obtained by providing values for the module's parameters and, correspondingly, by instantiating the free variables of the associated set of clauses.

This programming discipline permits also to model forms of encapsulation and scoping over the clauses contained in a program. Moreover, other authors studied alternative characterisations of implication goals in the attempt to capture stronger notions of scope, such as *lexical* scoping. The idea was to provide a richer support for programming-in-the-small and then to tailor those mechanisms to attack the problems of programming-in-the-large.

Outline

In this tutorial, we provide a uniform reconstruction of the above approaches to modularity. Both theoretical and implementation issues will be considered.

In particular, the tutorial will cover the following topics:

- Presentation of the algebraic approach in the different formulations it has been proposed. We will consider three basic operators (namely *union, overriding-union* and *closure*), and show that they suffice to model a rich set of mechanisms for program composition. We will then discuss the notions of program equivalence that arise for the different operators, and finally describe the extension of this framework with import/export facilities.

- Presentation of the different modular languages defined as linguistic extensions of Horn clauses with implication goals. We will present them mainly on the basis of the associated proof system, given in a sequent-style notation, so as to analyse differences and synthesise analogies. We will show, wherever this is possible, how the object-level logical connectives of this approach can be mapped onto the compositional operators of the algebraic one. Moreover, we will show through examples how the language of embedded implications (and its variations) has been adopted as the basis for implementing modules (possibly with parameters), blocks and objects in a logic language.

- The last part is devoted to describing implementation issues. The different forms of algebraic composition are realised in terms of corresponding binding policies for the local and non-local references to a predicate. The same principles apply to the modular languages based on the use of embedded implications. In this latter case, however, the design is complicated by the dynamic evolution of the structure of a program. Thus, the implementation must support the dynamic update of the binding for a predicate as well as provide adequate data structures for the run-time representation of a program. We will concentrate on implementations following a compilation approach as opposed to the meta-interpretative and the transformational approach. In particular, we will shortly present existing implementations which extends the Warren's Abstract Machine with new instructions and data structures to support the modular languages under consideration.

Abduction and Abductive Logic Programming

A.C. Kakas
Department of Computer Science
University of Cyprus
Kallipoleos 75
P.O. Box 537, Nicosia, Cyprus.
Email: antonis@jupiter.cca.ucy.cy

P. Mancarella
Dipartimento di Informatica
Università di Pisa
Corso Italia, 40
I-56125 Pisa, Italy.
Email: paolo@di.unipi.it

Abstract

Abduction is concerned with hypothetical reasoning. It is a form of reasoning that generates a set of hypotheses that often explain some observed facts according to some known theory and constraints describing the domain of the observation. Abduction is most appropriate when we need to reason about problems for which we have incomplete information as for example in the case of common sense reasoning. Incomplete knowledge is handled by designating some relations as abducibles. These can then be assumed, whenever needed, thus extending the background theory, provided it is consistent to do so. At a later stage they may be retracted if new information makes them inconsistent or inappropriate. Abductive reasoning is thus used in many problems of Artificial Intelligence such as Diagnosis, Planning, Natural Language Understanding and Knowledge Assimilation.

The natural computational model of abduction that stems directly from its semantical definition is closely analogous to the basic computational model of Logic Programming (LP). Both models are goal oriented trying to succeed on a certain goal by making assumptions (in the case of LP these are equality assumptions), that are not given explicitly in the underlying theory (program) under some constraints (e.g. the equality theory in LP) governing the validity of the assumptions. It is thus very natural and relatively easy to integrate the two paradigms to obtain the enhanced framework of Abductive Logic Programming (ALP). We note here that, for basically the same reason, it is also easy to integrate abduction with another important extension of LP, namely Constraint Logic Programming.

As a form of reasoning appropriate for handling incomplete information, abduction is also closely related to non-monotonic reasoning. It provides a framework where different forms of non-monotonic reasoning, e.g. default reasoning, counterfactual reasoning and belief revision, can be accommodated. In particular, in the case of LP, Negation as Failure can be understood and generalised using abduction.

Abduction thus appears as a principle or method that can unify many different aspects of Logic Programming. As a result the framework of ALP is a simple yet powerful and useful framework for many interesting and important problems.

The tutorial provides an introduction to abduction with particular emphasis on Abductive Logic Programming. It covers semantic and computational issues and examines the connection of abduction to other forms of reasoning such as non-monotonic, default and temporal reasoning. The relation of ALP to other extensions of Logic Programming, such as Constraint Logic Programming and Inductive Logic Programming, is also examined. The tutorial includes a discussion of the use of abduction and ALP in Databases and in various application problems of Artificial Intelligence. An effort will be made to provide an extensive bibliography of past and recent work in the field.

Semantics I

Splitting a Logic Program

Vladimir Lifschitz
Department of Computer Sciences and Department of Philosophy
University of Texas at Austin
Austin, TX 78712
vl@cs.utexas.edu

Hudson Turner
Department of Computer Sciences
University of Texas at Austin
Austin, TX 78712
hudson@cs.utexas.edu

Abstract

In many cases, a logic program can be divided into two parts, so that one of them, the "bottom" part, does not refer to the predicates defined in the "top" part. The "bottom" rules can be used then for the evaluation of the predicates that they define, and the computed values can be used to simplify the "top" definitions. We discuss this idea of splitting a program in the context of the answer set semantics. The main theorem shows how computing the answer sets for a program can be simplified when the program is split into parts. The programs covered by the theorem may use both negation as failure and classical negation, and their rules may have disjunctive heads. The usefulness of the concept of splitting for the investigation of answer sets is illustrated by several applications. First, we show that a conservative extension theorem by Gelfond and Przymusinska and a theorem on the closed world assumption by Gelfond and Lifschitz are easy consequences of the splitting theorem. Second, (locally) stratified programs are shown to have a simple characterization in terms of splitting. The existence and uniqueness of an answer set for such a program can be easily derived from this characterization. Third, we relate the idea of splitting to the notion of order-consistency.

1   Introduction

In many cases, a logic program can be divided into two parts, so that one of them, the "bottom" part, does not refer to the predicates defined in the "top" part. The "bottom" rules can be used then for the evaluation of the predicates that they define, and the computed values can be used to simplify the "top" definitions.

This idea of *splitting a logic program into parts* has a rather long history. Although it is applicable even to positive programs, it turned out to be particularly useful when negation as failure is involved. The best known application of splitting is found in the notion of a stratification [Apt *et al.*, 1988]. In a stratified program P, the first stratum is a bottom part that does not contain negation as failure. Having substituted the values of the bottom predicates in the bodies of the remaining rules, we reduce P to a program with fewer strata. By applying the splitting step several times, and computing every time the "minimal model" of a positive bottom, we will arrive at the "intended model" of P. In fact, this step-by-step reduction to a series of positive programs is sometimes applicable even when P is not stratified. This observation leads to the notion of a weakly stratified program [Przymusinska and Przymusinski, 1988].

The notion of a stratification has been also extended in two other directions. First, it may be possible to split a program into an infinite—or even transfinite—sequence of parts, instead of a finite number. This is what happens in locally stratified programs [Przymusinski, 1988]. (As observed above, splitting a program into finitely many parts can be achieved by repeatedly splitting into two; introducing infinite splittings is a nontrivial generalization.) Second, the bottom does not need to be a positive program. This idea has led Schlipf [1992] to the definition of a "stratified pair," and Dix [1992] to the definitions of "relevance" and "modularity."

In this paper, we discuss splitting in the context of the "answer set semantics" of [Gelfond and Lifschitz, 1991]. The main theorem shows how computing the answer sets for a program can be simplified when the program is split into parts. The programs covered by the theorem may use both negation as failure and classical negation, and their rules may have disjunctive heads.

The usefulness of the concept of splitting for the investigation of answer sets is illustrated by several applications. First, we generalize a conservative extension theorem from [Gelfond and Przymusinska, 1991] and the theorem on the closed world assumption from [Gelfond and Lifschitz, 1991], and show that these generalizations can be easily proved as consequences of the splitting theorem. Second, (locally) stratified programs are shown to have a simple characterization in terms of splitting. This characterization leads to a new proof of the existence and uniqueness of an answer set for a stratified program. Third, we relate the idea of splitting to the syntactic property of programs called "order-consistency"; that property is important in view of the fact that it implies the existence of at least one answer set [Fages, 1994]. Order-consistent programs can be characterized in terms of splitting also.

After a brief review of the syntax and semantics of (disjunctive) programs (Section 2), we state the special case of the main theorem that deals with splitting a program into two parts (Section 3) and show how it can be applied to the study of conservative extensions (Section 4) and of the closed world assumption (Section 5). Then the main theorem is stated in full generality (Section 6); it allows us to split a program into a transfinite sequence of parts. The theorem is applied to stratified programs in Section 7 and to order-consistent programs in Section 8. We conclude with Section 9.

2 Programs

We begin with a brief review of the syntax and semantics of disjunctive logic programs. Consider a nonempty set of symbols called *atoms*. A *literal* is an atom possibly preceded by the classical negation symbol ¬. A *rule* is determined by three finite sets of literals—the set of *head literals*, the set of *positive subgoals* and the set of *negated subgoals*. The rule with the head literals $L_1, \ldots, L_l$, the positive subgoals $L_{l+1}, \ldots, L_m$ and the negated subgoals $L_{m+1}, \ldots, L_n$ is written as

$$L_1 \mid \ldots \mid L_l \leftarrow L_{l+1}, \ldots, L_m, not\ L_{m+1}, \ldots, not\ L_n.$$

We will denote the three parts of a rule r by $head(r)$, $pos(r)$ and $neg(r)$; $lit(r)$ stands for $head(r) \cup pos(r) \cup neg(r)$.

A *program* is a set of rules. For any program P, by $lit(P)$ we denote the union of the sets $lit(r)$ for all $r \in P$; the literals in this set are said to *occur* in P.

Note that this description of the syntax of programs is in some ways different from what is usually found in the literature. First, a program is a *set* of rules, rather than a list; similarly, the literals in the head and in the body of a rule are not supposed to be ordered. The order of rules and subgoals is essential for query evaluation, but it is irrelevant as long as we are interested in the declarative semantics of the program. Second, we accept an abstract view of what atoms are and say nothing about their internal structure. The most important case is when the set of atoms is defined as the set of ground atoms of a first-order language; then a large (even infinite) set of rules can be specified by a single "schematic rule" with variables. Here again, the difference between a "schematic rule" and the set of its "ground instances," fundamental for the procedural view, is irrelevant for the study of declarative properties.

A program P is *positive* if, for every rule $r \in P$, $neg(r) = \emptyset$. The notion of an answer set is first defined for positive programs, as follows. A set X of literals is *closed* under a positive program P if, for every rule $r \in P$ such that $pos(r) \subset X$, $head(r) \cap X \neq \emptyset$. (We write $X \subset Y$ when X is a subset of Y, not necessarily proper.) A set of literals is *logically closed* if it is consistent or contains all literals. An *answer set* for a positive program P is a minimal set of literals that is both closed under P and logically closed.

Now let P be an arbitrary program. Take a set X of literals. For each rule $r \in P$ such that $neg(r) \cap X = \emptyset$, consider the rule r' defined by

$$head(r') = head(r),\ pos(r') = pos(r),\ neg(r') = \emptyset.$$

The positive program consisting of all rules r' obtained in this way is the *reduct* of P relative to X, denoted by P^X. We say that X is an *answer set* for P if X is an answer set for P^X.

For example, $\{a\}$ is an answer set for the program

$$a \leftarrow not\ b,$$
$$b \leftarrow not\ a,$$

because the reduct of this program relative to $\{a\}$ is $\{\ a \leftarrow\ \}$, and $\{a\}$ is an answer set for this reduct. The only other answer set for this program is $\{b\}$.

A literal L is a *consequence* of a program P if L belongs to all answer sets for P.

For future reference, we will summarize here some simple facts about answer sets.

Fact 1. *If X is a consistent answer set for a program P, then every literal in X belongs to the head of one of the rules of P.*

Fact 2. *If a program P has a consistent answer set, then all answer sets for P are consistent.*

Fact 3. *A literal L is a consequence of a program P if and only if L belongs to all consistent answer sets for P.*

3 Splitting Sets

A *splitting set* for a program P is any set U of literals such that, for every rule $r \in P$, if $head(r) \cap U \neq \emptyset$ then $lit(r) \subset U$. If U is a splitting set for P, we also say that U *splits* P. The set of rules $r \in P$ such that $lit(r) \subset U$ is called the *bottom* of P relative to the splitting set U and denoted by $b_U(P)$. The set $P \setminus b_U(P)$ is the *top* of P relative to U. It is clear that the head literals of all rules in $P \setminus b_U(P)$ belong to $lit(P) \setminus U$.

Every program P is split, trivially, by the empty set and by $lit(P)$. For an example of a nontrivial splitting, consider the following program P_1:

$$a \leftarrow b, not\ c,$$
$$b \leftarrow c, not\ a,$$
$$c \leftarrow\ .$$

The set $U = \{c\}$ splits P_1; the last rule of P_1 belongs to the bottom, and the first two rules form the top.

A splitting set for a program P can be used to break the task of computing the answer sets for P into several tasks of the same kind for smaller programs. This process involves the "partial evaluation" of the top of P with respect to each of the answer sets for the bottom of P.

Consider, for instance, the unique answer set for the bottom of P_1, which is $\{c\}$. The "partial evaluation" of the top part of P_1 consists in dropping its first rule, because the negated subgoal c makes it "useless," and in dropping the "trivial" positive subgoal c in the second rule. The result of simplification is the program consisting of one rule:

$$b \leftarrow not \ a. \qquad (1)$$

The only answer set for P_1 can be obtained by adding the only answer set for (1), which is $\{b\}$, to the answer set for the bottom used in the evaluation process, $\{c\}$.

To define how this procedure works in general, we need the following notation. Consider two sets of literals U, X and a program P. For each rule $r \in P$ such that $pos(r) \cap U$ is a part of X and $neg(r) \cap U$ is disjoint from X, take the rule r' defined by

$$head(r') = head(r), \ pos(r') = pos(r) \setminus U, \ neg(r') = neg(r) \setminus U.$$

The program consisting of all rules r' obtained in this way will be denoted by $e_U(P, X)$. For example,

$$e_U(P_1 \setminus b_U(P_1), \{c\}) = \{ \ b \leftarrow not \ a \ \}.$$

Let U be a splitting set for a program P. A *solution* to P (with respect to U) is a pair $\langle X, Y \rangle$ of sets of literals such that

- X is an answer set for $b_U(P)$,

- Y is an answer set for $e_U(P \setminus b_U(P), X)$,

- $X \cup Y$ is consistent.

For example, $\langle \{c\}, \{b\} \rangle$ is the only solution to P_1 (with respect to $\{c\}$).

Every literal occurring in $b_U(P)$ belongs to $lit(P) \cap U$, and every literal occurring in $e_U(P \setminus b_U(P), X)$ belongs to $lit(P) \setminus U$. In view of Fact 1 (Section 2), it follows that, for any solution $\langle X, Y \rangle$ to P,

$$X \subset lit(P) \cap U,$$
$$Y \subset lit(P) \setminus U,$$

and consequently $X \cap Y = \emptyset$.

Splitting Set Theorem. *Let U be a splitting set for a program P. A set A of literals is a consistent answer set for P if and only if $A = X \cup Y$ for some solution $\langle X, Y \rangle$ to P with respect to U.*

In Section 6, this theorem is extended to sequences of splitting sets.

In view of Fact 2 (Section 2), we conclude:

Corollary 1. *Let U be a splitting set for a program P, such that there exists at least one solution to P with respect to U. Program P is consistent, and a set A of literals is an answer set for P if and only if $A = X \cup Y$ for some solution $\langle X, Y \rangle$ to P with respect to U.*

As another example, take the following program P_2:

$$c \leftarrow a,$$
$$c \leftarrow b,$$
$$a \leftarrow not\ b,$$
$$b \leftarrow not\ a.$$

Let $U = \{a, b\}$. The bottom consists of the last two rules and has two answer sets, $\{a\}$ and $\{b\}$. Program $e_U(P_2 \setminus b_U(P_2), \{a\})$ consists of one rule, $c \leftarrow$, and has one answer set, $\{c\}$. Thus the first solution to P_2 is $\langle \{a\}, \{c\} \rangle$. Similarly, the second solution is $\langle \{b\}, \{c\} \rangle$. By Corollary 1, the answer sets for P_2 are $\{a, c\}$ and $\{b, c\}$.

In view of Fact 3 (Section 2), the Splitting Set Theorem implies:

Corollary 2. *Let U be a splitting set for a program P. A literal L is a consequence of P if and only if, for every solution $\langle X, Y \rangle$ to P with respect to U, $L \in X \cup Y$.*

The next example illustrates the role of the consistency condition in the definition of a solution. Let P_3 be the program

$$\neg b \leftarrow ,$$
$$a \mid b \leftarrow .$$

The only solution to P_3 with respect to $\{a, b\}$ is $\langle \{a\}, \{\neg b\} \rangle$. The pair $\langle \{b\}, \{\neg b\} \rangle$ is not a solution, because the set $\{b, \neg b\}$ is inconsistent. This set is not an answer set for P_3.

The proof of the Splitting Set Theorem is based on the following observations. The statement of the theorem can be reformulated as follows: If U is a splitting set for P, then a consistent set X of literals is an answer set for P^X if and only if

- $X \cap U$ is an answer set for $b_U(P)^{X \cap U}$,

- $X \setminus U$ is an answer set for $e_U(P \setminus b_U(P), X \cap U)^{X \setminus U}$.

Since these reducts have no common literals, the last two conditions can be combined into one: X is an answer set for

$$b_U(P)^{X \cap U} \cup e_U(P \setminus b_U(P), X \cap U)^{X \setminus U}. \qquad (2)$$

On the other hand, it is easy to see that P^X is the same as

$$b_U(P)^{X \cap U} \cup (P \setminus b_U(P))^X. \qquad (3)$$

In the proof, we verify that X is an answer set for (2) if and only if it is an answer set for (3).

4   Application: Conservative Extensions

If we extend a program P by rules whose heads do not occur in P, then, typically, we do not expect to see any new consequences of the program among the literals occurring in P. This conservative extension property (called "the weak principle of stratification" by Schlipf [1992] and "relevance" by Dix [1992]) is not valid without additional restrictions, however. For instance, after we extend a program by the contradictory rules $a \leftarrow$ and $\neg a \leftarrow$, every literal in the language will become its consequence.

One case when the conservative extension property does hold is described in [Gelfond and Przymusinska, 1991], Proposition 2.1. In this section, we state a slightly more general fact and prove it as a corollary to the Splitting Set Theorem.

A program is *nondisjunctive* if the head of each of its rules is a singleton.

Proposition 1. *Let P be a program, and let C be a consistent set of literals that do not occur in P and whose complements also do not occur in P. Let Q be a nondisjunctive program such that, for every rule $r \in Q$, $head(r) \subset C$ and $neg(r) \subset lit(P)$. For any literal $L \notin C$, L is a consequence of $P \cup Q$ if and only if L is a consequence of P.*

For instance, after adding the first two rules of program P_2 to its last two rules, a and b cannot turn into its consequences (take $C = \{c\}$).

The theorem by Gelfond and Przymusinska mentioned above is the special case when, additionally, P is assumed to be nondisjunctive, neither P nor Q uses classical negation, and $pos(r) \subset lit(P)$ for every $r \in Q$.

Proof of Proposition 1. Let $U = lit(P)$. From the fact that no literal in C occurs in P, we conclude that U splits $P \cup Q$, with the bottom P and the top Q. Take any consistent answer set X for P. The program $e_U(Q, X)$ is nondisjunctive and positive, and the heads of all its rules are contained in C. Since C is consistent, it follows that this program has a unique answer set Y, and $Y \subset C$. Furthermore, since no literal in C has its complement in $lit(P)$, and since $X \subset lit(P)$, the set $X \cup Y$ is consistent. Thus, $\langle X, Y \rangle$ is a solution to $P \cup Q$ with respect to U. Consequently, for every consistent answer set X for P there exists a set $Y \subset C$ such that $\langle X, Y \rangle$ is a solution to $P \cup Q$; moreover, if $\langle X, Y \rangle$ is a solution to $P \cup Q$, then $Y \subset C$. By Corollary 2 to the Splitting Set Theorem, it follows that a literal $L \notin C$ is a consequence of $P \cup Q$ if and only if it is a consequence of P.

5   Application: Closed World Assumption

The *closed world assumption rule* for a literal L is the rule

$$L \leftarrow not\ \overline{L},$$

where $\overline{L}$ stands for the literal complementary to L. Rules of this kind play an important part in knowledge representation ([Gelfond and Lifschitz, 1991], Section 3).

The following theorem describes the effect of adding a set of closed world assumption rules to a program:

Proposition 2. *Let P be a program, let C be a consistent set of literals that do not occur in P, and let P' be the program obtained from P by adding the closed world assumption rules for all literals in C. If X is a consistent answer set for P, then*

$$X \cup \{L \in C : \overline{L} \notin X\} \tag{4}$$

is a consistent answer set for P'. Moreover, every consistent answer set for P' can be represented in form (4) for some consistent answer set X for P.

This theorem can be illustrated by the following example. Let the set of atoms be $\{p(1), p(2), q(1), q(2)\}$, let P_4 be the program

$$
\begin{aligned}
p(1) &\leftarrow \quad, \\
\neg q(2) &\leftarrow \quad,
\end{aligned}
$$

and let P'_4 be obtained from P_4 by adding the closed world assumption rules

$$
\begin{aligned}
\neg p(x) &\leftarrow \quad not\ p(x), \\
q(x) &\leftarrow \quad not\ \neg q(x),
\end{aligned}
$$

$(x \in \{1, 2\})$. Since the only answer set for P_4 is $\{p(1), \neg q(2)\}$, Proposition 2 shows that the only answer set for P'_4 is

$$\{p(1), \neg q(2)\} \cup \{\neg p(2), q(1)\}.$$

Proposition 4 from [Gelfond and Lifschitz, 1991] is the special case of Proposition 2 in which P is a nondisjunctive program without classical negation, and C is the set of all negative literals.

Proof of Proposition 2. Let $U = lit(P)$. From the fact that no literal in C occurs in P we conclude that U splits P' and $b_U(P') = P$. Take any consistent answer set X for P. The program $e_U(P' \setminus b_U(P'), X)$ consists of the rules $L \leftarrow$ for all literals $L \in C$ such that $\overline{L} \notin X$. Obviously, the only answer set Y for this program is $\{L \in C : \overline{L} \notin X\}$. Since X and C are consistent, $X \cup Y$ is consistent also. It follows that the solutions to P' are the pairs $\langle X, \{L \in C : \overline{L} \notin X\}\rangle$, where X is an answer set for P. Now the assertion of Proposition 2 follows from the Splitting Set Theorem.

6 Splitting Sequences

A *(transfinite) sequence* is a family whose index set is an initial segment of ordinals, $\{\alpha : \alpha < \mu\}$. The ordinal μ is the *length* of the sequence. A sequence $\langle U_\alpha \rangle_{\alpha < \mu}$ of sets is *monotone* if $U_\alpha \subset U_\beta$ whenever $\alpha < \beta$, and *continuous* if, for each limit ordinal $\alpha < \mu$, $U_\alpha = \bigcup_{\eta < \alpha} U_\eta$.

A *splitting sequence* for a program P is a monotone, continuous sequence $\langle U_\alpha \rangle_{\alpha < \mu}$ of splitting sets for P such that $\bigcup_{\alpha < \mu} U_\alpha = lit(P)$.

For instance, if U_0 is a splitting set for P, then $\langle U_0, lit(P) \rangle$ is a splitting sequence for P of length 2. Consider the well-known "even number" program P_5:

$$p(0) \leftarrow \ ,$$
$$p(S(x)) \leftarrow \ not \ p(x)$$

$(x = 0, S(0), S(S(0)), \ldots)$. The following sequence of length ω is a splitting sequence for P_5:

$$\langle \{p(0)\}, \{p(0), p(S(0))\}, \{p(0), p(S(0)), p(S(S(0)))\}, \ldots \rangle. \tag{5}$$

The definition of a solution with respect to a splitting set is extended to splitting sequences as follows. Let $U = \langle U_\alpha \rangle_{\alpha < \mu}$ be a splitting sequence for a program P. A *solution* to P (with respect to U) is a sequence $\langle X_\alpha \rangle_{\alpha < \mu}$ of sets of literals such that

- X_0 is an answer set for $b_{U_0}(P)$,

- for any α such that $\alpha + 1 < \mu$, $X_{\alpha+1}$ is an answer set for

$$e_{U_\alpha}(b_{U_{\alpha+1}}(P) \setminus b_{U_\alpha}(P), \bigcup_{\nu \le \alpha} X_\nu),$$

- for any limit ordinal $\alpha < \mu$, $X_\alpha = \emptyset$,

- $\bigcup_{\alpha < \mu} X_\alpha$ is consistent.

It is easy to see that the solutions to P with respect to a splitting sequence $\langle U_0, lit(P) \rangle$ are the same as the solutions to P with respect to the splitting set U_0. The only solution $\langle X_0, X_1, \ldots \rangle$ to P_5 with respect to (5) is defined by the equations:

$$X_n = \begin{cases} \{p(S^n(0))\}, & \text{if } n \text{ is even,} \\ \emptyset, & \text{otherwise.} \end{cases}$$

This is easy to check by induction on n.

Let $U = \langle U_\alpha \rangle_{\alpha < \mu}$ be a splitting sequence for a program P, and let $\langle X_\alpha \rangle_{\alpha < \mu}$ be a sequence of sets of literals. Every literal occurring in $b_{U_0}(P)$ belongs to $lit(P) \cap U_0$, and every literal occurring in

$$e_{U_\alpha}(b_{U_{\alpha+1}}(P) \setminus b_{U_\alpha}(P), \bigcup_{\nu \le \alpha} X_\nu)$$

$(\alpha + 1 < \mu)$ belongs to $lit(P) \cap (U_{\alpha+1} \setminus U_\alpha)$. In view of Fact 1 (Section 2), it follows that, if $\langle X_\alpha \rangle_{\alpha < \mu}$ is a solution, then

$$X_0 \subset lit(P) \cap U_0,$$
$$X_{\alpha+1} \subset lit(P) \cap (U_{\alpha+1} \setminus U_\alpha).$$

It follows that the members of any solution are pairwise disjoint.

The following propositions generalize the Splitting Set Theorem and its corollaries.

Splitting Sequence Theorem. *Let $U = \langle U_\alpha \rangle_{\alpha < \mu}$ be a splitting sequence for a program P. A set A of literals is a consistent answer set for P if and only if $A = \bigcup_{\alpha < \mu} X_\alpha$ for some solution $\langle X_\alpha \rangle_{\alpha < \mu}$ to P with respect to U.*

Corollary 1. *Let $U = \langle U_\alpha \rangle_{\alpha < \mu}$ be a splitting sequence for a program P, such that there exists at least one solution to P with respect to U. Program P is consistent, and a set A of literals is an answer set for P if and only if $A = \bigcup_{\alpha < \mu} X_\alpha$ for some solution $\langle X_\alpha \rangle_{\alpha < \mu}$ to P with respect to U.*

Corollary 2. *Let $U = \langle U_\alpha \rangle_{\alpha < \mu}$ be a splitting sequence for a program P. A literal L is a consequence of P if and only if, for every solution $\langle X_\alpha \rangle_{\alpha < \mu}$ to P with respect to U, $L \in \bigcup_{\alpha < \mu} X_\alpha$.*

By Corollary 1, it follows that the only answer set for P_5 is

$$\{p(S^n(0)) : n \text{ is even}\}.$$

The proof of the Splitting Sequence Theorem is based on the Splitting Set Theorem.

7 Components

Let $U = \langle U_\alpha \rangle_{\alpha < \mu}$ be a splitting sequence for a program P, and let $\langle X_\alpha \rangle_{\alpha < \mu}$ be a sequence of sets of literals. Some applications of the Splitting Sequence Theorem depend on the syntactic form of the programs whose answer sets can be members of a solution:

$$\begin{aligned} & b_{U_0}(P), \\ & e_{U_\alpha}(b_{U_{\alpha+1}}(P) \setminus b_{U_\alpha}(P), \textstyle\bigcup_{\nu \le \alpha} X_\nu) \qquad (\alpha + 1 < \mu). \end{aligned} \tag{6}$$

It is clear that each rule of each of these programs is obtained from a rule of P by removing some of its subgoals. A more specific claim regarding the structure of programs (6) can be made, using the following terminology.

For any program P and any set X of literals, let $rm(P, X)$ be the part of P obtained by removing all subgoals that belong to X, both positive and negated, from each of the rules of P. For any program P and any splitting sequence $U = \langle U_\alpha \rangle_{\alpha < \mu}$ for P, the programs

$$\begin{aligned} & b_{U_0}(P), \\ & rm(b_{U_{\alpha+1}}(P) \setminus b_{U_\alpha}(P), U_\alpha) \qquad (\alpha + 1 < \mu) \end{aligned}$$

will be called the *U-components* of P.

For example, the U-components of P_5 are the programs $\{ p(S^n(0)) \leftarrow \}$ for all n.

It is easy to see that for any set X of literals, $e_{U_\alpha}(b_{U_{\alpha+1}}(P) \setminus b_{U_\alpha}(P), X)$ is a subset of $rm(b_{U_{\alpha+1}}(P) \setminus b_{U_\alpha}(P), U_\alpha)$. Consequently, each program in (6) is a subset of a U-component of P.

To demonstrate the usefulness of the notion of a U-component, we will show now that it leads to a simple characterization of the class of stratified programs.

A *level mapping* is a function from literals to ordinals. A program P is *stratified* if there exists a level mapping f such that, for every rule $r \in P$ and any literals L_1, L_2,

- if $L_1, L_2 \in head(r)$ then $f(L_1) = f(L_2)$,

- if $L_1 \in head(r)$ and $L_2 \in pos(r)$ then $f(L_1) \geq f(L_2)$,

- if $L_1 \in head(r)$ and $L_2 \in neg(r)$ then $f(L_1) > f(L_2)$.

For instance, every positive program is stratified: take $f(L) = 0$ for every literal L. Program P_5 is a stratified program: take $f(p(S^n(0))) = n$. Programs P_1 and P_2 are not stratified.

The definition given above is equivalent to the usual definition of a "locally stratified" program [Przymusinski, 1988] when the set of atoms is defined as the set of ground atoms of a first-order language, and there is no classical negation. (A "nonlocal stratification" does not make sense in the context of the abstract view of atoms accepted here.)

A rule r is a *constraint* if $head(r) = \emptyset$. Clearly, if a program is stratified, this property will not be affected by adding or deleting constraints.

Proposition 3. *A program P that does not contain constraints is stratified if and only if it has a splitting sequence U such that all U-components of P are positive.*

Proof. Assume that P is stratified, and let f be the corresponding level mapping. Take μ to be the smallest ordinal that is greater than all values of f, and define, for every $\alpha < \mu$,

$$U_\alpha = \{L \,:\, f(L) < \alpha\}.$$

It is easy to check that $U = \langle U_\alpha \rangle_{\alpha < \mu}$ is a splitting sequence for P, and that all U-components of P are positive. Conversely, if $U = \langle U_\alpha \rangle_{\alpha < \mu}$ is a splitting sequence for P such that all U-components of P are positive, then we can define $f(L)$ as the smallest α such that $L \in U_\alpha$.

Proposition 3 leads to a new proof of a familiar property of stratified nondisjunctive programs without classical negation ([Gelfond and Lifschitz, 1988], Corollary 1):

Proposition 4. *Every stratified, nondisjunctive program without classical negation has a unique answer set.*

Proof. Let P be a stratified, nondisjunctive program without classical negation, and let $U = \langle U_\alpha \rangle_{\alpha < \mu}$ be a splitting sequence for P such that all U-components of P are positive. Then, for any sequence $\langle X_\alpha \rangle_{\alpha < \mu}$ of sets of literals, every program in (6) is a positive nondisjunctive program without classical negation. Consequently, each of these programs has a unique answer set. It follows that the definition of a solution can be reformulated in this case as follows: $\langle X_\alpha \rangle_{\alpha < \mu}$ is a solution to P if

- X_0 is the answer set for $b_{U_0}(P)$,

- for any α such that $\alpha + 1 < \mu$, $X_{\alpha+1}$ is the answer set for

$$e_{U_\alpha}(b_{U_{\alpha+1}}(P) \setminus b_{U_\alpha}(P), \bigcup_{\nu \le \alpha} X_\nu),$$

- for any limit ordinal $\alpha < \mu$, $X_\alpha = \emptyset$,

- $\bigcup_{\alpha < \mu} X_\alpha$ is consistent.

The first three conditions provide a recursive definition of $\langle X_\alpha \rangle_{\alpha < \mu}$. Consequently, there is exactly one sequence satisfying these conditions. Every element of every member of this sequence is an atom, so that the last condition is satisfied also.

8   Splitting and Order-Consistency

The notions of a "signed" program (program with a signing) [Kunen, 1989] and an "order-consistent" program [Sato, 1990] can be defined as follows. In the definitions, P is assumed to be a nondisjunctive program without classical negation.

We say that P is *signed* if there exists a set S of atoms such that, for every rule r in P,

$$head(r) \cup pos(r) \subset S, \ neg(r) \cap S = \emptyset$$

or

$$(head(r) \cup pos(r)) \cap S = \emptyset, \ neg(r) \subset S.$$

To define the much wider class of order-consistent programs, we need the following notation. For any atom A, P_A^+ and P_A^- are the smallest sets of atoms such that $A \in P_A^+$ and, for every rule $r \in P$,

- if $head(r) \subset P_A^+$ then $pos(r) \subset P_A^+$ and $neg(r) \subset P_A^-$,

- if $head(r) \subset P_A^-$ then $pos(r) \subset P_A^-$ and $neg(r) \subset P_A^+$.

Program P is called *order-consistent* if there exists a level mapping f such that $f(B) < f(A)$ whenever $B \in P_A^+ \cap P_A^-$.

The following theorem describes the relationship between these classes of programs:

Proposition 5. *Let P be a nondisjunctive program without classical negation. Program P is order-consistent if and only if it has a splitting sequence U such that all U-components of P are signed.*

For instance, the following program P_6 is order-consistent, but not signed:

$$a \leftarrow b,$$
$$a \leftarrow not\ b.$$

Let U be the sequence $\langle \{b\}, \{a,b\} \rangle$. This sequence splits P_6, and the U-components of P_6 are the signed programs $\{\, a \leftarrow \}$ and $\emptyset$.

Using Proposition 5 and the Splitting Sequence Theorem, we can derive Fages's theorem [Fages, 1994] on the existence of an answer set for an order-consistent program from a similar—and easier—theorem for signed programs.

Proof of Proposition 5 (sketch). Let P be a program with a splitting sequence $U = \langle U_\alpha \rangle_{\alpha < \mu}$ such that all U-components of P are signed. A level mapping f required in the definition of order-consistency can be defined as follows: For each atom A, $f(A)$ is the least ordinal α such that $A \in U_\alpha$. Assume, on the other hand, that P is order-consistent, and let f be the corresponding level mapping. Arrange all atoms in a transfinite sequence $\langle A_\alpha \rangle_{\alpha < \mu}$ so that $f(A_\alpha) < f(A_\beta)$ whenever $\alpha < \beta$. A splitting sequence for P can be defined by $U_\alpha = \bigcup_{\beta < \alpha}(P^+_{A_\beta} \cup P^-_{A_\beta})$. For this sequence U, all U-components of P are signed.

9 Conclusion

The usefulness of splitting is illustrated in this paper by several applications. The Splitting Set Theorem is also employed in the paper "Language Independence and Language Tolerance in Logic Programs" [McCain and Turner, 1993], which appears in this volume. It is used there to prove one of the central results—Theorem 6.1, which shows that, under some conditions, one can ignore the fact that the language of a logic program is many-sorted. We expect that, in the future, the idea of splitting will find many other uses.

Acknowledgements

The authors would like to thank Norman McCain for useful discussions on the subject of this paper. We are also grateful to Enrico Giunchiglia and G. N. Kartha for their comments. This work was partially supported by National Science Foundation under grants IRI-9101078 and IRI-9306751.

References

[Apt *et al.*, 1988] Krzysztof Apt, Howard Blair, and Adrian Walker. Towards a theory of declarative knowledge. In Jack Minker, editor, *Foundations of Deductive Databases and Logic Programming*, pages 89–148. Morgan Kaufmann, San Mateo, CA, 1988.

[Dix, 1992] Jürgen Dix. Classifying semantics of disjunctive logic programs (extended abstract). In Krzysztof Apt, editor, *Proc. Joint Int'l Conf. and Symp. on Logic Programming*, pages 798–812, 1992.

[Fages, 1994] François Fages. Consistency of Clark's completion and existence of stable models. *Journal of Methods of Logic in Computer Science*, 1(1):51–60, 1994. To appear.

[Gelfond and Lifschitz, 1988] Michael Gelfond and Vladimir Lifschitz. The stable model semantics for logic programming. In Robert Kowalski and Kenneth Bowen, editors, *Logic Programming: Proc. of the Fifth Int'l Conf. and Symp.*, pages 1070–1080, 1988.

[Gelfond and Lifschitz, 1991] Michael Gelfond and Vladimir Lifschitz. Classical negation in logic programs and disjunctive databases. *New Generation Computing*, 9:365–385, 1991.

[Gelfond and Przymusinska, 1991] Michael Gelfond and Halina Przymusinska. Definitions in epistemic specifications. In Anil Nerode, Wiktor Marek, and V. S. Subramanian, editors, *Logic Programming and Non-monotonic Reasoning: Proceedings of the First International Workshop*, pages 245–259, 1991.

[Kunen, 1989] Kenneth Kunen. Signed data dependencies in logic programs. *Journal of Logic Programming*, 7(3):231–245, 1989.

[McCain and Turner, 1993] Norman McCain and Hudson Turner. Language independence and language tolerance in logic programs. Submitted for publication, 1993.

[Przymusinska and Przymusinski, 1988] Halina Przymusinska and Teodor Przymusinski. Weakly perfect model semantics for logic programs. In Robert Kowalski and Kenneth Bowen, editors, *Logic Programming: Proc. of the Fifth Int'l Conf. and Symp.*, pages 1106–1120, 1988.

[Przymusinski, 1988] Teodor Przymusinski. On the declarative semantics of deductive databases and logic programs. In Jack Minker, editor, *Foundations of Deductive Databases and Logic Programming*, pages 193–216. Morgan Kaufmann, San Mateo, CA, 1988.

[Sato, 1990] Taisuke Sato. Completed logic programs and their consistency. *Journal of Logic Programming*, 9:33–44, 1990.

[Schlipf, 1992] John Schlipf. Formalizing a logic for logic programming. *Annals of Mathematics and Artificial Intelligence*, 5:279–302, 1992.

Language Independence and Language Tolerance in Logic Programs

Norman McCain and Hudson Turner
Department of Computer Sciences
University of Texas at Austin
Austin, TX 78712
{mccain,hudson}@cs.utexas.edu

Abstract

The consequences of a logic program depend in general upon both the rules of the program and its language. However the consequences of some programs are independent of the choice of language, while others depend on the language of the program in only a restricted way. In this paper, we define notions of language independence and language tolerance corresponding to these two cases. Furthermore, we show that there are syntactically-defined classes of programs that are language independent and language tolerant. A primary application of these results is to guarantee that for some programs it is permissible to ignore the fact that the language of the program is many-sorted. This is useful to know, since query evaluation procedures generally take no account of sorts.

1 Introduction

The consequences of a logic program depend in general upon both the rules of the program and its language. For instance, consider the program P_1 whose only rule is

$$p(X) \leftarrow .$$

If the language of P_1 is unsorted and contains, as its only ground terms, the constant symbols a and b, then its consequences are $p(a)$ and $p(b)$. However, if b is replaced by c, then instead its consequences are $p(a)$ and $p(c)$. As a second example, consider the program P_2,

$$p(a) \leftarrow \ not \ q(X),$$
$$q(a) \leftarrow .$$

Suppose the language of P_2 is the unsorted language that includes only the symbols used in the program; so the only ground term in the language is the constant symbol a. Then $p(a)$ is not a consequence of P_2. However, if the language of P_2 includes in addition the constant symbol b, then $p(a)$ is a consequence of P_2.

Both programs illustrate the fact that the consequences of a program may depend on its language, but the programs differ in one important respect. In the case of P_1, the consequences of the program taken with respect to any pair of languages inevitably agree in their intersection; for example, wrt the two languages discussed in relation to P_1, the consequences agree on $\{p(a)\}$. However, in the case of P_2, this is not so. For example, $p(a)$ is in the intersection of the languages discussed in relation to P_2, but it is a consequence wrt only one of them. Therefore, P_1 is, in a sense, more tolerant of language changes than P_2. In this paper, we will define a notion of *language tolerance* such that P_1 is language tolerant but P_2 is not.

The consequences of some language tolerant programs do not depend at all on what language is taken as the language of the program.[1] As an example, consider the program P_3,

$$p(X) \leftarrow r(X), \, not \, q(X),$$
$$r(a) \leftarrow \, .$$

The consequences of P_3 remain $p(a)$ and $r(a)$, regardless of the language of the program. We will define a notion of *language independence*, generalizing the definition in [Martens and De Schreye, 1992], such that P_3 is language independent but P_1 (and of course, P_2) are not.

Our main purpose in this paper is to identify syntactically-defined classes of programs that are language independent and language tolerant. One reason for desiring such results is suggested in the following paragraph.

In applications of logic programming to knowledge representation, it is often convenient to use a language with many sorts. For instance, a program that represents knowledge about actions in the situation calculus might include such sorts as; *action, fluent* and *situation*. Since the standard query evaluation procedures for logic programs take no special account of sorts, this raises a basic question: What is the effect on the declarative meaning of a program when we ignore the fact that its language is many-sorted and replace the language of the program by an unsorted language with the same signature? For a language independent program, it is clear that the consequences are not affected at all, while for a language tolerant program, the result is a conservative extension of the program, with identical consequences in the original many-sorted language.

The question of when it is acceptable to "ignore sorts" in logic programs was the original motivation for these investigations, and it remains the primary application of our results.

In the following section, we specify the syntax and semantics of logic programs. We then define the notion of language independence (Section 3)

---

[1]Of course, any candidate language must include the symbols that actually occur in the program, and, if the language is many-sorted, must specify the sorts of these symbols in ways that are compatible with their use.

and a syntactic class of language independent programs (Section 4). We do the same for the notion of language tolerance in Sections 5 & 6. In Section 7 we show that ignoring sorts in a language tolerant program yields a conservative extension, and we apply this result to a program for reasoning about actions. We discuss related work in Section 8 and present conclusions in Section 9. Proofs and proof sketches are given in Section 10.

2 Languages, Programs and Answer Sets

To specify a language $\mathcal{L}$ for logic programs, we specify a signature $\Sigma_{\mathcal{L}}$, a nonempty set $I_{\mathcal{L}}$, whose members are called sorts, and a sort specification for each symbol of $\Sigma_{\mathcal{L}}$ as follows.

A *signature* $\Sigma_{\mathcal{L}}$ for a language $\mathcal{L}$ is a triple consisting of disjoint sets of predicate symbols (with arities), function symbols (with arities), and variables. (Constant symbols appear in the signature as zero-ary function symbols.) $\mathcal{L}$ is said to be *one-sorted* (or *unsorted*), if $I_{\mathcal{L}}$ contains exactly one sort. When the language is clear from the context, we may drop the subscript, writing Σ or I.

We assign a *sort specification* to each symbol of Σ as follows. Each variable is assigned a sort in I. Each n-ary function symbol is assigned an $n + 1$-tuple $\langle s_1, \ldots, s_n, s_{n+1} \rangle$, where for each i, $1 \leq i \leq n + 1$, $s_i \in I$. Each n-ary predicate symbol is assigned an n-tuple $\langle s_1, \ldots, s_n \rangle$, where for each i, $1 \leq i \leq n$, $s_i \in I$. It is stipulated that there must be at least one constant symbol of each sort in I.[2] The terms and atomic formulas (or atoms) of $\mathcal{L}$ are recursively defined in the usual way, respecting the sort specifications of the symbols. Given the atoms, we define the set of literals of $\mathcal{L}$ as the set including, for each atom A, both the atom A and the negated atom $\neg A$. Finally, the rules of $\mathcal{L}$ are the expressions of the form

$$L_1 \mid \ldots \mid L_l \;\; \leftarrow \;\; L_{l+1}, \ldots, L_m, \; not\ L_{m+1}, \ldots, \; not\ L_n \qquad (1)$$

with $0 \leq l \leq m \leq n$, where each L_i $(1 \leq i \leq n)$ is a literal.

A *program* P is a set of rules in a language $\mathcal{L}_P$, which may be one-sorted or many-sorted.[3] The rules of P inevitably belong to a host of other languages as well. These languages may differ from $\mathcal{L}_P$ in their symbols or in their sorts (or both). We will be concerned with how the declarative meaning of a program is affected by choices among these languages.

Definition. Let $\mathcal{L}$ be an arbitrary language, and let P be a program. If every rule in P is a rule of $\mathcal{L}$, we say that $\mathcal{L}$ is *permissible* for P. When the program P is clear from the context, we say simply that $\mathcal{L}$ is permissible.

---

[2]This stipulation is analogous to the stipulation in classical logic that domains are nonempty.

[3]So by a program, unless we say otherwise, we shall mean an extended disjunctive logic program [Gelfond and Lifschitz, 1991].

For every program P, $\mathcal{L}_P$ is permissible for P.

Definition. Given a program P and a language $\mathcal{L}$ that is permissible for P, $\mathcal{H}(P, \mathcal{L})$ is the ground program, consisting of all ground instances, in the language $\mathcal{L}$, of rules in P. The language of the ground program $\mathcal{H}(P, \mathcal{L})$ obtained in this manner is $\mathcal{L}$.

In most declarative semantics of logic programs, including the answer set semantics, we take a program P with variables to be essentially a shorthand specification of the ground program $\mathcal{H}(P, \mathcal{L}_P)$, where $\mathcal{L}_P$ is the (often un-specified) language of P.[4] Thus, the answer sets for a program P are the answer sets for the ground program $\mathcal{H}(P, \mathcal{L}_P)$.

In order to finish defining the answer set semantics, we introduce a few more definitions and notational conventions. Given a rule r as in (1), by the subgoals of r we mean

$$L_{l+1}, \ldots, L_m, \; not \; L_{m+1}, \ldots, \; not \; L_n.$$

We define the following: $head(r) = \{L_1, \ldots, L_l\}$, $body(r) = \{L_{l+1}, \ldots, L_n\}$, $pos(r) = \{L_{l+1}, \ldots, L_m\}$, and $neg(r) = \{L_{m+1}, \ldots, L_n\}$. A program P is a *positive program* if, for every rule r in P, $neg(r) = \emptyset$. For a program P, by $Lit(P)$ we denote the set of ground literals that occur in P. For a language $\mathcal{L}$, by $Lit(\mathcal{L})$ we denote the set of ground literals of $\mathcal{L}$.

Now, let P be a positive ground program, with $\mathcal{L}$ a language permissible for P. Let B be a subset of $Lit(\mathcal{L})$. B is *closed under* the rules of P if for all rules r in P, $head(r) \cap B \neq \emptyset$ whenever $body(r) \subset B$. B is *consistent* if B does not contain a pair of complementary literals. B is *logically closed* (wrt $\mathcal{L}$) if either B is consistent or $B = Lit(\mathcal{L})$.

An *answer set* for a positive ground program P is a minimal subset of $Lit(\mathcal{L}_P)$ that is both closed under P and logically closed (wrt $\mathcal{L}_P$).

Let P be a ground program. Let X be a subset of $Lit(\mathcal{L}_P)$. The *reduct* of P wrt X is the positive program P^X, where

$$P^X = \left\{ \begin{array}{l} r' : \exists r \in P . \; neg(r) \cap X = \emptyset \wedge head(r') = head(r) \\ \qquad \wedge pos(r') = pos(r) \wedge neg(r') = \emptyset \end{array} \right\}.$$

Given a ground program P, with $B \subset Lit(\mathcal{L}_P)$, B is an *answer set* for P iff B is an answer set for P^B.

Example. Consider the program P_4,

$$p(X, Y) \leftarrow r(X), \; not \; q(X, Y),$$
$$r(a) \leftarrow,$$
$$q(a, 0) \leftarrow,$$

---

[4] By convention, when the language $\mathcal{L}_P$ of a program P is not otherwise specified, we assume that $\mathcal{L}_P$ is the minimal unsorted language that (i) is permissible for P, and (ii) includes the constant symbol a if no constant symbol occurs in P.

where the signature $\Sigma_{\mathcal{L}_{P_4}}$ is $(\{p/2, r/1, q/2\}, \{a/0, 0/0, 1/0, 2/0\}, \{X, Y\})$, the set of sorts $I_{\mathcal{L}_{P_4}}$ is $\{letter, num\}$, and the sort specifications for the symbols of $\mathcal{L}_{P_4}$ are $sort(X) = letter$, $sort(Y) = num$, $sort(p) = sort(q) = \langle letter, num \rangle$, $sort(r) = \langle letter \rangle$, $sort(a) = \langle letter \rangle$, and $sort(0) = sort(1) = sort(2) = \langle num \rangle$.

The ground program $\mathcal{H}(P_4, \mathcal{L}_{P_4})$ is

$$p(a, 0) \leftarrow r(a), \; not \; q(a, 0),$$
$$p(a, 1) \leftarrow r(a), \; not \; q(a, 1),$$
$$p(a, 2) \leftarrow r(a), \; not \; q(a, 2),$$
$$r(a) \leftarrow,$$
$$q(a, 0) \leftarrow.$$

Let $A = \{p(a, 1), p(a, 2), r(a), q(a, 0)\}$. The reduct P_4^A is the positive program

$$p(a, 1) \leftarrow r(a),$$
$$p(a, 2) \leftarrow r(a),$$
$$r(a) \leftarrow,$$
$$q(a, 0) \leftarrow.$$

Since A is a minimal set that is both closed under the rules of P_4^A and logically closed, A is an answer set for P_4. It is, in fact, the only answer set, and of course it is consistent.

A program P *entails* exactly those literals from $Lit(\mathcal{L}_P)$ that are included in every answer set for P. We denote the set of literals entailed by P by $Cn(P)$. A program P is *consistent* if $Cn(P)$ is consistent, and *inconsistent* otherwise.

We make two simple observations: (i) for a program P, $Cn(P)$ is the set of literals from $Lit(\mathcal{L}_P)$ that are included in every consistent answer set for P, and (ii) if a program P is inconsistent, then either it has no answer set or its only answer set is $Lit(\mathcal{L}_P)$.

We will at times be interested in the class of normal programs. A program P is a *normal* program if every rule in P has the form
$$A_0 \leftarrow A_1, \ldots, A_m, \; not \; A_{m+1}, \ldots, \; not \; A_n$$
with $0 \le m \le n$, where all A_i $(i = 0, \ldots, n)$ are atoms of $\mathcal{L}_P$.

3 Language Independence

In this section we define the notion of language independence and state a simple proposition regarding the consequences of language independent programs.

Definition. A program P is *language independent* if, for any two languages $\mathcal{L}_1, \mathcal{L}_2$ that are permissible for P, the ground programs $\mathcal{H}(P, \mathcal{L}_1)$ and $\mathcal{H}(P, \mathcal{L}_2)$ have the same consistent answer sets.

Proposition 3.1 *Let P be a language independent program, and let $\mathcal{L}_1, \mathcal{L}_2$ be permissible languages for P. Then $Cn(\mathcal{H}(P, \mathcal{L}_1)) = Cn(\mathcal{H}(P, \mathcal{L}_2))$.*

Ground programs are trivially language independent. Let P be a ground program. For any language $\mathcal{L}$ that is permissible for P, we have $P = \mathcal{H}(P, \mathcal{L})$. Hence, for any two languages $\mathcal{L}_1, \mathcal{L}_2$ that are permissible for P, $\mathcal{H}(P, \mathcal{L}_1) = \mathcal{H}(P, \mathcal{L}_2)$. So P is language independent. Thus, for the purpose of determining answer sets and consequences, there is no need to specify the language of a consistent ground program.

We will be interested in identifying additional classes of language independent and language tolerant programs.

4 Allowed Programs are Language Independent

In this section we present a theorem which states that *allowed* programs are language independent. The class of allowed programs is syntactically-defined and was studied in [Lloyd and Topor, 1986] in connection with the problem of floundering in SLDNF. The same class of programs is also known as *range-restricted*.

We begin by generalizing the definition of an allowed program, which was originally defined for normal programs only.

Definition. Let P be a program. A rule $R \in P$ is *allowed* if every variable in R occurs in $pos(R)$. The program P is *allowed* if every rule in P is allowed.

The program P_3 is allowed, but the programs P_1, P_2 and P_4 are not. We can now state the following theorem.

Theorem 4.1 *Every allowed program is language independent.*

The theorem shows that for allowed programs, as for ground programs, consistent answer sets are unaffected by the choice of language. However, the reason for this is different in the case of allowed programs, since the choice of language $\mathcal{L}$ for an allowed program P generally does affect $\mathcal{H}(P, \mathcal{L})$. As an example, suppose that $\mathcal{L}_1$ and $\mathcal{L}_2$ are permissible languages for P_3, with a as the only ground term in $\mathcal{L}_1$, and a and b as the only ground terms in $\mathcal{L}_2$. Then, although the ground program $\mathcal{H}(P_3, \mathcal{L}_1)$ is

$$p(a) \leftarrow r(a), \; not \; q(a),$$
$$r(a) \leftarrow ,$$

and the ground program $\mathcal{H}(P_3, \mathcal{L}_2)$ is

$$p(a) \leftarrow r(a), \; not \; q(a),$$
$$p(b) \leftarrow r(b), \; not \; q(b),$$
$$r(a) \leftarrow ,$$

the answer sets and consequences for the two programs are identical. Theorem 4.1 implies that the same result holds for all allowed programs and their permissible languages.

5   Language Tolerance

In this section we define the notion of language tolerance and state a simple proposition regarding the consequences of language tolerant programs.

Definition.   A program P is *language tolerant* if, for any two languages $\mathcal{L}_1, \mathcal{L}_2$ that are permissible for P the following holds: If A_1 is a consistent answer set for the ground program $\mathcal{H}(P, \mathcal{L}_1)$, then there is a consistent answer set A_2 for the ground program $\mathcal{H}(P, \mathcal{L}_2)$ s.t. $A_1 \cap Lit(\mathcal{L}_2) = A_2 \cap Lit(\mathcal{L}_1)$.

Proposition 5.1 *Let P be a language tolerant program, and let $\mathcal{L}_1, \mathcal{L}_2$ be permissible languages for P. Then $Cn(\mathcal{H}(P, \mathcal{L}_1)) \cap Lit(\mathcal{L}_2) = Cn(\mathcal{H}(P, \mathcal{L}_2)) \cap Lit(\mathcal{L}_1)$.*

Let $X = Lit(\mathcal{L}_1) \cap Lit(\mathcal{L}_2)$. Since the answer sets for $\mathcal{H}(P, \mathcal{L}_1)$ are subsets of $Lit(\mathcal{L}_1)$ and the answer sets for $\mathcal{H}(P, \mathcal{L}_2)$ are subsets of $Lit(\mathcal{L}_2)$, the equality expressions in the previous definition and proposition can be replaced by $A_1 \cap X = A_2 \cap X$ and $Cn(\mathcal{H}(P, \mathcal{L}_1)) \cap X = Cn(\mathcal{H}(P, \mathcal{L}_2)) \cap X$, respectively. Thus, if P is language tolerant, the consequences of P, determined wrt any pair of permissible languages, agree in the intersection of the languages.

Clearly, every language independent program is language tolerant, but the converse does not hold. This is illustrated by the programs P_1 and P_4. It is easy to show that these programs are not language independent.

Example.   [cont.] Let $\mathcal{L}$ be the language that differs from $\mathcal{L}_{P_4}$ by including an additional constant symbol b of sort *letter* and by replacing the constant symbol 1 in $\mathcal{L}_{P_4}$ by 4. The ground program $\mathcal{H}(P_4, \mathcal{L})$, which contains eight rules, has the unique answer set $\{p(a, 2), p(a, 4), r(a), q(a, 0)\}$. The unique answer set for $\mathcal{H}(P_4, \mathcal{L}_{P_4})$ is $\{p(a, 1), p(a, 2), r(a), q(a, 0)\}$, as given in Section 2. Since these answer sets differ, P_4 is not language independent. However, the two answer sets agree in the intersection of the two languages.

It will be easy to show that P_1 and P_4 are language tolerant, using the results obtained in the next section.

6   Some Stable Programs are Language Tolerant

The class of stable programs [Stroetman, 1993] properly includes the class of allowed programs. Under a rather strong restriction, we can show that stable programs are language tolerant. The restriction is stated after the following definition.

Definition. A program Q is a *part* of a program P if Q can be obtained from P by (i) selecting a subset of the rules in P and (ii) deleting zero or more subgoals from each selected rule.

We can show that a stable program is language tolerant if, for every language $\mathcal{L}$ that is permissible for P, every part of $\mathcal{H}(P, \mathcal{L})$ has a consistent answer set. In general of course it may be difficult determine whether a program has this property, but there are some easily recognized classes of programs that do; for instance, stratified normal programs. Later in this section we will define a larger class of normal programs with this property, namely, the class of predicate-order-consistent programs.

We begin our discussion of stable programs by generalizing a number of definitions given originally in [Stroetman, 1993] in the framework of normal programs.

An I/O specification σ for a program P is a function that maps every n-ary predicate symbol Q that occurs in P to a pair of modes — σ_Q and $\sigma_{\neg Q}$ — each of which is a function from the set $\{1, \ldots, n\}$ to $\{+, -\}$. [5]

The mode σ_Q can be conveniently written as $Q(\sigma_Q(1), \ldots, \sigma_Q(n))$. For example, $\neg Holds(-, +)$ means that $\sigma_{\neg Holds}(1) = -$ and $\sigma_{\neg Holds}(2) = +$.

Definition. Let P be a program with I/O specification σ and permissible language $\mathcal{L}$. For any expression E from $\mathcal{L}$, by $FV(E)$ we designate the set of free variables that occur in E. For any atom $Q(t_1, \ldots, t_n)$ in $\mathcal{L}$ s.t. Q occurs in P,

$$FV^+(Q(t_1, \ldots, t_n)) = \bigcup\{FV(t_i) : i \in \{1, \ldots, n\} \text{ and } \sigma_Q(i) = +\}$$
$$FV^-(Q(t_1, \ldots, t_n)) = \bigcup\{FV(t_i) : i \in \{1, \ldots, n\} \text{ and } \sigma_Q(i) = -\}.$$

For any negated atom $\neg Q(t_1, \ldots, t_n)$ in $\mathcal{L}$, s.t. Q occurs in P,

$$FV^+(\neg Q(t_1, \ldots, t_n)) = \bigcup\{FV(t_i) : i \in \{1, \ldots, n\} \text{ and } \sigma_{\neg Q}(i) = +\}$$
$$FV^-(\neg Q(t_1, \ldots, t_n)) = \bigcup\{FV(t_i) : i \in \{1, \ldots, n\} \text{ and } \sigma_{\neg Q}(i) = -\}.$$

Definition. Let P be a program. A rule $R \in P$ is *stable wrt* an I/O specification σ if there exists an ordering $L_1, \ldots, L_k$ of $pos(R)$ such that at least one of the following conditions is satisfied for every variable x that occurs in R:

(i) $head(R) \neq \emptyset \wedge \forall L \in head(R)[x \in FV^+(L)]$,

(ii) $\exists i \in \{1, \ldots, k\}[x \in FV^-(L_i) \wedge \forall j \in \{1, \ldots, i\}[x \notin FV^+(L_j)]]$.

---

[5] Intuitively, if $\sigma_Q(i) = +$, then i is an input position for any atom with the predicate Q, and if $\sigma_Q(i) = -$, then i is an output position. Similarly, if $\sigma_{\neg Q}(i) = +$, then i is an input position for any negated atom with the predicate Q, and if $\sigma_{\neg Q}(i) = -$, then i is an output position. An input position is an argument place that should be a ground term in any call to Q. An output position need not be ground. These concepts are associated with the procedural semantics of normal logic programs.

Program P is *stable wrt* σ if every rule in P is stable wrt σ, and P is *stable* if for some σ, P is stable wrt σ.

The programs P_1, P_3, and P_4 are stable. P_1 is stable wrt the I/O specification $p(+)$. P_3 is stable wrt $p(-)$, $q(-)$, and $r(-)$. P_4 is stable wrt $p(-,+)$, $q(-,-)$, and $r(-)$. The program P_2 is not stable.

It is easy to see that a program P is allowed iff it is stable wrt the I/O specification that maps every argument place to $-$. So the class of stable programs is a superset of the class of allowed programs.

The preceding definition generalizes the definition in [Stroetman, 1993] to the class of extended disjunctive programs. But even in the special case of normal programs, the definition is more general. In [Stroetman, 1993] the body of a rule is an ordered sequence rather than a set, and whether or not a rule is stable may depend on this ordering. For instance, according to the original definition, the rule $p \leftarrow not\ r(X), q(X)$ is not stable. By the definition given here, on the other hand, the rule is stable wrt any I/O specification σ such that $\sigma_q(1) = -$.

It is not the case that every stable program is language tolerant, as the following program P_5 illustrates,

$$p(X) \leftarrow\ not\ p(X),$$
$$p(a) \leftarrow\ .$$

P_5 is stable wrt the I/O specification $p(+)$. Suppose that $\mathcal{L}_1$ is the minimal unsorted permissible language for P_5 and that $\mathcal{L}_2$ is the same as $\mathcal{L}_1$ except that it contains the additional constant symbol b. Then $\mathcal{H}(P_5, \mathcal{L}_1)$ has a single answer set $\{p(a)\}$, but $\mathcal{H}(P_5, \mathcal{L}_2)$ is inconsistent and has no answer sets at all. This shows that P_5 is not language tolerant.

It is also not the case that every stable program that is consistent wrt every permissible language is language tolerant. This is illustrated by the program P_6.

$$p(X) \leftarrow d,\ not\ p(X),$$
$$p(a) \leftarrow,$$
$$c \mid d \leftarrow\ .$$

P_6 is stable wrt the I/O specification $p(+)$, and for every permissible language $\mathcal{L}$ for P_6, $\{p(a), c\}$ is an answer set for $\mathcal{H}(P_6, \mathcal{L})$. Suppose that $\mathcal{L}_1$ is the minimal unsorted permissible language for P_6 and that $\mathcal{L}_2$ is the same as $\mathcal{L}_1$ except that it contains the additional constant symbol b. Then $\mathcal{H}(P_6, \mathcal{L}_1)$ has two answer sets $\{p(a), c\}$ and $\{p(a), d\}$, but $\mathcal{H}(P_6, \mathcal{L}_2)$ has only the answer set $\{p(a), c\}$. This shows that P_6 is not language tolerant and motivates the stronger condition stated in the following theorem.

Theorem 6.1 *If a program P is stable and, for every permissible language $\mathcal{L}$ for P, every part of $\mathcal{H}(P, \mathcal{L})$ has a consistent answer set, then P is language tolerant.*

As given, Theorem 6.1 is difficult to apply because of the consistency condition in the statement of the theorem. We now turn to the problem of defining a general syntactic class of programs that satisfy this condition. For this purpose, we define the property of predicate-order-consistency in a manner analogous to the definition of order-consistency in [Fages, 1994]. Unlike the definition of order-consistency, the definition of predicate-order-consistency does not refer to the language of the program, but only to the predicate symbols that occur in the program.

Let P be a normal program. The property of predicate-order-consistency is defined in terms of the *predicate dependency graph* $G(P)$ of P. The nodes of the graph are the predicate symbols that occur in P.

Let p, q be predicate symbols that occur in P. There is a positive edge in $G(P)$ from p to q if there is a rule $R \in P$ with p occurring in $pos(R)$ and q occurring in $head(R)$, and there is a negative edge in $G(P)$ from p to q if there a rule $R \in P$ with p occurring in $neg(R)$ and q occurring in $head(R)$.

Definition. Given $G(P)$, we define two relations. For all predicate symbols p, q that occur in P,

(i) $p \leq_+ q$ if there is a path in $G(P)$ from p to q with an even number of negative edges,

(ii) $p \leq_- q$ if there is a path in $G(P)$ from p to q with an odd number of negative edges.

Finally, a third relation $\leq_\pm$ is defined in terms of the previous two: For all predicate symbols p, q that occur in P, $p \leq_\pm q \equiv [p \leq_+ q$ and $p \leq_- q]$.

Definition. A normal program P is *predicate-order-consistent* if the relation $\leq_\pm$ in $G(P)$ is well-founded and there is no predicate symbol p that occurs in P s.t. $p \leq_\pm p$.

The following proposition is proved by using the result from [Fages, 1994] which states that every order-consistent normal program has an answer set.

Proposition 6.1 *If P is a predicate-order-consistent normal program, then for every permissible language $\mathcal{L}$ for P, every part of $\mathcal{H}(P, \mathcal{L})$ has a consistent answer set.*

Theorem 6.2 *If normal program P is stable and predicate-order-consistent, then P is language tolerant.*

Since the programs P_1 and P_4 clearly satisfy the conditions of Theorem 6.2, they are language tolerant.

7 Ignoring Sorts

In this section, we define the notion of "ignoring sorts" and state a theorem that justifies ignoring sorts in language tolerant programs.

Definition. Let P and P' be ground programs such that $P \subset P'$. We say that P' is a *conservative extension* of P if the following condition holds: A is a consistent answer set for P iff there is a consistent answer set A' for P' such that $A = A' \cap Lit(\mathcal{L}_P)$.

Proposition 7.1 *If a program P' is a conservative extension of a program P, then $Cn(P) = Cn(P') \cap Lit(\mathcal{L}_P)$.*

Definition. Let $\mathcal{L}, \mathcal{L}'$ be languages. We say that $\mathcal{L}'$ is obtained from $\mathcal{L}$ by *ignoring sorts* if $\Sigma_{\mathcal{L}} = \Sigma_{\mathcal{L}'}$ and $\mathcal{L}'$ is one-sorted.

Proposition 7.2 *Let P be a language tolerant program. If $\mathcal{L}$ is obtained from $\mathcal{L}_P$ by ignoring sorts, then $\mathcal{H}(P, \mathcal{L})$ is a conservative extension of $\mathcal{H}(P, \mathcal{L}_P)$.*

We now apply Proposition 7.2 to a program for reasoning about actions from [Lifschitz *et al.*, 1993]. The language of the program is a many-sorted language with four sorts: *fluent*, *action*, *truth-value*, and *situation*. The language contains the following constant symbols: *Loaded* and *Alive* of sort *fluent*; *Load*, *Wait*, and *Shoot* of sort *action*; 0 and 1 of sort *truth-value*; and *S0* of sort *situation*. In addition, the language contains the function symbol *Result*, where

$$sort(Result) \ = \ \langle action, situation, situation \rangle \,,$$

and the predicate symbols, *Holds*, *Holds'*, *Noninertial*, and *Rel*, where

$$sort(Holds) \ = \ sort(Holds') = \langle fluent, situation \rangle$$
$$sort(Noninertial) \ = \ \langle fluent, action, situation, truth\text{-}value \rangle$$
$$sort(Rel) \ = \ \langle situation \rangle \,.$$

The sorts of the variables, f, a, and s, can be inferred from their use.

The program P_7 is the *positive form* of an extended program given in [Lifschitz *et al.*, 1993].[6] It formalizes the so-called Murder Mystery variant of the Yale Shooting Problem [Hanks and McDermott, 1987].

1. *Holds(Alive, S0)*.

2. *Holds'(Alive, Result(Wait, Result(Shoot, S0)))*.

2a. *Rel(Result(Wait, Result(Shoot, S0)))*.

2b. *Rel(Result(Shoot, S0))*.

3. *Holds(Loaded, Result(Load, s))*.

---

[6]The positive form was obtained by replacing each literal of the form $\neg Holds(\_,\_)$ by an atom of the form $Holds'(\_,\_)$, where *Holds'* is a new predicate symbol. See [Gelfond and Lifschitz, 1991].

4. $Noninertial(Loaded, Load, s, 1)$.

5. $Holds'(Alive, Result(Shoot, s)) \leftarrow Holds(Loaded, s)$.

6. $Noninertial(Alive, Shoot, s, 0) \leftarrow not\ Holds'(Loaded, s)$.

7. $Holds'(Loaded, s) \leftarrow Rel(Result(Shoot, s)), Holds(Alive, Result(Shoot, s))$.

8. $Holds(Loaded, s) \leftarrow Rel(Result(Shoot, s)), Holds(Alive, s),$
$$Holds'(Alive, Result(Shoot, s)).$$

9. $Holds'(Loaded, Result(Shoot, s))$.

10. $Noninertial(Loaded, Shoot, s, 0)$.

11. $Holds(f, Result(a, s)) \leftarrow Holds(f, s),\ not\ Noninertial(f, a, s, 0)$.

12. $Holds'(f, Result(a, s)) \leftarrow Holds'(f, s),\ not\ Noninertial(f, a, s, 1)$.

13. $Holds(f, s) \leftarrow Rel(Result(a, s)), Holds(f, Result(a, s)),$
$$not\ Noninertial(f, a, s, 1).$$

14. $Holds'(f, s) \leftarrow Rel(Result(a, s)), Holds'(f, Result(a, s)),$
$$not\ Noninertial(f, a, s, 0).$$

The program is not allowed, because in each of the rules 3, 4, 6, 9, 10, 11 and 12 there is a variable that does not occur in the positive part of the body.

Let σ be the following I/O specification: $Holds(-, +)$, $Holds'(-, +)$, $Noninertial(+, +, +, +)$, and $Rel(-)$. It is easy to check that the program is stable wrt σ. Also, it is easy to see that the program is predicate-order-consistent; in fact, the relation $\leq_\pm$, which is defined wrt the predicate dependency graph $G(P_7)$, is empty. Thus, by Theorem 6.2, P_7 is language tolerant.

Let $\mathcal{L}'_{P_7}$ be the language that is obtained from $\mathcal{L}_{P_7}$ by ignoring sorts. By Proposition 7.2, $\mathcal{H}(P_7, \mathcal{L}'_{P_7})$ is a conservative extension of $\mathcal{H}(P_7, \mathcal{L}_{P_7})$. So ignoring sorts in $\mathcal{L}_{P_7}$ has no effect on whether or not an atom in the original many-sorted language is a consequence of the program. For P_7, this justifies the use of query evaluation procedures that take no account of sorts.

8   Discussion

A notion of *language independence* is defined for stratified normal programs in [Martens and De Schreye, 1992] as follows: "A stratified program P with underlying language $\mathcal{L}_P$ is called *language independent* iff for any extension $\mathcal{L}'$ for $\mathcal{L}_P$, its perfect $\mathcal{L}'$-Herbrand model is equal to its perfect $\mathcal{L}_P$-Herbrand model." (Here $\mathcal{L}_P$ is the minimal (unsorted) permissible language for P.) Furthermore, the following result is stated as Proposition 2.5: "Let P be a stratified program. If P is range-restricted then P is language-independent." Note that the class of allowed programs and the class of range-restricted programs are the same.

Since the perfect model semantics and the answer set semantics agree for the class of stratified normal programs, it is possible to compare the preceding proposition with our Theorem 4.1. First, our theorem applies to sorted as well as unsorted languages. Secondly, it applies to non-stratified normal programs and more generally to the entire class of extended disjunctive programs. In these respects, Theorem 4.1 is more general than Proposition 2.5. Since our notion of language independence considers all pairs of permissible languages, not only the minimal unsorted permissible language and each of its unsorted extensions, Theorem 4.1 is at least as strong as Proposition 2.5. There is no definition in [Martens and De Schreye, 1992] analogous to our notion of language tolerance.

To our knowledge, the closest analogues to our definition of language tolerance appear in [Topor and Sonenberg, 1988] and [Ross, 1994]. In [Topor and Sonenberg, 1988], a concept called "domain independence" is defined as follows: "A stratified database D is *domain independent* if, for all languages $\mathcal{L}_1$ and $\mathcal{L}_2$ extending that of D, and for all atoms A in $\mathcal{L}_1$ and $\mathcal{L}_2$, $ans(A, D, \mathcal{L}_1) = ans(A, D, \mathcal{L}_2)$." (Here $ans(A, D, \mathcal{L})$ may be taken to be the set of ground instances of A that are consequences of $\mathcal{H}(D, \mathcal{L})$ according to any of the various semantics that coincide on stratified programs.) This definition resembles our definition of language tolerance in its focus on the intersections of pairs of languages. However, sorted languages and extended or disjunctive programs are not covered, and the largest syntactic class of programs shown to be domain independent is the class of allowed stratified programs.

In [Ross, 1994], definitions and results bearing a family resemblance to ours are presented, but in the framework of HiLog languages rather than sorted first-order languages. While it is clear that these ideas are related to our notions of language tolerance and stability, we are not yet able to describe the relationships precisely. This is a topic for further study.

9   Conclusion

The classes of allowed and stable programs have been previously studied in connection with the problem of floundering in SLDNF. We have generalized these classes to include extended disjunctive programs and shown results relating them to the notions of language independence and language tolerance. We have applied these results to show that the practice of "ignoring sorts" when evaluating queries wrt a logic program in a many-sorted language can sometimes be justified declaratively, in the sense that the program that results from ignoring sorts is a conservative extension of the original program.

It is interesting to note that the class of stable programs does not include all positive programs, which intuitively are also language tolerant. It should be possible, therefore, to find yet larger classes of programs that are language tolerant. This is a topic for further study.

10 Proofs

Definition. Given a ground program P, a permissible language $\mathcal{L}$, and a set $X \subset Lit(\mathcal{L})$, we say that a rule $r \in P$ is *confined to X* if either $pos(r) \not\subset X$ or $head(r) \subset X$. We say that P is *confined to X*, if every rule in P is confined to X.

Definition. For ground program P and $X \subset Lit(P)$, let $c_X(P) = \{r \in P : pos(r) \subset X\}$.

Proposition 10.1 *If ground program P is confined to X, then the consistent answer sets for P are the consistent answer sets for $c_X(P)$.*

The proof of this proposition is straightforward. The following lemma is asserted without proof. Note that $FV(L)$ denotes the set of free variables in the literal L, as defined in Section 6.

Lemma 10.1 *Let $\mathcal{L}_1, \mathcal{L}_2$ be languages. If $A_1, \ldots, A_k, B$ are literals of $\mathcal{L}_1$ and $\mathcal{L}_2$, θ is a substitution in $\mathcal{L}_1$, and*

$$FV(B) \subset \bigcup_{i=1}^{k} FV(A_i),$$

then if $A_1\theta, \ldots, A_k\theta \in Lit(\mathcal{L}_2)$ then $B\theta \in Lit(\mathcal{L}_2)$.

Lemma 10.2 *Let P be an allowed program with permissible languages $\mathcal{L}_1$ and $\mathcal{L}_2$. Let $X = Lit(\mathcal{L}_1) \cap Lit(\mathcal{L}_2)$. Programs $\mathcal{H}(P, \mathcal{L}_1)$ and $\mathcal{H}(P, \mathcal{L}_2)$ are each confined to X.*

Proof. Suppose $r \in \mathcal{H}(P, \mathcal{L}_1)$. Then there is a rule $R \in P$ and a substitution θ in $\mathcal{L}_1$ s.t. $r = R\theta$. We will show that if $pos(r) \subset X$ then $head(r) \subset X$. Suppose $pos(r) \subset X$. Clearly, $head(r) \subset Lit(\mathcal{L}_1)$. It remains to show that $head(r) \subset Lit(\mathcal{L}_2)$. So, suppose $L \in head(r)$. Then for some literal B in $head(R)$, $L = B\theta$. Let $A_1, \ldots, A_k$ be the literals in $pos(R)$. Since $\mathcal{L}_1, \mathcal{L}_2$ are permissible, $A_1, \ldots, A_k, B$ are literals of $\mathcal{L}_1, \mathcal{L}_2$. Since $r \in \mathcal{H}(P, \mathcal{L}_1)$, $A_1\theta, \ldots, A_k\theta \in Lit(\mathcal{L}_1)$. Since R is allowed,

$$FV(B) \subset \bigcup_{i=1}^{k} FV(A_i).$$

Since $A_1\theta, \ldots, A_k\theta \in pos(r) \subset X \subset Lit(\mathcal{L}_2)$, we conclude by Lemma 10.1 that $B\theta \in Lit(\mathcal{L}_2)$. It follows that $head(r) \subset Lit(\mathcal{L}_2)$. So $\mathcal{H}(P, \mathcal{L}_1)$ is confined to X. By symmetry, $\mathcal{H}(P, \mathcal{L}_2)$ is confined to X. $\square$

Lemma 10.3 *Let P be a program with permissible languages $\mathcal{L}_1$ and $\mathcal{L}_2$. Let $X = Lit(\mathcal{L}_1) \cap Lit(\mathcal{L}_2)$. If P is allowed, then $c_X(\mathcal{H}(P, \mathcal{L}_1)) = c_X(\mathcal{H}(P, \mathcal{L}_2))$.*

Proof. Suppose $r \in c_X(\mathcal{H}(P, \mathcal{L}_1))$. Then $pos(r) \subset X$. By Lemma 10.2, $\mathcal{H}(P, \mathcal{L}_1)$ is confined to X, so $head(r) \subset X$. It remains to show that $neg(r) \subset X$. This is proved, using Lemma 10.1, in a manner similar to that used in proving the previous lemma. So $head(r) \cup body(r) \subset X \subset Lit(\mathcal{L}_2)$. So $r \in \mathcal{H}(P, \mathcal{L}_2)$. Since $pos(r) \subset X$, $r \in c_X(\mathcal{H}(P, \mathcal{L}_2))$. Thus, $c_X(\mathcal{H}(P, \mathcal{L}_1)) \subset c_X(\mathcal{H}(P, \mathcal{L}_2))$. By symmetry, $c_X(\mathcal{H}(P, \mathcal{L}_2)) \subset c_X(\mathcal{H}(P, \mathcal{L}_1))$. $\square$

Proof. (of Theorem 4.1) Suppose P is an allowed program. To show that P is language independent, we show that for any two permissible languages $\mathcal{L}_1, \mathcal{L}_2$, $\mathcal{H}(P, \mathcal{L}_1)$ and $\mathcal{H}(P, \mathcal{L}_2)$ have the same consistent answer sets. Let $X = Lit(\mathcal{L}_1) \cap Lit(\mathcal{L}_2)$. By Lemma 10.3, $c_X(\mathcal{H}(P, \mathcal{L}_1)) = c_X(\mathcal{H}(P, \mathcal{L}_2))$. By Proposition 10.1, the consistent answer sets for $\mathcal{H}(P, \mathcal{L}_1)$ are the consistent answer sets for $c_X(\mathcal{H}(P, \mathcal{L}_1))$, and the consistent answer sets for $\mathcal{H}(P, \mathcal{L}_2)$ are the consistent answer sets for $c_X(\mathcal{H}(P, \mathcal{L}_2))$. It follows that $\mathcal{H}(P, \mathcal{L}_1)$ and $\mathcal{H}(P, \mathcal{L}_2)$ have the same consistent answer sets. Therefore, P is language independent. $\square$

The following definitions and theorem from [Lifschitz and Turner, 1994] are used in the proof of Theorem 6.1.

Definition. Given a rule r, $lit(r)$ stands for $head(r) \cup body(r)$. A *splitting set* for a ground program P is any set U of ground literals such that, for every rule $r \in P$, if $head(r) \cap U$ is nonempty then $lit(r) \subset U$. The set of rules $r \in P$ such that $lit(r) \subset U$ is called the *bottom* of P relative to the splitting set U and denoted by $b_U(P)$. The set $t_U(P)$ is the *top* of P relative to U. Consider two sets of literals U, X and a program P. For each rule $r \in P$ such that $pos(r) \cap U$ is a subset of X and $neg(r) \cap U$ is disjoint from X, take the rule r' defined by

$$head(r') = head(r), \ pos(r') = pos(r) \setminus U, \ neg(r') = neg(r) \setminus U.$$

The program consisting of all rules r' obtained in this way will be denoted by $e_U(P, X)$. Let U be a splitting set for a program P. A *solution* to P (with respect to U) is a pair $\langle X, Y \rangle$ of sets of literals such that

- X is an answer set for $b_U(P)$,

- Y is an answer set for $e_U(t_U(P), X)$,

- $X \cup Y$ is consistent.

Splitting Set Theorem [Lifschitz and Turner, 1994]. *Let U be a splitting set for a program P. A set A of literals is a consistent answer set for P if and only if $A = X \cup Y$ for some solution $\langle X, Y \rangle$ to P with respect to U.*

We prove the following corollary to the Splitting Set Theorem.

Corollary 10.4 *Let P be a ground program with splitting set U s.t. every literal in U has its complement in U. If every part of P has a consistent answer set, then the sets $\{A \cap U : A$ is a consistent answer set for $P\}$ and $\{B : B$ is a consistent answer set for $b_U(P)\}$ coincide.*

Proof. Left-to-right follows immediately from the Splitting Set Theorem. To see the other direction, assume that B is a consistent answer set for $b_U(P)$. We must show that there is a consistent answer set A for P s.t. $A \cap U = B$. Since every part of P has a consistent answer set, and since $e_U(t_U(P), B)$ is a part of P, $e_U(t_U(P), B)$ has a consistent answer set. Let C be a consistent answer set for $e_U(t_U(P), B)$. Let $A = B \cup C$. We need to show that A is a consistent set. We know that every consistent answer set for a program is a subset of the literals in the program. So, since $Lit(b_U(P)) \subset U$ and $Lit(e_U(t_U(P), X)) \subset Lit(\mathcal{L}_P) \setminus U$, we conclude that $B \subset U$ and $C \subset Lit(\mathcal{L}_P) \setminus U$. Because every literal in U has its complement in U, we know that every literal in B has its complement in U, and it follows that no literal in B has its complement in C. So $B \cup C = A$ is a consistent set, and we have shown that $\langle B, C \rangle$ is a solution to P with respect to U. By the Splitting Set Theorem we conclude that A is a consistent answer set for P. Furthermore, $A \cap U = B$. $\square$

Definition. A ground program P is *stable wrt* (U, X), $U \subset X \subset Lit(\mathcal{L}_P)$, if for every rule $r \in P$, at least one of the following three conditions holds:

(i) $head(r) \cup body(r) \subset U$

(ii) $head(r) \subset X \setminus U$

(iii) $pos(r) \not\subset X$.

Lemma 10.5 *A ground program P is stable wrt (U, X) iff P is confined to X and U splits $c_X(P)$.*

Proof. To prove the left-to-right direction, suppose P is stable wrt (U, X). Let r be a rule in P. If r satisfies condition (iii) then r is trivially confined to X. If r satisfies condition (i) or (ii) then $head(r) \subset X$, so again r is confined to X. So P is confined to X. Every rule in $c_X(P)$ satisfies either condition (i) or (ii). These rules are clearly split by U. To prove the right-to-left direction, suppose P is confined to X and U splits $c_X(P)$. We must show that each rule in P satisfies one of the three conditions in the definition of stable wrt (U, X). Suppose r is a rule in P. If r satisfies condition (iii), we are done. So suppose it does not. Then since P is confined to X, $head(r) \subset X$. Since U splits $c_X(P)$, either $head(r) \cap U = \emptyset$ or $head(r) \cup body(r) \subset U$. If $head(r) \cap U = \emptyset$ then r satisfies condition (ii). If $head(r) \cup body(r) \subset U$ then r satisfies condition (i). $\square$

Proposition 10.2 *Let P be a ground program. Let $U \subset X \subset Lit(\mathcal{L}_P)$ s.t. every literal in U has its complement in U. If P is stable wrt (U, X), and if every part of P has a consistent answer set, then B is a consistent answer set for $b_U(P)$ iff there is a consistent answer set A for P s.t. $A \cap U = B$.*

Proof. Suppose P is stable wrt (U, X) and that every part of P has a consistent answer set. By Lemma 10.5, P is confined to X and U splits

$c_X(P)$. Since $c_X(P) \subset P$, every part of $c_X(P)$ has a consistent answer set. By Corollary 10.4, the sets $\{A \cap U : A \text{ is a consistent answer set for } c_X(P)\}$ and $\{B : B \text{ is a consistent answer set for } b_U(c_X(P))\}$ coincide. Furthermore, $b_U(c_X(P)) = b_U(P)$, since

$$
\begin{aligned}
b_U(c_X(P)) &= \{r \in c_X(P) : head(r) \cup body(r) \subset U\} \\
&= \{r \in P : pos(r) \subset X \wedge head(r) \cup body(r) \subset U\} \\
&= \{r \in P : head(r) \cup body(r) \subset U\} \\
&= b_U(P).
\end{aligned}
$$

The third step is justified by the definition of stable wrt (U, X), which requires that $U \subset X$, and by the fact that $pos(r) \subset body(r)$. By Proposition 10.1, the consistent answer sets for $c_X(P)$ are the consistent answer sets for P. So we've shown that B is a consistent answer set for $b_U(P)$ iff there is a consistent answer set A for P s.t. $A \cap U = B$. $\square$

Definition. Let x be a variable and t be a ground term in $\mathcal{L}_1$. Then $same\text{-}sort_{\mathcal{L}_2}(x, t)$ if x is a variable in $\mathcal{L}_2$, t is a ground term in $\mathcal{L}_2$ and t has the same sort in $\mathcal{L}_2$ as x does.

Definition. Let $[\neg]Q(t_1, \ldots, t_n) \in Lit(\mathcal{L}_1)$. For all i $(1 \leq i \leq n)$, $well\text{-}sorted_{\mathcal{L}_2}([\neg]Q(t_1, \ldots, t_n), i)$ if there is a literal $[\neg]Q(t'_1, \ldots, t'_n) \in Lit(\mathcal{L}_2)$ s.t. $t_i = t'_i$.

Intuitively, $well\text{-}sorted_{\mathcal{L}_2}([\neg]Q(t_1, \ldots, t_n), i)$ holds if Q is an n-ary predicate symbol of $\mathcal{L}_2$ and t_i is a term of $\mathcal{L}_2$ of the proper sort for the ith argument of Q in $\mathcal{L}_2$.

Definition. Let P be a program with I/O specification σ. Let $\mathcal{L}_1, \mathcal{L}_2$ be permissible languages for P.

$$
G_\sigma^+(\mathcal{H}(P, \mathcal{L}_1), \mathcal{L}_2) = \left\{
\begin{array}{l}
[\neg]Q(t_1, \ldots, t_n) \in Lit(\mathcal{H}(P, \mathcal{L}_1)) : \\
\text{for all } i \ (1 \leq i \leq n), \text{ if } \sigma_{[\neg]Q}(i) = +, \\
\text{then } well\text{-}sorted_{\mathcal{L}_2}([\neg]Q(t_1, \ldots, t_n), i)
\end{array}
\right\}
$$

Intuitively, $G_\sigma^+(\mathcal{H}(P, \mathcal{L}_1), \mathcal{L}_2)$ is the set of literals in $\mathcal{H}(P, \mathcal{L}_1)$ that are well-sorted in $\mathcal{L}_2$ in all argument places that are assigned $+$ by σ.

Lemma 10.6 *Let P be a program that is stable wrt I/O specification σ, with permissible languages $\mathcal{L}_1, \mathcal{L}_2$. Let $U = Lit(\mathcal{L}_1) \cap Lit(\mathcal{L}_2)$. Let $X = U \cup (Lit(\mathcal{L}_1) \setminus G_\sigma^+(\mathcal{H}(P, \mathcal{L}_1), \mathcal{L}_2))$. Program $\mathcal{H}(P, \mathcal{L}_1)$ is stable wrt (U, X).*

Proof. Assume $r \in \mathcal{H}(P, \mathcal{L}_1)$ s.t. $head(r) \cup body(r) \not\subset U$ and $head(r) \not\subset X \setminus U$. We must show that $pos(r) \not\subset X$. There is a rule $R \in P$, which is stable wrt σ, and for some ground substitution θ in $\mathcal{L}_1$, $r = R\theta$. Since $head(r) \cup body(r) \subset Lit(\mathcal{L}_1)$ but $head(r) \cup body(r) \not\subset U$, we conclude that there is a variable z in R s.t. $\neg same\text{-}sort_{\mathcal{L}_2}(z, z\theta)$. Since $head(R\theta) \not\subset X \setminus U$, there is a literal $L \in head(R)$ s.t. $L\theta \notin X \setminus U$. Thus, $L\theta \notin X$ or $L\theta \in U$. If

$L\theta \notin X$, then $L\theta \in G_\sigma^+(\mathcal{H}(P, \mathcal{L}_1), \mathcal{L}_2)$. If $L\theta \in U = Lit(\mathcal{L}_1) \cap Lit(\mathcal{L}_2)$, then clearly, by the definition of G_σ^+, we again have $L\theta \in G_\sigma^+(\mathcal{H}(P, \mathcal{L}_1), \mathcal{L}_2)$. We can conclude that $z \notin FV^+(L)$, since $\neg same\text{-}sort_{\mathcal{L}_2}(z, z\theta)$. By the definition of stable wrt σ, there is an ordering $L_1, \ldots, L_k$ of the literals of $pos(R)$ s.t.

$$[head(R) \neq \emptyset \wedge \forall b \in head(R)[z \in FV^+(b)]]$$
$$\vee$$
$$\exists i \in \{1, \ldots, k\}[z \in FV^-(L_i) \wedge \forall j \in \{1, \ldots, i\}[z \notin FV^+(L_j)]] .$$

Since we have shown that $z \notin FV^+(L)$ and $L \in head(R)$, it follows that

$$\exists i \in \{1, \ldots, k\}[z \in FV^-(L_i) \wedge \forall j \in \{1, \ldots, i\}[z \notin FV^+(L_j)]] .$$

Thus, we have shown that z occurs in some literal in $pos(R)$ and also that $\neg same\text{-}sort_{\mathcal{L}_2}(z, z\theta)$. Now, let L_i be the leftmost literal from $L_1, \ldots, L_k$ with a $y \in FV(L_i)$ s.t. $\neg same\text{-}sort_{\mathcal{L}_2}(y, y\theta)$. Clearly $L_i\theta \notin Lit(\mathcal{L}_2)$, so $L_i\theta \notin U$. It remains to show that $L_i\theta \in G_\sigma^+(\mathcal{H}(P, \mathcal{L}_1), \mathcal{L}_2)$. Since L_i is a literal in $\mathcal{L}_2$, if, for every $x \in FV^+(L_i)$, $same\text{-}sort_{\mathcal{L}_2}(x, x\theta)$, then $L_i\theta \in G_\sigma^+(\mathcal{H}(P, \mathcal{L}_1), \mathcal{L}_2)$, and we are done. So suppose there is an $x \in FV^+(L_i)$ s.t. $\neg same\text{-}sort_{\mathcal{L}_2}(x, x\theta)$. By the definition of stable, we can conclude that $\exists i' \in \{1, \ldots, i-1\}[x \in FV^-(L_{i'})]$, which contradicts our choice of L_i, since L_i is the leftmost literal from $L_1, \ldots, L_k$ with a $y \in FV(L_i)$ s.t. $\neg same\text{-}sort_{\mathcal{L}_2}(y, y\theta)$. So $L_i\theta \in G_\sigma^+(\mathcal{H}(P, \mathcal{L}_1), \mathcal{L}_2)$. We have shown that $L_i\theta \notin U$ and also that $L_i\theta \notin Lit(\mathcal{L}_1) \setminus G_\sigma^+(\mathcal{H}(P, \mathcal{L}_1), \mathcal{L}_2)$. That is, $L_i\theta \notin X$. Since $L_i\theta \in pos(r)$, we've shown that $pos(r) \not\subset X$, which was our goal. $\square$

Lemma 10.7 *Let P be a stable program such that, for every permissible language $\mathcal{L}$ for P, every part of $\mathcal{H}(P, \mathcal{L})$ has a consistent answer set. Let $\mathcal{L}_1, \mathcal{L}_2$ be permissible languages for P, and let $U = Lit(\mathcal{L}_1) \cap Lit(\mathcal{L}_2)$. Then B is a consistent answer set for $b_U(\mathcal{H}(P, \mathcal{L}_1))$ iff there is a consistent answer set A for $\mathcal{H}(P, \mathcal{L}_1)$ s.t. $A \cap U = B$.*

Proof. Suppose P is stable wrt the I/O specification σ. Let $X = U \cup (Lit(\mathcal{L}_1) \setminus G_\sigma^+(\mathcal{H}(P, \mathcal{L}_1), \mathcal{L}_2))$. By Lemma 10.6, $\mathcal{H}(P, \mathcal{L}_1)$ is stable wrt (U, X). Since for every permissible language $\mathcal{L}$ for P, every part of $\mathcal{H}(P, \mathcal{L})$ has a consistent answer set, every part of $\mathcal{H}(P, \mathcal{L}_1)$ has a consistent answer set. Since $U = Lit(\mathcal{L}_1) \cap Lit(\mathcal{L}_2)$, it is clear that every literal in U has its complement in U. So, by Proposition 10.2, B is a consistent answer set for $b_U(\mathcal{H}(P, \mathcal{L}_1))$ iff there is a consistent answer set A for $\mathcal{H}(P, \mathcal{L}_1)$ s.t. $A \cap U = B$. $\square$

Proof. (of Theorem 6.1) Suppose P is stable and for every permissible language $\mathcal{L}$ for P every part of $\mathcal{H}(P, \mathcal{L})$ has a consistent answer set. Let $\mathcal{L}_1, \mathcal{L}_2$ be permissible languages for P. Let $U = Lit(\mathcal{L}_1) \cap Lit(\mathcal{L}_2)$. Then $b_U(\mathcal{H}(P, \mathcal{L}_1)) = b_U(\mathcal{H}(P, \mathcal{L}_2))$. Suppose A_1 is a consistent answer set for $\mathcal{H}(P, \mathcal{L}_1)$. By Lemma 10.7, $A_1 \cap U$ is a consistent answer set for

$b_U(\mathcal{H}(P, \mathcal{L}_1))$. Since $b_U(\mathcal{H}(P, \mathcal{L}_1)) = b_U(\mathcal{H}(P, \mathcal{L}_2))$, $A_1 \cap U$ is a consistent answer set for $b_U(\mathcal{H}(P, \mathcal{L}_2))$. By Lemma 10.7, there is a consistent answer set A_2 for $\mathcal{H}(P, \mathcal{L}_2)$ s.t. $A_2 \cap U = A_1 \cap U$. Since $A_1 \subset Lit(\mathcal{L}_1)$ and $A_2 \subset Lit(\mathcal{L}_2)$, it follows that $A_1 \cap Lit(\mathcal{L}_2) = A_2 \cap Lit(\mathcal{L}_1)$. So P is language tolerant. $\square$

The following straightforward lemmas are used in the proof of Proposition 6.1 and are given here without proof.

Lemma 10.8 *If P is a predicate-order-consistent normal program, then for every permissible language $\mathcal{L}$ for P, $\mathcal{H}(P, \mathcal{L})$ is an order consistent normal program.*

Lemma 10.9 *Every part of an order-consistent normal program is also an order-consistent normal program.*

Proposition 10.3 *([Fages, 1994]) Every order-consistent normal program has an answer set.*

Proof. (of Proposition 6.1) Suppose P is a predicate-order-consistent normal program. By Lemma 10.8, for every permissible language $\mathcal{L}$ for P, $\mathcal{H}(P, \mathcal{L})$ is an order-consistent normal program. By Lemma 10.9, every part of $\mathcal{H}(P, \mathcal{L})$ is also an order-consistent normal program. So, by Proposition 10.3, for every permissible language $\mathcal{L}$, every part of $\mathcal{H}(P, \mathcal{L})$ has an answer set. Since normal programs have only consistent answer sets, the proposition is proved. $\square$

Proof. (of Theorem 6.2) The theorem follows immediately by Proposition 6.1 and Theorem 6.1. $\square$

Proof. (of Proposition 7.2) Let P be a language tolerant program, and let $\mathcal{L}$ be the language that is obtained from $\mathcal{L}_P$ by ignoring sorts. For the left-to-right direction, suppose that A is a consistent answer set for $\mathcal{H}(P, \mathcal{L}_P)$. By the definition of language tolerance, there is a consistent answer set A' for $\mathcal{H}(P, \mathcal{L})$ s.t. $A \cap Lit(\mathcal{L}) = A' \cap Lit(\mathcal{L}_P)$. Since $A \subset Lit(\mathcal{L}_P) \subset Lit(\mathcal{L})$, $A \cap Lit(\mathcal{L}) = A$. So $A = A' \cap Lit(\mathcal{L}_P)$. For the right-to-left direction, suppose there is a consistent answer set A' for $\mathcal{H}(P, \mathcal{L})$, and let $A = A' \cap Lit(\mathcal{L}_P)$. Since P is language tolerant, there is a consistent answer set A'' for $\mathcal{H}(P, \mathcal{L}_P)$ s.t. $A' \cap Lit(\mathcal{L}_P) = A'' \cap Lit(\mathcal{L})$. Since $A'' \subset Lit(\mathcal{L}_P) \subset Lit(\mathcal{L})$, $A' \cap Lit(\mathcal{L}_P) = A''$. So, $A = A''$. Thus, A is a consistent answer set for $\mathcal{H}(P, \mathcal{L}_P)$. $\square$

Acknowledgements

The authors are grateful to Vladimir Lifschitz for useful discussions on the subject of this paper. We are also grateful to Enrico Giunchiglia and G. N. Kartha for their comments. This work was partially supported by the National Science Foundation under grants IRI-9101078 and IRI-9306751.

References

[Fages, 1994] François Fages. Consistency of Clark's completion and existence of stable models. *Journal of Methods of Logic in Computer Science*, 1(1):51–60, 1994. To appear.

[Gelfond and Lifschitz, 1991] Michael Gelfond and Vladimir Lifschitz. Classical negation in logic programs and disjunctive databases. *New Generation Computing*, 9:365–385, 1991.

[Hanks and McDermott, 1987] Steve Hanks and Drew McDermott. Nonmonotonic logic and temporal projection. *Artificial Intelligence*, 33(3):379–412, 1987.

[Lifschitz and Turner, 1994] Vladimir Lifschitz and Hudson Turner. Splitting a logic program. In *Logic Programming: Proceedings of the Eleventh International Conference for Logic Programming*, 1994.

[Lifschitz et al., 1993] Vladimir Lifschitz, Norman McCain, and Hudson Turner. Automated reasoning about actions: a logic programming approach. Manuscript, 1993.

[Lloyd and Topor, 1986] John Lloyd and Rodney Topor. A basis for deductive database systems II. *Journal of Logic Programming*, 1:55–67, 1986.

[Martens and De Schreye, 1992] Bern Martens and Danny De Schreye. A perfect Herbrand semantics for untyped vanilla meta-programming. In *Logic Programming: Proceeding of the Joint International Conference and Symposium*, pages 511–525. MIT Press, 1992.

[Ross, 1994] Kenneth A. Ross. On negation in HiLog. *Journal of Logic Programming*, 18:27–53, 1994.

[Stroetman, 1993] Karl Stroetman. A completeness result for SLDNF resolution. *Journal of Logic Programming*, 15(4):337–355, 1993.

[Topor and Sonenberg, 1988] Rodney Topor and E.A. Sonenberg. On domain independent databases. In Jack Minker, editor, *Foundations of Deductive Databases and Logic Programming*, pages 217–240. Morgan Kaufmann, San Mateo, CA, 1988.

Computing Stable Models by Program Transformation

Jürgen Stuber
Max-Planck-Institut für Informatik
Im Stadtwald
D-66123 Saarbrücken
Germany
juergen@mpi-sb.mpg.de

Abstract

In analogy to the Davis-Putnam procedure we develop a new procedure for computing stable models of propositional normal disjunctive logic programs, using case analysis and simplification. Our procedure enumerates all stable models without repetition and without the need for a minimality check. Since it is not necessary to store the set of stable models explicitly, the procedure runs in polynomial space.

We allow clauses with empty heads, in order to represent truth or falsity of a proposition as a one-literal clause. In particular, a clause of form $\sim A \to$ expresses that A is constrained to be true, without providing a justification for A. Adding this clause to a program restricts its stable models to those containing A, without introducing new stable models. Together with $A \to$ this provides the basis for case analysis.

We present our procedure as a set of rules which transform a program into a set of solved forms, which resembles the standard method for presenting unification algorithms. Rules are sound in the sense that they preserve the set of stable models. A subset of the rules is shown to be complete in the sense that for each stable model a solved form can be obtained. The method allows for concise presentation, flexible choice of a control strategy and simple correctness proofs.

1 Introduction

Stable models have been introduced by Gelfond and Lifschitz [6] as a semantics for logic programs. After some early approaches [10, 4] recently the interest in their computation has grown [5, 7, 11, 1]. In particular, the stable model semantics is suitable for implementing nonmonotonic deductive databases.

In this paper we present a new procedure which computes the stable models of a normal disjunctive logic program (a normal deductive database). For infinite Herbrand bases the problem is known to be infeasible in general.

There may exists continuum many stable models, and the problem of deciding whether a recursively enumerable interpretation is a stable model is Π_2^0-hard [9]. Therefore we limit ourselves to the finite case, like all other currently known methods for computing stable models. This still includes the practically important case of datalog programs.

Several methods build stable models bottom-up, using clauses in the forward direction. For clauses whose premises are satisfied in a partially built interpretation, one proposition of the head is made true, which requires a case split for disjunctive clauses. The propositions of the negative premises are recorded to be false, either by collecting them in a separate set or by adding special literals to the interpretation. An interpretation is discarded if an inconsistency is detected. Saccà and Zaniolo [10] give a procedure which finds a single stable model of a normal non-disjunctive program. Nevertheless it can easily be modified to allow enumerating all stable models. However, because clauses with independent assumptions may be considered in any order, a stable model may be generated many times. Fernandez and Minker [5] and Inoue et al. [7] compute stable models of normal disjunctive programs. To cope with disjunction they explicitly store sets of models in order to test for minimality, which may require exponential space in the worst case.

Subrahmanian et al. [11] use case analysis on the truth or falsity of atoms to compute stable models of normal programs. Candidates for stable models are stored and explicitly tested for minimality. The well-founded semantics, which can be computed efficiently, is used to approximate the stable models; thereby the number of cases which need to be considered is reduced. Bell et al. [1] compute models of the Clarke completion $comp(P)$ of a normal program P, which are then tested for being stable. The advantage of this approach is that techniques for solving classical satisfiability problems—in their case cutting planes for integer programming problems—are well developed and efficient. Eshghi [4] uses the Assumption-based Truth Maintenance System (ATMS) for computing stable models of non-disjunctive programs. It starts with inconsistent assumptions and relaxes them until stable models are reached. Its representation of minimal sets of inconsistent assumptions (nogoods) and minimal sets of assumptions needed to derive a certain proposition (environments) may also require exponential space in the worst case.

Our procedure uses case analysis with respect to the truth-value of propositions, in analogy to Davis and Putnam [2]. This enables it to enumerate the stable models for finite propositional normal disjunctive logic programs without repetitions and without the need to explicitly test for minimality. Rather than testing afterwards, we take care to preserve minimality during computation. Each model is generated only once because cases do not overlap.

Eiter and Gottlob [3] have shown that deciding whether a stable model exists is Σ_2-complete in the polynomial hierarchy. Our procedure reflects this result; it uses nondeterministic polynomial time, and the disjunction rule uses *SAT* from *NP* as an oracle.

Our procedure tries to transform a normal disjunctive logic program into sets of clauses in solved form which for each proposition contain exactly one of the clauses $A \to$ or $\to A$.[1] This makes determining its stable model trivial. One-literal clauses play a special role in our procedure, since they are used to represent truth or falsity of a proposition, as specified by the following table.

$A \to$	A is false
$\to A$	A is true and justified
$\sim A \to$	A is true but not justified

A true but unjustified proposition acts as a constraint; it does not help in the construction of a stable model, but is used to check the truth of A after the model has been constructed. Operationally, if $A \to$ is ever added to a program containing $\sim A \to$, an inconsistency results. $A \to$ or $\to A$ are used to simplify the program, removing all other occurrences of A. With $\sim A \to$ we may remove clauses containing $\sim A$—these are subsumed—and we may reduce positive premises A from clauses with an empty head. Other simplifications are not possible because we have to be careful not to add unwarranted justification for A. Another use of $\sim A \to$ is to block case analysis on A, since then its truth-value is already known. The basis for case analysis is the observation that adding alternatively $A \to$ or $\sim A \to$ to a program P splits its set of stable models exactly into the two sets of stable models of the new programs. One contains all stable models of P where A is false while the other contains those where A is true.

Case analysis and simplification are sufficient to compute all stable models of non-disjunctive programs. For disjunctive programs only a very restricted case remains open, where the constraints specify exactly one possible stable model. It remains to test whether the disjunctions provide justification for all propositions constrained to true. To this end it is necessary to prove the validity of certain classical implications. Any procedure for tautology checking in classical propositional logic may be employed, for instance classical Davis-Putnam.

We prove the soundness of some other rules which are not needed for completeness but which may speed up the computation, namely Tautology elimination, Factoring and Default negation. Default negation corresponds to the Purity rule of the classical Davis-Putnam procedure for the case of propositions which don't appear positively. It is our only nonmonotonic rule.

For programs without a stable model Inoue et al. [7] distinguish between *inconsistent* and *incoherent* programs. Incoherent programs are those which do not allow to derive an inconsistency, but which have no stable model for lack of justification. Suppose we do not use the Default negation rule. Then an incoherent program is transformed into at least one program which is reduced with respect to our rules, not solved and does not contain the

---

[1] Note that we allow clauses with empty heads.

empty clause. The distinction between solved forms and reduced incoherent programs will then be the only source of nonmonotonicity. If incremental computation is desired, one may store these reduced incoherent programs and resume the computation when new clauses are added.

We present our procedure as a set of rules which transform a program into a set of solved forms, which resembles the standard method for presenting unification algorithms. Rules are sound in the sense that they preserve the set of stable models. Subsets of the rules are shown to be complete for non-disjunctive and disjunctive programs, in the sense that for each stable model a solved form can be obtained. This presentation has several advantages. Soundness, termination and completeness can be proven with relative ease. It is made precise which transformations are necessary to achieve completeness, while more sound transformation may be used where appropriate. Any inference system between these boundaries is sound and complete. We also make precise which choices can be made eagerly, and where alternative cases have to be considered.

2 Preliminaries

See Lloyd [8] for an introduction to logic programming. $\uplus$ denotes disjoint union. We assume a fixed set of propositions $Prop$. A (normal disjunctive) clause C is a triple $\langle Prem^+(C), Prem^\sim(C), Concl(C)\rangle$ of sets of propositions $Prem^+(C) = \{A_1, \ldots, A_n\}$, $Prem^\sim(C) = \{B_1, \ldots, B_m\}$ and $Concl(C) = \{D_1, \ldots, D_k\}$, which is written

$$A_1, \ldots, A_n, \sim B_1, \ldots, \sim B_m \to D_1, \ldots, D_k.$$

Given $\Gamma = A_1, \ldots, A_n$ we write $\sim \cdot \Gamma$ for $\sim A_1, \ldots, \sim A_n$. A clause C is *non-disjunctive* if $k \leq 1$ and *negation-free* if $m = 0$. A (normal disjunctive logic) program is a set of clauses. A program is *non-disjunctive* if all its clauses are non-disjunctive. We write $Prog$ for the set of programs, and $NProg$ for the set of non-disjunctive programs.

An *interpretation* I is a set of propositions. I satisfies a negation-free clause C, written $I \models C$, iff $Prem^+(C) \not\subseteq I$ or $Concl(C) \cap I \neq \emptyset$. I satisfies a negation-free program P, written $I \models P$, iff it satisfies all clauses in P. In this case we also say that I is a *model* of P. The set of models of P is denoted by $Mod(P)$. P' is a *logical consequence* of P, written $P \models P'$, if $Mod(P) \subseteq Mod(P')$. An $I \in Mod(P)$ is *minimal* if there exists no $J \in Mod(P)$ such that J is a proper subset of I. $Min(P)$ denotes the set of minimal models of a program P. For a program P let $\tilde{P}$ be the program where each literal $\sim A$ is replaced by a new proposition $\tilde{A}$. Analogously define $\tilde{C}$ for a clause C. Let $\widetilde{Prop} = \{\tilde{A} \mid A \in Prop\}$.

Gelfond and Lifschitz [6] define a transformation on logic programs which eliminates all literals $\sim A$ from a program P based on an interpretation I, where $\sim A$ is treated as true if A is not in I. For an interpretation I, a clause C and a program P let

$$GL_I(C) = \begin{cases} \{Prem^+(C) \to Concl(C)\} & \text{if } Prem^\sim(C) \cap I = \emptyset \\ \emptyset & \text{otherwise} \end{cases}$$

$$GL_I(P) = \bigcup_{C \in P} GL_I(C)$$

If $GL_I(C) = \emptyset$ we say GL_I *eliminates* C. $GL_I(P)$ is called the *Gelfond-Lifschitz transformation* of P with respect to I. An interpretation I is called a *stable model* of P if I is a minimal model of $GL_I(P)$. We write $Stab(P)$ for the set of stable models of P. If we restrict this to the case of non-disjunctive clauses we get the original notion of stable model as defined by Gelfond and Lifschitz [6].

3   Transformation rules

To describe our procedure we will use transformation rules on programs. They allow to take whole program into account, which is necessary to make nonmonotonic inferences. A program will be transformed into a set of solved forms, which correspond to the programs stable models.

A program P is *in solved form* if it consists of clauses of form $A \to$ or $\to A$ with exactly one clause for each proposition A. For a program P in solved form we define the corresponding interpretation I_P as $\{\, A \mid \to A \in P \,\}$. On the other hand an interpretation I corresponds to the program in solved form $P_I = \{\, \to A \mid A \in I \,\} \cup \{\, A \to \mid A \in Prop - I \,\}$.

Lemma 3.1 *Let P be a program. If P is in solved form then $Stab(P) = \{I_P\}$.*

A *transformation relation* is a subset $\vdash$ of $Prog \times Prog$. We write $\vdash^*$ for its reflexive-transitive closure. A transformation rule r is a set of instances $\rho = \frac{P}{P_1|\dots|P_n}$. An instance ρ defines a transformation relation $\vdash_\rho$ where $P \vdash_\rho P'$ if $\rho = \frac{P}{\dots|P'|\dots}$. To a rule r the associated transformation relation is $\vdash_r = \bigcup_{\rho \in r} \vdash_\rho$. Similarly, for a set of rules R we define $\vdash_R = \bigcup_{r \in R} \vdash_r$. We also say ρ is an instance of R.[2] We say P is *R-reduced* if there exists no P' such that $P \vdash_R P'$.

A *strategy* $\vdash_S$ for R is a subrelation of $\vdash_R$ such that if P is not R-reduced then $(\vdash_\rho) \subseteq (\vdash_S)$ for some instance ρ of R. I.e., it is sufficient to eagerly apply some arbitrarily chosen rule. Rules with more than one conclusion encode the control information that several alternatives must be considered, either by backtracking or in parallel.

Let $\vdash$ be a transformation relation, R a set of transformation rules and $\mathcal{P}$ a class of logic programs. $\vdash$ is *sound* if $P \vdash P'$ implies $Stab(P) =$

---

[2]We do this two-step construction, since we want to keep track which instances belong to the same rule, without specifying formally how to instantiate the schemas defining rules.

$\bigcup_{P \vdash P'} Stab(P')$. $\vdash$ is complete with respect to $\mathcal{P}$ if $Stab(P) = \{ I_{P'} \mid P \vdash^* P' \text{ and } P' \text{ is in solved form} \}$ for all P in $\mathcal{P}$. $\vdash$ is *terminating* if there exists no infinite sequence $P_0 \vdash P_1 \vdash P_2 \vdash \dots$. $\vdash$ *preserves* $\mathcal{P}$ if $P \in \mathcal{P}$ and $P \vdash P'$ implies $P' \in \mathcal{P}$. R preserves $\mathcal{P}$ if $\vdash_R$ preserves $\mathcal{P}$. R is *sound, terminating* or *complete* if every strategy for R is sound, terminating or complete, respectively. A set of transformation rules R is *independent* with respect to $\mathcal{P}$ if there is no proper subset R' of R such that R' is complete with respect to $\mathcal{P}$.

Lemma 3.2 *Let R be a set of transformation rules.*

1. *If $\vdash_r$ is sound for all r in R then $\vdash_R$ is sound.*

2. *R is sound if and only if $\vdash_\rho$ is sound for all instances ρ of R.*

Proof: (1) If $\vdash_r$ is sound for all r in R then $Stab(P) = \bigcup_{P \vdash_r P'} Stab(P')$ for all r in R. Hence $\bigcup_{P \vdash_R P'} Stab(P') = \bigcup_{r \in R} \bigcup_{P \vdash_r P'} Stab(P') = \bigcup_{r \in R} Stab(P) = Stab(P)$.

(2) Suppose $\vdash_r$ is sound for all r in R, then $\vdash_R$ is sound by (1). By definition $P \vdash_S P'$ implies $P \vdash_R P'$. Thus $\bigcup_{P \vdash_S P'} Stab(P') \subseteq \bigcup_{P \vdash_R P'} Stab(P') = Stab(P)$. On the other hand, $\{ P' \mid P \vdash_\rho P' \} \subseteq \{ P' \mid P' \vdash_S P' \}$ for some instance ρ of R, and thus $Stab(P) = \bigcup_{P \vdash_\rho P'} Stab(P') \subseteq \bigcup_{P \vdash_S P'} Stab(P')$.

For the converse, assume that R is sound, but $\vdash_\rho$ is not sound for some instance $\rho = \frac{P}{P_1 | \dots | P_n}$ of R. Then $Stab(P) \neq \bigcup_{1 \leq i \leq n} Stab(P_i)$. We may choose $\vdash_S$ such that $P \vdash_S P'$ iff $P \vdash_r P'$, which makes $\vdash_S$ unsound. $\qquad \square$

4   Sound program transformations

We first state the soundness of some general program transformation rules. Later we will use this to show soundness of the specific transformation rules of our procedure for computing stable models.

We call clauses of form $A, \Gamma \rightarrow A, \Delta$ *standard tautologies* and clauses of form $A, \sim A, \Gamma \rightarrow \Delta$ *constraint tautologies*. Tautologies are always satisfied and do not contribute to the meaning of a program. We may remove tautologies.

Tautology elimination $\dfrac{\{C\} \uplus P}{P}$ if C is a tautology.

We have two different inference rules for resolution. We may resolve a negative literal either with a positive or a constraint literal. In the latter case a first approach might be the following inference rule.

Naïve constraint resolution $\dfrac{\sim A, \Gamma \rightarrow \Delta \qquad A, \Lambda \rightarrow \Pi}{\Gamma, \Lambda \rightarrow \Delta, \Pi}$

But with this rule it is possible to create new justification for the propositions in Π. The simplest example is the program $P = \{\sim p \rightarrow ; p \rightarrow p\}$, which has no stable model. Naïve constraint resolution would add the clause $\rightarrow p$, which leads to the stable model $\{p\}$. Therefore we will adopt the following inference rules for resolution.

Standard resolution
$$\frac{\Gamma \rightarrow \Delta, A \qquad A, \Lambda \rightarrow \Pi}{\Gamma, \Lambda \rightarrow \Delta, \Pi}$$

Constraint resolution
$$\frac{\sim A, \Gamma \rightarrow \Delta \qquad A, \Lambda \rightarrow \Pi}{\Gamma, \Lambda, \sim \cdot \Pi \rightarrow \Delta}$$

The conclusion of such a resolution inference is called a *resolvent* of the premises. We may add resolvents.

Resolution $\qquad \dfrac{P}{\{C\} \cup P} \qquad$ if C is a resolvent of two clauses in P.

Subsumption is useful to remove clauses which are already implied by the program, in order to reduce the size of the program. Moreover, we will use it to explicitly remove clauses which are satisfied. Note the interaction between positive and constraint literals. In particular, $\rightarrow A$ subsumes $\sim A \rightarrow$. A clause C' *subsumes* a clause C if $Prem^+(C') \subseteq Prem^+(C)$, $Prem^\sim(C') \subseteq Prem^\sim(C)$ and $Concl(C') \subseteq Concl(C) \cup Prem^\sim(C)$. We may remove subsumed clauses.

Subsumption $\qquad \dfrac{\{C, C'\} \uplus P}{\{C'\} \uplus P} \qquad$ if C' subsumes C.

A clause $\sim A, \Gamma \rightarrow \Delta$ is called a *factor* of $\sim A, \Gamma \rightarrow A, \Delta$. Note that a proposition cannot appear twice in the same role in a clause, since for each clause the positive premises, the negative premises and the conclusions form sets. Hence we do not have other factoring rules.

Factoring $\qquad \dfrac{P}{\{C\} \cup P} \qquad$ if C is a factor of a clause in P.

We can explain the effect of a clause with negative loop like $\sim p \rightarrow p$ by observing that it can be factored to $\sim p \rightarrow$. Hence it constrains p to be true. The classical Davis-Putnam procedure has a Purity-rule, which stipulates a propositions to be true if it only appears in positive positions and false if it only appears in negative positions. Since we need to preserve minimality, we can only do the latter here. In fact, if a proposition does not appear in any head of a clause it cannot be true in a stable model.[3]

Default negation $\qquad \dfrac{P}{\{A \rightarrow\} \cup P} \qquad$ if no head of a clause in P contains A.

---

[3]In practice it would be useful to have a better criterion, like being false in the least model of some definite program approximating the normal disjunctive one under consideration [11].

In contrast to the other rules in this section, Split is not an equivalence transformation on programs, but generates two programs whose combined semantics is equivalent to the original. The two cases correspond to A being either true or false.

Split
$$\frac{P}{\{A \to\} \uplus P \quad | \quad \{\sim A \to\} \uplus P}$$

Unlike in the classical Davis-Putnam procedure, case analysis is not sufficient to cope with disjunctive programs in the case of stable semantics. We can remove all false disjuncts by resolution with the negative fact $A \to$, but if in a minimal model more than one disjunct is true the constraint $\sim A \to$ is too weak to remove the disjunction.

Disjunction
$$\frac{\{\to A_1, \ldots, A_n\} \uplus P}{\{\to A_1; \ldots; \to A_n; \to A_1, \ldots, A_n\} \cup P}$$
if $n \geq 2$ and $\tilde{P} \cup \{\to A_1, \ldots, A_n\} \models \{\to A_1; \ldots; \to A_n\}$.

Disjunction factors out the problem, thereby enabling us to apply any suitable method to it. For instance, we may check if $\tilde{P} \cup \{\to A_1, \ldots, A_n\} \cup \{A_1, \ldots, A_n \to\}$ is inconsistent by using a classical Davis-Putnam procedure.

Theorem 4.1 *Subsumption, Tautology elimination, Factoring, Resolution, Default negation, Disjunction and Split are sound transformation rules.*

Proof: (Sketch) Except for the case of Split we have two programs P_1 and P_2 with $P_1 \subseteq P_2$. Given an interpretation I, one shows that I is a minimal model of $GL_I(P_1)$ if and only if it is a minimal model of $GL_I(P_2)$. This can be done by showing that J is a model of $GL_I(P_2)$ from the assumptions that I is a model of $GL_I(P_1)$, J is a not necessarily proper subset of I and J is a minimal model of $GL_I(P_1)$. The proof for Split is straightforward. $\square$

5 The Davis-Putnam procedure

Factoring, Disjunction and certain Resolution transformations add clauses which subsume a clause in their premise. We may remove this clause by subsumption. In combination this yields simplification rules which decrease the size of the program. Moreover, we will also use Tautology elimination and Subsumption for simplification, and in particular subsumption with respect to one-literal clauses, as this can be implemented most efficiently.

Split, Disjunction, Default negation and Constraint propagation add one-literal clauses, thereby decreasing the number of propositions whose truth value is unknown. When proving termination, we will give this decrease precedence over the increase in size. Also, the increase in size is at most linear in the number of propositions. We call a proposition A *unknown* in P if it doesn't appear in a one-literal clause in P.

Subsumption-true (SubT)

$$\frac{\{\Gamma \to \Delta, A; \to A\} \uplus P}{\{\to A\} \uplus P}$$

Subsumption-false (SubF)

$$\frac{\{\Gamma, A \to \Delta; A \to\} \uplus P}{\{A \to\} \uplus P}$$

Subsumption-constraint (SubC)

$$\frac{\{\Gamma, \sim A \to \Delta; \sim A \to\} \uplus P}{\{\sim A \to\} \uplus P}$$

GL-Subsumption (SubGL)

$$\frac{\{\Gamma, \sim A \to \Delta; \to A\} \uplus P}{\{\to A\} \uplus P}$$

Reduction-true (RedT)

$$\frac{\{\Gamma, A \to \Delta; \to A\} \uplus P}{\{\Gamma \to \Delta\} \cup \{\to A\} \cup P}$$

Reduction-false (RedF)

$$\frac{\{\Gamma \to \Delta, A; A \to\} \uplus P}{\{\Gamma \to \Delta\} \cup \{A \to\} \cup P}$$

Reduction-constraint (RedC)

$$\frac{\{\Gamma, A \to; \sim A \to\} \uplus P}{\{\Gamma \to\} \cup \{\sim A \to\} \cup P}$$

GL-Reduction (RedGL)

$$\frac{\{\Gamma, \sim A \to \Delta; A \to\} \uplus P}{\{\Gamma \to \Delta\} \cup \{A \to\} \cup P}$$

Split (Split)

$$\frac{P}{\{A \to\} \uplus P \quad | \quad \{\sim A \to\} \uplus P}$$

if A is unknown in P.

Disjunction (Disj)

$$\frac{\{\to A_1, \ldots, A_n\} \uplus P}{\{\to A_1; \ldots; \to A_n\} \cup P}$$

if $n \geq 2$, for some $1 \leq i \leq n$ neither $A_i \to$ nor $\to A_i$ is in P and $\tilde{P} \cup \{\to A_1, \ldots, A_n\} \models \{\to A_1; \ldots; \to A_n\}$.

Constraint propagation (CP)

$$\frac{\{A_1, \ldots, A_n \to B; \sim A_1 \to; \ldots; \sim A_n \to\} \uplus P}{\{\sim B \to; A_1, \ldots, A_n \to B; \sim A_1 \to; \ldots; \sim A_n \to\} \uplus P}$$

if B is unknown in P.

Default negation (DN)

$$\frac{P}{\{A \to\} \uplus P}$$

if P contains no clause of form $\Gamma \to \Delta, A$ and $A \to$ is not already in P.

Tautology elimination (TE)

$$\frac{\{C\} \uplus P}{P} \qquad \text{if } C \text{ is a tautology.}$$

Factoring (F)
$$\frac{\{\sim A, \Gamma \to A, \Delta\} \uplus P}{\{\sim A, \Gamma \to \Delta\} \cup P}$$

Let *Full* be the set of all transformation rules defined in this section. Furthermore we define the following particular subsets of *Full*:

$$Norm = \{SubF, SubGL, RedT, RedGL, Split\}$$
$$Disj = Norm \cup \{SubT, RedF, Disj\}$$

We will show that these are complete and independent for their respective classes of programs. Note that the Gelfond-Lifschitz transformation essentially uses the transformation rules $GL = \{SubGL, RedGL\}$, i.e., $P \cup P_I \vdash_{GL}^*$ $GL_I(P) \cup P_I$.

Theorem 5.1 *Every subset of Full is sound.*

Proof: It is sufficient to show $Stab(P) = \bigcup_{1 \le i \le n} Stab(P_i)$ for every rule instance $\frac{P}{P_1 | \dots | P_n}$ of *Full*. The subsumption rules are instances of the general subsumption rule. The reduction rules can be obtained from Resolution followed by Subsumption. Disjunction and Factoring can be obtained from the general rules followed by Subsumption. Constraint propagation is an instance of Resolution. Default negation, Tautology elimination and Split are exactly the general rules. Thus soundness follows from theorem 4.1. $\square$

Theorem 5.2 *Every subset R of Full is terminating. Moreover, the length of a derivation $P \vdash \dots \vdash P'$ is polynomial in the size of P for any $(\vdash) \subseteq$ $(\vdash_{Full})$.*

Proof: To each program we associate a complexity measure $c(P) = 2U(P) + 2U'(P) + |P|$ where $U(P)$ is the set of unknown propositions in P, $U'(P)$ is the set of propositions A such that P neither contains $A \to$ nor $\to A$ and $|P|$ is the number of literal occurrences in P. All subsumption and reduction rules, Tautology elimination and Factoring don't increase $2U(P) + 2U'(P)$ and strictly decrease $|P|$. Disjunction, Default negation, Split and Constraint propagation strictly decrease $2U(P) + 2U'(P)$ by at least two, while Disjunction doesn't increase $|P|$ and Default negation, Split and Constraint propagation increase $|P|$ by one. Thus every rule strictly decreases $c(P)$ and every derivation in $\vdash_{Full}$ starting from P can have at most length $c(P)$. Since any strategy for a subset of *Full* is a subset of $\vdash_{Full}$ we conclude that every subset of *Full* is terminating. $\square$

Our transformation rules allow a great variety of strategies, but only a few will be reasonable in a practical sense. Tautology elimination and Factoring need to be used only at the beginning, since no rule introduces a tautology or a factorable clause. The simplification rules, Constraint propagation and Default negation should be used exhaustively before applying Split. For the selection of the literal to use for splitting, heuristics known from classical Davis-Putnam procedures, like selecting propositions from short clauses, should be useful. We conjecture that in practice Disjunction will be applicable rarely. Since it is expensive to test its condition, it is reasonable to try it only if no other rule is applicable. In this case for a disjunction $\rightarrow A_1, \ldots, A_n$ there exist clauses $\sim A_1 \rightarrow; \ldots; \sim A_n \rightarrow$ and a stable model can only be reached if all A_i become true. We may abort a branch of our computation once the empty clause signals an inconsistency. For instance, to determine the stable models of $P = \{\rightarrow p, q; \sim p \rightarrow p; p, \sim q \rightarrow r\}$ the following would be a typical computation.

$$
\begin{array}{l}
\quad\quad\quad\quad\quad \mathrm{F} \dfrac{\{\rightarrow p, q; \sim p \rightarrow p; p, \sim q \rightarrow r\}}{\{\rightarrow p, q; \sim p \rightarrow; p, \sim q \rightarrow r\}} \\[4pt]
\text{Split} \;\; \overline{\rule{0pt}{10pt}} \\[-2pt]
\text{RedF} \;\; \dfrac{\{q \rightarrow; \rightarrow p, q; \sim p \rightarrow; p, \sim q \rightarrow r\}}{\{q \rightarrow; \rightarrow p; \sim p \rightarrow; p, \sim q \rightarrow r\}} \quad\Big|\quad
\dfrac{\{\sim q \rightarrow; \rightarrow p, q; \sim p \rightarrow;}{} \\
\text{SubGL} \;\; \\
\text{RedGL} \;\; \dfrac{\{q \rightarrow; \rightarrow p; p, \sim q \rightarrow r\}}{\{q \rightarrow; \rightarrow p; p \rightarrow r\}} \\
\text{RedT} \;\; \dfrac{}{\{q \rightarrow; \rightarrow p; \rightarrow r\}}
\end{array}
$$

Split
RedF
SubGL
RedGL
RedT

Left branch:

$$\mathrm{F}\ \dfrac{\{\rightarrow p, q; \sim p \rightarrow p; p, \sim q \rightarrow r\}}{\{\rightarrow p, q; \sim p \rightarrow; p, \sim q \rightarrow r\}}$$

$$\dfrac{\{q \rightarrow; \rightarrow p, q; \sim p \rightarrow; p, \sim q \rightarrow r\}}{\{q \rightarrow; \rightarrow p; \sim p \rightarrow; p, \sim q \rightarrow r\}}$$

$$\dfrac{\{q \rightarrow; \rightarrow p; p, \sim q \rightarrow r\}}{\{q \rightarrow; \rightarrow p; p \rightarrow r\}}$$

$$\{q \rightarrow; \rightarrow p; \rightarrow r\}$$

solved, $I_P = \{p, r\}$

Right branch:

$$\dfrac{\{\sim q \rightarrow; \rightarrow p, q; \sim p \rightarrow; p, \sim q \rightarrow r\}}{\{\sim q \rightarrow; \rightarrow p, q; \sim p \rightarrow\}} \;\; \text{SubC}$$

$$\dfrac{}{\{r \rightarrow; \sim q \rightarrow; \rightarrow p, q; \sim p \rightarrow\}} \;\; \text{DN}$$

incoherent, no model

We get the result $Stab(P) = \{\{p, r\}\}$.

The other procedures for computing stable models of disjunctive programs do a case analysis with respect to which proposition of the conclusion becomes true. As a consequence some implied proposition may also become true, and the resulting model need not be minimal. Hence they need an explicit minimality check. We do case analysis whether an atom is false or constrained to true. With a false proposition we can reduce a disjunction while preserving minimality. However, we cannot reduce a disjunction with respect to a clause $\sim A \rightarrow$, hence we get a residual case where all atoms in the disjunction are constrained to be true. The Disjunction rule is then used to handle this special situation. The following derivations illustrates what happens for two critical example programs. First consider $P = \{\rightarrow p, q; p \rightarrow q\}$.

$$
\begin{array}{ll}
\text{Split} & \dfrac{\{\rightarrow p, q; p \rightarrow q\}}{} \\[6pt]
\text{RedF} & \dfrac{\{p \rightarrow; \rightarrow p, q; p \rightarrow q\}}{\{p \rightarrow; \rightarrow q; p \rightarrow q\}} \quad\Big|\quad \dfrac{\{\sim p \rightarrow; \rightarrow p, q; p \rightarrow q\}}{\{\sim q \rightarrow; \sim p \rightarrow; \rightarrow p, q; p \rightarrow q\}} \;\; \text{CP} \\[6pt]
\text{SubF} & \dfrac{}{\{p \rightarrow; \rightarrow q\}}
\end{array}
$$

solved, $I_P = \{q\}$ \qquad incoherent, no model

In the right branch Disjunction is not applicable, since p is not a consequence of P. By adding the clause $q \rightarrow p$ we get an example where Disjunction is needed. Note that this computation is an extension of the previous one, which illustrates the possibility of incremental computation.

$$
\begin{array}{l}
\text{Split} \ \dfrac{\{\to p, q; p \to q; q \to p\}}{} \\[2pt]
\text{RedF} \ \dfrac{\{p \to; \to p, q; p \to q; q \to p\} \quad | \quad \{\sim p \to; \to p, q; p \to q; q \to p\}}{} \ \text{CP} \\[2pt]
\text{RedT} \ \dfrac{\{p \to; \to q; p \to q; q \to p\}}{} \qquad \dfrac{\{\sim q \to; \sim p \to; \to p, q;}{} \\[2pt]
\text{RedT} \ \dfrac{\{p \to; \to q; p \to q; \to p\}}{} \qquad \dfrac{p \to q; q \to p\}}{} \ \text{Disj} \\[2pt]
\{\Box; \to q; p \to q; \to p\} \qquad \{\sim q \to; \sim p \to; \to p; \to q;
\end{array}
$$

inconsistent, no model

$$
\dfrac{p \to q; q \to p\}}{\vdots}
$$

$$
\overline{\{\to p; \to q\}}
$$

solved, $I_P = \{p, q\}$

5.1   Completeness

Lemma 5.3 *Full preserves NProg.*

Proof: Observe that no transformation rule introduces new literals into the conclusion. $\qquad\Box$

Theorem 5.4 *Norm is complete and independent for NProg.*

Proof: To prove completeness it suffices to show that a *Norm*-reduced program which is not in solved form has no stable models. Then we will eventually obtain the solved forms for all stable models since every strategy has to apply some rule for non-reduced programs, and since *Norm* is terminating and sound.

Suppose P is *Norm*-reduced. Then Split assures that for every proposition A either $A \to$, $\to A$ or $\sim A \to$ is in P. Assume that for each proposition there exists one clause of form $A \to$ or $\to A$, but that P is not in solved form because P contains some additional clause C. If $C = \Box$ then $Stab(P) = \emptyset$ and we are done. P doesn't contain both $A \to$ and $\to A$ since Reduction-true is not applicable. Hence the premise of C cannot be empty, and we can apply some rule according to the following table, contradicting that P is reduced.

	$A \to$	$\to A$
$A, \Gamma \to \Delta$	Subsumption-false	Reduction-true
$\sim A, \Gamma \to \Delta$	GL-Reduction	GL-Subsumption

Hence we may now assume that the set of all propositions A such that P contains neither $A \to$ nor $\to A$ is nonempty. Let us call this set U. From the table above we also know that the premises of clauses in P which are not of form $A \to$ or $\to A$ contain only propositions from U, since otherwise some transformation is possible. Since the Split rule is not applicable, P contains a clause $\sim A \to$ for each A in U. Hence P has the form

$$
\underbrace{\begin{matrix} L_{11}, \ldots, L_{1k_1} \to \Delta_1 \\ \vdots \\ L_{n1}, \ldots, L_{nk_n} \to \Delta_n \end{matrix}}_{P'} \quad \underbrace{\begin{matrix} \sim B_1 \to \\ \vdots \\ \sim B_m \to \end{matrix}}_{P_U} \quad \underbrace{\begin{matrix} \to B_1' \\ \vdots \\ \to B_{m'}' \end{matrix}}_{P_T} \quad \underbrace{\begin{matrix} B_1'' \to \\ \vdots \\ B_{m''}'' \to \end{matrix}}_{P_F}
$$

where $n, m', m'' \geq 0$, $m \geq 1$, $|\Delta_i| \leq 1$, $k_i + |\Delta_i| \geq 2$, $U = \{B_1, \ldots, B_m\}$, $T = \{B_1', \ldots, B_{m'}'\}$ and $F = \{B_1'', \ldots, B_{m''}''\}$ are pairwise disjoint, and all L_{ij} are of form B or $\sim B$ for B in U. Then P has at most the stable model $I = T \cup U$. $P_1 = GL_I(P)$ eliminates all clauses with negative literals. We will show that $J = T$ is a model of P_1. It satisfies $GL_I(P_T) = P_T$, $GL_I(P_F) = P_F$ and $GL_I(P_U) = \emptyset$. To see that J satisfies $GL_I(P')$, observe that any clause in $GL_I(P')$ has at least one positive premise from U. We conclude that I is not minimal and $Stab(P) = \emptyset$.

To prove independence we exhibit for each rule r in $Norm$ a program in $NProg$ which is $(Norm - \{r\})$-reduced, not in solved form and has a stable model.

Rule	Program	Stable models
Reduction-true (RedT)	$\{p \to q; \to p; \to q\}$	$\{p, q\}$
GL-Reduction (RedGL)	$\{\sim p \to q; p \to; \to q\}$	$\{q\}$
Subsumption-false (SubF)	$\{p, q \to; p \to; q \to\}$	$\emptyset$
GL-Subsumption (SubGL)	$\{\sim p \to; \to p\}$	$\{p\}$
Split	$\{\sim p \to q; \sim q \to p\}$	$\{p\}, \{q\}$

$\square$

Theorem 5.5 *Disj is complete and independent for Prog.*

Proof: As in the completeness proof for *Norm* we will show that a *Disj*-reduced program which is not in solved form has no stable model. Suppose P is a *Disj*-reduced program. Then it is also *Norm*-reduced, and has the following form.

$$
\underbrace{\begin{matrix} L_{11}, \ldots, L_{1k_1} \to \Delta_1 \\ \vdots \\ L_{n1}, \ldots, L_{nk_n} \to \Delta_n \end{matrix}}_{P'} \quad \underbrace{\begin{matrix} \sim B_1 \to \\ \vdots \\ \sim B_m \to \end{matrix}}_{P_U} \quad \underbrace{\begin{matrix} \to B_1' \\ \vdots \\ \to B_{m'}' \end{matrix}}_{P_T} \quad \underbrace{\begin{matrix} B_1'' \to \\ \vdots \\ B_{m''}'' \to \end{matrix}}_{P_F}
$$

where $n, m', m'' \geq 0$, $m \geq 1$, $k_i + |\Delta_i| \geq 2$, $U = \{B_1, \ldots, B_m\}$, $T = \{B_1', \ldots, B_{m'}'\}$ and $F = \{B_1'', \ldots, B_{m''}''\}$ are pairwise disjoint, and all L_{ij} are of form B or $\sim B$ for B in U. Moreover, SubT and RedF ensure that $\Delta_i \subseteq U$. Then P has at most the stable model $I = T \cup U$ and $GL_I(P) = GL_I(P') \cup P_T \cup P_F$, where $GL_I(P')$ contains exactly the negation-free clauses of P'.

Now suppose Disjunction is not applicable. If $k_i > 0$ for all i then $J = T$ is a model of $GL_I(P)$, hence I is not minimal.

If there exists a clause with $k_i = 0$, but $\tilde{P} \cup \{\to A_1, \ldots, A_l\} \not\models \{\to A_1; \ldots;$ $\to A_l\}$ then there exists an interpretations M of $\tilde{P} \cup \{\to A_1, \ldots, A_l\}$ such that $A_j \notin M$ for some $1 \leq j \leq l$. Because of P_U all propositions $\tilde{B}$ for B in U are false in M. Let $J = M \cap Prop$, then $J \models GL_I(P)$, $J \subseteq (T \cup U) \setminus \{A_j\} \subset T \cup U = I$ and I is not minimal. We conclude $Stab(P) = \emptyset$.

For independence we augment the proof for the non-disjunctive case by programs which are $(Disj - \{r\})$-reduced for $r \in \{RedF, Disj\}$. All the programs of the previous proof are reduced with respect to these rules, hence they carry over to this proof.

Rule	Program	Stable models
Subsumption-true (SubT)	$\{\to p, q; \to p; \to q\}$	$\{p, q\}$
Reduction-false (RedF)	$\{\to p, q; p \to; \to q\}$	$\{q\}$
Disjunction (Disj)	$\{\to p, q; p \to q; q \to p;$ $\sim p \to; \sim q \to\}$	$\{p, q\}$

$\square$

6 Further work

Datalog. For the case of Datalog programs it would be desirable to avoid explicitly representing all false propositions and all instances of rules. This requires a more general notion of solved form and some modifications of the procedure since the original clauses will not be subsumed by their instances arising during computation. Moreover, Split and Disjunction may only be used on ground atoms, otherwise they are not sound. For the case of range-restricted programs, where all variables of a clause appear in its positive premises, this can be guaranteed.

Querying. Normally the interest is not so much in computing models but in query answering. It is possible to use a refutational approach for stable semantics. Consider a query $Q = A_1 \wedge \ldots \wedge A_n \wedge \neg B_1 \wedge \ldots \wedge \neg B_m$ and let $neg(Q) = A_1, \ldots, A_n, \sim B_1, \ldots, \sim B_m \to$. Then for any program P

$$P \models_{Stab} Q \quad \text{iff} \quad Stab(P \cup \{neg(Q)\}) = \emptyset$$

It remains to develop a procedure which is specifically tailored to query answering. For that purpose it is not necessary to actually compute the stable models, but it suffices to test for satisfiability.

7 Discussion

In this section we will investigate whether the theoretical advantage of our procedure using only polynomial space vs. exponential space of the other known procedures can also result in a practical advantage. Since the space is used to store the stable models or some kind of candidates, the advantage will manifest itself only if the set of stable models or the set of candidates at some intermediate stage becomes large. Most of the known examples are not of this type; they possess at most a few stable models. It is however conceivable that such examples exist and are of practical importance. For instance using default negation to express nondeterminism, as Saccà and Zaniolo [10] suggest, would result in such a large set of stable models. Subrahmanian et al [11] also give some artificial examples of this type. If almost all branches lead to a stable model then recomputing a large set could even be more efficient than retrieving it from (secondary) storage.

If the cost of storing candidates is acceptable, other methods are probably superior. Take for instance the procedure of Subrahmanian et al [11], which also does case analysis with respect to truth values. Because the explicit check of minimality allows stronger simplifications in the case of assuming an atom to be true, the search space will be smaller than with our approach.

Since our current implementation is very inefficient, we cannot provide benchmarks to support these assumptions.

8 Conclusion

We have presented a new procedure for computing stable models of normal disjunctive logic programs. In analogy to the well-known Davis-Putnam procedure for classical propositional logic we used case analysis on the truth value of a proposition. It was crucial to allow clauses with empty heads. Then $\sim A \rightarrow$ could represent that A is constrained to be true, without justifying A. Together with $A \rightarrow$ this allowed case analysis. We have shown the soundness of several transformation rules on programs, which allow to transform a program into an equivalent one. These may be interesting in their own right, either to develop different procedures for reasoning with stable models, or because they provide more insight into the nature of stable semantics. For instance, Factoring allowed to notice that $\sim p \rightarrow p$ is equivalent to $\sim p \rightarrow$, hence its only effect is to constrain p to be true. From sets of sound rules we built our procedures and showed them to be complete, in the sense that they enumerate all stable models and terminate. We showed that for completeness only a subset of the rules was needed, while the others could be useful to improve performance. An actual implementation is free to choose which of these additional rules it uses.

We presented our procedure as a set of transformation rules, which resembled the standard method for presenting unification algorithms. Rules were sound in the sense that they preserved the set of stable models. The method allowed for concise presentation, flexible choice of a control strategy and simple correctness proofs.

Acknowledgements I would like to thank Harald Ganzinger for his helpful remarks on an earlier version of this paper and Ullrich Hustadt and Yannis

Dimopoulos for many discussions and for their general support.

This research was funded by the German Ministry for Research and Technology (BMFT) under grant ITS 9103. The responsibility for the contents of this publication lies with the author.

References

[1] Colin Bell, Anil Nerode, Raymond Ng, and V. S. Subrahmanian. Mixed integer programming methods for computing nonmonotonic deductive databases. To appear in the Journal of the ACM. Preliminary version in LPNMR'93, 1994.

[2] Martin Davis and Hilary Putnam. A computing procedure for quantification theory. *Journal of the ACM*, 7:201–215, 1960.

[3] Thomas Eiter and Georg Gottlob. Complexity results for disjunctive logic programming and applications to nonmonotonic logics. In *Proc. Int. Logic Programming Symp.*, pages 266–278, 1993.

[4] Kave Eshghi. Computing stable models by using the ATMS. In *Proc. AAAI-90*, pages 272–277, Boston, 1990.

[5] José Alberto Fernández and Jack Minker. Disjunctive deductive databases. In *Int. Conf. on Logic Programming and Automated Reasoning*, pages 332–356, St. Petersburg, July 1992. Springer LNCS 624.

[6] M. Gelfond and V. Lifschitz. The stable model semantics for logic programming. In *Proc. Logic Programming Conf.*, Seattle, 1988.

[7] Katsumi Inoue, Miyuki Koshimura, and Ryuzo Hasegawa. Embedding negation as failure into a model generation theorem prover. In Deepak Kapur, editor, *11th International Conference on Automated Deduction*, pages 400–415, Saratoga Springs, NY, June 1992. Springer LNAI 607.

[8] J. W. Lloyd. *Foundations of Logic Programming*. Springer, 1987.

[9] W. Marek and V. S. Subrahmanian. The relationship between stable, supported, default and autoepistemic semantics for general logic programs. *Theoretical Computer Science*, 103:365–386, 1992.

[10] D. Saccà and C. Zaniolo. Stable models and non-determinism in logic programs with negation. In *Proc. 9th ACM Symp. on Principles of Database Systems*, pages 205–229, Nashville, TN, 1990.

[11] V. S. Subrahmanian, Dana Nau, and Carlo Vago. WFS + branch and bound = stable models. Technical Report TR-92-83, Univ. of Maryland, Inst. for Systems Research, July 1992. Submitted to IEEE Trans. on Knowledge and Data Engineering.

Declarative Interpretations Reconsidered

Krzysztof R. Apt
Centre for Mathematics and Computer Science
Kruislaan 413, 1098 SJ Amsterdam, The Netherlands
and
Faculty of Mathematics and Computer Science
University of Amsterdam, Plantage Muidergracht 24
1018 TV Amsterdam, The Netherlands
apt@cwi.nl

Maurizio Gabbrielli
Centre for Mathematics and Computer Science
Kruislaan 413, 1098 SJ Amsterdam, The Netherlands
gabbri@cwi.nl

Abstract

Three semantics have been proposed as the most promising candidates for a declarative interpretation for logic programs and pure Prolog programs: the least Herbrand model, the least term model, i.e. the C-semantics, and the S-semantics. Previous results show that a strictly increasing information ordering between these semantics exists for the class of all programs. In particular, the S-semantics allows us to model computed answer substitutions, which is not the case for the other two.

We study here the relationship between these three semantics for specific classes of programs. We show that for a large class of programs (which is Turing complete) these three semantics are isomorphic. As a consequence, given a query, we can extract from the least Herbrand model of the program all computed answer substitutions. This result is applied to propose a method for proving partial correctness of programs based on the least Herbrand model.

1 Introduction

1.1 Motivation

The basic question we are trying to answer in this paper is: can one reason about partial correctness (that is about the computed answer substitutions) of "natural" pure Prolog programs using the least Herbrand semantics? We claim that the answer to this question is affirmative by showing that many logic and pure Prolog programs satisfy a property which implies that various declarative semantics of them are isomorphic.

Usually the declarative semantics is identified with the least Herbrand model. When considering the class of all logic programs there are a number of problems associated with this choice. First, this model depends on the underlying first-order language. For certain choices of this language this model is equivalent with the least term model, and for others not. Secondly, in general it matches the procedural interpretation of logic programs only for ground queries. So the procedural behaviour of the program cannot be completely "retrieved" from this model.

The least term model of Clark [6] (or C-semantics of Falaschi et al. [8]) is another natural candidate for the declarative semantics, and in fact it has been successfuly used in the probably most elegant and compact proof of the strong completeness of the SLD-resolution due to Stärk [12]. However, it shares with the least Herbrand model the same deficiencies.

The last choice is the S-semantics proposed by Falaschi et al. in [7]. This semantics provides a precise match with the procedural interpretation of logic programs. So it captures completely the procedural behaviour of the program. However, for specific programs it is rather laborious to construct and difficult to reason about.

We show here that for a large class of programs, called subsumption free programs, these three semantics are in fact isomorphic. This allows us to reason about partial correctness of subsumption free programs using the least Herbrand model. To prove that a program is subsumption free we apply a result of Maher and Ramakrishnan [10]. Using it we checked that several standard pure Prolog programs are subsumption free.

1.2   A Word on Terminology

In principle, we use the standard notation of logic programming. We consider here finite programs and queries w.r.t. a first-order language defined by a signature Σ. Given two expressions E_1, E_2, we say that E_1 *is more general than* E_2, and write $E_1 \leq E_2$, if there exist a substitution θ such that $E_1\theta = E_2$. $\leq$ is called the subsumption ordering. If $E_1 \leq E_2$ but not $E_2 \leq E_1$, we write $E_1 < E_2$, and when both $E_1 \leq E_2$ and $E_2 \leq E_1$, we say that E_1 and E_2 are *variants*. Finally we denote by $Var(E)$ the set of all variables occurring in the expression E.

A substitution if called *grounding* if all terms in its range are ground. A substitution is called a *renaming* if it is a permutation of the variables in its domain. We say that substitutions θ_1 and θ_2 are *variants* if for some renaming η we have $\theta_1 = \theta_2\eta$. Below we shall freely use the well-known result that all mgu's of two expressions are variants and that E_1 and E_2 are variants iff for some renaming η we have $E_1 = E_2\eta$. Further, we denote by $\mathcal{B}$ the set of all atoms (the *base* of the language) and by $\mathcal{B}_{\mathcal{H}}$ the set of all ground atoms.

For a number of reasons, we found it more convenient to work here with the concept of a query, correct and computed instance, and most general instance, instead of, respectively, the concepts of a goal, correct and computed answer substitution, and most general unifier.

In short, a query is a finite sequence of atoms, denoted by letters $Q, \mathbf{A}, \mathbf{B}, \mathbf{C}, \ldots$. Given a program P, Q' is a *correct instance* of Q, if $P \models Q'$ and $Q' = Q\theta$ for a substitution θ; Q' is a *computed instance* of Q, if there exists a successful SLD-derivation of Q with a computed answer substitution θ such that $Q' = Q\theta$.

Our interest here is in finding for a given program P the set of computed instances of a query. In analogy to the case of imperative programs, we write $\{Q\}\, P\, \mathcal{Q}$ to denote the fact that $\mathcal{Q}$ is the set of computed instances of the query Q, and denote the set of computed instances of the query Q by $sp(Q, P)$ (for *strongest postcondition* of Q w.r.t. P). Given two queries Q and Q' we write

$$mgi(Q, Q') = \{Q\theta \mid \theta \text{ is an mgu of } Q \text{ and } Q'\}.$$

So $mgi(Q, Q')$ is the set of most general instances of Q and Q'.

A query is called *separated* if the atoms forming it are pairwise variable disjoint. Given a set of atoms I we denote by I^* the set of separated queries formed from the atoms of I. Given a query Q and a set of atoms I we write

$$mgi(Q, I) = \{Q\theta \mid \exists Q' \in I^*(Var(Q) \cap Var(Q')) = \emptyset \text{ and } \theta \text{ is an mgu of } Q \text{ and } Q')\}.$$

So $mgi(Q, I)$ is the set of most general instances of Q and any query from I^* variable disjoint with Q. Finally, an atom is called *pure* if it is of the form $p(x_1, \ldots, x_n)$ where $x_1, \ldots, x_n$ are different variables.

2 Background - Three Declarative Semantics

Three semantics of logic programs, each yielding a single model, were introduced in the literature and presented as "declarative". We review them now briefly and discuss their positive and problematic aspects.

2.1 The Least Herbrand Model, or $\mathcal{M}$-semantics

This semantics was introduced by van Emden and Kowalski [15]. It associates with each program its least Herbrand model. Identifying each Herbrand model with the set of ground atoms true in it, we can equivalently define this semantics as

$$\mathcal{M}(P) = \{A \in \mathcal{B}_H \mid P \models A\}.$$

As is well-known this semantics completely characterizes the operational behaviour of a program on ground queries because (see Apt and van Emden [4]), for a ground Q a successful SLD-derivation of Q exists iff $Q \in \mathcal{M}(P)^*$. However, for non-ground queries the situation changes as the following example of Falaschi et al. in [7] shows.

Example 2.1 Consider the two programs $P_1 = \{\text{p(X) .}\}$ and $P_2 = \{\text{p(a) ., p(X) .}\}$. Then $\mathcal{M}(P_1) = \mathcal{M}(P_2)$ but the query p(X) yields different computed answer substitutions w.r.t. to each program. □

So in general, the $\mathcal{M}$-semantics is not a function of the operational behaviour of a program.

2.2 The Least Term Model, or $\mathcal{C}$-semantics

This semantics was introduced by Clark [6] and more extensively studied in Falaschi et al. [8]. It associates with each program its least term model. Identifying each term model with the set of atoms true in it, we can equivalently define this semantics as

$$\mathcal{C}(P) = \{A \in \mathcal{B} \mid P \models A\}.$$

As we shall see in Section 4, when the signature contains infinitely many constants, this semantics is equivalent to $\mathcal{M}$-semantics, so it cannot model the operational behaviour of a program either.

2.3 $\mathcal{S}$-semantics

This semantics was introduced in Falaschi et al. [7]. Its aim is to provide a *precise match* between the procedural and declarative interpretation of logic programs. Ideally, we would like to be able to "reconstruct" the procedural interpretation from the declarative one. Now, a procedural interpretation of a program P can be identified with the set of all pairs (Q, θ) where θ is a computed answer substitution for Q, or, equivalently with the set of all statements of the form $\{Q\} \ P \ \mathcal{Q}$.

The $\mathcal{S}$-semantics assigns to a program P the set of atoms [1]

$$\mathcal{S}(P) = \{A \in \mathcal{B} \mid A \text{ is a computed instance of a pure atom}\}.$$

It seems at first sight that the restriction to pure atoms results in a "loss of information" and as a result the operational interpretation cannot be reconstructed from $\mathcal{S}(P)$. But it is not so, as the following theorem of Falaschi et al. [7] shows.

Theorem 2.2 (Strong Completeness) *For a program P and a query Q*

$$\{Q\} \ P \ mgi(Q, \mathcal{S}(P)).$$

$\square$

Consequently, by the form of $\mathcal{S}(P)$ we have

Corollary 2.3 (Full abstraction) *For all programs P_1, P_2*

$$\mathcal{S}(P_1) = \mathcal{S}(P_2) \text{ iff } sp(Q, P_1) = sp(Q, P_2) \text{ for all queries } Q.$$

$\square$

An important property of the $\mathcal{S}$-semantics is that it can be defined by means of a fixpoint construction. More precisely, Falaschi et al. [7] introduced the following operator on term interpretations

$$T_P^{\mathcal{S}}(I) = \{H\theta \mid \ \exists \ \mathbf{B}, \mathbf{C} \ (H \leftarrow \mathbf{B} \in P, \ \mathbf{C} \in I^*, \ Var(H \leftarrow \mathbf{B}) \cap Var(\mathbf{C}) = \emptyset, \\ \theta \text{ is an mgu of } \mathbf{B} \text{ and } \mathbf{C}) \qquad \}$$

and proved the following.

Theorem 2.4

(i) *$T_P^{\mathcal{S}}$ is continuous on the complete lattice of term interpretations ordered with $\subseteq$.*

(ii) *$\mathcal{S}(\mathcal{P})$ is the least fixpoint and the least pre-fixpoint of $T_P^{\mathcal{S}}$.*

(iii) *$\mathcal{S}(\mathcal{P}) = T_P^{\mathcal{S}} \uparrow \omega$.*

$\square$

3 Relating Them

In what follows we wish to clarify the relationship between these three semantics for various classes of programs. To this end we introduce the following definition, where we view semantics as a function from the considered class of programs to some further unspecified semantic domain $\mathcal{D}$.

---

[1] In the original proposal actually the sets of equivalence classes of atoms w.r.t. to the "variant of" relation are considered. We found it more convenient to work with the above definition.

Definition 3.1 Consider a class of programs **C**. We say that two semantics $\mathcal{S}_1$: **C** → $\mathcal{D}_1$ and $\mathcal{S}_2$: **C** → $\mathcal{D}_2$ are *isomorphic* on **C** iff there exist two functions, $\phi_1 : Range(\mathcal{S}_1) \to Range(\mathcal{S}_2)$ and $\phi_2 : Range(\mathcal{S}_2) \to Range(\mathcal{S}_1)$ such that, for any program $P \in \mathbf{C}$

$$\mathcal{S}_1(P) = \phi_2(\mathcal{S}_2(P)) \text{ and } \mathcal{S}_2(P) = \phi_1(\mathcal{S}_1(P)).$$

□

Alternatively, two semantics $\mathcal{S}_1 : \mathbf{C} \to \mathcal{D}_1$ and $\mathcal{S}_2 : \mathbf{C} \to \mathcal{D}_2$ are isomorphic on **C** iff there exists a bijection $\phi : Range(\mathcal{S}_1) \to Range(\mathcal{S}_2)$ such that, for any program $P \in \mathbf{C}$, $\mathcal{S}_2(P) = \phi(\mathcal{S}_1(P))$.

Every semantics $\mathcal{T}$ for **C** induces an equivalence relation $\approx_\mathcal{T}$ on programs from **C** defined by $P_1 \approx_\mathcal{T} P_2$ iff $\mathcal{T}(P_1) = \mathcal{T}(P_2)$. Note that the notion of isomorphism can be also equivalently given in terms of equivalences, by defining two semantics isomorphic on **C** if they induce the same equivalence relation on **C**. When constructing isomorphisms between the semantics the following operators will be useful.

Definition 3.2 Let I be a set of atoms. We define

(i) $Variant(I) = \{A \in \mathcal{B} \mid \exists B \in I \text{ s.t. } B \leq A \text{ and } A \leq B\}$, the set of variants,

(ii) $Up(I) = \{A \in \mathcal{B} \mid \exists B \in I \text{ s.t. } B \leq A\}$, the set of instances,

(iii) $Ground(I) = \{A \in \mathcal{B}_H \mid \exists B \in I \text{ s.t. } B \leq A\}$, the set of ground instances,

(iv) $Min(I) = \{A \in I \mid \neg \exists B \in I \text{ s.t. } B < A\}$, the set of minimal (i.e. most general) elements,

(v) for I a set of ground atoms
$True(I) = \{A \in \mathcal{B} \mid I \models A\}$, the set of atoms true in the Herbrand interpretation I.

□

Note that $Variant, Up, Ground$ and Min are all idempotent. Moreover, the following clearly holds.

Note 3.3 *For all I, $Min(Up(I)) = Min(I)$.* □

4 Relating $\mathcal{M}$-semantics and $\mathcal{C}$-semantics

We begin by clarifying the relationship between $\mathcal{M}(P)$ and $\mathcal{C}(P)$. The following result is an immediate consequence of the definitions.

Note 4.1 $\mathcal{M}(P) = Ground(\mathcal{C}(P))$. □

So the $\mathcal{M}$-semantics can be reconstructed from the $\mathcal{C}$-semantics. The converse does not hold in general as the following argument due to Falaschi et al. [8] shows.

Example 4.2 Consider the two programs $P_1 = \{\mathtt{p(X).}\}$ and $P_2 = \{\mathtt{p(a).}, \mathtt{p(b).}\}$ defined w.r.t. the language with the signature $\Sigma = \{\mathtt{a}/0, \mathtt{b}/0\}$. Then $\mathcal{M}(P_1) = \mathcal{M}(P_2) = \{\mathtt{p(a)}, \mathtt{p(b)}\}$, while $\mathcal{C}(P_1) = \{\mathtt{p(X)}, \mathtt{p(a)}, \mathtt{p(b)}\}$ and $\mathcal{C}(P_2) = \{\mathtt{p(a)}, \mathtt{p(b)}\}$.

□

In case the signature contains infinitely many constants, the situation changes, as the following result due to Maher [9] shows.

Theorem 4.3 *Assume that Σ contains infinitely many constants. Then $C(P) = True(\mathcal{M}(P))$.*

Proof. We provide here an alternative, direct proof based on the theory of SLD-resolution. The implication $C(P) \subseteq True(\mathcal{M}(P))$ always holds, since $\mathcal{M}(P)$ is a model of P. Take now $A \in True(\mathcal{M}(P))$. Let $x_1, \ldots, x_n$ be the variables of A and $c_1, \ldots, c_n$ distinct constants which do not appear in P or A. Let $\theta = \{x_1/c_1, \ldots, x_n/c_n\}$. Then $A\theta \in \mathcal{M}(P)$. By the completeness of SLD-resolution there exists a successful SLD-derivation of $A\theta$ with the empty computed answer substitution. By replacing in it c_i by x_i for $i \in [1, n]$ we get a successful SLD-derivation of A with the empty computed answer substitution. Now by the soundness of SLD-resolution $A \in C(P)$.
$\square$

Consequently, when the signature contains infinitely many constants, the semantics $\mathcal{M}(P)$ and $C(P)$ are isomorphic. We shall exploit this fact later.

5 Relating C-semantics and S-semantics

Next, we clarify the relationship between $C(P)$ and $S(P)$. First, we have the following result of Falaschi et al. [8].

Theorem 5.1 $C(P) = Up(S(P))$. $\square$

So the C-semantics can be reconstructed from the S-semantics. The converse does not hold in general as the following argument due to Falaschi et al. [7] shows.

Example 5.2 Consider the programs P_1 and P_2 of Example 2.1. Then $C(P_1) = C(P_2) = Up(\{\text{p}(\text{X})\})$, while $S(P_1) = Variant(\{\text{p}(\text{X})\})$ and $S(P_2) = Variant(\{\text{p}(\text{X}), \text{p}(\text{a})\})$. Note that the signature of the language was immaterial here. $\square$

Thus on the class of all programs the C-semantics and the S-semantics. are not isomorphic. In what follows we show that for a large class of programs they are in fact isomorphic. First, we have the following result.

Lemma 5.3 $Min(C(P)) \subseteq S(P)$.

Intuitively, it states that all most general atoms true in $C(P)$ belong to $S(P)$.

Proof. By Theorem 5.1 $Min(C(P)) = Min(Up(S(P)))$ and the claim follows by Note 3.3, since for all I we have $Min(I) \subseteq I$.
$\square$

In general, the converse inclusion does not hold.

Example 5.4 Consider the following program $P = \{\text{p}(\text{a})., \text{p}(\text{X}).\}$ defined w.r.t. the language with the signature $\Sigma = \{\text{a}/0\}$. Then $S(P) = Variant(\{\text{p}(\text{Y})\}) \cup \{\text{p}(\text{a})\}$, whereas $Min(C(P)) = Variant(\{\text{p}(\text{Y})\})$. $\square$

A closer examination of the situation reveals the following. By the soundness of SLD-resolution we always have $S(P) \subseteq C(P)$. The above example shows that the stronger inclusion $S(P) \subseteq Min(C(P))$ does not need to hold. The reason is that

$\mathcal{S}(P)$ can contain a pair A, B such that A strictly subsumes B (i.e. $A < B$). This cannot happen when $\mathcal{S}(P)$ contains only minimal elements. So we are brought to the following definition due to Maher and Ramakrishnan [10].

Definition 5.5 A set of atoms I is called *subsumption free* if $Min(I) = I$. A program P is called *subsumption free* if $\mathcal{S}(P)$ is. □

We now show that that the notion of a subsumption free program is a key for establishing the converse of Lemma 5.3.

Theorem 5.6 $\mathcal{S}(P) = Min(\mathcal{C}(P))$ *iff P is subsumption free.*

Proof. ($\Rightarrow$) We have

$$
\begin{aligned}
Min(\mathcal{S}(P)) &= &\{\text{assumption}\} \\
Min(Min(\mathcal{C}(P))) &= &\{\text{idempotence of } Min\} \\
Min(\mathcal{C}(P)) &= &\{\text{assumption}\} \\
\mathcal{S}(P). & &
\end{aligned}
$$

($\Leftarrow$) We have

$$
\begin{aligned}
\mathcal{S}(P) &= &\{\text{assumption}\} \\
Min(\mathcal{S}(P)) &= &\{\text{Note 3.3}\} \\
Min(Up(\mathcal{S}(P))) &= &\{\text{Theorem 5.1}\} \\
Min(\mathcal{C}(P)). & &
\end{aligned}
$$

□

Consequently, the $\mathcal{C}$-semantics and $\mathcal{S}$-semantics are isomorphic on subsumption free programs. Additionally, when the signature contains infinitely many constants, all three semantics are isomorphic. Combining Theorems 2.2, 4.3 and 5.6 we thus obtain.

Corollary 5.7 *Assume that Σ contains infinitely many constants. Then for a subsumption free program P and a query Q*

$$\{Q\} \ P \ mgi(Q, Min(True(\mathcal{M}(P)))).$$

□

It shows that partial correctness of subsumption free programs can be fully reconstructed from the least Herbrand model, using unification. In the next section we shall identify a smaller class of programs for which this characterization of partial correctness does not involve unification.

Of course, if we do not make any assumption on the class of programs **C**, subsumption freedom is only a sufficient condition for the isomorphism of the $\mathcal{C}$-semantics and $\mathcal{S}$-semantics. Indeed, when the class of programs consists of just the program from Example 5.4, which is not subsumption free, then the $\mathcal{C}$-semantics and $\mathcal{S}$-semantics are obviously isomorphic. However, for a "reasonably large" class of programs subsumption freedom turns out to be also a necessary condition for isomorphism of programs.

Definition 5.8 A class of programs **C** is *$\mathcal{S}$-closed* if for every program P in **C** every finite subset of $\mathcal{S}(P)$ is in **C**. □

Indeed, we have the following result.

Note 5.9 *For an S-closed class* **C** *of programs, the* **C***-semantics and* S*-semantics are isomorphic on* **C** *iff* **C** *is a class of subsumption free programs.*

Proof. ($\Rightarrow$) Suppose that some $P \in$ **C** is not subsumption free. Then for some atoms $A, B \in S(P)$ we have $A < B$. By the definition of S-closedness both $P_1 = \{A, B\}$ and $P_2 = \{A\}$ are in **C**. Now $C(P_1) = Up(\{A, B\}) = Up(\{A\}) = C(P_2)$, whereas $S(P_1) = Variant(\{A, B\}) \neq Variant(\{A\}) = S(P_2)$. Contradiction. ($\Leftarrow$) This is the contents of Theorems 5.1 and 5.6. $\qquad \square$

This shows that the notion of subsumption freedom is crucial for our considerations. In what follows we provide some means of establishing that a program is subsumption free.

6 S-Unification Free Programs

We begin by studying a subclass of subsumption free programs.

Definition 6.1 A program P is called S-unification free iff $S(P)$ does not contain a pair of non-variant unifiable atoms. $\qquad \square$

We prefer to use the qualification "S-" in order to avoid confusion with the class of unification free programs studied in Apt and Etalle [2]. Clearly, S-unification freedom implies subsumption freedom, since $S(P)$ is closed under renaming and $A < B$ implies that A and a variant B' of B are non-variant and unifiable. The converse does not hold.

Example 6.2 Consider the following program $P = \{\text{p(X,a)}.\,,\ \text{p(a,X)}.\}$ defined w.r.t. the language with the signature $\Sigma = \{\text{a}/0\}$.
Then $S(P) = Variant(\{\text{p(X, a)}, \text{p(a, X)}\})$, so P is not S-unification free. However, it is clearly subsumption free, because the atoms p(X, a) and p(a, X) are not comparable in the subsumption ordering. $\qquad \square$

The following theorem summarizes the difference between the subsumption free and S-unification free programs in a succinct way. Let us extend the Min operator in an obvious way to sets of queries.

Theorem 6.3

   (i) P is subsumption free iff for all pure atoms A, $Min(sp(A, P)) = sp(A, P)$.

   (ii) P is S-unification free iff for all queries Q, $Min(sp(Q, P)) = sp(Q, P)$.

Proof.
(i) Note that for some variables $x_1, x_2, \ldots$, $S(P)$ is a disjoint union of sets of the form $sp(p(x_1, \ldots, x_{arity(p)}), P)$ and that atoms belonging to different such sets are incomparable in the $\leq$ ordering. Thus $Min(S(P))$ is a disjoint union of sets of the form $Min(sp(p(x_1, \ldots, x_{arity(p)}), P))$.

(ii) ($\Rightarrow$) Consider two computed instances Q_1 and Q_2 of Q. By Theorem 2.2 there exist $\mathbf{C}_1$ and $\mathbf{C}_2$ in $S(P)^*$ such that for $i \in [1, 2]$ Q and $\mathbf{C}_i$ are variable disjoint and

$$Q_i \in mgi(Q, \mathbf{C}_i). \qquad (1)$$

In particular $\mathbf{C}_1 \leq Q_1$ and $\mathbf{C}_2 \leq Q_2$.

Suppose now that $Q_1 < Q_2$. Then $\mathbf{C}_1 \leq Q_2$, so Q_2 is an instance of both $\mathbf{C}_1$ and $\mathbf{C}_2$. Since we may assume that $\mathbf{C}_1$ and $\mathbf{C}_2$ are variable disjoint, we conclude that $\mathbf{C}_1$ and $\mathbf{C}_2$ are unifiable. By assumption about P and the fact that $\mathbf{C}_1$ and $\mathbf{C}_2$ are separated queries, $\mathbf{C}_1$ and $\mathbf{C}_2$ are variants. This implies by (1) that Q_1 and Q_2 are variants, as well. Contradiction.

($\Leftarrow$) Suppose that $\mathcal{S}(P)$ does contain a pair A, B of non-variant unifiable atoms. Let $C \in mgi(A, B)$. Then $A \leq C$ and $B \leq C$ and at least one of these subsumption relations, say the first one, is strict. So $A < C$. Take now a variant A' of A variable disjoint with A and B. By Theorem 2.2 $A, C \in sp(A', P)$. So $Min(sp(A', P)) \neq sp(A', P)$. Contradiction.

$\square$

For $\mathcal{S}$-unification free programs we can simplify the formulation of Corollary 5.7.

Corollary 6.4 *For a $\mathcal{S}$-unification free program P and a query Q*

$$\{Q\} \ P \ Min(\{Q\theta \mid P \models Q\theta\}).$$

Proof. This result follows from Theorem 6.3(ii) and the following two claims.

Claim 1 *For an arbitrary program P and a query Q*

$$Min(\{Q\theta \mid P \models Q\theta\}) \subseteq sp(Q, P) \subseteq \{Q\theta \mid P \models Q\theta\}.$$

Proof. Take $Q_1 \in Min(\{Q\theta \mid P \models Q\theta\})$. By the Strong Completeness of SLD-resolution there exists a computed instance Q_2 of Q_1 such that $Q_2 \leq Q_1$. By the choice of Q_1, $P \models Q_2$, so by the minimality of Q_1, Q_1 and Q_2 are variants. Thus Q_1 is also a computed instance of Q, i.e. $Q_1 \in sp(Q, P)$. $\square$

Claim 2 *For sets of queries $\mathcal{Q}_1$ and $\mathcal{Q}_2$, if $Min(\mathcal{Q}_1) \subseteq \mathcal{Q}_2 \subseteq \mathcal{Q}_1$ and $Min(\mathcal{Q}_2) = \mathcal{Q}_2$, then $\mathcal{Q}_2 = Min(\mathcal{Q}_1)$.*

Proof. Immediate.

$\square$

So for $\mathcal{S}$-unification free programs the sets of computed instances can be defined without the use of unification. In Corollary 6.4 we can always replace "$P \models$" by "$\mathcal{C}(P) \models$", and also by "$\mathcal{M}(P) \models$" if Σ contains infinitely many constants.

Maher and Ramakrishnan [10] studied subsumption free programs in the context of the bottom up computation in deductive databases and showed that for these programs this computation can be performed more efficiently. They also provided a method allowing us to conclude that a program is $\mathcal{S}$-unification free, so a fortiori subsumption free. Using this method they proved that the class of $\mathcal{S}$-unification free programs is Turing complete.

Their method is equally applicable in our situation. To formulate it the following notation is useful. By $hground(P)$ we denote the set of instances of clauses of P whose head is ground. Given a Herbrand interpretation I and a query $\mathbf{B}$ we write

$$I \models \exists \leq 1\mathbf{B}$$

if at most one sequence of ground $t_1, \ldots, t_n$ exists such that $I \models \mathbf{B}\{x_1/t_1, \ldots, x_n/t_n\}$, where $x_1, \ldots, x_n$ are the variables occurring in $\mathbf{B}$.

Theorem 6.5 (Maher and Ramakrishnan [10]) *Suppose that the following conditions hold for a program P:*

SEM1. *If c, d are different clauses in P, then no pair $A \in T^{\mathcal{S}}_{\{c\}}(\mathcal{S}(P))$ and $B \in T^{\mathcal{S}}_{\{d\}}(\mathcal{S}(P))$ is unifiable.*

SEM2. *For every clause $H \leftarrow \mathbf{B}$ in $hground(P)$*

$$if \; \mathcal{M}(P) \models H \; then \; \mathcal{M}(P) \models \exists \leq 1\mathbf{B}.$$

Then P is $\mathcal{S}$-unification free.

Proof. To keep the paper self-contained we provide here a direct proof. By Theorem 2.4(iii) it suffices to show that, for $n \geq 0$, $T^{\mathcal{S}}_P \uparrow n$ does not contain a pair of non-variant unifiable atoms. The proof is by induction on n.
($n = 0$) Obvious.
($n > 0$). Denote $T^{\mathcal{S}}_P \uparrow n$ by I and consider $A, B \in T^{\mathcal{S}}_P(I)$. Two cases arise.

Case 1 A and B are generated by the different clauses, say c and d. Then $A \in T^{\mathcal{S}}_{\{c\}}(I)$ and $B \in T^{\mathcal{S}}_{\{d\}}(I)$ and the claim follows by condition SEM1 since by Theorem 2.4 $I \subseteq \mathcal{S}(P)$ and $T^{\mathcal{S}}_P$ is monotonic.

Case 2 A and B are generated by the same clause, say $H \leftarrow \mathbf{B}$. Then for some $\mathbf{C}_1 \in I^*$, $\mathbf{C}_2 \in I^*$ and ϑ_1, ϑ_2

$$A = H\vartheta_1, \; Var(H \leftarrow \mathbf{B}) \cap Var(\mathbf{C}_1) = \emptyset, \; \vartheta_1 \text{ is an mgu of } \mathbf{B} \text{ and } \mathbf{C}_1, \tag{2}$$

$$B = H\vartheta_2, \; Var(H \leftarrow \mathbf{B}) \cap Var(\mathbf{C}_2) = \emptyset, \; \vartheta_2 \text{ is an mgu of } \mathbf{B} \text{ and } \mathbf{C}_2 \tag{3}$$

Suppose A and B are unifiable. Then there exists a grounding η whose domain includes the variables of $(H \leftarrow \mathbf{B})\vartheta_1$ and $(H \leftarrow \mathbf{B})\vartheta_2$, such that both $\vartheta_1\eta$ and $\vartheta_2\eta$ are grounding and $H\vartheta_1\eta = H\vartheta_2\eta$. So $\vartheta_1\eta$ and $\vartheta_2\eta$ coincide on the variables of H. Denote their common restriction to $Var(H)$ by δ. Then $(H \leftarrow \mathbf{B})\delta$ is in $hground(P)$.

By the soundness of SLD-resolution $\mathcal{M}(P) \models H\delta$, since $A \in \mathcal{S}(P)$ and $H\delta = A\vartheta_1\eta$. Thus by condition SEM2

$$\mathcal{M}(P) \models \exists \leq 1 \; \mathbf{B}\delta. \tag{4}$$

Now, for some grounding δ_1 and δ_2 we have $\vartheta_1\eta = \delta \overset{.}{\cup} \delta_1$ and $\vartheta_2\eta = \delta \overset{.}{\cup} \delta_2$, so $\vartheta_1\eta = \delta\delta_1$ and $\vartheta_2\eta = \delta\delta_2$. This implies by (2) that

$$\mathbf{B}\delta\delta_1 = \mathbf{B}\vartheta_1\eta = \mathbf{C}_1\vartheta_1\eta = \mathbf{C}_1\delta\delta_1, \tag{5}$$

and similarly by (3)

$$\mathbf{B}\delta\delta_2 = \mathbf{C}_2\delta\delta_2. \tag{6}$$

Again by the soundness of SLD-resolution $\mathcal{M}(P) \models \mathbf{C}_1\delta\delta_1$ and $\mathcal{M}(P) \models \mathbf{C}_2\delta\delta_2$, since $\mathbf{C}_1 \in \mathcal{S}(P)^*$ and $\mathbf{C}_2 \in \mathcal{S}(P)^*$. By (4) $\mathbf{B}\delta\delta_1 = \mathbf{B}\delta\delta_2$, so by (5) and (6) $\mathbf{C}_1\delta\delta_1 = \mathbf{C}_2\delta\delta_2$. Thus $\mathbf{C}_1$ and $\mathbf{C}_2$ are unifiable, since we may assume that they are variable disjoint. By the induction hypothesis and the fact that $\mathbf{C}_1$ and $\mathbf{C}_2$ are separated, $\mathbf{C}_1$ and $\mathbf{C}_2$ are variants. Thus by (2) and (3) $H\vartheta_1$ and $H\vartheta_2$, i.e. A and B are variants. This concludes the proof of the induction step. □

In certain situations the conditions of the above theorem can be ensured by means of syntactic restrictions. Namely, condition SEM1 is obviously implied by condition

SYN1. If $H_1 \leftarrow \mathbf{B}_1$ and $H_2 \leftarrow \mathbf{B}_2$ are different clauses in P, then H_1 and H_2 do not unify,

and condition SEM2 is automatically satisfied when condition

SYN2. If $H \leftarrow \mathbf{B} \in P$, then $Var(\mathbf{B}) \subseteq Var(H)$

holds.

It is worth noting that an immediate proof of Turing completeness for S-unification free programs can be obtained by using the encoding of two register machines into pure logic programs given in Shepherdson [11]. In fact, conditions SYN1 and SYN2 readily apply to programs obtained by such an encoding. In the next section we assess the applicability of Theorem 6.5.

7 Applications

We first provide 4 illustrative uses of Theorem 6.5.

Example 7.1
(i) Consider the APPEND program:

```
append([], Ys, Ys).
append([X | Xs], Ys, [X | Zs]) ← append(Xs, Ys, Zs).
```

Here the syntactic conditions SYN1 and SYN2 readily apply.

(ii) Consider the SUFFIX program:

```
suffix(Xs, Xs).
suffix(Xs,[Y | Ys]) ← suffix(Xs,Ys).
```

Note that the heads of the clauses unify, so we cannot use condition SYN1. To prove condition SEM1 we reason as follows. Denote by OCC the set of atoms of the form $\text{suffix}(\mathtt{Z},t_{\mathtt{Z}})$ where $\mathtt{Z}$ is a variable and $t_{\mathtt{Z}}$ a term containing $\mathtt{Z}$. By definition of T_P^S, $T_{\text{SUFFIX}}^S(OCC) \subseteq OCC$, i.e. OCC is a pre-fixpoint of T_{SUFFIX}^S. By Theorem 2.4 $S(\text{SUFFIX}) \subseteq OCC$. So because of the occur-check $\text{suffix}(\mathtt{Xs}, \mathtt{Xs})$ does not unify with any $A \in OCC$ of the form $\text{suffix}(\mathtt{Z},t)$ with t a proper term. Thus SEM1 holds.

The clauses of SUFFIX do not contain local variables, so condition SYN2 applies.

(iii) Consider now the naive REVERSE program:

```
reverse([ ],[ ]).
reverse([X | Xs], Zs) ← reverse(Xs,Ys), append_t(Ys,[X],Zs)
```

augmented by the "well-typed" APPEND_T program:

```
append_t([X | Xs], Ys, [X | Zs]) ← append_t(Xs, Ys, Zs).
append_t([], Ys, Ys) ← list(Ys).

list([H | Ts]) ← list(Ts).
list([].
```

The heads of different clauses do not unify, so condition SYN1 applies. However, due to presence of the local variable Ys in the second clause, condition SYN2 does not apply. To prove condition SEM2 we analyze the least Herbrand model

$\mathcal{M}($REVERSE$)$. Using the techniques of Apt and Pedreschi [3] it is straightforward to check that

$$\mathcal{M}(\texttt{REVERSE}) \quad = \{\texttt{reverse(s,t)} \mid \texttt{s,t} \text{ are ground lists and } \texttt{t=rev(s)}\}$$
$$\cup \, \mathcal{M}(\texttt{APPEND\_T}) \qquad \text{where}$$

$$\mathcal{M}(\texttt{APPEND\_T}) \quad = \{\texttt{append\_t(s,t,u)} \mid \texttt{s,t,u} \text{ are ground lists and } \texttt{s*t=u}\}$$
$$\cup \, \{\texttt{list(s)} \mid \texttt{s} \text{ is a ground list }\}$$

where given a list s, rev(s) denotes its reverse, and $*$ denotes the operation of concatenating two lists. Take now an instance
reverse([x | xs], zs) ← reverse(xs,ys), append_t(ys,[x],zs)
of the second clause with reverse([x|xs], zs) ground and in $\mathcal{M}($REVERSE$)$. Then reverse(xs, ys) $\in \mathcal{M}($REVERSE$)$ implies ys = rev(xs), so condition SEM2 holds for this clause. For other clauses condition SYN2 applies. We conclude that REVERSE is $\mathcal{S}$-unification free.

(iv) Finally, consider the following program HANOI from Sterling and Shapiro [13] which, for the query hanoi(n,a,b,c,Moves), solves the "Towers of Hanoi" problem with n disks and three pegs a, b and c giving the sequence of moves forming the solution in Moves:

```
hanoi(s(0),A,B,C,[A to B]).
hanoi(s(N),A,B,C,[A to B]) ←
   hanoi(N,A,C,B,Ms1)
   hanoi(N,C,B,A ,Ms2)
   append_t(Ms1,[A to B|Ms2],Moves).
```

augmented by the APPEND_T program.

Note that conditions SYN1 and SYN2 do not apply here. First observe that for any I, if hanoi(t1,t2,t3,t4,t5) $\in T^{\mathcal{S}}_{\texttt{HANOI}}(I)$ then t1 $\neq 0$. So by Theorem 2.4, hanoi(t1,t2,t3,t4,t5) $\in \mathcal{S}(\texttt{HANOI})$ implies t1 $\neq 0$ and consequently condition SEM1 holds.

To prove SEM2 we use the methodology of Maher and Ramakrishnan [10] based on functional dependencies. First we need a definition.

Definition 7.2 Let p be an n-ary relation symbol. A functional dependency is a construct of the form $p[I \to J]$ where $I, J \subseteq \{1, \dots, n\}$. Let M be a set of ground atoms. We say that $p[I \to J]$ *holds over* M if for all $p(s_1, \dots, s_n), p(t_1, \dots, t_n) \in M$, the following implication holds:

$$(\forall i \in I. \; s_i = t_i) \Rightarrow (\forall j \in J. \; s_j = t_j).$$

A set F of functional dependencies holds over M iff each of them holds over M. $\square$

We now show that the set of functional dependencies

$$F = \{\texttt{hanoi}[\{1, 2, 3, 4\} \to \{5\}], \texttt{append\_t}[\{1, 2\} \to \{3\}]\}$$

holds over $\mathcal{M}($HANOI$)$. By the fixpoint definition of $\mathcal{M}(P)$, if $A \in \mathcal{M}(P)$ then A is a ground instance of the head of a clause in P. Then a simple syntactic check on the heads of the clauses in HANOI reveals that hanoi$[\{1, 2, 3, 4\} \to \{5\}]$ holds over $\mathcal{M}($HANOI$)$. The other functional dependency can be directly established by considering the explicit definition of $\mathcal{M}($APPEND_T$)$ previously given.

Using the information given by F it is now straightforward to prove the implication required by SEM2. The only clause that we have to consider is the non unit clause for `hanoi`. Consider an instance

```
hanoi(s(n),a,b,c,[a to b]) ←   hanoi(n,a,c,b,ms1),hanoi(n,c,b,a,ms2),
                               append_t(ms1,[a to b|ms2],moves)
```

of such a clause with `hanoi(s(n),a,b,c,[a to b])` ground and in $\mathcal{M}(\text{HANOI})$.

Since $\text{hanoi}[\{1,2,3,4\} \rightarrow \{5\}]$ holds over $\mathcal{M}(\text{HANOI})$, if `hanoi(n,a,c,b,ms1)` $\in \mathcal{M}(\text{HANOI})$ then there exists no `hanoi(n,a,c,b,ms1')` $\in \mathcal{M}(\text{HANOI})$ such that `ms1` $\neq$ `ms1'`. Analogously for `ms2` and, using the dependency $\text{append\_t}[\{1,2\} \rightarrow \{3\}]$, for `moves`. Consequently, SEM2 holds and HANOI is $\mathcal{S}$-unification free.

A general method for establishing functional dependencies on $\mathcal{M}(P)$, based on an extended version of Amstrong axioms (see Ullman [14]), is given in Maher and Ramakrishnan [10]. □

Note that Theorem 6.5 only provides sufficient conditions for $\mathcal{S}$-unification freedom. Indeed, the program $\{\text{p}(\text{X}) \leftarrow \text{q}(\text{X},\text{Y})., \text{q}(\text{a},\text{b})., \text{q}(\text{a},\text{c}).\}$ is easily seen to be $\mathcal{S}$-unification free but condition SEM2 does not hold. Moreover, for certain natural programs Theorem 6.5 cannot be used to establish their subsumption freedom, simply because they are not $\mathcal{S}$-unification free. An example is of course the program considered in Example 6.2. But more natural programs exist. In such situations we still can use a direct reasoning.

Example 7.3 Consider the MEMBER program:

```
member(X,[X | Xs]).
member(X,[Y | Xs]) ← member(X,Xs).
```

We now prove that MEMBER is subsumption free. By Theorem 2.4 it suffices to show that if I is subsumption free then $T^{\mathcal{S}}_{\text{MEMBER}}(I)$ is subsumption free. Denote the first clause by c_1 and the second one by c_2. Consider a pair $A_1, A_2 \in T^{\mathcal{S}}_{\text{MEMBER}}(I)$. The following two cases arise.

Case 1 $A_1 \in T^s_{\{c_1\}}(I)$ and $A_2 \in T^s_{\{c_2\}}(I)$.

By definition of $T^{\mathcal{S}}_P$, $A_1 = \text{member}(\text{X},[\text{X}|\text{Xs}])\rho$ for a renaming ρ and $A_2 = \text{member}(\text{X},[\text{Y}|\text{Xs}])\vartheta$ where ϑ is an mgu of $\text{member}(\text{X},\text{Xs})$ and B for a B such that $\text{Y} \notin Var(B)$. This implies $\text{X}\vartheta \not\equiv \text{Y}\vartheta$ and hence $A_1 \not\preceq A_2$ and $A_2 \not\prec A_1$.

Case 2 $A_1, A_2 \in T^s_{\{c_2\}}(I)$.

By definition, $A_i = \text{member}(\text{X},[\text{Y}|\text{Xs}])\vartheta_i$ where ϑ_i is an mgu of $\text{member}(\text{X},\text{Xs})$ and B_i for $i = 1,2$. Assuming $B_i = \text{member}(\text{t}_i,\text{l}_i)$ we have $\vartheta_i = \{\text{X}/t_i, \text{Xs}/l_i\}$ (up to renaming). Then the assumption $B_1 \not\prec B_2$ implies $\text{member}(\text{X},\text{Xs})\,\vartheta_1 \not\prec \text{member}(\text{X},\text{Xs})\vartheta_2$ and hence $A_1 \not\prec A_2$. Analogously for the symmetric case.

Note that MEMBER is not $\mathcal{S}$-unification free. □

The results contained in the previous sections can be applied to prove partial correctness of logic programs by using the least Herbrand model. Given a program P and a query Q, we wish to prove assertions of the form $\{Q\}\, P\, \mathcal{Q}$. This can be done by performing the steps listed below, which extend a methodology introduced in Apt [1] to the case of "non-ground" inputs (or more precisely to queries with "non-ground" computed instances). We illustrate our technique by means of an example. Consider the program REVERSE of Example 7.1 and the query $Q = \text{reverse}(\text{s},\text{X})$, where s is a (possibly non-ground) list and X is a variable. In the following, we assume an infinite signature.

1. *Construct $\mathcal{M}(P)$.*

   Usually, the "specification" of the program limited to its ground queries coincides with $\mathcal{M}(P)$. The techniques of Apt and Pedreschi [3] are useful for verifying validity of such a guess.

2. *Prove that P is $\mathcal{S}$-unification (subsumption) free* (see Example 7.1).

3. *Find a correct instance Q' of Q,* i.e. such that $\mathcal{M}(P) \models Q'$. Note that by definition

$$\mathcal{M}(P) \models Q' \text{ iff } Ground(Q') \subseteq \mathcal{M}(P)^*. \tag{7}$$

   In our case, by definition of $\mathcal{M}(\text{REVERSE})$, if Q'' is a ground instance of `reverse(s,rev(s))` then $Q'' \in \mathcal{M}(\text{REVERSE})$ holds. Therefore by (7)

$$\mathcal{M}(\text{REVERSE}) \models \text{reverse(s,rev(s))}.$$

4. *By suitably generalizing from 3. find a minimal correct instance Q' of Q,* i.e. such that $\mathcal{M}(P) \models Q\gamma$ implies $Q' \leq Q\gamma$. (In general, find the set of minimal correct instances of Q). Here the following implication which holds for any pair of expressions E_1, E_2 can be useful

$$(\forall \eta \text{ s.t. } (E_1 = E_2)\eta \text{ is ground . } E_1\eta = E_2\eta) \Rightarrow E_1 = E_2. \tag{8}$$

   Assume in our case that

$$\mathcal{M}(\text{REVERSE}) \models \text{reverse(s,X)}\gamma.$$

   By (7), for any η s.t. `reverse(s,X)`$\gamma\eta$ is ground, $X\gamma\eta = rev(s\gamma\eta) = $ (by definition of rev) $rev(s)\gamma\eta$. Then by (8) $X\gamma = rev(s)\gamma$ and hence

$$\text{reverse(s, rev(s))} \leq \text{reverse(s, X)}\gamma$$

   holds.

5. *Apply Corollary 6.4 (or Corollary 5.7 for programs which are not $\mathcal{S}$-unification free).* For REVERSE we obtain

$$\{\text{reverse(s, X)}\} \text{ REVERSE } Variant(\{\text{reverse(s,rev(s))}\}).$$

8 Conclusions

We now present a list of example programs from the book of Sterling and Shapiro [13] for which we proved that $\mathcal{S}$-semantics and $\mathcal{M}$-semantics are isomorphic. For each program it is indicated by what method the result was established. For example SEM1-SYN2 means that condition SEM1 of Theorem 6.5 and condition SYN2 following it were used. DP stands for a "direct proof". In all cases condition SEM2 was established by means of the functional dependency analysis.

To deal with programs which use arithmetic relations we assumed that each such relation is defined by infinitely many ground unit clauses which form its true ground instances. Note that such ground unit clauses obviously satisfy the conditions SYN1 and SYN2. It should be noted that the results of this paper hold for programs with infinitely many clauses provided we modify the assumption "the signature has infinitely many constants" to "the signature has infinitely many constants which do not occur in the program".

Finally, it should be made clear that none of the considered semantics deals with the problem of errors which can arise in presence of arithmetic relations. To handle properly this issue, the results concerning partial correctness (so Corollaries 5.7 and 6.4) have to be restricted to the queries whose evaluation cannot yield an error. Apt [1] provides a method for proving absence of errors for pure Prolog programs augmented by arithmetic relations.

program	page	sub.free	S-unif. free	method
member	45	yes	no	DP
prefix	45	yes	yes	SYN1-SYN2
suffix	45	yes	yes	SEM1-SYN2
naive reverse	48	yes	yes	SYN1-SEM2
reverse_accum.	48	yes	yes	SYN1-SYN2
delete	53	yes	yes	SEM1-SYN2
select	53	yes	no	DP
permutation	55	yes	no	DP
permutation sort	55	yes	no	DP
insertion sort	55	yes	yes	SEM1-SEM2
partition	56	yes	yes	SEM1-SYN2
quicksort	56	yes	yes	SEM1-SEM2
tree_member	58	yes	no	DP
iso_tree	58	yes	yes	SEM1-SYN2
substitute	60	yes	yes	SEM1-SYN2
pre_order	60	yes	yes	SYN1-SEM2
in_order	60	yes	yes	SYN1-SEM2
post_order	60	yes	yes	SYN1-SEM2
polynomial	62	yes	no	DP

This provides a strong indication that for most "natural" pure Prolog programs the S-semantics is isomorphic to the M-semantics. For such programs it is possible to reason about their partial correctness using the least Herbrand model only. This might suggest that S-semantics is not needed. This would be, however, a too hastily drawn conclusion. First of all, S-semantics has other uses than the ones investigated in this paper – for example in the area of abstract interpretations (see e.g. Bossi et al. [5] for an overview). Secondly, to formulate and prove the key results, namely Corollary 5.7 and Theorem 6.5, we did use the S-semantics. It would be interesting to find proofs of these results by means of the M-semantics.

Acknowledgments

We thank the referees of the paper for useful comments. The research of the first author was partly supported by the ESPRIT Basic Research Action 6810 (Compulog 2). The research of the second author was supported by the Italian National Research Council (CNR).

References

[1] K. R. Apt. Declarative programming in Prolog. In Dale Miller, editor, *Proc. Int'l Symposium on Logic Programming*, pages 12–35. The MIT Press, Cambridge, Mass., 1993.

[2] K. R. Apt and S. Etalle. On the unification free Prolog programs. In A. Borzyszkowski and S. Sokolowski, editors, *Proc. of the Conference on Mathematical Foundations of Computer Science (MFCS 93), Lecture Notes in Computer Science*, pages 1–19. Springer-Verlag, Berlin, 1993.

[3] K. R. Apt and D. Pedreschi. Reasoning about Termination of Pure Prolog Programs. *Information and Computation*, 106(1):109–157, 1993.

[4] K. R. Apt and M.H. van Emden. Contributions to the theory of logic programming. *Journal of the ACM*, 29(3):841–862, 1982.

[5] A. Bossi, M. Gabbrielli, G. Levi, and M. Martelli. The s-semantics approach: Theory and applications. Technical Report TR 9/93, Dipartimento di Informatica, Università di Pisa, 1993. To appear in the *Journal of Logic Programming*.

[6] K. L. Clark. Predicate logic as a computational formalism. Res. Report DOC 79/59, Imperial College, Dept. of Computing, London, 1979.

[7] M. Falaschi, G. Levi, M. Martelli, and C. Palamidessi. Declarative Modeling of the Operational Behavior of Logic Languages. *Theoretical Computer Science*, 69(3):289–318, 1989.

[8] M. Falaschi, G. Levi, M. Martelli, and C. Palamidessi. A Model-Theoretic Reconstruction of the Operational Semantics of Logic Programs. *Information and Computation*, 102(1):86–113, 1993.

[9] M. J. Maher. Equivalences of Logic Programs. In J. Minker, editor, *Foundations of Deductive Databases and Logic Programming*, pages 627–658. Morgan Kaufmann, Los Altos, Ca., 1988.

[10] M. J. Maher and R. Ramakrishnan. Déjà Vu in Fixpoints of Logic Programs. In E. Lusk and R. Overbeek, editors, *Proc. North American Conf. on Logic Programming*, pages 963–980. The MIT Press, Cambridge, Mass., 1989.

[11] J.C. Shepherdson. Unsolvable problems for SLDNF resolution. *Journal of Logic Programming*, 10(1):19–22, 1991.

[12] R. Stärk. A direct proof for the completeness of SLD-resolution. In Börger, H. Kleine Büning, and M.M. Richter, editors, *Computation Theory and Logic 89*, volume 440 of *Lecture Notes in Computer Science*, pages 382–383. Springer-Verlag, 1990.

[13] L. Sterling and E. Y. Shapiro. *The Art of Prolog*. The MIT Press, Cambridge, Mass., 1986.

[14] J. D. Ullman. *Principles of Database and Knowledge-base Systems*, volume I. Computer Science Press, 1988.

[15] M. H. van Emden and R. A. Kowalski. The semantics of predicate logic as a programming language. *Journal of the ACM*, 23(4):733–742, 1976.

Parallelism

ACE: <u>A</u>nd/Or-parallel <u>C</u>opying-based <u>E</u>xecution of Logic Programs

Gopal Gupta[†]
Manuel Hermenegildo[‡]
Enrico Pontelli[†]
Vítor Santos Costa[§]

abstract

In this paper we present a novel execution model for parallel implementation of logic programs which is capable of exploiting both independent and-parallelism and or-parallelism in an efficient way. This model extends the stack copying approach, which has been successfully applied in the Muse system to implement or-parallelism, by integrating it with proven techniques used to support independent and-parallelism. Recomputation is used to deal with non-determinism, as in Prolog, i.e., solutions of and-parallel goals are not *shared*. We propose a scheme for the efficient management of the address space in a way that is compatible with the apparently incompatible requirements of both and- and or-parallelism. We also show how the full Prolog language, with all its extra-logical features, can be supported in our and-or parallel system so that its sequential semantics is preserved. The stack copying scheme together with our proposed memory management scheme can also be used to implement models that combine dependent and-parallelism and or-parallelism, such as Andorra and Prometheus.

1 Introduction

Recently, stack copying has been demonstrated to be a very successful alternative for representing multiple environments in or-parallel execution of logic programs [1]. In this approach, stack frames are explicitly copied from the stack(s) of one processor[1] to that of another whenever the latter processor needs to share a branch of the or-parallel tree of the former. In practice, by having an identical logical address space for all processors and allocating the stack(s) of each processor in identical locations of this address space, the copying of stack frames can be reduced to copying large contiguous blocks of memory from the address space of one processor to that of the other—an operation which most multiprocessor architectures perform quite efficiently—without requiring any sort of pointer relocation. The chief advantage of the stack copying approach is that program execution in a single processor is exactly the same as in a sequential system. This considerably simplifies the building of parallel systems from existing sequential systems, as was shown by MUSEwhich was built using the sequential SICStus Prolog System.

[†]Laboratory for Logic, Database, and Advanced Programming, Dept. of Computer Science, New Mexico State University, Las Cruces, NM, USA.

[‡]Facultad de Informática, U. Madrid (UPM), Madrid - Spain.

[§]LIACC, Universidade do Porto, Porto, Portugal.

[1]Throughout the paper we will often refer to the "stack" of a "processor" meaning the *memory areas* that a *computing agent* is using.

Similar arguments can also be made for the design of independent and-parallel systems based on *program annotation* (i.e. using Conditional Graph Expressions) and *recomputation of subgoals* (i.e. non-deterministic and-parallel subgoals are recomputed and not shared), as proven by &-Prolog [13]. Briefly, a program annotated for independent and-parallelism contains expressions of the form $\cdots, (\langle conditions \rangle \Rightarrow literal_1 \& \cdots \& literal_n), \cdots$ where $literal_1, ..., literal_n$ will be executed in (and-) parallel only if the (optional) $\langle conditions \rangle$ are satisfied.

A long standing goal of parallel logic programming systems designers has been to obtain more general systems by combining different forms of parallelism into a single framework in an efficient way. In particular, one would expect that independent and-parallelism and or-parallelism, that have been exploited successfully in Prolog, could naturally be exploited together. In fact, this is a hard problem, as the difficulties (e.g. supporting full Prolog) faced by several previous proposals [10, 18, 16] do show. Recently an abstract model, called the Composition Tree [8], has been designed that allows efficient realization of systems that combine both forms of parallelism while supporting full Prolog. In this paper we design a novel model, a realization of the C-tree, exploiting or- and independent and-parallelism, which subsumes both the stack copying approach (for or-parallelism) and the subgoal recomputation approach (for and-parallelism).

The resulting and-or parallel system, called ACE, is in the same category as PEPSys [18], ROPM [16] and the AO-WAM System [10]. However, our system is arguably better than the above systems in many respects, the chief ones being ease of implementation, sequential efficiency, and better support for the full Prolog language, in particular being able to incorporate side-effects in a more elegant way. These advantages are due to several factors. One of them is that ACE *recomputes* independent and-parallel goals, rather than *sharing* their solutions (solution sharing was adopted in all the previously proposed models [10, 18, 16]). Recomputation means that, given a goal a(X) & b(Y), where the two subgoals a and b are independent, the solutions for the subgoal b will be recomputed for every solution found for subgoal a. Recomputation has important advantages (they are are discussed at length in [8]), and was fundamental in the design of the C-Tree model. In this paper we show how the complete independent and- and or-parallel system based on the C-Tree can be constructed using stack-copying.

ACE subsumes both MUSE and &-Prolog in terms of execution behaviour. One of our aims is to have ACE subsume performance characteristics of MUSE and &-Prolog, namely, their low parallel overhead, their considerable speedups for interesting applications, and their support for the full Prolog language. To accomplish this we need to carefully address the many issues that arise in combining both forms of parallelism. These issues are:

- Coordination between independent and-work and or-work: that is, deciding when should the alternatives created by goals working in independent and-parallel be made available for or-parallel processing. In ACE we lay down a set of *sharing requirements* that a choicepoint should satisfy before a processor can pick an or-parallel alternative from it.

- Memory management: for or-parallel execution in MUSE the stacks of one processor *should not be* visible to the other processors (except during copying), while in independent and-parallel execution in &-Prolog the stacks of one processor *should be* visible to all other processors. In ACE processors are organized into *teams* [3] to get around these conflicting requirements for or- and independent and-parallelism respectively.

- Scheduling: ACE can use the existing schedulers of MUSE and &-Prolog for scheduling or- and independent and-parallelism respectively. However, in addition, it should also balance the amount of resources allocated for exploiting or- and independent and-parallelism.

- Efficient implementation of copying: while MUSE copies stacks of a single processor at a time, ACE needs to copy stacks of multiple processors. Therefore, developing optimized copying techniques is even more fundamental for ACE.

- Implementation of Prolog's extra-logical features (such as cuts and side-effects): Both MUSE and &-Prolog have developed techniques for supporting full Prolog. In ACE we need to extend these techniques to support sequential Prolog semantics in the presence of both or- and independent and-parallelism. Here we can benefit from the principles designed for the C-tree abstraction [6].

In designing the solutions to these problems, our aim is to obtain a full Parallel Prolog system that will have low sequential overheads and good parallel speedups. Also, we try to follow the techniques that have been used for &-Prolog and MUSE as much as possible, as they have proven to be effective in practice.

Our perspective so far of ACE has been as a concretization of the C-tree framework for combining independent and- and or-parallelism using stack copying. Once ACE is fully described, it will be apparent that ACE can be seen in quite a different perspective. In this new perspective, ACE generalizes the principle of copying, from the copying used in MUSE to obtain or-parallelism between sequential computations, to *copying to obtain or-parallelism between and-parallel computations*. In the paper we show that this principle, *Generalized Copying*, not only gives a way to understand ACE, but it applies, and should be useful, to combine or-parallelism with many forms of and-parallelism, such as parallelism between determinate and-goals as exploited in Andorra-I [3], or with dependent and independent and-parallelism as exploited in DDAS [17].

The paper is organized as follows. We first present the ACE model. Although the C-tree abstraction is implicit to our reasoning, it is not needed for understanding the rest of the paper. We in fact describe the ACE copying approach directly in order to give a more intuitive feel for the model. We then enter the more specific problems of memory management, and how copying can be implemented between stack sets. We give a brief overview of the new scheduling problems that arise, and present and discuss two schemes for the optimization of copying in ACE. We also propose a scheme to support cut and side-effects in ACE. We finally discuss the effectiveness of ACE and show how our scheme can be generalized to dependent and-parallel systems. Throughout the paper, we assume some familiarity with the implementation of Prolog, &-Prolog, and MUSE.

Also, we assume that programs are annotated to express the and-parallelism using &-Prolog's Conditional Graph Expressions (CGEs) before execution commences.

2 Stack Copying for And-Or Parallelism

In ACE, the multiple environments that are needed to implement or-parallelism are supported through explicit stack copying. We first summarize the stack copying approach (as used by the MUSE system). In a stack-copying or-parallel system several processors explore different alternatives in the search tree independently (modulo side-effect synchronization). The execution of each processor is identical to a sequential Prolog execution. Whenever a processor P1 exhausts its branch and wants to share work with another processor P2 it selects an untried alternative from a choice point `cp` in P2's stack. It then copies the entire stack of P2, backtracks up to the choice point `cp` in order to undo all the conditional bindings made below `cp`, and starts executing one of the untried alternatives. In this approach, provided there is a mechanism for copying stacks, the only cells that need to be shared during execution are those corresponding to the choice points. Shared choice points are thus copied from P2's private memory to shared memory where they can be accessed from both P1's and P2's private memory via pointers[2] (these choice points are said to have been made *public*, following MUSE's terminology).

If we consider the presence of and-parallelism in addition to or-parallelism, then, depending on the actual types of parallelism appearing in the program and the nesting relation between them, a number of cases can be distinguished. The simplest two cases are of course those where the execution is purely or-parallel or purely and-parallel, which do not require any special intervention.

Two forms of intermixing of or- and and-parallelism can be recognized [17]. *"And Under Or"* refers to cases where or-parallelism present inside and-parallel goals is not exploited. Thus, only alternatives in those choice points that are not nested inside any CGE, i.e., not created during processing of and-parallel goals, are made available for or-parallel processing. If the choice point is not preceded by any and-parallel computation we are exactly in the same situation as in normal stack-copying based or-parallelism (e.g. in a MUSE execution). Otherwise the part of the computation tree preceding the choice point from which an alternative is going to be taken contains a completed and-parallel computation, possibly spread over the stacks of different workers. All these portions need to be copied, since they may contain variables accessed by the subsequent execution. The copying process is straightforward, since it is related to subgoals whose execution has already been completed.

"Or Under And" refers to the cases where the untried alternatives of choice points created within and-parallel goals in CGEs are also made available for or-parallel processing. One could simplify, and disallow or-parallel processing of such alternatives, trying them sequentially via backtracking instead, but there is experimental evidence that a considerable amount of or-parallelism may be lost [17]. Therefore, ACE does support or-under-and parallelism. When an alternative created within and-parallel goals in a CGE is selected, one needs to carefully decide which portions of the stacks to copy. Our guiding principle is the following: copy all branches that would be copied in an equivalent or-parallel (MUSE in this case) execution, and recompute all those branches that would be recomputed in an equivalent pure and-parallel computation. As far as the and-parallel execution is concerned, we want to be as close as possible to the recomputation approach hence implementing the PWAM "point backtracking" strategy [12] used in &-Prolog. As we will see, our strategy results in copying only parts that &-Prolog reuses during backtracking and recomputing those that &-Prolog (and also MUSE and Prolog) recomputes.

Consider a CGE $(g_1 \& \ldots g_i \ldots \& g_n)$ that is encountered during execution, and whose goal g_i has an untried alternative in one of the choice points in its search tree. Assume a processor picks up this untried alternative for or-parallel processing. Then this processor will have to copy all the stack portions in the branch from the root to the CGE including the *CGE descriptor* (called *C-node* in [8] and *parcall frame* in &-Prolog [13]). It will also have to copy the stack portions corresponding to the goals $g_1 \ldots g_{i-1}$ (i.e. goals to the left of g_i). The stack portions up to the

---

[2]To be precise, shared choice points are not copied but a *record* representing the choice point is created in the shared area.

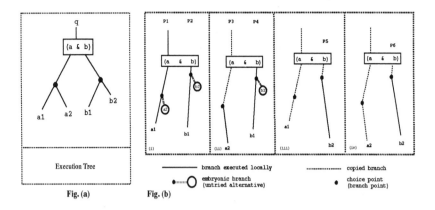

Figure 1: Execution of an Or Under And computation

CGE need to be copied because each different alternative within g_i might produce a different binding for any variable defined in an ancestor goal of the CGE. The stack portions corresponding to goals g_1 through g_{i-1} have to be copied because execution of the goals following the CGE may need to access some of the bindings generated by the goals $g_1 \ldots g_{i-1}$. The stack portions corresponding to the goals $g_{i+1} \ldots g_n$ *need not be copied*, because these goals would be recomputed. The issue is further illustrated with a simple example.

Figure 1.(a) shows the and-or tree for the query q containing a CGE (`true =>` `a(X) & b(Y)`), each of whose goals leads to two solutions. For sake of simplicity, we have only shown the path from the root of the tree to the CGE.

Execution in ACE begins with processor P1 executing the top level query q. When P1 encounters the CGE, it picks the subgoal a for execution, leaving b for some other processor. Let us assume that processor P2 picks up goal b for execution (Figure 1.(b).(i)). As execution continues P1 finds solution a1 for a, generating a choice point along the way. Likewise, P2 finds solution b1 for b.

Since we allow for full or-parallelism within and-parallel goals, a processor can steal the untried alternative in the choice point created during execution of a by P1 (to this end P1 has to move the choicepoint into the shared area). Let us assume that processor P3 now steals this alternative, and sets itself up for executing it. To begin execution of this untried alternative P3 copies the stack of processor P1 (Figure 1.(b).(ii) shows this process; see index at the bottom of Figure 1 for explanation of the symbols). P3 then simulates failure to remove conditional bindings made below the choice point, and restarts the goals to its right (i.e. the goal b). Processor P4 picks up the restarted goal b and finds a solution, b1, for it. In the meantime, P3 finds the solution a2 for a (see Figure 1.(b).(ii)).

Note that before P3 can commence with the execution of the untried alternative and P4 can execute the restarted goal b, they have to make sure that any conditional bindings made by P1 after the selected choice point have been cleared, as in Muse. The same applies now to any bindings made by P2 while executing b have been cleared. The former can be implemented by either (i) P4 copying b from P2 and completely backtracking over it[3]; or, (ii) P3 (or P4) getting a copy of the trail stack

---

[3] An optimization could be that P4 choses not to backtrack over b or recompute it again, rather

of P2 and resetting all the variables that appear in it.

At this point, two copies of b are being executed in or-parallel, one for each solution of a. Note that the process of finding the solution b1 for b leaves a choice point behind. The untried alternative in this choice point can be picked up for execution by another processor. This is indeed what is done by processors P5 and P6 for each copy of b that is executing. These processors copy the stack of P2 and P4 respectively, up to the choice point. The stack portions corresponding to goal a are also copied (Figures 1.(b).(iii), 1.(b).(iv)) from processors P1 and P3, respectively. The processors P5 and P6 then proceed to find the solution b2 for b. If no processors are available to steal unexplored alternatives, the successive solutions will be found using &-Prolog backtracking. In the above example, all other operations that are performed during and-parallel execution remain the same as in &-Prolog. We place a restriction (called the *sharing requirement*) on choice points inside a CGE that can be made available for or-parallel processing: given a goal g_i in a CGE, choice points arising in it can be made available for or-parallel processing only if the goals to the left of g_i in that CGE have reached a solution. If the CGE containing g_i is nested inside another CGE, then all goals to the left of the goal leading to the inner CGE should also have found a solution, and so on. Thus, in the example above (Fig. 1.(b).(i)), the alternative b2 of b cannot be picked up by any team until the solution a1 has been found. The sharing requirement allows to keep scheduling very close to the scheduling strategy employed by MUSE and to avoid possible speculative or-parallelism. We could go one step further, and stipulate that choice points inside CGEs will be made available only if *all* goals in the CGE have found at least one solution. Although this will keep us closer to &-Prolog and enable us to do a limited form of intelligent backtracking (the kind that is also present in &-Prolog), this will overly restrict the amount of or-parallelism.

3   Memory Management in ACE

One of the main features of stack-copying based or-parallel systems which greatly facilitates stack copying is that each processor has an identical logical memory address space. This enables one processor to copy (part of) the stack of another without relocating any pointer. In the presence of and-parallelism this feature may be hard to ensure, as each goal in a CGE may be executed in and-parallel by a different processor. In other words, as far as and-parallel execution is concerned, all the participating processors should work on separate segments of a common address space, whereas for or-parallel execution each processor should have an identical but independent logical address space (so that stack portions can be copied without any pointer relocation). Thus, the requirements for or- and and-parallelism seem to be antithetical to each other. The problem can be resolved by dividing all the available processors into *teams* (as proposed, for other purposes, in the Andorra-I system [3]) such that and-parallel work can only be shared between processors of the same team, and or-parallel work can only be shared between teams. All processors in a team thus share the same logical address space, but each team has its own independent logical address space (which must be identical to the address space of all other teams to allow copying without any pointer relocation).

P4 simply copies b and reuses it. This optimization is only valid if b has not yet generated a solution (or at least, execution of the continuation of the CGE, which may bind variables conditionally in b, should not have begun). Some problems may also arise with extra-logical predicates in b, and in general only the part before such an extra-logical predicate can be copied into P4.

To implement and-parallelism, the address space of each team is divided up into *k memory segments* (as happens in &-Prolog), where k is the maximum number of processors allowed in any given team. Each processor of the team allocates its stack set (heap, local stacks, trail etc.) in one of the segments. The sizes of the k different memory segments in the address space of a team are not required to be the same. However, once one team's address space has been divided into segments using some scheme for division, the address spaces of all other teams should be divided into segments in an identical way, so that during copying of stacks no pointer relocation is needed. Processors belonging to other teams are allowed to join a different team as long as there is a memory segment available for them to allocate their stacks in the new team's address space.

Consider the simple scenario where a choice point, belonging to a team T1 and *outside the scope of any CGE*, is picked by a team T2. Let i be the memory segment number in T1 in which this choice point lies. For simplicity, we assume that the root of the Prolog execution tree also lies in memory segment i. T2 will thus copy the stack from the ith memory segment of T1 into its own ith memory segment. Since the logical address space of each team is identical and is divided into identical segments, no pointer relocation is needed. Failure is then simulated and the execution of the untried alternative of the stolen choice point begun.

Now consider the more interesting scenario where a choice point, created by a team T1 and which lies within the scope of a CGE, is picked up by a processor in a team T2. Let this CGE be $(g_1 \& \ldots \& g_n)$ and let g_i be the goal in the CGE whose sub-tree contains the stolen choice point. T2 needs to copy the *stack segments* corresponding to the computation from the root up to the CGE and the stack segments corresponding to the goals g_1 through g_i. Let us assume these stack segments lie in the memory segments numbered $i_1, \ldots, i_k$ of team T1. They will be copied, at the same position, into the memory segments numbered $i_1, \ldots, i_k$ of team T2. (Section 5.2 describes a strategy for incremental copying). Failure would then be simulated on g_i. We further need to remove the conditional bindings made during the execution of the goal $g_{i+1} \ldots g_n$ by team T1. Let $i_{k+1} \ldots i_l$ be the stack segments where $g_{i+1} \ldots g_n$ are executing in team T1. Once removal of conditional bindings is done the execution of the untried alternative of the stolen choice point is begun. The execution of the goals $g_{i+1} \ldots g_n$ is reinitiated (since we are following a recomputation approach) and these can be executed by other processors which are members of the team (some of this re-computation can be avoided, as mentioned earlier). Note that whereas copied stack segments occupy the same memory segments as the original stack segments, restarted goals can be executed in any of the available memory segments (clearly, if T2 decides to copy the computations done by team T1 for goals g_{i+1} through g_n to save recomputation or for untrailing, as mentioned earlier, then the corresponding stack segments will have to be copied in the same memory segments, i.e. i_{k+1} through i_l, of T2). Figure 2 illustrates the process of performing sharing between teams.

Note also that each memory segment in a team's address space has a complete set of stacks for a processor to work on corresponding to the "stack set" of &-Prolog [13]. Thus, the segmented memory management proposed can also be viewed as each team having a number of stack sets on which different processors ("agents") can work on. This view allows the immediate application of standard memory management techniques developed for independent and-parallelism [13] within each team.

This leads to a layering of the parallelism exploitation in ACE: at the lower layer, within each team, the computation is purely and-parallel, as in a group of

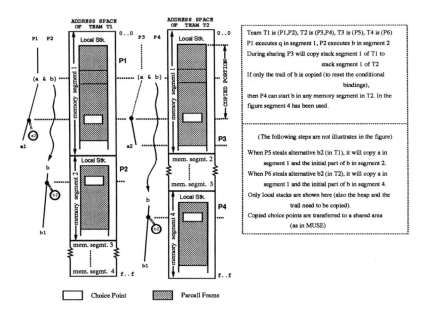

Figure 2: Illustration of Stack Copying

"stack sets" in &-Prolog to which a number of "agents" are attached; at the higher layer, among the teams, the computation is purely or-parallel (as in MUSE). Thus, it is easy to see that in the presence of only and-parallelism our system would be as efficient as &-Prolog, while in the presence of only or-parallelism it would be as efficient as the MUSE system.

An interesting property of ACE also related to memory management is that it adapts quite naturally to a hybrid multiprocessor in which parts of the address space are shared among subsets of processors, as, for example, in a system containing multiple shared-memory multiprocessors connected by a message passing or broadcast local network. In this kind of system each shared-memory multiprocessor would be a natural host for a team, its processors sharing the common addressing space. The various teams would then be spread over the different multiprocessors communicating over the message-passing or broadcast local network. And-parallelism would be exploited within the shared-memory system while or-parallelism would be exploited over the distributed network of these shared memory systems. The argument above has been based on locality of addressing space issues, but a perhaps even more important factor involved is that of the location dependent, non uniform memory access time in the system. It also makes sense from this point of view to keep processors in a team, which communicate more often, within the fast communication area and put different teams, which communicate less often, at a larger distance from the point of view of communication. Similar principles apply and a similar approach can be taken for implementing and-or parallel systems on general NUMA (Non Uniform Memory Access) Machines even if they have a global addressing space.

4 Scheduling

The need to schedule work arises at two independent levels: (i) and-parallel work at the level of processors within a team and, (ii) or-parallel work at the level of teams. A processor can steal and-parallel work only from members of its own team. An idle team can steal an untried alternative from a choice point (which has been moved to the public area in another team). This suggests that separate schedulers can be used for managing the and-parallel and or-parallel work respectively. Schedulers developed for &-Prolog and for MUSE can be used for this purpose. The only main element that has to be taken into account during or-scheduling is the fact that new alternatives can be taken only out of choice points satisfying the sharing requirement.

Finally, one has the new problem of balancing the number of teams and the number of processors in each team, in order to fully exploit all the and- and or-parallelism available in a given Prolog program. In order to solve this problem dynamically, processors can migrate from one team to another or start new teams. An idle processor first looks for and-parallel work in its own team. If no and-parallel work is found, it can decide to migrate to another team where there is work, provided (a) it is not the last remaining processor in that team, and (b) there is a free memory segment in the memory space of the team it joins. If no such team exists it can start a new team of its own, perhaps with idle processors of other teams, provided there is a free address space available for the new team. The new team can now steal or-parallel work from other teams. Some of the 'flexible scheduling' techniques [4] that are being developed for deciding when a processor should switch teams etc. in the Andorra-I system can also be used in ACE.

5 Implementation of ACE

The discussion so far has aimed at providing a general, high-level description of the ACE execution model. In this section we will present a number of practical issues which arise in the implementation of the model and propose a number of solutions for efficiently resolving them. The two main issues we study are related to memory management (and how copying of stack sets between teams can be efficiently implemented by only copying parts of such stack sets), and how full Prolog can be supported in ACE. (Further details on implementation of ACE, that are not included here for lack of space, can be found in [9]).

5.1 Goal Execution Order in CGEs

Memory management is a complex problem in the implementation of parallel logic programming systems, one that is closely related to scheduling.

Memory management is simplified in MUSE because each processor manipulates a separate Prolog stack set. In contrast, in ACE a team manipulates multiple stack sets that may have to be copied when teams fetch work from other teams. Furthermore, depending on and-scheduling, only parts of such stack sets may be needed: the order in which stack frames are pushed on the processor's stack may not obey the order in which they would have been pushed in a sequential Prolog implementation, and thus a stack segment may contain "trapped" stack frames (actually, whole "stack sections") that are not part of the computation surrounding it [13]. As a result of this, when copying stack segments we may copy sections that are unrelated to the branch we need. We can completely avoid copying these non-relevant parts, but then many small fragments of the stack will have to be copied making the copying operation somewhat inefficient [9], and, in any case, the hole created by the trapped goal would remain in the copying stacks because copying is address-to-address to avoid pointer relocation. Incremental copying is also made difficult by this potential lack of order.

Ideally, we would prefer that a parallel stack-based system implementing Prolog semantics would obey the *seniority constraint* [14]: Given two stack frames, f_1 and f_2, corresponding to two nodes in the Prolog search tree, then f_1 should be allowed to appear above f_2 (there might be other intervening nodes between f_1 and f_2) if and only if f_1 will appear above f_2 in the stack in standard sequential execution of Prolog. Thus frames of descendent nodes in the execution tree must appear on top of frames of their ancestors. This would allow to have a perfect matching between the backtracking order and the order in which stack frames are allocated on the stack.

Enforcing this constraint for an independent and-parallel system such as &-Prolog (or ACE) may severely constrain the way and-parallel goals can be scheduled, causing a considerable loss of parallelism (as illustrated in [13]). Ignoring the seniority constraint leads to the creation of holes in the stack (and trapped subgoals), that will be reclaimed once everything above has been removed. This creates many problems in ACE, because now when we copy a stack set, we may copy many trapped goals that are not part of the current alternative stolen. These trapped goals may need to be identified before execution can begin in the copying team. This problem and our solutions are further discussed in the next section in the context of techniques for *incremental copying* of stacks.

5.2   Incremental Copying in ACE

An optimization that significantly improves the performance of stack-copying or-parallel systems, like MUSE, is *incremental copying*, i.e., when a processor copies a stack of another, only those parts are copied in which the two processors differ. This is illustrated in Figure 3.(i) (only local stacks are shown). Assume processor P1 is working on branch 1, and P2 on branch 2. At this point both P1 and P2 have a common stack up to the branch node a (modulo conditional bindings). Assume now that after exploring branch 2, P2 decides to pick an alternative from P1 (along branch marked 3) in node b. To do so it backtracks up to node a and steals the second alternative from b in P1. Therefore, before P2 can proceed, it needs to create on its stacks the state that existed in P1 at the time the choicepoint corresponding to b was created. To do so it copies P1's stacks. The copying and restoring of state can be done in three ways [1] (Figure 3.(i)):

(i) Total: copy the entire stacks of P1 (everything from the root to the bottom most node along branch 1), then backtrack until choicepoint b is reached. Thus, the hatched, gray, and black shaded segments of P1's stack in Figure 3.(i) will be copied;

(ii) Incremental: copy only frames below choice point a (those above a are already on P2's stack), then backtrack until choice point b. Thus, only the gray and black segments in P1's stack in Figure 3.(i) will be copied);

(iii) Optimized incremental: copy only the stack segments between choice points b and a because those above a are already on P2's stack, and those below b are not needed for execution. Thus, only the gray shaded portion of P1's stack in Figure 3.(i) will copied. The exception is that the entire trail stack below a is copied,

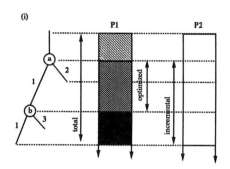 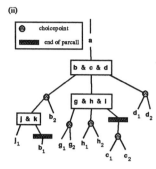

Figure 3: Incremental Copying

so that the parts of the trail stack below choice point b can be used for removing conditional bindings.

Clearly, option (i) involves unnecessary copying[4] because there are copied parts that are immediately backtracked over and reclaimed. Option (ii) also does unnecessary copying, unless the black shaded part of the stack in Figure 3.(i) is very small in size. In MUSE the difference between Incremental and Optimized is almost irrelevant, since in most of the cases there will be hardly anything on the stack below the choice point (assuming the stack is growing downward as in Figure 3.(i)) from which the new alternative is taken. This is a consequence of the scheduling policy adopted by MUSE, in which alternatives are always taken from the bottommost choice point (known as dispatching-on-bottommost [1]).

In ACE, however, things are different due to the presence of and-parallelism. Referring again to the and-or tree shown in Figure 3.(ii), suppose that a team, T2, was working on alternative g_2 of goal g in the inner CGE (which it stole from a team, T1, earlier). It finds a solution, looks for more work, and decides to pick an alternative h_2 from node h (corresponding to solution g_1 from T1). T2 and T1 have a common stack up to the CGE labeled (g & h & i). The stack frames leading up to choicepoint g are also present in both. Applying the idea of incremental copying, T2 will have to copy the difference between T1 and itself. As before, there are two ways of copying incrementally: (i) blindly copying the difference between corresponding stacks (of different processors of the two teams) on T2's stacks (Incremental Copying); (ii) copying only those parts which will be useful for T2, i.e. leaving out the parts that will be immediately backtracked over (e.g. the frames corresponding to h_1, i, c_1 and d_1) copying only the trail for such parts. Incremental copying proceed as follows: team T2, initially positioned at choice point b, steals alternative g2, does blind incremental copying, backtracks over d, c, i, g1, and h (the shaded area indicates the holes left), computes g2, and restarts all goals to the right (h, i, and d). .

While in MUSE Incremental copying (rather than Optimized incremental copying) results in very little space being copied that gets immediately backtracked over, in ACE this may not be the case, as ACE supports and-parallelism and follows the *sharing requirement* to make nodes public. Consider the following scenario: suppose

---

[4]Experiments on the Sequent Symmetry have shown that for memory chunks larger than 4K the copying time is proportional to the size of the memory chunk being copied [9].

as before that T2 tries to steal alternative h_2 from choicepoint h, and that T1 has not yet found a solution for goal i. In this case, T1 will not make the choice points of all the branches to the right of i public (that is, choice points created from the goal d in the example). This is for two main reasons. Firstly, and as mentioned when presenting the sharing requirement, work available from these choice points will be very speculative, as i may yet fail (possibly after computing for a long time) and all the work in copying these branches and picking work from them may therefore be wasted. Second, making these choice points public will lead to mixing of public and private parts of the logical search tree.[5] This mixing of public and private areas of the logical search tree will result in complications in scheduling. Hence, choice points in goals to the right of an incomplete goal in a CGE are never made public. As a consequence of this, incremental copying will end up copying all the private goals, that may form a large part of the tree, and immediately discarding them (by backtracking over them), which is clearly a waste.

It is not very clear, on the other hand, which incremental copying approach (Incremental or Optimized) will reduce the synchronization time between teams T1 and T2. However, it is obvious that Incremental copying is the simpler of the two: in the case of Incremental copying T1 has to synchronize for the duration of the copying of the difference, while in the Optimized case we first have to figure out the limits of copying for each processor stack in T1 (which may require a complete traversal of the and-parallel tree computed by T1) and then do the copying. Further details on how optimized incremental copying is realized can be found in [9]. In ACE we propose to use both Incremental and Optimized incremental copying depending on the situation. The following heuristic tries to balance the excessive unnecessary copying (Incremental copying) and the excessive synchronization time (Optimized copying) by dynamically detecting which of the two options may give the best results. If the choicepoint from which the alternative is being stolen is outside the scope of any CGE, or it is in the scope of some CGEs and all these CGEs have found a solution (i.e. each subgoal of each CGE has already found a solution) in the team from which the alternative is being stolen, then Incremental copying will be adopted. Otherwise, Optimized incremental copying will be used. Finally, note that all processors in a team can cooperate to speed up detecting the areas to be copied and actually performing the copy of stack segments from one team to another.

5.3 Implementing Side-effects and Cuts in the ACE Model

One advantage of an and-or parallel model that recomputes independent goals is that since it closely mirrors traditional Prolog execution it can quite easily support full Prolog, i.e., support the execution of order sensitive predicates such as side-effect predicates (e.g. read, write, assert, retract, and calls to dynamic predicates) and cut (!).

Essentially, a side-effect predicate (sep for brevity) should be executed only after the sep "preceding" it (preceding in the sense of left-to-right, top-to-bottom Prolog order) has finished execution. If the preceding sep has not been executed, the current sep should suspend, and resume after the execution of the preceding sep is over. However, given a sep, determining the sep that "precedes" it is a nontrivial problem, and therefore the knowledge that the preceding sep has finished, in general, has to be approximated.

For example, consider supporting seps in purely or-parallel systems [11]. Here,

---

[5]Note that they are already mixed in the physical stacks.

the preceding **sep** is assumed to be finished if the or-branch containing it has finished execution. In other words, a **sep** is executed only when the branch containing it becomes the leftmost in the or-parallel tree. Likewise, in a purely independent and-parallel system, such as &-Prolog, a simple approach is to make a **sep** encountered in an independent and-parallel goal g in a CGE C be executed only after all the independent and-parallel goals to the left of g in the CGE C have finished execution. If the CGE C containing the goal g is nested inside a goal h, which is an independent and-parallel goal in another CGE D, then all the independent and-parallel goals in D that are to the left of h should have finished, and so on.[6]

We can combine the conditions for executing **seps** in a purely or-parallel system with those for a purely and-parallel system to generate the conditions for executing a **sep** in an and-or parallel system such as ACE. Given a CGE $(cond \Rightarrow g_1 \ \& \ \ldots \ \& \ g_i \ \& \ \ldots \ \& \ g_n)$, where we assume that the parallel execution of goal g_i leads to a side-effect, the conditions under which this side-effect will be executed are given below. Note that the goal g_i is being recomputed in response to solutions $s_1 \ldots s_{i-1}$ that will be found for goals $g_1 \ldots g_{i-1}$ respectively. Let $b_1 \ldots b_{i-1}$ be the or-branches in respective search trees of goals $g_1 \ldots g_{i-1}$ that lead to these solutions. The conditions are as follows:

(i) The or-branch that contains the **sep** in the search tree of goal g_i should become leftmost.[7]

(ii) The computation of solutions $s_1 \ldots s_{i-1}$ should have finished; and the or-branches $b_1 \ldots b_{i-1}$ should be leftmost in the search tree of their respective goals $g_1 \ldots g_{i-1}$.

(iii) If the CGE containing g_i is nested inside another CGE then conditions (i) and (ii) must recursively hold for the inner CGE with respect to the outer CGE. If the CGE is not nested inside other CGEs, then the or-branch in which it appears should be leftmost with respect to the root of the whole computation tree.

In the rest of this section we present a concrete technique for determining when a **sep**'s turn for execution has come during and-or parallel execution. The technique makes use of those developed for &-Prolog [2], MUSE [1], and Aurora [5]. For simplicity, and without loss of generality, we assume that when a processor reaches a **sep** it repeatedly performs the above check until it succeeds (thus the processor busy-waits rather than suspends). However, suspension would be used in practice[8] so that the processor that encountered the **sep**, rather than busy-waiting and wasting cpu-cycles, can do useful work elsewhere.

5.3.1 Side-Effects in ACE

Note that while verifying the above conditions to check if a side-effect can be executed, processors need to access shared choice points recorded in the shared memory (to do the leftmost check). This can be expensive, especially in a non-shared memory or a hybrid multiprocessor system. One can reduce the number of accesses to shared memory by first requiring a processor that has reached a side-effect to: (a) check if all goals to the left of g_i in the current CGE, and those to the left in all the ancestor CGEs have produced a solution (first part of condition (ii), and condition

---

[6]Note, however, that more sophisticated synchronization mechanisms can also be implemented [15].

[7]With respect to the local search tree of g_i.

[8]Implementation of suspension does not present problems in &-Prolog. Techniques for implementing suspension more efficiently in MUSE by storing the difference between the suspended branch and the one that the processor switches to have recently also been developed by the MUSE group. These techniques can be adapted for ACE.

(iii)); (b) check if the side-effect is in the leftmost branch, and the solutions to preceding goals in all the CGEs are in leftmost branches (condition (i), second part of condition (ii), and condition (iii)). Note that check (a) does not require access to the shared area, it is performed wholly within the address space of the team executing the side-effect. Check (b) will be made only after check (a) succeeds, thus reducing the number of accesses to shared area. The above decomposition also neatly separates the and-parallel and the or-parallel components of the check. Both checks (a) and (b) must be implemented efficiently, particularly check (a) since it is going to be performed more often.[9]

The presence of the sharing requirements allows separating the side-effect checks for or and and-parallelism in a different way. In fact the sharing requirements guarantee that all the branches to the left of a public choice point are completed (otherwise the choice point would not satisfy the requirements during the sharing operation). Because of this we need not perform check (a) in the public part of the tree. Furthermore, in the private part of the tree check (b) is unnecessary since no sharing operations have been performed (the side effect is for sure in the leftmost branch). Thanks to these observations, if P is the bottommost public node in the current branch, then we can organize the side-effect check as follows: (1) apply check (a) only to the subtree rooted at P; (2) apply check (b) only to the public part of the tree above P. Check (a) can be performed using any of the algorithms suggested for and-parallel systems [15, 2].

To check if a given node is in the leftmost branch of a given subtree, we need access to the left sibling nodes of the immediate ancestor choice point nodes (given a node, if the choice point node above it doesn't have any left siblings, the node is in the leftmost branch of the subtree rooted at that choice point). However, the sibling-nodes of a choice point are not directly accessible to a team doing the check, therefore we have to use some other technique to determine this. An algorithm based on the MUSE approach (using bitmaps to keep track of the agents working below a choice point) has been developed. Full details can be found in [9].

Techniques to deal with *cuts* for the ACE system can be obtained quite easily adapting those developed for or-parallel systems (like those for MUSE and Aurora). A detailed treatment of this topic can be found in [9].

6   Efficiency and Generality of the ACE Model

We believe that an implementation of the ACE model will be quite an efficient realization of an or- and independent and-parallel system. This is primarily because, as may already be evident, in the presence of only or-parallelism ACE will be as efficient as MUSE, while in the presence of only independent and-parallelism it will be as efficient as &-Prolog. Therefore, it is clear that having an ACE system would be, at least, as powerful and efficient as having both a MUSE and an &-Prolog system, in the sense that now a single system will run or-parallel only programs and and-parallel only programs with similar performance as the MUSE and &-Prolog systems respectively. ACE should also combine speedups from programs where both or- and independent and-parallelism are available, hence performing even better than the best of MUSE or &-Prolog for such applications. Note that with respect to MUSE, the parts that are copied in and-or parallel execution in

---

[9]Indeed, check (a) can be implemented quite efficiently since the appropriate information about the status of and-parallel goals is maintained in the CGE's descriptor, and therefore, performing check (a) involves a simple look-up of the corresponding parcall frame(s).

ACE for a given program are exactly those that will be copied by MUSE in an equivalent purely or-parallel execution of the same program, but, whereas MUSE will copy one large stack segment at any given time, by exploiting independent and-parallelism, ACE may spread this segment over many memory segments in the address space of the team. This may in principle add some overhead to the copying cost (since many small segments rather than one large segment may have to be copied). However, because each team has multiple processors, the copying of multiple segments can be done in parallel. With respect to &-Prolog, ACE does not introduce any new overheads. The only inefficiency present in the ACE model is with respect to memory consumption, but that cannot be avoided if we want to use stack-copying for representation of multiple environments. Given that memory is inexpensive, we hope that this will not be such a big bottleneck.

Another important point that should be noted is that the approach outlined in this paper for implementing and-or parallel systems, while presented in terms of combining the types of parallelism present in MUSE and &-Prolog, is actually quite general, and can be applied to the implementation of other systems that exploit and- and or-parallelism, such as Andorra-I [3], Prometheus [17], and IDIOM [7]. It is quite easy to see how Andorra-I, a system that exploits or-parallelism and determinate dependent and-parallelism, can be implemented (the implementation of Andorra-I by Yang, Santos Costa, and Warren is based on binding arrays) using stack-copying. In Andorra-I there is no or-parallelism within and-parallel goals since only deterministic goals can be processed in and-parallel (thus it reduces to the case described in section 2). And-parallel execution can be performed by each team locally. Or-parallelism will be implemented using stack-copying and the memory-management scheme described above. Likewise, Prometheus [17], a system that exploits or-parallelism and non-determinate dependent and-parallelism (with no coroutining) by extending CGEs, can be easily implemented using the ACE scheme. In fact, since the DAS-WAM abstract machine on which Prometheus is based is itself based on that of &-Prolog, no extra measures need to be taken apart from those needed to support dependent and-parallelism, which are for the most part orthogonal to the issues dealt with by ACE. IDIOM, which adds independent and-parallelism to Andorra-I, can also be implemented using the ACE approach. Its implementation can be thought of as a combination of the ACE and Andorra-I implementations, and, again, is straightforward to derive.

7 Conclusions

In this paper, we presented ACE, a model capable of exploiting both non-deterministic and-parallelism and or-parallelism. We have discussed both high-level and low level implementation issues and shown how using recomputation the scheme can incorporate side-effects and support Prolog as the user language easily.

We have shown how ACE subsumes two of the most successful approaches for exploiting parallelism in logic programming (MUSE and &-Prolog).

We have argued how the resulting system has a good potential for low sequential overhead, can be implemented in a reasonably easy way by extending existing systems, and retains the advantages of both purely or-parallel systems as well as (even non-deterministic) purely and-parallel systems. A collaborative implementation of ACE on Sequent and other multiprocessors is under way at New Mexico State University and University of Madrid (UPM).

8 Acknowledgements

The research presented in this paper has benefited from discussions with Khayri Ali, Manuel Carro, Roland Karlsson, Kish Shen, and David H.D. Warren, all of whom we would like to thank. Ongoing work is supported by NSF Grants CCR 92-11732 and HRD 93-53271, Grants AE-1680 and AI-1929 from Sandia National Labs, by an Oak Ridge Associated Universities Faculty Development Award, by NATO Grant CRG 921318, by ESPRIT/CICYT project PARFORCE, by a fellowship from the European Commission to V. Santos Costa, while he was at the University of Bristol, and by a fellowship from Phillips Petroleum to Enrico Pontelli.

References

[1] K.A.M. Ali and R. Karlsson. The muse or-parallel prolog model and its performance. In *1990 N. American Conf. on Logic Prog.* MIT Press, 1990.

[2] S.-E. Chang and Y. P. Chiang. Restricted AND-Parallelism Execution Model with Side-Effects. In *Proceedings of NACLP89*, pages 350–368, 1989.

[3] V. Santos Costa, D.H.D. Warren, and R. Yang. Andorra-I: A Parallel Prolog System that Transparently Exploits both And- and Or-parallelism. In *Proc. 3rd ACM SIGPLAN PPoPP*, 1990.

[4] Inês Dutra. A Flexible Scheduler for the Andorra-I System. In *ICLP'91 Pre-Conference Workshop on Parallel Execution of Logic Programs*, 1991.

[5] E. Lusk et al. The aurora or-parallel prolog system. *New Generation Computing*, 7(2,3), '90.

[6] G. Gupta and V. Santos Costa. Cut and Side-Effects in And-Or Parallel Prolog. In *4th IEEE Symp. on Parallel and Distr. Processing*, '92.

[7] G. Gupta, V. Santos Costa, R. Yang, and M. Hermenegildo. IDIOM: A Model Intergrating Dependent-, Independent-, and Or-parallelism. In *ILPS91*, MIT Press, '91.

[8] G. Gupta, M. Hermenegildo, V. Santos Costa. And-Or Parallel Prolog: a Recomputation based Approach. In *Journal of New Generation Computing*, Vol. 11(3-4), 1993.

[9] G. Gupta, M. Hermenegildo, E. Pontelli, and V. Santos Costa. Ace: And/or-parallel copying-based execution of logic programs. NMSU-CSTR-9402, New Mexico State University, March 1994.

[10] G. Gupta and B. Jayaraman. Compiled And-Or Parallelism on Shared Memory Multiprocessors. In *1989 NACLP89*, pages 332–349. MIT Press, 1989.

[11] Bogumił Hausman. *Pruning and Speculative Work in OR-Parallel PROLOG*. PhD thesis, The Royal Institute of Technology, Stockholm, 1990.

[12] M. V. Hermenegildo. An Abstract Machine for Restricted AND-parallel Execution of Logic Programs. In *Proc. 3rd ICLP, LNCS 225*, pages 25–40. Springer-Verlag, 1986.

[13] M. Hermenegildo and K. Greene. &-Prolog and its Performance: Exploiting Independent And-Parallelism. In *ICLP90*, pages 253–268. MIT Press,1990.

[14] M. V. Hermenegildo and R. I. Nasr. Efficient Management of Backtracking in AND-parallelism. In *3rd ICLP*, pages 40–55. Springer-Verlag LNCS 225, 1986.

[15] K. Muthukumar and M. Hermenegildo. Efficient Methods for Supporting Side Effects in Independent And-parallelism and Their Backtracking Semantics. In *1989 International Conference on Logic Programming*. MIT Press, June 1989.

[16] B. Ramkumar and L. V. Kale. Compiled Execution of the Reduce-OR Process Model on Multiprocessors. In *NACLP'89*, pages 313–331. MIT Press, 1989.

[17] K. Shen. *Studies in And/Or Parallelism in Prolog*. PhD thesis, U. of Cambridge, 1992.

[18] H. Westphal and P. Robert. The PEPSys Model: Combining Backtracking, AND- and OR- Parallelism. In *IEEE ISLP*, pages 436–448, 1987.

Hybrid tree search in the Andorra model

Remco Moolenaar and Bart Demoen
Department of Computer Science
Celestijnenlaan 200 A, 3001 Heverlee, Belgium
e-mail: {remco, bimbart}@cs.kuleuven.ac.be

Abstract: In this paper two techniques are described to further limit the amount of nondeterminism in the Andorra model. The first technique is to enhance the nondeterministic step with intelligent selection criteria, instead of doing plain left-most selection. The other technique is to remove nondeterministic alternatives that are inconsistent with the surrounding environment. Implementation results show that for ParAKL the amount of nondeterminism is reduced and stabilized (independent of the order of the goals) by these techniques.

1. Introduction

During the last couple of years several solutions have been proposed to extend the Prolog left-to-right depth-first search strategy. One solution is to introduce the notion of determinism in the search strategy itself. The Andorra Model [11] uses this notion to delay construction of nondeterministic parts of the computation tree until all deterministic computations are finished. The major advantage of this model is that it decreases the amount of nondeterminism of a logic program and thus improves overall efficiency, because backtracking search is inefficient, compared to forward deterministic execution [5].

One disadvantage of the Andorra Model is the use of the Prolog left-to-right depth-first selection of nondeterministic goals if no deterministic computations are available. In other words, the Andorra Model improves deterministic computation, but keeps the old-style Prolog search order.

One way to improve this, is to change the order of goals during backward execution [1]. Goals that would probably fail again are moved to the left part of the computation tree. This increases the priority of this goal at nondeterministic goal selection.

In this paper, we describe another approach: instead of using the left-to-right depth-first selection for nondeterministic goals, an intelligent, heuristic based selection mechanism is used, applying some analogous techniques known from database systems and constraint logic programs.

On top of this approach, a forward checking algorithm has been implemented to remove alternatives from the selected nondeterministic goal before copying is done. Both techniques are implemented in our parallel implementation of AKL, called ParAKL [6], and the first results (running the system sequentially) show that these techniques improve search in AKL and, in general, in the Andorra Model.

The rest of the paper is organized as follows: section 2 gives a short introduction to AKL, in particular about the copying involved in the non-deterministic promotion step; section 3 gives an overview of the different heuristics that can be used to select a goal; section 4 describes the forward checking algorithm actually implemented and in section 5 and 6 conclusions and plans for future work are formulated.

2. The Andorra Kernel Language.

In this section we present a short introduction of the Andorra Kernel Language (AKL), mainly to define the terminology used in the rest of the paper. For a more detailed review of AKL we refer to [2].

2.1. The Andorra Kernel Language syntax

AKL contains the following syntactic categories:

<guarded clause> ::= <head> :- <guard><guardoperator><body>
     <head> ::= <program atom>
 <guard>,<body> ::= <sequence of atoms>
     <atom> ::= <program atom> | <constraint atom>
<guard operator> ::= '?' | '->' | '|'   (wait, cut, commit)

For reasons of simplicity, the constraint system of Prolog and GHC is used. This means that, a constraint atom is of the form $X = t$ or $X = Y$ and is called a binding. A definition of a predicate is a finite sequence of guarded clauses with the same head atom and the same guard operator, defining the predicate of the head atom. Cut and commit are pruning guards operators. The wait-operator is used for all-solutions search. The body of a guarded clause is evaluated after the completion of the guard and promotion of the clause (see the rules in the next paragraph).

2.2. *The computation model*

The computation model can be captured in a number of rewrite rules, that describe a single execution step: one configuration is rewritten to the next configuration. A configuration is a nested expression built from atoms and boxes. The syntax is defined as follows:

<configuration> ::= <and-box> | <or-box>

    <and-box> ::= **and**(<sequence of local goals>)$_{<set\ of\ variables>}$

    <or-box> ::= **or**(<sequence of configurations>)

    <local goal> ::= <atom> | <choice-box>

    <choice-box> ::= **choice**(<sequence of guarded goals>)

    <guarded goal> ::= <configuration><guard operator><sequence of atoms>

In this paper only the so-called nondeterministic promotion rule is of interest. This rule is an essential part of AKL and is necessary to do nondeterministic computation steps (i.e. search).

This rule is defined in the following way:

and$(P,$ **choice**$(R,\ (C_v?\ B),\ S),\ T)w$
$$\Rightarrow$$
or(**and**$(P,\ C,\ B,\ T)v \cup w,$ **and**$(P,$ **choice**$(R,\ S),\ T)w)$

> Condition: the and-box is stable, i.e. no other rule is applicable to any subgoal of the and-box and there are no bindings in this and-box to variables outside the local variables of the and-box. P, R, S and denote a possibly empty sequence of local goals, B denotes a sequence of atoms, C denotes a sequence of constraint atoms and the letters V and W denote sets of variables.

The difference between AKL and Prolog is that the former uses copying and the latter uses choicepoint creation and backtracking. This copying can be visualized using an example:

```
:- a(X), b(X).


a(1).
a(2).
a(3).


b(X) :- X > 2 -> write(X).
```

The configuration before applying the nondeterministic promotion rule is:
and(
      choice(and(X=1) ? true, **and**(X=2) ? true, **and**(X=3) ? true),
      choice(and(X > 2) -> write(X)))

After applying the nondeterministic promotion rule, the configuration is as follows:
or(
      and(X=1, true, **choice(and**(X > 2) -> write(X)))
      and(
            choice(and(X=2) ? true, **and**(X=3) ? true),
            choice(and(X > 2) -> write(X))))

The surrounding and-box of a/1 is copied (that is, the choice-box of b/1 is copied) and thus creates two independent computations, each exploring a different part of the search tree.

The following remarks can be made:
- the nondeterministic promotion rule is rather expensive and the amount of copying depends on the size of the surrounding and-box (which can be large)
- decreasing the amount of nondeterministic promotion rule applications would increase the overall efficiency of the implementation.

3. Goal selection in the nondeterministic promotion rule

Current implementations of the Andorra Model [3][8] use the left-to-right depth-first rule to select the candidate which is allowed to promote one of its alternatives nondeterministically. This means that these implementations have a Prolog-like behavior for search programs.

But as the order of execution of goals, in the deterministic phase, is not defined, due to the fact that deterministic goals are selected first, there is no good reason to use the old style Prolog selection rule for *nondeterministic* goals. Moreover, insisting on a left-most selection, violates the programming in logic idea where procedural considerations should be of less concern to programmers.

It is quite obvious that criteria for goal selection used in database systems [9] and constraint logic programming [10] can be used here too. However, because of the different behavior of search in the Andorra Model, some other criteria must be used as well.

3.1. Selection criteria

The selection algorithm is a combination of known techniques [9][10] and specialized criteria. The known techniques, that are included in the algorithm, are the following:

- Select the predicate with the least number of alternatives. This criterion still holds if only one of the alternatives is promoted and the rest is kept in the choice-box, because this goal is still a good candidate after failure of the first promoted alternative.
- Select the goal which is the most constrained goal[1], that is, the goal with the largest number of constraints on every argument.

These general techniques are an important part of the selection algorithm, but, because in the Andorra Model, goals with plain variable unification (equality constraints) can be subject to selection as well, an extra selection criterion is necessary to select goals with *useful* bindings (variable-to-atom, etc... instead of variable-to-variable unification). This additional selection criterion prevents the computation to enter some infinite branches as can be shown by the following example:

```
delete(X, [X|L], L).
delete(X, [Y|L1], [Y|L2]) :- delete(X, L1, L2).

:- delete(X, [1,2,3,4], R), delete(Y, R, R1), constraints(X, Y).
```

If, for instance, the variable 'Y' is more constrained than variable 'X', the criterion based on the constraints, would select the second delete/3 goal. But, as can be seen

---

1. This is an instantiation of the first failure principle.

from the equality constraints stored in the alternatives of the second delete/3 goal[1], no useful binding is available. If the second delete/3 goal is selected systematically, the computation would enter an infinite branch of the computation tree.

The solution to this problem consists in counting the number of non-var arguments for a candidate goal and to lower the priority for such a candidate if there are variable-to-variable unifications stored in the alternatives. If the number of non-var arguments of a candidate goal is equal to the arity of this goal then its priority is raised. Such a goal can be seen as a test goal: no local bindings are stored, no computation can be restarted after promotion of an alternative. Such a goal has a big chance to be deterministic[2] and must be selected as soon as possible.

3.2. The selection algorithm

The selection algorithm, which consists of the previous described criteria, is implemented in the sequential version of our parallel AKL system called ParAKL [6]. It is our intension to upgrade the parallel version to include this algorithm as well. For this we need a parallel version of the nondeterministic promotion rule.

To be able to efficiently make a selection, all the available candidate goals are saved in a linked list during the deterministic phase of the execution. That is, if a wait guard suspends and there is a choice-box for this alternative and this choice-box is not yet a candidate, a reference to this choice-box is saved in the candidate list.

At application of the nondeterministic promotion rule, the selection algorithm calculates the priorities of all the candidate goals in the candidate list and selects the candidate goal with the highest priority. Then one of the alternatives of this goal is promoted nondeterministically.

The priority of a candidate goal is the sum of two priorities: the first one is based on the known techniques, the second one on the additional selection criterion, which takes into account the unification on and the instantiation of the arguments of a candidate goal.

---

1. The first clause of delete/3 unifies 'Y' with the local variable 'X', 'R' with the list [X|L] and 'R1' with the local variable 'L'. The second clause unifies 'R' and 'R1' with lists sharing the same head variable 'Y'.
2. The call 'member(1,[1,2])' is deterministic, but a nondeterministic promotion rule must be applied to resolve this.

The first priority: looking at constraints on a variable

The first priority of a goal is the sum of the priority calculations for every argument of the candidate goal that is a constrained variable.

The priority of a single constrained variable is calculated as follows (for every constraint on this variable):

- If the constraint is an equality constraint and the choice-box of the alternative that created the constraint is not equal to the candidate choice-box: raise the priority of the candidate (another choice-box has a binding for this variable as well).
- If the constraint is not an equality constraint and the number of variables on which this constraint is suspended is equal to one[1]: raise the priority (the nondeterministic promotion of the candidate will solve the constraint).
- If, of all the choice-boxes that created a binding for this argument, the choice-box of the candidate goal has the least number of alternatives: raise its priority (this is calculated when the complete constraint list has been traversed).

The amount of calculation needed for this is limited. It is bound by the arity of the candidate goal times the average number of constraints on a variable. In practice, this is an upper bound, because only output arguments will be constrained. This will approximately halve the total number of constraints.

The second priority: looking at the bindings of the arguments

The second priority is calculated as follows: first search for useful bindings made in one of the alternatives of the candidate goal. If none is found or the number of useful bindings is too low, the lowest priority is returned as the result of this calculation.

Otherwise, if all the arguments of the candidate goal are known (i.e. all arguments are bound), raise the priority of the candidate goal.

The complexity of this calculation depends on the arity of the candidate goal plus the total number of bindings made in all the alternatives.

The biggest problem is to combine those two calculations and to find the best weights for every step of the calculation. The algorithm that is implemented assigns a weight of 50 to a ground candidate goal, a weight of 20 for every solvable

---

1. This means: the constraint is suspended on just one variable.

constraint[1], a weight of 20 for the candidate with the least number of alternatives (only if there is more than one candidate to assign a binding to a variable), a weight of 1 for every constraint that is not solvable and a weight of 10 for every binding in another branch. These weights were obtained by running ParAKL with four different values for each of the weights: more than 4000 runs were created each with a different weight calculation.

The weights we choose, actually gave the lowest number of nondeterministic rule applications for all benchmarks, except for Zebra, whose minimum was 255 for a different set of weights. So it seems that the chosen weights are near to optimal for a range of test programs and that a general selection algorithm is practical.

The following results can be found (using the general weight calculation, i.e. without forward checking):

Benchmark	ParAKL	SICS AKL
Money_1	84	127
Money_2	84	76284
Queens(8)_1	18	23
Queens(8)_2	146	336
Zebra	258	540

Table 1: Number of nondeterministic rule applications

Money_1 and money_2 are the same program using member/2 (to assign values to the variables) and difflist/1 (to make sure that all the values assigned to the variables are unequal to each other), but money_1 has the goals in a different order to make sure that the carry selection for the leftmost carry is the leftmost goal in the clause and, thus, will be selected first using the left-to-right strategy used by SICS AKL.

Queens_1 is the famous queens program but creates constraints for the rows, columns and diagonals to make sure that maximum one field is occupied. The second queens program is the usual version with the delete/3 predicate. Zebra is the usual zebra program in which difflist/1 creates the inequality constraints between the different program variables.

---

1. A weight of 5 is assigned if the constraint is an inequality constraint.

SICS AKL is a sequential AKL implementation by SICS (version 0.8), which uses left-most selection for nondeterministic promotion.

The results show that a big improvement can be made with a simple selection criterium. It is also clear that the selection algorithm stabilizes the execution: the reordering of goals in the Send-More-Money puzzle has no effect on the number of nondeterministic promotion steps.

4. Forward checking

The selection algorithm, described in the previous section, can be extended by adding some sort of forward checking *after* the selection algorithm is applied, but *before* the copying algorithm. Using this forward checking some alternatives of the selected candidate goal can be removed, because a nondeterministic promotion of one of the alternatives would definitely lead to a failure. For example:

```
a(1).
a(2).

b(2).
b(3).

:- a(X), b(X).
```

If the first alternative of a/1 is promoted nondeterministically, the corresponding or-branch would fail, leaving one alternative for a/1 which is promoted deterministically. However, if forward checking is performed on the first alternative of a/1, it would remove that alternative without applying the (rather expensive) nondeterministic promotion rule, because there is no corresponding binding for the variable 'X' in b/1. So, instead of doing a nondeterministic promotion, a forward check is performed making a/1 deterministic.

4.1. The forward checking algorithm

Forward checking algorithms are very well known in the area of solving constraint satisfaction problems [4][7]. In this area forward checking algorithms are used to remove values from the domain of a variable. This is similar to the way our forward checking algorithm works: instead of removing values from a domain, alternatives from a candidate goal are removed. The similarity is clear, because the domain of a variable can be represented by a goal with as many clauses as there are domain values. For example, the domain of variable 'X', which is equal to [1..4], can be represented as follows:

domain_X(1).   domain_X(2).   domain_X(3).   domain_X(4).

It is clear, however, that our algorithm is different from an ordinary forward checking algorithm: our algorithm has to check for unification consistency. The different structure of the computation tree (for AKL) alters the basic algorithm as well.

The forward checking algorithm is defined as follows:
>   **ForEach** binding made in the alternative to an external variable **DO**
>>   **IF** binding inconsistent with surrounding and-box **THEN**
>>>   Remove alternative from candidate
>>   **FI**
>   **OD**

Checking of the consistency of a binding with its surrounding and-box is testing whether all the constraints of the variable are consistent. This means, if a constraint is from the surrounding and-box and is inconsistent, then the binding is inconsistent. On the other hand, if a constraint is from an alternative whose choice-box is directly allocated under the surrounding and-box and all alternatives from this choice-box are inconsistent with the binding, then the binding is inconsistent[1]. If a binding is created (because of the successful application of a constraint in the consistency algorithm, for instance), this binding is checked as well. This was very useful, especially for programs with complex constraints (like, for instance, the Send-More-Money puzzle).

4.2. The implementation results

The algorithm was implemented in ParAKL and the same programs as in the previous section were run. The results are summarized in table 2: the ParAKL and SICS AKL columns have not changed. The reason why the inclusion of the forward

---

1. This was shown in the example.

check does not lower the number of nondeterministic rule applications for 'Queens(8)_1' and 'Zebra', is not clear at the moment.

Benchmark	ParAKL + forward checking	ParAKL	SICS AKL
Money_1	49	84	127
Money_2	49	84	76284
Queens(8)_1	18	18	23
Queens(8)_2	52	146	336
Zebra	258	258	540

Table 2: Number of nondeterministic rule applications

4.3. Overhead of the algorithms

For the two versions of ParAKL (with and without forward checking) the relative overhead compared to the complete execution time for every part of the nondeterministic promotion step was investigated as well (using the queens_2 program):

Algorithm	ParAKL + forward checking	ParAKL
Selection algorithm	18.5%	10.0%
Forward checking	14.5%	-
Copying algorithm	23.4%	50.4%
Total overhead:	56.4%	60.4%

Table 3: Relative overheads compared to total execution

These results show that the amount of overhead is limited, especially if the forward checking algorithm is included. The reason for the higher overhead for the selection algorithm in the left column is that the number of selections is greater than the number of copying steps because the forward checking algorithm removes some selected alternatives before they are copied: the result is a 4-fold speedup in absolute time for this benchmark, while ParAKL is about the same speed as SICS

AKL. We have also tried to run the program with two simple selection criteria: always select the first goal in the list of available goals and randomly select a goal from this list. With these criteria, the program took too long (it ran out of heap).

5. Conclusions

There are two observations that can be made: first, an intelligent selection algorithm improves the execution of search programs in AKL by a factor of 2 to 3 in terms of the number of nondeterministic rule applications. We believe that this improvement can be obtained, generally speaking, in the Andorra model as well.

Second, the use of these techniques stabilizes the execution time of search programs, i.e. it becomes more independent of the order of the goals in a conjunction (this was shown in the two Send-More-Money programs).

If one looks at the overhead of the two described algorithms, it is obvious that the price that is payed, due to the extra computation of the priorities, is compensated by the smaller number of copying steps.

There is a disadvantage to the described techniques: the programmer loses the ability to direct the search by changing the ordering of goals in a conjunction. This is an advantage as well if one looks at it from a different angle: the programmer is freed from the necessity to have knowledge of the underlying execution model. In this context, the described selection criteria are useful for any logic programming paradigm, not just Andorra.

6. Future work

As ParAKL is a parallel execution model for AKL it is obvious that the described techniques must be parallellised as well. This is one of our major tasks that has to be performed to have a fully functional, parallel implementation for AKL.

The described techniques can be further optimized and evaluated. Especially the weights, that are used in the selection algorithm, can be fine-tuned to satisfy a large class of search programs.

Both the algorithms must be further optimized (as well as the copying algorithm), because the overhead for the algorithms will increase when the number of copying steps decreases.

One of the ideas for improvement is to maintain some sort of threshold for the priority calculation: if an inspected candidate goal has a calculated priority that is greater than the threshold, select this goal. This threshold can be used as a memory cell as well: the priority calculated for the selected candidate goal is saved in the threshold. This means that, if a candidate goal is found, in the next nondeterministic promotion step, which has a priority greater than the priority of the currently selected goal, select this goal; its priority is large enough (but probably not the largest). This idea could decrease the number of inspected candidate goals.

Finally, there are possibilities for reducing the overhead of the calculation of the priorities: global analysis can deduce freeness of variables and whether they are constrained or not, so that not all arguments of a goal must be inspected during the calculation of the first priority. And the forward checking priority calculation can be sped up by generating a form of interprocedural indexing code.

7. Acknowledgments

The authors wish to thank the 'Diensten voor de Programmatie van Wetenschapsbeleid' of the Belgium Ministry for support through project IT/4 and the European Community for support through Esprit Project ACCLAIM (07195).

8. References.

[1]   S. Abreu, L.M. Pereira and P. Codognet, "Improving backward execution in the Andorra Family of Languages", in *Proceedings of the Joint International Conference and Symposium on Logic Programming*, pp. 384-398, ed. Krzysztof Apt, MIT Press, Cambridge, Massachusetts, 1992.

[2]   Sverker Janson, Seif Haridi, "Programming Paradigms of the Andorra Kernel Language", in *Proceedings of the International Logic Programming Symposium*, pp. 167-183, ed. V. Saraswat, The MIT Press, Cambridge, Massachusetts, 1991.

[3]   Sverker Janson and Johan Montelius, "Design of a sequential prototype implementation of the Andorra Kernel Language", Technical Report, SICS, september 1991.

[4]   Alan K. Mackworth, "Consistency in Networks of Relations", Artificial Intelligence, Volume 8, pp. 99-118, 1977.

[5]   A. Marien, B. Demoen, "Findall without findall/3", in *Proceedings of the Tenth International Conference on Logic Programming*, pp. 408-423, ed. David S. Warren, MIT Press, Cambridge, Massachusetts, 1993.

[6]   Remco Moolenaar and Bart Demoen, "A parallel implementation for AKL",

in *Programming Language Implementation and Logic Programming: PLILP '93*, pp. 246-261, Tallinn, Estonia, 1993.

[7]   Bernard A. Nadel, "Constraint satisfaction algorithms", Computational Intelligence, Volume 5, pp. 188-224, 1989.

[8]   Vitor Santos Costa, David H.D. Warren, and Rong Yang, "Andorra-I: A Parallel Prolog System that Transparently Exploits both And- and Or-Parallelism", in *Proceedings of the Third ACM SIGPLAN Symposium on Principles & Practice of Parallel Programming, PPOPP'91*, SIGPLAN NOTICES, vol. 26, no. 7, pp. 83-93, ACM Press, Baltimore, July 1991.

[9]   Jeffrey D. Ullman, "Principles of Database Systems", Computer Science Press, Rockville, 1982.

[10]   Van Hentenryck, "Constraint Satisfaction in Logic Programming", The MIT Press, Cambridge, Massachusetts, 1989.

[11]   Warren, David H.D., "The Andorra principle", Internal report, Gigalips Group, 1988.

Parallel CLP on Heterogeneous Networks

Shyam Mudambi and **Joachim Schimpf**
European Computer-Industry Research Centre
Arabellastr. 17, D-81925 Munich
Germany

Email: mudambi@ecrc.de, joachim@ecrc.de

Abstract

The combination of Or-Parallelism and Constraint Logic Programming (CLP) has proven to be very effective in tackling large combinatorial problems in real-life applications. However, existing implementations have focused on shared-memory multiprocessors. In this paper, we investigate how we can efficiently implement Or-Parallel CLP languages on heterogeneous networks, where communication bandwidth is much lower and heterogeneity requires all communication to be in a machine-independent format. Since a recomputation-based system has the potential to solve these problems, we analyse the performance of a prototype using this approach. On a representative set of CLP programs we show that close to optimal speedups can be obtained on networks for programs generating large search spaces and that the overhead of recomputation is surprisingly low. We compare this approach with that of stack-copying and also discuss how side-effects can be dealt with during recomputation. The main conclusion of the paper is that *incremental* recomputation is a clean and efficient execution model for Or-Parallel CLP systems on heterogeneous networks.

Keywords: Parallel Logic Programming, CLP, Heterogeneous computing, Recomputation, Or-Parallelism.

1 Motivation

Networks of personal workstations are now ubiquitous and the idea of using such networks as high-performance compute servers has stimulated a great deal of interest. Often, these networks are heterogeneous, i.e. they link together machines that vary widely in terms of hardware and software. In this paper, we will investigate how we can efficiently implement Or-Parallel Constraint Logic Programming (CLP) languages on this type of hardware platform.

CLP is a generalization of logic programming where the basic operation of unification is replaced by constraint solving. CLP has been used to tackle a number of real-life combinatorial problems, where the basic paradigm is that of "constrain and generate". Since even after the constrain phase the remaining search space can be quite large, Or-Parallel CLP systems attempt to explore this remaining space in parallel. The combination of Or-Parallelism and CLP has first been suggested in [10]. Later the ElipSys system [11] which combines finite domain constraints with Or-parallelism has proven rather successful in practical applications.

However, existing implementations have focused on shared memory multiprocessors where communication is cheap and data structures can easily be shared. In a loosely coupled network of workstations, both assumptions are no longer true. First, any sharing of state between the processors has to be simulated by explicit communication, which is limited by the *bandwidth* of the interconnection network[1]. Second, a heterogeneous platform requires all communication to be done in a *machine independent* format, which adds conversion overhead and usually increases the amount of data to be transferred.

Our approach is to avoid all state sharing and instead rely on the *recomputation* of states[2, 9, 8]. This allows for both low bandwidth requirements and machine independency, thus solving the problems outlined above. We have implemented a prototype on a network of workstations based on the ECL^{i}PS^e CLP system developed at ECRC. The results of running a number of representative CLP programs on the prototype are very encouraging and indicate that such an approach is a clean and efficient way to implement Or-Parallel CLP systems on heterogeneous networks.

The rest of the paper is organized as follows: Section 2 introduces the Or-parallel task switching problem and describes how it is solved by the recomputation model and its competitors. Section 3 presents the prototype we have implemented and analyzes the benchmark results. Section 4 discusses some additional issues that will have to be tackled by a full implementation of such a programming environment, especially the problem of impure language features, and how to better exploit a network of multiprocessors. Section 5 concludes the paper.

2 The Task Switching Problem

An Or-Parallel system is one where alternatives of a nondeterministic program are explored in parallel. We can represent this as an Or-tree where the arcs represent deterministic computation and the nodes represent nondeterministic choices (figure 1).

The processors, called *workers*, work on different parts of the tree in parallel. When a worker has explored a subtree (task) completely, it is assigned to another subtree. Since every node in the tree corresponds to a certain state of computation, taking a task from another node means the

---

[1]Recent work on optimizing a distributed version of the ElipSys system ([7]) has brought some progress in this respect. Nevertheless, the overheads associated with the use of virtual shared memory are still significant.

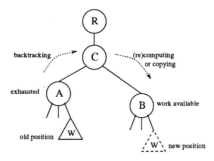

Figure 1: Moving a worker in the Or-tree

worker has to set up the corresponding state. Only then can the worker start exploring a subtree of this node. The main problem we investigate in this paper is how to efficiently achieve this state setup in a distributed environment.

In a WAM-based CLP system, the computation state is mainly represented by the (four) stacks[2] of the abstract machine. There are essentially three ways of setting up the computation state (i.e. the stacks): stack-sharing [6, 11], stack–copying[5] and recomputation [2, 8, 9].

The stack–sharing approach implies that all the stacks have to be potentially sharable and hence have to reside in (possibly virtually) shared memory. This direct sharing of a data structure is not viable in a heterogeneous setting, hence we will not discuss it further. Thus we are in particular interested in the comparison between the copying and the recomputation approaches, since in both these models each worker has its own copies of the stacks and so engine execution does not rely on shared data structures.

2.1 Stack-copying

In stack–copying, a state is set up by connecting to a worker that has a similar state and copying the stacks from there. The overhead consists in the actual transmission of the stack data, as well as in the fact that the sending worker has to interrupt its work while the copying is in progress. The amount of transmitted data is usually reduced by employing an *incremental* copying strategy. It consists of first identifying which old parts of the stacks the workers have already in common and then only copying the difference in the states of the two workers. Moreover, an appropriate scheduling strategy can also contribute to reduce the number of copying sessions by scheduling more than one node at a time. This approach has led to efficient Or-Parallel Prolog implementations on both UMA and NUMA shared memory machines [5].

Unfortunately, it is questionable whether a copying-based CLP system

---

[2]For our purposes we can treat all stacks alike.

can be efficiently implemented on a network of workstations for the following reasons:

1. The copying overhead will be considerably higher due to much lower communication bandwidth and because CLP programs typically generate larger stacks than conventional Prolog programs.

2. Though each worker has its own copy of the WAM stacks, some global data (such as atom and functor tables) has to be maintained, which can have severe performance penalties in a distributed setting.

3. Lastly, in a heterogeneous setting, copying stacks is not straightforward, as they will have to be transmitted in some device-independent format.

2.2 Recomputation

Instead of copying a state of computation, it can as well be recomputed. This is trivial as long as things are deterministic[3]: One just starts with the same initial goal and does the computation again. If the program contains nondeterministic paths, then we must make sure we take the right one if we want to reach a certain state. This can be achieved by using *oracles*, i.e. by keeping track of nondeterministic choices during the original execution and by using this recorded information (the oracle) to guide the recomputation.

The idea of using oracles and recomputation for parallelism was first implemented in the DELPHI system [2]. Their results indicated that such an approach was well suited to exploiting Or-Parallelism in coarse-grain Prolog programs on networks of workstations. [9] also describes a recomputation based algorithm and its prototype implementation in Flat Concurrent Prolog.

A striking advantage of the recomputation model is its implementational simplicity:

- The workers can be completely separated and do not have to share any state.

- The workers communicate by exchanging simple data (mainly oracles, which are just sequences of integers).

2.3 Incremental Recomputation

The incrementality optimizations used in a stack-copying [5] or stack-sharing [6] systems to reduce the amount of data to be copied can also be used in a recomputation-based approach to reduce the amount of recomputation and communication. For example to move a worker from node A to node B (figure 1) a naive system would backtrack to the root node R and recompute

---

[3]We ignore side effects for the moment.

the path from R to B. The incremental system will only backtrack to C and recompute from C to B. This is the same idea as in incremental stack copying. An incremental stack section corresponds to the incremental oracle which is needed to recompute it. Incremental recomputation has been successfully used in PARTHEO, a parallel theorem prover[8].

2.4 Comparison

The recomputation scheme has the potential to overcome both fundamental problems mentioned in the introduction: limited communication bandwidth and heterogeneity. Since oracles are a more compact representation of state than stacks, the size and volume of messages needed should be rather low. Secondly, since the workers do not share any state nor do they communicate internal representations of data structures (as is the case in stack copying), the recomputation scheme is suitable for heterogeneous networks.

Of course, recomputation can be computationally expensive for certain classes of programs. If we want to compare it with a stack copying scheme, we are interested in the difference between recomputing a piece of stack and copying it from another worker. Unfortunately, there is no fixed relation between the two. Reconstructing a piece of stack can be very expensive or quite cheap, depending on the program. A simple Prolog program can build up stacks at a rate of several Megabytes per second. On the other hand, a program may spend a lot of time while creating no (useful) stack data at all, e.g. computing a value of the Ackermann-function. Hence one of the issues we examined with our prototype were the incremental stack sizes generated by typical CLP programs.

The problem of global state and impure language features is often neglected when parallel declarative systems are discussed. With a stack copying approach, a solution to this problem would involve implementing some virtually shared data structures or a central manager for side effects. The recomputation idea, while holding out the promise to render this unnecessary, introduces new semantic problems that we discuss in section 4.2.

3 Results

The question we wanted to have answered was: Given similar scheduling strategies, would a recomputation-based CLP system be competitive with a copying-based system in a distributed setting? The main goal of implementing a prototype was therefore to gain a better understanding of the computational overhead of recomputation. Since the idea was to do it as quickly as possible, the prototype deals only with pure Prolog code and essentially returns all solutions to a particular query. The extensions necessary to deal with pruning and side effects are discussed later. First we describe the prototype implementation and then analyze the behaviour of six CLP programs and one plain Prolog program.

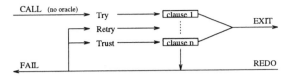

Figure 2: Backtracking in WAM

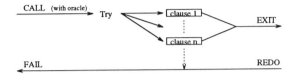

Figure 3: Oracle following in WAM

3.1 Prototype

Our results were obtained on a prototype which was implemented in three stages. First, the ECL^{i}PS^e WAM engine was extended to support recomputation, which is basically the ability to create and follow oracles. Secondly, the concept of parallel choicepoints was introduced, together with a flexible interface to control the parallel execution. This interface allows one to specify (via Prolog-coded event handlers) how the alternatives of a parallel choicepoint are executed. Lastly, on top of these features, a centralized scheduling scheme was developed in Prolog. The system was run on Sun IPC workstations connected via Ethernet.

3.1.1 Oracle Handling

The abstract machine has been extended for oracle handling. There are two modes of operation: in normal mode the machine executes as usual (figure 2) but builds up a record of which alternatives were taken at each choicepoint. In recomputation mode, the execution follows a given oracle (figure 3), i.e. the machine just deterministically takes the same alternatives that were successful while the oracle was recorded. This requires modifications of the WAM's choicepoint instructions (Try, Retry, Trust).

Oracles are implemented as a list on the global stack. The new ORC register points either to the end of the oracle list (during oracle recording) or to the current position in the oracle list (during oracle following). A small set of builtins is provided to manipulate oracles.

3.1.2 Scheduler Interface

To have a realistic prototype, it was necessary to introduce the distinction between sequential and parallel choicepoints. As in ElipSys[11], this

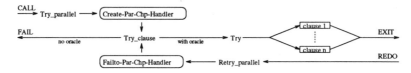

Figure 4: Parallel predicate implementation

is implemented by annotating a predicate as parallel, using the **parallel/1** declaration.

To make experiments with scheduling easy, we decided to provide a Prolog-level interface to the parallel choicepoints, rather than hard-wiring the scheduler interaction into the abstract machine. We have used the ECL^{i}PS^e event-mechanism to implement this, so that it is possible to control the parallel search with a Prolog-coded event handler. The following two events are associated with parallel choicepoints:

1. CREATING_PAR_CHP: This event is raised just before the parallel predicate is entered. The first argument to the event handler is the number of alternatives it is going to create. The handler now has the responsibility of managing these alternatives. Typically, some alternatives would be given to other workers, while the local worker takes one alternative itself. The handler forces the local worker to take a particular alternative by binding the second argument to a partial oracle. For example, in the following handler the local worker takes the first alternative.

   ```
   create_par_chp(NumAlt, ContOracle) :-
       inform_scheduler(NumAlt),
       ContOracle = [1|_].
   ```

2. FAIL_TO_PAR_CHP: This event is raised when a worker fails to a parallel choicepoint. The first argument to the handler is the number of the failed alternative. The handler can either return a new oracle and force the worker to explore another alternative (by binding the second argument to the appropriate oracle) , or force it to fail across the parallel choicepoint (by not binding the second argument). Thus a simple handler would be:

   ```
   fail_to_par_chp(FailedAlt, ContOracle) :-
       get_job_from_scheduler(ContOracle).
   ```

On the WAM level, this functionality has been implemented by prefixing the normal sequential choice instructions with the 3 new instructions Try_parallel, Retry_parallel and Try_clause (figure 4). The Try_parallel instruction creates a choicepoint, determines the number of alternatives, and raises the CREATING_PAR_CHP event. After the event handler returns, the Try_clause instruction is executed. If no oracle is given by the handler, it will cause the parallel predicate to fail. Otherwise it proceeds to the Try instruction which will just follow the oracle and execute a single clause deterministically. When the clause fails, the Retry_parallel instruction is executed, which raises the FAIL_TO_PAR_CHP event. After the event handler returns, Try_clause is executed as above.

3.1.3 The Scheduler

The Prolog implementation is made up of N ECL^{i}PS^e processes performing useful work (i.e. workers) and one ECL^{i}PS^e process which runs the central scheduler. As noted earlier, the scheduler code (in both the worker and central scheduler processes) is written in Prolog. The scheduler and the workers communicate with each other via sockets using normal Prolog reads and writeq's. The scheduler reads in a goal and returns all possible solutions to the goal. There is no special treatment of side effects, cut or commit. Thus the prototype can only be used to run "pure" programs or programs where the scope of the cut is limited to the "private" part of the stack (which is the section of the stack below the most recently created parallel choicepoint).

The worker processes read goals and oracles from the scheduler and run them. When a worker runs out of work, it informs the central scheduler. If the central scheduler has jobs, it sends a job (i.e. the corresponding oracle) to the idle worker. Otherwise, the scheduler process sends a request-work message to all busy workers. We have implemented a simple top-most scheduling strategy, where workers keep track of all parallel choicepoints seen so far and when requested for work, release the topmost (the one closest to the root) choicepoint to the scheduler. *Releasing* a choicepoint in this context means sending the scheduler the oracle (a list of integers) that leads up to the choicepoint. The workers poll for a request-work message each time either parallel choicepoint handler is called (i.e. when a parallel choicepoint is created or failed back to).

We have implemented a partial incrementality optimization in the prototype, which eliminates repeatedly computing the initial deterministic path that leads to the first parallel choicepoint in the program. Thus when a worker runs out of work, it fails back to the first parallel choicepoint of the goal, rather than failing completely out of the goal, and starting all over again from the root.

3.2 Performance Analysis

We used seven programs to analyze the performance of the prototype.

1. N-queens - A naive pure Prolog n-queens program which has been used as a benchmark for most Or-Parallel Prolog systems[6, 5].

2. K-puzzle - A number puzzle which uses finite domain constraints.

3. Ncar1, Ncar2 - The car sequencing program first implemented in CHIP[3]. Ncar1 is the original program and ncar2 is the same program, except that the `atmost/3` predicate was recoded using `delay/2`, which had the effect of increasing the granularity of parallelism.

4. cbse1-14, cbse1-18 - The protein topology prediction benchmark from ICRF [1] with 14 and 18 strands.

5. qg2-8 - A finite algebra theorem proving benchmark[4].

3.2.1 Overall Benchmark Results

The sequential execution in our prototype is somewhat slower than in the original ECL^{i}PS^e system. There are two sources of overhead: oracle recording and the prototype's event mechanism for managing parallel choicepoints. Their effect is shown in table 1. The first column is the efficiency of the original ECL^{i}PS^e system, the second column shows the slowdown due to oracle recording only, and the last column shows the effect of both. Note that the latter is the speed of the actual parallel prototype operating sequentially with a single worker. The 9-queens benchmark turns out to be particularly sensitive to the overheads we have introduced. The reason is that the dominant operation in this benchmark is the creation of parallel choicepoints, and this operation is slowed down by an order of magnitude in the prototype due to the Prolog handler calls.

For an optimized implementation we would, however, expect efficiency close to the second column, since the event handler overhead would disappear with a tighter integration.

Goal	ECL'PS^e	ECL'PS^e with Oracles	Prototype
9-queens	1.0	0.88	0.42
k-puzzle	1.0	0.99	0.93
ncar1	1.0	0.97	0.85
ncar2	1.0	0.93	0.81
cbse1-14	1.0	0.94	0.69
cbse1-18	1.0	0.94	0.71
qg2-8	1.0	0.99	0.75

Table 1: Overhead of oracle recording and parallel choicepoint handling

The speedups obtained with up to 12 workers for each of the above programs is shown in table 2 below. We should note that though an extra process was used by the central scheduler for ease of programming, the cpu time used by this process was negligible. All the timings were performed on Sun IPC machines, though the memory configurations and work loads were not identical, hence there was slight variation in the sequential running times on the various machines. The parallel timings shown are the best of four runs and speedups were computed by comparing the best parallel run with the best sequential run. There was a big variance between runtimes (especially in the short runs) which was due to network load caused by other jobs. Since the average values reflect these variances which have nothing to do with our prototype, we chose to use the best runs for our performance analysis.

Goals	Workers				
	1	2	4	8	12
9-queens	69.7	35.0 (1.99)	17.9 (3.90)	9.3 (7.50)	6.6 (10.64)
k-puzzle	995.0	557.0 (1.79)	269.1 (3.70)	145.6 (6.83)	98.3 (10.12)
ncar1	22.7	12.7 (1.78)	7.1 (3.19)	4.9 (4.60)	4.2 (5.37)
ncar2	63.2	34.0 (1.86)	18.6 (3.41)	10.70 (5.91)	8.4 (7.57)
cbse1-14	45.6	24.0 (1.91)	13.7 (3.34)	8.9 (5.13)	7.6 (6.01)
cbse1-18	801.9	403.4 (1.99)	229.9 (3.49)	111.0 (7.22)	74.4 (10.79)
qg2-8	23244.5	11926.3 (1.95)	6247.2 (3.72)	3074.1 (7.56)	2165.9 (10.73)

Table 2: Elapsed times (in seconds) and speedups of the Benchmarks

As can be seen, the k-puzzle, 9-queens, cbse1-18 and qg2-8 speedups are quite good[4], whereas the ncar1, ncar2 and cbse1 speedups fall once the number of workers is above four. One of the main reasons for this drop off in speedups for the shorter programs is the high startup time required for running jobs on a network. For example, it can take nearly a second before all the workers have tasks to work on. In a small job, a second is a significant portion of the runtime.

3.2.2 Parallel Execution Overheads

The main parallel execution overheads are due to recomputation and communication. A rough measure of the communication overhead can be obtained by examining the total number of oracles (jobs) sent out by the scheduler and their lengths. Table 3 provides these figures for the programs on the 12 worker runs. As we would expect the oracle lengths are quite small for the 9-queens query, implying that the communication overhead is quite low.

However, the oracle lengths for the CLP program are much higher - over a thousand entries, in the case of the ncar and qg2-8 queries. If we assume that an oracle entry takes up one byte, the minimum amount of data that must be communicated for these programs is over 80 Kbytes.

We should note here that a naive implementation of oracles can lead to even larger lengths. For example, many CLP programs follow the general

---

[4]It should be noted that due to the variation in sequential runtimes on the machines and the fact that we chose to compute speedups using the best sequential times, perfect speedups were not possible.

Goal	Jobs	Oracle Lengths	
		Min	Max
9-queens	229	1	20
k-puzzle	216	6	99
ncar1	135	1128	1374
ncar2	82	1146	1770
cbse1-14	302	329	525
cbse1-18	450	417	677
qg2-8	416	8678	8904

Table 3: Number of jobs and oracle lengths (12 workers)

strategy of setting up the constraints and then exploring the constrained search space. Though setting up the constraints is usually deterministic, in practice the code creates choicepoints which are cut away later, but still fill up the oracle. A solution is not to record the oracle for a deterministic path but only record its length, since another worker recomputing this section does not need any more information. Thus an oracle would consist of alternative numbers, representing which alternative to take from the next choicepoint and lengths fields (if the path is deterministic). If a length field is seen, it is decremented each time a new choicepoint is created and once it is zero, the rest of the oracle is followed (as before). We have implemented this optimization in the prototype and preliminary results show that the oracle lengths are reduced by 10% to 90%. This is of course at the expense of some recomputation time (due to useless sequential backtracking).

Tables 4 and 5 show the percentage of elapsed time spent in various activities by all the workers for the cbse1-14 and k-puzzle queries respectively. We see that the idle times for the cbse1-14 query are quite high. The main reason for this is high network startup costs and the simple work release mechanism used in the prototype. The "other" row in these tables reflects overheads such as scheduling (reading in oracles and releasing work) and garbage collecting[5]. The scheduling overhead should decrease with tighter integration.

The most interesting statistic here is of course the percentage of time spent recomputing. This overhead is not very large when compared to the total elapsed time of the query (less than 10% for both queries), which is quite encouraging. One of the reasons why this overhead is so low, is the partial incrementality optimization, which eliminated repeatedly computing the initial deterministic prefix of a goal. Since this initial segment in CLP programs is used to set up the constraints, it can be quite time consuming. For example, without this optimization the time spent recomputing in the

---

[5]Because oracle following does not create any choicepoints, the incremental garbage collector ends up repeatedly scanning such stack sections. Hence the gc time in the parallel runs was higher than the sequential gc times.

cbse1-14 program goes up from 8.5% to 25% for 12 workers. In addition, it also reduced the communication overhead significantly, since the oracles sent out by the scheduler could omit the initial deterministic prefix. The minimum oracle length column of table 3 shows the lengths of these prefixes.

Activity	Workers				
	1	2	4	8	12
Working	100.0	90.0	78.7	60.5	47.3
Idle	0.0	1.5	12.3	26.5	33.0
Recomputation	0.0	0.5	3.0	5.9	8.5
Other	0.0	8.0	6.0	7.1	11.2

Table 4: % Time spent in working and recomputing for cbse1-14

Activity	Workers				
	1	2	4	8	12
Working	100.0	88.9	92.0	85. 0	83.9
Idle	0.0	3.0	1.7	2.9	4.9
Recomputation	0.0	0.1	0.4	1.0	1.4
Other	0.0	8.0	5.9	11.1	9.8

Table 5: % Time spent in working and recomputing for k-puzzle

Table 6 gives the recomputation percentages of all the queries analysed in this paper. With the exception of the ncar1 program, all the other times are below 10%. The relatively larger percentage of time spent recomputing in the ncar1 program is due to the presence of fine-grain parallelism deep in the search tree. A more complete incrementality optimization, where a worker is given work which requires the least amount of recomputation to reach relative to its current position should allow the system to better exploit such parallelism.

Workers	2	4	8	12
queen9	0.1	0.2	0.7	1.0
k-puzzle	0.1	0.4	1.0	1.4
ncar1	2.1	6.0	17.8	16.3
ncar2	1.4	4.1	8.9	9.2
cbse1-14	0.5	3.0	5.9	8.5
cbse1-18	0.0	0.3	1.2	1.7

Table 6: Recomputation overhead of all benchmarks

3.2.3 Oracle Lengths versus Stack sizes

As we stated earlier, one of the goals of this investigation was to compare the merits of copying the state versus recomputing it. We have already seen that the oracle lengths for CLP programs are quite large, thus increasing the communication overhead. In order to see how this overhead would compare with the stack copying approach, we computed the ratio of the incremental stack sizes to the incremental oracle lengths. The maximum and minimum ratios are shown below for the benchmarks. We computed the ratio in two modes - one with the garbage collector turned off and the other in which garbage collection was forced at every parallel choice point (just before the incremental stack changes were computed). The forced garbage collection figures gives us the best case scenario for stack copying and the no garbage collection gives us close to the worst-case[6]. The ratios again seem to be quite encouraging for the recomputation scheme - the lowest ratio is 40, which means that even in the best case one oracle entry corresponds to 40 bytes of stack.

	Stack size (bytes)			Ratio to oracle length		
Goal	Average	Min	Max	Average	Min	Max
queen9 nogc	711	376	2164	100	71	376
queen9 gc	306	224	352	43	35	256
k-puzzle nogc	11321	384	35808	3046	128	13398
k-puzzle gc	6276	100	26092	1689	33	5218
ncar1 nogc	19554	448	135252	848	120	17228
ncar1 gc	5877	196	65400	255	49	4642
ncar2 nogc	19756	432	132408	295	93	18802
ncar2 gc	6612	100	65688	99	40	4626
cbse1-14 nogc	4114	880	66848	341	73	3323
cbse1-14 gc	1241	324	31676	103	30	984
cbse1-18 nogc	4778	880	97792	398	73	4192
cbse1-18 gc	1240	324	44284	103	30	1277
qg2-8 nogc	105776	8148	1119652	9178	129	71708
qg2-8 gc	30393	228	735388	2637	85	7538

Table 7: Incremental Stack sizes compared to oracle lengths

Of course, using recomputation one has the additional overhead of recomputing, but we have shown this overhead to be quite small for these programs. The actual incremental stack size data for the programs show that the stacks can get quite large for the four CLP queries(see Table 7). For the forced gc runs, the largest incremental changes were seen between the root and the creation of the first parallel choicepoint. This is what we

---

[6]The worst-case figure would actually be the sum of these two figures, since it could be the case that a worker X shares its state with another worker Y just before performing garbage collection. X then performs garbage collection immediately afterwards. Y then requests work from X again and this time has to copy the garbage collected state.

expected to see as it reflects the space used to set up the initial constraints. However, when no garbage collection was performed, this was not always the case. As the figures indicate, there is a wide variation between the gc and no gc runs. We see that for the CLP programs between 1 to 30 K-Bytes of stack has to be copied per task (when garbage collection is turned on). Unfortunately, it is difficult to estimate the frequency of these task migrations, without simulating parallel execution.

4 Full System

For a scalable, real implementation of a recomputation system, a number of optimizations are necessary, as well as support for impure language constructs.

4.1 Optimizations

A centralized scheduler would become a bottleneck when running on a large number of processors. Thus a distributed scheduler should be used, consisting of sub-schedulers each of which is only responsible for a subset of the parallel choice points. When moving from a centralized scheme to a distributed one, the main difference will be that the message volume will increase, since a request-work message might have to traverse all the busy workers before work is found. This increase is, however, not specific to the recomputation model. In fact it will be seen on every distributed Or-Parallel system.

The prototype used a simple site-based topmost scheduling policy out of necessity, since it did not keep any representation of the search tree. The results show that a topmost strategy works sufficiently well for programs with large grain parallel jobs. Though simple, such a strategy does not allow one to easily exploit incrementality optimizations. In a real implementation, it would be preferable to use a tree-based scheduling strategy which will try to match idle workers with the closest possible task. "Closeness" would be measured in terms of the amount of recomputation necessary.

4.2 Impure Language Features

Impure language features cause problems for all parallel implementations of Prolog. We will distinguish three different classes: pruning operators (cut and commit), side effects affecting the state of the environment (e.g. file system) and side effects affecting the internal state of the Prolog system (e.g. assert, record)

4.2.1 Pruning Operators

The implementation of the pruning operators in the recomputation system is basically the same for as for other Or-Parallel models (the scheduler handles pruning that affects parallel choicepoints). During recomputation, the cuts can just be ignored. We will therefore not consider this topic further.

4.2.2 Environment side effects

When, during recomputation, the system encounters a side effect predicate of the write-type, then execution of this predicate would duplicate the side effect (e.g. writing to a file) because it has already been done in the original computation. This can be relatively easily eliminated by suppressing this kind of side effects whenever a worker is in re-execution mode.

On the other hand, side-effects of the read-type need to be re-executed (because they have to return a result). But the environment state may not be the same as it was during the original execution. Non–critical examples are e.g. re-execution of compile-predicates, since the source files are not expected to change. But in general, read-type side effects may yield different results on re-execution, consider for instance a call to cputime/1 or a read/2 on a file that has been changed in the meantime. The solution is to record the results of such predicates together with the oracle during the original execution. On re-execution, the predicate is not executed, but the recorded result is used instead. This amounts to an extended notion of oracle: It predicts not only the correct branch of a nondeterminate choice, it also predicts the results of certain built-in calls. The cost of such a solution is a larger oracle.

4.2.3 Internal side effects

For internal side effects there are two sources of problems: the lack of shared state between distributed workers, and the repeated re-execution of side effect predicates during recomputation.

As long as internal side effects are not used to communicate between Or-branches, they pose no problems. They are just re-executed on recomputation and can be treated like pure logical code. The re-execution is in fact necessary because the internal state is not shared between workers and therefore has to be re-established.

The main problem is when such predicates are used to communicate between Or-branches (or in sequential terms: communicate across failures). There are three possible semantics for these predicates in an Or-Parallel setting and there is a gradual degradation of what one can do in terms of communication between Or-branches using this type of side-effects in the three different models:

1. sequential — the sequential Prolog semantics (imposing an order on the Or-branches)

2. parallel-shared — global data is (physically or virtually) shared, but no special precautions to preserve the sequential order of side effects

3. parallel-private — no data shared between Or-branches

We will not consider the first model further, since we believe that the ordering of Or-branches is an artifact from sequential implementations and should not be imposed on a parallel system. We note however, that it is default semantics implemented in [6, 5].

The parallel-shared model is implemented in ElipSys and behaves such that side effects executed in Or-Parallel branches are interleaved in some unspecified order which may be different in different runs.

In the parallel-private model without any shared state there is the additional effect that a side effect which is done in one Or-branch may never become visible in another Or-branch (when they are computed in parallel by different workers).

The simulation of the parallel-sharing semantics on a non-sharing recomputation model is quite expensive. It would be necessary to have a global manager to synchronize access to all dynamic predicates and recorded structures. This would be costly and remove the main attraction of a recomputation-based system, which is its simplicity. This problem is closely related to the issue of implementing a distributed dictionary in a copying-based scheme.

The other way is to make it impossible to use the internal side-effect primitives of sequential Prolog for Or-branch communication. The most pragmatic method would be to keep the current implementation and restrict their use to purely sequential parts of the search space.

To compensate for the lost feature of communicating information over Or-branches, we envisage a language construct that associates a non-logical object (a *bag*) with an Or-subtree. Inside this subtree, terms can be copied into this bag. The content is only retrieved once the subtree is exhausted. The content is the result of the subgoal and is also recorded in the extended oracle. On recomputation, the subtree is not searched again, but the recorded bag is taken from the oracle instead. An all-solutions predicate could then be written as:

```
findall(Goal, Bag) :-
    call_with_bag((Goal, bag_enter(Handle,Goal)), Handle, Bag).
```

The differences compared to the classical primitives are: The concept of a bag implies that the order of entries is unspecified, which maps naturally onto the parallel implementation. The handle-concept instead of global names simplifies disposal of the object on failure and garbage collection. Linking the bag to an Or-subtree solves the recomputation problem.

4.3 Hybrid Model

A realistic scenario of a common computing environment in the near future is a network of workstations where some or all workstations are multiprocessors with a small number $(2 - 8)$ of CPUs. Using a pure recomputation model on such a network would result in inefficient use of the multiprocessor workstations, since the basic tenet of recomputation is that it is cheaper to recompute than to communicate. As this will probably not hold on a shared-memory multiprocessor, a hybrid copying/recomputation scheme would be ideal in such a setting.

Such a model would use stack-copying when sharing work between processes on the same machine and use oracles across machines. The main issue in such a system would be the complexity of the scheduler, which would have to decide on the fly whether stack-copying or recomputation is the most appropriate work installation mechanism. The obvious advantage of such a system is that it would be able to exploit fine-grain parallelism within a cluster.

5 Conclusions

The main question investigated in this paper was whether an incremental recomputation-based scheme would be as efficient as a copying based scheme for implementing a CLP system in a distributed, heterogeneous setting.

Towards this end we implemented a recomputation-based prototype and analysed its performance on a set of representative CLP programs. The analysis revealed that the overhead of recomputation was between 1% and 18% per worker, which was surprisingly low, given that only partial incrementality optimizations were implemented in the prototype. As expected, this figure is higher than than the 3% to 9% overhead of copying reported for incremental stack-copying implemented on a shared-memory multiprocessor[5]. However, we also found that even the *incremental* stack sizes generated by the CLP queries were quite large and in fact even in the best case, a single oracle entry corresponded to 40 bytes of stack, while for some programs the average was well over a thousand bytes. Given these two results - reasonable recomputation overhead and the much lower bandwidth requirements of incremental recomputation, our conclusion is that such an approach will be as or more efficient than copying stacks in a distributed setting. In addition, since oracles are just sequences of integers, device independent communication is simple to implement (in contrast to stack-copying), making it easy to exploit heterogeneous networks.

In order to take advantage of cluster-based architectures (e.g. a network of multiprocessors) a hybrid model would be ideal. We are currently in the process of designing and implementing such a system.

Acknowledgements

Liang-Liang Li, Kees Schuerman and Alexander Herold's insightful comments on earlier versions of this paper were very helpful. Special thanks are due to Peter Kacsuk who initiated the idea of using a recomputation-based scheme for Parallel-ECL^{i}PS^e . This research was partially supported by the CEC under ESPRIT III project 6708 "APPLAUSE".

References

[1] D. Clark et al. Solving large combinatorial problems in molecular biology using the ElipSys parallel constraint logic programming system. *Computer Journal*, 36(4), 1993.

[2] W.F. Clocksin. The DelPhi Multiprocessor Inference Machine. In *Proc. of the 4th U.K. Conf. on Logic Prog.*, pages 189–198, 1992.

[3] M. Dincbas, H. Simonis, and P. Van Hentenryck. Solving the car-sequencing problem in Constraint Logic Programming. Technical Report TR-LP-32, ECRC, 1988.

[4] M. Fujita, J. Slaney, and F. Bennett. Automatic generation of some results in finite algebra. In *Proc. of IJCAI'93*, volume 1, pages 52–57, 1993.

[5] Roland Karlsson. *A high performance OR-Parallel Prolog system*. SICS Dissertation Series 07, Kista, Sweden, 1992.

[6] Ewing Lusk et al. The Aurora Or-Parallel Prolog system. In *Proceedings of the International Conference on Fifth Generation Computer Systems 1988*. ICOT, 1988.

[7] Kees Schuerman and Liang-Liang Li. Tackling false sharing in a parallel logic programming system. In *Proc. of the International Workshop on Scalable Shared Memory Systems*, 1994.

[8] J. Schumann and R. Letz. PARTHEO : A high-performance parallel theorem prover. In *Proc. of CADE'90*, pages 40–56. MIT press, 1990.

[9] Ehud Shapiro. Or-Parallel Prolog in Flat Concurrent Prolog. *Journal of Logic Programming*, 6(3):243–267, 1989.

[10] P. Van Hentenryck. Parallel constraint satisfaction in logic programming: Preliminary results of chip within PEPSys. In *Proceedings of the Sixth International Conference on Logic Programming*, pages 165–180, Lisbon, 1989. The MIT Press.

[11] A. Veron, K. Schuerman, M. Reeve, and L. Li. Why and how in the ElipSys Or-Parallel CLP system. In *Proc. of Parle '93*, pages 291–302. Springer-Verlag, 1993.

PDP: Prolog Distributed Processor for Independent_AND\OR Parallel Execution of Prolog [1]

Lourdes Araujo
Jose J. Ruz
Dpto.Informática y Automática
Universidad Complutense de Madrid
Madrid 28040, Spain
{lurdes, jjruz}@dia.ucm.es

Abstract

PDP (Prolog Distributed Processor) is a multisequential system for Independent_AND\OR parallel execution of Prolog. The system is composed of a set of workers controlled hierarchically. Each worker operates on its own private memory and interprocessor communication is performed only by the passing of messages. Independent AND_parallelism is exploited following a *fork-join* scheme and OR_parallelism is exploited following a multisequential approach. Both kinds of parallelism are implemented using closed environments. To exploit OR_parallelism, the parent worker environment is reconstructed in a new worker by *recomputing* the initial goal without backtracking, following the *success path* obtained from the parent worker. PDP deals with OR_under_AND parallelism producing the solutions of a set of parallel goals in a distributed way, that is, creating a new task for each element of the cross product. This approach has the advantage of avoiding both storing partial solutions and synchronizing workers, resulting in a largely increased performance. PDP has been implemented on a transputer network and performance results show that PDP introduces very little overhead into sequential programs, and provides a high speedup for coarse grain parallel programs.

1 Introduction

There are a considerable number of approaches proposed for the parallel execution of Prolog, dealing with OR_parallelism [1, 4, 5, 2], Independent AND_parallelism [10, 12, 14, 7], and recently combining AND-OR parallelism [19, 3, 11]. Since most of these approaches are implemented on systems with totally or partially shared memory, we are interested in investigating the possibilities of a completely distributed model of processing, that eliminates the shared memory contention.

---

[1]Supported by the Prontic project TIC92-0793-C02-01.

In this paper we present the Prolog Distributed Processor, a multise-quential system supporting both Independent_AND and OR_parallelism. In order to reduce the communications overhead, PDP has been designed with a hierarchic control. PDP is composed of a set of clusters, each of them consisting of a *controller* and a set of *workers*. Controllers are responsible for the distribution of pending work among idle workers. When every worker in a cluster is busy, the work may be sent to other clusters. Each worker operates on its own private memory and interprocessor communication is performed only by the passing of messages. In order to reduce communica-tion overhead, each worker follows a *closed environment approach* [6], that is, there are no variables in a worker defined in terms of variables that belong to other worker.

The goals and clauses to be executed in parallel (*parallel goals* and *parallel clauses*) are supposed to be annotated in the program, either by the compiler [7, 15] in AND_parallelism or by the user in OR_parallelism. The execution model has been developed as an extension of the Warren Abstract Machine (WAM) [18], maintaining both the optimization of the sequential Prolog techniques and the speedup of the Independent AND_parallel system and the multisequential OR_parallel system.

In the case of AND_parallelism, parallel goals are sent along with their variable bindings, to the idle worker indicated by the controller and an an-swer is then awaited by the parent worker. In order to control the execution of a parallel call, we have modified the shared memory model developed by Hermenegildo [12] for a distributed system.

The exploitation of OR_parallelism is based on the multisequential ex-ecution of the branches of the search tree, splitting the work dynamically. When a worker finds a parallel clause, it makes the new work available for idle workers, by sending a warning to the controller. Since each processor works in its own environment, the parent worker environment has to be re-constructed by the worker which assumes the new work. Instead of copying the environment as MUSE [1], PDP *recomputes* [2] the initial goal without backtracking, following the *success path* obtained from the parent worker (Figure 1). The amount of data communicated with this approach is smaller than that of the copying approach, which in turn speeds up the execution on a distributed system.

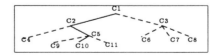

Figure 1: Recomputation following the success path C2,C5,C10

For programs presenting OR_under_AND parallelism the different solu-tions of each goal in a *parallel call* (set of parallel goals) have to be combined.

In the AND-parallelism approach the task carrying out a parallel goal reaches the successive solutions sequentially, when they are required because of backtracking. Therefore, if there is OR-parallelism in a parallel goal, maintaining the AND-parallelism approach requires the storing of the different solutions until required for building a new combination. The PDP approach avoids storing partial solutions and synchronizing workers. The idea is to create a new computation for each combination of solutions, recomputing the success path from the initial goal of the program until the parallel call is reached. In this way, the exploitation approach of AND-parallelism becomes that of OR-parallelism, which creates independent computations. This avoids the communications overhead of the AND-parallelism approach which is due to both the sending of solutions to the parent task and the requirements of new solutions from the offspring tasks. This is the reason why the speedup achieved by exploiting both kinds of parallelism may be greater than the product of the speedup achieved by exploiting each kind of parallelism separately. To avoid repeating solutions, we have introduced a *combination rule* to set the combinations corresponding to each new task.

The rest of the paper proceeds as follows: section 2 presents the execution model. Section 3 describes the parallel tasks of PDP. Section 4 presents a PDP execution scheme. Section 5 describes the scheduling policy. Results are presented in section 6 and finally conclusions drawn in section 7.

2   Execution Model

PDP exploits pure AND-parallelism, pure OR-parallelism and the combination of both, producing *OR_tasks* which explore the search tree branches from the root, and *AND_tasks* which execute parallel goals. The PDP approach to exploit combined parallelism – when it appears in the form OR_under_AND – is based upon the fact that the recomputation allows the AND-tasks to exploit OR-parallelism by creating OR-tasks. Therefore in the combined model both kinds of parallelism are joined in a very natural way. Another important point is that the search tree is automatically distributed among the workers by means of a distribution rule, so that no worker is in charge of the distribution. The model is outlined as follows:

- The execution of a program begins as an OR-task, that records the success path.

- If AND or OR-parallelism appear, new AND or OR-tasks are created, respectively.

- If an AND-task finds OR-parallelism, it creates a new OR-task to deal with the parallel clauses and transfers to it the success path leading to the parallel call. Notice that the AND-task at this point has received this information for this purpose only. In this way, **the**

exploitation approach of AND_parallelism becomes that of
OR_parallelism, and this reduces the exchange of information.

- Once the recomputation of this OR_task arrives to the parallel call
  from where it originates, if the operation were to blindly exploit the
  OR_parallelism, the result would be the simple repetition of solutions.
  In order to avoid this we have introduced a *combination rule* which
  decides the branch to be explored to solve each parallel goal. Let us
  call any goal which presents OR_parallelism and causes the creation
  of OR_tasks, the ancestor goal of these tasks. The key point of this
  rule is to fix the solution of the goals on the left of the ancestor goal
  and to combine them with every solution of the remaining goals. The
  combination rule is as follows:

  - If the goal is on the left of the ancestor goal, the branch to be
    explored is *fixed* to that explored by the previous "forefather"
    OR_task.

  - If the goal is the ancestor goal, the branch to be explored is the
    next one to that explored by the AND_task.

  - If the goal is on the right of the ancestor goal, the branch to be
    explored is the one leading to the first solution.

A new structure is introduced to specify the untried clauses: the *cross product
environment* (CPE), associated to each parallel call. It is composed of
a pointer marking the beginning of the success path corresponding to each
goal in a parallel call.

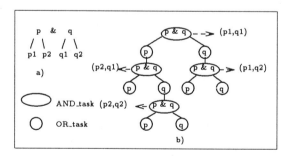

Figure 2: OR_under_AND parallelism in PDP

In order to visualize this process consider the program represented in
Figure 2a), whose execution is shown in Figure 2b). When the AND_tasks
which execute the parallel goals p and q find OR_parallelism, the first alternative clauses $p1$ and $q1$ are explored to give the answer to the parent
task, and new OR_tasks are created to explore $p2$ and $q2$. For the OR_task

corresponding to $(p2, q1)$ p is the ancestor goal and therefore, the branch to be explored so as to solve p corresponds to $p2$ ($p1$ is already being explored by the parent AND_task). Since q is on the right of the ancestor goal, the branch to be explored is $q1$, the first one. For the OR_task corresponding to $(p2, q2)$ the ancestor goal is q and therefore, the branch to be explored to solve p (which is on the left) is $p2$, the same as that explored by the previous forefather OR_task, i.e. that corresponding to $(p2, q1)$. For q the branch to be explored is $q2$, the following branch to the one explored by the parent AND_task.

3   Parallel Tasks in PDP

The PDP approach to exploit OR_under_AND parallelism leads to the distinction between different kinds of OR and AND_tasks depending both on the kind of task it arose from and on the ancestor goal position. The kinds of tasks are:

- **Primary OR_task:**
  This arises from the OR_parallelism exploitation in an OR_task. When the recomputation of the received success path is completed, the execution follows in the normal way.

- **Secondary OR_task:**
  This arises from the OR_parallelism exploitation in an AND_task. When the recomputation of the success path leading to the parallel call is finished, a new combination of solutions is created.

- **Primary AND_task:**
  This arises from the AND_parallelism exploitation in an AND_task, a primary OR_task or a secondary OR_task provided the latter does not correspond to a goal on the left of the ancestor goal. Primary AND_tasks exploit OR_parallelism appearing during the execution.

- **Secondary AND_task:**
  This arises from the AND_parallelism exploitation in a secondary OR_task corresponding to a goal on the left of the ancestor goal. According to the combination rule, this task must ignore any OR_parallelism appearing during the execution.

Producer and consumer relationships of the tasks can be shown pictorially as a *task tree*. In general, the task tree and the search tree are different, since it is not always possible, neither suitable to exploit all the potential parallelism of the program. Figure 3 shows a PDP execution example corresponding to the following program.

```
:- p & q.
p :- p1.        q :- q1.
p :- p2.        q :- q2.
p :- p3.
```

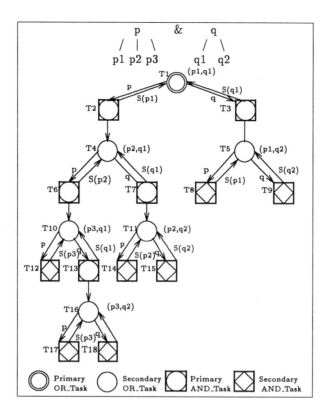

Figure 3: PDP execution example

The first solution of the parallel call $p\&q$ is obtained with the clauses $p1$ and $q1$ of p and q respectively. If a failure occurs or new solutions are required, there is a number of pending alternatives to obtain the solutions, corresponding to the cross product of p and q: $(p1, q2)$, $(p1, q3)$, $(p2, q1)$, etc. The execution begins as a primary OR_task that finds a parallel call and creates the AND_tasks T2 and T3. When the goal p is executed, T2 finds OR_parallelism, then it takes the first clause $p1$, explores it by itself and creates a new secondary OR_task, T4, for exploring a new solution. T1 builds the CPE $(p1, q1)$, that is passed to T2 and T3. T2 builds the CPE $(p1*, q1)$ because the ancestor goal $(*)$ is the first one. The next combination corresponding to this CPE is passed to T4 which takes the next clause, $p2$, for the goal marked as the ancestor one, and the first one for every goal on the right, $q1$. T5 receives $(p1, q2*)$, indicating that the alternative clause to exploit for p is the first one and for q it is the second one.

```
type res_type = (success, fail);
type task_type = (primary_AND, secondary_AND, primary_OR, secondary_OR);
process AND_task(p:program; Q:goal; V:substitution;
                 C:success path; CPE: cross product env.; tasktype: task_type);
var
    R: resolvent; result: res_type; S: backtracking stack;
begin
    R := [Q]; S := ∅; C := C[CPE[Q]];
    recomputation(p, R, S, V, C, CPE);
    if R <> ∅ then
        execution(p,R,S,V,C,CPE,tasktype,result); end
    else result := success; end
    if result = success then send_success(parent_task, restriction(V,Q), alternative);
    else send_fail(parent_task);
end
```

Figure 4: AND_task creation

The scheme of creation of an AND_task is shown in Figure 4. The entry to
an AND_task consists of a goal along with its variable bindings V, the success
path C and the CPE corresponding to the received goal. The program and
the kind of AND_task to be created are also received. The *resolvent* R and
the *backtracking stack* S (where the state is saved) are initialized. The new
AND_task takes from the received success path C the part which corresponds
to the goal to be executed, starting at the point indicated in the CPE. The
success path of the goal may be empty, incomplete or complete, depending
on both the kind of task and on the position of the goal in the parallel call.
If after the recomputation of the success path of the goal the resolvent is not
empty, the pending execution is performed. The answer obtained is sent to
the parent task.

```
process OR_task(p:program;Q:goal; C:success path;
                CPE: cross product env.; tasktype: task_type)
var
    S : backtracking stack; V: substitution; R: resolvent;
begin
    R := [Q]; S := ∅;
    recomputation(p,R,S,V,C,CPE);
    execution(p,R,S,V,C,CPE,tasktype,result);
    if result = success then
        V := restriction(V,Q);
    display(V,result);
end
```

Figure 5: OR_task creation

The scheme of creation of an OR_task is shown in Figure 5. An OR_task receives as entry the success path and the CPE of the parent task. The program along with the goal to be executed and the kind of OR_task to be created are also received. After initializing the resolvent and the backtracking stack, the recomputation of the success path is performed. This recomputation produces an environment consisting of a resolvent, a backtracking stack and a substitution. Then, the execution of the pending resolvent is performed. Once it is finished the result is presented to the user.

4 PDP Execution Scheme

Figure 6 shows the PDP execution scheme. Following the resolution algorithm, the resolvent is transformed until it becomes empty (successful execution) or a failure occurs. In each resolution step, a set of independent goals is taken from the resolvent (AND_parallelism). Each independent goal is solved by a different *AND_task* except the first one which is executed by the parent task itself. If the created AND_task is *primary*, the CPE is updated to a new combination, and the answers corresponding to goals executed by other tasks are awaited (*waited_answer* $= 0$). For the goals whose computation succeeds, the computed answer substitution obtained is received and composed with the computed answer substitution of the current task. If all computations succeed, the resolution process continues. The resolution of an only goal ($r = 1$) *unifies* the goal with the head of a clause of the associated predicate. If there is OR_parallelism, *OR_tasks* are created to perform the unification of the goal with other clauses, removing these pending alternative clauses in the parent processor. If the created OR_task is *secondary* the CPE is updated to a new combination. If the execution of the goal succeeds, the state is *saved* in the backtracking stack, the substitution obtained and the previous one are *composed*, the goal is *replaced* by the body of the clause in the resolvent, and the alternative clause considered is recorded in the *success path*. If the execution fails, backtracking will be performed taking a previous state out the backtracking stack.

5 Scheduling Policy

The controllers are responsible for the distribution of pending work among idle workers. At initialization time, each worker is loaded with the same program and the execution starts in one of them. A worker will be in one of the three states: *idle* (without work), *busy* (working) or *offering* (with pending work). The controller is warned about idle and offering workers informing to the idle workers which offering worker has to be requested for work. To optimize the communications, the workers do not report every change in

```
procedure execution(℘:program; R:resolvent; S:backtracking stack; V:substitution
    C: success path; CPE: cross product env.; tasktype:task_type; result:res_type);
var
    a: goal; Pₐ: associated procedure to goal a;
    c: clause; V': substitution; r: integer;
begin
  repeat
      [A₁, ..., Aᵣ] := independent_set(R); r = size([A₁, ..., Aᵣ]);
      if r > 1 then begin
        waited_answers := 0;
        for i := 2 to r  /* AND PARALLELISM */
            if tasktype = primary_OR_task or
            tasktype = primary_AND_task or
            tasktype = secondary_OR_task and ancestor_goal(CPE) <= i then
                AND_task(℘,Aᵢ,restriction(V,(Aᵢ)),C,new_comb(CPE),primary);
            else
                AND_task(℘,Aᵢ,restriction(V,(Aᵢ)),C,CPE, secondary);
            waited_answers := waited_answers + 1; end
        execution(℘, [A₁], S, V, C, CPE, tasktype, result);
        while waited_answers > 0 and result = success do begin
            result := receive_answer(i,θᵢ);
            waited_answers := waited_answers - 1;
            if result = success then begin
                R := apply(θᵢ,R);
                V := V ∘ θᵢ; end
        end
      end
      else begin /* r = 1 */
        a := R[1] /* The first atom in the resolvent is taken */
        search_procedure(a,℘,Pₐ); /* associated procedure to the goal a */
        repeat
            c := Pₐ[1]; /* The first pending clause in the procedure is taken */
            Pₐ := Pₐ - c;
            if OR_parallelism(c) then
                if tasktype = AND_task or tasktype = secondary_OR_task then
                    OR_task(℘,R,V,C,new_comb(CPE),secondary);
                else
                    OR_task(℘,R,V,C,CPE,primary);
                Pₐ := Pₐ - Pₐ[1]; end
            result := unify(a,c,V');
        until (Pₐ = []) or result = success;
        if result = success then begin
            if Pₐ <> [ ] then save(Pₐ,R,V,S);
            V := compose(V,V');
            replace(R,a,c); /* In R, replace a by c body */
            push(c,C); end /* The explored alternative is write in C */
      end
      if result = fail then backtracking(℘,S,R,V,C,result);
  until (R = [ ]) or result = fail;
end
```

Figure 6: PDP execution scheme

program	strategy A	strategy B	strategy C
query	3.4	3.2	3.3
zebra	3.9	3.5	3.6
mm	4.5	4.3	4.3
queen(8)	12.9	11.9	12.6
queen(9)	14.2	13.5	13.8
queen(10)	14.7	14.5	14.5

Table 1: Speed-up for different scheduling policies

their work load. The controller has exact information about idle workers and offering workers, and approximate information about the workers load.

In order to choose the offering worker which is going to share work with an idle worker, several strategies previously used by different systems [16, 13] have been tested.

- strategy A: Choose the nearest (physical distance) idle worker to the offering worker

- strategy B: Choose the most loaded offering worker

- strategy C: Choose the oldest offer

Table 1 shows the speedup on a system with 15 workers for each strategy. Since the measured times differ from run to run, all speedups given are computed using the average times of three runs. The example programs examined are standard benchmarks for AND_parallel systems, the *queen* problem, *query*, a database problem, *zebra*, a puzzle and *mm*, the mastermind program. The results show that the best strategy is A, choosing the nearest idle worker to the offering worker. This strategy optimizes the traffic in the network and favours exchanges between workers which have shared work previously, optimizing OR_parallelism exploitation. The worst strategy is B, since it is the most expensive one (it requires more information exchange than the other), while strategy C, choosing the oldest request is almost as good as A, since it is the cheapest one in that it doesn't need any analysis by the controller.

Because of the overhead associated with the parallel execution, the *granularity* of a job, i.e. an estimate of the amount of work needed to solve it, should be taken into account [8, 9, 17] when deciding whether or not to execute a job as a separate task. PDP applies control mechanisms based on heuristic observations about memory occupation.

Measurements have shown the similarity of the amount of data in the stack when each solution is reached. Therefore, it is possible to estimate how

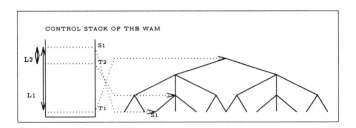

Figure 7: Granularity estimation of OR_parallelism exploitation

close a worker is to reaching the next solution and therefore if it is worthwhile to share the work that leads to the next solution. PDP performs a granularity control for the exploitation of OR_parallelism based on this observation. When a worker obtains a solution, it records the value of the backtracking stack top. The pending OR_tasks are associated to a *choice point* in the backtracking stack. A pending OR_task is sent to an idle worker only if the distance between the choice point and the top of the stack when the last solution was reached is greater then a critical value that is experimentally set. This test does not introduce run time overhead since only a comparison is needed. Figure 7 shows the stack size when solution $S1$ is reached. This point is very close to the choice point associated to the pending task $T2$ and therefore the distance $L2$ is smaller than the critical value C. This means, as the search tree shows, that $T2$ has a fine grain and therefore the task is kept in the worker. On the other hand, the task $T1$, that corresponds to a choice point in the bottom of the stack, has a high granularity and is sent to an idle worker.

program	3 proc.		8 proc.		15 proc.	
	no c.	with c.	no c.	with c.	no c.	with c.
query	2.6	2.6	2.8	2.9	3.0	3.4
zebra	1.8	1.8	3.5	3.7	3.6	3.9
mm	2.1	2.1	3.2	3.4	4.1	4.5
queen(8)	2.9	2.8	7.0	7.3	12.3	12.9
queen(9)	2.4	2.4	7.5	7.7	13.8	14.2
queen(10)	3.0	3.1	7.8	7.9	14.5	14.7

Table 2: Speed-up achieved controlling OR_parallelism granularity

Measurements have been taken to investigate the critical value C. On a system with 8 and 15 workers, this value, that depends on the system size is about *stack_size*/6, where *stack_size* is the size of the backtracking stack when the last solution was reached. The speedup achieved by performing this procedure is shown in Table 2. For 3 workers the granularity control has no effect. For 8 workers the speedup increases for programs with a lot of parallel work (queen10). The greatest effect of the control is achieved on the system with 15 workers.

6 Performance Results

Our current implementation has been made in Parallel ANSI C on a Supernode (Parsys) with 16 T800 transputers connected in a torus network. In each processor the computation and communication functions have been split. There are three processes controlling the input, output and computation respectively.

The system does not support *cut* and database predicates yet, so the programs used to evaluate the system does not present these predicates. Some sequential programs have been tried in order to evaluate the overhead due to the parallel mechanism. The experiments demonstrate that the overhead when sequential programs are run on PDP is less than 5%. Results show that the overhead due to the writing down of the success path is less than 5%.

program	3 workers		8 workers		15 workers	
program	copying	recomp.	copying	recomp.	copying	recomp.
query	2.8	2.6	3.0	2.9	3.4	3.4
zebra	1.9	1.8	3.6	3.7	3.1	3.9
mm	2.2	2.1	3.4	3.4	4.5	4.5
queen(8)	3.1	2.8	7.4	7.3	12.9	12.9
queen(9)	2.4	2.4	7.7	7.7	14.1	14.2
queen(10)	3.0	3.1	8.0	7.9	14.0	14.7

Table 3: OR_parallelism speed-up with copying and recomputation approaches

We have compared speedup obtained exploiting OR_parallelism using stack copying and recomputation approaches. All benchmarks have been executed in a "program, fail" way. The results obtained are shown in table 3. These results show significant speedup for all tested programs. Though the achieved speedup using stack copying and recomputation is quite similar, it is slightly greater with the copying approach using a smaller number of workers, and for programs with smaller granularity. On the other hand, it becomes greater with the recomputation approach when the system size increases. The reason for this is the smaller amount of information exchange in the recomputation approach. For queen10 the copying approach is more efficient on a 3 or 8-worker system, while on a 15-worker system more efficiency is gained using the recomputation approach.

program	3 workers	8 workers	15 workers
qsort(700)	2.3	2.8	3.4
merge(500)	2.3	2.5	2.7

Table 4: AND-parallelism speed-up

The exploitation of AND-parallelism in PDP requires high granularity programs, since the workers sharing a job, exchange more messages than in the case of OR-parallelism. Table 4 shows the speedup for *mergesort* and *qsortsort* programs, standard benchmarks used for AND-parallel systems. For programs with more fine grain parallelism no speedup is achieved by exploiting AND-parallelism.

In order to evaluate the behavior of PDP for programs with both kinds of parallelism, synthetic benchmarks with coarse grain parallelism have been run. The first one (synthetic 1) presents AND-under-OR parallelism:

```
:- check.
check :- times1(X),(p(X) & p(X) & p(X)).
check :- times2(X),(p(X) & p(X) & p(X)).
check :- times3(X),(p(X) & p(X) & p(X)).
times1(2000). times2(1000). times3(500).
p(0).
p(X) :- X > 0, X1 is X - 1, p(X1).
```

There is OR-parallelism in the procedure *check* while AND-parallelism appears in the body clauses of this procedure. The following benchmark (synthetic 2) presents OR-under-AND parallelism:

```
:- check(X).
check([Xs,Ys,Zs]) :- times(X), times(Y), times(Z), (p(X,Xs) & p(Y,Ys) & p(Z,Zs)).
p(X,Xs) :- p1(X,Xs).
p(X,Xs) :- p2(X,Xs).
p1(0,a).
p1(X,Xs) :- X > 0, X1 is X-1, p1(X1,Xs).
p2(0,b).
p2(X,Xs) :- X > 0, X1 is X-1, p2(X1,Xs).
times(1000).
```

There is AND-parallelism in the body of the *check* clause, while the procedure *p* presents OR-parallelism. Table 5 presents the speedup achieved by exploiting each kind of parallelism with 15 workers. Results show signifi-

program	OR_par.	AND_par.	Comb. par.
synthetic 1	1.5	2.9	4.5
synthetic 2	2.4	1.7	4.4

Table 5: OR, AND and Combining parallelism speed-up

cant speedup for all executions exploiting parallelism. The benchmark 1 has been chosen to show the advantages of exploring at the same time different solutions since the first solution explored by the sequential machine can be the slower to reach (the second clause of *check* is computed in a shorter time that the first one). It may be observed from the table that when both kinds of parallelism are exploited, the performance has been improved in all cases. The speedup achieved when exploiting both kinds of parallelism is greater than the product of the speedups achieved by exploiting each kind of parallelism separately. The reason is that the exploration of the different solutions when AND_parallelism is exploited requires a number of messages exchanges between the parent worker and the worker exploring each goal in the parallel call (new solution requests and answers) that are avoided when OR_under_AND parallelism is exploited.

7 Conclusions

A system, PDP, to execute Prolog programs on distributed memory systems exploiting both, Independent_AND and OR_parallelism, has been presented. The execution model is based on multisequential Prolog engines that work independently under a hierarchic control. PDP deals with OR_under_AND parallelism producing in a distributed way the cross product of the solutions of the goals in a parallel call and creating a new computation for each combination. This avoids both the storage of partial solutions and the synchronization of workers. Results show that the overhead introduced to sequential execution is quite small. The overhead due to the exploitation mechanism of each kind of parallelism is also small. Different scheduling policies have been tested. The best result have been achieved when the nearest idle worker was chosen. This strategy is expected to yield even better results when the system size increases. Granularity controls have been introduced, showing a performance improvement when the system size increases. Significant speedup is achieved for coarse grain benchmark programs with each kind of parallelism. For some programs presenting both kinds of parallelism PDP achieves better results than the product of both. In the future the system will be extended to a larger number of workers and real applications will be tried.

Acknowledgements

We would like to thank Mario Rodriguez Artalejo and Jose Cuesta for their helpful comments.

References

[1] Ali, K. A. M, Karlsson, R.. *The Muse Approach to Or-Parallel Prolog.* Int. J. of Parallel Programming, Vol 19 No. 2 (1990), pp. 129-162.

[2] Araujo, L. and Ruz, J.J. *OR-Parallel Execution of Prolog on a Transputer-based System.* Transputers and Occam Research: New Directions. IOS Press (1993), pp. 167-181.

[3] Biswas P., Su S., Yun D. *A Scalable Abstract Machine Model to Support Limited-OR(LOR)/Restricted-AND Parallelism(RAP) in Logic Programs.* Proc. ICLP (1988), pp. 1160-1179.

[4] Calderwood A., Szeredi, P. *Scheduling Or-parallelism in Aurora - the Manchester scheduler* Proc. ICLP (1989), pp. 419-435.

[5] Clocksin W. F., Alshawi H. *A Method for Efficiently Horn Clause Programs Using Multiple Processors* New Generation Computing,5 (1988), pp. 361-376.

[6] Conery, J. S. *Binding Environments for Parallel Logic Programs in Non-Shared Memory Multiprocessors* Int. J. of Parallel Programming 17(2), (1988), pp. 125-152.

[7] Chang, J. -H., Despain, A. and Degroot, D. *AND-parallelism of logic programs based on a static dependency analisys,* Proc. Spring Compcon, IEEE, (1985), pp. 218-225.

[8] Debray, S.K., Lin, N.-W., Hermenegildo, H. *Task Granularity Analysis.* SIGPLAN'90 Conf. on Programming Language Design and Implementation, (1990), pp. 174-188.

[9] Debray, S.K., Lin, N. *Automatic complexity Analysis of Logic Programs* Proc. ICLP. (1991), pp. 599-613.

[10] Degroot, D., *Restricted AND-Parallelism.* Proc. of Int. Conf. Fifth Gen. Comp. Sys., ICOT (1984), pp. 471-478

[11] Gupta, G., Hermenegildo, M. *ACE:And/Or-parallel Copying-based Execution of Logic Programs.* Tech. Report TR-91-25, Department of Computer Science, University of Bristol, Oct 1991.

[12] Hermenegildo, M., *An abstract Machine Based Execution Model for Computer Architecture Design and Efficient Implementation of Logic Program in Parallel.* PhD thesis, U. of Texas at Austin (1986).

[13] Kuchen, H., Wagener, A. *Comparison of Dynamic Load Balancing Strategies* Tech. Report 90-5 . Aachener Informatik-Berichte.

[14] Lin, Y.-J. and Kumar, V., *AND-parallel execution of Logic Programs on a Shared-Memory Multiprocessor.* The J. of Logic Programming, (1991):10:, pp. 155-178.

[15] Muthukumar, K., Hermenegildo, M. *Determination of Variable Dependence Information at Compile-Time Through Abstract Interpretation* North American Conf. LP (1989) pp. 166-185.

[16] Sugie, M. Yoneyama, M., Tarui, T. *Load-Dispatching Strategy on Parallel Inference Machine* Proc. Int. Conf. on Fifth Generation Computer System (1988), pp. 987-993.

[17] Tick, E. *Compile-Time Granularity Analysis for Parallel Logic Programming Languages* New Generation Computing, 7 (1990), pp. 325-337.

[18] Warren, D.H.D., *An Abstract Prolog Instruction Set.* Tech. Note 309, SRI International, (1983).

[19] Westphal, H, Robert, P, Chassin, J, Syre, J. *The PEPsys model: Combining Backtracking, AND- and OR-parallelism.* Proc. Symp. of LP (1987), pp. 436-448.

Implementation

On the Scheme of Passing Arguments in Stack Frames for Prolog

Neng-Fa Zhou
Faculty of Computer Science and Systems Engineering
Kyushu Institute of Technology, 680-4 Kawazu, Iizuka, Fukuoka, Japan
zhou@mse.kyutech.ac.jp

Abstract

The scheme of passing arguments in argument registers has been commonly considered as one of the most important features of WAM (Warren Abstract Machine). Nevertheless, as argument registers are not a part of the frames of callees, the argument registers have to be saved and restored in many cases. In this paper, we consider the scheme of passing arguments in stack frames, which is usually adopted in compilers for procedural languages, and present a new abstract machine, called NTOAM, that adopts this scheme. This scheme has the following three advantages over the argument passing scheme of WAM: (1) as the arguments of a call need not be saved and restored for backtracking and delay, backtracking and delay become simpler; (2) a larger class of predicates can be classified as determinate and be optimized; and (3) tail recursion can be converted into iteration easily. Empirical data show that all these advantages are important for speeding up Prolog programs.

1 Introduction

WAM [2, 12] passes arguments from a calling predicate (caller) to a called predicate (callee) through argument registers. It first transfers arguments of a call from the caller's frame or some other argument registers to appropriate argument registers, and then, when necessary, it transfers them into the callee's frame. WAM uses two kinds of frames for storing information associated with predicate calls. One is called *environment*, which stores the continuation program point and local variables, and the other is called *choice point*, which stores the machine status and the argument registers. The scheme of passing arguments in argument registers has been commonly considered as one of the most important features of WAM. It has mainly the following two advantages. Firstly, manipulating registers is much faster than manipulating slots in frames.[1] Secondly, storing information about a call into two frames seems to be space efficient, because in some cases only

---

[1] This depends on the implementation methods. In an emulator-based implementation, argument registers are actually simulated using memory. In a native-compiler-based implementation on some computers, frames can be mapped into register windows in most cases.

an environment frame, and in some other cases only a choice point frame is needed.

However, as argument registers are not a part of the frames of callees, the argument passing scheme of WAM may cause data to be moved often between registers and slots in frames in many cases. For a nondeterminate predicate, it has to first save and then repeatedly restore the argument registers in order to find all the answers to a call of the predicate. Even for some determinate predicates, it still has to create choice points for saving the argument registers [6]. The scheme also makes the execution of delay primitives expensive [3]. Before waking and executing a delayed call, it has to save the argument registers of the current call to be suspended.

In this paper, we consider the scheme of passing arguments in stack frames, which is usually used in compilers for procedural languages [1], and present a new abstract machine called NTOAM, a successor to the TOAM [13], that adopts this scheme. In NTOAM, each time before a predicate is invoked by a call, a frame is allocated or an old frame is reused for the call, and the arguments of the call are passed directly to the frame. The structure of frames, which is quite similar to that used in the PLM [11], are the same for all types of predicates. Depending on whether the callee is binary, flat, determinate or nondeterminate, different slots are used.

Compared with the scheme adopted in WAM, the scheme of passing arguments in stack frames has the following advantages. Firstly, as the arguments of a call need not be saved and restored for backtracking and delay, backtracking and delay become simpler. This advantage is especially important for improving the efficiency of constraint programs [9] as they use backtracking and delay primitives frequently. Secondly, a larger class of predicates can be classified as determinate and be optimized. In the TOAM [13], the heads and inline tests at the beginning of bodies of clauses are the sources for determining determinism. In contrast, in NTOAM, some user-defined predicates at the beginning of bodies are also used as a source for determining determinism. Thirdly, tail recursion elimination converts tail recursion into iteration and thus makes it possible for tail calls to reuse not only the space but also some information in the frames of head predicates. Tail call optimization in the WAM deallocates the environment frame of the head predicate of a clause before the tail call of the clause is executed. It only makes the space but not the information in the frame of the head predicate reusable. Meier's method [8] for converting tail recursion into iteration in the WAM requires argument registers be saved in environment frames at the entry points.

Empirical data show that these advantages are really important for speeding up Prolog programs and the space efficiency of NTOAM is also better than that of the WAM in general.

In Section 2, we describe the preliminary concepts. In Section 3, we present the architecture of NTOAM. In Section 4, we describe how programs are compiled. In Section 5, we show how tail recursion elimination can be implemented easily in NTOAM. In section 6, we give the empirical results, and in Section 7, we give the conclusion.

2 Preliminaries

A given Prolog program is first transformed equivalently into its *standard form*. In a standard form program, each clause takes one of the following two forms:

$$H:-G : B. \quad (1)$$
$$H:-G ? B. \quad (2)$$

where H is called the *head*, G the *guard*, and B the *body* of the clause. The $' :'$ and $'?'$ are called *choice operators*. The $' :'$ is called a *determinate choice operator* and the $'?'$ is called a *nondeterminate choice operator*. Execution can not backtrack over a determinate choice operator. In other words, when B in clause (1) fails, the next clause defining the same predicate as H will not be tried.

For a predicate, if all the choice operators in it are determinate, then it is said to be *determinate*; otherwise, if at least one choice operator is nondeterminate, then it is said to be *nondeterminate*. A call is said to be *inline* if its evaluation does not invoke any predicate. A predicate is said to be *binary* if the guard of any clause in it consists only of inline calls and the body of any clause consists of at most one non-inline call to the left of which there may exist some inline calls. A predicate is said to be *flat* if the guard of any clause in it consists only of inline calls. A predicate is said to be *globally determinate* if all the predicates it calls directly or indirectly are determinate. A *chunk* is defined to be a non-inline call in the guard or body of a clause to the left of which there may exist a sequence of inline calls.

A call is said to be *globally determinate* if it does not leave any choice points behind after it succeeds. The condition for globally determinate predicates is stronger than that for globally determinate calls. A call of a globally determinate predicate is globally determinate, but not vice versa.

In each standard form clause, the head and the guard represent conditions on a call for it to be reduced by the body. A call C satisfies the head condition H if it matches the head ($H\theta = C$), i.e., it becomes the same with the head after a substitution is performed on the head. The guard G must be a sequence of calls to globally determinate predicates. It cannot bind any variable in the head unless it succeeds and the $' :'$ follows it. In G, the one directional matching predicate $X <= Y$, which succeeds if Y matches X ($X\theta = Y$), can be used. Suppose the matching substitution of a call with the head of a clause is θ, then the call satisfies the guard G if $G\theta$ succeeds. The body B is a sequence of calls of any type, including the '!'. In B, the assignment predicate $X := Y$, which assigns the term Y to the variable X, can be used. The predicate $X <= Y$ and $X := Y$ are specialized unification generated by compilers.

For example, consider the following predicate that computes the intersection of two sets represented as unordered lists:

```
intersect([],S,[]).
intersect([X|Xs],S2,[X|Ys]):-
    membchk(X,S2),!,
    intersect(Xs,S2,Ys).
intersect([X|Xs],S2,S3):-
    intersect(Xs,S2,S3).
```

Assume that the first two arguments of the predicate are inputs and the third argument is output, then the compiler transforms this predicate automatically into:

```
intersect([],S2,S3):-true :
    S3:=[].
intersect([X|Xs],S2,S3):-
    membchk(X,S2) :
    S3:=[X|Ys],
    intersect(Xs,S2,Ys).
intersect([X|Xs],S2,S3):-true :
    intersect(Xs,S2,S3).
```

Due to space limitation, we will not explore further the techniques for transforming programs into their standard forms. Previous program analysis techniques for inferring predicate modes and detecting determinism [6] will be useful but not sufficient as standard form predicates may not be flat.

Backtracking is classified into three different types. The backtracking caused by the failure of an inline call in a guard is treated as a *jump*, the backtracking caused by the failure of a user-defined call in a guard is called *shallow* backtracking and the backtracking caused by the failure of other calls is called *deep* backtracking. For a jump, no computation state needs to be saved. For shallow backtracking, only a part of the computation state needs to be saved and restored. For deep backtracking, the whole computation state needs to be saved and restored.

Standard form predicates are transformed into *matching trees* as is done for the TOAM [13]. The matching tree for a predicate consists of a root, test nodes, and leaves. The root corresponds to the beginning of the predicate, test nodes correspond to the guards, and leaves correspond to the bodies of the clauses in the predicate. For each node in a matching tree, the node to go to when it fails is called the *alternative node* of the node.

3 NTOAM

This section describes the data areas and instruction set of NTOAM.

3.1 Data Areas

NTOAM uses all the data areas used by WAM. The *program code* stores the instructions compiled from programs. The *heap* stores terms created during execution. The *trail* stack stores those variables that must be unbound upon backtracking. The *control* stack stores frames associated with predicate calls. Each time when a predicate is invoked by a call, a frame (see Figure 1) is placed on top of the control stack unless the frame currently on top of the control stack can be reused.

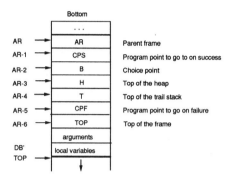

Figure 1: The structure of a frame.

The AR slot points to the frame of the caller. The CPS slot stores the continuation program point to go to after the call succeeds. The B slot points to the frame of the latest predecessor of the call that has alternative nodes in its matching tree to be tried. The H slot points to the top of the heap. The T slot points to the top of the trail stack. The CPF slot stores the alternative program point to go to after a branch in the matching tree of the predicate fails. The TOP slot points to the top of the frame. The arguments of the call and the local variables in the callee are denoted Y_1, Y_2, and so on. The frame of a call to a nondeterminate predicate that has alternative nodes to be tried in its matching tree is called a *deep choice point*, and the frame of a call to a nonflat determinate predicate that has alternative nodes to be tried in its matching tree is called *shallow choice point*.

The current machine status is indicated by the following group of registers.

P:	Current program pointer
TOP:	Top of the control stack
PA:	Pointer to the position of the next argument
AR:	Current frame
H:	Top of the heap
T:	Top of the trail stack
DB:	Latest deep choice point
SB:	Latest shallow choice point
HB:	H slot of the latest deep choice point

DB':   Pointer to the top of the latest deep choice point

The last four registers need further explanation. The DB register points to the latest deep choice point. The SB register points to the lastest shallow choice point. When a failure occurs, the contents of DB and SB are compared. If DB is younger than SB (DB<SB), then deep backtracking is invoked; otherwise, shallow backtracking is invoked. DB and SB never have the same contents.

The HB and DB' registers are used in checking whether or not a variable needs to be trailed. The HB register always holds the content of the H slot in the latest deep choice point. The DB' register points to the top of the latest deep choice point. When a variable is bound, if it is older than HB or DB', then it is trailed.

The two registers named S and RW of WAM are also used. The S register points to the next component of a compound term to be processed, and the RW denotes the mode of read or write.

3.2 Instructions

This subsection describes the instructions of NTOAM. The instructions are classified into basic and control instructions. The basic instructions consist of *jump, hash, fetch, move, assign, build, unify, unify argument*, and *parameter passing* instructions. The control instructions consist of *call, allocate, return* and *backtracking* instructions.

We use the same notation for registers and frame slots as that used in WAM. The operand X denotes a register and Y denotes a frame slot in the current frame.

3.2.1 Basic Instructions

- **Conditional jump** These instructions correspond to inline tests. A conditional jump instruction tests a condition and moves control to the destination if the condition is satisfied.

- **Hash** It moves control to a child node in a matching tree directly according to the content of a frame slot or a register.

- **Fetch** A fetch instruction fetches the next component of a compound term into a frame slot or a register.

- **Move** A move instruction moves an operand to a frame slot or a register, or moves data between frame slots and registers.

- **Assign** An assign instruction assigns a term to a variable stored in a frame slot or a register. It never fails.

- **Build** These instructions are responsible for building components of a compound term on top of the heap.

```
call q
    *TOP = AR;
    AR = TOP;
    *(AR-1) = P;
    P = entrypoint(q);
execute q
    P = entrypoint(q)
```

Figure 2: Definition of call instructions.

- **Unify** These instructions correspond to calls of the $' ='$. Unlike assign instructions, unify instructions set the RW and S registers when unifying a register or a frame slot with a compound term.

- **Unify argument** These instructions behave differently according to the content of the RW register. In write mode, they act like build instructions, whereas in read mode, they unify the next component pointed to by the S register with the operand.

- **Parameter passing** A parameter passing instruction passes an argument to the frame of the callee by placing it in the position pointed to by the PA register.

3.2.2 Call Instructions

Call instructions correspond to calls in guards and bodies of the clauses in a predicate.

- **call q** It fills in the AR and CPS slots of the frame for q and moves control to q.

- **execute q** It corresponds to such a tail call in a clause that can reuse the frame of the head predicate. It just moves control to q.

Figure 2 gives the complete definitions of these two instructions in pseudo-C.

3.2.3 Allocate Instructions

Allocate instructions are responsible for allocating frames for predicates.

- **allocate_flat N** It is responsible for allocating a frame for those determinate predicates that are flat, but not binary. It allocates N locations in the current frame, and lets the PA register point to the correct location.

- **allocate_nonflat N** It is responsible for allocating a frame for those determinate predicates that are not flat. It allocates N locations in the current frame, fills in the B slot with the content of the SB register, fills in the TOP slot, and updates the SB and PA registers accordingly.

```
allocate_flat N
    TOP = AR-N;
    PA = TOP-7;
allocate_nonflat N
    TOP = AR-N;
    PA = TOP-7;
    *(AR-2) = SB;
    *(AR-6) = TOP;
    SB = AR;
allocate_nondet N
    TOP = AR-N;
    PA = TOP-7;
    DB' = TOP;
    HB = H;
    *(AR-2) = DB;
    *(AR-3) = H;
    *(AR-4) = T;
    *(AR-6) = TOP;
    DB = AR;
```

Figure 3: Definition of allocate instructions.

- **allocate_nondet N** It is responsible for allocating a frame for nondeterminate predicates. It allocates N locations in the current frame, fills in the B slot with the content of the DB register, fills in the H, T, and TOP slots, and updates the DB, PA, HB and DB' registers accordingly.

Figure 3 shows the complete definition of these three instructions. The code for checking stack overflow and reseting the program counter is omitted.

3.2.4   Return Instructions

Return instructions are responsible for returning control to callers.

- **return_a** It is responsible for handling the return from those predicates whose frames are no longer useful after control is returned to the caller.

- **return_b** It returns control to the caller without discarding the current frame.

Figure 4 shows the definition.

3.2.5   Backtracking Instructions

Backtracking instructions are responsible for treating failures.

- **fork L** It lets the CPF slot of the current frame hold L.

- **fail** It first determines the type of the failure. If SB is younger than DB, then it invokes shallow backtracking; otherwise, it invokes deep backtracking. For shallow backtracking, it lets the latest shallow choice

```
return_a
    TOP = AR;
    PA = TOP-7;
    P = *(AR-1)
    AR = *AR;
return_b
    PA = TOP-7;
    P = *(AR-1)
    AR = *AR;
```

Figure 4: Definition of return instructions.

```
fail
    if (SB<DB) {
        AR = SB;    /* shallow backtracking */
        P = *(AR-5);
        TOP = *(AR-6);
        PA = TOP-7;
        } else {        /* deep backtracking */
        AR = DB;
        H = *(AR-3);
        P = *(AR-5);
        TOP = *(AR-6);
        PA = TOP-7;
        while (T > *(AR-4)) unbind(--T);
    }
```

Figure 5: Definition of *fail*.

point pointed to by the SB register to be the current frame and sets the P register to hold the address stored in the CPF slot of the choice point. For deep backtracking, besides the things done for shallow backtracking, it also restores the H and T registers, and unbinds those variables trailed after the choice point is created. Figure 5 gives the definition.

- **save_b** It saves the content of the DB register in the B slot of the current frame.

- **commit** It sets the SB register to hold the content of the B slot in the current frame.

- **cut** It sets the DB register to hold the content of the B slot in the current frame, and updates HB and DB' accordingly.

3.3   Remarks

In this design, the PA register is reset to point to the appropriate position when the top of the control stack changes. An alternative method is to reset PA just before passing the first argument of the next call to be executed.

Although this method makes some resets unnecessary due to backtracking, it requires special instructions for passing first arguments.

The DB' register points to the top of the latest deep choice point. It would be more efficient to make DB' point to the lowest local variable shared by more than one clause. In this way, some variables that are not shared in the latest deep choice point need not be trailed when being assigned values.

4 Compilation

Most of the compilation algorithms developed for the TOAM [13] can be still used in the compiler for NTOAM. We will not describe the whole algorithm, but instead illustrate the compilation through examples.

The instructions generated for the standard form intersect predicate are listed in Figure 6. When the predicate is invoked, the caller should have allocated a frame for it with the AR and CPS fields and the arguments filled in. The *allocate_nonflat* instruction completes the job of allocating a frame for the predicate. It allocates a frame with eleven slots among which four slots are used for storing arguments and local variables, and lets the frame to be the latest shallow choice point. It also fills in the TOP slot such that the top of the control stack can be restored after membchk(X,S2) in the guard fails. The *switch_on_list Y1,C2,COM_FAIL* instruction moves control to the next instruction if $Y1$ is a nil; to $C2$ if $Y1$ is a list; otherwise, to COM_FAIL, the label of a *commit* instruction followed by a *fail* instruction. Each *commit* instruction corresponds to a ' :' choice operator in the predicate. The two arguments [X|Xs] in the heads of the last two clauses are transformed into a test node in the matching tree, and thus X and Xs are fetched only once for each call. The *fork C3* instruction sets the alternative program pointer. After membchk(X,S2) fails, control will be moved to C3. The return_a instruction reclaims the current frame before moving control to the caller. The *execute* instructions correspond to the tail calls. The frame of the head predicate is reused by the tail calls.

The following rules for allocating variables are used:

- Rule-1: Variables that are shared by more than one branch in a matching tree are stored in frame slots.

- Rule-2: Variables occurring in more than one chunk are stored in frame slots.

- Rule-3: Variables occurring in only one chunk in only one branch in a matching tree are stored in registers except when allocating frame slots to them can reduce data movements.

- Rule-4: Frame slots and registers allocated to variables are reclaimed and reused for other variables as early as possible.

```
intersect/3 :
    allocate_nonflat 11
    switch_on_list Y1,C2,COM_FAIL
    commit
    assign_nil Y3
    return_a
C2: fetch_var Y4
    fetch_var Y1
    fork C3
    para_value Y4
    para_value Y2
    call membchk/2
    commit
    assign_list Y3
    build_value Y4
    build_var Y3
    execute intersect/3
C3: commit
    execute intersect/3
```

Figure 6: Code for intersect.

From the code for intersect, it is not difficult to understand how these rules are followed. Rule-1 is important for avoiding components of compound terms being fetched many times. For example, the variables X and Xs in the intersect predicate occur in both of the last two clauses and thus are allocated frame slots. Rule-2 is also obeyed by the compilers for WAM. Rule-3 is important for reducing data movements. For example, it is possible to allocate a register to the variable Ys since the variable occurs in only one chunk. However, allocating Y3 to it is better than allocating a register because the variable will have to be placed in Y3 eventually. Rule-4 is important for minimizing the sizes of frames and the number of registers used.

For determinate predicates that are binary, no *allocate* instruction is necessary because the part of the frame created by the the caller is adequate for the execution of them. For determinate predicates that are flat but not binary, the *allocate_flat* instruction is generated as the first instruction. For this type of determinate predicates, no instruction is generated for any ' :' choice operator. For nondeterminate predicates, the *allocate_nondet* instruction is generated as the first instruction and a *cut* instruction is generated for each ' :' choice operator.

It is an important problem to determine whether or not the frame of a predicate can be reused by the tail calls in the predicate. Suppose H is the head, and $'B_1, \ldots, B'_n$ the body of a clause. The frame of H can be reused by B_n if (1) the choice operator of the clause is ' :' and $'B_1 \ldots B'_{n-1}$ are globally determinate calls, or (2) some $B_i(1 < i < n)$ is a cut and $'B_{i+1} \ldots B'_{n-1}$

are globally determinate calls. For those predicates that do not satisfy this condition, the compiler generates two sequences of instructions for each tail call. One sequence reuses the current frame and the other not. Before these two sequences of instructions, there is an instruction called *jump_on_det L* that determines which sequence should be executed. For example, suppose q(X) is not known to be globally determinate, then the predicate

p(X):-true : q(X),r(X).

is transformed into the following code:

```
p/1:
      allocate_flat 8
      para_value Y1
      call q/1
      jump_on_det L
      para_value Y1
      call r/1
      return_b
   L:  execute r/1
```

The *jump_on_det L* instruction checks whether the latest deep choice point is older than the current frame. If so, it moves control to L; otherwise, it moves control to the next instruction following it.

5   Tail Recursion Elimination

Tail recursion elimination is a technique for converting tail recursion into iteration. The scheme of passing arguments in stack frames makes it easy to implement this technique.

Consider the clause

H:-G : B1,...,Bn

in a predicate where Bn is the same predicate as H and Bn can reuse the frame of H. In the naive code for the predicate, the *execute* instruction for Bn will move control to the entry point of the predicate of H. The first instruction in the code for the predicate may be an allocate instruction which will allocate a new frame that is the same or almost the same as the old one. When H is a determinate predicate, we can safely replace the *execute* instruction with a *jump* instruction. When H is a binary determinate predicate, the *jump* instruction jumps to the first instruction in the code for the predicate; otherwise, it jumps to the instruction just below the allocate instruction.

When H is a nondeterminate predicate, we replace the *execute* instruction with a *save_ht_jump* instruction which saves the H and T registers into the current frame and jumps to the instruction below the *allocate_nondet* instruction.

We must pay special attention to the ' :'. When H is a flat determinate predicate, no instruction will be generated for the ' :'. However, when H

```
intersect/3 :
      allocate_nonflat 11
C1:   switch_on_list Y1,C2,COM_FAIL
      commit
      assign_nil Y3
      return_a
C2:   fetch_var Y4
      fetch_var Y1
      fork C3
      para_value Y4
      para_value Y2
      call membchk/2
      assign_list Y3
      build_value Y4
      build_var Y3
      jump C1
C3:   jump C1
```

Figure 7: Optimized code for intersect.

is a nonflat or a nondeterminate predicate, there should be a *commit* or *cut* instruction generated for the $'\;:'$. If $'B_1 \ldots B'_{n-1}$ never fail, then the *commit* or *cut* instruction is removed; otherwise, it is replaced by a *fork COM_FAIL* or *fork CUT_FAIL* instruction. The *CUT_FAIL* is the label of a *cut* instruction followed by a *fail* instruction.

It is in general impossible to decide whether or not a call may fail. However, many built-in predicates such write/1 do not fail. Using this information, the compiler is able to decide that some user-defined predicates never fail.

For example, Figure 7 shows the optimized code for the intersect predicate. As there is no call to the left of the tail calls in the tail recursive clauses that may fail, the two *commit* instructions are removed.

6 Evaluation

In this section, we compare the performance of a byte-code compiler for NTOAM with three WAM-based systems: SB-Prolog (Version 3.1) [5], SICStus-Prolog (Version 2.1) [10], and Eclipse (Version 3.3) [7]. The following programs are tested.

- member: Select all the elements of a list of size 10^5 one by one by backtracking.

- queens: Find all solutions to the 8-queens problem.

- color: Color the graph by Gardner that consists of 110 vertices.

No.	program	NTOAM(bc)	SB(bc)	SICS(bc)	SICS(nc)	Eclipse(bc)
1	member	(0.80)1	1.98	1.93	0.64	2.73
2	queens	(0.35)1	2.34	1.65	0.66	2.43
3	color	(57.32)1	5.14	1.76	1.01	1.75
4	nrev	(2.73)1	1.44	0.94	0.30	2.09
5	intersect	(2.36)1	2.63	1.83	0.82	2.17
6	boyer	(7.14)1	2.40	0.92	0.41	0.87
7	compiler	(2.35)1	2.42	1.73	0.97	2.44

Table 1: Comparison of execution time (SPARC-2).

- nrev: Reverse a list of integers whose length is 10^3.

- intersect: Find the intersection of two identical sets of size 10^3.

- boyer: A theorem prover.

- compiler: Compile the *boyer* program into NTOAM instructions.

Table 1 depicts the ratios between the execution time of the WAM-based systems and that of NTOAM. *bc* indicates a byte-code compiler and *nc* indicates a native-code compiler. The numbers in the parentheses are execution time in seconds. NTOAM is faster than SB for all programs and faster than the byte-code compiler of SICS for all programs except for *nrev* and *boyer*.

It is difficult to tell to what extent the argument passing scheme affects the execution speed because the four systems compared are very different. SB is the simplest. SICS is a complicated system. The emulator is well tuned and some built-in predicates such as *read* and *write* are written in C. In addition, the scheme of unifying some nested compound terms without flattening them [4] also favors SICS, especially for *boyer*. Eclipse uses two words to represent a data cell, one holding the tag and the other holding the value. NTOAM takes advantage of mode and determinacy declarations to generate efficient standard form programs. Its performance is affected by not only the argument passing scheme but also by the sophisticated indexing scheme. Nevertheless, the data do reflect the advantages of the scheme of passing arguments in stack frames. For example, for *member*, the NTOAM code is faster than the WAM code because backtracking in NTOAM is simpler than that in WAM and tail recursion elimination makes it possible to reuse many frame slots. For *intersect*, NTOAM code is faster than the WAM code because it involves no deep backtracking.

To understand clearly the effect of the argument passing scheme, we need to neglect the effect of indexing and specialization. For this purpose, we replace each nonvariable term T at the head of every clause with a new variable X and place the call unify(X,T) at the beginning of the body. The results show that NTOAM is 30% to 90% faster than the byte-code compiler of SICS. This results are due to the following two facts: Firstly, most

program no.	1	2	3	4	5	6	7
NTOAM	1	1	1	1	1	1	1
WAM(SB)	1.73	1.56	1.12	0.46	1.86	0.72	1.56

Table 2: Comparison of control stack space.

predicates in the transformed programs are neither determinate nor binary. In WAM, almost all arguments transferred into argument registers need be further stored in a choice point or an environment or both, and thus passing arguments into registers loses its advantages. Secondly, a large portion of tail recursion is transformed into iteration in NTOAM.

Table 2 shows the ratios between the control stack space required by SB and that by NTOAM. To the contrary of expectations, the results are not bad to NTOAM. In the benchmarks, only for *nrev* and *boyer*, does WAM require less local stack space than NTOAM. WAM requires more control stack space than NTOAM for other programs because some predicates require both a choice point and an environment to be created, and the space for the choice point can not be reclaimed in forward execution even if a cut discards the choice point.

7 Conclusion

In this paper, we presented a new abstract machine called NTOAM. Unlike WAM, it passes arguments in stack frames and uses only one frame for each predicate call. NTOAM has the following advantages over the WAM: (1) backtracking and delay are simpler; (2) a large class of predicates can be classified as determinate and be optimized; (3) tail recursion is converted into iteration easily; (4) in an emulator-based implementation, the destination to which the next argument is to be passed is stored in the PA register and the emulator needs not to fetch and interpret it. The disadvantages of the NTOAM include: (1) a frame that is large enough for executing all clauses in a predicate has to be allocated at the beginning of the predicate; (2) it needs be checked at runtime whether or not the frame of a predicate can be reused when no information is available about the determinacy of the calls in the predicate. The empirical data show that, in emulator-based implementations, NTOAM outperforms WAM concerning both execution time and space in general.

Acknowledgement

The author would like to thank Bart Demoen, Saumya K. Debray, Kenichi Kakizaki and the anonymous reviewers for their helpful comments.

References

[1] Aho, A.V., Sethi, R. and Ullman, J.D. : Compilers – Principles, Techniques, and Tools, Addison-Wesley, 1986.

[2] Ait-Kaci, H. : Warren's Abstract Machine, The MIT Press, 1991.

[3] Carlsson, M. : Freeze, Indexing, and other Implementation Issues in the WAM, Proc. of the 4th International Conference on Logic Programming, 40-58,1987.

[4] Carlsson, M. : Design and Implementation of an OR-Parallel Prolog Engine, Doctoral Dissertation, Swedish Institute of Computer Science, 1990.

[5] Debray, S.K. (ed.) : The SB-Prolog System, A User Manual, Dept. of Computer Science, University of Arizona, Tucson, 1988.

[6] Debray, S.K. and Warren, D.S. : Functional Computation in Logic Programs, ACM Trans. on Programming Languages and Systems, 11, 451-481,1989.

[7] ECLIPS : ECRC Common Logic Programming System, Release 3.3, International Computers Limited and ECRC GmbH, 1993.

[8] Meier, M. : Recursion Vs. Iteration in Prolog, Proc. of the 8th International Conference on Logic Programming, 156-169, 1991.

[9] Van Hentenryck, P. : Constraint Satisfaction in Logic Programming, The MIT Press, 1989.

[10] SICStus Prolog User's Manual, Swedish Institute of Computer Science, 1991.

[11] Warren, D.H.D. : Implementing Prolog-Compiling Predicate Logic Programs, Tech. Rep. 39 and 40, Dept. of Artif. Intell., Univ. of Edinburgh, 1977.

[12] Warren, D.H.D. : An Abstract Prolog Instruction Set, SRI International No. 309, 1983.

[13] Zhou, N.F. : Global Optimizations in a Prolog Compiler for the TOAM, J. Logic Programming, 15, 265-294, 1993.

Output Value Placement in Moded Logic Programs

Peter A. Bigot   David Gudeman   Saumya Debray
Department of Computer Science
University of Arizona
Tucson, AZ 85721, USA
{pab, gudeman, debray}@CS.Arizona.EDU

Abstract

Most implementations of logic programming languages treat input and output arguments to procedures in a fundamentally asymmetric way: input values are passed in registers, but output values are returned in memory. In some cases, placing the outputs in memory is useful to preserve the opportunity for tail call optimization. In other cases, this asymmetry can lead to a large number of unnecessary memory references and adversely affect performance. When input/output modes for arguments are known it is often possible to avoid much of this unnecessary memory traffic via a form of interprocedural register allocation. In this paper we discuss how this problem may be addressed by returning output values in registers where it seems profitable to do so. The techniques described have been implemented in the jc system, but are also applicable to other moded logic programming languages, such as Parlog, as well as languages like Prolog when input/output modes have been determined via dataflow analysis.

1   Introduction

In the Warren Abstract Machine (WAM), which is used as the basis for a large number of implementations of Prolog and other logic programming languages, there is a fundamental asymmetry in the treatment of the input and output values of a procedure: input values are passed in argument registers, while output values are returned in memory. The reason for this is clear in the context of Prolog, for which the WAM was originally designed: Prolog procedures do not, in general, have any notion of input and output arguments, and a particular argument to a procedure can be an input argument in one invocation and an output argument in another. Because of this, it is simplest to pass all arguments into a procedure in registers, with each uninstantiated variable—usually corresponding to an output argument— passed by reference, as a pointer to the cell occupied by that variable. An output value is returned by binding an uninstantiated variable to a value, i.e., by writing to the corresponding memory location.

While this scheme is simple and works in general, it may incur unnecessary overheads. To see this, consider the following procedure to compute the factorial of a given number:

```
:- mode fact(in, out).
fact(0, 1).
fact(N, F) :- N > 0, N1 is N-1, fact(N1, F1), F is N*F1.
```

At each level of recursion, the variable F1, which corresponds to the output argument of the recursive call, is allocated a slot in the stack frame (which must be initialized as an unbound variable), and a pointer to the slot is passed into the recursive call. When the call returns, the value of F1 is retrieved from memory, used to compute the expression N*F1, and the result stored back into memory. This sequence of events is repeated all the way up the chain of recursion. This leads to two sources of overhead: a space overhead because environments on the stack must allocate space for the output variables of procedures, and a time overhead because of the increased memory traffic. It is not difficult to see that the repeated loads and stores of the output argument in the example above are not necessary: it can be computed into a register at each level of recursion and returned in that register. Indeed, since implementations of functional languages typically put the return value of a function in a (hardware) register (see, for example, [4, 8]), the behavior described above can be a source of performance disadvantage for logic programming languages compared to functional languages. Finally, since the number of procedure returns at runtime must be equal to the number of procedure calls, the benefits of reducing the cost of procedure returns, in particular via careful management of registers, can be significant.

It is obvious that knowledge about which arguments of a procedure are output arguments is necessary for this optimization to be carried out: this information may be obtained user from user annotations, or via dataflow analysis (e.g., see [6, 11]). However, a number of other issues must also be addressed in order to carry out the kind of interprocedural register allocation discussed in the fact/2 example above, including how the merits of alternative output placements should be compared, and how output placement decisions interact with the ability to carry out tail call optimization. The remainder of the paper discusses these and related issues and describes how they have been addressed in the context of jc, a sequential implementation of a variant of Janus [7].[1] However, the techniques we have developed are not peculiar to Janus in any way, and are applicable also to other logic programming languages where mode information about procedure arguments is available. To minimize syntactic hurdles for the reader, we will use a Prolog-like syntax for our examples, with input and output arguments of procedures indicated by mode declarations as in the fact/2 example above.

2 Output Value Placement: Implementation Considerations

There are a variety of implementation concerns which interact with output value placement. If an output placement algorithm is chosen naïvely, the overhead of extra work induced by unfortunate placements can overwhelm any benefits of returning values in registers. Some of those concerns are considered here.

2.1 Interactions with Tail Call Optimization

While program performance can be improved significantly by returning output values in registers rather than in memory, the situation is complicated by the interaction of this optimization with *tail call optimization* (TCO). This optimization collapses procedure returns when the last body goal is a call, immediately followed

---

[1] An alpha release of the system is available by anonymous ftp from ftp.cs.arizona.edu, file janus/jc/jc-2.0.tar.

by a procedure return. By replacing this *tail call* with a jump to the called procedure and re-using the caller's frame, one avoids a redundant return and frame allocation. The interaction problem arises when an ill-chosen placement blocks this optimization by requiring move instructions to be inserted after the tail call, to reconcile the return locations of caller and callee. The cost of this "de-optimization" must be weighed against the expected savings accruing from returning output values in registers when deciding whether or not the outputs of a procedure should be returned in registers.[2] In general, if output arguments are returned in registers, then it is impossible to avoid deoptimizing some tail calls in some clauses, regardless of what approach is taken for output register assignment and code generation. The problem is illustrated by the following example:

Example 2.1 Consider a procedure defined by the clauses

```
:- mode p(out, out).
p(X,Y) :- q(X,Y).
p(X,Y) :- q(Y,X).
```

It is not difficult to see that if either p/2 or q/2 returns either of its outputs in registers, at least one of the clauses defining p/2 will have to give up tail call optimization. □

2.2   Interactions with Procedure Suspension

Committed choice languages such as GHC [12] and Janus [10] typically require that if a procedure activation cannot make progress because its inputs are not adequately instantiated, it should suspend until its inputs are available. Many modern Prolog systems also provide facilities whereby an activation can be made to suspend until certain of its arguments become instantiated. Since a procedure that suspends cannot return an output value, it is necessary to take such suspension behavior into account when considering whether to return output values in registers. As an example, consider the following clause:

```
p(X,Y) :- q(X,Z), Y is Z+X.
```

Suppose that the procedure q/2 has the mode q(in, out), and we choose to return the output Z of the call q(X,Z) in a register r. If the execution of this call suspends, then it is necessary to ensure that r is set to a value that causes the computation Y is Z+X to suspend as well. Moreover, the suspension structure for the goal Y is Z+X has to be set up in such a way that this computation is resumed when the computation of q(X,Z) eventually computes a value for Z. This can complicate handling procedure suspension and resumption considerably. One can imagine various baroque schemes for dealing with these problems; it was not clear to us that the complications and runtime overhead incurred were justified by the benefits of returning in registers the output values of procedures that may suspend, especially given the already high cost of suspension and resumption. For this reason, we have chosen to return output values of a call to a procedure p in registers only if all of the computation underneath that call can be guaranteed to not suspend: such calls

---

[2]However, the cost of this de-optimization may not be as bad as one might expect: our experimentally-determined cost model, summarized in Table 1, suggests that the cost of sacrificing a tail call optimization where an environment has already been allocated (C_{tn}) is roughly twice the total time cost of returning a value in memory, including the cost of initialization, assignment, and loading the value ($C_p + C_a + C_l$). Losing a tail call where an environment must be allocated (C_{ta}) costs only 25–35% more than the cost of returning the value in memory.

are said to be *transitively non-suspending*. Since the suspension behavior of a particular call depends on its arguments, we create two copies of candidate procedures: one that can be guaranteed to not suspend and may return its outputs in registers, and another that may or may not suspend and returns its outputs in memory in the traditional way. At compile time, calls are routed to one or the other of these copies, depending on the results of dataflow analysis. If the analysis determines that only one of these versions is used, only that version is kept.

3 Output Value Placement Methods

A variety of placement algorithms exist, each with its own advantages and disadvantages. We will discuss several of these methods in turn, using them both as examples to highlight features that are to be sought or avoided, and to introduce various components of the cost model we will ultimately use to choose a placement for return values.

3.1 Homogeneous Placements

The simplest way to assign output value locations is to choose one fixed form of return, and use it throughout the program. This obviates the need to make complicated decisions about the best location to hold a return value, thereby speeding and simplifying compilation, possibly at the expense of run-time performance. Several homogeneous schema are plausible.

3.1.1 Memory

The classical place to return output values is in memory. As noted above, returning a value in memory is necessary in the absence of mode information, or when the suspension behavior of a procedure cannot be predicted. It has the added advantage of never preventing a tail call optimization, since one memory location is as good as any other, and no moves to preferred locations need be inserted.

The disadvantage of returning values in memory is exemplified by the factorial program discussed in Section 1: the processor will store a value into memory, only to reload it immediately on return to the caller. The cost of returning a value in memory can be broken down into several components: (i) allocating space for the return value on the stack or heap; (ii) preparing the return value slot (storing an "uninitialized variable" marker); (iii) at the callee, dereferencing the variable before assignment; (iv) assigning the value into memory; and (v) loading it from memory again at the use-point. For a homogeneous return scheme, the time taken to allocate space for a variable is not a major concern, since space can be reserved in the activation record of the clause which uses the value.

There are three reasons for initializing the return location by storing within it some special marker that indicates that it contains an uninitialized variable: first, for the correct working of general-purpose unification routines; second, so that garbage collection routines can recognize every item on the heap; and third, because a computation may attempt to use a logical variable before a value has been computed for it. This initialization is usually slightly more expensive than a simple register-to-memory store, since some sort of tagging operation must be performed on the value to be stored.

Dereferencing a pointer chain to reach the final unassigned memory slot is relatively expensive, since it requires at least a load from memory, a test, and a conditional branch. In our cost model, we combine the cost of determining the address and performing the store into one parameter, because the two correspond to one virtual machine instruction. The load of the value at the point of its use corresponds to a simple memory load.

There are other cases where simple memory stores and loads are required, such as when saving a value across a procedure call. We separate these two costs into two parameters, because reading and writing memory may require different overheads, especially on shared or distributed memory parallel architectures (due to overhead of memory-consistency mechanisms).

For each assignment of a return value into memory, we must do two memory writes (the initialization and the eventual assignment) and at least one memory read (for dereferencing), and possibly other operations such as tagging and untagging; in addition, there will be a read at the use point which might otherwise be avoided. Since memory operations can be expensive, and having the value in memory is often unnecessary, it is natural to consider returning all values in registers instead.

3.1.2 Fixed Register Placement

The simplest way to assign registers to output values is to adopt a fixed mapping from outputs to registers. For example, we may use a convention similar to that used for the input arguments, with the first output argument being returned in register 1, the second in register 2, and so on. While simple, this scheme has the problem that it may require additional data movement to get the output values into the registers where they are needed. This is illustrated by the following example.

Example 3.1 Consider the following procedure, taken from a program to compute and evaluate Chebyshev polynomials:

```
:- mode cheb(in,in,out,out).
cheb(0,_,Y1,Y2) :- Y1=1, Y2=0.
cheb(1,X,Y1,Y2) :- Y1=X, Y2=1.
cheb(N,X,Y1,Y2) :- N > 1, N1 is N-1, cheb(N1,X,Z1,Z2),
                   c1(X,Z1,Z2,Y1,Y2).
```

The third and fourth arguments of cheb/4 are output arguments. Suppose that we use the convention that the first output argument of a procedure is returned in register 1, the second in register 2, and so on. In this case, this means that in the literal cheb(N,X,Z1,Z2) in the body of the recursive clause, the value of Z1 is returned in register 1 while that of Z2 is returned in register 2. However, given the parameter passing convention of the WAM, the call c1(X,Z1,Z2,Y1,Y2) requires that Z1 should be in register 2 and Z2 in register 3. Thus, two additional register-to-register moves are necessary at each level of recursion to set up the arguments to the next call correctly. ☐

In most functional languages, where a function has only a single value, this scheme does not suffer from the problem of sometimes being unable to use tail call optimization. Even in functional languages where a function may return multiple values, such as Common Lisp, the simplicity of this scheme makes it the approach of choice: for example, the S-1 Common Lisp implementation returns up to 8 numeric output values in registers reserved for that purpose [2]. Unfortunately, this scheme interferes with tail call optimization in the presence of any of a number of features that are common in logic programming languages, such as multiple outputs as in Example 2.1, or returning structures as in the following example, where the tail call is blocked to store q/1's output into the cons cell and reload its address for p/1's return.

Example 3.2

```
:- mode p(out).
p([a|X]) :- q(X).
```

□

3.1.3 Varied Register Placements

Many of the problems noted in the fixed scheme are a result of the rigidity of register assignment (and the ensuing need to move values to the desired location, as in Example 3.1). A natural extension is to consider choosing the appropriate return register to avoid as many of those moves as possible, by seeing where the value will be needed by calling procedures. We did not examine homogeneous varied schemes of this sort directly because (*i*) they require estimation of execution frequencies to determine which of several use points is the most important to satisfy, hence become much more complicated than a fixed scheme; (*ii*) choosing a return location for one procedure may require recomputation of preferred locations for a previously assigned procedure (especially in the presence of non-trivial strongly connected components in the call graph), resulting in an iterative computation which may not reach a fixpoint; and (*iii*) there are still cases, such as that in Example 2.1, where no homogeneous register return scheme will preserve opportunities for tail call optimization. This last problem is avoided by adopting a heterogeneous output placement method, which allows different procedures to return values in either memory or registers, depending on their callers. The machinery involved in our method of deciding whether to use memory or register for the return location naturally extends to indicate which register will require the fewest additional moves, addressing the first concern as well. By applying the heterogeneous scheme in a bottom-up order (assigning return locations to the most frequently executed candidates first), we avoid the second problem while preserving good savings overall.

3.2 Heterogeneous Assignments

Perhaps the best-known heterogeneous return location assignment is that used in the Aquarius Prolog compiler, and described by Van Roy in [13]. The Aquarius scheme can be considered a fixed register heterogeneous method, in which all return values of non-suspending procedures are candidates for being returned in a register, and are removed from candidacy (placed into memory) when some condition is no longer met. Candidates that survive the winnowing process are then returned in the register in which the unassigned variable pointer would have been passed. This fixed assignment avoids the need to re-visit previously assigned procedures as the candidacy of return values from called procedures changes, as would be required with the policy described in Section 3.1.2.

The Aquarius method does not take into account frequency of execution, and may unwittingly choose to return values in memory in a frequently called procedure in order to retain a tail-call optimization opportunity in a rarely called one. Nor does it consider relative costs of losing a tail call optimization versus storing values into memory: the overhead of preparing memory slots and dereferencing chains can make the two costs fairly close. Our implementation of this method in `jc`, which matches the Aquarius implementation on the test programs, shows varied but often good speedups for small programs, but more negligible improvement over homogeneous memory for more complicated programs where few outputs satisfy the restrictions for register placement (see Tables 2 and 3).

Pass 1: Local Cost Computation
For all non-suspending procedures
    Reset the per-clause costs and output/placement TCO block flags
    For all call sites to procedure and the resulting output values
        add costs for placements based on use point of value
    For all clauses of the procedure and their output values
        add costs for placements based on definition point

Pass 2: Assigning Output Placements
For all non-suspending procedures by most frequently called
    For each clause that can still do a TCO
        update flags to note potential blocking output placements
    While some output is not placed
        compute costs for all placements for all unplaced outputs
        assign output whose cheapest placement is most expensive
        update flags of blocked tail calls

Figure 1: Overview of Placement Algorithm

---

4 An Algorithm for Output Value Placement

The discussion of the previous section suggests that a good return location assignment should have the following characteristics: (*i*) it should be *heterogeneous*, so as to avoid both losing tail call optimization opportunities and excess memory accesses; (*ii*) it should be *varied* in register assignment, so that values are placed in registers where they will be needed next; (*iii*) it should take into account the expected frequency of execution of various procedures, so that rarely executed code is not optimized at the expense of frequently executed code; and (*iv*) it should be parameterized for the costs of certain primitive operations, so that it can be implemented in compilers for a variety of architectures which can have drastically different memory subsystem behaviors.

This section describes an algorithm we have developed that has these characteristics and that has been implemented in the jc system [7]. It assumes that information about input/output modes and relative execution frequencies for procedures and clauses has been obtained separately. It also assumes that dataflow analysis has been used to determine which variables can be returned in registers: this involves a global analysis to identify transitive non-suspension of calls, and one to identify variables that will not be used before bindings are computed for them. (Due to space limitations, the analyses are not described here; see [1] for an overview.) The algorithm has two passes: the first pass assigns costs to various output locations based on the amount of work that would have to be done if those locations were chosen without assuming anything about placements in other procedures, and the second pass does a bottom-up assignment, choosing at each point the (apparently) best return location while avoiding tail call deoptimizations that would overwhelm the benefits of previous choices. A high-level overview of the method appears in Figure 1. What is most interesting about the algorithm is the reasoning involved in determining the cost incurred by a particular placement, and this is treated in depth below by considering the features of the various contexts in which values are defined and used.

4.1 Pass 1: Determining Output Location Costs

The first pass determines the costs associated with each potential return location for each output value of a procedure without assuming anything about other procedures. This involves looking at two program points separately: the point where the returned value is used, and the point in a clause where a return value is defined.

Output values are defined either by calls or via explicit assignment operations;[3] definitions by calls ultimately are grounded in assignment operations. Assignments compute the value to be assigned into a register, and we assume that the local code generator can arrange to place the value in any specified register without incurring additional cost. We follow the terminology of Van Roy [13] and classify body goals as either *survive* goals, which preserve the contents of registers, or *non-survive* goals, which can destroy the contents of registers. If a clause body contains a non-survive goal following a definition into a register, the value of that register has to be saved over the non-survive goals and restored at the clause end, possibly preventing tail call optimization.

The first pass of the algorithm associates a vector of cost information, indexed by potential placement (memory and registers), with each output of a particular procedure. The costs are incremental, in the sense that they characterize the additional expense of choosing a particular location over the best case, and distributed, in the sense that they associate the components of a cost induced by choosing a particular location with the program point at which the cost is paid.

Example 4.1 Consider the following code:

```
:- mode p(out, out).      :- mode q(out).     :- mode r(out).
p(A, B) :- q(A), r(B).     q(A) :- A = 3.      r(A) :- A = 4.
```

Assume that p/2 is to return its first value (A) in a register. Because calls are non-survive goals, A must be saved into memory across the call to r/1. If q/1 returns its value in a register, then this causes an incremental cost of one load and save within p/2. If the value is returned from q/1 in memory, p/2 adds the cost of allocating and initializing a memory slot for the value, then loading the value again at the end. The cost of doing the actual assignment into memory is associated with the assignment statement in q/1. No matter where q/1 returns its value, the tail call to r/1 cannot be optimized, because the return result of q must be reloaded afterwards.

On the other hand, if p/2 is to return its value in memory, then it has been passed a pointer to a memory location by some ancestor: the program point where that location was reserved accrued the cost of allocation and initialization. If q/1 returns its value in a register, then p/2 incurs the cost of doing the pointer dereference and assignment after control returns from q/1. If q/1 returns its value in memory, then p/2 incurs no additional cost at all, since the cost of doing the assignment is attached to q/1. □

Costs associated with a particular program point are multiplied by the estimated execution frequency of the clause in which the point occurs, so that we get an estimate of the overall time spent by the program as a whole due to the choice of a particular return location.

It is important to point out that the costs associated with deoptimizing a tail call are incurred only once for each clause, no matter how many potential decisions might

---

[3]In general, variables are given bindings via unification, but since we assume a moded language, this degenerates to assignment.

separately force this deoptimization. For example, the code in Example 3.2 may block TCO for two reasons: q/1 returning its value in a register, or p/1 returning its value in a register. Either is sufficient to block TCO and incur the corresponding cost, but the cost should not be charged twice if both conditions hold. Therefore, rather than add tail call deoptimization costs into the cost vectors now, we simply set, for each potential output placement for a clause, a flag that indicates whether choosing that location for that value will prevent a tail call optimization in that clause. In the second pass, tail call opportunities are further constrained as return locations are assigned in other procedures, and the flags are updated accordingly. At the final assignment for a particular output in the second pass, the cost of losing a tail call opportunity is added exactly once for each placement that would force such a loss where the opportunity existed before.

4.1.1 Cost Considerations at Use Point

The costs of preparing for and using a returned value depend on the contexts of the definition and use in a clause body. At a particular call site that defines a variable, there are several possible places for the use of that variable: (i) in a body goal following the definition point (assignment statement or output instance in a call), (ii) in a body goal prior to the definition point, or (iii) returned from the clause. There is also the potential that it is not used at all, or that it is used multiple times in different ways. We consider each of these cases in turn below. In the discussion that follows, cost vectors are summarized using the following notation, which indicates the cost due to a program point that must be added to the total cost of using the given placement for the output of interest: r_i refers to (an arbitrary) register i, M refers to memory, and the cost parameters are as described in Table 1.

Consider the following sequence of body goals:

$$g(\vec{t}) :\text{-} p_1, d(\ldots, x, \ldots), p_3, u(\ldots, x, \ldots), p_5. \tag{1}$$

where the p_i encapsulate zero or more body goals (survive or non-survive), d is a procedure call which defines some variable x, and u is either a procedure call or an expression which uses the value of x computed in the call d.

- If u is an expression and p_3 contains no non-survive goals, then d can return x in any register, and it will be available for use in u at no additional cost. For memory returns, the cost is that of preparing a memory space for d to assign into, and loading the memory value back into a register for use at u.

$$r_i : 0 \qquad M : C_p + C_l$$

- If u is a call and p_3 contains no non-survive goals, then the returned value x will be passed to u in the register corresponding to its argument position, say r_k, known at analysis time. If d returns x in register r_k, the cost is zero. If it returns x in a register r_i, where $i \neq k$, the cost is that of moving a value from one register to another. If d returns x in memory, the cost is the same as in the previous case, since the load can be made into the desired register.

$$r_k : 0 \qquad r_{i(i \neq k)} : C_x \qquad M : C_p + C_l$$

- If p_3 contains non-survive goals, then the return value must be saved over those goals, no matter where the value is returned. The incremental cost for memory

Parameter	Description	Typical Value cc	cc -O2
C_x	Move a value from one register to another	1	1
C_s	Store a value from a register into memory	101	100
C_l	Load a value from memory into a register	50	50
C_a	Deref variable and assign register to memory	202	201
C_p	Initialize an unassigned variable slot	148	148
C_{ta}	Call and return plus environment allocation	800	601
C_{tn}	Call and return, no environment allocation	724	507

Table 1: Parameters to cost model

over registers is that of initialization, and the cost of any register is a store (the store for memory is accounted for at the definition point).

$$r_i : C_s \qquad M : C_p$$

An appearance of an output value before its use point cannot actually reference the value, because this is precluded by the dataflow analyses that identify which variables can be returned in registers. However, such an appearance may occur, for example when the variable occurs within a compound term (as in Example 3.2): in that case, register returns block TCO. If the value is unused in the body, but returned through the head, the preferred location depends on where the callee wants it, and cannot be determined locally. Values that are computed and unused induce no preference on their output placement; values that are used multiple times are placed according to the preference of their first use.

4.1.2 Cost Considerations at Definition Point

A definition point for an output of a clause looks like:

$$g(\ldots, x, \ldots) :- p_1, d(\ldots, x, \ldots), p_2. \tag{2}$$

where x is an output of g, d is an assignment to x or a procedure call with x in an output position, and the p_i are again zero or more body goals. If x is to be returned in memory, one of the inputs to g is a pointer to its storage cell. If p_1 contains any non-survive goals, this pointer must be saved across them in the activation record, so memory costs an additional $C_s + C_l$. (We assume that non-survive goals in non-tail position induce a frame allocation to save information such as return location, so there is no incremental cost for allocating the storage space).

If d defines the value by an assignment statement, then we assume the value to be assigned is computed into a register, and it doesn't matter which one, so we can arrange for it to be computed into whichever register is most useful. As such, returning a value in any register costs nothing, unless there is a non-survive goal in p_2, in which case the value must saved and reloaded, potentially deoptimizing a last call. If the value is returned in memory, the cost is that of dereferencing the variable chain and performing the store (C_a).

$$r_i : 0 \text{ or } C_s + C_l \qquad M : C_a$$

If d defines the value by a call (the "chained definition" of the previous section), then the cost of each return location depends on where the defining call returns the value. Since this information isn't available yet and no alternative seems more likely than another, we do nothing in this case, adding in what costs we can in the final pass where some of the callee return locations will have already been assigned.

4.2 Pass 2: Choosing Output Locations

At the end of the first pass, we have defined all the costs that are independent of particular output value placements. We can now visit each procedure in turn, and assign to each output the location that yields the smallest incremental cost to the program as a whole.

As noted previously, fixing a choice for one procedure affects the optimal choice for another (e.g., in tail calls). One way to avoid the difficulties that arise from this is to use an iterative approach, going back to reconsider previous decisions when an assignment that might affect them is made. It is not immediately clear that such iteration will reach a fix-point. We have opted for a greedy approach that processes procedures, and clauses within procedures, in order of decreasing execution frequency. We start by augmenting the flags originally defined in the first pass that indicate that particular output placements will cause a tail call deoptimization. Each clause of the procedure is examined: any output defined prior to a potentially optimizable tail call will cause a loss of TCO if it is returned in a register, so register placements for all such outputs are tagged as preventing this optimization. We can also take advantage of the fact that other procedures may have already determined their output placements. Therefore, if a clause ends in a tail call to a procedure whose outputs have already been assigned, the flags are updated to indicate loss of optimization for mismatched locations that will require cleanup code to move values. When we have a tail call to an unassigned procedure, we have no way of telling which locations will eventually cause loss of optimization, so leave the flags unmodified.

The cost for assigning a particular output of the procedure to a particular location is initially set to the cost computed in the first pass. For each clause that has the potential for tail call optimization, each placement that would prevent that optimization gets an additional cost corresponding to the expense of losing the opportunity, scaled by the frequency of the clause. Furthermore, for each tail call from an already-placed procedure, placements which would force a deoptimization in the caller incur the corresponding tail call optimization loss cost (either C_{ta} or C_{tn}, depending on context), associated with the callee so they are counted.

Within a particular procedure, there may be multiple outputs, each of which has a choice of return locations. The assignments for these outputs can also interfere, for example when an assignment of a particular register to one output at a small savings prevents use of that register for another output, incurring an overwhelming cost for the next best choice. To lessen the effect of this interference, we look for the output value whose minimum cost location is the most expensive amongst all minimum cost output placements: placing any other output will certainly not decrease this output's minimum cost, and may well increase it if the former assignment prevents the preferred location from being chosen when this output is finally assigned. In the case of ties between locations, memory is chosen over registers of the same cost because memory will less often destroy a tail call opportunity. This assignment is then set: tail calls that must be followed by cleanup code resulting from the assignment are marked as no longer potential sites for tail call optimization (so the corresponding costs are not charged multiple times), and the search and assignment is repeated until all outputs have an assigned location.

Assuming that p is an upper bound on the number of output arguments of any procedure in the program, the complexity of the first pass is $O(p(S + C))$ and the second pass $O((1 + p^2)(S + C))$, where S is the number of call sites in the program and C is the number of clauses. Hence, the algorithm is essentially linear in the size of the program.

5 Tuning and Testing the Model

As noted in Table 1, there are seven parameters to the cost model, which are system and compiler specific, on which the algorithm depends. Before using the location assignment algorithm, appropriate values must be found for these parameters for a given system. This is done by an iterative process on a small set of test programs. After parameters have been chosen that yield good behavior on the tuning programs, the model must be checked against other programs to verify that a projection of its performance is generalizable.

To avoid the tedium of implementing an assembly-level back end, and to increase portability across architectures, jc translates Janus programs into C text, which is then compiled by the system C compiler. The current version of jc translates programs into one large function, in which "registers" are C local variables (which are often cached in hardware registers by the C compiler). As such, we do not have to be concerned about register windows making register-returned values inaccessible or slowing operations. While this means that some of the work of putting values in hardware registers rather than memory is done by the C compiler rather than jc directly, there is still a significant benefit from avoiding allocating and initializing memory locations in the heap. An implementation which did hardware register allocation itself would only increase the performance benefits.

Tuning and performance evaluation were done experimentally, by compiling Janus programs with various location assignment policies, and measuring the time taken to execute a query with the resulting executable. Timing tests were done on a Sun IPX (40MHz SPARC) with 32MB physical memory, running SunOS 4.1.1, using the gettimeofday(2) system call to obtain microsecond-resolution measurements of execution time, with the testing being the only active process. The system was tested using the Sun C compiler bundled with SunOS 4.1.1, with no optimizations and with -O2 optimizations.

The first step in using the method requires estimating values for the cost parameters in Table 1. This can be done in several ways: one could count the number of machine instructions required, or attempt to measure them experimentally by comparing programs that differ only by those instructions. The values in Table 1 were computed with the latter method: except for C_x, which was given a minimal value simply to choose one register over another, they may be interpreted in nanoseconds. After an initial set of parameters is generated, a tuning set of small benchmarks whose performance has a strong dependence on output placement is run with the placement policies described in section 3. The tuning benchmarks are small, so the given policies tend to cover the possible output placements. In any case where our method chooses an inferior placement (usually between register and memory, rather than an incorrect register), we can examine a trace of the algorithm's choices and tweak the parameters until we get a global optimum placement on the tuning tests. This tweaking has not been necessary with the experimentally-derived estimations in Table 1, though it was useful with earlier, less accurate estimates.

Table 2 indicates performance results on the tuning benchmarks for both sets of parameters, compared with the fixed placement of section 3.1.2 and our implementation of the Aquarius algorithm of section 3.2, all implemented within jc and available with compiler options. The values are the median of five runs of each

Benchmark Name	#OP	Sun cc, no opt			Sun cc -O2		
		jc	Fixed	Aquarius	jc	Fixed	Aquarius
array_qs	8	1.08 [b:8]	1.09 [c:8]	**1.01** [a:5]	**0.90** [b:8]	**0.90** [c:8]	1.00 [a:5]
binomial	9	**0.68** [b:9]	0.70 [c:9]	0.83 [a:7]	**0.72** [b:9]	**0.72** [c:9]	0.85 [a:7]
combB	4	**1.00** [b:2]	1.33 [c:4]	**1.00** [a:1]	**0.99** [b:2]	1.37 [c:4]	1.00 [a:1]
dnf	3	**0.99** [b:3]	**0.99** [b:3]	1.00 [a:2]	**0.97** [b:3]	**0.97** [b:3]	0.99 [a:2]
dotprodB	5	**1.00** [b:2]	1.26 [c:5]	**1.00** [a:1]	**1.00** [b:2]	1.26 [c:5]	**1.00** [a:1]
fact2	2	**0.67** [b:2]	0.69 [c:2]	0.83 [a:2]	**0.70** [b:2]	**0.70** [c:2]	0.83 [a:2]
fact3	2	**1.00** [b:2]	**1.00** [b:2]	**1.00** [a:2]	**1.00** [b:2]	**1.00** [b:2]	**1.00** [a:2]
fib	2	**0.66** [b:2]	0.70 [c:2]	0.77 [a:2]	**0.56** [b:2]	0.57 [c:2]	0.68 [a:2]
hanoi	4	**0.86** [b:4]	0.87 [c:4]	**0.86** [a:3]	**0.83** [b:4]	**0.83** [c:4]	0.84 [a:3]
lclocal	2	**1.00** [m:0]	1.51 [a:2]	**1.00** [m:0]	**1.00** [m:0]	1.27 [a:2]	**1.00** [m:0]
list_qs	5	**0.97** [b:3]	1.34 [c:5]	**0.97** [a:3]	**0.96** [b:3]	1.36 [c:5]	**0.96** [a:3]
long1	3	**0.57** [b:3]	**0.57** [b:3]	0.67 [a:3]	**0.52** [b:3]	**0.52** [b:3]	0.56 [a:3]
nr	3	**1.00** [a:1]	1.63 [b:3]	**1.00** [a:1]	**1.00** [a:1]	1.73 [b:3]	**1.00** [a:1]
pascalB	11	**1.00** [b:5]	1.39 [c:11]	**1.00** [a:1]	**0.99** [b:5]	1.36 [c:11]	1.00 [a:1]
queen	8	**0.88** [b:4]	0.93 [c:8]	1.01 [a:1]	**0.81** [b:4]	0.86 [c:8]	1.03 [a:1]
short	3	**0.49** [b:3]	**0.49** [b:3]	0.55 [a:3]	**0.50** [b:3]	**0.50** [b:3]	0.51 [a:3]
short-2	2	**0.51** [b:2]	**0.51** [b:2]	0.53 [a:2]	**0.51** [b:2]	**0.51** [b:2]	**0.51** [a:2]
tak	1	**0.59** [b:1]	0.62 [c:1]	0.62 [a:1]	**0.53** [b:1]	0.54 [c:1]	0.54 [a:1]
Global	77	**0.80** [56]	0.91 [77]	0.85 [40]	**0.78** [56]	0.87 [77]	0.82 [40]

Table 2: Tuning test results for various policies, normalized to homogeneous memory

benchmark, normalized to the time required by a homogeneous memory placement. Following each number, in brackets, is a letter used to distinguish the output placements chosen for the program, and a number indicating the number of candidate outputs that were put into memory. Due to vagaries of experimental analysis, there are cases (such as nr for cc -O2) where two algorithms resulted in the same set of placements (a), but one apparently performed slightly better than the other (perhaps due to a side effect of different hashing of atoms in the procedure tables; the code is the same): differences with the same placement should be ignored. The number of outputs placed in registers indicates approximately how frequently this optimization is effective. The total number of candidate outputs (outputs for procedures that were determined to be nonsuspending) appears in the second column of the table, for reference.

The performance of an algorithm on simple benchmarks for which it may have been tuned is no indication of what sort of performance we can expect on other and more complicated programs. Therefore, after tuning was completed, a separate set of benchmarks which tended to be more complicated were run with the same policies. Note that #OP is not a clear indicator of the actual complexity of the program—for example, although deriv has only one output, the program consists of 10 clauses which define a symbolic differentiation procedure, which has 13 call sites to the one procedure.

Table 3 gives the results of various policies using the same performance model and compiler options as in Table 2. For three programs—deriv, list_qs2, and merge—our algorithm chose to return values in memory rather than registers. This is appropriate because these programs all work on structures with little scalar computation—returning values in registers would be a mistake, as exhibited by the results using the fixed placement for those programs. On the seven (of ten) programs where our algorithm found an opportunity to make a register placement,

Benchmark	#OP	Sun cc, no opt			Sun cc -O2		
Name		jc	Fixed	Aquarius	jc	Fixed	Aquarius
bessel	13	0.89 [b:11]	**0.87** [c:13]	1.04 [a:6]	0.91 [b:13]	**0.90** [c:13]	0.94 [a:6]
cheb	5	**0.49** [a:5]	0.52 [b:5]	1.00 [m:0]	**0.44** [a:5]	**0.44** [b:5]	1.00 [m:0]
cheb-2	4	**0.94** [b:3]	0.95 [c:4]	1.03 [a:3]	**0.96** [b:3]	0.98 [c:4]	1.03 [a:3]
deriv	1	**1.00** [m:0]	1.11 [a:1]	**1.00** [m:0]	**1.00** [m:0]	1.12 [a:1]	**1.00** [m:0]
disj2	19	**0.76** [b:16]	0.77 [c:19]	0.86 [a:1]	**0.77** [b:16]	0.79 [c:19]	0.91 [a:1]
factsq	2	**0.96** [b:2]	**0.96** [b:2]	1.03 [a:1]	**0.98** [b:2]	**0.98** [b:2]	1.00 [a:1]
list_qs2	4	**1.00** [m:0]	1.21 [a:4]	**1.00** [m:0]	1.02 [m:0]	1.23 [a:4]	**1.00** [m:0]
merge	1	**1.00** [m:0]	1.54 [a:1]	**1.00** [m:0]	1.02 [m:0]	1.53 [a:1]	**1.00** [m:0]
prime1	7	**1.00** [b:2]	1.33 [c:7]	**1.00** [a:1]	1.01 [b:2]	1.28 [c:7]	**1.00** [a:1]
queenk	3	**0.94** [b:3]	**0.94** [b:3]	0.95 [a:2]	**0.94** [b:3]	**0.94** [b:3]	0.95 [a:2]
Global	59	**0.88** [42]	0.98 [59]	0.99 [14]	**0.88** [44]	0.97 [59]	0.98 [14]

Table 3: Performance evaluation test results

the average improvement was 17%. However, the degree of improvement is highly dependent on the actual code being compiled, so the "global" average should not be used to predict improvements for a particular program.

Even though our algorithm may occasionally choose to give up tail call optimization in order to put output values in registers, no program does significantly worse than the traditional approach of returning outputs via memory using our scheme. Overall, and recognizing the variance in applicability, we find that our algorithm for output placement produces an average performance improvement of about 12–18%, depending on compiler and benchmarks—this compares favorably with execution time reductions that have been reported for optimizations that are recognized as effective within the compiler construction community, such as procedure inlining (12% [5], 10% [3]), register allocation (20% [9]), and loop-invariant code motion (13% [9]).

6 Conclusions

While most implementations of logic programming languages return the output arguments of procedures via memory, this can be a source of unnecessary overhead and can cause a performance degradation. Returning outputs in registers is an attractive alternative, but the situation is complicated by the fact that this may lead to a loss of tail call optimization. In this paper, we examined a variety of plausible schemes for returning output arguments, and gave an algorithm for output argument placement that uses cost estimates for various alternatives, weighted by execution frequency estimates, to determine a "good" output location assignment for each procedure in a program. Our experiments indicate that for programs where the outputs are best returned in memory, this algorithm usually makes the right decisions, and the performance of the resulting code is no worse than that of the traditional scheme for returning outputs via memory; for programs where registers can be used advantageously for output arguments, our algorithm produces code that is significantly faster than the traditional scheme. Although our algorithm can take advantage of additional information such as frequency estimates to yield even better speedups, the bulk of the improvement arises from careful preservation of opportunities to return values in registers and use of cost estimates for different alternatives, resulting in code that is frequently better than any homogeneous return policies or the heterogeneous policy used in the Aquarius compiler.

Acknowledgements

This work was supported in part by the National Science Foundation under grant number CCR-9123520. The first author was also supported by graduate fellowships from the U.S. Office of Naval Research and AT&T Bell Laboratories.

References

[1] Peter A. Bigot, Saumya K. Debray, and David Gudeman. Output value placement in moded logic programs. Technical Report TR 94-03, University of Arizona, Computer Science Department, Jan. 1994.

[2] R. A. Brooks, R. P. Gabriel, and G. L. Steele, Jr., "S-1 Common Lisp Implementation", *Proc. ACM Symp. on Lisp and Functional Programming*, Pittsburgh, PA, Aug. 1982, pp. 108–113.

[3] F. C. Chow, "A Portable Machine-Independent Global Optimizer: Design and Measurements", Ph.D. Dissertation, Stanford University, Dec. 1983. Technical Report No. 83-254.

[4] W. Clinger, "The Scheme 311 Compiler: An Exercise in Denotational Semantics", *Proc. 1984 ACM Symp. on Lisp and Functional Programming*, Austin, TX, Aug. 1984, pp. 356–364.

[5] J. W. Davidson and A. M. Holler, "A Study of a C Function Inliner", *Software Practice and Experience* vol. 18, pp. 775–790, 1988.

[6] S. K. Debray, "Static Inference of Modes and Data Dependencies in Logic Programs", *ACM Transactions on Programming Languages and Systems* vol. 11, no. 3, June 1989, pp. 419-450.

[7] D. Gudeman, K. De Bosschere, and S.K. Debray, "jc: An Efficient and Portable Sequential Implementation of Janus", *Proc. Joint International Conference and Symposium on Logic Programming*, Washington DC, Nov. 1992, pp. 399–413. MIT Press.

[8] B. Hausman, "Turbo Erlang: An Efficient Implementation of a Concurrent Programming Language", manuscript, Ellemtel Telecommunications Systems Labs., Sweden, March 1993.

[9] M. L. Powell, "A Portable Optimizing Compiler for Modula-2", *Proc. SIGPLAN-84 Symp. on Compiler Construction*, Montreal, June 1984, pp. 310–318. SIGPLAN Notices vol. 19 no. 6.

[10] V. Saraswat, K. Kahn, and J. Levy, "Janus: A step towards distributed constraint programming", in *Proc. 1990 North American Conference on Logic Programming*, Austin, TX, Oct. 1990, pp. 431-446. MIT Press.

[11] K. Ueda, "The Mode System of Moded Flat GHC", *Proc. ILPS-93 Post-conference Workshop on Global Compilation of Logic Programs*, Vancouver, Canada.

[12] K. Ueda, "Guarded Horn Clauses", in *Concurrent Prolog: Collected Papers*, vol. 1, ed. E. Shapiro, pp. 140-156, 1987. MIT Press.

[13] P. Van Roy. *Can Logic Programming Execute as Fast as Imperative Programming?* PhD thesis, University of California at Berkeley, 1990.

Native Code Compilation in SICStus Prolog

Ralph Clarke Haygood

Swedish Institute of Computer Science[1]

Abstract: SICStus Prolog is a sequential Prolog implementation built around a version of the Warren Abstract Machine (WAM). For several years, SICStus has supported WAM-to-native code compilation for Sun workstations. This old scheme is neither as portable nor as open to experiments as would be desirable. With the support of my colleagues in the SICStus group, I have developed a new scheme that is more of both and performs slightly better too. Portability enhancement is achieved by introducing a new abstract machine, a fragment of an idealized general-purpose architecture, between the WAM and native code targets. This allows most of the complexity of native code compilation to be in phases containing only well-encapsulated target dependencies. Moreover, it allows the run-time library for native code to be substantially target-independent. For RISC targets, a derivative of the new abstract machine allows quasi-target-independent instruction scheduling to be performed. This paper explains the SICStus approach to native code compilation, presents the new scheme in detail, and evaluates it with respect to portability and performance.

Descriptors: Prolog, Compilation, Native Code, Abstract Machines.

1 Introduction

SICStus Prolog is the sequential Prolog implementation developed at the Swedish Institute of Computer Science since 1986 [And93]. SICStus offers: extensive functionality - not only the "Edinburgh standard" but also extensions, including indefinite precision integer arithmetic, interoperability with C, and coroutining; portability to a variety of platforms, especially workstations running some version of UNIX; and performance high enough for practical applications. These qualities, along with a low price to academic institutions, have made SICStus popular in universities and research institutes.

Like most Prolog implementations in use today [Van94], SICStus is built around a version of the Warren Abstract Machine (WAM). Prolog is compiled to WAM code, which is executed by an emulator written in C. Performance of emulated code is good; however, better performance is attainable by compiling to native code. For several years, SICStus has supported native code compilation for Sun workstations. This old scheme is neither as portable nor as open to experiments as would be desirable. With the support of my colleagues in the SICStus group, I have developed a new scheme that is more of both and performs slightly better too. Little has been published about the old scheme[2], so this paper describes some features shared by the two schemes, e.g., a strategy for compiling compound term unifications. Mostly, however, this paper is about the new scheme. It should be of interest to implementors of Prolog and other logic languages and maybe to implementors of nonlogic languages who are interested in native code compilation.

The organization of the paper is as follows. In section 2, I consider a number of issues pertaining to programming language implementation in general and native code compilation in particular, explaining the SICStus approach. In section 3, I present the new scheme - its abstract machines, compilation phases, and run-time library - in detail. And in section 4, I evaluate the new scheme with respect to portability and performance. Throughout, I assume familiarity with Prolog and the WAM. Some acquaintance with the SPARC, 68k, and/or MIPS architectures would be helpful.

---

[1] mail: Box 1263, S-164 28 Kista, Sweden; telephone: +46 8 752 15 69; fax: +46 8 751 72 30; electronic mail: rch@sics.se.
[2] There is a technical report in Swedish [Boo91].

2   Native Code Compilation

Of the general approaches open to a programming language implementor, the simplest is interpretation. Interpreters are typically fast to write but slow to run. Moreover, for languages like Prolog, they have bad memory behavior, if written naively, due to heavy recursion. SICStus uses interpretation for dynamic predicates, whose clause sequences may be incrementally altered. However, in SICStus, as in programming language implementations generally, the desire for efficiency in time and space alike dictates some form of compilation as the normal usage.

The simplest form of compilation is to an abstract machine, designed with respect to the language to be implemented and free of many complications typical of concrete machines (pipelining, interrupts, etc.). The abstract machine must be realized in terms of some concrete machine; emulation is doing this without further compilation. An implementor has great freedom of choice about the abstract machine - its level of abstraction, the techniques used in compiling to it, and the techniques used in emulating it. Loosely speaking, if the level of abstraction is low enough, a vast assortment of compilation techniques is available for generating efficient code; and if it is high enough, the abstract machine is amenable to emulation techniques that make the implementation portable to many concrete machines.

SICStus partakes of both advantages. The core of SICStus is an emulator for a version of the Warren Abstract Machine (WAM) [Car91]. Over the last decade, the WAM has become paradigmatic for implementors of Prolog and other logic languages [Van94]. It serves performance by specializing unification (**get_***, **put_***, **unify_***), reducing nondeterminism (**switch_***), and a judicious memory strategy (registers and stack-allocated memory); and it serves portability in that its instruction set is coarse-grained, and its architecture is otherwise simple. Of course, it is possible to go further in either direction, especially toward performance - ideas abound in the literature (e.g., [Van90]). However, for the most part, SICStus does not go further. The SICStus compiler [Car90], *pl_wam*, operates predicate-by-predicate. There is no global analysis. Clause selection is by first-argument indexing only. Despite this naiveté, performance has proved high enough for many purposes. The emulator, written in C, has proved portable to many platforms. SICStus has an active user community of several hundred people throughout the world, many of whom depend on emulated code.

Despite the advantages of emulation, it is natural to look beyond it. For high performance, it seems obvious that one should compile to a concrete machine; this is native code compilation.[3] However, there are a number of issues to consider; I consider them here with respect to SICStus.

First, how much higher performance should one expect? SICStus is a mature implementation, the product of many person-years of skilled labor, much of it directed at tuning *pl_wam* and the emulator. This means that emulated code is not so easy to improve upon as one might suppose.[4] Moreover, real applications spend time in built-in predicates that in SICStus are written in C and in garbage collection, likewise in C. Native code compilation need not reduce this; attention to Amdahl's Law is appropriate. A rough analysis of these factors suggests that, for SICStus, well-crafted native code compilation should yield a speed-up between one and something like three for most programs, but one should not expect a greater speed-up for almost any program, unless maybe one alters the SICStus approach to compilation radically (e.g., by adding global analysis).

Second, what about portability? The last phase of native code compilation cannot be target-independent, and there is tension between keeping the earlier phases target-independent and generating efficient code. Indeed, efficiency is likely to engender target dependencies throughout. Portability loss is reduced if target dependencies in the earlier phases are well-encapsulated. Another way of reducing portability loss is compiling to C and using a C compiler as a back-end. There has been a

---

[3] Of course, there are degrees of concreteness. E.g., for a microcoded processor with a writeable control store, the standard instruction set architecture is not the bottom level for programming. I shall ignore such distinctions, an imprecision that seems unlikely to mislead.

[4] E.g., there is a program, not written as a benchmark, for which SICStus emulated code runs about twice as fast as native code in Aquarius Prolog, an implementation using far more sophisticated compilation techniques [Van90]. The reason is a register allocation flaw, which makes Aquarius do badly on a critical predicate. This is unusual - Aquarius is competitive with SICStus native code for most programs - but it suggests the point: SICStus emulated code is good enough that native code compilation must be well-crafted to improve upon it.

lot of interest in this approach recently (e.g., [Chi94, Hau93, Gud92]). For reasons given below, it is not appropriate for SICStus, but it may be appropriate for many logic language implementations. SICStus users are mostly academic and industrial researchers. The prevalence of workstations from Sun, DEC, etc. among these people means that SICStus native code compilation is valuable, even if available for these platforms only. However, to allow for new trends in the workstation market and to ease the maintenance burden, it is desirable for SICStus native code compilation to be as portable as possible, consistent with other requirements.

The other requirements pertain to implementation effort and functionality. As usual in engineering, these are somewhat at odds. On one hand, high performance is the basic goal. On the other hand, the SICStus group is small, and its members have other responsibilities. Moreover, SICStus is not a research prototype - though we do not guarantee it, our attitude is that anything we add to it should be robust. This led us to the conclusion that our native code compilation should use as much as possible of the existing implementation, at least to begin with. In particular, *pl_wam* has been retained as the first phase, with minor alterations for native code relative to emulated code. This decision implies that it is natural for native code compilation to operate predicate-by-predicate, unlike native-code-via-C schemes, which must compile whole programs or modules at a time to attain high performance.

This incrementality is one aspect of a general commitment, namely, that native code should behave just like emulated code, except that it may take somewhat more time to generate, it may take somewhat more space to store, and hopefully, it will run faster. "Somewhat" is vague, of course, and both program- and target-dependent; we are content with factors of something like three or less. Besides incrementality, this commitment entails transparent interoperability between native code and emulated code. Broadly speaking, this means that native code compilation is convenient for development as well as "production" usage. The value of this flexibility is a matter of opinion. However, several users have expressed appreciation for it. Also, it has been helpful for debugging native code compilation, since it is easy to compile any portion of a program to native code and the rest to emulated code.

As mentioned in section 1, for several years, SICStus has supported native code compilation for Sun workstations. This old scheme fulfills the foregoing desiderata acceptably, except that it is not as portable as desired. For one thing, the WAM-to-native code phases for the two targets, the 68k[5] and SPARC, are disjoint and permeated with target-dependencies. For another, native code continually refers to a run-time library, the kernel, written in assembly language - about 2000 lines of it. The necessity of providing all this for a new target is a major barrier. Therefore, I have built a new scheme, in two stages. In the first stage, I rebuilt the WAM-to-native-code phases so that most of the complexity is in phases containing only well-encapsulated target dependencies. In the second stage, I rebuilt the kernel in the same fashion. Having finished the new scheme for the 68k and SPARC, I extended it to the MIPS[6], mainly for use on DECstations. The basic goal of my work has been portability enhancement. However, I have sought to improve performance too. Moreover, with the new scheme, it should be easier to perform experiments toward further performance improvement.

3   The New Scheme

The new scheme is built around a new abstract machine, the SICStus Abstract Machine (SAM). The WAM is first compiled to the SAM, using essentially the same compiler, regardless of the native code target, and the SAM is then compiled to the desired target. Moreover, the kernel is written largely in SAM code, and this too is compiled to native code. For RISC[7] targets, commonality is practical even further down the machine hierarchy. Between the SAM and such targets, the new scheme places a "RISCified" SAM, the RISS. Quasi-target-independent instruction scheduling is performed on RISS code.

---

[5] In full, the MC680X0 family with $X \geq 2$.

[6] In full, the MIPS R2000 and R3000; R4000 and R6000 extensions are not generated at present.

[7] I am using "RISC" in the colloquial sense: a pipelined load/store architecture.

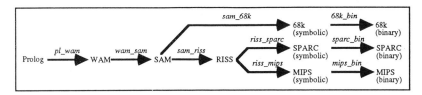

Figure 1: The Prolog Compilation Path

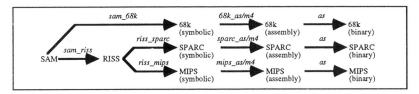

Figure 2: The Kernel Compilation Path

Figures 1 and 2 show the Prolog and kernel compilation paths. Apart from the standard utility *m4* and the standard assembler *as* (at the end of the kernel compilation path), each phase is written in Prolog and constitutes a self-contained module. WAM, SAM, RISS, and target instructions are represented by terms in a straightforward way, and each interior phase consumes a list of instructions from the preceding phase and produces one for the following phase. The result of a Prolog compilation may be loaded immediately or written to a file for subsequent loading. The result of a kernel compilation is an object file, which is linked (along with object files for the emulator, the garbage collector, etc.) into the SICStus executable. There are target dependencies from the WAM level down. However, in *wam_sam*, *sam_riss*, and the kernel, they are well-encapsulated.

The following subsections discuss the SAM, *wam_sam*, the kernel, the RISS, and *sam_riss* in detail. A further subsection discusses *riss_sparc* as an example of final compilation to a target. Since the 68k is no longer in fashion, I shall say little about *sam_68k*. Also, since they are mundane, I shall say little about **_bin*, the assembly phases of Prolog compilation, or **_as*, the target-level syntax-transformation phases of kernel compilation.

3.1 The SAM

The SAM instruction set architecture is presented in Figure 3. Concisely, it is a fragment of an idealized general-purpose architecture. It is load/store with three-operand arithmetic instructions and self-contained conditional branches. Loads, stores, and control transfers are undelayed. The major idealizations are that any number of registers are available, and any datum may be an immediate.

This design was shaped by the WAM and a set of targets: primarily, the SPARC and the 68k, to which SICStus was committed, and secondarily, prospective RISC targets, especially the MIPS. The SAM was to be something to which the WAM could be compiled satisfactorily and which in turn could be compiled satisfactorily to the targets, with most of the complexity in the former step. In detail, this meant the following. Generally, native code compilation realizes WAM instructions partly instance-by-instance and partly in the kernel, i.e., partly in-line and partly in subroutines. This was true in the old scheme, and the rationale for it remains valid in the new scheme. The SAM was to be such that all the in-line parts could be in SAM code. The SAM was also to be used for the kernel, but

Data are binary words. The number of bits is unspecified.

I denotes an immediate operand. Any datum may be an immediate operand - there are no size restrictions.

R, *R1*, or *R2* denotes a register operand. The number of registers is unspecified. Registers are generic with respect to instructions, with two exceptions: there is a register **zero** that always contains binary zero, and there is a register **link** that is implicitly defined by the **jmpl** instruction. Each register holds exactly one binary word.

S, *S1*, or *S2* denotes a source operand, which may be an immediate or a register.

The number of memory locations is unspecified. Memory locations are generic with respect to instructions. Each memory location has a unique binary word address and holds exactly one binary word.

L denotes a label operand, which is an immediate specifying an address.

Instructions are denoted by a term syntax. The destination operand, if any, is right-most. Instructions use and define binary words - there are no partial- or multiple-word operations. Instruction behaviors are presented informally - they are largely implicit in the names. Synthetic forms are defined for convenience.

---

memory instructions

instructions

ld(*R1*,*S*,*R2*)	load
st(*S1*,*R*,*S2*)	store

- **ld** loads *R2* from the memory location whose address is *R1* plus *S*.
- **st** stores *S1* to the memory location whose address is *R* plus *S2*.

synthetic forms

ld(*R1*,*R2*)	≡	**ld**(*R1*,zero,*R2*)
ld(*I*,*R*)	≡	**ld**(zero,*I*,*R*)
st(*S*,*R*)	≡	**st**(*S*,*R*,zero)
st(*S*,*I*)	≡	**st**(*S*,zero,*I*)
stz(*R*,*S*)	≡	**st**(zero,*R*,*S*)
stz(*S*)	≡	**st**(zero,*S*)

arithmetic instructions

instructions

add(*R1*,*S*,*R2*)	add
sub(*R1*,*S*,*R2*)	subtract
and(*R1*,*S*,*R2*)	and
or(*R1*,*S*,*R2*)	or
xor(*R1*,*S*,*R2*)	exclusive or
sll(*R1*,*S*,*R2*)	shift left logical
srl(*R1*,*S*,*R2*)	shift right logical
sra(*R1*,*S*,*R2*)	shift right arithmetic

- **add** and **sub** are insensitive to overflow. Should sensitivity be desired, it is suggested that the instruction set be extended with **addt** and **subt** that trap on signed integer overflow.
- The behavior of **sll**, **srl**, and **sra** for a negative shift count or a shift count greater than the datum size is undefined.

synthetic forms

Op(*S*,*R*)	≡	*Op*(*R*,*S*,*R*)
neg(*R1*,*R2*)	≡	**sub**(zero,*R1*,*R2*)
neg(*R*)	≡	**neg**(*R*,*R*)
mov(*S*,*R*)	≡	**or**(zero,*S*,*R*)
movz(*R*)	≡	**mov**(zero,*R*)

- *Op* denotes one of {**add, sub, and, or, xor, sll, srl, sra**}.

control transfer instructions

instructions

br(*C*,*R*,*S*,*L*)	branch
jmp(*L*)	jump
jmpl(*L*)	jump and link
jmpr(*R*)	jump register

- Branches are conditional, jumps are unconditional.
- *C* denotes one of {**e, ne, l, le, g, ge, lu, leu, g u, g e u**}, which signify the usual signed and unsigned integer comparisons.
- **br**(*C*,*R*,*S*,*L*) branches to *L* when *R C S* - the order is the usual one.
- **jmpl** puts the address of the instruction after itself in **link**.

synthetic forms

br(*Cz*,*R*,*L*)	≡	**br**(*C*,*R*,zero,*L*)

- *C* denotes one of {**e, ne, l, le, g, ge**}.
- *Cz* denotes the concatenation of *C* and **z**.

Figure 3: The SAM Instruction Set Architecture

it did not need to be complete for the kernel. Anything SAM code could not do could be done using inclusions of assembly language. As long as most of the kernel were in SAM code, a few assembly inclusions would not impair portability greatly. Omission from the SAM of capabilities needed only in the kernel would simplify the post-SAM compilation phases (*sam_riss, sam_68k*, etc.).

wam_sam uses all but a few of the features in Figure 3, and these are sufficient for it - assembly inclusions are unnecessary.[8] The kernel uses the remaining features. However, the SAM is not complete for the kernel. E.g., the kernel contains one instance of integer multiplication and two of integer division. Neither operation is needed in-line. The simplicity gained by omitting them from the SAM is significant, since different targets implement them in quite different ways.

Compiling the SAM to any target involves bounding the register set, and it usually involves bounding immediate sizes. Both tasks require that one or more temporary registers be set aside for the post-SAM compilation phases. E.g., if the target is load/store, and the destination of a SAM instruction is a SAM register that is mapped to a target memory location, then the corresponding target instruction must write to a temporary register, which is in turn stored to the memory location. For RISC targets, the other major issue is instruction scheduling. The SAM is otherwise enough like the SPARC and MIPS that it compiles to them easily.

Compiling the SAM to the 68k is not so easy. Though the 68k is obsolete, it is instructive to describe how the new scheme treats it as a target unlike the SAM in some ways the SPARC and MIPS are not. The 68k has two-operand arithmetic instructions, two register classes, and assorted memory addressing modes, many usable in arithmetic instructions. Problems with the first two characteristics are largely avoided by judicious assignments of SAM registers to 68k registers and otherwise solved, for the most part, by setting aside one address register for *sam_68k*. The third characteristic makes it possible to avoid using a temporary register in the 68k for many SAM instructions that require one in other targets. However, the postincrement and predecrement modes, which are valuable, e.g., for building terms on the global stack, are incongruous with the SAM as presented so far. To exploit them, the SAM itself is conditionally extended with postincrement and/or predecrement loads and stores. Conceptually, the SAM is broadened from a single abstract machine to an abstract machine schema, instances of which are specified by parameters abstracted from targets. This notion recurs in the RISS.

Based on knowledge of the old scheme, experiments in compiling WAM to SAM and SAM to targets, and discussions with colleagues, I formulated an initial design for the SAM.[9] This design evolved over the course of the project, as it became clearer to me what was necessary and comfortable. E.g., the initial design had SPARC-like condition codes. However, I found that I had to reset them immediately prior to nearly every branch, i.e., I was hardly ever able to do multiple branches on a single compare or test. Moreover, they were somewhat awkward to implement in full generality for targets other than the SPARC. Therefore, I scrapped them in favor of self-contained branches.

3.2 *wam_sam*

wam_sam is actually two modules, one for predicate code (indexing instructions) and one for clause code (everything else). *wam_sam_predicate* is a one-pass macro-expansion. *wam_sam_-clause* is likewise, plus peephole optimizations to get rid of superfluous jumps. The WAM **x** registers map to SAM registers, along with the usual WAM pointer registers (**h**, **s**, etc.). Also, *wam_sam* introduces **u** registers to serve as temporaries. Three suffice for *wam_sam*; a fourth is used in the kernel. These are managed "by hand" per WAM instruction.

The most interesting aspect of *wam_sam* is how it compiles unification of a variable with a compound term. Compound term unification in the context of the WAM has attracted a lot of attention (e.g., [Mei90, Umr90, Mar91]). See the literature for general analyses; I shall merely present the

---

[8] A few are used, purely as optimizations. Various pseudo-ops, not shown in Figure 3, are also necessary.
[9] Patterson and Hennessy's [Hen90] chapter on instruction set design helped me to consider the possibilities systematically.

strategy. *pl_wam* generates **get_*** and **unify_*** largely as in the original WAM, and *wam_sam* expands these to SAM instructions realizing a version of what has become known as the two-stream algorithm [Van94]. There are two code streams, one for **read** mode and one for **write** mode, with branches between them. The compound term, regarded as a tree with a node per compound subterm, is traversed, unifying with the term that was represented by the variable at compile time. As long as this is nonvariable, execution proceeds in the **read**-mode stream. When a variable is encountered where a compound subterm is to be, execution branches to the **write**-mode stream, which builds the compound subterm. Afterward, execution returns to the **read**-mode stream. Each subterm corresponds to exactly one sequence of instructions in each stream - code size is linear in term size. **Write** mode is propagated to subterms. The order of traversal is the traditional depth-first - subterms are not reordered. Given this order, an economical branch apparatus is generated.

The strategy is best explained by an example; Figure 4 presents one, which also appears in [Mar91]. WAM and SAM instructions are represented essentially as in *wam_sam*. Refinements associated with indexing are omitted, and other items irrelevant to the example are omitted from the SAM code. The SAM code is for a target other than the 68k; for the 68k, postincrement loads on **s** and stores on **h** are generated. I shall not explain the example exhaustively; the highlights are as follows:

- **unify_temp_variable / get_temp_structure**: These propagate **write** mode to compound subterms. **unify_temp_variable**(X) is identical to **unify_variable**(X), except that it tells *wam_sam* that the argument is a compound subterm - there will be one use of X. **get_temp_structure**(F,X) is identical to **get_structure**(F,X), except that it tells *wam_sam* that the structure is a subterm and X was defined by **unify_temp_variable**(X) - this is the one use of X. In **read** mode, the extra information makes no difference, but in **write** mode, it enables *wam_sam* to avoid first creating X unbound, then dereferencing, trail-checking, and binding it. This is the only change the strategy imposes on the WAM or *pl_wam*.

- kernel calls: The meat of the unification instructions is in the kernel, for reasons given in section 3.2. NATIVE_GET_STRUCTURE etc. are mnemonics for kernel routine numbers. These numbers pass into binary code, where the loader recognizes them and fills in the appropriate addresses. The difference between NATIVE_GET_* and NATIVE_GET_SUB* is that the latter assumes its term is not a local variable, since it has been loaded from the global stack; this saves a little time. NATIVE_GET_[SUB]STRUCTURE dereferences its term (**u**(**1**)). If the result is a variable, it is bound to a structure-tagged pointer to the global stack, the functor (**u**(**0**)) is pushed, and the return is to **write** mode. Otherwise, the result must be a structure with the correct functor, or failure occurs; if this succeeds, **s** is set to point to the functor, and the return is to **read** mode. The presence of **s** in *wam_sam* and the kernel embodies the fact that SICStus tags occupy the top of the word. For most targets, this means that untagging cannot be folded into the displacement of a load or store - hence **s** is desirable.

- **fix_offset** pseudo-ops: These enable two-way returns from NATIVE_GET_[SUB]STRUCTURE. WRETURN_RRETURN_OFFSET is a target-dependent parameter. A **write**-mode return is to the point immediately after the call; a **read**-mode return is to that point plus WRETURN_-RRETURN_OFFSET. Guided by **fix_offset** pseudo-ops, the assemblers (**_bin*) insert no-ops if necessary to make this work.[10] E.g., the **write**-mode return from the NATIVE_GET_-STRUCTURE call is **local**(A), and the **read**-mode return is **local**(B); the **fix_offset** pseudo-op separates these by WRETURN_RRETURN_OFFSET.

- branch apparatus (marked ‡): **s** is free in **write** mode, so it is used to control returns from **write** mode to **read** mode after building compound subterms. Before the jump to **write** mode, **s** is set to what **h** will be after the subterm has been built. The condition for return is simply **h** = **s**. **s** is set if and only if it will be compared with **h**. A single branch instruction is always enough.

This strategy resembles that of [Mar91]. However, it was invented by Kent Boortz for SICStus. The algorithm *wam_sam* uses to generate the SAM code may be formalized in terms of a push-down automaton. I shall not present this here; interested readers should contact me.

---

[10] This is trivial for RISC targets and tedious for the 68k.

In Figure 4, **mov(x(2),u(0))** under **local(B)** is superfluous, since **ld(s,word(1),x(2))** preceding it could as well be **ld(s,word(1),u(0))**. An optimization pass could deal with this, of course. However, early in this project, I tried something more ambitious. **x(2)** is introduced here by *pl_wam* and **u(0)** by *wam_sam*. If instead of assigning it to **x(2)**, *pl_wam* would let the argument of the first **unify_temp_variable** be a virtual register, then it could be assigned to **u(0)** by a register allocation at the SAM level. I implemented such a register allocation, using a graph coloring algorithm. However, though it certainly dealt with cases like the one considered here, the benefit was disappointing for most programs. Typical speed-ups were less than two percent. Moreover, compilation time typically increased significantly. The texture of the SAM code is one reason for the lackluster results. Most computations must survive kernel calls - cases like the one considered here are relatively uncommon. Most kernel calls may define the **u** registers. Consequently, most computations ended up in **x** registers - where *pl_wam* would have put them anyway. It follows that an implementation that did more in-line would probably benefit more from such a register allocation.

Two software engineering techniques used in *wam_sam* may be of interest. First, target dependencies, e.g., whether to generate postincrement loads on **s**, are handled using the *m4* macro preprocessor. *m4* is run on a configuration file that defines macros appropriate to the target, e.g., POSTINC_S for the 68k, followed by the source code of *wam_sam*, yielding true Prolog. Thus *wam_sam* wastes no time determining dependencies when it runs. Other global parameters, e.g., WRETURN_- RRETURN_OFFSET, are neatly handled in this fashion too. Second, concurrent accumulation of multiple code streams, e.g., for compound term unifications, is handled using an extended definite clause grammar syntax. The syntax and a version of **term_expansion/2** that interprets it were developed by Peter Van Roy [Van89]. These techniques are used in *wam_sam* and throughout the new scheme.

3.3 The Kernel

Kernel routines belong to four classes. Unification routines encompass not only general unification but also the meat of **get_constant**, **get_list**, and **get_structure**. Nondeterminism routines include failure and try, retry, and trust routines that manage choicepoints. Built-in routines support common built-in predicates for which *pl_wam* generates a **builtin_*** or **function_*** instruction instead of a standard call; most of these routines pertain to arithmetic expressions, but there are also routines for term comparison, **arg/3**, and **functor/3**. Finally, linkage routines handle transfers between native code and emulated code, garbage collection, etc.

The primary purpose of the kernel is to moderate code size; this issue is significant, because SICStus is supposed to run real applications. A secondary purpose is to simplify the SAM and hence the post-SAM compilation phases. Calling a kernel routine costs something, so these purposes are in tension with the goal of high performance. Deciding what to put in-line and what to put in the kernel is a matter of judgment, preferably informed by experiments. The goals of this project include making experiments easier by making it easier to evaluate the consequences for all targets of a change in the division between the kernel and code compiled from Prolog. E.g., arithmetic operations are always handled in the kernel at present; it might be interesting to try handling in-line the common case of dereferenced small integer operands.

Within the kernel, common and simple cases are handled in SAM code, with assistance from assembly inclusions as needed. Other cases are passed to routines written in C; the same routines handle these cases for emulated code. Error reporting is deferred to these routines too. E.g., many built-in routines pertaining to arithmetic expressions check whether their arguments dereference to small integers. If so, the appropriate operation is performed immediately. If not, a C routine is called to handle large integer or floating point arguments or report an error.

The SAM-to-target phases of the kernel compilation path are the same as those of the Prolog compilation path. This is good for portability. Of course, minor differences could be parameterized, but this happens to be unnecessary for any target so far. The results of *sam_68k* and *riss_** are lists of target instructions represented by terms. For the kernel, **_as* followed by *m4* turn these into a file of target instructions in syntax acceptable to the standard assembler *as*. Use of *as* is not inevitable. It is to

```
Prolog:     head(f(g(a),h(foo))).

WAM:        get_structure(f/2,x(0)).
            unify_temp_variable(x(2)).
            unify_temp_variable(x(1)).
            get_temp_structure(g/1,x(2)).
            unify_constant(a).
            get_temp_structure(h/1,x(1)).
            unify_constant(foo).
            proceed.

SAM:        mov(functor(f/2),u(1)).                          % get_structure(f/2,x(0))
            mov(x(0),u(0)).                                  % "
            jmpl(kernel(NATIVE_GET_STRUCTURE)).              % "
     fix_offset(local(A),local(B),word(WRETURN_RRETURN_OFFSET)).
            label(local(A)).                                 % " [enter write mode]
                add(h,word(7),s).                            % " ‡
                jmp(local(H)).                               % " ‡
            label(local(B)).                                 % ••• read-mode stream •••
                ld(s,word(1),x(2)).                          % unify_temp_variable(x(2))
                ld(s,word(2),x(1)).                          % unify_temp_variable(x(1))
                mov(functor(g/1),u(1)).                      % get_temp_structure(g/1,x(2))
                mov(x(2),u(0)).                              % "
                jmpl(kernel(NATIVE_GET_SUBSTRUCTURE))%       "
     fix_offset(local(C),local(D),word(WRETURN_RRETURN_OFFSET)).
            label(local(C)).                                 % " [enter write mode]
                add(h,word(2),s).                            % " ‡
                jmp(local(I)).                               % " ‡
            label(local(D)).                                 % " [continue read mode]
                mov(tagged(a),u(1)).                         % unify_constant(a)
                ld(s,word(1),u(0)).                          % "
                jmpl(kernel(NATIVE_GET_SUBCONSTANT)).%       "
            label(local(E)).                                 % get_temp_structure(h/1,x(1))
                mov(functor(h/1),u(1)).                      % "
                mov(x(1),u(0)).                              % "
                jmpl(kernel(NATIVE_GET_SUBSTRUCTURE))%       "
     fix_offset(local(F),local(G),word(WRETURN_RRETURN_OFFSET)).
            label(local(F)).                                 % " [enter write mode]
                jmp(local(J)).                               % " ‡
            label(local(G)).                                 % " [continue read mode]
                mov(tagged(foo),u(1)).                       % unify_constant(foo)
                ld(s,word(1),u(0)).                          % "
                jmpl(kernel(NATIVE_GET_SUBCONSTANT)).%       "
            jmpr(1).                                         % proceed
            label(local(H)).                                 % ••• write-mode stream •••
                add(h,mask(STR_MASK)+word(3),u(0)).          % unify_temp_variable(x(2))
                st(u(0),h,word(1)).                          % "
                add(h,mask(STR_MASK)+word(5),u(0)).          % unify_temp_variable(x(1))
                st(u(0),h,word(2)).                          % "
                add(word(3),h).                              % get_structure(f/2,x(0)) [end]
                st(functor(g/1),h,word(0)).                  % get_temp_structure(g/1,x(1))
            label(local(I)).                                 % "
                st(tagged(a),h,word(1)).                     % unify_constant(a)
                add(word(2),h).                              % get_temp_structure(g/1,x(1)) [end]
                br(e,h,s,local(E)).                          % " ‡ [maybe return to read mode]
                st(functor(h/1),h,word(0)).                  % get_temp_structure(h/1,x(1))
            label(local(J)).                                 % "
                st(tagged(foo),h,word(1)).                   % unify_constant(foo)
                add(word(2),h).                              % get_temp_structure(h/1,x(1)) [end]
                jmpr(1).                                     % proceed
```

Figure 4: A compound term unification example

‡ marks the branch apparatus.

some extent a relic of the old scheme, where the kernel was written directly in assembly language. At the cost of complicating *_bin, the kernel could be assembled like code compiled from Prolog. Assembly would occur at installation time and loading at run time; much of SICStus is already processed this way. I have not pursued this possibility, but it might be worthwhile. It would avoid the quirks of some standard assemblers.[11]

3.4 The RISS

Like the SAM, the RISS is an abstract machine schema. The parameters specifying an instance are meant to make the RISS correspond closely to the RISC target. Generally, the RISS differs from the SAM as follows:

- The number of registers is specified. A proper subset of SAM registers map to RISS registers, and the rest to memory locations.

- Immediates are size-restricted. The restrictions may be instruction-dependent. SAM immediates map to RISS immediates if they are small enough. If not, it is necessary to construct them in RISS registers, or maybe to map them to RISS registers, if they are heavily used.[12] Construction may be done in typical RISC fashion. The word is split into high and low parts, the low part being small enough for any instruction. The RISS has an instruction **sethi**(I,R) that assigns immediate I to the high part of register R.[13]

- Control transfers have delay slots. The instruction in the delay slot, known as the delay instruction, of a **jmp**, **jmpl**, or **jmpr** is always executed. By default, this applies to **br** too; however, the RISS may be extended with annulling branches. When this is done, branches have the form **br**(A,C,R,S,L), where A is one of $\{n, y\}$. If A is **n**, the delay instruction is always executed; but if A is **y**, the delay instruction is not executed when the branch is not taken. **jmpl** puts the address of the instruction after its delay instruction in **link**. The set of instructions that may be delay instructions is a parameter of the RISS.

For some targets, there may be other differences. E.g., for the SPARC and MIPS, the source of a **st** must be a RISS register, since these architectures do not have a store with an immediate source.

The purpose of this design is to make the mapping of RISS instructions to target instructions as one-to-one as possible - hence RISS registers should map to target registers, RISS high and low part splitting should be as in the target, and the RISS should have annulling branches if and only if the target has them. The mapping is not perfectly one-to-one, due to things like branches that different targets realize in different ways, usually involving multiple instructions. However, it is close enough to make it reasonable to perform instruction scheduling at the RISS level. This is the most complex aspect of *sam_riss*; if it were done at the target level, it would be the most complex aspect of the target-level phases.

3.5 *sam_riss*

sam_riss has two passes. The first bounds the register set and immediate sizes, and the second performs instruction scheduling, which consists of introducing a delay slot per control transfer and trying to fill it with something useful. Other kinds of instruction scheduling might be worthwhile, e.g., separating a load to a register from a following instruction using the register; at present, however, *sam_riss* merely fills delay slots. There are two obvious places to look for something useful: first, prior to the control transfer in the basic block it terminates; second, in the basic block commencing with the target of the control transfer. *sam_riss* tries both, trying the second if the first fails to find something useful, the control transfer is a **jmp**, **jmpl**, or annulling **br**, and the target is local. The procedure is prolix to explain but intuitively straightforward; two aspects of it merit further discus-

---

[11] E.g., MIPS *as* fails to provide the primitive **div** instruction of the basic machine; the synthetic instruction provided in its place performs a 32-bit overflow check, which is superfluous in the kernel.

[12] E.g., for the SPARC and MIPS, *sam_riss* maps the structure tag mask to a RISS register.

[13] There are subtleties associated with high and low part splitting - but this paper too is size-restricted.

sion. First, a RISS instruction is suitable for a delay slot if and only if it is context-independent and compiles to exactly one target instruction. E.g., **jmpl** is excluded because it is context-dependent, and **br** is likely to be excluded because it compiles to a pair of target instructions. *sam_riss* is guided by a predicate defined per target that succeeds if and only if its single argument is a RISS instruction suitable for a delay slot. Second, copying an instruction from a basic block to the delay slot of a control transfer to that basic block leads to multiple copies of the instruction. It may be desirable in the post-RISS phases for all copies to be linked together somehow. It is easy for *sam_riss* to supply a link in the form of an unbound variable attached to all copies of a given instruction. Section 3.6 explains how *riss_sparc* uses this "tag".

3.6 *riss_sparc*

riss_sparc is an instructive example of what final compilation to a target may involve. It has two passes, a macro-expansion and a peephole optimization. By design, the RISS code it compiles is much like SPARC code to begin with, but a couple of issues remain to be resolved, both pertaining to control transfers.

One issue is compiling RISS **jmp** to a nonlocal label.[14] The available single-instruction control transfer to an unrestricted label is SPARC **call**. This implicitly defines **o(7)** and is the natural choice for RISS **jmpl**, mapping **link** to **o(7)**. It would be nice to use it for RISS **jmp** to a nonlocal label too, in order to use just one instruction. Of course, this is safe only if **link** is dead at the **jmp**. In SICStus usage, this requirement happens to be satisfied most of the time: **jmpl** is used to call the kernel, so **link** is usually live only in the kernel. *riss_sparc* takes advantage of this, assuming **link** is dead at **jmp** to a nonlocal label, except in certain contexts, which it recognizes. This is satisfactory but nongeneric, i.e., it depends on SICStus usage.

The other issue is using the SPARC condition codes. *riss_sparc* macro-expansion compiles RISS **br** to SPARC **cmp** or **tst** followed by **bicc** (branch on integer condition code). In an instance of **tst** / **bicc**, the **tst** is usually superfluous if the preceding instruction is an arithmetic that defines the operand of the **tst**, since most arithmetics can set the condition codes as a side-effect. The main task of *riss_sparc* peephole optimization is to take advantage of this. It is simple, apart from one complication: what if the arithmetic is the first instruction in a basic block and has been copied to one or more delay slots by *sam_riss*? Then each copy must set the condition codes. The tags supplied by *sam_riss* offer a means of arranging this. *riss_sparc* uses the tag of an arithmetic to specify whether the arithmetic should set the condition codes. Fixing the tag in one copy fixes it in all copies, since all copies share the tag. Of course, the problem could be solved by having all arithmetics set the condition codes, but this seems clumsy. The solution adopted is elegant.

4   Evaluation

I shall focus on the SPARC and MIPS in preference to the antiquated 68k. Results for the 68k are qualitatively consistent with results for the SPARC.

4.1 Portability

The basic goal of the new scheme relative to the old is portability enhancement. Portability is resistant to quantification, but some measures suggest that the new scheme achieves significant enhancement. Table 1 presents the sizes of the post-WAM compilation phases, in lines of source code, excluding comments and blanks. According to this admittedly crude measure, most of the complexity is in *wam_sam*, as desired. Table 2 presents the amounts of SAM and assembly code in the kernel, again in lines of source code, excluding comments and blanks.[15] Since almost all target-dependencies in the kernel are in the form of assembly inclusions, this measure implies a substantial degree of target-independence for the kernel. In both respects, the new scheme improves upon the old.

---

[14] RISS **jmp** to a local label compiles to SPARC **ba** (branch always).

[15] The amount of MIPS assembly code is inflated by quirks of MIPS *as*.

	SPARC			MIPS	
phase	lines	percentage	phase	lines	percentage
wam_sam	2117	62	*wam_sam*	2109	60
sam_riss	589	17	*sam_riss*	583	16
riss_sparc	184	6	*riss_mips*	179	5
sparc_bin	_515_	_15_	*mips_bin*	_656_	_19_
	3405	100		3527	100

Table 1: Sizes of Post-WAM Compilation Phases

	SPARC			MIPS	
language	lines	percentage	language	lines	percentage
SAM	1629	89	SAM	1663	83
assembly	_197_	_11_	assembly	_330_	_17_
	1826	100		1993	100

Table 2: Amounts of SAM and Assembly Code in the Kernel

A less objective but maybe more meaningful indicator is my experience with extending the new scheme to the MIPS. I spent a bit over a week roughing in working versions of *riss_mips*, *mips_bin*, and *mips_as* and dealing with target-dependencies in *wam_sam*, the kernel, and *sam_riss*, as well as other parts of SICStus like the loader. Then I spent a bit under a week on debugging and polishing specific to the MIPS. Thus the total was about two weeks. I believe it would have taken considerably longer to extend the old scheme. However, three factors must be taken into account. One is that, as the designer of the new scheme, I know it well - this surely helped me in extending it. Another is that I designed it with the MIPS in mind - it might not accommodate even another RISC target as easily. Finally, no optimizations specific to the MIPS are performed - I believe there are some that would be worthwhile. To mitigate the knowledge factor, I kept a log of my MIPS experience, and I have added to it general explanations and advice, so that it amounts to a rudimentary "porting manual". Undoubtedly, the best test of portability would be for someone other than myself to extend the new scheme to a new target. Unfortunately, this has not been possible yet, but the SICStus group hopes it may be soon.

4.2 Performance

Benchmarking the new scheme versus the old for a target they share, the SPARC, reveals how well the new scheme measures up. For the new target, the MIPS, benchmarking native versus emulated code reveals how well the new scheme realizes the potential of native code. Not only performance but also compilation time and space are of interest.

Tables 3 and 4 present measurements of the well-known Warren benchmarks [Van94].[16] Compile time and size are for the program only, i.e., the benchmark minus the query. Compile size includes not only code but also auxiliary memory that SICStus allocates whenever it compiles the program.[17] Run time is for multiple repetitions as follows: **derivative**: 100000; **naive_reverse**: 10000; **query**: 1000; **quicksort**: 10000; **serialise**: 10000. Repetitions are performed using a failure-driven loop; the overhead of this arrangement is low, and memory is recovered per repetition, so garbage collection never occurs. Times are in milliseconds, and sizes are in bytes.

---

[16] **derivative** is the sum of **divide10**, **log10**, **ops8**, and **times10**.

[17] Code size is not conveniently accessible at present.

	compile time (ms)		compile size (b)		run time (ms)	
	old	new	old	new	old	new
derivative	130	170	3088	3552	15301	15130
naive_reverse	30	40	896	944	4770	4030
quicksort	50	80	1216	1264	8400	7890
query	240	339	8416	8192	6760	6650
serialise	110	180	3408	3568	6230	6020

Table 3: Warren Benchmarks - Old Scheme Versus New for the SPARC

	compile time (ms)		compile size (b)		run time (ms)	
	emulated	native	emulated	native	emulated	native
derivative	191	340	2240	3872	53993	23342
naive_reverse	43	94	496	992	15288	5878
quicksort	75	125	672	1376	25459	13335
query	266	621	5648	7568	21745	7839
serialise	172	320	1776	3792	19682	9378

Table 4: Warren Benchmarks - Emulated Versus Native Code for the MIPS

Table 3 compares the old scheme to the new for the SPARC. The platform is a Sun 10/30 with 32 megabytes of memory. In all cases, compile time is longer for the new scheme, typically about half again as long. This is reasonable, since the new scheme has more passes.[18] As would be expected, the lengthening is approximately linear in the compile size. In all but one case, compile size is somewhat larger for the new scheme. I believe this is largely due to changes in the division between the kernel and code compiled from Prolog. On the whole, the new scheme puts somewhat more in-line. In all cases, run time is slightly shorter for the new scheme. My impression is that slightly faster first-argument indexing and dispatching in the kernel account for most of this. It seems that enhancing portability has not diminished performance.

Table 4 compares emulated to native code for the MIPS. The platform is a DECstation 5000/240 with 48 megabytes of memory. Emulated code is measured in the standard version of SICStus and native code in my version. In the standard version, the compilation phases, along with many built-in predicates, are in emulated code, but in my version, they are in native code; this is a "hidden" benefit of native code. In Table 4, compile time is about twice as long and compile size about twice as large for native code, well within the factors of three mentioned in section 2. Run time is shorter for native code by factors of between 1.9 (**quicksort**) and 2.8 (**query**), a satisfactory reduction. However, I have made this comparison for the SPARC too. Apart from **query**, which compiles atypically well for the MIPS, code expansions are 5-10% less and speed-ups 5-20% more for the SPARC. This suggests a need for MIPS-oriented code improvements. More sophisticated instruction scheduling might be especially helpful. Measurements show that *sam_riss* fills more branch delay slots for the SPARC, which gives the RISS annulling branches, than for the MIPS, which does not. Giving the RISS load delay slots would also be desirable for the MIPS.

---

[18] This does not increase garbage collection or paging overhead, since compilation is a failure-driven loop, recovering memory per clause.

	compile time (ms)		compile size (b)		run time (ms)		memory time (ms)	
	old	new	old	new	old	new	old	new
bamspec	4330	5760	128736	131488	10140	9920	1300	1180
freplan	7740	11990	314896	338208	190630	183440	19590	19250
mixtus	15560	23310	604448	618896	39140	38360	280	290

Table 5: Applications - Old Scheme Versus New for the SPARC

	compile time (ms)		compile size (b)		run time (ms)		memory time (ms)	
	emulated	native	emulated	native	emulated	native	emulated	native
bamspec	6855	10499	84656	141856	35181	18217	2152	2657
freplan	10616	20944	185568	363888	406720	278400	31552	31826
mixtus	21471	42325	398800	653072	75875	57803	613	797

Table 6: Applications - Emulated Versus Native Code for the MIPS

The Warren benchmarks are tiny programs requiring almost no built-in predicates - only integer arithmetic - and no garbage collection. Consequently, benchmarking with them may be misleading with respect to real applications. Tables 5 and 6 present measurements of three substantial programs: **bamspec**, by Peter Van Roy, is the executable specification of the Berkeley Abstract Machine, the core of Aquarius Prolog [Van90], executing the Warren benchmark **query**; **freplan**, by Mats Carlsson and Mats Grindal, solves a frequency assignment problem for a cellular telephone grid using a graph coloring algorithm; **mixtus**, by Dan Sahlin, is a partial evaluator for Prolog, evaluating the Warren benchmark **serialise**. Table 5 corresponds to Table 3 and Table 6 to Table 4, with the difference that garbage collection and other memory overflow handling is nontrivial; it is included in run time but also tabulated as memory time. Space does not permit a detailed discussion of these statistics. I shall limit myself to noting that, for these more-or-less real applications[19], native code compilation is worthwhile, but generally not as much so as for the Warren benchmarks, not surprisingly. The speed-ups for MIPS native versus emulated code, excluding memory time, are 112% for **bamspec**, 52% for **freplan**, and 32% for **mixtus**; the speed-up for **bamspec** is the greatest I have seen for a substantial program.

4.3 Future Work

There are two obvious directions for future work: more targets and more optimizations. The new scheme should be extended to several more targets. Candidates include the newly-introduced Pow-erPC, the HP PA-RISC, and the DEC Alpha. The SICStus group hopes to undertake at least one of these during the next few months. Beyond improving instruction scheduling, there are two categories encompassing many potential improvements. First in importance are changes in memory strategy. SICStus has a number of frequently-referenced control words that at present are independent global variables, e.g., the global stack limit word, which is the trigger for garbage collection. A reference to one of these costs two instructions in the RISS or a RISC target: **sethi** followed by **ld** or **st**. These should at least be put in a table, where they could be referenced using base-displacement loads and stores. A suitable table already exists in SICStus. Maybe some of these or other items in the table, e.g., the WAM **hb** register, should be mapped to registers for some native code targets. The other category of improvements is changes in the distribution of labor between the kernel and code generated by *wam_sam*. There is scope for this, though care is necessary to keep code size under control. The new scheme makes it easier than before to experiment with these and other possibilities. Some of them seem likely to yield significant benefits. The next release of SICStus, containing the new scheme for native code compilation, should improve upon the performance reported in this paper.

---

[19] The **freplan** program has been applied to industrial problems.

5 Acknowledgments

I am grateful for the support of the SICStus group: Stefan Andersson, Kent Boortz, and Mats Carlsson; I find them most agreeable colleagues. Huge thanks to Mats for inviting me to SICS, proposing this project, and being endlessly helpful throughout it. Likewise, huge thanks to Kent for pioneering the old scheme, suggesting the possibility of a "RISCified" SAM, and prototyping *sam_riss* and *riss_sparc*. Finally, I appreciate the encouragement of Seif Haridi. This project was sponsored in part by Ellemtel Utvecklings AB.

6 References

[And93]   J. Andersson et al., *SICStus Prolog User's Manual*, SICS Technical Report T93:01.

[Boo91]   Kent Boortz, *SICStus Maskinkodscompilering*, SICS Technical Report T91:13, 1991. (In Swedish.)

[Car90]   Mats Carlsson, *A Prolog Compiler and its Extension for OR-Parallelism*, SICS Research Report R90006, 1990.

[Car91]   Mats Carlsson, *The SICStus Emulator*, SICS Technical Report T91:15, 1991.

[Chi94]   Takashi Chikayama, Tetsuro Fujise, and Daigo Sekita, *A Portable and Reasonably Efficient Implementation of KL1*, preprint, 1994.

[Gud92]   David Gudeman, Koen De Bosschere, and Saumya K. Debray, *jc: An Efficient and Portable Sequential Implementation of Janus*, in *Joint International Conference and Symposium on Logic Programming 1992*, pp. 399-413.

[Hau93]   Bogumil Hausman, *Turbo Erlang: An Efficient Implementation of A Concurrent Programming Language*, preprint, 1993.

[Hen90]   John L. Hennessy and David A. Patterson, *Computer Architecture: A Quantitative Approach*, Morgan Kaufmann, 1990.

[Mar91]   André Mariën and Bart Demoen, *A new Scheme for Unification in WAM*, in *International Logic Programming Symposium 1991*, pp. 257-271.

[Mei90]   Micha Meier, *Compilation of Compound Terms in Prolog*, in *North American Conference on Logic Programming 1990*, pp. 63-79.

[Umr90]   Zerksis Umrigar, *Finding Advantageous Orders for Argument Unification for the Prolog WAM*, in *North American Conference on Logic Programming 1990*, pp. 80-96.

[Van89]   Peter Van Roy, *A Useful Extension to Prolog's Definite Clause Grammar Notation*, in *ACM SIGPLAN Notices*, pp. 132-134, November 1989.

[Van90]   Peter Van Roy, *Can Logic Programming Execute as Fast as Imperative Programming?*, Ph.D. dissertation, University of California, Berkeley Computer Science Division Technical Report UCB/CSD 90/600, 1990.

[Van94]   Peter Van Roy, *1983-1993: The Wonder Years of Sequential Prolog Implementation*, to appear in *Journal of Logic Programming*, 1994.

Actions

Representing Actions in Equational Logic Programming

Michael Thielscher
Intellektik, Informatik, TH Darmstadt
Alexanderstraße 10, D–64283 Darmstadt, Germany
E-mail: `mit@intellektik.informatik.th-darmstadt.de`

Abstract

A sound and complete approach for encoding the action description language $\mathcal{A}$ developed by M. Gelfond and V. Lifschitz in an equational logic program is given. Our results allow the comparison of the resource-oriented equational logic based approach and various other methods designed for reasoning about actions, most of them based on variants of the situation calculus, which were also related to the action description language recently.

A non-trivial extension of $\mathcal{A}$ is proposed which allows to handle uncertainty in form of non-deterministic action descriptions, i.e. where actions may have alternative randomized effects. It is described how the equational logic programming approach forms a sound and complete encoding of this extended action description language $\mathcal{A}_{ND}$ as well.

1   Introduction

Understanding and modelling the ability of humans to reason about actions, change, and causality is one of the key issues in Artificial Intelligence and Cognitive Science. Since logic appears to play a fundamental rôle for intelligent behavior, many deductive methods for reasoning about change were developed and thoroughly investigated. It became apparent that a straightforward use of classical logic lacks the essential property that facts describing a world state may change in the course of time. To overcome this problem, the truth value of a particular fact has to be associated with a particular state. This solution brings along the famous technical frame problem which captures the difficulty of expressing that the truth values of facts not affected by some action are not changed by the execution of this action.

Many deductive methods for reasoning about change are based on the ideas underlying the situation calculus. These approaches require one or more axioms accounting for the frame problem, e.g. a set of frame axioms as in [26, 11, 20], successor state axioms as in [27], a nonmonotonic law of inertia as in [25] and [10], or persistence assumptions as in [21]. Recently, three resource-oriented deductive methods were proposed which do not require additional frame axioms, namely the linear connection method [3], the use of a certain fragment of linear logic [24], and an approach based on equational logic programs [15]. The three approaches treat logic formulas as resources which can be produced and consumed through the execution of actions [14]. It has been proved that they are equivalent for conjunctive planning problems, i.e. problems where situations as well as conditions and effects of actions are conjunctions of atomic facts [12, 29].

In spite of the equivalence result for the resource-oriented approaches, the expressiveness of the equational logic approach, say, appears not to be satisfactorily clarified as there is a much deeper rift between this approach and methods based on the situation calculus. Recently, M. Gelfond and V. Lifschitz initiated a comparison of a variety of deductive frameworks for reasoning about change wrt a semantical approach based on the action description language $\mathcal{A}$ [10]. This language overcomes some restrictions of former work in so far as it supports reasoning about the past as well as handling partial information about situations. Furthermore, [10] presents a sound encoding of $\mathcal{A}$ in terms of extended logic programs with two kinds of negation. In [8], a logic program including a single law of inertia is used to encode $\mathcal{A}$. It is shown that, by using a partial completion semantics, the program is sound and complete wrt the semantics of $\mathcal{A}$. Independently, a similar sound and complete abductive logic program is constructed in [7]. [19] showed soundness and completeness as regards $\mathcal{A}$ for, among others, a circumscription based method [2] and R. Reiter's formalism [27].

Recently, the expressiveness of the resource-oriented equational logic approach was substantially enhanced by introducing the concept of specificity which allows to handle several descriptions of one and the same action, depending on the particular situation in which this action is performed [16, 17]. In this paper, we show how this extended approach can be used as a sound and complete method for encoding $\mathcal{A}$. This result bridges the gap between the resource-oriented approaches and all the methods enumerated in the previous paragraph as it rigorously shows the equivalence with regard to the problem class determined by $\mathcal{A}$.

A broad spectrum of characteristic examples for reasoning about change is presented in [28]. Many of them are covered by $\mathcal{A}$. However, some more complicated domains require indeterminism in form of randomized effects of actions. As a second major contribution of this paper, we extend the action description language $\mathcal{A}$ such that this kind of reasoning can be performed. We illustrate how the equational logic approach can be used to encode it as well. The extended action description language $\mathcal{A}_{ND}$ can be considered as a basis for investigating if and how the various methods which were already related to $\mathcal{A}$ can cope with problems of indeterminism and uncertainty.

A recapitulation of the equational logic programming based approach augmented by the notion of specificity is given in the following Section 2. The action description language $\mathcal{A}$ is briefly described in Section 3, and a formalization in terms of equational logic programming is presented in Section 4. The proofs of the various results are omitted due to lack of space. They can be found in a detailed technical report [31]. In Section 5 we extend the action description language to express uncertainty regarding the effects of actions, and in Section 6 we briefly illustrate how this extended version $\mathcal{A}_{ND}$ can be modelled using the particular equational logic program developed in Section 2. Finally, in Section 7 we shall discuss some merits of our approach and outline conceivable future extensions as regards $\mathcal{A}$.

2 The Equational Logic Programming Approach

Throughout this paper we illustrate the various basic notions and results with the help of the Yale Shooting scenario [13] and some of its variants such as the Stanford Murder Mystery [1] or the Russian Turkey domain [28].

The most significant feature of the equational logic based approach is that a complete situation is represented by a single term using a binary function symbol $\circ$ which connects the various atomic facts, called *resources*, which hold in this situation. For example, the term[1]

$$loaded \circ dead. \tag{1}$$

describes a situation where the gun is loaded and the turkey is already shot dead. Intuitively, the order of the various subterms describing a situation should be irrelevant. To this end, the function $\circ$ is required to be associative, i.e. $X \circ (Y \circ Z) = (X \circ Y) \circ Z$, commutative, i.e. $X \circ Y = Y \circ X$, and to have a unit element $\emptyset$ which denotes the situation where nothing is known, i.e. $X \circ \emptyset = X$. These three axioms (AC1) essentially define the data structure multiset, i.e. the so-called *AC1-term* (1) can be adequately interpreted as the multiset $\mathcal{S} = \{\!\{loaded, dead\}\!\}$.[2] Based on this concept, actions are defined by a multiset of conditions along with a multiset of effects. For instance, the *shoot* action can be specified by the triple

$$\langle \{\!\{loaded\}\!\}, shoot, \{\!\{unloaded\}\!\} \rangle \tag{2}$$

where $\{\!\{loaded\}\!\}$ denotes the multiset of conditions, *shoot* is the name of the action, and $\{\!\{unloaded\}\!\}$ denotes the multiset of effects. Such a description $\alpha = \langle \mathcal{C}, a, \mathcal{E} \rangle$ of an action a is applicable in a situation $\mathcal{S}$ iff $\mathcal{C} \dot{\subseteq} \mathcal{S}$. If an action description is applicable then it is executed by removing the conditions from the actual situation and adding the effects afterwards, i.e. applying the action description α to a situation $\mathcal{S}$ yields the new situation $(\mathcal{S} \dot{-} \mathcal{C}) \dot{\cup} \mathcal{E}$.[3] In our example, (2) is applicable in the situation represented by (1) since $\{\!\{loaded\}\!\} \dot{\subseteq} \{\!\{loaded, dead\}\!\}$. The resulting situation is $(\{\!\{loaded, dead\}\!\} \dot{-} \{\!\{loaded\}\!\}) \dot{\cup} \{\!\{unloaded\}\!\} = \{\!\{unloaded, dead\}\!\}$. No additional axioms for solving the technical frame problem are needed since each resource which is not affected by an action — here the resource *dead* — is available after having applied the two multiset operations.

In [16] it is argued that there is often more than simply a single specification such as (2) of one action because the effects of a particular action may vary from situation to situation. For example, (2) is formally applicable also in case of $\{\!\{loaded, alive\}\!\}$. Its application yields $\{\!\{unloaded, alive\}\!\}$ which is undesired since shooting with a previously loaded gun should cause *alive* to be replaced by *dead* . (It possibly could be that turkeys do not fully agree with this view.) The notion of *specificity* accounts for this problem. First, another action description for *shoot* is introduced, viz.

$$\langle \ \{\!\!|\ loaded, alive\ |\!\!\} \ , \ shoot \ , \ \{\!\!|\ unloaded, dead\ |\!\!\} \ \rangle . \qquad (3)$$

Now, (3) is applicable whenever the original action description (2) is applicable but not vice versa. Hence, (3) is said to contain a *more specific* information and, thus, should be preferred whenever it can be used in a particular situation. To this end, we formally define a partial ordering on a set of action descriptions with regard to specificity as follows. An action description $\alpha_1 = \langle C_1, a_1, \mathcal{E}_1 \rangle$ is said to be *more specific* than an action description $\alpha_2 = \langle C_2, a_2, \mathcal{E}_2 \rangle$ iff $a_1 = a_2$ and $C_1 \supset C_2$. Taking into consideration this definition, an action description should be applied only if there is no more specific description which is also applicable. If an action description can be applied to a situation S on this condition then we say that it is *most specific wrt* S. Note that this requirement does not rule out the existence of more than one most specific action description. In Section 6 we illustrate how multiple most specific descriptions capture the problem of indeterminism.

A second useful application of specificity is to avoid inconsistencies via the so-called *completion* mechanism. For instance, one of the action descriptions of *load* should be

$$\langle \ \{\!\!|\ |\!\!\} \ , \ load \ , \ \{\!\!|\ loaded\ |\!\!\} \ \rangle . \qquad (4)$$

This works fine in situations like $\{\!\!|\ alive\ |\!\!\}$ or $\{\!\!|\ dead\ |\!\!\}$, i.e. if nothing is known about the state of the gun. However, the application of (4) to $\{\!\!|\ unloaded\ |\!\!\}$, say, yields the unintended situation $\{\!\!|\ unloaded, loaded\ |\!\!\}$. This can be avoided by *completing* (4) to obtain the additional action description $\langle \{\!\!|\ unloaded\ |\!\!\}, load, \{\!\!|\ loaded\ |\!\!\} \rangle$ which is more specific than (4). The Yale Shooting scenario is discussed more thoroughly in Section 4.

The reasoning process described so far can be encoded using the equational logic program depicted in Figure 1 (see [16, 17]): The various action descriptions of a domain are encoded using a ternary predicate *action* . The ternary predicate $causes(i, [a_1, \ldots, a_n], g)$ expresses the fact that the application of the sequence $[a_1, \ldots, a_n]$ of actions to the initial situation i yields the goal situation g. If $n \geq 1$ then an action description α of a_1 with conditions c is selected such that c is contained in i — i.e. $\exists V. c \circ V =_{\mathrm{AC1}} i$ —, α is most specific wrt i, and the recursive call uses the resulting situation after applying α to i, along with the sequence $p = [a_2, \ldots, a_n]$. Finally, the notion of specificity is encoded using the predicate $non\_specific(a, c, i)$ which expresses the fact that there is a description of action a which is more specific wrt the situation i than the particular description with conditions c. Following the definition of specificity, such a more specific action description must have conditions c' such that c' is applicable in i and the multiset corresponding to c' is a strict superset of the multiset corresponding to c. In terms of AC1-representation this is true iff $\exists V. c' \circ V =_{\mathrm{AC1}} i$ and $\exists W \neq_{\mathrm{AC1}} \emptyset. c \circ W =_{\mathrm{AC1}} c'$ hold.

$action(c_1, a_1, e_1).$

$\qquad \vdots$

$action(c_m, a_m, e_m).$

$causes(I, [\,], I).$

$causes(I, [A|P], G) \leftarrow action(C, A, E), \quad C \circ V =_{\text{AC1}} I,$
$\qquad\qquad\qquad\qquad\qquad \neg non\_specific(A, C, I), \quad causes(V \circ E, P, G).$

$non\_specific(A, C, I) \leftarrow action(C', A, E'), \quad C' \circ V =_{\text{AC1}} I,$
$\qquad\qquad\qquad\qquad\qquad C \circ W =_{\text{AC1}} C', \quad W \neq_{\text{AC1}} \emptyset.$

Figure 1: The equational logic program P_A used to reason about change, where $A = \{\langle C_i, a_i, \mathcal{E}_i \rangle \mid 1 \leq i \leq m\}$ is a finite set of action descriptions and c_i (resp. e_i) are AC1-terms representing C_i (resp. $\mathcal{E}_i$). The binary predicate $=_{\text{AC1}}$ denotes equality modulo our equational theory (AC1).

Our equational program includes negative literals. Therefore, the adequate computation mechanism is *SLDENF-resolution*, i.e. SLD-resolution augmented by negation-as-failure along with an extended unification procedure which unifies wrt a concrete equational theory [30, 17, 32]. Moreover, we sometimes employ *constructive negation* [5] to avoid the problem of floundering. Semantics is defined by K. Clark's *completion* [6] along with a so-called *unification complete* theory AC1* which allows to derive inequality of two terms whenever they are not unifiable [18, 30, 17]. Let $(P_A^*, \text{AC1}^*)$ denote the completion of our program depicted in Figure 1.

In [17] it is argued that we can restrict ourselves to models of $(P_A^*, \text{AC1}^*)$ where terms which are built up from the AC1-function $\circ$ are interpreted as multisets. Let $\mathcal{I}$ denote such an interpretation. In [17] it is shown that $(P_A^*, \text{AC1}^*)$ models actions, change, and specificity as intended:

Theorem 2.1 *Let A be a finite set of action descriptions and P_A be as in Figure 1. Then, $(P_A^*, \text{AC1}^*) \models causes(i, [a_1, \ldots, a_n], g)$ iff there are multisets $S_0, \ldots, S_n$ such that $S_0 \doteq i^{\mathcal{I}}$, $S_n \doteq g^{\mathcal{I}}$, and $S_j \doteq (S_{j-1} \dot{-} C_j) \dot{\cup} \mathcal{E}_j$, where $\langle C_j, a_j, \mathcal{E}_j \rangle \in A$ is most specific wrt S_{j-1} ($1 \leq j \leq n$).*

3 The Action Description Language $\mathcal{A}$

In this section we give a brief introduction to the ideas underlying the semantical approach described in [10] which is based on an action description language called $\mathcal{A}$. We use the Stanford Murder Mystery domain [1] to illustrate the expressiveness of $\mathcal{A}$ regarding reasoning about the past and handling incomplete information about the initial situation. This example describes the reasoning process which has to be performed to conclude that the gun must have been loaded if the turkey was alive at the beginning and is observed to be dead after shooting and waiting.

The basic elements of $\mathcal{A}$ are action names, e.g. *load*, *wait*, and *shoot*, and fluent names, e.g. *loaded* and *alive*, along with expressions like

$$
\begin{array}{llll}
load & \textbf{causes} & loaded & \\
shoot & \textbf{causes} & \neg alive & \textbf{if} \quad loaded \\
shoot & \textbf{causes} & \neg loaded &
\end{array}
\tag{5}
$$

These expressions describe the effect of a particular action, e.g. *shoot*, on a single fluent, e.g. *alive*, provided a number of conditions, e.g. *loaded*, hold. In general, these so-called *e-propositions* (i.e. *effect* propositions) are of the form a **causes** e **if** $c_1, \ldots, c_n$, where a is an action name, e is a fluent name occurring either affirmatively or negatively, and $c_1, \ldots, c_n$ are affirmative or negated fluent names ($n \geq 0$). The set of e-propositions describing a domain is used to define a *transition function* which maps states into states given a particular action name. A *state* σ is a set of fluent names, and a positive fluent f (resp. a negative fluent $\neg f$) is said to *hold* in σ iff $f \in \sigma$ (resp. $f \notin \sigma$). For instance, $\{alive\}$ describes the state where *alive* and $\neg loaded$ hold, and the transition function Φ determined by (5) is

$$
\begin{array}{lll}
\Phi(load, \sigma) & = & \sigma \cup \{loaded\} \\
\Phi(shoot, \sigma) & = & \begin{cases} \sigma - \{loaded, alive\}, & \text{if } loaded \in \sigma \\ \sigma, & \text{otherwise.} \end{cases} \\
\Phi(wait, \sigma) & = & \sigma
\end{array}
\tag{6}
$$

In general, Φ is designed such that (a) if there is an e-proposition describing the effects of a on a positive fluent f (resp. a negative fluent $\neg f$) whose conditions hold in σ then $f \in \Phi(a, \sigma)$ (resp. $f \notin \Phi(a, \sigma)$) and (b) if there is no such e-proposition then $f \in \Phi(a, \sigma)$ iff $f \in \sigma$. It is noteworthy that given a set of e-propositions either the corresponding transition function is definitely determined or there is no transition function satisfying (a) and (b). The reader is invited to verify that the transition function (6) satisfies these conditions as regards the e-propositions (5).

Apart from defining the effects of actions there is a possibility to describe the value of a single fluent in a particular state using so-called *v-propositions* (i.e. *value* propositions). For example,

$$
\begin{array}{l}
\textbf{initially} \ alive \\
\neg alive \ \textbf{after} \ [shoot, wait]
\end{array}
\tag{7}
$$

describe the facts that the turkey is alive in the initial state and is dead after executing the sequence of actions $[shoot, wait]$, respectively, which precisely corresponds to the Stanford Murder Mystery scenario. In general, a v-proposition is of the form f **after** $[a_1, \ldots, a_n]$ where $a_1, \ldots, a_n$ are action names, and if $n = 0$ then the expression **initially** f is used instead.

A set of e-propositions and v-propositions is called a *domain*. A *structure* consists of an *initial* state σ_0 and a transition function Φ. A structure

(σ_0, Φ) is a *model* of a domain $\mathcal{D}$ iff Φ is determined by the e-propositions in $\mathcal{D}$, and Φ together with σ_0 satisfy the v-propositions occurring in $\mathcal{D}$: A v-proposition **initially** f is satisfied in (σ_0, Φ) iff f holds in σ_0, and a v-proposition f **after** $[a_1, \ldots, a_n]$ is satisfied iff f holds in $\Phi([a_1, \ldots, a_n], \sigma_0)$, which abbreviates $\Phi(a_n, \Phi(a_{n-1}, \ldots, \Phi(a_1, \sigma_0) \ldots))$. A domain is called *consistent* if it admits at least one model.

In our example, Φ is defined as in (6) and — due to (7) — (σ_0, Φ) is a model of the Stanford Murder Mystery iff *alive* $\in \sigma_0$ and *alive* $\notin$ $\Phi([shoot, wait], \sigma_0)$. It is easy to verify that *loaded* $\in \sigma_0$ holds in each such model due to (6), i.e. we are allowed to conclude that the gun was necessarily loaded in the initial state. In other words, the v-proposition **initially** *loaded* is said to be *entailed* by the domain description $\mathcal{D}$ given by (5) and (7); this is written $\mathcal{D} \models$ **initially** *loaded*.

4 Encoding $\mathcal{A}$

The first step towards the formalization of a particular domain via the equational logic approach consists in the definition of an underlying set of resources. As the equational logic approach does not support explicit negation, we need two different resources for each fluent name of a domain description in $\mathcal{A}$. Thus, in case of the Yale Shooting scenario we deal with the set $\{loaded, \overline{loaded}, alive, \overline{alive}\}$, where the independent resource $\overline{f}$ should be interpreted as the negation of resource f, i.e. $\overline{loaded}$ and $\overline{alive}$ take the rôle of *unloaded* and *dead*, respectively, used in Section 2. A situation S built up from these resources is said to *correspond* to a state σ (and vice versa) iff for each fluent name f we find that if $f \in \sigma$ then $f \in S$ and if $f \notin \sigma$ then $\overline{f} \in S$. For instance, $\{\!|alive, \overline{loaded}|\!\}$ corresponds to $\{alive\}$.

The second step in formalizing a domain consists in fixing consistency criteria. In view of the fact that states in $\mathcal{A}$ are sets, no resource should occur more than once in a situation. Moreover, no resource together with its negation may occur, and each fluent name occurs either affirmatively or negatively in a situation. [4] This is formalized by the clauses depicted in Figure 2.

The third and final step consists in creating a set of action descriptions. Given a set of action names along with a set of e-propositions the following Algorithm 1 automatically generates such a set. For notational simplicity, it is assumed that the e-propositions are given in terms of our method, i.e. whenever a negated fluent name $\neg f$ occurs then it is replaced by the term $\overline{f}$.

Algorithm 1 For each action name a let

$$\left\{ \begin{array}{llll} a & \textbf{causes} & e_1 & \textbf{if} \quad F_1 \\ & & \vdots & \\ a & \textbf{causes} & e_m & \textbf{if} \quad F_m \end{array} \right\}$$

be the set of all e-propositions wrt action name a, where each F_i is a sequence of resources $f_{i1}, \ldots, f_{in_i}$ ($1 \leq i \leq m$). Note that this set may be

$inconsistent(f_i \circ f_i \circ V)$.

$inconsistent(\overline{f_i} \circ \overline{f_i} \circ V)$.

$inconsistent(f_i \circ \overline{f_i} \circ V)$.

$inconsistent(S) \leftarrow \neg holds(f_i, S), \neg holds(\overline{f_i}, S)$.

$holds(F, F \circ V)$.

Figure 2: The clauses defining inconsistency, where $F = \{f_i \mid 1 \le i \le m\}$ is a finite set of fluent names and the first four clauses are generated separately for each member of F.

empty, e.g. in case of a being *wait*. In what follows, a multiset is called consistent iff it contains no multiple occurrences of an element and no f along with its negation $\overline{f}$.

1. For all (possibly empty) consistent combinations

$$\mathcal{C} := F_i \cup \ldots \cup F_j \tag{8}$$

where $\{i, \ldots, j\}$ is a subset of $\{1, \ldots, m\}$, let $\mathcal{E}$ contain the effects determined by the conditions $\mathcal{C}$, along with those conditions which are not affected by the action, i.e. [5]

$$\mathcal{E} := \{\!| e_k \mid F_k \subseteq \mathcal{C} |\!\} \cup \{\!| f \in \mathcal{C} \mid \overline{f} \notin \{\!| e_k \mid F_k \subseteq \mathcal{C} |\!\} |\!\}$$

where $\overline{\overline{f}}$ should be interpreted as f. Then, create the action description $\langle \mathcal{C}, a, \mathcal{E} \rangle$. All action descriptions generated in this step are called *pure*.

For instance, as regards the *shoot* action there are two possible combinations of conditions, viz. $\mathcal{C}_1 = \{\!| |\!\}$ and $\mathcal{C}_2 = \{\!| loaded |\!\}$ determining the effects $\mathcal{E}_1 = \{\!| \overline{loaded} |\!\}$ and $\mathcal{E}_2 = \{\!| \overline{alive}, \overline{loaded} |\!\}$, respectively (c.f. (5)).

2. Apply the following completion procedure (c.f. the paragraph below equation (4) in Section 2) to each pure action description $\alpha = \langle \mathcal{C}, a, \mathcal{E} \rangle$ of a: Let $\mathcal{F}$ be the set of "free" effects, i.e. those elements of $\mathcal{E}$ which neither occur affirmatively nor negatively in $\mathcal{C}$, along with their negations, i.e.

$$\mathcal{F} := \{\!| e \mid e \in \mathcal{E} \wedge e \notin \mathcal{C} \wedge \overline{e} \notin \mathcal{C} |\!\} \cup \{\!| \overline{e} \mid e \in \mathcal{E} \wedge e \notin \mathcal{C} \wedge \overline{e} \notin \mathcal{C} |\!\}$$

Then, for each consistent non-empty subset $F \subseteq \mathcal{F}$ create the *completion* $\langle \mathcal{C} \cup F, a, \mathcal{E} \rangle$ of $\alpha = \langle \mathcal{C}, a, \mathcal{E} \rangle$ — provided there is no pure action description generated in Step 1 of the same action and with conditions $\tilde{\mathcal{C}}$ such that $\mathcal{C} \cup F \supseteq \tilde{\mathcal{C}} \supset \mathcal{C}$ (this will be clarified below).

For example, for the pure description $\langle \{\!| loaded |\!\}, shoot, \{\!| \overline{alive}, \overline{loaded} |\!\} \rangle$ we have $\mathcal{F} = \{\!| \overline{alive}, alive |\!\}$ which has two consistent non-empty subsets. Hence, we obtain the completions $\langle \{\!| loaded, \overline{alive} |\!\}, shoot, \{\!| \overline{alive}, \overline{loaded} |\!\} \rangle$ and $\langle \{\!| loaded, alive |\!\}, shoot, \{\!| \overline{alive}, \overline{loaded} |\!\} \rangle$, respectively. ∎

Given a domain description $\mathcal{D}$ we refer to the set of action descriptions generated via Algorithm 1 by $A_{\mathcal{D}}$. For instance, applying this algorithm to the Yale Shooting domain which consists of the action names *load*, *shoot*, and *wait* along with the e-propositions (5) yields four pure action descriptions, viz.

$$\langle \{\!\!\{\,\}\!\!\}, wait, \{\!\!\{\,\}\!\!\} \rangle \qquad\qquad \langle \{\!\!\{\,\}\!\!\}, shoot, \{\!\!\{\overline{loaded}\}\!\!\} \rangle$$
$$\langle \{\!\!\{\,\}\!\!\}, load, \{\!\!\{loaded\}\!\!\} \rangle \qquad \langle \{\!\!\{loaded\}\!\!\}, shoot, \{\!\!\{\overline{alive}, \overline{loaded}\}\!\!\} \rangle \tag{9}$$

Step 2 then yields the following completions:

$$\langle \{\!\!\{loaded\}\!\!\}, load, \{\!\!\{loaded\}\!\!\} \rangle \qquad \langle \{\!\!\{\overline{loaded}\}\!\!\}, shoot, \{\!\!\{\overline{loaded}\}\!\!\} \rangle$$
$$\langle \{\!\!\{\overline{loaded}\}\!\!\}, load, \{\!\!\{loaded\}\!\!\} \rangle \quad \langle \{\!\!\{loaded, \overline{alive}\}\!\!\}, shoot, \{\!\!\{\overline{alive}, \overline{loaded}\}\!\!\} \rangle \tag{10}$$
$$\langle \{\!\!\{loaded, alive\}\!\!\}, shoot, \{\!\!\{\overline{alive}, \overline{loaded}\}\!\!\} \rangle$$

The restriction at the end of Step 2 prevents us from using the pure action description $\langle \{\!\!\{\,\}\!\!\}, shoot, \{\!\!\{\overline{loaded}\}\!\!\} \rangle$ to create $\langle \{\!\!\{loaded\}\!\!\}, shoot, \{\!\!\{\overline{loaded}\}\!\!\} \rangle$ because a pure description of *shoot* with conditions $\tilde{C} = \{\!\!\{loaded\}\!\!\}$ is already included in (9). This is in fact desired since after shooting we definitely know that the turkey is dead whenever the gun was loaded before.

Some observations concerning the output of Algorithm 1 are necessary to obtain our first main result: The set $A_{\mathcal{D}}$ does not contain two action descriptions for one and the same action with the same multiset of conditions and different effects. The most important consequence of this observation is that given a situation and an action name there is always a single most specific description of this action wrt this particular situation. (Note that there is always at least one applicable action description since C in (8) can be empty.) Furthermore, the application of this most specific action description to a consistent situation again yields a consistent situation with regard to the consistency criterion defined in Figure 2, provided the original domain $\mathcal{D}$ is not inconsistent itself. Now, the following equivalence result for the transition function of a domain description and our approach can be proved. For a more thorough discussion we must refer the reader to [31].

Proposition 4.1 *Let $\mathcal{D}$ be a consistent domain description with transition function Φ, σ be a state, a an action name, and S_σ the situation corresponding to σ. Then, $(S_\sigma \doteq C) \dot{\cup} \mathcal{E}$ corresponds to $\Phi(a, \sigma)$, where $\alpha = \langle C, a, \mathcal{E} \rangle \in A_{\mathcal{D}}$ is the most specific action description of a wrt S_σ.*

Beside translating the e-propositions into a set of action descriptions we have to consider the v-propositions which describe a particular scenario. To this end, we use a unary predicate *observations* with the intended meaning that *observations*(i) is true if i represents a consistent situation such that each v-proposition is satisfied wrt i. Furthermore, the binary predicate *satisfiable*$(f, [a_1, \ldots, a_n])$ is used to express the fact that the additional v-proposition f `after` $[a_1, \ldots, a_n]$ holds in some model of the domain. The clauses defining these two predicates are depicted in Figure 3.

$$observations(I) \leftarrow \neg inconsistent(I),$$
$$causes(I, [a_{11}, \ldots, a_{1n_1}], f_1 \circ V_1),$$
$$\vdots$$
$$causes(I, [a_{m1}, \ldots, a_{mn_m}], f_m \circ V_m).$$

$$satisfiable(F, P) \leftarrow observations(I),$$
$$causes(I, P, F \circ V).$$

Figure 3: The given v-propositions $\{f_i \text{ after } a_{i1}, \ldots, a_{in_i} \mid 1 \leq i \leq m\}$ are collected in a single clause defining the unary predicate *observations* which is used in the definition of the predicate *satisfiable*.

For example, the two value propositions (7) are encoded via

$$observations(I) \leftarrow \neg inconsistent(I), \ causes(I, [\,], alive \circ V_1),$$
$$causes(I, [shoot, wait], \overline{alive} \circ V_2).$$

If $\mathcal{D}$ is a domain description then let $P_{\mathcal{D}}$ consist of the clauses depicted in Figure 1, Figure 2, and Figure 3. Then, $(P_{\mathcal{D}}, AC1)$ can be shown to form a sound and complete encoding of $\mathcal{A}$ wrt the completion semantics:

Theorem 4.2 (Soundness & Completeness) *If $\mathcal{D}$ is a consistent domain description then $\mathcal{D} \models f \text{ after } [a_1, \ldots, a_n]$ iff*

$$(P_{\mathcal{D}}^*, AC1^*) \models \neg \, satisfiable(\overline{f}, [a_1, \ldots, a_n]) \,. \tag{11}$$

Proof (sketch): Let Φ be the transition function determined by $\mathcal{D}$. If i is a term representing a situation $\mathcal{I}$ then, according to Theorem 2.1, Proposition 4.1, and Figure 3, $(P_{\mathcal{D}}^*, AC1^*) \models observations(i)$ if and only if there is a state σ_0 corresponding to $\mathcal{I}$ such that (σ_0, Φ) is a model of $\mathcal{D}$. Hence, (11) is true iff there is no model of $\mathcal{D}$ such that $\overline{f}$ holds in $\Phi([a_1, \ldots, a_n], \sigma_0)$, i.e. iff $\mathcal{D} \models f \text{ after } [a_1, \ldots, a_n]$. ∎

For the complete proof the reader is referred to [31].

The part of the consistency criterion in Figure 2 where a situation is required to be complete in the sense that it must contain either the positive or the negative version of each fluent seems not particularly satisfactory. Fortunately, this condition can be omitted in many applications, e.g. in all of the various examples in [10]. However, the requirement is necessary to obtain completeness in examples like

$$
\begin{array}{llll@{\qquad}llll}
a & \text{causes} & f_1 & \text{if } h & b & \text{causes} & g & \text{if } f_1 \\
a & \text{causes} & f_2 & \text{if } \neg h & b & \text{causes} & g & \text{if } f_2
\end{array}
$$

These e-propositions entail $g \text{ after } [a, b]$ which cannot be obtained in our approach until each initial situation is forced to either contain h or $\overline{h}$.

It is noteworthy that when using schema (11) to decide the entailment of a v-proposition, this proposition is encoded within the query. Thus, one might object that v-propositions have to be guessed before proving their entailment. However, this is not necessary in general since the various answers to the query $\exists I.\ observations(I)$ provide the set of possible initial situations.

5 $\mathcal{A}$ + Non-Determinism = $\mathcal{A}_{ND}$

A basic assumption underlying $\mathcal{A}$ is that the effects of an action are always completely known and deterministic. Surely, one cannot adhere to this idealistic view of the real world in general since it is impractical, and even impossible due to a theoretical result of physics, to refine descriptions of the world until the effects of an arbitrary action can always be explicitly computed. The ability of humans to handle uncertainty, indeterminism, surprising effects etc. very flexibly contrasts sharply with the necessity of completely determining the effects of actions.

In this section we extend the action description language $\mathcal{A}$ such that effect propositions can express indeterminism. This approach is, of course, again idealistic as it is assumed that all possible alternatives are known and can be enumerated, and that stating priorities in form of, say, probabilistic values for the individual alternatives is not supported. Rather the extended action description language $\mathcal{A}_{ND}$ should be regarded as a first step in the large and open area of uncertainty, indeterminism, and disjunctive planning.

As the running example of this section we use the Russian Turkey scenario as formalized in [28]. The set of actions is augmented by the action *spin* with the intended meaning that spinning causes the gun to become randomly loaded or unloaded regardless of its state before. This action can be formalized in $\mathcal{A}_{ND}$ using the two expressions

$$
\begin{aligned}
&spin \;\; \textbf{alternatively causes} \;\; loaded \\
&spin \;\; \textbf{alternatively causes} \;\; \neg loaded
\end{aligned}
\tag{12}
$$

In general, a **alternatively causes** $e_1, \ldots, e_m$ **if** $c_1, \ldots, c_n$ is called an *extended* effect proposition in $\mathcal{A}_{ND}$. The intended meaning is as follows: Let

$$
\left\{
\begin{array}{l}
a \;\; \textbf{alternatively causes} \;\; E_1 \;\; \textbf{if} \;\; C_1 \\
\qquad\qquad\qquad\vdots \\
a \;\; \textbf{alternatively causes} \;\; E_k \;\; \textbf{if} \;\; C_k
\end{array}
\right\}
\tag{13}
$$

be the set of all extended e-propositions such that $C_1, \ldots, C_k$ simultaneously hold in a particular state σ. If a is executed in σ then exactly one of the various sets of effects $E_1, \ldots, E_k$ will become true in the resulting state.

Recall that a set of e-propositions in the language $\mathcal{A}$ determines a transition function Φ. Now, the possibility of alternative effects forces a redefinition of the notion of transition. At first glance one might suggest for allowing the existence of several different transition functions, each of them modelling one of the various alternative effects of an action. Consider the e-propositions (5) of Section 3 and (12) for the Russian Turkey scenario. Φ

could be designed as in (6) augmented by either $\Phi(spin, \sigma) = \sigma \cup \{loaded\}$ or $\Phi(spin, \sigma) = \sigma - \{loaded\}$ for each σ separately. However, this idea does not correctly capture the intuition: If Φ is such a transition function in a particular model then the result of spinning the gun, say, will be fixed forever regarding a particular state, e.g. it would be impossible to find a model where **initially** $\neg loaded$, $\neg loaded$ **after** $[spin]$, and $loaded$ **after** $[spin, spin]$ are simultaneously true. This is of course unintended.

For this reason, we propose to drop the idea of Φ being a function and use the notion of Φ as a *relation* between a pair of states and an action name instead, such that two states σ, σ' and action name a are related whenever the application of a to σ might yield σ'. For instance, for the Russian Turkey scenario we obtain the following transition relation Φ:

$$(\sigma, spin, \sigma') \in \Phi \quad \text{iff} \quad \sigma' = \sigma \cup \{loaded\} \quad \text{or} \quad \sigma' = \sigma - \{loaded\}$$

$$(\sigma, load, \sigma') \in \Phi \quad \text{iff} \quad \sigma' = \sigma \cup \{loaded\}$$

$$(\sigma, shoot, \sigma') \in \Phi \quad \text{iff} \quad \sigma' = \begin{cases} \sigma - \{loaded, alive\}, & \text{if } loaded \in \sigma \quad (14) \\ \sigma, & \text{otherwise.} \end{cases}$$

$$(\sigma, wait, \sigma') \in \Phi \quad \text{iff} \quad \sigma' = \sigma$$

In general, Φ is designed such that a triple (σ, a, σ') is element of Φ if and only if the following conditions are satisfied:

(a) If a **causes** f **if** $c_1, \ldots, c_n$ (resp. a **causes** $\neg f$ **if** $c_1, \ldots, c_n$) is an effect proposition such that $c_1, \ldots, c_n$ hold in σ then f (resp. $\neg f$) holds in σ'.

(b) Let (13) be the set of all extended e-propositions such that each element occurring in $C_1, \ldots, C_k$ holds in σ. If $k > 0$ then it is possible to select a $\lambda \in \{1, \ldots, k\}$ such that the members of E_λ hold in σ.

(c) Let f be a fluent name such that neither f nor $\neg f$ is forced to hold in σ' by (a) or (b) then $f \in \sigma'$ iff $f \in \sigma$.

The reader is invited to verify that the transition relation (14) satisfies these conditions wrt the e-propositions (5) and (12).

Having defined the notion of transition, we now concentrate on defining models in $\mathcal{A}_{ND}$. The issue of models is, in general, to provide a view of the real world. Usually, there exist several models which all satisfy some fundamental properties, observations, and maybe subjective impressions, but which differ in unknown or uninteresting things. All these models describe possible worlds although reality is captured by only one of them. In $\mathcal{A}$, where no indeterministic and randomized effects are allowed, the only task left to nature is to design the initial state. Now, however, the rôle of nature is much more appreciable because it has to decide which effects occur whenever alternatives are allowed. To this end, we employ an additional component for each model, namely a function φ which states the behavior of nature in this model in case of alternative effects. For instance, if the initial state is

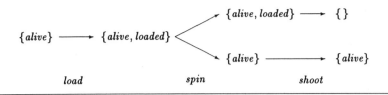

Figure 4: The possible developments in the Russian Turkey scenario.

known to be $\{alive\}$ and we are interested in the consequences of executing the sequence of actions $[load, spin, shoot]$ then the set of models of this domain can be divided into two classes: either the gun remains loaded after spinning, or it becomes unloaded. Hence, if we additionally observe that the turkey is as lively as before after loading, spinning, and shooting then no model of the former class can explain this. Thus it is reasonable to conclude that the gun was necessarily unloaded after $[load, spin]$. This is illustrated in Figure 4.

In the sequel we extend the formal definitions concerning $\mathcal{A}$ to $\mathcal{A}_{ND}$. A *structure* is a triple $(\sigma_0, \Phi, \varphi)$ where σ_0 denotes the initial state as before, Φ is a transition relation, and φ is a mapping from pairs consisting of a finite sequence of actions and a state into the set of states. A structure $(\sigma_0, \Phi, \varphi)$ is a *model* of a domain $\mathcal{D}_{ND}$ iff Φ is determined by the e-propositions in $\mathcal{D}_{ND}$, φ satisfies the two conditions

1. $\varphi([\,], \sigma_0) = \sigma_0$ and
2. $(\varphi([a_1, \ldots, a_{n-1}], \sigma_0), a_n, \varphi([a_1, \ldots, a_n], \sigma_0)) \in \Phi$,

and φ together with σ_0 satisfy the v-propositions of $\mathcal{D}_{ND}$: A v-proposition **initially** f is satisfied in $(\sigma_0, \Phi, \varphi)$ iff f holds in σ_0, and a v-proposition f **after** $[a_1, \ldots, a_n]$ is satisfied iff f holds in $\varphi([a_1, \ldots, a_n], \sigma_0)$. A domain description in $\mathcal{A}_{ND}$ is *consistent* if it admits at least one model $(\sigma_0, \varphi, \Phi)$ such that for any σ and any a there is at least one σ' such that $(\sigma, a, \sigma') \in \Phi$. For instance, a structure $(\sigma_0, \Phi, \varphi)$ is a model of (5) and (12) along with the two v-propositions

$$\begin{aligned}&\textbf{initially } alive\\&alive \textbf{ after } [load, spin, shoot]\end{aligned} \qquad (15)$$

iff Φ is as in (14), φ is appropriately defined, and $alive \in \sigma_0$ as well as $alive \in \varphi([load, spin, shoot], \sigma_0)$. Obviously, $\neg loaded \in \varphi([load, spin], \sigma_0)$ holds in each such model, i.e. $\mathcal{D}_{ND} \models \neg loaded$ **after** $[load, spin]$ (see again Figure 4).

At the very end of [7], the authors suggest a similar way of handling indeterminism using propositions of the form a **possibly causes** f **if** $c_1, \ldots, c_n$ but without giving a formal description of transition and entailment. A detailed examination and a comparison to our approach remains to be done.

6 Encoding $\mathcal{A}_{ND}$

In this section, we briefly illustrate how the equational logic program described in Section 2 can just as well be used to encode domain descriptions in the extended language $\mathcal{A}_{ND}$. Recall that the set of action descriptions generated by Algorithm 1 is designed such that for each action and each situation there is exactly one most specific description. Now, the existence of several most specific action descriptions addresses the existence of alternatives. In our example, we generate the pure descriptions

$$\langle\ \{\!|\ |\!\},\ spin\,,\ \{\!|loaded|\!\}\ \rangle \quad \text{and} \quad \langle\ \{\!|\ |\!\},\ spin\,,\ \{\!|\overline{loaded}|\!\}\ \rangle \tag{16}$$

according to (12). In general, Algorithm 1 can be straightforwardly modified such that each possible alternative for a fixed set of conditions determines a unique pure action description. The completion step simply remains as it stands.

Nonetheless, the kind of reasoning illustrated with the Russian Turkey domain cannot be modelled yet. If the query $\neg satisfiable(loaded, [load, spin])$ is used to prove entailment of $\neg loaded$ **after** $[load, spin]$ in the spirit of Theorem 4.2 then a negative answer is obtained. The reason for this undesired result is that we are free to choose the effect of spinning independently such that both $alive$ **after** $[load, spin, shoot]$ as well as $loaded$ **after** $[load, spin]$ can be satisfied by applying different most specific action description of $spin$.

The crucial point is that we have to take into account the reaction of nature, which is implicitly determined by the observations (15). Our solution to this problem is as follows: Instead of using simply the action name such as $spin$, we add an argument to denote a particular effect of this action such as in $spin(1)$. The additional argument is intended to take the rôle of the index λ used in the definition of transition in $\mathcal{A}_{ND}$ (see the paragraph below equation (14)). All actions are extended in this way.

In our running example, the following list includes all such action descriptions of $spin$, i.e. the two descriptions (16) — augmented by the additional argument — along with their completions:

$$
\begin{array}{ll}
\langle\{\!|\ |\!\},\ spin(1)\,,\{\!|loaded|\!\}\ \rangle & \langle\{\!|\ |\!\},\ spin(2)\,,\{\!|\overline{loaded}|\!\}\rangle \\[4pt]
\langle\{\!|loaded|\!\},\ spin(1)\,,\{\!|loaded|\!\}\rangle & \langle\{\!|loaded|\!\},\ spin(2)\,,\{\!|\overline{loaded}|\!\}\rangle \\[4pt]
\langle\{\!|\overline{loaded}|\!\},\ spin(1)\,,\{\!|loaded|\!\}\rangle & \langle\{\!|\overline{loaded}|\!\},\ spin(2)\,,\{\!|\overline{loaded}|\!\}\rangle
\end{array} \tag{17}
$$

The other action descriptions (9) and (10) are extended in a similar way.

The two predicates $observations$ and $satisfiable$ make use of these additional arguments. In our example (15) they are defined as follows:

$$
\begin{aligned}
observations(I, X_1, X_2, X_3) \leftarrow\ & \neg inconsistent(I),\ causes(I, [\,], alive \circ V_1), \\
& causes(I, [load(X_1), spin(X_2), shoot(X_3)], alive \circ V_2).
\end{aligned}
$$

$$
\begin{aligned}
satisfiable(F, P, X_1, X_2, X_3) \leftarrow\ & observations(I, X_1, X_2, X_3), \\
& causes(I, P, F \circ V).
\end{aligned}
$$

Now, let $P_{\mathcal{D}_{ND}}$ consist of the clauses depicted in Figure 1 — where the set of action descriptions is given as described above — and Figure 2 along with the clauses above. Then it is easy to prove that

$$\neg \exists X_1, X_2, X_3.\ satisfiable(loaded, [load(X_1), spin(X_2)], X_1, X_2, X_3)$$

is a logical consequence of $(P^*_{\mathcal{D}_{ND}}, \text{AC1}^*)$. A more detailed analysis and a formal proof of a result similar to Theorem 4.2 can be found in [31].

7   Discussion

The soundness and completeness of the equational logic approach with respect to the action description language developed by M. Gelfond and V. Lifschitz constitutes the main result of this paper. This achievement illustrates that our approach is not only suitable for temporal projection but can also be used to reason about former situations, to find explanations for observations, and to deal with incomplete knowledge about situations. In particular the way incompletely specified situations are modelled appears to be very elegant: We merely have to add a variable to an AC1-term describing a situation. Nonetheless, an important aspect of incomplete information has not been discussed yet. Suppose nothing is known about the state of the gun then our program answers **no** when asked whether the v-proposition $\neg alive$ **after** $[shoot]$ is entailed. This appears to be too optimistic but can be easily improved. Recall that our program entails a v-proposition only if the contrary cannot be consistently assumed. Instead of answering **no** if this is not the case the answer could be **maybe** whenever both the v-proposition itself and the contrary are satisfiable wrt the domain description.

Probably the most important application of approaches to reasoning about actions is the field of planning. Our equational logic program can be directly used to search for plans: One simply employs an appropriate instance of the predicate *causes* with the middle argument left uninstantiated, i.e. an answer to the query $\exists P.\ causes(i, P, g)$ provides a plan whose application to i yields g (see [15]). In addition, as our approach can handle partial information about the initial situation, say, it is able to deal with questions such as *what do I need to achieve a certain goal?* Furthermore, values can be assigned to the various available resources so that the system is required to find an initial situation which is as cheap as possible (wrt the cost of the chosen resources). All these features are available in a quite compact logic program where no additional frame axioms increase the search space or make derivations more difficult in general.

The way planning is performed in our approach suggests an extension of $\mathcal{A}$ which provides a new kind of reasoning about the past. Hitherto, $\mathcal{A}$ supports reasoning about facts in former situations. But suppose we observe a lively turkey which suddenly drops dead, then it seems to be reasonable to conclude, from all of our knowledge, that a *shoot* action must have been performed. This can be easily obtained by using the query

$\exists A, I, V. (\neg inconsistent(I \circ alive) \land causes(I \circ alive, [A], \overline{alive} \circ V))$ yielding a single solution, namely $\{A \mapsto shoot, I \mapsto loaded, V \mapsto \overline{loaded}\}$.

Planning with uncertainty and incomplete information about the effects of actions is somewhat more difficult. The ideas presented in Section 6 cannot be directly adopted because if the additional argument of each action name is left variable then the system is always free to choose the desired effect. This is, of course, too optimistic. Rather, a *cautious agent* should be defined who is content only if solutions to the planning problem in each possible alternative can be found. This may require the creation of different subplans, each of them solving the problem in only some of the several alternatives, which is not feasible in our equational logic program of Section 2. In [4] it is shown how a cautious agent can be modelled in our method. The basic idea is to introduce a second function symbol, again embedded in a particular equational theory, which denotes a *disjunctive* connection of AC1-terms, each of them describing a possible situation. This can be regarded as the first step in view of weakening our restriction that situations are represented by conjunctions of atomic facts.

There are a variety of other aspects concerning upgrades of existing approaches such as concurrent actions, multiple agents, complex and non-inertial actions, probabilistic values for alternative effects etc. We have hopes that the equational logic based approach enables us to carry out experiments with respect to these and other ontological aspects as well.

Acknowledgements

The author would like to thank Wolfgang Bibel, Stefan Brüning, Steffen Hölldobler, Vladimir Lifschitz, and Aaron Rothschild for valuable comments on an earlier version of this paper. The author was partially supported by ESPRIT within basic research action MEDLAR-II under grant no. 6471 and by the German Research Community (DFG) within project KONNEK-TIONSBEWEISER under grant no. Bi 228/6-2.

Notes

1. Throughout this paper, we use a PROLOG–like syntax, i.e. constants and predicates are in lower cases whereas variables are denoted by upper case letters. Moreover, free variables are assumed to be universally quantified and, as usual, the term $[h \,|\, t]$ denotes a list with head h and tail t.

2. Multisets are depicted using the brackets $\{\!|\ |\!\}$, and $\dot{\cup}$, $\dot{-}$, $\dot{\subseteq}$, $\dot{=}$, etc. denote the multiset extensions of the usual set operations and relations.

3. Thus, planning in this approach is closely related to planning in STRIPS [9, 22] except that multisets are used instead of sets and that planning is performed in a purely deductive context. As argued in [12] multisets are more adequate solutions to the frame problem. We therefore do not require the function symbol $\circ$ to be idempotent. The fundamental difference, however,

is that STRIPS was designed for planning only and cannot be used to perform the kind of general reasoning which is necessary for modelling $\mathcal{A}$, say.

4. The latter is a rather strict assumption which is required by $\mathcal{A}$ and therefore necessary to obtain completeness. We will take up this problem later.

5. Observe that $\mathcal{C}$ as well as $\mathcal{E}$ are multisets although set operations such as $\cup$ and $\subseteq$ are used to define them, which is to ensure that neither $\mathcal{C}$ nor $\mathcal{E}$ contain elements more than once.

References

[1] A. B. Baker. A simple solution to the Yale shooting problem. In *Proceedings of the Int.'l Conf. on Knowledge Representation and Reasoning*, 11–20, 1989.

[2] A. B. Baker. Nonmonotonic reasoning in the framework of situation calculus. *Artificial Intelligence*, 49:5–23, 1991.

[3] W. Bibel. A Deductive Solution for Plan Generation. *New Generation Computing*, 4:115–132, 1986.

[4] S. Brüning, S. Hölldobler, J. Schneeberger, U. Sigmund, and M. Thielscher. Disjunction in Resource–Oriented Deductive Planning. In D. Miller, ed., *Proc. of the ILPS*, page 670, Vancouver, 1993. MIT Press. (Poster presentation.)

[5] D. Chan. Constructive Negation Based on the Completed Database. *Proc. of the IJCSLP*, 111–125, 1988.

[6] K. L. Clark. Negation as Failure. In H. Gallaire and J. Minker, ed.'s, *Workshop Logic and Data Bases*, 293–322. Plenum Press, 1978.

[7] M. Denecker and D. de Schreye. Representing Incomplete Knowledge in Abductive Logic Programming. In D. Miller, ed., *Proc. of the ILPS*, 147–163, Vancouver, 1993. MIT Press.

[8] P. M. Dung. Representing Actions in Logic Programming and its Applications in Database Updates. In D. S. Warren, ed., *Proc. of the ICLP*, 222–238, Budapest, 1993. MIT Press.

[9] R. E. Fikes and N. J. Nilsson. STRIPS: A new approach to the application of theorem proving to problem solving. *Artificial Intelligence*, 5(2):189–208, 1971.

[10] M. Gelfond and V. Lifschitz. Representing Action and Change by Logic Programs. *Journal of Logic Programming*, 17:301–321, 1993.

[11] C. Green. Application of theorem proving to problem solving. In *Proc. of the IJCAI*, 219–239, Los Altos, CA, 1969. Morgan Kaufmann Publishers.

[12] G. Große, S. Hölldobler, J. Schneeberger, U. Sigmund, and M. Thielscher. Equational Logic Programming, Actions, and Change. In K. Apt, ed., *Proc. of the IJCSLP*, 177–191, Washington, 1992. MIT Press.

[13] S. Hanks and D. McDermott. Nonmonotonic logic and temporal projection. *Artificial Intelligence*, 33(3):379–412, 1987.

[14] S. Hölldobler. On Deductive Planning and the Frame Problem. In A. Voronkov, ed., *Proc. of the Int.'l Conf. on Log. Prog. and Autom. Reasoning (LPAR)*, 13–29. Springer, volume 624 of LNAI, 1992.

[15] S. Hölldobler and J. Schneeberger. A New Deductive Approach to Planning. *New Generation Computing*, 8:225–244, 1990.

[16] S. Hölldobler and M. Thielscher. Actions and Specificity. In D. Miller, ed., *Proc. of the ILPS*, 164–180, Vancouver, 1993. MIT Press.

[17] S. Hölldobler and M. Thielscher. Computing Change and Specificity with Equational Logic Programs. *Annals of Mathematics and Artificial Intelligence*, special issue on Processing of Declarative Knowledge, 1994. (To appear.)

[18] J. Jaffar, J.-L. Lassez, and M. J. Maher. A theory of complete logic programs with equality. *Journal of Logic Programming*, 1(3):211–223, 1984.

[19] G. N. Kartha. Soundness and Completeness Theorems for Three Formalizations of Actions. In R. Bajcsy, ed., *Proc. of the IJCAI*, 724–729, Chambéry, France, 1993. Morgan Kaufmann.

[20] R. Kowalski. *Logic for Problem Solving*, volume 7 of *Artificial Intelligence Series*. Elsevier, 1979.

[21] R. Kowalski and M. Sergot. A logic based calculus of events. *New Generation Computing*, 4:67–95, 1986.

[22] V. Lifschitz. On the Semantics of STRIPS. In M. P. Georgeff and A. L. Lansky, ed.'s, *Proc. of the Workshop on Reasoning about Actions & Plans*. Morgan Kaufmann, 1986.

[23] J. W. Lloyd. *Foundations of Logic Programming*. Series Symbolic Computation. Springer, second, extended edition, 1987.

[24] M. Masseron, C. Tollu, and J. Vauzielles. Generating Plans in Linear Logic. In *Foundations of Software Technology and Theoretical Computer Science*, 63–75. Springer, volume 472 of LNCS, 1990.

[25] J. McCarthy. Applications of circumscription to formalizing common-sense knowledge. *Artificial Intelligence*, 28:89–116, 1986.

[26] J. McCarthy and P. J. Hayes. Some Philosophical Problems from the Standpoint of Artificial Intelligence. *Machine Intelligence*, 4:463–502, 1969.

[27] R. Reiter. The frame problem in the situation calculus: A simple solution (sometimes) and a completeness result for goal regression. In V. Lifschitz, ed., *Artificial Intelligence and Mathematical Theory of Computation*, 359–380. Academic Press, 1991.

[28] E. Sandewall. Features and Fluents. Technical Report LiTH-IDA-R-92-30, University of Linköping, Sweden, 1992.

[29] J. Schneeberger. *Plan Generation by Linear Deduction*. PhD thesis, FG Intellektik, TH Darmstadt, 1992.

[30] J. C. Shepherdson. SLDNF–Resolution with Equality. *Journal of Automated Reasoning*, 8:297–306, 1992.

[31] M. Thielscher. Modelling theories of actions by Equational Logic Programs. Technical Report AIDA-93-18, FG Intellektik, TH Darmstadt, 1993. Available via anonymous ftp from 130.83.26.1 in /pub/AIDA/Tech-Reports/1993.

[32] M. Thielscher. SLDENF–Resolution. 1994 (submitted). Available via anonymous ftp from 130.83.26.1 in /pub/AIDA/Tech-Reports/OTHER.

Representing Continuous Change in the Abductive Event Calculus

Kristof Van Belleghem, Marc Denecker, Danny De Schreye
Department of Computer Science, K.U.Leuven,
Celestijnenlaan 200A, B-3001 Heverlee, Belgium.
{kristof, marcd, dannyd}@cs.kuleuven.ac.be

Abstract

In this paper we extend the Abductive Event Calculus, a variant and extension of the Event Calculus of Kowalski and Sergot, with a representation for continuous change. We assume the change is not exactly known and use constraints to represent the available knowledge. The resulting logic program can be executed by the SLDNFA abductive procedure of Denecker and De Schreye. We show how our representation of continuous change combines with solutions to other problems in temporal reasoning, like indeterministic effects of actions, and how it can be used not only for temporal projection, but also to solve planning and diagnosis problems or any combination thereof.

1 Introduction

The Event Calculus (see [12]) is one of the many formalisms used for representing a changing world. The basic concepts are events and properties, events initiating and terminating periods of time during which properties hold.

Several modified versions of the Event Calculus have been used, for example in [19], [9] and [15], mostly to simplify the ontology and to eliminate problems occuring because of bidirectional persistence of properties (forward as well as backward in time). Extensions were introduced to improve the expressive power in several ways. One of the most important of these was the introduction of abduction, for example in [8], [15] and [5], which made it possible to use the Event Calculus for planning and for diagnosis ([7]) as well as for temporal projection.

In the original Event Calculus, as in most other versions, all change is supposed to be discrete. Recently there have been proposals ([19], [16]) to incorporate continuous change in the Event Calculus, describing changing quantities as exactly known functions of time. In this paper we propose an extension of the Abductive Event Calculus that does not require such complete knowledge about the change, and which is closer to the qualitative reasoning point of view. One other qualitative approach to representing continuous change in the Event Calculus is described in [20], but as the author points out, that work was never really completed.

We will apply our formalism to a number of examples and show how it can be used to solve projection, planning and diagnosis problems and problems in which indeterminism occurs.

2   The Event Calculus

In the Event Calculus, information is represented in Horn clauses augmented with *negation as failure*. The following axioms define a simplified version of the Event Calculus, which we use as a basis for introducing our extension:

$$holds\_at(P, T) \quad \leftarrow \quad happens(E), E << T, initiates(E, P),$$
$$not\ clipped(E, P, T).$$
$$clipped(E, P, T) \quad \leftarrow \quad happens(C), in(C, E, T),$$
$$terminates(C, P).$$
$$in(C, E, T) \quad \leftarrow \quad E << C, C << T.$$

happens(E) holds if the event E occurs. We allow only one event to occur at any one time point, which makes it possible to represent events directly by their time of occurrence. This does not limit the expressive power of the formalism, since it is possible for more than one action to take place during one event. We consider events to be just special time points, on which for example actions may occur. A strict chronological order $<<$ is defined on all time points, including events.

The actions associated with an event determine which properties are initiated or terminated by it. This is formulated through domain dependent rules which are represented in the form

$$initiates(E, P) \quad \leftarrow \quad act(E, A), Precond(A, P).$$
$$terminates(E, P) \quad \leftarrow \quad act(E, B), Precond(B, P).$$

where the optional $Precond(A, P)$ consists of a number of preconditions for the action, mostly in the form of *holds_at* and *not holds_at* expressions.

To represent problems in which an initial state is given, a *start* event is introduced. This event initiates all properties that are true in the initial state:

$$happens(start).$$
$$initiates(start, P) \quad \leftarrow \quad initially(P).$$

No events are allowed to occur before *start*.

3   SLDNFA in the Event Calculus

The Event Calculus can be used as a logic program under Clark completion semantics ([2]) to solve temporal projection (prediction) problems. This can be done deductively using the well-known SLDNF procedure. However, Clark completion semantics assumes complete knowledge about the problem domain. Any form of incomplete knowledge — like actions with indeterministic effects — can not be dealt with. Furthermore, postdiction (diagnosis) and planning problems can not be solved using deduction in this form of the Event Calculus.

These problems can be overcome in the following way: on the representational level, we use the Console completion semantics for abductive logic programs of [3], augmented with general first order logic constraints. This semantics allows for the use of *undefined* predicates: predicates with an unknown truth value. Thus, incomplete knowledge can be represented.

On the level of problem solving, we will use *abduction* as well as deduction, which requires an abductive proof procedure: given a set of logic formulas F (facts and rules about the problem domain) and a number of conclusions G, an abductive procedure attempts to find a set of additional facts Δ such that

- $F + \Delta$ is consistent.

- $F + \Delta \models G$.

- Δ is minimal: no subset of Δ exists that satisfies the first two conditions.

The minimality condition is not always added. The facts allowed in Δ will be constrained by the user to obtain useful results.

Abduction can be used to deal with indeterministic effects and to solve diagnosis and planning problems, by constraining the facts in Δ in the appropriate way. In general the predicates allowed in Δ are those we have incomplete knowledge about, in other words the undefined predicates. In the sequel we refer to these as the *abducible* predicates. For example, in planning problems we have incomplete knowledge about the actions occurring in the plan and the time relations that connect them, so *happens*, *act* and $<<$ will be abducible. We try to find the sequence of actions necessary to prove the goal, which is the desired end state. In a similar way postdiction problems and indeterminism can be modeled.

For our experiments we have used an implementation of the SLDNFA (SLD resolution with Negation as Failure and Abduction) procedure described in [6] and [7]. This procedure allows for a better treatment of abducible atoms containing variables compared to other procedures. A proof of the soundness and completeness of the procedure with respect to Console completion semantics can be found in the aforementioned papers.

An important feature of this procedure is that it keeps track of both a list of goals for which a successful derivation is needed, and a list of goals for which finite failure must be proven. Therefore it is quite easy to handle constraints of the form

$$false \leftarrow A_1, \ldots A_n.$$

by adding $\leftarrow A_1, \ldots A_n.$ to the latter list of goals. The use of this kind of constraints proved very helpful in many situations, not in the least in our proposal for modeling continuous change. In general we can transform any logic formula into one or more rules of this form ([14]), thereby extending the expressiveness of the formalism considerably. Given the program F including the set of constraints, and the goal "$\neg false$ & G", the SLDNFA procedure finds a Δ such that

$$Comp(F + \Delta) \models \neg false \ \& \ G$$

where $Comp(P)$ is the Clark completion of P. Note that the atom $false$ should not be interpreted as simply $\neg true$: it actually means "a constraint is violated", and the goal $\neg false$ is then used to ensure satisfaction of all constraints.

4   Continuous Change

Like most other formalisms developed for temporal reasoning, the Event Calculus originally did not take the possibility of continuous change into account. Every property takes on a number of discrete values (most often just booleans), and changes of these values occur at certain isolated time points. In many cases such an approach is sufficient: many properties have a boolean value or can only take on a limited number of discrete values. It is even possible to model a continuously changing value at a high level of abstraction using discrete values. One can for example use the properties $on(X, A)$, $on(X, B)$ and $between(X, A, B)$ to model the location of X, even though that location is in fact a continuous variable.

But for some problems this level of abstraction is too high: it can be used to model the continuous value, but it is insufficient if we want to model the change itself. An example where we need to model continuous change is the problem of a tank that can be filled with water, as introduced in [19]. This is a simple problem, yet it shows many of the complications that arise when continuous change occurs. The most important of these is the problem of autotermination, also introduced in [19]. It is possible that the change of a property over time gets terminated by itself, without the occurrence of any external event. This happens for example when the rising water in a tank reaches its rim. At that moment, the change in water level causes the event of its own termination.

Other complications of this form can occur if the water triggers events when it reaches certain levels, like the ringing of a warning bell. In general, a changing property can cause a number of other events to happen at different time points.

The water tank problem can be extended in several ways, and we can use it to demonstrate a number of different types of problem solving. For example, it is possible to introduce a number of taps and plugs (open taps fill the tank, open plugs empty it) that can be opened or closed simultaneously. We can introduce several warning bells, as discussed earlier, and allow for the possibility that some of these bells are broken (indeterministic aspect). We can then open a tap without closing it later, and ask why no bell has rung (diagnosis : the bell must be broken). We can ask whether the opening of the tap will result in bells ringing (two solutions: no if they are broken, yes otherwise). We can open a tap and ask to avoid the ringing of any bells, even though they are not broken (planning: the tap must be closed, or a plug opened, or maybe the bell turned off).

When looking for a representation of continuous change, two approaches can be distinguished. The first one assumes complete knowledge about the change: the changing quantity is exactly known as a function of time, or can be calculated from other data (like the flow through a certain tap). This approach is taken by most authors, for example in [17], [19] and [16].

But in the case of continuous change — even more than in other cases — it seems necessary to allow for incomplete knowledge. For example, while it is easy to check whether a turkey is dead or alive, determining the water level in a filling tank as an exact function of time is non-trivial. Most probably the only real knowledge available is that the level is rising. We will show that even such very limited knowledge contains important information that can be used in several types of problem solving.

5 Representation of continuous change in the Abductive Event Calculus

We propose a representation of continuous change that only requires qualitative knowledge. For example, in the case of a filling water tank such knowledge might be that the water level is rising, that it is rising in a continuous way, that autotermination will occur when the water reaches the rim, etc. We want this solution to fit in with the general framework of the Abductive Event Calculus, so that it can be combined with discrete changes, indeterminism, and planning and diagnosis problems.

We present our proposal in two stages: in a first step we allow only one influence to exist on a changing variable at the same instant in time. In the second step we extend this solution with simultaneous influences. We illustrate the formalism by modeling a filling water tank and using the representation for problem solving.

5.1 Solution without simultaneous influences

In our first step we introduce two new predicates. $cont\_change(P, Sort, T)$ holds if at time point T the property P is subject to a continuous change of sort $Sort$. $Sort$ is a parameter used to distinguish different kinds of change, where each kind has certain unique properties. How many and which kinds of change are to be distinguished, depends on the amount of available knowledge as well as on the relevance of the observed differences between two kinds. A lot of work on this topic of making useful and adequate abstractions exists in the qualitative physics community (see for example [10] and [13]). One simple and obvious abstraction, which is often used in qualitative physics, is the distinction between positive and negative change. We will use this distinction in our examples.

$state\_in\_change(P, T)$ is a predicate describing the value of P as a function of time during periods of change. We add the following axiom to the Event Calculus to express this:

$$holds\_at(P, T) \leftarrow cont\_change(P, Sort, T),$$
$$state\_in\_change(P, T).$$

So, if P is changing, its value is defined by $state\_in\_change$. The following axioms describe when a continuous change is in effect.

$$cont\_change(P, Sort, T) \leftarrow happens(E), E << T,$$
$$init\_change(E, P, Sort),$$
$$not\ change\_clipped(E, P, T, Sort).$$
$$change\_clipped(E, P, T, Sort) \leftarrow happens(C), in(C, E, T),$$
$$term\_change(C, P, Sort).$$

where *init_change*, *term_change* and *change_clipped* correspond to *initiates*, *terminates* and *clipped* for discrete properties.

During periods of change, the *state_in_change* function determines the value of properties. This approach is similar to the definition of trajectories in [19], but where trajectories are defined as exactly known functions, we leave *state_in_change* undefined (abducible). Instead we define constraints on the *state_in_change* function to represent the available knowledge, for example monotonicity or continuity of the change. These constraints will be described later on. We will show that they provide the expressiveness needed to handle all aforementioned applications.

The original axioms of the Event Calculus still apply, and describe the state of properties while they are not undergoing any change. To ensure correct interaction between periods of change and periods of rest, we add the following axioms:

$$terminates(E, P) \quad \leftarrow \quad init\_change(E, P, Sort).$$
$$initiates(E, P) \quad \leftarrow \quad holds\_at(P, E), term\_change(E, P, Sort).$$

meaning that the start of a change terminates a period of rest, while termination of the change initiates a new period of rest. In particular, the case in which a change has terminated and no new change initiated, is now properly dealt with by the *holds_at* rule for discrete change.

We will illustrate the use of this formalism by describing a filling water tank. The constraints we define are problem specific, since they depend on the actual knowledge available about the change. However, most of them represent quite common properties, like continuity of change, and can be generalized or adapted to other problem descriptions.

The tank contains a tap and a plug. An open tap results in rising water level, an open plug in dropping level. The tap and the plug can not be open simultaneously, since in this first step we do not allow multiple influences on one property at the same moment:

$$init\_change(E, level(L), +) \quad \leftarrow \quad act(E, open\_tap).$$
$$term\_change(E, level(L), +) \quad \leftarrow \quad act(E, close\_tap).$$
$$init\_change(E, level(L), -) \quad \leftarrow \quad act(E, open\_plug).$$
$$term\_change(E, level(L), -) \quad \leftarrow \quad act(E, close\_plug).$$
$$false \quad \leftarrow \quad cont\_change(E, P, -), cont\_change(E, P, +).$$

In this example we choose to distinguish only two kinds of continuous change: rising and dropping water level, denoted by sorts $+$ and $-$. As indicated earlier, this is a very simple abstraction, but we will show its usefulness. The changing property we consider is $level(L)$, the water level in the tank. We know the following:

- The water level is rising (dropping) monotonically.

- At any instant in time, there can be only one level.

- The change is continuous (if the water reaches two different levels during one period of change, then it will also reach all levels between them).

- If the tap is opened, and nothing happens that stops the rising of the water, then the water will eventually reach the rim of the tank (we assume the water will not do strange things like rise asymptotically to the rim). Similarly the tank will eventually become empty if the plug is open.

- When the rising (dropping) water reaches the rim (bottom) of the tank, the change is automatically terminated.

This information is expressed in a number of constraints, written in the form required by SLDNFA. In order to be able to write these constraints, we first specify when two time points belong to a same period of change:

$$same\_change(P, Sort, T_1, T_2) \leftarrow happens(C),\ C \leq T_1,\ T_1 << T_2,$$
$$init\_change(C, P, Sort),$$
$$not\ change\_clipped(C, P, T2, Sort).$$

where $\leq$ is defined in the usual way.

Next, we define a linear order on the set of water levels. A special constraint module has been added to our SLDNFA-implementation to efficiently keep track of any number of such ordered sets, ensuring they have a strict linear order defined on them. The formula $isa(X, O)$ is used to indicate that X belongs to set O. The linear order is described by the predicate $smaller/3$: $smaller(O, X, Y)$ holds if X is smaller than Y with respect to the order on O. From a declarative point of view, $smaller/3$ is an undefined predicate satisfying antireflexivity, antisymmetry, transitivity and linearity constraints.

Moreover, if a scenario asserts $isa(bottom(O), O)$ and/or $isa(top(O), O)$, these are the extrema of O. Otherwise no extrema exist. The set O does not need to be completely determined: it is possible to make isa abducible (satisfying certain constraints of course). For example, this allows us to consider only the relevant levels in a tank, with the possibility to introduce more levels if (and only if) needed.

In fact, the order $<<$ on events is a variant of this general linear order, with start being the minimum of the set and no maximum defined. Similarly $happens$ is a special case of isa.

We refer to the set of water levels as l_type, and add the constraint

$$false \leftarrow holds\_at(level(X), T),\ not\ isa(X, l\_type).$$

Now we can formulate our constraints on changes. The constraints are written in terms of $holds\_at$, but actually — through the rules for $holds\_at$ in terms of $state\_in\_change$ — constrain this undefined predicate. The first of the constraints, concerning monotonicity, ensures that for every two time points during the same period of positive change, the level on the later time point is greater than the level on the earlier one. The opposite holds for negative change.

$$false \leftarrow same\_change(level(L), +, T_1, T_2), holds\_at(level(X), T_1),$$
$$holds\_at(level(Y), T_2), T_1 << T_2, smaller(l\_type, Y, X).$$
$$false \leftarrow same\_change(level(L), +, T_1, T_2), holds\_at(level(X), T_1),$$
$$holds\_at(level(X), T_2), T_1 << T_2, not\ X = top(l\_type).$$
$$false \leftarrow same\_change(level(L), -, T_1, T_2), holds\_at(level(X), T_1),$$
$$holds\_at(level(Y), T_2), T_1 << T_2, smaller(l\_type, X, Y).$$
$$false \leftarrow same\_change(level(L), -, T_1, T_2), holds\_at(level(X), T_1),$$
$$holds\_at(level(X), T_2), T_1 << T_2, not\ X = bottom(l\_type).$$

We allow for the level to remain constant once the water reaches the rim. This, together with the restriction that the rim is the maximum existing level, captures the meaning of autotermination: when the tank is full, the level stops rising. We choose this representation rather than introducing a terminating event caused by the change like Shanahan does. Such autoterminating event would not distinguish the case in which the tap is closed just when the tank is full from the case in which the tank overflows. However, there are differences, like the floor getting wet. Moreover, in our next step we will allow for multiple simultaneous influences on a changing variable. In that case, the introduction of an autoterminating event leads to erroneous conclusions, as we will discuss later. In our representation the tank being full does not terminate the period of change, even though the level remains constant.
The other constraints look like this:

- no two levels at the same instant:
$$false \leftarrow holds\_at(level(X), T_1), holds\_at(level(Y), T_1), not\ X = Y.$$

- continuity:
$$false \leftarrow same\_change(level(L), Sort, T_1, T_2), T_1 << T_2,$$
$$holds\_at(level(X), T_1), holds\_at(level(Y), T2), isa(Z, l\_type),$$
$$between(l\_type, Z, X, Y), not\ reach\_between(l\_type, Z, T_1, T_2).$$
$$reach\_between(l\_type, Z, T_1, T_2) \leftarrow happens(T_3), T_1 << T_3, T_3 << T_2,$$
$$holds\_at(level(Z), T_3).$$
$$between(O, Z, X, Y) \leftarrow smaller(O, X, Z), smaller(O, Z, Y).$$
$$between(O, Z, X, Y) \leftarrow smaller(O, Y, Z), smaller(O, Z, X).$$

- water eventually reaches the rim:
$$false \leftarrow happens(E), init\_change(E, level(X), +),$$
$$not\ change\_clipped\_after(E, level(X), +),$$
$$isa(top(l\_type), l\_type), not\ reach\_after(E, top(l\_type)).$$
$$false \leftarrow happens(E), init\_change(E, level(X), -),$$
$$not\ change\_clipped\_after(E, level(X), -),$$
$$isa(bottom(l\_type), l\_type), not\ reach\_after(E, bottom(l\_type)).$$
$$reach\_after(E, L) \leftarrow happens(E_2), E << E_2, holds\_at(level(L), E_2).$$
$$change\_clipped\_after(E, P, Sort) \leftarrow happens(E_2), E << E_2,$$
$$term\_change(E_2, P, Sort).$$

5.2 Applications

This version of our proposal can already handle a variety of problems. First we study a simple scenario in the water tank world. We define three levels: the bottom of the tank, the top, and a level halfway. The tank is initially empty, and then a tap is opened.

Although in practice we can and most often will make *happens* and $<<$ abducible, this usually implies that infinitely many solutions to a given query exist. Using an iterative deepening control in the SLDNFA implementation, solutions with a minimal number of abduced events can be generated first. Since we do not want to elaborate on this implementation in the current paper, we instead assume that the necessary number of events is added to the scenario. We emphasize, however, that this is not a limitation of the approach. In this scenario, we add two additional events.

$$happens(start). \quad happens(e_1). \quad happens(e_2). \quad happens(e_3).$$
$$start << e_1. \quad e_1 << e_2. \quad e_2 << e_3.$$
$$isa(bottom(l\_type), l\_type). \quad isa(half, l\_type). \quad isa(top(l\_type), l\_type).$$
$$initially(level(bottom(l\_type))). \quad act(e_1, open\_tap).$$

We want to know if, and under which conditions, this scenario is possible. So we try to solve the query "$\leftarrow not\ false$". We obtain the following abduced facts:

$$state\_in\_change(level(half), e_2).$$
$$state\_in\_change(level(top(l\_type)), e_3).$$

and a couple of facts ordering the l_type set. This order is trivial, since there is only one level apart from the minimum and maximum of the set.

This solution is indeed correct: because the tap is never closed, the water reaches the top. This can happen no later than at time e_3, since e_3 is the last time point we defined. Now, since the water reaches the top, we know it also reaches all levels between bottom and top. So, the water must reach the level halfway sometime between e_1 and e_3, which can only be at e_2, the only other event we provided. Of course, if other events existed between e_1 and e_3, and especially if happens were abducible, there would be other solutions as well.

In a second example we add a bell that rings when the water reaches the level halfway. This shows how we can handle events that are caused by the change. At the same time we add an indeterministic aspect, by making it possible for the bell to be broken. We do not know whether the bell is broken or not, so we declare *broken_bell* to be an abducible predicate, as in [7]. We only have to add the rule

$$initiates(E, ring\_bell) \leftarrow holds\_at(level(half), E), not\ broken\_bell.$$

With the bell and the indeterminism added, we can demonstrate how diagnosis problems are handled. To diagnose why the bell is not ringing at e_3, we use the query

$$\leftarrow not\ false, not\ holds\_at(ringbell, e_3).$$

The additional abduction of *broken_bell* is made, since the level halfway has to be reached at e_2. A solution without *broken_bell* does not exist.

Postdiction problems, where facts about an earlier time point are derived given information about a later one, are a special form of diagnosis problem where *initially* is the abducible predicate.

Finally we can use this representation with the SLDNFA procedure for planning in the context of continuous change. As an example, we generate a plan of actions that explains the fact that, after opening a tap, the bell does not ring even though it is not broken. We have the general rules

$$init\_change(E, level(X), +) \quad \leftarrow \quad act(E, open\_tap).$$
$$term\_change(E, level(X), +) \quad \leftarrow \quad act(E, close\_tap).$$
$$initiates(E, ring\_bell) \quad \leftarrow \quad holds\_at(level(half), E), not\ broken\_bell.$$

The definitions of *happens*, *isa*, *initially* and $<<$ are identical to those in our first application, and *state_in_change*, *smaller*, *act* and *broken_bell* are abducible. If we want to solve

$$\leftarrow not\ false, act(e_1, open\_tap), not\ holds\_at(ringbell, e_3), not\ broken\_bell.$$

we find one solution with abduced facts $act(e_1, open\_tap)$ and $act(e_2, close\_tap)$, and a second one with the close_tap action on e_3 instead of e_2. Because the tap is now closed at a certain point in time, the water is no longer guaranteed to reach the rim, or even the level halfway. The level at time e_3 will be somewhere between $bottom(l\_type)$ and *half*.

5.3 Extension for multiple influences

If we want to allow for multiple simultaneous influences to exist on the same changing variable, we need to extend our proposal. Where the notion of *influence*, or in fact the distinction between change and influence was unimportant in our previous version, it is now of vital importance. We introduce a new predicate *influence*/4. $influence(I, P, Sort, T)$ holds if at time point T, P is subject to the influence I of sort *Sort*.

Changes are now defined in terms of the existing influences, while the effect of actions is the initiation and/or termination of these influences. The predicates *init_change*, *term_change* and *change_clipped* will be eliminated and replaced by a set of new predicates *init_influ*, *term_influ*, *influ_clipped*, *influ_started* and *influenced*. The following new definitions apply:

$$influence(I, P, S, T) \quad \leftarrow \quad happens(E), E << T, init\_influ(E, I, P, S),$$
$$\qquad\qquad\qquad\qquad not\ influ\_clipped(I, E, P, T).$$
$$influ\_clipped(I, E, P, T) \quad \leftarrow \quad happens(C), in(C, E, T), term\_influ(C, I, P, S).$$
$$influ\_started(I, E, P, T) \quad \leftarrow \quad happens(C), in(C, E, T), init\_influ(C, I, P, S).$$
$$influenced(T_1, P, T_2) \quad \leftarrow \quad influ\_clipped(I, T_1, P, T_2).$$
$$influenced(T_1, P, T_2) \quad \leftarrow \quad influ\_started(I, T_1, P, T_2).$$

We redefine *cont_change* in terms of influences, and leave our frame axioms and constraints unchanged. We choose to distinguish two kinds of influence:

positive and negative. This leads to three kinds of change: if all influences on a variable are positive, the change is positive ($+$). If all influences are negative, the change is negative ($-$). If there are both positive and negative influences, the change is continuous but with unknown direction (?). This is expressed in the following rules:

$$cont\_change(P, +, T) \leftarrow influence(I, P, +, T), not\ any\_influ(P, -, T).$$
$$cont\_change(P, -, T) \leftarrow influence(I, P, -, T), not\ any\_influ(P, +, T).$$
$$cont\_change(P, ?, T) \leftarrow influence(I, P, +, T), influence(J, P, -, T).$$
$$any\_influ(P, Sort, T) \leftarrow influence(J, P, Sort, T).$$

where the last rule is introduced to avoid floundering.

As in the first proposal, the types of change and influence are chosen because of their generality. They can be modified if the problem domain requires this, for example when a distinction can be made between slow change and fast change. We choose to stick with this very general set of types, to show that even with a small amount of knowledge several problems can be handled.

The interaction between periods of rest and periods of change is ensured by the following rules:

$$terminates(E, P) \leftarrow init\_influ(E, I, P, S).$$
$$initiates(E, P) \leftarrow holds\_at(P, E), term\_influ(E, I, P, S),$$
$$not\ unterminated\_influ(P, E).$$
$$unterminated\_influ(P, E) \leftarrow init\_influ(E, I, P, Sort).$$
$$unterminated\_influ(P, E) \leftarrow happens(E^*), influence(I, E^*, P, Sort),$$
$$not\ term\_influ(E, I, P, Sort).$$

where $unterminated\_influ(P, E)$ holds if there are influences on P that will continue to exist after E.

We can now model the water tank in the following way, adding the possibility of multiple taps and plugs:

$$init\_influ(E, tap(Y), level(X), +)) \leftarrow act(E, open\_tap(Y)).$$
$$init\_influ(E, plug(Y), level(X), -)) \leftarrow act(E, open\_plug(Y)).$$
$$term\_influ(E, tap(Y), level(X), +)) \leftarrow act(E, close\_tap(Y)).$$
$$term\_influ(E, plug(Y), level(X), -)) \leftarrow act(E, close\_plug(Y)).$$

using the name or number of the tap to identify the influence. In this way, it is easy to determine which influence is initiated or terminated by an action.

The monotonicity, continuity and unique level constraints do not need to be modified. However, the constraints indicating that the water eventually reaches the top or the bottom — when rising or dropping — get more complicated because of the possibility of many influences: if, at a certain point in time, there are unterminated positive influences while no negative influences remain, and if after that time point there is no change of influence anymore, then the water will eventually reach its maximum level. Again a similar conclusion holds about the water reaching its minimum level if only negative influences exist.

$$false \quad \leftarrow \quad happens(E), \; unterminated\_influ(E, level(L), +),$$
$$not \; unterminated\_influ(E, level(L), -),$$
$$not \; influenced\_after(E, level(L)),$$
$$isa(top(l\_type), l\_type), \; not \; reach\_after(E, top(l\_type)).$$
$$false \quad \leftarrow \quad happens(E), \; unterminated\_influ(E, level(L), -),$$
$$not \; unterminated\_influ(E, level(L), +),$$
$$not \; influenced\_after(E, level(L)), \; isa(bottom(l\_type), l\_type),$$
$$not \; reach\_after(E, bottom(l\_type)).$$

with *reach_after* as before, and *influenced_after* defined as

$$influenced\_after(E, P) \quad \leftarrow \quad happens(E_2), \; E << E_2, \; term\_influ(E, I, P, S).$$
$$influenced\_after(E, P) \quad \leftarrow \quad happens(E_2), \; E << E_2, \; init\_influ(E, I, P, S).$$

which completes our proposal for continuous change with multiple influences. Basically it can handle the same kinds of problems as our first proposal, but it eliminates the unrealistic restriction to one influence. An example that shows how even changes with unknown direction provide us with useful information, is the following scenario: we open a tap and a plug, resulting in an unknown change. We know nothing about the initial water level. We observe the water level at t_1 and t_2, and see it is below halfway at t_1 and above halfway at t_2. In this case, the bell should be ringing at t_2 if it is not broken. Apart from the general rules descibed above, we have

$$initiates(E, ring\_bell) \quad \leftarrow \quad holds\_at(level(half), E), \; not \; broken\_bell.$$

$isa(bottom(l\_type), l\_type).$	$happens(start).$	$start << e_1.$
$isa(x, l\_type).$	$happens(e_1).$	$e_1 << t_1.$
$isa(half, l\_type).$	$happens(t_1).$	$t_1 << e$
$isa(y, l\_type).$	$happens(e).$	$e << t_2.$
$isa(top(l\_type), l\_type).$	$happens(t_2).$	
$act(e_1, open\_tap(tap_1)).$	$act(e_1, open\_plug(plug_1)).$	

We add an extra event e between t_1 and t_2. If happens were abducible, this event would always be abduced, as the constraints can never be satisfied otherwise. For the reasons indicated earlier we choose to simply add this necessary event to the scenario. Of course we do not give any information about what is going on at time e, it is just there to be used if needed. Similarly we add two new levels x and y. We ask

$$\leftarrow \quad not \; false, \; holds\_at(level(x), t_1), \; holds\_at(level(y), t_2),$$
$$smaller(l\_type, x, half), \; smaller(l\_type, half, y),$$
$$not \; holds\_at(ring\_bell, t_2).$$

and again, we find *broken_bell* is abduced. Indeed, the change is not required to be monotonic, and we do not know how the water level behaves between t_1 and t_2, whether it reaches the top or the bottom, or how many times it passes the level halfway. Yet we do know, because of continuity, that it passes the level halfway at least once between t_1 and t_2. Therefore, if the bell is not ringing, it has to be broken.

We conclude this section by indicating why autoterminating events would lead to erroneous results in the extended version of our proposal. Suppose we use autoterminating events. If we open a tap and wait until the tank is full, such event would occur. Suppose then we do not close the tap, but open a plug. We could then conclude that there is a negative influence from the plug, but no positive one from the tap, since that influence was (auto)terminated by the event. Therefore we could conclude that the tank would empty.

However, in reality the positive influence of the tap still exists. Though it has no effect if it is the only influence present, it is not terminated and can still show itself by counteracting other influences.

This does not mean, however, that autoterminating events are a worthless notion: they can indeed occur in reality. As an example, there could be a sensor at the rim of the tank that detects the water level reaching it. This could provoke the closing of all taps. In that case, we have a real autoterminating event, and it has to be represented as such.

6 Discussion

We have incorporated a representation of continuous change in the Abductive Event Calculus, assuming that we have no complete knowledge about that change. We have used constraints in combination with abduction to represent the available knowledge. We have made a distinction between the influences on a changing value and the change of that value itself. This distinction is necessary if we want to model any but the most simple problem domains.

A few other authors have addressed the problem of representing continuous change in a temporal reasoning formalism. Allen's theory of time ([1]) was modified in [11] to fix certain problems arising when continuous change was considered in the original theory. Sandewall ([17], [18]) describes a framework that uses differential equations combined with logic and a form of chronological minimisation.

In an approach based like ours on the Event Calculus, Shanahan extends the formalism with *trajectories*([19]). These trajectories describe periods of continuous change, assuming the change is exactly known as a function of time. The extension fits in nicely with the Event Calculus, as periods of rest — described by the basic Event Calculus axioms — and periods of motion — described by the axioms for trajectories — interact without a problem. This solution is further refined in [16] to make reasoning at different levels of time granularity possible, and to allow for the parameters of the change to be modified while the change is in effect.

This approach assumes that each trajectory is exactly known. To avoid this, in [20] a qualitative version of trajectories is proposed, based on the naive physics theory of confluences described in [4]. Confluences are, simply stated, a form of qualitative differential equations. They can be used to describe the world in terms of the signs of certain quantities and the signs of their derivatives, without knowing any exact values. Shanahan combines these confluences with trajectories. These trajectory do not need to be exactly known anymore, but are quqlitative.

However, there are many differences between this approach and ours. Shanahan distinguishes certain *landmark values* through which the changing value can pass. This corresponds in a sense to our definition of levels, but the set of landmarks is always fixed while our levels and their order can be incompletely known. This results in a greater flexibility of our approach.

Another difference lies in Shanahan's treatment of autotermination using a caused event, which leads to the problems we indicated earlier. Finally, Shanahan does not distinguish influences from changes, where we argue that this distinction is necessary for handling simultaneous influences on the same variable.

Shanahan's proposal is presented in Horn clause logic, and as a logic theory provides a valid representation, but it is not intended to run as a logic program. Shanahan indicates that it still contains many loops and inefficiencies.

Our representation is compatible with the aspects of the Abductive Event Calculus that have been developed to represent indeterminism and to solve problems involving planning and diagnosis. This is probably the most important aspect of the proposal, since as far as we know all representations of continuous change to date, be it qualitative or quantitative, are only intended to solve prediction problems (if problem solving is at all possible), and can certainly not deal with indeterminism. The advantage of our proposal is that it combines the extensions for planning, diagnosis, indeterminism and continuous change in one framework.

Our theories can be — and are — actually executed by means of the SLD-NFA procedure. Because of the use of many constraints and of the very high level implementation, that execution is still rather inefficient (though certain optimisations, using constraint logic programming techniques, have been included). One of our further research goals is the improvement of the abductive proof procedure, besides further representational issues.

Acknowledgements

Kristof Van Belleghem is partly supported by ESPRIT BR project Compulog II and partly by the Belgian IWONL. Marc Denecker is supported by Dienst Onderzoekscoordinatie, K.U.Leuven. Danny De Schreye is a senior research associate of the Belgian NFWO. We thank anonymous referees for valuable comments.

References

[1] J. F. Allen. Towards a General Theory of Action and Time. *Artifical Intelligence*, 23(11):123, 1984.

[2] K. Clark. Negation as failure. In H. Gallaire and J. Minker, editors, *Logic and databases*, pages 293–322. Plenum Press, 1978.

[3] L. Console, D. Theseider Dupre, and P. Torasso. On the relationship between abduction and deduction. *Journal of Logic and Computation*, 1(5):661–690, 1991.

[4] J. de Kleer and J. S. Brown. A qualitative physics based on confluences. In J. Hobbs and R. Moore, editors, *Formal Theories of the Commonsense World*, pages 109–183. Ablex, 1985.

[5] M. Denecker. *Knowledge Representation and Reasoning in Incomplete Logic Programming*. PhD thesis, Department of Computer Science, K.U.Leuven, 1993.

[6] M. Denecker and D. De Schreye. SLDNFA; an abductive procedure for normal abductive programs. In K. Apt, editor, *Proceedings of the International Joint Conference and Symposium on Logic Programming, Washington*, 1992.

[7] M. Denecker, L. Missiaen, and M. Bruynooghe. Temporal reasoning with abductive event calculus. In *Proceedings of ECAI 92, Vienna*, 1992.

[8] K. Eshghi. Abductive planning with event calculus. In R. Kowalski and K. Bowen, editors, *Proceedings of the 5th ICLP*, 1988.

[9] C. Evans. The Macro-Event Calculus: Representing Temporal Granularity. In *Proceedings of PRICAI, Tokyo*, 1990.

[10] K. Forbus. Qualitative Process Theory. *Artifical Intelligence*, 24:85–168, 1984.

[11] A. Galton. A critical examination of allen's theory of action and time. *Artifical Intelligence*, 42:109–188, 1990.

[12] R. A. Kowalski and M. Sergot. A logic-based calculus of events. *New Generation Computing*, 4(4):319–340, 1986.

[13] B. Kuipers. Qualitative Simulation. *Artifical Intelligence*, 29:289–338, 1986.

[14] J. Lloyd and R. Topor. Making prolog more expressive. *Journal of logic programming*, 1(3):225–240, 1984.

[15] L. Missiaen. *Localized abductive planning with the event calculus*. PhD thesis, Department of Computer Science, K.U.Leuven, 1991.

[16] A. Montanari, E. Maim, E. Ciapessoni, and E. Ratto. Dealing with Time Granularity in the Event Calculus. In *Proceedings of FGCS, Tokyo*, pages 702–712, 1992.

[17] E. Sandewall. Combining logic and differential equations for describing real-world systems. In *Proceedings 1989 Knowledge Representation Conference*, page 412, 1989.

[18] E. Sandewall. Filter preferential entailment for the logic of action in almost continuous worlds. In *Proceedings of IJCAI 89*, page 894, 1989.

[19] M. Shanahan. Representing continuous change in the event calculus. In *Proceedings of the 9th ECAI*, page 598, 1990.

[20] M. Shanahan. Towards a calculus for temporal and qualitative reasoning. In *Proceedings of AAAI Symposium, Stanford, 1991*, 1991.

Concurrency and plan generation in a logic programming language with a sequential operator

Alessio Guglielmi
Dipartimento di Informatica, Corso Italia 40, 56125 Pisa, Italy
ph.: +39 (50) 887 248   fax: +39 (50) 887 226
guglielm@di.unipi.it

ABSTRACT *In this paper we define a logic programming language, called* SMR, *whose main computational mechanism is multiset rewriting. It features a guarded choice capability and, above all, a sequential and-like operator. The language is defined starting from a core language,* LM, *a subset of Andreoli and Pareschi's* LO, *which is directly derived from linear logic.* LM *is minimal in a certain sense we will specify. The language* SMR *admits a translation into* LM *through a uniform "continuation" mechanism. We show how* SMR *could be interesting in two diverse areas, viz. concurrency and plan generation.*

KEYWORDS *Logic programming, linear logic, concurrency, planning.*

1 Introduction

Linear logic [13, 10] is widely recognized as a logic of concurrency, meaning that the proof theory underlying it faithfully represents some aspects of concurrent computations. Recently it has been pointed out that the same logic is suited for carefully modeling concepts of action and change in planning problems [19, 16]. In particular linear logic offers a very elegant solution to the so-called "frame problem" [20].

The aim of our work is to investigate the use of linear logic as the underlying formal system of *linear* logic programming languages, and in particular to study the expressiveness of the languages obtained wrt the two fields mentioned above: concurrency and planning. We claim that, when we come to logic programming, both computational paradigms have a natural interpretation in terms of a common language, called LM, which we use as a kernel language for further enrichments. The difference between the two paradigms completely lies on the control imposed on the computations. The planning case requires a "proof search as computation" mechanism, while the concurrency one is better fitted into the "proof as computation" one. The former case corresponds to the "don't know" type of nondeterminism (where backtracking is admitted), the latter to the "don't care" one (where backtracking is not admitted).

The foundation of logic programming languages by means of proof theory has been investigated by Miller *et al.* in the seminal work [23], where the concept of *uniform proof* is defined. In the case of logic programming languages based on linear logic, the concept has been further explored in [22, 1, 3, 17]. The use of a clean proof theory as a foundational tool has been proved very effective for studying semantics, analysis, transformation and verification issues.

Following these guidelines we define the language LM. It is made up of the linear implication connective ∘– (written reversed, as usual in logic programming) and the "par" connective ⅋. The ⅋ connective is used as a sort of "and", except for the termination condition, as we will see. In the concurrency framework it enables us to represent multiple processes in the same environment, allowing synchronization and communication. Atoms connected by ⅋ are considered as resources. In planning, atoms connected by ⅋ are states, conditions which hold at a certain time, subject to disappear or change as the computation evolves. The mechanism which makes the computation to proceed is provided by $\circ\!-$, which relates in *methods* (multiple headed clauses) two multisets of atoms connected by $\bfseries ?\!?$. The program is a set of methods and is itself expressed in linear logic, but it enjoys a "classical" treatment, in that methods can be freely reused.

This computational framework is essentially pattern-based multiset rewriting. We use a first-order theory and pattern matching is achieved through unification. As the fundamental technical tool we use the *sequent calculus* [12, 15, 11, 14], where at the left of the sequents we will put the program and at the right the status of the computation. We exploit of course the ability of linear logic of taking into account the multiplicity of atoms, and the absence of the weakening and the contraction rule, which in our case is applied only to the right of the sequents.

Having defined LM we show how we can enrich it with a sequentiality mechanism, which embodies in three features: a sequential operator (a sort of sequential "and"), a very general guard mechanism, and a global termination condition. The great expressiveness obtained this way is shown through examples. The language we define, called SMR, directly derives from Monteiro's *distributed logic* [24, 25]. Sequentialization is achieved by means of a "continuation" mechanism, that allows us to uniformly translate programs in SMR into programs in LM. This mechanism allows us to cope with the above mentioned features of SMR in a straightforward and uniform way. The full power of the underlying language LM is exploited and it is our belief that SMR obtains great expressive power at the price of a little departure from a purely proof theoretical frame. It still retains enough simplicity and cleanliness that should be of great benefit to the study of its computational behavior, analysis, semantics and so on.

The paper is organized as follows: in section 2 the language LM is defined; in section 3 it is defined SMR and in section 4 the translation from SMR to LM is shown. Two theorems are given which relate the two steps we make: from linear logic to LM and from LM to SMR. They state the fact that we do not loose correctness and completeness passing from one to the other.

2 *Multiset rewriting and linear logic: The language* LM

We will show now a characterization of multiset rewriting in terms of linear logic, obtaining a logic programming language. Let $\mathcal{A}$ be the set of atoms, of the form $p^n(t_1, \ldots, t_n)$, where p^n is a predicate name of arity n and t_1, ..., t_n are terms. We want to give logical structure to the following situation: a *multiset* of atoms is subject to rewriting until a certain termination condition is reached, and the possible rewritings are specified by rules.

2.1 LM *and its relation with linear logic*

Let us call LM (*Linear Methods*) our logic programming language: it is made up of atoms of $\mathcal{A}$, a distinguished atom $\top$ and the two connectives $?\!?$ and $\circ\!-$. The set $\mathcal{M}$ has generic element M, defined this way:

$$H = A \mid H \bfseries ?\!? H,$$
$$B = A \mid \top \mid B \bfseries ?\!? B,$$
$$M = H \circ\!- B,$$

where A is an element of $\mathcal{A}$. The set $\mathcal{P}_{\text{LM}}$ of programs of LM is the class of finite subsets of $\mathcal{M}$. A method is a formula of type *head* $\circ\!-$ *body*, and is the specification of a rule by which a multiset is possibly rewritten. When some atoms in the multiset match the head of a method (*i.e.* there is a unifying substitution), they are all replaced by an instance of the atoms in the body of the method. A program is a collection of rules of this kind, and every rule may be applied an unlimited number of times.

In the following we will use *sequents*, *i.e.* expressions of the form $\Gamma \vdash \Delta$, where Γ and Δ are multisets of atoms [12, 15, 11, 14]. In particular, we will consider partitioned the atoms at the right of the $\vdash$. We then have sequents of the kind $\mathcal{P} \vdash \mathcal{C}, \mathcal{G}$, where $\mathcal{P}$, the *program*, is a finite set of methods, $\mathcal{C}$ is called the *context* and $\mathcal{G}$ is the *goal*. We keep at the right of the $\vdash$ the multiset upon which we do the rewriting, and $\mathcal{G}$ is a distinguished multiset of atoms which match the head of one of the methods in $\mathcal{P}$. Considering a program either a set or a multiset of methods does not make any difference, as will be clear in the following. We prefer to consider it a set because there is no point in having twice the same method, and the contraction rule of linear logic applies to programs.

The following proof rules hold for LM:

$$\top \frac{}{\mathcal{P} \vdash \mathcal{C}, \top};$$

$$\mathsf{R} \frac{\mathcal{P} \vdash \mathcal{C}\sigma, A_1''\sigma, \ldots, A_n''\sigma}{\mathcal{P} \vdash \mathcal{C}\sigma, A_1\sigma, \ldots, A_m\sigma}, \text{ where } A_1' \,\mathbin{\invamp}\, \cdots \,\mathbin{\invamp}\, A_m' \,\mathbin{\circ\!\!-}\, A_1'' \,\mathbin{\invamp}\, \cdots \,\mathbin{\invamp}\, A_n'' \text{ is a method}$$

in $\mathcal{P}$, σ is a substitution and $(A_1, \ldots, A_m)\sigma = (A_1', \ldots, A_m')\sigma$.

The rule R is called *reaction*.

A computation in LM is strictly related to the formation of a proof starting from the bottom. This process is as follows. We start with a query $\mathcal{P} \vdash \mathcal{G}_0$, *i.e.* we ask whether the goal $\mathcal{G}_0$ is derivable from the program $\mathcal{P}$. Suppose we can find in $\mathcal{G}_0$ a subgoal $\mathcal{G}_1$ which matches the head of a method in $\mathcal{P}$, that is a substitution σ_1 exists such that $\mathcal{G}_1\sigma_1 = \mathcal{H}_1\sigma_1$ for a method $\mathcal{H}_1 \,\mathbin{\circ\!\!-}\, \mathcal{B}_1$ in $\mathcal{P}$. Then we can write, if $\mathcal{G}_0 = \mathcal{C}_1, \mathcal{G}_1$:

$$\mathsf{R} \frac{\mathcal{P} \vdash \mathcal{C}_1\sigma_1, \mathcal{B}_1\sigma_1}{\mathcal{P} \vdash \mathcal{G}_0\sigma_1}.$$

We could find in $\mathcal{C}_1\sigma_1, \mathcal{B}_1\sigma_1$ a subgoal $\mathcal{G}_2$, that is $\mathcal{C}_1\sigma_1, \mathcal{B}_1\sigma_1 = \mathcal{C}_2, \mathcal{G}_2$, such that $\mathcal{G}_2$ matches the head of a method $\mathcal{H}_2 \,\mathbin{\circ\!\!-}\, \mathcal{B}_2$ with substitution σ_2. Now we have

$$\mathsf{R} \frac{\mathsf{R} \dfrac{\mathcal{P} \vdash \mathcal{C}_2\sigma_2, \mathcal{B}_2\sigma_2}{\mathcal{P} \vdash \mathcal{C}_1\sigma_1\sigma_2, \mathcal{B}_1\sigma_1\sigma_2}}{\mathcal{P} \vdash \mathcal{G}_0\sigma_1\sigma_2}.$$

The search proceeds upwards until a $\top$ appears in the multiset, and the $\top$ rule is applied. Of course which multiset is to be matched with which method's head is a matter of choice.

A proof generated from a query $\mathcal{P} \vdash \mathcal{G}$ is then a chain of applications of reactions, starting with a $\top$ rule and ending with a $\mathcal{P} \vdash \mathcal{G}\sigma$ sequent. We can take σ as an *answer* generated from the program $\mathcal{P}$ to our query $\mathcal{G}$. The proof-theoretic point of view hides the potential parallelism inherent in this computational framework. Parallelism here is related to the possibility of exchanging, in a proof, the application of two distinct reactions: this is possible when they are applied to disjoint multisets' goals, sharing no variables, or at least without conflicts on them. We write $\mathcal{P} \vdash_{\mathsf{LM}} \mathcal{G}$ to state the fact that a proof for $\mathcal{P} \vdash \mathcal{G}$ exists using LM's proof rules.

In the rest of the subsection we will briefly show how the proof rules for LM are related to the proof rules of linear logic, and how provability in LM relates to provability in linear logic.

We will refer to the following fragment of linear logic, where F and G stand for formulae and Γ, Δ, Σ and Θ stand for finite multisets of formulae.

Axioms: left contraction:

$$\mathsf{I}\ \frac{}{F \vdash F}, \qquad \top\ \frac{}{\Gamma \vdash \Delta, \top}; \qquad\qquad >_l \frac{!F, !F, \Gamma \vdash \Delta}{!F, \Gamma \vdash \Delta};$$

cut rule: left "of course:"

$$\bowtie \frac{\Gamma \vdash \Delta, F \quad F, \Sigma \vdash \Theta}{\Gamma, \Sigma \vdash \Delta, \Theta}; \qquad\qquad !_l \frac{F, \Gamma \vdash \Delta}{!F, \Gamma \vdash \Delta};$$

multiplicative rules:

$$\multimap_l \frac{\Gamma \vdash \Delta, F \quad G, \Sigma \vdash \Theta}{G \multimap F, \Gamma, \Sigma \vdash \Delta, \Theta}, \qquad \mathbin{\bindnasrepma}_l \frac{F, \Gamma \vdash \Delta \quad G, \Sigma \vdash \Theta}{F \mathbin{\bindnasrepma} G, \Gamma, \Sigma \vdash \Delta, \Theta}, \qquad \mathbin{\bindnasrepma}_r \frac{\Gamma \vdash \Delta, F, G}{\Gamma \vdash \Delta, F \mathbin{\bindnasrepma} G};$$

universal quantification:

$$\forall_l \frac{F[t/x], \Gamma \vdash \Delta}{\forall x F, \Gamma \vdash \Delta}, \text{ where } t \text{ is any term.}$$

As usual in logic programming, $\multimap$ is the linear implication connective written reversed.

First, we note that the $\mathbin{\bindnasrepma}$ connective and the comma are completely interchangeable at the right of the $\vdash$. In fact we can introduce the rule

$$\mathbin{\bindnasrepma}_r^{-1} \frac{\Gamma \vdash \Delta, F \mathbin{\bindnasrepma} G}{\Gamma \vdash \Delta, F, G} \quad \equiv \quad \bowtie \frac{\Gamma \vdash \Delta, F \mathbin{\bindnasrepma} G \quad \mathbin{\bindnasrepma}_l \dfrac{\mathsf{I}\ \dfrac{}{F \vdash F} \quad \mathsf{I}\ \dfrac{}{G \vdash G}}{F \mathbin{\bindnasrepma} G \vdash F, G}}{\Gamma \vdash \Delta, F, G}.$$

Now, given M a method in $\mathcal{M}$, let us write $!\forall M$ to indicate the formula obtained by M by universally quantifying every variable in M and then prefixing by $!$ the formula obtained. By $!\forall\mathcal{P}$ we mean the set composed of formulae $!\forall M$, for every method M in $\mathcal{P} \in \mathscr{P}_{\mathrm{LM}}$.

In the same hypotheses as above, the rule R can be decomposed in our fragment of linear logic as follows:

$$\mathbin{\bindnasrepma}_r^{-1\star} \frac{>_l \dfrac{!_l \dfrac{\forall_l^{\star} \dfrac{\multimap_l \dfrac{\mathbin{\bindnasrepma}_r^{\star} \dfrac{!\forall\mathcal{P} \vdash \mathcal{C}\sigma, A_1''\sigma, \ldots, A_n''\sigma}{!\forall\mathcal{P} \vdash \mathcal{C}\sigma, A_1''\sigma \mathbin{\bindnasrepma} \cdots \mathbin{\bindnasrepma} A_n''\sigma} \quad \mathsf{I}\ \dfrac{}{A_1'\sigma \mathbin{\bindnasrepma} \cdots \mathbin{\bindnasrepma} A_m'\sigma \vdash A_1\sigma \mathbin{\bindnasrepma} \cdots \mathbin{\bindnasrepma} A_m\sigma}}{A_1'\sigma \mathbin{\bindnasrepma} \cdots \mathbin{\bindnasrepma} A_m'\sigma \multimap A_1''\sigma \mathbin{\bindnasrepma} \cdots \mathbin{\bindnasrepma} A_n''\sigma, !\forall\mathcal{P} \vdash \mathcal{C}\sigma, A_1\sigma \mathbin{\bindnasrepma} \cdots \mathbin{\bindnasrepma} A_m\sigma}}{\forall(A_1' \mathbin{\bindnasrepma} \cdots \mathbin{\bindnasrepma} A_m' \multimap A_1'' \mathbin{\bindnasrepma} \cdots \mathbin{\bindnasrepma} A_n''), !\forall\mathcal{P} \vdash \mathcal{C}\sigma, A_1\sigma \mathbin{\bindnasrepma} \cdots \mathbin{\bindnasrepma} A_m\sigma}}{!\forall(A_1' \mathbin{\bindnasrepma} \cdots \mathbin{\bindnasrepma} A_m' \multimap A_1'' \mathbin{\bindnasrepma} \cdots \mathbin{\bindnasrepma} A_n''), !\forall\mathcal{P} \vdash \mathcal{C}\sigma, A_1\sigma \mathbin{\bindnasrepma} \cdots \mathbin{\bindnasrepma} A_m\sigma}}{!\forall\mathcal{P} \vdash \mathcal{C}\sigma, A_1\sigma \mathbin{\bindnasrepma} \cdots \mathbin{\bindnasrepma} A_m\sigma}}{!\forall\mathcal{P} \vdash \mathcal{C}\sigma, A_1\sigma, \ldots, A_m\sigma},$$

where the * means repeated application of the rule to which it is applied.

We write $\Gamma \vdash_{\text{LL}} \Delta$ if a proof in linear logic exists for the sequent $\Gamma \vdash \Delta$. Provability in LM and provability in linear logic are substantially equivalent, as the following proposition holds:

THEOREM   *Given $\mathcal{P} \in \mathcal{P}_{\text{LM}}$ and $\mathcal{G}$ a multiset of atoms in $\mathcal{A}$, then $\mathcal{P} \vdash_{\text{LM}} \mathcal{G}$ if and only if $!\forall \mathcal{P} \vdash_{\text{LL}} \mathcal{G}$.*

2.2   *Expressiveness of* LM

In the following we discuss two examples aimed at showing the expressive power of LM: the first is a simple planning problem taken from [19], the second is the specification of two processes communicating through a buffer. The reader should keep in mind that LM is not meant to be a real programming language, but rather a kernel language which richer languages may be built upon.

In the rest of the paper we will stick to the convention of writing variables with all-lowercase letters, and constants with a leading capital.

1)   *A block world problem*   We have a world in which three blocks can be moved on a table by a robot hand. We want to express and solve the problem of finding a sequence of actions that make the world evolve from the situation on the left to that on the right:

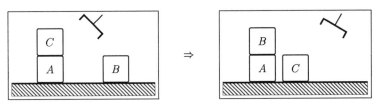

The following predicates describe the world: $clear(x)$: the block x has nothing on top; $empty\_hand$: the hand of the robot is empty; $hold(x)$: x is held by the hand; $on(x, y)$: x is on top of y; $on\_table(x)$: the block x is on the table.

Four possible actions are specified in the program by means of these four methods (labeled for convenience):

$$Put(x): \quad empty\_hand \,\mathcal{B}\, on\_table(x) \,\mathcal{B}\, clear(x) \circ\!\!- hold(x);$$
$$Remove(x, y): \quad hold(x) \,\mathcal{B}\, clear(y) \circ\!\!- empty\_hand \,\mathcal{B}\, clear(x) \,\mathcal{B}\, on(x, y);$$
$$Stack(x, y): \quad empty\_hand \,\mathcal{B}\, on(x, y) \,\mathcal{B}\, clear(x) \circ\!\!- hold(x) \,\mathcal{B}\, clear(y);$$
$$Take(x): \quad hold(x) \circ\!\!- empty\_hand \,\mathcal{B}\, clear(x) \,\mathcal{B}\, on\_table(x).$$

Note that, in the above formulation, the frame problem is solved in a very elegant way. Take for instance the $Put(x)$ action: before it is applied the hand holds x. After the action, of course, the hand no more holds x, and this is reflected by the atom $hold(x)$ disappearing from the multiset. This is due to the fact that linear logic has greater control than classical logic over the application of the contraction and weakening rules.

A possible solution to the problem is the sequence of actions: $Remove(C, A)$, $Put(C)$, $Take(B)$, $Stack(B, A)$. We can express the initial status as:

$$on\_table(A) \,\mathcal{B}\, on\_table(B) \,\mathcal{B}\, on(C, A) \,\mathcal{B}\, clear(B) \,\mathcal{B}\, clear(C) \,\mathcal{B}\, empty\_hand \circ\!\!- \top,$$

and the target status as the goal

$$on\_table(A) \,\mathcal{B}\, on\_table(C) \,\mathcal{B}\, on(B, A) \,\mathcal{B}\, clear(B) \,\mathcal{B}\, clear(C) \,\mathcal{B}\, empty\_hand.$$

Now, it is easy to see that the given solution corresponds to a proof of the goal, considering the reactions involved from top to bottom in the proof. It should be noted that a dual translation of the problem into LM could be given by reversing the linear implications in the methods and exchanging the initial and the final status. In this case the order in which the actions are to be performed is from bottom to top in the proofs so obtained.

We are here in the "proof search as computation" paradigm. The computation is the *search* for a proof, and the proof found corresponds to the plan required.

2)   *Two concurrent processes and a buffer*   Suppose we have a process *prod* which writes in the first position of a buffer, when it is empty. There is a process *cons* which consumes the elements in the last position of the buffer. When the buffer is empty and *prod* has finished writing, the whole computation stops. Here are *prod* and *cons*:

$$prod([x \mid y]) \ \mathbin{\rotatebox[origin=c]{180}{\&}} \ free\_first \ \mathbin{\rotatebox[origin=c]{180}{\&}} \ count(z) \circ\!\!- \ prod(y) \ \mathbin{\rotatebox[origin=c]{180}{\&}} \ pos\_first(x) \ \mathbin{\rotatebox[origin=c]{180}{\&}} \ count(s(z));$$
$$prod([]) \ \mathbin{\rotatebox[origin=c]{180}{\&}} \ count(0) \circ\!\!- \ \top;$$
$$cons(x) \ \mathbin{\rotatebox[origin=c]{180}{\&}} \ pos\_last(x) \ \mathbin{\rotatebox[origin=c]{180}{\&}} \ count(s(y)) \circ\!\!- \ cons(z) \ \mathbin{\rotatebox[origin=c]{180}{\&}} \ free\_last \ \mathbin{\rotatebox[origin=c]{180}{\&}} \ count(y).$$

In a modular way we can define the buffer process, with the desired number of positions. Here is a buffer with four positions:

$$pos\_first(x) \ \mathbin{\rotatebox[origin=c]{180}{\&}} \ free\_two \circ\!\!- \ pos\_two(x) \ \mathbin{\rotatebox[origin=c]{180}{\&}} \ free\_first;$$
$$pos\_two(x) \ \mathbin{\rotatebox[origin=c]{180}{\&}} \ free\_three \circ\!\!- \ pos\_three(x) \ \mathbin{\rotatebox[origin=c]{180}{\&}} \ free\_two;$$
$$pos\_three(x) \ \mathbin{\rotatebox[origin=c]{180}{\&}} \ free\_last \circ\!\!- \ pos\_last(x) \ \mathbin{\rotatebox[origin=c]{180}{\&}} \ free\_three.$$

We can have some degree of parallelism in computations with the above program, and this is reflected in the possibility of exchanging in the proofs the application of some reactions. Termination in the above program is completely determined by the termination of the producer process. Alternatively, we could eliminate the counter in the buffer: this way we may obtain greater parallelism between producer and consumer, but are forced to propagate the termination of the producer through the buffer. It is interesting to note that the $\mathbin{\rotatebox[origin=c]{180}{\&}}$ connective behaves as an "and" with respect to reactions, but it is like an "or" when we come to the termination condition.

Here we assume to have a "proof as computation" control mechanism. The computation is the proof itself, and our program is correct (wrt to our requirements) if *every* proof obtainable is correct. This is customary in the logical view of concurrent computations, and corresponds to the "don't care" nondeterminism in concurrent logic programming languages.

2.3   *Relations with other formal systems*

The work [19] relates a set-theoretical notion of action to a fragment of linear logic. Our approach above is essentially equivalent (through some transformations) but has the advantage of being a logic programming language. It is not a big difference from the computational point of view, but our presentation is more suited to be enriched and compared to other works in the logic programming field.

Petri nets [26] have strong relationships with linear logic too, as shown, for instance, in [18]. A computation on a Petri net is essentially multiset rewriting too, and again our formalism can express it faithfully.

Another formalism related to ours is the GAMMA model of computation [4]. Its fundamental computational mechanism is the Γ operator. Given a multiset $\mathcal{M}$ and a set of couples reaction-action (R_i, A_i), the command $\Gamma(R_1, A_1) \dots (R_n, A_n)\mathcal{M}$ has the following operational semantics: if, for any i, the relation $R_i(x_1, \dots, x_{m_i})$

holds for $x_1, \ldots, x_{m_i} \in \mathcal{M}$, then substitute $x_1, \ldots, x_{m_i}$ with $A_i(x_1, \ldots, x_{m_i})$; proceed until no reaction R_i is applicable. For example $\Gamma(x \geqslant y, \{x\})\mathcal{M}$ finds the maximum element in the (multi)set $\mathcal{M}$: until no couple of elements is present, the lesser is eliminated; at last the maximum element remains. Our formalism differs from GAMMA in that our termination condition is local, *i.e.* methods cannot have a global vision of the multiset they rewrite. The GAMMA formalism has given rise to the so-called *chemical metaphor* [2, 5], in which a program is viewed as the specification of possible *chemical reactions* to occur in a *solution*, *i.e.* a multiset of *molecules* (data, processes) which, thanks to *brownian motion*, can combine together to form new molecules. The parallelism inherent in the formalism provides for an asynchronous concurrent computation.

Multiple heads Horn clauses have been studied in the past out of linear logic (with set-theoretical characterizations in mind instead of the monoidal ones proper of linear logic, semantically speaking), in particular in [6, 9]. A recent linear logic programming (object oriented) language, which is a superset of ours, is LO [3].

3 Adding a sequentiality mechanism: the language SMR

Multiset rewriting is a powerful computational formalism. In this section we present SMR (*Structured Multiset Rewriting*), a language whose operational semantics is a reelaboration of Monteiro's distributed logic [24, 25]. SMR enhances significantly the expressive power of LM while retaining its substantial simplicity. We will show that every program in SMR can be translated into an equivalent program in LM, this way inheriting the proof theory underlying LM.

The language SMR enhances LM essentially in three aspects:

1) it has a *guard* mechanism;
2) there is a provision to *sequentialize* the applicable reactions;
3) a computation terminates when *all* of the atoms in the multiset are reduced.

3.1 Syntax and operational semantics of SMR

Let $\mathcal{A}$ be the set of atoms, of the form $p^n(t_1, \ldots, t_n)$, with $n \geqslant 0$. Consider the two mutually recursive sets of *sequential* and *parallel* goals:

$$\mathcal{G}_s = \{ (G_1 \bullet \cdots \bullet G_n) \mid n \geqslant 2, G_i \in \{\Lambda\} \cup \mathcal{A} \cup \mathcal{G}_p, 1 \leqslant i \leqslant n \};$$
$$\mathcal{G}_p = \{ (G_1 + \cdots + G_n) \mid n \geqslant 2, G_i \in \{\Lambda\} \cup \mathcal{A} \cup \mathcal{G}_s, 1 \leqslant i \leqslant n \}.$$

Λ is the empty goal and is subject to the following normalization rules:

$$(\Lambda + G), (G + \Lambda) \Rightarrow G;$$
$$(\Lambda \bullet G), (G \bullet \Lambda) \Rightarrow G.$$

We take $\tilde{\mathcal{G}} = \{\Lambda\} \cup \mathcal{A} \cup \mathcal{G}_s \cup \mathcal{G}_p$ as the set of non-normalized goals, and the set of goals $\mathcal{G}$ is the set obtained by $\tilde{\mathcal{G}}$ by normalizing its elements with the two rules above. Given $G \in \tilde{\mathcal{G}}$, we write $|G|$ to indicate the goal obtained by normalizing G. To save on parentheses, we assume that $\bullet$ takes precedence over $+$. Then we can write the goal $(((A + B) \bullet C) + D)$ as $(A + B) \bullet C + D$ without any ambiguity. The $\bullet$ is called the *sequential operator* and, as it will be clear in the following, states that in $G \bullet G'$ the resolution of the goal G must be completed *before* the resolution of G' begins. The operator $+$ (*parallel*) specifies that in $G + G'$ the two subgoals G and G' are resolved upon concurrently. Furthermore, we consider $+$ a commutative operator, *i.e.* $G + G'$ is the same as $G' + G$.

The set $\mathcal{D}$ of clauses is defined as:

$$\mathcal{D} = \{\, A_1, \ldots, A_n \Leftarrow G_0 \to G_1, \ldots, G_n \mid n \geqslant 1,\ A_i \in \mathcal{A},\ G_i \in \mathcal{G},\ 0 \leqslant i \leqslant n \,\}.$$

A clause is then of the form *head* $\Leftarrow$ *guard* $\to$ *body*, and states the conditional replacement of n atoms with as many normalized goals in a parallel and simultaneous way; this is the mechanism which synchronization is achieved through. The set $\mathcal{P}_{\mathrm{SMR}}$ of programs is the family of finite subsets of $\mathcal{D}$. We write the unconditional clause $A_1, \ldots, A_n \Leftarrow \Lambda \to G_1, \ldots, G_n$ as $A_1, \ldots, A_n \Leftarrow G_1, \ldots, G_n$.

To build an operational semantics, let us define the *top* multiset of atoms of a given (not necessarily normalized) goal (notation: $\{\ldots\}_+$ is a multiset and $\uplus$ is multiset union):

$$\mathrm{top}(G) = \begin{cases} \varnothing & \text{if } G = \Lambda; \\ \{G\}_+ & \text{if } G \in \mathcal{A}; \\ \mathrm{top}(G') & \text{if } G = G' \bullet G''; \\ \mathrm{top}(G') \uplus \mathrm{top}(G'') & \text{if } G = G' + G''. \end{cases}$$

In the following, with a slight abuse of language, by $\mathrm{top}(G)$ we will indicate the occurrences in the goal G of the atoms which concur to form $\mathrm{top}(G)$.

Given $G, G_1, \ldots, G_n \in \tilde{\mathcal{G}}$ and $A_1, \ldots, A_n \in \mathcal{A}$, then $G[G_1/A_1, \ldots, G_n/A_n]$ is the goal obtained from G by substituting the occurrences (if any) of $A_1, \ldots, A_n$ in $\mathrm{top}(G)$ respectively with the goals $G_1, \ldots, G_n$. In this substitution multiplicity matters, for example if $G = A \bullet A \bullet G' + B + A$, then $G[C/A]$ is either $C \bullet A \bullet G' + B + A$ or $A \bullet A \bullet G' + B + C$. To simplify the notation we suppose to know which atoms in the top the substitutions refer to.

Now let us define the transition $C_1, \ldots, C_h, G \xrightarrow[\sigma]{\mathcal{P}} C'_1, \ldots, C'_h, G'$, where $h \geqslant 0$, $\mathcal{P} \in \mathcal{P}_{\mathrm{SMR}}$, σ is a substitution and $C_1, \ldots, C_h, C'_1, \ldots, C'_h, G, G' \in \mathcal{G}$. With this relation we want to capture the *resolution* by a clause of $\mathcal{P}$ over the goal G in the *context* $C_1 + \cdots + C_h$. We suppose to have, for every application of the resolution rule, a set $\{X_1, \ldots, X_n\}$ of pairwise distinct atoms, which do not appear in $\mathcal{P}$ nor in any other resolution. Purpose of these atoms is to prevent the participation, in the resolution of the guard, of atoms which match the head of the clause with which the resolution is accomplished. They are only used as placeholders. Note that it is not required that the atoms in $\mathrm{top}(G)$ participate in the resolution step. The relation $\xrightarrow[\sigma]{\mathcal{P}}$ is recursively defined this way:

$$\frac{\begin{array}{l} \{A_1, \ldots, A_n\}_+ \subseteq \mathrm{top}(C_1 + \cdots + C_h + G) \\ A'_1, \ldots, A'_n \Leftarrow G_0 \to G_1, \ldots, G_n \in \mathcal{P} \\ (A_1, \ldots, A_n)\sigma' = (A'_1, \ldots, A'_n)\sigma' \\ C''_i = (C_i[X_1/A_1, \ldots, X_n/A_n])\sigma', \text{ for } 1 \leqslant i \leqslant h \\ G'' = (G[X_1/A_1, \ldots, X_n/A_n])\sigma' \\ C''_1, \ldots, C''_h, G'', G_0\sigma' \xrightarrow[\sigma'']{\mathcal{P}}^\star C'''_1, \ldots, C'''_h, G''', \Lambda \\ \sigma = \sigma' \circ \sigma'' \\ C'_i = |C'''_i[G_1\sigma/X_1, \ldots, G_n\sigma/X_n]|, \text{ for } 1 \leqslant i \leqslant h \\ G' = |G'''[G_1\sigma/X_1, \ldots, G_n\sigma/X_n]| \end{array}}{C_1, \ldots, C_h, G \xrightarrow[\sigma]{\mathcal{P}} C'_1, \ldots, C'_h, G'},$$

where $\xrightarrow[\sigma]{\mathcal{P}}^\star$ is the transitive closure of $\xrightarrow[\sigma]{\mathcal{P}}$. Note that we require nothing about σ, apart from the fact that it must be a unifying substitution; in particular it is not necessarily a mgu.

The sequential operator imposes an order on atoms to participate in resolutions: if $G \cdot G'$ is a goal in the multiset, then we can use G' in a resolution only after G has been reduced to Λ. Looking at a computation we can recognize some tree structures. For example in $(G_1, G_2) \xrightarrow[\sigma]{p} (G_1', G_2' + G_2'')$ we see the two trees $\begin{smallmatrix} G_1' \\ \uparrow \\ G_1 \end{smallmatrix}$ and $\begin{smallmatrix} G_2' & & G_2'' \\ \nwarrow & & \nearrow \\ & G_2 & \end{smallmatrix}$. This will be clearer in the examples. Let us call these trees *resolution trees*, without pretending to be precise and with the sole purpose of giving some intuition.

The above presented system is a variant of Monteiro's distributed logic. The guard-evaluation mechanism here is more general than Monteiro's one: a clause's guard is evaluated in the same context of the atoms which match the head of the clause, and the guard can modify that context. This mechanism is suited for having communications in the guards. The body's goals are kept in place of the matching atoms only when the guard has been successfully reduced to Λ. Unlike distributed logic, we have no special mechanism for handling termination. If $G \xrightarrow[\sigma]{p}{}^\star \Lambda$, we write $\mathcal{P} \vDash_{\text{SMR}} G\sigma$.

In the following section we will give logical soundness to this notion in the framework of linear logic.

3.2 *Examples*

1) *Making a business trip without going bankrupt*   A (traveling) salesman has to decide which trip to undertake between two. The trips consist in visiting, in different order, four towns: a, b, c and d. In every town the salesman buys and sells something, in an order to be decided. He begins the voyage with a starting capital of, say, 1 \$. At the end of the voyage he wants to know how much he has earned. The goal is:

$$\Leftarrow start\_tour \cdot budget + capital(1) + earnings(x);$$

Being in a town is expressed by a propositional atom of the same name of the town. The process of traveling is inherently sequential. Here are the two possible trips the salesman can choose between:

$$tour \Leftarrow a \cdot b \cdot c \cdot d;$$
$$tour \Leftarrow d \cdot c \cdot b \cdot a.$$

In every town he has to buy and to sell something before leaving, spending or earning a specified sum correspondingly. It is a matter of choice which of the two actions has to be performed before. A natural implementation is the following, where the amounts of the commercial transactions are specified:

$$a \Leftarrow sells(5) + buys(2);$$
$$b \Leftarrow sells(2) + buys(2);$$
$$c \Leftarrow sells(2) + buys(3);$$
$$d \Leftarrow sells(1) + buys(2).$$

Here are the rules relative to the financial situation. Of course, the main constraint of the problem is the fact that to buy something the salesman must have the money!

$$sells(x), capital(y) \Leftarrow \Lambda, add(x, y, z) \cdot capital(z);$$
$$buys(x), capital(y) \Leftarrow ge(y, x) \rightarrow \Lambda, sub(x, y, z) \cdot capital(z).$$

We suppose to have already defined the three predicates $ge(\ldots)$, $add(\ldots)$ and $sub(\ldots)$, with the obvious meaning.

The following are the rules relative to the beginning and the end of the business trip:

$$start\_tour, capital(x) \Leftarrow tour, capital(x) + start\_capital(x);$$
$$budget, capital(x), start\_capital(y), earnings(z) \Leftarrow sub(y, x, z), \Lambda, \Lambda, \Lambda.$$

Being the above a planning problem, we are in the "proof search as computation" paradigm, that is we suppose to have some backtracking mechanism in the control. In this case it happens that the tour $d \bullet c \bullet b \bullet a$ cannot be undertaken, because in c a bankrupt is for sure. The tour $a \bullet b \bullet c \bullet d$ is ok, provided that in a the salesman sells something before buying. Without the sequential operator we have to "simulate" the sequentiality with some more complicated machinery involving terms.

2) *Finding the maximum in a multiset of integers*   Here is an example with a "chemical" flavor. It will be used in the following to show the translation of SMR into LM.

Let us consider the problem of finding the maximum in a multiset of integers, given *à la* Peano, *i.e.* as repeated applications of a successor function to 0. We have a "greater than or equal" predicate, defined as:

$$ge(s(x), s(y)) \Leftarrow ge(x, y);$$
$$ge(x, 0) \Leftarrow \Lambda.$$

The goal is of the form:

$$\Leftarrow el(N_1) + \cdots + el(N_M) + count(M) + max(m),$$

where every el atom contains an element, $count$ takes the arity of the multiset and max will bound m with $\max\{N_1, \ldots, N_M\}_+$. Here is the program that solves the problem:

$$el(x), el(y), count(s(z)), max(m) \Leftarrow ge(x, y) \rightarrow el(x), \Lambda, count(z), max(m);$$
$$el(x), count(s(0)), max(x) \Leftarrow \Lambda, \Lambda, \Lambda.$$

Our solution consists in putting a *catalyzer*, the $max(m)$ atom, into the bag of elements. It randomly provokes reactions which eliminate the smaller between two elements. In principle, this mechanism can achieve great parallelism. Note, in fact, that the atom $max(m)$ is not changed by the application of the first clause, nor variable m is in any way affected. So we could think of applying simultaneously many instances of the same reaction to the multiset. There is an obvious problem with the $count(\ldots)$ atom, which *is* affected by the reaction, and imposes some sequentialization. The problem could be solved with a slightly more complex version of the above program, where atoms specifying the necessity of decreasing $count(\ldots)$ are put in the multiset, and they are nondeterministically merged together and subtracted from $count(\ldots)$ in units greater than one.

3) *A partition problem*   Suppose we have two multisets, s_0 and t_0, and we want to produce two multisets s and t such that $s \uplus t = s_0 \uplus t_0$, $|s| = |s_0|$, $|t| = |t_0|$ and every element of s is smaller than every element of t. We want to define a predicate $partition(s_0, t_0, s, t)$ stating this fact. Suppose now we have two predicates $clear\_max(b, max, b')$ and $clear\_min(b, min, b')$ which eliminate, respectively, the maximum and the minimum elements max and min from the multiset b, yielding b'. The predicate $add(b, el, b')$ states that b' is obtained by b by adding to it the element el. In this example we hide in the definition of $clear\_max$, $clear\_min$ and

add the treatment of the real multisets and concentrate ourselves on the partition algorithm. A possible solution to the problem is to have two processes, one over s and the other over t, which repeatedly exchange the maximum element of s with the minimum element of t, until $\max(s) \leqslant \min(t)$. Here is this algorithm expressed in SMR:

$$partition(s_0, t_0, s, t) \Leftarrow$$
$$clear\_max(s_0, max, s_1) \bullet exc(max, min) \bullet proc\_s(s_1, s, max, min)$$
$$+ \, clear\_min(t_0, min, t_1) \bullet exc(max, min) \bullet proc\_t(t_1, t, max, min);$$
$$proc\_s(s_1, s, max, min) \Leftarrow max \leqslant min \rightarrow add(s_1, max, s);$$
$$proc\_s(s_1, s, max, min) \Leftarrow max > min \rightarrow$$
$$add(s_1, min, s_2) \bullet clear\_max(s_2, max_1, s_3) \bullet exc(max_1, min_1)$$
$$\bullet \, proc\_s(s_3, s, max_1, min_1);$$
$$proc\_t(t_1, t, max, min) \Leftarrow max \leqslant min \rightarrow add(t_1, min, t);$$
$$proc\_t(t_1, t, max, min) \Leftarrow max > min \rightarrow$$
$$add(t_1, max, t_2) \bullet clear\_min(t_2, min_1, t_3) \bullet exc(max_1, min_1)$$
$$\bullet \, proc\_t(t_3, t, max_1, min_1);$$
$$exc(max, min), exc(max, min) \Leftarrow \Lambda, \Lambda.$$

In this example we have two communicating processes. Here a certain degree of sequentiality is imposed; for example we exchange the maximum and the minimum when we have them, *i.e.* only after the variables are instantiated.

4   *Translation of* SMR *into* LM

4.1   *The translation*

We now give an algorithm to transform a given program $\mathcal{P} \in \mathscr{P}_{\text{SMR}}$ into a program in $\mathscr{P}_{\text{LM}}$. To do that we need some technical definitions and to introduce some classes of special predicates.

Given F a goal or a clause, we indicate by $\text{var}(F)$ the set of variables which appear in F. Let us suppose that on the set of variables a total order $\leqslant_v$ exists. By $(\!|V|\!)$ we indicate the term $[x_1, \ldots, x_n]$, such that $V = \{x_1, \ldots, x_n\}$ and $x_1 \leqslant_v \cdots \leqslant_v x_n$.

To be able to translate into LM the language SMR given above, and in particular the guard's and sequential operator's mechanism, we will use a "continuation" technique. We will introduce two classes of binary predicate names, namely $\{g_G\}$ and $\{s_G\}$, corresponding respectively to guards and sequential goals. These names are all pairwise distinct and do not appear in the program to be transformed. The atoms built on them are introduced in correspondence with certain goals G which appear in the clauses of the original program, and we call them *continuation* atoms. Continuation predicate names relative to goals which are the same but in different clauses or in different parts of the same clause are to be considered distinct. These atoms are placeholders for corresponding goals waiting for the successful execution of other goals. They carry with them two pieces of information: a list of variables common to parts of a clause linked by the placeholder and a unique identifier of the actual branch of the computation (here "branch" refers to the informal concept of resolution tree introduced earlier). A special unary predicate name eb is introduced. Purpose of an $eb(x)$ atom is to signal the successful resolution, in branch x, of some goal. The simultaneous presence of an $eb(x)$ and a continuation atom can fire the execution of goals which were to be executed afterwards. Finally, we introduce a class of unary predicate names $\{p_G\}$, pairwise distinct and which do not appear in the program to be transformed. Purpose of a $p_G(x)$ atom is to promote the production of an $eb(x)$ atom when all parallel subgoals of G, in branch x, are successfully executed. We hope this will be clearer in the following formal definitions and in the example.

We recursively define the function $t_p \colon \mathcal{P}_{\mathrm{SMR}} \to \mathcal{P}_{\mathrm{LM}}$:

$$t_p(\mathcal{P}) = \begin{cases} \varnothing & \text{if } \mathcal{P} = \varnothing; \\ t_c(C) \cup t_p(\mathcal{P}') & \text{if } \mathcal{P} = \{C\} \cup \mathcal{P}'. \end{cases}$$

The function $t_c \colon \mathcal{D} \to \mathcal{P}_{\mathrm{LM}}$ generates from every clause one main method, plus one method for handling the continuation of the guard, plus a set of additional methods for the guard and for every goal in the body of the clause. Being $C = A_1, \ldots, A_n \Leftarrow G_0 \to G_1, \ldots, G_n$ a clause, with $G_0 \neq \Lambda$, then:

$$\begin{aligned} t_c(C) = \{ & t_a(A_1, x_1) \,\mathbin{\rotatebox{45}{8}}\, \cdots \,\mathbin{\rotatebox{45}{8}}\, t_a(A_n, x_n) \\ & \mathbin{\circ\!\!-} t_g((\!|\mathrm{var}(C)|\!), G_0, [x_1, \ldots, x_n]) \,\mathbin{\rotatebox{45}{8}}\, g_{G_0}((\!|\mathrm{var}(C)|\!), [x_1, \ldots, x_n]) \} \\ \cup \{ & eb([x_1, \ldots, x_n]) \,\mathbin{\rotatebox{45}{8}}\, g_{G_0}((\!|\mathrm{var}(C)|\!), [x_1, \ldots, x_n]) \\ & \mathbin{\circ\!\!-} t_g((\!|\mathrm{var}(C)|\!), G_1, x_1) \,\mathbin{\rotatebox{45}{8}}\, \cdots \,\mathbin{\rotatebox{45}{8}}\, t_g((\!|\mathrm{var}(C)|\!), G_n, x_n) \} \\ \cup \, & t_g'((\!|\mathrm{var}(C)|\!), G_0) \cup \cdots \cup t_g'((\!|\mathrm{var}(C)|\!), G_n). \end{aligned}$$

If the clause to translate is of the form $C = A_1, \ldots, A_n \Leftarrow G_1, \ldots, G_n$, the above translation is simplified as in:

$$\begin{aligned} t_c(C) = \{ & t_a(A_1, x_1) \,\mathbin{\rotatebox{45}{8}}\, \cdots \,\mathbin{\rotatebox{45}{8}}\, t_a(A_n, x_n) \\ & \mathbin{\circ\!\!-} t_g((\!|\mathrm{var}(C)|\!), G_1, x_1) \,\mathbin{\rotatebox{45}{8}}\, \cdots \,\mathbin{\rotatebox{45}{8}}\, t_g((\!|\mathrm{var}(C)|\!), G_n, x_n) \} \\ \cup \, & t_g'((\!|\mathrm{var}(C)|\!), G_1) \cup \cdots \cup t_g'((\!|\mathrm{var}(C)|\!), G_n). \end{aligned}$$

The variables x_1, ..., x_n are pairwise distinct and do not appear in the original clause.

Purpose of the newly introduced variables is to keep track of the branches of the tree their atoms belong to. They are driven inside atoms in a straightforward way:

$$t_a(p(y_1, \ldots, y_n), x) = p(y_1, \ldots, y_n, x).$$

The arity of the involved predicate names is increased accordingly. To atoms in $\mathcal{P}$ with the same predicate name correspond in $t_p(\mathcal{P})$ atoms with the same name, too.

In the following s and 1, 2, ... are term constructors, and are used to keep track of the ramifications of the resolution tree. The goals in the body of the clauses are translated according to:

$$t_g(V, G, x) = \begin{cases} eb(x) & \text{if } G = \Lambda; \\ t_a(G, x) & \text{if } G \in \mathcal{A}; \\ t_g(V, G', s(x)) \,\mathbin{\rotatebox{45}{8}}\, s_G(V, x) & \text{if } G = G' \cdot G'' \text{ and } G' \notin \mathcal{G}_s; \\ t_g(V, G_1, 1(x)) \,\mathbin{\rotatebox{45}{8}}\, \cdots \,\mathbin{\rotatebox{45}{8}}\, t_g(V, G_n, n(x)) \,\mathbin{\rotatebox{45}{8}}\, p_G(x) \\ \qquad \text{if } G = G_1 + \cdots + G_n \\ \qquad \text{and } G_1, \ldots, G_n \notin \mathcal{G}_p. \end{cases}$$

Now let us see the transformation t_g', that is responsible for introducing rules to carry over continuations and to signal the resolution of a successful parallel goal:

$$t_g'(V, G) = \begin{cases} \varnothing & \text{if } G \in \{\Lambda\} \cup \mathcal{A}; \\ \{ eb(s(x)) \,\mathbin{\rotatebox{45}{8}}\, s_G(V, x) \mathbin{\circ\!\!-} t_g(V, G'', x) \} \cup t_g'(V, G') \cup t_g'(V, G'') \\ \qquad \text{if } G = G' \cdot G'' \text{ and } G'' \notin \mathcal{G}_s; \\ \{ eb(1(x)) \,\mathbin{\rotatebox{45}{8}}\, \cdots \,\mathbin{\rotatebox{45}{8}}\, eb(n(x)) \,\mathbin{\rotatebox{45}{8}}\, p_G(x) \mathbin{\circ\!\!-} eb(x) \} \\ \cup t_g'(V, G_1) \cup \cdots \cup t_g'(V, G_n) \\ \qquad \text{if } G = G_1 + \cdots + G_n \text{ and } G_1, \ldots, G_n \notin \mathcal{G}_p. \end{cases}$$

If $G = A_1 \otimes \cdots \otimes A_n$, where $A_1, \ldots, A_n \in \mathcal{A}$, let us indicate by $\wr G \wr$ the multiset $\{A_1, \ldots, A_n\}_+$. Now we can state the following proposition:

THEOREM *Given* $\mathcal{P} \in \mathcal{P}_{\mathrm{SMR}}$ *and* $G \in \mathcal{G}$ *then* $\mathcal{P} \vDash_{\mathrm{SMR}} G\sigma$ *if and only if*

$$t_p(\mathcal{P}) \cup t'_g(\mathrm{var}(\wr G \wr), G) \cup \{eb(0) \circ\!\!- \top\} \vDash_{\mathrm{LM}} \wr t_g(\mathrm{var}(\wr G \wr), G, 0) \wr \sigma,$$

where σ *is a substitution.*

4.2 Example

We refer here to the second example in subsection 3.2. The whole program and the goal are translated in LM, yielding:

$$ge(s(x), s(y), x_1) \circ\!\!- ge(x, y, x_1);$$
$$ge(x, 0, x_1) \circ\!\!- eb(x_1);$$
$$el(x, x_1) \otimes el(y, x_2) \otimes count(s(z), x_3) \otimes max(m, x_4)$$
$$\circ\!\!- ge(x, y, [x_1, x_2, x_3, x_4]) \otimes g_{G_1}([m, x, y, z], [x_1, x_2, x_3, x_4]);$$
$$eb([x_1, x_2, x_3, x_4]) \otimes g_{G_1}([m, x, y, z], [x_1, x_2, x_3, x_4])$$
$$\circ\!\!- el(x, x_1) \otimes eb(x_2) \otimes count(z, x_3) \otimes max(m, x_4);$$
$$el(x, x_1) \otimes count(s(0), x_2) \otimes max(x, x_3) \circ\!\!- eb(x_1) \otimes eb(x_2) \otimes eb(x_3);$$
$$eb(1(x)) \otimes \cdots \otimes eb((M{+}2)(x)) \otimes p_{G_2}(x) \circ\!\!- eb(x);$$
$$eb(0) \circ\!\!- \top;$$
$$\circ\!\!- el(N_1, 1(0)) \otimes \cdots \otimes el(N_M, M(0)) \otimes count(M, (M{+}1)(0))$$
$$\otimes max(m, (M{+}2)(0)) \otimes p_{G_2}(0).$$

Here is one of the possible derivations for the goal

$$\Leftarrow el(5) + el(8) + el(9) + count(3) + max(m),$$

where we use arabic numerals as an abbreviation for numerals in Peano's form:

$$
\begin{array}{l}
\mathrm{R} \dfrac{\top - \top}{eb(0)} \\[4pt]
\mathrm{R} \dfrac{}{eb(1(0)) \otimes eb(2(0)) \otimes eb(3(0)) \otimes eb(4(0)) \otimes eb(5(0)) \otimes p_{G_2}(0)} \quad m = 9 \\[4pt]
\mathrm{R} \dfrac{}{eb(1(0)) \otimes eb(2(0)) \otimes el(9, 3(0)) \otimes count(1, 4(0)) \otimes max(m, 5(0)) \otimes p_{G_2}(0)} \\[4pt]
\mathrm{R} \dfrac{}{eb(1(0)) \otimes eb([3(0), 2(0), 4(0), 5(0)]) \otimes g_{G_1}([m, 9, 8, 1], [3(0), 2(0), 4(0), 5(0)]) \otimes p_{G_2}(0)} \\[4pt]
\mathrm{R}^\star \dfrac{}{eb(1(0)) \otimes ge(9, 8, [3(0), 2(0), 4(0), 5(0)]) \otimes g_{G_1}([m, 9, 8, 1], [3(0), 2(0), 4(0), 5(0)]) \otimes p_{G_2}(0)} \\[4pt]
\mathrm{R} \dfrac{}{el(8, 2(0)) \otimes el(9, 3(0)) \otimes eb(1(0)) \otimes count(2, 4(0)) \otimes max(m, 5(0)) \otimes p_{G_2}(0)} \\[4pt]
\mathrm{R} \dfrac{}{el(8, 2(0)) \otimes eb([3(0), 1(0), 4(0), 5(0)]) \otimes g_{G_1}([m, 9, 5, 2], [3(0), 1(0), 4(0), 5(0)]) \otimes p_{G_2}(0)} \\[4pt]
\mathrm{R}^\star \dfrac{}{el(8, 2(0)) \otimes ge(9, 5, [3(0), 1(0), 4(0), 5(0)]) \otimes g_{G_1}([m, 9, 5, 2], [3(0), 1(0), 4(0), 5(0)]) \otimes p_{G_2}(0)} \\[4pt]
\mathrm{R} \dfrac{}{el(5, 1(0)) \otimes el(8, 2(0)) \otimes el(9, 3(0)) \otimes count(3, 4(0)) \otimes max(m, 5(0)) \otimes p_{G_2}(0)}.
\end{array}
$$

In the above derivation we have omitted the left part of the sequents and every substitution produced, except where the variable m is bound to 9, the required value. Successful derivations of $ge(\ldots)$ goals (the guards) are omitted, too.

5 Conclusions

SMR is a direct sprout of a small and well studied fragment of linear logic. It enriches it in a direction not yet sufficiently explored by proof theory, *viz.* sequentialization of the form seen above. It seems to us that what is needed from proof theory is a mix of parallel and sequential operators. At the best of the author's knowledge only the work [28, 27] exists. There, a calculus in which a noncommutative connective, intermediate between $\otimes$ and $\otimes$, is studied. The calculus is very complex, and involves ordered sequents and other structures more general than the usual ones. Nonetheless, the purely proof theoretical direction of research is very interesting, and we hope to find some useful relations between it and our language.

SMR is a powerful language, and we have shown three examples of different nature: a complex planning problem, a typical multiset rewriting application with a "chemical" flavor and the specification of two concurrent communicating processes. By the way, SMR is an obvious extension of HCL, in that a HCL clause $H \leftarrow B_1, \ldots, B_n$ is translated into SMR as $H \Leftarrow B_1 + \cdots + B_n$.

Compared to LO [3] (which uses the same underlying fragment of linear logic plus the & connective) we have only one "object." This is not necessarily a limit in the expressive power of the language, and is the only way in the linear logic framework to obtain a "non-tree" structure in the evolution of concurrent processes. In particular, here processes have complete view of other processes and very different forms of interaction are possible, not only communication through variable sharing.

SMR is completely realizable in LinLog [1] (which is a superset of LM), and in particular in the asynchronous fragment of linear logic.

We plan to fit SMR in a categorical construction we are presently pursuing in order to give a very general semantical characterization to multiset rewriting languages, following the approaches of [7, 8, 21].

Acknowledgments

We wish to thank Antonio Brogi, Paola Bruscoli, Paolo Ciancarini, Pietro Di Gianantonio, Giorgio Levi, Dale Miller and Paolo Volpe for the many helpful comments.

References

[1] Jean-Marc Andreoli. Logic programming with focusing proofs in linear logic. *Journal of Logic and Computation*, 2(3):297–347, 1992.

[2] Jean-Marc Andreoli, Paolo Ciancarini, and Remo Pareschi. Interaction Abstract Machines. In G. Agha, P. Wegner, and A. Yonezawa, editors, *Trends in Object-Based Concurrent Computing*. The MIT Press, 1993.

[3] Jean-Marc Andreoli and Remo Pareschi. Linear Objects: Logical processes with built-in inheritance. *New Generation Computing*, 9:445–473, 1991.

[4] Jean-Pierre Banâtre and Daniel Le Métayer. The Gamma model and its discipline of programming. *Science of Computer Programming*, 15(1):55–77, November 1990.

[5] Gérard Berry and Gérard Boudol. The Chemical Abstract Machine. In *Proc. of the 17th ACM Symp. on Principles of Programming Languages*, pages 81–93, 1990.

[6] Antonio Brogi. And-parallelism without shared variables. In David H.D. Warren and Peter Szeredi, editors, *Logic Programming, Proceedings of the Seventh International Conference*, pages 306–321. The MIT Press, 1990.

[7] Andrea Corradini and Andrea Asperti. A categorical model for logic programs: Indexed monoidal categories. In *Proceedings of the REX Workshop, Beekbergen (NL)*, pages 110–137, 1992.

[8] Andrea Corradini and Ugo Montanari. An algebraic semantics for structured transition systems and its application to logic programs. *Theoretical Computer Science*, 103:51–106, 1992.

[9] Moreno Falaschi, Giorgio Levi, and Catuscia Palamidessi. A synchronization logic: Axiomatics and formal semantics of generalized Horn clauses. *Information and Control*, 60:36–69, 1984.

[10] Jean Gallier. Constructive logics. Part II: Linear logic and proof nets. Available by anonymous ftp from ftp.cis.upenn.edu, July 1992.

[11] Jean Gallier. Constructive logics. Part I: A tutorial on proof systems and typed λ-calculi. *Theoretical Computer Science*, 110:249–339, 1993. Available by anonymous ftp from ftp.cis.upenn.edu.

[12] Gerhard Gentzen. Investigations into logical deduction. In M.E. Szabo, editor, *The Collected Papers of Gerhard Gentzen*. North-Holland Publishing Co., 1969.

[13] Jean-Yves Girard. Linear logic. *Theoretical Computer Science*, 50:1–102, 1987.

[14] Jean-Yves Girard. *Proof Theory and Logical Complexity, Volume I*, volume 1 of *Studies in Proof Theory*. Bibliopolis, 1987. Distributed by Elsevier Science Publishing Co.

[15] Jean-Yves Girard, Yves Lafont, and Paul Taylor. *Proofs and Types*, volume 7 of *Cambridge Tracts in Theoretical Computer Science*. Cambridge University Press, 1990.

[16] Gerd Große, Steffen Hölldobler, Josef Schneeberger, Ute Sigmund, and Michael Thielscher. Equational logic programming, actions, and change. In Krzysztof Apt, editor, *Proceedings of the Joint International Conference and Symposium on Logic Programming*, pages 177–191. The MIT Press, 1992.

[17] J.A. Harland and D.J. Pym. A uniform proof-theoretic investigation of linear logic programming. To appear in the Journal of Logic and Computation, 1993.

[18] Narciso Martí-Oliet and José Meseguer. From Petri nets to linear logic through categories: A survey. Technical Report SRI-CSL-91-07, SRI International, April 1991.

[19] M. Masseron, C. Tollu, and J. Vauzeilles. Generating plans in linear logic I. Actions as proofs. *Theoretical Computer Science*, 113:349–370, 1993.

[20] J. McCarthy and P.J. Hayes. Some philosophical problems from the standpoint of artificial intelligence. *Machine Intelligence*, 4:463–502, 1969.

[21] José Meseguer. Conditional rewriting logic as a unified model of concurrency. *Theoretical Computer Science*, 96:73–155, 1992.

[22] Dale Miller. The π-calculus as a theory in linear logic: Preliminary results. In Evelina Lamma and Paola Mello, editors, *Proceedings of the 1992 Workshop on Extensions to Logic Programming*, Lecture Notes in Computer Science, pages 242–265. Springer-Verlag, 1993. Available by anonymous ftp from ftp.cis.upenn.edu and as technical report MS-CIS-92-48 from the Computer Science Department, University of Pennsylvania.

[23] Dale Miller, Gopalan Nadathur, Frank Pfenning, and Andre Scedrov. Uniform proofs as a foundation for logic programming. *Annals of Pure and Applied Logic*, 51:125–157, 1991.

[24] Luís Monteiro. Distributed logic: A logical system for specifying concurrency. Technical Report CIUNL-5/81, Departamento de Informática, Universidade Nova de Lisboa, 1981.

[25] Luís Monteiro. Distributed logic: A theory of distributed programming in logic. Technical report, Departamento de Informática, Universidade Nova de Lisboa, 1986.

[26] Wolfgang Reisig. *Petri Nets. An Introduction*, volume 4 of *EATCS Monographs on Theoretical Computer Science*. Springer-Verlag, 1985.

[27] Christian Retoré. Pomset logic. Available by anonymous ftp from cma.cma.fr, December 1993.

[28] Christian Retoré. *Réseaux et Séquents Ordonnés*. PhD thesis, Université Paris 7, February 1993.

Semantics II

Computing Annotated Logic Programs

Sonia M. Leach, James J. Lu
Bucknell University
Lewisburg, PA 17837
{leach,lu}@pleiades.cs.bucknell.edu

Abstract

Annotated Logics is a formalism that has been applied to a variety of situations in knowledge representation, expert systems, quantitative reasoning, and hybrid databases [3, 11, 12, 13, 14, 15, 21, 24, 25]. Annotated Logic Programming is a subset of Annotated Logics that can be used directly for programming Annotated Logic applications. In this paper, we investigate an approach to top-down query processing in Annotated Logic Programs that contains elements of constraint solving. The key to our approach is in observing that satisfaction, as introduced originally for Annotated Logic Programming (cf. [3, 15]), may be naturally generalized. Computationally, our method uses constraints in a way that differs from the Constraint Logic Programming scheme introduced by Jaffar, Lassez, and Lassez [8] in that constraints maintained within a proof need not be satisfied at each deduction step. Our approach simplifies a number of previous proposals and also improves on their efficiency. We describe a first computer implementation of the Annotated Logic Programming system. Overall, this paper offers new insights into the proof theory of Annotated Logic Programming, as well as an understanding of certain key implementation issues.

Keywords. Annotated Logic Programming, Constraint Solving, Query Processing

1 Introduction

Annotated Logics is a formalism that has been applied to a variety of situations in knowledge representation, expert systems, quantitative reasoning, and hybrid databases [3, 11, 12, 13, 14, 15, 21, 24, 25]. The distinguishing feature of annotated logics is the incorporation of names for truth values directly into the language of the logics. Such signing of formulas has been considered elsewhere including by [20, 7] for analyzing multiple-valued logics, by [2] for evidential reasoning, and by [26] for fuzzy reasoning.

As the utility of Annotated Logics becomes more apparent, the next important set of research questions to address includes the development of proof procedures for automated reasoning in Annotated Logics, and the examination of issues related to implementing such procedures. A subset of Annotated Logics that has been considered most frequently is Annotated Logic Programming, which focuses on *Annotated Horn Clauses* (cf. [11, 3,

14, 15]). Due to the procedural interpretation naturally associated with Horn Clauses, Annotated Logic Programming can be used to directly implement many Annotated Logic applications.

The current paper investigates a query processing method for Annotated Logic Programming, and presents a prototype interpreter based on the method. The key to the development of our procedure is in observing that the semantics of Annotated Logic Programs can be naturally generalized. In [19], a variant of this generalization was introduced, which simplified the resolution proof procedure given in [13] for Annotated Logics. However, the proposal of [19] does not consider annotation variables and functions, and the direct application of the method is not amenable to computer implementation. Our procedure possesses the advantage of the simplified rule, yet it works with succinctly representable atoms where annotation variables and functions may occur.

Our procedure contains elements of constraint programming [16]. The inclusion of constraint solving mechanisms into logic programming is a topic of considerable interest in recent years [4, 10, 22]. In [15], the semantics of Annotated Logic Programs extended with constraints have been studied. Here, we discuss how the mechanism developed in [15] corresponds to *local propagation* [16], and can be used to solve queries in our system.

There is an interesting difference between our uses of constraints and the typical Constraint Logic Programming (CLP) scheme. In CLP, Horn clauses are augmented by constraints. At each step of a computation, the interpreter must ensure the solvability of the constraint. Unsolvable constraints cause backtracking. On the other hand, in our system, the solvability of constraints *defines* the satisfiability of a query. Constraints are associated with atoms in the query; they do not exist independently of the atoms. An unsolvable constraint does not cause backtracking, but instead, prompts further searches until a solvable constraint is found. Therefore constraints are continually *modified* until a solvable constraint is constructed. In CLP, an existing constraint does not change. Additional constraints, however, may be added.

We describe what we believe is a first implementation of an Annotated Logic Programming system. Compared to ordinary logic programming, the search space for a query in Annotated Logic Program is more complex. Certain issues absent in classical Horn clause programming surface in Annotated Logics programming. We illustrate these complexities and discuss possible strategies for reducing the search space.

2 Annotated Logic Programs

Throughout this paper, we assume that Δ is a fixed complete lattice with the associated ordering $\preceq$. The least upper bound and the greatest lower bound operators are denoted $\sqcup$ and $\sqcap$, respectively. For reasons that will become apparent, the operators $\sqcup$ and $\sqcap$ are required to be computable. The set

Δ constitutes those objects that are used for signing formulas in Annotated Logics. As described in [15], elements in Δ may be thought of as confidence factors, as degrees of belief, or as truth values. The requirement that Δ forms a lattice stems from the desire to use Δ for modeling certain epistemic concepts such as inconsistency. Other formalisms where an underlying algebraic structure forms the basis of logic programming semantics include the work of Fitting [6]. Signed formulas as considered in [20, 7], however, do not impose any structure on the set of annotations.

The simplest lattice, used in the original study on logic programming for reasoning with inconsistent information [3], is the lattice FOUR, which consists of the four elements $\top, \mathbf{t}, \mathbf{f}$, and $\bot$. The ordering $\preceq$ is the transitive reflexive closure of the relation $\prec$ where $\mathbf{t} \prec \top$, $\mathbf{f} \prec \top$, $\bot \prec \mathbf{t}$, and $\bot \prec \mathbf{f}$. Based on a lattice Δ, we may define an annotated logic $\mathbf{Q}_\Delta$. We assume that we have a language L consisting of finite sets of constant symbols, function symbols (with associated arities), predicate symbols (with associated arities), and infinitely many variables, called *object variables*, denoted $O\mathcal{V}$. Atoms are defined in the usual way (cf. [17]).

For each $i \geq 1$, we assume a set $\mathcal{F}_i$ of total continuous computable functions, called annotation functions, each of type $\Delta^i \to \Delta$. We use $A\mathcal{V}$ to denote the set of *annotation variables*, disjoint from $O\mathcal{V}$. An *annotation* is either an element of Δ, an element of $A\mathcal{V}$, or is an expression $f_i(\alpha_1, ..., \alpha_i)$ where $f_i \in \mathcal{F}_i$ and α_j, $1 \leq j \leq i$ are annotations.

Suppose A is an atom, and α is an annotation. Then $A : \alpha$ is an *annotated atom*. To maintain consistency with the terminology used in [15], an annotated atom $A : \alpha$ is *c-annotated* (constant annotated) if $\alpha \in \Delta$. It is *v-annotated* (variable annotated) if $\alpha \in A\mathcal{V}$. Otherwise, it is *t-annotated* (term annotated). If $A : \alpha$ is an annotated atom and $B_1 : \mu_1, ..., B_k : \mu_k$ are c- or v-annotated atoms, then

$$A : \alpha \leftarrow B_1 : \mu_1, ..., B_k : \mu_k$$

is an *annotated clause*. $A : \alpha$ is called the *head* of the clause, and $B_1 : \mu_1, ..., B_k : \mu_k$ is called the *body* of the clause. All variables (object or annotation) appearing in the clause are implicitly universally quantified at the beginning of the clause. A set of annotated clauses is called an *Annotated Logic Program*. Suppose $A : \mu$ is the head of an annotated clause where μ is a t-annotation that does not contain any annotation variables. Since each annotation function is computable, we may replace μ by the lattice element that is the result of carrying out the computation of all functions in μ on their arguments. Throughout this paper, we make the assumption that such a replacement is always made whenever possible.

Definition (Satisfaction). An interpretation I is a mapping from the set of ground atoms to Δ. It is said to satisfy

1. the ground c-annotated atom $A : \mu$ iff $\mu \preceq I(A)$.

2. the ground c-annotated conjunction $F_1, ..., F_n$ if it satisfies each of F_1 through F_n.

3. the ground c-annotated clause $A \leftarrow B_1, ..., B_n$ if whenever it satisfies $B_1, ..., B_n$, it also satisfies A.

4. the c-annotated clause $A \leftarrow B_1, ..., B_n$ if it satisfies each ground instance, obtained by replacing each object variable by a term. Different occurrences of the variable must be replaced with the same term.

5. the annotated clause $A \leftarrow B_1, ..., B_n$ if it satisfies each c-annotated instance, obtained by replacing each annotation variable by an element in Δ. Different occurrences of the variable must be replaced with the same object.

We use the symbol $\models$ to denote both satisfaction and logical consequence.

Example 1 ([15]) Let Δ be the lattice FOUR. Take P to be the ALP

$P_1 \quad p : V \leftarrow q(X) : V$

$P_2 \quad q(a) : \mathbf{t} \leftarrow$

$P_3 \quad q(b) : \mathbf{f} \leftarrow.$

Among the ground c-annotated instances of P_1 are:

$p : \mathbf{t} \leftarrow q(a) : \mathbf{t}$

$p : \mathbf{f} \leftarrow q(b) : \mathbf{f}.$

According to the definition for satisfaction, any interpretation that satisfies the program must assign to p an element in FOUR that is greater than or equal to $\mathbf{t}$ and $\mathbf{f}$. Clearly, the only such element is $\top$ itself. Hence $P \models p : \top$.

Variables that occur in the head but not in the body of clauses are called *free variables*. Conversely, variables occurring only in the body but not in the head of a clause are called *local variables*. The following proposition states it is without loss of generality to consider only ALPs absent of local and free variables.

Proposition 1 Suppose P is an ALP. Let P_1 be the ALP obtained from P by first eliminating from each clause each annotated atom that contains a local annotated variable, and then replacing each free variable by $\top$. Then P and P_1 have the same models. ∎

3 Query Processing in ALPs

The most popular technique for answering queries in Logic Programs is based on SLD-resolution [17]. The main advantage in using an SLD-style proof procedure is, as noted in [15], the choice of clauses that need to be considered at each deduction step is restricted to the current goal and the program clauses. Unfortunately thus far, finding an SLD-style proof procedure has proven elusive for ALPs [14, 15]. The difficulty lies in the need to compute *reductants* (defined below). We illustrate this in the next example. First we give some necessary definitions.

To handle complex annotation terms and annotation variables, Kifer and Subrahmanian introduced the notion of constrained queries [15]. A *lattice constraint* Ξ is an expression of the form

$$\kappa_1 \preceq \tau_1, ..., \kappa_m \preceq \tau_m$$

where each κ is a c- or v-annotation, and each τ is an annotation. In the case that Ξ does not contain any annotation variables, then Ξ is said to be *solvable with respect to* Δ if each $\kappa_i \preceq \tau_i$ holds. Otherwise let $\{v_1, ..., v_n\}$ be all the annotation variables that occur in Ξ. Then Ξ is solvable with respect to Δ iff there is a set of lattice elements $\{\beta_1, ..., \beta_n\}$ such that $\Xi(\beta_1/v_1, ..., \beta_n/v_n)$ holds in Δ. Here, the expression $\Xi(\beta_1/v_1, ..., \beta_n/v_n)$ represents the variable free constraint obtained by simultaneously replacing each occurrence of v_i by β_i, for $1 \le i \le n$.

An expression of the form $\leftarrow \Xi \| A_1 : \mu_1, ..., A_n : \mu_n$ where Ξ is a lattice constraint is called a *constrained query*. In [15], the constraint part of a constrained query need not be restricted to lattice constraints. However, we focus only on lattice constraints in this paper since they must be handled for any system that includes an ALP component [3, 15, 21, 25]. The notion of satisfaction for constrained queries is immediate. Following are two inference rules for query answering in ALPs, introduced in [15].

Definition (Annotated resolution). Suppose $C = A : \rho \leftarrow B_1, ..., B_n$ is a clause and $Q = \leftarrow \Xi \| A_1 : \alpha_1, ..., A_m : \alpha_m$ is a constrained query with no variables in common with C. Moreover, suppose that for some $1 \le i \le m$, A_i is unifiable with A via mgu θ. Then the annotated resolvent of Q and C with respect to A_i is the query

$$\leftarrow \alpha_i \preceq \rho, \Xi \| (A_1 : \alpha_1, ..., A_{i-1} : \alpha_{i-1}, B_1, ..., B_n,$$
$$A_{i+1} : \alpha_{i+1}, ..., A_m : \alpha_m)\theta.$$

Definition (Reduction). Assume two annotated clauses

$A_1 : \mu_1 \leftarrow B_1 : \beta_1, ..., B_n : \beta_n$
$A_2 : \mu_2 \leftarrow C_1 : \gamma_1, ..., C_m : \gamma_m$

where A_1 and A_2 are unifiable via mgu θ. The *reductant* of the two clauses is the clause

$$(A_1 : \sqcup\{\mu_1, \mu_2\} \leftarrow B_1 : \beta_1, ..., B_n : \beta_n, C_1 : \gamma_1, ..., C_m : \gamma_m)\theta.$$

In terms of resolution theorem proving, an SLD-proof procedure does not exist for ALPs due to the incompatibility of the two rules of inference, annotated resolution and reduction, with the linear restriction strategy [18]. Kifer and Subrahmanian circumvent this difficulty by specifying that a deduction consists of only applications of annotated resolution. However, each inference may involve a resolution with an annotated clause obtained by implicit applications of the reduction procedure.

Example 2 Consider the program from Example 1. We have shown that the program entails $p : \top$. Hence the query $\leftarrow \| p : \top$ should have a refutation. Observe that if we do not use the reduction inference rule, the only possible annotated resolvent that can be obtained from the query is $\leftarrow \top \preceq V \| q(X) : V$. Resolving the new query with P_2 yields the query that contains the unsolvable constraint $\top \preceq V, V \preceq t$. Similarly, resolving with P_3 produces an unsolvable constraint. Hence no proof can be found.

Using the reduction inference on the other hand, we may first compute the reductant $p : \sqcup\{V_1, V_2\} \leftarrow q(X_1) : V_1, q(X_2) : V_2$ from two variants of P_1. This resolves with the original query, resulting in the constrained query $\leftarrow \top \preceq \sqcup\{V_1, V_2\} \| q(X_1) : V_1, q(X_2) : V_2$. Resolving the new query with P_2 and P_3 in succession yields the constrained query $\leftarrow \top \preceq \sqcup\{V_1, V_2\}, V_1 \preceq t, V_2 \preceq f \|$. As the constraint in the query is solvable, we have a refutation.

Unfortunately, the implicit use of reduction causes difficulties since a proof, which consists of only annotated resolution steps, may contain many deductions with clauses that are not in the original program. This makes the proof difficult to read. Moreover, application of the reduction inference is expensive since it must be allowed to occur any time during a deduction, thus greatly expanding the search space. This situation is analogous to the use of the restart rule in Disjunctive Logic Programming [23].

3.1 Regular Representation

The two inference rules, annotated resolution and reduction, appear to be very different in nature and as Example 2 illustrates, we must apply both in order to retain completeness. However, in [19], it was observed that the apparent disparity in the two rules vanishes under an appropriate translation of annotated clauses (along with an appropriate redefinition of satisfaction). Thus, a single unified inference rule exists. In turn, this enables a definition of a top-down (i.e. SLD-like) query processing procedure that has, up to this point, been absent.

The translation considered in [19] requires the replacement of each annotation by a subset of Δ. The resulting clauses are called *regular representations*. It can be shown that using regular representations, the only inference rule required for query processing is based on computing set intersection on the annotation sets.

Unfortunately, the explicit replacement of annotations by sets is not practical for implementation purposes. In most cases, the storage requirement for the set annotation is very large, and in some cases, it is impossible since the set is infinite. It follows that an alternative solution amenable to computer implementation is needed. We introduce next the notion of *constrained annotated atoms* to address precisely this issue. Constrained annotated atoms, unlike regular representations, have the advantage of being succinctly representable. Moreover, the proof procedure that we will introduce handles annotation variables and functions, which were not considered in [19].

3.2 Constrained Annotated Atoms and CA-Resolution

A *constrained annotation* is a pair $\langle \mu, S \rangle$ where μ is an annotation and S is a finite set of annotations. A *constrained annotated atom* is an expression $A : \mathcal{C}$ where A is an atom and $\mathcal{C}$ is a constrained annotation.

Definition (Satisfaction of Constrained Atom). An interpretation I satisfies a ground constrained annotated atom $A : \langle \mu, S \rangle$ iff $I(A) \in (\uparrow \mu) \cup (\uparrow \sqcup S)'$.

Given a lattice element γ, $\uparrow\gamma$ denotes the upset of γ (cf. [5]). In other words, $\uparrow\gamma = \{\delta \in \Delta | \gamma \preceq \delta\}$. Set complementation of a set A is denoted A'. Intuitively, a constrained annotated atom says that the truth value of A is either greater than or equal to μ, or is not greater than or equal to the least upper bound of S.

Example 3 Suppose I is the interpretation that assigns to p the value $\mathbf{t}$ in FOUR. Then I satisfies the constrained annotated atom $p : \langle \mathbf{t}, \{\}\rangle$, but it does not satisfy $p : \langle\top, \{\mathbf{t}\}\rangle$ since $(\uparrow\top) \cup (\uparrow \sqcup \{\mathbf{t}\})' = \{\top, \mathbf{f}, \bot\}$, which does not contain $\mathbf{t}$.

The following is immediate from the definition since $\mu \preceq \sqcup S$ iff $\uparrow \mu \cup (\uparrow \sqcup S)' = \Delta$, for any $\mu \in \Delta$ and $S \subseteq \Delta$.

Proposition 2 Let I be an interpretation and let $A : \langle\mu, S\rangle$ be a ground constrained atom such that $\mu \preceq \sqcup S$. Then I satisfies $A : \langle\mu, S\rangle$.

The definition of satisfaction of constrained atoms is the key generalization in the semantics of ALPs that enables us to introduce our proof procedure below. Note that the original definition of satisfaction of annotated atoms naturally fits into this more general definition. Since Δ is a lattice, $\sqcup\{\} = \bot$. If we have a ground constrained annotated atom $A : \langle\mu, \{\}\rangle$, then a satisfying interpretation I must assign, according to definition, an element in $(\uparrow \mu) \cup (\uparrow \bot)'$ to A. As $\uparrow \bot = \Delta$, it follows that $(\uparrow \bot)' = \{\}$. Hence $(\uparrow \mu) \cup (\uparrow \bot)' = \uparrow \mu$ and $I(A) \in \uparrow \mu$, the same condition as $\mu \preceq I(A)$.

Based on this observation, we see that constrained annotated atoms generalize ordinary annotated atoms since $A : \mu$ may be regarded equivalently as the special constrained annotated atom $A : \langle\mu, \{\}\rangle$. A query $\leftarrow A_1 : \mu_1, ..., A_n : \mu_n$ can therefore be rewritten

$$\leftarrow A_1 : \langle\mu, \{\}\rangle, ..., A_n : \langle\mu_n, \{\}\rangle$$

without changing its meaning. In general, we call a query consisting of only constrained annotated atoms a ca-query (constrained annotation query).

Let C be a conjunction of constrained annotated atoms $A_1 : \langle\mu_1, S_1\rangle, ..., A_n : \langle\mu_n, S_n\rangle$. The *constraint associated with* C, denoted $C_\mathcal{N}$, is the lattice constraint

$$\mu_1 \preceq \sqcup S_1, ..., \mu_n \preceq \sqcup S_n.$$

The following relates the solvability of $Q_\mathcal{N}$ and the unsatisfiability of $\leftarrow Q$.

Proposition 3 A ca-query $\leftarrow Q$ is unsatisfiable iff $Q_\mathcal{N}$ is solvable with respect to Δ. ∎

Definition (CA-Resolution). Let $A : \mu \leftarrow B_1 : \beta_1, ..., B_n : \beta_n$ be an annotated clause that does not share any object or annotation variables with the ca-query $\leftarrow A_1 : \mathcal{D}_1, ..., A_m : \mathcal{D}_m$, and suppose A_i and A are unifiable via mgu θ, for some $i \in \{1, ..., m\}$. Assuming that $\mathcal{D}_i$ is the constrained annotation $\langle\gamma, T\rangle$, then the ca-query

$$\leftarrow (A_1 : \mathcal{D}_1, ..., A_{i-1} : \mathcal{D}_{i-1}, A_i : \langle\gamma, T \cup \{\mu\}\rangle, B_1 : \langle\beta_1, \{\}\rangle, ...,$$

$$B_n : \langle\beta_n, \{\}\rangle, A_{i+1} : \mathcal{D}_{i+1}, ..., A_m : \mathcal{D}_m)\theta$$

is a ca-resolvent of the given clause and ca-query.

Observe that in creating the ca-resolvent, we first translate each annotated atom from the body of the annotated clause into an equivalent constrained annotated atom.

A deduction of a ca-query from a given ALP and an initial ca-query using ca-resolution is defined in the usual way. We call such a deduction a *ca-deduction*. A ca-deduction of a ca-query from an ALP is a *ca-proof* if the last clause in the deduction is unsatisfiable.

Example 4 Recall the program in Example 2. The initial query $\leftarrow p : \top$ may be represented equivalently as $\leftarrow p : \langle \top, \{\} \rangle$. A ca-proof of the query is shown below. The constraint associated with each ca-query is displayed below the query.

$Q_0 :\leftarrow p : \langle \top, \{\} \rangle$ (Initial Query)
     Constraint: $\top \preceq \perp$

$Q_1 :\leftarrow p : \langle \top, \{V_1\} \rangle, q(X_1) : \langle V_1, \{\} \rangle$ (ca-resolvent of Q_0 and P_1)
     Constraint: $\top \preceq V_1, V_1 \preceq \perp$

$Q_2 :\leftarrow p : \langle \top, \{V_1\} \rangle, q(a) : \langle V_1, \{t\} \rangle$ (ca-resolvent of Q_1 and P_2)
     Constraint: $\top \preceq V_1, V_1 \preceq t$

$Q_3 :\leftarrow p : \langle \top, \{V_1, V_2\} \rangle, q(X_2) : \langle V_2, \{\} \rangle, q(a) : \langle V_1, \{t\} \rangle$ (ca-resolvent of Q_2 and P_1)
     Constraint: $\top \preceq \sqcup\{V_1, V_2\}, V_1 \preceq t, V_2 \preceq \perp$

$Q_4 :\leftarrow p : \langle \top, \{V_1, V_2\} \rangle, q(b) : \langle V_2, \{f\} \rangle, q(a) : \langle V_1, \{t\} \rangle$ (ca-resolvent of Q_3 and P_2)
     Constraint: $\top \preceq \sqcup\{V_1, V_2\}, V_1 \preceq t, V_2 \preceq f$

We may verify that of the constraints associated with each of the queries in the above deduction, only the last one is solvable with respect to FOUR. Indeed, this is exactly the same constraint derived using reduction and annotated resolution shown in Example 2. Therefore we can see that, in one sense, the use of ca-resolution amounts to an incremental computation of reduction.

A point of interest that was emphasized in the introduction is how constraints are used differently in our system as compared to conventional CLP systems. Similar to classical logic programming, a ca-proof in ALP is obtained when an unsatisfiable query is derived. In a ca-deduction, the determination of whether a query $\leftarrow A_1 : \langle \mu_1, S_1 \rangle, ..., A_n \langle \mu_n, S_n \rangle$ is unsatisfiable depends on the solvability of the associated constraint $\mu_1 \preceq \sqcup S_1, ..., \mu_n \preceq \sqcup S_n$ (cf. Proposition 3). The unsolvability of this constraint does not cause backtracking, as can be seen in the example above. The first ca-resolvent of the proof is a satisfiable ca-query since there is no solution to the lattice constraint $\top \preceq \sqcup\{V_1\}, V_1 \preceq \perp$. In CLP, only solvable constraints are allowed to appear in each query of a deduction. A related difference in our approach is that constraints are modified during a deduction. The above unsolvable constraint associated with the first ca-resolvent in the example is modified to $\top \preceq \sqcup\{V_1\}, V_1 \preceq t$ in the second ca-resolvent. The goal of a ca-deduction therefore can be viewed as searching for a satisfiable constraint. In CLP, an existing constraint remains throughout a deduction.

3.3 Completeness Issues

The completeness result below holds under the condition that the given program possesses the *fixpoint reachability property*, discussed in [15]. The condition ensures that the least model of a given ALP is recursively enumerable. Hence any annotated atom that is a logical consequence of the program has a proof. Due to space limitation, we do not elaborate on this condition.

Theorem 1 CA-resolution is sound and complete for ALPs. ∎

Using ca-resolution, it is not necessary to compute reductants. This enhances the readability of proofs as they contain only program clauses, and increases efficiency by eliminating the expensive reduction inference rule. Moreover, using constrained annotated atoms, we need not explicitly represent set annotations as in [19], hence making it amenable for implementation. Annotation functions and variables are also not considered in [19]. CA-resolution thus represents the first complete top-down procedure for handling ALPs in its full generality.

In classical logic programming, an important theoretical result regarding SLD-resolution is the *independence of the computation rule* [17]. A computation rule specifies the literal in a query to resolve on at each step of a deduction. The result tells us that any computation rule will suffice. This enables for example, Prolog to safely choose the leftmost literal to resolve on at each step. (Of course, Prolog is still incomplete due to its use of depth-first search.) Unfortunately, in the case of ca-resolution, selecting systematically the leftmost or the rightmost literal causes incompleteness, even if we select clauses fairly.

Example 5 Suppose we adopt the selection rule of choosing the leftmost literal in a query. Consider the ALP over the lattice $[0, 1]$, where the ordering $\preceq$ is the usual relation $\leq$ on reals,

$$q : (V + W) \leftarrow p : V, r : W$$
$$p : 0.2 \leftarrow$$
$$r : 0.2 \leftarrow$$

and the ca-query $\leftarrow q : \langle 0.4, \{\} \rangle$. The first ca-resolvent is $\leftarrow q : \langle 0.4, \{(V + W)\} \rangle, p : \langle V, \{\} \rangle, r : \langle W, \{\} \rangle$. The associated constraint $0.4 \preceq (V + W), V \preceq 0, W \preceq 0$ is not solvable with respect to $[0, 1]$. It is easy to see that one may continue to resolve the leftmost literal with the first clause, but never obtain a solvable constraint.

Suppose on the other hand, we select the rightmost literal to resolve on. From the first ca-resolvent we obtain the ca-resolvent $\leftarrow q : \langle 0.4, \{(V + W)\} \rangle, p : \langle V, \{\} \rangle, r : \langle W, \{0.2\} \rangle$. Again the associated constraint $0.4 \preceq (V + W), V \preceq 0, W \preceq 0.2$ is not solvable. Resolving on the rightmost literal in the next deduction step yields the same ca-query.

One can see that no systematic selection of literals in this case can produce a proof of the original query, even though clearly $q : \langle 0.4, \{\} \rangle$ is a logical consequence of the program. Thus the independence of the computation rule does not hold for ca-resolution. One must select literals "fairly", in the sense that each literal will be tried eventually. This will be considered in Section 4.2 when the ALP interpreter is discussed.

3.4 Unsatisfiability of CA-queries and Normal Constraints

The key to implementing ca-resolution lies in determining solvability of constraints (with respect to Δ) associated with queries. Kifer and Subrahmanian have devised an algorithm for determining satisfiability of the class of *normal constraints* [15]. It turns out that normal constraints are exactly the class of lattice constraints we need to consider. A *normal constraint* is a lattice constraint

$$\kappa_1 \preceq \tau_1, ..., \kappa_n \preceq \tau_n$$

where if κ_i is a variable, then it does not occur in $\tau_1, ..., \tau_i$. For example, the constraint $V \preceq f(W), W \preceq g(V)$ is not a normal constraint since any ordering of the inequalities violates the required condition.

According to definition, annotations that occur in a query must be either c- or v-annotations. A ca-resolution of a query with a clause adds a constraint onto the literal resolved on in the query, and may introduce additional literals. The following is straightforward.

Proposition 4 Suppose $\leftarrow Q$ is a ca-query where $Q_{\mathcal{N}}$ is a normal constraint and P is an ALP. Let $\leftarrow R$ be any ca-resolvent of Q with a clause in P. Then $R_{\mathcal{N}}$ is a normal constraint. ∎

We call a ca-query $\leftarrow Q$ a *normal ca-query* if $Q_{\mathcal{N}}$ is a normal constraint. Since solvability of normal constraint is decidable [15], we may adopt Kifer and Subrahmanian's algorithm to test unsatisfiability of ca-queries. In order to make the paper self-contained, we include below their algorithm, which we have incorporated into our interpreter, and will analyze further in the next section.

Algorithm 1 *Input: A normal constraint $C = \kappa_1 \preceq \tau_1, ..., \kappa_n \preceq \tau_n$. Output: Boolean*

1. *If C is an empty constraint, return True;*

2. *Find $i_0 \geq 1$ such that i_0 is the maximal integer where κ_{i_0} is the same expression as κ_1 and substitute $\top$ for all variables that occur in $\tau_1, ..., \tau_{i_0}$.*

3. *If κ_1 is a constant then if $\kappa_1 \preceq \tau_1, ..., \kappa_{i_0} \preceq \tau_{i_0}$ is false in Δ, return False*
   Set C to $\kappa_{i_0+1} \preceq \tau_{i_0+1}, ..., \kappa_n \preceq \tau_n$, rearrange the indices of the constraints so that they start with 1, and goto step 1.

4. */* κ_1 is a variable */*
   Let $v = \sqcap\{\tau_1, ..., \tau_{i_0}\}$.
   Set C to $\kappa_{i_0+1}(v/\kappa_1) \preceq \tau_{i_0+1}(v/\kappa_1), ..., \kappa_n(v/\kappa_1) \preceq \tau_n(v/\kappa_1)$ and goto 1.

4 An ALP Interpreter

We have implemented in C an interpreter for ALPs based on ca-resolution. In this section, we focus on the important modules in our interpreter. Following the approach of [9], our interpreter for ALP consists of a Prolog-like inference engine and a constraint solver. A third module distinct to our system is a function to select the next literal to resolve on. In Prolog, the usual method is to apply resolution to the leftmost literal of the query in each step of a deduction. The theoretical issue of the independence of computation rule was considered in Section 3.3. In Section 4.2, we discuss strategies for selecting literals within a query.

The inference engine performs ca-resolution. Thus its task includes performing unification on object variables, and constructing and modifying constraints associated with each ca-query in a deduction. The constraint solver is used to determine unsatisfiability of a ca-query. Efficient lattice algorithms exist for computing greatest lower bounds and least upper bounds (e.g. [1]) of finite lattices and they will be incorporated into our interpreter. Currently, the algorithm used by the constraint solver is adapted from Algorithm 1.

4.1 The Constraint Solver

The constraint $Q_\mathcal{N}$ associated with each ca-query $\leftarrow Q$ can be represented graphically. For example, the normal constraint $U \preceq \top, V \preceq \mathbf{t}, V \preceq \mathbf{f}, \mathbf{t} \preceq \sqcup\{U, V\}$ associated with the ca-query

$$\leftarrow p_1 : \langle \mathbf{t}, \{U, V\}\rangle, p_2 : \langle V, \{\mathbf{f}\}\rangle, p_3 : \langle V, \{\mathbf{t}\}\rangle, p_4 : \langle U, \{\top\}\rangle$$

has the graphical representation shown in Figure 1. Circular nodes represent operators. Constants are operators that require no arguments. Square nodes represent variables. We call the nodes occurring on the far left *origins* of the graph, and the single node occurring on the far right the *destination* of the graph. This representation allows us to view constraints associated with ca-queries as constraint graphs (cf. [16]), which may be solved by *local propagation*. A constraint graph is satisfiable when the variables take on values that make the specified relation true. The relation implicitly specified by the graph above is that the value associated with the arc that terminates at the destination is greater than or equal to the value of the destination. In the given example, the graph in Figure 1 is satisfied since the value that emanates from the $\sqcup$ node is $\top$.

Representing normal constraints as constraint graphs in the above manner, one can see that Algorithm 1 corresponds to local propagation. In step 4, the algorithm computes the values of the origins, and propagates the results along the arcs to the right to fill in the values for the variables. When the least upper bound left of the destination is eventually computed, the result is checked against the value of the destination in step 3. The order in which values are computed is thus strictly left to right, delineated by operator nodes. In particular, to compute the value for each of the nodes

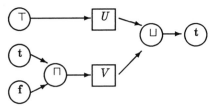

Figure 1: A Constraint Graph

containing $\sqcup$ and $\sqcap$, all nodes whose arcs terminate at the operator node must first be evaluated, and the resulting values propagated.

The node labeled with $\sqcap$ is obtained from the two inequalities $V \preceq \mathbf{t}$ and $V \preceq \mathbf{f}$, since any lattice element γ that satisfies both inequalities must satisfy $\gamma \preceq \sqcap\{\mathbf{t}, \mathbf{f}\}$. Note this is also the basis behind step 4 of Algorithm 1, which can be stated in the next proposition.

Proposition 5 Given a normal constraint $\Xi = \kappa_1 \preceq \tau_1, ..., \kappa_n \preceq \tau_n$. Suppose for some $1 \leq i < j \leq n$, κ_i and κ_j are the same variable. Then the constraint

$$\kappa_1 \preceq \tau_1, ..., \kappa_{i-1} \preceq \tau_{i-1}, \kappa_{i+1} \preceq \tau_{i+1}, ..., \kappa_j \preceq \sqcap\{\tau_i, \tau_j\}, ..., \kappa_n \preceq \tau_n$$

is solvable iff Ξ is solvable. ∎

Typically a constraint associated with a ca-query consists of several disjoint constraint graphs. For example, the constraint associated with the query

$$\leftarrow p : \langle \mathbf{t}, \{V\}\rangle, q : \langle V, \{\top\}\rangle, r : \langle \mathbf{t}, \{\mathbf{f}\}\rangle$$

contains two disjoint constraint graphs. The first is formed by the constraints associated with the p and q atoms, namely $\mathbf{t} \preceq V, V \preceq \top$. The second is formed from the r atom with the single inequality $\mathbf{t} \preceq \mathbf{f}$. We refer to each set of atoms that forms an independent constraint graph as a *network*. Equivalently, a network of a ca-query $\leftarrow Q$ is an element in the partition π of the atoms in Q where for each pair $N_1, N_2 \in \pi$, no annotation variable occurs in both N_1 and N_2. Thus the two networks in the above ca-query are $N_1 = \{p : \langle \mathbf{t}, \{V\}\rangle, q : \langle V, \{\top\}\rangle\}$, and $N_2 = \{r : \langle \mathbf{t}, \{\mathbf{f}\}\rangle\}$. A result that parallels the independence of computation rule in classical logic programming is that for ALPs, networks can be solved independently.

Proposition 6 Suppose $\leftarrow Q$ is a query that contains networks $N_1, ..., N_k$. Then $\leftarrow Q$ has a ca-proof iff each of $\leftarrow N_1, \leftarrow N_2, ..., \leftarrow N_k$ has a ca-proof, and the resulting substitutions of the object variables are compatible. ∎

4.2 Literal Selection Strategies

Example 5 demonstrated the importance of eventually trying each literal in a network. In this subsection, we analyze possible strategies for selecting literals. Interestingly, each literal selection strategy relates to how the constraint graph is modified. Recall the earlier discussion on the difference

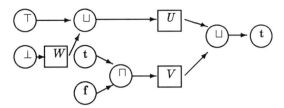

Figure 2: A Modified Constraint Graph

between how constraints are used in our system as compared to their use in conventional CLP systems. In a ca-deduction, a constraint is continually modified until a solvable constraint is constructed. As constraints can be represented by constraint graphs, it is therefore not surprising that the order in which literals are selected for performing ca-resolution determines how the associated constraint graph changes. We illustrate this point with an example.

Example 6 Let us reconsider the constraint graph corresponding to the query

$$\leftarrow p_1 : \langle t, \{U, V\}\rangle, p_2 : \langle V, \{f\}\rangle, p_3 : \langle V, \{t\}\rangle, p_4 : \langle U, \{\top\}\rangle$$

shown in Figure 1.

If we select the atom $p_4 : \langle U, \{\top\}\rangle$ to perform ca-resolution, and if our program contains the clause $p_4 : W \leftarrow p_5 : W$, then the ca-resolvent is

$$\leftarrow p_1 : \langle t, \{U, V\}\rangle, p_2 : \langle V, \{f\}\rangle, p_3 : \langle V, \{t\}\rangle, p_4 : \langle U, \{\top, W\}\rangle, p_5 : \langle W, \{\}\rangle.$$

The constraint graph that represents the associated constraint is shown in Figure 2. One sees that the origin of the graph has been modified, and the overall depth of the graph is increased since the longest path now is of length five. Suppose on the other hand, the atom $p : \langle t, \{U, V\}\rangle$ is chosen first for applying ca-resolution. This does not change the depth of the graph, but instead modifies the graph by adding new arcs that terminate at the node ⊔ left of the destination.

For our interpreter, we have classified constrained atoms into four categories, which has enabled the development of literal selection strategies. With respect to the constraint graph, one of the literal selection strategies corresponds to modifying the graph in a "depth-first" manner, where the length of some path in the graph is increased, as illustrated in the previous example. Orthogonally, literals may be selected so as to modify the constraint graph "breadth-first". Each of these strategies for selecting literals is a *guidance strategy*, in the same spirit as guidance strategies are used in theorem proving [27]. Such a strategy imposes an ordering on the search space, but does not eliminate any part of it. It is generally accepted in theorem proving that the usefulness of guidance strategies typically can only be supported experimentally. We are currently experimenting with several literal selection strategies to determine their effectiveness.

5 Discussion

The ability to answer queries in ALPs using constraints is not a novelty. Kifer and Subrahmanian developed the first query processing procedure through constraint solving [14, 15]. However, existing proof procedures requires complex machinery, namely both annotated resolution and reduction, for constructing the necessary normal constraints. The bottleneck rests with the restrictive semantics currently defined for satisfaction of annotated atoms. In this paper, we presented a top-down resolution procedure with constraint solving for processing queries in ALPs based on the observation that the semantics of annotated atoms may be naturally generalized to set membership. The new procedure captures the effect of earlier approaches through a considerably smaller search space. However, constraints within our procedure are handled differently from conventional CLP systems, and certain completeness issues absent in classical Horn clause programming surface with the new procedure. All the theoretical development in this paper has been driven by practical implementation concerns.

Acknowledgement: We are grateful to the National Science Foundation for supporting this work under the RUI-Grant CCR9225037.

References

[1] H. Aït Kaci, R. Boyer, R. Lincoln, R. Nasr, Efficient Implementation of Lattice Operations, *ACM Transactions on Programming Language and Systems*, 11, 1, 115– 146, 1989.

[2] J.F. Baldwin, Evidential Support Logic Programming, *Fuzzy Sets and Systems*, 24, 1–26, 1987.

[3] H.A. Blair, V.S. Subrahmanian, Paraconsistent Logic Programming, *Theoretical Computer Science*, 68, 135–154, 1989.

[4] J. Cohen, Constraint Logic Programming Languages, *Communications of the ACM*, 33, 7, 52–68, 1990.

[5] B.A. Davey and H.A. Priestley, *Introduction to Lattices and Order*, Cambridge University Press, 1990.

[6] M. Fitting, Bilattices and the Semantics of Logic Programming, *Journal of Logic Programming*, 11, 91–116, 1991.

[7] R. Hähnle, Uniform Notation Tableau Rules for Multiple-valued Logics, *Proceedings of the International Symposium on Multiple-Valued Logic*, 26–29, 1991.

[8] J. Jaffar, J-L Lassez, C. Lassez, Constraint Logic Programming, tutorial notes given in the Fourth IEEE Symposium on Logic Programming, 1987.

[9] J. Jaffar, S. Michaylov, Methodology and Implementation of a CLP System, tutorial notes given in the Fourth IEEE Symposium on Logic Programming, 1987.

[10] J. Jaffar, S. Michaylov, P. Stuckey, R. Yap, The CLP(R) Language and System, *ACM Transactions on Programming Languages and Systems*, 14, 3, 339-395, 1992.

[11] M. Kifer, A. Li, On the Semantics of Rule-based Expert Systems with Uncertainty, *Proceedings of the 2nd International Conference on Database Theory*, 102–117, 1988.

[12] M. Kifer, E. Lozinskii, RI: A Logic for Reasoning with Inconsistency, *IEEE Symposium on Logic in Computer Science*, 253–262, 1989.

[13] M. Kifer, E. Lozinskii, A Logic for Reasoning with Inconsistency, *Journal of Automated Reasoning*, 9, 179–215, 1992.

[14] M. Kifer, V.S. Subrahmanian, On the Expressive Power of Annotated Logics, *Proceedings of the North American Conference on Logic Programming*, 1069–1089, 1989.

[15] M. Kifer, V.S. Subrahmanian, Theory of Generalized Annotated Logic Programming and its Applications, *Journal of Logic Programming*, 12, 335–367, 1992.

[16] W. Leler, *Constraint Programming Languages: Their Specification and Generation*, Addison-Wesley, 1988.

[17] J.W. Lloyd, *Foundations of Logic Programming*, 2nd ed., Springer, 1988.

[18] D.W. Loveland, A Unifying View of some Linear Herbrand Procedures, *Journal of the ACM*, 19, 366–384, 1972.

[19] J.J. Lu, N.V. Murray, E. Rosenthal, Signed Formulas and Annotated Logics, *Proceedings of the 23rd International Symposium on Multiple-Valued Logics*, 48–53, 1993.

[20] N.V. Murray, E. Rosenthal, Signed Formulas: A Liftable Meta-Logic for Multiple-Valued Logics, *Proceedings of International Symposium on Methodologies for Intelligent Systems*, 275–284, 1993.

[21] R. Ng, V.S. Subrahmanian, A Semantical Framework for Supporting Subjective and Conditional Probabilities in Deductive Databases, *Journal of Automated Reasoning*, 10, 191–235, 1993.

[22] P. Van Hentenryck, *Constraint Satisfaction in Logic Programming*, MIT Press, 1989.

[23] D.W. Reed, D.W. Loveland, Near-Horn Prolog and the Ancestry Family of Procedures, presented at the symposium *Logic in Databases, Knowledge Representation and Reasoning* at the University of Maryland Institute for Advanced Computer Studies, Nov. 1993.

[24] V.S. Subrahmanian, Paraconsistent Disjunctive Databases, *Theoretical Computer Science*, 93, 115–141, 1992.

[25] V.S. Subrahmanian, Amalgamating Knowledge Bases, manuscript. Accepted to appear in ACM Transactions on Database Systems.

[26] T.J. Weigert, J-P. Tsai, X. Liu, Fuzzy Operator Logic and Fuzzy Resolution, *Journal of Automated Reasoning*, 10, 59–78, 1993.

[27] L. Wos, *Automated Reasoning: 33 Research Problems*, Prentice Hall, 1988.

Conditional Logic Programming

D.Gabbay Department of Computing
Imperial College of Science and Technology
180 Queen's Gate - London SW7 2BZ, UK
e-mail: dg@doc.ic.ac.uk

L.Giordano, A.Martelli, N. Olivetti
Dipartimento di Informatica
Università di Torino
C.so Svizzera 185 - 10149 Torino, ITALY
e-mail: {laura,mrt,olivetti}@di.unito.it

Abstract

In this paper we propose a logic programming language which supports hypotetical updates together with integrity constraints. The language makes use of a revision mechanism, which is needed to restore consistency when an update violates some integrity constraint. The revision policy adopted is based on the simple idea that more recent information is preferred to earlier one. We show how this language can be used in planning applications, non-monotonic and counter-factual reasoning. We also define a model-theoretic semantics for it and we point out some connections with belief revision.

1 Introduction

This paper lies in the common ground of belief revision (or database updates) and logic programming. We aim at defining a logic programming language which is able to deal with hypothetical reasoning when integrity constraints are present. The language, called *CondLP* (for *Conditional Logic Programming*), is an extension of NProlog [GaRe84, Gabbay85]. As in NProlog and in other similar logic programming languages [Miller86, Miller89, McCa88a, McCa88b], Horn clause logic is extended to allow embedded implications both in goals and in clause bodies. Embedded implications are implications of the form $D \Rightarrow G$, where G is a goal and D is a set of clauses local to G. Operationally in NProlog, an embedded implication $D \Rightarrow G$ succeeds from a program P if G succeeds from the enlarged program $P \cup \{D\}$. D can be regarded as an *update* to the current program, that only affects the proof of G.

Here we will consider the case when D contains a single fact, and hence we will write the embedded implications as $A \Rightarrow G$, where A is an atom. Moreover, we allow in the program integrity constraints of the form $G \rightarrow \bot$, whose meaning is that G must be false ($\bot$ is a distinguished symbol denoting falsity).

In our language, as a difference with respect to NProlog, when an implication goal $A \Rightarrow G$ has to be proved, the fact A may be inconsistent with the actual program P, i.e. adding A to P may produce the violation of one or more constrains. When this happens, a *revision* of the program is needed in order to restore consistency.

To revise the current program in face of an update, we follow a *formula-based approach*, that is, the semantics of an update is based on the formulas present in the programs, rather than on the models of the program as it happens in the model-based approach (see [Winslett90]). Moreover, we consider the program to be composed of a protected part and a removable part. All clauses and integrity constraints belong to the protected part so that they cannot be removed to restore consistency. Only facts in the removable part of the program can be given up. Also, we keep track of the order in which facts have been introduced in the program and we make the assumption that older facts are more likely to be removed than more recent facts. The set of removable facts is assumed to be totally ordered (by a time ordering). With this assumption, we can always obtain a uniquely revised program. It must be observed, however, that the actual choice of the temporal ordering and of the revision function (remove the oldest facts) is motivated only by some possible applications we have in mind, such as planning, default and counterfactual reasoning. In principle the choice could be different and our operational semantics can be thought of as being parametric with respect to these choices.

We finish this preliminary discussion by presenting an example (from [GaRe84]):

Example 1 Let P be the program, containing the clauses and constraints:
$$british\_citizen(X,T) \leftarrow born\_in\_UK(X) \wedge father(X,Y)$$
$$\wedge(alive(Y,T) \Rightarrow british\_citizen(Y,T))$$
$$british\_citizen(Z,T_2) \leftarrow british\_citizen(Z,T_1) \wedge less\_than(T_1,T_2)$$
$$\wedge alive(Z,T_2)$$
$$dead(X) \wedge alive(X) \rightarrow \perp,$$

and the list of facts:
$$L = born\_in\_UK(bob), father(bob,tom), british\_citizen(tom,1950),$$
$$dead(tom,1984), less\_than(1950,1984).$$
The clauses and constraints belong to the protected part of the program, while all facts are removable and ordered as they are listed. The goal
$$G = british\_citizen(bob,1984)$$
succeeds. In fact, the subgoals $born\_in\_UK(bob)$ and $father(bob,tom)$ succeed from P. The subgoal $alive(tom,1984) \Rightarrow british\_citizen(tom,1984)$ succeeds from P since $british\_citizen(tom,1984)$ succeeds from the revised program $P_{alive(tom,1984)}$, obtained from P by adding $alive(tom,1984)$ and removing $dead(tom,1984)$ (which is the oldest fact inconsistent with the addition

alive(tom, 1984*))*.

While an embedded implication can be interpreted as an update operation that adds the implication antecedent temporarily to the program, an embedded implication together with integrity constraints can be used to model an update operation that removes a fact temporarily: deletion is performed implicitly by restoring consistency after addition. For instance, let us assume that a fact q is derivable from a program P and that we want to prove a goal G in a revised program where q is deleted. In order to allow this, it is sufficient to have in the program the integrity constraint $q \wedge not_q \rightarrow \bot$, where not_q is a new proposition, and prove the goal $not_q \Rightarrow G$. Adding not_q to the program produces an inconsistency, which is removed by deleting the oldest facts in P supporting q.

The problem of maintaining consistency in face of new contradictory information has been widely studied in belief revision and in database theory (see [Winslett90] for a survey), in the context of view updates [FUV83, FKUV88, RN89] and, more specifically, concerning logical databases in [MW87, NR90, GL90]. In particular, [NR90] provides a procedure for reasoning over inconsistent data, with the aim of supporting temporal, hypothetical and counter-factual queries. As in [NR90] we adopt the idea that earlier information is superseded by later information. As a difference, we provide update operations in the language itself, by making use of embedded implications. Hence, our proposal is on the same line of [MW87, FH88], which provide update operations within the language.

In [FH88] a logic containing a modal operator *assume[L]* (where L is a literal) is defined, to represent addition and deletion of atomic formulas. Differently from us they follow a model-based approach to revision.

The paper by Manchanda and Warren [MW87] presents the language DLP, based on a dynamic logic of updates. DLP extends logic programs with update goals of the form $< +p > G$ or $< -p > G$, whose meaning is that the goal G should be proved in a new database updated by adding (deleting) the fact p to the extensional part. This language has some similarities with ours, since also in CondLP we update the database by adding facts, but there are also substantial differences. In fact, DLP does not cope with integrity constraints, and so the addition or deletion of a fact does not affect all other facts in the database. Instead, CondLP only allows for the addition of facts, though, as mentioned above, *deletion* of facts can be implicitly represented.

The problem of belief revision in logic programming has also been stuidied for logic programs with default and explicit negation in [PAA91], and for Truth Maintenance Systems in [GM90].

The outline of the paper is the following. In Section 2 we define the language and its operational semantics in the propositional case. In Section 3 we show some examples. In Section 4 we define a model-theoretic semantics and we give soundness and completeness results with respect to the operational semantics. In Section 5 we explore some connections with belief revision. Finally, in Section 6 we sketch the extension to the first order case.

2   The Operational Semantics

In this section we define the syntax of CondLP and we define its operational semantics. We will deal with the propositional case, the first order estension will be sketched in Section 6.

Let *true* and $\perp$ be distinguished propositions (true and false) and let A denote atomic propositions different from $\perp$. The syntax of the language is the following:

$$\text{G:= } true \mid \text{A} \mid G_1 \wedge G_2 \mid A \Rightarrow G$$
$$\text{D:= } G \rightarrow A$$
$$\text{I:= } G \rightarrow \perp.^1$$

In this definition G stands for a goal, D for a clause and I for an integrity constraint.

Notice that, in a clause $G \rightarrow A$ and in a constraint $G \rightarrow \perp$, G can contain embedded implications of the form $A \Rightarrow G'$. Moreover, we have used two different arrows $\rightarrow$ and $\Rightarrow$ for the implication in clause definitions and in embedded implications (we will often call them *implication goals*).

Let us define the operational semantics of the language. Since we want to keep track of the order in which facts have been introduced in the program, we represent a program P as follows: $P = \Delta \parallel L$, where $\Delta = S \cup IC$ is a set of clauses (S) and integrity constraints (IC), and $L = A_1, \ldots, A_n$ is a list of facts. While the facts in L can be removed from the program when an inconsistency arises, the clauses in Δ cannot be removed, they are *protected*. Note that we can represent a protected atom A in Δ by the clause $true \rightarrow A$. Thus in the following we will assume that Δ can contain clauses, atoms and constraints. The ordering of facts in the list is a time ordering: A_i is regarded to be older (and hence less preferable) than A_{i+1}. Thus lists represent ordered sets of atoms with respect to a temporal ordering. Lists are assumed to be without repetitions, so that when adding an atom A to a list $L = A_1, \ldots, A_n$, the atom A is appended to the end of L and if, for some i, $A_i = A$, then A_i is removed. Given a program $\Delta \parallel L$, and an atom A we write $\Delta \parallel L, A$ to denote the result of adding A to L.

---

[1] Our interpretation and use of falsity requires some comment. The fragment of N-Prolog containing implication and conjunction is based on intuitionistic logic, which for this fragment is identical with minimal logic. When falsity $\perp$ is added, we can define $\neg A$ as $A \rightarrow \perp$ and we have two options. One is to regard $\perp$ as a constant without any special properties, in which case we have adopted the minimal logic negation. The other is to regard $\perp$ as implying anything (ie $\perp \vdash B$ for any B) in which case we adopted intuitionistic logic negation. Since we will use $\perp$ to record integrity constraints in the program, and we do not want to derive everything from the violation of integrity constraints, then we will adopt minimal logic, and we will give no special meaning to the constant $\perp$.

To define the operational semantics for this language we need to define the following:

1. *derivability of a goal from a program,*

2. *a consistency check procedure,*

3. *the updating function*: this will take care of revising a program $P = \Delta \parallel L$ with respect to an atom A. We select the *maximal* subset M of L such that $M \wedge A \wedge \Delta$ is consistent. Thus we must define:

4. *an ordering relation* between subsets of L, with respect to which we take the maximal elements.

(1) The derivability relation

The operational derivability of a given goal G from a program $P = \Delta \parallel L$ (written $\Delta \parallel L \vdash_o G$) is defined by the following proof rules:

1. $\Delta \parallel L \vdash_o true$;

2. $\Delta \parallel L \vdash_o A$ if $A \in L$, or there is a clause $G \to A \in \Delta$ such that $\Delta \parallel L \vdash_o G$;

3. $\Delta \parallel L \vdash_o G_1 \wedge G_2$ if $\Delta \parallel L \vdash_o G_1$ and $\Delta \parallel L \vdash_o G_2$;

4. $\Delta \parallel L \vdash_o A \Rightarrow G$ if $(\Delta \parallel L)_A \vdash_o G$,

   where $(\Delta \parallel L)_A$ is the program P updated with A (to be defined below).

(2) The consistency check procedure

Given a set of clauses, facts, and integrity constraints Γ we define when $\Gamma \vdash_c \bot$. The relation $\Gamma \vdash_c \bot$, means that $\bot$ succeeds from Γ; in this case, we say that Γ is inconsistent. The relation $\vdash_c$ is defined as in standard propositional NProlog. Integrity constraints are treated as ordinary clauses.

1. $\Gamma \vdash_c true$;

2. $\Gamma \vdash_c Q$ if $Q \in \Gamma$ or there is a clause $G \to Q \in \Gamma$ such that $\Gamma \vdash_c G$,
   (where $Q = A$ or $Q = \bot$);

3. $\Gamma \vdash_c G_1 \wedge G_2$ if $\Gamma \vdash_c G_1$ and $\Gamma \vdash_c G_2$;

4. $\Gamma \vdash_c A \Rightarrow G$ if $\Gamma \cup \{A\} \vdash_c G$;

Notice that when evaluating an implication goal $A \Rightarrow G$, A is simply added to Γ. The relation $\vdash_c$ corresponds to derivability in minimal logic.

(3) The updating function

We now define the updating function $(\Delta \parallel L)_A$:

$$(\Delta \parallel L)_A = \begin{cases} \Delta \parallel M, A & \text{if } M \subseteq L \text{ is the } \preceq_L\text{-maximal subset of } L \text{ s.t.} \\ & \Delta \cup M \cup \{A\} \not\vdash_c \bot \\ \Delta \parallel L, A & \text{if } \Delta \cup \{A\} \vdash_c \bot \end{cases}$$

Notice that, when the update A is inconsistent with the protected part Δ, A is simply added to the program. A plausible motivation for this choice is that, when A is inconsistent with the protected part, nothing can be removed to restore consistency. The only reasonable alternative in this case would be not to add A, but this would violate one basic property we want: the update A always makes A true (so that the goal $A \Rightarrow A$ always succeeds).

(4) The ordering relation

A list $L = A_1, \ldots, A_n$ may be seen as a totally ordered set of atoms, where $A_i < A_{i+1}$. We recursively define a (total) ordering $\preceq_L$ between subsets of L as follows:

- $\emptyset \preceq_L S$ for every subset S;

- $R \preceq_L S$ if either $max(R) < max(S)$, or $max(R) = max(S)$ and
  $$(R - \{max(R)\}) \preceq_L (S - \{max(S)\}).$$

where, for each subset S of L, $max(S)$ is the atom in S with maximal index. For instance, given $L = A, B, C, D, E, F$, we have that:

$$\{A, B, C, F\} \prec_L \{C, D, F\}$$

where $R \prec_L S$ is defined as $R \preceq_L S$ and $R \neq S$.

From the definition of updating function and of $\preceq_L$-maximality, when $\Delta \cup L \cup \{A\} \not\vdash_c \bot$, we have $M = L$. This means that if $\Delta \cup L \cup \{A\}$ is consistent, then A is simply added to the program.

The definition of the operational semantics depends on the updating function. In turn, the definition of the updating function uniformly depends on the consistency check procedure, and on the $\preceq_L$-ordering relation. Changing one of these items, we would obtain a different revision function. Thus we may think of our operational semantics as parametric with respect to the revision function, and the latter as parametric with respect to the consistency check procedure and the $\preceq_L$- ordering relation.

In order to compute the revised program, given an update, we need a function which inputs a program $P = \Delta \parallel L$, and an atom A, and outputs the $\preceq_L$-maximal subset M of L such that

$$\Delta \cup M \cup \{A\} \not\vdash_c \bot.$$

We assume that $\Delta \cup \{A\} \not\vdash_c \bot$. In what follows, we offer two simple ways of using the proof procedure $\vdash_c$ to compute such a set M.

The first method is very simple. Let $P = \Delta \parallel L$, with $L = A_1, \ldots, A_k$, and let A be the atom we want to add to the program. The set M can be computed as follows.

At the beginning we set M to be empty. For each $A_i \in L$, starting from the newest one (A_k), add A_i to M; if the resulting program $\Delta \cup \{A\} \cup M$ is inconsistent then delete A_i from M; otherwise, keep A_i in M and step to the next (older) fact A_{i-1}.

Algorithm $MAX1(P, A)$:

$M := \emptyset$;
for $i = k$ to 1
  if $\Delta \cup M \cup \{A, A_i\} \not\vdash_c \perp$ **then** $M := M \cup \{A_i\}$
end for

It is easy to see that the set $M = MAX1(P, A)$, built up by the algoritm $MAX1$, is the $\preceq_L$- maximal consistent subset of L, and if such a set exists it will be computed by $MAX1$.

Proposition Let $P = \Delta \parallel L$, be a program and A be an atom. Suppose that $\Delta \cup \{A\} \not\vdash_c \perp$. Then $M = MAX1(P, A)$ is the $\preceq_L$-maximal subset of L, such that $\Delta \cup M \cup \{A\} \not\vdash_c \perp$.

When the current program P is known to be consistent, the consistency of an update A with P can be checked in a more efficient way than looking backward for a proof of $\perp$. The integrity checking method proposed by Sadri and Kowalski [SaKo87] is based on the idea of reasoning forward from the update A to derive the contradiction. To this purpose, they define an extension of SLDNF proof procedure, which allows arbitrary clauses (not only goals) to be used as top clause and makes use of an extended resolution step for reasoning forward from negated facts. Their language also admits negation as failure. A similar method for consistency checking could be defined for our language that contains embedded implications and used in the above algorithm to perform the consistency check.

An alternative method for computing M, the $\preceq_L$-maximal consistent subset of L, is based on the idea of finding all the possible $\vdash_c$-proofs of $\perp$ from $\Delta \cup L \cup \{A\}$, recording for each derivation $\mathcal{D}_l$, the set of atoms $F_l \subseteq L$ used in that derivation of $\perp$. Following ATMS-terminology [DeKleer86], we call the sets F_l *nogoods*. Suppose we determine in some way all nogoods $F_1, \ldots, F_n$, for a given program P and update A. Let F be the set of the oldest elements of each F_i. Since atoms are totally ordered there is a unique minimal subset R of F such that removing R, no inconsistency is derivable anymore. The following algorithm computes such R and removes it from L. In the following, for each subset S of L, we denote by *min(S)* the atom in S with the minimal index (i.e., the oldest atom in S).

Algorithm $MAX2$

Step 1 Compute all nogoods for P and A. Let such nogoods be $F_1, \ldots F_n$.
Let $F = \{min(F_l) : l = 1 \ldots n\}$;

Step 2 compute M by the following procedure:

1. let $K = F$, $H = [1, \ldots, n]$, and $R = \emptyset$;
2. Let B $= max(K)$;
3. for each $l \in H$, if $B \in F_l$, then remove l from H;
4. add B to R;
5. **if** $H = \emptyset$ **then** set $M := L - R$ and STOP;
   else set $K = \{min(F_l) : l \in H\}$ and go to step (2).

It can be proved that the algoritm is correct and complete, i.e. the set M computed by $MAX2(P, A)$ is the $\preceq_L -maximal$ consistent subset of L.

Proposition
Let $P = \Delta \parallel L$, be a program and A be an atom. Suppose that $\Delta \cup \{A\} \not\vdash_c \perp$. Then $M = MAX2(P, A)$ is the $\preceq_L$-maximal subset of L, such that $\Delta \cup M \cup \{A\} \not\vdash_c \perp$.

3 Some Examples

Example 2 (Planning Application)
Consider the blocks world, where states are described with the predicates $on(X, Y)$, $clear(X)$ and $ontable(X)$. Though so far we have only discussed the propositional case, in this example we will make use of a first order language. The predicate case will be discussed in some detail in Section 6.
We have the integrity constraints
$$on(X, Y) \wedge on(X, Z) \wedge diff(Y, Z) \to \perp$$
$$clear(X) \wedge on(Y, X) \to \perp$$
$$on(X, Y) \wedge ontable(X) \to \perp$$
The initial state is represented by a list of facts. Consider, for instance, the list
$$L = on(a, b), clear(a), clear(c), ontable(b), ontable(c)$$

that describes the state in which a is on b, both b and c are on the table, and nothing is on a and c. In order to find a plan to achieve a goal G, we define a predicate $holds(G, S)$, where S is a sequence of operators which have to be applied to the initial state to reach a state satisfying the goal G. The rules for holds are the following:

$$holds(G, []) \leftarrow G.$$

$$holds(G, [move(X,Y)|S]) \leftarrow clear(X) \wedge clear(Y) \wedge diff(X,Y) \wedge on(X,Z) \wedge$$
$$(on(X,Y) \Rightarrow (clear(Z) \Rightarrow holds(G,S))).$$

$$holds(G, [move\_to\_table(X)|S]) \leftarrow clear(X) \wedge on(X,Y) \wedge$$
$$(ontable(X) \Rightarrow (clear(Y) \Rightarrow holds(G,S))).$$

$$holds(G, [move\_from\_table(X,Y)|S]) \leftarrow clear(X) \wedge ontable(X) \wedge$$
$$clear(Y) \wedge diff(X,Y) \wedge (on(X,Y) \Rightarrow holds(G,S)).$$

The first rule is used when G holds in the current state. The second rule describes the operator $move(X,Y)$, for moving a block X on top of block Y. If the preconditions $clear(X)$, $clear(Y)$, $diff(X,Y)$, $on(X,Z)$ hold, then the operator can be applied, and the derivation continues in a new state, where the facts $on(X,Y)$ and $clear(Z)$ are added, and all inconsistent facts of the previous state are automatically removed. Similarly, the other rules describe other operators. For instance, starting with the previous list L and the goal

$$holds(on(a,c), S),$$

the second rule can be applied with the bindings

$$X = a, Y = c, Z = b, S = [move(a,c)|S']$$

Then the goal

$$holds(on(a,c), S')$$

succeeds with S '= [] from the updated list

$$L' = clear(a), ontable(b), ontable(c), on(a,c), clear(b)$$

where $on(a,c)$, $clear(b)$ have been added to L, whereas $on(a,b)$ and $clear(c)$ have been deleted because they are inconsistent with the more recent facts.

Similarly, the derivation of

$$holds((on(a,b), on(b,c)), S)$$

succeeds from L with

$$S = [move\_to\_table(a), move\_from\_table(b,c), move\_from\_table(a,b)]$$

It is clear that this language with updates and constraints supports some form of non-monotonic reasoning. The following example shows how it can be used to represent simple default inferences.

Example 3 Let $P = \Delta \parallel normal_{bird}$ be a program with protected part
$\Delta = \{bird \wedge normal_{bird} \rightarrow fly.$
     $true \rightarrow bird.$
     $penguin \rightarrow bird.$

$$penguin \rightarrow notfly.$$
$$fly \wedge notfly \rightarrow \bot.\}$$

The goals $G_1 = fly$ and $G_2 = penguin \Rightarrow notfly$ both succeed from P. Let us consider the goal G_2. We have that $\Delta \cup \{normal_{bird}, penguin\} \vdash_c \bot$ and $F = \{normal_{bird}, penguin\}$ is the unique nogood. Hence, $P_{penguin} = \Delta \parallel penguin$ (the fact $normal_{bird}$ is deleted), and $P_{penguin} \vdash_o notfly$. Therefore, the goal G_2 succeeds from P.

4 Semantics

In this section we present a first attempt to define a logical intepretation of our language. We will define a simple model-theoretic semantics and we will show its equivalence with the operational semantics of section 2. Since the operational semantics makes use of two procedures, we expect that the model-theoretic semantics will involve two notions of validity: one is the counterpart of the consistency-check procedure and the other of the top-level derivability relation. As we have already remarked the former is intended to mean validity in minimal logic. Firstly, we review minimal logic Kripke structures. In minimal logic models, there is no need of interpreting in a different way goal implication $\Rightarrow$ from clause implication $\rightarrow$; thus, their interpretation will be the same.

Definition Given a propositional language $\mathcal{L}$, with connectives $\{\wedge, \rightarrow, \Rightarrow, true, \bot\}$, an interpretation M is a triple (W, R, I), where W is a non-empty set, R is a reflexive-transitive relation on W, I is a function which assigns sets of propositional atoms (i.e subsets of $Atom_{\mathcal{L}}$) to elements of W. Moreover, function I satisfies the following condition:

$$\forall w, w' \in W(wRw' \Rightarrow I(w) \subseteq I(w')).$$

Truth in an interpretation $M = (W, R, I)$ is defined as follows:

$M, w \models true,$
$M, w \models A$ if A is an atom and $A \in I(w),$
$M, w \models F \wedge H$ if $M, w \models F$ and $M, w \models H,$
$M, w \models F \rightarrow H$ (the same for $F \Rightarrow H$) if for all $w' \in W$ such that wRw' it holds that:

$$\text{if } M, w' \models F \text{ then } M, w' \models H.$$

Falsum $\bot$ is regarded as any other atom, so that for some w it is possible that $\bot \in I(w)$. Next we define:

$$M \models F \text{ iff } \forall w \in W, \ M, w \models F,$$

and for any set of formulas Δ:

$$M \models \Delta \text{ iff } \forall H \in \Delta, \ M \models H.$$

We finally define, for any set Δ and formula F:

$$\Delta \models F \text{ iff } \forall M,\ M \models \Delta \Rightarrow M \models F.$$

This concludes the description of minimal logic semantics. With respect to the operational semantics, we have the following result ([Gabbay85, Miller86, McCa88a]).

Theorem (Soundness and Completeness of the consistency-check procedure) For all sets of formulas Δ and formulas F, it holds that:

$$\Delta \vdash_c F \text{ iff } \Delta \models F.$$

Now we turn to the logical interpretation of the top level operational semantics. To this purpose, given a propositional language $\mathcal{L}$ (over the logical constants $\{true, \wedge, \Rightarrow, \rightarrow\}$) let $\Sigma_{\mathcal{L}}^{\#}$ be the set of finite sequences of atoms of $\mathcal{L}$ *without repetitions*. On $\Sigma_{\mathcal{L}}^{\#}$ we introduce the operation $+$. Let $\alpha = A_1 \dots A_n \in \Sigma_{\mathcal{L}}^{\#}$, then for any atom B:

$$\alpha + B = \begin{cases} A_1 \dots A_{i-1} A_{i+1} \dots A_n B & \text{if, for some } i,\ A_i = B \\ \alpha B & \text{otherwise.} \end{cases}$$

Definition Given a program Δ, a Δ-*structure* is a triple $(\Sigma_{\mathcal{L}}^{\#}, I, S_\Delta)$, where

- I is a function of type $\Sigma_{\mathcal{L}}^{\#} \rightarrow 2^{Atom_{\mathcal{L}}}$ which satisfies the following condition: for each $\alpha \in \Sigma_{\mathcal{L}}^{\#}$, if A occurs in α then

$$A \in I(\alpha).$$

- S_Δ is a function of type $\Sigma_{\mathcal{L}}^{\#} \times Atom_{\mathcal{L}} \rightarrow \Sigma_{\mathcal{L}}^{\#}$ satisfying the following conditions

  1. for each α and B, $S_\Delta(\alpha, B) = \gamma + B$, where γ is a subsequence of α;
  2. if $S_\Delta(\alpha, B) = \gamma + B$ then $\Delta \cup \{B\} \not\models \bot$ implies $\Delta \cup \gamma \cup \{B\} \not\models \bot$.

We define truth (of clauses and goals) in any Δ- structure $M = (\Sigma_{\mathcal{L}}^{\#}, I, S_\Delta)$ as follows:

$M, \alpha \Vdash_{op} true,$
$M, \alpha \Vdash_{op} A$ if A is an atom and $A \in I(\alpha)$;
$M, \alpha \Vdash_{op} F \wedge H$ if $M, \alpha \Vdash_{op} F$ and $M, \alpha \Vdash_{op} H$;
$M, \alpha \Vdash_{op} F \rightarrow H$ iff for all $\beta \in \Sigma_{\mathcal{L}}^{\#}$, $M, \beta \Vdash_{op} F$ implies $M, \beta \Vdash_{op} H$;
$M, \alpha \Vdash_{op} A \Rightarrow H$ (where A is an atom) if $M, S_\Delta(\alpha, A) \Vdash_{op} H$.

We also write $M, \alpha \Vdash_{op} S$, where S is a set of formulas if $M, \alpha \Vdash_{op} H$, for every $H \in S$.

Notice, in the above definition, that the two implications $\Rightarrow$ and $\rightarrow$ have a completely different interpretation. Furthermore, we may observe that the definition of truth in a Δ-structure depends on the underlying minimal logic only through the conditions on the function S_Δ which is intended to represent the revision function. Thus, changing the conditions on S_Δ, would leave the definiton of truth formally unaltered.

We next define a preorder relation on Δ structures.

Definition Given two Δ-structures $M = (\Sigma_{\mathcal{L}}^\#, I, S_\Delta)$ and $N = (\Sigma_{\mathcal{L}}^\#, I', S'_\Delta)$, we say that M is *less preferred* than N (denoted by $M \preceq N$) iff for all $\alpha \in \Sigma_{\mathcal{L}}^\#, B \in Atom_{\mathcal{L}}$ it holds that:

$$S_\Delta(\alpha, B) \preceq_\alpha S'_\Delta(\alpha, B),$$

where the relation $\preceq_\alpha$ is that one defined in section 2. Having defined such a preorder among Δ-structures the notion of *most preferred* Δ-structures is defined as well.

Given a database $\Delta = S \cup IC$, (where S is a set of clauses not involving $\perp$, IC is a set of integrity constants,) a string of atoms $\alpha \in \Sigma_{\mathcal{L}}^\#$, and a goal G we say that $\Delta \parallel \alpha$ *entails* G, denoted by:

$$\Delta \parallel \alpha \Vdash_{op} G,$$

if and only if for every *most preferred* Δ-structure M, if $M, \alpha \Vdash_{op} S$ then $M, \alpha \Vdash_{op} G$.

Now we come to the main result of this section, namely soundness and completeness of the operational semantics with respect to the semantic entailment defined above.

Theorem (Soundness and completeness of the operational semantics) For any database Δ, string $\alpha \in \Sigma_{\mathcal{L}}^\#$ and goal G, we have:

$$\Delta \parallel \alpha \vdash_o G \text{ if and only if } \Delta \parallel \alpha \Vdash_{op} G.$$

(Proof is omitted because of lack of space.)

The semantics we have presented is simple and tailored for the operational semantics. However, it may be thought of as an instance of a more general semantic framework, since it depends in a uniform way on the properties of the revision function S_Δ, and on the relation $\preceq$ among Δ-structures. This parametric character of the model-theoretic semantics matches the corresponding feature of the operational semantics presented in section 2.

As a further step we will study a more abstract semantics for this language in the style of *sphere semantics* of conditional logics. This would be important in order to establish a precise link between our language and conditional logics.

5   Connections with Belief Revision

We have seen that updates can be expressed in the language by using implication goals. Since the addition of new information by updates can produce
inconsistencies, updating a program containing constraints involves a revision process. As mentioned above, in the previous section we have followed
a *formula-based* approach to revision. Given a program P and an update formula A, the revised program P_A is obtained from P by deleting the minimal
set of oldest facts sufficient to restore consistency. The revision produces a
uniquely revised program.

The kind of revision we have proposed is a special case of *priorized base
revision* presented by Nebel in [Nebel91]. Priorized base revision is a form of
syntax based revision in which the belief base Z, to which revision is applied,
is partitioned into disjoint *priority classes* Z_i, $i \geq 1$. In our case, priority
classes are singletons: each class contains a fact, A_i, so that the set of facts
$A_1, \ldots, A_n$ plays the role of Z.

Let us reformulate, within the context of minimal logic, the definition
of priorized base revision of finite belief bases, given in [Nebel91]. Let $\vdash$
be derivability in minimal logic and $Cn(S)$, for a set of formulas S, be the
set of logical consequences of S in minimal logic. Let Z be a belief base
partitioned into disjoint priority classes Z_i, $i \geq 1$ and let x be a formula.
The *priorized removal of x* (written $Z \Downarrow x$) is the set of all maximal subsets
of Z not implying x, where the sentences in Z_i have higher priority than
those in Z_j if $i < j$:

$$Z \Downarrow x = \Big\{ Y \subseteq Z \mid Y \nvdash x, Y = \bigcup_{i \geq 1} Y_i,$$
$$\forall i \geq 1 : (Y_i \subseteq Z_i \text{ and}$$
$$\forall X : Y_i \subset X \subseteq Z_i \Rightarrow (\textstyle\bigcup_{j=1}^{i-1} Y_j \cup X) \vdash x \Big) \Big\}.$$

When the belief base Z is finite, the priorized base revision operation, denoted by $\oplus$, can be defined as follows:

$$Z \oplus x = \begin{cases} Cn\left(\left(\bigvee(Z \Downarrow \neg x)\right) \wedge x\right), & \text{if } \nvdash \neg x \\ Z \wedge x, & \text{otherwise.} \end{cases}$$

The correspondence between our definition of P_A and the notion of priorized base revision can be stated as follows.

Proposition Let $P = \Delta \parallel A_1, \ldots, A_n$ and let $Z = \{A_1, \ldots, A_n\}$ be a belief
base with priority classes $Z_j = \{A_{n-j+1}\}$, $j \geq 1$. For all atoms A and B,
$\quad P_A \vdash B$ iff $B \in Z \oplus (A \wedge \Delta)$.

Note that the class $\{A_{i+1}\}$, has higher priority than $\{A_i\}$. Updating with
an atom A a program P with protected part Δ, corresponds to updating the
revisable part of P with A and Δ.

Given a program P and un update A, the revised program P_A satisfies the conditions below, that roughly correspond to the Gärdenfors postulates for revision [Gärdenfors88] (those which do not explicitly involve conjunctive updates):

1. $A \in Cn[(\Delta \parallel L)_A]$

2. $Cn[(\Delta \parallel L)_A] \subseteq Cn[\Delta \parallel L, A]$

3. if $\perp \notin Cn[\Delta \parallel L, A]$, then $Cn[(\Delta \parallel L)_A] \supseteq Cn[\Delta \parallel L, A]$

4. if $\perp \in Cn[(\Delta \parallel L)_A]$, then $\perp \in Cn[\Delta \parallel A]$.

6 The Predicate Case

In this section we outline how to extend the operational semantics presented in section 2 to a first order language. The syntax of goals and clauses is extended by allowing universally quantified clauses, as follows:
$$D ::= G \rightarrow A \mid \forall x D.$$
Notice that a clause, and hence a program may contain *free variables* (i.e. unquantified variables) to be thought of as parameters. A fact is an atom, and variables in a fact are assumed to be free; thus an atom $q(z)$ is different from a unit clause $\forall z q(z)$. In the following, given a program $P = \Delta \parallel L$, we will assume that L is a list of facts. We will also assume that the initial program in any derivation is closed.

The first order extension is subject to several difficulties. The first problem is that the operational semantics of the language makes use of a consistency check procedure, and consistency of a set of first order formulas is *not decidable*. Hence we must expect that the consistency check procedure sometimes fails to give an answer.

Another problem concerns *existential variables* that can be introduced in a program because of embedded implications. Indeed, in order to prove a goal $D(X) \Rightarrow G(X)$, the clause $D(X)$ (containing the free variable X) has to be added to the program. Existential variables in the program make difficult to define a revised program with respect to a given update, since inconsistency may arise or not according to how free variables will be instantiated.

In the following we outline a possible way to deal with this problem. On the other hand, at the end of this section we also discuss how the introduction of existentially quantified variables in the program can be prevented by putting some syntactic condition on programs.

Consider the following example. Let
$$P = \Delta \parallel natural\_haired(tom), natural\_haired(fred)$$
be a program with protected part Δ:
$$\Delta = \begin{cases} \forall X (fair(X) \wedge dark(X) \rightarrow \perp). \\ \forall Y (greek(Y) \wedge natural\_haired(Y) \rightarrow dark(Y)). \\ \forall U (albino(U) \rightarrow fair(U)). \\ albino(tom). \end{cases}$$

The goal $G_1 = greek(fred) \Rightarrow dark(fred)$ succeeds from P. We have that $greek(fred)$ can be consistently added to the program and $dark(fred)$ can be proved from the resulting program. On the contrary, the goal $G_2 = greek(tom) \Rightarrow dark(tom)$ fails from P. In fact, adding $greek(tom)$ to the program gives an inconsistency: the program is revised by removing $natural\_haired(tom)$, and $dark(tom)$ fails from the resulting program.

Let us now consider the goal $G_3 = greek(Z) \Rightarrow dark(Z)$. The variable Z is implicitly existentially quantified in G_3, and, hence, we would expect that G_3 also succeeds from P with answer more general than $Z = fred$. In order to prove G_3 the program must be revised by adding the fact $greek(Z)$. If Z is bound to tom, we get an inconsistency with P, so that we want the fact $natural\_haired(tom)$ to be removed from the program. Otherwise, we do not want this fact to be removed.

A possible way to update the program with the nonground fact $greek(Z)$, is as follows: add $greek(Z)$ to the database and record (to preserve consistency), that Z must be different from tom. This can be done by adding to the query $dark(Z)$ the constraint $(Z \neq tom)$. Then the goal $dark(Z)$ is resolved with the first clause in Δ, so that the new goal to be proved is $greek(Z) \wedge natural\_haired(Z) \wedge (Z \neq tom)$. The first two subgoals succeed with answer $Z = tom$, which does not satisfy the constraint, and with the answer $Z = fred$, which satisfies the constraint $(Z \neq tom)$. Thus, the initial query succeeds with $Z = fred$.

In this way, the computation proceeds, by accumulating constraints on the variables free in the program, which have to be satisfied for the computation to succeed.

In general, given a program $P = \Delta \parallel L$ and an implication goal $G' = A(Z) \Rightarrow G(Z)$, let us assume that $\Delta \cup \{L, A(Z)\} \vdash_c \bot$ with (a finite number of) answer substitutions $\theta_1, \ldots, \theta_k$. These substitutions give the bindings for the variables free in G' and in P, which make $A(Z)$ inconsistent with the current program. Given $\theta_1, \ldots, \theta_k$, it is possible to compute an *equality formula* $\neg E_\bot$ (a formula built from equalities and inequalities), which represents all variable bindings that make $\Delta \cup \{L, A(Z)\}$ consistent. Then, the goal G' succeeds if the following happens: either (i) the goal $G(Z)$ succeeds for some answer substitution θ, satisfying the equality formula $\neg E_\bot$, so that $A(Z)\theta$ is consistent with the current database; or (ii) there is a substitution θ_i (which makes $A(Z)$ inconsistent with the current database) such that the goal $G(Z)\theta_i$ succeeds from the revised program $(\Delta \parallel L\theta_i)_{A(Z)\theta_i}$.

The assumption that the set of answer substitutions $\theta_1, \ldots, \theta_k$ for which $\Delta \cup \{L, A(Z)\} \vdash_c \bot$ is finite is essential. Under this assumption, it is possible to determine an equality formula which represents the whole answer to the query $\bot$. In particular, each answer substitution θ_i can be viewed as an equality formula

$$E_i \equiv (x_1 = x_1\theta_i) \wedge \ldots \wedge (x_n = x_n\theta_i)$$

where $x_1, \ldots, x_n$ are the free variables in $\Delta \cup \{L, A(Z)\}$, and the whole answer to the query $\bot$ is given by the disjunction

$$E_\perp \equiv E_1 \vee \ldots \vee E_k.$$

The negation of the formula $E_\perp$ is the equality formula $\neg E_\perp \equiv \neg E_1 \wedge \ldots \wedge \neg E_k$ which represents the variable bindings that make $\Delta \cup \{L, A(Z)\}$ consistent.

Of course, to deal with such equalities and inequalities the proof procedure must be extended. The whole matter is quite similar to the so-called *constructive negation* in logic programming [Chan88, Przy89, Stuckey91]. In [Przy89] a notion of *equality-definable programs* is introduced to design the class of programs for which all answers to a query can be represented by an equality formula. Not all programs have this property. For instance, the program containing the two clauses $p(a)$ and $\forall X(p(X) \rightarrow p(f(X)))$ has an infinite set of answer substitutions, which cannot be represented by an equality formula.

We have mentioned above that it is possible to prevent the introduction of existentially quantified variables in the program, by putting some syntactic restrictions on programs. The syntactic condition that is needed happens to be quite similar to the *allowedness condition* defined for general logic programs, i.e., logic programs with negation as failure. The usual allowedness condition [Lloyd84, Kunen89] forces all negative literals in a goal to be ground, when all the positive literals have been selected. In this way, in a computation starting from an allowed program and an allowed goal, it cannot happen that a goal contains only nonground negative literals (this is called a floundering situation, since in this case a safe computation rule cannot select any literal). In a similar way, to prevent the introduction of existential variables in the program, here we do not want implication goals $A \Rightarrow G$ to be selected when the antecedent A is not ground. Hence, we need a condition which guarantees that, during a computation, if a goal contains only embedded implications, then there is at least one of them, $A \Rightarrow G$, such that A is ground. Such a condition, still called *allowedness*, has been defined in [GiOl92] for a logic programming language containing both embedded implications and negation as failure. Obviously, that allowedness condition works as well for this language with embedded implications, but without negation as failure. In particular, the allowedness condition in [GiOl92] ensures that all answer substitutions to a query are ground.

7 Conclusions and Future Research

In this paper we have defined a logic programming language which is an extension of NProlog and supports hypotetical updates together with integrity constraints. The language makes use of a revision mechanism, which is needed to restore consistency when an update violates some integrity constraint in the database. The revision policy adopted here is based on the simple idea that more recently introduced information is preferred to earlier one. However, different policies could be adopted, by modifying the ordering relations between the revisable facts, with respect to which both the operational and the model-theoretic semantics are parametric.

In our proposal, each time an update is performed in the proof of a given goal and an inconsistency arises, the database is modified by deleting some facts. An alternative approach, which has been pursued in [Cholvy93, NR90], is to keep all possibly inconsistent information, so that the proof procedure itself maintains the consistency of logical consequences of the database according to the priority among fact. We believe that this alternative proposal is worth to be further investigated in the context of an hypotetical language like ours.

Acknowledgement

This work has been partially supported by the ESPRIT Basic Research Project 6471, Medlar II.

References

[Cholvy93] L.CHOLVY, Proving Theorems in a Multi-source Environment, *in* Proc. IJCAI93, Chambery, vol. 1, pp. 66-71, 1993.

[Chan88] D.CHAN, Constructive Negation Based on the Completed Database, *in* Proc. Fifth Logic Programming Symposium, MIT Press, 1988.

[DeKleer86] J. DE KLEER, An Assumption-Based TMS, *in* Artificial Intellingence 28, pp. 127-162 (1986).

[FKUV88] R.FAGIN, G.KUPER, J.ULLMAN, M.VARDI, Updating Logical Databases, *in* Advances in Computing Research, P.Kanellakis ed., Morgan-Kaufman, Los Altos, CA, 1988.

[FUV83] R.FAGIN, J.ULLMAN, M.VARDI, On the Semantics of Updates in Databases, *in* Proc. of the 2nd ACM Symp. on Principles of Database Systems, 1983

[Gärdenfors88] P.GÄRDENFORS, *Knowledge in Flux: Modelling the Dynamics of Epistemic States*, The MIT Press, 1988.

[GaRe84] D.M. GABBAY, U. REYLE, N-Prolog: an Extension of Prolog with Hypothetical Implications.I, *in* J. Logic Programming 4:319-355 (1984).

[Gabbay85] D.M. GABBAY, N-Prolog: an Extension of Prolog with Hypothetical Implications.II. Logical Foundations and Negation as Failure, *in* J. Logic Programming 4:251- 283 (1985).

[FH88] L. FARIÑAS DEL CERRO, A. HERZIG, An Automated Modal Logic for Elementery Changes, *in* Non-Standard Logics for Automated Reasoning, (P.Smets et al. ed.) Academic Press, 1988, pp.63-79.

[GM90] L. GIORDANO, A. MARTELLI, Generalized Stable Models, Truth Maintenance and Conflict Resolution, *in* Proc. 7th Int. Conf. on Logic Programming, Jerusalem, 1990, pp.427-441.

[GiOl92] L. GIORDANO, N. OLIVETTI, Negation as Failure in Intuitionistic Logic Programming, *in* Proc. Int. Joint. Conf. and Symp. on Logic Programming, Washington, 1992, pp.431-445.

[GL90] A. GUESSOUM, J.W. LLOYD, Updating Knowledge Bases, *in* New Generation Computing, 8(1), pp.71-89, 1990.

[Kunen89] K. KUNEN, Signed Data Dependencies in Logic Programs, *in* J. Logic Programming 7:231-245 (1989).

[Lloyd84] J.W. LLOYD, *Foundations of Logic Programming*, Springer, Berlin, 1984.

[McCa88a] L.T. MCCARTY, Clausal Intuitionistic Logic. I. Fixed-Point Semantics, *in* J. Logic Programming 5(1):1-31 (1988).

[McCa88b] L.T. MCCARTY, Clausal Intuitionistic Logic. II. Tableau Proof Procedures, *in* J. Logic Programming 5(2):93-132 (1988).

[Miller86] D. MILLER, A Theory of Modules for Logic Programming, *in* IEEE Symposium on Logic Programming, Sept. 1986, pp.106-114.

[Miller89] D. MILLER, A Logical Analysis of Modules in Logic Programming, *in* J. Logic Programming, 6:79-108 (1989).

[MW87] S. MANCHANDA, D.S. WARREN, A Logic-based Language for Database Updates, *in* Foundation of Deductive Databases and Logic Programming, (J.Minker, ed.), Morgan Kaufman, Palo Alto, Ca, 1987.

[Nebel91] B. NEBEL, Belief Revision and Default Reasoning: Syntax-Based Approaches, *in* 2nd Int. Conf. on Principles of Knowledge Representation and Reasoning, 1991, pp.417-428.

[NR90] S. NAQVI, F. ROSSI, Reasoning in Inconsistent Databases, *in* Proc. of the 1990 North American Conf. on Logic Programming, pp. 255-272, 1990.

[PAA91] L.M.PEREIRA, J.J.ALFERES, J.N.APARICIO, Contradiction Removal within Well Founded Semantics, *in* Proc. Logic Programming and Non-Monotonic Reasoning'91, A.Nerode et al., ed., pp. 115-119, MIT Press, 1991.

[Przy89] T.C. PRZYMUSINSKI, On Constructive Negation in logic Programming, *in* Proceedings North American Conf. on Logic Programming, 1989, preprint.

[RN89] F. ROSSI, S. NAQVI, Contribution to the View Update Problem, *in* Proc. of the 6th Int. Conf. on Logic Programming, 1989.

[SaKo87] F. SADRI, R. KOWALSKI, A Theorem-Proving Approach to Database Integrity, *in* Foundation of Deductive Databases and Logic Programming, (J.Minker, ed.), Morgan Kaufman, Palo Alto, Ca, 1987.

[Stuckey91] P.STUCKEY, Constructive Negation for Constraint Logic Programming, *in* Proc. LICS, pp.328-339, 1991.

[Warren84] D.S. WARREN, Database Updates in Pure Prolog, *in* Proc. Int. Conf. on Fifth Generation Computer Systems, Tokyo, 1984, pp.244-253.

[Winslett90] M. WINSLETT, *Updating Logical Databases*, Cambridge University Press, 1990.

Causal Models of Disjunctive Logic Programs

Jürgen Dix
Department of Computer Science
University of Koblenz
Rheinau 1, 56075 Koblenz, Germany
dix@informatik.uni-koblenz.de

Georg Gottlob
Institut für Informationssysteme
Technische Universität Wien
Paniglgasse 14, 1040 Wien, Austria
gottlob@vexpert.dbai.tuwien.at

Viktor Marek
Department of Computer Science
University of Kentucky
Lexington, KY 40506, USA
marek@cs.uky.edu

Abstract

We present a new semantics for disjunctive logic programs. The idea is
to extract a class of programs, *causal* programs, where the disjunction can
be simulated by negation-as-failure: disjunctive programs are reduced to
stratified nondisjunctive programs by a series of *shift-operations*. A similar
approach has been recently defined by Schaerf and the complexity of testing
causality was stated as an open question. We solve this problem by proving its NP-completeness and we give a simple syntactic condition to define
a subclass which is polynomial. We define *causal* models and consider the
semantics induced by these models. We show that our *causal* semantics has
very attractive computational behaviour: it belongs to the first level of the
polynomial hierarchy unlike the minimal model semantics (GCWA), which
is even for positive disjunctive programs Π_2^P-complete. In addition, causal
semantics satisfies interesting abstract properties: it is *cumulative* and *rational*. The class of *positive causal* programs also extends the class of *positive
head-cycle-free* programs, recently defined by Ben-Eliahu and Dechter. We
also compare our semantics with Schaerf's approach.

1   Introduction

One is often tempted to consider as desired models of a theory T only *intended models*. But what is an *intended model*? Clearly, such model depends

on the possible applications that the programmer has in mind while writing a theory. Various intentions lead to different results. For instance, the analysis of the frame problem leads to the acceptance of minimal models as the class of desired models and, subsequently to the notion of *circumscription* ([McC80]). The analysis of closed systems of *beliefs* leads to the acceptance of *supported* models of programs ([Cla78, MT93]).

In this paper we are looking at logical theories (described by means of a disjunctive program, possibly with negation in the body) as expressing a possible *causal* relationship between various atoms of the underlying language. Moreover we want to express the interpretation of negation as *negation by failure to prove*. The idea is that when we observe a *state of affairs*, we write a program describing it, and we want to find the possible ways of causal interplay of atoms.

We give a *stratified* interpretation to causality. That is, when a program is stratified, it imposes on atoms of the underlying language an ordering; some atoms are decided earlier than other atoms. Such ordering, together with the program itself leads to the unique model which can be viewed as a description of the causal relationship. The way it went in the earlier strata (together with the program) determines the way the matters stand in the next stratum. A theory (that is a disjunctive program) may or may not admit a transformation to a stratified logic program. We are interested in the theories which admit such representation. It will be shown that not all theories possess such representation. Moreover, like in the case of stratified programs, theories logically equivalent may be different from the point of view of causality.

Thus our idea is that some theories carry in their syntactic form one or more computational procedure that can be associated with that theory. In this we are taking a position similar to that of [ABW88, Prz88, vG88]. The difference is that we are interested in all the stratifications that can be obtained from the program.

We assign to a disjunctive program the *causal* models. Those are models obtained from the program by a series of *shifts* which move atoms from the head to the body (and negate them). The procedure is unidirectional – we cannot move a literal from the body to the head. Therefore we can keep an additional control over the way the causal models are produced – if we want an atom not to depend on other atoms we can move it to the body (providing it appears in a head consisting of a proper disjunction).

The paper is organized as follows. Section 2 contains some terminology used throughout the paper, the definition of the perfect model for stratified nondisjunctive programs and its complexity. In Section 3 the class of *causal* programs is defined. Its NP-completeness is shown and a smaller class, *simple* disjunctive programs, is shown to be polynomial. In Section 4 we define the notion of *causal* models for the class of programs introduced in the previous section and consider the induced entailment relation. We determine its complexity and show some interesting abstract properties of it. Section 5 compares our work to similar approaches by Schaerf and Ben-Eliahu/Dechter. We end in Section 6 with some conclusions.

2   Preliminaries

A *disjunctive rule* is a formula $a_1 \vee \ldots \vee a_n \leftarrow b_1, \ldots, b_m, \neg c_1, \ldots, \neg c_l$, where $n \geq 1$, $m, l \geq 0$ and a_i, b_i, c_i are arbitrary propositional atoms. As usual, the comma represents conjunction. We call such a rule *positive* if $l = 0$, *normal* if $n = 1$. One can think of a rule C as a pair of sets $\langle head(C), body(C) \rangle$, where $head(C) = \{a_1, \ldots, a_n\}$ and $body(C) = \{b_1, \ldots, b_m, \neg c_1, \ldots, \neg c_l\}$.

A *disjunctive logic program* is a set of disjunctive rules: it straightforwardly inherits the typology of rules. A normal logic program is often also called *general logic program*. The *Herbrand base* induced by a program P is denoted B_P.

Here we only deal with *finite* disjunctive logic programs. Since all the clauses of a disjunctive program have nonempty heads, a disjunctive logic program is always consistent (viewed as a first-order theory).

We say that a normal program P is *stratified* if there exists a *rank* function f, $f : At \rightarrow \mathbb{N}$ such that for every rule

$$C = p \leftarrow q_1, \ldots, q_n, \neg s_1, \ldots, \neg s_m \quad (p, q_1, \ldots, q_n, s_1, \ldots, s_m \text{ are atoms})$$

from P: $rk(p) \geq rk(q_i)$, $i \leq n$, and $rk(p) > rk(s_j)$, $j \leq m$.

Let P be a stratified normal logic program. We can assign to P a model, called the *perfect* model ([ABW88] as presented in [MT93]) as follows: first, split the program P into the union of programs P_i according to the ranks of heads. Let $P = \bigcup_{n \in \mathbb{N}} P_n$ be this decomposition. Define M_0 to be the least model of P_0 (notice that according to stratification condition, P_0, if nonempty, must be a Horn program). Next, assuming that $M_i, i < j$, are already computed proceed as follows: for every clause C in P_j perform the following *reduction*. If some atom p in $\bigcup_{i<j} M_i$ appears negatively in C then eliminate C. If all the atoms appearing negatively in the body of C do not belong to $\bigcup_{i<j} M_i$ then eliminate all these negated atoms. The resulting reduced program Q_j is a Horn program, and M_j is defined as the smallest model of $Q_j \cup \{a \leftarrow \ : a \in \bigcup_{i<j} M_i\}$.

The following fact is proved by Apt, Blair and Walker ([ABW88]):

Theorem 2.1 (Perfect Model for Stratified Normal Programs)
If P is a stratified normal logic program, then its perfect model is a minimal model of P. Moreover the perfect model of P does not depend on stratification: every stratification of P generates the same perfect model.

We also note the following well-known fact, which follows immediately from the quadratic complexity of the wellfounded semantics ([Sch92]):

Lemma 2.2 (Quadratic Complexity of the Perfect Model)
Let P be a stratified normal logic program. Then the perfect model of P can be computed in quadratic time.

3 Causal Disjunctive Programs

Our intention is to define a semantics on a certain subclass of disjunctive programs with good computational behaviour. Since the perfect model of a stratified normal program can be computed in quadratic time (see Lemma 2.2 in Section 2) it is promising to try to reduce a disjunctive program to a set of stratified nondisjunctive programs. The important notion to do this is a *shift*: a *shift* in a disjunctive logic program consists in moving a literal of a rule containing more than one literal in the head from the head to the body and negating it. Clearly, a shift does not change the classical models of a rule (viewed as a first-order formula). If C is a disjunctive rule and C' the result of a shift of some atom from the head to the body, then every model of C is a model of C' and conversely. But from a negation-as-failure viewpoint there is obviously a difference between "$a \vee b$" and "$a \leftarrow \neg b$".

In Section 3.1 we define the class of programs we are interested in and discuss some examples. Section 3.2 solves the complexity problem of testing causality: this has been stated as an open problem in [Sch93].

3.1 Reducing Disjunctive to Normal Programs by Shifts

The reduction consists in reducing the disjunctive program in all possible ways (any sequence of shifts) to a set of normal (nondisjunctive) programs and finally only considering the stratified ones.

Definition 3.1 (Causal Program)
A disjunctive logic program is called causal *if it can be transformed by a sequence of shift operations to a stratified normal logic program.*

There is a simple syntactic condition to ensure causality. Let us define $b(P) := \bigcup_{C \in P} \{a : \ a$ an atom s.t. a or $\neg a \in body(C)\}$. Then

Lemma 3.2 *Let P be a disjunctive logic program such that for every head $head(C)$ of a clause $C \in P$, $head(C) \setminus b(P) \neq \emptyset$. Then P is causal.*

Proof: Shift all the elements of $b(P)$ to the bodies. Notice that such elements may appear in the heads of clauses from P as well. Our assumption guarantees that after such sequence of shifts every clause will have at least one atom in the head. Next, order all the elements of $At \setminus b(P)$ in order $\prec$ of type at most ω. As before, leave at the head of the modified clause only the atom highest in the ordering $\prec$, shifting all the remaining atoms to the body. Now, assign to every atom the following rank: the elements of $b(P)$ are assigned the rank 0. Similarly, the atoms which do not appear in the heads of clauses of P are assigned 0 as well. For the remaining atoms p (these are precisely the atoms appearing in the heads of clauses after the initial shift) are assigned the rank $n + 1$ where n is the position of p in the ordering $\prec$. We claim that the resulting program P' is stratified. Indeed, let $C = p \leftarrow q_1, \ldots, q_n, \neg s_1, \ldots, \neg s_m$ be a clause of P'. First of all, the atoms q_i, $i \leq n$ must belong to $b(P)$, and therefore they have rank 0. Hence their rank is smaller than that of p. Concerning the remaining (negated) literals: they either come from $b(P)$ and then they have the rank 0 (whereas the rank of p is not zero) or they appear in the ordering $\prec$ before p and so they also have smaller rank. Thus P' is stratified. ∎

We notice that the program constructed in the proof of Lemma 3.2 is in fact *hierarchical* (see [Llo87]), not only stratified. A special instance of the previous Lemma is that all programs whose bodies are empty are causal. But not every disjunctive program is causal:

Example 3.3 (A Non-Causal Positive Disjunctive Program)
Let P be the following disjunctive logic program:

$$
\begin{aligned}
p \vee q &\leftarrow r \\
p \vee r &\leftarrow q \\
r \vee q &\leftarrow p
\end{aligned}
$$

Then P is not causal. Indeed, by symmetry we can shift p in the first clause. Then $rk(p) < rk(q)$, and $rk(r) \leq rk(q)$. This forces us to select r for the shift in the third clause. This implies that $rk(p) = rk(r)$ and $rk(q) < rk(p)$. Now, in the second clause, neither p nor r can be shifted to the body, for one of them has to have smaller rank than the other. On the other hand, every proper subprogram of P is causal.

3.2 Testing Causality

In [Sch93], Schaerf asked (in our terminology) to determine the complexity of testing causality and of determining tractable subclasses of programs. Theorem 3.4 and Lemma 3.5 are solutions to these problems.

Theorem 3.4 (NP-Completeness of Deciding Causality)
Testing whether a disjunctive logic program is causal is NP-complete.

Proof: The problem is obviously in NP: if the given disjunctive logic program is stratifiable we may nondeterministically guess a correct sequence of shifts and check in polynomial time by well-known methods that the resulting normal logic program is stratifiable. NP-hardness is shown by a polynomial transformation from EXACT HITTING SET, a well-known NP-complete problem.

An instance of EXACT HITTING SET consists of a finite set S and a family of subsets $S_1, \ldots, S_n$ of S. The question is whether there exists a set

$H \subseteq S$ such that $\forall i : 1 \le i \le n$ $|H \cap S_i| = 1$. If such a set exists it is called an *exact hitting set* of $S_1, \ldots, S_n$.

To each instance $\{S, S_1, \ldots, S_n\}$ of EXACT HITTING SET we define a disjunctive logic program P as follows

- The atoms of P are: $S \cup \{q\}$, where q is a new predicate symbol.

- P contains for each S_i a rule R_i of the form: $\bigvee_{x \in S_i} x \leftarrow q$.

- In addition, P contains an extra rule R of the form: $q \leftarrow \bigwedge_{x \in S} x$.

Obviously, P is causal if and only if the S_i have an exact hitting set.

Let us first show the if-direction. Assume the $S_1, \ldots, S_n$ have an exact hitting set H. Transform the disjunctive logic program P to a normal logic program P' by shifting each atom of each rule $R_1, \ldots, R_n$ not occurring in H to the right (i.e., to the rule body). First observe that P' is effectively a normal logic program, since each rule contains only one atom in its head (because H is an exact hitting set). Now observe that P' is stratified. Indeed, none of the negative literals that occur in the rule bodies occurs also in the rule head; this allows a stratification of two strata: the top stratum consists of $H \cup \{q\}$ and the bottom stratum consists of all other predicate symbols.

Let us now show the only-if direction. Assume P is causal. Then P can be transformed by shift operations to a stratified normal logic program P'. Obviously the special rule R remains unaffected by the shifts and is therefore also present in P'. Thus P' is of the form $\{R'_1, \ldots, R'_n, R\}$ where R'_i is the transform of R_i for $1 \le i \le n$. Let H be the set of all head-atoms of the rules $R'_1, \ldots, R'_n$. Obviously, H is a hitting set of the family $S_1, \ldots, S_n$, since H intersects each S_i. We claim that H is an *exact* hitting set of $S_1, \ldots, S_n$. Assume it is not. Then for some S_i it holds that $|S_i \cap H| \ge 2$, hence, there are at least two different atoms p and s in $H \cap S_i$. This means that during the *shift* from P to P', at least one of these atoms, say p, is shifted from the head to the rule body of R_i. Hence p occurs negatively in the body of R'_i. By definition of H, however, there must exist a rule R'_j whose head is p. Now it is easy to see that the existence of the three rules R'_i, R'_j, and R in P' constitutes a contradiction to our assumption that P' is stratified. Indeed, from R'_i we know that for some atom t (namely the head of R'_i), we have $t > p$; from R we further know that $q \ge t$, hence it follows $q > p$. But from the existence of R'_j we deduce that $p \ge q$, a contradiction. Therefore, H must be an exact hitting set. ∎

Observe that the program constructed in the last proof does not contain any negated literal (if written in implicational form of course). Hence, NP-completeness of causality-testing also holds for the restricted class of *positive* disjunctive logic programs. Actually, adding negated literals to the rule bodies makes things easier because some choices are prohibited.

If a disjunctive logic program has only negated literals in the rule bodies, then causality can be tested in polynomial time. Let us therefore call *simple disjunctive logic programs* those disjunctive logic programs whose rule bodies contain only negated literals.

Lemma 3.5 (Polynomial Complexity of Simple Programs)
There is a polynomial time algorithm for testing causality of simple disjunctive logic programs.

>   *Proof:* One first shows the following two claims:

1. If a simple disjunctive logic program P is causal, then there must exist an atom p in some rule head of P such that $\neg p$ does not occur in any rule body (exploiting the finiteness ...). Call such an atom a *top-atom*.

2. If a simple disjunctive logic program P contains a top-atom p then it is causal if and only if the program $P' \subset P$ consisting of all rules of P in which p does not occur is causal.

These claims imply that a polynomial algorithm for testing the causality of a simple disjunctive logic program P is easily derived by choosing top-atoms of smaller and smaller programs. If the algorithm ends-up with the empty program then the input-program is causal; if the algorithm gets stuck because at some level there is no top-atom, then the input-program is not causal. ■

4 Causal Entailment

In this section we first define the notion of a *causal* model (Section 4.1) and consider the induced entailment relation *truth in all causal models*. We determine its complexity (Section 4.2) and consider abstract properties introduced by Dix ([Dix91, Dix92b]) into logic programming (Section 4.3).

4.1 Causal Models

We have associated to every disjunctive program a set of stratified normal programs. Since there is general agreement about the right semantics for this class of programs, it is natural to define these perfect models as the causal models of the original disjunctive program:

Definition 4.1 (Causal Model)
We call a model M of a disjunctive logic program P causal if there exists a series of shifts such that the resulting program P' is a stratified normal logic program and M is the perfect model of P'.

Hence, we are looking at the possible stratifications of a disjunctive logic program and in this fashion a disjunctive logic program may possess none, unique, or several causal models. The following observations are obvious:

1. Every Horn program P possesses the unique causal model. This model coincides with the least model M_P of P.

2. Every stratified normal program P possesses its perfect model M_P^{supp} as the unique causal model. The causal semantics therefore extends the stratified semantics.

3. The disjunctive logic program $\{p \vee q\}$ possesses two causal models: $\{p\}$ and $\{q\}$.

Having defined the notion of causal model, it is natural to consider the induced entailment relation:

Definition 4.2 (Causal Entailment)
A literal l is causally entailed by P *if l is satisfied in all causal models of P.*

Let us compare this relation with the GCWA (introduced by Minker in [Min82]). For a positive disjunctive program P, the GCWA entails all literals true in all *minimal* models of P. Note that for *atoms* it makes no difference between considering (classical) entailment or minimal entailment. This is no longer the case for our causal entailment.

Example 4.3 (Minimal vs. Causal Entailment)
Let P be the following disjunctive logic program:

$$
\begin{array}{lcl}
p & \leftarrow & q \\
q & \leftarrow & p \\
p \vee q \vee r & &
\end{array}
$$

Clearly, P possesses two minimal models, one contains both p and q but not r, the other contains only r (but neither p nor q). When we look at the stratified programs obtained from P by shifts, then we see that there is only one such program, in which both p and q are shifted to the right. This is because both p and q are in the same stratum, so the shifts of the third clause must move them both. Therefore only the second of two minimal models is a causal model of P, and so P causally entails r. On the other hand, P does not minimally entail any atom.

In the last example the causal semantics is stronger than GCWA (more literals are derivable). On the other hand there are non-causal programs (see Example 3.3) where the causal semantics is not defined but the GCWA is. Another reason for the difference of GCWA and the causal semantics is its complexity: while GCWA is Π_2^P-complete ([CS90, EG93]), causal entailment is located one level below in the polynomial hierarchy as we will show in the next section.

4.2 Complexity

In the previous section we introduced causal entailment and noticed that this notion, even for atoms, is different from the usual entailment. We also found the complexity of the existence of causal model. In this section we use these results to analyze the complexity of causal entailment.

Let us define $S \vdash^{sc} \varphi$ ("φ follows *sceptically* from S") to denote that φ is true in *every* causal model of theory S. Similarly $S \vdash^{cr} \varphi$ ("φ follows *credulously* from S") denotes that φ is true in *some* causal model of S.

Theorem 4.4 (Complexity of Causal Entailment)

1. *Determining whether $S \vdash^{sc} \varphi$ is a co-NP-complete problem.*

2. *Determining whether $S \vdash^{cr} \varphi$ is an NP-complete problem.*

Proof: First, we need to prove that the problem complementary to our problem is in the class NP and that our problem is co-NP-hard.

1. To test that $S \vdash^{sc} \varphi$ can be done in NP time is done as follows: first we guess a stratification for S. Next, using Lemma 2.2 we compute the corresponding causal model. Finally we check that the constructed causal model of S does not satisfy φ.

2. Since S is a disjunctive logic program, S is consistent. Therefore, $S \vdash^{sc} \perp$ is equivalent to the fact that S is not causal. Hence there is a trivial polynomial reduction from the problem complementary to causality testing to testing of $S \vdash^{sc} \varphi$. Thus, by Theorem 3.4 our problem is co-NP-hard.

Second, we need to prove that our problem belongs to the class NP and that it is NP-hard.

1. To establish that our problem is in the class NP we proceed as above. We guess a stratification of S, compute the corresponding causal model of S and then check that that model satisfies φ. This is, of course, done in polynomial time.

2. Now, it is clear that S possesses a causal model if and only if $S \vdash^{cr} \top$. Thus we get a trivial reduction of stratifiability problem to the $\vdash^{cr}$ entailment problem. This, by Proposition 3.4 implies that our problem is NP-hard. ∎

Notice that $\perp, \top$ are atoms, so our problems are, respectively, co-NP-complete and NP-complete even for φ being atoms.

4.3 Abstract Properties

In [Dix91, Dix92b] the first author adapted various abstract conditions known in the context of general nonmonotonic reasoning to logic programming semantics. It was argued that the properties of *Cumulativity* and *Rationality*

> *Cumulativity:* If $P \mathrel{\vdash^{sc}} \alpha$ then: $P \mathrel{\vdash^{sc}} \varphi$ if and only if $P \cup \{\alpha\} \mathrel{\vdash^{sc}} \varphi$.

> *Rationality:* If <u>not</u> $P \mathrel{\vdash^{sc}} \neg\alpha$ then: $P \mathrel{\vdash^{sc}} \varphi$ implies $P \cup \{\alpha\} \mathrel{\vdash^{sc}} \varphi$.

(originally introduced by Gabbay and Makinson) are connected with the complexity of a semantics. This was supported by two famous examples: the wellfounded semantics WFS and the WGCWA. Both are cumulative and rational [Dix91, Dix92b] and have a lower complexity than their non-rational "competitors" STABLE and GCWA:

- While WFS is polynomial (this was already cited in Section 2), STABLE is at the first level of the polynomial hierarchy ([MT91]),

- While WGCWA is at the first level, GCWA is at the second level the polynomial hierarchy ([CS90]).

In addition, Fernandez defined in [Fer93] a semantics WICWA for general disjunctive programs which he claims to be cumulative and rational. He showed that WICWA is of lower complexity than PERFECT (which extends GCWA and is not rational). The same holds if we compare our causal semantics with GCWA: we have already shown that causal semantics has a lower complexity. Indeed, it shares with WFS the following nice properties:

Theorem 4.5 (Abstract Properties of Causal Semantics)
Sceptical causal entailment $\vdash^{sc}$ is cumulative and rational.

But this connection between abstract properties and computational complexity is not as obvious as it seems (as noted by Marco Schaerf). The first author defined (in the context of normal logic programs) semantics that are rational but of the same complexity as STABLE (co-NP-complete for propositional programs, see [Dix94]). Therefore the exact relationship between abstract properties and complexity still remains open.

One of the drawbacks of the causal semantics (shared with STABLE) is its inconsistency: non-causal programs have no meaning. Adding a useless rule like "$a \leftarrow \neg a$" to a causal program destroys its causality. Therefore the condition *Relevance* (introduced in [Dix92a]) is not satisfied. This can be repaired by looking at all wellfounded models of the transformations (they are always defined and coincide with the perfect model if the latter exists) or by modifying the definition and taking the *Relevance*-property seriously ([Dix94]).

Other weak or *well-behaved* properties especially tailored for disjunctive semantics are currently under investigation ([DM94]). Their impact on the causal semantics will be discussed in the forthcoming full paper. It seems, however, that most of them are true: this is because they are true for the *stratified* semantics and the fact that causal semantics reduces to it.

5   Relation to other approaches

Schaerf considered recently ([Sch93]) also the technique of shifting a disjunctive program into a normal one. His viewpoint is different from ours. Schaerf associates to any semantics for normal programs (WFS, STABLE, SUPPORTED) a corresponding semantics for disjunctive programs (Weak-WFS, Weak-STABLE, Weak-SUPPORTED) by taking the respective models of all shift-transformations: it is not required that the shift-transformations result in stratified programs (although he mentions that this is an interesting property). In addition, Schaerf considered all supported models of a program, not only the perfect one. Therefore even for stratified programs his semantics is different from ours. The complexity of his semantics, however, is identical to ours.

Another approach is due to Ben-Eliahu and Dechter [BED92]. They tried to find classes of programs where the complexity of the stable semantics is low. They defined the class of *head-cycle-free* programs and proved that the entailment relation ("truth in all stable models") is co-NP-complete for this class. A program is *head-cycle-free*, if any two literals that occur in the same head do not depend positively on each other. Here "A depends positively on B" is the transitive closure of "A depends immediately positively on B" (which means that there is a rule C containing A in its head and B positively in its body). Note that in this definition negative dependencies are ignored.

As an example "$A \vee B \leftarrow A, B$" is not *head-cycle-free* while "$A \leftarrow \neg A$" is. Therfore the classes of *head-cycle-free* programs and of *causal* programs are incomparable. But for positive programs we have:

Lemma 5.1 *The class of positive causal programs strictly includes the class of positive head-cycle free clauses.*

Therefore our semantics can be seen as an extension of the class of *positive head-cycle free clauses* retaining the attractive low complexity. But obviously both semantics are different even on the smallest class of head-cycle free programs. This is because causal semantics relies on *perfect* models while Ben-Eliahu and Dechter's semantics is based on *stable* models.

We also note that causal entailment is stronger than stable entailment (this was pointed out by Piero Bonatti):

Lemma 5.2 *Every causal model of P is also a stable model of P.*

The reason is that every causal model M of P is also a minimal model of P^M, the Gelfond-Lifschitz transform of P with respect to M. By definition, the minimal models M of P^M (a *positive* program) are exactly the stable models of P.

6   Conclusions

We found that some propositional theories S (we termed them *causal*) carry with them one or more computational procedures which determine the order of construction of atoms in some model of S. Once such a procedure is known, we can construct this model in polynomial time. We showed that the problem of existence of such order is itself *NP*-complete, thereby solving a problem recently raised by Schaerf.

We defined *causal* models and investigated the induced entailment relation. Causal entailment is different from all other semantics proposed in the literature and is of low complexity. In addition this semantics behaves in a nice way: sceptical entailment is *cumulative* and *rational*.

We gave simple syntactic conditions on the program that ensure the existence of causal models. In general, the problem of existence of a causal model is as complex as the satisfiability problem. We find a class of programs for which we can test the existence of a causal model in polynomial time.

We also compared our approach to work of Ben-Eliahu/Dechter and Schaerf.

Acknowledgements

We thank Piero Bonatti, Marco Schaerf and some anonymous referees for useful comments on the subject of the paper.

References

[ABW88] K. Apt, H. Blair, and A. Walker. Towards a theory of declarative knowledge. In Jack Minker, editor, *Foundations of Deductive Databases*, chapter 2, pages 89–148. Morgan Kaufmann, 1988.

[BED92] Rachel Ben-Eliahu and Rina Dechter. Propositional Semantics for Disjunctive Logic Programs. In K. Apt, editor, *LOGIC PROGRAMMING: Proceedings of the 1992 Joint International Conference and Symposium*. MIT Press, November 1992.

[Cla78] K. L. Clark. Negation as Failure. In H. Gallaire and J. Minker, editors, *Logic and Data-Bases*, pages 293–322. Plenum, New York, 78.

[CS90] Jan Chomicki and V.S. Subrahmanian. Generalized Closed World Assumption is Π_2^0-Complete. *Information Processing Letters*, 34:289–291, 1990.

[Dix91] Jürgen Dix. Classifying Semantics of Logic Programs. In Anil Nerode, Wiktor Marek, and V. S. Subrahmanian, editors, *Logic Programming and Non-Monotonic Reasoning, Proceedings of the first International Workshop*, pages 166–180. Washington D.C, MIT Press, July 1991.

[Dix92a] Jürgen Dix. A Framework for Representing and Characterizing Semantics of Logic Programs. In B. Nebel, C. Rich, and W. Swartout, editors, *Principles of Knowledge Representation and Reasoning: Proceedings of the Third International Conference (KR '92)*, pages 591–602. San Mateo, CA, Morgan Kaufmann, 1992.

[Dix92b] Jürgen Dix. Classifying Semantics of Disjunctive Logic Programs. In K. Apt, editor, *LOGIC PROGRAMMING: Proceedings of the 1992 Joint International Conference and Symposium*, pages 798–812. MIT Press, November 1992.

[Dix94] Jürgen Dix. Semantics of Logic Programs: Their Intuitions and Formal Properties. An Overview. In Andre Fuhrmann and Hans Rott, editors, *Logic, Action and Information. Proceedings of the Konstanz Colloquium in Logic and Information (LogIn '92)*. DeGruyter, 1994.

[DM94] Jürgen Dix and Martin Müller. An Axiomatic Framework for Representing and Characterizing Semantics of Disjunctive Logic Programs. In Pascal Van Hentenryck, editor, *Proceedings of the 11th Int. Conf. on Logic Programming, S. Margherita Ligure*. MIT, June 1994.

[EG93] Thomas Eiter and Georg Gottlob. Propositional Circumscription and Extended Closed World Reasoning are Π_2^P-complete. *Theoretical Computer Science*, 144(2):231–245, Addendum: vol. 118, p. 315, 1993, 1993.

[Fer93] Jose Alberto Fernandez. Weak Models for Disjunctive Logic Programs. In *Proceedings of Workshop on Logic Programming with Incomplete Information, Vancouver Oct. 1993, following ILPS' 93*, pages 190–205, 1993.

[Llo87] John Lloyd. *Foundations of Logic Programming*. Springer- Verlag, 2nd edition, 1987.

[McC80] John McCarthy. Circumscription: A Form of Nonmonotonic Reasoning. *Artificial Intelligence*, 13:27–39, 1980.

[Min82] Jack Minker. On indefinite databases and the closed world assumption. In *Proceedings of the 6th Conference on Automated Deduction, New York*, pages 292–308. Springer, 1982.

[MT91] Wiktor Marek and Mirek Truszczyński. Computing Intersection of Autoepistemic Expansions. In *Logic Programming and Non-Monotonic Reasoning, Proceedings of the first International Workshop*. MIT Press, 1991.

[MT93] Viktor M. Marek and Mirek Truszczyński. *Nonmonotonic Logics; Context-Dependent Reasoning*. Springer Verlag, Berlin-Heidelberg-New York, 1st edition, 1993.

[Prz88] Teodor Przymusinski. On the declarative semantics of deductive databases and logic programs. In Jack Minker, editor, *Foundations of Deductive Databases*, chapter 5, pages 193–216. Morgan Kaufmann, 1988.

[Sch92] John S. Schlipf. A Survey of Complexity and Undecidability Results in Logic Programming. In H. Blair, W. Marek, A. Nerode, and J. Remmel, editors, *Proceedings of the Workshop on Complexity and Recursion-theoretic Methods in Logic Programming, following the JICSLP'92*. informal, 1992.

[Sch93] Marco Schaerf. Negation and minimality in non-Horn databases. In Catriel Beeri, editor, *Proceedings of the Twelfth Conference on Principle Of Database Systems (PODS-93)*, pages 147–157. ACM Press, 1993.

[vG88] Allen van Gelder. Negation-as-failure using tight Derivations for General Logic Programs. In Jack Minker, editor, *Foundations of Deductive Databases*, chapter 1, pages 19–88. Morgan Kaufmann, 1988.

An Axiomatic Approach to Semantics of Disjunctive Programs

Jürgen Dix
Department of Computer Science
University of Koblenz, Rheinau 1
D-56075 Koblenz, Germany
dix@informatik.uni-koblenz.de

Martin Müller
Graduiertenkolleg Kognition and
German Research Center for AI (DFKI)
Stuhlsatzenhausweg 3
D-66123 Saarbrücken, Germany
mmueller@dfki.uni-sb.de

Abstract

In this paper we consider semantics for disjunctive logic programs and distinguish between an *inclusive* and an *exclusive* interpretation of "∨". We develop an axiomatic framework for classifying and characterizing disjunctive semantics. This framework comes in form of a number of *weak principles* which, as we claim, should be satisfied by any semantics: we then call it *well-behaved*. A similar axiomatic framework has been introduced in previous work for *normal* programs, but extending logic programs by disjunction adds various complications and gives rise to some new *principles*. While we claim that most of our conditions should be generally satisfied, we also state two principles to ensure a semantics to be an extension of GCWA (resp. WGCWA). These principles reflect the conviction that any semantics should coincide with PERFECT or WPERFECT (the analogue of PERFECT for the inclusive view of "∨") on stratified disjunctive programs. We also extend our definition of the semantics WDWFS and DWFS introduced in earlier work of ours. Our main results state that any semantics satisfying our weak principles already coincides for stratified disjunctive programs with WPERFECT (under the *inclusive* view) or with PERFECT (under the *exclusive* view). In addition, any such semantics is either an extension of the well-behaved semantics WDWFS or of DWFS.

1 Introduction

While there is only one canonical semantics for positive programs without disjunctions, the least Herbrand model M_P, the situation changes when disjunctive heads are allowed, since we can interpret "∨" *exclusive* or *inclusive*. The inclusive view leads to the "WGCWA" ([RLM89]) or, equivalently, the DDR-rule ([RT88]), and the exclusive view to the "GCWA", defined by Minker. Since both are widely accepted as the correct semantics for *positive programs* under the different readings of "∨", we shall use the notion of an exclusive (inclusive) semantics for one which coincides on positive programs with GCWA (WGCWA).

In both cases, it is an interesting question, and a field of active research, to ask for extensions of the respective semantics to larger classes of programs, e.g. to the class of *stratified* disjunctive programs or, finally, to the whole class of *all* disjunctive programs. Recently, various semantics have been proposed:

- the *perfect* "PERFECT" and "GCWAS" (see [Prz88], and [MLR91]) for *stratified* disjunctive programs (interpreting "∨" exclusive), the *weak perfect* "WPERFECT" ([Dix92b]) for *stratified* disjunctive programs (interpreting "∨" inclusive),

and some semantics defined for general disjunctive programs:

- the *stationary* semantics STN ([Prz91]) and the more recent *static* semantics ([Prz94]) of Przymusinski, "GCWA¬", "WGCWA¬" and the possible world semantics "PWA" ([SI93]),

- "GDWFS" and "WF³" of Baral/Lobo/Minker ([BLM91a, BLM91b]).

as well as an extension of "STABLE" to arbitrary disjunctive programs ([GL91]). The starting point of most of these semantics was a particular program that was, according to the intuitions of some researchers, not handled correctly by the existing semantics. The new semantics was then designed to give the desired conclusions.

Our approach (introduced in [Dix91, Dix92b]) consists in associating, uniform for all semantics, a consequence relation $\vdash_P$ between sets of atoms and sets of literals to each program P: for any semantics SEM and any program P, a relation $\vdash_P$ is canonically defined. We can now ask for the properties of this $\vdash$ relation. A semantics was considered as associating with any program P the set of all sceptically derivable literals. These results lead to two sorts of requirements on semantics SEM for *normal* logic ([Dix94a, Dix94b]):[1]

Weak Principles: Conditions, that, as we claim, should always be satisfied to guarantee that a semantics is *well-behaved*.

Strong Principles: Conditions, that can be used to distinguish between the various existing semantics. These properties might be useful in particular applications.

---

[1] These abstract properties seem to be related to the complexity of computing a semantics: we refer the reader to [MD93] where we focus on this point.

This paper is a continuation of [Dix92b] (which extends [Dix91] to disjunctive programs): we extend the results obtained in [Dix92a] for *normal* programs to the class of *general disjunctive* programs. The overall aim still is to get a better understanding of the various existing semantics of disjunctive logic programs, their mutual relations and potential new candidates.

We consider a semantics SEM as a mapping from the class of all programs to the powerset of all 3-valued Herbrand structures and its induced sceptical entailment relation SEM^{scept} to a subset of all *pure* disjunctions. This significantly extends our framework from [Dix92b]. We also extend our previously introduced *weak principles* to the disjunctive case and introduce some new ones. If we restrict it to *normal* programs, we get back our *weak principles* from [Dix94b] so that the results obtained there also apply here.

Among the existing semantics for the whole class of disjunctive programs, we have already shown that $\mathcal{STN}$ of Przymusinski as well as GDWFS and WF^3 of Baral, Lobo and Minker have serious shortcomings (they fail to satisfy our weak principles).

Previously [Dix92b], we have introduced WPERFECT, WDWFS and DWFS. We extend the definition of WDWFS and DWFS in this paper and we show, that all these semantics satisfy some of our reasonable principles. Indeed, it turns out that DWFS (resp. WDWFS) is the weakest possible semantics under the *exclusive* (resp. *inclusive*) view.

The paper is organized as follows. In Section 2 we introduce some terminology and introduce the sceptical entailment SEM_P^{scept} of a semantics SEM. In Section 3 we review some of our previous work which is important for the rest of the paper. We consider *positive, stratified* and *general disjunctive* programs and extend our definition of DWFS and WDWFS given earlier. Section 4 is the heart of the paper. We formulate a list of conditions and call any semantics satisfying these conditions *well-behaved*. We try to convince the reader of the plausibility of our conditions. Some of our conditions are inspired by shortcomings of semantics like STABLE (failure of *Relevance*), $\mathcal{STN}$ (failure of *Modularity*), or GWFS (failure of *PPE*) while others (*Subsumption, Tautology*) reflect and formalize some very convincing reasoning-modes. Theorems 4.15, 4.16, 4.17 and 4.18 are our main results. We conclude in Section 5 with some additional remarks.

2   Notation

A program clause or a rule is a formula $a_1 \vee \ldots \vee a_n \leftarrow b_1, \ldots, b_m, \neg c_1, \ldots \neg c_l$, where $n \geq 1$ and $m, l \geq 0$. We call it a *positive* or *definite* clause :iff $l = 0$, *normal* :iff $n = 1$, and *general disjunctive* :iff $n \geq 2$. A rule with $l = m = 0$ is called a *fact*. As usual, the comma denotes conjunction. We think of a clause C as a pair of sets $\langle head(C), body(C) \rangle$, where $head(C) = \{a_1, \ldots, a_n\}$ and $body(C) = \{b_1, \ldots, b_m, \neg c_1, \ldots, \neg c_l\}$, on the components of which we allow the usual set operations. A *program* P is a finite set of rules and it straightforwardly inherits the typology of clauses. Every program P induces a language $\mathcal{L}_P$ which contains exactly the predicate, function and constant symbols occurring in P. In general the a_i, b_j, c_l are arbitrary atomic formulæ. But here we follow common practice in restricting ourselves to fully grounded programs. If we have no function symbols, i.e. deal only with so-called (disjunctive) *datalog* programs, then the grounded program is finite if and only if the original program is. In the sequel *program* will mean *fully grounded program* (which may be infinite).

The *dependency graph* $\mathcal{G}_P$ captures the structure of a logic program P: the nodes of this graph are the predicate symbols from $\mathcal{L}_P$, and there is an edge (b, a) in $\mathcal{G}_P$ whenever $a \vee head \leftarrow c, body \in P$ where $c = b$ or $c = \neg b$. The edge is labelled "$-$" (resp."$+$") if there is a clause $a \vee head \leftarrow \neg b, body$ (resp. $a \vee head \leftarrow b, body$) in P. The dependency graph of a disjunctive program P contains additional "$+$" edges (a_i, a_j) for all $a_i, a_j \in head(C)$ for some $C \in P$. These dependencies can for the exclusive view be illustrated by the fact that the truth of a component in an *exclusive* disjunction may be used to derive the falsity of the others.

We say, an atom a *depends on* another one b if there is a path from b to a in $\mathcal{G}_P$. In addition we define for a program P:

- the *definition of a in P*: $P_{def}(a) := \{C \in P \mid a \in head(C)\}$, and

- the *clauses relevant for a in P*: $P_{rel}(a) := \bigcup\{P_{def}(c) \mid a \text{ depends on } c\}$

for which we obviously have: $P_{def}(a) \subseteq P_{rel}(a) \subseteq P$. Both definitions are easily extended to take sets as arguments ($P_{def}(A) := \bigcup\{P_{def}(a) \mid a \in A\}$). For an arbitrary clause C, $P_{def}(C)$ has the obvious meaning (where C is viewed as a set of literals).

In the sequel we mainly adopt notation from [LMR92]. The *Herbrand Universe* is the set of all ground terms which can be built over $\mathcal{L}_P$. The *Herbrand Base HB_P* is the set of ground atomic formulæ over $\mathcal{L}_P$. A disjunction built solely from either *negative* (denoted by D^-) or *positive* (denoted by D^+) literals only is called a *pure disjunction* (also denoted by $D^\pm$). The *Disjunctive Herbrand Base DHB_P* is the set of all positive disjunctions over HB_P. The *Conjunctive Herbrand Base CHB_P* is the set of all positive conjunctions over HB_P. We denote by $\neg \cdot CHB_P$ the set of all negative disjunctions.

A *positive Herbrand State $\mathcal{H}^+$* is an arbitrary subset of DHB_P. A *negative Herbrand State $\mathcal{H}^-$* is an arbitrary subset of $\neg \cdot CHB_P$. Thus, $\mathcal{H}^+$ is a set of *positive* disjunctions while $\mathcal{H}^-$ is a set of *negative* disjunctions. Given a set $S \subseteq DHB_P \cup \neg \cdot CHB_P$ we write $Lit(S)$ for the set of literals contained in S.

Given an arbitrary set of disjunctions $\mathcal{D}$ we denote by $can(\mathcal{D})$ the set of all disjunctions D of $\mathcal{D}$ such that there is no proper subclause D' of D in $\mathcal{D}$: $can(\mathcal{D})$ is called the *canonical form* of $\mathcal{D}$.

2.1 Sceptical Semantics $SEM^{scept}(P)$

In the case of nondisjunctive logic programs all the existing semantics can be defined as subsets of the set of three-valued Herbrand-models of the underlying language $\mathcal{L}_P$. For disjunctive semantics, such models are not always available. For example the semantics defined by Minker and his group are given by associating to a program P a pair $\langle \mathcal{H}^+, \mathcal{H}^- \rangle$ consisting of Herbrand states. While Herbrand states also play a distinguished role in Przymusinski's *stationary* semantics ([Prz91]), his new *static* semantics ([Prz94]) is defined as a closed theory in an extended language. DSTABLE (the extension of the stable semantics to disjunctive programs [GL90]), however, is given by a set of classical (two-valued) models.

But even if a semantics SEM is given by associating to any program P an arbitrary subset Φ of $GHB_P{}^2$ we can naturally view such a semantics by its set of 3-valued Herbrand models of $\Phi \cup P$. We therefore define:

Definition 2.1 (SEM)
A semantics SEM is a mapping from the class of all programs into the powerset of the set of all 3-valued Herbrand structures. SEM assigns to every program P a set of 3-valued Herbrand models of P:

$$SEM(P) \subseteq MOD_{3-val}^{Herb_{\mathcal{L}_P}}(P).$$

In the sequel, however, we will abstract from such a semantics and only consider its induced *sceptical* consequence relation. We will also focus only on the derivable *pure* disjunctions. Thus we are associating to any semantics SEM the following sceptical relation:

$$SEM^{scept}(P) := \bigcap_{\mathcal{M} \in SEM(P)} \{D^{\pm} : \ \mathcal{M} \models_3 D^{\pm}\}.$$

Sometimes it is useful to restrict this notion a bit further and to denote SEM^{scept} as a pair $\langle \mathcal{H}^+, \mathcal{H}^- \rangle$ where both $\mathcal{H}^+$ and $\mathcal{H}^+$ are in their (unique) canonical forms: $can(\mathcal{H}^+) = \mathcal{H}^+$, $can(\mathcal{H}^-) = \mathcal{H}^-$. This formulation is needed when we consider *strong* properties like *Cumulativity* and *Rationality* in the context of disjunctive programs. It is, however, not needed in this paper. From now on, if no confusion arises, we also simply use $SEM(P)$ instead of $SEM^{scept}(P)$.

For a pure disjunction $D^{\pm}$ we use $SEM(P)(D^{\pm})$ to denote the truthvalue (**t** "true", **f** "false" or **u** "undefined") of $D^{\pm}$ with respect to SEM(P). We extend the two notions of the *extension relation* between semantics from the normal to the disjunctive case. When we say that a semantics SEM_2 *extends* another semantics SEM_1, we have to distinguish between:

- $SEM_1 \leq_k SEM_2$: i.e. for all P: $SEM_1(P) \subseteq SEM_2(P)$,

---

[2] GHB_P is the *generalized Herbrand Base* consisting of all disjunctions (also mixed, not only pure) over HB_P.

- SEM_2 is defined for a class of programs that strictly includes the class of programs for which SEM_1 is defined and for all programs of the smaller class, both semantics coincide.

The first notion makes perfectly sense for semantics defined for the same class of programs, while the second intuitively compares a semantics for one class of programs with the projection of another one to this class.

3   From Positive to General Disjunctive Programs

All semantics defined for the whole class of general disjunctive programs, considered so far in the literature, e.g. Baral, Lobo and Minker's GDWFS ([BLM91a]), Baral, Lobo and Minker's WF^3 ([BLM91b]), the stationary and the static semantics of Przymusinski coincide on the class of *positive* disjunctive programs: the respective semantics was first considered by Minker and is given by the set of minimal models of P. It interprets "$\vee$" exclusive and is called GCWA. In [RT88] and [RLM89] two complementary approaches, interpreting "$\vee$" inclusive, were introduced and turned out to be equivalent: WGCWA. We shall investigate its properties in the next section.

3.1   GCWA, WGCWA

In [MR90] a fixpoint operator $T_P^{\mathcal{C}}$ is defined operating on the powerset of DHB_P. The authors showed that the set of atoms, the negations of which are derivable under GCWA, is exactly $HB_P \setminus \{$atoms in $can(T_P^{\mathcal{C}} \uparrow \omega(\emptyset)\}$.

Originally, WGCWA was defined by modifying the set of derivable negated atoms. Instead of considering $HB_P \setminus \{$atoms in $can(T_P^{\mathcal{C}} \uparrow \omega(\emptyset)\}$ Minker and Rajasekar declared $HB_P \setminus \{$atoms in $T_P^{\mathcal{C}} \uparrow \omega(\emptyset)\}$ to be the set of derivable negated atoms under WGCWA. The set of derivable *atoms* is for both semantics the same. In [RLM89], they gave an equivalent model-theoretic characterization by transforming any positive disjunctive program P into a certain definite program P^* and considering M_{P^*} for the derivation of negated atoms.

The difference between GCWA and WGCWA can be illustrated very nicely with our strong properties introduced in [Dix92b] (see also Figure 1).

Note that although originally both GCWA and WGCWA were only defined to derive *literals* (not *pure disjunctions*), we are treating them as semantics as defined in the first section. This is no problem because they are both defined as a set of certain models. The same reason makes it possible to apply both semantics not only to positive programs, but also to programs enlarged by arbitrary pure disjunctions.

Recently, even semantics different from GCWA for positive programs have been defined ([DGM94]). The main underlying feature is to reduce the complexity. Nevertheless, most of our axioms to be introduced in the next section (with the exception of *Relevance* and *GCWA-Extension*) seem to hold.

3.2 PERFECT and WPERFECT

Analogously to the situation for programs without disjunction, there is also the notion of a *stratified* disjunctive database together with canonical models associated to it: the *perfect* models defined by Przymusinski. The definition of stratification naturally extends from normal programs to disjunctive programs (see [Prz88]).

In [Dix92b] we defined a semantics WPERFECT. It is an extension of WGCWA to stratified programs and based on the following set of models $\{M : M$ is a perfect model of $P\} \cup \{M_{P*}^{supp}\}$. It is interesting to note that Sakama and Inoue ([SI93]) defined independantly the same semantics[3].

Recently, Fernandez [Fer93] defined extensions of WGCWA with a lower complexity than WPERFECT[4]. He derives "$\neg a$" from the program "$a \leftarrow \neg b$, $a \leftarrow \neg c$, $b \lor c$": this behaviour does not reflect an *inclusive* interpretation of "$\lor$". We think that only the *derivation* of a should be blocked.

3.3 General Disjunctive Programs

While, as mentioned above, all semantics for general disjunctive programs coincide on positive programs with GCWA (resp. WGCWA), the picture is not completely homogenous in the case of stratified programs. WF[3] and GDWFS ([BLM91a, BLM91b]) do not extend PERFECT (see Figure 1). The stationary semantics of Przymusinski ([Prz91]) extends PERFECT in the version employing an additional *disjunctive inference rule*. In the definition of the static semantics ([Prz94]) Przymusinski decided to be more cautious: the static semantics does not extend PERFECT.

In Section 4.4 we generalize our definition of DWFS and WDWFS originally defined in [Dix92b]. These semantics are cautiously constructed on top of (W)PERFECT. They reflect our belief in the appropriateness of (W)PERFECT.

4 The Axioms

In this section we give axioms which should be satisfied for any semantics for disjunctive programs. Some of them will be known to readers of the previous papers on the topic but have to be adapted to the disjunctive case. We shall also try to convince the reader of the plausibility of our axioms.

4.1 Tautology and Subsumption

The principle of Tautology comes in two versions, one for the *exclusive* and one for the *inclusive* reading. Both state that the semantics of a program P should not depend on a clause containing no information.

---

[3]The restriction of their WGCWA$^{\neg}$ to stratified programs coincides with WPERFECT.
[4]WPERFECT is easily seen to be of the same complexity as PERFECT.

Definition 4.1 (Principle of Exclusive Tautology)
Let P be a general disjunctive program, $C \in P$ with $head(C) \cap body(C) \neq \emptyset$
(i.e. an atom a appears both in the head and (positively) in the body). Then:
$SEM(P) = SEM(P \backslash \{C\})$.

For an inclusive semantics it would be incorrect to delete e.g. the single clause from $P = \{a \vee b \leftarrow a\}$, since we must not derive $\neg b$ from P while we get it from the empty program. The inclusive version thus is a weaker and subsumed by the exclusive version:

Definition 4.2 (Principle of Inclusive Tautology)
Let P be a general disjunctive program, $C \in P$ with $head(C) \subseteq body(C)$.
Then: $SEM(P) = SEM(P \backslash \{C\})$.

For a semantics defined for all disjunctive programs one could generalize these and the following principles by also allowing *to add clauses*. We stick to the weaker ones, because we may leave the class of stratified programs by freely adding clauses such that $SEM(P \cup \{C\})$ may become undefined. In addition we intend to use the principles as reductions transforming a general disjunctive program to a stratified one whose semantics is well-understood.

It is also understood that the underlying language for the computation of SEM is always that of the larger program to ensure that (e.g.) the literals in $HB_P \backslash HB_{P \backslash \{C\}}$ are correctly classified as false.

The *principles of Subsumption* state that the semantics of P should not depend on a clause which contains less information than another clause in P. The first principle is required for both exclusive and inclusive view, while the second one can only hold in the exclusive case.

Definition 4.3 (Principle of Subsumption)
Let P be a general disjunctive logic program, l a literal and $C_1, C_2 \in P$ with
$head(C_1) = head(C_2)$, $body(C_1) \subseteq body(C_2)$.
Then: $SEM(P) = SEM(P \backslash \{C_2\})$.

Definition 4.4 (Principle of Exclusive Subsumption)
Let P be a general disjunctive program, $C_1, C_2 \in P$ with $body(C_1) \subseteq body(C_2)$
and $head(C_1) \subseteq head(C_2)$. Then: $SEM(P) = SEM(P \backslash \{C_2\})$.

Note that neither the principle of tautology nor the subsumption principle claims the redundancy of clauses with *inconsistent bodies* in general. Otherwise, we could not even capture the well-founded semantics, as the example $a \leftarrow b, \neg b$; $b \leftarrow \neg b, a$ shows. WFS is empty on this program, but derives $\neg a$ from $b \leftarrow \neg b, a$ by negation as failure.

4.2 Relevance

The principle of Relevance is a precondition of the applicability of a calculus as a programming or specification language. Without it one could not perform a top-down evaluation of queries. The principle states that no program clause should have influence on the truth conditions of some obviously unrelated concept. Not all semantics have this intuitive property. The most prominent example for the failure of Relevance is STABLE: consider the program $P = \{ a \leftarrow \neg b \}$ and P' obtained from P by adding "$c \leftarrow \neg c$": $P' = \{ a \leftarrow \neg b, \; c \leftarrow \neg c \}$. While P has the unique stable model $\{a\}$, P' has no stable models and therefore does not derive $\neg b$ (or, depending on how one interprets the empty set, derives anything). We consider this a very undesirable feature of STABLE. It is important to note that the problem is not the inconsistency alone (see [DM93]).

Definition 4.5 (Principle of Relevance)
*Let P be a general disjunctive logic program, $D^{\pm} \in DHB_P \cup \neg \cdot CHB_P$.
Then: $SEM(P)(D^{\pm}) = SEM(P_{rel}(D^{\pm}))(D^{\pm})$.*[5]

A consequence of Relevance is that an atom a which does not appear in the head of any clause becomes false, since then $P_{rel}(a) = \emptyset$.

4.3 Reduction

The idea of *reducing P with a set of pure disjunctions $\mathcal{D}^{\pm}$* is to use the information of $\mathcal{D}^{\pm}$ *(i) to simplify the program P by modifying (or even cancelling) some rules of P and thereby (ii) to derive new pure disjunctions*. In the case of normal programs (where only derivable *literals* are considered), things are much easier: *P reduced by $M \subseteq HB_P \cup \neg \cdot HB_P$* is obtained by replacing in P every occurrence of a literal contained in M by its truthvalue and then evaluate (or simplify) the program. This reduction decreases the Herbrand base (see [MD93]) as literals contained in M do no longer occur in P^M!

Note that although our notion of reduction resembles the Gelfond-Lifschitz transformation in the definition of stable models we use it differently in two respects: *(i) our reduced program still contains negation (the Gelfond-Lifschitz transformation is a positive program), (ii) while Gelfond/Lifschitz reduce with a set N of atoms (and implicitly assume that all atoms not in N are false), we are more cautious and reduce only those literals that are explicitly contained in M.*

The principle of reduction given in [Dix92a] states that reduction *with literals* should not change the semantics (L stands for literals):

Definition 4.6 (Principle of L-Reduction)
*Let P be a general disjunctive program and M a set of literals over HB_P.
Then: $SEM(P \cup M) = SEM(P^M) \cup M$.*

---

[5]I.e.: the truthvalue of $D^{\pm}$ with respect to $SEM(P)$ coincides with the truthvalue of $D^{\pm}$ with respect to $SEM(P_{rel}(D^{\pm}))$.

While the addition of atoms to P has an obvious meaning, the addition of negative literals has not: in the normal case we mean with $P \cup \{\neg x\}$ the program obtained from P by deleting all clauses with x in their heads. In the disjunctive case this amounts to deleting x from all heads in which it appears and dropping the clauses whose heads become empty.

We are now generalizing this idea to disjunctive programs. Given a pure disjunction D, we can think of the following four cases of D *subsumes a clause* C:

Definition 4.7 (Syntactical D-Reductions)

Let $D^+ = a_1 \vee \ldots \vee a_n$, $D^- = \neg c_1 \vee \ldots \vee \neg c_k$, and C be a program clause. We say

1. D^- α-implies C :iff $C = head \leftarrow c_1, \ldots, c_k, body,$
2. D^+ β-implies C :iff $C = a_1 \vee \ldots \vee a_m \vee head \leftarrow \neg a_{m+1}, \ldots, \neg a_n, body,$
3. D^+ γ-implies C :iff $C = a_1 \vee \ldots \vee a_n \leftarrow body.$

Now let $\mathcal{D}^{\pm}$ be a set of pure disjunctions and C a program clause. Then the syntactical reduction $red(C; \mathcal{D}^{\pm})$ of C by $\mathcal{D}^{\pm}$ is defined as follows:

1. *Exclusive Case:*

$$
C^S = \begin{cases}
\mathbf{t}, & \text{if there is } D \in \mathcal{D}^{\pm} \text{ such that} \\
& D \text{ } \alpha\text{-, or } \beta\text{-implies } C \text{ } m \leq n, \\
C', & \text{otherwise, where} \\
& head(C') = head(C)\backslash\{\neg l \mid l \in Lit(\mathcal{D}^-)\}, \\
& body(C') = body(C)\backslash Lit(\mathcal{D}^{\pm}).
\end{cases}
$$

2. *Inclusive Case:*

$$
C^S = \begin{cases}
\mathbf{t}, & \text{if there is } D \in \mathcal{D}^{\pm} \text{ such that} \\
& D \text{ } \alpha\text{- or } \gamma\text{-implies } C, \\
C', & \text{otherwise, where} \\
& head(C') = head(C), \\
& body(C') = body(C)\backslash Lit(\mathcal{D}^{\pm}).
\end{cases}
$$

The syntactical reduction of a program P by $\mathcal{D}^{\pm}$ is explained clausewise: $red(P; \mathcal{D}^{\pm}) := \{red(C; \mathcal{D}^{\pm}) \mid C \in P\}.$

Unfortunately, this notion of reduction is not strong enough. Let us consider the following simple example

$$
\begin{array}{llll}
P: & x \leftarrow a & P': & x \leftarrow \neg a \\
& x \leftarrow b & & x \leftarrow \neg b \\
& x \leftarrow \neg x & & x \leftarrow \neg x
\end{array}
$$

We claim that any semantics should be able to derive x from $P \cup \{a \vee b\}$ and from $P' \cup \{\neg a \vee \neg b\}$.[6] Up to now, neither of our reductions allow us to simplify the program in such a way that x is derivable. For normal programs, all three-valued consequences (i.e. literals!) can be obtained by successively applying our reductions. In the disjunctive case, however, this is not possible as our examples show. In view of the fact that we consider semantics as given by a certain set of 3-valued Herbrand models, this amounts to require for a reasonable semantics to add (at least) all 3-valued (positive) consequences of a program.

Definition 4.8 (P reduced by $\mathcal{D}^{\pm}$: $P^{\mathcal{D}^{\pm}}$)
Let $\mathcal{D}^{\pm}$ be a set of pure disjunctions and C a program clause. Then we denote by $P^{\mathcal{D}^{\pm}}$ the "reduction of P with respect to $\mathcal{D}^{\pm}$" defined as follows:

> *1. Let $P' := red(P; \mathcal{D}^{\pm})$ and $P'' := P'^{Lit(\mathcal{D}^{\pm})}$.*

> *2. Finally: $P^{\mathcal{D}^{\pm}} := P'' \cup \{D^+ \mid D^+ \text{ a pos. disj. with } P'' \cup \mathcal{D}^{\pm} \models_3 D^+\}$.*

Once again, the reduction of a program P by $\mathcal{D}^{\pm}$ is explained clausewise:
$P^{\mathcal{D}^{\pm}} := \{C^{\mathcal{D}^{\pm}} \mid C \in P\}$.

Since we do not exploit the disjunctive knowledge contained in $\mathcal{D}^{\pm}$, $\mathcal{L}_{\mathcal{D}^{\pm}}$ and $\mathcal{L}_{P\mathcal{D}^{\pm}}$ are in general not disjoint. We require the following weak principle:

Definition 4.9 (Principle of D-Reduction)
Let P be a general disjunctive program and $\mathcal{D}^+ \subseteq DHB_P$.
Then: $SEM(P^{\mathcal{D}^+} \cup \mathcal{D}^+) = SEM(P \cup \mathcal{D}^+)$.

This principle is the analogue of the L-Reduction. It guarantees (together with some other principles) that if $P \cup SEM(P) \models_3 D^{\pm}$ then $D^{\pm} \in SEM(P)$.

4.4 DWFS and WDWFS

Here we generalize our definition of DWFS and WDWFS originally defined in [Dix92b]. First we need the definition of *ending in a negative loop*: an atom $x \in HB_P$ *ends in a negative loop* w.r.t. P, if x depends on an atom y that depends negatively on itself. We say that a pure disjunction *ends in a negative loop*, if some of its components do. We also denote by $P^{\#}$ the result of removing all program clauses from P, that contain in their bodies a literal that ends in a negative loop.

Note that $P^{\#}$ always is a stratified program. This allows us to construct a weak semantics DWFS (resp. WDWFS) by iteratively computing $P_{\alpha}^{\#}$ and using a given semantics for stratified programs in an appropriate way. The main notion is that of *reducing a program P by a set of pure disjunctions* $\mathcal{D}^{\pm}$. Suppose we already constructed $P_{\alpha}^{\#}$ and computed SEM_{α} (the final

---

[6]Note that this claim is different from requiring to derive x from $\{a \leftarrow \neg b; \ b \leftarrow \neg a; \ x \leftarrow a; \ x \leftarrow b\}$.

semantics will be the union $\bigcup_\alpha SEM_\alpha$). We first consider $P_\alpha^\#$ and compute $SEM(P_\alpha^\#)$. Then we reduce the program P_α by $SEM(P_\alpha^\#)$ and obtain $P_{\alpha+1}$. The construction eventually ends (in finitely many steps, if we consider propositional programs) and we are done.[7]

Definition 4.10 (DWFS and WDWFS)
Let $P_0 := P$ and

$$P_{\alpha+1} := P_\alpha^{\mathcal{D}_\alpha^+ \cup \mathcal{D}_\alpha^-}, \ where$$

$$\mathcal{D}_\alpha^- = \{D^- : \ D^- \in \neg \cdot CHB_{P_\alpha} \ does \ not \ end \ in \ a \ negative \ loop \ in \ P_\alpha \ an$$
$$D^- \in PERFECT_{\mathcal{L}_{P_\alpha}}(P_\alpha^\#)\},$$

$$\mathcal{D}_\alpha^+ = \{D^+ : \ D^+ \in DHB_{P_\alpha^\#} \ and \ D^+ \in PERFECT(P_\alpha^\#)\}.$$

Note that $\mathcal{L}_{P_{\alpha+1}} \subseteq \mathcal{L}_{P_\alpha}$. The construction ends, if $\mathcal{D}_\alpha^+ \cup \mathcal{D}_\alpha^- = \mathcal{D}_{\alpha+1}^+ \cup \mathcal{D}_{\alpha+1}^-$ and $\mathcal{L}_{P_{\lambda+1}} = \mathcal{L}_{P_\lambda}$. We therefore define:

$$SEM(P) = \bigcup_{\alpha=0}^{\lambda} \mathcal{D}_\alpha^+ \ \cup \ \bigcup_{\alpha=0}^{\lambda} \mathcal{D}_\alpha^-.$$

The semantics WDWFS for the inclusive interpretation of "$\vee$" is obtained by simply replacing "PERFECT" by "WPERFECT".

The notion of *reduction* (i.e. $P_\alpha^{\mathcal{D}_\alpha^+ \cup \mathcal{D}_\alpha^-}$) is crucial in the above definition: note that it depends on the *exclusive* or *inclusive* interpretation of "$\vee$".

4.5 Modularity

The dependency graph $\mathcal{G}_P$ of a program P induces a *modular structure* of P by the partial order given by its strongly connected components, where positive and negative edges of $\mathcal{G}_P$ are not distinguished. More formally: we say $a \approx b$:iff there is a path from a to b and vice versa in $\mathcal{G}_P$. Since $\approx$ is an equivalence relation it induces *(i) equivalence classes, which we call* modules *of P*, and *(ii) a partial order on these modules*. Let us call a program P *definitionally-closed* :iff for all $a \in HB_P : P_{rel}(a) \subseteq P$.

The principle of modularity states that we can compute the semantics of P bottom up following the modular structure of P:

Definition 4.11 (Principle of Modularity (see [Dix92a]))
Let $P = P_1 \dot\cup P_2$ such that P_2 is definitionally-closed. Then we have:

$$SEM(P_1 \cup P_2) = SEM(P_1^{SEM(P_2)} \cup P_2).$$

---

[7]As explained above, the notation $PERFECT_{\mathcal{L}_P}$ indicates that PERFECT is to be evaluated w.r.t. $\mathcal{L}_P$.

Note that - by Relevance - we may restrict P_2 to the for $P_1^{SEM(P_2)}$ relevant part $P_2' = \bigcup\{P_{rel}(a) \mid a \in P_1^{SEM(P_2)}\}$. Then we obtain: $SEM(P_1 \cup P_2) = SEM(P_1^{SEM(P_2)} \cup P_2') \cup SEM(P_2)$. As an example let us consider

$$
\begin{array}{llll}
P_1: & b & \leftarrow & y \\
 & y \vee x & \leftarrow & a \\
 & z \vee y & \leftarrow & a \\
 & m & \leftarrow & x, z, b \\
 & y & \leftarrow & \neg m
\end{array}
\qquad
\begin{array}{llll}
P_2: & a & \leftarrow & e, \neg g \\
 & a & \leftarrow & f, \neg g \\
 & a & \leftarrow & f, \neg e \\
 & a & \leftarrow & g, \neg e \\
 & e \vee f \vee g &
\end{array}
$$

$\mathcal{G}_{P_2}$ is a strongly connected component of $\mathcal{G}_{P_1 \cup P_2}$. As PERFECT derives a from P_2, we should have $SEM(P_1 \cup P_2) \mid_{\mathcal{L}_{P_1 \setminus \{a\}}} = SEM(P_1^{\{a\}})$ for any semantics extending PERFECT.

This formulation complements *Relevance* and expresses the wish to compute $SEM(P_2)$ exactly once and then percolate this definite knowledge into dependent modules. There is a strong relation between the principles of L-Reduction and Modularity. We can think of literals as *trivial modules* the semantics of which is fixed in advance.

4.6 PPE

In [Dix92a] we introduced the PPE, a principle related to partial evaluation. The failure of the PPE for GWFS can be illustrated with the following program P, which also applies to GDWFS and WF[3], since on this particular program all these semantics coincide.

$$
\begin{array}{llll}
P: & p & \leftarrow & \neg b \\
 & b & \leftarrow & c \\
 & c & \leftarrow & p, \neg a \\
 & a & \leftarrow & \neg b
\end{array}
\qquad
\begin{array}{llll}
P_c: & p & \leftarrow & \neg b \\
 & b & \leftarrow & p, \neg a \\
 & a & \leftarrow & \neg b
\end{array}
$$

Note that c has only been replaced by the rule defining it, but yet the semantics of P and P_c differ: P derives p and a while P_c does not.

The following generalizes the PPE to the disjunctive case (see also [Mül92])

Definition 4.12 (Disjunctive PPE)
Let P be a general disjunctive logic program and let $c \in HB_P$ appear only positively in P. Let $P_{def}(c) = \{c \vee head_1 \leftarrow body_1, \ldots, c \vee head_n \leftarrow body_n\}$, where for no i: $body_i$ contains c.[8] Define P_c as the program which consists of exactly the clauses

$$head \vee head_1 \leftarrow body, body_1$$
$$\vdots$$
$$head \vee head_n \leftarrow body, body_n$$

for every $head \leftarrow c, body \in P$. If any $a \in \bigcup_{i=1}^n head_i$ appears only positively in P as well, we require: $SEM(P_c) = SEM(P)$.

---

[8] Note that Tautology allows to satisfy this condition trivially.

Without the last proviso the transformation $P \rightsquigarrow P_c$ might destroy the stratifiability of P: the program $\{a \vee b; \ c \leftarrow \neg b, a\}$ is stratified, while $P_a = \{b \vee c \leftarrow \neg b\}$ is not. In the normal case this principle reduces to the one given in [Dix92a]. Repeated application of the PPE may drastically reduce the Herbrand Base induced by P while the number of clauses may grow very large.

4.7 GCWA- and WGCWA-Property

Our last property is designed to ensure a semantics to be either an extension of GCWA (exclusive interpretation of "$\vee$") or of WGCWA (inclusive interpretation of "$\vee$"). It reduces the semantics of a program P in some special cases to the computation of GCWA or WGCWA. Recall the difficulty to explain $P \cup \{D^-\}$ for an arbitrary semantics while it is straightforward in the model based GCWA (WGCWA).

Definition 4.13 (GCWA- (resp. WGCWA-) Extension)
Let $P = P_1 \cup P_2$ be a disjunctive logic program where P_2 is positive and definitionally-closed. We assume further that the only negative dependencies are of the form "a neg. depends on b" where $a \in HB_{P_1}$ and $a \in HB_{P_2}$. The principle of GCWA-Extension states:

$$SEM(P_1 \cup P_2) = GCWA(P_1^{shift} \cup SEM(P_2)),$$

where P_1^{shift} is the positive disjunctive program obtained from P_1 by putting every negative literal in the body of a clause to its head.

The principle of WGCWA-Extension is obtained by replacing GCWA by WGCWA.

The last property we need is the *Cut*. It states that "if $\mathcal{D}^+ \subseteq SEM(P)$ then $SEM(P \cup \mathcal{D}^+) \subseteq SEM(P)$.

4.8 Well-behaved Semantics

We are now in a position to define what a well-behaved semantics is:

Definition 4.14 (Well-behaved Semantics)
A well-behaved disjunctive semantics SEM under the exclusive view *is a mapping*
$$\{P : P \ a \ program\} \longrightarrow 2^{DHB_P \cup \neg \cdot CHB_P}$$
such that the following conditions are satisfied:

- *Exclusive Tautology, Subsumption, Exclusive Subsumption, Relevance, D-Reduction, Modularity, Disjunctive PPE, Cut, and GCWA-Extension*

A well-behaved disjunctive semantics SEM under the inclusive view *is obtained by dropping above the principle of "Exclusive Subsumption", replacing "Exclusive Tautology" by "Inclusive Tautology" and replacing "GCWA-Extension" by "WGCWA-Extension".*

Using the principles we have introduced so far, we are able to prove:

Theorem 4.15 (Well-behaved Excl. SEM's extend PERFECT)
Any well-behaved exclusive semantics coincides for stratified programs with PERFECT.

Theorem 4.16 (Well-behaved Incl. SEM's extend WPERFECT)
Any well-behaved inclusive semantics coincides for stratified programs with WPERFECT.

The proof for both theorems is along the lines for the proof given in [Dix94b, Theorem 5.18] that any well-behaved semantics already extends M^{supp}. The lowest stratum of a stratified disj. program is a positive disj. program. By iterated application of *D-Reduction*, *Modularity*, *Relevance* and *GCWA-Extension* (resp. *WGCWA-Extension*) we can reduce every stratified program to a positive disjunctive program (together with a set of pure disjunctions), the semantics of which is determined by GCWA (resp. WGCWA).

Theorem 4.17 (DWFS as weakest extension of PERFECT)
DWFS is a well-behaved exclusive semantics. In addition, it is the weakest one: any well-behaved excl. semantics is a $\leq_k$-extension of DWFS.

Theorem 4.18 (WDWFS as weakest extension of WPERFECT)
WDWFS is a well-behaved inclusive semantics. In addition, it is the weakest one: any well-behaved incl. semantics is a $\leq_k$-extension of WDWFS.

The proofs can again be generalized from the corresponding ones in [Dix94b]. Complete proofs and more illustrating examples will be given in the full paper. The newly introduced static semantics from Przymusinski seems to fulfill all of our principles, with the exception of *GCWA-Extension* (which is obvious since it does not extend PERFECT).

We end with Figure 1 that illustrates how most of the semantics discussed above are related. The exact definition of the *strong* properties like *Cumulativity*, *Rationality*, *OR* and *Converse of OR* in our extended framework (where arbitrary *pure* disjunctions are allowed to be derived) will be dealt with in a separate paper.

5 Conclusion

We have introduced an axiomatic approach of classifying and representing semantics of disjunctive logic programs. If we restrict to *normal* programs, our results reduce to those presented in [Dix92a, Dix94b]. Unlike in the normal case, where several reasonable semantics compete with each other, there are not many such candidates for general disjunctive programs. We do, however, strongly believe that any reasonable semantics for disjunctive

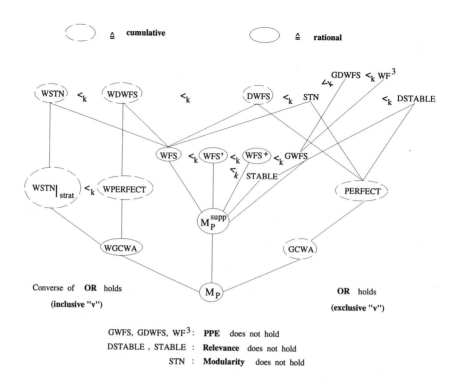

Figure 1: Semantics for Disjunctive Programs

programs should extend either PERFECT or WPERFECT. Theorems 4.17 and 4.18 illustrate that DWFS and WDWFS are indeed the weakest possible semantics.

The axiomatic approach may be used to derive reasonable semantics on the base of such with drawbacks. How for instance a well-behaved version of STABLE could be defined, is shown in [DM93].

Recently, Alferes et. al. ([ADP93]) noted the usefulness of our weak principles of *PPE*, *Modularity* and *Relevance* for defining Top-Down Query evaluation methods for normal logic programs. We believe that the extensions of these principles to the disjunctive case will also turn out to be interesting for implementation-theoretic purposes.

We also hope that our investigations help to find new and reasonable semantics defined for all disjunctive programs. Especially distinguishing between an *inclusive* and an *exclusive* meaning of "∨" might turn out to be useful in different application domains.

6 Acknowledgments

We would like to thank Roland Bol and two anonymous referees for suggestions how to improve the presentation of some principles and for clarifying comments.

References

[ADP93] J. J. Alferes, Carlos Viegas Damasio, and L. M. Pereira. Top-down query evaluation for well-founded semantics with explicit negation (draft). Technical report, CENTRIA, 1993.

[BLM91a] C. Baral, J. Lobo, and J. Minker. Generalized Disjunctive Well-founded Semantics for Logic Programs: Declarative Semantics. In Z.W. Ras, M. Zemankova, and M.L Emrich, editors, *Proceedings of the 5th Int. Symp. on Methodologies for Intelligent Systems, Knoxville, TN, October 1990*, pages 459–468, 1991.

[BLM91b] C. Baral, J. Lobo, and J. Minker. WF^3: A Semantics for Negation in Normal Disjunctive Logic Programs. In Z.W. Ras and M. Zemankova, editors, *Methodologies for Intelligent Systems*, pages 459–468. Springer, Lecture Notes in Artificial Intelligence 542, 1991.

[DGM94] Jürgen Dix, Georg Gottlob, and Viktor Marek. Causal Models for Disjunctive Logic Programs. In Pascal Van Hentenryck, editor, *Proceedings of the 11th Int. Conf. on Logic Programming, S. Margherita Ligure*. MIT, June 1994.

[Dix91] Jürgen Dix. Classifying Semantics of Logic Programs. In Anil Nerode, Wiktor Marek, and V. S. Subrahmanian, editors, *Logic Programming and Non-Monotonic Reasoning, Proceedings of the first International Workshop*, pages 166–180. Washington D.C, MIT Press, July 1991.

[Dix92a] Jürgen Dix. A Framework for Representing and Characterizing Semantics of Logic Programs. In B. Nebel, C. Rich, and W. Swartout, editors, *Principles of Knowledge Representation and Reasoning: Proceedings of the Third International Conference (KR '92)*, pages 591–602. San Mateo, CA, Morgan Kaufmann, 1992.

[Dix92b] Jürgen Dix. Classifying Semantics of Disjunctive Logic Programs. In K. Apt, editor, *LOGIC PROGRAMMING: Proceedings of the 1992 Joint International Conference and Symposium*, pages 798–812. MIT Press, November 1992.

[Dix94a] Jürgen Dix. A Classification-Theory of Semantics of Normal Logic Programs: I. Strong Properties. *Fundamenta Informaticae*, forthcoming, 1994.

[Dix94b] Jürgen Dix. A Classification-Theory of Semantics of Normal Logic Programs: II. Weak Properties. *Fundamenta Informaticae*, forthcoming, 1994.

[DM93] Jürgen Dix and Martin Müller. Extensions and Improvements of the Stable Semantics. Technical report, submitted, University of Koblenz, Department of Computer Science, 1993.

[Fer93]   Jose Alberto Fernandez. Weak Models for Disjunctive Logic Programs. In *Proceedings of Workshop on Logic Programming with Incomplete Information, Vancouver Oct. 1993, following ILPS' 93*, pages 190–205, 1993.

[GL90]   Michael Gelfond and Vladimir Lifschitz. Logic Program with Classical Negation. In David H.D. Warren and Peter Szeredi, editors, *Proceedings of the 7th Int. Conf. on Logic Programming*, pages 579–597. MIT, June 1990.

[GL91]   Michael Gelfond and Vladimir Lifschitz. Classical Negation in Logic Programs and Disjunctive Databases. *New Generation Computing*, 9, 1991.

[LMR92]   Jorge Lobo, Jack Minker, and Arcot Rajasekar. *Foundations of Disjunctive Logic Programming*. MIT-Press, 1992.

[MD93]   Martin Müller and Jürgen Dix. Implementing Semantics for Disjunctive Logic Programs Using Fringes and Abstract Properties. In Luis Moniz Pereira and Anil Nerode, editors, *Logic Programming and Non-Monotonic Reasoning, Proceedings of the Second International Workshop*, pages 43–59. Lisbon, MIT Press, July 1993.

[MLR91]   Jack Minker, Jorge Lobo, and Arcot Rajasekar. Circumscription and Disjunctive Logic Programming. In V. Lifschitz, editor, *Artificial Intelligence and Mathematical Theory of Computation. Papers in Honor of John McCarthy*, pages 281–304. Academic Press, 1991.

[MR90]   Jack Minker and Arcot Rajasekar. A fixpoint semantics for disjunctive logic programs. *Journal of Logic Programming*, 9:45–74, 1990.

[Mül92]   Martin Müller. Disjunctive Logic Programs: Characterization and Implementation. Master's thesis, Universität Karlsruhe, 1992. (in German).

[Prz88]   Teodor Przymusinski. On the declarative semantics of deductive databases and logic programs. In Jack Minker, editor, *Foundations of Deductive Databases*, chapter 5, pages 193–216. Morgan Kaufmann, 1988.

[Prz91]   Teodor Przymusinski. Stationary Semantics for Normal and Disjunctive Logic Programs. In C. Delobel, M. Kifer, and Y. Masunaga, editors, *DOOD '91, Proceedings of the 2nd International Conference*. Muenchen, Springer, LNCS 566, December 1991.

[Prz94]   Teodor Przymusinski. Static Semantics For Normal and Disjunctive Logic Programs. *Annals of Mathematics and Artificial Intelligence*, Special Issue on Disjunctive Programs:to appear, 1994.

[RLM89]   Arcot Rajasekar, Jorge Lobo, and Jack Minker. Weak Generalized Closed World Assumption. *Journal of Automated Reasoning*, 5:293–307, 1989.

[RT88]   Kenneth A. Ross and Rodney A. Topor. Inferring negative Information from disjunctive Databases. *Journal of Automated Reasoning*, 4:397–424, 1988.

[SI93]   Chiaki Sakama and Katsumi Inoue. Negation in Disjunctive Logic Programs. In D. Warren and Peter Szeredi, editors, *Proceedings of the 10th Int. Conf. on Logic Programming, Budapest*. MIT, July 1993.

Constraints I

Finding Conflict Sets and Backtrack Points in CLP($\Re$)

Jennifer Burg
Wake Forest University
Winston-Salem, NC 27109
burg@mthcsc.wfu.edu

Sheau-Dong Lang
Charles E. Hughes
University of Central Florida
Orlando, FL 32816
lang@cs.ucf.edu
ceh@cs.ucf.edu

Abstract

This paper presents a method for intelligent backtracking in CLP($\Re$). Our method integrates a depth-first intelligent backtracking algorithm developed for logic programming with an original constraint satisfaction algorithm which naturally generates sets of conflicting constraints. We prove that if CLP($\Re$) is assumed to cover strictly the domain of real numbers, then the constraint satisfaction algorithm provides minimal conflict sets to be used as a basis for intelligent backtracking. We then extend the backtracking method to cover a two-sorted domain, where variables can be bound to either structured terms or real numbers. We discuss a practical implementation of the algorithm using a generator-consumer approach to the recording of variable bindings, and we give an example of a CLP($\Re$) program which benefits significantly from intelligent backtracking.

1 Introduction

CLP($\Re$) is a constraint logic programming language in which constraints can be expressed in the domain of real numbers. Even when these constraints are restricted to linear equations and inequalities[1], this language has proven to be expressive enough for practical applications such as scheduling problems, options trading, critical path analysis, resolution of temporal constraints, and AI-type puzzles [8, 2]. However, the range of problems which are solved efficiently by CLP($\Re$) is limited by the possible explosion of the search space as well as the complexity of the constraint satisfaction algorithm. A number of approaches to speeding up execution of CLP($\Re$) programs have been

---

[1]with, optionally, a mechanism for "delaying" non-linear constraints until sufficient variables are bound to make them linear

explored, including the fine-tuning of simplex-based constraint satisfaction algorithms, compilation [10], parallelism [2], and intelligent backtracking, the subject of this paper.

Intelligent backtracking seems a particularly appropriate strategy for CLP($\Re$), since the real-number domain lends itself quite naturally to the identification of conflict sets. We can illustrate this point with the CLP($\Re$) program in Figure 1, which solves the following cryptarithmetic puzzle:

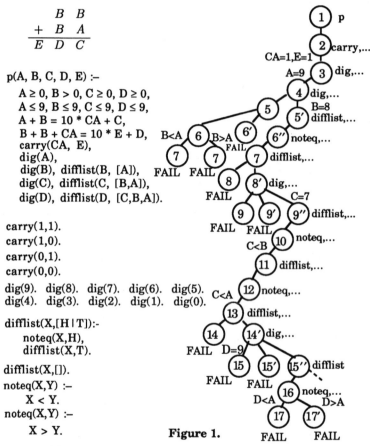

$$\begin{array}{ccc} & B & B \\ + & B & A \\ \hline E & D & C \end{array}$$

p(A, B, C, D, E) :–

   A ≥ 0, B > 0, C ≥ 0, D ≥ 0,
   A ≤ 9, B ≤ 9, C ≤ 9, D ≤ 9,
   A + B = 10 * CA + C,
   B + B + CA = 10 * E + D,
   carry(CA, E),
   dig(A),
   dig(B), difflist(B, [A]),
   dig(C), difflist(C, [B,A]),
   dig(D), difflist(D, [C,B,A]).

carry(1,1).
carry(1,0).
carry(0,1).
carry(0,0).

dig(9). dig(8). dig(7). dig(6). dig(5).
dig(4). dig(3). dig(2). dig(1). dig(0).

difflist(X,[H | T]):-
   noteq(X,H),
   difflist(X,T).

difflist(X,[]).
noteq(X,Y) :–
   X < Y.
noteq(X,Y) :–
   X > Y.

Figure 1.

When node 4 is exited, A is 9 and B is 8. Upon exit from node 8′, C is redundantly given the value 7. At node 15, we fail to find a consistent value for D. Clearly, this failure was inevitable as soon as A was given the value 9 and B the value 8, and trying new values for C is wasted effort. A useful intelligent backtracking algorithm should recognize this and backtrack directly to node 4.

The backtracking method which we propose for CLP($\Re$) prunes obvious failure paths from the search tree by identifying conflict sets during the constraint satisfiability check. The first time a failure occurs at node 17, the relevant constraints in the tableau are (assuming the unification of variables) (1) $A \geq 0$, (2) $B > 0$, (3) $C \geq 0$, (4) $D \geq 0$, (5) $A \leq 9$, (6) $B \leq 9$, (7) $C \leq 9$, (8) $D \leq 9$, (9) $A + B = 10 * CA + C$, (10) $B + B + CA = 10 * E + D$, (11) $E = 1$, (12) $CA = 1$, (13) $A = 9$, (14) $B = 8$, (15) $A - B > 0$, (16) $C = 7$, (17) $B - C > 0$, (18) $A - C > 0$, (19) $D = 9$, (20) $D < A$. A failure is signaled when D is given the value 9 but at node 16 the constraints $D < A$ and $D > A$ both fail. We will show that our constraint satisfaction algorithm can easily identify the source of the conflict (equations 20, 14, 13, 12, 11, 10, and 9), and as execution retreats from node 15 this information sends us directly back to the last node where one of the guilty equations was introduced, node 4.

The compatibility between CLP($\Re$) and intelligent backtracking has been recognized by DeBacker and Beringer [7], Hogger and Kotzamanidis [9], and Burg, Lang, and Hughes [2, 3]. The roots of the research can be traced to Bruynooghe and Pereira [1] and Cox [6], who developed strategies for intelligent backtracking in logic programming. More recent work includes generator-consumer approaches [12] and the DIB (depth-first intelligent backtracking) algorithm of Codognet, Codognet, Filé, and Sola [4, 5]. DeBacker and Beringer give a recursive formulation of the DIB algorithm in [7], pointing out that it is applicable to any constraint logic programming language in which conflict sets can be identified upon failure. However, they stop short of integrating the algorithm into CLP($\Re$) since they do not allow for the possibility of structured terms in the domain. With such a restriction, the CLP($\Re$) they assume is not the language originally conceived by Jaffar et al., who describe CLP($\Re$) as based upon a two-sorted domain of real numbers and structured terms [11]. The two-sorted domain yields a more interesting, expressive language, and it is worthwhile to extend intelligent backtracking to this context. Our contribution to this research area is to integrate intelligent backtracking into the two-sorted domain of CLP($\Re$), basing our method on an original constraint satisfaction algorithm and an accompanying proof that minimal conflict sets are generated directly.

2 Depth-First Intelligent Backtracking

We begin by sketching the DIB algorithm which forms the framework of our backtracking method. Consider the example in Figure 2. At each failure node i, we identify a set containing conflicting constraints associated with the failure. Call this set the *conflict set* for node i. The *source* of a constraint is defined as the node to which execution must return in order to remove the constraint from the tableau. The source of a goal literal is defined similarly. The *backtrack set* for failure node i is defined as the union of the source numbers for all the constraints in i's conflict set. The backtrack set tells us the nodes at which new execution paths ought to be tried. The idea is that if node i receives a failure message from its child node, but i is not in the accompanying backtrack set, then constraints introduced at i had nothing to do with the conflict, and trying another branch from there is useless.

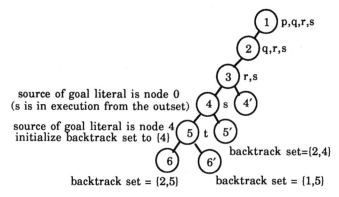

Figure 2.

Say that when we attempt to execute goal t at node 5, we fail on both branches. When the conflict is detected at node 6, the backtrack set $\{2, 5\}$ is passed up and stored at node 5. Then, node 5 tries another branch to execute goal t. Again, t fails, and the backtrack set $\{1, 5\}$ is returned to node 5, where it is unioned with $\{2, 5\}$. At this point, node 5 has no more paths to try, so 5 is deleted from the collected set. Note that before this backtrack set $\{1, 2\}$ can be sent up the tree, the source of node 5's leftmost goal must be included in it, yielding $\{1, 2, 4\}$. This is because it is goal t which failed, and when we go back to node 4 we remove t from execution. If 4 were not in the backtrack set returned to node 4, node 4 would not try another branch and a solution could be missed. In our example, re-execution of goal s at node $5'$ returns the backtrack set $\{2, 4\}$ to node 4. Since node 4's leftmost goal, s, was in execution from the root of the search tree, there is nothing to add to this backtrack set, and node 3 receives the set $\{1, 2\}$. At this point, node 3 knows that it is useless to try another branch, and it immediately fails, passing the backtrack set $\{1, 2\}$ up to node 2.

3   The Constraint Satisfaction Algorithm

The implementation of a CLP($\Re$) interpreter can be divided into two modules: an inference engine, which performs resolution; and a solver, which checks the satisfiability of linear constraints in the real number domain. To describe this algorithm, we use R and M to denote the tableau of constraints.[2] R represents the constraints as they first appeared to the

---

[2]For convenience, we speak interchangeably of the tableau as an ordered list of rows, a set of rows, or a matrix. M_i denotes the ith row in the tableau, while $M_{i,j}$ denotes the coefficient of the jth variable in the ith row.

solver, in their canonical input form. Before being given to the solver, inequalities are transformed to equations with slack variables, where each slack variable is constrained to take on only non-negative values. M is the "working copy" of the tableau, upon which Gaussian elimination and the simplex method are performed in order to maintain M in a solved form.

We call our constraint satisfaction algorithm *checksat*. Beginning with a tableau M of $m-1$ constraints which, taken together, are known to be satisfiable, *checksat* is given a new constraint to process, identical copies being placed in rows R_m and M_m. Each row M_i in the satisfiable tableau has a variable that is implicitly being "solved for" in the row. We call this variable the *basic variable* in the row. If the basic variable is a program variable (unconstrained), then it is the first variable in the row.[3] If the basic variable is a slack variable, then it does not appear in any other row which has only slack variables (*all-slack rows*). The constant in each row in the tableau is maintained as non-negative.

The tableau is maintained in this solved form in the following manner. First, basic unconstrained variables are substituted out of M_m until the first non-basic unconstrained variable is encountered, if one exists. Then there are four cases to consider. (1) If the equation has reduced to $0 = 0$, it is redundant and M_m and R_m are discarded. (2) Else, if it reduces to $a = b$ where a and b are constants and $a \neq b$, it is in conflict with the rest of the tableau. (3) Else, if a non-basic unconstrained variable has been encountered, it is made basic. (4) Else, if only slack variables remain, basic slack variables are substituted out of M_m, the all-slack rows are isolated, and we perform the first phase of the two-phase simplex method on them to determine if a slack variable can be made basic. We know that a slack variable cannot be made basic if we reach a state where the coefficients for all the slack variables in the new row are non-positive while the constant is positive. In this case, the tableau is unsatisfiable. We give the full algorithm and a proof of correctness in [2].

This algorithm has certain advantages over other algorithms proposed for CLP($\Re$). First, the operations of Gaussian elimination and the simplex method are cleanly separated, making the algorithm simple to describe, implement, and prove correct. The clean dichotomy also increases the algorithm's efficiency in that only the all-slack rows are involved in the simplex procedure. Furthermore, only the forward elimination part of Gaussian elimination is used to uncover linear dependencies in the tableau, back substitution being delayed until the end of a successful solution path. Forward elimination is often sufficient for the satisfiability check, and we are saved the expense of back substitution (which serves only to make the solution more explicit) on failure paths. Most importantly for our purposes here, we can show that this algorithm naturally generates minimal conflict sets.

---

[3]For efficiency reasons, variables are ordered according to their time of creation, newer variables placed before older ones, and program variables before slack variables. To avoid confusion, we do not show the newer-to-older ordering in the examples below.

4 Collecting Conflict Sets

To identify a conflict set when *checksat* uncovers a conflict, we keep a record of row operations. This process can easily be described with a matrix representation. Without loss of generality, we can assume that the solver is given m constraints to process, and it processes them one at a time, finding a conflict when it gets to the mth one. R is an $m \times n + 1$ matrix representing the original forms of the rows in the tableau. M is a dynamic $m \times n + 1$ matrix representing the rows as they change state during *checksat*. We will use an $m \times m$ matrix B to record the row operations which transform R to M. Initially, B is the identity matrix. Each time we add a multiple of one row to another during Gaussian elimination or simplex, as in $M_j \leftarrow c * M_i + M_j$ we also perform $B_j \leftarrow c * B_i + B_j$. By this means, we maintain the relation $M = B * R$. In particular, say that the last row of B is $[B_{m,1}, ..., B_{m,m}]$. Then we have the relation

$$M_m = B_{m,1} * R_1 + ... + B_{m,m} * R_m \tag{1}$$

(where $B_{m,m}$ is either 1 or -1). When a conflict is uncovered in M_m, we claim the set of rows $C = \{R_i \mid B_{m,i} \neq 0\}$ constitutes a conflict set.[4]

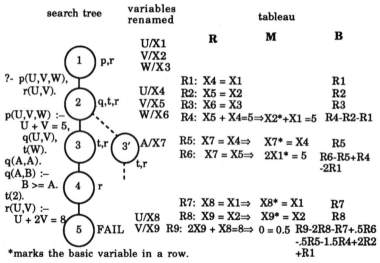

*marks the basic variable in a row.

Figure 3.

Figure 3 illustrates how the source of conflict can be identified by our method. Note that the ith program variable to be encountered during program execution (not including variables eliminated when redundancies or conflicts are uncovered) is renamed X_i at the time of creation. Note also

---

[4]Implicitly, the conflict set C also contains the inequality $s_i \geq 0$ for every slack variable s_i in the rows in C.

that unifications are entered as equations into the tableau. When the conflict is uncovered here, B_9 identifies M_9 as a linear combination of rows R_9, R_8, R_7, R_6, R_5, R_4, R_2, and R_1. The sources of these rows are nodes 4, 2, and 1, indicating that node 3 had nothing to do with the conflict. Thus, we can backtrack directly from node 4 to node 2.

5   Minimal Conflict Sets

We now show that the conflict set C identifiable through B is minimal; that is, no proper subset of C is also a conflict set. In the following, we will treat an equation, say $q_1x_1 + \ldots + q_nx_n = b$, as a row vector $[q_1, \ldots, q_n, b]$, and also as an algebraic expression $b - (q_1x_1 + \ldots + q_nx_n)$. The following lemma summarizes the end result in the tableau when a conflict is uncovered.

Lemma 5.1 *Suppose that during* checksat, *the current tableau* $Q = \{M_1, \ldots, M_{m-1}\}$ *is in solved form and is consistent, but the new row in its original form, denoted R_m, is found to be inconsistent with Q when R_m is transformed to its current form M_m. Then, writing M_m as an expression, $M_m = M_{m,1}x_1 + \ldots + M_{m,n}x_n + b$, the following holds: If the inconsistency is found during the forward elimination step, then all $M_{m,i} = 0$, $1 \leq i \leq n$, and $b > 0$; otherwise, if the inconsistency is found during simplex, then $b > 0$, $M_{m,i} \geq 0$ for all $1 \leq i \leq n$, and for all $M_{m,i} > 0$, the corresponding variable x_i must be a slack variable.*

As a result of Lemma 1, when the algorithm *checksat* uncovers a conflict in row M_m in either case, we have

$$M_m = \sum_{s_i \in D} c_i s_i + b \qquad (2)$$

where $c_i > 0$, D is either empty or contains slack variables only, and $b > 0$.

We illustrate equations (1) and (2) using an example in which a conflict is found during simplex. Consider the following tableau.

$R_1 : X_1 \geq 1$ $R_5 : X_5 \leq 1$
$R_2 : X_2 \geq 1$ $R_6 : X_1 + X_2 + X_3 = 5$
$R_3 : X_3 \leq 1$ $R_7 : X_3 + X_4 = 1$
$R_4 : X_4 \leq 1$ $R_8 : X_1 + X_5 = 7$

The five inequalities are converted to equations with slack variables. This tableau shows the resulting equations, with basic variables identified by $*$.

	X_1	X_2	X_3	X_4	X_5	S_1	S_2	S_3	S_4	S_5	b
R_1	1^*	0	0	0	0	-1	0	0	0	0	1
R_2	0	1^*	0	0	0	0	-1	0	0	0	1
R_3	0	0	1^*	0	0	0	0	1	0	0	1
R_4	0	0	0	1^*	0	0	0	0	1	0	1
R_5	0	0	0	0	1^*	0	0	0	0	1	1

To process R_6, we substitute out basic variables X_1, X_2, and X_3, The resulting all-slack row is kept in a separate tableau. Simplex chooses S_2 as a basic variable in it. Similarly, when R_7 is processed, the basic variables X_3 and X_4 are substituted out, resulting in an all-slack row $-S_3 - S_4 = -1$. Then, negating both sides yields the row $S_3 + S_4 = 1$. The following shows the tableau of all-slack rows with the basic variable identified.

	S_1	S_2	S_3	S_4	S_5	b
M_6'	1	1*	−1	0	0	2
M_7'	0	0	1	1*	0	1

At this point, the equations R_1 through R_7 are consistent. To process R_8, we first substitute out the basic variables X_1 and X_5, resulting in the all-slack row M_8' added to the tableau.

	S_1	S_2	S_3	S_4	S_5	b
M_6'	1	1*	−1	0	0	2
M_7'	0	0	1	1*	0	1
M_8'	1	0	0	0	−1	5

To determine the consistency of the system of R_1 through R_8, we need to apply simplex to the all-slack rows. The essence of the simplex procedure is to treat M_8' as an objective function to be minimized, given the solution space determined by M_6' and M_7'. When the standard pivoting procedure is applied twice, the tableau yields a minimized objective function $M_8 = 2 + S_2 + S_4 + S_5$.

	S_1	S_2	S_3	S_4	S_5	b
M_6	1*	1	0	1	0	3
M_7	0	0	1*	1	0	1
M_8	0	−1	0	−1	−1	2

Keeping track of the row operations, we obtain the following algebraic identity, treating each row $(LHS = RHS)$ as an expression, $RHS - LHS$.
$$M_8 = -M_6' - M_7' + M_8'$$
$$= -(-R_1 - R_2 - R_3 + R_6) - (R_3 + R_4 - R_7) + (-R_1 - R_5 + R_8)$$
$$= R_2 - R_4 - R_5 - R_6 + R_7 + R_8$$
$$= 2 + S_2 + S_4 + S_5$$

As noted in (1), M_m is a linear combination of rows in their original form. Combining (1) and (2) yields

$$M_m = \sum_{R_i \in C} B_{m,i} R_i = \sum_{s_i \in D} c_i s_i + b \tag{3}$$

Since any solution satisfying the equations $R_i \in C$, when substituted into (3), would yield

$$0 = \sum_{s_i \in D} c_i s_i + b > 0,$$

clearly the set $C = \{R_i | B_{m,i} \neq 0\}$ forms a set of conflicting equations. It is obvious that C contains equation R_m, because $\{R_1, \ldots, R_{m-1}\}$ is known to be satisfiable. To prove that the set is a minimal conflict set, we first note that since (3) is an algebraic identity, those slack variables s_i appearing on the righthand side must also appear on the lefthand side. Since a unique slack variable is introduced from its "source" inequality, the slack variables on the righthand side of (3) identify exactly those inequalities whose corresponding equations appear on the lefthand side of (3). We now prove that C forms a minimal conflict set.

Theorem 5.2 *Given a satisfiable tableau of $m - 1$ rows, if algorithm check-sat uncovers a conflict when it processes a new row R_m, then*
$C = \{R_i | B_{m,i} \neq 0\}$ *constitutes a minimal conflict set.*

Proof: Suppose that C is not minimal. That is, there exists a set C' which is a proper subset of C, where C' is also a conflict set. The set C' must contain R_m because the previous $m - 1$ rows $R_1, \ldots, R_{m-1}$ are satisfiable. Applying the algorithm *checksat* to C' will lead to a relation similar to (3), according to Lemma 1:

$$\sum_{R_i \in C'} B'_{m,i} R_i = \sum_{s_i \in D'} c'_i s_i + b' \qquad (4)$$

Without loss of generality, we assume that in both (3) and (4), the coefficient for R_m on the lefthand side is 1. Combining (3) and (4) yields

$$R_m = - \sum_{R_i \in C - \{R_m\}} B_{m,i} R_i + \sum_{s_i \in D} c_i s_i + b$$

$$= - \sum_{R_i \in C' - \{R_m\}} B'_{m,i} R_i + \sum_{s_i \in D'} c'_i s_i + b' \qquad (5)$$

The tableau $\{M_1, \ldots, M_{m-1}\}$ is in solved form when a conflict with M_m is uncovered; thus, the basic variables in $\{M_1, \ldots, M_{m-1}\}$ can be solved in terms of the non-basic variables. Substituting these solutions for the basic variables into (3), using the fact that $R = B^{-1}M$, all the expressions R_i, $1 \leq i \leq m-1$, would vanish. Thus, after substitution, equation (3) becomes

$$R_m{}^* = \sum_{s_i \in D} c_i s_i + b$$

where $R_m{}^* = (R_m$ after substitutions).

Note that the expression

$$\sum_{s_i \in D} c_i s_i + b$$

in (5) is not affected by the substitutions because the variables in D are non-basic. Similarly, the same set of substitutions into (4) yields

$$R_m{}^* = \sum_{s_i \in D'} c_i' s_i + b'$$

because these same substitutions erase all R_i's, $1 \leq i \leq m-1$. Therefore, we have

$$\sum_{s_i \in D} c_i s_i + b = \sum_{s_i \in D'} c_i' s_i + b' \tag{6}$$

Since (6) is an algebraic identity, the two sides must be identical expressions. Thus $D = D'$, $c_i = c_i'$, for each $s_i \in D$, and $b = b'$.

Substituting (6) into (5) yields

$$\sum_{R_i \in C - \{R_m\}} B_{m,i} R_i = \sum_{R_i \in C' - \{R_m\}} B'_{m,i} R_i$$

which results in a non-trivial dependency among the rows $R_i \in C$, because we assumed C' is a proper subset of C. This dependency relation contradicts the fact that there are no redundant rows in C, because there are no redundant rows in the tableau $\{M_1, \ldots, M_m\}$. This contradiction proves the theorem.

6   A Two-Sorted Domain

Some implicit assumptions were made in Figure 3 in order to simplify the initial discussion of our backtracking method. First, we assume that variable bindings are entered as equations in the tableau. If binding information is not integrated into the collection of conflict sets, solutions may be missed. In our example, $U + V = 5$ from clause p is in conflict with $U + 2V = 8$ from clause r, but only in the context of the bindings equating the original U and V, which occurred when goal q was executed. The presence of equations R_5 and R_6 in the conflict set ensures that node 2 is in the backtrack set, as it should be. A second simplifying assumption is that all variables are type *real*, so there is no need to check for type clashes, nor to account for the recursive unification of arguments to structured terms. In this section, we abandon this second assumption and deal with the two-sorted domain, temporarily retaining the method of recording variable bindings as equations.

To handle variables of two types in CLP($\Re$), we define an abstract supertype *term*, of which types *structured term* and *real number* are subtypes. Equality between terms is defined as follows:

If t is a structured term and c is a real number, then $t \neq c$. (An attempt to unify terms of different types is called a *type clash*.)

If t and u are structured terms and $t = u$, then their function symbols are identical, t and u both have n arguments ($n \geq 0$) and for $1 \leq i \leq n$, $v_i = w_i$, where v_i is the ith argument of t, and w_i is the ith argument of u.

Equality over real numbers is defined in the usual manner.

Since bindings are handed to the solver as equations, we now have equations over terms in the tableau. Each unification equation $v_i = w_i$ created between the ith pair of arguments to two unified structured terms is called a *recursive unification equation*. Equations and inequalities found in the body of a clause are referred to as *clause equations*.

We propose algorithm *enterclause* to generalize the work of the solver to a two-sorted domain. This algorithm initially processes all unifications and clause equations as equations over terms. *enterclause* uses a generalized process of forward elimination, making our method for collecting conflict sets directly applicable. Forward elimination is now divided into three stages. The first stage, applicable to unification equations, dereferences variables by following binding chains. The second and third stages are applied to equations with real number expressions on both sides after dereferencing, or clause equations which are input in this form. In the second stage, all variables are identified as type *real*. The third stage continues forward elimination in the domain of reals using *checksat*, applying simplex if necessary.

In all three stages, we maintain R, M, and B as before. It should be clear that in the simple case, where no recursive unification equations are involved, our method of collecting backtrack sets generalizes directly to the two-sorted domain. Consider the case where a type clash is uncovered during dereferencing. As long as we are processing equations over terms, we can view each structured term or real number expression simply as a constant. Say that X_1 is bound to 3, X_2 is bound to $g(X_3)$ and then we attempt to bind X_2 to X_1. This situation is represented by the following tableau:

R	M	B
$X_1 = 3$	$X_1^* = 3$	R_1
$X_2 = g(X_3)$	$X_2^* = g(X_3)$	R_2
$X_2 = X_1$	$g(X_3) = 3$	$R_3 - R_2 + R_1$

By our usual method of recording row operations, the conflict set is identified as $\{R_1, R_2, R_3\}$. In the case where an equation consists entirely of real number expressions, extending our method for recording row operations from the dereferencing step to the *checksat* algorithm is also straightforward.

We now must account for the presence of recursive unification equations in the tableau. Since a recursive unification equation can be introduced as a result of binding chains, we are interested in the *history* of such an equation, identifying nodes where bindings which eventually entailed the equation can be undone. Consider the example in Figure 4, where $f(X_2) = f(X_1)$ is the result of forward elimination on R_{11}. Since $f(X_2) = f(X_1)$ results from the linear combination of R_{11}, R_{10}, R_8, R_5, and R_4, these rows make up the history of the recursive unification equation $X_2 = X_1$.

More generally, the history of the mth row, $HIST(R_m)$, tells us the constraints which brought R_m into existence. Say that R_m is a recursive unification equation which arose when two structured terms were unified in M_i. Let $BROWS(i)$ denote $\{R_k | B_{i,k} \neq 0\}$. Then $HIST(R_m)$ is defined as

$$HIST(R_m) = \bigcup_{R_j \in BROWS(i)} HIST(R_j).$$

If R_m is a non-recursive unification equation or a clause equation, then $HIST(R_m) = \{R_m\}$. If a new row R_m is found to be inconsistent with the previous $m - 1$ rows, then we identify a conflict set containing R_m as

$$CONFL(R_m) = \bigcup_{R_j \in BROWS(m)} HIST(R_j).$$

If R_m is not in conflict with the rest of the tableau, $CONFL(R_m) = \{\}$.

It should be noted that $CONFL(R_m)$ is not necessarily minimal. (See [3] for an example.) However, it suffices to identify *any* conflict set to apply the DIB algorithm without missing a solution, and a significant degree of intelligent backtracking can be achieved without minimality.

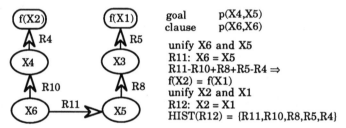

Figure 4.

7 A Generator-Consumer Approach

We have shown how our method for collecting conflict sets can be extended to account for structured terms. This method is based upon the recording of unifications as equations in the tableau, an admittedly inefficient strategy. We now offer a more efficient approach arising from the following observation.

Let the *ancestor path* of a goal literal p be defined as an ordered set of node numbers $\{n_0, n_1, \ldots, n_m\}$ where n_0 is the number of the node where p is the leftmost goal, and for $1 \leq i \leq m$, n_i is the node number of the source of the leftmost literal at node n_{i-1}. If the source of the leftmost literal at node n_i is 0, then $m = i + 1$. The *source of a variable* which is created when goal p is executed is the node where goal p is leftmost. The *ancestor path of a variable* is the ancestor path of the goal literal being executed when the variable is created. Consider the example in Figure 5. Here, the source of X_5 is node 7 and its ancestor path is $\{7, 3, 1\}$. Equations $X_1 + X_2 = 5$ and $X_5 + X_6 = 6$ are in conflict, but only in the context of the bindings which occurred at nodes 7 and 3. By our previous method, the equations representing the bindings would be part of the conflict set. However, putting the source of these equations in the backtrack set introduces redundant information. If we fail on all paths from node 7, the DIB algorithm requires that we place the source of goal p, node 3, in the backtrack set. If we fail at node 3, the source of the goal q, node 1, is placed in the backtrack set. As failure continues, we will always backtrack through the ancestor paths of the failing goals, precisely the nodes associated with the input bindings. Thus, we need only record extra "stopping places" along the way so as not to miss a solution. That is, we need to mark a variable binding only if that binding occurs at some node after the node where the variable was created. Such a situation is illustrated by Figure 3, where we need to mark the binding of X_2 to X_1 as having occurred at node 2.

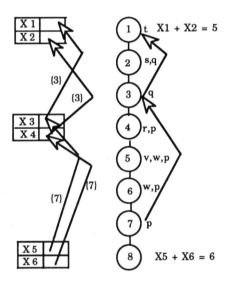

Figure 5.

By this reasoning, we can simplify our method for tracing bindings. Let us represent variable bindings by pointers through the variable space rather than equations. Using a dereferencing procedure analogous to our forward elimination procedure in *checksat*, we follow the binding chains of the variables being unified, and if there is at least one unbound variable at the ends of these chains, we bind the newer variable to the other term.

Analogous to our method of recording row operations during Gaussian elimination, we trace the reasons for each variable X_i's binding in a generator set (denoted $GEN(X_i)$), that is, a set of nodes where alternative paths can be tried in order to undo the binding. For any variable X_i, if X_i receives its binding at the node where it is first created, then $GEN(X_i)$ is the empty set. Otherwise, let p be the goal being executed when X_i receives its binding, let node n be the node where p is leftmost, and let V be the set of variables whose dereferencing led to the binding of X_i. In the case where X_i's binding is being changed during execution of some node after the node where X_i was created,

$$GEN(X_i) = (\bigcup_{X_k \in V} GEN(X_k)) \cup \{n\}$$

Thus, we collect generator sets during dereferencing and store the collected set with the variable which is eventually bound, if a binding is made. If dereferencing of a unification leads us to two structured terms requiring recursive unifications, we carry the generator set along with each recursive unification and continue the dereferencing in the same manner. If dereferencing eventually uncovers a conflict, the generator set thus collected tells us nodes not on the ancestor path of the literal being executed, but where we can try another path of execution with the possibility of finding a solution.

In Figure 6, X_2 is bound to X_1 when r is executed . Since X_2's binding is being changed, it is marked with the generator set $\{4\}$, containing only the source of r. When X_{10} is unified with 2 at node 6, we use the binding of X_2 to X_1 in the dereferencing, and the generator set is $\{4\} \cup \{6\} = \{4, 6\}$. We find a conflict when we later attempt to unify X_1 with 3, and the generator set becomes $\{4, 6, 8\}$, including the source of the goal just executed.

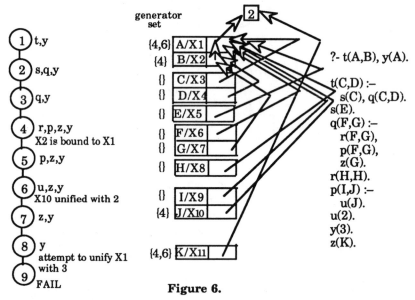

Figure 6.

This method takes a generator-consumer approach to intelligent backtracking, similar to [12], by identifying nodes which generate bindings for earlier nodes. Our method optimizes the generator-consumer approach by recognizing that bindings generated for a node by its "ancestor" nodes need not be recorded, since the ancestor nodes will automatically be included in the backtrack set by the DIB algorithm. We can integrate this approach into CLP($\Re$)'s constraint satisfaction algorithm by modifying our definition of the history of a clause equation so that it consists of node numbers rather than rows. When an equation is being prepared for the solver, the variables therein are dereferenced in the manner described above. Let V be the set of all the variables dereferenced when the equation is prepared for the solver. Then the history for the equation when it enters the tableau consists of

$$\bigcup_{X_k \in V} GEN(X_k) \cup \{n\}$$

where n is the node number of the source of the equation. With this definition for the history of an equation, we can again use B to identify a backtrack set when a conflict appears. If row R_m is found to be inconsistent with a satisfiable tableau of $m - 1$ rows, then we identify the backtrack set associated with the conflict as

$$\bigcup_{R_j \in BROWS(m)} HIST(R_j).$$

8 Implementation

We have implemented a CLP($\Re$) interpreter in C using *checksat*. The tableau is stored in R and a working copy of the solved form is maintained in M, with row operations recorded in B and conflict sets thereby generated. In a run of the Figure 1 program, equations 19, 14, 12, 11, and 10 are correctly identified as constituting a conflict set at node 15, while equations 20, 14, 13, 12, 11, 10, and 9 constitute the conflict set at node 17. We have also installed the DIB algorithm into the inference engine's backtracking mechanism and integrated the identification of conflict sets between the solver and the inference engine. Tests runs on the canonical cryptarithmetic problem show a 14% speedup despite the overhead. We note that the cost of our intelligent backtracking mechanism is reasonable. Only matrix B is required for storing row operations. If we further optimize the algorithm by employing the revised simplex method, we get minimal conflict sets at no added expense, since in the revised simplex method the tableau is represented by the operations performed on it rather than by its current state [13]. The tracing of variable bindings requires only (1) a comparison of the node number of the variable being bound to the current node number, (2) the storing of a generator set for each variable, and (3) the unioning of generator sets during dereferencing. In many cases, the generator sets will be empty. In the Figure 1 example, a small amount of extra bookkeeping results in a significant benefit in intelligent backtracking, since each of nodes 14, 12, 11, 10, $9''$, $8'$, 6 and $5'$ is a choice point. We conclude that our constraint satisfaction algorithm and technique for tracing variable bindings combine to form a feasible intelligent backtracking algorithm for the two-sorted domain of CLP($\Re$).

References

[1] Bruynooghe, M., and L. Pereira. Deduction revision by intelligent backtracking. In J. Campbell, ed. *Implementations of Prolog*, Ellis Horwood, 1984.

[2] Burg, J. Parallel execution models and algorithms for constraint logic programming over a real-number domain. PhD Dissertation, University of Central Florida, December 1992.

[3] Burg, J., S.-D. Lang, and C. Hughes. Finding conflict sets and backtrack points in CLP($\Re$). Technical Report TR-CS-93-01, Wake Forest University, Winston-Salem, NC. Nov. 1993.

[4] Codognet, C., P. Codognet, and G. Filé. Yet another intelligent backtracking method. *Proc. of the Fifth Int. Conf. and Symp. on Logic Programming*, (Seattle, 1988): 447-465.

[5] Codognet, P. and T. Sola. Extending the WAM for intelligent backtracking. *Proc of the Eighth Int. Conf. on Logic Programming*, (Paris, France, 1991): 127-141.

[6] Cox, P. Finding backtrack points for intelligent backtracking. In J. Campbell, ed. *Implementations of Prolog*, Ellis Horwood, 1984.

[7] DeBacker, B. and H. Beringer. Intelligent backtracking for CLP languages: An application to CLP($\Re$). *Proc. of the international symposium on logic programming.* (San Diego, Oct. 1991), 405-419.

[8] Heintze, et al. The CLP($\Re$) programmer's manual, Version 1.2. IBM Thomas J. Watson Research Center, Sept. 1992.

[9] Hogger, C., and A. Kotzamanidis. Aspects of failure analysis in a CLP($\Re$) system. Internal Report, Imperial College, London, June 1993.

[10] Jaffar, et al. An abstract machine for CLP($\Re$). *Proc. of SIGPLAN 92 conference on programming language description and implementation.* (San Francisco, May 1992), 128-139.

[11] Jaffar, et al. The CLP($\Re$) language and system. *ACM transactions on programming languages and systems* 14, 3 (July 1992), 339-395.

[12] Kumar, V., and Y.-J. Lin. An intelligent backtracking scheme for Prolog. *Proc. of the international symposium on logic programming.* (Sept. 1987), 406-414.

[13] Luenberger, D. *Linear and Nonlinear Programming.* 2nd ed. Reading, Mass.: Addison-Wesley.

Entailment of Finite Domain Constraints

Björn Carlson and **Mats Carlsson**
Swedish Institute of Computer Science
Box 1263, S-164 28 KISTA, Sweden
{bjornc,matsc}@sics.se

Daniel Diaz
INRIA-Rocquencourt
Domaine de Voluceau
78153 Le Chesnay, France
Daniel.Diaz@inria.fr

Abstract Using a glass-box theory of finite domain constraints, FD, we show how the entailment of user-defined constraints can be expressed by anti-monotone FD constraints. We also provide an algorithm for checking the entailment and consistency of FD constraints. FD is shown to be expressive enough to allow the definition of arithmetical constraints, as well as non-trivial symbolic constraints, that are normally built in to CLP systems. In particular, we use conditional FD constraints, which exploit entailment checking, to define symbolic constraints. Thus, we claim that a glass-box system such as FD is expressive enough to capture the essence of finite domain constraint programming.

Keywords: constraint logic programming, finite domain constraints, entailment, monotonicity.

1 Introduction

The glass-box approach to constraint logic programming consists in controlling the constraint solver at a more detailed level than what is possible in a system where the solver is provided as a black box. Constraints that are builtins of a black-box solver, are instead defined by programming primitives of the glass-box [5, 13, 4, 1]. Combinators of a glass-box system typically include conjunction, implication and disjunction.

The benefits of using glass-box systems are that the programmer is given *more freedom* of how to specify a problem, since the constraints can be tailored with respect to the problem at hand, and that the problem can be solved *more efficiently* since it need not be reduced to fit the constraints of the solver.

Furthermore, the implementation of a glass-box system lifts the complexity from the emulator level to the compiler level, as well as making available traditional compiler optimization techniques. The net result being that the implementations of glass-box systems can be made highly efficient [3, 13, 1].

In this paper we study how to use the glass-box system FD [12] to define non-trivial finite domain constraints and to check their entailment. We show that by using conditional reasoning, based on entailment, complex symbolic constraints can be defined in FD. Entailment has previously been recognized as the key to how concurrent and constraint programming can be merged [8, 10], but hence it serves an important function even within a constraint logic programming framework.

By exploiting the monotonicity of FD constraints we show that entailment checking can be done purely in terms of anti-monotone FD constraints. Hence, FD is expressive enough both to define complex constraints and to check their entailment.

The method we propose works by translating a constraint definition into a sufficient truth condition, where some attention is put into making the condition minimal. The condition is translated into an anti-monotone FD constraint, which can efficiently be checked by an algorithm we provide.

The paper is structured as follows: we begin by describing the FD theory (Section 2), including a section on how to define constraints in FD, where some non-trivial constraints are defined. We then show how a constraint definition is translated into a sufficient truth condition (Section 3). A section follows which describes a translation of the truth conditions into anti-monotone FD constraints, and which includes algorithms for checking the monotonicity and the entailment of FD constraints (Section 4). A short summary concludes the paper (Section 5).

2 FD: A Theory of Finite Domain Constraints

The constraint system FD [12] is a general purpose constraint framework for solving discrete constraint satisfaction problems in a concurrent constraint setting. The theory is based on unary constraints by which higher arity constraints are defined, so for example constraints such as $X = Y$ or $X \leq 2Y$ are *defined* by FD constraints, instead of being built in to the theory. The unary constraints of FD are thought of as propagation rules, i.e. rules for describing node and arc consistency propagation.

The unary constraints of FD can be used as the target language for compilers of arbitrary finite domain constraints [2], and in fact FD subsumes basically all existing finite domain constraint systems with preserved and sometimes improved efficiency [1, 3, 4].

2.1 The theory

FD is based on *domain constraints* $X \in I$, where I is a set of integers described by a finite union of intervals. The set I is the set of *possible values* of X, and X is said to be *constrained* to I. $X \in I$ is satisfied by assigning a value in I to X.

A set S of domain constraints, where any two domain constraints $X \in I$ and $X \in I'$ have been replaced by $X \in (I \cap I')$, is called a *store*. Hence,

$$
\begin{aligned}
N ::=&\ X \mid i, \text{ where } i \in \mathcal{Z} \\
T ::=&\ N \mid T + T \mid T - T \mid T * T \mid T/T \mid T \textbf{ mod } T \mid \\
&\ \textbf{min}(R) \mid \textbf{max}(R) \\
R ::=&\ T..T \mid T.. \mid ..T \mid R \ \& \ R \mid R : R \mid -R \mid \\
&\ R + T \mid R - T \mid R \textbf{ mod } T \mid \\
&\ \textbf{dom}(X) \\
C ::=&\ N \textbf{ in } R \mid C \rightarrow C \mid C \wedge C
\end{aligned}
$$

Figure 1: SYNTAX OF CONSTRAINTS IN FD

a store S is *consistent* if there is no domain constraint $X \in \emptyset$ in S. The set which X is constrained to in S is denoted by X_S in the following. X is *determined* in S if $X_S = \{n\}$.

Suppose S_1 and S_2 are two stores. Let $S_1 \sqsubseteq S_2$ if for any variable X it holds $X_{S_2} \subseteq X_{S_1}$.

The computational primitive of FD, X **in** r, is a partial function from stores to domain constraints, such that X **in** r applied to a store S evaluates to a domain constraint $X \in r_S$, where r_S is the value of r in S (see below). The expression r is called a *range* (defined by R in Figure 1), which denotes a partial function from stores to finite unions of intervals over the integers. We will refer to X **in** r as an *indexical* in the following [12].

The partial function r is evaluated in a store S as follows. Any variable V not occurring as **dom**(V) in r must be determined in S, and any variable V occurring as **dom**(V) in r must be constrained in S to make r in S well-defined. The *value of a range* r in S, r_S, is thus *a set of integers* defined as: the expression **dom**(Y) evaluates to Y_S, the expression $t_1..t_2$ is interpreted as the set $\{i \in \mathcal{Z} : t_{1_S} \leq i \leq t_{2_S}\}$, the expression $t..$ is interpreted as the set $\{i \in \mathcal{Z} : t_S \leq i\}$, the expression $..t$ is interpreted as the set $\{i \in \mathcal{Z} : i \leq t_S\}$, the operators : and & denote union and intersection respectively, the expressions $r + t$, $r - t$, and r **mod** t denote pointwise integer addition, subtraction, and modulo of r_S and t_S, where t cannot contain **max** or **min** terms, and finally the value of $-r$ in S is the set $\mathcal{Z} \backslash r_S$.

The *value of a term* t in S, t_S, is an *integer* defined as: a number is interpreted as itself, a variable is evaluated to its assignment, the interpretation of the arithmetical operators is the interpretation over the integers, and the expressions **min**(r) and **max**(r) evaluate to the infimum and supremum values of r_S. It is required that in a modulo expression t **mod** t_0, t_0 does not contain **max** or **min** terms. If every variable in t is determined in S, t is *determined* in S.

The set of FD constraints is the set of indexicals closed under (intuitionistic) implication and conjunction. In the following we sometimes refer to implications as *conditional constraints*.

Let S be a store, and c (d) be a constraint in FD. Thus define:

- S *entails* X **in** r if r is defined in S and $X_{S'} \subseteq r_{S'}$, for any S' such that $S \sqsubseteq S'$.

- S entails $c \wedge d$ if S entails c and S entails d.

- S entails $c \rightarrow d$ if for every S', $S \sqsubseteq S'$, if S' entails c then S' entails d.

- c is *consistent* in S if for some S', $S \sqsubseteq S'$, S' entails c.

- c is *inconsistent* in S if c is not consistent in S.

Finally, r is *monotone* if for every pair of stores S_1 and S_2 such that $S_1 \sqsubseteq S_2$, $r_{S_2} \subseteq r_{S_1}$. r is *anti-monotone* if for every pair of stores S_1 and S_2 such that $S_1 \sqsubseteq S_2$, $r_{S_1} \subseteq r_{S_2}$.

X **in** r is monotone (anti-monotone) if r is monotone (anti-monotone), $c \wedge d$ is monotone (anti-monotone) if c and d are monotone (anti-monotone), and $c \rightarrow d$ is monotone (anti-monotone) if d is monotone (anti-monotone). Monotone constraints are used for adding domain constraints to the store, and anti-monotone constraints are used for checking entailment (see Section 3).

In the following we will use $\mathbf{min}(X)$ as shorthand for $\mathbf{min}(\mathbf{dom}(X))$. Also we use the variable r for ranges, the variable t for terms, the variables n for natural numbers and i for integers, and the variable c for constraints, where all the symbols may be indexed.

2.2 Defining constraints in FD

We define n-ary (arithmetical) constraints as FD constraints, the intention being that the denotation of the n-ary constraint should be captured by the interpretation of the FD expression.

Put more formally: suppose p is an n-ary relation over the integers, let H be $p(X_1, \ldots, X_n)$, and let S be a store. Then $S \Rightarrow H$ if $\{\langle a_1, \ldots, a_n \rangle : a_i \in X_{iS}\} \subseteq p$. Furthermore, suppose c is a constraint in FD. We then require the following to make c a definition of p.

1. If S entails c, then $S \Rightarrow H$.

2. If S determines X_i and $S \Rightarrow H$, then S entails c, $1 \le i \le n$.

In the following we adapt to the clause syntax of Prolog and use ":-" for definitions and "," for conjunction.

Example 1. The constraint $X = Y + 1$ can be defined as:
$$X = Y + 1 \quad : -$$
$$X \text{ in } \mathbf{dom}(Y) + 1,$$
$$Y \text{ in } \mathbf{dom}(X) - 1.$$

or as
$$X = Y + 1 \quad : -$$
$$X \text{ in } (\mathbf{min}(Y)+1)..(\mathbf{max}(Y)+1),$$
$$Y \text{ in } (\mathbf{min}(X)-1)..(\mathbf{max}(X)-1).$$

Hence, X (Y) is constrained by either the domain of Y (X), or by the minimum and maximum of Y (X). The domain approximation performs stronger propagation than the interval approximation, but the interval version is more efficient to compute. For a careful examination of domain and interval approximations of constraints see elsewhere [6, 13, 14].

Note that operationally the constraint propagation implemented by the FD constraints may be weaker than what can be performed by a constraint solver for the n-ary constraint.

Example 2. The constraint $X \neq Y$ can be defined either as

$X \neq Y$ $:-$

$\quad\quad X$ **in** $-$ **dom**(Y),
$\quad\quad Y$ **in** $-$ **dom**(X).

or as

$X \neq Y$ $:-$

$\quad\quad X$ **in** $-$ $(\mathbf{max}(Y)..\mathbf{min}(Y))$,
$\quad\quad Y$ **in** $-$ $(\mathbf{max}(X)..\mathbf{min}(X))$.

thus either the constraint is defined to be anti-monotone or monotone (see Section 4.3).

Example 3. We define the constraint $(X = A) \equiv B$, where B is 0 iff $X \neq A$ is true, and B is 1 iff $X = A$ is true, as

$(X = A) \equiv B$ $:-$

$\quad\quad\quad X = A \rightarrow B = 1,$
$\quad\quad\quad B = 1 \rightarrow X = A,$
$\quad\quad\quad X \neq A \rightarrow B = 0,$
$\quad\quad\quad B = 0 \rightarrow X \neq A.$

Let us detail some symbolic constraints which need entailment detection, constraints that are normally built in to a CLP system but which can naturally be defined using conditionals.

Example 4. The magic series problem [11] consists in finding a sequence of numbers $\{X_0, \ldots, X_n\}$ such that i occurs X_i times in the sequence. The original formulation [11] used a `freeze` on each X_i. However, owing to entailment detection it is possible to simply encode the following relation [9]:

$$X_j = \sum_{i=0}^{n} (j)_i$$

where $(j)_i$ is 1 if $X_i = j$ and 0 if $X_i \neq j$. This is achieved by defining B_{ji} as $(X_i = j) \equiv B_{ji}$, and adding the constraints $\sum_{i=0}^{n} B_{ji} = X_j$, for each j between 0 and n.

Obviously, the constraint propagation obtained with this constraint is stronger than the propagation of the formulation using `freeze`. In [4] it is shown that the speedup with respect to the CHIP definition grows with n.

Finally, note that the constraint `atmost(N, L, V)`, which is true iff V occurs at most N times in L, can be defined by $\sum_{i=1}^{n} B_i \leq N$, where $L = [X_1, \ldots, X_n]$, and $(X_i = V) \equiv B_i$, $1 \leq i \leq n$.

Example 5. Similarly, the constraint `element(I,E,V)`, which holds iff the Ith element of E equals V, can be defined by conditional constraints as: let E be the list $[E_1, \ldots, E_k]$, and suppose $1 \leq I \leq k$ and B_i **in** $0 : i$ hold, for each i between 1 and k. The following constraints define the `element/3` relation:

- $I = i \rightarrow E_i = V$

- I **in** $\mathbf{dom}(B_1) : \cdots : \mathbf{dom}(B_k)$, where

- $E_i \neq V \rightarrow B_i = 0$, and

- $E_i = V \rightarrow B_i = i$.

However, note that this version of `element/3` does not exploit the full pruning possible from the denotation of the constraint [1].

3 Entailment Conditions

In this section we characterize the entailment of FD constraints by sufficient truth conditions.

3.1 Entailment of indexicals

The aim of this section is to show how to generate *logical* conditions to detect entailment and inconsistency of indexicals. The basic idea being that ranges are approximated by intervals, and thus entailment detection is made by reasoning over intervals. In later sections (Section 4 and 4.2) we use the conditions to generate anti-monotone indexicals which decide the conditions.

The general problem of deciding entailment of finite domain constraints belongs to **NP**, and thus we cannot expect to have efficient and complete entailment detection. Instead we choose to use entailment conditions which are efficient to compute (see Section 4.2), and in practice sufficiently strong.

In the following we consider only linear FD terms, which simplifies the presentation, but the tables can be generalized to hold for all FD terms.

Let *inf* (*sup*) be a function from linear terms to values which increases (decreases) as the computation progresses. That is, $inf(t)$ $(sup(t))$ is the smallest (largest) value that t can ever get (see Table 1).

Let m_k be the partial function such that $m_k(t) = t \bmod k$ when t is determined, let a_i be the function such that $a_i(t) = t + i$, let $f \circ g$ be defined as $(f \circ g)(t) = f(g(t))$, and let c be X **in** r, for some X and r. Let E_c (entailment condition) and D_c (inconsistency condition) be the two

t	$inf(t)$	$sup(t)$
i	i	i
$t_1 + t_2$	$inf(t_1) + inf(t_2)$	$sup(t_1) + sup(t_2)$
$t * n$	$inf(t) * n$	$sup(t) * n$
$t * (-n)$	$sup(t) * (-n)$	$inf(t) * (-n)$
$t_1 - t_2$	$inf(t_1) - sup(t_2)$	$sup(t_1) - inf(t_2)$
t/n	$inf(t)/n$	$sup(t)/n$
$t/(-n)$	$sup(t)/(-n)$	$inf(t)/(-n)$
i **mod** n	i **mod** n	i **mod** n
$\mathbf{min}(X)$	$\mathbf{min}(X)$	$\mathbf{max}(X)$
$\mathbf{max}(X)$	$\mathbf{min}(X)$	$\mathbf{max}(X)$

Table 1: UPPER AND LOWER BOUNDS OF LINEAR FD-TERMS

r	$E(X, r, f)$
$t..$	$\mathbf{min}(X) \geq sup(f(t))$
$..t$	$\mathbf{max}(X) \leq inf(f(t))$
$t_1..t_2$	$\mathbf{min}(X) \geq sup(f(t_1)) \wedge \mathbf{max}(X) \leq inf(f(t_2))$
$\mathbf{dom}(Y)$	$E(X, \mathbf{min}(Y)..\mathbf{max}(Y), f)$
$r_1 : r_2$	$E(X, r_1, f) \vee E(X, r_2, f)$
r_1 & r_2	$E(X, r_1, f) \wedge E(X, r_2, f)$
$-r$	$D(X, r, f)$
$r + t$	$E(X, r, f \circ a_t)$
$r - t$	$E(X, r, f \circ a_{-t})$
r **mod** t	$E(X, r, f \circ m_t)$

Table 2: DEFINITION OF $E(X, r, f)$

logical expressions defined by $E(X, r, a_0)$ and $D(X, r, a_0)$, where E and D are defined in Table 2 and Table 3.

Observe that if E_c (resp. D_c) is true in a store S then E_c (resp. D_c) is true in any store logically stronger than S. This follows from an inductive reasoning over the structure of c.

The *correctness* of the translation is shown by proving that if E_c (D_c) is true then c is entailed (inconsistent). This is done by induction over the structure of c. Thus, E_c and D_c are *sufficient* truth conditions for c.

Example 6. Let us consider the constraint (c) X **in** $\mathbf{min}(Y)..$, which can be used to impose $X \geq Y$. It follows from the above that $E_c \equiv \mathbf{min}(X) \geq \mathbf{max}(Y)$ and $D_c \equiv \mathbf{max}(X) < \mathbf{min}(Y)$. Thus, E_c is true (i.e. $X \geq Y$ is detected) as soon as all possible values of X are greater or equal to any possible value of Y, and D_c is true as soon as no possible value of X can be greater or equal to any possible value of Y.

r	$D(X, r, f)$
$t..$	$\mathbf{max}(X) < inf(f(t))$
$..t$	$\mathbf{min}(X) > sup(f(t))$
$t_1..t_2$	$\mathbf{max}(X) < inf(f(t_1))\vee$
	$\mathbf{min}(X) > sup(f(t_2))\vee$
	$inf(f(t_1)) > sup(f(t_2))$
$\mathbf{dom}(Y)$	$D(X, \mathbf{min}(Y)..\mathbf{max}(Y), f)$
$r_1 : r_2$	$D(X, r_1, f) \wedge D(X, r_2, f)$
$r_1 \,\&\, r_2$	$D(X, r_1, f) \vee D(X, r_2, f)$
$-r$	$E(X, r, f)$
$r + t$	$D(X, r, f \circ a_t)$
$r - t$	$D(X, r, f \circ a_{-t})$
$r \bmod t$	$D(X, r, f \circ m_t)$

Table 3: Definition of $D(X, r, f)$

3.2 Entailment of user defined constraints

To deal with user defined constraints we need to generalize the truth conditions (see Section 3.1) to FD constraints as follows. Let c be an FD constraint. Then E_c (D_c) is defined as

- $E_{X \textbf{ in } r} = E(X, r, a_0)$ and $D_{X \textbf{ in } r} = D(X, r, a_0)$.

- $E_{c \wedge d} = E_c \wedge E_d$ and $D_{c \wedge d} = D_c \vee D_d$.

- $E_{c \to d} = D_c \vee E_d$ and $D_{c \to d} = E_c \wedge D_d$.

However, in many typical definitions $E_{c \wedge d}$ $(D_{c \wedge d})$ can be reduced to E_c (D_c) since $E_c \equiv E_d$ $(D_c \equiv D_d)$.

Example 7. Let us consider the user constraint $X \geq Y$ defined as:
$X \geq Y \quad :-$
$(c_X) \qquad X$ **in** $\mathbf{min}(Y)..$,
$(c_Y) \qquad Y$ **in** $..\mathbf{max}(X)$.

From the above constraints it follows:

- $E_{c_X} \equiv E_{c_Y} \equiv \mathbf{min}(X) \geq \mathbf{max}(Y)$

- $D_{c_X} \equiv D_{c_Y} \equiv \mathbf{max}(X) < \mathbf{min}(Y)$

Hence, $E_{X \geq Y} = E_{c_X} \wedge E_{c_Y} \equiv E_{c_X}$, and $D_{X \geq Y} \equiv D_{c_X}$.

Example 8. Consider $X \neq Y$ defined as:
$X \neq Y \quad :-$
$(c_X) \qquad X$ **in** $-\mathbf{dom}(Y)$,
$(c_Y) \qquad Y$ **in** $-\mathbf{dom}(X)$.

The conditions detect when the domains of X and Y do *not overlap* anymore as:

$$E_{X \neq Y} \equiv E_X \text{ in } -\mathbf{dom}(Y) \ (c_X \text{ and } c_Y \text{ are equivalent})$$
$$\equiv D_X \text{ in } \mathbf{dom}(Y)$$
$$\equiv D_X \text{ in } \mathbf{min}(Y)..\mathbf{max}(Y)$$
$$\equiv \mathbf{max}(X) < \mathbf{min}(Y) \vee \mathbf{min}(X) > \mathbf{max}(Y)$$

For checking the equivalence of two entailment conditions a normalization procedure can be used. Let c be a (monotone) FD constraint, and Π_c its associated truth (E_c) or falsity (D_c) condition.

The *normalization* of Π_c is done by rewriting Π_c into a disjunctive normal form, where each term in Π_c is replaced by its additive normal form. The rewriting is done by applying rewrite rules defined below. A rewrite rule applies if its template matches a substrate expression, modulo associativity and commutativity for $\{:, \&, *, +, \wedge, \vee\}$, replacing the substrate expression by a rewritten expression.

Given the following list of rewrite rules we iterate in top-down order through the list, applying a rule if it applies anywhere in the condition. If a rule is applied, the iteration is restarted from the beginning of the list. When no rule in the list applies, the iteration is terminated.

DNF. The *disjunctive normal form* of a condition is computed by the following rule:

$$E \wedge (E_1 \vee E_2) \Rightarrow (E \wedge E_1) \vee (E \wedge E_2)$$

ANF. The following rules compute the *additive normal form* of a term:

$$t * (t_1 \cdot t_2) \Rightarrow t * t_1 \cdot t * t_2 \ (\cdot \in \{+, -\})$$

MS. Subtraction is moved across inequalities as:

$$t_1 - t \cdot t_2 \Rightarrow t_1 \cdot t_2 + t, \cdot \in \{\leq, \geq\}$$
$$t_1 \cdot t_2 - t \Rightarrow t_1 + t \cdot t_2, \cdot \in \{\leq, \geq\}$$

Let Π_{c_1} and Π_{c_2} be two normalized entailment conditions. Π_{c_1} and Π_{c_2} are *equal* up to commutativity and associativity of $\wedge$ and $\vee$, if each corresponding pair of inequalities in Π_{c_1} and Π_{c_2} are equal. Two inequalities $t_1 \leq t_2$ and $t_3 \leq t_4$ are equal iff t_1 equals t_3 and t_2 equals t_4, where equality between terms is defined as identity up to commutativity and associativity of $+$ and $*$.

The *correctness* of the algorithm is shown by proving that if Π_{c_1} and Π_{c_2} are decided equivalent then Π_{c_1} is true iff Π_{c_2} is true. This is done by proving the correctness of each rewrite rule, and that the equivalence relation defined for normalized conditions is true equivalence.

The normalization *terminates* since **DNF** replaces a conjunction with two smaller conjunctions, **ANF** replaces a product with two smaller products, and the **MS** rules decrease the number of subtractions each time applied.

X **in** r in S	r monotone	r anti-monotone
$X_S \cap r_S = \emptyset$	inconsistent	may become entailed
$X_S \subseteq r_S$	may become inconsistent	entailed
$X_S \neq (X_S \cap r_S) \neq \emptyset$	may become inconsistent	may become entailed

Table 4: ENTAILMENT/CONSISTENCY OF X **in** r IN A STORE S

Note that the algorithm is *incomplete* since for example the two constraints X **in** 1..0 and X **in** $\mathbf{dom}(Y)$ & $-\mathbf{dom}(Y)$ are logically equivalent, but are *not* decided such.

4 Entailment constraints

In this section we give a decision table for detecting entailment of indexicals, which is based on their monotonicity, and we show how to exploit this table to evaluate the entailment conditions (see Section 3.1). Furthermore we give an inductive definition of the monotonicity of X **in** r, which is needed to implement the entailment checking.

4.1 Entailment detection of X in r

Let c be X **in** r, and let S be the current constraint store. Suppose X is constrained in S to a (finite) set X_S, and let r_S be the value of r in S.

The entailment of c in S is checked using a case-analysis based on the value of X and r in S and on the monotonicity of r (see Table 4).

For example, suppose c is monotone and constrains X to the empty set in S. Then c is inconsistent in S since in any store stronger or equal to S, c will constrain X to the empty set. However, if c is anti-monotone and constrains X to the empty set in S, then there may be stores stronger than S in which c constrains X to something other than the empty set. Hence, c may or may not become entailed when S is strengthened.

If c is anti-monotone and X_S is a subset of r_S then c is entailed in S. Finally, if c is monotone and constrains X to something other than the empty set, c still may become inconsistent.

Computationally, whenever a constraint has become entailed it can be discarded, and whenever a constraint is inconsistent the computation fails. In all other cases the computation records (suspends) the constraint so that when the store is updated the constraint can be rechecked when necessary [1, 3]. If c is monotone, $X \in (X_S \cap r_S)$ is added to the store.

Example 9. Again we use disequality as an example. Suppose we define $X \neq Y$ as

$X \neq Y$: —
(c_X) $\quad$ X **in** $-\mathbf{dom}(Y)$,
(c_Y) $\quad$ Y **in** $-\mathbf{dom}(X)$.

r	$\nu_E(X, r, f)$
$t..$	$(sup(f(t)) - \min(X))..$
$..t$	$..(inf(f(t)) - \max(X))$
$t_1..t_2$	$(sup(f(t_1)) - \min(X))..(inf(f(t_2)) - \max(X))$
$\mathbf{dom}(Y)$	$\nu_E(X, \min(Y)..\max(Y), f)$
$r_1 : r_2$	$\nu_E(X, r_1, f) : \nu_E(X, r_2, f)$
$r_1 \, \& \, r_2$	$\nu_E(X, r_1, f) \, \& \, \nu_E(X, r_2, f)$
$-r$	$\nu_D(X, r, f)$
$r + t$	$\nu_E(X, r, f \circ a_t)$
$r - t$	$\nu_E(X, r, f \circ a_{-t})$
$r \bmod t$	$\nu_E(X, r, f \circ m_t)$

Table 5: $E(X, r, f)$ EXPRESSED AS A RANGE

Observe that c_X and c_Y are anti-monotone. Suppose the domains of X and Y are disjoint in a given store S. Hence, $X_S \subseteq -Y_S$ and $Y_S \subseteq -X_S$, i.e. the entailment of c_X and c_Y in S is detected (see Table 4).

The decision table is *incomplete* since for example in the store $\{X \in \{1, 2\}, Y \in \{3, 4\}\}$ the monotone constraint X **in** $..\max(Y)$ is entailed without being detected such by Table 4. Only when Y is determined the constraint will be decided entailed (see Section 4.3).

This scheme has been implemented in the AKL-system, developed at SICS [7], and preliminary results indicate an efficiency comparable with clp(FD), cc(FD), and CHIP [1].

4.2 Generating entailment checking indexicals

In this section we show how to use the entailment detection in Section 4 for checking the entailment conditions of Section 3.1. We adapt Table 2 and Table 3 to generate anti-monotone indexicals instead of conditions, and thus we can use the decision table (Table 4) for checking the conditions [1].

Two operators are defined, ν_E and ν_D (see Table 5 and 6), such that the indexical 0 **in** $\nu_E(X, r, a_0)$ is entailed iff the condition $E(X, r, a_0)$ is true and the indexical 0 **in** $\nu_D(X, r, a_0)$ is entailed iff the condition $D(X, r, a_0)$ is true, which can be proven by induction over r.

Furthermore, $\nu_E(X, r, a_0)$ and $\nu_D(X, r, a_0)$ are anti-monotone, since $t..$, $..t$, and $t_1..t_2$ are mapped onto anti-monotone ranges and anti-monotonicity is preserved by unions and intersections. Thus, if $E(X, r, a_0)$ $(D(X, r, a_0))$ is true then 0 **in** $\nu_E(X, r, a_0)$ (0 **in** $\nu_D(X, r, a_0)$) is decided entailed by Table 4.

Note that 0 **in** $\nu_E(X, r, a_0)$ (0 **in** $\nu_D(X, r, a_0)$) contains all variables in the indexical X **in** r. So these conditions will be (re)tested each time a variable of X **in** r is modified until the constraint is true or false.

Finally, let ν_{E_c} (ν_{D_c}) correspond to $\nu_E(X, r, a_0)$ $(\nu_D(X, r, a_0))$ in the following, where c is X **in** r for some X and r. Thus, $E_c \wedge E_d$ is mapped

r	$\nu_D(X, r, f)$
$t..$	$..(inf(f(t)) - \mathbf{max}(X) - 1)$
$..t$	$..(\mathbf{min}(X) - sup(f(t)) - 1)$
$t_1..t_2$	$..(inf(f(t_1)) - \mathbf{max}(X) - 1) :$
	$..(\mathbf{min}(X) - sup(f(t_2)) - 1) :$
	$..(inf(f(t_1)) - sup(f(t_2)) - 1)$
$\mathbf{dom}(Y)$	$\nu_D(X, \mathbf{min}(Y)..\mathbf{max}(Y), f)$
$r_1 : r_2$	$\nu_D(X, r_1, f)\ \&\ \nu_D(X, r_2, f)$
$r_1\ \&\ r_2$	$\nu_D(X, r_1, f) : \nu_D(X, r_2, f)$
$-r$	$\nu_E(X, r, f)$
$r + t$	$\nu_D(X, r, f \circ a_t)$
$r - t$	$\nu_D(X, r, f \circ a_{-t})$
$r \bmod t$	$\nu_D(X, r, f \circ m_t)$

Table 6: $D(X, r, f)$ EXPRESSED AS A RANGE

onto 0 in $\nu_{Ec}\ \&\ \nu_{Ed}$, $D_c \vee D_d$ is mapped onto 0 in $\nu_{Dc} : \nu_{Dd}$, $D_c \vee E_d$ is mapped onto 0 in $\nu_{Dc} : \nu_{Ed}$, and $E_c \wedge D_d$ is mapped onto 0 in $\nu_{Ec}\ \&\ \nu_{Dd}$.

4.3 Computing monotonicity of X in r

We now give an inductive definition of the monotonicity of X **in** r which is used as the basis of an algorithm for checking the monotonicity. We use mutually recursive definitions (Table 7 and 8) to compute when r is monotone, and when r is anti-monotone. The definitions state which variables occurring in r that must be determined before r is monotone ($\mathcal{M}_r$), and which variables in r which must be determined before r is anti-monotone ($\mathcal{A}_r$).

Intuitively, the monotonicity of a range is preserved under set arithmetical operations, union, intersection, and inverted by the complement operator. The monotonicity of the interval combinator $t_1..t_2$ depends on whether the terms t_1 and t_2 are increasing or decreasing expressions. The increase/decrease property of terms is preserved under addition and multiplication, and inverted in the second argument of subtraction and division. If r is monotone, the expression $\mathbf{min}(r)$ is an increasing expression, and the expression $\mathbf{max}(r)$ is a decreasing expression. If r is anti-monotone, the expression $\mathbf{min}(r)$ is a decreasing expression, and the expression $\mathbf{max}(r)$ is an increasing expression.

In the following we consider only linear FD terms, which simplifies the presentation.

Let t be a linear term. The sets $\mathcal{S}_t$ (shrinking) and $\mathcal{G}_t$ (growing) are two sets of variables defined by Table 7. The intuition being that if all variables in $\mathcal{S}_t$ ($\mathcal{G}_t$) are determined (constants), then t takes on decreasing (increasing) values. If $\mathcal{S}_t$ and $\mathcal{G}_t$ both are empty, t denotes a unique natural number.

Let r be a range. The sets $\mathcal{M}_r$ and $\mathcal{A}_r$ are defined by Table 8. The

t	$\mathcal{S}_t$	$\mathcal{G}_t$
n	$\emptyset$	$\emptyset$
$t_1 + t_2$	$\mathcal{S}_{t_1} \cup \mathcal{S}_{t_2}$	$\mathcal{G}_{t_1} \cup \mathcal{G}_{t_2}$
$t * n$	$\mathcal{S}_t$	$\mathcal{G}_t$
$t * (-n)$	$\mathcal{G}_t$	$\mathcal{S}_t$
$t_1 - t_2$	$\mathcal{S}_{t_1} \cup \mathcal{G}_{t_2}$	$\mathcal{G}_{t_1} \cup \mathcal{S}_{t_2}$
t/n	$\mathcal{S}_t$	$\mathcal{G}_t$
$t/(-n)$	$\mathcal{G}_t$	$\mathcal{S}_t$
$t_1 \bmod t_2$	$\mathcal{S}_{t_1} \cup \mathcal{S}_{t_2} \cup \mathcal{G}_{t_2}$	$\mathcal{G}_{t_1} \cup \mathcal{S}_{t_2} \cup \mathcal{G}_{t_2}$
$\mathbf{min}(r)$	$\mathcal{A}_r$	$\mathcal{M}_r$
$\mathbf{max}(r)$	$\mathcal{M}_r$	$\mathcal{A}_r$

Table 7: MONOTONICITY OF LINEAR TERMS

r	$\mathcal{M}_r$	$\mathcal{A}_r$
$t..$	$\mathcal{G}_t$	$\mathcal{S}_t$
$..t$	$\mathcal{S}_t$	$\mathcal{G}_t$
$t_1..t_2$	$\mathcal{G}_{t_1} \cup \mathcal{S}_{t_2}$	$\mathcal{S}_{t_1} \cup \mathcal{G}_{t_2}$
$\mathbf{dom}(V)$	$\emptyset$	$\{V\}$
$r_0 \cdot t \ (\cdot \in \{+, -, \mathbf{mod}\})$	$\mathcal{M}_{r_0} \cup \mathcal{S}_t \cup \mathcal{G}_t$	$\mathcal{A}_{r_0} \cup \mathcal{S}_t \cup \mathcal{G}_t$
$r_1 \cdot r_2 \ (\cdot \in \{ : , \& \})$	$\mathcal{M}_{r_1} \cup \mathcal{M}_{r_2}$	$\mathcal{A}_{r_1} \cup \mathcal{A}_{r_2}$
$-r_0$	$\mathcal{A}_{r_0}$	$\mathcal{M}_{r_0}$

Table 8: MONOTONICITY OF RANGES

intuition being that if all variables in $\mathcal{M}_r$ ($\mathcal{A}_r$) are determined (constants), then r denotes a monotone (anti-monotone) range. If $\mathcal{M}_r$ and $\mathcal{A}_r$ both are empty, r denotes a unique set.

Example 10.

- Let $r = 1..3$. Then $\mathcal{M}_r = \mathcal{A}_r = \emptyset$.

- Let $r = \mathbf{dom}(Y)$. Then $\mathcal{M}_r = \emptyset$ and $\mathcal{A}_r = \{Y\}$.

- Let $r = \mathbf{dom}(Y) : -\mathbf{dom}(Z)$. Then $\mathcal{M}_r = \{Z\}$ and $\mathcal{A}_r = \{Y\}$.

Hence, $X \ \mathbf{in} \ r$ is monotone if all variables in $\mathcal{M}_r$ are determined and anti-monotone if all variables in $\mathcal{A}_r$ are determined. The *complexity* of checking the monotonicity is the complexity of the union-procedure multiplied by the numbers of operators in r, i.e. basically $O(|r|v \log v)$, where v is the number of variables in r.

The *correctness* of the tables is shown by induction on r. Furthermore, by induction on r it can be proven that $\mathcal{A}_{\nu_E(X,r,a_0)} = \emptyset = \mathcal{A}_{\nu_D(X,r,a_0)}$. Hence, combining Table 8 with Table 4 gives an algorithm for checking the entailment conditions of section 3.

Observe that we do not have a complete decidability procedure for monotonicity. Ranges such as $\mathbf{dom}(Y) : -\mathbf{dom}(Y)$ and $\mathbf{dom}(Y)\ \&\ -\mathbf{dom}(Y)$ cannot be classified until Y is determined, even though they both denote a unique set in any store ($\mathcal{Z}$ and $\emptyset$ respectively).

5 Conclusion

In this paper we consider the entailment of finite domain constraints. Given a finite domain constraint c, defined by an FD constraint, an anti-monotone FD constraint is derived denoting a sufficient truth condition for c. We provide an efficient algorithm for checking the entailment of anti-monotone FD constraints.

Conditional finite domain constraints exploit entailment detection and are shown to be sufficient for defining some non-trivial symbolic constraints. Thus, this implies that many high-level constraints, builtins of existing CLP systems, can be user-defined in a system such as FD while still being efficient.

Current and future research concerns the entailment, compilation, and implementation of logical combinations of constraints, such as disjunctions and implications of finite domain constraints.

Acknowledgements: This work has partly been financed by ACCLAIM, ESPRIT Project 7195. We also owe Philippe Codognet at INRIA-Rocquencourt, Seif Haridi and Torkel Franzén at SICS many thanks for their assistance throughout the work. Finally, we would like to thank the anonymous referees for their helpful recommendations.

References

[1] B. Carlson, S. Janson and S. Haridi. Programming in AKL(FD). Forthcoming SICS Research Report, 1994.

[2] B. Carlson and M. Carlsson. Compiling Linear Integer Constraints. Forthcoming SICS Research Report, 1994.

[3] D. Diaz and P. Codognet. A Minimal Extension of the WAM for clp(FD). In *Proceedings of the 10th International Conference on Logic Programming*, 1993.

[4] D. Diaz and P. Codognet. Compiling Constraint in clp(FD). Technical report, INRIA-Rocquencourt, 1993.

[5] M. Dincbas, P. van Hentenryck, H. Simonis, A. Aggoun, T. Graf, and F. Berthier. The Constraint Logic Programming Language CHIP. In *Proceedings of the International Conference on Fifth Generation Computer Systems*, 1988.

[6] M. Dincbas, P. van Hentenryck, and H. Simonis. Constraint Satisfaction using constraint logic programming. In *Artifical Intelligence*, vol 58, 113-159, 1992.

[7] S. Janson and S. Haridi. Programming paradigms of the Andorra Kernel Language. In *Logic Programming: Proceedings of the 1991 International Symposium*, MIT Press, 1991.

[8] M. J. Maher. Logic semantics for a class of committed choice programs. In *Logic Programming: Proceedings of the Fourth International Conference*, MIT Press, 1987.

[9] W.J. Older and F. Benhamou. Programming in CLP(BNR). In *Position Papers of the First Workshop, PPCP*, Newport, Rhode Island, 1993.

[10] V. A. Saraswat. *Concurrent Constraint Programming*, MIT Press, 1993.

[11] P. van Hentenryck. *Constraint Satisfaction in Logic Programming*. MIT Press, 1989.

[12] P. van Hentenryck, V. Saraswat, and Y. Deville. Constraint processing in cc(FD). Unpublished manuscript, Computer Science Department, Brown University, 1991.

[13] P. van Hentenryck, V. Saraswat, and Y. Deville. Constraint Logic Programming over Finite Domains: the Design, Implementation, and Applications of cc(FD). Technical report, Computer Science Department, Brown University, 1992.

[14] P. van Hentenryck and Y. Deville. Operational Semantics of Constraint Logic Programming over Finite Domains. In *Proceedings of the 3rd Int. Symposium on Programming Language Implementation and Logic Programming*, 1991.

Notes on the Design of an Open Boolean Solver

Antoine Rauzy

LaBRI - CNRS - Université Bordeaux I
351, cours de la Libération
33405 Talence Cedex (France)
rauzy@labri.u-bordeaux.fr

Abstract

In this paper, we describe the implementation of an efficient, versatile and open Boolean solver using if-then-else DAGs as basic structure. The design of this solver is driven by a study of possible applications of Boolean constraints. We propose a new way to implement an if-then-else DAGs package as well as new algorithms that this implementation permits. We discuss the integration of this package in a CLP or cc system and we give some experimental results.

1 Introduction

Since their early versions, PrologIII [11], CHIP [16] and CAL [22] include Boolean solvers [1,8,19], and a number of works have been done on Boolean constraints handling in the last years. It is worthwhile to say that the CLP communauty has gained a great experience on the design of such solvers. Nevertheless, conversely to what happened for finite domains constraints, only few efforts have been done to find (and to deal with) "real-life" applications of Boolean constraints. Several reasons explain that: first, the SAT problem – satisfiability of a set of propositional clauses – is an active research field in itself (recall that it was the first problem to be shown NP-complete [12]). Second, "real-life" applications of Boolean constraints do not come from operational research and are not so easily available than optimization problems. It results that actually implemented Boolean solvers are more designed to solve mathematical puzzles than to be usefull in practice, even some interesting results have been obtained on hardware verification [15].

The aim of this paper is to propose a guideline for the implementation of the next generation of Boolean solvers. More precisely, we describe the implementation of an efficient, versatile and open Boolean solver using if-then-else DAGs as basic structure (if-then-else DAGs generalize the Bryant's Binary Decision Diagrams [6]).

The design of this solver is driven by a study of possible applications of Boolean constraints. As a case study, we examine the computation of prime implicants of a formula, which is of a special interest for implementing ATMS systems as shown in [13] and for safety analysis of embedded systems [14,21]. This application is very representative since it requires to manipulate sets of solutions of Boolean constraints as well as extra-logical operations that cannot be implemented by means of "black-box" solvers.

Our implementation follows the so-called "glass-box" approach proposed in [17]. The idea is to provide a restricted but complete set of instructions handling memory management of if-then-else DAGs. The remaining, i.e. algorithms that perform logical operations, variable ordering, ..., being left to the host system. For this purpose, we propose a new way to implement an if-then-else DAGs package as well as new algorithms that this implementation permits. Roughly speaking, this package differs from the usual ones by merging the tables in which if-then-else nodes and computation results are stored. As an example, we describe an algorithm that normalizes partially formulae and which is more efficient for testing the satisfiability than the computation of a full normal form.

The remaining of this paper is organized as follows: at section 2 we examine the desired functionalities for a Boolean solver. At section 3 we recall basic definitions and properties of if-then-else DAGs. At section 4, we describe our if-then-else DAGs package. Its integration in a CLP or cc system is discussed at section 5. Finally, we present the mentionned application at section 6.

2 Background

We assume the reader familiar with usual definitions and properties of the propositional calculus.

Boolean *formulae* are terms inductively built over the two constants 0 and 1, a denumerable set of variables X, and usual logical connectives $\land, \lor, \neg, \Rightarrow, \Leftrightarrow, \oplus$ whose semantics is given by the well known truth tables.

In the following, we assume that a *Boolean constraint* is any formula (even it is not exactly the case in implemented systems such as PrologIII).

Boolean solvers are to be considered from two points of view : first, the internal one, which is concerned in the way they encode constraints and algorithms they apply on this data structure. Second, the external one, which is concerned by the functionalities they provide.

In the CLP paradigm, any solver must fulfill at least the two following requirements:
– Each time a constraint is added to the store, the satisfiability of the extended store must be – at least partially – tested.
– When the computation process is successfully terminated, the store must be projected on the variables of the query in order to display the result.

Implemented solvers do not do really more than that. They can roughly classified as follows:

Resolution-based methods Such a method is implemented in the current version of PrologIII [1]. Constraints are encoded as set of clauses.

An extended SL-Resolution is used to produce clauses that have interesting morphological properties among those implied by the store. This technique, so-called "production fields" [3], permits to fulfill the two above requirements.

Methods maintaining a normal form Boolean solvers of CHIP [8,7] and CAL [19] implements such methods. The principle is to maintain the store under a normal form that ensures its satisfiability. In CHIP, this is realized by means of BDD package. We will describe this technique later. The projection of the store on the variables of the query can be performed either by existentially quantifying the other variables or by computing a most general unifier. Note that in this case, Boolean unification just permits a pretty presentation of results.

Enumerative methods These methods roughly consists in trying possible assignments and testing consistency in various sophisticated ways. The internal representation of constraints can be either clauses [4,5], bit vectors [18] or general formulae [20,9] following the chosen propagation scheme. The display of results can be performed either simply by enumerating solutions [18,9] or by using the production fields technique [5] or by computing a most general unifier [20].

In order to make a fair comparison of these methods, one must examine several aspects :

Efficiency Resolution-based methods are of several order of magnitude worst than the others. Marseilles' school has now a sufficiently good experience to be convince that there is no hope to improve them significantly. When they avoid to check consistency each time a constraint is added to the store, enumerative methods are in general several times faster than BDDs as shown in [9,23]. In practice it is always possible to avoid such a test, either by choosing the appropriate propagation scheme or by using an additional variable to delay the constraints [5].

Implementation cost This criterion must be understood in the following way : the implementation of a specific Boolean solver in a CLP or cc system must justify its implementation cost by providing functionalities that are useful and not available otherwise. In [9], P. Codognet and D. Diaz demonstrate that enumerative methods can be implemented on the top of a finite domains solver with no additional cost. Since it seems clear that Boolean unification and implied formulae production are not of particular interest in the CLP or cc paradigm, there is no reason to implement a specific enumerative Boolean solver. The same remark stands also for the – otherwise excellent – work by Bockmayr [2] on pseudo-boolean constraints.

Functionalities Finite domain solvers – that implement the enumeration/propagation scheme – are designed to find efficiently a solution to a problem, eventually the best one following a given criterion (objective function). Thus, the two requirements of the CLP paradigm are sufficient to handle a wide range of finite domains problems. On the contrary, all applications of Boolean constraints we know (circuit verification, safety analysis, model checking, abstract interpretation) require to manipulate constraints as *relations*, i.e. as sets of solutions. Enumerative methods do not support such manipulations. Conversely, BDDs and if-then-else DAGs provide the desired functionalities. We examine this technique in the next section.

3   Binary Decision Diagrams, If-Then-Else DAGs

3.1   Data Structure

Reduced Ordered Binary Decision Diagrams are the state-of-the-art structure for Boolean function manipulation. For an excellent survey see [6]. This structure is based on a single universal operator – the if-then-else (ite) operator.

Definition 3.1 $ite(F, G, H) = (F \wedge G) \vee (\neg F \wedge H)$

All binary functions are easily defined with the ite operator. For example, $F \wedge G \equiv ite(F, G, 0)$, $F \vee G \equiv ite(F, 1, G)$ and $F \oplus G \equiv ite(F, \neg G, G)$.

We divide if-then-else representations into two categories: Binary Decision Diagrams (BDD for short), in which the if-part is always a variable and if-then-else DAGs which may have arbitrary expressions in the if-part.

Definition 3.2 Binary Decision Diagrams
A Binary Decision Diagram is a rooted binary directed acyclic graph with two leaves 0 and 1 and which each non-leaf node is labeled with a variable x and has two out-edges pointing to the then-part and to the else-part. The meaning of a BDD is defined recursively as $ite(x, meaning(then\_part), meaning(else\_part))$.

The definition of if-then-else DAGs is the same, excepted that DAGs are ternary, the if-part being either a variable or a DAG.

A BDD is *free*, if each variable is encountered at most once on each path from the root to a terminal vertex. A BDD is *ordered*, if it is free and the variables are encountered in the same order on each path from the root to a terminal vertex. A BDD is *reduced* if it none of the two following operations remains possible:
– Identifying two nodes v and w where the sub-BDD rooted by v and w are isomorphic.
– Deleting a node v whose two outgoing edges point to the same node w and connect the incoming edges of v to w.

Example 3.1 Assume $F = (x \wedge y) \vee z$, then the corresponding reduced ordered BDD with respect to the order $x < y < z$ is given Fig. 1.

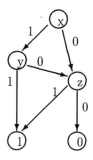

Figure 1: The BDD encoding $(x \wedge y) \vee z$

Property 3.1 canonicity
The BDD representation is canonical (for a given variable ordering).

This property is fundamental. In particular, it means that testing e-quality of two BDDs representations is reduced to testing equality of their addresses.

BDDs encoding a formula and its negation are isomorphic, up to the invertion of their leaves. To simplify negation operation, and to reduce the storage needed for representing expressions, one bit flags are introduced on edges indicating whether the BDD (or if-then-else DAG) must be considered positively or negatively. In order to maintain the canonicity of the representation, a triple $ite(F, G, H)$, where F is either a variable or a DAG is transformed in a equivalent triple $ite(F', G', H')$ such that F' and G' are positive. For example, $ite(F, \neg G, H) \rightarrow \neg ite(F, G, \neg H)$ and $ite(\neg F, G, H) \rightarrow ite(F, H, G)$.

In order to respect the optimal reduction property (i.e. canonicity), ite nodes are kept in an hashtable (called in the following ite-table). Each time a node $ite(F, G, H)$ must be created, a hashcode is computed (from F, G and H) and the node is actually created if it does not occur in the corresponding collision chain. The ite-table can be seen as a BDD forest.

3.2 Computation of the BDD associated with a formula

Let $F = F_1 \odot F_2$ be a formula, where $\odot$ is any binary connective. In order to compute the BDD B associated with F, the BDDs associated with F_1 and F_2 are computed, then they are composed by means of the following procedure (to do that, $\odot$ must be transformed in its *ite* form) :

```
ite(F, G, H) {
    if (terminal case) return result
    else if (computed_table has entry {F, G, H}) return result
    else {
        let x be the top variable of F, G and H,
        U ← ite(F_{x=1}, G_{x=1}, H_{x=1})
        V ← ite(F_{x=0}, G_{x=0}, H_{x=0})
        R = find_or_add_ite_table(x, U, V)
        insert_computed_table({F, G, H}, R)
        return R
    }
}
```

In the sequel, we will call this principle the bottom-up computation of the BDD associated with the formula.

Some explanations must be given on the above algorithm :

– A terminal case occurs when the value of $ite(F, G, H)$ can be trivially computed. For instance, $ite(F, G, G) \equiv G$.

– In the *computed_table*, 4-tuples $\langle \{F, G, H\}, R \rangle$ are kept, where F, G, H and R are BDDs such that $ite(F, G, H) \equiv R$. Before any computation of $ite(F, G, H)$, one checks if the result is not already in the table (*computed_table* has entry ...). The *computed_table* is, in general, implemented as a hash-based cach, that is to say that newer entries overwrite older ones.

– $F_{x=v}$ denotes the sub-BDD pointed by the outgoing edge of F labeled with v, if the top variable of F is x and the BDD F itself otherwise.

– Trivial simplifications may be performed on $ite(F, G, H)$. For instance, $ite(F, F, G) \equiv ite(F, 1, G)$ and $ite(F, G, \neg F) \equiv ite(F, G, 1)$.

Heuristics To conclude this short presentation of BDDs, we have to emphasize that the size of a BDD (and the computation time) depends critically on the variable ordering. For instance, the BDD representation of $F_n = (x_1 \wedge y_1) \oplus \ldots \oplus (x_n \wedge y_n)$ is linear for the order $x_1 < y_1 < x_2 < \ldots < x_n < y_n$) but exponential for the alphabetic order.

There are many heuristics to select a good ordering (to find the best is co-NP complete). In a glass-box solver, the programmer can choose his own heuristics, which is not possible in the black-box approach.

4 A unique table based Boolean solver

BDDs have two drawbacks when used in the CLP or cc paradigm. First, in order to test the satisfiability of a formula, one has to compute the whole BDD associated with this formula, which may be very costly. Second, there is no natural way to delay the treatment of a constraint (waiting for a instantiation of variables).

The aim of the implementation we propose is to remove these drawbacks. The idea is to merge the `ite-table` and the `computed-table` into an unique table. Each item (node) in the table encodes the following informations:
– Three pointers to the if-, then- and else-parts.
– The type of the node (BDD, if-then-else DAG, ...).
– A pointer to the next element in the collision chain and a reference count for garbage collection.
– Finally, and here stands the novelty, a pointer to the *value* of the encoded triple, in the same spirit than it is done in Colmerauer's unification algorithm for rational tree algebra [10].

In our implementation, a node is encoded by means of 6 words (we assume a 32 bits machine). Fields `value` permits to create chains of equivalent formulae that are more and more normalized, i.e. more and more close to a BDD, along the chain.

The computation of the BDD associated with a formula is performed in two steps:

1. The formula is inserted in the table, each binary connective being transformed into its equivalent if-then-else form. For example, the formula $a \vee b$ is transformed into $ite(ite(a, 1, 0), 1, ite(b, 1, 0))$ (a variable x is automatically encoded by means of the BDD $ite(x, 1, 0)$.

2. The BDD is computed from the stored if-then-else DAG.

The second part of this process may be only partial: it is possible to stops it when the formula has been transformed into a satisfiable equivalent formula which is not yet a BDD.

Basic instructions the unique table management are the following :
– `find_or_add_ite(type,if-part,then-part,else-part)`. If the node already exists in the table, this instruction returns its address, otherwise it creates a new node with a NULL value and returns its address.
– `bind_ite(node1,node2)` that sets the value of node1 to node2.
– `dereferenced_value(node)` that returns the dereferenced value of the given node.

The previous algorithm is rewritten for the new package as follows :

```
ite(F,G,H) { /* F, G, H are assumed to be BDDs */
    N ← derefenced_value(find_or_add_ite(ite_DAG, F, G, H))
    if (type(N) = BDD) return N
    else {
        let x be the top variable of F, G and H,
        U ← ite(F_{x=1}, G_{x=1}, H_{x=1})
        V ← ite(F_{x=0}, G_{x=0}, H_{x=0})
        R = find_or_add_ite(BDD, x, U, V)
        bind_ite(N, R)
        return R
    }
}
```

The algorithm that computes the BDD associated with a formula is s-ketched below. It is called "bottom-up" for it mimics the usual BDD computation.

```
bottom_up_normalization(N) {
        M ← derefenced_value(N)
        if (type(M) = BDD) return M
        else {
            F ← dereferenced_value(if_part(M))
            G ← dereferenced_value(then_part(M))
            H ← dereferenced_value(else_part(M))
            R = ite(F, G, H)
            bind_ite(M, R)
            return R
            }
    }
```

As said above, the interesting feature of the implementation we propose is that it allows other normalization or partial normalization methods than the previous one.

Let us introduce a new type of if-then-else DAG – the shannon DAGs – that are in the form $ite(x, F, G)$ where x is a variable and F and G are any if-then-else DAGs.

Given a formula N and x the least variable of N, it is possible to compute a formula $ite(x, U, V)$ equivalent to N, where U and V are formulae in which x doesn't occur :

```
shannon_form(N, x) {
        M ← derefenced_value(N)
        if (type(M) = BDD) return M
        else {
            F ← shannon_form(if_part(M), x)
            G ← shannon_form(then_part(M), x)
            H ← shannon_form(else_part(M), x)
            U ← find_or_add_ite(ite_DAG, F_{x=1}, G_{x=1}, H_{x=1})
            V ← find_or_add_ite(ite_DAG, F_{x=0}, G_{x=0}, H_{x=0})
            R = find_or_add_ite(shannon_DAG, x, U, V)
            bind_ite(M, R)
            return R
            }
    }
```

With this algorithm, it is possible to define a top-down computation of the BDD associated with a formula. This algorithm is depicted bellow. The idea is the following: in order to compute the BDD associated with the formula N whose least variable is x, first a shannon DAG $ite(x, F, G)$ equivalent to N is computed, second the algorithm is called on F and G.

```
top_down_normalization(N) {
    M ← derefenced_value(N)
    if (type(M) = BDD) return M
    else if (type(M) = shannon_DAG) {
        let x be the least variable of M,
        U ← top_down_normalization(then_part(M))
        V ← top_down_normalization(else_part(M))
        R = find_or_add_ite(BDD, x, U, V)
        bind_ite(M, R)
        return R
    }
    else {
        let x be the least variable of M,
        F ← shannon_form(M, x)
        bind_ite(M, F)
        return top_down_normalization(F)
    }
}
```

At this point, it is interesting to compare performances of normalization algorithms. We tried them on the well-known pigeon-hole problem that consists to put P pigeons into N holes in such way that there is at most one pigeons in each hole. We model the problem by means of $P \times N$ variables (a variable for each pair (pigeon,hole)) and $P + P \times (N \times (N-1))/2$ clauses. The formula is defined as the conjunction of the clauses. Variables are ordered lexicographically.

The following table gives the comparative results of 1) a classical BDD package, 2) the bottom-up computation in our package, 3) the top-down computation in our package.

P/H	5/5	6/5	6/6	7/6	7/7	8/7	8/8	9/8	9/9
solutions	120	0	720	0	5040	0	40320	0	362880
usual	0s13	0s23	0s56	0s86	2s16	3s43	7s86	10s65	30s40
bottom − up	0s16	0s28	0s70	1s10	2s75	4s05	10s06	14s35	38s86
top − down	0s76	1s75	16s63	?	?	?	?	?	?

The above table shows that the performances of our package are comparable to those of a classically implemented package for bottom-up computations. This result is true for all examples we tried. Space consumptions are also very similar. Performances of the top-down computation are catastrophic (at least on this example).

The real interest of the top-down principle is that it allows a partial normalization of formulae. In the previous algorithm, the two outedges of the root of a shannon DAG are normalized. But, in order to ensure the satisfiability of a formula, it suffices to normalize one of the two sub-DAGs. For this purpose, we introduce a new type of if-then-else DAGs, called satisfiable DAGs, that are inductively defined as follows :

– BDDs (different from the leaf 0) are satisfiable DAGs.

– If x is a variable, F is a satisfiable DAG whose least variable is greater than x and G is any if-then-else DAG whose least variable is greater than x, then $ite(x, F, G)$ and $ite(x, G, F)$ are satisfiable DAGs.

The algorithm computing a satisfiable DAG equivalent to a given if-then-else DAG is depicted below. Note that in this version, the **then-part** is systematically explored before the **else-part**. The choice of the first part to normalize could be driven by another (and more clever) heuristics.

$partial\_normalization(N)$ {
    $M \leftarrow derefenced\_value(N)$
    if $(type(M) = BDD\ or\ satisfiable\_DAG)$ return M
    else if $(type(M) = shannon\_DAG)$ {
        let x be the least variable of M,
        $U \leftarrow partial\_normalization(then\_part(M))$
        if $(U = 0)$ $V \leftarrow partial\_normalization(else\_part(M))$
        else $V \leftarrow else\_part(M)$
        $R = find\_or\_add\_ite(satisfiable\_DAG, x, U, V)$
        $bind\_ite(M, R)$
        return R
        }
    else {
        let x be the least variable of M,
        $F \leftarrow shannon\_form(M, x)$
        $bind\_ite(M, F)$
        return $partial\_normalization(F)$
        }
    }

Note finally that if-then-else DAGs can be used in order to store the result of an enumerative method with a minimal storage cost, thanks to isomorphic sub-DAGs sharing.

5 Integration into a CLP or cc system

In order to build an open solver, we propose to conceive it essentially as a memory manager. Its primitive constraints are the instructions used in the previous section and given below in a Prolog.

Decomposition constraints	Creation constraints
if_part(F,R)	find_or_add_ite(Type,F,G,H)
then_part(F,R)	unify_ite(F,G)
else_part(F,R)	
type(F,R)	
value(F,R)	

The remaining, including variable ordering and algorithms computing logical operations, can be written in the host language. For instance, the computation of the BDD associated with a formula can be defined as a high-level constraint i.e. as a prolog predicate, as shown below. This construction is very similar to those adopted in [17,9]. The various algorithms we have described in the previous section as well as many others (computation of prime implicants, BDD traversal, computation of Boolean unifier, ...) may constitute a toolbox for Boolean constraint programming.

```
bdd(N,R) :-
    deferenced_value(N,M),
    type(M,T),
    aux_bdd(M,T,R).

aux_bdd(R,bdd,R) :- !.
aux_bdd(M,_,R) :-
    if_part(M,F), then_part(M,G), else_part(M,H),
    ite(F,G,H,R),
    bind_ite(M,R).

dereferenced_value(F,F) :- value(F,NULL), !.
dereferenced_value(F,R) :- value(F,G), dereferenced_value(G,R).
```

The operational semantics of the **tell** operation (that adds a constraint to the store) can be either just to insert the given formula in the unique table, or to do this and then to perform a partial normalization of the store.

Note that in the latter case, it is still possible to delay the treatment of a constraint, as proposed in [5], by introducing a new variable of least index x and by writing the added constraint C as $x \vee C$. The partial normalization algorithm stops immediately since $ite(x, 1, C)$ is a satisfiable DAG. In order to start the treatment of delayed constraints, it suffices to add $\neg x$.

At a higher level, the propositional calculus has two interesting features:
– A formula can be equalize to a variable. It is thus possible to *name* constraints and stores $(x \Leftrightarrow f(y_1, \ldots, y_n))$, and to use these names as ordinary variables.
– A store S implies a constraint C iff $S \Rightarrow C$ is a tautology. Thus it is very easy to define an **ask** operation.

6 Minimal Cuts in Fault Trees

In this section, we present an application of Boolean constraints: the computation of minimal solutions (cuts) of fault trees. The fault trees method is one of the most used for safety analysis of industrial systems. Its principle is as follows: the studied system is decomposed into subsystems, then each subsystem is itself decomposed into subsystems, and so on until the desired granularity as been reached. Then, the possible faults of each (sub)system are described as a Boolean function of the possible faults in its subsystems.

A qualitative safety analysis of the embedded system requires to know the minimal sets of basic faults – called minimal cuts – that induce a fault of the whole system. In a logical point of view, it means that it requires to compute prime implicants of the formula.

In practice, most of the fault trees are monotone functions. A Boolean function f is said *monotone* if, for any solution σ of f such that $\sigma(x) = 0$, the assignment σ' is equal to σ everywhere except for x where $\sigma'(x) = 1$ is also a solution of f.

Example 6.1 The fault tree $(((a \vee b) \wedge (c \vee d)) \wedge ((c \vee d) \wedge e)))$ is monotone and has four minimal cuts: $\{\{a, c, e\}, \{a, d, e\}, \{b, c, e\}, \{b, d, e\}\}$

The computation of the minimal cuts in fault trees is, in our opinion, a good benchmark for Boolean solvers. First, it is a real industrial application, and second, the minimality of a cut cannot be expressed with the usual connectives (except if one enumerates, for any assignment, all the possible assignments included). With a "black-box" solver, it is not possible to perform this computation since one cannot create new basic operations.

The full algorithm is described in [21]. Its first part is depicted below.

```
% minimal_cuts(+T,-R)
minimal_cuts(T,T) :- one(T), !.
minimal_cuts(T,T) :- zero(T), !.
minimal_cuts(T,R) :-
    find_or_add_ite(minimal_cuts,T,NULL,S),
    minimal_cuts_aux(T,S,R).

minimal_cuts_aux(T,S,R) :-
    value(S,NULL), !,
    if_part(T,X), then_part(T,F), else_part(T,G),
    minimal_cuts(F,K),
    without(K,G,U),
    minimal_cuts(G,V),
    find_or_add_ite(BDD,X,U,V,R),
    bind_ite(G,R).
minimal_cuts_aux(F,G,R) :- value(G,R).
```

The predicate without(+F,+G,-R) computes the BDD R encoding the solutions of the BDD F which are not included (positively) in one solution of the BDD G. The main interest of these few lines of Prolog code is to demonstrate that a solver built over the basic constraints described in the section 5 permits the manipulation of BDD in many different ways, including operations that build BDDs in an extra-logical way and operations that memorize the results of these computations.

With our if-then-else DAGs package one can easily program extra-logical operations such as computing the minimal cuts, counting or displaying the solutions, projecting on subvocabulary, computing an unifier and so forth.

Benchmarks We have tested the algorithm on sixteen industrial fault trees. Ten were proposed by Dassault Aviation (da1–da10), four by Y. Dutuit from the Université Bordeaux I (chinese, euro1–euro3) and one by J.C. Madre and O. Coudert from BULL (edf1). In order to perform the tests, we have meta-programmed in SICSTUS prolog version 0.7 a CLP($\mathcal{B}$). Primitive constraints are written in C and linked with prolog predicates. The tables below give the number of variables, the number of connectives and the number of minimal cuts of each tree.

	da1	da2	da3	da4	da5	da6	da7	da8	da9	da10
var.	103	170	122	51	53	51	121	276	49	109
con.	145	257	82	30	30	20	112	324	36	73
sol.	8060	12143	14217	16200	16704	17280	19518	25988	27788	81.10^9

	chinese	euro1	euro2	euro3	edf1
var.	25	61	32	80	183
con.	36	84	40	107	132
sol.	392	46188	4805	24386	579720

The tables below give run-times for the two implementations: Prolog+C and Adia the software written in C for Dassault Aviation.

	da1	da2	da3	da4	da5	da6	da7	da8	da9	da10
Prolog + C	34s41	325s4	3s33	0s27	0s37	0s21	6s21	34s90	0s35	0s60
Adia	3s13	45s76	0s56	0s03	0s03	0s01	0s65	4s43	0s05	0s05

	chinese	euro1	euro2	euro3	edf1
Prolog + C	0s38	45s67	3s18	67s03	18s79
Adia	0s05	4s36	0s31	6s81	1s43

The mixed implementation Prolog+C is thus satisfactory — only about 10 times slower than the C code — since there are many optimizations possible.

7 Conclusion

In this paper, we have proposed a guideline for the implementation of a flexible, versatile and open Boolean solver. Our solver is

a memory manager, just a memory manager.

The generalization Binary Decision Diagrams permits the implementation of many algorithms. This opens CLP($\mathcal{B}$) or cc($\mathcal{B}$) systems to a wide range of real life problems.

It remains to include the solver and the associated toolbox into a CLP or cc system.

Note finally, that there is no semantics associated with the nodes in the table. It means that it is possible to interpret them for instance as

Reed-Muller expansion $< F, G, H >= (F \wedge G) \oplus H$ rather than as Shannon expansion $< F, G, H >= (F \wedge G) \vee (\neg F \wedge H)$. This approach has been shown interesting for circuit design. The same remarks holds also for non-free or non-ordered BDDs or to other normal forms implementable by means of if-then-else DAGs.

References

[1] F. Benhamou and J.M. Boï. *Le traitement des contraintes booléennes dans PrologIII*. PhD thesis, GIA - Université Aix-Marseille II, 1988.

[2] A. Bockmayr. Logic Programming with Pseudo-Boolean Constraints. Research report MPI-I-91-227, Max Planck Institut, Saarbrucken, Germany, 1991.

[3] J.M. Boï, E. Innocente, A. Rauzy, and P. Siegel. Production Fields: a New Approach to Deduction Problems and two Algorithms for Propositional Calculus. *Revue Française d'Intelligence Artificielle*, 06(3), 1992.

[4] J.M. Boï and A. Rauzy. Two algorithms for constraints system solving in propositional calculus and their implementation in prologIII. In P. Jorrand and V. Sugrev, editors, *Proceedings Artificial Intelligence IV Methodology, Systems, Applications (AIMSA'90)*. North-Holand, september 1990. Alba-Varna bulgarie.

[5] J.M. Boï and A. Rauzy. Using Boolean Constraints in Prolog. In *Proceedings of the Italian Conference on Logic Programming GULP'91*. GULP, 1991.

[6] R. Bryant. Symbolic Boolean Manipulation with Ordered Binary Decision Diagrams. *ACM Computing Surveys*, 1992.

[7] W. Buettner. Unification in Finite Algebras is Unitary (?). In 9th *Conference on Automatic Demonstration*, volume 310. LNCS, 1988.

[8] W. Buettner and H. Simonis. Embedding Boolean Expressions into Logic Programming. *Journal of Symbolic Computation*, 4:191–205, 1987.

[9] P. Codognet and D. Diaz. Boolean Constraint Solving Using clp(FD). In D. Miller, editor, *proceedings of the International Logic Programming Symposium, ILPS'93*. MIT Press, 1993.

[10] A. Colmerauer. Unification over Rational Trees. Technical report, Groupe d'Intelligence Artificielle, Université Aix-Marseille II, 1982.

[11] A. Colmerauer. An introduction to prologIII. *Communications of the ACM*, 28 (4), july 1990.

[12] S.A. Cook. The Complexity of Theorem Proving Procedures. In *Proceedings of the 3rd Ann. Symp. on Theory of Computing, ACM*, pages 151–158, 1971.

[13] O. Coudert and J.C. Madre. A Logically Complete Reasoning Maintenance System Based on Logical Constraint Solver. In *Proceedings of the International Join Conference on Artificial Intelligence, IJCAI'89*, August 1991.

[14] O. Coudert and J.C. Madre. METAPRIME, an Iteractive Fault Tree Analyser. In *Proceedings of the Annual Reliability and Maintenability Symposium*, 1992.

[15] Filkorn, Schmid, E. Tiden, and Warkentin. Experiences for a Large Industrial Circuit Application. In *proceedings of the International Logic Programming Symposium, ILPS'91*. MIT Press, 1991.

[16] P. Van Hentenryck. *Constraint Satisfaction in Logic Programming*. Logic Programming Series. MIT Press, 1989.

[17] P. Van Hentenryck, V. Saraswat, and Y. Deville. Constraint processing in cc(FD). personnal communication, 1992.

[18] J-L. Massat. Using Local Consistency Technics to Solve Boolean Constraints. In A. Colmerauer and F. Benhamou, editors, *Constraint Logic Programming: Selected Research*. MIT Press, 1993.

[19] S. Menju, K. Sakai, Y. Sato, and A. Aiba. A Study on Boolean Constraints Solvers. In A. Colmerauer and F. Benhamou, editors, *Constraint Logic Programming: Selected Research*. MIT Press, 1993.

[20] A. Rauzy. Boolean unification: an efficient algorithm. In A. Colmerauer and F. Benhamou, editors, *Constraint Logic Programming: Selected Research*. MIT Press, 1993.

[21] A. Rauzy. New Algorithms for Fault Trees Analysis. *Reliability Engineering & System Safety*, 05(59), 1993.

[22] Sakai and Aiba. CAL: a Theorical Background if Constraint Logic Programming and its Applications. In *Proceedings of the Workshop Languages and Constraints Providence*, 88.

[23] H. Simonis and M. Dincbas. Propositional Calculus Problems in CHIP. In A. Colmerauer and F. Benhamou, editors, *Constraint Logic Programming: Selected Research*. MIT Press, 1993.

Improved CLP Scheduling with Task Intervals

Yves Caseau
Bellcore, 445 South Street,
Morristown NJ 07960, USA.
caseau@bellcore.com

François Laburthe
Ecole Normale Supérieure
45, rue d'Ulm, 75005 PARIS
laburthe@clipper.ens.fr

Abstract

In this paper we present a new technique that can be used to improve performance of job scheduling with a constraint programming language. We show how, by focusing on some special sets of tasks, one can bring CLP in the same range of efficiency as traditional OR algorithms on a classical benchmark (MT10 [MT63]), thus making CLP both a flexible and an efficient technique for such combinatorial problems. We then present our programming methodology which we have successfully used on many problems, and draw conclusions on what features constraint programming languages should offer to allow its use.

1. Introduction

Real-life scheduling problems are often the composition of various well-identified hard problems. In the previous years, we have worked on applications such as task-technician assignments [CK92] or staff timetable scheduling [CGL93] and developed a methodology for solving such problems with an extensible constraint logic programming language. In both cases we have applied the same methodology that is to add, to a declarative constraint-based approach, algorithms taken from operational research (OR) that are used both as a search guide and as branch cutting heuristics. We have experienced a significant improvement in performance while retaining the flexibility of constraint logic programming (CLP). However, the nature of these problems makes it hard to perform serious comparisons with other competitive techniques. In this paper, we apply the same methodology to the job-shop scheduling problem. Although one can criticize such a choice by saying that real-life job-shop scheduling problems are more complex than the abstraction made by algorithm specialists, "simple" n × m scheduling problems have been thoroughly studied, and we can compare the results provided by our method with OR best algorithms and other CLP solutions for the same problem.

We started with a naive scheduling program, similar to the program used in [VH89], and which we had used for many years as a benchmark for our constraint satisfaction engine. To this program, we have simply added the notion of task intervals, which are sets of tasks sharing the same resource represented by the "earliest" and "latest" members of the sets. The next step is to add the set of obvious redundant constraints that one can write using these task intervals. The last step is to use these intervals to guide the search using a well-known technique of "edge finding" [AC91]. The program that we obtain is still fairly small and easily extensible, and it performs much better that the original naive one.

The fact that we obtain performance results that are comparable with the state-of-the-art of OR algorithms is important for CLP for two reasons. On the one hand, it shows that there is no reason why CLP cannot deliver high levels of performance and thus be applied to large and complex problems. In addition, performance is only one aspect of scheduling problems, and the flexibility provided by CLP makes it a programming paradigm of choice for "real-life" problems. On the other hand, these results confirm some of our previous findings, mainly that CLP constraint solvers need to be open and extensible. A user of a CLP language needs to be able to use techniques such as those presented in this paper in a fairly natural and readable manner.

The paper is organized as follows. Section 2 recalls what a job-shop scheduling problem is, and how it is usually solved with a CLP language. It also recalls some of our preliminary findings with other problems that guided us for job-shop scheduling. Section 3 describes a set of redundant dynamic constraints based on task intervals. We show how to represent and implement these constraints using logical rules. Section 4 shows how task intervals are used to guide the search, and gives some preliminary results using the bridge benchmark used in the CLP community [VH89] and the 10×10 problem [MT63] used in the OR community. Section 5 presents a comparison with related work and a "wish list" that we have derived from our experience as a CLP user.

2. Job-shop Scheduling and Constraint Logic Programming

2.1. Job-Shop Scheduling

A job scheduling problem is defined by a set of tasks T and a set of resources R. Tasks are linked through precedence relationships, which tell that a task must wait for another task to be completed before it can start (sometimes, as in the bridge scheduling problem, a delay may be added). Tasks that share a resource are mutually exclusive (we do not address here the case, frequent in real life, where a resource can handle more than one task at a time). The goal is to find an optimal schedule that is, a schedule that completes all the tasks in the minimum amount of time. A complete description of such a problem can be found in [VH89]: the bridge scheduling problem has become a classical benchmark for CLP solvers.

Job-shop scheduling is a special case where each task is part of a job, and where the only precedence relation is that a task must be performed after its predecessor in the job order. It is also assumed that each task in a job needs a different machine. Such problems are often called $n \times m$ problems, where n is the number of jobs and m the number of resources. The simplification does not come from the matrix structure (one could always add empty tasks to a scheduling problem) but rather from the fact that precedence is a functional relation. For instance, the bridge problem cannot be seen as a job-shop scheduling problem. The interest of $n \times m$ scheduling problems is the attention they have received in the last 20 years. For instance, the 10×10 problem of [MT63] was left unsolved until 1989 [CP89] and has been used as a benchmark for most OR algorithms since then.

2.2 CLP and Scheduling

Constraint Logic Programming, and more generally constraint satisfaction languages, are good candidates for job scheduling problems. In fact, a scheduling problem can be stated with two families of constraints. In the following, we will write $precede(t_1, t_2)$ when t_2 cannot be performed before t_1 is completed, $d(t)$ will denote the duration of the task t and $r(t)$ will denote the resource that it uses.

$$\forall\, t_1, t_2 \in T, \quad precede(t_1, t_2) \Rightarrow \quad time(t_2) \geq time(t_1) + d(t_1)$$
$$\forall\, t_1, t_2 \in T, \quad r(t_1) = r(t_2) \Rightarrow \quad time(t_2) \geq time(t_1) + d(t_1) \; \vee$$
$$time(t_1) \geq time(t_2) + d(t_2)$$

Most CLP languages offer a direct encoding of these constraints and a CHIP scheduling program can be less than 100 lines. The resolution is usually based on two simple ideas: representing the unknown domain associated with $time(t_i)$ as an interval, and getting rid of disjunctions first. To each task t_i (represented by a logical variable that denotes the starting time) the CLP solver associates an interval $\left[\underline{t_i}, \overline{t_i} - d(t_i)\right]$ where $\underline{t_i}$ is the minimal starting date and $\overline{t_i}$ is the maximal completion date (thus the starting date must be between $\underline{t_i}$ and $\overline{t_i} - d(t_i)$). Precedence constraints can be easily propagated using interval abstractions [Ca91]; when there are only precedence constraints, the resulting interval lower bounds are the optimal schedule. Therefore, the search strategy is to order each pair of tasks that share the same resource. There are many variations depending on which pair to pick, how to exploit the disjunctive constraint before the pair is actually ordered, etc., but the general strategy is almost always to order pairs of tasks [AC91].

Modern CLP solvers do a good job in implementing this general strategy efficiently. The bridge scheduling problem is solved in a second's range on a workstation, which compares well to special purpose algorithms built for this problem [VH89]. However, their performance on large n × m problems is still far from that of specialized algorithms such as those presented in [AC91]. A first step was proposed in CHIP with the notion of cumulative constraints that encapsulate some techniques from OR into the CHIP solver [AB92]. The approach that we follow in this paper is slightly different, since we do not extend the constraint solver (black-box approach) but rather the program (white-box approach); thus it can be used with languages other than the one we picked for our experiments.

2.3 Experience with complex scheduling problems

CLP is also a big winner over OR scheduling programs as far as flexibility is concerned. The same program can be used for job-shop scheduling or for the bridge scheduling. Adding domain-dependent constraints is easy and usually improves the performance. From our perspective, the biggest advantage of CLP solutions over algorithmic ones is that they can be combined easily. A scheduling algorithm can be combined with a traveling-salesman algorithm to obtain a time-constrained traveling-salesman algorithm [CK92]. This is much harder with a procedural algorithm. As mentioned earlier, we have developed a methodology for solving complex scheduling problems with LAURE [CGL93][1]. This methodology is the result of developing a few applications that turned out to be successful after a difficult start:

- Build a naive program by encoding all the problem constraints. Run with a large sample of test data and identify bottlenecks.
- Collect, from OR literature and previous experience, equations (redundant constraints and cutting heuristics) that can be used to reduce branching.
- Implement each technique derived from one of the previous equations using logical rules (production rules) as a glue.

The reason for using logical rules for additional heuristics is that rules can be combined easily. This allows us to experiment with various sets of heuristics. For each problem that we have solved, we have found improvements of more than two orders of magnitude by adding "domain-dependent expertise". Our motivation for the work described in this paper was to apply the same method to job-shop scheduling and see if we would obtain similar improvements.

3. Task Intervals and their Application to Scheduling

3.1 Intervals as Sets of Tasks

The most obvious redundant constraint that is used by anyone trying to solve the bridge scheduling problem [VH89] is the resource interval constraint. If we denote by $T(r)$ the set of tasks that uses the resource r, $\underline{T(r)} = \min\{\underline{t}, t \in T(r)\}$ the earliest starting time of any tasks of $T(r)$ and $\overline{T(r)} = \max\{\overline{t}, t \in T(r)\}$ the latest completion time of any tasks of $T(r)$, the task constraint

---

[1] LAURE [Ca91] is an object-oriented CLP language that combines constraints, rules, and objects. LAURE was designed to be flexible and extensible, which makes it a good platform for hybrid (constraint + procedural) algorithms. However, the techniques presented in this paper could have been used similarly with other CLP languages, such as PECOS [PA91].

$$\bar{t} - \underline{t} \geq d(t)$$

also applies to $T(r)$ (with $d(T(r)) = \sum\{d(t), t \in T(r)\}$):

$$\overline{T(r)} - \underline{T(r)} \geq d(T(r)) \tag{1}$$

This constraint actually applies to any set of tasks that share the same resource. This is quite powerful but would generate m × (2^n -1) equations in an n × m problem. Fortunately, we do not need to consider all sets of tasks, but simply task intervals. A task interval [t_1, t_2] represents the set of tasks t such that $\underline{t_1} \leq \underline{t}$ and $\bar{t} \leq \bar{t_2}$. To any set of task $s = \{t_1, t_2, ... t_i\}$ we can associate t_p, t_q such that $\underline{t_p} = \underline{s}$ and $\overline{t_q} = \overline{s}$; since d([$t_p$, t_q]) ≥ d(s) by construction, the equation (1) for [t_p, t_q] subsumes that for s. On all following figures, the time will be represented on a horizontal axis, each task t on a horizontal line with two brackets to denote its domain[2] $\left[\underline{t}, \bar{t}\right]$ and a box of length d(t) between both brackets. Figure 1 shows an example of task interval $s = [t_1, t_1]$ which domain is indicated by larger brackets.

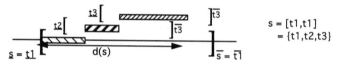

Figure 1: Task Intervals

We say that a task interval [t_1, t_2] is active when it is not empty (i.e., $\underline{t_1} \leq \underline{t_2} \wedge \overline{t_1} \leq \overline{t_2}$). By construction, there are at most m × n^2 task intervals to consider, which is only n times more than the number of tasks. It is possible to further reduce the number of intervals that must be considered if we notice that the same "time" interval may be represented by many pairs of tasks. We can use a total ordering on tasks to select a unique task interval to represent each time interval. However, the maintenance of such "critical intervals" has been shown to be too computationally expensive to gain any benefits from a reduced number of intervals.

Each task interval can be seen as the representation of a dynamic constraint. In addition to the two bounds t_1 and t_2 that do not change, we need to store for each interval [t_1, t_2] its duration (for the constraint (1)) and its set extension (for propagation [Section 3.2] and maintenance [Section 3.3]). To see if an interval is active, we simply check if its extension is not empty. Both durations and set extensions are dynamic values that will change throughout the search and that need to be backtracked. To avoid useless memory allocation, it is convenient to code the set extension with a bit vector mechanism. Task intervals are stored in a matrix with cross-access, so that we have direct access to [t,_] which is the set of intervals with t as a lower bound and [_,t] which is the set of intervals with t as an upper bound.

In addition to dynamic sets represented as intervals, we also need to consider static sets of tasks that are needed by a special task. If a task t needs a set of tasks $\{t_1,..., t_p\}$, then the following equation holds:

$$\underline{t} \geq \min\{\underline{t_1},...,\underline{t_p}\} + d(\{t_1,...,t_p\})$$

This is often better than what we get by only using precedence equations:

$$\underline{t} \geq \max\{\underline{t_i} + d(t_i), i = 1,...,p\}$$

---

[2] To avoid confusion, we will call domain of t the interval $\left[\underline{t}, \bar{t}\right]$ and will reserve the word "interval" for task intervals.

Each static set thus represents an additional redundant constraint. Notice that these static sets are not used for job-shop scheduling by definition, but they play an important role for the bridge problems, as we shall see in Section 4.2. In the rest of the paper, we shall call the slack of an interval i, written $\Delta(i)$, the value $\bar{i} - \underline{i} - d(i)$.

3.2 Reduction with Intervals

In addition to the constraints from the equation (1), we use three sets of reduction rules, corresponding respectively to ordering, edge finding and exclusion. Ordering rules use the precedence relation among tasks, the precedence relation with static set (as explained previously) and a dynamic ordering relation *order*, that will be build during the search (cf. Section 4.1). The precedence relation among tasks uses an extra argument that represents the delay between the two tasks. It is usually the duration of the first task, but it can be modified to represent additional waiting periods (e.g., the bridge example). The rules are as follows[3].

$$\forall t_1,t_2,(order(t_1,t_2) \wedge \underline{t_2} < \underline{t_1} + d(t_1)) \Rightarrow \underline{t_2} := \underline{t_1} + d(t_1))$$

$$\forall t_1,t_2,(precede(t_1,t_2,d) \wedge \underline{t_2} < \underline{t_1} + d) \Rightarrow \underline{t_2} := \underline{t_1} + d$$

$$\forall t,s,(precede(s,t) \wedge \underline{t} < \underline{s} + d(s)) \Rightarrow \underline{t} := \underline{s} + d(s)$$

Three other symmetrical rules apply to upper bounds.

The second set of rules, edge finding, determines if a task can be the first or the last in a given task interval. If t is a task belonging to an interval s, we look at $\bar{s} - \underline{t} - d(s)$. If it is strictly negative, we know that t cannot be the first, therefore t should start after the minimum of $(t_i + d(t_i))$ for t_i in s other than t (cf. Figure 2). Thus the rule that we apply is the following :

$$\forall t,s,(t \in s \wedge \bar{s} - \underline{t} - d(s) < 0) \Rightarrow \underline{t} \geq \min\{t_i + d(t_i), t_i \in s - \{t\}\}$$

Here also, a symmetrical rule applies to see if a task can or cannot be the last member of a given interval. Finding the first and last members of task intervals is known as "edge finding" [CC88] [AC91] and is a proven way to improve the search. We will complete these two rules in Section 4.1 with a search strategy that also focuses on edge finding.

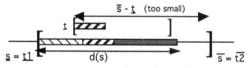

Figure 2: Edge Finding

The previous rule has one drawback, however, because it requires the computation of $\min\{t_i + d(t_i), t_i \in s - \{t\}\}$, which is expensive. If we implement this rule with a rule-based language, this rule is likely to be evaluated for many tasks for which it will not increase $\underline{t}$. Since using a rule-based implementation has many other advantages (readability, maintainability and flexibility), we improve the rule by using $\underline{t_1} + d(t_1)$ (the lower bound of the interval s) as an oracle for $\min\{t_i + d(t_i), t_i \in s - \{t\}\}$. The rule now becomes :

$$\forall t,s = [t_1,t_2],(t \in s \wedge \bar{s} - \underline{t} - d(s) < 0 \wedge \underline{t} \leq \underline{t_1} + d(t_1)) \Rightarrow \underline{t} \geq \min\{t_i + d(t_i), t_i \in s - \{t\}\}$$

The last set of rules, exclusion, tries to order tasks and intervals. More precisely, we check to see if a task can be performed before an interval to which it does not belong (but

---

[3]The precede relation with three arguments is used for precedence constraints with delays (e.g. in the bridge problem). *precede(t_1, t_2, d)* means that t_2 must wait d unit of time after the start of t_1 to start.

which uses the same resource). This is done by computing $\bar{s} - \underline{t} - d(s) - d(t)$ (same as previously but t no longer belongs to s). If the result is negative, then t cannot be executed before s. We then compute

$$packed?(s,t) := (d(t) > (\bar{s} - \underline{s} - d(s)))$$

If this value is true (cf. Figure 3), then it is not possible to insert t inside s, and thus t must be after s. Otherwise, t must be after the first member of s. Therefore, we use the following rule (and its symmetrical counterpart):

$$\forall t, s = [t_1, t_2], t \notin s \wedge \bar{s} - \underline{t} - d(s) - d(t) < 0 \Rightarrow$$

$$\textit{if } packed?(s,t)$$
$$\textit{then } \quad \underline{t} \geq \underline{s} + d(s) \wedge \forall t_i \in s, \bar{t_i} \leq \bar{t} - d(t)$$
$$\textit{else } \quad \underline{t} \geq \min\{\underline{t_i} + d(t_i), t_i \in s\}$$

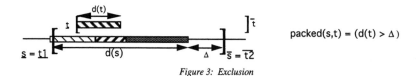

$$packed(s,t) = (d(t) > \Delta)$$

Figure 3: Exclusion

Note that we can also avoid computing $min(\underline{t_i} + d(t_i),\ t_i \in s)$ when $\underline{t} \geq \underline{t_i} + d(t_i)$. We have implemented these reduction rules with production rules in LAURE, following previous examples described in [CK92] and [CGL93].

3.3 Interval Maintenance

Taking task intervals into account is a powerful technique that allows focusing very quickly on bottlenecks. However, the real issue is the incremental maintenance of intervals. Resources are interdependent because of precedence relationship (As displayed in Figure 4, where the arrows symbolize the precedence constraints). While we are scheduling one resource, the changes of the domains of the tasks are propagated to other resources. We need to be able to compute the changes on intervals very quickly (new active intervals, intervals that are no longer active and changes to the sets associated with the intervals). More precisely, there are two types of events that we need to propagate: the increase of $\underline{t}$ and the decrease of $\bar{t}$.

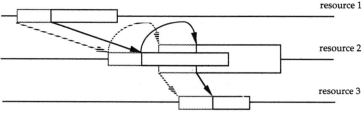

Figure 4: Resource Interdependence

The correct algorithm for updating $\underline{t}$ can be derived from the definition of the set extension of a task interval:

$$set([t_1, t_2]) = \{t, \underline{t_1} \leq \underline{t} \wedge \bar{t} \leq \bar{t_2}\}$$

From this definition, we see that, when increasing the values of $\underline{t}$ from n to m,

- we must deactivate intervals $[t,t_2]$ if the new value m is bigger than t_2,
- we must remove tasks t' from active intervals $[t,t_2]$ when $\underline{t'}$ is less than m,
- we must create new active intervals $[t_1, t]$ if m is bigger than t_1 and n was not,
- we must add t to active intervals $[t_1, t_2]$ if m is bigger than t_1 and n was not and if $\overline{t}$ is less than $\overline{t_2}$.

The interesting issue is the order in which we need to perform these operations, and when we are in a state good enough to propagate the changes and trigger the rules. It turns out that negative changes (removing tasks from set extension) do not need to be propagated, because all the rules we use always apply to subsets of intervals (i.e., if a rule can be applied to an interval, it could also be applied to any subset and would not yield more changes). Thus we perform the two "negative" actions first. Then we need to augment the other intervals, which requires triggering rules (as the size or the set extension of intervals changes). This requires that we have set $\underline{t}$ to its new value m (but not propagated this change yet because the intervals are not set up properly yet). We can legally propagate rules at that point because we know that all intervals have a set extension *that can only be smaller than what it should be.* Therefore, because of the sets of rules that we are using (monotonic with respect to set containance), we know that any conclusion we might draw will still be valid.

The last action is then to propagate the change to $\underline{t}$ and to update static sets (which we could also do with a propagation rule). To avoid duplicate work, we also need to check that $\underline{t}$ was not subsequently changed to a higher value by the propagation of a rule. Therefore, we are using two invariants H0 and H1 (cf. the following algorithm) to make sure that we stop all propagation work if m is no longer the new value for $\underline{t}$.

The algorithm that we use to increase $\underline{t}$ from n to the new value m is therefore as follows.

```
increase(t,n,m)                                              ;; m > n
    for i = [t,t₂] in [t,_],
        if ( n ≤ t₂ < m ) ∧ (t₂ ≠ t)  set(i) := ∅            ;; i is no longer active
        for t' in set(i),
            if ( n ≤ t' < m ) ∧ ( t' < t₂ )
                do        set(i) := set(i) - {t'}
                          d(i) := d(i) - d(t')     end
    t = m                                                    ;; H0 ⇔ (t = m)
    for all t₁ ≠ t such that r(t) = r(t₁),
        if ( n < t₁ ≤ m )                                    ;; H1 ⇔ (t₁ ≤ m)
            for i' = [t₁, t₂] in [t₁, _],
                if ( t ≤ t₂ ) ∧ H0 ∧ H1    do    set(i') := set(i') + {t'}l
                                                 d(i') := d(i') + d(t')  end
    for i = [t₁, t] in [_,t],
        if ( t₁ ≤ m ) ∧ ( t₁ ≤ t ) ∧ H0    do set(i) := {...}, d(i) := ... end
    if H0 do   propagate( t = m )
               for all static sets s that contain t,
                   if ( s = n )  s := min(...)
```

The algorithm for decreasing $\overline{t}$ is exactly symmetrical. We have tried two different variations of this algorithm. First, as mentioned earlier, we tried to restrict ourselves to "critical intervals", using a total ordering on tasks to eliminate task intervals that represented the same time interval (and thus the same set). It turns out that the additional complexity does not pay off. Moreover, the algorithm is so complex that it becomes very hard to prove. The other idea that we tried is to only maintain the extension of task intervals (represented by a bit vector) and use a function to compute the duration (using a pre-computed duration matrix of size 2^n and the bit vector). It turns out that the duration is used very heavily during the computation and that cashing its value improves performance substantially.

4. Application to Some Scheduling Problems

4.1 Search Strategy

As we mentioned previously, one of the best branching schemes for the job-shop is to order pairs of tasks that share the same resource [AC91]. The search algorithm, therefore, proceeds as follows. It picks a pair of tasks $\{t_1, t_2\}$ and a preferred ordering $t_1 \prec t_2$. The algorithm then explores sequentially the two branches ($t_1 \prec t_2$ and $t_2 \prec t_1$) recursively. This is what most CLP solvers do for scheduling (with simple strategies to pick the pair), and it is very easy to perform with such a language (since backtracking is implicit). To complete the description of our search algorithm, we simply need to describe how we pick the ordered pair (t_1, t_2). Note that this algorithm produces only a feasible schedule. To get the optimal schedule we must iterate the algorithm many times with decreasing lower bounds. There are, however, better alternatives as we shall discuss later (Section 4.3).

The choice of the task pairs is directly inspired from the edge-finding method[AC91], which is itself inspired from the work of Carlier & Pinson [CP89]. The idea is to pick the set of unscheduled tasks for a given resource, and pick a pair of tasks that could be both first (resp. last) in this set. The choice between first and last is based on cardinality. Our adaptation of this idea is to focus on the most constrained subset of tasks for the resource instead of the set of tasks that are currently unscheduled. This allows faster focusing on bottlenecks and takes advantage of the task intervals that we are carefully maintaining.

We select, therefore, the task interval i with the smallest slack $\Delta(i)$. We compute the set of tasks $\{t_1,..,t_p\}$ that could be the first tasks of i and the set of tasks $\{t'_1, ...,t'_q\}$ that could be last. We pick $\{t_1,..,t_p\}$ if $p \leq q$ and $\{t'_1, ...,t'_q\}$ otherwise. Let's assume from now on that we have picked $\{t_1,..,t_p\}$. Among this set, we need to pick two tasks t_a and t_b such that $(t_a \prec t_b)$ and $(t_b \prec t_a)$ will have the maximal impact (we try to reduce the entropy of the scheduling system, in a manner similar to what is described in [CGL93]). We use the immediate consequence of the ordering $(t_a \prec t_b)$:

$$t_a \prec t_b \Rightarrow \underline{t_b} := \max(\underline{t_b}, \underline{t_a} + d(t_a)) \wedge \overline{t_a} := \min(\overline{t_a}, \overline{t_b} - d(t_b))$$

We decided to pick t_a as the lower bound of the interval i. Therefore, if $t_b < t_a$, the slack $\Delta(i)$ will be reduced by $\delta = \min\{t, t \in i - \{t_a\}\} - \underline{t_a}$. Our goal is clearly to reduce $\Delta(i)$, $\Delta(t_a)$ and $\Delta(t_b)$ as much as possible. Thus, we need to give a value to the change $\Delta := \Delta - \delta$, so that we minimize $\Delta - \delta$ (the resulting slack) and maximize δ (the change). We have used the following function (where UB is the upper bound for the scheduling problem).

$f(\Delta, \delta) = $ if $(\delta = 0)$ UB else if $(\Delta < \delta)$ 0 else $(\Delta - \delta)^2 / \Delta$

Notice that our goal is to obtain a value of f that is as small as possible. Therefore, to evaluate the impact of the decision $(t_a \prec t_b)$, we compute

$$\delta(t_a) = \max(\overline{t_a}, \overline{t_b} - d(t_b)) - \underline{t_a},$$

$$\delta(t_b) = \overline{t_b} - \min(\underline{t_b}, \underline{t_a} + d(t_a)),$$

and use the value $f(t_a \prec t_b) = \min(f(\Delta(t_a), \delta(t_a)), f(\Delta(t_b), \delta(t_b)))$.

The value associated with the pair (t_a, t_b) is

$$value(t_a, t_b) = max(f(t_a \prec t_b), \ min(f(\Delta(i), \delta(i)), \ f(t_b \prec t_a)).$$

Notice that we take the change to $\Delta(i)$ into account in the case where we try $(t_b \prec t_a)$. We can now summarize how to select a pair of tasks for a given resource r.

find_pair(r)

    find i = [t_1, t_2] in intervals(r) such that Δ(i) is minimal,

    let S1 = {t | r(t) = r $\wedge$ t $\neq$ t_1 $\wedge$ not(order(t_1,t)) $\wedge$ $\underline{t} \leq \underline{t_1} + \Delta(i)$ }   ;; could be first

    S2 = {t | r(t) = r $\wedge$ t $\neq$ t_2 $\wedge$ not(order(t,t_2)) $\wedge$ $\overline{t} \geq \overline{t_2} - \Delta(i)$}   ;; could be last

    if |S1| $\leq$ |S2|

        do δ(i) := Min($\underline{t}$, t$\in$ i - {t_1}) - $\underline{t_1}$

                find t in S1 such that value(t_1, t) is minimal

                return (t_1,t) if f(t_1 < t) $\leq$ f(t < t_1) and (t,t_1) otherwise

                end

        else do δ(i) := $\overline{t_2}$ - max{$\overline{t}$, t $\in$ i - {t_2}}

                find t in S1 such that f(t, t_2) is minimal

                return (t,t_2) if f(t < t_2) $\leq$ f(t_2 < t) and (t_2,t) otherwise

                end

We use the same high-level strategy as in [AC91]: we choose the most difficult resource as the one with the task interval with the smallest slack. We first schedule this resource totally (i.e., we apply *find_pair* only to this resource). Then we apply *find_pair* to all other resources - we minimize break ties Δ(i) with min(|S1|,|S2|).

4.2 Bridge Scheduling

As we previously mentioned, the bridge scheduling, which used to be the benchmark of choice for CLP, is nowadays solved easily by most solvers. Typical run-times (CHIP[AB91], PECOS, LAURE) are in the 100 ms range for finding the optimal solution (104 days) and in the 1s for finding the proof of optimality. This proof of optimality is still the longest step, because it requires a number of backtracks (500 to 2000 depending on the search strategy). The first interesting result that we obtain with the previously described algorithm is that the proof of optimality is found with no backtrack (and no search). That means that by simply looking at the right task intervals and by applying the reduction rules that we gave, we can show that there is no solution in 103 or fewer days. A summary of the proof is given in Figure 5. Even for someone who is not familiar with the actual problem, this shows the few steps that allow us to show the optimality on a blackboard without a computer.

A consequence is that we are able to solve the problem faster than with previous approaches (cf Figure 6). By "pure CLP" we mean programs that just contain the scheduling constraints. The improved performance is a minor side effect compared to the fact that the whole resolution is done without backtracking. The absence of backtracking is a sign that the algorithm is more powerful and thus will perform better on larger problems. To a certain extent, the results on 10 x 10 job-shop scheduling problems confirm this expectation, but it would be more interesting to use a larger "complex scheduling problem", with complex precedence constraints. In fact, the bridge scheduling can no longer be considered a benchmark for our algorithm, since it does not really make use of the search strategy.

It must also be noticed that the search strategy that we have presented here is designed to optimize the proof of optimality (by minimizing entropy). Other strategies actually work better to simply produce a good solution. We will come back to this issue in the next section, but it is clear that better strategies exist to find the optimal solution (in 104 days) than our method, which is probably too complex here. On the other hand, this complexity provides a robustness (constant performance when the parameters of the problems are changed randomly) that we did not experience with the "pure" CLP solutions. Using a simple heuristic as a starting point, we have been able to reduce the time to obtain the optimal solution to 50ms.

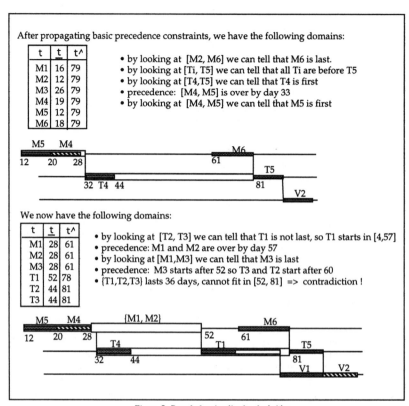

After propagating basic precedence constraints, we have the following domains:

t	$\underline{t}$	t^
M1	16	79
M2	12	79
M3	26	79
M4	19	79
M5	12	79
M6	18	79

- by looking at [M2, M6] we can tell that M6 is last.
- by looking at [Ti, T5] we can tell that all Ti are before T5
- by looking at [T4,T5] we can tell that T4 is first
- precedence: [M4, M5] is over by day 33
- by looking at [M4, M5] we can tell that M5 is first

We now have the following domains:

t	$\underline{t}$	t^
M1	28	61
M2	28	61
M3	28	61
T1	52	78
T2	44	81
T3	44	81

- by looking at [T2, T3] we can tell that T1 is not last, so T1 starts in [4,57]
- precedence: M1 and M2 are over by day 57
- by looking at [M1,M3] we can tell that M3 is last
- precedence: M3 starts after 52 so T3 and T2 start after 60
- {T1,T2,T3} lasts 36 days, cannot fit in [52, 81] => contradiction !

Figure 5: Proof of optimality for the bridge

	CHIP ([AB91]) pure CLP	LAURE([Ca91]) pure CLP	LAURE task intervals
find optimal solution	160ms	400ms	400ms
proof of optimality	3300ms	1500ms	50ms
total time	3.4 s	1.9s	0.45s

Figure 6: Preliminary results (SPARC-1)

4.3 The MT10 Problem

MT10 is a 10×10 job-shop scheduling problem that is described in [MT63]. As noticed in [AC91], it is not a very hard 10×10 problem, but it has resisted many efforts for a long time and thus has become an interesting benchmark. Using cumulative constraints [AB92], a CHIP program was able to find the optimal solution, after quite a long computation time. Similarly, MT10 was solved in 90 hours with the cc(fd) language [VHSD93], using constructive disjunctions. To our knowledge, no CLP approaches have yet found the proof of optimality in a reasonable time. Therefore, it is a good test for the method based on task intervals.

Our first experiment was to look for lower bounds. We use two techniques that we compared with the methods that are currently used in OR approaches [AC91]. First we determined what maximum lower bound value would cause a contradiction when we apply our reduction rules. This is the method that gave us a 104 lower bound for the bridge problem, so it had already shown to be powerful. For MT10, we obtained 858, which is much better than the lower bounds obtained with other methods (cf. Figure 7). We have also used a common technique, which is to compute the minimal schedule of one machine, but we left the propagation rules active. That is to say that we schedule only one machine, but decisions made on this machine are propagated to the other tasks, which can raise a contradiction. This gives us another lower bound, which is more expensive to obtain (but still less than complex Cuts methods [AC91]). For MT10, we obtained the surprisingly high value of 912.

	Preempt	1-Mach	Cuts 1	Cuts 3	Task Intervals	T. Int. 1-Mach
value	808	808	823	827	858	912
time	0.1	0.1	5.2	7000	5	200

Figure 7: Lower Bounds for MT10 (from AC91)

These results show the power of task intervals and their reduction rules as a cutting mechanism. We also found similar good results to obtain the proof of optimality (Figure 8). We obtained the proof of optimality in 730 s on a SPARC-1, which is only 2.3 times slower than the special-purpose algorithm of [AC91]. In addition, we explored only 6700 nodes, which is much smaller than the 16000 nodes used by [AC91]. The consequence of these differences will be developed in the next section. To find the optimal solution, we tried several approaches. It must first be noticed that if we use 930 as an upper bound, we find the solution very quickly (40 s). Starting with a high upper bound and reducing gradually produces the optimal solution in 540 s, where most of the time is lost lowering the upper bound to a nontrivial value. Therefore, this solution would need to be coupled with a heuristic, as in [AC91], to give better performance. Starting with the simplest heuristics proposed in [AC91], we can start the search at the value 952 and find the optimal solution in 300 s. We also tried to reduce the upper bound dynamically (instead of restarting the search after each solution). The results were very similar, in the sense that we got very good results if we had a good starting upper bound (e.g., 955), but that a lot of time was wasted when we started with a very high value (e.g., 1200). We tried to implement the shuffle procedure of [AC91] to improve the convergence, but we obtained very unstable results. Depending on the initial parameters, we would converge very quickly toward the optimal solution or quite slowly towards a suboptimal solution (935).

	LAURE - Task Intervals		[AC91]	
	time	nodes	time	nodes
MT10 - optimal solution	540		60	
MT10 - proof of optimality	730	6728	310	16000
LA19 - proof of optimality	610	6458	1300	93000
ORB2 - proof of optimality	1200	16400	2300	153000

Figure 8: Computational Results for three 10 × 10 Problems (SPARC-1)

These results are preliminary, and further work is needed. We have already confirmed some of our intuition about the low number of backtracks (number of nodes explored) by running the same program on other 10 × 10 problems that were found to be more difficult in [AC91]. LA19 is a problem from [La84] and ORB2 on the problems described in

[AC91]. In both cases, we obtained better results than those published in [AC91], using a surprisingly small number of nodes to establish the proof of optimality. The algorithm presented here was designed to build short proofs of optimality, and this shows in the computational results. On the other hand, we spent little time designing good strategies to obtain the optimal solution quickly. We now plan to turn to this important aspect and see how the search strategy could be modified. In addition, we believe that entropy should play a larger role in the selection of branching pairs for larger problems.

5. Application to the Design of CLP Languages

5.1 Comparison with Non-CLP Approaches

It is interesting to compare this approach with the OR approach as related in [AC91] (and also [CC88] and [CP89]) from two different standpoints. On the one hand, we can compare the algorithms, trying to factor out the implementation differences. On the other hand, we can compare the implementation techniques, trying to factor out the differences between the algorithms.

As far as algorithms are concerned, different approaches have been used. For instance, the problem can be seen as a linear programming instance and one can use a linear programmation package optimized with plane cuts to solve it (the cuts proposed in [DW90], [Ba69] are summarized in [AC91]). It can also be seen as a graph with symetric arrows that one wants to orient in order to minimize the length of the longest chain. Traditionnal graph techniques include division into smaller problems [Po 88], the use of Petri nets and branch and bound with explicit backtracking (for a complete survey, see [CC88]). More original methods have been proposed, such as [VLAL92] which is derived from statistical physics.

The algorithm that we use is actually similar to the one proposed by [CP89] and refined by [AC91]. The cutting equations used in [AC91] are all subsumed by the the propagation on task intervals caused by our rules (ordering, edge finding and exclusion) and by the basic equation *(1)*. The consistent use of reduction rules for all task intervals and not simply for selected ones as in [AC91] explains the lower number of nodes explored by our algorithm. The search strategy is very similar; the two differences are that we focus on the most constrained task interval instead of the wider intervals of unscheduled tasks (as in [AC91]) and we use a different cost function to pick the branching pairs of tasks. Our new heuristic function, based on entropy, seems to give better result that the one used in [AC91] (originally proposed in [ABZ83]).

The difference between the performance figures for MT10 are not significant from the algorithm point of view. The code used by [AC91] is hand-optimized C code that took a long time to write. A ratio of 2.3 with the C code generated by the LAURE compiler is a good result and we believe that if our algorithm was implemented directly in C, its performances would improve by such a factor. The real difference between the two algorithms is the lower number of backtracks of our approach, which pays off very strongly with the more complex 10×10 problems and is likely to have even more influence for larger problems. For instance, we have been able to improve the lower bound of of the 15×10 problem LA21 [La84] from 1039 [AC91] to 1041, which is, to our knowledge, the best value known so far for this open problem.

From an implantation point of view, the advantages of our CLP approach are obvious. First, our program can handle job shop problems as well as problems with more complex dependencies (e.g. the bridge scheduling). If we start with the jobshop program, we can add static sets with a few as 30 lines of LAURE code that are totally independent from the earlier code. This is much harder for hand-optimized algorithms written in C. The flexibility comes from the use of logical rules, which create a nonexplicit binding between components of the software and allow us to add new rules representing new constraints or new heuristics without changing a line of the original program.

The second advantage of the CLP approach is its simplicity. Through the use of a high-level programming language and a limited number of redundant constraints, we have kept the size of the LAURE program under 400 lines (without counting the data definition part). This is much longer than the 40 lines of the original CLP program from which we started, but much shorter than the 2000 lines of C code of the similar program from [AC91]. In addition, the use of high-level programming paradigms (such as sets, objects or rules) makes the code much easier to read and maintain. Another measure is that the program was written in a few days, then it was tuned and optimized within 2 weeks.

5.2 Comparison with Similar CLP Approaches

It is easy to compare this new LAURE program with the scheduling program that we used before. As stated previously, the program has lost its original simplicity since we went from 40 to 400 lines of code, but it has also gone from a naive and declarative style of programming to a more expert style. However, we have obtained an improvement in performance and robustness that make the new program able to compete with the best OR algorithm, which was definitely not the case for the simpler program. For instance, the MT10 problem cannot be solved with the simple, generic approach of our 40-line program. These remarks obviously apply to the similar programs that one could write with CHIP or PECOS, since we had previously shown LAURE to be among the best available finite-domain constraint solvers. It is interesting to notice that the new approach could also have been implemented with PECOS, which is a lower-level language than LAURE (i.e., it does not support logical rules), although with a bigger programming effort. On the other hand, CHIP is somehow a higher-level (of abstraction) language than LAURE, since it does not provide the same control and access to the data structures of the constraint solver. As a consequence, writing an efficient program that uses task intervals in CHIP is a much harder task.

CHIP has followed a different direction and included an additional type of *cumulative constraint* [AB92][4]. These constraints encapsulate some of the OR techniques that we have mentioned previously, although the exact behavior of the cumulative constraint is proprietary information. These techniques allowed CHIP to be the first CLP language to find the optimal solution of the MT10 problem, but they fell short of providing performances that are competitive with OR dedicated algorithms. For instance, the proof of optimality for MT10 is still out of reach within reasonable computation time. Cumulative constraints are more general than a simple one-machine scheduler, but these results show that a user of CHIP with cumulative constraint would get much better performance using task intervals.

This leads to the most interesting question: Should a technology such as task intervals be packaged into a closed component, such as a cumulative constraint, or should the user understand how it works and have access to its implementation ? If we go back to the CHIP example, we believe that the designers of the compiler can easily pick the ideas presented in this paper and make their system as efficient as the LAURE program presented here (and maybe more efficient, since they are implementing their code in a black-box manner). However, we do not believe that this solution would match the needs of the users. Our experience with large, real-life problems is that no generic search techniques (even as successful as task intervals) are powerful enough to solve them. It takes the domain-dependent expertise of the user to make the right combination of such techniques to solve the problem. This is why we were looking for a simple and powerful technique that could be explained to anyone, as opposed to a clever algorithm that we would implement into the

---

[4] There has been a lot of work about general search principles and handling of disjunctive constraints that is relevant to job shop scheduling (e.g. [dBB93], [VHSD93]), some of which was actually included into the generic LAURE solver. However, to our knowledge, using only generic techniques has not lead to performances comparable to OR algorithms on problems such as MT10.

LAURE system. It would be very easy to package resources with task intervals as a first-class LAURE constraint, which would allow us to claim much shorter programs with similar good performance. Our claim is that packaging it as a set of rules with associated methods [Ca91] makes it easier for the user to pick the components that are necessary for his problem.

5.3 A CLP User's Wish List

The previous postulate in favor of a "white-box" implementation of techniques such as task intervals has a profound impact on what a CLP language should offer. We have already addressed some of the issues in earlier papers [Ca91], but we believe that the previous findings on job-shop scheduling give more strength to these ideas. Here is a list of the three major features that we are expecting from a CLP language that should be self-evident from the algorithm proposed in Section 3.

- *Backtracking over user-defined structure.* All CLP languages provide automatic backtracking over the logical variables that define the problem. However, in most problems, additional data structures need to be maintained. In this example, we used task intervals. In a staff scheduling problem [CGL93], we used a min/max global matrix. Using additional data structures is enormously simplified if changes can be backtracked automatically. The only task left to the user is to describe how choices made by the constraint solver will impact the data structure.

- *Control over search strategy.* It is also clear that generic search strategies, such as the first-fail principle, are not a panacea. In many of the complex problems that we have solved, what is needed is a dynamic generation of branching goals. This means that we need more than being able to redefine the ordering of goals. We really need complete control over the search strategy.

- *Semi-explicit propagation.* Quite often, changes to the external data structure must be made when a (complex) logical condition is satisfied. The reduction rules that we gave in Section 3 are good examples. Being able to write this declaratively with a logical rule makes the programming task much easier. The alternative would be to examine the logical condition and determine all the cases when the conclusion must be evaluated, which is a tedious and error-prone process. This last feature is less critical, since we can always return to explicit propagation in a procedural way. However, rule-based propagation helps retain many of the desirable features of "naive" CL programming, such as readability and flexibility.

6. Conclusion

This new technique for job scheduling focusing on intervals of tasks gives a very good representation of the problem, and its incremental maintenance makes it efficient. The logical rules, although quite simple, subsume most cuts used by traditional OR techniques ([Ba69], [CP89], [DW90], [AC91]). The search heuristic is efficient because it focuses on bottlenecks. Using logical rules brings much flexibility: the authors were surprised by how fast they could adapt the program from the bridge problem to n × m scheduling problems. More results are expected soon. From the results on the bridge problem and on MT10, we draw two conclusions:

- First, CLP is a technology of choice for these hard combinatorial problems because it can combine efficiency and flexibility. As a matter of fact, we now project incorporating this algorithm in other programs that involve, among other things, job scheduling.

- Second, our methodology (refining step by step a naive logical description of the problem) has brought, up to now, tremendous results. Thus it seems very important that constraint logic language designers give programmers the necessary transparency to allow such programming.

Acknowledgments

This paper and the work on job-shop scheduling has been strongly influenced by conversations with Bill Cook, Francois Fages, Jean-Francois Puget and Pascal Van Hentenryck.

References

[ABZ83]   J.Adams, E. Balas & D. Zawak. *The Shifting Bottleneck Procedure for Job Shop Scheduling.* Management Science 34, p391-401. 1983

[AB91]   A. Aggoun, N. Beldiceanu. *Overview of the CHIP Compiler.* Proc. of the 8th ICLP, Paris, 1991.

[AB 92]   A. Aggoun, N. Beldiceanu. *Extending CHIP in order to Solve Complex Scheduling and Placement Problems.* Proc. of JFPL'92 (Journées Francophones sur la Programmation Logique), Lille (France), May 1992.

[AC91]   D. Applegate & B. Cook. *A Computational Study of the Job Shop Scheduling Problem.* Operations Research Society of America vol 3, no 2, 1991

[Ba 69]   E. Balas. *Machine Sequencing via Disjunctive Programming: an Implicit Enumeration Algorithm.* Operations Research 17, p 941-957. 1969

[Ca91]   Y. Caseau: *A Deductive Object-Oriented Language.* Annals of Mathematics and Artificial Intelligence, Special Issue on Deductive Databases, March 1991.

[CC88]   J. Carlier & P. Chretienne. *Problemes d'ordonnancement.* col. ERI, Masson, Paris 1988

[CGL93]   Y. Caseau, P.-Y. Guillo, E. Levenez. *A Deductive and Object-Oriented Approach to a Complex Scheduling Problem.* Proc. of DOOD'93, Phoenix, December 1993.

[CK92]   Y. Caseau, P. Koppstein. *A Cooperative-Architecture Expert System for Solving Large Time/Travel Assignment Problems.* International Conference on Databases and Expert Systems Applications, Valencia, Spain, September 1992.

[CP89]   J. Carlier & E. Pinson. *An Algorithm for Solving the Job Shop Problem.* Management science, vol 35, no 2, february 1989

[dBB93]   B. de Backer, H. Beringer. *A CLP language handling disjunctions of linear constraints.* Proc. of 10th ICLP, The MIT Press,1993.

[DW90]   M. Dyer & L.A. Wolsey. *Formulating the Single Machine Sequencing Problem with Release Dates as a Mixed Integer Program.* Discrete Applied Mathematics 26, p255-270. 1990

[La84]   S. Lawrence. *Resource Constrained Project Scheduling: an Experimental Investigation of Heuristic Scheduling Techniques.* GSIA, Carnegie Mellon University 1984

[MT63]   J.F. Muth & G.L. Thompson *Industrial scheduling.* Prentice Hall, Englewood Cliffs, NJ, 1963

[PA91]   J.F. Puget, P. Albert. *PECOS: programmation par contraintes orientée objets.* Génie Logiciel et Systèmes Experts, vol. 23, 1991.

[Po88]   M.C. Portmann. *Methodes de Decomposition Spatiale et Temporelles en Ordonancement de la Production.* RAIRO vol 22, no 5, 1988

[VLA92] P. Van Laarhoven, E.Aarts & J.K. Lenstra. *Job Shop by Simmulated Annealing.* Operations Research vol 40, no 1, 1992

[VH89]   P. Van Hentenryck: *Constraint Satisfaction in Logic Programming.* The MIT press, Cambridge, 1989.

[VHSD93]   P. Van Hentenryck, V. Saraswat, Y. Deville. *The Design, Implementation, and Applications of the Constraint Language cc(FD).* Brown University Technical Report, 1993.

Higher-order and Meta Programming

Ambivalent logic as the semantic basis of metalogic programming: I

Yuejun Jiang[1]
Department of Computing
Imperial College, London SW7 2AZ
email: yj@uk.ac.ic.doc

Abstract

Current formalizations of metalogic programming usually involve either a *ground representation* of formulae or a standard Herbrand semantics that treats predicates in the scope of another predicate as functions. In this paper however, we shall take a radically different approach by proposing an *ambivalent logic* as the semantic basis of metalogic programming. In addition to allowing any formula to be treated as a term via *self-naming*, the proposed logic can also treat any term as a formula. The logic thus allows formulae of the form $demo(john, jim \leftarrow mary)$, $\forall T \forall X(demo(T, X) \leftarrow X)$ and $\forall T \forall X \forall Y(demo(T, X) \leftarrow demo(T, X \leftarrow Y) \wedge demo(T, Y))$. Unlike some existing ambivalent logics, the proposed logic satisfies Herbrand Theorem and strong completeness for finite theories. The major advantages of the ambivalent logic are its simple *nonground* naming scheme, its natural *amalgamation* of object-level reasoning and metalevel reasoning and its flexibility in metaprogramming due to the logic's undistinguished treatment among terms, formulae, predicates and functions. We apply the logic to show the soundess and completenes of the Vanilla metainterpreter. We also suggest two ways to formalise quantification within the scope of a predicate for the proposed ambivalent logic. One is the *functional* encoding of quantification in the form of $exists(X, \phi)$ or $forall(X, \phi)$ which allows ϕ to be substituted by an "open" wff, eg. p(X). The other is to represent quantifications within a predicate by quantified variables, eg. $demo(\exists X \phi)$ which does not allow ϕ to be substituted by p(X).

Keywords : Ambivalent Logic, Amalgamated Metalogic Programming, Higher-order Syntax without Higher-order Semantics, Herbrand Theorem, Strong Completeness, Vanilla Metainterpreter and Quantifications inside a predicate

1 Introduction

Since the pioneering work of Bowen & Kowalski [82], metalogic programming has continued to blossom over the years. Metalogic programming provides a *syntactical* treatment of modality *without* modal logic which often suffers

---

[1]SERC Advanced Fellow

from the *logical omniscience* problem [Vardi 86]. Metalogic programming also provides an *indirect* formulation of higher order reasoning *without* higher order logic which is generally *incomplete* [Turner 90]. Metalogic programming can also deal with self-references and reflections without paradoxes [Attardi & Simi 94]. Furthermore, metalogic programming presents a powerful paradigm for knowledge representation such as hypothetical reasoning and object-oriented programming [Brogi & Turini 92].

The focus of this paper is on the semantics of metalogic programming. Conventional wisdom in such a semantics usually adopts a *ground* representation of formulae that are treated as terms in some form of quoted strings. To allow the quantification of variables inside such a representation, complex operations on strings are often required [Perlis 85]. This approach is essentially taken by Hill & Lloyd [88]. Ground representation is the most powerful way of naming a formula. It can reason about variable names (eg. in defining a substitution operation) as well as the syntactical properties (eg. "This sentence has 5 words") of the representation. However despite the fact that partial evaluation can improve its effectiveness, the ground representation in metalogic programs often leads to more complex and less efficient specifications in many applications.

A promising alternative is to treat logical connectives, quantifiers and predicates as functions (e.g. bel(a,exists(X,and(p(X),q(X))))) in the naming of a formula. The resultant language can then be formalised via a standard Herbrand semantics. This approach is advocated by De Schreye & Martens [92]. It is followed by Levi & Ramundo [93] who additionally extends the *standard* Herbrand semantics to accommodate *non-ground atoms* in the spirit of S-semantics [Falaschi et al 88]. This approach is very attractive as its naming scheme is simple and its semantics is essentially standard. Nevertheless it overloads the Herbrand semantics with function symbols for logical connectives and quantifiers. Furthermore, the approach still carries over the *incompleteness problem* [Lloyd 84] of the standard Herbrand semantics. For example, the theory $\{p(a), \forall X(p(f(X)) \leftarrow p(X))\}$ logically implies $\forall X p(X)$ under the standard Herbrand semantics, however the theory cannot derive $\forall X p(X)$. As noted by Subramaniam [88], the corresponding metatheory of the example $\{$ demo(p(a)), $\forall X \, demo(p(f(X))) \leftarrow demo(p(X))\}$ will not be continous since it leaves a gap on $demo(\forall X p(X))$.

In this paper, we shall take a radically different approach to the semantics of metalogic programming based on an ambivalent logic. An ambivalent logic allows formulae to be treated as terms via *self-naming*. It is *ambivalent* in the sense that there is *no syntactical distinction* between formulae as terms and formulae as formulae. The motivations of our position are

1. an ambivalent logic is close to the use of Prolog as a metalanguage

2. an ambivalent logic is naturally amalgamated; there is no object-level and metalevel distinction

3. an ambivalent logic names a formula via self-naming which is very
simple and allows the variables in the name to be easily quantified.

Consider for example in [Bowen & Kowalski 82], the statement "an individual
is innocent unless proven guilty". It can be represented in an ambivalent
language as follows

$$\forall X(innocent(X) \leftarrow \neg proven(guilty(X))).$$

Here the naming of guilty(X) is simply a *non-ground* representation in the
same way as the use of guilty(X) as a formula; and X can be quantified
by both the "object level" formula $innocent(X)$ and "metalevel" formula
$\neg proven(guilty(X)))$ in a natural amalgamation. More importantly, an ambivalent representation corresponds well with existing Prolog practice.

Richards [74] was perhaps the first one to develop an ambivalent logic. It
provides a valuable basis towards formalising an amalgamated metalanguage.
However Richards' logic does not satisfy the *Herbrand Theorem* which is
essential to logic programming where *Robinson's resolution principle* and
unification is based on the theorem. The logic is also not complete for
finite theories. Furthermore, neither the logic can represent *variables as
formulae* nor can it reason about *"open" formulae*. Both issues are essential
in metalogic programming. For example, in the Vanilla metainterpreter, the
metaclause

$$\forall T \forall X \forall Y(demo(T, X \wedge Y) \leftarrow demo(T, X) \wedge demo(T, Y))$$

represents variables as formulae. While in Sato's metaprogram [92] that
reasons about quantified formulae, the metaclause[2]

$$\forall X \forall F(demo(exists(X, F)) \leftarrow some formula)$$

is intended to substitute X by a variable name such as y and to substitute F
by an *"open" formula* such as $p(y)$ to achieve the effect of reasoning about
existentially quantified formulae. Allowing variables to represent formulae
is also important to reason about axiom schemata such as the reflection rule

$$\forall X(demo(john, X) \leftarrow X)$$

which are useful in commonsense reasoning [Kowalski & Kim 91].

However a pure ambivalent language may not handle correctly all cases
of quantification within the scope of a predicate. Consider the formula
$\forall \phi demo(\exists X \phi)$ for example. Since $\exists X$ binds X, we cannot substitute ϕ by
an open formula like p(X)? Sometimes, we would like to have such a sub-
stitution based on the *usual* metalogic programming practice such as Sato's
metaprogram as mentioned earlier. However such substitution would violate
the general restriction that the substitution must be *free* for the variable

---

[2]We omit the substitution environment here.

to be substituted in a formula[3] because p(X) contains the variable X that is bound by $\exists X$. These problems will vanish if we replaces $\exists X\phi$ by the functional encoding $exists(X, \phi)$ in the above formula. However the functonal encoding may not always behave correctly in metareasoning. Consider for example we represent the statement "Everyone is believed by John to like someone" by $\forall Y\, bel(john, exists(X, likes(Y, X)))$. Since this allows the substitution of Y by X which is free for X in the formula, then we would incorrectly conclude that $bel(john, exists(X, likes(X, X)))$.

The purpose of this paper is to propose a new ambivalent logic that deals with all the above problems. In addition to allowing formulae to be treated as terms, the new logic also allows terms to be treated as formulae. Syntactically, unlike Hilog [Chen et al 93] which identifies *atomic* formulae with terms, the proposed ambivalent language identifies *arbitrary* formulae with terms. Like the standard Herbrand semantics, the semantics of the ambivalent logic is still Herbrand-based except that its Herbrand Universe consists of all the closed formulae of the language and it satisfies strong completeness for *finite* theories in addition to the Herbrand Theorem. We shall show that Vanilla metainterpreter under the semantics of the proposed logic is sound and complete with respect to *definite* object logic programs. To deal with the problems of quantification inside a predicate, we propose to allow the functional encoding of a quantified formula inside a predicate as long as this is what is intended. From the viewpoint of expressiveness, an ambivalent logic allows both the functional encoding and the pure ambivalent naming of a formula.

The paper is organised as follows. In Section 2, the syntax and semantics of the new ambivalent logic is proposed. The formal properties of the logic is analyzed with respect to Richards' logic and Hilog in Section 3. Section 4 applies the logic to establish the soundness and completeness results of the Vanilla Metainterpreter with respect to definite object logic programs. Section 5 addresses the problem of reasoning about *"open" formulae* and *quantifiers* inside the scope of a predicate in metalogic programming.

2 A new ambivalent logic - AL

In this section, we first present the language of the proposed logic followed by its motivation and comparisons with some similar languages. We then develop the semantics of the logic.

2.1 Language

The new ambivalent language (AL) can be inductively defined as follows.

Terms: • The variables X,Y,Z,.. and individual constants a,b,c,.. are terms.

---

[3]See **Definition 2**.

- Every expression of the form $t(t_1, ..., t_n)$ is a term where t is a term and $t_1, ..., t_n$ are terms.
- The wffs are terms.

Well-formed formula (wff): • If A and B are wffs, then so are $\neg A$, $A \wedge B$, $A \vee B$, $A \leftarrow B$, $A \rightarrow B$ and $A \equiv B$.

- If A is a wff and X is variable, then $\forall X A$ and $\exists X A$ are wffs
- If t is a term, then t is a wff

Predicate and function A term is a predicate and a function.

Atomic wff An atomic wff is an expression of the form $t(t_1, ..., t_n)$ where t is a term and $t_1, ..., t_n$ are terms.

Unlike Richards's ambivalent language which allows wffs to be treated as terms, the new ambivalent language *additionally* allows terms to be treated as wffs. In particular, a variable can denote a wff. Furthermore, unlike Richards' language, the new language makes no distinction between predicates, functions, terms and wffs. In this respect, it is similar to Hilog except that AL identifies arbitrary wffs with terms while Hilog only identifies *atomic* wffs with terms. For example, in Hilog, p(a) is a term, but not $\neg p(a)$, $p(a) \wedge q(b)$ or $\exists X p(X)$ which can also be treated as terms in the proposed ambivalent language.

It can be seen that the new language becomes more ambivalent in the sense that there is *no syntactical distinction* among a term, a wff, a predicate and a function. Such an indistinction is naturally justified by Prolog. Despite this, it is reassuring to know that there is *no semantic ambiguity* between wffs, terms and predicates/functions since the *context* of an occurrence can always determine whether the occurrence should be semantically evaluated as a term or a wff or a predicate/function [Jiang 93c]. As we shall see, we also do not semantically distinguish between a predicate and a function. For this reason, we write predicate/function to mean either a predicate or a function.

Theorem 2.1 (Unique Readability) *For any occurrence of an expression in a wff, it is semantically evaluated as a unique element of the set $\{a \ term, \ a \ wff, \ a \ predicate/function\}$ in AL.*

For example, if $c \wedge c(c)$ is a wff, then the occurrence c in the first conjunct is semantically evaluated as a wff; while the first occurrence c in the second conjunct is semantically evaluated as a predicate/function and the second occurrence c in the second conjunct is semantically evaluated as a term.

Allowing terms to represent wffs is in fact already present *indirectly* in Richards' language. For example, in the formula $\forall X believe(john, X)$, X can be substituted with constants as well as sentences. The new language further allows formulae of the form $believe(tom, john \leftarrow mary)$ which could mean something like "Tom believes that John knows more than Mary". Perhaps more usefully, the extension corresponds to the Vanilla Metainterpreter. For example, the metaclause $\forall X \forall Y (demo(T, X \wedge Y) \leftarrow demo(T, X) \wedge demo(T, Y))$ allows both the substitution of terms and formulae into the variables of the clause. Hilog also allows a term to denote a formula but restrict to the atomic case. For example, in Hilog, X in $demo(X) \leftarrow X$ can only be substituted by atomic wffs not for example $p \wedge q$. Gabbay's metalogic [92] does allow a variable to denote any wff except that he types between a variable term and a variable wff.

Allowing variables to represent sentences is also practically important for expressing axiom schemata (eg. those of modal logics) in the metalogic such as the reflection axioms. Allowing reflection principles to be expressed as axioms rather than rules of inference enables one to reason about them without changing the underlying inference system.

$$\forall X (demo(X) \leftarrow X)$$
$$\forall X (X \leftarrow demo(X))$$
$$\forall X \forall Y (X \rightarrow Y \rightarrow X)$$

The motivation of a higher order syntax for the ambivalent logic AL can be drawn from the inspirations of Hilog. For example, under the following representation

$$\forall X \forall Y (involved(X)(Y) \leftarrow Y(X))$$

the query involved(john)(Y)? will return all the unary predicates (eg. societies) that John is involved with. Here, involved(X) and Y are syntactically second-order notions. The difference with Hilog in this respect is that the ambivalent language also allows complex higher order predicates constructed from logical connectives and quantifiers. For example, we can have the following representation

$$\forall X \forall Y ((involved(X) \wedge \exists Z wantKnow(Z, X))(Y) \leftarrow Y(X))$$

which, given the query $(involved(john) \wedge \exists Z wantKnow(Z, john))(Y)$? will return all the unary predicates (eg. societies) that John is involved with and someone is interested in John.

Despite a higher-order syntax, it is important to emphasize that the ambivalent logic is still characterized by a first order (Herbrand) semantics. This is easy to see since syntactically we can transform all higher order formulae into a first order formula by representing all the higher order notions as arguments of some predicates.

Since terms are identified with wffs (even with predicates and functions) in AL, the "freeness" of variables in the ambivalent language need only be defined against one of the notions. We will use *expressions* to jointly refer terms, wffs and predicates/functions throughout the paper.

The set of free variables of an expression t, FV(t) is defined similarly to that of a formula in a standard way except that it is additionally defined through every argument of a function and a predicate.

Definition 1

$FV(X) = \{X\}$

$FV(constant) = \emptyset$

$FV(wff1 \wedge wff2) = FV(wff1) \cup FV(wff2)$

$FV(\neg wff) = FV(wff)$

$FV(\exists X wff) = FV(wff) - \{X\}$

$FV(t(t_1, .., t_n)) = FV(t) \cup FV(t_1) \cup .. \cup FV(t_n)$

Other connectives and the universal quantifier are similarly defined

We say a variable X in an expression t is bound *in t if $X \notin FV(t)$.*

For example, X is not free in $B(\exists X p(X))$ because X is not free in the argument $\exists X p(X)$ of predicate B.

Definition 2 *A closed term is a term that contains no free variable. A sentence is a closed wff. A universally quantified sentence is a sentence in the form of QA where Q is a sequence of universal quantifiers and A is a wff that contains no other quantifiers except those appear within the scope of a predicate. We use $A(t/X)$ to denote the result of replacing every free occurrence of X in A by t. We say an expression t is free for a variable X in a wff A iff t does not contain any free variable that is bound by some quantifiers in A when every free occurrence of X in A is replaced by t.*

2.2 Semantics

The semantics of AL is Herbrand-based except that its Herbrand Universe is formed of all the closed terms of the AL language. Formally, an interpretation structure M=(D,F) of AL is defined as follows.

1. D is the set of *closed* terms of the language

2. F is a denotation function that assigns to

   - each predicate/function[4] t: a set of tuples (of possibly varying arities) closed under the renaming of any variables of any tuple in the set where the domain of each field of any tuple is D

   - each term t of D: F(t)=t; i.e. the denotation of each closed term is an identity mapping

The satisfiability relation for an AL sentence in an interpretation structure M=(D,F) is inductively defined as follows:

---

[4]Constants are viewed as zero-placed functions.

1. M $\models_{AL} t(t_1, .., t_n)$ iff $[F(t_1), ..., F(t_n)] \in F(t)$

2. M $\models_{AL} A \wedge B$ iff M $\models_{AL} A$ and M $\models_{AL} B$

3. M $\models_{AL} \neg A$ iff M $\not\models_{AL} A$

4. M $\models_{AL} \exists X\ A$ iff there exists d of D, M $\models_{AL} A(d/X)$

5. Disjunction, implications, equivalence and universal quantification are defined in the standard way.

From the semantics, it can be seen that there is no semantic distinction between function and predicate symbols. This is mainly because we use a Herbrand interpretation for a *closed* term which is just an identical mapping. Furthermore, all predicates and functions can have varying arity of extensions. Both features correspond to the current practice of metalogic programming in Prolog.

Definition 3 *Let A and S be sets of AL sentences. We say A is satisfiable in AL iff there exists an interpretation M such that M $\models_{AL} \phi$ for all $\phi \in A$. M is called a model of A in this case. A. We say A is valid in AL, denoted by $\models_{AL} A$, iff $\neg A$ is not satisfiable in AL. We say A is a logical consequence of S, denoted by $S \models_{AL} A$, iff A is satisfiable in every model of S.*

Let $\vdash_{AL}$ denote the derivability of the AL logic. We identify it with a standard first order predicate calculus except that the definition of terms in the substitution axioms or rules of the calculus is that of the ambivalent logic.

Definition 4 *We say a logic L is weakly complete if it satisfies: $\models_L B$ iff $\vdash_L B$ for any sentence B. We say a logic is strongly complete if it satisfies: $S \models_L B$ iff $S \vdash_L B$ for any set S of sentences and for any sentence B.*

With these definitions, we can formally examine some of the properties of AL with respect to Richards' logic and Hilog to highlight the significance of the logic.

3 Formal results

In Richards' ambivalent logic, the evaluation of a function is different between the context where the function is evaluated inside a wff-term[5] and the context where the function is evaluated as a non-wff term. As a consequence, Herbrand Theorem is not satisfied. Consider for example the following set of sentences in Richards' ambivalent lnguage

$black(mayor(newyork))$
$\neg demo(jiang, black(mayor(newyork)))$

---

[5] By a wff-term, we mean a wff that is treated as a term.

$$\forall X(black(X) \rightarrow demo(jiang, black(X)))$$

This set is satisfiable in Richards' model M=(D,F)[6] where F(mayor(newyork)) is equal to tom, F(black)={[tom]} and F(demo)={[jiang,black(tom)]}. But the substitution of X by mayor(newyork) in the third sentence makes the resultant theory unsatisfible.

The loss of Herbrand Theorem is *expected* in a metalogic where modality can be modelled. The theorem is usually *not* satisfied in modal logics anyway [Jiang 93a]. Richards' motivation to remove the Herbrand Theorem is to avoid the blind substitution of equalities inside wff-terms of a predicate. For example, from bel(a,likes(father(john),b)) and father(john)=tom, it is not always correct to conclude that bel(a,likes(tom,b)).

The loss of Herbrand Theorem however is a problem for metalogic programming where Robinson's resolution with unification is based on the Herbrand Theorem. While Hilog does satisfy Herbrand Theorem with its single Herbrand interpretation of terms in various contexts, the way it is achieved does not seem to be satisfactory for a metalogic[7] since it allows the blind substitution of terms inside any predicate. If we consider Prolog as a meta-language as well, Hilog in this respect will not be a completely appropriate semantics for Prolog.

In contrast, because its Herbrand interpretation is identity-mapping, the AL logic satisfies Herbrand Therorem without the problem of blind substitution.

Theorem 3.1 (Jiang 93c) *In AL, a set of universally quantified sentences is unsatisfiable iff some finite ground substitutions of the set is unsatisfiable.*

To represent equality, we propose to treat it *syntactically* using a special binary predicate *eq*. The semantics of *eq* is evaluated in the same way as any other predicates except that we restrict $(t, t) \in F(eq)$ for every element t of D in any interpretation M=(D,F). Substitutions on equalities can now only be defined syntactically by *nonlogical* axioms. For example, one such axiom could be

$$\forall X \forall Y(bel(a, eq(X, Y)) \wedge bel(a, p(X)) \rightarrow bel(a, p(Y)))$$

although normally we do not have the axiom

$$\forall X \forall Y(eq(X, Y) \wedge bel(a, p(X)) \rightarrow bel(a, p(Y)))$$

This approach is coherent with Prolog's syntactical treatment of beliefs which in many ways deals with the logical omniscience problem of a modal logical treatment of beliefs [Vardi 86].

Another possible problem of Richards' logic is that it is not weakly complete with respect to a standard first order predicate calculus. This is exposed by the following theorem.

---

[6]In Richards' logic, D is formed only of the constants and sentences of the language and functions are not evaluated by identity mapping if they are not inside a wff-term.

[7]Of course Hilog is not meant to be a metalogic.

Theorem 3.2 *In Richards' logic, the following axiom is valid*

$$\forall X A \rightarrow A(t/X)$$

where t is a function-free *term that is* free for X *in A. But the following axiom is not valid in Richards' logic.*

$$\forall X A \rightarrow A(t/X)$$

where t is any *term that is* free for X *in A.*

In contrast, we have

Theorem 3.3 (Jiang 93c) *The following axiom is valid in the proposed ambivalent logic.*

$$\forall X A \rightarrow A(t/X)$$

where t is any *term that is* free for X *in A.*

Theorem 3.4 (Jiang 93c) *AL is weakly complete.*

In general, the new ambivalent logic still does not satisfy the strong completeness result. The unsatisfaction of strong completeness is just a consequence of restricting the semantic domains to the syntax of the language. Herbrand interpretation is such a restriction. Whether a FOL language allows formulae as terms or not, a Herbrand interpretation will never ensure strong completeness [Jiang 93c].

Example 1 *Let $t_1, .., t_{infinite}$ range over the entire closed terms of the AL language. Clearly, $\{t_1, ..., t_{infinite}\} \models \forall X X$, however there is no finite derivation for $\{t_1, ..., t_{infinite}\} \vdash \forall X X$*

Nevertheless if the ambivalent logic is restricted to a finite theory which is always the case in metalogic programming, the strong completeness result is satisfied.

Theorem 3.5 *AL is strongly complete for finite theories.*

The intuition behind the theorem is that the Herbrand Universe of an AL theory is identified with all the wffs that can be constructed with the language of the theory. This universe is not finitely recursive enumerable. Consider the following example from Lloyd [84].

Example 2 *Let $T = \{p(a), \forall X (p(f(X)) \leftarrow p(X))\}$.*

Under the Herbrand interpretation of a non-ambivalent logic such as those of [Martens & De Schreye 93] and S-semantics, T implies $\forall X p(X)$ and yet Robinson's resolution method cannot prove it. However under the Herbrand interpretation of the proposed ambivalent logic, T does not imply $\forall X p(X)$ in the first place, because X also ranges over all the *closed terms*. For example, $p(\exists X p(X))$ is not a logical consequence of T.

4 Soundness and completeness of Vanilla Metainterpreter

One immediate application of the proposed ambivalent logic is to show that the Vanilla metainterpreter based on the proposed semantics is sound and complete with respect to the standard Herbrand semantics of definite object logic programs. Similar results have also been achieved in [De Schreye & Marten 92] and [Kalsbeek 93]. In [De Schreye & Marten 92], the result is however not proved with respect to an ambivalent logic, but with respect to the standard Herbrand semantics of a metalogic which encodes logical connectives and quantifiers as functions in the process of naming a wff. As we have noted earlier, such a logic not only overloads the syntax of the Herbrand base of the logic, but also suffers from the completeness problem of the standard Herbrand semantics.

Although these problems are remedied slightly in Kalsbeek's logic, her approach still treats $\leftarrow$ and $\wedge$ as syntactical functions when they are used to construct variable wffs as terms. For example, Kalsbeek's logic can represent $demo(john, p \wedge q)$ without encoding $\wedge$ as a function. However when representing variable wffs such as $\forall X \forall Y demo(A, X \wedge Y)$, her approach still has to encode it as something like $\forall X \forall Y demo(A, and(X, Y))$. This again overloads the syntax in the same fashion as De Schreye & Marten's logic.

In contrast, the proposed new semantics treats variable wffs in a pure ambivalent fashion without any syntactical encoding. For example, $\wedge$ in $\forall X \forall Y demo(A, X \wedge Y)$ in the proposed language is just a logical connective, not some kind of function symbols.

Definition 5 *We define the Vanilla metainterpreter (VM) in AL as follows*

$$\forall T \forall P \forall Q (demo(T, P) \leftarrow demo(T, P \leftarrow Q) \wedge demo(T, Q))$$
$$\forall T \forall P \forall Q (demo(T, P \wedge Q) \leftarrow demo(T, P) \wedge demo(T, Q))$$

Theorem 4.1 (Jiang 93c) *Let A be the set of clauses of a definite object logic program T and p be any ground object-level atom. Let $\models_H$ denote the logical consequence operator of the standard Herbrand semantics. Let the encoding of an object-level formula in the proposed ambivalent logic be performed by the following rule*

$$if \; \forall X_1..\forall X_n Clause \in A, \; then \; \forall X_1..\forall X_n demo(T, Clause) \in T^{Meta}$$

Then we have the following soundness and completeness results between T and its metalogic counterpart.

$$A \models_H p \; iff \; (VM \cup T^{Meta}) \models_{AL} demo(T, p)$$

It should be noted that the theorem only relates an object-level program with its metalogic counterpart on *ground object-level atoms*[8]. The metaprogram itself is of course always more powerful than its object-level counterpart. For example, it can answer goals such as $\exists X demo(a, p \leftarrow X)$ and it allows higher order programming in the sense that formulae (or program) can be passed as arguments.

5 Quantification within the scope of a predicate

As noted in the introduction, a purely ambivalent representation of quantifications within the scope of a predicate present a dilemma to the substitution of "open" wffs in metalogic programming. To solve this problem, we propose to use a functional encoding of quantification for this problem. This encoding involves two special functions *exists* and *forall* which are semantically evaluated just like any other function symbols. Although the intended meanings of these functions are close to $\exists$ and $\forall$ respectively, however there are two crucial differences between them.

1. exists(X,ϕ) (cf. forall(X,ϕ)) does not bind X; while $\exists X \phi$ (cf. $\forall X \phi$) does.

2. $\forall X exists(X, \phi)$ (cf. $\forall X forall(X, \phi)$) logically implies exists(t,ϕ(t/X)) (cf. forall(t,ϕ(t/X))) for any closed term t; while $\forall X \exists X \phi$ (cf. $\forall X \forall X \phi$) logically reduces to $\exists X \phi$ (cf. $\forall X \phi$).

Whether to use a functional encoding of a quantification or just the quantification itself depends on the particular application in hand. For example, if we want to achieve the effect of substituting an "open" wff in reasoning about existentially quantified wff, then we should use the functional encoding for the quantification. The corresponding metaclause in this case would be represented as something like:

$$\forall X \forall \phi (demo(exists(X, \phi)) \leftarrow some formula)$$

In this representation, $\forall X$ can quantify over X in $exists(X, \phi)$ from which we can derive $demo(exists(y, \phi))$ where y can be seen as a variable name. Since $exists(y, \phi)$ does not bind Y, we can substitute ϕ with a wff such as p(y) to indirectly achieve the effect of substituting an "open" wff. In contrast, if we had used a purely ambivalent representation of quantification

$$\forall \phi (demo(\exists X \phi) \leftarrow some formula)$$

then we cannot substitute ϕ with p(X) because p(X) is not *free* [9] for X in the formula; ie. it violates the substitution restriction that the substituted term should not contain a **variable** that is bound in the formula.

---

[8]Some researchers relax this restriction (eg. [Marten& De Schreye 92], [Levi & Ramundo 93]). These relaxations still in effect guarantee that any atom that satisfies the above kind of theorem must be an object level atom.

[9]See **Definition 2**.

However in general, we cannot always use the functional encoding of a quantification in place of the quantification. Consider for example the knowledge that "For everyone, John believes that someone likes him/her". If we use the functional encoding, then we would have the following representation

$$\forall X \forall Y (believe(john, exists(X, likes(X, Y))) \leftarrow var(X))$$

Assuming z is a variable name, this representation logically implies that believe(john,exists(z, likes(z,z))), ie. "John believes that someone likes himself" which is clearly not valid. In contrast, if we use the quantification itself, then the representation would be

$$\forall Y \, believe(john, \exists X \, likes(X, Y))$$

Because X is bound by $\exists X$, we cannot substitute Y by X which is not free for Y in $believe(john, \exists X \, likes(X, Y))$. $believe(john, \exists X \, likes(X, X))$ is thus not logically implied.

6   Conclusion

In this paper, we have proposed an ambivalent logic as the semantic basis of metalogic programming. We have identified formulae with terms in this logic. We have demonstrate some formal results such as strong completeness for finite theory and Herbrand theorem for the logic. We have applied the logic to show the soundness and completeness of the Vanilla Metainterpreter. We have also proposed two representations of quantified wff-terms.

Due to space reason, we have not included many issues such as reasoning about substitution, self-referential formulae and paradoxes which are discussed in [Jiang 93c]. There we noted that ground representation of a wff term is in general more powerful than a simple ambivalent approach. We also showed that the strength of the ambivalent logic lies in its combination of expressive power, simplicity and paradox-freeness. We also indicated that typing is not orthogonal to the ambivalent logic. In fact, we can easily have a typed ambivalent logic to explicitly distinguish various roles (predicate, function, term, formula) an expression plays in different context.

One important issue we have not addressed is negative introspection which is important for nonmonotonic reasoning [Jiang 93b]. One way to solve this problem is to have an autoepistemic semantics (e.g. in the spirit of [Bonanti 92]) on top of the ambivalent semantics we have just developed. We can even extend nonmonotonic reasoning to multiagents so that we can have negative introspection within the scope of nested and agent-indexed demo predicates, e.g. demo(a, p:- not demo(b,c)). These issues are partially addressed in [Jiang 94] in the context of autoepistemic logics and require further investigation in the context of metalogic programming.

Finally, it is worth noting that the ambivalent approach presented in this paper can be seen as another justification of Kowalski's thesis on logic without model theory [Kowalski 94]. It has enforced the view that you can do higher-order reasoning and modal reasoning without any non-first order semantics for them. In particular, the semantics for them is best to be handled by a Herbrand semantics which is still syntactical in the sense that Herbrand models are constructed from the syntax of the language.

Acknowledgements

This work is inspired by ideas from Bob Kowalski and has been greatly benefited by many fruitful discussions with Barry Richards. I am also grateful to helpful discussions with Bern Martens (Leuven), Marianne Kalsbeek (Amsterdam), Piero Bonanti (Piza), John Lloyd and Pat Hill (Bristol). Special thanks are also to the four referees who made critical and helpful remarks to the technical clarity and presentation of the paper. This research is supported by the Compulog project on metareasoning.

References

G. Attardi & M. Simi (1992) *Proofs in Context* KR 94.

A. Brogi & F. Turini (1992) *Metalogic for knowledge representation* KR 92.

P. Bonanti (1992) *Model-theoretic semantics for demo* Meta 92.

K. Bowen & R. Kowalski (1982) *Amalgamating languages and metalanguage in logic programming* in Logic Programming, eds. K. Clark & S. Tarnlund, Academic Press.

W. Chen, M. Kifer & D. S. Warren (1993) *Hilog: A foundation for higher order logic programming* Journal of Logic Programming 15 (3).

K. Clark (1978) *Negation as failure* in logic and database eds. H. Galliare and J. Minker, Plenum, New York, 293-322.

D. De Schreye & B. Martens (1993) *A sensible least Herbrand semantics for untyped Vanilla metaprogramming and its extension to a limited form of amalgamation* Meta 92.

M. Falaschi, G. Levi, M. Martelli & C. Palamidessi (1988) *A new declarative semantics for logic languages* ICLP 1988.

D. Gabbay (1992) *Metalevel features in the object level: modal and temporal logic programming III* in Intensional logics for programming, Eds L. Farinas del Cerro and M. Penttonen, Clarendon Press.

P. Hill & J. Lloyd (1989) *Analysis of meta-programs* Meta88.

P. Hill & J. Lloyd (1993) *The Godel language* MIT press, to appear.

Y. Jiang (1990) *An epistemic model of logic programming* New Generation Computing Vol 8, No 5.

Y. Jiang (1993a) *An intensional epistemic logic and equality* Studia Logica Vol 52, No 2, 1993.

Y. Jiang (1993b) *On the autoepistemic reconstruction of logic programming* New Generation Computing Vol 11, No 8.

Y. Jiang (1993c) *Ambivalent logic as the semantics of metalogic programming: I* Tech. Report, Dept. of Computing, Imperial College.

Y. Jiang (1994) *On multiagent autoepistemic logic - an extrospective view* KR 94

M. Kalsbeek (1993) *The Vanilla metainterpreter for definite logic programs and ambivalent syntax* ILLC CT-93-01, University of Amsterdam.

R. Kowalski & J. Kim (1991) *A metalogic programming approach to multiagent knowledge and belief* in Art. Intel. and Math. Theory of Computation, ed. V. Lifschitz, Academic Press.

R. Kowalski (1994) *Logic without a model theory* in What is a logical system, ed. Dov Gabbay, Oxford University Press, 1994.

G. Levi & Davide Ramundo (1993) *A formalization of metaprogramming for real* ICLP 93.

J. Lloyd (1984) *Foundations of logic programming* Springer Verlag.

B. Martens & D. De Schreye (1992) *A perfect Herbrand semantics for untyped Vanilla Metaprogramming* JICSLP 92.

B. Martens & D. De Schreye (1993) *Why untyped non-ground meta-programming is not (much of) a problem* to appear in Journal of Logic Programming.

D. Perlis (1985) *On self-referential languages I* AI 25

B. Richards (1974) *A point of self-reference* Synthese 28.

T. Sato (1992) *Metaprogramming through a truth predicate* ICLP 92.

V. Subrahmanian (1988) *A simple formulation of the theory of metalogic programming* Meta 88.

R. Turner (1990) *Truth and modality for knowlede representation* Pitman Pub.

M. Vardi (1986) *On epistemic logic and logical omniscience* TARK I.

Higher-order Aspects of Logic Programming (Summary)

Uday S. Reddy

University of Illinois at Urbana-Champaign
Urbana, IL 61801
Net: reddy@cs.uiuc.edu

Abstract

Are higher-order extensions to logic programming needed? We answer this question in the negative by showing that higher-order features are already available in pure logic programming. It is demonstrated that higher-order lambda calculus-based languages can be compositionally embedded in logic programming languages preserving their semantics and abstraction facilities. Further, we show that such higher-order techniques correspond to programming techniques often practiced in logic programming.

Keywords: Higher-order features, functional programming, lambda calculus, logic variables, concurrent logic programming, types, semantics.

1   Introduction

In an early paper [30], Warren raised the question whether higher-order extensions to Prolog were necessary. He suggested that they were not necessary by modelling higher-order concepts in logic programs. His proposal modelled functions and relations *intensionally* by their names. As is well-known in Lisp community, such an encoding does not obtain the full power of higher-order programming. In particular, lambda abstraction and "upward" function values are absent.

An entirely different approach to the issue was pursued by Miller et. al. in Lambda Prolog [15]. The objective here seems to be not higher-order logic programming, but logic programming over higher-order terms. While this approach has many interesting applications, particularly in meta-logical frameworks, it still leaves open the question of whether higher-order programming is possible in a standard logic programming setting. A similar comment applies to other higher-order languages like HiLog [5].

In this paper, we return to Warren's question and suggest a negative answer. Using new insights obtained from the connection between linear logic and logic programming [11, 1, 2, 21], we contend that idealized logic programming is "already higher-order" in its concept, even though one might wish to add some syntactic sugar to obtain convenience. A similar answer is also suggested by Saraswat's work [23] showing that concurrent logic programming is higher-order in a categorical sense.

We argue that idealized logic programming is higher-order by presenting two

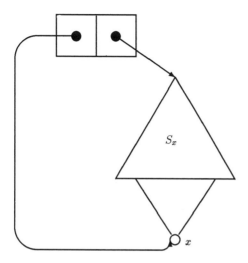

Figure 1: Difference structures

forms of evidence:

- We exhibit a compositional, semantics-preserving translation from higher-order lambda calculus-based languages to logic programs.

- We show that higher-order programming techniques are already in use in logic programming (albeit in a limited form) and that these can be generalized.

Two features of logic programming play important role is in this modelling: *logic variables* and *concurrency*. Using logic variables, one often constructs data structures with multiple occurrences of variables, e.g., difference lists [6]. Typically, one of the occurrences of the variable is designated for input, i.e., a binding is given to the variable via this occurrence, and other occurrences are used as output. If we form a pair (x, S_x) consisting of a variable x and a structure S_x with embedded occurrences of x (see Fig. 1), we have essentially formed a "function" value. The function is "applied" to an argument by binding the variable x and the result of application is obtained via S_x. Whereas this scheme allows S_x to be a data structure, using concurrency, one can similarly build *computational* structures with shared variables. S_x is then thought of as a "process" and a pair of variables involved in the process is viewed as a function value. All this provides "functions" that are good for only one function application. General functions that can be used multiple times are modelled by generating entire streams of such pairs, again using a process-oriented view. The streams are generated in a demand-driven fashion so that the user of the stream can terminate the stream at will. Mathematically, such streams are best viewed as *finite sets*.

It should be noted that our modelling of higher-order functions is not a trivial "Turing tarpit" form of translation. We do not turn higher-order programs into data and then interpret them by an interpreter in logic programming. Such a translation would not model the *abstractions* of the higher-order language and would be of little practical value owing to the interpretation overhead. Rather, our translation is characterized by the properties *compositional* and *semantics-preserving*. The former means that the translation of a compositie term is made up of the translations of its parts. The latter means that equivalent terms are translated into equivalent programs. (Neither of these properties would be satisfied by a "Turing tarpit" translation.) These properties capture the intuition that the abstractions of the source language are truly present in the target language.

Concurrency is often thought of as an extraneous feature of logic programming. However, idealized logic programs executed with *fair* SLD-resolution [14] are necessarily concurrent. Under a fair resolution scheme, no goal can be delayed forever. So, each goal of a query must be thought of as a separate process which cooperates with other processes to solve the problem. Our modelling of higher-order concepts in this framework. This cannot be duplicated in sequential logic programming languages like Prolog due to the crucial role of concurrency already mentioned. However, our scheme is applicable to almost all concurrent logic programming languages such as Concurrent Prolog [27], Parlog [8] and Guarded Horn clauses [28] as well as languages with coroutine facilities like Mu-Prolog [17].

1.1 Related work

From a theoretical point of view, the fact that higher-order features can be simulated by relations seems to have been folklore in category theory for some time. See [3] for an explicit presentation. Within the programming language theory, it is implicit in the work of [11, 1, 21] which shows that linear logic proofs can be modelled as logic programs. Another piece of related work is Milner's embedding of lambda calculus in pi-calculus [16]. His embedding only uses a subset that has a direct correspondence to concurrent logic programming languages. Thus, our presentation documents what has been implicitly known in various programming language circles.

Many of our ideas are also implicit in Shapiro's work on modelling objects in concurrent logic programming [27, 26]. Since objects provide collections of operations to their clients, modelling objects involves modelling function values as well. In fact, our translations easily extend to higher-order imperative programs (object-based programs) using the same ideas as Shapiro's. Somewhat more explicit is the work of Saraswat [23] where it is shown in that the semantic model of concurrent constraint programs forms a cartesian closed category.

2 The framework

We find it convenient to treat logic programs as defining *binary* relations. So, a predicate definition looks like:

$$R : A \leftrightarrow B$$
$$R(x, y) \Leftrightarrow \psi$$

where A and B are types, and ψ is a formula built from predicate applications, equality, conjunction, disjunction and existential quantification. (We often suppress the existential quantifiers and disjunctions by using Horn clause notation $R(x, y) \leftarrow \psi$). Typically, the type A is a finite product type, in which case we write:

$$R : A_1 \times \ldots \times A_k \leftrightarrow B$$
$$R(x_1, \ldots, x_k, y) \Leftrightarrow \psi$$

Note that we suppress the parentheses around the tuple $(x_1, \ldots, x_k)$, to avoid clutter. The special case of $k = 0$ appears as:

$$R : unit \leftrightarrow B$$
$$R(y) \Leftrightarrow \psi$$

Types include

- primitive types such as *int* and *bool*,

- finite products, including the nullary product called *unit*, and

- finite disjoint unions, including the nullary version $\emptyset$.

We often write disjoint unions with *constructor* symbols for injections, *e.g.*,

type *result* = fail(*unit*) + succ(*int*)

which is syntactic sugar for *unit* + *int*. All symbols other than constructors of this kind are variables (usually x, y, z and X, Y, Z). We do not use a case convention for variables. We also allow polymorphic type constructions with recursive definitions, *e.g.*,

type *list*(α) = nil(*unit*) + α.*list*(α)

which denotes the least set L such that $L = unit + \alpha \times L$. All these constructions have well-defined semantics. See, for example, [13].

3 Embedding PCF

PCF (Programming Language for Computable Functions), due to Scott [24], is a higher-order functional programming language. (See [20] and [9, 4.1] for published descriptions.) PCF is a typed lambda calculus with a single primitive type for integers. (The boolean type can be omitted without loss of expressiveness.) In this section, we show how PCF can be embedded in a logic programming language. The modelling of functions being the crux of the problem, extension to other kinds of data structures is more or less immediate.

Another issue is the parameter passing mechanism. We treat PCF with call-by-name parameter passing in the main body of the paper. The modelling can be easily adapted to call-by-value PCF as indicated in Section 3.2.

Examples We start by showing some examples. First, consider "linear" functions, *i.e.*, functions that use their arguments exactly once. This restriction allows us to introduce a simpler model first. Here is an example:

$$inc : int \triangleright int \qquad inc : int \leftrightarrow int$$
$$inc(x) = x + 1 \qquad inc(x, y) \Leftrightarrow add(x, 1, y)$$

On the left, we have a term $x + 1$ treated as a function of x. We always use the symbol $\triangleright$ to denote this kind of implicit function that occurs at the top level. This function is modelled as a relation between integers. Such modelling of functions by relations is elementary for any one with some knowledge of set theory.

In lambda calculus, one can abstract over x to form a function term:

$$succ : \; \triangleright int \rightarrow int \qquad succ : unit \leftrightarrow (int \times int)$$
$$succ = \lambda x. \; x + 1 \qquad succ((x, y)) \Leftrightarrow add(x, 1, y)$$

The function space $int \rightarrow int$ is modelled by the product $int \times int$. If this seems surprising, consider the fact that a relation $A \leftrightarrow B$ is really like a function $A \rightarrow \mathbb{P}B$. Due to the implicit power set construction, smaller cardinalities suffice in the second argument position of the relation. The point of this example is to illustrate that lambda-abstraction is modelled by *pair formation* in a logic program. This is the same kind of pair formation as that shown in Fig. 1 except that the "difference" between the input and output is a computation rather than a data structure.

A generic function composition term is modelled as follows:

$compose : (A \rightarrow B) \times (B \rightarrow C) \,\triangleright\, (A \rightarrow C)$
compose(f, g) = λx. g (f x)

$\quad\quad compose : (A \times B) \times (B \times C) \leftrightarrow (A \times C)$
$\quad\quad$compose(f, g, (x, z)) $\leftarrow$ f = (x, y), g = (y, z)

Notice that a function application, such as fx, is modelled by pair decomposition: $f = (x, y)$. We can use *compose* to make a twice composition of the *succ* function as follows:

$\quad$succ(f), succ(g), compose(f, g, h)

Note that h denotes the required composition: $h = (x, z)$ if and only if $z = x + 2$. This would correspond to the PCF term $compose(succ, succ) = \lambda x.(\lambda x'. x' + 1)((\lambda x'.x' + 1)x)$. Abstraction over f and g yields a composition "function" as a term:

$comp : \,\triangleright\, (A \rightarrow B) \rightarrow ((B \rightarrow C) \rightarrow (A \rightarrow C))$
comp = λf. λg. λx. g (f x)

$\quad\quad comp : unit \leftrightarrow (A \times B) \times ((B \times C) \times (A \times C))$
$\quad\quad$comp((f, (g, (x, z)))) $\leftarrow$ f = (x, y), g = (y, z)

Consider the PCF term *comp succ*. This denotes a higher-order function which, when applied to any function $g : int \rightarrow int$, yields the function $\lambda x. g(x + 1)$. Its effect is obtained by the logic programming query:

$\quad$succ(f), comp(f, h)

Note that $h = (g, (x, z))$ if and only if $g = (x + 1, z)$. Thus, the above scheme of translation works for functions of any order as long as the arguments of functions are used linearly.

Control Let us pause to examine the control issues. A query involving higher-order values, e.g., $succ(f), succ(g), compose(f, g, h), h = (1, z)$, must not be evaluated sequentially. Notice that $succ(f)$ reduces to $add(x, 1, y)$ which has an infinite number of solutions. The best order of evaluation would be the following:

$\quad\leftarrow$ succ(f), succ(g), compose(f, g, h), h = (1, z)
$\quad\leftarrow$ succ(f), succ(g), compose(f, g, (1, z))
$\quad\leftarrow$ succ(f), succ(g), f = (1, y), g = (y, z)
$\quad\leftarrow$ succ((1, y)), succ((y, z))
$\quad\leftarrow$ add(1, 1, y), add(y, 1, z)
$\quad\leftarrow$ add(2, 1, z)
$\quad\leftarrow$

This order of evaluation is achieved if

- every goal literal is suspended until it matches (becomes an instance of) the head of a clause, and

- literals of primitive predicates, like *add*, are suspended until their input arguments are instantiated.

In essence, we wish to treat our clauses as *Guarded Horn clauses* [28]. While most of our clauses have empty guards, the translation of conditional expressions will involve guards as well. It is interesting that the translation of functional programs should automatically give rise to GHC programs.

General functions To model general functions, we must handle multiple uses of arguments. Keeping in mind that arguments are often themselves functions, we model such multiple-use arguments as finite sets of values. For example, here is the *twice* function that composes its argument with itself:

$$twice : (A \to A) \rhd (A \to A)$$
$$\text{twice(f)} = \lambda \text{x. f (f x)}$$

$$twice : \mathbb{F}(A \times A) \leftrightarrow (A \times A)$$
$$\text{twice(F, (x, z))} \leftarrow \text{F} = \{\text{f1, f2}\}, \text{f1} = (\text{x, y}), \text{f2} = (\text{y, z})$$

Here, the input to the *twice* relation is a finite set of pairs, *i.e.*, a finite piece of a function graph. The *twice* function extracts two (not necessarily distinct) pairs from such a piece.

How do we make such pieces of function graphs? We first illustrate it for the *succ* function:

$$mksucc : unit \leftrightarrow \mathbb{F}(int \times int)$$
$$\text{mksucc(\{\})} \leftarrow$$
$$\text{mksucc(\{(x, y)\})} \leftarrow \text{add(x, 1, y)}$$
$$\text{mksucc(F1} \cup \text{F2)} \leftarrow \text{mksucc(F1), mksucc(F2)}$$

Note that *mksucc* makes as many pairs of the *succ* function as needed. In particular, the query *mksucc(F)*, $F = \{f1\} \cup \{f2\}$ is equivalent to:

$$\text{f1} = (\text{x1, y1}), \text{add(x1, 1, y1)}, \text{f2} = (\text{x2, y2}), \text{add(x2, 1, y2)}$$

Now, we can create the twice composition of the *succ* function by the following simpler goal:

$$\text{mksucc(F), twice(F, h)}$$

which corresponds to the PCF term *twice(succ)*. If we would like to use one portion of the *succ* function graph for use with *twice* and keep the rest for other purposes, that is easy enough to do too:

$$\text{mksucc(F} \cup \text{F'), twice(F, h), \dots F' \dots}$$

We now generalize the idea involved in *mksucc* to make finite portions of any graph. Notice that the relations of interest to us are, in general, of the form:

$$R : A_1 \times \dots \times A_n \leftrightarrow C$$
$$R(\bar{x}, u) \leftarrow \bar{x} = \bar{t}, \psi$$

The terms $\bar{t}$ decompose the inputs $\bar{x}$, the goal ψ performs some computation using the inputs and u is the output term. We assume that existential quantification is used in ψ such that $FV(\psi) \subseteq FV(\bar{t}) \cup FV(u)$. We can denote such relations compactly as input-computation-output triples written as $\bar{t} \mid \psi \mid u$.

Suppose $R = (\bar{t} \mid \psi \mid u)$ is a relation of type $\mathbb{F}A_1 \times \ldots \times \mathbb{F}A_n \leftrightarrow C$. Then, define a generic definition scheme (or "macro") for making graphs of the outputs as follows:

$$\mathbf{mkgraph}[\bar{t} \mid \psi \mid u] : \mathbb{F}A_1 \times \ldots \times \mathbb{F}A_n \leftrightarrow \mathbb{F}C$$
$$\mathbf{mkgraph}[\bar{t} \mid \psi \mid u] = P \text{ where}$$
$$P(\bar{x}, \{\}) \leftarrow \bar{x} = \{\}$$
$$P(\bar{x}, \{u\}) \leftarrow \bar{x} = \bar{t}, \psi$$
$$P(\bar{x}, y_1 \cup y_2) \leftarrow \bar{x} = \bar{x}_1 \cup \bar{x}_2, P(\bar{x}_1, y_1), P(\bar{x}_2, y_2)$$

Here, $\bar{x} = \{\}$ as well as $\bar{x} = \bar{x}_1 \cup \bar{x}_2$ mean their component-wise expansions.

Using the **mkgraph** scheme, we can represent the translations of PCF terms compactly. For example:

succ = λx. x + 1
$\quad$ **mkgraph**[| add(x, 1, y) | (x, y)]
comp = λf. λg. λx. g (f x)
$\quad$ **mkgraph**[| $\exists$y. F = {(x, y)}, G = {(y, z)} | (F, (G, (x, z)))]
twice = λf. comp f f
$\quad$ **mkgraph**[Comp | Comp = {(F1, (F2, h))} | (F1 $\cup$ F2, h)]

One is often tempted to ask the somewhat meaningless question, "how many elements are there in a finite set produced by an instance of **mkgraph**"? Well, the answer is "as many as needed". A **mkgraph** predicate is able to produce *all* possible subsets of a graph. A client procedure can determine which subset it wishes to use. In fact, treating a **mkgraph** procedure as a GHC program allows the procedure to be suspended until a client process determines the surface structure of the finite set. The **mkgraph** procedure then fills in the elements of the finite set.

Finite sets Our translation makes use of a finite set type which is not usually in the standard repertoire of logic programming. However, the unification problem for finite set-terms is decidable and it is certainly possible to add finite sets to a logic programming language. (See, for example, [7].)

On the other hand, a more modest method suffices for the purposes of this paper. Our use of finite sets is only via the **mkgraph** scheme and, within the scheme, a set constructor always appears with variable arguments. Therefore, the general set-unification algorithm is not needed. We can treat finite sets as a constructor data type of the following form:

$$\mathbf{type} \ \mathbb{F}(\alpha) = null + single(\alpha) + union(\mathbb{F}(\alpha), \mathbb{F}(\alpha))$$

The symbols *null, single* and *union* are constructors for finite sets. For readability, we continue to write *null* as $\{\}$, *single(t)* as $\{t\}$, and *union(X, Y)* as $X \cup Y$. We also use the short hand $\{t_1, \ldots, t_n\}$ for $\{t_1\} \cup \ldots \cup \{t_n\}$.

This simplification would be valid only if our use of the above constructor terms is consistent with the properties of finite sets. We verify such consistency as follows. Let $\equiv$ be the least congruence relation generated by the following theory of finite sets:

$$\begin{aligned}
\mathrm{union}(X, \mathrm{null}) &\equiv X \\
\mathrm{union}(\mathrm{null}, X) &\equiv X \\
\mathrm{union}(X_1, \mathrm{union}(X_2, X_3)) &\equiv \mathrm{union}(\mathrm{union}(X_1, X_2), X_3) \\
\mathrm{union}(X_1, X_2) &\equiv \mathrm{union}(X_2, X_1) \\
\mathrm{union}(X, X) &\equiv X
\end{aligned}$$

Then:

Lemma 3.1 *Let* $P : \mathbb{F}A_1 \times \ldots \times \mathbb{F}A_k \leftrightarrow \mathbb{F}C$ *be an instance of the* **mkgraph** *scheme, and* $y_1, y_2 \in \mathbb{F}C$ *such that* $y_1 \equiv y_2$. *Then, for all* $\bar{x}_1 \in \mathbb{F}A_1 \times \ldots \times \mathbb{F}A_k$ *such that* $P(\bar{x}_1, y_1)$, *there exists* $\bar{x}_2 \in \mathbb{F}A_1 \times \ldots \times \mathbb{F}A_k$ *such that* $\bar{x}_1 \equiv \bar{x}_2$ *and* $P(\bar{x}_2, y_2)$.

Proof: induction on the derivation of $y_1 \equiv y_2$. We show two of the base cases. The remaining cases are similar.

- If $y_1 = Y \cup \{\}$ and $y_2 = Y$ then $\bar{x}_1 = \bar{X} \cup \{\}$, for some $\bar{X}$, and $P(\bar{X}, Y)$. Let $\bar{x}_2 = \bar{X}$.

- If $y_1 = Y \cup Y'$ and $y_2 = Y' \cup Y$ then $\bar{x}_1 = \bar{X} \cup \bar{X}'$, for some $\bar{X}$, $\bar{X}'$, and $P(\bar{X}, Y)$ and $P(\bar{X}', Y')$. Let $\bar{x}_2 = \bar{X}' \cup \bar{X}$.

For the induction step of monotonic extension, let $y_1' \equiv y_2'$ and $y_1'' \equiv y_2''$. If $\bar{x}_1 \in \mathbb{F}A_1 \times \ldots \times \mathbb{F}A_k$ such that $P(\bar{x}_1, y_1' \cup y_1'')$ then $\bar{x}_1 = \bar{x}_1' \cup \bar{x}_1''$, $P(\bar{x}_1', y_1')$ and $P(\bar{x}_1'', y_1'')$ for some $\bar{x}_1'$ and $\bar{x}_1''$. Then, by induction hypothesis, there exist $\bar{x}_2'$ and $\bar{x}_2''$ such that $\bar{x}_1' \equiv \bar{x}_2'$, $\bar{x}_1'' \equiv \bar{x}_2''$, $P(\bar{x}_2', y_2')$ and $P(\bar{x}_2'', y_2'')$. Let $\bar{x}_2 = \bar{x}_2' \cup \bar{x}_2''$. $\square$

Another method, available in a committed-choice language, is to represent finite sets by streams. Union is then obtained by merge. Here is the definition of the **mkgraph** scheme using this representation:

$$\begin{aligned}
&\mathbf{mkgraph}[\bar{t} \mid \psi \mid u] : list(A_1) \times \ldots list(A_n) \leftrightarrow list(C) \\
&\mathbf{mkgraph}[\bar{t} \mid \psi \mid u] = P \text{ where} \\
&\quad P(\bar{x}, [\,]) \leftarrow \bar{x} = [\,] \\
&\quad P(\bar{x}, u.ys) \leftarrow merge(\bar{x}_1, \bar{x}_2, \bar{x}), \bar{x}_1 = \bar{t}, \psi, P(\bar{x}_2, ys)
\end{aligned}$$

This makes no essential change to the **mkgraph** scheme except for linearizing the recursion. We can profitably use Shapiro's metaphor [27] and think of a **mkgraph** predicate as an "object" and the finite set argument as a stream of "messages" sent to the object.

3.1 Translation

Table 1 gives a description of PCF types, terms and the type rules for terms. The type rules are expressed in terms of judgements of the form

$$x_1 : A_1, \ldots, x_n : A_n \, \triangleright \, M : C$$

where $x_1, \ldots, x_n$ are the free variables of M. We use $\Gamma, \Delta, \ldots$ to range over sequences of variable typings $x_1 : A_1, \ldots, x_n : A_n$ (called "type contexts"). All the variables in a type context must be distinct. The first type rule (called Exchange rule) allows the typings in a type context to be freely rearranged. So, the order of typings is essentially insignificant. The type rules of Table 1 look different from the usual formulations, but they are equivalent to them. They are designed to give the cleanest possible translation.

Types : A, B, C
$$A ::= int \mid A_1 \to A_2$$
Variables : x, y, z
Numbers : $n ::= 0 \mid 1 \mid \ldots$
Terms : M, N, V
$$M ::= x \mid n \mid M + N \mid M - N \mid \text{if } M \, N_1 \, N_2 \mid \lambda x.\, M \mid MN \mid \text{rec } M$$
Type rules :

$$\frac{\Gamma, x : A, y : B, \Gamma' \,\triangleright\, M : C}{\Gamma, y : B, x : A, \Gamma' \,\triangleright\, M : C} \qquad \frac{\Gamma, y_1 : A, y_2 : A \,\triangleright\, M : C}{\Gamma, x : A \,\triangleright\, M[x/y_1, x/y_2] : C} \qquad \frac{\Gamma \,\triangleright\, M : C}{\Gamma, x : A \,\triangleright\, M : C}$$

$$\frac{}{x : A \,\triangleright\, x : A} \qquad \frac{\Gamma \vdash M : A \quad \Delta, x : A \vdash N : C}{\Gamma, \Delta \vdash N[M/x] : C}$$

$$\frac{}{\triangleright n : int} \qquad \frac{\Gamma \,\triangleright\, M : int \quad \Delta \,\triangleright\, N : int}{\Gamma, \Delta \,\triangleright\, M + N : int} \qquad \frac{\Gamma \,\triangleright\, N_1 : A \quad \Gamma \,\triangleright\, N_2 : A}{\Gamma, x : int \,\triangleright\, \text{if } x \, N_1 \, N_2 : A}$$

$$\frac{\Gamma, x : A \,\triangleright\, M : B}{\Gamma \,\triangleright\, \lambda x.\, M : A \to B} \qquad \frac{\Gamma \,\triangleright\, M : A \to B}{\Gamma, x : A \,\triangleright\, Mx : B} \qquad \frac{}{x : A \to A \,\triangleright\, \text{rec } x : A}$$

Table 1: Definition of PCF

The translation of PCF programs to logic programs as follows. The types are translated by the mapping $(\ )^\circ$:

$$int^\circ = int$$
$$(A \to B)^\circ = \mathbb{F}A^\circ \times B^\circ$$

The translations represents the intuitions explained earlier in this section.

A term with a typing of the form $x_1 : A_1, \ldots, x_n : A_n \,\triangleright\, M : C$ is translated to a relation R of type $\mathbb{F}A_1^\circ \times \ldots \times \mathbb{F}A_n^\circ \leftrightarrow C^\circ$. We denote such relations using the notation $\bar{t} \mid \psi \mid u$ where $\bar{t}$ is a tuple of terms of type $\mathbb{F}A_1^\circ \times \ldots \times \mathbb{F}A_n^\circ$, u a term of type C° and ψ a formula. This is meant to denote a relation R defined by

$$R(x_1, \ldots, x_n, u) \leftarrow x_1 = t_1, \ldots, x_n = t_n, \psi$$

The translation will be defined by induction on type derivations. For each type rule, we give a translation rule in terms of relation triples. Using these one can construct a derivation tree of relations, each relation corresponding to a PCF term in the type derivation. Each use of the **mkgraph** primitive generates a recursive predicate definition. The collection of such predicate definitions forms a logic program and the relation triple corresponding to the overall term becomes the query.

The translations for the first three rules (called the structural rules of Exchange,

Contraction and Weakening) are straightforward:

$$\frac{\Gamma, x:A, y:B, \Gamma' \triangleright M:C}{\Gamma, y:B, x:A, \Gamma' \triangleright M:C} \qquad \frac{\bar{t}, u_1, u_2, \bar{t'} \mid \psi \mid v}{\bar{t}, u_2, u_1, \bar{t'} \mid \psi \mid v}$$

$$\frac{\Gamma, y_1:A, y_2:A \triangleright M:C}{\Gamma, x:A \triangleright M[x/y_1, x/y_2]:C} \qquad \frac{\bar{t}, u_1, u_2 \mid \psi \mid v}{\bar{t}, u_1 \cup u_2 \mid \psi \mid v}$$

$$\frac{\Gamma \triangleright M:C}{\Gamma, x:A \triangleright M:C} \qquad \frac{\bar{t} \mid \psi \mid v}{\bar{t}, \{\} \mid \psi \mid v}$$

The next two rules (called Identity and Cut) are translated as follows:

$$\frac{}{x:A \triangleright x:A} \qquad \frac{}{\{z\} \mid true \mid z}$$

$$\frac{\Gamma \vdash M:A \quad \Delta, x:A \vdash N:C}{\Gamma, \Delta \vdash N[M/x]:C} \qquad \frac{\bar{t}_1 \mid \psi_1 \mid u \quad \bar{t}_2, u' \mid \psi_2 \mid v}{\bar{x}_1, \bar{t}_2 \mid \mathbf{mkgraph}[\bar{t}_1 \mid \psi_1 \mid u](\bar{x}_1, u'), \psi_2 \mid v}$$

The complexity of the Cut rule is due to the fact that the term u in the first premise is of type A° whereas u' in the second premise is of type $\mathbb{IF}A^\circ$. Therefore, we must generate a graph of u's and match it to u'.

The primitives are translated as follows:

$$\frac{}{\triangleright n:int} \qquad \frac{}{\mid true \mid n}$$

$$\frac{\Gamma \triangleright M:int \quad \Delta \triangleright N:int}{\Gamma, \Delta \triangleright M+N:int} \qquad \frac{\bar{t}_1 \mid \psi_1 \mid u_1 \quad \bar{t}_2 \mid \psi_2 \mid u_2}{\bar{t}_1, \bar{t}_2 \mid \psi_1, \psi_2, add(u_1, u_2, z) \mid z}$$

$$\frac{\Gamma \triangleright N_1:A \quad \Gamma \triangleright N_2:A}{\Gamma, x:int \triangleright \mathbf{if}\, x\, N_1\, N_2:A} \qquad \frac{\bar{t}_1 \mid \psi_1 \mid v_1 \quad \bar{t}_2 \mid \psi_2 \mid v_2}{\bar{x}, \{x\} \left| \begin{array}{l} (x=0, \bar{x}=\bar{t}_1, \psi_1, y=v_1) \vee \\ (x \neq 0, \bar{x}=\bar{t}_2, \psi_2, y=v_2) \end{array} \right| y}$$

Notice that the translation of the conditional gives rise to a disjunction. In a concurrent logic programming language, one must treat $x=0$ and $x \neq 0$ as guards of the two branches.

Finally, the higher-order terms are translated by:

$$\frac{\Gamma, x:A \triangleright M:B}{\Gamma \triangleright \lambda x.\, M:A \to B} \qquad \frac{\bar{t}, u \mid \psi \mid v}{\bar{t} \mid \psi \mid (u, v)}$$

$$\frac{\Gamma \triangleright M:A \to B}{\Gamma, x:A \triangleright Mx:B} \qquad \frac{\bar{t} \mid \psi \mid u}{\bar{t}, X \mid \psi, u=(X, z) \mid z}$$

$$\frac{}{x:A \to A \triangleright \mathbf{rec}\, x:A} \qquad \frac{}{F \mid recurse(F, z) \mid z}$$

Notice that abstraction is pair formation and application is pair decomposition. The *recurse* predicate used in the last rule is defined as follows:

recurse : $\mathbb{IF}(\mathbb{IF}A \times A) \leftrightarrow A$
recurse(F, x) $\leftarrow$ F = $\{(X, x)\} \cup$ F', $\mathbf{mkgraph}[$F $\mid$ recurse(F, x) $\mid$ x$]($F', X$)$

As an example of the translation, consider the *succ* function:

$$\frac{x:int \triangleright x:int \quad \triangleright 1:int}{\frac{x:int \triangleright x+1:int}{\triangleright \lambda x.\, x+1:int}} \qquad \frac{\{x\} \mid true \mid x \quad \mid true \mid 1}{\frac{\{x\} \mid add(x,1,y) \mid y}{\mid add(x,1,y) \mid (\{x\}, y)}}$$

The translation triple of this term denotes a relation $succ : \mathbb{F}\,int \leftrightarrow int$ defined by:

$$succ((\{x\}, y)) \leftarrow add(x, 1, y)$$

This differs from the translation given at the beginning of Sec. 3 in that there we did not model the input of $succ$ as of type $\mathbb{F}\,int$. The translation given here treats all types uniformly. But, int being a pure data type with ·no higher-order values, the use of $\mathbb{F}$ can ·be dropped. This and other optimizations are discussed in Sec. 3.4 below.

We show the correctness of the translation as follows:

Lemma 3.2 (type soundness) *The translation of a PCF term* $x_1 : A_1, \ldots, x_n : A_n \,\triangleright\, M : C$ *is a relation of type* $\mathbb{F}A_1^\circ \times \ldots \times \mathbb{F}A_n^\circ \leftrightarrow C^\circ$.

Theorem 3.3 *The following equivalences of lambda terms are preserved by the translation:*

$$
\begin{aligned}
(\lambda x.\, M)\, N &\equiv M[N/x] \\
\lambda x.\, M\, x &\equiv M \\
rec\, M &\equiv M\,(rec\, M)
\end{aligned}
$$

Proof: For $(\lambda x.\, M)\, N$ we have a translation of the following form:

$$
\cfrac{\Gamma \,\triangleright\, N : A \quad \cfrac{\cfrac{\Delta, x : A \,\triangleright\, M : B}{\Delta \,\triangleright\, \lambda x.\, M : A \to B}\quad \Delta, y : A \,\triangleright\, (\lambda x.\, M)y : B}{}}{\Gamma, \Delta \,\triangleright\, (\lambda x.\, M)N : B}
$$

$$
\cfrac{\bar{t}' \mid \psi' \mid u' \quad \cfrac{\cfrac{\bar{t}, u \mid \psi \mid v}{\bar{t} \mid \psi \mid (u, v)}}{\bar{t}, X \mid \psi, (u, v) = (X, z) \mid z}}{\bar{x}', \bar{t} \mid \mathbf{mkgraph}[\bar{t}'|\psi'|u'](\bar{x}', X), \psi, (u, v) = (X, z) \mid z}
$$

By unifying (u, v) with (X, z) and substituting for X and z, we obtain the translation of $M[N/x]$:

$$
\cfrac{\Gamma \vdash N : A \quad \Delta, x : A \vdash M : C}{\Gamma, \Delta \vdash M[N/x] : C} \qquad \cfrac{\bar{t}' \mid \psi' \mid u' \quad \bar{t}, u \mid \psi \mid v}{\bar{x}', \bar{t} \mid \mathbf{mkgraph}[\bar{t}'|\psi'|u'](\bar{x}', u), \psi \mid v}
$$

The preservation of the *eta* equivalence follows similarly from the properties of unification and the recursion equivalence follows from the definition of the *recurse* predicate. □

3.2 Call by value

The translation of a call-by-value version of PCF would follow the same general ideas as above, but it differs in where finite sets are formed. In particular, it is based on the following translation $(\ )^*$ at the level of types:

$$
\begin{aligned}
int^* &= int \\
(A \to B)^* &= \mathbb{F}(A^* \times B^*)
\end{aligned}
$$

The translation of a term $x_1 : A_1, \ldots, x_n : A_n \,\triangleright\, M : C$ is a relation of type $A_1^* \times \cdots A_n^* \leftrightarrow C^*$. This modelling represents the intuition that both the inputs and outputs of CBV functions are "values".

3.3 Data structures

The translation can be readily extended to deal with data structures. Product and sum types of a functional language are translated as follows:

$$
\begin{aligned}
unit^\circ &= \emptyset \\
(A \times B)^\circ &:= \mathrm{fst}(A^\circ) + \mathrm{snd}(B^\circ) \\
(c(A) + d(B))^\circ &= c(\mathbb{F}A^\circ) + d(\mathbb{F}B^\circ)
\end{aligned}
$$

In the case of product types, *fst* and *snd* are assumed to be constructor symbols not used elsewhere. Notice that the translation of product types exhibits the same kind of reduction in the cardinality as encountered with function types previously. Think of a pair-typed value as a process that responds to *fst* and *snd* messages.

The translations of terms can be easily derived using the translation of types as a heuristic. For binary products:

$$
\frac{\Gamma \vartriangleright M : A \quad \Gamma \vartriangleright N : B}{\Gamma \vartriangleright (M,N) : A \times B} \qquad \frac{\bar{t}_1 \mid \psi_1 \mid u_1 \quad \bar{t}_2 \mid \psi_2 \mid u_2}{\bar{x} \left|\begin{array}{l} (y = \mathrm{fst}(u_1), \bar{x} = \bar{t}_1, \psi_1) \vee \\ (y = \mathrm{snd}(u_2), \bar{x} = \bar{t}_2, \psi_2) \end{array}\right| y}
$$

$$
\frac{}{x : A \times B \vartriangleright \mathrm{fst}\ x : A} \qquad \frac{}{\{\mathrm{fst}(z)\} \mid true \mid z}
$$

The relation for the pair has two clauses. One of them will get exercised when a component is selected. Similarly, the translation of terms of sum types is:

$$
\frac{\Gamma \vartriangleright M : A}{\Gamma \vartriangleright c(M) : c(A) + d(B)} \qquad \frac{\bar{t} \mid \psi \mid u}{\bar{t} \mid \psi \mid c(u)}
$$

$$
\frac{\Gamma, x_1 : A \vartriangleright M : C \quad \Gamma, x_2 : B \vartriangleright N : C}{\Gamma, x : c(A) + d(B) \vartriangleright \mathbf{case}\,x\,\mathbf{of}\,c(x_1) \Rightarrow M \mid d(x_2) \Rightarrow N : C}
$$

$$
\frac{\bar{t}_1, t_1 \mid \psi_1 \mid u_1 \quad \bar{t}_2, t_2 \mid \psi_2 \mid u_2}{\bar{x}, \{x\} \left|\begin{array}{l} (x = c(t_1), \bar{x} = \bar{t}_1, z = u_1) \vee \\ (x = d(t_2), \bar{x} = \bar{t}_2, z = u_2) \end{array}\right| z}
$$

Many data structures occurring in practice take the form of sum-of-products. For example, lists are given by a type definition of the form:

type list $=$ nil(unit) $+$ cons(int $\times$ list)

In translating such a type to the logic programming context, we can make use of the isomorphisms:

$$
\mathbb{F}(A + B) \cong \mathbb{F}A \times \mathbb{F}B \qquad \mathbb{F}\emptyset \cong unit
$$

So, the translation of the list type can be given as:

$$
list^\circ = \mathrm{nil(unit)} + \mathrm{cons}(\mathbb{F}\ \mathrm{int} \times \mathbb{F}\ list^\circ)
$$

3.4 Optimizations

The type $\mathbb{F}int$ denotes finite sets of integers. Since functional programs give determinate results, such a set contains at most one integer. The empty set, $\{\}$, appears when a program ignores its integer input. A singleton set appears when the program uses the input. The use of finite sets for data values thus allows "lazy" data. Similarly, the above type $list^\circ$ makes available lazy lists within a concurrent logic program.

If we are not interested in lazy data structures, we can eliminate all uses of IF in data structures. To model this, we use the following translation:

$$
\begin{aligned}
int^* &= int \\
unit^* &= unit \\
(A \times B)^* &= A^* \times B^* \\
(c(A) + d(B))^* &= c(A^*) + d(B^*)
\end{aligned}
$$

For example,

$$
list^* = nil(unit) + cons(int \times list^*)
$$

The function type $A \to B$ is then translated to $A^* \times B^\circ$ instead of $\text{IF}\,A^\circ \times B^\circ$. We will see applications of this translation in the next section.

Another opportunity for optimization occurs when the argument of a function is used *linearly*, i.e., if the function uses its argument precisely once. In this case, we can simplify the translation of functions to

$$
(A \to B)^\circ = A^\circ \times B^\circ
$$

This optimization is already illustrated in the examples at the beginning of Sec. 3.

4 Example applications

The results of Sec. 3 establish a close correspondence between the higher-order programming techniques of functional programming and those of logic programming. Two features of logic programming play a role in this correspondence:

- logic variables, and

- concurrency.

The higher-order programming techniques are available only to a limited extent in sequential logic programming due to the crucial role of concurrency in this correspondence. However, they are still available and logic programmers frequently make use of them. In this section, we draw a correspondence between some of the common programming techniques used in functional and logic programming paradigms in the light of our translation. We hope that this will lead to a reexamination of the logic programming techniques in the light of "higher-order programming" and pave the way for further exchange of ideas and techniques between the two paradigms.

Difference lists form a familiar logic programming technique which allow for constant time concatenation [6]. A very similar technique was developed in functional programming using function values [10]. Our correspondence identifies the two techniques, i.e., if we translate the functional programming representation of difference lists using the translation of Sec. 3, we obtain the logic programming representation.

The functional programming technique is shown in Table 2. A difference list is represented as a function from lists to lists. The representation of an ordinary list $[x_1, \ldots, x_n]$ is the function $\lambda l.\, x_1.x_2.\ldots.x_n.l$. (See the function *rep*.) Concatenation is then just function composition, which works in constant time.

The logic programming technique is shown in Table 3. Here, a difference list is a pair of lists, but one of the lists is typically a logic variable which is shared in the

```
type diff_list = list → list
rep : list → diff_list
rep [ ] = λl. l
rep x.xs = λl. x.((rep xs) l)
concat : diff_list → diff_list → diff_list
concat x y = λl. x (y l)
```

Table 2: Difference lists in functional programming

```
type diff_list = list × list
rep : list ↔ diff_list
rep([ ], (l',l)) ← l = l'
rep(x.xs, (l',l)) ← rep(xs, (m, l)), l' = x.m
concat : diff_list × diff_list ↔ diff_list
concat(x, y, (l', l)) ← y = (m, l), x = (l', m)
```

Table 3: Difference lists in logic programming

other list. The representation of a list $[x_1, \ldots, x_n]$ is a pair $(x_1.x_2.\ldots.x_n.l, l)$ where l is a variable.

To see the correspondence between the two versions, notice that the functional difference list uses its list argument linearly. Thus, as noted in Sec. 3.4, *list → list* can be translated to *list × list* in the logic programming context. (The second component corresponds to the input list and the first component to the output list.) A close examination of the two programs is quite striking. They correspond operator by operator according to the translation of Sec. 3.

A difference structure, in general, involves some data or computational structure with a place-holder inside the structure captured by a logic variable. That is essentially what a function is. It is a computation with a place holder for the argument. Thus, the example we found here is an instance of a general concept.

Difference lists of Table 3 can only be used linearly. Our technique also allows us to build difference lists that can be used multiple times. The procedure **mk-graph**[rep] of type *list ↔ IF diff_list* produces multiple copies of the difference list representation.

Another important application for function values is in abstract syntax. Consider a language that has variable-binding operators, e.g., lambda calculus or predicate calculus. In writing a processor for such a language (evaluator, theorem prover *etc.*), there arise delicate issues of variable renaming, substitution *etc.* Pfenning and Elliott [19] proposed that such issues can be treated in modular fashion by using higher-order abstract syntax, i.e., syntactic representations that involve function values. To see how this works, consider the first-order and higher-order representations for lambda terms:

term = varF(symbol) + lamF(symbol × term) + apF(term × term)
hoterm = varH(hoterm) + lamH(hoterm → hoterm) + apH(hoterm × hoterm)

The higher-order representation (*hoterm*) is symbol-free. The variable binding operator, *lamH*, takes a function mapping terms (the arguments) to terms (the result of embedding the argument in the body of the abstraction). For example, the Church numeral $\mathbf{2} = \lambda s. \lambda x. s(sx)$, has the following representations:

first-order: lamF("s", lamF("x", apF(varF("s"), apF(varF("s"), var("x"))))))

higher-order: lamH(λt. lamH(λu. apH(varH(t), apH(varH(t), varH(u)))))

The difference between the two representations is illustrated by the following function *apply* (for carryingout a function application in an evaluator) in the two cases:

apply lamF(sym, body) arg = compute (substitute sym arg body)

apply lamH(f) arg = compute (f arg)

Notice that substitution is elided by the use of higher-order representation.

The higher-order representation is also available in logic programming. A simplified version of the representation is:

hoterm = varF(hoterm) + lamH(hoterm × hoterm) + apH(hoterm × hoterm)

It results in a similar simplification of the processing:

apply(lamF(sym, body), arg, result) ←
    substitute(sym, arg, body, newbody), compute(newbody, result)

apply(lamH(param, body), arg, result) ←
    param = arg, compute(body, result)

Higher-order representations of this kind have been used used for polymorphic type terms in the Typed Prolog typechecker [13, 12]. See [22] for further details regarding the application of higher-order abstract syntax.

Many other programming techniques of higher-order functional programming can be similarly adapted to the logic programming context. See [4, 18, 29]. The reader is invited to try some of these using the translation scheme of Section 3.

5 Conclusion

We have demonstrated the expressive power of logic programming by modelling higher-order programming features in pure logic programs. Further, these programming techniques, in a limited context, correspond to well-known techniques of logic programs.

However, the significant abstraction facilities made possible by higher-order techniques are not available in sequential logic programming. Thus, we believe that sequential logic programming is a poor approximation to logic programming and that efforts must be made to incorporate concurrency and fairness. Concurrent logic programming languages as well as coroutining facilities [17] are an important step in this direction. These systems need to be extended to deal with backtracking nondeterminism. Formal semantics and type systems must be developed to place them on a firm foundation.

The correspondences drawn in this work are only a first step in exploiting the richness of the logic programming paradigm. These techniques must be further explored and applied to practical contexts.

Acknowledgements This paper is a revised (and abridged) version of a workshop paper of the same title [22]. I thank Roy Dyckhoff, Dale Miller and anonymous referees for several useful comments which led to the improved presentation here.

References

[1] S. Abramsky. Computational interpretation of linear logic. Tutorial Notes, International Logic Programming Symposium, San Diego, 1991, 1991.

[2] S. Abramsky. Computational interpretations of linear logic. *Theoretical Comp. Science*, 111(1-2):3–57, 1993.

[3] M. Barr. *-Autonomous categories and linear logic. *Math. Structures in Comp. Science*, 1:159–178, 1991.

[4] R. Bird and P. Wadler. *Introduction to Functional Programming*. Prentice-Hall International, London, 1988.

[5] W. Chen, M. Kifer, and D. S. Warren. HiLog: A first-order semantics for higher-order logic programming constructs. In L. Lusk, E and R. A. Overbeek, editors, *Logic Programming: Proc. of the North American Conf. 1989*, pages 1090–1144. MIT Press, 1989.

[6] K. L. Clark and S. A. Tarnlund. A first-order theory of data and programs. In *Information Processing*, pages 939–944. North-Holland, 1977.

[7] A. Dovier, E. G. Omodeo, E. Pontelli, and G. F. Rossi. {log}: A logic programming langugae with finite sets. In K. Furukawa, editor, *Logic Programming: Proceedings of the Eigth International Conference*. MIT Press, 1991.

[8] S. Gregory. *Parallel Logic Programming in PARLOG: The Language and its Implementation*. Addison-Wesley, Reading, Mass., 1987.

[9] C. A. Gunter. *Semantics of Programming Languages: Structures and Techniques*. MIT Press, 1992.

[10] R. J. M. Hughes. A novel representation of lists and its application to the function "reverse". *Information Processing Letters*, 22:141–144, Mar 1986.

[11] Y. Lafont. Linear logic programming. In P. Dybjer, editor, *Porc. Workshop on Programming Logic*, pages 209–220. Univ. of Goteborg and Chalmers Univ. Technology, Goteborg, Sweden, Oct 1987.

[12] T. K. Lakshman. Typed prolog: Type checking/type reconstruction system (version 1.0). Software available by anonymous FTP from cs.uiuc.edu, 1991.

[13] T.K. Lakshman and U. S. Reddy. Typed Prolog: A Semantic Reconstruction of the Mycroft-O'Keefe Type System. In V. Saraswat and K. Ueda, editors, *Logic Programming: Proceedings of the 1991 International Symposium*, pages 202 – 217. MIT Press, Cambridge, Mass., 1991.

[14] J.-L. Lassez and M. J. Maher. Closures and fairness in the semantics of programming logic. *Theoretical Computer Science*, pages 167–184, May 1984.

[15] D. A. Miller and G. Nadathur. Higher-order logic programming. In *Intern. Conf. on Logic Programming*, 1986.

[16] R. Milner. Functions as processes. In *Proceedings of ICALP 90*, volume 443 of *Lect. Notes in Comp. Science*, pages 167–180. Springer-Verlag, 1990.

[17] Lee Naish. *Negation and control in Prolog*, volume 238 of *Lect. Notes in Comp. Science*. Springer-Verlag, New York, 1986.

[18] L. C. Paulson. *ML for the Working Programmer*. Cambridge Univ. Press, Cambridge, 1991.

[19] F. Pfenning and C. Elliott. Higher-order abstract syntax. In *ACM SIGPLAN '88 Conf. Program. Lang. Design and Impl.*, pages 22–24. ACM, 1988.

[20] G. D. Plotkin. LCF considered as a programming language. *Theoretical Comp. Science*, 5:223–255, 1977.

[21] U. S. Reddy. A typed foundation for directional logic programming. In E. Lamma and P. Mello, editors, *Extensions of Logic Programming*, volume 660 of *Lect. Notes in Artificial Intelligence*, pages 282–318. Springer-Verlag, 1993.

[22] U. S. Reddy. Higher-order aspects of logic programming. In R. Dyckhoff, editor, *Extensions of Logic Programming*, Lect. Notes in Artificial Intelligence. Springer-Verlag, 1994. (to appear).

[23] Vijay Saraswat. The category of constraint systems is Cartesian-closed. In *Proceedings, Seventh Annual IEEE Symposium on Logic in Computer Science*, pages 341–345, Santa Cruz, California, 22–25 June 1992. IEEE Computer Society Press.

[24] D. S. Scott. A type theoretical alternative to CUCH, ISWIM and OWHY. Unpublished manuscript, Oxford University, 1969.

[25] E. Shapiro. *Concurrent Prolog: Collected Papers*. MIT Press, 1987. (Two volumes).

[26] E. Shapiro and A. Takeuchi. Object-oriented programming in Concurrent Prolog. *New Generation Computing*, 4(2):25–49, 1986. (reprinted in [25].).

[27] E. Y. Shapiro. A subset of Concurrent Prolog and its interpreter. Technical Report TR-003, ICOT- Institute of New Generation Computer Technology, January 1983. (Reprinted in [25].).

[28] K. Ueda. Guarded Horn clauses. In E. Wada, editor, *Logic Programming*, pages 168–179. Springer-Verlag, 1986. (reprinted in [25].).

[29] P. Wadler. The essence of functional programming. In *ACM Symp. on Princ. of Program. Lang.*, 1992.

[30] D. H. D. Warren. Higher-order extensions to Prolog: Are they needed? In D. Michie, editor, *Machine Intelligence, 10*, pages 441–454. Edinburgh University Press, 1982.

Higher-Order Polymorphic Unification for Logic Programming

Luis Caires and Luis Monteiro

Dept. de Informática - Universidade Nova de Lisboa, Portugal
Email: {lxc,lm}@fct.unl.pt

Abstract

The motivation for logic programming in a domain of functional values represented by terms of a lambda calculus has been presented in the literature. Languages of the λ-Prolog family use the simply-typed lambda calculus of Church as term domain. Since a logic programming language must present some form of polymorphism to be of practical utility, most implementations of such languages use variants of ML-like type systems. However, most approaches do not avoid problems due to the interaction of variable types with higher-order unification, and some lack a theoretical analysis. With the motivation to overcome some of these problems we present Π^*, a subset of the second-order lambda calculus, and develop for it a complete unification procedure in the Huet style. The procedure is presented in a form adequate for integration into a λ-Prolog like a logic programming language allowing quantification over values and types. Such integration will be sketched at the end of the paper.

1   Introduction

The motivation for higher-order logic programming (HOLP) in general, and in particular of logic programming in a domain of functional values represented by terms of a lambda calculus, has been presented in the literature. Languages of the λ-Prolog family [15, 11] are based on a subset of higher-order intuitionistic logic and use the simply-typed lambda calculus of [2] as the basic term domain. However, a (logic) programming language must present some form of polymorphism to be of practical utility. Hence most implementations of λ-Prolog use variants of a ML like [13] type system defined in [16] that displays some forms of parametric and ad-hoc polymorphism. Similar needs have been pointed out in [17] wrt the Isabelle [18] unification algorithm, where a formal treatment of unification is acomplished for a λ-calculus with type variables. However, these approaches do not avoid some problems related to the interaction of variable types with higher-order unification, and yield incomplete algorithms and do not support type-parametric terms.

With the motivation to overcome some of these problems we present a suitably defined subset of the second-order lambda calculus of Girard-Reynolds [6, 20], herein designated by Π^*, and develop for it a complete unification procedure similar to Huet's. The procedure is presented in a form adequate for integration into a logic programming language in the λ-Prolog style with universally quantified goals over values and types.

Several reasons may be put forward for considering the polymorphic lambda calculus (Λ_Π) as a term language for HOLP. In the first place, the obvious reason is that it yields a natural embedding of polymorphism into HOLP, by being a natural enrichment of the simply-typed lambda calculus with type variables. Second, it provides a framework in which the presence of polymorphism in HOLP can be analysed and evaluated. This could lead to the development of a formal basis for discussing the effects of the presence of variable types on semantics, interpretation and pragmatical (ie. user oriented) concerns of HOLP. Note also that adopting Λ_Π as a data domain provides the possibility of explicit reference to type information in the course of computation.

The main obstacle to the introduction of polymorphic lambda terms in a logic programming language is related to the unification operation required for the proof procedure. In fact, Huet's higher-order unification algorithm [8] depends in an essential way on type information that may not be available in terms with free type variables. Such circumstance contributes to make the general unification problem in Λ_Π hard to solve. Proposed solutions have been either to sacrifice completeness of the unification algorithm [17, 15] or to consider some restriction of the full language, as does [19] by adapting the argument-restricted terms of L_λ to the Calculus of Constructions, a language that contains Λ_Π as a proper subset. This approach works well since unification in L_λ does not depend on types. However, it is very excluding, since it does not allow for every term of the simply typed calculus. Concerning unification in λ-calculi with type variables but without type quantification, we should also mention the work of [4] that proceeds by translating λ-terms into combinatory logic, and the system of [9] that is complete but not goal-directed.

Our approach will be to restrict the basic language of Λ_Π, although we consider every simply-typed term and a large class of polymorphic (and type-parametric) terms. Note that HOLP is a convenient domain in relation to which restrictions of the full language admitting complete unification algorithms could be evaluated and compared, since one of the principal applications of unification is in proof procedures and these are at the heart of logic programming.

The paper is structured as follows. In Sec.2 we review some notions concerning typed λ-calculi. In Sec.3 unification in Λ_Π is discussed and some problems with adapting Huet's algorithm exposed. In Sec.4 the restricted language Π^* and its unification algorithm is presented. In Sec.5 we sketch the integration of our algorithm into a logic programming language. Finally, some conclusions are drawn.

2 Preliminaries

Here we review some notions concerning typed λ-calculi and present the notation adopted. For a comprehensive introduction to the subject see [10, 7].

The set K of *kinds* of Λ_Π is defined as the set of nonempty words over the alphabet $\{\bullet\}$. Assume given a set $\mathcal{KC}$ of *type constants*. A *kind signature* χ is a mapping assigning to each $c \in \mathcal{KC}$ a kind $\chi(c) \in K$. Those $k \in \mathcal{KC}$ with $\chi(k) = \bullet$ will be called *ground types*.

The set $\mathcal{T}$ of *types* of Λ_Π is defined as the smallest set built from a denumerable supply $\mathcal{V}_T$ of type variables, the type constants of ground type, and closed under arrow $(A \Rightarrow B)$, universal quantification $(\Pi X.B)$ and the following formation rule. Given any $k \in \mathcal{KC}$ with $\chi(k) = \bullet^{n+1}$, and $T_1, T_2, \ldots, T_n$ arbitrary types of Λ_Π, we may form the type $k(T_1, \ldots, T_n)$.

The subset of $\mathcal{T}$ containing but types built from constants of $\mathcal{KC}$ and arrow $\Rightarrow$ will be called the set of *simple types* over χ. Any type variable or type of the form $k(\overline{T_n})$ will be called an *atomic type*.

We now define value terms. Assume given a set $\mathcal{TC}$ of *term constants*. A *type signature* Σ is a mapping assigning to each $c \in \mathcal{TC}$ a closed type $\Sigma(c) \in \mathcal{T}$. The set P_Π of the raw terms of Λ_Π is defined inductively as the smallest set containing the types, the value variables from $\mathcal{V}_t$, constants from $\mathcal{TC}$ and closed under application (ab), value abstraction $(\lambda x : A.a)$ and type abstraction $(\Lambda X.a)$. The smallest subset of P_Π containing only constants and variables of simple type and closed under application and value abstraction will be called the set of *simply-typed raw terms* over $\chi - \Sigma$. By $\equiv$ we denote the equality relation on Λ_Π modulo a renaming of bound variables (ie. we take α-conversion as primitive equality between terms). By $FV(b)$ we shall denote the set of free variables of a term b. Any term b such that $FV(b) = \emptyset$ will be called a *closed term*, otherwise *open*. We shall write $b[x/a]$ for the (free variable capture avoiding) replacement of every free occurrence of x in b by a.

In order to make notation more uniform we will sometimes write $X^\Pi \Rightarrow B$ instead of $\Pi X.B$: this will allow us to write any type T in the form $A_1 \Rightarrow \ldots \Rightarrow A_n \Rightarrow B$ with B atomic. This B will be called *target* of the type T (written $tgt(T)$). We will also write $\lambda X : \bullet.b$ instead of $\Lambda X.b$: in this way we can write a sequence of type and term abstractions as $\lambda \overline{x_n : T_n}$ with each T_i a type or just $\bullet$.

We now present a type system for raw terms. A typing environment Δ of domain $\overline{x_n}$ is a finite sequence of pairs $\{x_1 : X_n \ldots x_n : X_n\}$ with $\overline{x_n}$ a set of distinct value and type variables. Such an environment assigns to each $x_i \in \mathcal{V}_t$ a type X_i such that $FV(X_i) \subseteq \{x_1, \ldots, x_{i-1}\}$ and to each $x_i \in \mathcal{V}_T$ the kind $\bullet$. If Δ is an environment, T a type and $x \notin Dom(\Delta)$, we shall write $\Delta(x : T)$ for the environment obtained from Δ by appending the pair $x : T$ to Δ. We will sometimes write just $x \in \Delta$ for $x \in Dom(\Delta)$ and $\Delta(x) = T$ whenever Δ has the form $\Delta'(x : T)\Delta''$ for some Δ' and Δ''. The structure of environments also enables us to write a term $\lambda \overline{x_n : X_n}.m$ simply as $\lambda \Delta.m$. If T is a type with all of its free variables declared in Δ we will call T a Δ-*type*. Thus one has $\Delta(x_i)$ a Δ-type for every value variable $x_i \in \Delta$.

The following natural deduction proof system defines validity of typing judgements of the form $\Delta \triangleright t : T$, where Δ is an environment, t a value term and T a type term. A valid judgement asserts that t is well-typed with type T in Δ.

$$[R_1] \; \Delta \triangleright c : \Sigma(c) \qquad [R_2] \; \Delta \triangleright x : \Delta(x) \quad \text{whenever } x \in \mathcal{V}_t$$

$$[\Rightarrow_E] \; \frac{\Delta \triangleright a : A \Rightarrow B \quad \Delta \triangleright b : A}{\Delta \triangleright (ab) : B} \qquad [\Rightarrow_I] \; \frac{\Delta x : A \triangleright b : B}{\Delta \triangleright (\lambda x : A.b) : A \Rightarrow B}$$

$$[\Pi_I] \; \frac{\Delta(X : \bullet) \triangleright b : B}{\Delta \triangleright (\Lambda X.b) : \Pi X.B} \qquad [\Pi_E] \; \frac{\Delta \triangleright a : \Pi X.B}{\Delta \triangleright (aT) : B[X/T]}$$

In rule $[\Pi_E]$, T is any Δ-type. If $\Delta \triangleright t : T$ is a valid typing judgement we write $\Delta \vdash t : T$. If $\Delta \vdash b : B$ then we call b a Δ-term.

We assume the usual notions of β and η reduction and conversion in Λ_Π and recall that strong normalization and confluence holds for well-typed terms.

Besides the usual concepts concerning η-expansion and rigid and flexible terms due to [8], we will assume the following further conventions and notations. A term is in *canonical form* (cform) if and only if its β-normal and η-expanded. Given a term t, we will denote by $t\downarrow_\beta$ the β-nf of t and by $t\downarrow$ the canonical form of t. Given a term u in β-nf, its cform can be obtained by just performing η-expansion; this we shall denote by $\uparrow^\eta(u)$.

When writing $\lambda \overline{x_m}.m$ we assume m not an abstraction unless otherwise stated. When writing $\lambda \overline{x_m}.h(v_1 \ldots v_p)$ we assume h not an application. A term $u_x =_\eta x$ for a variable x is called a *simple* occurrence of x. For a type variable X a *simple* occurrence is an occurrence in a type $T \equiv X$ (ie. an occurrence not embedded in a more complex type term). We now introduce substitutions.

Let Δ and Δ' be environments. A well-typed substitution of domain Δ and codomain Δ' is a function $\theta : \mathcal{V}_T \cup \mathcal{V}_t \to P_\Pi$ subject to the following conditions: 1. $\theta(x) \neq x$ only at a finite number of points. 2. If $X \in \Delta$ is a type variable then $\theta(X)$ is a Δ'-type. 3. If x is a value variable such that $\Delta \vdash x{:}X$ then $\Delta' \vdash \theta(x){:}\theta(X)$.

To make explicit the domain Δ and codomain Δ' of a substitution θ we shall use the notation $\theta : \Delta \to \Delta'$. By ι_Δ we shall denote the identity substitution on Δ. We extend a substitution to all terms is the usual way. Hence a substitution $\theta : \Delta \to \Delta'$ when applied to a term $\Delta \vdash t{:}T$ yields a term $\Delta' \vdash \theta(t){:}\theta(T)$.

Two substitutions θ and θ' are $\beta\eta$-equivalent (written $\theta = \theta'$) if they have the same domain Δ and $\theta(x) =_{\beta\eta} \theta'(x)$ for every $x \in \Delta$. We compose $\theta : \Delta \to \Delta'$ with $\theta' : \Delta' \to \Delta''$ to obtain a substitution $\theta' {\circ} \theta : \Delta \to \Delta''$ defined by $(\theta' {\circ} \theta)(x) = \theta'(\theta(x))$ for every $x \in \Delta$. The action $\theta[t]$ of a substitution θ on a term t is defined to be $\theta(t){\downarrow}$. Note that $\theta(x) =_{\beta\eta} \theta'(x)$ if and only if $\theta[x] \equiv \theta'[x]$. If θ and θ' are substitutions then θ is more general than θ' (written $\theta \leq \theta'$) whenever $\rho \circ \theta =_{\beta\eta} \theta'$ for some substitution ρ.

3   Towards Unification in Λ_Π

In this section we discuss the problem of unifying terms of Λ_Π. The higher-order unification problem addressed is the one of finding a substitution θ such that $\theta(a) =_{\beta\eta} \theta(b)$ for given terms a and b. We assume here familiarity with Huet's pre-unification algorithm HU [8, 21] and address the problem of adapting it from the simply-typed calculus to Λ_Π. Our methodology will be to define a suitable and statically determinable restriction of Λ_Π that while being sufficiently expressive to provide a basis for a polymorphic higher-order programming language, could admit a complete (pre-)unification (semi-)algorithm in the style of HU and still contain as a proper subset the simply-typed calculus.

1. When we consider variable types, a problem occurs wrt the generation of projection bindings when either T or the target type of some U_i is a free variable (therefore subject to instantiation). For example, consider $\chi = [i \mapsto \bullet, j \mapsto \bullet]$, $\Sigma = [c \mapsto i]$ and $\Delta = \{X{:}\bullet, u{:}X, F{:}i \Rightarrow X \Rightarrow i\}$, and the pair of Δ-terms

$$F(c, u) \doteq c \tag{1}$$

Suppose that θ unifies (1). Note that independently of the type X' that θ assigns to X, $\theta(F)$ may have the form (of a projection binding) $\lambda y{:}i\lambda z{:}X'.y$. However, if (say) $\theta(X) = i$ one may also consider $\theta(F) = \lambda y{:}i\lambda z{:}i.z$. As a matter of fact, one can see that for each substitution assigning to X some type of the form $X' \equiv T_1 \Rightarrow \ldots \Rightarrow T_n \Rightarrow i$ one must consider for F a binding term of the form $\lambda y{:}i\lambda z{:}X'.z(H_1, H_2 \ldots H_n)$. Hence,

$$\{\theta | \theta = [u/\lambda \overline{y_n{:}i}.y_n, F/\lambda y{:}i.\lambda z{:}T.z(\overbrace{y, \ldots, y}^{n}), X/T] \text{ where } T \equiv \overbrace{i \Rightarrow \ldots i}^{n} \Rightarrow i\}$$

is a set of independent unifiers for (1). Therefore, an infinite number of choices for projection bindings (depending on appropriate type) for which there is no suitable finite set of approximating substitutions may exist, just like in the flexible-flexible of HU. The approaches of [17, 16] tackle this problem by commiting (at runtime) the target types in question to be atomic and are therefore not complete. We suggest requiring that whenever a rigid-flexible pair like

$$F(\overline{u_m}) \doteq c(\overline{v_n}) \tag{2}$$

is encountered in the course of unification the type T of the matrix $F(\overline{u_m})$ be such that it could not be instantiated to an $\Rightarrow$ or Π type. To insure the invariance of this property during unification, we require both components of a disagreement pair to have the same type, and every rigid-matrix in the original unification problem to be of Π_L type[1]. However, this simpler condition is not sufficient, some additional requirements are required to enable the projection terms to be finitely determined. To be precise, we require that for every value[2] term u_i appearing as argument to the free variable F either its target type is a Π_L, in which case we can test if u_i is a candidate for projection based on type information, or else u_i must have the simple structure of a bound variable. In this last case, we can project u_i if and only if $u_i =_\eta c$. Note that requiring rigid matrices to have non-extensible type makes the absence of type information for determining projection bindings coincide with the presence of flexible-flexible pairs in a unification problem. Since we are only aiming at pre-unification, this turns out to be very convenient.

2. Another point concerns the order by which arguments of rigid terms are pairwise unified. Note that HU does not depend on any particular order by which rules (ie. decomposition, imitation, projection) are actually applied. Since we require (like HU does) both components of a disagreement pair to have the same type, one cannot maintain such a freedom when unifying terms of Λ_Π. For instance, let χ be as above, $\Sigma = [c \mapsto \Pi X.(X \Rightarrow i)]$ and $\Delta = \{X:\bullet, Y:\bullet, x:X, y:Y\}$. One cannot decompose the homogeneous pair of Δ-terms $c(X,x) \doteq c(Y,y)$ into $X \doteq Y, x \doteq y$ because $x \doteq y$ is a heterogeneous pair. However, if we first unify the types of x and y by solving $X \doteq Y$ by say $\tau = [X/Z, Y/Z] : \Delta \to \Delta'$ where $\Delta' = \{Z:\bullet, x:Z, y:Z\}$, then we can proceed with the homogeneous pair $x \doteq y$ of Δ'-terms. It is crucial here that we can always decide locally the unifiability of type terms and compute mgus whenever they exist. This contrasts with the solution of [5] for a similar problem with unification in λ_Π (the λ-calculus with dependent types of the LF system).

3. Another problem that must be tackled concerns the treatment of arguments of flexible terms, due to their intimate role in projection. We first address type arguments. Consider again (2) and let $u_{p_1}, \ldots, u_{p_v}$ and $u_{q_1}, \ldots, u_{q_t}$ be enumerations of respectively the value and type arguments to F. Likewise let $v_{r_1}, \ldots, v_{r'_v}$ and $v_{s_1}, \ldots, v_{s'_t}$ be enumerations of respectively the value and type arguments to c. Now consider the general form of an imitation binding for F: it must have the form $\lambda x_m:\overline{U_m}.c(\overline{A_n})$ where $A_{s_1} \ldots A_{s'_t}$ are type terms and $A_{r_1} \ldots A_{r'_v}$ are value terms. Since each of $x_{q_1} \ldots x_{q_t}$ is a type variable, we conclude that

$$A_{s_i}[\overline{x_{q_t}/\theta(u_{q_t})}] \equiv \theta(v_{s_i}) \tag{3}$$

If a substitution is allowed to act on each u_{q_t}, since each A_n is also determined by θ, we see that for each instance $\theta(v_{s_i})$ of v_{s_i} there are in general many ways of satisfying (3) be varying A_{s_i} and $\theta(u_{q_j})$ for $1 \leq j \leq t$. Such makes the search for general solutions of a unifier very undirected, much like in the flexible-flexible case for value terms. Obviously we cannot prohibit every occurrence of type terms as arguments to free variables, not only because of their contribution to the expressive power of the language, but because they turn out to be necessary (just consider the cform of a free variable of polymorphic type). However, it is clear from preceding remarks that some restriction is needed. Therefore, both to avoid such type terms to be instantiated, and to obtain a deterministic and decidable type unification problem, we find convenient adopting the L_λ restriction [11] to type terms. That means that

---

[1] These *non-extensible* types (Π_L types) will be formally defined later.
[2] Some of the u_j may be type terms.

type arguments to free variables are required to be distinct bound variables. This approach also has the advantage of being smoothly integrable into an algorithm for computing unifiers in the context of embedded existential and universal quantifiers [12], as required for logic programming languages with universally quantified goals, and also it enables the basic language of Λ_Π to be sligthly enriched.

We now turn to value arguments. To motivate the discussion, we present the following example. Let χ be as previously, $\Sigma = [r \mapsto \Pi Y.i]$, $\Delta = \{F : \Pi X.((\Pi Y.i) \Rightarrow i)\}$ and the flexible Δ-term $a \equiv \Lambda Z.F(Z, \Lambda X.F(X, r))$.

Note that $\rho = [F/\Lambda Z \lambda f : (\Pi Y.i).f(HZ)] : \Delta \to \Delta'$ with $\Delta' = \Delta(H : \bullet^2)$ is an appropriate projection binding for F, and that both a and $\rho(F)$ satisfy every restriction suggested until now. However, $\rho(a)$ β reduces to the Δ'-term $\Lambda Z.F(HZ, r)$. Clearly, this term does not satisfy the conditions required for type arguments to flexible terms, since the type HZ occurring as argument to the free variable F is not a bound variable. But we must surely require our restricted language to be closed under substitution and normalization. Therefore we cannot permit at argument places of flexible terms the occurrence of terms that upon projection can place arbitrary types at argument places of flexible terms, like does $\Lambda X.F(X, r)$ in the above example. Hence we restrict value arguments of flexible terms to *determining* (FD) terms, to be formally defined later. Essentially, FD terms insure the closure of Π^* under substitution and normalization by placing all their type and extensible type value parameters at argument places of rigid matrices.

4 Unification in Π^*

In this section we present the restricted language Π^* and its (pre)-unification algorithm. See [1] for full proofs of the presented results. As justified above, we need to extend in a non essential way the type language $\mathcal{T}$ defined in Sec.2 in order to cope with variables of 'higher kind'. To that end, assume for every kind k a set V_k of type variables of kind k. In particular, let $V_\bullet = \mathcal{V}_T$. By 'type variable' we will usually mean of kind $\bullet$, unless otherwise stated.

4.1 The language of Π^*

Our definition of Π^* (type and value) terms will be relativized to certain *quantifier prefixes*[3]. Prefixes record scopes of variables in the course of proof searching. A quantifier prefix $\mathcal{P}$ is a environment $\mathcal{P}_{cx}$ plus an assignment to each variable X in the domain of $\mathcal{P}$ of a quantifier $\mathbf{Q} \in \{\Pi, \Sigma\}$. Those variables annotated with Π (resp. Σ) will be called universal (resp. existential) in $\mathcal{P}$. To make explicit the structure of a prefix we sometimes write $(\mathbf{Q}x_1 : X_1) \ldots (\mathbf{Q}x_n : X_n)$ for a prefix, and refer $\mathcal{P}_{cx}$-terms by just $\mathcal{P}$-terms. The notations $(\mathbf{Q}x : X) \in \mathcal{P}$ and $X \in \mathcal{P}$ with $\mathcal{P}$ a prefix will be used in the obvious sense. We can also extend the notions of rigid/flexible to $\mathcal{P}$-terms. A $\mathcal{P}$-term $\lambda \Delta.h(\overline{v_n})$ is called $\mathcal{P}$-rigid if h is either a constant, a variable in Δ or a universal variable in $\mathcal{P}$. The same $\mathcal{P}$-term is called $\mathcal{P}$-flexible if h is a existential variable in $\mathcal{P}$. Given a prefix $\mathcal{P}$, define the ordering $\prec_\mathcal{P}$ among variables in the domain of $\mathcal{P}$ by: $x \prec_\mathcal{P} y$ if and only if $\mathcal{P}$ has the form $\mathcal{L}(\mathbf{Q}x : X)\mathcal{M}(\mathbf{Q}'y : Y)\mathcal{R}$ for some prefixes $\mathcal{L}$, $\mathcal{M}$ and $\mathcal{R}$ and quantifiers $\mathbf{Q}$ and $\mathbf{Q}'$. We are finally in a position to introduce the Π^* types.

Let $\mathcal{P}$ be a prefix. Then $\Pi_\mathcal{P}$ is the class of types such that: If $(\mathbf{Q}X : \bullet) \in \mathcal{P}$ then $X \in \Pi_\mathcal{P}$. If $\mathcal{P} = \mathcal{L}(\Sigma F : \bullet^{n+1})\mathcal{R}$ and $\overline{X_n}$ are distinct and universal in $\mathcal{R}$ then

---

[3]Most of the prefix-related concepts presented here are due to [12].

$F\overline{X_n} \in \Pi_{\mathcal{P}}$. If $A_i \in \Pi_{\mathcal{P}}$ and $k \in \mathcal{KC}$ with $\chi(k) = \bullet^{n+1}$ then $k(\overline{A_i}) \in \Pi_{\mathcal{P}}$. If $A \in \Pi_{\mathcal{P}}$ and $B \in \Pi_{\mathcal{P}}$ then $(A \Rightarrow B) \in \Pi_{\mathcal{P}}$. If $A \in \Pi_{\mathcal{P'}}$ with $\mathcal{P'} = \mathcal{P}(\Pi X : \bullet)$ then $\Pi X.A \in \Pi_{\mathcal{P}}$ and $\Lambda X.A \in \Pi_{\mathcal{P}}$. Thus the $\Pi_{\mathcal{P}}$ types are but the types of Sec.2 but now we also allow existential type variables of higher kind to occur in some circumstances. Note also the definition of types with the form $\Lambda X.A$. These higher kind types are needed to define substitution terms for generalized type variables. For the sake of simplicity we will refer from now by Π^* types the $\Pi_{\mathcal{P}}$ types, abstracting over the prefixes $\mathcal{P}$.

Since our main concern will be with the Π^* types we shall restrict ourselves to well formed prefixes in the following sense: for every value variable $x \in \mathcal{P}$, $T \in \Pi_{\mathcal{P}}$ whenever $\mathcal{P} \vdash x : T$. Now we can define the Π_L types alluded to in Sec.3.

Let $\mathcal{P}$ be a prefix. Define $\Pi^L_{\mathcal{P}}$ to be the smallest subclass of $\Pi_{\mathcal{P}}$ closed under the following formation rules. 1. If X is a type variable universal in $\mathcal{P}$ then $X \in \Pi^L_{\mathcal{P}}$. 2. If $A_i \in \Pi_{\mathcal{P}}$ and $k \in \mathcal{KC}$ with $\chi(k) = \bullet^{n+1}$ then $k(\overline{A_n}) \in \Pi^L_{\mathcal{P}}$. 3. If $A \in \Pi^L_{\mathcal{P}}$ and $B \in \Pi^L_{\mathcal{P}}$ then $A \Rightarrow B \in \Pi^L_{\mathcal{P}}$. 4. If $A \in \Pi^L_{\mathcal{P'}}$ with $\mathcal{P'} = \mathcal{P}(\Pi X : \bullet)$ then $\Pi X.A \in \Pi^L_{\mathcal{P}}$.

Any $\Pi^L_{\mathcal{P}}$ type constructed using only rules (2-3) above will be called a *simple* $\Pi^L_{\mathcal{P}}$ type. Given a type T, an occurrence defined by a context $E\langle\rangle$ of a type variable X in $T \equiv E\langle X \rangle$ is said to be *neutral* if and only if it is not an occurrence as an argument of some variable of higher kind and $E\langle\rangle \equiv F\langle k(\dots G\langle\rangle \dots)\rangle$ for some contexts $F\langle\rangle$ and $G\langle\rangle$. Note that every occurrence of an existential variable in a $\Pi^L_{\mathcal{P}}$ type is neutral. The point for neutrality is the following: Let $\mathcal{P} = \mathcal{L}(\Pi X)\mathcal{R}$. If $A \in \Pi^L_{\mathcal{P}}$ and some universal variable X of $\mathcal{P}$ is neutral in A then $A \in \Pi^L_{\mathcal{P'}}$ where $\mathcal{P'} = \mathcal{L}(\Sigma X)\mathcal{R}$. In other words, the non-extensibility of a type does not depend on neutral occurrences of universal variables (compare with a case where X is not neutral, say $A \equiv X \to X \in \Pi^L_{\mathcal{P}}$).

We now define the *determining* terms motivated in Sec.3.

Definition 4.1 *Let Δ be a set of universal variables in $\mathcal{P}$.*
A $\mathcal{P}$-term $m \equiv \lambda\overline{y_n}.u_0(\overline{u_p})$ is $\mathcal{P}$-Δ-FD if : (a) Every free occurrence of $x \in \Delta$ in m is in a simple occurrence u_x of x, with u_x an argument of a $\mathcal{P}$-rigid matrix, unless x is of simple $\Pi^L_{\mathcal{P}}$ type. (b) Every free occurrence of $X \in \Delta$ in the type of a matrix inside some u_j is neutral, unless that matrix occurs inside a simple occurrence of some $x \in \Delta$. A cform $\mathcal{P}$-term $\lambda\Delta.m$ is determining (FD) in $\mathcal{P}$ if its matrix m is $\mathcal{P}(\Pi\Delta)$-Δ-FD, has $\Pi^L_{\mathcal{P}(\Pi\Delta)}$ type and has as argument a simple occurrence of every type variable $X \in \Delta$.

The reason for requiring type and value parameters of FD terms not of simple Π_L type to occur but as arguments of rigid matrices was already justified in Sec.3. The restriction to neutral occurrences of type parameters is needed so that rigid matrices inside the FD term are kept of non-extensible type when a projection occurs. We also required every type parameter to a FD term to occur simple in its toplevel (rigid) matrix to permit type arguments of projection bindings to be locally decided (see *Rigid-Flex-Proj-II* rule in next section).

For simple examples of determining terms (in any prefix) take any simply-typed term or any constant $c \in \Sigma$ in cform. We finally define the value terms of Π^* (ie. $\Pi_{\mathcal{P}}$ for some $\mathcal{P}$). The definition essentially integrates the ideas of Sec.3. The structure of Π^* terms will be formally presented by a proof system. The system actually defines G-indexed classes $\mathbf{C}^G_{\mathcal{P}}$ of $\mathcal{P}$-terms, where G is a set of universal (type or value) variables of $\mathcal{P}$. Let b be a value term. Then $b \in \Pi_{\mathcal{P}}$ whenever $b \in \mathbf{C}^{\emptyset}_{\mathcal{P}}$ has a proof in the system below.

Abstraction   *Rigid* (h constant or universal variable in $\mathcal{P}$)

$$\frac{m \in \mathbf{C}^G_{\mathcal{P}(\Pi x:T)}}{\lambda x{:}T.m \in \mathbf{C}^G_{\mathcal{P}}} \qquad \frac{T \in \Pi^L_{\mathcal{P}} \quad v_{\lambda_i} =_\eta z \in G \text{ or } v_{\lambda_i} \in \mathbf{C}^G_{\mathcal{P}} \text{ for } 1 \le i \le r}{h(v_1, v_2, \dots, v_m) \in \mathbf{C}^G_{\mathcal{P}}}$$

Flexible (h existential in $\mathcal{P}$)

$$\frac{v_{\lambda_i} =_\eta z \text{ universal in } \mathcal{P} \text{ or } v_{\lambda_i} \ \mathcal{P}\text{-}G\text{-admissible for } 1 \le i \le r}{h(v_1, v_2, \dots, v_m) \in \mathbf{C}^G_{\mathcal{P}}}$$

In each rule above assume $\mathcal{P} \vdash t : T$ with $T \in \Pi_{\mathcal{P}}$ for each term t in the conclusion. Let Λ_i for $1 \le i \le t$ enumerate the type arguments of $h(\overline{v_m})$ and λ_j for $1 \le j \le r$ its value arguments. In *Rigid* we require $v_{\Lambda_j} \in \Pi_{\mathcal{P}}$ for $1 \le j \le t$. In *Flexible*, by $v_{\lambda_i} \equiv \lambda \nabla .m$ to be $\mathcal{P}$-G-admissible we mean v_{λ_i} determining in $\mathcal{P}$ and also the inductive condition $m \in \mathbf{C}^{G'}_{\mathcal{P}'}$ where $G' = G \cup Dom(\nabla)$ and $\mathcal{P}' = \mathcal{P}(\Pi \nabla)$. In the same rule it is also required that $v_{\Lambda_1} \dots v_{\Lambda_t}$ are distinct universally quantified type variables in $\mathcal{P}$ to the right of (Σh). In *Abstraction*, m can be any term. Note that for every simply-typed term t one has $t \in \Pi_{\mathcal{P}}$ for every $\mathcal{P}$.

Having defined Π^*, we can now present the essential property of FD terms.

Lemma 4.2 *Let* $f = \lambda \overline{x_n{:}T_n}.m \in \Pi_{\mathcal{P}}$ *be* FD*, and* $\overline{u_n}$ *any* $\Pi_{\mathcal{P}}$ *terms. Then* $(f u_1 u_2 \dots u_n) \!\downarrow\, \in \Pi_{\mathcal{P}}$.

We now turn to substitution in Π^*, and start by noting that we need to modify and complement some of previous definitions. Condition 2 in the definition of well-typed substitution must be replaced by: 2′. If $F{:}\bullet^{n+1} \in \Delta$ then $\theta(F) = \Lambda \overline{X_n}.A$ for some $\Delta'\{X_1{:}\bullet, \dots, X_n{:}\bullet\}$-type A and $n \ge 0$. Also, if θ is such that $\theta(F) = \Lambda \overline{Y_n}.A$ and $F\overline{X_n}$ a $\Pi_{\mathcal{P}}$ type, then by $\theta(F\overline{X_n})$ we mean $A[\overline{Y_n}/\overline{X_n}]$.

One of the motivations for prefixes is to make explicit scoping constraints for substitutions. We now make this comment precise, defining a *prefix substitution* $\theta : \mathcal{P} \to \mathcal{P}'$ to be a well-typed substitution $\theta : \mathcal{P}_{cx} \to \mathcal{P}'_{cx}$ such that:

1. Every universal variable x of $\mathcal{P}$ is universal in $\mathcal{P}'$ and $\theta(x) = x$. 2. If x is existential in $\mathcal{P}$ then $\theta(x)$ does not contain occurrences of universal variables z_i of $\mathcal{P}$ such that $x \prec_{\mathcal{P}} z_i$. 3. If $x \prec_{\mathcal{P}} y$ and y is universal in $\mathcal{P}$ then $z \prec_{\mathcal{P}'} y$ for every $z \in FV(\theta(x))$ existential in $\mathcal{P}'$.

Since our concern is with Π^* call Π^*-substitution to a prefix substitution $\theta : \mathcal{P} \to \mathcal{P}'$ such that $\theta(x) \in \Pi_{\mathcal{P}'}$ for every value variable $x \in \mathcal{P}$ and $\theta(X) \in \Pi_{\mathcal{P}'}$ for every type variable $X \in \mathcal{P}$.

We now present the following fundamental result, concerning the closure of Π^* under substitution and reduction to canonical form.

Theorem 4.3 *Let* $b \in \Pi_{\mathcal{P}}$ *and* $\theta : \mathcal{P} \to \mathcal{Q}$ *a prefix* Π^*-*substitution. Then* $\theta[b] \in \Pi_{\mathcal{Q}}$.

We now define unification problems.

A *type unification problem* is a pair $\mathcal{P} \triangleright S$ where $\mathcal{P}$ is a prefix and S is a multiset of equations of the form $A \doteq B$ where A and B are $\mathcal{P}$-types. Let $\mathcal{P} \triangleright S$ be a type unification problem. A $\mathcal{P}$-*unifier* of S is a $\mathcal{P}$-substitution $\theta : \mathcal{P} \to \mathcal{P}'$ such that $\theta(A) \equiv \theta(B)$ for every equation $A \doteq B \in S$. A *value unification problem* is a pair $\mathcal{P} \triangleright S$ where $\mathcal{P}$ is a prefix and S is a multiset of equations of the form $a \doteq b$ with a and b value $\mathcal{P}$-terms of the same type such that $a, b \in \mathbf{C}^\emptyset_{\mathcal{P}}$.

Let $\mathcal{P} \triangleright S$ be a (value) unification problem. The following usual notions also apply. A $\mathcal{P}$-*unifier* of S is a $\mathcal{P}$-substitution $\theta : \mathcal{P} \to \mathcal{P}'$ such that $\theta(a) =_{\beta\eta} \theta(b)$

(ie. $\theta[a] \equiv \theta[b]$) for every $a \doteq b \in S$. A *most general $\mathcal{P}$-unifier* of S is a $\mathcal{P}$-unifier θ of S such that $\theta \leq \theta'$ for every $\mathcal{P}$-unifier θ' of S. A *$\mathcal{P}$-preunifier* of S is a $\mathcal{P}$-substitution $\theta : \mathcal{P} \to \mathcal{P}'$ such that $\theta(S)$ consists of equations between flexible terms. The notion of *most general $\mathcal{P}$-preunifier* also applies. In is possible to show that every $\mathcal{P}$-preunifier $\theta : \mathcal{P} \to \mathcal{P}'$ can be extended to a $\mathcal{P}$-unifier $\xi\theta$ by composition with a certain substitution $\xi : \mathcal{P}' \to \mathcal{P}''$.

The presentation of the unification algorithm follows.

The algorithm is structured into two main components, an algorithm to perform type unification, and a semi-algorithm to perform value unification.

The type unification algorithm is based on a system of transition rules on type unification problems. Each transition rule has the form $\mathcal{P} \vartriangleright L \longrightarrow_\theta \mathcal{P}' \vartriangleright R$ where $\mathcal{P} \vartriangleright L$ and $\mathcal{P}' \vartriangleright R$ are type unification problems and $\theta : \mathcal{P} \to \mathcal{P}'$ a Π^* substitution. A computation with these transition rules consists in a sequence $\mathcal{P}_1 \vartriangleright L_1 \longrightarrow_{\theta_1} \mathcal{P}_2 \vartriangleright L_2 \longrightarrow_{\theta_2} \cdots \longrightarrow_{\theta_n} \mathcal{P}_{n+1} \vartriangleright L_{n+1}$ of transitions. Such n step transition sequences will be written $\mathcal{P} \vartriangleright L \xrightarrow{n}_\theta \mathcal{P}' \vartriangleright R$ with $\theta = \theta_n\theta_{n-1}\ldots\theta_1$.

RR $\quad : \mathcal{P} \vartriangleright k(\overline{A_n}) \doteq k(\overline{B_n}), S \longrightarrow_{\iota_\mathcal{P}} \mathcal{P} \vartriangleright A_1 \doteq B_1, \ldots, A_n \doteq B_n, S$

U $\quad : \mathcal{P} \vartriangleright X \doteq X, S \longrightarrow_{\iota_\mathcal{P}} \mathcal{P} \vartriangleright S$

Q $\quad : \mathcal{P} \vartriangleright \Pi X.A \doteq \Pi X.B, S \longrightarrow_{\iota_\mathcal{P}} \mathcal{P}(\Pi X) \vartriangleright A \doteq B, S$

FRU $\quad : \mathcal{L}(\Sigma F)\mathcal{R} \vartriangleright F\overline{X_n} \doteq X, S \longrightarrow_\rho \mathcal{L}\mathcal{R}' \vartriangleright \rho(S)$

FRQ $\quad : \mathcal{L}(\Sigma F)\mathcal{R} \vartriangleright F\overline{X_n} \doteq \Pi Z.A, S \longrightarrow_\rho \mathcal{L}(\Sigma G)\mathcal{R}'(\Pi Z) \vartriangleright G\overline{X_n}Z \doteq A, \rho(S)$

FRC $\quad : \mathcal{L}(\Sigma F)\mathcal{R} \vartriangleright F\overline{X_n} \doteq k(\overline{A_m}), S \longrightarrow_\rho \mathcal{L}\mathcal{M}\mathcal{R}' \vartriangleright \overline{H_m\overline{X_n}} \doteq A_m, \rho(S)$

FFD $\quad : \mathcal{L}(\Sigma F)\mathcal{M}(\Sigma G)\mathcal{R} \vartriangleright F\overline{X_n} \doteq G\overline{Y_m}, S \longrightarrow_\rho \mathcal{L}(\Sigma H)\mathcal{R}' \vartriangleright \rho(S)$

FFS $\quad : \mathcal{L}(\Sigma F)\mathcal{R} \vartriangleright F\overline{X_n} \doteq F\overline{Y_n}, S \longrightarrow_\rho \mathcal{L}(\Sigma H)\mathcal{R}' \vartriangleright \rho(S)$

For brevity, we have ommited kinds of variables in prefixes. In rule RR we also include the arrow $\Rightarrow$. In rule FRU let $\rho = [F/\Lambda\overline{X_n}.X]$ and $\mathcal{R}' = \rho(\mathcal{R})$: if X is universal in $\mathcal{R}$ raise failure (bound variable capture). In rule FRC let $\rho = [F/\Lambda\overline{X_n}.k(H_1\overline{X_n}\ldots H_m\overline{X_n})]$, $\mathcal{M} = (\Sigma\overline{H_n})$ and $\mathcal{R}' = \rho(\mathcal{R})$. If F occurs free in $k(\overline{A_m})$ raise failure (occurs-check). In rule FRQ let $\rho = [F/\Lambda\overline{X_n}.\Pi Z.G\overline{X_n}Z]$. In rule FFD, let $\rho = [F/\Lambda\overline{X_n}.H\overline{Z_p}, G/\Lambda\overline{Y_m}.H\overline{Z_p}]$ where $\overline{Z_p} = \overline{X_n} \cap (\overline{U_q} \cup \overline{Y_m})$, $\overline{U_q}$ are the universal type variables in $\mathcal{M}$ and $\mathcal{R}' = \rho(\mathcal{M}\mathcal{R})$. In rule FFS, let $\rho = [F/\Lambda\overline{X_n}.H\overline{Z_p}]$ where $\overline{Z_p} = \{X_i | X_i \equiv Y_i\}$ and $\mathcal{R}' = \rho(\mathcal{M}\mathcal{R})$.

A detailed exposition of this algorithm cannot be included here. However, note that this is simply a simple adaptation of Miller's L_λ unification algorithm [11]. For the above algorithm we can prove

Theorem 4.4 *1. Let $\mathcal{P} \vartriangleright S$ be unifiable by a $\mathcal{P}$-unifier σ. Then every sequence of unification transitions for $\mathcal{P} \vartriangleright S$ can be extended to a sequence of the form $\mathcal{P} \vartriangleright S \xrightarrow{*}_\theta \mathcal{P}' \vartriangleright \emptyset$ with $\theta : \mathcal{P} \to \mathcal{P}'$ a $\mathcal{P}$-unifier of S more general that σ. 2. Let $\mathcal{P} \vartriangleright S$ be a unification problem. If there is no $\mathcal{P}$-unifier of S then every sequence of transitions can only be extended to sequences $\mathcal{P} \vartriangleright S \xrightarrow{n}_\theta \mathcal{P}' \vartriangleright S'$ such that S' is non-empty and no rule applies.*

We proceed with the presentation of the semi-algorithm for unification of values, also by means of a system of transition rules on unification problems. Each transition rule has either the form $\mathcal{P} \vartriangleright L \Longrightarrow_\theta \mathcal{P}' \vartriangleright R$ or the form

$$\frac{\dagger}{\mathcal{P} \vartriangleright L \Longrightarrow_\theta \mathcal{P}' \vartriangleright R}$$

where $\mathcal{P} \rhd L$ and $\mathcal{P}' \rhd R$ are unification problems, $\theta : \mathcal{P} \to \mathcal{P}'$ a Π^* $\mathcal{P}$-substitution and $\dagger$ some prerequisite on the application of the rule expressed by a computation of the type unification algorithm. Computation with these transition rules is similar to those of the type unification algorithm, as well as the way of extracting its result. We now present the system of rules. In each one assume c a constant or universal variable in $\mathcal{P}$ and F an existential variable in $\mathcal{P}$.

Abs-Abs simply pushes the binders into the prefix.

Abs-Abs:

$$\mathcal{P} \rhd \lambda \overline{x_n : A_n}.a \doteq \lambda \overline{x_n : A_n}.b, S \Longrightarrow_{\iota_p} \mathcal{P}(\Pi x_1 : A_1) \dots (\Pi x_n : A_n) \rhd a \doteq b, S$$

Rig-Rig pairwise unifies the value arguments u_{λ_j} and v_{λ_j} after performing pairwise unification of type arguments u_{Λ_j} and v_{Λ_j} as shown to be required in Sec.3.

Rig-Rig:

$$\frac{\mathcal{P} \rhd u_{\Lambda_1} \doteq v_{\Lambda_1}, \ \dots \ , u_{\Lambda_k} \doteq v_{\Lambda_k} \overset{*}{\longrightarrow}_\theta \mathcal{P}' \rhd \emptyset}{\mathcal{P} \rhd c(\overline{u_m}) \doteq c(\overline{v_m}), S \Longrightarrow_\theta \mathcal{P}' \rhd \theta(u_{\lambda_1}) \doteq \theta(v_{\lambda_1}), \ \dots \ , \theta(u_{\lambda_n}) \doteq \theta(v_{\lambda_n}), \theta(S)}$$

We will consider from now on flexible-rigid pairs of the form $F(\overline{u_n}) \doteq c(\overline{v_m})$. Assume $\mathcal{P} \vdash F : T_1 \Rightarrow \dots T_n \Rightarrow T$ and $\mathcal{P} \vdash c : C_1 \Rightarrow \dots C_m \Rightarrow C$. We shall refer by u_{λ_q} (u_{Λ_r}) the value (type) arguments of F and by v_{λ_t} (v_{Λ_p}) the the value (type) arguments of c. *Rig-Flex-Imit* is similar to the imitation rule of HU.

Rig-Flex-Imit:

$$\frac{\mathcal{P}' \rhd v_{\Lambda_1} \doteq H_1 \overline{u_{\Lambda_r}}, \dots, v_{\Lambda_p} \doteq H_p \overline{u_{\Lambda_r}} \longrightarrow_\tau \mathcal{P}'' \rhd \emptyset}{\mathcal{P} \rhd F(\overline{u_n}) \doteq c(\overline{v_m}), S \overset{*}{\Longrightarrow}_\theta \mathcal{P}'' \rhd \theta(G_1(\overline{u_n})) \doteq \theta(v_{\lambda_1}) \dots \theta(G_j(\overline{u_n})) \doteq \theta(v_{\lambda_j}), \theta(S)}$$

where $\mathcal{P} = \mathcal{L}(\Sigma F)\mathcal{R}$, $\mathcal{P}' = \mathcal{L}(\Sigma \overline{H_p : \bullet^r})(\Sigma \overline{G_t : T_t^G})\mathcal{R}$ and

$$\theta : \mathcal{P} \to \mathcal{P}'' = \tau \circ [F/\lambda \overline{x_n : T_n}.c(\overline{A_m})]$$

$$A_{\lambda_j} \equiv G_j(\overline{x_n}) \ 1 \le j \le t \quad A_{\Lambda_i} \equiv H_i \overline{x_{\Lambda_r}} \ 1 \le i \le p$$

Note the introduction of the new variables $\overline{H_p}$ (each of kind $\bullet^r$) and $\overline{G_t}$ (each of type $T_j^G \equiv T_1 \Rightarrow \dots T_n \Rightarrow C_{\lambda_j}[C_{\Lambda_p}/A_{\Lambda_p}]$). These variables have the same role as the fresh variables introduced in HU in order for substitutions to be built incrementally. Note also the use of type unification in determining the correct types $\tau(A_{\Lambda_p})$ to appear in the binding term ρ as arguments to c. We now turn to projection rules *Rig-Flex-Proj-I* and *Rig-Flex-Proj-II*. In both assume $\mathcal{P} \vdash c(\overline{v_m}) : A$ and $\mathcal{P} \vdash u_\pi : T_\pi$ with $T_\pi = U_1 \Rightarrow \dots U_k \Rightarrow P$ for the projected term u_π.

In *Rig-Flex-Proj-I* type information is actually used to select projection terms. This rule is used to project a determining term u_π that do not take type parameters.

Rig-Flex-Proj-I:

$$\frac{\mathcal{P} \rhd A \doteq P \overset{*}{\longrightarrow}_\tau \mathcal{P}' \rhd \emptyset}{\mathcal{P} \rhd F(\overline{u_n}) \doteq c(\overline{v_m}), S \Longrightarrow_{\rho\tau} \mathcal{P}'' \rhd \rho\tau(F(\overline{u_n}) \doteq c(\overline{v_m}), S)}$$

where $\mathcal{P} = \mathcal{L}(\Sigma F)\mathcal{R}$, $\mathcal{P}' = \mathcal{L}'(\Sigma F)\mathcal{R}'$, $\mathcal{P}'' = \mathcal{L}'(\Sigma \overline{G_k : T_k^G})\mathcal{R}'$ and

$$\rho : \mathcal{P}' \to \mathcal{P}'' = [F/\lambda \overline{x_n : T_n'}.x_\pi(\overline{t_k})] \quad t_i \equiv G_i(\overline{x_n}) \ 1 \le i \le k$$

Assume that no U_i corresponds to a type quantification (ie. u_π does not take type arguments). Each of the new variables $\overline{G_k}$ have type $T_j^G \equiv T_1' \Rightarrow \ldots T_n' \Rightarrow U_i'$ where $T_i' \equiv \tau(T_i)$ and $U_i' \equiv \tau(U_i)$. Note that the target types A and P can be safely unified since they are known to be of (atomic) Π_P^L type and therefore admit but instantiations to atomic types.

Rule *Rig-Flex-Proj-II* is used to project either determining terms u_π that actually take types as parameters or terms that are simple occurrences of bound variables. Note that both sorts of such terms have $\mathcal{P}$-rigid heads. So we can use just the head of u_π as guiding information to select the valid projection terms.

Rig-Flex-Proj-II:

$$\frac{\mathcal{P}' \rhd a_{f_1} \doteq v_{f_1} \ldots a_{f_l} \doteq v_{f_l}, H_1 \overline{u_{\Lambda_r}} \doteq v_{\phi(V_1)} \ldots H_p \overline{u_{\Lambda_r}} \doteq v_{\phi(V_p)} \xrightarrow{\ *\ }_\tau \mathcal{P}'' \rhd \emptyset}{\mathcal{P} \rhd F(\overline{u_n}) \doteq c(\overline{v_m}), S \Longrightarrow_\rho \mathcal{P}'' \rhd \rho(F(\overline{u_n}) \doteq c(\overline{v_m}), S)}$$

where $\mathcal{P} = \mathcal{L}(\Sigma F)\mathcal{R}$, $\mathcal{P}' = \mathcal{L}(\Sigma \overline{H_p : \bullet^r})(\Sigma \overline{G_s : T_s^G})\mathcal{R}$ and

$$u_\pi \equiv \lambda \overline{y_k : U_k}.c(\overline{a_h}) \quad \rho : \mathcal{P} \to \mathcal{P}'' = \tau \circ [F/\lambda \overline{x_n : T_n}.x_\pi(A_1 \ldots A_v)] \quad v = m + (k - h)$$

$$A_{g_j} \equiv G_i(\overline{x_n}) \ \ 1 \le i \le s \quad A_{V_i} \equiv H_i \overline{x_{\Lambda_r}} \ \ 1 \le i \le p$$

Let V_i for $1 \le i \le p$ mark the position of the type arguments of u_π (in other words, the position of type quantifications in T_π) and g_i for $1 \le i \le s$ the position of its value arguments. Let ϕ be the injection mapping the index i of every type variable y_i into the index $\phi(i)$ of its simple occurrence $a_{\phi(i)}$ in the topmost matrix of u_π (see Def.4.1), and f_l enumerate the other type arguments of u_π. The new variables $\overline{H_p}$ and $\overline{G_j}$ (each of type $T_i^G \equiv T_1 \Rightarrow \ldots T_n \Rightarrow U_{v_i}[\overline{U_{V_p}/A_{V_p}}]$) have the same role as in previous rules. Note that this rule can be seen as a combination of imitation and projection. For the above rule system one can prove the following result establishing soundness and completeness for unification in Π^*.

Theorem 4.5 *Let $\mathcal{P} \rhd S$ be a well formed Π^* unification problem. 1. If $\mathcal{P} \rhd S$ admits no unifier then the presented algorithm either reaches a problem $\mathcal{P}' \rhd S'$ with at least one rigid-flexible pair to which none of the above rules apply or fails to terminate. 2. If $\mathcal{P} \rhd S$ admits some preunifier σ then there is a computation of the algorithm above that yields a Π^*-preunifier $\theta \ge \sigma$.*

We now present an example of execution of the unification algorithm. Let $\chi = [i \mapsto \bullet]$ and $\Sigma = [o \mapsto \Pi X.(X \Rightarrow X), a \mapsto \Pi X.(X \Rightarrow i), add \mapsto i \Rightarrow i \Rightarrow i, 0 \mapsto i]$. Consider then the problem

$$(\Sigma X : \bullet)(\Sigma F : i \Rightarrow (\Pi Z.Z \Rightarrow Z) \Rightarrow X)$$
$$\rhd$$
$$a \ X \ (F \ 0 \ (\Lambda X.\lambda y : X.o \ X \ y)) \doteq a \ (i \Rightarrow i) \ \lambda x : i.(add \ 0 \ (o \ i \ 0))$$

after applying Rig-Rig (note the use of the type unification algorithm) we get to

$$(\Sigma F : i \Rightarrow (\Pi Z.Z \Rightarrow Z) \Rightarrow i \Rightarrow i)$$
$$\rhd$$
$$\lambda x : i.(F \ 0 \ (\Lambda X.\lambda y : X.o \ X \ y) \ x) \doteq \lambda x : i.(add \ 0 \ (o \ i \ 0))$$

We then apply Abs-Abs, what leads to

$$(\Sigma F : i \Rightarrow (\Pi Z.Z \Rightarrow Z) \Rightarrow i \Rightarrow i)(\Pi x : i) \rhd F \ 0 \ (\Lambda X.\lambda y : X.o \ X \ y) \ x \doteq add \ 0 \ (o \ i \ 0)$$

Imitation with $\rho = [F/\lambda x\!:\!i.\lambda f\!:\!(\Pi Z.Z \Rightarrow Z).\lambda y\!:\!i.add\,(H_1\,x\,f\,y)\,(H_2\,x\,f\,y)]$,

$$(\Sigma H_1\!:\!i \Rightarrow (\Pi Z.Z \Rightarrow Z) \Rightarrow i \Rightarrow i)(\Sigma H_2\!:\!i \Rightarrow (\Pi Z.Z \Rightarrow Z) \Rightarrow i \Rightarrow i)(\Pi x:i)$$
$$\triangleright$$
$$add\,(H_1\,0\,(\Lambda X.\lambda y\!:\!X.o\,X\,y)\,x)\,(H_2\,0\,(\Lambda X.\lambda y\!:\!X.o\,X\,y)\,x) \doteq add\,0\,(o\,i\,0)$$

Apply again Rig-Rig to get

$$(\Sigma H_1\!:\!i \Rightarrow (\Pi Z.Z \Rightarrow Z) \Rightarrow i \Rightarrow i)(\Sigma H_2\!:\!i \Rightarrow (\Pi Z.Z \Rightarrow Z) \Rightarrow i \Rightarrow i)(\Pi x:i)$$
$$\triangleright$$
$$H_1\,0\,(\Lambda X.\lambda y\!:\!X.o\,X\,y)\,x \doteq 0,\,H_2\,0\,(\Lambda X.\lambda y\!:\!X.o\,X\,y)\,x \doteq o\,i\,0$$

By Rig-Flex-Proj-I with $\rho = [H_1/\lambda x\!:\!i\lambda f\!:\!(\Pi Z.Z \Rightarrow Z)\lambda y\!:\!i.x]$, and Rig-Rig again we get

$$(\Sigma H_2\!:\!i \Rightarrow (\Pi Z.Z \Rightarrow Z) \Rightarrow i \Rightarrow i)(\Pi x:i)\; \triangleright\; H_2\,0\,(\Lambda X.\lambda y\!:\!X.o\,X\,y)\,x \doteq o\,i\,0$$

We now apply Rig-Flex-Proj-II. Here we show in detail what happens. The type unification algorithm computes

$$(\Sigma V\!:\!\bullet)(\Sigma H_3\!:\!i \Rightarrow (\Pi Z.Z \Rightarrow Z) \Rightarrow i \Rightarrow V)(\Pi x:i)\; \triangleright\; V \doteq i \longrightarrow_\tau (\Pi x:i)\; \triangleright\; \emptyset$$

yielding $\tau = [V/i]$. Hence $\rho = \tau \circ [H_2/\lambda x\!:\!i\lambda f\!:\!(\Pi Z.Z \Rightarrow Z)\lambda y\!:\!i.(f\,V\,(H_3\,x\,f\,y))]$, that is $\rho = [H_2/\lambda x\!:\!i\lambda f\!:\!\Pi Z.Z \Rightarrow Z)\lambda y\!:\!i.(f\,i\,(H_3\,x\,f\,y))]$. Therefore we obtain

$$(\Sigma H_3\!:\!i \Rightarrow (\Pi Z.Z \Rightarrow Z) \Rightarrow i \Rightarrow i)(\Pi x:i)\; \triangleright\; o\,i\,(H_3\,0\,(\Lambda X.\lambda y\!:\!X.o\,X\,y)\,x) \doteq o\,i\,0$$
$$(4)$$

a problem the reader can easily solve using the rules above. Composing the partial bindings above we obtain the unifier (supposing (4) is solved by imitation)

$$\theta = [X/i \Rightarrow i, F/\lambda x\!:\!i.\lambda f\!:\!(\Pi Z.Z \Rightarrow Z)\lambda y\!:\!i.add\,x\,(f\,i\,0)]$$

5   Logic Programming

In this section we sketch the integration of the Π^* unification procedure into a logic programming language similar to λ-Prolog. We start from the proof system I_Π obtained essentially from the addition to intuitionistic higher-order logic of the rules Π-L and Π-R.

$$\frac{P, A[X/T] \vdash C}{P, \Pi X\!:\!\bullet^n.A \vdash C}\;[\Pi\text{-L}] \qquad \frac{P \vdash A}{P \vdash \Pi X\!:\!\bullet^n.A}\;[\Pi\text{-R}]$$

Then we define valid data and goal formulas by the following proof system.

$$\frac{A \in \Pi_P}{P \Rightarrow_{d/g} A} \qquad \frac{P \Rightarrow_g G_1\; P \Rightarrow_g G_2}{P \Rightarrow_g G_1 \wedge G_2} \qquad \frac{P \Rightarrow_g G\; P \Rightarrow_d A}{P \Rightarrow_d A \leftarrow G} \qquad \frac{P \Rightarrow_g G\; P \Rightarrow_d D}{P \Rightarrow_g G \leftarrow D}$$

$$\frac{P(\Pi x\!:\!T) \Rightarrow_g G}{P \Rightarrow_g \forall x\!:\!T.G} \qquad \frac{P(\Sigma x\!:\!T) \Rightarrow_d D}{P \Rightarrow_d \forall x\!:\!T.D} \qquad \frac{P(\Pi X\!:\!\bullet) \Rightarrow_g G}{P \Rightarrow_g \Pi X\!:\!\bullet.G} \qquad \frac{P(\Sigma X\!:\!\bullet^n) \Rightarrow_d D}{P \Rightarrow_d \Pi X\!:\!\bullet^n.D}$$

Here G, G_1 and G_2 stand for goal formulas, D, D_1 and D_2 for data formulas and A for atomic formulas. In the first rule we assume A to be P-rigid. The data (goal) sentences are those D such that there is a proof of $\emptyset \Rightarrow_d D$ ($\emptyset \Rightarrow_g D$). A program is a set of closed data sentences. Note that only existential type variables of higher kind are allowed, as expected. In relation to this language of programs and goals one can prove

Theorem 5.1 *Let P be a program and G a goal formula. Then $P \vdash_{I_\Pi} G$ iff there is an uniform proof of $P \vdash_{I_\Pi} G$.*

A uniform proof [3] is a proof in which each occurrence in the succedent of a sequent of a non-atomic formula corresponds to the conclusion of the introduction rule for its toplevel connective. Uniform proofs interpret the search behavior of the logical connectives. The following transition system describes a proof procedure similar to the one [14] presented to first-order hereditary harrop formulas for our Π^*-based language (although we use an explicit quantifier prefix instead of the universe-labelling function). Each transition has the form $L \Rightarrow R$ where L and R represent states of an abstract interpreter. Each state has the form $\mathcal{P} \triangleright S$ were $\mathcal{P}$ is a quantifier prefix and S is a multisets of triples of the form $[G, x, P]$ with x a universal variable in $\mathcal{P}$, G is a $\mathcal{P}$-term with all of its free variables quantified in x-prefix of $\mathcal{P}$, and P a set of data $\mathcal{P}$-terms with the same property, or of singletons $[A \doteq B]$ with A and B being $\mathcal{P}$-terms. By the x-prefix of $\mathcal{P}$ we mean the prefix $\mathcal{P}_{[x]} = \mathcal{L}(\Pi x : T)(\Sigma \overline{x_n : T_n})$ of $\mathcal{P} = \mathcal{P}_{[x]}\mathcal{R}$ with $\mathcal{R}$ not starting by an existential quantification.

$\wedge$-transition $\qquad \mathcal{P} \triangleright [G_1 \wedge G_2, y, P], S \Rightarrow \mathcal{P} \triangleright [G_1, y, P], [G_2, y, P], S$

Π (there is a similar $\forall$) $\mathcal{P}_{[y]}\mathcal{Q} \triangleright [\Pi X.B, y, P], S \Rightarrow \mathcal{P}_{[y]}(\Pi X : \bullet)\mathcal{Q} \triangleright [B, X, P], S$

$\leftarrow \qquad\qquad \mathcal{P} \triangleright [G \leftarrow D, y, P], S \Rightarrow \mathcal{P} \triangleright [G, y, P \cup \{D\}], S$

Reduction $\mathcal{P}_{[y]}\mathcal{Q} \triangleright [A, y, P], S \Rightarrow \mathcal{P}_{[y]}(\Sigma \overline{y_n : Y_n})\mathcal{Q} \triangleright [A \doteq H], [B, y, P], S$

Unification $\qquad \mathcal{P} \triangleright [A \doteq B], S \Rightarrow_\sigma \mathcal{P}' \triangleright R, \sigma(S)$

This last rule depends on a subsidiary computation $\mathcal{P} \triangleright A \doteq B \overset{*}{\longrightarrow}_\sigma \mathcal{P}' \triangleright R$ of the Π^* unification algorithm. In the Goal-Reduction transition, we assume there is a rule $\mathbf{Q}\overline{y_n : X_n}(H \leftarrow B) \in P$. For this system of transition rules we can show the following soundness and completeness result [1].

Theorem 5.2 *Let P be a program and G a goal with free variables $\overline{x_n}$. 1. If there is a computation $(\Pi t : \bullet)(\Sigma \overline{x_n : T_n}) \triangleright [G, t, P] \overset{*}{\Rightarrow}_\sigma \mathcal{P}' \triangleright S$, and S is constituted only by elements of the form $[a \doteq b]$ with a and b flexible $\mathcal{P}'$-terms, then there is a substitution $\rho : \mathcal{P}' \to \mathcal{Q}$ such that $P \vdash_{I_\Pi} \rho\sigma(G)$. 2. If $P \vdash_{I_\Pi} \theta(G)$ then there is a computation $(\Pi t : \bullet)(\Sigma \overline{x_n : T_n}) \triangleright [G, t, P] \overset{*}{\Rightarrow}_\sigma \mathcal{P}' \triangleright S$, such that S is constituted only by elements of the form $[a \doteq b]$ with a and b flexible $\mathcal{P}'$-terms, and σ a $\mathcal{P}$-substitution more general than θ.*

As an example, we show a simple program specifying a proof system for a fragment of second order intuitionistic propositional logic using a coding of propositions into types, that delivers (representations of) terms of system $\mathcal{F}$ as proof terms.

```
kind and * -> * -> *                      /* theorem prover */
kind or * -> * -> *
kind true * -> *
type impint   Pi [A:*] [B:*] (true(A) -> true(B)) -> true(A -> B)
type impelim  Pi [A:*] [B:*] true(A -> B) -> true(A) -> true(B)
type allint   Pi [A:*] A -> o
type p        Pi [A:*] A -> o

p true(A -> B) (impint A B F) :-
    pi [X:true(A)] (p true(A) X -: p true(B) (F X)).
```

```
p true(B) (impelim A B F b) :- p true(A -> B) F, p true(A) b.
p true(Pi [X:*] (F X)) (allint (Pi [X:*] (F X)) G) :-
    pi [X:*] p true(F X) (G X).
```

This last program when given goal p true(Pi [X:*] Pi [Y:*] X -> (Y -> X)) Z will instantiate Z to a representation of a proof of $\Pi X.\Pi Y.X \Rightarrow (Y \Rightarrow X)$.

6 Conclusions and Further Work

We presented an unification algorithm for the polymorphic λ-calculus Λ_Π designed to be integrated into a logic programming language. To obtain a complete algorithm we have made some restrictions to the full language of Λ_Π. These restrictions turn out to integrate well with pre-unification and support a large class of polymorphic terms without excluding any simply-typed term as do other approaches. On the other hand, consider the following example.

```
type map Pi [X:*] Pi [Y:*] (X->Y)->list(X)->list(Y)->o
map A B F (nil A) (nil B).
map A B F (cons A X L) (cons B (F X) T) :- map A B F L T.
```

This program is not allowed wrt previous definitions, since in the second clause for map, the term X given as argument to the flexible term (F X) is not determining (in fact the target type of X is the existential variable A). We can of course cure the problem by defining type-specific versions of the application (F X), say

```
map A B F (nil A) (nil B).
map A B F (cons A X L) (cons B Z T) :- apply A B F X Z, map A B F L T.
apply A int F X (F X).
apply A list(B) F X (F X).
```

However, we are currently studying a version of the programming language that through a suitable restriction on occurrences of just type terms will allow programs such as the first version of map above. Essentially we will insure toplevel type arguments of predicates to be instantiated to Π_L types, by redefining the notion of goal formula. We believe that this last formulation will provide a very useful polymorphic HO logic programming language, if we choose to give up some of the type-manipulation ability in exchange for an even more extensive term language.

In many applications the presence of explicit type information is cumbersome. Thus we expect to relieve the programmer from having to always provide explicit types by means of a type-argument synthesis algorithm. Another application we would like to achieve is a logical foundation for modules with local types.

Acknowledgements

We would like to thank JNICT for partial support of this work and the anonymous referees for their useful suggestions and references.

References

[1] L. Caires and L. Monteiro. Higher-order polymorphic logic programming. Technical report, DI-FCT, Universidade Nova de Lisboa, forthcoming.

[2] A. Church. A formulation of the simple theory of types. *J. Symbolic Logic*, (5):56–68, 1940.

[3] F. Pfenning D. Miller, G. Nadathur and A. Scedrov. Uniform proof as a foundation for logic programming. *Annals of Pure and Applied Logic*, (51):125–157, 1991.

[4] Daniel Dougherty. Higher-order unification via combinators. *Theoretical Computer Science*, 114(114):273–298, 1993.

[5] C. Elliot. Higher-order unification with dependent function types. In Springer Verlag, editor, *in LNCS : Rewriting Techniques and Applications*, volume 355, 1989.

[6] J-Y. Girard. Une extension de l'interpretation de Gödel a l'analyse, et son application a l'elimination de coupures dans l'analyse et la theorie des types. In J.E. Fenstad North-Holland, editor, *Proc. of the Second Scandinavian Logic Symposium*, 1971.

[7] Carl Gunter. *Semantics of Programming Languages: Structures and Techniques*. MIT Press, 1992.

[8] G. Huet. *Resolution d'equations dans des languages d'ordre 1,2,...,ω*. PhD thesis, Université Paris VII, 1976.

[9] Ulrich Hustadt. A complete transformation system for polymorphic higher-order unification. In Boston University DCS, editor, *Proc. 6th Int. Workshop on Unification*, 1993.

[10] J.C. Mitchell. Type systems for programming languages. In J. van Leewen, editor, *Handbook of Theoretical Computer Science*, 1990.

[11] D. Miller. A logic programming language with lambda-abstraction, function variables, and simple unification. *J. Logic and Computation*, 1(4), 1991.

[12] D. Miller. Unification under a mixed prefix. *J. of Symbolic Systems*, 14:321–358, 1992.

[13] R. Milner. A theory of type polymorphism in programming. *J. Computer and System Sciences*, 17(3), 1978.

[14] G. Nadathur. A proof procedure for the logic of hereditary harrop formulas. Technical report, DCS, Duke University, 1992.

[15] G. Nadathur and D. Miller. An overview of λ-prolog. In *Proc. of the Fifth International Logic Programming Conference*, pages 810–827, 1988.

[16] G. Nadathur and F. Pfenning. The type system of a higher-order programming language. Technical Report CS-1992-02, DCS, Duke University, 1992.

[17] T. Nipkow. Higher-order unification, polymorphism, and subsorts. In *LNCS*, volume 516, 1991.

[18] L. Paulson. Introduction to Isabelle. Technical report, Computer Laboratory, University of Cambridge, 1993.

[19] F. Pfenning. Unification and anti-unification in the calculus of constructions. In Lars Hallnas LNCS, editor, *LICS 91*, 1991.

[20] J. Reynolds. Towards a theory of type structure. In 19 LNCS, editor, *Proc. Paris Symp. on Programming*, 1974.

[21] W. Snyder and J. Gallier. Higher-order unification revisited: Complete sets of transformations. Technical report, DCIS, University of Pennsylvania, 1992.

Databases

A Database Interface for Complex Objects

Marcel Holsheimer[†]
Centrum voor Wiskunde en Informatica (CWI)
Postbus 4079
1009 AB Amsterdam
The Netherlands
marcel@cwi.nl

Rolf A. de By
Computer Science Department
University of Twente
P.O. Box 217
7500 AE Enschede
The Netherlands
deby@cs.utwente.nl

Hassan Aït-Kaci[‡]
School of Computing Science
Simon Fraser University
Burnaby, British Columbia
V5A 1S6, Canada
hak@cs.sfu.ca

Abstract

We describe a formal design for a logical query language using ψ-terms as data structures to interact effectively and efficiently with a relational database. The structure of ψ-terms provides an adequate representation for so-called complex objects. They generalize conventional terms used in logic programming: they are sorted attributed structures, ordered thanks to a subsort ordering. Unification of ψ-terms is an effective means for integrating multiple inheritance and partial information into a deduction process. We define a compact database representation for ψ-terms, representing part of the subsorting relation in the database as well. We describe a retrieval algorithm based on an abstract interpretation of the ψ-term unification process and prove its formal correctness. This algorithm is efficient in that it incrementally retrieves only additional facts that are actually needed by a query, and never retrieves the same fact twice.

> The difficulty lay in the form and economy of it, so to dispose such a multitude of materials as not to make a confused heap of incoherent parts but one consistent whole.
>
> EPHRAIM CHAMBERS, *Cyclopaedia*

[†] Work done at University of Twente.

[‡] Work done at Digital's Paris Research Laboratory.

1 Introduction

1.1 Motivation and contribution

The combination of logic programming languages and database systems has been a research theme for the last decade in both logic programming and database communities. The interest from a logic programming perspective came when the need was felt for manipulating large sets of facts. Usually Prolog was coupled with a relational database. In [9], Ceri *et al.* provide an excellent overview of work in this area. In the database community, it was felt that the logic programming paradigm offers interesting opportunities as a database query language. This resulted in logical query languages like $\mathcal{LDL}$ [14] and NAIL! [13].

So-called complex objects have recently been studied for use in database systems [7, 8]. Much of what has been proposed in those studies is derived from earlier work extending first-order terms to ψ-terms [1]. The latter notion has had a more direct application in programming language design [4, 2, 6] than in database systems. Still, the functionality and naturalness of deductive queries over ψ-terms is a strong motivation for providing a logic programming language using ψ-terms with an effective means to access large volumes of data and knowledge stored in a database (see [5] for a convincing example).

We propose a formal design for an effective coupling of such a language with a relational database. For the purpose of our presentation and experimentation, we use the specific language LIFE [2], but this implies no loss of generality. Indeed, although we formulate it using ψ-terms, our design is directly applicable to any logical query language with complex objects represented as Prolog terms or as data structures *à la* [7, 8], since all these models turn out to be special cases of ψ-terms. We present the theoretical view of our proposed database support of that language and discuss the results. Our theoretical design was put into practice as the basis of an experimental implementation [12].

Although our experiment may be categorized as providing database support to a logic programming language, it goes beyond previous research in that it considers a language with sorts and attributed terms, which can be arbitrarily nested, and provide multiple inheritance. As will be shown, due to the specific characteristics of LIFE's sort system, our experiment has yielded a form of database support that not only allows querying for facts, but also posing abstract queries, that is, queries that ask for general knowledge as opposed to factual knowledge.

1.2 Organization of paper

Before we delve into technicalities, here is a brief introductory overview of the paper. Our system is organized as sketched in Figure 1 and consists of three subsystems; namely, the LIFE system, an interface written in LIFE, and an external relational database. The coupled system is intended to represent the facts of LIFE in the database and to retrieve these facts, when needed by the LIFE system.

Hence, the functionality of the interface is twofold. Firstly, it provides a compact database representation for logical facts. As we shall see in Section 2, these facts are ordered by a subsumption relation induced by a subsort ordering

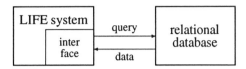

Figure 1. Architecture of the system.

on functors. In Section 3, we propose to group facts into what we call *qualified segments*, such that the subsort relationships involving symbols in these facts are implicitly represented. We also compress segments before storage in the database.

Secondly, for the retrieval of facts, we use a *tight coupling* [15, 16], where facts are loaded when needed by the LIFE system. In Section 4, we describe an abstraction of the unification process, where qualified segments in the database are approximated by a set of generalizations, called *qualifier*. If facts from the database are requested, we use the qualifier and the current goal, a term, to construct a *candidate*: a selection condition on the segment, retrieving all facts that unify with this goal. In Section 5, we show that not all subsort relationships need to be stored in the LIFE-system, since some are implicitly represented in the database. In Section 6, we optimize the retrieval process, by storing loaded facts in the internal database and retrieving each fact only once. We conclude with Section 7, with a recapitulation of our work and a brief overview of the perspectives it offers. No particular background is required to understand the technical contents of this paper other than elementary discrete algebra, shreds of logic programming, and basic notions of relational and deductive databases.

2   The facts of LIFE

LIFE (*Logic, Inheritance, Functions, Equations*) is a logic programming language extending Prolog terms as described in [2, 4, 6]. The user can specify inclusion relationships between functor symbols, thus enabling the direct representation and use of taxonomic information. Thus, functors are called sorts and no longer differentiated from values. For example, we can state that *apples* is a subsort of *food*, so that a fact *likes*(*mary*, *food*), stating that mary likes food, implies that mary likes apples as well.

To make use of a subsorting relation in à logic programming language, the unification operation must be redefined. The subsorting relation generates a partial order on the set of all terms called *term subsumption*. Unification of two terms computes their *greatest lower bound* (GLB) with respect to term subsumption. Failure of unification is denoted by a special term: the symbol $\perp$ (*"bottom"*).

For the purpose of our presentation, it will suffice to assume that a LIFE program P consists of the specification of the subsort ordering, and logical rules in the form of Horn-clauses. The essential point to keep in mind is that the literals making up a program's clauses are ψ-terms rather than conventional Prolog terms. Hence, as is the case in deductive database languages, the Horn clauses are separated into the *extensional* database (EDB)---*i.e.*, the facts containing no variables---and the *intensional* database (IDB)---the rest.

Our idea is to represent the (presumably numerous) facts of a LIFE program's EDB as flat relations to store in an external relational database. Then, designing an interface amounts to defining an intermediate representation allowing to translate from facts of LIFE (*i.e.*, ψ-terms) to database tuples and back. To be correct, a database retrieval algorithm responding to a LIFE query through this interface must be sound (*i.e.*, retrieve *no irrelevant* tuples) and complete (*i.e.*, retrieve *all relevant* tuples). Hence, the interface design and the correctness of retrieval depend in some essential way on the formalization of ψ-terms. This section is meant to give all the preliminary formalities that we use, introducing basic and disjunctive ψ-terms, sort signatures, subsumption, and related notions. From this point on, whenever we say ''term'' we shall mean (possibly disjunctive) ''ψ-term.''[1]

2.1 Terms

A *basic* term is built out of *sort symbols* and *attribute labels*. Let $\mathcal{L}$ be the set of all attribute labels, and $\mathcal{S}$ the set of all sort symbols, including $\top$ (*''top''*) and $\bot$ (*''bottom''*).

Definition 1 (Basic term) *A* basic term p *is an expression of the form:*

$$s(l_1 \Rightarrow p_1, \dots, l_n \Rightarrow p_n), \quad n \geq 0,$$

where:

- $s \in \mathcal{S}$ *is the* root symbol *of* p, *denoted by* **root**(p).

- $l_1 \dots, l_n \in \mathcal{L}$ *are pairwise distinct* attribute labels.

- $p_1, \dots, p_n$ *are terms: the* subterms *of* p.

If $n = 0$, p is is said to be *atomic*, and simply written as s. Otherwise, p is said to be *attributed*. The attribute-subterm list is unordered. A term with at least one occurrence of the symbol $\bot$ is considered to be equal to the term $\bot$. We call Ψ the set of all basic terms that can be constructed from sort symbols in $\mathcal{S}$ and labels in $\mathcal{L}$.

Example 2.1 An example of a basic term is:

likes(who $\Rightarrow$ mary,
born $\Rightarrow$ date(day $\Rightarrow$ 24,
month $\Rightarrow$ january,
year $\Rightarrow$ 1965),
what $\Rightarrow$ apples).

---

[1] More precisely, we shall mean ψ-terms *without variables* since only EDB facts will be considered.

The root symbol is *likes*; it has three subterms with attribute labels *who*, *born* and *what*. The sort symbols are *likes*, *mary*, *date*, 24, *january*, 1965, and *apples*. The attribute labels are *who*, *born*, *day*, *month*, *year*, and *what*. □

We shall use a more convenient mathematical characterization of a basic term that is formally equivalent to their syntactic representation of Definition 1. It sees a term as a mapping from a set of *occurrences* (*i.e.*, strings of labels in the free monoid $\mathcal{L}^*$) to $\mathcal{S}$, assigning sort symbols to each of these occurrences.

Definition 2 (Occurrence) *An* occurrence *is a string formed by concatenating labels, separated by '.'. The root label is denoted by the empty string ε. The set of all occurrences $\mathcal{L}^*$ is inductively defined as $\mathcal{L}^* := \varepsilon \mid \mathcal{L}.\mathcal{L}^*$, where $a.\varepsilon = \varepsilon.a = a$ for any occurrence a.*

In what follows, every time we refer to term p, we mean the generic one in Definition 1.

Definition 3 (Occurrence domain) *The set of occurrences actually appearing in a term p is the* occurrence domain Δ_p: *the smallest subset of $\mathcal{L}^*$ for which:*

- $\varepsilon \in \Delta_p$ *and*

- $l_i.a \in \Delta_p$ *iff l_i is the label in p denoting the subterm p_i, and $a \in \Delta_{p_i}$.*

Definition 4 (Sort function) *To each term p there corresponds a* sort function $\psi_p : \mathcal{L}^* \rightarrow \mathcal{S}$ *which assigns a sort symbol to each occurrence:*

$$\psi_p(a) = \begin{cases} \top & \text{if } a \notin \Delta_p \\ \mathbf{root}(p) & \text{if } a = \varepsilon \\ \psi_{p_i}(a') & \text{if } a = l_i.a' \end{cases}$$

Hence, a basic term is formally characterized as a pair $p = \langle \Delta_p, \psi_p \rangle$.

Example 2.2 Referring to the term in Example 2.1, the domain is $\{\varepsilon,$ *who*, *born*, *born.day*, *born.month*, *born.year*, *what*$\}$. The sort function is defined as: $\psi(\varepsilon) = likes, \psi(who) = mary, \psi(born) = date, \psi(born.day) = 24$, etc. Note that the sort function returns the $\top$-symbol for any occurrence not in the occurrence domain, for example $\psi(day.what) = \top$. □

2.2 A short terminological digression

For the sake of self-containment and to settle some terminology, we indulge in a brief *intermezzo* defining a few general basic order-theoretic notions that we shall use in the rest of this paper. All definitions in this short digression will refer to a partially-ordered set, or *poset*, $\langle S, \leq \rangle$.

Recall that a chain of S is a totally ordered subset of S. Let us also recall the notion of *cochain*, a dual of the more familiar notion of chain:

Definition 5 (Cochain) *A* cochain *C of S is a subset of S where all distinct elements are mutually incomparable. Formally, $C \times C \cap\ \leq\ =\ \mathbf{1}_C$.*[2]

---

[2]Where $\mathbf{1}_X = \{\langle x, x \rangle | x \in X\}$ is the identity relation on X.

The set of all cochains of S is denoted as $\mathbf{coc}(S)$. The set $\mathbf{coc}(S)$ is itself partially ordered as follows.

Definition 6 (Cochain ordering) $\forall C_1, C2 \in \mathbf{coc}(S), \quad C_1 \sqsubseteq C_2 \quad \textit{iff} \quad \forall x_1 \in C_1, \exists x_2 \in C_2 : x_1 \leq x_2.$

Note that the empty set $\varnothing$ is a cochain. In particular, the empty set is the *least* element in $\mathbf{coc}(S)$; that is, $\forall C \subseteq S : \varnothing \sqsubseteq C$.

Note also that singletons of elements of S are cochains too. In fact, the cochain ordering $\sqsubseteq$ coincides with $\leq$ on singletons; namely, $\forall x, x' \in S : \{x\} \sqsubseteq \{x'\}$ iff $x \leq x'$. For this reason, an element x of S may be identified with the singleton $\{x\}$. Hence, the cochain ordering $\sqsubseteq$ is a "natural" extension of the base ordering $\leq$ and so we shall use only one symbol $(\leq)$ indifferently on base elements or cochains of S without risk of confusion.

It will be convenient to refer, for a given element of S, to specific subsets of its upper bounds or lower bounds. The following definitions introduce a few that we will use. In what follows, x and x' denote elements of such a set S.

Definition 7 (Ancestors) *The set of ancestors of x is the set $\mathbf{anc}(x)$ of elements greater than, or equal to x:*

$$\mathbf{anc}(x) = \{x' \in S \mid x \leq x'\}.$$

Definition 8 (Descendants) *The set of descendants of x is the set $\mathbf{des}(x)$ of elements smaller than, or equal to x:*

$$\mathbf{des}(x) = \{x' \in S \mid x' \leq x\}.$$

Given $S' \subseteq S$, let $\lceil S' \rceil$ (resp., $\lfloor S' \rfloor$) denote the set of all its maximal (resp., minimal) elements.[3] We define *parents* and *children*, as well as *maximal common lower bounds* and *minimal common upper bounds*, in terms of ancestors and descendants as follows.

Definition 9 (Parents and children) *The* parents *of x are its immediate upper bounds; i.e., the minimal ancestors, excluding x itself:*

$$\mathbf{par}(x) = \lfloor \mathbf{anc}(x) \setminus \{x\} \rfloor$$

Dually, the children *of x are its immediate lower bounds; i.e.,*

$$\mathbf{chi}(x) = \lceil \mathbf{des}(x) \setminus \{x\} \rceil$$

Definition 10 (Maximal common lower bounds) *The set of* maximal common lower bounds *of x and x' is denoted as $x \sqcap x'$, and defined as:*

$$x \sqcap x' = \left\lceil \mathbf{des}(x) \cap \mathbf{des}(x') \right\rceil.$$

---

[3]To be well-defined, this requires that S not contain infinitely ascending (resp., descending) chain. So we shall implicitly assume this. In fact, all the posets on which we will use these operations will be finite.

Definition 11 (Minimal common upper bounds) *Dually, the set of minimal common upper bounds of s and s′ is denoted $x \sqcup x'$, and defined as:*

$$x \sqcup x' = \lfloor \mathbf{anc}(x) \cap \mathbf{anc}(x') \rfloor.$$

Note that all the sets introduced by the four previous definitions are cochains.

Finally, given two functions f and f' from a set A to a poset $\langle S, \leq \rangle$, we say that $f \leq f'$ whenever $\forall a \in A : f(a) \leq f'(a)$.

This concludes our terminological digression. We now return to our topical considerations.

2.3 Sort signature

The set of sort symbols S comes with a subsort ordering $\leq$. The set S and the ordering form a *sort signature*, a poset $\Sigma = \langle S, \leq \rangle$. We may assume the sort signature to be fixed.

Definition 12 (Sort signature) *A sort signature Σ is a poset $\langle S, \leq \rangle$, where:*

- *S is the set of sort symbols, containing top symbol $\top$ and bottom symbol $\bot$.*

- *$\leq \subseteq S \times S$ is a partial order---the subsorting---on S such that $\forall s \in S$: $\bot \leq s \leq \top$.*

Example 2.3 All the examples to follow will use a sort signature consisting of a set $S = \{\top, \bot, student, emp, mary, likes, food, apples, sweets, cookies, chocolate\}$, and for subsorting the least ordering such that $apples \leq food$, $sweets \leq food$, $cookies \leq sweets$ and $chocolate \leq sweets$, expressing that apples and sweets are food, and cookies and chocolate are sweets; and such that $mary \leq student$ and $mary \leq emp$, expressing that mary is both a student and an employee. This sort signature will be referred to as Σ and is depicted in Figure 2. □

2.4 Term subsumption

The partial order $\leq$ on sort symbols extends to the set of all terms as follows:

Definition 13 (Basic term subsumption) *The basic term subsumption relation $\trianglelefteq$ on the set of all basic terms Ψ is defined as $p \trianglelefteq p'$ iff $p = \bot$ or $\psi_p \leq \psi_{p'}$.*

Example 2.4 The term $p_1 = likes(who \Rightarrow mary, what \Rightarrow apples)$ is subsumed by the term $p_2 = likes(who \Rightarrow mary, what \Rightarrow food)$ since $apples \leq food$. Term p_1 is also subsumed by the term $p_3 = likes(who \Rightarrow mary)$ since the sort symbol is $\top$ for any occurrence that is not in the occurrence domain; *i.e.*, $\psi_{p_1}(what) = apples \leq \psi_{p_3}(what) = \top$. Thus any basic term is subsumed by $\top$ and subsumes $\bot$. □

Note since S is a subset of Ψ, $\trianglelefteq$ coincides with $\leq$ on it. Therefore, $\trianglelefteq$ can be seen as a "natural" extension of the subsort ordering $\leq$ and therefore we shall again use only one symbol $(\leq)$ indifferently on sort symbols or basic terms without risk of confusion.

As expected, we now extend terms to cochains of terms.

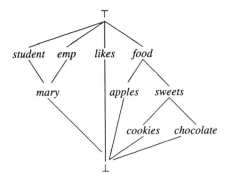

Figure 2. The sort signature Σ.

Definition 14 (Disjunctive terms) *A disjunctive term is a cochain of basic terms.*

Term subsumption is naturally extended to disjunctive terms as the cochain ordering of basic term subsumption. Hence, by "term" we now shall mean basic or possibly disjunctive term.

As usual, a singleton disjunctive term $\{p\}$ is identified with the basic term p. In particular, the singleton set $\{\top\}$ is identified with the basic term $\top$. This is natural since they are both greatest elements for term subsumption. Similarly, $\{\bot\}$ is identified with the basic term $\bot$. Note that this is natural since they are both least elements. However, the empty set $\varnothing$ is also the least element of $\mathbf{coc}(\Psi)$, and hence we can identify all three: $\bot = \{\bot\} = \varnothing$.

The following is a particular case of a more general result in [1].

Theorem 1 *The poset $\langle \mathbf{coc}(\Psi), \leq \rangle$ is a lattice.*[4]

Proof Greatest lower bounds are constructed as follows. For basic terms p and p', the (possibly disjunctive) term $p \wedge p'$ is the set of maximal elements of the set of all basic terms $u = \langle \Delta_u, \psi_u \rangle$ such that:

- $\Delta_u = \Delta_p \cup \Delta_{p'}$,

- $\forall a \in \Delta_u : \psi_u(a) \in \psi_p(a) \sqcap \psi_{p'}(a)$.

For (possibly singleton) disjunctive terms C, C', it is given by $C \wedge C' = \lceil \{p \wedge p' \mid p \in C, p' \in C'\} \rceil$.

Dually, least upper bounds (LUB) are constructed as follows. For basic terms p and p', the (possibly disjunctive) term $p \vee p'$ is the set of minimal elements of the set of all basic terms $u = \langle \Delta_u, \psi_u \rangle$ such that:

---

[4]Recall that a lattice L is a poset where a unique greatest lower bound and a unique least upper bound both exist in L for any finite non-empty subset of L.

- $\Delta_u = \Delta_p \cap \Delta_{p'}$,

- $\forall a \in \Delta_u : \psi_u(a) \in \psi_p(a) \sqcup \psi_{p'}(a)$.

For (possibly singleton) disjunctive terms C, C', it is given by $C \vee C' = \lfloor \{p \vee p' \mid p \in C, p' \in C'\} \rfloor$.

It is easy to verify that these operations are lattice operations with respect to term subsumption. ∎

Note that if the sort signature Σ is a lattice, then so is Ψ, and moreover, it is then a sublattice of $\mathbf{coc}(\Psi)$.

Example 2.5 The GLB of terms p_1 and p_2 in Example 2.4 is p_1, since $p_1 \leq p_2$. The GLB of $likes(who \Rightarrow student)$ and $likes(who \Rightarrow emp)$ is $likes(who \Rightarrow mary)$. Their LUB is $likes(who \Rightarrow \top)$. The GLB of atomic terms $food$ and $student$ is $\perp$; *i.e.*, we cannot unify these. □

3 Representation in a database

We now discuss the storage of facts in an external relational database.

3.1 Qualified segments

In a relational database, identically formed objects are grouped together in a relation. We must define a similar grouping on facts that we store in the external database. We must also find a way to represent subsort information relevant to sort symbols in these facts in the database as well as there is no evident way to express subsumption in relational algebra. Therefore, if a fact is stored in a database relation, it should imply that particular subsort relationships are defined for symbols in this fact. Thus we should group facts with similar subsort relationships for its symbols, for example symbols with the same parents or children or both. However, there is a trade-off: the more subsort information is implicitly represented, the more database relations are needed to store all facts.

We choose to group facts with the *same set of parents* for all symbols at each given occurrence. It turns out that this is a natural choice since sharing parents is the most immediate commonality, akin to values being of the same sort. These sets are called *qualified segments*:

Definition 15 (Qualified segment) *A qualified segment Q is a set of non-bottom facts such that all facts have the same set of parents for the sort symbol at each occurrence:*

$$\forall f, f' \in Q, \forall a \in \Delta_f : \mathbf{par}(\psi_f(a)) = \mathbf{par}(\psi_{f'}(a))$$

With some easy thinking, one can convince oneself that all facts in Q must necessarily be identically formed. Indeed, the occurrence domain is the same for all facts in a qualified segment, since parents are the same for symbols at each occurrence. For a qualified segment Q, the common occurrence domain of all facts is denoted Δ_Q.

For a program P, we can use multiple qualified segments to store part of the facts in P in the database. We store each qualified segment in a separate database relation, and in the interface we store a description of the contents of each segment, called the *qualifier*. A qualifier is a set of terms, that are generalizations of all facts in the qualified segment:

Definition 16 (Qualifier) *To a qualified segment Q corresponds a qualifier, denoted* **qua**(Q), *which is the LUB of all facts in Q.*

Example 3.1 Let us assume the two facts of LIFE *likes*$(who \Rightarrow mary, what \Rightarrow sweets)$ and *likes*$(who \Rightarrow mary, what \Rightarrow apples)$. Since both facts have the same parents for all sort symbols, we can represent them in a qualified segment $Q = \{likes(who \Rightarrow mary, what \Rightarrow sweets), likes(who \Rightarrow mary, what \Rightarrow apples)\}$. The qualifier is **qua**$(Q) = likes(who \Rightarrow mary, what \Rightarrow food)$. □

An important remark is that the qualifier of a qualified segment is alway a *strict* generalizer of all facts of the segment. This is a consequence of having grouped facts in the same qualified segment if and only if the sort symbols at all their occurrences shared the same parents.[5] And thus, as we will see in Section 5, a qualifier and the terms in the corresponding segment, implicitly represent subsort relationships.

3.2 Database relations

A relational database consists of database relations:

Definition 17 (Database relation) *A database relation R_T is a set $\{r_1, r_2, \ldots, r_m\}$, $(m \geq 0)$ of n-ary tuples $(n \geq 1)$ and is identified by its relation name R and a set of attribute names $T = \{t_1, t_2, \ldots, t_n\}$. For a particular tuple r, the value of attribute t is denoted as r.t.*

We store a qualified segment Q in database relation R_T by representing each fact in Q as a tuple in R_T. We represent fact f as a tuple r by *flattening* the fact; *i.e.*, we define a bijective function v---called *attribute function*---that maps occurrences in the occurrence domain Δ_f to attribute names in T. Then, for each occurrence $a \in \Delta_f$, we store sort symbol $\psi_f(a)$ in attribute $v(a)$ in tuple r.

This representation is sound, but it can be compressed by recognizing that for particular occurrences in the occurrence domain, symbols are the same in all facts in the segment. For example, the symbol at the *who* occurrence in Example 3.1 is *mary* for all facts in Q. This (possibly empty) set of occurrences is the *fixed symbol set*:

Definition 18 (Fixed symbol set) *For qualified segment Q we define the* fixed symbol set $D_Q \subseteq \Delta_Q$ as:

$$D_Q = \{a \in \Delta_Q \mid \forall f, f' \in Q : \psi_f(a) = \psi_{f'}(a)\}$$

---

[5]More precisely, this is true if the qualified segment is not reduced to only one fact. But then, as we shall see, there is no relation to store in the database.

Symbols at occurrences in the fixed occurrence set D_Q are the same for all facts in qualified segment Q, hence, we do not have to store them in the database. We only store symbols at occurrences not in D_Q and use any basic term in the qualifier to represent the missing symbols. Indeed, for each basic term q in the qualifier, the sort symbol $\psi_q(a)$ for each occurrence a in the fixed symbol set D_Q is their LUB and thus the same as the symbol at this occurrence for all facts in Q.

The correspondence between qualified segment Q and database relation R_T is defined by a *data definition*:

Definition 19 (Data definition) *Given segment Q, the corresponding database relation R_T is defined by a* data definition *given by the quadruple* $\langle \mathbf{qua}(Q), R, v, D_Q \rangle$.

Data definitions are stored in the interface, thus enabling the representation of facts in segment Q as tuples in R_T. With each fact $f = \langle \Delta_f, \psi_f \rangle \in Q$ corresponds a unique tuple $r \in R_T$, defined by:

$$\forall t \in T : \; r.t = \psi_f(v^{-1}(t))$$

Conversely, each database tuple $r \in R_T$ represents a fact $f = \langle \Delta_Q, \psi_f \rangle$, where the sort function ψ_f is defined as:

$$\psi_f(a) = \begin{cases} \top & \text{if } a \notin \Delta_Q \\ \psi_q(a) & \text{if } a \in D_Q \\ r.v(a) & \text{otherwise} \end{cases}$$

where $q \in \mathbf{qua}(Q)$.

Example 3.2 The qualifier for qualified segment Q from Example 3.1 is $\{likes(who \Rightarrow mary, what \Rightarrow food)\}$, and the fixed symbol set is $D_Q = \{\varepsilon, who\}$. If we represent Q as a database relation R_T, we only need to store the symbols at occurrence *what*, so we need a relation with a single column, say $T = \{foodname\}$.

We define the attribute function v as: $v(what) = foodname$. The representation of Q as a database relation is $R_T = \{\langle sweets \rangle, \langle apples \rangle\}$. □

Note, for the sake of consistency, that in the already mentioned degenerate case of a qualified segment reduced to only one fact, all the information goes into the fixed address set and the qualifier, leaving nothing to be stored in the external database.

4 Retrieval algorithm

For the retrieval of facts from the database, we use a tight coupling, where we load facts from the database whenever needed by the inference engine. For a particular goal g, we load the subset $Q[g]$ from segment Q, containing all facts in Q that unify with g:

$$Q[g] = \{f \in Q \mid f \wedge g \neq \bot\}$$

Qualified segment Q is stored in the database, so we do not know its actual contents, hence we cannot compute $Q[g]$ by simply unifying all facts in Q with the goal. So, we need another technique to compute $Q[g]$, independent of the contents of Q. We use an *abstract interpretation* [11] of the inference process, where we use qualifiers instead of facts. In this abstraction, unification of facts in Q with goal g is an operation on the qualifier and the goal, resulting in a term---called the *candidate*---which approximates the subset of Q of all facts unifiable with g. We describe the construction of candidates. First, we define the *unifiable set* $U(s)$, the set of all sort symbols that unify with symbol s; *i.e.*, symbols for which the maximal common subsort with s is non-bottom:

Definition 20 (Unifiable set) *For a sort symbol s in $\mathcal{S}$, we define the* unifiable set $U(s)$ *as:*

$$U(s) = \{s' \in \mathcal{S} \mid s \sqcap s' \neq \{\bot\}\}$$

A candidate is defined such that any fact in the qualified segment subsumed by a basic term in the candidate, unifies with goal g:

Definition 21 (Candidate) *Given a goal g, a basic term, the* candidate C *is the set of all maximal terms $c = \langle \Delta_Q, \psi_c \rangle$ that can be constructed from a term q in the qualifier* **qua**(Q) *that is unifiable with g, as follows.* $\forall a \in \Delta_Q$:

$$\psi_c(a) \begin{cases} = & \top \quad \text{if } a \in D_Q, \text{ or } \psi_q(a) \leq \psi_g(a), \\ \in & \textbf{chi}(\psi_q(a)) \cap U(\psi_g(a)) \quad \textit{otherwise.} \end{cases}$$

Example 4.1 Assume the goal $g_1 = likes(what \Rightarrow cookies)$ and qualified segment Q as in Example 3.2. By Definition 21, we construct a candidate $C_1 = \top(who \Rightarrow \top, what \Rightarrow sweets)$. For goal $g_2 = likes(who \Rightarrow student, what \Rightarrow food)$, we construct candidate $C_2 = \top(who \Rightarrow \top, what \Rightarrow \top)$. For goal $g_3 = likes(who \Rightarrow peter, what \Rightarrow apples)$, we construct candidate $C_3 = \emptyset$. $\quad\square$

Thus a candidate contains terms, identically formed to the facts in the segment, and consisting of $\top$-symbols and immediate subsorts of symbols in the qualifier; *i.e.*, symbols that appear in facts in Q. If candidate C is empty, the symbols in the terms in the qualifier and the goal do not unify, then the qualified segment does not contain any facts that unify with the goal. We have to prove that any fact f in qualified segment Q that unifies with goal g, is subsumed by a basic term c in candidate C.

Theorem 2 *A fact f in qualified segment Q unifies with goal g iff it is subsumed by a basic term c in candidate C; namely,*

$$f \wedge g \neq \bot \Leftrightarrow f \leq c$$

Proof By Definition 13 and Theorem 1, we can rewrite the above to a condition on sort symbols, $\forall a \in \mathcal{L}^*$:

$$\psi_f(a) \sqcap \psi_g(a) \neq \{\bot\} \Leftrightarrow \psi_f(a) \leq \psi_c(a)$$

We first prove that if the maximal common subsort of two symbols $\psi_f(a)$ and $\psi_g(a)$ is non-bottom, then we can construct a term c such that $\psi_f(a)$ is smaller than the corresponding symbol $\psi_c(a)$ in c.

Symbols $\psi_f(a)$ and $\psi_g(a)$ unify, so $\psi_f(a)$ is in the unifiable set $U(\psi_g(a))$. Symbol $\psi_q(a)$ is larger than $\psi_f(a)$, and thus unifies with $\psi_g(a)$ as well: $\psi_g(a) \in U(\psi_g(a))$. So, by definition, $\psi_c(a)$ is not the symbol $\bot$. Assume that occurrence a is in the fixed occurrence set D_Q. By definition, $\psi_c(a) = \top$ and thus symbol $\psi_f(a)$ is smaller than the symbol $\psi_c(a)$ in c. Alternatively, if occurrence a is not in the fixed symbol set D_Q, symbol $\psi_f(a)$ in fact f is a child of $\psi_q(a)$. We also know that $\psi_f(a)$ is in $U(\psi_g(a))$, thus we can construct a term c where $\psi_c(a) = \psi_f(a)$. So we can construct a term c larger than any fact f that unifies with goal g.

We also prove that if fact f in Q does *not* unify with goal g, we cannot construct a term c larger than f. Fact f and term g do not unify, so for at least one occurrence a, the maximal common subsort of $\psi_f(a)$ and $\psi_g(a)$ is the bottom symbol. We prove that, for this occurrence, we cannot construct a candidate c with $\psi_f(a) \leq \psi_c(a)$.

The symbol $\psi_q(a)$ is a supersort of $\psi_f(a)$. If q and g do not unify, the candidate is empty. Thus, it does not subsume any fact. If q and g unify then $\psi_q(a)$ is in $U(\psi_g(a))$, for all occurrence a in Δ_Q. Symbol $\psi_g(a)$ cannot be a supersort of $\psi_q(a)$, otherwise, $\psi_g(a)$ would be a supersort of $\psi_f(a)$ as well, and their maximal common subsort would be $\psi_f(a)$. Moreover, occurrence a cannot be in the fixed symbol set D_Q, otherwise $\psi_f(a) = \psi_q(a)$, contradicting that $\psi_q(a)$ is not in the unifiable set $U(\psi_g(a))$. Hence, the symbol $\psi_c(a)$ in c is not $\top$.

If we can construct a term c larger than f, symbol $\psi_c(a)$ would be a child of $\psi_q(a)$ and a member of the unifiable set $U(\psi_g(a))$. Since occurrence a is not in the fixed occurrence set, $\psi_f(a)$ is also a child of $\psi_q(a)$. So the only child of $\psi_q(a)$, larger than $\psi_f(a)$, is $\psi_f(a)$ itself. However, $\psi_f(a)$ is not in the unifiable set $U(\psi_g(a))$, so we cannot construct a term c, where $\psi_c(a) \in \mathbf{chi}(\psi_q(a)) \cap U(\psi_g(a))$, that is larger than fact f. $\blacksquare$

Corollary 1 *If fact f is subsumed by a basic term c in candidate C, all symbols in c are either the top symbol, or equal to the corresponding symbol in fact f.*

Proof Follows directly from the above proof, since $\psi_c(a)$ is either $\top$, or a child of the symbol $\psi_q(a)$ in the qualifier. For these symbols, occurrence a is not in the fixed occurrence set, thus symbol $\psi_f(a)$ in term f is also a child of $\psi_q(a)$. $\blacksquare$

The corollary is important, since it states that we can compute $Q[g]$ by a selection with the candidates, where $\top$ is the wild card argument and non-top symbols are selection arguments. With a candidate C for data definition $D = \langle F, R_T, v, D_Q \rangle$, there corresponds a selection condition $T[C]$ that is true for all elements of the set $Q[g]$ and false for any other element of Q:

$$T[C] = \big(T[c_1]\big) \text{ or } \ldots \text{ or } \big(T[c_p]\big)$$

where $C = \{c_1, \ldots, c_p\}$. For each term c_i we construct a selection condition:

$$T[c_i] = \qquad (v(a_1) = \psi_c(a_1))$$
$$\mathbf{and} \quad \ldots$$
$$\mathbf{and} \quad (v(a_n) = \psi_c(a_n))$$

where $a_1, \ldots, a_n$ are the occurrences with non-top symbols in term c_i. We select the tuples that represent facts in $Q[g]$ with a simple SQL-query:

select $t_1, \ldots, t_n$
from R
where $T[C]$

The retrieved tuples are then translated to facts, as stated in Section 3.2.

Example 4.2 For the candidate C_1 of Example 4.1, we construct a selection condition $T[C_1] = (v(what) = \psi_{c_1}(what)) = (foodname = sweets)$. The query is:

select *foodname*
from R
where *foodname* $=$ *'sweets'*

and returns the tuple $\langle sweets \rangle$, which is transformed to the fact *likes(who* $\Rightarrow$ *mary, what* $\Rightarrow$ *sweets)*. □

5 Reduced sort signature

For the construction of candidates, we use sort signature Σ. Part of the subsort relationships are implicitly represented in the database, that is, for each fact in a qualified segment, the parents of all symbols at occurrences not in the fixed symbol set D_Q are stored in the qualifier. We do not store these 'implicit' subsort relationships in the LIFE system, but add them when facts are loaded.

The remaining subsort relationships have to be stored in the LIFE system, since we have to be able to reconstruct the entire sort signature. However, part of the subsort relationships implicitly stored in the database are needed to construct candidates. Thus we should either retrieve these relationships at run-time from the database, or simply duplicate the necessary relationships in the LIFE system, or use a combination of both techniques.

We will adopt the second strategy, which is simple, and probably non-optimal: we store sufficient subsort relationships in the LIFE system to compute candidates for any goal and qualifier in program P. We construct a *reduced sort signature* $\Sigma' = \langle S', \le' \rangle$, where $S' \subseteq S$ and $\le' \subseteq \le$.

Definition 22 (Reduced sort signature) *Given* $\Sigma = \langle S, \le \rangle$, *the* reduced sort signature $\Sigma' = \langle S', \le' \rangle$ *is such that* S' *is the subset of* S, *where we may exclude least sorts (parents of bottom) with a single parent, stored in a database relation, and not in a term in a qualifier. The* reduced subsort relation $\le'$ *is the subset of* $\le$, *induced by the set* S' :

$$\le' = \le \cap S' \times S'.$$

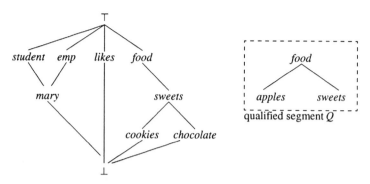

Figure 3. Reduced sort signature Σ'.

Example 5.1 The reduced sort signature Σ' is depicted in Figure 3. The least sorts with a single parent are the symbols *likes, mary, apples, cookies* and *chocolate*. The symbols in the database are *apples* and *sweets*. The symbols not in a qualifier are *student, emp, apples, sweets, cookies* and *chocolate*. Hence, the only symbol that is a least sort, in a database relation and not in a qualifier is *apples*. □

We have to prove that the reduced sort signature is complete; that is, all subsort relationships are represented either in the database or in the reduced sort signature. Moreover, we have to prove that we construct the same candidates with the reduced sort signature.

Theorem 3 *All subsort relationships are either represented in the LIFE system or implicitly in the database.*

Proof Assume a subsort relation $s \leq s'$ where s is not in $\mathcal{S}'$. By definition, s is a symbol in a database relation, and not a symbol in a qualifier. So there is a symbol $s'' \in \mathcal{S}'$ at the corresponding occurrence in the qualifier for this database relation, so $s \leq s''$ is a relation implied by this segment. Since s and s'' are in $\mathcal{S}'$, $s'' \leq' s'$. So we can reconstruct $s \leq s'$, since $s \leq s''$ and $s'' \leq' s'$.

Now assume the relation $s \leq s'$ where s' is not in $\mathcal{S}'$. Since only least sorts are not stored in $\mathcal{S}'$, s must be the bottom symbol, and $\bot \leq s'$ is implicitly defined by the sort signature for any $s' \in \mathcal{S}$. ∎

Theorem 4 *If we exchange Σ for Σ', we construct the same candidates for a goal g and a qualifier* **qua**(Q).

Proof To construct candidates, we compute the unifiable set $U(s)$ for any symbol s in the goal. We define $U'(s)$ as the set containing all symbols in $\mathcal{S}'$ that unify with $s \in \mathcal{S}'$, as defined by the subsort relation $\leq'$. For the correct construction of candidates, $U'(s)$ should contain all symbols in $U(s)$ that are also in $\mathcal{S}'$, that is:

$$\forall s, s' \in \mathcal{S}' : s' \in U'(s) \;\Leftrightarrow\; s' \in U(s)$$

Symbol s' is in $U(s)$ if the maximal common subsort of s and s' is non-bottom. We prove that for any s, s' in $\mathcal{S}'$, maximal common subsorts $s \sqcap s'$ form a subset of $\mathcal{S}'$, and thus that s' is in $U'(s)$ if s' is in $U(s)$. The set $s \sqcap s'$ is either $\{s\}$ or $\{s'\}$, or a set of symbols, smaller than both s and s'. These symbols are all in $\mathcal{S}'$, since we excluded only symbols with a single parent, thus symbols that can never be a maximal common subsort of two other symbols.

Moreover, if $s \sqcap s' = \{\bot\}$ (*i.e.*, $s' \notin U(s)$), than s' is not in the unifiable set $U'(s)$ as well, since the subsort relation $\leq'$ in the reduced sort signature form a subset of the subsort relation $\leq$. ∎

As can be seen in Example 5.1 and Figure 3, simply duplicating all necessary subsorting information works fine for qualified segments containing a large number of facts with least sort symbols (*i.e.*, data typically found in databases), since these symbols are not stored in the reduced sort signature. However, we stress that the above solution is non-optimal, since the reduced sort signature Σ' contains more subsort information than actually needed. We believe it is possible to further 'strip-down' the reduced sort signature. We think of a technique called *segment guessing*, where less subsort information is needed, and the retrieval algorithm queries any database relation that might contain unifiable facts, based on available subsort information.

6 Optimization

To reduce database interaction, we assert loaded facts in the internal LIFE database, instead of retrieving the same facts over and over again. However, if we assert facts in the internal database, we should retrieve each fact only once. Thus when querying the database for all unifiable facts for goal g_i in segment Q, we should exclude all facts loaded from Q for previous goals $g_1, \ldots, g_{i-1}$.

As we stated in Section 4, we can describe each subset $Q[g_i]$ with a selection condition $T[C_i]$. Thus we can exclude any subset with the negation of its selection condition. We select the tuples from the database with an SQL-query:

```
select   t_1, ..., t_n
from     R
where    T[C_i]  and  not (T[C_1])
                 and  ...
                 and  not (T[C_{i-1}])
```

The set of all candidates for previous goals forms an *abstract cache*, storing the results of previous abstract computations; *i.e.*, all constructed candidates. This is also known as the *caching of queries*, as described by Ceri *et al.* in [10]. However, storing all these candidates is expensive, and therefore we will shortly mention a few optimizations.

Instead of storing all previous candidates, we use a single set---called *look-up set* to represent that part of the qualified segment that has been loaded:

Definition 23 (Look-up set) *For a segment Q, we define the* look-up set *$L[i]$ as the set, formed of the maximal terms in the union of candidates $c_1, \ldots, c_i$.*

A look-up set is an equivalent, but more compact notation for a set of candidates, since any term subsumed by another term, is removed. The SQL-query reduces to:

> **select** $t_1, \ldots, t_n$
> **from** R
> **where** $T[C_i]$ **and not** $\left(L[i-1] \right)$

Another optimization consists of posing only queries that might retrieve any tuples, that is, we exclude queries with a contradicting selection condition. This occurs when the current query is subsumed by a previous query, as described in [10]. The subsumption of queries is defined by the subsort relation $\leq$ on candidates. That is, all facts for goal g_i have been loaded if any term c in candidate C_i is subsumed by some term c' in the look-up set: $\forall c \in C_i, \exists c' \in L[i-1] : c \leq c'$.

A third optimization is the partial exclusion of previous queries. If we retrieve a set from the database, we only need to exclude previously retrieved sets that overlap with the current set; *i.e.*, $Q[g_i] \cap Q[g_j] \neq \emptyset$.

We further like to mention that, since candidates are wild card selections, testing subsumption and overlapping reduces to simple comparison operations on the respective sort symbols.

7 Conclusion

We have overviewed a formal design for interfacing a logical query language with complex objects to a relational database. Our system is an improvement on previous systems in that it provides database storage for objects ordered thanks to a subsort hierarchy, representing part of this hierarchy in the database as well. The representation of the objects is flexible; arbitrarily nested objects can be represented in a maximally compressed format, where compressing and decompressing is handled by the interface. The loading algorithm is quite efficient in that it loads only objects actually needed by the LIFE system, and never loads the same object twice, thus improving results in [10]. In addition, our design also improves on previous work by providing for free the ability, intrinsic to ψ-terms, to store and query partial information. For example, if all facts in LIFE's EDB stipulate that all students are happy, a query requesting to list happy things will avoid itemizing *in extenso* all 12,452 tuples of students, giving only the one tuple corresponding to the *intensional* LIFE fact *happy(student)*.

LIFE is an extension of logic programming: first-order logic programs are LIFE programs with a *flat* sort signature; *i.e.*, all sort symbols---except for $\top$ and $\bot$ are incomparable. Hence, the retrieval algorithm holds for languages using Prolog terms as objects as well.

Part of the system described in this paper has been implemented: the LIFE--WISDOM system (*LIFE With Inheritance Supported Data Object Management*) implements a database interface for an implementation of LIFE called Wild_LIFE [3], to an ORACLE relational database [12]. The current system implements both database retrieval and updates, but only for single inheritance and facts consisting of least sorts.

As for the future, we want to extend this approach to goals with variables. For example, a goal such as $name(X, X)$ must only unify with facts with identical arguments and should generate database queries retrieving only tuples with identical values in columns. Then, we may translate entire LIFE rules to complex join operations on the database. The translation of recursive LIFE rules to extended relational algebra expressions must also be explored. Another direction of research consists of weakening the restrictions for the reduced sort signature, by redefining qualified segments and using other search strategies, such as *segment guessing*. Also, we may consider iterating our construction, building multiple levels of abstractions; *i.e.*, the storage of qualifiers themselves in *higher-level* qualified segments.

Acknowledgements

The authors wish to thank Herman Balsters, Jean-Pic Berry, Maurice van Keulen, and Andreas Podelski for their support and useful remarks.

References

1. Hassan Aït-Kaci. An algebraic semantics approach to the effective resolution of type equations. *Theoretical Computer Science*, 45:293--351 (1986).

2. Hassan Aït-Kaci. An introduction to LIFE---programming with logic, inheritance, functions, and equations. In Dale Miller, editor, *Proceedings of the International Symposium on Logic Programming (Vancouver, BC)*, pages 52--68, Cambridge, MA (October 1993). MIT Press.

3. Hassan Aït-Kaci, Bruno Dumant, Richard Meyer, and Peter Van Roy. The Wild_LIFE handbook. PRL Research Report (forthcoming), Digital Equipment Corporation, Paris Research Laboratory, Rueil-Malmaison, France (1994).

4. Hassan Aït-Kaci and Roger Nasr. LOGIN: A logic programming language with built-in inheritance. *Journal of Logic Programming*, 3:185--215 (1986).

5. Hassan Aït-Kaci, Roger Nasr, and Jungyun Seo. Implementing a knowledge-based library information system with typed Horn logic. *Information Processing & Management*, 26(2):249--268 (1990).

6. Hassan Aït-Kaci and Andreas Podelski. Towards a meaning of LIFE. *Journal of Logic Programming*, 16(3-4):195--234 (July-August 1993).

7. François Bancilhon and Setrag Khoshafian. A calculus for complex objects. *Journal of Computer and System Sciences*, 38(2):326--340 (April 1989).

8. O. Peter Buneman, Susan D. Davidson, and Aaron Watters. A semantics for complex objects and approximate answers. *Journal of Computer and System Sciences*, 43(1):170--218 (August 1991).

9. Stefano Ceri, Georg Gottlob, and Letizia Tanca. *Logic Programming and Databases*. Springer Verlag, Berlin, Germany (1990).

10. Stefano Ceri, Georg Gottlob, and Gio Wiederhold. Interfacing relational databases and Prolog efficiently. In Larry Kerschberg, editor, *Proceedings of the 2nd International Conference on Expert Database Systems*, pages 141--153, Menlo Park, CA (1987). Benjamin-Cummings.

11. Patrick Cousot and Radhia Cousot. Abstract interpretation and application to logic programs. *Journal of Logic Pogramming*, 13(2-3):103--179 (1992).

12. Marcel Holsheimer. LIFE--WISDOM, a database interface for the LIFE system. Master's thesis, Computer Science, University of Twente, Enschede, The Netherlands (September 1992).

13. Katherine Morris, Jeffrey D. Ullman, and Allen Van Gelder. Design overview of the Nail! system. In Ehud Shapiro, editor, *Proceedings of the 3rd International Conference on Logic Programming*, pages 544--568, Berlin, Germany (1986). LNCS 225, Springer-Verlag.

14. Shamim Naqvi and Shalom Tsur. *A Logical Language for Data and Knowledge Bases.* Computer Science Press, Rockville, MD (1989).

15. Yannis Vassiliou, James Clifford, and Matthias Jarke. How does an expert system get its data? In *Proceedings of the International Conference on Very Large Databases*, pages 70--72 (1983). Extended abstract.

16. Yannis Vassiliou and Matthias Jarke. Databases and expert systems: Opportunities and architectures for integration. In *New Applications of Databases*, pages 185--201, London, UK (1984). Academic Press.

A slick procedure for integrity checking in deductive databases

Hendrik Decker* and Matilde Celma**

* Siemens ZFE ST SN 33, D-81730 München, hendrik@ztivax.zfe.siemens.de
** DSIC, Univ. Politéc., PO box 22 012, E-46071 Valencia, mcelma@dsic.upv.es

Abstract

We present a resolution-based proof procedure called SLIC, for integrity check-ing in deductive databases. Sadri and Kowalski's meta-level rules are replaced in SLIC by much simpler inference steps. SLIC optimizes the tradeoff between focusing the evaluation of integrity constraints on the difference of consecutive database states, on one hand, and the cost of generating that difference with sufficient precision, on the other. SLIC is sound. It is complete in each case for which also SLDNF is complete. SLIC terminates in a large class of cases. We present a sufficient condition for ensuring the termination of SLIC and also SLDNF, by generalizing the class of acyclic databases and bounded queries.

Introduction

In [SK], a theorem proving approach to integrity checking in deductive databases is proposed. The approach, in short: It is assumed that the current state satisfies integrity. By rooting the reasoning process at clauses from a given update, integrity check-ing is focused on the facts, rules and constraints that are actually affected by the update. That way, a considerable simplification is achieved. Generally, that has been established as a principle in [Ni], for relational databases.

Several other approaches also simplify integrity checking by fo-cusing on affected data, e.g. [Del] [LST] and others. In any of these approaches, two kinds of steps can be distinguished. Firstly, there are steps of *generation*, for capturing the effective difference be-fore and after the update; clauses in that difference are then used to generate simplified instances of affected integrity constraints. Secondly, there are steps of *evaluation* of such instances, which determine satisfaction or violation of integrity. As opposed to other methods, no additional meta-programming is necessary in [SK]. But for processing deletions, a significant amount of extra work is merely encapsulated in meta-level inference rules in [SK]. (For convenience, we identify the method in [SK] with [SK].)

After some preliminaries, we present SLIC, a Selection-driven Linear resolution procedure for Integrity Checking in deductive databases. It is conceived along the lines of [SK]. The latter's meta-level rules are considerably simplified by SLIC inference steps, which are all performed directly on the resolution level. Each SLIC step which replaces the application of a meta-level rule in [SK] merely consists of a single negation-as-failure run. SLIC always operates on the updated state only. As opposed to that, meta-level rules of [SK] have to run several derivations, both in the "old" state (before the update) and in the "new" state (after the update), for determining the precise set of facts that are effectively deleted by an update.

We present soundness, completeness and termination results for SLIC. (For non-definite databases, proving completeness and termination of [SK] is problematic, although such results have been brought about in [Nü] [NDCC].) We argue that SLIC optimizes the tradeoff between focusing the evaluation of constraints on the difference of old and new state, and generating that difference with sufficient precision.

1 Preliminaries

In [SK], "extended clauses" (roughly, clauses in implication form, possibly with a negative literal in the head) are used for representing databases, integrity theories, updates and their consequences. We use a subclass of extended clauses, called "SLIC clauses": A *SLIC clause* is of form $L \leftarrow B$, where the *head* L (if not empty) is a literal, the *body* B (if not empty) is a conjunction of literals, and if L is negative then $B = L$. Each variable in $L \leftarrow B$ is supposed to be universally quantified at the front. SLIC clauses may contain function symbols. A *database clause* is a SLIC clause with a positive literal in the head. A *(deductive) database* is a finite set of database clauses. An *integrity theory* is a finite set of integrity constraints. An *integrity constraint* (shortly, *constraint*) is a *denial*, i.e., a SLIC clause with empty head. Using transformations as described in [Ll] [De3], a representation of constraints as denials is always possible. A *(normal) clause* is either a database clause or a denial. An integrity theory IC is *satisfied in* D if *comp*(D) ∪ IC is a consistent set of formulae, where *comp*(D) is the well-known *completion* of D [Cl] [Ll]. Conversely, IC is *violated in* D if *comp*(D) ∪ IC is inconsistent.

An *update* (often called *transaction* in the literature) is a bi-partite set $U = U_{del} \cup U_{ins}$ of clauses such that no variant of any clause in U_{del} is in U_{ins} and vice-versa. For a database D, an integrity theory IC and an update U, the *updated database* D' and the *updated integrity theory* IC' are obtained by deleting each database clause in U_{del} from D, deleting each denial in U_{del} from IC, inserting each database clause in U_{ins} to D and inserting each denial in U_{ins} to IC, by an indivisible operation.

For a clause $C = A \leftarrow B$ in U_{del}, it may well happen that some consequence of C is still derivable in the updated database, via clauses other than C. Therefore, representing the deletion of C by $\neg C$ or $\neg A \leftarrow B$ (as in [SK] [CCD] and others) is not very accurate. We are going to see that deletions are captured more conveniently by:

Definition For an update $U = U_{del} \cup U_{ins}$, the *operational update* U^* contains each clause in U_{ins}. For each database clause $A \leftarrow B$ in U_{del}, U^* contains the SLIC clause $\neg A \leftarrow \neg A$. Nothing else is contained in U^*. Each SLIC clause in U^* is called an *update clause*. □

Intuitively, a SLIC clause of form $\neg A \leftarrow \neg A$ reads: *Any ground instance A' of A is deleted if all attempts to prove A' in the updated state fail.* SLIC does not care whether any instance of A was true before the update or not. This is similar to the treatment of potential deletions in [LT] [LST], i.e., the meta-rules of [SK] which generate the negation of all facts that hold before the update but no more afterwards, are replaced by checking whether potentially deleted facts are actually no more derivable in the updated state.

2 SLIC resolution

We are going to define SLIC refutations and finitely failed SLIC trees. A SLIC refutation in an updated database, rooted at either an update clause or an integrity constraint, indicates violation of integrity. Conversely, the finite failure of all attempts to refute any update clause or any constraint implies satisfaction. For convenience, we first define what we mean with "resolvent".

Definition Let $C_1 = L_1 \leftarrow B_1$, $C_2 = L_2 \leftarrow B_2$ be two SLIC clauses that do not share any variable, and L a literal in B_1 such that L and L_2 unify by some mgu θ. Then, the SLIC clause $L_1\theta \leftarrow (B \& B_2)\theta$ is a *resolvent of C_1 and C_2 on L and L_2* (as well as a *resolvent of C_2 and C_1 on L_2 and L*) *using* θ, where B is obtained from B_1 by dropping L. □

Definition Let D be a database, IC an integrity theory and C a SLIC clause. A *SLIC refutation of* C *in* D $\cup$ IC is a sequence $C_0 = C$, ..., C_n = [ ] of SLIC clauses, a sequence L_0, ..., L_{n-1} of literals and a sequence θ_1, ..., θ_n of substitutions such that, for each i < n, one of the three points below is applied.

① L_i is selected in the head (resp., body) of C_i, and there is a clause C' in D $\cup$ IC such that C_{i+1} is a resolvent of C_i and a fresh variant C'' of C' on L_i and some literal L in the body (resp., head) of C'', using θ_{i+1} which is an mgu of L and L_i.

② L_i is selected in the body of C_i, L_i is negative and ground, and there is a finitely failed SLIC tree of $\leftarrow$ A in D (of subsidiary rank), where A is the atom of L_i, C_{i+1} is obtained by dropping L_i from C_i and θ_{i+1} is the identity substitution.

③ L_i is selected in the head of $C_i = L_i \leftarrow$ B, and there is a fresh variant $A' \leftarrow B'$ of some database clause in D with a literal L in B' such that the polarities of L and L_i are opposed (i.e., L is negative if L_i is not and vice-versa), θ_{i+1} is an mgu of the atoms of L and L_i and $C_{i+1} = (\neg A' \leftarrow \neg A')\theta_{i+1}$. $\square$

Point ① corresponds to an ordinary, logic-programming-style resolution step; polarities of literals L and L_i are the same. Point ② corresponds to negation-as-failure in SLDNF resolution. (For simplicity, we have not introduced explicit ranks of subsidiary SLIC computations, as in [Ll], by which circularity in the definitions of 'refutation' and 'finitely failed tree' is avoided.)

Now, point ③: As in ①, selecting in the head means to propagate a SLIC clause in forward direction through the bodies of clauses via which consequences of the update are inferred. As opposed to ①, the polarities of the two literals on which the inference step is taken are opposed. Propagating a SLIC clause with positive (resp., negative) literal in the head through a negative (resp., positive) literal in the body of another SLIC clause always yields a SLIC clause with negative literal in the head as resolvent.

The literal $\neg A'\theta_{i+1}$ in the head of C_{i+1} (point ③), which indicates a possible deletion of $A'\theta_{i+1}$, also appears in the body of C_{i+1}, in order to support that $\neg A'\theta_{i+1}$ is deduced if $A'\theta_{i+1}$ cannot be proved. In [SK] and [Del], such tests of (non-) provability are done in separate, rather circumstantial meta-level steps that have to run several derivations on both old and new state.

Since point ③ does not apply if C_i is a denial, a SLIC refutation of a denial C in $D \cup IC$ coincides with an SLDNF refutation of $D \cup \{C\}$. Moreover, the subsidiary SLIC tree of $\leftarrow A$ in D required in point ② is always an SLDNF tree, in effect. Thus, SLIC and SLDNF coincide for checking integrity the "blind" way, i.e., evaluate each constraint as it stands after each update. However, according to [SK], it is in general much more efficient to root integrity checking at update clauses, rather than at (unsimplified) constraints.

In point ③, C_{i+1} is always a tautology. Hence, each step in a SLIC derivation is correct, in the sense that, for a SLIC clause C, a database D and an integrity theory IC, each SLIC clause in a SLIC derivation of C in $D \cup IC$ is a logical consequence of $comp(D) \cup \{C\}$.

At first, it may seem that trivial tautologies of form $\neg A \leftarrow \neg A$ are redundant, since deriving them seems to be the weakest possible gain of knowledge that can be obtained by any inference rule. However, there is more to SLIC clauses of form $\neg A \leftarrow \neg A$ that are either in some operational update U^* or inferred by forward reasoning from some update clause in U^*: They focus the search for detecting integrity violation. For example, let $U_{del} = \{q(a)\}$ and $I = \leftarrow p(x) \,\&\, \neg q(x)$ a constraint. Then, evaluating I as it stands may be quite expensive (e.g., because of a large extension of p). However, SLIC infers, with a single "forward" step from $\neg q(a) \leftarrow \neg q(a)$, the focused constraint $\leftarrow p(a) \,\&\, \neg q(a)$, the evaluation of which is less costly than evaluating the original constraint I. The subgoal $\neg q(a)$ is necessary, since $q(a)$ might still be derivable after the update, in which case $\neg q(a)$ causes SLIC to fail.

According to the distinction mentioned in the introduction, SLIC steps that select in the head (resp., body) are *forward generation* (resp., *backward evaluation*) steps.

Next, we define finitely failed SLIC trees. For brevity, we skip definitions for describing the search space of SLIC. They can be obtained along the lines of similar definitions for SLDNF [LI].

Definition Let D be a database, IC an integrity theory and C_0 a SLIC clause. A *finitely failed SLIC tree of* C_0 *in* $D \cup IC$ is a finite tree such that each of its nodes is a non-empty SLIC clause, its root is C_0 and the following holds.

- Let C be a non-leaf node in the tree and suppose a literal L is selected in C. Then, each SLIC clause derived in one SLIC step from C on L, as defined in the definition of SLIC refutations, modulo variants, is a child node of C.

- Let C be a leaf node in the tree and suppose a literal L is selected in C. Then, none of the three points in the definition of SLIC refutations applies, i.e. no SLIC step can be taken from C. Moreover, if L is negative, ground and selected in the body of C, then there is a SLIC refutation of ← A in D (of subsidiary rank), where A is the atom of L. □

3 An example

The following example is due to [NDCC]. Each fact in the relation room, below, consists of the number of a room (first argument) belonging to a certain department (second argument). Each fact in the relation course consist of its subject (first) and the organizing department (second), i.e., either maths or comp(uting). Each fact in the relation lect(ure) contains course subject (first), room number (second), weekday (third) and start time (fourth). The relation r-equipment records pieces of equipment (second) in rooms (first), and c-equipment specifies equipment (second) needed for courses (first).

The three rules declare certain rooms to be either inadequate or acceptable for certain courses. Note that (perhaps because of scarcity of space) a room may have to be considered acceptable for some course, even though it might qualify as inadequate for that course. Also note that the maths and the computer science departments may use each other's rooms if acceptable and consistent with the integrity constraints. The first constraint denies that there may be two different lectures in the same room at the same time of the same day. The second one forbids that any lecture be held in a room that is not acceptable for the respective course. Integrity is satisfied in the given state.

All variable symbols are represented by (possibly subscribed) capital letters. All constants are strings of digits or lower case characters. The symbol "←" is omitted in clauses that are facts. An expression of form $X \neq Y$, as used in one of the constraints below, is an abbreviation for the literal $\neg \text{equal}(X, Y)$, where the predicate equal is supposed to be defined by the (possibly built-in) clause equal$(X, X) \leftarrow$. For later reference, clauses are numbered.

1 room(5, maths)   4 course(logic, maths)   7 lect(logic, 5, mo, 9)

2 room(6, maths)   5 course(prolog, comp)   8 lect(prolog, 6, tue, 9)

3 room(7, comp)   6 course(lisp, comp)   9 lect(lisp, 7, wed, 10)

10 r-equipment(5, board)   15 c-equipment(logic, board)

11 r-equipment(5, coffee)   16 c-equipment(logic, coffee)

12 r-equipment(6, board)   17 c-equipment(prolog, overhead)

13 r-equipment(6, overhead)   18 c-equipment(prolog, board)

14 r-equipment(7, video)   19 c-equipment(lisp, overhead)

20 inadequate(R, C) ← room(R, X) & course(C, Y) &
                         c-equipment(C, E) & ¬r-equipment(R, E)

21 acceptable(R, C) ← room(R, X) & course(C, X)

22 acceptable(R, C) ← ¬inadequate(R, C)

23   ← lect(C_1, R, W, S) & lect(C_2, R, W, S) & $C_1 \neq C_2$

24   ← lect(C, R, W, S) & ¬acceptable(R, C)

U = U_{del} = {r-equipment(6, overhead)}

The SLIC refutation below shows that the update U (removing the overhead projector from room number 6) violates integrity. Its root is the only element in U*. Used input clauses are identified by their respective numbers. Selected literals are underlined, if there is a choice. Selection proceeds from left to right, in the head first, but delays non-ground negative literals in the body. Substitutions are understood.

<u>¬r-equipment(6, overhead)</u> ← ¬r-equipment(6, overhead)
                    | 20
<u>inadequate(6, C)</u> ← ¬r-equipment(6, overhead) & room(6, X) &
                    course(C, Y) & c-equipment(C, overhead)
                    | 22
          <u>¬acceptable(6, C)</u> ← ¬acceptable(6, C)
                    | 24
     ← ¬acceptable(6, C) & <u>lect(C, 6, W, S)</u>
                    | 8
     ← ¬acceptable(6, prolog)
                    | *negation-as-failure, see tree below*
          [ ]

$\leftarrow$ acceptable(6, prolog)

/ 21   \ 22

$\leftarrow$ <u>room(6, X)</u> & course(prolog, X) $\leftarrow$ ¬inadequate(6, prolog)

| 2   *negation-as-|failure, see below*

$\leftarrow$ course(prolog, maths)   *failure*

|

failure

$\leftarrow$ inadequate(6, prolog)

| 20

$\leftarrow$ <u>room(6, X)</u> & course(prolog, Y) &
c-equipment(prolog, E) & ¬r-equipment(6, E)

| 2

$\leftarrow$ <u>course(prolog, Y)</u> &
c-equipment(prolog, E) & ¬r-equipment(6, E)

| 5

$\leftarrow$ <u>c-equipment(prolog, E)</u> & ¬r-equipment(6, E)

| 17

$\leftarrow$ ¬r-equipment(6, overhead)

| *negation-as-failure*

[ ]

Processing U with [SK] takes some more effort: Before propagating the literal ¬r-equipment(6, overhead) through clause 20 (as done in the first SLIC step above), [SK] checks whether r-equipment(6, overhead) is true in the old and false in the new state. (SLIC does none of that.) If, in the next step, [SK] would propagate inadequate(6, C) through clause 22 (as SLIC does), then [SK] would end up floundering when trying to check whether ¬acceptable(6, C) is true in the new state. Thus, [SK] is forced to select in the body, such that inadequate(6, prolog)$\leftarrow$ is eventually generated. (SLIC ignores the four literals in the body of the first resolvent all together.) Before propagating inadequate(6, prolog) through clause 22, [SK] checks that acceptable(6, prolog) is true in the old and false in the new state. (SLIC only checks the latter, as shown in the subsidiary computations above.)

4 Soundness, completeness and termination of SLIC

For brevity, proofs of the following results are omitted (but are available in the unabridged version of this paper).

Theorem 1 (Soundness of SLIC)

Let D be a database, IC an integrity theory that is satisfied in D, U an update, D' the updated database and IC' the updated integrity theory.

a)   If, for some update clause C in U*, there is a SLIC refutation of C in D' ∪ IC', then IC' is violated in D'.

b)   If, for each update clause C in U*, there is a finitely failed SLIC tree of C in D' ∪ IC', then IC' is satisfied in D'. □

Roughly, the next result says that SLIC is complete whenever SLDNF is. That is, integrity checking with SLIC preserves completeness, relative to SLDNF.

Theorem 2 (Completeness of SLIC)

Let D be a database, IC an integrity theory that is satisfied in D, U an update, D' the updated database and IC' the updated integrity theory. Further, suppose that, for some I ∈ IC', there is an SLDNF refutation of D' ∪ {I}. Then, there is an update clause C ∈ U* and a SLIC refutation of C in D' ∪ IC'. □

In general, both SLDNF and SLIC are not refutation-complete, i.e., violation of integrity is not necessarily detected, no matter if integrity is rooted at constraints or update clauses. Hence, sufficiently large and practically relevant classes of databases and integrity theories that ensure the completeness of the two procedures are of interest. For SLDNF, such classes have been identified, e.g., in [CL] [Ca] [De4]. By theorem 2, each completeness result for SLDNF carries over to SLIC.

According to theorem 1, satisfaction of integrity is shown by the failure of all attempts of SLIC to refute an update clause. However, neither SLDNF nor SLIC do always terminate. Moreover, SLIC does not necessarily terminate whenever SLDNF does. For example, the insertion of $p(f(x)) \leftarrow p(x)$ causes an infinite number of SLIC forward steps, while the evaluation of each constraint with SLDNF may terminate.

On the other hand, SLIC terminates conclusively (i.e., with success or failure) in some cases, while SLDNF does not. For example, suppose that $p(f(x)) \leftarrow p(x)$ is the only clause about p before the update, $I = \leftarrow p(x)$ is a constraint and $U = U_{ins} = \{q\}$. Then, SLIC is likely to terminate with failure when attempting to refute q, while SLDNF will loop infinitely when trying to refute I. Another example is a database without an occurrence of p in the body of any database clause, the integrity constraint $\leftarrow \neg p(x)$ and the update $U = U_{ins} = \{p(a)\}$. Then, SLIC immediately terminates with failure when trying to refute $p(a)$, while SLDNF flounders when tryinging to refute I.

Despite such odds, SLIC terminates for a large class of databases and constraints, for which SLDNF has been shown to always terminate, too. For describing that class, the following definition is convenient. For technical reasons, parts a and b differ slightly from the original definitions in [AB] [Ca], while corresponding consequences are preserved. Parts c and d are adapted from [Nü]. Dependency of clauses is defined by the transitive closure of "direct dependency": A clause C *depends directly* on a clause C' if the head of C' unifies with some atom in the body of C.

Definition Let P be a set of normal clauses and $\underline{P}$ the set of ground instances of clauses in P.

$a)$ P is *acyclic* if there is a mapping $|.|$ assigning each clause in $\underline{P}$ a natural number such that the following holds: For each pair C, C' of clauses in $\underline{P}$ such that C depends on C', $|C'| < |C|$.

$b)$ A denial C is *bounded in* P if $P \cup \{C\}$ is acyclic by a mapping $|.|$ such that the least upper bound of $\{ |\underline{C}| : \underline{C}$ is a ground instance of $C\}$ is a natural number.

$c)$ A clause C is *confined in* P if $P \cup \{C\}$ is acyclic and, for each variable x in C, there is a positive literal L in the body of C such that x occurs in L and $\leftarrow L$ is bounded in P.

$d)$ P is *confined* if each clause in P is confined in P. $\square$

Clearly, if a denial C is bounded in a database D, then $D \cup \{C\}$ is acyclic; if C is range-restricted and bounded in D, then C is confined in D. If a clause C is confined in D, then C is range-restricted and $D \cup \{C\}$ is acyclic. The implications are proper. For example, $\{q(0), q(f(x)) \leftarrow q(x)\} \cup \{\leftarrow q(x)\}$ is acyclic, but $\leftarrow q(x)$ (though range-restricted) is not bounded (let alone confined) in the given database; $\leftarrow p(x) \, \& \, q(x)$ is confined but not bounded in $\{p(0), q(f(x)) \leftarrow q(x)\}$.

The proposition below generalizes results in [AB] [Ca] which, in terms of the definition above, say that, for a denial C which is bounded in a database D, each SLDNF derivation of D ∪ {C} is finite; if, additionally, each clause in D ∪ {C} is range-restricted, then each SLDNF derivation of D ∪ {C} terminates conclusively.

Proposition Let D be a database and C a denial such that C is confined in D. Then, each fair SLDNF derivation of D ∪ {C} is finite. Hence, if D is also range-restricted, then each fair SLDNF derivation of D ∪ {C} terminates with success or failure. □

In the proposition, fairness of selection is essentially the simple condition in [Ll], not the impractical one in [CL]: Since each clause in D ∪ {C} is range-restricted and C is confined in D, it follows that selecting among positive literals in a fair manner (which never is a problem) eventually grounds all variables. Acyclicity, groundness of all variables and range-restrictedness entail that each literal is "potentially failable" [CL]. Hence, also selecting negative literals in a fair manner is no problem. Moreover, acyclicity and groundness of all variables entail termination and, together with range-restrictedness, conclusivity of evaluating a confined query.

Acyclicity and boundedness are backward-oriented, in the sense that these properties cater for the termination of backward derivations. Since SLIC may also reason forwards, confinedness or even boundedness of denials does not suffice for termination. However, if all constraints and all database clauses are confined, then we obtain conclusive termination, as expressed below.

Theorem 3 (Termination of SLIC)
Let D be a database, IC an integrity theory and C a SLIC clause. Further, suppose that D ∪ IC is confined. Then, each fair SLIC derivation of C in D ∪ IC terminates with success or failure. Hence, if C is an update clause from some update that has led to D and IC, and if IC is satisfied in D, then there is a finitely failed SLIC tree of C in D ∪ IC, and each SLIC tree of C in D ∪ IC constructed with a safe and fair selection of literals is finitely failed. □

5 Comparisons and conclusion

SLIC is the result of a development that started with [De0] [De1]. It proceeded via intermediate stages as documented in [De2] [BDM] [NDCC] [CCD] [CD], which took the developments of [LT], [SK], [LST] and discussions with all authors into account.

Now, let us identify each reference with the respective procedure. The essential difference between SLIC and [Del] is that [Del] always attempts to generate the precise difference of literals that are false in the old and true in the new state. As opposed to that, the difference generated by SLIC is in general less precise. In particular, SLIC does not care to exclude "idle" consequences in the difference, while [Del] does. (A literal in the difference is *idle* if it is true in the new state and also already true in the old state).

Also [Del] and [SK] are distinguished by the degree of precision with which the difference of consecutive states is generated: With regard to positive literals that are consequences of a given update, [SK] is less precise than [Del]. However, that does not necessarily entail a loss of focus for evaluation steps. Only in case of idle positive consequences, which are not taken care of in [SK], the higher precision of [Del] may yield a better performance. For generating negative literals in the difference, [Del] and [SK] essentially coincide. Thus, also [SK] is more precise than SLIC with regard to negative literals in the difference. However, as in [Del], the higher precision of [SK] w.r.t. negative literals is obtained only at the expense of additional meta-level reasoning that alternates between two consecutive database states, and therefore tends to be quite costly.

The difference generated by [LST] w.r.t. positive consequences is the least precise of all procedures mentioned so far. For negative literals in the difference, [LST] essentially coincides with SLIC. An advantage of [LST] and SLIC is that both reason exclusively on the new state, while [Del] and [SK] also reason on the old state.

To summarize, SLIC takes advantage of the precision of positive consequences in the difference as generated by [SK]. On the other hand, SLIC profits, similar to [LST], from the lack of potential overhead for generating a precise difference of negative consequences. So, SLIC takes the best of [SK] and [LST] while avoiding their respective flaws, thus attaining a relative optimum between the two: SLIC is more likely to perform better than any of the other procedures, the less idle consequences there are. And even if there are idle consequences, SLIC performs better in most practical cases. Higher precision as obtained by possibly costly meta-level reasoning in [Del] [SK] (which may pay off only sometimes, if at all; e.g., if idle consequences are detected early) is not striven for in SLIC, while the precision of [LST] is improved practically without any additional cost. More on generating a precise difference of consecutive database states can be found in [Kü] [Ol] [Ce] [CCD] [De5]. A more detailed comparison of several of the integrity checking methods mentioned above, including one which corresponds to SLIC with a fixed selection function, is undertaken in [CGMD].

References

[AB] K.R. Apt and M. Bezem, Acyclic Programs, in D.H.D. Warren and P. Szeredi (eds), *Proc. 7th ICLP*, 617-633, MIT Press, 1990.

[BDM] F. Bry, H. Decker and R. Manthey, A uniform approach to constraint satisfaction and constraint satisfiability in deductive databases, in J. Schmidt et al (eds), *Proc. 1st Int'l Conf. Extending Database Technology (EDBT)*, 488-505, Springer LNCS 303, 1988.

[Ca] L. Cavedon, Acyclic logic programs and the completeness of SLDNF-resolution, *Theoretical Computer Science* 86, 81-92, 1991.

[Ce] M. Celma, *Comprobation de la Integridad en Bases de Datos Deductivas*, PhD thesis, DSIC, Universidad Politécnica de Valencia (Spain), 1992.

[CCD] M. Celma, J.C. Casamayor and H. Decker, Improving integrity checking by compiling derivation paths, in M.E. Orlowska and M. Papazoglou (eds), *Advances in Database Research, Proc. 4th Australian Database Conf.*, 145-160, World Scientific, 1993.

[CD] M. Celma and H. Decker, Integrity checking in deductive databases – the ultimate method?, in R. Sacks-Davis (ed), *Proc. 5th Australasian Database Conf.*, 136-146, Global Publications Services, 1994.

[CGMD] M. Celma, C. García, L. Mota and H. Decker, Comparing and synthesizing integrity checking methods for deductive databases, *Proc. 10th IEEE Conf. Data Engineering*, 214-222, 1994.

[CL] L. Cavedon and J.W. Lloyd, A completeness theorem for SLDNF-resolution, *J. Logic Programming* 7, 177-191, 1989.

[Cl] K.J. Clark, Negation as failure, in H. Gallaire and J. Minker (eds), *Logic and Databases*, 293-322, Plenum Press, 1978.

[De0] H. Decker, Expression and enforcement of integrity constraints in Prolog KB version 0, *TR-KB-3*, ECRC, München (Germany), 1985.

[De1] H. Decker, Integrity enforcement on deductive databases, in L. Kerschberg (ed), *Expert Database Systems*, 381-395, Benjamin-Cummings, 1987.

[De2] H. Decker, A note on enforcing integrity with a resolution-like proof procedure, *WP-KB-2*, ECRC, 1987.

[De3] H. Decker, The range form of databases and queries, or: How to avoid floundering, in J. Retti und K. Leidlmair (eds), *Proc. 5. Österreichische Artificial-Intelligence-Tagung*, 114-123, Springer Informatik-Fachberichte 208, 1989.

[De4] H. Decker, On generalized cover axioms, in K. Furukawa (ed), *Proc. 8th ICLP*, 693-707, MIT Press, 1991.

[De5] H. Decker, Knowledge engineering in deductive databases, tutorial handout, *9th IEEE Conf. Data Engineering*, 1993.

[Kü] V. Küchenhoff, On the efficient computation of the difference between consecutive database states, in C. Delobel et al (eds), *Proc. DOOD '91*, 478-502, Springer LNCS 566, 1991.

[Ll] J.W. Lloyd, *Foundations of Logic Programming*, Springer, 1987.

[LST] J.W. Lloyd, E.A. Sonenberg and R.W. Topor, Integrity constraint checking in stratified databases, *J. Logic Programming* 4, 331-343, 1987.

[LT] J.W. Lloyd and R.W. Topor, A basis for deductive database systems, *J. Logic Programming* 2, 93-109, 1985.

[NDCC] G. Nüssel, H. Decker, M. Celma and J.C. Casamayor, A complete proof procedure for efficient integrity checking in deductive databases, in A. Olivé (ed), *Proc. 3rd Int'l Workshop on the Deductive Approach to Information Systems and Databases*, LSI-92-19, Univ. Politèc. Catalunya, Barcelona, 199-216, 1992.

[Ni] J.M. Nicolas, Logic for improving integrity checking in relational data bases, *Acta Informatica* 18, 227-253, 1982.

[Nü] G. Nüssel, Integritätstests in deduktiven Datenbanken – ein beweistheoretischer Ansatz, *Diplomarbeit*, Mathematische Fakultät, LMU München, 1991.

[Ol] A. Olivé, Integrity constraints checking in deductive databases, *Proc. 17th VLDB*, 1991.

[SK] F. Sadri and R.A. Kowalski, A theorem-proving approach to database integrity, in J. Minker (ed), *Foundations of Deductive Databases and Logic Programming*, 313-362, Morgan Kaufman, 1988.

Acknowledgements

We appreciate to have received several helpful referee comments. The second author was supported by CICYT grant TIC93-0475.

LPDA : Another look at Tabulation in Logic Programming

Eric Villemonte de la Clergerie and **Bernard Lang**
INRIA Rocquencourt - BP 105
78153 LE CHESNAY France
{Eric.Clergerie, Bernard.Lang}@inria.fr

Abstract

The Logic Push-Down Automaton (LPDA) is introduced as an abstract operational model for the evaluation of logic programs. The LPDA can be used to describe a significant number of evaluation strategies, ranging from the top-down OLD strategy to bottom-up strategies, with or without prediction. Two types of dynamic programming, i.e. tabular, interpretation are defined, one being more efficient but restricted to a subclass of LPDAs. We propose to evaluate a logic program by first compiling it into a LPDA according to some chosen evaluation strategy, and then applying a tabular interpreter to this LPDA. This approach offers great flexibility and generalizes Magic Set transformations. It explains in a more intuitive way some known Magic Set variants and their limits, and also suggests new developments.

Keywords: logic programs, tabulation, memoing, magic-set, dynamic programming, push-down automata.

1 Introduction

The recent years have seen the popularity of (at least) two approaches to introduce tabulation in Logic Programming, for answer completeness, termination (on DATALOG programs), or efficiency through computation sharing. The first approach consists in adding a memoing mechanism to a standard PROLOG evaluator [TS86, Vie87, War89, LCMVH91]. We will not discuss this approach in this paper. The second approach is provided by the so called Magic Set transformation and its extensions [BR87, BMSU86, Ram88, Sek89]. It relies on a semi-naïve (i.e. with tabulation) bottom-up evaluation of a transformed version of the original program that includes "magic" predicates to restrict the computation to a "useful" part of the search space.

We propose a third approach which, we believe, generalizes and explains Magic Set transformations. Rather than mixing into a single logic program, both data and resolution mechanisms, we introduce a distinct formalism of Logic Push-Down Automata [Lan88a, Lan91] which we believe to be an appropriate operational formalism to express logic programs computations.

The key idea is that the operational proof-tree exploration strategy (e.g. bottom-up, top-down, predictive, ...) is naturally expressed, as for context-free grammars (CFG), by a non-deterministic push-down machine or automaton (PDA). Different types of interpreters can be used to actually execute the code of a PDA, with backtrack, breadth first, or dynamic programming (tabulation). The execution of a logic program is thus decomposed into a compilation phase of the program into a Logical PDA (LPDA), and an interpretation phase of the LPDA code.

The combination of various compilation and interpretation strategies allows us to express uniformly a wide range of logic program evaluation techniques. This paper presents some of that spectrum. It shows in particular that the well known Magic Set techniques may be seen as the application of a particular dynamic programming interpreter to an LPDA that mimics the predictive bottom-up tree exploration proposed first by Earley in the CFG case, and extended by Pereira and Warren to Definite Clause Grammars.

A notable advantage of this approach is the separation of concerns between compilation and interpretation phase, which results in a decomposition and hence a significant simplification of correctness proofs.

After defining our notations in section 2, we give in section 3 a brief account of the Magic Set techniques. Section 4 introduces the logic pushdown automaton (LPDA) and some techniques for compiling logic programs into LPDAs. In section 5 we present two dynamic programming (i.e. tabular) interpretations of LPDAs, and then show in section 6 that the Magic Set construction is equivalent to a combination of the second interpretation technique, dubbed $\mathcal{S}1$, with a specific family of predictive compilers.

2 Notations

We consider pure first order Horn clause programs (without any limitation such as DATALOG or range-restricted clauses). The clause γ_k of a program P is noted "$A_{k.0} :- A_{k.1}, \ldots, A_{k.n_k}.$" where $A_{k.i}$ is an atom.

A query "$?A_1, \ldots, A_n.$" is implicitly normalized by adding
$$\text{``}\gamma_0 : \text{query}(\vec{X}) :- A_1, \ldots, A_n.\text{''}.$$

We also introduce the new set of predicates $\nabla_{k.i}$ which will be used to denote "analysis points"[1] The meaning of the atom $\nabla_{k.i}(\vec{X}_{k.i})\sigma$ is usually that "the first i literals of clause γ_k have been proved for substitution σ." It may also be viewed as an environment where bindings are stored while refuting the head of γ_k. Multiple definitions of variable tuples $\vec{X}_{k.i}$ may be given, but to simplify this presentation[2], we use $\vec{X}_{k.i} = \vec{X}_k = \text{Var}(\gamma_k) = \text{Var}(A_{k.0}) \cup \text{Var}(A_{k.1}) \cup \ldots \cup \text{Var}(A_{k.n_k})$.

---

[1] These predicates were introduced in [Lan88b, Lan88a], and are similar to the supplementary predicates of the Magic Set construction [BR87]. They are the logic counterpart of the dotted-rules of Earley's algorithm [Ear70], which are the crucial step for achieving the $\mathcal{O}(n^3)$ CF parsing complexity.

[2] In section 4, we keep in each tuple only the variables needed to carry information further, as in the Magic Set technique. Reordering literals to minimize this number of variables may have a drastic effect on the complexity of the evaluation, since in the DATALOG case it affects the exponent of the polynomial complexity. However optimal reordering of

$$\nabla_{k.i}(\vec{X}_{k.i})$$
$$\downarrow$$
$$\gamma_k \;:\; A_{k.0} :- A_{k.1}, \ldots, A_{k.i}, A_{k.i+1}, \ldots, A_{k.n_k}.$$

The (meta) atoms call(A) (resp. ret(A)), where A is any atom (or variable ranging over atoms), is used to denote that A is being queried (resp. that A has been proved). Note that call(X) where X is a variable means that every possible atom is being queried.

We recall that an atom A subsumes (or generalizes) an atom B iff there exists a substitution σ such that $B = A\sigma$. By extension, $A_1, \ldots, A_n$ subsumes $B_1, \ldots, B_n$ iff there exists σ such that, for all i, $B_i = A_i\sigma$.

Throughout this paper, the **ancestor** program is our running example:

$$[\textbf{ancestor}] \begin{cases} \gamma_0 : \text{query}(Y) :- a(a, Y). & \gamma_3 : p(a, b). \\ \gamma_1 : a(X, Y) :- p(X, Y). & \gamma_4 : p(b, c). \\ \gamma_2 : a(X, Y) :- a(X, Z), p(Z, Y). \end{cases}$$

3 Magic Set

3.1 Presentation

The Magic Set technique is a rewriting of logic programs so as to guide the bottom-up evaluation with a top-down predictive control, thus reducing the number of useless intermediate results produced. It can be seen as a goal-oriented bottom-up evaluation. There is however a price to be paid in the added predictive control, and one must be careful that it remains smaller than the gain it procures [Shi85].

The better known description of this technique is the Magic Set transformation for DATALOG programs [BMSU86, BR87, Ram88]. It has been extended to PROLOG programs as the "Magic Templates" transformation [Ram88] and the "Alexander Templates" transformations [RLK86, Sek89].

The formulation of the transformation rules differs slightly from [BR87] and takes after [Nil91]. In particular, the atoms call(A) (resp. ret(A)) are used in place of magic(A) (resp. of A).

1. Each clause γ_k of P is replaced by the $n_k + 1$ following clauses:

(α) $\qquad\qquad$ ret($A_{k.0}$) :- call($A_{k.0}$), ret($A_{k.1}$), ..., ret($A_{k.n_k}$).
(β) $\quad \forall i \in [0, n_k - 1]$, call($A_{k.i+1}$) :- call($A_{k.0}$), ret($A_{k.1}$), ..., ret($A_{k.i}$).

2. The initial query is replaced by the fact: "call($A_{0.0}$).".

3. The answer substitutions σ are extracted from the facts "ret($A_{0.0}$)σ.".

---

a rule is a register allocation problem, which is NP hard in the size of the rule.

The (α) clauses propagate pseudo-facts $ret(A)$ on condition that they be associated with a pseudo-query $call(A)$. The (β) clauses are used to initiate the pseudo-queries $call(A_{k.i})$ as the rule γ_k is being reduced.

For instance, here is the compilation of γ_2 for the program **ancestor** :

$$\left\{ \begin{array}{l} ret(\text{a}(X,Y)) :\!-call(\text{a}(X,Y)), ret(\text{a}(X,Z)), ret(\text{p}(Z,Y)). \\ call(\text{a}(X,Z)) :\!-call(\text{a}(X,Y)). \\ call(\text{p}(Z,Y)) :\!-call(\text{a}(X,Y)), ret(\text{a}(X,Z)). \end{array} \right.$$

3.2 Supplementary Magic Templates

A second version of the construction, called "Supplementary Magic Templates" [BR87, SR93], is closer to the ideas presented in this paper. It uses the "supplementary predicates" $\nabla_{k.i}$ to identify partial refutations, and thus avoids redoing them in a tabulating evaluation.

$$\begin{array}{lll} (\boldsymbol{\alpha}) & & ret(A_{k.0}) :\!-\nabla_{k.n_k}(\vec{X}_k). \\ (\boldsymbol{\beta}) & \forall i \in [0, n_k - 1], & call(A_{k.i+1}) :\!-\nabla_{k.i}(\vec{X}_k). \\ (\boldsymbol{\gamma}) & & \nabla_{k.0}(\vec{X}_k) :\!-call(A_{k.0}). \\ (\boldsymbol{\eta}) & \forall i \in [0, n_k - 1], & \nabla_{k.i+1}(\vec{X}_k) :\!-\nabla_{k.i}(\vec{X}_k), ret(A_{k.i+1}). \end{array}$$

Note In practice, for each k, the α and η rules are merged for $i = n_k$, thus producing the rule $(\boldsymbol{\alpha\eta})$ $ret(A_{k.0}) :\!-\nabla_{k.n_k-1}(\vec{X}_k), ret(A_{k.n_k})$.

We illustrate these rules on the clause γ_2 of the **ancestor** example.

(γ_2) $\nabla_{2.0}(X,Y,Z) :\!-call(\text{a}(X,Y)).$ (α_2) $ret(\text{a}(X,Y)) :\!-\nabla_{2.2}(X,Y,Z).$
$(\beta_{2.1})$ $call(\text{a}(X,Z)) :\!-\nabla_{2.0}(X,Y,Z).$ $(\eta_{2.1})$ $\nabla_{2.1}(X,Y,Z) :\!-\nabla_{2.0}(X,Y,Z), ret(\text{a}(X,Z)).$
$(\beta_{2.2})$ $call(\text{p}(Z,Y)) :\!-\nabla_{2.1}(X,Y,Z).$ $(\eta_{2.2})$ $\nabla_{2.2}(X,Y,Z) :\!-\nabla_{2.1}(X,Y,Z), ret(\text{p}(Z,Y)).$

3.3 Technical points

Magic Set techniques were initially intended for semi-naïve bottom-up evaluators working with ground atoms. This imposes in practice (1) to consider only "range restricted" programs, and (2) to use predicate specialization techniques based on the mode of their arguments (adornments). Extensions of Magic Set transformations to compute with non-ground complex terms generally require (1) a subsumption mechanism to eliminate redundant results, (2) a mechanism for indexing large sets of non-ground atoms, and (3) structure sharing techniques to reduce the tabulation costs, as well as speed up subsumption [VdlC93b, SR93].

4 Logic Push-Down Automata

4.1 History

The approach presented here takes its roots in the work on context-free (CF) parsing. First it extends the concept of push-down automaton, the standard operational model used to described parsing strategies, known to be one of the more natural devices for exploring tree structures — proof trees in our case. It also extends "Chart Parsing" [Ear70] which, by using dynamic programming techniques, i.e. tabulation, can achieve the best known complexity bounds for practical parsers[3].

The principle of our approach — compilation of the grammar/program into PDA code, and dynamic programming interpretation of that code on actual data — was first proposed for CF parsing [Lan74], thus allowing the optimization of chart parsers through the use of well known PDA construction techniques [BL89], as well as providing a common theoretical justification to a variety of general CF parsers. It was later extended for DATALOG [Lan88b] and then for PROLOG, or more precisely for full first order Horn Clauses [Lan88a].

4.2   Logic Push Down Automata

Resolution strategies (OLD, bottom-up, Earley deduction, ...) can be decomposed into a non-deterministic proof-tree exploration strategy, and a strategy to handle the non-determinism. Most tree exploration strategies can be expressed by PDA construction techniques which are the object of this section. Section 5 will consider the handling of non-determinism when interpreting the PDA.

A PDA in the classical CF sense is usually an automaton consisting of a finite state memory and a pushdown memory that determine the state of the automaton, together with a finite set of transitions (that may scan an input string) that defines the possible successive states changes in computations starting from some standard initial state. One essential characteristic is that each transition can observe or change the pushdown stack only to a bounded depth from its top.

Without loss of generality, the PDA model we consider has no finite state memory, since it can always be encoded in the top of the stack (which is on the left in our horizontal notation). We have three kinds of transitions, namely PUSH: $B \mapsto CB$, POP: $BD \mapsto C$ and replacement SWAP: $B \mapsto C$, where B, C, D are pushdown stack symbols, ignoring the input scanning for simplicity. Note that the POP transitions replace two stack symbols by a single one, which is necessary to do away with the finite memory. The well known LR parsers are a typical example of this formalization of PDAs. Classical parsing technology **compiles** grammars into PDAs which are then interpreted (at least when deterministic) on the sentences to be parsed. This strategy is also applicable to non-deterministic PDAs [Lan74].

The Logic PDA (LPDA) follows exactly the same structure, but stack symbols are replaced by logic atoms on some sets of predicate, function and variable symbols[4]. Transitions are as in the above PDA model, but with (usually non-ground) atoms in place of symbols, and are applied to stack

---

[3] Better bounds are known for CF recognizers.

[4] Predicate symbols need not be distinguished from function symbols.

elements modulo a unification process, as illustrated in figure 1. A full formal definition is given in [Lan88a, VdlC93a]. A notable point is that the substitution σ produced by the unification is to be applied to the whole stack. It is however easy to preserve the bounded depth property of classical PDAs by appropriately delaying the application of this substitution. A computation starts from a standard *initial* stack, and the results, i.e. answer substitutions, may be simply extracted from *final* stacks (characterized by the predicate appearing at the top).[5]

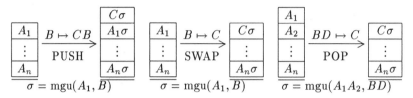

Figure 1: Application of a transition on $[A_1, \ldots, A_n]$

4.3 Compilation

Following the CF parser methodology, we now show some techniques, i.e. *compilation schemes*, for compiling a logic program (including the query) into a LPDA $\mathcal{A}$ that gives the same results. Formalization and correctness proofs for these constructions may be found in [Lan88a, VdlC93a].

With the 3 types of transitions defined above, a wide variety of compilation schemes may be defined. However, to preserve space within this paper, we shall consider only instantiations of the following generic scheme that covers a number of strategies found in the literature. Actual compilation schemes will be then defined by specifying the meta-symbols $C_{k.i}$ and $R_{k.i}$.

Recall that a program is a collection of rules γ_k: $A_{k.0} :- A_{k.1}, \ldots, A_{k.n_k}$. with $k \in [0, n]$. The transitions to be produced by the compiler are:

- **[I]**nit : starts the computation on the initial stack.

$$\$_{\text{init}}() \mapsto \nabla_{0.0}(\vec{X}_0)\$_{\text{init}}()$$

- **[C]**all : calls a sub-query from a calling environment.

$$[\mathbf{C}]_{k.i+1} \qquad \nabla_{k.i}(\vec{X}_k) \mapsto \text{call}(C_{k.i+1})\nabla_{k.i}(\vec{X}_k) \qquad \forall k, i \in [0, n_k - 1]$$

- **[S]**elect : selects a rule for refutation.

$$[\mathbf{S}]_l \qquad \text{call}(A_{l.0}) \mapsto \nabla_{l.0}(\vec{X}_l) \qquad \forall l \neq 0$$

- **[T]**abulate : tabulate a computed fact resulting from a successful refutation.

---

[5]It is straightforward to show that transition application is monotonic w.r.t. the subsumption order, i.e. when $\xi \preceq \theta$ for two stacks ξ and θ , then for any transition τ we have $\tau\xi \preceq \tau\theta$ whenever τ is applicable to θ.

[T]$_l$ $\qquad$ $\nabla_{l.n_l}(\vec{X}_l) \mapsto \text{ret}(A_{l.0})$ $\quad \forall l \neq 0$

- **[R]**eturn : returns to the calling environment after tabulation.

[R]$_{k.i+1}$ $\qquad$ $\text{ret}(R_{k.i+1})\nabla_{k.i}(\vec{X}_k) \mapsto \nabla_{k.i+1}(\vec{X}_k)$ $\quad \forall k, i \in [0, n_k - 1]$

The initial stack is $[\$_{\text{init}}()]$ and we call "*LPDA answer substitution*" any substitution α such that the final stack $\left[\nabla_{0.n_0}(\vec{X}_0)\alpha, \$_{\text{init}}()\right]$ is (non-deterministically) reachable.

Figure 2 illustrates graphically the computation steps corresponding to this generic scheme.

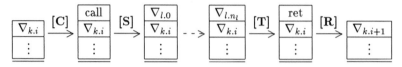

Figure 2: Intuitive view of some computation steps

This generic compilation scheme is parameterized by the set of atoms (or possibly variables) $C_{k.i}$ and $R_{k.i}$ which must only verify the relation:

$$\text{mgci}(\frac{C_{k.i+1}}{\nabla_{k.i}(\vec{X}_k)}, \frac{R_{k.i+1}}{\nabla_{k.i}(\vec{X}_k)}) \equiv \frac{A_{k.i+1}}{\nabla_{k.i}(\vec{X}_k)} \qquad \forall k, i \qquad (1)$$

where $\text{mgci}(x, y)$ denotes the most general common instance of its 2 arguments, and $\frac{A}{B}$ represents a pair of atoms.

Intuitively, this criterion means that the information (or constraints) existing between $\nabla_{k.i}(\vec{X}_k)$ and $A_{k.i+1}$ are well distributed between the call and return steps.

Theorem 4.1 *LPDA correctness*: Any LPDA built according to the above generic scheme from a logic program P and a query Q, is correct. It computes non-deterministically the same answer substitutions as P on query Q, for any choice of the $C_{k.i}$ and $R_{k.i}$ that meets condition (1).

The choice of $C_{k.i}$ and $R_{k.i}$ gives fine control over the information flow -1- in the sub-queries for the $C_{k.i}$ (top-down flow), and -2- in the propagation of computed facts for the $R_{k.i}$ (bottom-up flow). The following table 1 shows the choices corresponding to some classical resolution strategies (with X denoting a fresh variable).

Thus the purely top-down OLD strategy of PROLOG imposes maximal prediction, but no bottom-up propagation of computed facts. Pure bottom-up resolution imposes no restriction on sub-queries, which can actually be optimized away, but checks bottom-up propagation of computed facts. Earley resolution [Por86, PW83] does maximal prediction and bottom-up check. Intermediate strategies are possible as suggested by [Shi85].

Scheme	OLD	Earley	Bottom-Up
$C_{k.i}$	$A_{k.i}$	$A_{k.i}$	X
$R_{k.i}$	X	$A_{k.i}$	$A_{k.i}$

$$(X \notin \vec{X}_k)$$

Table 1: Some specializations of the generic compilation scheme

The (unoptimized) Earley compilation of clause γ_2 of the **ancestor** example gives the following transitions:

$$\gamma_2 \begin{cases} [\mathbf{S}]_2 & \mathrm{call}(\mathrm{a}(X,Y)) \mapsto \nabla_{2.0}(X,Y,Z) \\ [\mathbf{C}]_{2.1} & \nabla_{2.0}(X,Y,Z) \mapsto \mathrm{call}(\mathrm{a}(X,Z))\nabla_{2.0}(X,Y,Z) \\ [\mathbf{R}]_{2.1} & \mathrm{ret}(\mathrm{a}(X,Z))\nabla_{2.0}(X,Y,Z) \mapsto \nabla_{2.1}(X,Y,Z) \\ [\mathbf{C}]_{2.2} & \nabla_{2.1}(X,Y,Z) \mapsto \mathrm{call}(\mathrm{p}(Z,Y))\nabla_{2.1}(X,Y,Z) \\ [\mathbf{R}]_{2.2} & \mathrm{ret}(\mathrm{p}(Z,Y))\nabla_{2.1}(X,Y,Z) \mapsto \nabla_{2.2}(X,Y,Z) \\ [\mathbf{T}]_2 & \nabla_{2.2}(X,Y,Z) \mapsto \mathrm{ret}(\mathrm{a}(X,Y)) \end{cases}$$

Optimizations:

1. Some transitions may be merged. For example the return of the last literal $[\mathbf{R}]_{k.n_k}$ and the following tabulation transition $[\mathbf{T}]_k$ may be merged into a transition $\mathrm{ret}(R_{k.n_k})\nabla_{k.n_k-1}(\vec{X}_k) \mapsto \mathrm{ret}(R_{k.0})$. It is similarly possible to better compile facts, clauses of length 1, and the merge of $[\mathbf{S}]_k$ and $[\mathbf{C}]_{k.1}$ transitions.

2. It is not necessary to keep all variables of a clause γ_k during the whole refutation process. One can keep with each $\nabla_{k.i}$ only a vector $\vec{X}_{k.i}$ of useful variables, i.e. those already carrying bindings that will be needed later. The definition of these vectors is however often complex due to the spread of bindings propagation between bottom-up and top-down phases. Table 2 gives the variables in $\vec{X}_{k.i}$ for the OLD, Bottom-Up and Earley schemes, for $k \neq 0$.[6] Table 3 contains the actual vector for an example (with $\vec{A}_{k.i} = \mathrm{Var}(A_{k.i})$).

3. Some choices of the $C_{k.i}$ and $R_{k.i}$ atoms allow simplifications. For example, for the OLD scheme, the tabulation transition $[\mathbf{T}]$ may be simplified into $\nabla_{l.n_l}(\vec{X}_l) \mapsto \mathrm{ret}(X)$, since in the absence of constraints on fact propagation, tabulation is useless. Similarly, in the bottom-up case, the selection transition $[\mathbf{S}]$ simplifies into $\mathrm{call}(X) \mapsto \nabla_{l.0}(\vec{X}_l)$. More generally, if a subterm of an atom is systematically generalized during prediction, the corresponding subterm in the selection transition can also be generalized. The same principle applies for tabulation and return transitions.[7]

---

[6] The case $k = 0$ is different since we want to get the answer substitutions at the end of the refutation of γ_0.

[7] This suggests a higher abstraction level for the generic scheme, by parameterizing further the selection and tabulation transitions.

Scheme	$\vec{X}_{k.i}$
OLD	$\left(\bigcup_{j=0}^{j=i} \vec{A}_{k.j} \cap \vec{A}_{k.i+1}\right) \cup \left(\bigcup_{j=0}^{j=i+1} \vec{A}_{k.j} \cap \bigcup_{j=i+2}^{j=n_k} \vec{A}_{k.j}\right)$
Earley	$\left(\bigcup_{j=1}^{j=i} \vec{A}_{k.j} \cap \left[\vec{A}_{k.0} \cup_{j=i+1}^{j=n_k} \vec{A}_{k.j}\right]\right) \cup \left(\vec{A}_{k.0} \cap \bigcup_{j=1}^{j=n_k} \vec{A}_{k.j}\right)$
Bottom-Up	$\left(\bigcup_{j=1}^{j=i} \vec{A}_{k.j}\right) \cap \left(\vec{A}_{k.0} \cup_{j=i+1}^{j=n_k} \vec{A}_{k.j}\right)$

Table 2: Definition of the $\vec{X}_{k.i}$

Scheme	$\vec{X}_{k.0}$	$\vec{X}_{k.1}$	$\vec{X}_{k.2}$	$\vec{X}_{k.3}$
OLD	X,Y,V	Y,V	V	$\emptyset$
Earley	X,Y	X,Y,V	X,Y,V	X,Y
Bottom-Up	$\emptyset$	X,V	X,Y,V	X,Y

Table 3: Definition of the $\vec{X}_{k.i}$ for $\gamma_k : a(X,Y,Z) :- b(X,V), c(Y,W), d(V)$.

5 Dynamic Programming Interpretation of LPDA

So far LPDAs are abstract non-deterministic devices, intended as an abstract operational model of logic programs computations. Actual interpretation of LPDA requires in particular the choice of an implementation strategy to handle non-determinism. This could be backtrack as in PROLOG or breadth-first. We describe here two *Dynamic Programming (DP)*, or tabular, techniques $\mathcal{S}1$ and $\mathcal{S}2$ that generalize CF chart parsing, and use a semi-naïve saturation.

The key idea is that a LPDA computation never uses information below the top of the stack until the top is POPped. Hence, computations can be factorized w.r.t. stack tops. Stack tops, called here *items*, are the basic data structure used by our DP interpreters. In the $\mathcal{S}2$ interpretation an item consists of the top two stack elements $<A_1|A_2>$ (topmost on the left), while an $\mathcal{S}1$ item consists only of the topmost stack element $<A_1|$. Starting from an initial item[8], corresponding to the initial stack, transitions are applied to already computed items and produce new items, or *derived SWAP transitions* in the case of POP.[9] Table 4 describes, for both interpretations, the application of a transition τ to a (renamed) item. All possible items (up

---

[8] where $\diamond$ denotes the stack bottom.

[9] Strictly speaking, a POP transition applies to pairs of items, but partial application on the first item returns a SWAP transition. For uniformity reasons, we describe this partial application explicitly.

The following table shows how to apply directly $BD \mapsto C$ on a pair of items.

	$\sigma =$	$\mu =$	output
$\mathcal{S}2$-items $<A_1|A_2><E_1|E_2>$	$\mathrm{mgu}([A_1, A_2], [B, D])$	$\mathrm{mgu}(B\sigma, E_1)$	$<C\sigma\mu|E_2\mu>$
$\mathcal{S}1$-items $<A_1|\ <E_1|$	$\mathrm{mgu}(A_1, B)$	$\mathrm{mgu}(D\sigma, E_1)$	$<C\sigma\mu|$

to subsumption) are computed, and answers are extracted from *final items* corresponding to the tops of final stacks.

τ	S2-item $<A_1\|A_2>$		S1-item $<A_1\|$	
	$\sigma =$	output	$\sigma =$	output
$B \mapsto CB$	$\text{mgu}(A_1, B)$	$<C\sigma\|A_1\sigma>$	$\text{mgu}(A_1, B)$	$<C\sigma\|$
$B \mapsto C$	$\text{mgu}(A_1, B)$	$<C\sigma\|A_2\sigma>$	$\text{mgu}(A_1, B)$	$<C\sigma\|$
$BD \mapsto C$	$\text{mgu}([A_1, A_2], [B, D])$	$D\sigma \mapsto C\sigma$	$\text{mgu}(A_1, B)$	$D\sigma \mapsto C\sigma$
initial item	$<\$_{\text{init}}()\|\diamond>$		$<\$_{\text{init}}()\|$	
final items	$<\nabla_{0.n_0}(\vec{X}_0)\alpha\|\$_{\text{init}}()>$		$<\nabla_{0.n_0}(\vec{X}_0)\alpha\|$	

Table 4: Application of τ on a S2 or S1 item

Note that transition application is monotonic in both interpretations.

Theorem 5.1 *Correctness of S2 interpretation:* The S2 interpretation of a LPDA is sound and complete w.r.t. the abstract non-deterministic stack interpretation. This means that:[10]

1. for any derivable stack $[A_1, A_2, \ldots]$, there exists a derivable S2-item $<B_1\|B_2>$ such that $<B_1\|B_2> \preceq <A_1\|A_2>$

2. for any derivable S2-item $<B_1\|B_2>$, there exists a derivable stack $[A_1, A_2, \ldots]$ such that $<A_1\|A_2> \preceq <B_1\|B_2>$

Theorem 5.2 *Correctness of S1 interpretation:* The S1 interpretation of a LPDA is complete w.r.t. the abstract non-deterministic stack interpretation. It is sound for any LPDA $\mathcal{A}$ satisfying the following *bottom-up property*:

Bottom-Up property:
For every POP transition $BD \mapsto C$ of LPDA $\mathcal{A}$, if there are two non-deterministic computations: $[\$_{\text{init}}()] \vdash^{\ast} [D_1, D_2, D_3, \ldots]$
and $[\$_{\text{init}}()] \vdash^{\ast} [B_1, B_2, B_3, \ldots]$
such that $\sigma = \text{mgu}(\langle B, D \rangle, \langle B_1, D_1 \rangle)$,
then there is a computation $[D\sigma] \vdash^{\ast} [A, D\sigma]$ such that $A \preceq B\sigma$.

Despite its apparent complexity, this property simply states that the possible results of the non-deterministic computation are constrained only by return constraints, i.e. by bottom-up propagation of computed facts. These results would not be changed by weakening the constraints on top-down propagation of information.

In the case of our generic compilation scheme, the bottom-up property is equivalent to the condition $R_{k.i} = A_{k.i}$ for every (k, i). The Earley and Bottom-up schemes are S1 correct, but in general the OLD scheme is not.

It is actually possible to mix S1 and S2, in order to take advantage of the greater simplicity of S1 only where its use is sound.

---

[10]Actually answer correctness requires the stated correspondence only between final stacks and items. However, it comes as a corollary of the existence of the stated correspondence between stacks and items at every step of the computations.

5.1   DyALog : a fixed-point based implementation

The simplicity of derived items (and of derived transitions) makes their tabulation tractable. Since transitions applications, and hence computations, are monotonic w.r.t. both the transitions and the items, it is possible to discard any derived object that is subsumed by a more general derived object (this is a generalization of the elimination of already known facts in ground semi-naïve evaluation). We call *representative* of a derivable object any derivable object that is more general.

The architecture of an efficient complete evaluator for logic program, called DyALog, has been based on these results. It uses a fixed-point saturation algorithm, with tabulation and subsumption (i.e. semi-naïve) to compute a representative of all derivable items (which represent all computable stacks). DyALog works for both dynamic programming interpretations $S1$ and $S2$ (and also for their combinations), because it relies on a uniform and simple execution model described in Figure 3.

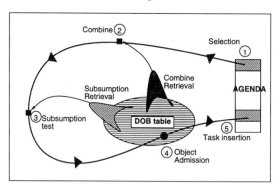

Figure 3: An execution model for DyALog

A characteristic of this implementation model is that it manages both items and transitions in a uniform way. Hence we call *Dynamic Object (DOB)* any object manipulated by DyALog, whether transitions , or items for $S1$ and $S2$ interpretations.

The main two components of DyALog are (1) a table where all DOBs are tabulated[11], and (2) an agenda which keeps a collection of DOBs to be processed and decides on the order of their processing.[12] An execution cycle goes as follows (cf. Figure 3):

(step 1) A DOB O_1 is selected in the agenda, and **(step 2)** a search is done in the table ("combination retrieval") to retrieve each tabulated DOBs

---

[11]In practice, some DOBs may not be tabulated, but this is beyond the scope of this paper.

[12]The DOB ordering strategy of the agenda must be *fair* to ensure answer completeness. It is however possible to consider also unfair agendas to mimic other types of computations, such as pure backtrack.

O_2 that can be combined with O_1. **(step 3)** The combination of O_1 and O_2 (always an item and a transition) produces a new DOB O_3, that is then checked for subsumption against all tabulated DOBs (new "subsumption retrieval"). **(step 4)** If O_3 survives the subsumption check, it is tabulated, and **(step 5)** scheduled in the agenda.

With a fair agenda, the algorithm is complete and terminates when the DOB domain is finite modulo subsumption (i.e. any set of DOBs has a finite number of most general elements). This is the case for DATALOG. The subsumption test may be weakened to an equivalence test, or in the ground case to syntactic equality, generally at some cost in efficiency or termination. The implantation problems we face with DyALog are very similar to those already mentioned in section 3.3 for non-ground evaluators, viz. the indexation and the storage of the DOB table. Presently, DyALog indexes on all first level atom arguments and uses an efficient structure-sharing mechanism [VdlC93b, VdlC93a].

6 Magic Set transformations vs LPDAs

6.1 Equivalence of Magic Set and Earley constructions

In the $\mathcal{S}1$ interpretation of LPDAs, we can observe that items may be viewed as facts already proved, and transitions as clauses as follows:

Transition τ	$B \mapsto C\,B$	$B \mapsto C$	$BD \mapsto C$
Clause	$C :- B.$	$C :- B.$	$C :- D, B.$

The $\mathcal{S}1$ interpretation of an LPDA is identical (up to notations) to a bottom-up evaluation of the clauses corresponding to its transitions. Applying this correspondence to transitions of the Earley LPDA obtained by compiling a logic program, we obtain:

$$
\begin{array}{lll}
[\mathbf{T}] \mapsto (\boldsymbol{\alpha}) & & \mathrm{ret}(A_{k.0}) :- \nabla_{k.n_k}(\vec{X}_k). \\
[\mathbf{C}] \mapsto (\boldsymbol{\beta}) & \forall i \in [0, n_k - 1], & \mathrm{call}(A_{k.i+1}) :- \nabla_{k.i}(\vec{X}_k). \\
[\mathbf{S}] \mapsto (\boldsymbol{\gamma}) & & \nabla_{k.0}(\vec{X}_k) :- \mathrm{call}(A_{k.0}). \\
[\mathbf{R}] \mapsto (\boldsymbol{\eta}) & \forall i \in [0, n_k - 1], & \nabla_{k.i+1}(\vec{X}_k) :- \nabla_{k.i}(\vec{X}_k), \mathrm{ret}(A_{k.i+1}).
\end{array}
$$

Those rules are no other than those produced by the Magic Set construction,[13] as presented in section 3.2. The two techniques are thus computationally isomorphic. More generally, variants of the Magic Set construction describes call-return strategies which can be adequately described with $\mathcal{S}1$-correct LPDAs.

Our purpose here is not to rediscover via a different path the well established Magic Set techniques. Rather we wish to show that a different formal paradigm, based on a fairly natural construction, which is a direct extension

---

[13] Compare the transitions for the Earley LPDA of `ancestor` in Section 4 with the corresponding Magic Set clauses in Section 3.2.

of classical formal languages technology, is computationally isomorphic to the Magic Set approach. We believe that it gives a new and probably more intuitive understanding of the structures involved, which should help both theory and implementation.

The explanatory power of the LPDA approach is further illustrated in the next section.

6.2   From $\mathcal{S}2$ to $\mathcal{S}1$

The examination of the $\mathcal{S}1$ interpretation shows that it amounts to forgetting the push-down store structure of the LPDA. The equivalence between $\mathcal{S}1$ interpretation and Magic Set transformation thus suggests that Magic Set is ill-adapted to the representation of phenomena related to the push-down store structure, even though it is possible to contrive it as we see below.

For example, it is quite easy to define a variant of the OLD compilation scheme which does tail-recursion elimination by freeing environments while making the last call to a sub-query of a clause. One simply has to replace transitions $[\mathbf{C}]_{k.n_k}$, $[\mathbf{R}]_{k.n_k}$ and $[\mathbf{T}]_k$ by a new transition $[\mathbf{lCT}]$:[14]

$[\mathbf{lCT}]$ $\qquad\qquad \nabla_{k.n_k-1}(\vec{X}_k) \mapsto \mathrm{call}(A_{k.n_k}) \quad \forall k \neq 0$

However, like the pure OLD scheme, this modified version does not have the bottom-up property and is not $\mathcal{S}1$-correct. Hence we can expect that this kind of "last call optimization" will be hard to express in the Magic Set framework. The discussion below gives a general framework to explains the method followed by [RS91] to achieve this optimization.

The problem of the $\mathcal{S}1$ interpretation is that it does not preserve the stack structure. In order to preserve this structure, we have to consider pairs of stack elements as in the $\mathcal{S}2$ interpretation, but we will encode those pairs directly in the transitions, so as to be able to $\mathcal{S}1$ interpret them, i.e. we consider transitions on a stack of pair $\langle A, A' \rangle$ of atoms.[15] We achieve this by transforming the LPDA, defining for each transition τ a new transition $\tilde{\tau}$, according to the following table, where X denotes a new variable not occurring in τ :

τ	$B \mapsto CB$	$B \mapsto C$	$BD \mapsto C$
$\tilde{\tau}$	$\langle B, X \rangle \mapsto \langle C, B \rangle \langle B, X \rangle$	$\langle B, X \rangle \mapsto \langle C, X \rangle$	$\langle B, D \rangle \langle D, X \rangle \mapsto \langle C, X \rangle$

It is quite clear that this transformation encodes the pairs of $\mathcal{S}2$ interpretation directly in the transitions, by memorizing the second topmost stack element in the variable X. Thus the items computed by an $\mathcal{S}1$ interpreter of the transformed transitions are really the pair items computed by an $\mathcal{S}2$ interpretation of the original LPDA transitions.

---

[14]This implies that $n_k \geq 1$, i.e. γ_k is not a fact.

[15]Such pairs may be seen as atoms by considering the pairing operator $\langle \ , \ \rangle$ as a new predicate.

Theorem 6.1 Given an LPDA $\mathcal{A}$, let $\tilde{\mathcal{A}}$ be the LPDA produced from $\mathcal{A}$ with the above transformation. The LPDA $\tilde{\mathcal{A}}$ is $\mathcal{S}1$-correct, and its $\mathcal{S}1$ interpretation is equivalent to the $\mathcal{S}2$ interpretation of $\mathcal{A}$, i.e.:

1. $\vdash^{\mathcal{A}}_{\star} [A, B \mid \xi]$ iff $\vdash^{\tilde{\mathcal{A}}}_{\star} [\langle A, B \rangle \mid \tilde{\xi}]$ where ξ and $\tilde{\xi}$ are stack tails.

2. $\tilde{\mathcal{A}}$ is $\mathcal{S}1$-correct.

If we apply this transformation to the OLD compilation scheme, we get the transitions given below (omitting the i and k quantifications). The corresponding LPDAs are $\mathcal{S}1$-correct, but equivalent to those produced by the original OLD scheme.

[I] $\langle \$_{\text{init}}(), X \rangle \mapsto \left\langle \nabla_{0.0}(\vec{X}_0), \$_{\text{init}}() \right\rangle \langle \$_{\text{init}}(), X \rangle$

[C] $\left\langle \nabla_{k.i}(\vec{X}_k), X \right\rangle \mapsto \left\langle \text{call}(A_{k.i+1}), \nabla_{k.i}(\vec{X}_k) \right\rangle \left\langle \nabla_{k.i}(\vec{X}_k), X \right\rangle$

[S] $\langle \text{call}(A_{l.0}), X \rangle \mapsto \left\langle \nabla_{l.0}(\vec{X}_l), X \right\rangle$

[T] $\left\langle \nabla_{l.n_l}(\vec{X}_l), X \right\rangle \mapsto \langle \text{ret}(A_{l.0}), X \rangle$

[R] $\left\langle \text{ret}(\_), \nabla_{k.i}(\vec{X}_k) \right\rangle \left\langle \nabla_{k.i}(\vec{X}_k), X \right\rangle \mapsto \left\langle \nabla_{k.i+1}(\vec{X}_k), X \right\rangle$

These results remain true when we use the variant with the "last call optimization", and the **[lCT]** transition then becomes:

[lCT] $\left\langle \nabla_{k.n_k-1}(\vec{X}_k), X \right\rangle \mapsto \langle \text{call}(A_{k.n_k}), X \rangle$ $\qquad \forall k \neq 0$

The LPDAs produced by this transformed OLD scheme are $\mathcal{S}1$-correct. Thus we can read their transitions as clauses, as we did in the previous section. The result is precisely the Magic Template with tail recursion removal (MT-TR) construction proposed in [RS91].

The fundamental point here is that the above transformation of LPDAs to make them $\mathcal{S}1$-correct is totally independent of the kind of stack related optimization we may be interested in. In all cases, we can produce an $\mathcal{S}1$-correct LPDA, and thus a corresponding Magic Set transformation. Direct explicitation of proof-tree exploration strategies and of stack management makes the constructions more intuitive, and sometimes more general, without changing the end result. An optimized OLD compilation of clause γ_2 of **ancestor** gives the following non $\mathcal{S}1$-correct transitions:

$$\gamma_2 \begin{cases} \textbf{[S]}_2 & \text{call}(\text{a}(X, Y)) \mapsto \nabla_{2.0}(X, Y, Z) \\ \textbf{[C]}_{2.1} & \nabla_{2.0}(X, Y, Z) \mapsto \text{call}(\text{a}(X, Z)) \nabla_{2.0}(X, Y, Z) \\ \textbf{[lCT]} & \text{ret}(\_) \nabla_{2.0}(X, Y, Z) \mapsto \text{call}(\text{p}(Z, Y)) \end{cases}$$

The transformation of these transitions into $\mathcal{S}1$-correct transitions, followed by a transformation into clauses gives the following result, which is similar to the MT-TR transformation.

$$\begin{cases} \langle \nabla_{2.0}(X, Y, Z), P \rangle :- \langle \text{call}(\text{a}(X, Y)), P \rangle. \\ \langle \text{call}(\text{a}(X, Z)), \nabla_{2.0}(X, Y, Z) \rangle :- \langle \nabla_{2.0}(X, Y, Z), P \rangle. \\ \langle \text{call}(\text{p}(Z, Y)), P \rangle :- \langle \nabla_{2.0}(X, Y, Z), P \rangle, \langle \text{ret}(\_), \nabla_{2.0}(X, Y, Z) \rangle. \end{cases}$$

7 Conclusion

Like the work on Magic Set and on tabulation techniques, the main motivation for this paper is of an operational nature, with the ultimate goal of building logic evaluators with adequate properties (performance, completeness, ...) for various purposes. However, we believe that the development of an operational technology should be built on formal operational models of the evaluation of logic programs.

Logic programming remains fundamentally based on the construction of proofs and hence of proof trees. Since the early developments of formal languages theory, and more specifically of Context-Free languages theory, it is known that the push-down engine is one of the more natural devices for describing a large family of tree exploration/construction strategies. A large body of knowledge and techniques has been developed around this idea, which can probably be generalized at least in part to logic programming. Indeed, CF languages have long be known as a subfamily of logic programs, and the very first version of the Magic Set strategy was developed early on by Pereira and Warren as an extension of Earley's parsing algorithm [PW83], even though in a fully interpreted rather than compiled form.

The ideas presented in this paper are more than mere hindsight and reconstruction, since several were developed independently of the corresponding work in the Magic Set setting. Other variants, not considered here, can be naturally expressed in our formalization. We feel that the PDA model is a very intuitive support for understanding these phenomena and constructions, even more than exhibited here, since for brevity we had to present mainly the generic scheme which is more abstract than each specific construction.

Since the pushdown engine model also underlies most implementations of PROLOG, we expect the LPDA to be the proper framework for bridging the backtrack technology of PROLOG and the semi-naïve saturation techniques more in favor in the database community. The LPDA model also lends itself nicely to other extensions, such as the Subsumption-oriented Push-Down Automata [BVdlC92, VdlC93a], which extends our techniques to non Herbrand domains, with applications to such areas as constraint logic programming, natural language parsing or abstract interpretation.

Acknowledgements

This work has been partially supported by the Eureka Software Factory (ESF) project.

References

[BL89] S. Billot and B. Lang. The structure of shared forests in ambiguous parsing. In *Proc. of the 27 Annual Meeting of the Association for Computational Linguistics*, June 1989.

[BMSU86]   F. Bancilhon, D. Maier, Y. Sagiv, and J. Ullman. Magic–set and other strange ways to implement logic programs. In *Proc. of the 5th ACM symp. on Principles of Database Systems (PODS)*, 1986.

[BR87]   C. Beeri and R. Ramakrishnan. On the power of magic. In *Proc. of the 6th ACM symp. on Principles of Databases Systems (PODS)*, 1987.

[Bry90]   F. Bry. Query evaluation in recursive databases : Bottom-up and top-down reconciled. In *Data and Knowledge Engineering*, 1990.

[BVdlC92]   F. P. Barthélemy and E. Villemonte de la Clergerie. Subsumption-oriented Push–Down Automata. In Springer-Verlag, editor, *Proc. of PLILP'92*, pages 100–114, 1992.

[Ear70]   S.W. Earley. An efficient context-free parsing algorithm. In *Communications ACM 13(2)*, pages 94–102. ACM, 1970.

[Lan74]   B. Lang. Deterministic techniques for efficient non-deterministic parsers. In *Proc. of the 2nd Colloquium on automata, languages and Programming*, pages 255–269, Saarbrücken (Germany), 1974. Springer-Verlag (LNCS 14).

[Lan88a]   B. Lang. Complete evaluation of Horn clauses: an automata theoretic approach. Technical Report 913, INRIA, Rocquencourt, France, nov 1988.

[Lan88b]   B. Lang. Datalog automata. In *Proc. of the 3 Int. Conf. on Data and Knowledge Bases*, June 1988.

[Lan91]   B. Lang. Towards a uniform formal framework for parsing. In Masaru Tomita, editor, *Current issues in Parsing Technology*, chapter 11. Kluwer Academic Publishers, 1991. also appear in the Proc. of Int. Workshop on Parsing Technologies – IWPT89.

[LCMVH91]   B. Le Charlier, K. Musumbu, and P. Van Hentenryck. A generic abstract interpretation algorithm and its complexity analysis. In *Proc. of ILCP'91*, 1991.

[Nil91]   U. Nilsson. Abstract interpretation : A kind of magic. In *Proc. of PLILP'91*, 1991.

[Por86]   H. H. III Porter. Earley deduction. Technical Report CS/E-86-002, Oregon Graduate Center, Beaverton, Oregon, March 10 1986.

[PW83]   F.C.N. Pereira and D.H.D. Warren. Parsing as deduction. In *Proc. of the 21st Annual Meeting of the Association for Computationnal Linguistic*, pages 137–144, Cambridge (Massachussetts), 1983.

[Ram88]   R. Ramakrishnan. Magic templates: A spellbinding approach to logic programs. CS Tech Report 771, University of Wisconsin-Madison, June 1988. To appear in Proc. of ICLP'88.

[RS91]   R. Ramakrishnan and S. Sudarshan. Top–down vs. bottom–up revisited. In *Logic Programming, Proc. of the 1991 Int. Symposium*, pages 321–336, 1991.

[RLK86] J. Rohmer, R. Lescoeur, and J. M. Kerisit. The Alexander method — a technique for the processing of recursive axioms in deductive database queries. *New Generation Computing*, 4:522–528, 1986.

[Sek89] H. Seki. On the power of alexander templates. In *Proc. of the 8th ACM symps. on principles of Databases Systems*, 1989.

[Shi85] S. M. Shieber. Using restriction to extend parsing algorithms for complex–feature–based formalisms. In *Proc. of the 23rd Annual Meeting of the Association for Computationnal Linguistic*, pages 145–152, 1985.

[SR93] S. Sudarshan and R. Ramakrishnan. Optimizations of bottom-up evaluation with non-ground terms. In Dale Miller, editor, *Proc. of the 1993 Int. Symp. on Logic Programming (ILPS)*, pages pp. 557–574, 1993.

[TS86] H. Tamaki and T. Sato. OLD resolution with tabulation. In E Shapiro, editor, *Proc. of Third Int. Conf. on Logic Programming*, pages 84–98, London, 1986. Springer–Verlag.

[VdlC93a] E. Villemonte de la Clergerie. *Automates à Piles et Programmation Dynamique. DyALog : Une application à la programmation en Logique*. PhD thesis, Université Paris 7, 1993.

[VdlC93b] E. Villemonte de la Clergerie. Layer Sharing : an improved structure–sharing framework. In *Proc. of POPL'93*, pages 345–356, 1993.

[Vie87] L. Vieille. Database-complete proof procedures based on SLD resolution. In *Proc. of the 4 int. Conf. on Logic Programming*, May 1987.

[War89] D.S. Warren. The XWAM : A machine that integrates prolog and deductive database query evaluation, October 1989.

Several self-references by the authors are available by anonymous FTP from:
`ftp.inria.fr:/INRIA/publication/ChLoE`

Abduction and Negation

On the Equivalence between Disjunctive and Abductive Logic Programs

Chiaki Sakama
ASTEM Research Institute of Kyoto
17 Chudoji Minami-machi
Shimogyo, Kyoto 600 Japan
sakama@astem.or.jp

Katsumi Inoue
Department of Information and Computer Sciences
Toyohashi University of Technology
Tempaku-cho, Toyohashi 441 Japan
inoue@tutics.tut.ac.jp

Abstract

This paper presents the equivalence relationship between disjunctive and abductive logic programs. We show that the generalized stable model semantics of abductive logic programs can be translated into the possible model semantics of disjunctive programs, and vice versa. It is also proved that abductive disjunctive programs can be expressed by abductive logic programs under the possible model semantics. Furthermore, when considering the disjunctive stable model semantics instead of the possible model semantics, it is unlikely that disjunctive programs can be efficiently expressed in terms of the generalized stable model semantics. The results of this paper reveal that disjunctive programs and abductive logic programs are just different ways of looking at the same problem if we choose the appropriate semantics.

1 Introduction

Disjunctive programs and abductive logic programs are two extensions of logic programming which draw much attention recently. Disjunctive programs provide us with the framework of reasoning with indefinite information. The framework was firstly studied by Minker [Min82] in which he introduced the *minimal model semantics* of positive disjunctive programs. In the last decade, various extensions of this framework have been studied for disjunctive programs with negation. On the other hand, abductive logic programs supply the ability to perform reasoning with hypotheses. Such a framework was firstly investigated by Eshghi and Kowalski [EK89] and then generalized by Kakas and Mancarella [KM90] who extended Gelfond and Lifschitz's stable model semantics [GL88] to the *generalized stable model semantics*. Further extensions have been studied by several researchers in the last few years [KKT92].

Disjunctive programs and abductive logic programs have been independently developed and have different syntax and semantics from each other. However, in disjunctive programs, each disjunction is considered to represent knowledge about possible alternative beliefs, and such beliefs can also be regarded as a kind of hypotheses. In abductive logic programs, on the other hand, each candidate hypothesis is examined whether it is adopted or not, and this situation can be considered as meta-level disjunctive knowledge that either a hypothesis is true or not. Thus, each formalism appears to deal with very similar problems from different viewpoints. Then the question naturally arises whether there is any formal correspondence between these two frameworks.

There are some works which can be related to the above question. Dung [Dun92] presents a program transformation from acyclic disjunctive programs to normal logic programs under the stable model semantics and uses Eshghi and Kowalski's abductive proof procedure for such programs. However, Dung's transformation is restricted to acyclic disjunctive programs and not applicable in general. Inoue and Sakama [IS93] present a program transformation from abductive logic programs to disjunctive programs under the stable model semantics and use a bottom-up model generation proof procedure for computing abduction. While their transformation is fairly general, it is a one-way transformation from abductive logic programs to disjunctive programs.

This paper investigates a general correspondence between disjunctive programs and abductive logic programs. For the part from abductive logic programs to disjunctive programs, we show that the generalized stable models of an abductive logic program are characterized by the *possible models* [Sak89, SI93] of the transformed disjunctive program. Conversely, from disjunctive programs to abductive logic programs, we show that the possible models of a disjunctive program are exactly the generalized stable models of the transformed abductive logic program. Moreover, if the *disjunctive stable model semantics* [Prz91] is taken as the underlying semantics instead of the possible model semantics, it is unlikely that disjunctive programs can be efficiently expressed in terms of the generalized stable model semantics. It is also shown that abductive disjunctive programs can be expressed by abductive logic programs under the possible model semantics.

The rest of this paper is organized as follows. In Section 2, we introduce notations used in this paper. In Section 3, we present a program transformation from abductive logic programs to disjunctive programs and show that the generalized stable models of an abductive logic program are characterized by the possible models of the transformed disjunctive program. In

Section 4, we present that a converse transformation is also possible and show that the possible models of a disjunctive program are the generalized stable models of the transformed abductive logic program. In Section 5, abductive disjunctive programs are also translated into disjunctive programs and it is shown that abductive logic programs are as expressive as abductive disjunctive programs under the possible model semantics. Section 6 discusses the relation between disjunctive programs and abductive logic programs from the complexity point of view. Section 7 concludes this paper.

2 Definitions

A *normal disjunctive program* is a finite set of clauses of the form:

$$A_1 \vee \ldots \vee A_l \leftarrow B_1 \wedge \ldots \wedge B_m \wedge not\, B_{m+1} \wedge \ldots \wedge not\, B_n \quad (l \geq 0,\ n \geq m \geq 0) \quad (1)$$

where A_i's and B_j's are atoms and *not* denotes *negation as failure*. The left-hand side of the clause is called the *head*, while the right-hand side of the clause is called the *body*. In this paper, we often use the Greek letter Γ to denote the conjunction in the body of a clause. A clause is called *disjunctive* (resp. *normal*) if its head contains more than one atom (resp. exactly one atom). A clause with the empty head is called an *integrity constraint*. A normal disjunctive program containing no *not* is called a *positive disjunctive program*, while a program containing no disjunctive clause is called a *normal logic program*. As usual, we semantically identify a program with its *ground program*, which is the possibly infinite set of all ground clauses from the program.

An *interpretation* of a program P is a subset of the Herbrand base $\mathcal{HB}_P$ of the program. An interpretation I is called a *disjunctive stable model* [Prz91] of P if I coincides with a minimal model of the positive disjunctive program P^I defined as

$$P^I \quad = \quad \{\, A_1 \vee \ldots \vee A_l \leftarrow B_1 \wedge \ldots \wedge B_m \mid \text{there is a ground clause}$$
$$\text{of the form (1) from } P \text{ such that } \{B_{m+1}, \ldots, B_n\} \cap I = \emptyset \,\}.$$

In particular, when P is a normal logic program, I is called a *stable model* of P [GL88].

The *possible model semantics* proposed in [Sak89, SI93][1] is an alternative semantics for disjunctive programs. It is introduced to enable one to specify both inclusive and exclusive disjunctions in a program.

Given a normal disjunctive program P, a *split program* is defined as a ground normal logic program obtained from P by replacing each ground disjunctive clause of the form (1) with the following ground normal clauses (called *split clauses*):

$$A_i \leftarrow B_1 \wedge \ldots \wedge B_m \wedge not B_{m+1} \wedge \ldots \wedge not B_n \quad \text{for every } A_i \in S$$

---

[1]In [SI93], it is called the *possible world semantics*.

where S is some non-empty subset of $\{A_1, \ldots, A_l\}$. Then a *possible model* of P is defined as a stable model of any split program of P. Clearly, possible models reduce to stable models in normal logic programs. In positive disjunctive programs, the notion of possible models also coincides with the *possible worlds* presented in [Cha93].

Example 2.1 Let P be the program:

$$\{\, a \vee b \leftarrow not\, c, \quad d \leftarrow a \wedge b \,\}.$$

Then the split programs of P are

$$\{\, a \leftarrow not\, c, \quad d \leftarrow a \wedge b \,\},$$

$$\{\, b \leftarrow not\, c, \quad d \leftarrow a \wedge b \,\},$$

$$\{\, a \leftarrow not\, c, \quad b \leftarrow not\, c, \quad d \leftarrow a \wedge b \,\},$$

and $\{a\}$, $\{b\}$, $\{a, b, d\}$ are the possible models of P. $\square$

Note that $\{a\}$ and $\{b\}$ are also disjunctive stable models, while $\{a, b, d\}$ is not. Thus the disjunctive stable models exclude the possibility of an inclusive interpretation of the disjunction in the above example, while the possible models consider both exclusive and inclusive interpretations. Notice that if one does not want the inclusive interpretation $\{a, b, d\}$ under the possible model semantics, it is enough to insert the integrity constraint $\leftarrow a \wedge b$ in P. Intuitively speaking, each possible model presents an interpretation in which each atom has its possible justification in a program, and both exclusive and inclusive interpretations of disjunctions are considered whenever there is no integrity constraint to inhibit inclusive ones. In [Sak89, SI93], it is shown that the possible model semantics can provide a flexible mechanism for inferring negation in disjunctive programs.

An *abductive logic program* is a pair $\langle P, \mathcal{A} \rangle$ where P is a normal logic program and $\mathcal{A}$ is a finite set of atoms called the *abducibles*.[2] Let $\langle P, \mathcal{A} \rangle$ be an abductive logic program and E be a subset of $\mathcal{A}$. An interpretation I is a *generalized stable model* of $\langle P, \mathcal{A} \rangle$ if I is a stable model of the normal logic program $P \cup E$. A generalized stable model I is called $\mathcal{A}$-*minimal* if there is no generalized stable model J such that $J \cap \mathcal{A} \subset I \cap \mathcal{A}$. Clearly, ($\mathcal{A}$-minimal) generalized stable models coincide with stable models if $\mathcal{A} = \emptyset$.

Let $\langle P, \mathcal{A} \rangle$ be an abductive logic program and O be an atom which represents *observation*.[3] Then a set $E \subseteq \mathcal{A}$ is an *explanation* of O if there is a generalized stable model I of $\langle P, \mathcal{A} \rangle$ such that I satisfies O and $E = I \cap \mathcal{A}$. An explanation E of O is *minimal* if no $E' \subset E$ is an explanation of O.

---

[2] We slightly modified the original definition of [KM90] by including integrity constraints in a program and considering abducible atoms instead of abducible predicates. Here, an abducible containing variables is identified with its ground instances.

[3] As discussed in [IS93], without loss of generality an observation is assumed to be a non-abducible ground atom.

Note that the problem of finding explanations is essentially equivalent to the problem of finding generalized stable models since E is a (minimal) explanation of O with respect to $\langle P, \mathcal{A} \rangle$ iff I is a ($\mathcal{A}$-minimal) generalized stable model of $\langle P \cup \{ \leftarrow not\, O \}, \mathcal{A} \rangle$ such that $I \cap \mathcal{A} = E$ [IS93].

Example 2.2 Let $\langle P, \mathcal{A} \rangle$ be an abductive logic program such that

$$P = \{ \, p(x) \leftarrow q(x) \wedge not\, r(x), \quad q(x) \leftarrow s(x), \quad q(x) \leftarrow t(x) \, \}$$

and $\mathcal{A} = \{ \, s(x), \, t(b) \, \}$. Then, for a given observation $O = p(a)$, the ($\mathcal{A}$-minimal) generalized stable model $I = \{ \, p(a), \, q(a), \, s(a) \, \}$ of $\langle P, \mathcal{A} \rangle$ satisfies O and its (minimal) explanation is $E = I \cap \mathcal{A} = \{ \, s(a) \, \}$. Here, I is also the unique generalized stable model of $\langle P \cup \{ \leftarrow not\, p(a) \}, \mathcal{A} \rangle$. □

3 Generalized Stable Models are Possible Models

In this section, we present a program transformation from abductive logic programs to normal disjunctive programs and show that the generalized stable models of an abductive logic program can be expressed by the possible models of the transformed normal disjunctive program.

In an abductive logic program, each candidate hypothesis is either assumed or not. Such a situation is naturally expressed by disjunctions in a program.

Definition 3.1 Let $\langle P, \mathcal{A} \rangle$ be an abductive logic program. Then its *dlp-transformation* is defined by a normal disjunctive program $dlp(\langle P, \mathcal{A} \rangle)$ which is obtained from P by adding the following disjunctive clauses for each abducible $A \in \mathcal{A}$:

$$A \vee \varepsilon \leftarrow \tag{2}$$

where ε is an atom not appearing elsewhere in P. □

The intuitive meaning of the *dlp*-transformation is that when an abducible A is assumed in an abductive logic program $\langle P, \mathcal{A} \rangle$, the corresponding disjunct A is chosen from (2) in the transformed normal disjunctive program $dlp(\langle P, \mathcal{A} \rangle)$. Else when A is not assumed, the newly introduced atom ε is chosen from (2). Thus the *dlp*-transformation specifies meta-level knowledge representing whether each abducible is assumed or not.[4]

Now we express the generalized stable model semantics in terms of $dlp(\langle P, \mathcal{A} \rangle)$. Let I be a possible model of a normal disjunctive program P. We say that I is $\mathcal{A}$-*minimal* if there is no possible model J of P such that $J \cap \mathcal{A} \subset I \cap \mathcal{A}$. In the following, an atom A is identified with the unit clause $A \leftarrow$ in E.

---

[4] A similar transformation is also presented in [IS94] in the context of extended disjunctive programs with *positive occurrences of negation as failure*.

Theorem 3.1 Let $\langle P, \mathcal{A} \rangle$ be an abductive logic program. Then,

(i) $I \setminus \{\varepsilon\}$ is a generalized stable model of $\langle P, \mathcal{A} \rangle$ iff I is a possible model of $dlp(\langle P, \mathcal{A} \rangle)$.

(ii) $I \setminus \{\varepsilon\}$ is an $\mathcal{A}$-minimal generalized stable model of $\langle P, \mathcal{A} \rangle$ iff I is an $\mathcal{A}$-minimal possible model of $dlp(\langle P, \mathcal{A} \rangle)$.

Proof: (i) Let I' be a generalized stable model of $\langle P, \mathcal{A} \rangle$. Then I' is a stable model of $P \cup E$ for some E from $\mathcal{A}$. Now let us consider the transformed program $dlp(\langle P, \mathcal{A} \rangle)$. Then there is a split program P' of $dlp(\langle P, \mathcal{A} \rangle)$ such that for each disjunctive clause (2), $A \leftarrow$ is in P' if $A \in E$; $\varepsilon \leftarrow$ is in P', otherwise. When $\varepsilon \leftarrow$ is in P', $I' \cup \{\varepsilon\}$ is a stable model of P' and also a possible model of $dlp(\langle P, \mathcal{A} \rangle)$. Else when $\varepsilon \leftarrow$ is not in P', I' is a stable model of P' and also a possible model of $dlp(\langle P, \mathcal{A} \rangle)$. Hence the result of only-if part follows.

Conversely, when I is a possible model of $dlp(\langle P, \mathcal{A} \rangle)$, it is a stable model of some split program P' of $dlp(\langle P, \mathcal{A} \rangle)$. Let E be the set of all split clauses included in P'. Then I is a stable model of $P \cup E$. Since $E \setminus \{\varepsilon \leftarrow\}$ consists of instances from $\mathcal{A}$, $I \setminus \{\varepsilon\}$ is a generalized stable model of $\langle P, \mathcal{A} \rangle$.

(ii) The result directly follows from (i) and the definitions of $\mathcal{A}$-minimal generalized stable models/$\mathcal{A}$-minimal possible models. $\square$

Corollary 3.2 Let $\langle P, \mathcal{A} \rangle$ be an abductive logic program. Then, for a given observation O, there is a (minimal) explanation E of O iff there is an ($\mathcal{A}$-minimal) possible model I of $dlp(\langle P, \mathcal{A} \rangle)$ satisfying O and $I \cap \mathcal{A} = E$. $\square$

Example 3.1 Let $\langle P, \mathcal{A} \rangle$ be an abductive logic program such that

$$P \quad = \quad \{ \; wet\text{-}shoes \leftarrow wet\text{-}grass \wedge not\, driving\text{-}car,$$
$$wet\text{-}grass \leftarrow rained,$$
$$wet\text{-}grass \leftarrow sprinkler\text{-}on \; \},$$

and $\mathcal{A} = \{ \; rained, \; sprinkler\text{-}on \; \}$. Then,

$$dlp(\langle P, \mathcal{A} \rangle) = P \cup \{ \; rained \vee \varepsilon \leftarrow, \quad sprinkler\text{-}on \vee \varepsilon \leftarrow \; \}$$

which has the five possible models:

$$\{rained, \; sprinkler\text{-}on, \; wet\text{-}grass, \; wet\text{-}shoes\},$$
$$\{\varepsilon\},$$
$$\{\varepsilon, \; rained, \; wet\text{-}grass, \; wet\text{-}shoes\},$$
$$\{\varepsilon, \; sprinkler\text{-}on, \; wet\text{-}grass, \; wet\text{-}shoes\},$$
$$\{\varepsilon, \; rained, \; sprinkler\text{-}on, \; wet\text{-}grass, \; wet\text{-}shoes\}.$$

Thus, the generalized stable models of $\langle P, \mathcal{A} \rangle$ coincide with the sets which are obtained by removing ε from each possible model. In particular, $\{\varepsilon\}$ is the $\mathcal{A}$-minimal possible model and it corresponds to the $\mathcal{A}$-minimal generalized stable model $\emptyset$ of $\langle P, \mathcal{A} \rangle$. $\square$

The result of this section indicates that abductive logic programs are also considered as disjunctive programs. In the next section, we present that the converse also holds.

4 Possible Models are Generalized Stable Models

As presented in introduction, indefinite information in disjunctive programs is viewed as possible hypotheses in a program. Then it is natural to represent disjuncts in terms of abducibles in an abductive logic program. However, the problem is that disjunctive clauses possibly have conditions in their bodies, while abductive logic programs introduced in Section 2 lack the ability of expressing assumptions with preconditions. Then our first task is to extend the framework of abductive logic programs to possibly include such hypothetical rules.

An abductive logic program considering in this section is a pair $\langle P, C \rangle$ where P is a normal logic program and C is a finite set of normal clauses called the *abducible rules*. The abducible rule intuitively means that if the rule is abduced then it is used for inference together with the background knowledge from P. In this sense, abductive logic programs presented in the previous sections are considered as a special case where each abducible rule has the empty precondition. The generalized stable model semantics of such an extended framework is defined as follows.

Definition 4.1 Let $\langle P, C \rangle$ be an abductive logic program and F be a subset of C. An interpretation I is a *generalized stable model* of $\langle P, C \rangle$ if it is a stable model of the normal logic program $P \cup F$. □

The generalized stable models introduced above are a direct extension of those presented in the previous sections, and they reduce to the usual notion when $C = A$.

Next we provide a program transformation which translates normal disjunctive programs into abductive logic programs. For a normal disjunctive program P, we define $P = disj(P) \cup \overline{disj}(P)$ where $disj(P)$ is the set of all disjunctive clauses from P and $\overline{disj}(P)$ is the set of all normal clauses and integrity constraints from P.

Definition 4.2 Given a normal disjunctive program P, let us consider the set of normal clauses

$$C = \{ A_i \leftarrow \Gamma \mid A_1 \vee \ldots \vee A_l \leftarrow \Gamma \in disj(P) \text{ and } 1 \leq i \leq l \} \tag{3}$$

and the integrity constraints

$$IC = \{ \leftarrow \Gamma \wedge notA_1 \wedge \ldots \wedge notA_l \mid A_1 \vee \ldots \vee A_l \leftarrow \Gamma \in disj(P) \}. \tag{4}$$

Then we define the *alp-transformation* of P by $alp(P) = \langle \overline{disj}(P) \cup IC, C \rangle$. □

The intuitive meaning of the *alp*-transformation is that each disjunctive clause in a program is replaced with a set of abducible rules (3) in $\mathcal{C}$. The integrity constraints (4) in IC impose the condition that at least one of disjuncts are chosen as an abducible whenever the body of a disjunctive clause is true. In this way, by the *alp*-transformation each disjunctive clause is rewritten by a set of abducible rules.

Now we present the relationship between the possible models of a normal disjunctive program P and the generalized stable models of the transformed abductive logic program $alp(P)$.

Theorem 4.1 Let P be a normal disjunctive program. Then I is a possible model of P iff I is a generalized stable model of $alp(P)$.

Proof: Let I be a possible model of P. Then there is a split program P' of P such that I is a stable model of P'. Suppose that each ground disjunctive clause $C^k : A_1 \vee \ldots \vee A_{l_k} \leftarrow \Gamma_k$ from P is replaced with the split clauses in $C_S^k = \{A_i \leftarrow \Gamma_k \mid A_i \in S\}$ in P' where S is a non-empty subset of $\{A_1, \ldots, A_{l_k}\}$. Then I is a stable model of $\overline{disj}(P) \cup \bigcup_k C_S^k$. Since $\bigcup_k C_S^k$ consists of instances from $\mathcal{C}$ and I satisfies integrity constraints IC, I is also a generalized stable model of $alp(P)$.

Conversely, let I be a generalized stable model of $alp(P)$. Then I is a stable model of $P \cup F$ where F is a subset of $\mathcal{C}$. For each normal clause $A_i \leftarrow \Gamma$ in F, there is a corresponding disjunctive clause $C : A_1 \vee \ldots \vee A_l \leftarrow \Gamma$ in $disj(P)$ such that $1 \leq i \leq l$. Also, since I satisfies integrity constraints IC, when I satisfies Γ, at least one normal clause $A_i \leftarrow \Gamma$ is included in F. In this case, there is a split program P' of P in which each ground instance of a disjunctive clause C is split into a corresponding ground instance of a normal clause $A_i \leftarrow \Gamma$. Thus I is also a stable model of P', hence a possible model of P. $\square$

Example 4.1 [Cha93] Let

$$P = \{ \textit{violent} \vee \textit{psychopath} \leftarrow \textit{suspect},$$
$$\textit{dangerous} \leftarrow \textit{violent} \wedge \textit{psychopath},$$
$$\textit{suspect} \leftarrow \}.$$

Then, $alp(P) = \langle \overline{disj}(P) \cup IC, \mathcal{C} \rangle$ where

$$\overline{disj}(P) \cup IC = \{ \textit{dangerous} \leftarrow \textit{violent} \wedge \textit{psychopath},$$
$$\textit{suspect} \leftarrow,$$
$$\leftarrow \textit{suspect} \wedge \textit{not violent} \wedge \textit{not psychopath} \},$$
$$\mathcal{C} = \{ \textit{violent} \leftarrow \textit{suspect}, \quad \textit{psychopath} \leftarrow \textit{suspect} \}.$$

Thus, $alp(P)$ has three generalized stable models:

$$\{\textit{suspect, violent}\},$$

$\{suspect,\ psychopath\}$,

$\{suspect,\ violent,\ psychopath,\ dangerous\}$,

which coincide with the possible models of P. □

Note that in the above example there is no minimal model of P containing *dangerous*. By contrast, $alp(P)$ has a generalized stable model in which *dangerous* is true, which corresponds to a possible model in which the disjunction is inclusively true.

The abductive logic programming framework presented in this section is also introduced by Inoue [Ino91] in the context of the *knowledge system* for *extended logic programs* [GL90]. He also shows that an abductive logic program $\langle P, \mathcal{C} \rangle$ can be translated into a semantically equivalent usual abductive logic program $\langle P, \mathcal{A} \rangle$. Given an abductive logic program $\langle P, \mathcal{C} \rangle$, let us consider a program P' which is obtained from P by including the clause $A \leftarrow A' \wedge \Gamma$ for each abducible rule $A \leftarrow \Gamma$ in $\mathcal{C}$. Here A' is a newly introduced atom not appearing elsewhere in P and is uniquely associated with each A. Also let $\mathcal{A}'$ be a set of abducibles which consists of every newly introduced atom A'. Then he proves that there is a one-to-one correspondence between the generalized stable models of $\langle P, \mathcal{C} \rangle$ and the generalized stable models of $\langle P', \mathcal{A}' \rangle$. This fact implies that the possible models of a normal disjunctive program are also expressed by the generalized stable models of a usual abductive logic program.

5 Generalized Possible Models are Generalized Stable Models

This section presents a connection between abductive disjunctive programs and abductive logic programs.

Abductive disjunctive programs are normal disjunctive programs with abducibles. The definition of an *abductive disjunctive program* $\langle P, \mathcal{A} \rangle$ is the same as an abductive logic program except that P is a normal disjunctive program. For a given set $E \subseteq \mathcal{A}$, an interpretation I is a *generalized disjunctive stable model* of $\langle P, \mathcal{A} \rangle$ if it is a disjunctive stable model of the normal disjunctive program $P \cup E$. On the other hand, I is a *generalized possible model* of $\langle P, \mathcal{A} \rangle$ if it is a possible model of the normal disjunctive program $P \cup E$. A generalized disjunctive stable model (resp. generalized possible model) I is $\mathcal{A}$-*minimal* if there is no generalized disjunctive stable model (resp. generalized possible model) J such that $J \cap \mathcal{A} \subset I \cap \mathcal{A}$.

The above definitions are direct extensions of the previously proposed notions. In fact, generalized disjunctive stable models (resp. generalized possible models) reduce to disjunctive stable models (resp. possible models) in normal disjunctive programs with $\mathcal{A} = \emptyset$, and both generalized disjunctive stable models and generalized possible models reduce to generalized stable models in abductive logic programs.

A difference between generalized disjunctive stable models and generalized possible models is illustrated in the following example.

Example 5.1 Let $\langle P, \mathcal{A} \rangle$ be an abductive disjunctive program such that

$$P = \{ a \vee b \leftarrow c, \quad d \leftarrow a \wedge b \}$$

and $\mathcal{A} = \{ c \}$. Then, $\emptyset$, $\{c, a\}$, $\{c, b\}$, $\{c, a, b, d\}$ are all generalized possible models, while $\{c, a, b, d\}$ is not a generalized disjunctive stable model. Thus, for a given observation $O = d$, it has an explanation c under the generalized possible models, while no explanation is available under the generalized disjunctive stable models. □

In this way, the generalized possible model semantics can provide explanations which come from inclusive disjunctions, while the generalized disjunctive stable model semantics cannot in general.

Inoue and Sakama [IS93] present that generalized disjunctive stable models of abductive disjunctive programs are translated into disjunctive stable models of normal disjunctive programs. That is, normal disjunctive programs are as expressive as abductive disjunctive programs under the disjunctive stable model semantics. We first show that this fact also holds for the possible model semantics.

For an abductive disjunctive program $\langle P, \mathcal{A} \rangle$, we define its *dlp-transformation* $dlp(\langle P, \mathcal{A} \rangle)$ in the same manner as presented in Definition 3.1. Then the following results hold.

Theorem 5.1 Let $\langle P, \mathcal{A} \rangle$ be an abductive disjunctive program. Then,

(i) $I \setminus \{\varepsilon\}$ is a generalized possible model of $\langle P, \mathcal{A} \rangle$ iff I is a possible model of $dlp(\langle P, \mathcal{A} \rangle)$.

(ii) $I \setminus \{\varepsilon\}$ is an $\mathcal{A}$-minimal generalized possible model of $\langle P, \mathcal{A} \rangle$ iff I is an $\mathcal{A}$-minimal possible model of $dlp(\langle P, \mathcal{A} \rangle)$.

Proof: Similar to the proof of Theorem 3.1. □

The above theorem, together with Theorem 4.1, implies the following result.

Corollary 5.2 Let $\langle P, \mathcal{A} \rangle$ be an abductive disjunctive program. Then $I \setminus \{\varepsilon\}$ is a generalized possible model of $\langle P, \mathcal{A} \rangle$ iff I is a generalized stable model of $alp(dlp(\langle P, \mathcal{A} \rangle))$. □

By Theorem 5.1, normal disjunctive programs are also as expressive as abductive disjunctive programs under the possible model semantics. Moreover, Corollary 5.2 presents that abductive disjunctive programs can be expressed even by abductive logic programs under the generalized possible model semantics.

6 Discussion

In this section, we discuss relationships between disjunctive programs and abductive logic programs from the computational complexity point of view. Throughout this section, programs are assumed to be propositional programs.

When abductive logic programs do not contain negation as failure, Selman and Levesque [SL90] and Eiter and Gottlob [EG92] show that the decision problem of the existence of explanations for a given observation in an abductive Horn program is NP-complete. In other words, in an abductive Horn program, deciding whether there is a generalized stable model satisfying an observation is NP-complete.

Inoue [Ino91] and Satoh and Iwayama [SI91] show that an abductive logic program can be translated into a semantically equivalent normal logic program. For an abductive logic program $\langle P, \mathcal{A} \rangle$, consider a normal logic program obtained from P by adding the following clauses for each abducible A in $\mathcal{A}$:

$$A \leftarrow not\ A',$$
$$A' \leftarrow not\ A,$$

where A' is a newly introduced atom not appearing elsewhere in P and is uniquely associated with each A. Then these authors show that there is a one-to-one correspondence between the generalized stable models of $\langle P, \mathcal{A} \rangle$ and the stable models of the transformed normal logic program. Since it is known that deciding whether an atom is true in a stable model is NP-complete [MT91], the above translation implies that deciding whether there is a generalized stable model satisfying a given observation is also NP-complete.[5]

Sakama and Inoue [SI93] have shown that possible models of a normal disjunctive program can be efficiently expressed by stable models of a normal logic program. For a normal disjunctive program P, let us consider a normal logic program obtained from P by replacing each disjunctive clause:

$$A_1 \vee \ldots \vee A_l \leftarrow \Gamma$$

in P with the following normal clauses and an integrity constraint:

$$A_i \leftarrow \Gamma \wedge not\ A_i' \quad \text{for } i = 1, \ldots, l,$$
$$A_i' \leftarrow \Gamma \wedge not\ A_i \quad \text{for } i = 1, \ldots, l,$$
$$\leftarrow \Gamma \wedge A_1' \wedge \ldots \wedge A_l',$$

---

[5]More precisely, the generalized stable models include the stable models as a special case, then its set-membership problem is NP-hard. Since the polynomial-time transformation translates the decision problem for a generalized stable model into the corresponding problem for a stable model which is in NP, the membership in NP also follows.

Table 1: Comparison of Computational Complexity

Program	Semantics	Complexity
Abductive LP	Horn Abduction	NP-complete
	Generalized Stable Model	NP-complete
Normal DLP	Possible Model	NP-complete
	Disjunctive Stable Model	Σ_2^P-complete
Abductive DLP	Generalized Possible Model	NP-complete
	Generalized Disjunctive Stable Model	Σ_2^P-complete

where each A_i' is a new atom not appearing in P and is uniquely introduced for each A_i in $\mathcal{HB}_P$. Then they show that there is a one-to-one correspondence between the possible models of P and the stable models of the transformed normal logic program. Therefore, deciding the existence of a possible model satisfying a given atom is NP-complete. Furthermore, from discussion presented in Section 5, since generalized possible models can be efficiently translated into possible models, the corresponding decision problem for generalized possible models is also NP-complete.

On the other hand, deciding the existence of a disjunctive stable model containing a given atom is known to be Σ_2^P-complete [EG93a]. Inoue and Sakama [IS93] present a polynomial-time transformation from abductive disjunctive programs to normal disjunctive programs under the disjunctive stable model semantics. Therefore, deciding whether there is a generalized disjunctive stable model satisfying a given observation is also Σ_2^P-complete. These results are summarized in Table 1.

The above complexity measures verify the results of this paper that the generalized stable model semantics of abductive logic programs can be expressed in terms of the possible model semantics of normal disjunctive programs by a polynomial-time transformation, and vice versa. Moreover, we can observe that *there is no efficient way to express the disjunctive stable model semantics in terms of the generalized stable model semantics unless the polynomial hierarchy collapses*. This observation extends the fact that disjunctive stable models cannot be expressed by stable models of a normal logic program in polynomial time [EG93b]. This explains the reason why we have chosen the possible model semantics in this paper. Also we can observe that when considering to extend the framework of abductive logic programs to abductive disjunctive programs, *the generalized possible model semantics enables us to extend the framework without increasing computational complexity, while this is not the case for the generalized disjunctive stable model semantics.* The fact that the complexity of the (generalized) disjunctive stable model semantics is higher than the complexity of the (generalized) possible model semantics is explained as follows: computation of disjunctive stable models introduces an additional source of complexity for its minimality-checking, while this is not the case for computation of possible models due to its "non-minimal" feature.

The possible model semantics is originally introduced in order to provide a flexible mechanism for closed world assumptions in disjunctive programs. However, the results of this paper reveal that the possible model semantics also contributes to bridge the gap between disjunctive programs and abductive logic programs. As presented earlier in this section, under the possible model semantics normal disjunctive programs are reducible to normal logic programs. Since abductive disjunctive programs are reducible to normal disjunctive programs, abductive disjunctive programs are also reducible to normal logic programs under the possible model semantics. Moreover, in [SI93] we have shown that normal disjunctive/logic programs are also transferable to semantically equivalent positive disjunctive programs. These facts, together with the results presented in this paper, indicate a somewhat surprising fact that *all "extensions" of logic programming, i.e., normal logic programs, disjunctive programs, and abductive logic programs, are essentially equivalent under the possible model semantics. That is, negation as failure, disjunctions, and abducibles can be used interchangeably under the possible model semantics.*

7 Conclusion

This paper has investigated the relationship between disjunctive programs and abductive logic programs. The contributions of this paper are summarized as follows.

1. A program transformation from abductive logic programs to normal disjunctive programs was presented. It was shown that the generalized stable models of an abductive logic program are characterized by the possible models of the transformed normal disjunctive program.

2. A converse transformation from normal disjunctive programs to abductive logic programs was presented. It was shown that the possible models of a normal disjunctive program are exactly the generalized stable models of the transformed abductive logic program.

3. Normal disjunctive programs were proved to be as expressive as abductive disjunctive programs. Moreover, it was shown that abductive disjunctive programs, normal disjunctive programs, abductive logic programs, and normal logic programs are all equivalent under the possible model semantics.

4. From the computational complexity point of view, we have argued that expressing the disjunctive stable model semantics in terms of generalized stable models is most unlikely possible in polynomial time. Also, it was shown that the generalized possible model semantics can extend

the framework of abductive logic programs to abductive disjunctive programs without increasing the computational complexity.

Disjunctive knowledge in disjunctive programs and abductive hypotheses in abductive logic programs appear to deal with very similar problems from different viewpoints. This paper verified this conjecture and revealed close relationships between disjunctive programs and abductive logic programs. That is, *both formalisms are just different ways of looking at the same problem if we choose the appropriate semantics*. The results of this paper verify the usefulness of the possible model semantics as a theoretical tool not only for disjunctive programs but also for abductive logic programs. Moreover, we have argued that the possible model semantics can provide a unifying framework for various extensions of logic programming, and in spite of its usefulness, it does not increase the computational complexity more than the classical propositional satisfiability. The possible model semantics also has a close relation to autoepistemic logic [IS94].

Acknowledgements

We are grateful to anonymous referees for their helpful comments.

References

[Cha93] Chan, E. P. F., A Possible World Semantics for Disjunctive Databases, *IEEE Trans. on Data and Knowledge Engineering* 5(2), 282-292, 1993.

[Dun92] Dung, P. M., Acyclic Disjunctive Logic Programs with Abductive Procedure as Proof Procedure, *Proc. Int. Conf. on Fifth Generation Computer Systems*, 555-561, 1992.

[EG92] Eiter, T. and Gottlob, G., The Complexity of Logic-Based Abduction, Research Report CD-TR 92/35, Technical University Vienna, 1992, to appear in *J. ACM*. Extended abstract in *Proc. 10th Ann. Symp. on Theoretical Aspects of Computer Science*, LNCS 665, 70-79, 1993.

[EG93a] Eiter, T. and Gottlob, G., Complexity Aspects of Various Semantics for Disjunctive Databases, *Proc. 12th ACM SIGACT-SIGMOD-SIGART Symp. on Principles of Database Systems*, 158-167, 1993.

[EG93b] Eiter, T. and Gottlob, G., Complexity Results for Disjunctive Logic Programming and Application to Nonmonotonic Logics, *Proc. Int. Logic Programming Symp.*, 266-278, 1993.

[EK89] Eshghi, K. and Kowalski, R. A., Abduction Compared with Negation by Failure, *Proc. 6th Int. Conf. on Logic Programming*, 234-254, 1989.

[GL88] Gelfond, M. and Lifschitz, V., The Stable Model Semantics for Logic Programming, *Proc. 5th Int. Conf./Symp. on Logic Programming*, 1070-1080, 1988.

[GL90] Gelfond, M. and Lifschitz, V., Logic Programs with Classical Negation, *Proc. 7th Int. Conf. on Logic Programming*, 579-597, 1990.

[Ino91] Inoue, K., Extended Logic Programs with Default Assumptions, *Proc. 8th Int. Conf. Logic Programming*, 490-504, 1991. Extended version: Hypothetical Reasoning in Logic Programs, *J. Logic Programming* 18, to appear, 1994.

[IS93] Inoue, K. and Sakama, C., Transforming Abductive Logic Programs to Disjunctive Programs, *Proc. 10th Int. Conf. on Logic Programming*, 335-353, 1993.

[IS94] Inoue, K. and Sakama, C., On Positive Occurrences of Negation as Failure, *Proc. 4th Int. Conf. on Principles of Knowledge Representation and Reasoning*, to appear, 1994.

[KM90] Kakas, A. C. and Mancarella, P., Generalized Stable Models: A Semantics for Abduction, *Proc. 9th European Conf. on Artificial Intelligence*, 385-391, 1990.

[KKT92] Kakas, A. C., Kowalski, R. A. and Toni, F., Abductive Logic Programming, *J. Logic and Computation* 2(6), 719-770, 1992.

[MT91] Marek, W. and Truszczynski, M., Autoepistemic Logic, *J. ACM* 38(3), 588-619, 1991.

[Min82] Minker, J., On Indefinite Data Bases and the Closed World Assumption, *Proc. 6th Int. Conf. on Automated Deduction*, Lecture Notes in Computer Science 138, Springer-Verlag, 292-308, 1982.

[Prz91] Przymusinski, T. C., Stable Semantics for Disjunctive Programs, *New Generation Computing*, 401-424, 1991.

[Sak89] Sakama, C., Possible Model Semantics for Disjunctive Databases, *Proc. 1st Int. Conf. on Deductive and Object-Oriented Databases*, 337-351, 1989.

[SI93] Sakama, C. and Inoue, K., An Alternative Approach to the Semantics of Disjunctive Logic Programs and Deductive Databases. Research Report, ASTEM Research Institute of Kyoto. Shorter version: Negation in Disjunctive Logic Programs, *Proc. 10th Int. Conf. on Logic Programming*, 703-719, 1993.

[SI91] Satoh, K. and Iwayama, K., Computing Abduction by using the TMS, *Proc. 8th Int. Conf. on Logic Programming*, 505-518, 1991.

[SL90] Selman, B. and Levesque, H. J., Abductive and Default Reasoning: A Computational Core, *AAAI-90*, 343-348, 1990.

The Acceptability Semantics for Logic Programs

A. C. Kakas
Dept. of Computer Science
University of Cyprus
Kallipoleos 75
Nicosia, Cyprus
antonis@jupiter.cca.ucy.cy

P. Mancarella
Dipartimento di Informatica
Università di Pisa
Corso Italia, 40
56125 Pisa, Italy
paolo@di.unipi.it

Phan Minh Dung
Division of Computer Science
Asian Institute of Thechnology
GPO Box 2754
Bangkok 10501, Thailand
dung@cs.ait.ac.th

Abstract

We present a simple yet powerful semantics for Negation as Failure (NAF) in logic programming, called the acceptability semantics. This is based on the idea that NAF literals represent possible extensions of a given logic program, provided that these satisfy an appropriate criterion, namely the acceptability criterion. The importance of this semantics and the way it is formulated lies in the fact that it allows us to abstract away NAF from the object-level syntax of our representation language. This has two significant consequences. First, it introduces a new more general, yet simpler, style of logic programming which is closer to the logical specification of non-monotonic problems, with the same basic computational paradigm of logic programming. Additionally, the understanding of the NAF principle through acceptability provides us with a general encapsulation of this non-monotonic reasoning principle that can be applied to other, richer in language, representation frameworks.

1 Introduction

This paper is concerned with the semantics of Negation as Failure (NAF) in Logic Programming [2] and the extension of this non-monotonic reasoning principle to more general representation frameworks. It proposes a way of understanding NAF that can be adopted more generally to provide a simple and natural representation framework close to the logical specification of problems requiring non-monotonic reasoning.

The basic motivation behind this work is the view that NAF is first and foremost a reasoning principle rather than a form of object-level negation. We are thus interested in providing a direct formalization of the intuitive principle "*not p* holds iff *p* fails to hold". The resulting semantics is called the acceptability semantics. We will show that this encompasses most of the existing semantics for NAF and thus it can help to unify and simplify the study of NAF in logic programming (LP, for short). More importantly, this formalization of the NAF principle provides a more general encapsulation of the principle that can be applied to other (richer in language) representation frameworks outside normal LP. In fact, many of the existing non-monotonic reasoning frameworks can be understood via this general NAF principle. In LP itself this allows us to remove NAF from the object-level syntax of the language, and thus the problem of the existence of two types of negation (explicit negation and NAF) in the language disappears: NAF is elevated into the semantics.

The work in this paper follows a series of recent works on related ideas. It builds on the basic idea originating in [6] that NAF can be regarded as hypotheses that can be added to a given logic program, provided that they satisfy appropriate criteria. Whereas in [6] the criteria were expressed as integrity constraints, in later work [3] the basic criterion takes the form of acceptance relative to other possible conflicting extensions. The new approach of [3] was extended in [12]. The complexity aspects of this new approach have been studied in [22]. In particular, the paper [12] ends with the suggestion of the acceptability criterion as a simple and general semantics for NAF that can encompass other previously studied semantics. The current paper aims at presenting a proper formalization of the acceptability semantics for NAF in LP and then at applying it to define more general non-monotonic reasoning frameworks. The connection of these works to the notion of acceptability has been studied in [11], where an argumentation theoretic description of acceptability is proposed which we will be adopting in this paper. Also, in [5] a weaker notion of acceptability in LP is studied and shown that it encompasses various semantics for NAF such as the well-founded model and partial stable model semantics. The possibility of extending the acceptability semantics outside LP has been studied in [10] using the argumentation theoretic description of [11]. In particular it is shown that Default Logic [18] can be understood in this way. Similar results of understanding Default Logic and other existing non-monotonic frameworks in terms of different criteria for accepting hypotheses which are closely related to the acceptability have been obtained in [1]. An abstract framework for argumentation is proposed in [4], in which it is possible to place these previous approaches, although the criteria proposed in [4] are different from the acceptability criterion used in this paper.

2 Acceptability Semantics in Logic Programming

In this section we will present and study the acceptability semantics for normal LP, as proposed in [12], using the argumentation theoretic view suggested in [11]. Our study starts from the object-level realization of NAF in LP, which will point out the need of elevating back the NAF principle at the semantics level, aiming at developing a framework where NAF is not explicit in the language.

2.1 Motivation

In the LP framework, NAF is basically a realization of the Closed World Assumption. Informally, it can be explained by the statement that, given a logic program P, "*not p* holds (in P) iff p fails to hold (in P)". In many examples of its use in LP we can indeed see that NAF is not an object level negation. Consider the rule

$fly \leftarrow bird, not\ abnormal.$

Here the negative condition *not abnormal* is used as a test that *abnormal* fails. It is a realization of the statement *unless abnormal* rather than a representation of an object-level negative condition needed for *fly* to hold. As a result, this negative condition would be absent in any framework that aims to be closer to the natural representation of this default rule.

On the other hand, there are examples where NAF is used in place of an object-level negation and therefore negative conditions should need to be present in the representation. Examples of this are the following programs for the even numbers and game playing, respectively:

$even(0) \leftarrow$ $win(x) \leftarrow move(x, y), not\ win(y)$
$even(s(x)) \leftarrow not\ even(x).$

Using NAF in this way, we cannot represent fully complex problems. For example, in the *even* program we do not capture that $s(d)$, for any d which is not a natural number, is also not even. On the contrary we can conclude (incorrectly) $even(s(d))$. Also, we the above *game* rule we can not represent games in which there are draw positions. If y is a draw position, and so *not win(y)* holds, we will be able to derive (incorrectly) that any position x from which a move to y exists is a winning position. The problem here stems from the fact that NAF, which is to be understood as a form of CWA to form negative assumptions, is used in place of the explicit object-level negation $\neg win(y)$. Although it is possible to modify the program suitably to handle these cases, our aim is to study how this can be done by remaining as close as possible to the natural representation of the problem.

This discussion indicates that, even in the case of normal LP, there is the need for two types of negations, which must be properly separated one at the object level and the other (NAF) at the metal-level. In section 4 we will see one way to achieve this.

2.2 Acceptability Semantics of Normal Logic Programs

A series of recent works [3, 5, 6, 12] have studied NAF as a form of default hypothesis that can be used to extend a given logic program. Thus, given a normal logic program P we regard the set of negation as failure literals (naf literals, for short)

$$\mathcal{B}^* = \{not\ p \mid p \in \text{Herbrand Base of } P\}$$

as a set of (default) hypotheses with which we can extend the program P. (We will assume that a logic program containing variables is a representation of all its variable-free instances over its Herbrand Universe.)

In an extension $P \cup H$, $H \subseteq \mathcal{B}^*$, we reason using definite Horn logic, where the naf literals $not\ p$ appearing in P and H are treated as positive atoms. The question of whether a subset H of $\mathcal{B}^*$ can be accepted as an extension of P depends on whether it obeys the NAF principle "$not\ p$ holds if and only if p fails to hold".

The acceptability semantics, as suggested in [12], can be seen as a proposal for the formalisation of this principle. The first thing to notice is that the acceptability of the hypothesis $not\ p$ depends on the possibility of deriving (or not) the contrary information p. Hence $not\ p$ is in conflict with any other set A of naf literals that, together with P, allows one to conclude p. We say that such a set *attacks not p*. More generally, the notion of attack between two sets of naf literals is the following.

Definition 2.1 Let P be a normal logic program and $A, H \subseteq \mathcal{B}^*$. Then A attacks H iff there exists $not\ p \in H$ such that $P \cup A \vdash p$.   □

In the above definition, $\vdash$ stands for the usual provability relation of Horn clause logic (recall that here naf literals are viewed as positive atoms). Then, the acceptability of a set $H \subseteq \mathcal{B}^*$ depends on the ability or not to derive conflicting information from $\mathcal{B}^*$, i.e. it depends on the possible attacks against it. There are two cases for which it is easy to determine whether a hypothesis $not\ p$ is acceptable. When the program contains no rules for p, there are no attacks against $not\ p$. Hence, $\{not\ p\}$ is acceptable. Conversely, if p is provable from the rules of the program without any further negative assumptions, i.e. $A = \{\}$ is an attack against $not\ p$, then $\{not\ p\}$ is not acceptable. In fact, with this interpretation of "p holds" as "there is an acceptable attack against $\{not\ p\}$" and further with the interpretation of "p fails to hold" not simply as "there is no attack to $\{not\ p\}$" but rather as "any attack against $\{not\ p\}$ is not acceptable", we arrive at a recursive interpretation of the NAF principle as acceptability given by

"H is acceptable iff any attack A against H is not acceptable."

This interpretation has been formalised and studied in [5] in terms of the fix points of an associated monotonic operator. This work has shown that the least fix point of this operator corresponds to the well-founded model [23] and the greatest fix points correspond to the preferred extensions [3] (and therefore to any other semantics equivalent to this, e.g. partial stable models [19].) This formalization can be generalised to cover extensions of these semantics while, at the same time, avoiding the need to consider greatest fix points. In fact, we can define the semantics fully in terms of the least fix point of a more general acceptability operator, that defines an acceptability relation satisfying the following specification.

Definition 2.2 (*Specification of Acceptability for LP*)
Let P be a normal logic program and $H_0, H \subseteq \mathcal{B}^*$. Then:

$Acc(H, H_0)$ iff for any attack A against $(H \setminus H_0) : \neg Acc(A, H \cup H_0)$. □

It is important to notice that acceptability is a binary relation on $\mathcal{B}^*$, i.e. that the central notion is "H is acceptable w.r.t. H_0", where H_0 is regarded as a given choice or context of hypotheses. The basic idea is to consider the acceptability of a set H as a property relative to itself, i.e. in the context where H is to be assumed. This context is defined non-deterministically when we choose a set H among the whole set $\mathcal{B}^*$ of hypotheses. We can then use the hypotheses in H to justify themselves, i.e. to make themselves acceptable by rendering attacking sets of hypotheses not acceptable.

Notice also that the attacks A against H that must be considered are only those that attack the new part of H, namely $H \setminus H_0$. This subtraction of H_0 is important as it is needed to ensure that attacks are not against hypotheses in H_0, which we are in fact trying to adopt. In other words, the notion of attack must be *relative to* a given set of hypotheses (namely "A attacks H rel. to H_0") that limits the attacks only to those that are against the new hypotheses in H (a more detailed discussion regarding this issue can be found in [12].) Before defining formally the acceptability relation, we illustrate it with an example.

Example 2.3

$P:$ $p \leftarrow not\ q$
         $q \leftarrow not\ p$

$H_1 = \{not\ p\}$ is an acceptable extension of P, since any attack against H_1 must contain $\{not\ q\}$. But any set containing $not\ q$ is counter-attacked by H_1, which is trivially acceptable to itself. This shows how a set of hypotheses is used as its own defence to render itself acceptable. Similarly, $H_2 = \{not\ q\}$ is also an acceptable extension of P.   □

2.3 A fix point definition of Acceptability

The acceptability relation is defined formally as the least fix point of a suitable operator $\mathcal{F}$, obtained by unfolding its recursive specification above.

Definition 2.4
Let P be a logic program and R be the set of binary relations on $2^{\mathcal{B}^*}$. Then $\mathcal{F} : R \to R$ is defined as follows, for any $Acc \in R$ and $H, H_0 \in 2^{\mathcal{B}^*}$:

$\mathcal{F}(Acc)(H, H_0)$ iff for any attack A against $(H \setminus H_0)$
there exists an attack D against $(A \setminus (H \cup H_0))$
s.t. $Acc(D, A \cup H \cup H_0)$.

$\square$

It is easy to show that this operator is monotonic with respect to $\subseteq$.

Definition 2.5 (*Acceptability relation and acceptable extensions*)
Let P be a logic program and $\mathcal{F}$ the operator as in Def. 2.4. Then:

(i) the acceptability relation Acc of P is the least fix point of $\mathcal{F}$

(ii) given $H \subseteq \mathcal{B}^*$, $P \cup H$ is an *acceptable extension* of P iff $Acc(H, \{\})$. $\square$

Proposition 2.6 [1] *Let P be a normal logic program and Acc its acceptability relation. Then:*

(i) there exists at least one acceptable extension of P

(ii) if $H \subseteq H_0$ then $Acc(H, H_0)$

(iii) if $Acc(H, \{\})$ then $P \cup H$ is consistent, i.e. for no p both not $p \in H$ and $P \cup H \vdash p$. $\square$

Proposition 2.6(ii) shows how Def. 2.5 effects the desired property of taking a set of hypotheses H_0 as an a-priori given set under which we want to investigate the acceptability of some other set of hypotheses. Proposition 2.6(iii) shows that inconsistency is understood as self-attack. Let us illustrate the above definitions with an example that emphasizes the recursive nature of acceptability.

Example 2.7

P:	$p \leftarrow not\ q$	$r \leftarrow not\ p$
	$q \leftarrow not\ r$	$s \leftarrow r$

---

[1]All the proofs are omitted and are reported in [13].

We note here that a program like the previous one can be generated by the stable-marriage problem presented and discussed in [4] (see also [13]). The set $H = \{not\ p\}$ is not acceptable since, in the context of H, its attack $\{not\ q\}$ becomes acceptable. In fact, any attack against $\{not\ q\}$ must contain $\{not\ r\}$ and therefore can itself be attacked by H (since it derives r) which is acceptable to itself. Now the set $\{not\ s\}$ is acceptable, since its attacks must contain $H = \{not\ p\}$ and hence are not acceptable. □

Theorem 2.8 *Let P be a logic program. Then any stable model [8], partial stable model [19], stationary expansion [17], preferred extension [3] and stable theory [12] corresponds to an acceptable extension of P.* □

Furthermore, there are programs for which the acceptability semantics gives additional extensions which are not captured by these other semantics, such as example 2.7. Theorem 2.8 deals with the credulous semantics for logic programs. Turning to the skeptical semantics, it can be shown (see [12]) that the well-founded model [23] of any logic program corresponds to an acceptable extension. More importantly, we can define a strong form of acceptability that captures and extends the well-founded semantics.

Definition 2.9 Let P be a logic program and $H \subseteq \mathcal{B}^*$. Then H is defined to be *strongly acceptable* to P, (denoted by $Acc_{ST}(H)$) if:

$Acc_{ST}(H)$ iff for any attack A of H : $\neg Acc(A, \{\})$,

where Acc is the (credulous) acceptability relation of Def. 2.5. □

Essentially, a set H is strongly acceptable if there is no possible non-deterministic choice of hypotheses that is acceptable and attacks H.

Definition 2.10 The skeptical acceptable semantics of P is given by its maximal strongly acceptable extension. □

Example 2.7 shows that the skeptical acceptability semantics can be seen as an extension of the well-founded semantics. Its skeptical acceptability semantics is given by $H = \{not\ s\}$ whereas the well-founded semantics does not assign a value to s or $not\ s$. Note that to capture the well-founded semantics exactly (see [5]) we need to restrict our notion of strongly acceptable as follows:

$Acc_{WF}(H)$ iff for any attack A of H, $\neg Acc_{WF}(A)$.

We note here that in many cases it is sufficient to work with approximations of the acceptability semantics given by the various iterations (or approximations of these iterations) of the fix point operator defined in Def. 2.4. An important example of such an approximation is given by admissibility [3]. This will be used in Section 4 to show and motivate the connection between ordinary LP with NAF in the object-level syntax and the new framework of LP that we are proposing, where NAF is absent from the language.

3 General Theory of Acceptability

The acceptability semantics for normal LP can be applied to more general representation frameworks. To do this we need to abstract some of the central notions of the semantics, as applied to LP, and then apply the same ideas referring to a different underlying representation framework. The central notions in the LP case are the notions of attack and acceptability. In our generalization, we keep the notion of acceptability fixed and simply use the attacking relation as a parameter on which acceptability depends.

Definition 3.1 A *non-monotonic reasoning framework* is given by a monotonic background logic $\mathcal{L}$ along with a binary attacking relation $attack(T, T')$ between sets of sentences (theories) in $\mathcal{L}$. □

Given a theory T in a non-monotonic reasoning framework, we have the following defining axioms for acceptability.

Definition 3.2 *(Axioms of acceptability)*
Let $\mathcal{T}$ be a theory in a non-monotonic reasoning framework. Then the acceptability relation Acc on $\mathcal{T}$ is specified via the following axioms. For any $T, T_0 \subseteq \mathcal{T}$:

(a1) $Acc(T, T_0)$ if $T \subseteq T_0$

(a2) $Acc(T, T_0)$ if for any attack T' against T rel. to T_0, $\neg Acc(T', T \cup T_0)$.

□

Note that (a2) requires the notion of attack *relative to* a given subtheory T_0 of sentences. This is a generalization of the subtraction $(H \setminus H_0)$ that we have in the Def. 2.4 for the LP case, where the sentences in H and H_0 are simple assertions of NAF literals. This notion captures the fact that T_0 should be considered as given, and consequently any attack T' against T should not at the same time be an attack against T_0. In other words T' should not attack T_0 in exactly the same way it attacks T. To see the importance of this notion consider $Acc(T, \{\})$. For T to be acceptable to $\{\}$, it is necessary, for any attack T' against T (rel. to $\{\}$), that T counter-attacks T' (rel. to T). Now, if T' contains statements that belong to T, the required counter-attack against T' must be a genuine attack against T', that is it can not be isolated as an attack against the part of T' that also belongs to T.

We will thus require that this notion of relative attack has the following properties:

(1) if T' attacks T and T' does not attack T_0 then T' attacks T rel. to T_0

(2) if $T \subseteq T_0$ then there exists no T' s.t. T' attacks T rel. to T_0.

The existence of the acceptability relation and semantics in a general non-monotonic reasoning framework follows in exactly the same way as for the special case of normal LP in Proposition 2.6. The associated fix point operator is defined in the same way as in Def. 2.4, where we replace the specific form of relative attack with its general form.

Definition 3.3 Let $\mathcal{T}$ be a theory in a non-monotonic reasoning framework and R be the set of binary relations on $2^{\mathcal{T}}$. Then $\mathcal{F} : R \to R$ is defined as follows, for any $Acc \in R$ and $T, T_0 \in 2^{\mathcal{T}}$:

$$\mathcal{F}(Acc)(T, T_0) \quad \text{iff} \quad \text{for any attack } T' \text{ against } T \text{ rel. to } T_0,$$
$$\text{there exists an attack } T'' \text{ against } T' \text{ rel. to } (T \cup T_0)$$
$$\text{s.t. } Acc(T'', T' \cup T \cup T_0).$$

□

Definition 3.4 The (credulous) semantics for a theory $\mathcal{T}$ is the set of acceptable extensions of $\mathcal{T}$, i.e. the set of $T \subseteq \mathcal{T}$ s.t. $Acc(T, \{\})$, Acc being the least fix point of the operator $\mathcal{F}$ of Def. 3.3. □

The skeptical semantics of a non-monotonic reasoning framework can be defined as in the LP case through a strong acceptability relation, as in Def. 2.9 and 2.10. As for LP, the definition of acceptability captures the following informal abstraction of the NAF principle. Given a theory $\mathcal{T}$ that may typically contain incompatible information, the acceptability relation gives us suitable subsets T of $\mathcal{T}$ such that $Acc(T, \{\})$, which we can reason with. Such a set T has the property that it can defend itself from any subset of $\mathcal{T}$ that would render it incompatible, i.e. it can defend itself from any attack. The acceptability semantics for a general non-monotonic reasoning framework is based on an attacking relation among theories. It is important to relate this attacking relation to the background logic of the framework or, in other words, to use an attacking relation that is *naturally* derived from the background logic itself. For the case of LP, as analysed in the previous section, the background logic is definite Horn logic and the notion of attack is the one of Def. 2.1, that is it is defined through the conflict between *not p* and p. Like in LP, we often have some natural notion of conflicting information and then, roughly speaking, we can say that a theory T' attacks another theory T iff they derive conflicting information. The typical example of such conflicting information is of course the case of a sentence and its explicit (or classical) negation.

Definition 3.5 *(Complements/Consistency)*
Let $\mathcal{L}$ be a background logic, ϕ a wff formula and ϕ^c a complement of ϕ. We say that ϕ and ϕ^c are in conflict. A theory T is inconsistent (or incompatible) iff $T \vdash \phi, \phi^c$ for some formula ϕ. Otherwise, we say that T is consistent (or conflict-free). □

We thus assume that a non-monotonic framework comes with some notion of complements and consistency of its theories. We then require that the attacking relation obeys the following properties.

Property 3.6 (Properties of Attacks)
Let T' and T be two theories in $\mathcal{L}$:

  (i) if T' attacks T then there exists a wff ϕ such that $T \vdash \phi$ and $T' \vdash \phi^c$;

  (ii) if T' attacks T then T' attacks any superset of T;

  (iii) if T is inconsistent, then T attacks T. $\square$

Property 3.6(iii) ensures that any acceptable extension of a given theory T is consistent.

Theorem 3.7 *Let $\mathcal{T}$ be a theory and $T \subseteq \mathcal{T}$ such that $Acc(T, \{\})$. Then T is consistent.* $\square$

Another important observation is that, if the attacking relation is symmetric, then the acceptability semantics always reduces to consistency as the following result shows. This can occur for example if the complement relation is symmetric, i.e. $(\phi^c)^c = \phi$.

Proposition 3.8 *Let $\mathcal{T}$ be a theory in a non-monotonic reasoning framework whose attacking relation is symmetric. Then $T \subseteq \mathcal{T}$ is acceptable to $\{\}$ iff T is consistent.* $\square$

The most interesting cases of the acceptability semantics occurs when the attacking relation is not symmetric. Informally, in order to allow T' to attack T we need to localise the incompatibility of T and T' within T. For example, in the case of LP, where the given theory $\mathcal{T} = P \cup \mathcal{B}^*$, the attacking relation is not symmetric. We can understand this breaking of the symmetry in different ways. One simple way is to regard the complement relation as non-symmetric, namely the complement of *not* p is p but the reverse does not hold. This understanding is not completely satisfactory in view of the fact that it can not be applied to other frameworks where the conflicts are given through explicit or classical negation (a symmetric form of complement.) Another way of understanding this asymmetric attacking relation of LP is based on the separation of any given theory $\mathcal{T}$ into the program P and the set $\mathcal{B}^*$. This is defined as follows.

Definition 3.9 *(Attack for logic programming)*
Let P be a normal logic program and $<$ the priority relation on $P \cup \mathcal{B}^*$ that assigns any sentence in $\mathcal{B}^*$ lower priority than any sentence in P. Then, for any $H, A \subseteq P \cup \mathcal{B}^*$, A attacks H iff there exist a literal L and $A' \subseteq A$, $H' \subseteq H$ such that:

(i) $H' \vdash_{min} L$ and $A' \vdash_{min} L^c$, and

(ii) there is no rule ϕ in A' such that $\phi < \psi$ for some rule ψ in H'

where $T \vdash_{min} L$ denotes the fact that $T \vdash L$ and no proper subset T' of T is such that $T' \vdash_{min} L$. □

Notice that L stands for a positive or negative literal (p or $not\ p$ resp.) and L^c denotes its symmetric complement ($not\ p$ or p resp.). It is easy to see that this attacking relation is equivalent to the one in Def 2.1.

This relatively simple alternative view of the attacking relation in LP is very important as it will motivate the definition of a general non-monotonic reasoning framework that can extend LP and, at the same time, allows us to remove NAF from the object-level language.

Before presenting these issues, we mention here that that the general theory of acceptability developed in this section can be applied in a straightforward way (see [13]) to give a semantics to extensions of LP such as disjunctive LP and extended LP with classical negation.

4 Logic Programming without negation as failure

In this section we present a concrete framework for non-monotonic reasoning, based on the general ideas and theory developed in section 3, which encompasses and extends the frameworks of normal LP and its various extensions. We saw in section 3 that, in order to specify a non-monotonic reasoning framework, we need to define its background logic, complements and attacking relation.

Definition 4.1 *(Background logic)*
Formulae in the language of the framework are defined as $L \leftarrow L_1, \ldots, L_n$, where $L, L_1, \ldots, L_n$ are positive or explicit negative literals. The only inference rule is the modus ponens rule

$$\frac{L \leftarrow L_1, \ldots, L_n \qquad L_1, \ldots, L_n}{L} \qquad (n \geq 0) \qquad \square$$

We assume that, together with the set of sentences T, we are given a priority relation $<$ on these sentences (where $\phi < \psi$ means that ϕ has lower priority than ψ). The role of the priority relation is to encode locally the relative strength of rules in the theory, typically between contradictory rules. We will require that $<$ is irreflexive and antisimmetric.

Definition 4.2 *(Non-Monotonic Theory or Program)*
A theory $(T, <)$ is a set of sentences T in $\mathcal{L}$ together with a priority relation $<$ on the sentences of T. □

Let us now proceed to define an appropriate notion of attack on these theories. The only source of conflict that we have in a theory $\mathcal{T}$ is between a literal L and its explicit negation $\neg L$, which is a symmetric form of complement. The presence of the priority relation $<$ on $\mathcal{T}$ allows us to define a notion of attack which is in general non-symmetric.

Definition 4.3 *(Attacks)*
Let $(\mathcal{T}, <)$ be a theory and $T, T' \subseteq \mathcal{T}$. Then T' attacks T iff there exists L, $T_1 \subseteq T'$ and $T_2 \subseteq T$ such that

(i) $T_1 \vdash_{min} L$ and $T_2 \vdash_{min} \neg L$

(ii) $(\exists r' \in T_1, r \in T_2 \text{ s.t. } r' < r) \Rightarrow (\exists r' \in T_1, r \in T_2 \text{ s.t. } r < r')$. $\qquad\square$

$T \vdash_{min} L$ means that $T \vdash L$ and that L can not be derived from any proper subset of T. This definition is a generalization of the corresponding notion of attack for LP as given in Def. 3.9. Notice also that the property "if T is inconsistent then T attacks T" is trivially satisfied by this attacking relation.

In this way, we have completed the definition of our non-monotonic reasoning framework according to Def. 3.1. Its semantics is given by acceptability within the argumentation theoretic framework of section 3. As mentioned in section 3, we can work with any suitable approximation of the acceptability semantics. In this spirit, we will now consider the approximation given by *admissibility* and show how logic programs with object-level NAF can be equivalently understood as a specific type of theories in the above non-monotonic reasoning framework.

Definition 4.4 *(Admissibility)*
Let $(\mathcal{T}, <)$ be a theory and $T \subseteq \mathcal{T}$. Then T is *admissible* iff for any $T' \subseteq \mathcal{T}$ if T' attacks T then T attacks T' rel. to T. $\qquad\square$

This can be expressed equivalently as "T is admissible iff T is consistent and for any $T' \subseteq \mathcal{T}$ if T' attacks T then T attacks T'" which is a form closer to the original definition in [3].

Given a logic program, P, we define a corresponding theory $\mathcal{D}(P)$. This transformation is motivated (see section 2) from the interpretation of *not p* as *unless p*. For example, if we have a rule "$p \leftarrow q, not\ r$" then this is understood as "p holds if q holds unless r holds, in which case this way of deriving p can not apply". The rule is then transformed into two sentences "$p \leftarrow q$"and "$\neg p \leftarrow r$", and the second is assigned higher priority than the first.

Definition 4.5 Let P be a logic program and r be a rule in P of the form $A \leftarrow L_1, \ldots, L_n$. Then $\mathcal{D}(r)$, the default theory associated to r, is $(T_r, <_r)$ defined as follows. T_r contains only the sentences generated by 1,2 and 3 below:

(1) $A \leftarrow A_r$ belongs to T_r;

(2) $A_r \leftarrow A_1, \ldots, A_m$ belongs to T_r, where $A_1, \ldots, A_m$ is the conjunction of all the positive atoms in $L_1, \ldots, L_n$;

(3) for each *not B* in the conjunction $L_1, \ldots, L_n$, the rule $\neg A_r \leftarrow B$ belongs to T_r

where A_r is a new propositional letter. The priority relation, $<_r$, contains only the pairs $r' <_r r''$, where r' is the rule introduced in (2) and r'' is any rule introduced in (3). □

Definition 4.6 Let P be a normal logic program. Then the corresponding theory, $\mathcal{D}(P)$, is the non-monotonic theory $(T_P, <)$ defined as follows:

(1) T_P is the union of T_r, for every rule r in the program P

(2) for any r', r'' in T_P, $r' < r''$ iff $r' <_r r''$ for some rule r in P. □

We assume that the new propositional symbols introduced in $\mathcal{D}(P)$ associated with two different rules are distinct, even when these two rules have the same head. In fact, this is the reason for introducing these new symbols so that we can separate different rules in P for the same atom.

Example 4.7 The theory $\mathcal{D}(P)$ associated with the program P of example 2.3 is the following:

$$\mathcal{D}(P): \quad \begin{array}{ll} p \leftarrow & q \leftarrow \\ \neg p \leftarrow q & \neg q \leftarrow p \end{array}$$

$$<: \quad \{(p \leftarrow) < (\neg p \leftarrow q), \ (q \leftarrow) < (\neg q \leftarrow p)\}$$

where we have not introduced new symbols here since there is only one rule for each propositional symbol of the original program. □

We note that a related transformation has been proposed in [14] to transform extended logic programs with explicit negation and NAF to normal logic programs containing only NAF. With this transformation of logic programs into non-monotonic theories we can show that admissibility in the two frameworks coincides.

Theorem 4.8 *Let P be a normal logic program, $\mathcal{D}(P) = (T_P, >)$ its corresponding theory, and a any positive atom in the original language of P. Then for each admissible extension $P \cup H$ there exists an admissible subtheory T of T_P such that*
 (i) $P \cup H \vdash a$ iff $T \vdash a$ and   (ii) if not $a \in H$ then $T \nvdash a$.
Conversely, for each admissible subtheory T of T_P there exists an admissible extension $P \cup H$ such that:
 (i) $T \vdash a$ iff $P \cup H \vdash a$ and   (ii) if $T \nvdash a$ then not $a \in H$. □

In the above example 4.7 the admissible set of hypotheses $\{not\ p\}$ corresponds to the admissible subtheory $\{(q \leftarrow), (\neg q \leftarrow p)\}$ of T_P.

Hence LP with NAF in the object language can be simulated exactly in terms of a subclass of non-monotonic theories that contain only explicit negation. We also note that we can apply a Closed World Assumption within an admissible (or more generally acceptable) subtheory T of $\mathcal{D}(P)$ by assuming the negation of any atom a that does not follow from T. The resulting theory will always be consistent.

This subclass of theories corresponding to ordinary logic programs is very specific, since it requires that all conditions of the rules in a theory are positive atoms and the priority relation on the theory is of the form given in Def. 4.6. In the new style of LP that we are advocating, both restrictions can be lifted thus providing a more general representation framework.

Let us illustrate this new framework with a few examples. The usual non-monotonic problem of "flying birds" can be represented by the theory

$r_1 :\ fly \leftarrow bird$ $\qquad\qquad r_1 < r_2$
$r_2 :\ \neg fly \leftarrow penguin$ $\qquad r_2 < r_3$
$r_3 :\ fly \leftarrow superpenguin$
$r_4 :\ bird \leftarrow penguin$
$r_5 :\ penguin \leftarrow superpenguin$

This theory has acceptable extensions that can derive separately fly or $\neg fly$. If we add to the theory "$r_6 : superpenguin \leftarrow$" then there is no acceptable extension that derives $\neg fly$.

The theory for representing the even numbers will now be written as

$r_1 :\ even(0) \leftarrow$
$r_2 :\ even(s(x)) \leftarrow \neg even(x)$
$r_3 :\ \neg even(s(x)) \leftarrow even(x)$

with an empty priority relation. This does not suffer from the same problems encountered in the program with NAF as discussed in section 2. The previous examples can be handled satisfactorily within the admissibility approximation of the acceptability semantics. There are however problems where this approximation is not sufficient. One such example is the game problem with draw positions, as discussed in section 2. The game program is now represented as

$r_1 :\ win(x) \leftarrow move(x, y), \neg win(y)$
$r_2 :\ \neg win(x) \leftarrow move(x, y), win(y)$

with extra rules for $move$ and an empty priority relation. Again this does not suffer from the problems discussed in section 2. Other examples can be found in [13].

5 Conclusions

We have proposed a framework for non-monotonic reasoning based on a general encapsulation, within an argumentation theoretic set up, of the NAF principle in LP. The semantics of these frameworks is given via the acceptability relation. One of the results of adopting this approach is a new non-monotonic framework based on LP where NAF is elevated to the semantics with only explicit negation needed in the object-level language. The acceptability relation and the corresponding semantics have a naturally associated proof theory that stems directly from their definition. This has been developed in [21] and applied to the special case of LP with object-level NAF as defined in section 2. This proof procedure shares all the basic characteristics of the computational model of ordinary LP with NAF.

We believe that a suitable domain of application of the new LP framework is the area of legislation [20]. This stems from the fact that the specification of problems in this domain, where some of the rules (laws) act as exceptions to other rules (laws), has naturally the form of the non-monotonic theories in the proposed framework.

The framework we have proposed relies heavily on the existence of a priority relation on its theories. The use of priorities and preference relations for non-monotonic reasoning has been the subject of study of many other previous works, e.g [7, 9, 15, 16] and further work is needed to study the relation between our work and these earlier works.

Acknowledgements

The authors have benefited from discussions with R. A. Kowalski and F. Toni, and from comments and suggestions of the anonymous referees. This research was partly supported by the ESPRIT BRA 6810 (Compulog 2), and PFI Sistemi Informatici e Calcolo Parallelo under grant no. 92.01564.PF69. The second and third author acknwoledge support from the EEC activity KIT011 - LPKRR. The third author was partly supported by the abduction group at Imperial College, under a grant from Fujitsu.

References

[1] Bondarenko A., Toni F. and R.A. Kowalski. An assumption-based Framework for Non-monotonic Reasoning. *Proc. 2nd Int. Workshop on Logic Programming and Non-Monotonic Reasoning*, Lisbon, 1993.

[2] Clark K.L. Negation as Failure. *Logic and Databases* (H. Gallaire and J. MInker, eds.), Plenum, New York, 1978.

[3] Dung P. M. Negation as Hypothesis: An Abductive Foundation for Logic Programming. *Proc. 8th ICLP*, MIT Press, Paris, 1991.

[4] Dung P. M. On the Acceptability of Arguments and its fundamental role in Non-Monotonic Reasoning and logic programming. *Proc. 13th IJCAI*, 1993.

[5] Dung P. M., Kakas A.C. and P. Mancarella. Negation as Failure Revisited. Technical Report, University of Pisa, 1992.

[6] Eshghi K. and R. A. Kowalski. Abduction Compared with Negation by Failure. *Proc. 6th ICLP*, Lisbon, (1989) 234-255.

[7] Geffner H. *Default Reasoning: Causal and Conditional Theories.* MIT Press, 1992.

[8] Gelfond M. and V. Lifschitz. The Stable Model Semantics for Logic Programming. *Proc. 5th ICLP*, MIT Press, Seattle, 1988.

[9] Hunter A. Using priorities in non-monotonic proof theory. Technical report, Imperial College, London, 1993.

[10] Kakas A.C. Default Reasoning via Negation as Failure *Proc. ECAI'92 Workshop on The theoretical foundations of Knowledge Representation and Reasoning*, (G. Lakemeyer and B. Nebel, eds), 1993.

[11] Kakas A.C., Kowalski R.A. and F. Toni. Abductive Logic Programming. *Journal of Logic and Computation*, 2(6):719-770, 1993.

[12] Kakas A.C. P. Mancarella. Stable theories for Logic Programs. *Proc. Int. Symp. of Logic Programming*, MIT Press, San Diego, 1991.

[13] Kakas A.C., Mancarella P. and P.M. Dung. The Acceptability Semantics for Logic Programming. Technical Report, University of Cyprus, 1994.

[14] Kowalski R.A. and F. Sadri. Logic Programs with Exceptions. *Proc. 7th ICLP*, MIT Press, Jerusalem, 1990.

[15] Laenens E., Saccà D. and D. Vermeir. Extending Logic Programming. *Proc. ACM SIGMOD Conference*, Atlantic City, 1990.

[16] Pereira L.M., Aparicio J.N. and J.J. Alferes. Non-Monotonic Resoning with well-founded semantics. *Proc. 8th ICLP*, Paris, 1991.

[17] Przymusinski T.C. Stationary Semantics for Disjunctive Logic Programs and Deductive Databases *Proc. NACLP 90* (S. Deabray and M. Hermenegildo, eds.), MIT Press, 40-60, 1990.

[18] Reiter R. A Logic for Default Reasoning. *Journal of AI*, 13:81-132, 1980.

[19] Saccà D. and C. Zaniolo. Stable Models and Non-Determinism for Logic Programs with Negation. *Proc. ACM SIGMOD-SIGACT Symp. on Principles of Database Systems*, 205-217, 1990.

[20] Sergot M.J. et al. The British Nationality Act as a Logic Program, *Communication of the ACM*, 29, 1986.

[21] Toni F. and A. C. Kakas. Computing the Acceptability Semantics. Technical report, Imperial College, 1993.

[22] A. Torres. Negation as Failure to Support. *Proc. 2nd Int. Workshop on Logic Programming and Non-Monotonic Reasoning*, Lisbon, 1993.

[23] Van Gelder A., Ross K.A. and J. S. Schlipf. Unfounded sets and the well-founded Semantics for General Logic Programs. *Proc. ACM SIGMOD-SIGACT Symp. on Principles of Database Systems*, 221-230, 1988.

A Bottom-up Semantics for Constructive Negation

Annalisa Bossi
Dip. di Matematica Pura ed Applicata, Università di Padova,
Via Belzoni 7, 35131 Padova, Italy,

Massimo Fabris
Dip. di Matematica Pura ed Applicata, Università di Padova,
Via Belzoni 7, 35131 Padova, Italy,

Maria Chiara Meo
Dipartimento di Informatica, Università di Pisa,
Corso Italia 40, 56125 Pisa, Italy,

Abstract

The constructive negation rule has been introduced by Chan [5, 6] to overcome the main drawbacks of the negation-as-failure rule: the unsoundness of floundering programs and, consequently, the inability of providing answers for non-ground negative queries. In this paper we define a bottom-up semantics for constructive negation which we prove sound and complete with respect to the three-valued completion of the program. The semantics describes answers as well as undefined computations for both positive and negative queries. Its construction closely follows the basic idea of constructive negation whereby answers to a negative query are obtained by negating a *frontier* of the computation tree for the corresponding positive query. Therefore, the proposed semantics can be considered as a natural base for reasoning on the operational semantics for constructive negation defined in the literature. Moreover, we show how the semantics can be effectively used to perform a bottom-up computation of the answers of a normal query.

1 Introduction

The standard rule for dealing with negation in logic programming is the "negation as failure" rule. Its main drawback is that *computing* by negation as failure, actually means *testing* by negation as failure, that is no answers are produced except for the yes/no ones.

To overcome this limitation Chan [5, 6] introduced the *constructive negation* rule which subsumes negation as failure and extends it by allowing non-ground negative subgoals to bind variables in the same way as positive ones. The basic idea which is formalized by SLD-CNF resolution is that, to handle a negative subgoal, one first considers its positive version and then negates all its answers. Answers to negative goals are described by first-order formulas which are interpreted in CET, the equality theory defined by Clark.

Stuckey [24] pointed out how constraint logic programming provides a much more natural setting for describing constructive negation and described a setting for constructive negation for constraint logic programming over arbitrary structures. He gave a new operational schema and proved its soundness and completeness with respect to the three-valued completion of the program.

Recently, Drabent [11, 10] proposed a method for deriving (constrained) answers for (constrained) normal queries in normal programs called SLDFA-resolution, an extension of SLDNF-resolution. The basic notions of SLDFA-resolution are SLDFA-refutation and finitely failed SLDFA-tree; they are mutually defined as the corresponding notions of SLDNF-resolution. Comparisons between Drabent's method and those defined by Chan and Stuckey suggest that the first may have practical advantages over the other two.

In this paper we follow a semantical approach to constructive negation. We develop a semantics in the style of [13]: we construct a denotation which directly characterizes the program behaviour on all most general atomic queries (positive or negative) and contains enough information to represent the program behaviour on all queries.

We consider CLP normal programs as defined by [16]. Our denotations (*uncertain interpretations*) extend both those defined in [8, 9, 1] for the semantics of definite programs, and those in [14] for modeling answer constraints in CLP normal programs. They contain four kinds of objects which represent the four different computational aspects of a program we are interested in. Three of them have a logical reading in the three-valued completion of the program. They are: *positive constrained atoms*, which represent success answers for positive general queries; *negative constrained atoms*, which represent success answers for negative general queries or, symmetrically, finite failures of positive general queries; *uncertain negative atoms*, which represent undefined answers on both negative and positive queries, they entail undefined values in three-valued logic. Besides a fourth kind of object (*uncertain positive atom*) is used to represent divergent computations of positive queries. Since a positive query may have both successful and divergent computations, uncertain positive atoms do not necessary entail undefined values.

To illustrate this point consider the definite program $\{p(a)., \; p(X) \leftarrow p(X).\}$. The success constraint for the query $p(X)$ is $X = a$, but its negation, $(X \neq a)$, is not a success for the query $\neg p(X)$. Note that the three valued model is $\{p(a)\}$. Our semantic denotation will contain: the positive constrained atom $X = a \,\Box\, p(X)$, the uncertain negative atom $X \neq a \,\Box\, ?p(X)$ and the uncertain positive atom $true \,\Box\, \widehat{p(X)}$. The last one models the divergent computation for the query $p(X)$.

Actually, the positive components in an uncertain interpretation are sufficient to determine the negative ones. For instance, observe that the absence of success answers for negative general queries in the above program can be derived by the fact that there is no way of negating both the constraint in the positive constrained atom $(X = a)$ and that in the uncertain positive atom $(true)$. On the other hand, the uncertain negative atom can be obtained by negating the success and asserting the divergence.

The semantics is obtained by iterating an operator Ψ_P which maps uncertain interpretations to uncertain interpretations. Our construction agrees with Fitting's Φ_P operator [12] in the sense that at each iteration step there is a one-to-one correspondence between the solutions represented by the uncertain interpretation and the three-valued interpretation constructed by Fitting's operator. There are obvious analogies between Ψ_P and $\Phi_P^{\mathcal{A}}$, the non-ground (constrained) version of Φ_P defined by Stuckey in [24]. The main difference is that instead of deriving information on success and failure we derive information on success and divergent computations.

Note that our information is richer than the former. In fact, by negating both successes and failures we obtain only a subset of divergent computations, while by negating both successes and divergent computations all failures can be obtained. Moreover the second construction conforms much better with the basic idea of constructive negation whereby an answer to a negative query is obtained by negating a *frontier* of the computation tree for the corresponding positive query.

The paper is organized as follows. In Section 2 we give the basic notations on CLP normal programs. In Section 3 we introduce our semantic domain and the notions of uncertain base and uncertain interpretations. The bottom-up semantics is defined in Section 4. In Section 5 we discuss and compare some other approaches to constructive negation. We dedicate special attention to Drabent's work and those properties of SLDFA-resolution captured by our semantics.

Due to the lack of space, all the proofs are omitted; they can be found in [2].

2 Preliminaries

We assume the reader is familiar with the basic concept of logic programming. We recall the basic CLP concepts as defined in [16] and [20]. A first order language is defined on a function symbols set denoted by Σ, a predicate symbols set denoted by Π and a collection of variables denoted by V. The predicate symbols are partitioned into two sets: Π_C which are pre-defined predicates and Π_B which are the predicates to be defined by the program. We assume that Π_C contains the predicate symbol $=$. $\tau(\Sigma \cup V)$ and $\tau(\Sigma)$ denote the set of terms and ground terms (i.e. terms without variables) built on Σ and V. An *atom* is of the form $p(t_1, \ldots, t_n)$ where p is an n-ary symbol in Π_B and $t_i \in \tau(\Sigma \cup V)$, $i = 1, \ldots, n$. A *literal* is either an atom or the negation of an atom. A *constraint* is a well formed formula over the alphabets Π_C and Σ. In the following, $\tilde{t}$, $\tilde{X}$ will denote tuple of terms and *distinct* variables, while $\tilde{L}$ denotes a (possibly empty) conjunction of literals. If o is a syntactic object, $FV(o)$ is the set of variables which are not explicitly quantified in o. Given a formula f, $\exists f$ and $\forall f$ denote its existential and universal closure respectively. $\exists_{-\tilde{X}} f$ denotes the existential closure of the formula f except for the variables $\tilde{X}$, which remain unquantified. Let F be a set of formulas, we use the notations $\bigvee F$ and $\bigwedge F$ as shorthands for the formulas $(\bigvee_{f \in F} f)$ and $(\bigwedge_{f \in F} f)$ respectively, where, $(\bigvee_{f \in \emptyset} f) = false$ and $(\bigwedge_{f \in \emptyset} f) = true$.

Definition 2.1 (*CLP normal programs*) *[16] A normal program is a finite set of clauses of the form $H \leftarrow c \,\square\, \tilde{L}$. where c is a constraint, H (the head) is an atom and $\tilde{L}$ (the body) is a (possibly empty) conjunction of literals. A normal goal is a program clause with no head and with a non-empty body.*

In the following we will consider clause heads of the form $p(\tilde{X})$, where $\tilde{X}$ is a sequence of distinct variables and we will denote by P^* the completed definitions of the predicates in a normal program P.

Moreover we will often use *normal queries* instead of normal goals, where given a normal goal $\leftarrow c \,\square\, \tilde{L}$ the corresponding (normal) query is $c \,\square\, \tilde{L}$.

Definition 2.2 *A constrained atom is of the form $c \,\square\, p(\tilde{X})$, where c is a constraint, $FV(c) \subseteq \{\tilde{X}\}$ and $p(\tilde{X})$ is an atom.*

A *structure* $\mathcal{D}$ over the alphabets Π_C and Σ, consists of a non empty set (D) and any interpretation of each function and predicate symbol according to its arity. The structures considered in CLP are the "solution compact" ones as defined in [16, 15]. A *domain theory* T *corresponding* to the structure $\mathcal{D}$ is a first-order consistent theory containing only predicate symbols from Π_C, such that $\mathcal{D}$ is a model of T and for every constraint c, $\mathcal{D} \models c$ iff $T \models c$. Moreover we require that for every constraint c either $T \models \exists c$ or $T \models \neg \exists c$ (namely, T is *satisfaction complete* [20]). A domain theory axiomatizes the particular domain $\mathcal{D}$ on which we wish to compute. We do not make any assumption on Σ. Rather we require that the domain theory T contains the standard theory CET, given in [7] to axiomatize unification. Moreover if the set of function symbols Σ is finite we assume the (weak) domain closure axiom (DCA) be added to CET, thus achieving the completeness of the theory CET in the case of a language with finite set of function symbols. Informally the axiom DCA [19] ensures that in the interpretation domain of any model of the theory, every object is a value of a non-variable term. A *valuation* is a mapping from the variables to D. The notion of valuation is extended in the obvious way to terms and constraints. A negation of an equation $s = t$ (a *disequation* or *inequality*) will be written as $s \neq t$. If $\tilde{t} = (t_1, \ldots, t_n)$ and $\tilde{s} = (s_1, \ldots, s_n)$ are two sequences of terms, $\tilde{t} = \tilde{s}$ will denote the set of equations $\{t_1 = s_1, \ldots, t_n = s_n\}$.

A constraint c is *satisfiable* in the theory T iff there exists a valuation θ such that $T \models c\theta$. θ is called a *solution* of c. If $C = \bigwedge_{i \in I} c_i$ is a possibly infinite conjunction of constraints, $T \models C\theta$ iff $\forall i \in I$, $T \models c_i\theta$. Analogously, if $C = \bigvee_{i \in I} c_i$ is a possibly infinite disjunction of constraints, $T \models C\theta$ iff $\exists i \in I$, such that $T \models c_i\theta$.

We also introduce the following $[\ ]$ operator on constrained atoms, which returns the set of "domain instances".

Definition 2.3 *[16] The set of "domain instances"* $[c \,\square\, p(\tilde{X})]$ *of a constrained atom* $c \,\square\, p(\tilde{X})$ *is defined as* $[c \,\square\, p(\tilde{X})] = \{p(\tilde{X})\theta \mid \theta \text{ is a solution of } c\}$. *Let S be a set of constrained atoms. Then* $[S] = \bigcup_{A \in S} [A]$.

Next we define a preorder $\preceq$ on constraints, and a preorder $\sqsubseteq$ on sets of constraints and the induced equivalence relations.

Definition 2.4 *Let c_1 and c_2 be constraints and let C_1 and C_2 be sets of constraints. Then*

- $c_1 \preceq c_2$ *iff* $T \models \forall(c_1 \rightarrow c_2)$. *We denote by $\equiv$ the equivalence relation induced by $\preceq$.*

- $C_1 \sqsubseteq C_2$ *iff for any $c_1 \in C_1$ such that $c_1 \not\equiv false$ there exists $c_2 \in C_2$ such that $c_1 \preceq c_2$. We denote by $\approx$ the equivalence relation induced by $\sqsubseteq$.*

Finally, if $\sim$ is an equivalence relation defined on a set $\mathcal{S}$ and $S \in \mathcal{S}$, we denote by $S_\sim$ the equivalence class in $\mathcal{S}/\sim$ which contains S.

3 Uncertain interpretations

We extend the notion of π-interpretation as introduced in [14] in order to provide three-valued models of the completion of a CLP normal program. First of all, a *partial* interpretation, as defined in [17], is any total function F from the set of all ground atoms into $\{\mathbf{t}, \mathbf{f}, \mathbf{u}\}$, where $\{\mathbf{t}, \mathbf{f}, \mathbf{u}\}$ are interpreted as *true*, *false* and *undefined*. According to our notation, we will represent such a function F as a set of ground literals $F^+ \cup F^-$, where $F^+ = \{p(\tilde{t}) \mid p(\tilde{t}) \text{ is a ground atom and } F(p(\tilde{t})) = \mathbf{t}\}$ and $F^- = \{\neg p(\tilde{t}) \mid p(\tilde{t}) \text{ is a ground atom and } F(p(\tilde{t})) = \mathbf{f}\}$. The extension of a partial interpretation to ground constraints and to ground formulas is defined in [24], by the following rules.

- Let c be a ground constraint. c is *true* in F iff $T \models c$ and c is *false* in F iff $T \models \neg c$.

- We assume the usual strong three-valued interpretation of the symbols $\wedge, \vee, \neg$, $\forall, \exists, \rightarrow$, and following Kunen, we use Lukasiewicz's truth table for the connective $\leftrightarrow$. Moreover the symbols '$\square$' and ',' will be interpreted as $\wedge$.

All the following definitions are related to a given $\mathcal{D}$ (and therefore to a given (Π_C, Σ)).

Before giving the definition of uncertain base we extend the preorder on constraints to constrained atoms. It represents the notion of "being more constrained". The equivalence induced by such a preorder is used in the semantic domain in order to abstract from syntactical differences among constrained atoms.

Definition 3.1 *Let $c_1 \square p(\tilde{X})$ and $c_2 \square p(\tilde{X})$ be constrained atoms. Then $c_1 \square p(\tilde{X}) \preceq c_2 \square p(\tilde{X})$ iff $c_1 \preceq c_2$. The equivalence induced by $\preceq$ on the set of atoms is still denoted by $\equiv$. The quotient set of all the constrained atoms w.r.t. the equivalence relation $\equiv$ will be denoted by $\mathcal{A}$.*

It is easy to see that the above equivalence $\equiv$ on constrained atoms corresponds to set equality on domain instances.

Lemma 3.2 *Let $c_1 \square p(\tilde{X})$ and $c_2 \square p(\tilde{X})$ be constrained atoms. Then $c_1 \square p(\tilde{X}) \equiv c_2 \square p(\tilde{X})$ iff $[c_1 \square p(\tilde{X})] = [c_2 \square p(\tilde{X})]$.*

For the sake of simplicity, we let the constrained atom $c \square p(\tilde{X})$ denote the equivalence class $(c \square p(\tilde{X}))_{\equiv}$ in $\mathcal{A}$ and, conversely, any $B \in \mathcal{A}$ will be considered also as a constrained atom obtained by selecting any (arbitrary) representative element in B. It is easy to verify that all our definitions are independent from the choice of such an element. The ordering induced by $\preceq$ on $\mathcal{A}$ will still be denoted by $\preceq$.

We now introduce the uncertain base.

Definition 3.3 (uncertain base) *Let P be a normal program. The uncertain base of interpretations, $\mathcal{B}$, is the union of the following sets.*

$$
\begin{array}{llll}
\mathcal{B}^+ & = & \mathcal{A} & \text{positive component} \\
\mathcal{B}^- & = & \{c \square \neg p(\tilde{X}) \mid c \square p(\tilde{X}) \in \mathcal{A}\} & \text{negative component} \\
\mathcal{B}^{\widehat{+}} & = & \{c \square \widehat{p(\tilde{X})} \mid c \square p(\tilde{X}) \in \mathcal{A}\} & \text{uncertain positive component} \\
\mathcal{B}^? & = & \{c \square ?p(\tilde{X}) \mid c \square p(\tilde{X}) \in \mathcal{A}\} & \text{uncertain negative component.}
\end{array}
$$

In the following, given $J \subseteq \mathcal{B}$ and $o \in \{+, -, \widehat{+}, ?\}$ we shall use the notations J^o for $J \cap \mathcal{B}^o$ and $J_{|A}$ for $\{c \mid c \square A \in J\}$. Intuitively any subset I of $\mathcal{B}$ conveys both *certain* and *uncertain* information. The certain information is contained in I^+ and I^- while the uncertain one is contained in the two other components $I^{\widehat{+}}$ and $I^?$.

We are interested in particular subsets of $\mathcal{B}$, called *consistent*. They have the property that the components $^-$ and $^?$ are completely determined by the two others: $^-$ is the complement of $^+$ and $^{\widehat{+}}$, while $^?$ is the difference between $^{\widehat{+}}$ and $^+$. The following definition formalizes these concepts.

Definition 3.4 (consistent set) *Let $I \subseteq \mathcal{B}$. We say that I is consistent if*

$$I^- = \mathrm{neg}(I) \ and \ I^? = \mathrm{unc}(I),$$

where

i) $\mathrm{neg}(I) = \{ \bigwedge\{\neg c \mid c \in I_{|p(\tilde{X})} \cup I_{|\widehat{p(\tilde{X})}}\} \Box \neg p(\tilde{X}) \mid p \in \Pi_B\}$

ii) $\mathrm{unc}(I) = \{ \bigwedge\{\neg c \mid c \in I_{|p(\tilde{X})}\} \wedge d \Box ?p(\tilde{X}) \mid p \in \Pi_B \ and \ d \Box \widehat{p(\tilde{X})} \in I\}$

We denote by $\mathcal{R}$ the set of consistent subsets of $\mathcal{B}$.

Example 3.5 *The set $I = \{(X = a) \Box p(\tilde{X}), \ (X = b) \Box \widehat{p(\tilde{X})}, \ (X \neq a) \wedge (X \neq b) \Box \neg p(\tilde{X}), \ (X = b) \Box ?p(\tilde{X})\}$ is consistent.*

Note that, for any consistent set I, $[I^+] \cup [I^-]$ is a standard three-valued interpretation. The following lemma shows that $[I^?]$ are exactly the undefined elements in $[I^+] \cup [I^-]$.

Lemma 3.6 *Let I be a consistent set. Then,*

$$\bigvee I_{|?p(\tilde{X})} \equiv \neg \bigvee (I_{|p(\tilde{X})} \cup I_{|\neg p(\tilde{X})})$$

Proof. The proof is immediate by definition of neg(I) and unc(I). $\qquad\square$

We propagate and extend the information contained in a consistent set I through a program P by means of an unfolding operation. The result of such an unfold is a consistent set too.

Definition 3.7 (I-unfolding) *Let P be a normal program and $I \in \mathcal{R}$ a consistent set. Moreover, let $C = p(\tilde{X}) \leftarrow c_0 \Box q_1(\tilde{t}_1), \ldots, q_n(\tilde{t}_n), \neg r_1(\tilde{s}_1), \ldots, \neg r_m(\tilde{s}_m)$ be a clause in P and*

$\psi_C^{+,\widehat{+}}(I) = \{\exists_{-\tilde{X}}.c \Box A \mid \ for \ i = 1, .., n, \ and \ for \ j = 1, .., m, \ there \ exist$

$\qquad c_i \Box Q_i \in I^+ \cup I^{\widehat{+}}, \ such \ that \ either \ Q_i = q_i(\tilde{X}_i) \ or \ Q_i = q_i(\widehat{\tilde{X}_i}) \ and$
$\qquad d_j \Box R_j \in I^- \cup I^?, \ such \ that \ either \ R_j = \neg r_j(\tilde{Y}_j) \ or \ R_j = ?r_j(\tilde{Y}_j),$
$\qquad\qquad renamed \ apart,$
$\qquad c = (c_0 \wedge \bigwedge_{i=1}^n (c_i \wedge \tilde{X}_i = \tilde{t}_i) \wedge \bigwedge_{j=1}^m (d_j \wedge \tilde{Y}_j = \tilde{s}_j)),$
$\qquad A = p(\tilde{X}) \ if \ for \ i = 1, .., n, \ j = 1, .., m, \ Q_i = q_i(\tilde{X}_i) \ and \ R_j = \neg r_j(\tilde{Y}_j)$
$\qquad A = \widehat{p(\tilde{X})} \ otherwise$ $\qquad\qquad\qquad\qquad\qquad\qquad\qquad \}$

The I-unfolding of P is the consistent set $\psi_P(I)$ whose positive components are
$$\psi_P(I)^{+,\widehat{+}} = \bigcup_{C \in P} \psi_C^{+,\widehat{+}}(I).$$

Observe that the previous unfolding operation returns certain information if the only information it uses is certain, otherwise it returns uncertain information.

Example 3.8 *Let P be the following normal program:*

$C_1 = p(X,Y){:}\text{-} \ X = f(V) \Box q(V).$ $\qquad$ $C_4 = r(X){:}\text{-} \ X = b \Box r(X).$
$C_2 = p(X,Y){:}\text{-} \ Y = g(W) \Box \neg r(W).$ $\qquad$ $C_5 = r(X){:}\text{-} \ X = c \Box r(X).$
$C_3 = q(X){:}\text{-} \ X = a.$ $\qquad\qquad\qquad\qquad$ $C_6 = r(X){:}\text{-} \ X = c.$

Consider the consistent set I_0 whose positive components are

$$I_0^+ = \emptyset \quad and \quad I_0^{\widehat{+}} = \{true \Box \widehat{p(X,Y)}, true \Box \widehat{r(X)}, true \Box \widehat{q(X)}\}$$

and consequently,

$$I_0^- = \{false \,\square\, \neg p(X,Y), false \,\square\, \neg r(X), false \,\square\, \neg q(X)\} \text{ and}$$
$$I_0^? = \{true \,\square\, ?p(X,Y), true \,\square\, ?r(X), true \,\square\, ?q(X)\}$$

Then

$$\psi_{C_1}^{+,\widehat{+}}(I_0) = \{\exists V. X = f(V) \,\square\, p(\widehat{X,Y})\} \qquad \psi_{C_4}^{+,\widehat{+}}(I_0) = \{(X=b) \,\square\, \widehat{r(X)}\}$$
$$\psi_{C_2}^{+,\widehat{+}}(I_0) = \{\exists W. Y = g(W) \,\square\, p(\widehat{X,Y})\} \qquad \psi_{C_5}^{+,\widehat{+}}(I_0) = \{(X=c) \,\square\, \widehat{r(X)}\}$$
$$\psi_{C_3}^{+,\widehat{+}}(I_0) = \{(X=a) \,\square\, q(X)\} \qquad \psi_{C_6}^{+,\widehat{+}}(I_0) = \{(X=c) \,\square\, r(X)\}$$

Hence the I_0-unfolding of P is composed by:

$$\psi_P^{+,\widehat{+}}(I_0) = \{\exists V. X = f(V) \,\square\, p(\widehat{X,Y}), \; \exists W. Y = g(W) \,\square\, p(\widehat{X,Y}),$$
$$(X=a) \,\square\, q(X), \; (X=c) \,\square\, r(X), \; (X=c) \,\square\, \widehat{r(X)}, \; (X=b) \,\square\, \widehat{r(X)} \}$$

$$\psi_P(I_0)^- = \{\forall VW. \; X \neq f(V) \wedge Y \neq g(W) \,\square\, \neg p(X,Y),$$
$$(X \neq a) \,\square\, \neg q(X), \; (X \neq c \wedge X \neq b) \,\square\, \neg r(X) \}$$

$$\psi_P(I_0)^? = \{\exists V. X = f(V) \,\square\, ?p(X,Y), \; \exists W. Y = g(W) \,\square\, ?p(X,Y),$$
$$false \,\square\, ?r(X), \; (X=b) \,\square\, ?r(X) \}$$

Next we introduce a preorder $\leq$ on $\mathcal{R}$. It is intended to represents the increasing of the amount of information relative to the two components $^+$ (which contains certain information) and $\widehat{+}$ (which contains uncertain information). The certain information should not decrease while the uncertain should not increase. Our third requirement in the definition of $\leq$ expresses also the fact that the increase of certain information should result from the relaxation of previous uncertain information.

Definition 3.9 *Let $I, J \in \mathcal{R}$ be two consistent sets. $I \leq J$ iff for any predicate symbol $p \in \Pi_B$, the following conditions hold*

1. $I_{|p(\check{X})} \sqsubseteq J_{|p(\check{X})}$.

2. $J_{\widehat{|p(\check{X})}} \sqsubseteq I_{\widehat{|p(\check{X})}}$.

3. $\bigvee J_{|p(\check{X})} \preceq \bigvee (I_{|p(\check{X})} \cup I_{\widehat{|p(\check{X})}})$.

The equivalence relation induced by $\leq$ will be denoted by $\simeq$.

The following lemma shows how the preorder $\leq$ is reflected to I^- and $I^?$. This supports our construction which derives negative and uncertain information from positive and divergent one.

Lemma 3.10 *Let $I, J \in \mathcal{R}$. If $I \leq J$ then for any predicate symbol $p \in \Pi_B$,*

1. $I_{|\neg p(\check{X})} \sqsubseteq J_{|\neg p(\check{X})}$

2. $J_{|?p(\check{X})} \sqsubseteq I_{|?p(\check{X})}$.

3. $\bigvee J_{|\neg p(\check{X})} \preceq \bigvee (I_{|\neg p(\check{X})} \cup I_{|?p(\check{X})})$.

Example 3.11 *Consider the consistent sets I_0 and $\psi_P(I_0)$ of Example 3.8. We have that $I_0 \leq \psi_P(I_0)$.*

The next proposition shows that the unfold operation ψ_P is monotonic wrt $\leq$.

Proposition 3.12 (monotony of ψ_P) *Let I, J be consistent sets such that $I \leq J$. Then, $\psi_P(I) \leq \psi_P(J)$.*

Take two consistent sets I and J such that $I \simeq J$. Then, from $I \leq J$ and $J \leq I$ we derive that for any $p \in \Pi_B$, $I_{|p(\tilde{X})} \approx J_{|p(\tilde{X})}$, $I_{|\neg p(\tilde{X})} \approx J_{|\neg p(\tilde{X})}$, $I_{|\widehat{p(\tilde{X})}} \approx J_{|\widehat{p(\tilde{X})}}$, $I_{|?p(\tilde{X})} \approx J_{|?p(\tilde{X})}$.

Two equivalent consistent sets conveys the same information. We identify them by taking equivalence classes of consistent sets as elements of our semantic domain.

Definition 3.13 (uncertain interpretation) *The set of uncertain interpretation is the quotient set of $\mathcal{R}$ wrt the equivalence $\simeq$.*

$$\mathcal{I} = \mathcal{R}/\simeq = \{I_\simeq \mid I \in \mathcal{R}\}$$

The ordering induced by $\leq$ on $\mathcal{I}$ will still be denoted by $\leq$.

All the subsequent definitions, lemmas and propositions will be given by selecting any representative element in equivalence class $I_\simeq$.

An uncertain interpretation $I_\simeq$ is just a denotation which conveys both certain and uncertain information present in every representative I. Definition 3.9 and Lemma 3.10 show how the partial order $\leq$ defined on $\mathcal{I}$ captures the increasing of the amount of information contained in an uncertain interpretation. Let $I_\perp$ the consistent set, whose positive components are

$$I_\perp^{+,\hat{+}} = \{false \,\Box\, p(\tilde{X}) \mid p \in \Pi_B\} \cup \{true \,\Box\, \widehat{p(\tilde{X})} \mid p \in \Pi_B\}.$$

It is easy to see that $\mathcal{I}_\perp = (I_\perp)_\simeq$ is the the least uncertain interpretation wrt $\leq$.

4 Bottom-up semantics

The bottom-up semantics of a normal program is the the set containing all the uncertain interpretations obtained by finite iterations of an immediate consequence operator Ψ_P. Such an operator is the natural extension to equivalence classes of the unfolding operator ψ_P.

Definition 4.1 (immediate consequence operator) *Let P be a program and $I_\simeq$ be an uncertain interpretation. Then*

$$\Psi_P(I_\simeq) = (\psi_P(I))_\simeq$$

Note that by Proposition 3.12 Ψ_P is well defined and monotonic wrt $\leq$.

Definition 4.2 (semantics) *Let P be a normal program. The semantics $[\![P]\!]^{\mathcal{CN}}$ is defined as*

$$[\![P]\!]^{\mathcal{CN}} = \{\Psi_P\!\uparrow^k \mid k \geq 0\}$$

where $\Psi_P\!\uparrow^0 = \mathcal{I}_\perp$ and $\Psi_P\!\uparrow^{k+1} = \Psi_P(\Psi_P\!\uparrow^k)$.

Observe that, as in ([1]), this semantics is the fixpoint of the monotonic and continuous operator $\mathcal{CN} : \mathcal{P}(\mathcal{I}) \mapsto \mathcal{P}(\mathcal{I})$ on the complete lattice of sets of uncertain interpretations $\mathcal{P}(\mathcal{I})$, defined as follows: $\mathcal{CN}(S) = \{\Psi_P(I_\simeq) \mid I_\simeq \in S\} \cup \{\mathcal{I}_\perp\}$.

Example 4.3 *Let P be the program of Example 3.8 and I_0 the consistent set there defined. Observe that $\mathcal{I}_\perp = (I_0)_\simeq$. Therefore $\psi_P(I_0)$ is a representative of $\Psi_P\!\uparrow^1$. Let us calculate $\Psi_P\!\uparrow^2$. For the sake of simplicity, we consider each predicate separately and let a set of constraints C denote the equivalence class $C_\simeq$. Observe that $\Psi_P\!\uparrow^2$ projected on $p(X,Y)$ can be calculated using $(\Psi_P\!\uparrow^1)_{|q(X)}$ and $(\Psi_P\!\uparrow^1)_{|\widehat{q(X)}}$ on the first clause, $(\Psi_P\!\uparrow^1)_{|\neg r(X)}$ and $(\Psi_P\!\uparrow^1)_{|?r(X)}$ on the second:*

$$\begin{aligned}
(\Psi_P\!\uparrow^2)_{|p(X,Y)} &= \{X = f(a),\ \exists W.\ Y = g(W) \wedge W \neq b \wedge W \neq c\}, \\
(\Psi_P\!\uparrow^2)_{|\widehat{p(X,Y)}} &= \{Y = g(b)\}.
\end{aligned}$$

Hence

$$\begin{aligned}
(\Psi_P\!\uparrow^2)_{|\neg p(X,Y)} &= \{X \neq f(a) \wedge (Y = g(c) \vee \forall W.\ Y \neq g(W))\}, \\
(\Psi_P\!\uparrow^2)_{|?p(X,Y)} &= \{X \neq f(a) \wedge Y = g(b)\}.
\end{aligned}$$

It is easy to see that the projections on q and r are the same in $\Psi_P\!\uparrow^1$ and $\Psi_P\!\uparrow^2$. At the third level of iteration also the projections on p of $\Psi_P\!\uparrow^3$ and $\Psi_P\!\uparrow^2$ are equal.

The next proposition shows soundness and completeness of the semantics wrt the completion of the normal program. Let $\langle I_\simeq \rangle$ be the partial interpretation associated to $I_\simeq$, namely $\langle I_\simeq \rangle = [I^+] \cup [I^-]$, and Φ_P be the operator defined by Fitting [12]. We prove that, for any finite k, there is a one-to-one correspondence between $\langle \Psi_P \uparrow k \rangle$ and $\Phi_P \uparrow k$.

Proposition 4.4 (soundness and completeness) *Let P be a normal program and Φ_P be Fitting's operator [12]. Then*

$$\langle \Psi_P \uparrow k \rangle = \Phi_P \uparrow k, \quad \text{for any finite } k.$$

4.1 Computing success and failure answers

The aim of this section is to show that our semantics can also be used to perform an effective bottom-up computation of the answers of a normal query. Given a normal query, we can derive both a success set and a failure set of constraints from every element of the chain $\Psi_P\!\uparrow^k$.

First, we define the success set of a query G wrt a representative I of an uncertain interpretation $I_\simeq$.

Definition 4.5 (success set) *Let $I \in \mathcal{R}$ be a representative of an uncertain interpretation, and G be a query. Moreover, let ans be a new predicate symbol, $ans \notin \Pi_B$, and $\{\tilde{X}\} = FV(G)$. Then the success set of G wrt I, $\mathcal{S}_G(I)$, is defined as*

$$\mathcal{S}_G(I) = \{c \mid c \,\square\, ans(\tilde{X}) \in \psi^+_{ans(\tilde{X}) \leftarrow G}(I)\}$$

The next lemma shows that we may extend definition 4.5 to interpretations.

Lemma 4.6 *Let I and J be representatives of uncertain interpretations such that $I \leq J$ and let G be a query. Then, $\mathcal{S}_G(I) \sqsubseteq \mathcal{S}_G(J)$.*

Then, by using the equivalence $\approx$ on sets of constraints introduced in Section 2, we define: $\mathcal{S}_G(I_\simeq) = \mathcal{S}_G(I)_\approx$, and, with the convention that a set of constraints C denotes the equivalence class $C_\approx$, we just write $\mathcal{S}_G(I)$.

Example 4.7 *Consider the program of Example 3.8. The constraint* $\forall V. \ X \neq f(V) \wedge Y = c$ *is in the success set of the query* $true \ \square \ \neg p(X,Y), r(Y)$ *wrt the interpretation* $\Psi_P\uparrow^1$.

The failure set of a query G wrt a representative of an uncertain interpretation $I_{\simeq}$ contains the negation of the constraint of the query as well as all the constraints in the success set of the negation of one of the literals in G. (Note that we simplify double negations).

Definition 4.8 *Let I be a representative of an uncertain interpretation and $G = c_0 \ \square \ L_1, \ldots, L_n$ be a query. The failure set of G wrt I, $\mathcal{F}_G(I)$ is defined as*
$$\mathcal{F}_G(I) = \{c \mid c = \neg c_0 \ or \ \exists i = 1, \ldots, n, \ such \ that \ c \in \mathcal{S}_{\neg L_i}(I)\}$$

The next lemma shows that we may extend definition 4.8 to interpretations.

Lemma 4.9 *Let I and J be representatives of uncertain interpretations such that $I \leq J$ and let G be a query. Then, $\mathcal{F}_G(I) \sqsubseteq \mathcal{F}_G(J)$.*

Then, we define, $\mathcal{F}_G(I_{\simeq}) = \mathcal{F}_G(I)/_{\approx}$.

Example 4.10 *Consider the program of Example 3.8. The constraint $Y \neq c \wedge Y \neq b$ is in the failure set of the query* $true \ \square \ \neg p(X,Y), r(Y)$ *wrt the interpretation* $\Psi_P\uparrow^1$.

The following proposition proves soundness and completeness of the previous definitions of success and failure sets.

Proposition 4.11 (extended soundness and completeness) *Let P be a normal program, Φ_P be Fitting's operator and $G = c_0 \ \square \ \tilde{L}$ be a query. Then*

- *if $c \in \mathcal{S}_G(\Psi_P\uparrow^n)$ (resp. $c \in \mathcal{F}_G(\Psi_P\uparrow^n)$) then for any $G' \in [c \ \square \ \tilde{L}]$, $\Phi_P\uparrow^n(G') = true$ (resp. $\Phi_P\uparrow^n(G') = false$)*

- *if $G' \in [c_0 \ \square \ \tilde{L}]$ and $\Phi_P\uparrow^n(G') = true$ (resp. $\Phi_P\uparrow^n(G') = false$) then there exists $c \in \mathcal{S}_G(\Psi_P\uparrow^n)$ (resp. $c \in \mathcal{F}_G(\Psi_P\uparrow^n)$) such that $G' \in [c \ \square \ \tilde{L}]$*

where $[c \ \square \ \tilde{L}]$ denotes the set of formulas $\{\tilde{L}\vartheta \mid \vartheta$ is a solution of $c\}$.

After proving that our semantics captures all the correct success and failure constraints, we show how this bottom-up computation can be made effective. The idea is that every element of the chain conveys correct information that is refined by the next element of the chain. This is proved by the next corollary of Lemmas 4.6 and 4.9:

Corollary 4.12 *Let P be a normal program and G be a query. Then for any $k \geq n$,*

$$\mathcal{S}_G(\Psi_P \uparrow n) \sqsubseteq \mathcal{S}_G(\Psi_P \uparrow k) \ and \ \mathcal{F}_G(\Psi_P \uparrow n) \sqsubseteq \mathcal{F}_G(\Psi_P \uparrow k)$$

The last point is to show how we can recognize that we have reached full information and hence stop. For any uncertain interpretation $I_{\simeq}$, $\Psi_P(I_{\simeq})_{|ans(\bar{X})} = \mathcal{S}_G(I_{\simeq})$ and $\Psi_P(I_{\simeq})_{|\neg ans(\bar{X})} = \bigvee \mathcal{F}_G(I_{\simeq})$. Then by Lemma 3.6 the bottom-up computation stops as soon as: $\Psi_P(I_{\simeq})_{|?ans(\bar{X})} = \{false\}$.

Let us apply the previous ideas to a couple of examples.

Example 4.13 *Consider the program of Example 3.8 and the query*

$$G = \neg p(g(Z), f(Z)), q(Z).$$

It is easy to see that $\mathcal{S}_G(\Psi_P\uparrow^1) = \{Z = a\}$, $\mathcal{F}_G(\Psi_P\uparrow^1) = \{Z \neq a\}$ *and* $(\Psi_P\uparrow^2)_{|?ans(Z)}$
$= \{false\}$. *Hence the first step is completely informative and then* $Z = a$ *is the only answer to the query* G *while* $Z \neq a$ *is the only answer to the query* $\neg G$.

Example 4.14 *Consider again the program of Example 3.8 and the query*

$$G' = p(S, g(T)), q(T).$$

The first steps gives $\mathcal{S}_{G'}(\Psi_P\uparrow^1) = \{false\}$ *and* $(\Psi_P\uparrow^2)_{|?ans(S,\,T)} = \{\exists V.S = f(V) \wedge T = a;\ T = a\}$. *Then we exploit also the second step that gives us* $\mathcal{S}_{G'}(\Psi_P\uparrow^2) = \{S = f(a) \wedge T = a;\ T = a\}$ *and* $(\Psi_P\uparrow^3)_{|?ans(S,\,T)} = \{false\}$. *This terminates the computation.*

5 Comparison with other approaches

We comment the information present in our semantics by relating it to some other approaches to constructive negation. We shall give the intuition that $[\![P]\!]^{\mathcal{CN}}$ captures and models computational features (like termination properties or answer substitutions as in [8, 1]) of some operational semantics for constructive negation recently proposed.

First we consider the operational semantics defined in [5, 22]. These semantics exploit a generalization to normal programs of the following idea: in a definite program, if the atomic query A has a finite set of answers $\delta_1, \ldots, \delta_n$ then $A \leftrightarrow \delta_1 \vee \ldots \vee \delta_n$ is a consequence of Clark's completion. Thus also $\neg A \leftrightarrow \neg \delta_1 \wedge \ldots \wedge \neg \delta_n$ is a consequence of Clark's completion, and if we "normalize" $\neg \delta_1 \wedge \ldots \wedge \neg \delta_n$ into an equivalent disjunction $\sigma_1 \vee \ldots \vee \sigma_m$ then each σ_i is an answer for the query $\neg A$. This method is correct with respect to the completion of the program, it is a natural generalization of negation as failure and its implementation is very simple: every time a negated atom $\neg A$ is found, the complete tree for A is built and the answers are negated. Unfortunately it is uncomplete: if the tree is infinite then the program enters an infinite loop and correct solutions are missed. To see that, consider the query $true \,\square\, \neg r(X)$ in the program of Example 3.8. The SLD-tree of the query $true \,\square\, r(X)$ is infinite with an infinite set of answers $X = c$. The answer $X \neq b \wedge X \neq c$ (which is captured by $(\Psi_P\uparrow^1)_{|\neg r(X)}$) is a consequence of the program completion but is missed by the previous method. Notice that $\Psi_P\uparrow^3_{|\widehat{r(X)}} = \{X = c;\ X = b\}$ captures the divergent computations of the predicate r: a query $\sigma \,\square\, r(Y)$ has an infinite derivation in every SLD-tree if and only if the constraint $\sigma \wedge (X = c \vee X = b)$ is satisfiable [1].

A second group of methods has been proposed to deal also with infinite trees and it can be understood as using the completion of a program instead of the program itself. The basic concept of [25, 18, 6, 24, 23, 21, 3, 4] is, roughly speaking, that in a derivation step for $\neg p(\tilde{t})$ the completed definition of the predicate p is used: literal $\neg p(\tilde{t})$ can be replaced by the negated right hand side of the completed definition of the predicate itself (with an appropriate mgu applied). Another extension of [6, 24] is that not only literals can be selected but also some negated formula. Both

---

[1]This property follows by the fact that if we deal with definite programs, the Ψ functional is equivalent to the one proposed by Delzanno and Martelli in [8].

previous rules are defined in details and in fact Chan has already implemented its rule in the Sepia Prolog compiler. Stuckey proves the completeness of his rule (in the more general framework of constraint logic programming) wrt the three-valued consequences of the completion of the program.

We sketch Stuckey's method, so to explain it and to introduce some motivations to Drabent's subsequent work. Stuckey's rule states that if a negative query $\neg G$ is selected, then the subsidiary tree for G is exploited till a fixed depth (depth 1 if the rule is the Depth Front one). If $F = \{\sigma_1 \,\Box\, \tilde{B}_1, \ldots, \sigma_n \,\Box\, \tilde{B}_n\}$ is the frontier of this tree then $P^* \wedge \mathcal{T} \models_3 G \leftrightarrow \exists_{-\tilde{X}}(\sigma_1 \wedge \tilde{B}_1) \vee \ldots \vee \exists_{-\tilde{X}}(\sigma_n \wedge \tilde{B}_n)$, where $\tilde{X} = FV(G)$ and hence $P^* \wedge \mathcal{T} \models_3 \neg G \leftrightarrow \neg\exists_{-\tilde{X}}(\sigma_1 \wedge \tilde{B}_1) \wedge \ldots \wedge \neg\exists_{-\tilde{X}}(\sigma_n \wedge \tilde{B}_n)$. In order to simplify the right hand side of the previous formula into a normal disjunctive form while retaining completeness, Stuckey propose to separate the constraints in the following way:

$$\neg\exists_{-\tilde{X}}(\sigma \wedge \tilde{B}) \quad \leftrightarrow \quad \neg\exists_{-\tilde{X}}\sigma \ \vee \ \neg\exists_{-\tilde{X}}(\sigma \wedge \tilde{B})$$

If we consider the formula obtained so far

$$\neg G \quad \leftrightarrow \quad (\neg\exists_{-\tilde{X}}\sigma_1 \vee \neg\exists_{-\tilde{X}}(\sigma_1 \wedge \tilde{B}_1)) \ \wedge \ \ldots \ \wedge \ (\neg\exists_{-\tilde{X}}\sigma_n \vee \neg\exists_{-\tilde{X}}(\sigma_n \wedge \tilde{B}_n))$$

we can see that computing the disjunctive form of the right hand side and adding every disjunct as a son of the query $\neg G$ in its derivation tree is correct and complete. The problem pointed out by Drabent is that doing so we add (in general) 2^n sons. Even worse, each $\neg\exists_{-\tilde{X}}(\sigma_i \wedge \tilde{B}_i)$ occurs in 2^{n-1} of them, producing in general repeated computations. Moreover, subqueries can become really very complex, and the method seem to produce a lot of redundant solutions. The method of Chan shares the same problems.

A solution to these drawbacks might be found in the approach recently proposed by Drabent [11, 10] for arbitrary normal programs. It is based on the construction of failed trees. If finitely failed trees are concerned then it is sound and complete wrt Clark completion in 3-valued logic. His idea is a generalization of Chan's first method: since correct answers for $true \,\Box\, \neg G$ are constraints σ such that $\sigma \,\Box\, G$ has a finitely failed tree, Drabent proposes to "build" such trees. Every time the selected literal is negative, $\neg A$, a constraint γ is searched such that $\gamma \,\Box\, A$ has a (subsidiary) failed SLDFA-tree. Hence γ is an answer for the query $true \,\Box\, \neg A$. The (subsidiary) failed SLDFA-tree for $\gamma \,\Box\, A$ is a finitely failed tree built in this way: if the selected literal is positive, then the usual step of SLD-derivation is applied. If the selected literal in the node $\theta \,\Box\, \neg B, \tilde{D}$ is the negative literal $\neg B$, then this node has children $\sigma_1 \,\Box\, \tilde{D}; \ldots; \sigma_m \,\Box\, \tilde{D}$ provided that there exist $\delta_1, \ldots, \delta_n$ SLDFA-computed-answers for the query $\theta \,\Box\, B$, and $CET \models \theta \rightarrow \delta_1 \vee \ldots \vee \delta_n \vee \sigma_1 \vee \ldots \vee \sigma_m$. The justification of this step is the following: since our aim is to falsify $\theta \,\Box\, \neg B, \tilde{D}$, then each δ_i is rejected because it implies $\theta \,\Box\, B$ and hence it already implies falsity of $\theta \,\Box\, \neg B, \tilde{D}$. If we build a failed subtree for each $\sigma_i \,\Box\, \tilde{D}$ then each σ_i implies $\neg\tilde{D}$ which implies falsity of $\theta \,\Box\, \neg B, \tilde{D}$. Drabent does not fully specify how to find the constraint γ, but he informally describes a method based on the construction of a pre-failed tree for A: a tree built using the two derivation steps of a failed SLDFA-tree, but not necessarily failed or fully expanded. Thus γ is the constraint that cuts all successful and unexpanded branches at a finite depth. Let us give the intuition of his idea applying SLDFA-resolution to the query $true \,\Box\, \neg p(X, Y)$. We start the subsidiary pre-failed tree for the query $true \,\Box\, p(X, Y)$. After expanding every branch of one level, we obtain the frontier of depth one:

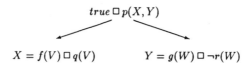

Since the negation of the disjunction of the constrains of the frontier is the satisfiable constraint $\{\forall VW.\ X \neq f(V) \wedge Y \neq g(W)\}$, we can already build a failed SLDFA-tree and add a successful son to $true \,\Box\, \neg p(X, Y)$:

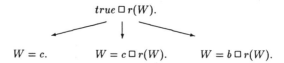

Notice that the first frontier of the tree for the query $true \,\Box\, p(X, Y)$ corresponds to $(\Psi_P{\uparrow}^1)_{|p(\widehat{X,Y})}$, while the first answer to $true \,\Box\, \neg p(X, Y)$ is in $(\Psi_P{\uparrow}^1)_{|\neg p(X,Y)}$. Notice also that according to our semantics $X \neq f(a) \wedge (Y = g(c) \vee \forall W.Y \neq g(W)) \in (\Psi_P{\uparrow}^2)_{|\neg p(X,Y)}$ is an answer for the query $true \,\Box\, \neg p(X, Y)$. To find it, we must expand the subsidiary pre-failed tree to another level. The first branch finds the success constraint $X = f(a)$. In the second branch the negative atom $\neg r(W)$ is selected and hence we begin the tree for $r(W)$ which is exploited till the first frontier:

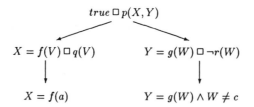

Since $W = c$ is an answer to the query $true \,\Box\, r(W)$ and $CET \models true \rightarrow W = c \vee W \neq c$ then the following is a pre-failed tree for the query $true \,\Box\, p(X, Y)$:

$$true \,\Box\, p(X, Y)$$

$$X = f(V) \,\Box\, q(V) \qquad Y = g(W) \,\Box\, \neg r(W)$$

$$X = f(a) \qquad Y = g(W) \wedge W \neq c$$

The negation of the disjunction of the constrains of the frontier of this pre-failed tree is the satisfiable constraint $X \neq f(a) \wedge \forall W.(Y \neq g(W) \vee W = c)$. Since it produces a failed SFDFA-tree, it is added to the tree $true \,\Box\, \neg p(X, Y)$ as a new successful son:

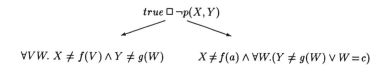

$$\forall VW. \ X \neq f(V) \wedge Y \neq g(W) \qquad X \neq f(a) \wedge \forall W.(Y \neq g(W) \vee W = c)$$

Now we continue to expand the tree $true \,\square\, r(W)$ so to find new (pre-)failed tree for $true \,\square\, p(X,Y)$ and hence new answers to the query $true \,\square\, \neg p(X,Y)$, and we enter an infinite loop. Note that this loop is captured by $(\Psi_P\uparrow^2)_{|?p(X,Y)} = \{X \neq f(a) \wedge Y = g(b)\}$. In fact, $\Psi_P\uparrow^2$ is the least fixpoint of Ψ_P, hence all elements in $[X \neq f(a) \wedge Y = g(b) \,\square\, p(X,Y)]$ are undefined in the completion of the program. Then any sound computation rule should produce an infinite derivation on all queries $\sigma \,\square\, \neg p(X,Y)$ such that $\sigma \wedge X \neq f(a) \wedge Y = g(b)$ is satisfiable.

We end up this section with a conjecture that is also our future work. This conjecture expresses our belief about the existence of a strong relationship between this bottom-up semantics and the SLDFA-derivation.

Conjecture 5.1 *Let P be a normal program, G the query $c_0 \,\square\, \tilde{L}$, and $c \,\square\, p(\tilde{X})$ an atomic query. For any representative $\psi_P\uparrow^n$ of $\Psi_P\uparrow^n$, $n \geq 0$,*

1. $\{c \mid$ *there exists an SLDFA-refutation for $P \cup \{G\}$, with answer c*$\}$
   $\approx \bigcup_{n \geq 0} \mathcal{S}_G(\psi_P\uparrow^n).$

2. $\{c \mid$ *there exists a finitely failed SLDFA-tree for $P \cup \{c_0 \wedge c \,\square\, \tilde{L}\}$* $\}$
   $\approx \bigcup_{n \geq 0} \mathcal{F}_G(\psi_P\uparrow^n).$

3. $c \,\square\, p(\tilde{X})$ *has an infinite SLDFA-derivation under any computation rule iff for every $n \geq 0$ there exists $c' \in (\psi_P\uparrow^n)_{\widetilde{|p(\tilde{X})}}$ such that $c \wedge c'$ is satisfiable.*

4. $c \,\square\, \neg p(\tilde{X})$ *has an infinite SLDFA-derivation under any computation rule iff for every $n \geq 0$ there exists $c' \in (\psi_P\uparrow^n)_{|?p(\tilde{X})}$ such that $c \wedge c'$ is satisfiable.*

References

[1] A. Bossi, M. Bugliesi, and M. Fabris. A New Fixpoint Semantics for Prolog. In D. Warren, editor, *Proceeding of the Tenth Int. Conf. on Logic Programming, ICLP'93*, pages 374–389. The MIT Press, 1993.

[2] A. Bossi, M. Fabris and M. C. Meo. A Bottom-up Semantics for Constructive Negation. Technical Report N.6, Università di Padova, Italy, December 1993.

[3] A. Bottoni, G. Levi. Computing in the Completion. In D. Saccá, editor, *Proceeding of the Eight Italian Conf. on Logic Programming*, pages 375–389. Mediterranean Press, 1993.

[4] A. Bottoni, G. Levi. The Inverse of Fitting's Functional. In G. Gottlob, A. Leitsch and D. Mundici, editors, *Proceeding Third Kurt Gödel Colloquium, Computational and Proof Theory, KGC'93*, pages 132–143. Springer-Verlag, 1993.

[5] D. Chan. Constructive Negation Based on the Completed Database. In R. A. Kowalski and K. A. Bowen, editors, *Proc. Fifth Int'l Conf. on Logic Programming*, pages 111–125. The MIT Press, Cambridge, Mass., 1988.

[6] D. Chan. An Extension of Constructive Negation and its Application in Coroutining. In E. Lusk and R. Overbeek, editors, *Proc. North American Conf. on Logic Programming'89*, pages 477–493. The MIT Press, Cambridge, Mass., 1989.

[7] K. L. Clark. Negation as Failure. In H. Gallaire and J. Minker, editors, *Logic and Data Bases*, pages 293–322. Plenum Press, New York, 1978.

[8] G. Delzanno and M. Martelli. A bottom-up characterization of finite success. Technical Report, Università di Genova, DISI, 1992.

[9] G. Delzanno and M. Martelli. S-semantica per modellare insiemi di soluzioni. In S. Costantini, editor, *Proc. Seventh Italian Conference on Logic Programming*, pages 191–205, 1992.

[10] W. Drabent. SLS-resolution without floundering. In L. M. Pereira and A. Nerode, editors, *Proc. of the Workshop on Logic Programming and Non-monotonic reasoning*, pages 82–98, 1993.

[11] W. Drabent. What is Failure? An Approach to Constructive Negation. *Acta Informatica*, 1993. To appear.

[12] M. Fitting. A Kripke-Kleene semantics for logic programs. *Journal of Logic Programming*, 2:295–312, 1985.

[13] M. Falaschi, G. Levi, M. Martelli, and C. Palamidessi. A new Declarative Semantics for Logic Languages. In R. A. Kowalski and K. A. Bowen, editors, *Proc. Fifth Int'l Conf. on Logic Programming*, pages 993–1005. The MIT Press, Cambridge, Mass., 1988.

[14] M. Gabbrielli and G. Levi. Modeling Answer Constraints in Constraint Logic Programs. In K. Furukawa, editor, *Proc. Eighth Int'l Conf. on Logic Programming*, pages 238–252. The MIT Press, Cambridge, Mass., 1991.

[15] J. Jaffar and J.-L. Lassez. Constraint Logic Programming. In *Proc. Fourteenth Annual ACM Symp. on Principles of Programming Languages*, pages 111–119. ACM, 1987.

[16] J. Jaffar and J.-L. Lassez. Constraint Logic Programming. Technical Report, Department of Computer Science, Monash University, June 1986.

[17] K. Kunen. Negation in logic programming. *Journal of Logic Programming*, 4:289–308, 1987.

[18] D. Lugiez. A Deduction Procedure for First Order Programs. In *Proc. of Sixth International Conf. on Logic Programming*, Lisbon, pages 585–599, MIT Press, 1989.

[19] P. Mancarella, S. Martini, and D. Pedreschi. Complete Logic Programs with Domain Closure Axiom. *Journal of Logic Programming*, 5(3):263–276, 1988.

[20] M.J. Maher. Logic Semantics for a Class of Committed-Choice Programs. In *Proc. of Fourth International Conf. on Logic Programming*, pages 858–876, MIT Press, 1987.

[21] J. A. Plaza. Fully Declarative Logic Programming. In *Programming Language Implementation and Logic Programming, Proceedings 1992*, pages 415–427, Springer-Verlag, 1992, LNCS 631.

[22] T. Przymusinsky. On Constructive Negation in Logic Programming. In *Proc. North American Conference on Logic Programming*, Addendum. MIT Press, 1989.

[23] T. Sato, and F. Motoyoshi. A Complete Top-down Interpreter for First Order Logic Programs. In *Logic Programming, Proc. of the 1991 International Symposium*, pages 35–53, MIT Press, 1991.

[24] P. J. Stuckey. Constructive Negation for Constraint Logic Programming. In *Proc. Sixth IEEE Symp. on Logic In Computer Science*, pages 328–339. IEEE Computer Society Press, 1991.

[25] M. Wallace. Negation by Constraints: a Sound and Efficient Implementation of Negation in Deductive Databases. In *Proc. 1987 Symposium on Logic Programming*, San Francisco, pages 253–263, August 1987.

Default Rules: An Extension of Constructive Negation for Narrowing-based Languages

Juan José Moreno-Navarro

U. Politécnica, Facultad de Informática, Campus de Montegancedo, Boadilla del Monte, 28660 Madrid, Spain, jjmoreno@fi.upm.es

Abstract

In this paper an extension of narrowing-based functional logic languages is proposed: Every partial definition of a function can be completed with a default rule. In a concrete function call, the default rule is applicable when the normal ones determine that they cannot compute the value of the call. The use of the default rule, in the presence of a goal with variables, is constructive. The operational semantics provides constraints to the variables to make the default rule applicable. Narrowing semantics are modified extending the technique of constructive negation [3, 4, 17].

1 Introduction

Narrowing is a unification based parameter passing mechanism which subsumes rewriting and SLD resolution. Different versions of narrowing have been used as the operational semantics of programming languages. In particular, so called *functional logic languages* retain functional syntax but use narrowing as operational semantics. They have been proposed to combine the functional and logic programming paradigms.

As in pure functional programming, the functions defined by the program can be partially defined. A computation fails when a function call cannot be solved. "Exceptions" (see [14] for their use in ML) allows to handle these cases, giving, for instance, a default value. However this solution is not so easy to achieve in the case of functional logic languages because the logical component of the language allows to search values for applying the function. The default value can be returned only if the other rules cannot apply what imposes some constraints on the calling parameters.

The definition of partial functions is implicitly used in PROLOG to carry out negation. Under the Closed World Assumption (CWA) a predicate p is *false* for all the tuples which are not positively defined by the clauses of p.

In this paper we extend this notion of completion for a functional logic language. Every (partial) definition of a function with a number of rules can be completed by an extra default rule. The default rule establishes the function value for all the tuples that are not finitely defined by the previous rules. In particular we have incorporated the default value feature to BABEL [15] with disequality constraints over the Herbrand Universe [10], resulting a new language called Def-BABEL. However, it is clear that the techniques are independent of the chosen narrowing based language.

In order to manage default rules, symbolic constraints are needed to express that the arguments have not the shape required by the normal rules. The default rules also impose universal quantifications over the free variables of the normal rules.

The operational mechanism is a natural extension of *constructive negation* proposed for PROLOG [3, 4, 17] which incorporates constraints as the answers into negative subgoals. The narrowing mechanism can be adapted to compute default values: in order to detect if a function call $f(e_1, \ldots, e_n)$ is defined we start a narrowing computation with $f(e_1, \ldots, e_n)$ as goal. Any frontier of this computation defines where the expression is defined, hence the complement of this frontier defines where it is undefined.

The paper also includes the formal meaning of these default rules by defining the declarative semantics of Def-BABEL programs. The domain distinguishes between finite failure and the $\perp$ value, which denotes divergence, in the style of Kunen's 3-valued semantics [11]. This semantics allows us to express soundness and completeness results.

2 A Functional Logic Language with Default Rules

This section defines Def-BABEL programs and gives some examples. We assume a ranked set $TC = \cup_{n \in N} TC^n$ of *type constructors* (e.g. $nat/0, list/1$) and a countably infinite set $TVar$ of *type variables* α, β, etc. (denoted in programs by capital letters). Any algebraic term τ built from type constructors and type variables – e.g. $list(nat), list(\alpha)$ – is a *data type*. A data type is *polymorphic* if it includes type variables, and *monomorphic* otherwise. We also assume a set DC of *data constructors* d/n with declared principal types: $d : \tau_1 \times \ldots \times \tau_n \to \tau$, e.g. s: $nat \to nat$. In practice, type constructors and data constructors can be introduced through type declarations and some types like $list$, nat or $bool = true|false$ are assumed to be predefined. Next, we assume a countably infinite set VS of (typed) data variables (denoted by capital letters) and a set FS of *function symbols* f/n with declared principal types: $f : \tau_1 \times \ldots \times \tau_n \to \tau$, for example $subs : nat \times nat \to nat$. Terms t and expressions e are defined as follows:

$$
\begin{array}{lll}
t ::= & X & \% \ X \in VS \\
\mid & d(t_1, .., t_n) & \% \ d/n \in DC
\end{array}
\qquad
\begin{array}{lll}
e ::= & X & \\
\mid & d(e_1, .., e_n) & \% \ d/n \in DC \\
\mid & f(e_1, .., e_n) & \% \ f \in FS
\end{array}
$$

and all of them must be well typed (following Milner's type system).

The syntax allows to build expressions involving some *primitive function symbols*: $\neg b$ (negation), (b_1 , b_2) (conjunction), $(b_1 ; b_2)$ (disjunction), $(b \to e)$ (guarded expression, meaning: **if** b **then** e **else** undefined), $(b \to e_1 \Box e_2)$ (conditional, meaning: **if** b **then** e_1 **else** e_2), and $(e_1 = e_2)$ (weak equality, both expressions denote the same object), where b is a boolean expression.

BABEL programs consist of declarations of types and *defining* or *default* rules for every function symbol $f : \tau_1 \times \ldots \times \tau_n \to \tau$, with the following shape, where guards are optional:

Defining rules	*Default rules*
$\underbrace{f(t_1, \ldots, t_n)}_{\text{left hand side}} := \underbrace{\{b \to\}}_{\text{guard}} \overbrace{\underbrace{e}_{\text{body}}}$ $\underbrace{\phantom{f(t_1, \ldots, t_n) := \{b \to\} e}}_{\text{right hand side}}$	$\textbf{default } f(X_1, \ldots, X_n) := b \to e$

BABEL functions are functions in the mathematical sense. In order to ensure confluence, some syntactical restrictions are imposed:

1. *Data Patterns and Left Linearity*: t_i's are terms and every *lhs* does not contain multiple variable occurrences.

2. *Restrictions on free variables*: Variables occurring in the *rhs* but not in the *lhs* are only allowed in the guard.

3. *Well Typedness*: It must be possible to check the types τ_i for each t_i $(1 \leq i \leq n)$, the type *bool* for b, and the type τ for e.

4. *Nonambiguity*: Given two different defining rules in the same function, either their left hand sides are not unifiable or if the *lhs*'s unify with m.g.u. σ, after applying σ to both bodies, either they are identical or their guards are incompatible[1].

Now, we can intuitively define the meaning of a function definition. The left column shows a set of function rules and the right column their meaning:

$$f(\overline{t}^1(\overline{X}^1)) \quad := b_1(\overline{X}^1, \overline{Y}^1) \to e_1$$
$$\cdots$$
$$f(\overline{t}^n(\overline{X}^n)) \quad := b_n(\overline{X}^n, \overline{Y}^n) \to e_n$$
$$\mathbf{default}\ f(\overline{X}) := b(\overline{X}, \overline{Y}) \to e$$

$$f(\overline{Z}) = \left\{ \begin{array}{ll} e_1 & \text{if } \exists \overline{X}^1 (\overline{Z} = \overline{t}^1 \wedge \exists\, \overline{Y}^1 b_1) \\ \cdots & \\ e_n & \text{if } \exists \overline{X}^n (\overline{Z} = \overline{t}^n \wedge \exists\, \overline{Y}^n b_n) \\ e & \text{if } \exists \overline{Y} b \wedge \delta\, (f(\overline{Z})) \end{array} \right.$$

where δ is the definitionless operator that means that the defining rules for f do not define $f(\overline{Z})$.

Example 2.1 *The following program computes the substraction of natural numbers. The partially defined version is completed with a default rule in order to return an integer. Integers are defined as signed numbers.*

type nat := 0 | s(nat).	**fun** subs : nat × nat → int.
type int := + nat | – nat.	subs (Y, 0) := + Y.
fun invert: int → int.	subs (s (Y),s (X)) := subs (Y, X).
invert(+ Y) := – Y.	**default** subs (Y, X) :=
invert(– Y) := + Y.	invert (subs (X, Y)).

eval subs (s (0), X).
> *result* + s (0)   *answer* X = 0
> *result* + 0   *answer* X = s (0)
> *result* – X'   *answer* X = s (X'), X' ≠ 0
> no (more) solutions.

Example 2.2 *The second example involves variable quantification. A natural number is even if it is the double of another natural number. Otherwise the number is odd. This last statement correspond to a default rule which involves an implicit universal quantification.*

type list A := []|[A|list A].	**fun** plus: nat × nat → nat.
type parity_type := even|odd.	plus (0, Y) := X.
fun <: nat × nat → bool.	plus (s (X), Y) := s (plus (X, Y)).
% Some rules for <.	

    fun parity: nat → parity_type.
    parity (X) := (Y < X, plus (Y, Y) = X) → even.
    default parity (X) := odd.

---

[1]Incompatibility [10] is a decidable syntactical property between two boolean expressions in order to ensure that they cannot be simultaneously reduced to true.

eval [parity (1), parity (2), parity (3), parity (4)].
$>$ *result* [odd, even, odd, even] $>$ no (more) solutions.

3   Declarative Semantics of Default Rules

This section is devoted to the declarative semantics of Def-BABEL. Since pure BABEL is a subset of our language some technical details (present in [15]) will be skipped or simplified. We start with the definition of the domain. Polymorphism is treated in the simplest way: every polymorphic function is replicated for each particular monomorphic application.

Definition 3.1 Herbrand Universe
$\mathcal{H}$ is the correctly typed Herbrand universe built up with the constructors of the types defined in the program These terms are called concrete elements. We also add to $\mathcal{H}$ two values for failure: fail (to indicate finite failure) and $\perp$ (for divergence). We assume the following ordering in $\mathcal{H}$

- *$\perp \sqsubseteq d$ for every d*   - *fail $\sqsubseteq d$ for every concrete element d*

Notice the similarities between our model and Kunen's 3-valued semantics [11]. However, our semantics needs two values for failure because *false* is a correct result for functions and predicates. Now we proceed with the definition of interpretations.

Definition 3.2 Interpretations and environments
A Herbrand interpretation I is a collection of well typed monotonic functions $f_I : \mathcal{H}^n \to \mathcal{H}$, one for every function f/n in FS such that $f_I(\perp) = \perp$ and $f_I(fail) = fail$. Interpretations can be equipped with the partial ordering:

$$I \sqsubseteq J \text{ iff for all } f/n \in FS \ f_I(\bar{s}) \sqsubseteq f_J(\bar{s}) \text{ for all } \bar{s} \in \mathcal{H}^n$$

The domain of Herbrand interpretations is noted $\mathcal{H}-\mathcal{INT}$.
An environment is any mapping $\rho : VS \to \mathcal{H} - \{fail, \perp\}$ such that $\rho(X)$ has the same type of the variable X.

Now, we just can define the valuation $[\![e]\!]_I(\rho)$ for a given well typed expression e into a concrete interpretation I under an environment ρ by induction on the syntactical structure of the expression.

Definition 3.3 Valuation
$$
\begin{aligned}
[\![X]\!]_I(\rho) &= \rho(X) \quad \text{for } X \in VS \\
[\![d\,(e_1,..,e_n)]\!]_I(\rho) &= d\,([\![e_1]\!]_I(\rho),..,[\![e_n]\!]_I(\rho)) \quad \text{for } d/n \in CS, n \geq 0 \\
[\![f\,(e_1,..,e_n)]\!]_I(\rho) &= f_I\,([\![e_1]\!]_I(\rho),..,[\![e_n]\!]_I(\rho)) \quad \text{for } f/n \in FS, n \geq 0 \\
[\![e_1 = e_2]\!]_I(\rho) &= eq([\![e_1]\!]_I(\rho), [\![e_2]\!]_I(\rho)) \\
[\![\neg b]\!]_I(\rho) &= not([\![b]\!]_I(\rho)) \\
[\![b_1, b_2]\!]_I(\rho) &= and([\![b_1]\!]_I(\rho), [\![b_2]\!]_I(\rho)) \\
[\![b_1; b_2]\!]_I(\rho) &= or([\![b_1]\!]_I(\rho), [\![b_2]\!]_I(\rho)) \\
[\![b \to e]\!]_I(\rho) &= if([\![b]\!]_I(\rho), [\![e]\!]_I(\rho)) \\
[\![b \to e_1 \Box e_2]\!]_I(\rho) &= if\_else([\![b]\!]_I(\rho), [\![e_1]\!]_I(\rho), [\![e_2]\!]_I(\rho))
\end{aligned}
$$
where the semantics functions and, not, or, if, if_else, and eq are defined as follows:

and	$\perp$	$fail$	false	true
$\perp$	$\perp$	$\perp$	$\perp$	$\perp$
$fail$	$\perp$	$fail$	$fail$	$fail$
false	$\perp$	$fail$	false	false
true	$\perp$	$fail$	false	true

or	$\perp$	$fail$	false	true
$\perp$	$\perp$	$\perp$	$\perp$	$\perp$
$fail$	$\perp$	$fail$	$fail$	$fail$
false	$\perp$	$fail$	false	true
true	$\perp$	$fail$	true	true

not	
$\perp$	$\perp$
$fail$	$fail$
false	true
true	false

$$eq(s_1, s_2) = \begin{cases} true & \text{if } s_1, s_2 \text{ concrete} \land s_1 = s_2 \\ false & \text{if } s_1, s_2 \text{ concrete} \land s_1 \neq s_2 \\ fail & \text{if } s_1 = s_2 = fail \\ \perp & \text{otherwise} \end{cases}$$

$$if(b, s) = \begin{cases} s & \text{if } b = true \\ fail & \text{if } b = false \\ & \text{or } b = fail \\ \perp & \text{otherwise} \end{cases} \qquad if\_else(b, s_1, s_2) = \begin{cases} s_1 & \text{if } b = true \\ s_2 & \text{if } b = false \\ fail & \text{if } b = fail \\ \perp & \text{otherwise} \end{cases}$$

Knowing how to evaluate expressions, any defining rule can be interpreted as the statement whose value for the *lhs* is always as least as defined as the *rhs* value. To formally define the meaning of a default rule we need some auxiliary definitions:

Definition 3.4 Definitionless function
Given a function f/n, a program Π, and a Herbrand interpretation I we define the functions $T_I(f)$, $\widehat{T}_I(f) : \mathcal{H}^n \to \mathcal{P}(\mathcal{H})$ as follows:

$$T_I(f)(s_1, .., s_n) = \{[\![R]\!]_I(\rho)/f\ (t_1, .., t_n) := R \in \Pi, \rho(t_i) = s_i\}$$
$$\widehat{T}_I(f)(s_1, .., s_n) = \{[\![R]\!]_I(\rho)/\mathbf{default}f\ (t_1, .., t_n) := R \in \Pi, \rho(t_i) = s_i\}$$

where ρ is an environment.
We also define the definitionless function $\delta_I(f) : \mathcal{H}^n \to bool$ such that

$$\delta_I(f)(\overline{s}) = \begin{cases} true & \text{if } T_I(f)(\overline{s}) = \emptyset \text{ or } T_I(f)(\overline{s}) = \{fail\} \\ \perp & \text{if } \perp \in T_I(f)(\overline{s}) \\ false & \text{otherwise.} \end{cases}$$

The δ function establishes where the function f has not a definition using the defining rules. Notice that the definitions of T_I and δ involve some implicit universal quantification if a defining rule contains free variables in the guard.

Now, we can define when an interpretation is a model of a program.

Definition 3.5 Models
An interpretation I is a model of a program Π (in symbols $I \models \Pi$) if

a).- I is a model of every defining rule in Π, and

b).- for every default rule $f\ (X_1, \ldots, X_n) := e$ in Π $\quad f_I(\rho(\overline{X})) = [\![e]\!]_I(\rho)$ if $\delta_I(f)(\rho(\overline{X})) = true$ for any environment ρ.

I is a Herbrand model of a defining rule $L := R$ iff $[\![L]\!]_I(\rho) \sqsupseteq [\![R]\!]_I(\rho)$ for all environments ρ.

We can prove now the existence of a least Herbrand model for any given program. As it is done in classical logic programming, minimal models are obtained as least fixpoints of monotonic interpretation transformers.

Definition 3.6 *The interpretation transformer associated to* Π *is the mapping* $\mathcal{T}_\Pi : \mathcal{H}-\mathcal{INT} \to \mathcal{H}-\mathcal{INT}$ *defined as follows: for any interpretation* I, $\mathcal{T}_\Pi(I)$ *is the Herbrand interpretation* J *such that for any* $f/n \in FS$ *and well typed elements* $s_1, \ldots, s_n \in \mathcal{H}$

$$f_J(\overline{s}) = \begin{cases} m & \text{if } m \sqsupset \text{fail} & \text{where} \\ n & \text{if } \delta_I(f)(\overline{s}) = \text{true} & m = \max T_I(f)(\overline{s}) \\ \bot & \text{otherwise} & n = \max \widehat{T}_I(f)(\overline{s}) \end{cases}$$

Proposition 3.1 $\mathcal{T}_\Pi$ *is well defined and monotonic.*

Proof: $\mathcal{T}_\Pi$ *is well defined as an immediate consequence of the confluence property, syntactically established. As the set* $T_I(f)(\overline{s})$ *can only have a single concrete value, then the maximum exists. Monotonicity can be easily proven from the definition of the transformer. The distinction between* $fail$ *and* $\bot$ *means the key point in the proof. The unknown values are denoted by* $\bot$ *and they cannot be used in a default rule. Only when a finite failure is calculated the value* $fail$ *is used and the default rules can be applied.*

The main result of the declarative semantics establishes the existence of a least Herbrand model I_Π for every BABEL program Π. It is deduced from Proposition 3.1 by using the well known Tarski's theorem.

Theorem 3.1 *There exists a least fixpoint* I_Π *of* $\mathcal{T}_\Pi$, *that can be computed as the limit of the sequence*

$$I_\Pi^0 = I_\bot \quad \text{and} \quad I_\Pi^{i+1} = \mathcal{T}_\Pi(I_\Pi^i)$$

where $I_\bot$ *is the interpretation that assigns* $\bot$ *as denotational value for every function. Moreover,* I_Π *is the least Herbrand model in* $\mathcal{H}-\mathcal{INT}$.

Once the existence of I_Π has been proven, some of the definitions for interpretations can be instantiated for it. In particular we will call, simply, δ to the function δ_{I_Π}. We will also use the complement of this function, called Δ. Intuitively $\Delta(f(e_1, \ldots, e_n))$ means that the expression $f(e_1, \ldots, e_n)$ is positively defined, i.e. can be calculated without the default rule. More formally: $\Delta(f(\overline{s})) = \text{not } \delta(f)(\overline{s})$

4   Operational Semantics

For simplicity of presentation, we restrict ourselves to an innermost version of narrowing working with symbolic constraints. In order to provide a stepwise definition for all the concepts we will first present how innermost narrowing works with constraints. In the next subsection the definition of innermost narrowing will be extended in order to cope with default rules. The main idea is to obtain the δ function syntactically. Finally we will describe the simplification of symbolic constraints.

4.1   Innermost Narrowing with Constraints over the Herbrand Universe

A computation involves a constraint c and an expression e. The constraint c contains equalities and disequalities of terms. The equalities collected into the constraint can be seen as the substitutions in usual narrowing, similarly as it is done within the CLP scheme [9]. A more abstract and general description of the operational semantics of the constraint functional logic programming paradigm can be found in [12].

To obtain a formal definition of BABEL's *innermost narrowing semantics* we need a notion of expression *normal form* (nf): the canonical representation of values. We say that an expression e is in nf iff

- e is a variable X,   • e is a nullary constructor d, or
- e is of the form $d(e_1, .., e_m)$, where $d/n \in DC$ and $e_1, .., e_m$ are in nf

Moreover, we need a notion of normal form also for constraints. A disequation $d(X, a) \neq d(b, Y)$ implies a disjunction $X \neq b \vee Y \neq a$. So, we use conjunctions of disjunctions of disequations as normal forms. On the other hand, we will produce disequations by means of the negation of an equation $X = t(\overline{Y})$. This fact produces the universal quantification of the free variables $\overline{Y}$, unless a more external quantification affects them. The negation of such equation is $\forall \overline{Y} \; X \neq t(\overline{Y})$. Also, universally quantified disequations are allowed in the constraints. More precisely, the normal form of constraints is:

$$\underbrace{\bigwedge_i (X_i = t_i)}_{\text{positive information}} \quad \underbrace{\wedge \bigvee_j \forall \overline{Z_j^1} \, (Y_j^1 \neq s_j^1) \wedge \ldots \wedge \bigvee_l \forall \overline{Z_j^n} \, (Y_l^n \neq s_l^n)}_{\text{negative information}}$$

where each X_i appears only in $X_i = t_i$, none s_k^r is equal to Y_k^r and the universal quantification could be empty (leaving a simple disequality).

The notation $c \vdash c'$ indicates that the constraint c' is the simplification (normal form) of c. $c \vdash false$ means that the constraint c is unsatisfiable. The rules for $\vdash$ will be presented in subsection 4.3.

The *one step narrowing relation* is denoted $c \parallel e \implies c' \parallel e'$, where c' is not *false*. It is specified by the following rules[2]:

1. *Rule application* $c \parallel f(e_1, \ldots, e_n) \implies c' \parallel e'$

    if • $e_1, \ldots, e_n$ are in nf, there is a variant $f(t_1, \ldots, t_n) := \{b \to\} e$ of one rule in the program (sharing no variables with the goal) such that $f(t_1, \ldots, t_n)$ and $f(e_1, \ldots, e_n)$ are unifiable with m.g.u. $\sigma = \sigma_{in} \dot{\cup} \sigma_{out}$ (where σ_{in} collects the bindings for variables in the t_i and σ_{out} records the bindings for variables in the e_i), and e' is $(\{b \to\} e)_{\sigma_{in}}$

    • $c \wedge \bigwedge (X_i = s_i) \vdash c'$, where $\sigma_{out} = \{\ldots, X_i/s_i, \ldots\}$

2. *Inner narrowing step* $\dfrac{c \parallel e_i \overset{*}{\implies} c' \parallel e_i'}{c \parallel k(e_1, .., e_i, .., e_n) \implies c'' \parallel k(e_1, .., e_i', .., e_n)}$

    if $k/n \in DC \cup FS, 1 \leq i \leq n$ and $c \wedge c' \vdash c''$.

3. *Rules for guards and conditionals*

    $c \parallel (true \to e) \implies c \parallel e$

    $c \parallel (true \to e_1 \square e_2) \implies c \parallel e_1$

    $c \parallel (false \to e_1 \square e_2) \implies c \parallel e_2$

    $\dfrac{c \parallel b \overset{*}{\implies} c' \parallel b'}{c \parallel (b \to e) \implies c'' \parallel (b' \to e)}$
    if b is not in nf and $c \wedge c' \vdash c''$

    $\dfrac{c \parallel b \overset{*}{\implies} c' \parallel b'}{c \parallel (b \to e_1 \square e_2) \implies c'' \parallel (b' \to e_1 \square e_2)}$
    if b is not in nf, $c \wedge c' \vdash c''$

---

[2]The rules assume that the condition holds, i.e. the resulting constraint is not *false*

4. *Rules for the equality*

$$c \parallel (e_1 = e_2) \implies c' \parallel true \quad \text{if } e_1, e_2 \text{ are in } nf, \text{ and } c \wedge (e_1 = e_2) \vdash c'$$

$$c \parallel (e_1 = e_2) \implies c' \parallel false \quad \text{if } e_1, e_2 \text{ are in } nf, \text{ and } c \wedge (e_1 \neq e_2) \vdash c'$$

$$\frac{c \parallel e_1 \overset{*}{\implies} c' \parallel e_1'}{c \parallel (e_1 = e_2) \implies c'' \parallel (e_1' = e_2)} \quad \text{if } e_1 \text{ is not in } nf \text{ and } c \wedge c' \vdash c''$$

$$\frac{c \parallel e_2 \overset{*}{\implies} c' \parallel e_2'}{c \parallel (e_1 = e_2) \implies c'' \parallel (e_1 = e_2')} \quad \text{if } e_2 \text{ is not in } nf \text{ and } c \wedge c' \vdash c''$$

The rest of the primitive functions can be computed by some predefined rules (see [15]) or, alternatively, by including some explicit narrowing rules. It allows to have a lazy (short-circuit) definition of the logical connectives.

The notation $c \parallel e \equiv c_0 \parallel e_0 \implies \ldots c_i \parallel e_i \ldots \implies c_n \parallel e_n \equiv c' \parallel e'$, or simply $c \parallel e \overset{*}{\implies} c' \parallel e'$ denotes the *narrowing relation* (composition of several narrowing steps).

There is some degree of freedom in the previous scheme. A *redex* is the point where one of the previous rules is applicable. The selected expression to be reduced into a construction (rule 2) or an equality (rule 4) should be fixed by a *computation rule* $\mathcal{R}$. The usual implemented rule is the selection of the left-most redex that it is not yet in normal form. However, this is not the only cause of nondeterminism: several applicable rules for a given expression could be done.

Definition 4.1 Children and Narrowing Tree

Given a constraint expression $c \parallel e$, a program Π and a computation rule $\mathcal{R}$ we call any possible application of the one step narrowing relation guided by R a child of $c \parallel e$ on Π.

All the possible narrowing reductions of a constraint expression $c \parallel e$ given a program Π and a computation rule $\mathcal{R}$ form the narrowing tree *for $c \parallel e$. Every node is labelled with a constraint expression[3].*

Performing narrowing with a BABEL goal expression $c \parallel e$ may lead to several situations, which classify the paths into the narrowing tree:

- *Success:* $c \parallel e \overset{*}{\implies} c' \parallel t$ with $t \in Term$ and c' satisfiable.
- *Failure:* $c \parallel e \overset{*}{\implies} c' \parallel e'$, $e' \notin Term$ and e' is not further narrowable or c' unsatisfiable.
- *Nontermination:* In this case we may still have $c \parallel e \overset{*}{\implies} c' \parallel e'$ where $e' \notin Term$ and e''s constructors give a partial result.

When a succesful narrowing relation reaches a term $c' \parallel t$ we speak of a *computation* for the *goal $c \parallel e$* with *result t* and *answer c'*.

A very important notion for our purpose is the concept of *frontier* of a narrowing tree.

---

[3] In the following we will omit the reference to the program Π and the computation rule $\mathcal{R}$ when no ambiguity is possible.

Definition 4.2 Frontier

A frontier of $c \parallel e$ is a finite set of nodes of the narrowing tree such that every narrowing reduction of $c \parallel e$ is either a failure or passes through exactly one node in the set. We will denote a frontier F as a set $\{c_1 \parallel e_1, \ldots, c_m \parallel e_m\}$.

Example 4.1 *A frontier of the expression $true \parallel subs(s(0), X)$ in example 1.1 could be $\{X = 0 \wedge Y = s(0) \parallel + s(0), Y = 0 \wedge X = s(X') \parallel subs(0, X')\}$ following the narrowing tree:* $true \parallel subs(s(0), X)$

$$X = 0 \wedge Y = s(0) \parallel + s(0) \qquad Y = 0 \wedge X = s(X') \parallel subs(0, X')$$

4.2 Narrowing for default rules

The next step is the computation of default rules. The main idea is to manage the δ function syntactically. However, let us remember that the semantical definition of the δ function includes an implicit universal quantification. They are moved to explicit $\forall$-quantifications. We will work with expressions of the form $\forall \overline{X} \, \delta(c \parallel e)$ (where $c \parallel e$ is a constraint expression) that must be read "under the constraint c, e is undefined using the defining rules".

In the previous section we have defined how an expression is computed with the defining rules by using narrowing. We can narrow the expression in every possible way until we get all the solutions and then we can negate them. This yields to a condition that is equivalent to the δ function. However, the narrowing tree could be infinite and the process will not terminate. An effective solution consists of the use of a frontier of the narrowing tree (which is always finite) to produce a condition equivalent to the δ function. The process is based in the following result:

Proposition 4.1 *If Π is a BABEL program and $F = \{c_1 \parallel e_1, \ldots, c_n \parallel e_n\}$ is a frontier of $c \parallel e$ then*

$$\Delta(c \parallel e) \leftrightarrow \exists \, \overline{X}^1 \, (c_1 \wedge \Delta(e_1)) \vee \ldots \vee \exists \, \overline{X}^n \, (c_n \wedge \Delta(e_n))$$

where $\overline{X}^i$ are the free variables in $c_i \parallel e_i$ which are not in $c \parallel e$.

As the δ function is the negation of the Δ function, this result can be used to calculate a δ expression by the negation of the right hand side formula. The notion of *complement* of a frontier is used for this purpose.

Definition 4.3 Complement of a frontier

Let $F = \{c_1 \parallel e_1, \ldots, c_n \parallel e_n\}$ be the frontier of a constraint expression $c \parallel e$ and V a set of variables (denoting the free variables in the goal expression). The complements of F under V are all the possible conjunctions of complements of each $c_i \parallel e_i$ under V: $c'_1 \wedge \ldots \wedge c'_m \parallel b_1, \ldots, b_m$ is a complement of F iff each $c'_i \parallel b_i$ is a complement of $c_i \parallel e_i$ under V.

In order to define the complement of a constraint expression $c \parallel e$, let us briefly discuss the quantification of variables. First, we only need to focus on those useful variables, i.e. those that are free in the goal expression. We collect them in the set V. A variable X appearing in the positive part of the constraint as $X = t$ can be eliminated. If t is a variable $X' \in V$ we substitute X for X' in $c \parallel e$. Otherwise, the equation is irrelevant.

Next, we identify the variables that will have a universal quantification when the complement is calculated. They are the free variables in e that are neither in V nor in the positive part (that have an implicit quantification). We collect them in the set U. The disjunction of inequalities with variables in U cannot be separated from e. The rest of the disjunctions can be negated separately from e. When a disjunction of disequalities is negated it is moved into a conjunction of equalities. These equalities have not quantification even if the original disequation are not quantified because the free variables are (implicitly) quantified outside. In summary, we can organize the simplification of c as:

$$c = \bigwedge_{i=1}^{m}(X_i = t_i) \wedge \bigwedge_{j=1}^{n} \bigvee_{k=1}^{n_j} \forall \, \overline{Z}_k^j \, (Y_k^j \neq s_k^j) \wedge c'$$

where c' collects all the inequalities with a variable in U.

Definition 1.1 Complements of a constraint expression
The complements of $c \parallel e$ under V are:

- $\bigvee_{1=1}^{m} \forall \, \overline{Z}_i \, (X_i \neq t_i) \parallel true$, where $\overline{Z}_i$ are the variables of t_i that are not quantified outside, i.e. $var(t_i) \cap V$.

- $\bigwedge_{i=1}^{m}(X_i = t_i) \wedge \bigwedge_{k=1}^{n_l}(Y_l^k = s_l^k) \; \wedge \; \bigwedge_{j=1}^{l-1} \bigvee_{k=1}^{n_j} \forall \, \overline{Z}_k^j \, (Y_k^j \neq s_k^j) \parallel true$, for all $l < n$.

- $\bigwedge_{i=1}^{m}(X_i = t_i) \wedge \bigwedge_{j=1}^{n} \bigvee_{k=1}^{n_j} \forall \, \overline{Z}_k^j \, (Y_k^j \neq s_k^j) \parallel \forall \, \overline{Z} \, \delta(c' \parallel e)$, where $\overline{Z}$ are the variables in U.

The last component in the definition 4.4 includes the computation of the definitionless operation δ. This δ-expression can be simplified when the expression e is a constructor application or a predefined function. Due to the lack of space we omit some rules for the simplification. Some examples are: $\forall \, \overline{X} \, \delta(c \parallel \neg b) \equiv \forall \, \overline{X} \, \delta(c \parallel b), \forall \, \overline{X} \, \delta(c \parallel (b \rightarrow e)) \equiv \delta(c \parallel b); \forall \, \overline{X} \, \delta(c \parallel b \rightarrow e \Box true)$, if $\overline{X}$ is empty or they appear only in e, or $\forall \, \overline{X} \, \delta(c \parallel (e_1 = e_2)) \equiv \forall \, \overline{X} \, \delta(c \parallel e_1); \forall \, \overline{X} \, \delta(c \parallel e_2)$. The simplification rules try to minimize the computational effort. For instance, in the case of the equality rule avoids to compute the real value of the equality and it just computes the definitionless operation of both expressions. Usually a very big expression generates a complicate search space, and it is better to consider the definitionless of the subexpressions one by one.

Example 1.1 *In order to compute the complement of the frontier of example 4.1, the complement of each constraint expression of the frontier is computed. X is the single goal variable, so the equations for the variable Y are eliminated.*

The complements of $X = 0 \parallel + s(0)$ are: $X \neq 0 \parallel true$ and $X = 0 \parallel \delta(true \parallel + s(0))$ but the second one is equivalent to false after applying δ-simplification rules. The complements of $X = s(X') \parallel subs(0, X')$ are: $\forall X' \ X \neq s(X') \parallel true$ and $X = s(X') \parallel \delta(true \parallel subs(0, X'))$.

Finally, the complements of the frontier of true $\parallel subs(s(0), X)$ are obtained by combining the previous complements:

1. $X \neq 0 \parallel true, \forall X'(X \neq s(X') \parallel true$
2. $X \neq 0 \parallel true, X = s(X') \parallel \delta(subs(0, X'))$

As we will see, the first expression yields to a constraint that is unsatisfiable in the domain of the natural number and will be discarded.

Now, we complete the narrowing rules to use the default rule (if present) and to compute a $\delta(c \parallel e)$ expression. The new rules are:

5. *Default rule*
$$\frac{\delta(c \parallel f(e_1, \ldots, e_n) \overset{*}{\Longrightarrow} c' \parallel true}{c \parallel f(e_1, \ldots, e_n) \Longrightarrow c'' \parallel e\sigma}$$

where **default** $f(X_1, \ldots, X_n) := e \in \Pi$ and $e_1, \ldots, e_n$ are in *nf*, $\sigma = \{.., X_i/e_i, ..\}$ and $c \wedge c' \vdash c''$.

6. *Definitionless expressions rule*

Let F be a frontier of the narrowing tree of $c \parallel e$ using rules $1, \ldots, 4$ for the first step, and let V be the set of free variables of $c \parallel e$ that are not in $\overline{X}$.

$$\forall \overline{X} \ \delta(c \parallel e) \Longrightarrow true \quad \text{if } F = \emptyset$$

$\forall \overline{X} \ \delta(c \parallel e) \Longrightarrow c \parallel b$ if $F \neq \emptyset$ and $(c \parallel b)$ is a complement of F under V

For each complement of F we have a different child in the narrowing tree.

4.3 Management of symbolic constraints

This subsection discusses how to check the satisfiability of constraints and how to maintain their normal forms. In the literature there are also simpler normal forms as a simple conjunction of equalities and disequalities (see [5, 13, 4] for papers devoted to this and related subjects). Disjunctions of disequality constraints can be handled by backtracking. We have used a more compact representation to simplify the search space.

The most complicate part in the simplification of a constraint is the addition of an equality or a disequality. The unification algorithm can be used to detect if they are satisfiable and to help in this simplification.

Another important point is the fact that our domains (types) for constraints have a finite number of constructors. We need to add a rule to detect inconsistencies like $X \neq 0 \ \wedge \ \forall Y \ (X \neq s(Y))$ for the *nat* type. To apply this rule we need some previous notions.

Definition 4.5 Covering

A set of terms $t_1, \ldots, t_n$ (none a variable) is complete for a variable X on a monomorphic type τ iff for all the concrete elements $s \in \mathcal{H}$ with type τ there exists i and a substitution θ such that $s = t_i\theta$.

A covering for τ on X is the constraint built as the negation of a complete set of terms $\ldots, t_i(\overline{Y^i}), \ldots$ for X on τ: $\ldots \wedge \forall \overline{Y^i} X \neq t_i \wedge \ldots$

Example 4.3

- $X \neq 0 \wedge \forall Y \, (X \neq s(Y))$
- $X \neq 0 \wedge X \neq s(0) \wedge \forall Y \, (X \neq s(s(Y)))$ are coverings for *nat* on X.

A covering is unsatisfiable on $\mathcal{H}$, what means that every constraint with a covering can be reduced to *false*.

Now, we define the rules to combine a constraint in normal form with a new constraint. In the following the substitution σ denotes the positive part of the constraint, i.e. $\sigma = \{X_1/t_1, \ldots, X_n/t_n\}$.

- *Addition of an equation*

$$t = s \wedge \bigwedge (X_i = t_i) \wedge c \vdash false \qquad \text{if} \quad \bullet \ c \text{ has only disequalities,}$$
$$\bullet \ t\sigma, s\sigma \text{ are not unifiable}$$

$$t = s \wedge \bigwedge (X_i = t_i) \wedge c \vdash \bigwedge (X_i = t_i)\theta \wedge \bigwedge (X'_j = t'_j) \wedge c'$$

$$\text{if} \quad \bullet \quad c \text{ has only disequalities,}$$
$$\bullet \quad \theta = m.g.u.(t\sigma, s\sigma) = \{X'_1 = t'_1, \ldots, X'_m = t'_m\},$$
$$\bullet \quad c\sigma\theta \vdash c'$$

- *Addition of a disequation*

$$\forall \overline{Z}\, t \neq s \wedge \bigwedge (X_i = t_i) \wedge c \vdash \bigwedge (X_i = t_i) \wedge c$$

$$\text{if } c \text{ has only disequalities and } t\sigma, s\sigma \text{ are not unifiable}$$

$$\forall \overline{Z}\, t \neq s \wedge \bigwedge (X_i = t_i) \wedge c \vdash \bigwedge (X_i = t_i)\theta \wedge \bigvee (X'_j \neq t'_j) \wedge c'$$

$$\text{if } c \text{ has only disequalities, and } \theta = m.g.u.(t\sigma, s\sigma) = \{.., X'_i = t'_i, ..\}$$

$$\forall \overline{Z}\, t \neq s \wedge \bigwedge (X_i = t_i) \wedge c \vdash false$$

$$\text{if } c \text{ has only disequalities and } \theta = m.g.u.(t\sigma, s\sigma) \text{ only binds variables in } \overline{Z}$$

Note: The universall quantification on $\overline{Z}$ should be empty.

- *Simplification rules*

$$true \wedge c \vdash c \qquad false \wedge c \vdash false \qquad c_1 \ldots \wedge c_n \vdash false \text{ if it contains a covering}$$

$$c \wedge c_1 .. \wedge c_n \vdash c \wedge c'_1 \wedge .. \wedge c'_n \quad \text{if} \quad \bullet \ c \text{ contains the equalities and } c_i\text{'s the}$$
$$\text{disequalities of the whole constraint}$$
$$\bullet \ c \wedge c_i \vdash c'_i, \text{ for each } i$$

$$c \wedge c_1 \vee .. \vee c_n \vdash c \wedge c'_1 \wedge .. \wedge c'_n \quad \text{if} \quad \bullet \ c \text{ has equalities and the } c_i\text{'s}$$
$$\text{are single disequalities}$$
$$\bullet \ c \wedge c_i \vdash c'_i, \text{ for each } i$$

Example 4.4 *In previous examples we have computed the complements of a frontier of the expression true $\| \, subs(s(0), X)$. Now, rule 5. can be applied to obtain:*

$$\delta(true \, \| \, subs(s(0), X)) \Longrightarrow_{\text{Rule } 7} X \neq 0 \, \| \, true, X = s(X') \, \| \, \delta(true \, \| \, subs(0, X'))$$
$$\overset{*}{\Longrightarrow}_{\text{Rules for}} \, , \vdash \ X = s(X') \, \| \, \delta(true \, \| \, subs(0, X'))$$

The only frontier for $\delta(true \, \| \, subs(0, X'))$ is $\{X' = 0 \, \| \, +0\}$, which has an unique useful complement $X' \neq 0$.

$$X = s(X') \, \| \, \delta(true \, \| \, subs(0, X')) \Longrightarrow_{\text{Rule } 6} X = s(X') \wedge X' \neq 0 \, \| \, true$$

Now, the narrowing sequence can be completed as follows:

$$\ldots \Longrightarrow_{\text{Rule } 5} X = s(X') \wedge X' \neq 0 \, \| \, invert(subs(s(X'), s(0))) \overset{*}{\Longrightarrow} -X'$$

4.4 Soundness and Completeness

Finally, we can establish the soundness and completeness of our narrowing semantics. Due to the lack of space we will omit the proofs.

Theorem 4.1 Soundness

Let Π be a program. Any narrowing sequence $c \parallel e \stackrel{*}{\Longrightarrow} c' \parallel e'$ computes a sound outcome in the sense that

$$[\![c, c' \to e]\!]_{I_\Pi}(\rho) \sqsupseteq [\![c' \to e']\!]_{I_\Pi}(\rho) \qquad \text{for all environments } \rho.$$

Notice that if e' is a term its valuation corresponds with the term itself (except the variables), giving the expected soundness result for succesful computations. The interpretation of a constraint c as an expression is obvious.

Theorem 4.2 Completeness

Let Π be a program, e an expression, c a constraint, s an element in $\mathcal{H}$ and θ a substitution that binds any variable of c, e into a ground term (ground substitution). If $[\![(c \to e)\theta]\!] \sqsupseteq s$ then there exists a narrowing sequence $c \parallel e \stackrel{*}{\Longrightarrow} c' \parallel t$, (with t a term), and a ground substitution σ such that $t\sigma = s$, and $c_\sigma \wedge c_\theta \wedge c'$ is satisfiable (where c_σ, c_θ denote the constraints with positive part σ, θ and no negative part).

Proof Idea: *The proof combines the ideas of the completeness of innermost narrowing, using the $\mathcal{T}_\Pi$ operator, with the completeness proof of [17]. In fact the result is, in some sense, a corollary of this last one.*

5 Related work

The work uses some of the techniques developed for constructive negation [3, 4, 17]. However, they are adapted to a more general framework. Our more complex notion of constraint normal form forces us to redefine the notion of complement used in Chan's papers. Chan's method to obtain constraint information from a frontier relies in the following property:

$$\neg \exists \overline{Y}, \overline{Z}(X = s \wedge Q) \leftrightarrow \forall \overline{Y}(X \neq s) \vee \exists \overline{Y}(X = s \wedge \neg \exists \overline{Z})Q$$

while Stuckey abstracts, into the CLP framework, to:

$$\neg \exists \overline{Y}, c \wedge Q \leftrightarrow (\neg \exists \overline{Y}c) \vee (\neg \exists \overline{Y}c \wedge Q)$$

(see [17]). Our method uses a mixture of both of them, adding the rules for simplification of δ-expressions. These rules generalize the double negation simplification of Chan (which cannot be used in Stuckey's approach).

The narrowing rule for default rules has an advantage with respect to Chan's work: The whole constraint is passed to the definitionless expression, what reduces the search space. This idea was pointed by Stuckey instead of the use only of the positive constraint (substitution) in Chan's paper.

Only some few papers have been devoted to the combination of constructive negation with narrowing. [16] treats a different problem: to compute the answers to a disequation $f(t) \neq s$ by computing the results for $f(t) = s$ and then negating the resulting formula. The undefined values for $f(t)$ are not taken into account (or f must be total). In our framework we can compute all the values for $f(t)$, by bactracking, and then compare them with s. It is valid even if $f(t)$ is undefined, by adding a default rule **default** $f(X) := r$, with $r \neq s$. However, if $f(t)$ has infinitely many solutions the method is not effective, while negating a frontier of $f(t) = s$ is.

[6] defines a narrowing procedure to compute disunification (i.e. disequations over the Herbrand universe modulo an equational theory). It is complete when the equational theory is defined by a basic term rewriting system. The problem is also different from the treated in this paper.

Another trend of work which makes use of innermost narrowing and negative information is present in the languages SLOG [7] and ALF [8]. Narrowing is combined with *simplification* using some rules by pure rewriting. In some cases, under the CWA, it is possible to define a rewriting rule indicating when a function fails. This could optimize the computation and also can transform an infinite computation ($\perp$) into a finite failure (*fail*). The technique is independent of our work an can be used to optimize it.

Another interesting approach to negation in PROLOG is the transformational one [1, 2]. New predicates are added in order to express the negative information. Informally, the *complement* of head terms of the positive clauses are computed and they are used later as the head of the negated predicate. However, in some cases, the new program contains some kind of universal quantification construct hard to be efficiently implemented.

In our case, this approach can be adapted when the program has no guards or guards without free variables. The default rule can be expressed as a normal rule. For instance, in the *subs* example, the new rule is:

$$\text{subs } (0, \, Y) := Y \neq 0 \rightarrow - \, Y.$$

However, in the presence of a constraint $X \neq Y$ the program will produce infinitely many solutions (if the type has a non constant constructor).

6 Conclusion

In this paper we have studied the completion of partial functions with a default rule in functional logic languages. The narrowing rule has been modified to cope with these new rules. The used techniques are an extension of constructive negation: subderivations are used to detect when a function call will finitely fail by using the defining rules.

Pure PROLOG can be interpreted as a subset of BABEL when predicates are implemented as boolean functions. By using default rules, PROLOG programs with negation are subsumed by Def-BABEL. The negated part of a predicate is obtained by using a default rule with body *false*.

Furthermore, in our language, the programmer can freely use explicit negation and negation as failure. Kowalski pointed out the advantages of this distinction for knowledge representation.

The paper has focused on the extension of narrowing based languages using a constructor discipline. This restricts our constraint system to the Herbrand Universe. However, we agree [17] that it is more general (and natural) to study the problem in a CLP framework. Although there are few paper addressing the integration of functions, predicates and constraints, we believe that default rules can be best described in the context of Constraint Functional Logic Programming [12].

As a future work, we plan to incorporate these techniques to lazy narrowing. The coroutining implementation technique reported in [3, 4] can be seen as an application of lazy evaluation.

Acknowledgements

This research was supported in part by the spanish project TIC/93-0737-C02-02.

References

[1] R. Barbuti, D. Mancarella, D. Pedreschi, F. Turini. Intensional Negation of Logic Programs. *Proc. TAPSOFT'87, Springer LNCS* 250, 96-110, 1987.

[2] R. Barbuti, D. Mancarella, D. Pedreschi, F. Turini. A Transformational Approach to Negation in Logic Programming. *Journal of Logic Programming*, 8(3):201-228, 1990.

[3] D. Chan. Constructive Negation Based on the Complete Database *Proc. Int. Conference on Logic Programming'89, The MIT Press*, 111-125, 1988.

[4] D. Chan. An Extension of Constructive Negation and its Application in Coroutining. *Proc. NACLP'89, The MIT Press*, 477-493. 1989.

[5] H. Comon, P. Lescanne. Equational Problems and Disunification. *Journal of Symbolic Computation*, 7:371-425, 1989.

[6] M. Fernández. Narrowing Based Procedures for Equational Disunification. *Applicable Algebras in Eng. Communications and Computing*, 3:1-26, 1992.

[7] L. Fribourg. SLOG: A Logic Programming Language Interpreter based on Clausal Superposition and Rewriting. *Proc. Symp. on Logic Programming, IEEE Comp. Soc. Press*, 1985.

[8] M. Hanus. Compiling Logic Programs with Equality. *Proc. PLILP'90, Springer LNCS*, 1990.

[9] J. Jaffar, J.L. Lassez. Constraint Logic Programming. *Proc. 14th ACM Symp. on Princ. of Prog. Lang.*, 114-119, 1987.

[10] H. Kuchen, F. López-Fraguas, J.J. Moreno-Navarro, M. Rodríguez-Artalejo. Implementing a Lazy Functional Logic Language with Disequality Constraints. *Joint International Conference and Symposium on Logic Programming, The MIT Press*, 189-223, 1992.

[11] K. Kunen. Negation in Logic Programming. *Journal of Logic Programming* 4:289-308, 1987.

[12] F.J. López-Fraguas. A General Scheme for Constraint Functional Logic Programming. *Proc. ALP'92, Springer LNCS*, 1992.

[13] M. Maher. Complete Axiomatization of the Algebras of Finite, Rational and Infinite Trees. *Proc. 3rd Symp. on Logic in Computer Science*, 348-357, 1988.

[14] R. Milner, M. Tofte, R. Harper. The Definition of Standard ML. *The MIT Press*, 1990.

[15] J.J. Moreno Navarro, M. Rodríguez Artalejo. Logic Programming with Functions and Predicates: The Language BABEL. *Journal of Logic Programming* 12:189-223, 1992.

[16] M.J. Ramírez, M. Falaschi. Conditional Narrowing with Constructive Negation. *Proc. 3rd Int'l Workshop on Extension of Logic Programming ELP'92, Springer LNCS* 660, 59-79, 1993.

[17] P. Stuckey. Constructive Negation for Constraint Logic Programming *Proc. IEEE Symp. on Logic in Computer Science, IEEE Comp. Soc. Press*, 1991.

Analysis

Depth-k Sharing and Freeness

Andy King
Computing Laboratory,
University of Kent, Canterbury, CT2 7NF, UK.

Paul Soper
Department of Electronics and Computer Science,
University of Southampton, Southampton, SO17 1BJ, UK.

Abstract

Analyses for variable sharing and freeness are important both in the automatic parallelisation and in the optimisation of sequential logic programs. In this paper, a new analysis is described which can infer sharing and freeness information to an unusually high degree of accuracy. By encoding structural properties of substitutions in a sharing group fashion, a powerful depth-k sharing and freeness analysis is synthesised which exploits the synergy between tracing sharing information and tracking term structure. The analysis propagates groundness with the accuracy of sharing groups and yet can precisely infer sharing and freeness. Correctness is formally proven.

1   Introduction

Abstract interpretation for possible sharing is an important topic of logic programming. Sharing (or aliasing) analysis conventionally infers which program variables are definitely grounded and which variables can never be bound to terms containing a common variable. Applications of sharing analysis are numerous: the sound removal of the occur-check [15]; specialisation of unification [17]; and the detection [12] and efficient exploitation [9, 13] of independent and-parallelism [8].

This paper is concerned with a semantic basis for sharing and freeness analysis, and in particular, the justification of a precise abstract unification algorithm. The abstract unification algorithm finitely traces unification by representing substitutions with sharing and freeness abstractions. The accuracy of the analysis depends, in part, on the substitution properties that the sharing abstractions capture. For instance, a knowledge of freeness can improve sharing (and *vice versa*) [12]. Freeness [3, 12, 16] relates to the structure of a term or binding. Freeness information distinguishes between a free variable, a variable which is definitely not bound to a non-variable term; and a non-free variable, a variable which is possibly bound to a non-variable term. Without exploiting freeness (or linearity [5, 15]), analyses have to assume that aliasing is transitive. Freeness information, in addition, is essential in the detection of non-strict and-parallelism [8].

Conventional sharing and freeness analyses [2, 3, 6, 7, 12, 16] typically adopt a coarse-grained approach to analysis and do not always adequately reason about the fine-grained sharing and freeness interactions between sub-terms. In some circumstances, however, accuracy can pivot on the ability of an analysis to reason about the sharing and freeness of sub-terms. Put another way, for the required precision, it may be necessary to trace sharing and freeness to depth-k [14].

This paper presents a new approach to sharing and freeness analysis that is capable of reasoning about sharing and freeness to depth-k. The analysis explains how structural properties of substitutions can be represented in a sharing group format [9, 13]. In effect, this is a two-fold win: first, groundness and sharing is improved; second, freeness can be refined. The analysis has also been proven correct. This is important because subtle errors and omissions have been reported [6] in some of the more recent proposals for freeness analysis [3, 12, 16]. Thus formal proof is useful, indeed necessary, to instill confidence. The exposition is structured as follows. Section 2 describes the notation and preliminary definitions which will be used throughout. The depth-k analysis is constructed in two parts to ease its development and justification. Section 3 develops a depth-∞ framework for sharing and (possible) freeness analysis. The framework explains how to abstract structural properties of substitutions with sharing groups. The framework, alas, can lead to unterminating computations. Section 4 is thus concerned with finiteness, detailing how to collapse the depth-∞ framework into a tractable and practical depth-k analysis. To trace definite freeness, possible groundness must additionally be traced. Section 5 briefly comments on this refinement. Finally, sections 6 and 7 discuss related work, future work and present the conclusions. For reasons of brevity and continuity, the formal proofs are not included in the paper, but can be found in [10].

2 Notation and preliminaries

To introduce the analysis some notation and preliminary definitions are required. The reader is assumed to be familiar with the standard constructs used in logic programming [11] such as a universe of all variables $(u, v \in) Uvar$; the set of terms $(t \in) Term$ formed from the set of functors $(f, g, h \in) Func$ (of the first-order language underlying the program); and the set of program atoms $Atom$. Let $Pvar$ denote a finite set of program variables – the variables that are in the text of the program; and let $var(o)$ denote the set of variables in a syntactic object o.

2.1 Substitutions

A substitution ϕ is a total mapping $\phi : Uvar \rightarrow Term$ such that its domain $dom(\phi) = \{u \in Uvar \mid \phi(u) \neq u\}$ is finite. The application of a substitution ϕ to a variable u is denoted by $\phi(u)$. Thus the codomain is given by $cod(\phi) = \bigcup_{u \in dom(\phi)} var(\phi(u))$. A substitution ϕ is sometimes represented as a finite set of variable and term pairs $\{u \mapsto \phi(u) \mid u \in dom(\phi)\}$. The identity mapping on $Uvar$ is called the empty substitution and is denoted by ϵ. Substitutions, sets of substitutions, and the set of all substitutions are denoted by lower-case Greek letters, upper-case Greek letters, and $Subst$.

Substitutions are extended in the usual way from variables to functions, from functions to terms, and from terms to atoms. The restriction of a substitution ϕ to a set of variables $U \subseteq Uvar$ and the composition of two substitutions ϕ and φ are respectively defined by: $\phi \restriction U = \{u \mapsto \phi(u) \mid u \in dom(\phi) \cap U\}$ and $(\phi \circ \varphi)(u) = \phi(\varphi(u))$. The preorder $Subst$ $(\sqsubseteq)$, ϕ is more general than φ, is defined by: $\phi \sqsubseteq \varphi$ if and only if there exists a substitution $\psi \in Subst$ such that $\varphi = \psi \circ \phi$. The preorder induces an equivalence relation $\approx$ on $Subst$, that is: $\phi \approx \varphi$ if and only if $\phi \sqsubseteq \varphi$ and $\varphi \sqsubseteq \phi$. The equivalence relation $\approx$ identifies substitutions with consistently renamed codomain variables which, in turn, factors $Subst$ to give the poset $Subst/\approx$ $(\sqsubseteq)$ defined by: $[\phi]_\approx \sqsubseteq [\varphi]_\approx$ if and only if $\phi \sqsubseteq \varphi$.

2.2 Equations and most general unifiers

An equation is an equality constraint of the form $a = b$ where a and b are terms or atoms. Let $(E \in) Eqn$ denote the set of finite sets of equations. The equation set $\{e\} \cup E$, following [5], is abbreviated by $e : E$. The set of most general unifiers of E, $mgu(E)$, is defined operationally in terms of a predicate mgu. The predicate $mgu(E, \phi)$ is true if ϕ is a most general unifier of E.

Definition 1 (*mgu*) *The set of most general unifiers $mgu(E) \in \wp(Subst)$ is defined by:* $mgu(E) = \{\phi \mid mgu(E, \phi)\}$ *where*

$$mgu(\emptyset, \epsilon)$$
$$mgu(v = v : E, \zeta) \, if \, mgu(E, \zeta)$$
$$mgu(t = v : E, \zeta) \, if \, mgu(v = t : E, \zeta)$$
$$mgu(v = t : E, \zeta \circ \eta) \, if \, mgu(\eta(E), \zeta) \wedge v \notin var(t) \wedge \eta = \{v \mapsto t\}$$
$$mgu(f(t_1 \ldots t_n) = f(t_1' \ldots t_n') : E, \zeta) \, if \, mgu(\{t_i = t_i'\}_{i=1}^n : E, \zeta)$$

By induction it follows that $dom(\phi) \cap cod(\phi) = \emptyset$ if $\phi \in mgu(E)$, or put another way, that the most general unifiers are idempotent [4].

The semantics of a logic program is formulated in terms of a single $unify$ operator. To construct $unify$, and specifically to rename apart program variables, an invertible substitution [4], Υ, is introduced. It is convenient to let $Rvar \subseteq Uvar$ denote a set of renaming variables that cannot occur in programs, that is $Pvar \cap Rvar = \emptyset$, and suppose that $\Upsilon : Pvar \to Rvar$.

Definition 2 (*unify*) *The partial mapping unify* : $Atom \times Subst/\approx \times Atom \times Subst/\approx \to Subst/\approx$ *is defined by:* $unify(a, [\phi]_\approx, b, [\psi]_\approx) = [(\varphi \circ \phi) \restriction Pvar]_\approx$ *where* $\varphi \in mgu(\{\phi(a) = \Upsilon(\psi(b))\})$.

2.3 Sub-terms and paths

To reason about sharing and freeness to depth-k it is necessary to introduce some notation to identify the sub-terms of a term. Finite sequences of integers, paths, are used to distinguish the different occurrences of a sub-term within a term. Formally, the set of paths, $(p, q, r \in P \subseteq) Path$, is defined to be the least set such that: $\lambda \in Path$ and $n \cdot p \in Path$ if $p \in Path$ and $n \in \mathcal{N}$ $= \{1, 2, \ldots\}$ (for n less or equal to the maximum arity of $Func$). Each sub-term, and therefore each variable occurrence, can be identified by a path, which navigates the way from the root of the term, to the sub-term. For instance, the paths $2 \cdot 1 \cdot \lambda$, $1 \cdot \lambda$, λ respectively identify the v, u and $f(u, g(v))$ sub-terms of $f(u, g(v))$.

The set of valid paths for a term t is denoted by $path(t)$ where $path(v) = \{\lambda\}$ if $v \in Uvar$; otherwise $path(f(t_1 \ldots t_n)) = \{\lambda\} \cup \{i \cdot p_i \mid p_i \in path(t_i) \wedge 1 \leq i \leq n\}$. It is convenient to regard $\cdot$ as concatenation and thus $(1 \cdot 2 \cdot \lambda) \cdot (3 \cdot \lambda) = 1 \cdot 2 \cdot 3 \cdot \lambda$. Formally the sub-term of t at p is denoted by $term_p(t)$, that is, $term_\lambda(t) = t$ and $term_{i \cdot p}(f(t_1 \ldots t_n)) = term_p(t_i)$. Hence, $term_{2 \cdot 1 \cdot \lambda}(f(u, g(v))) = v$, whereas $term_{1 \cdot \lambda}(f(u, g(v))) = u$, and $term_\lambda(f(u, g(v))) = f(u, g(v))$. The mapping $term_p(t)$ is partial since it is only defined for $p \in path(t)$.

3 Depth-∞ framework for sharing

Abstract interpretation can provide focus for developing an analysis by emphasising the importance of abstracting data and illuminating the relationship between data, operations, and their abstract counterparts. In section 3.1, an abstraction for substitutions, the data, is proposed which represents structural properties of substitutions to arbitrary depth. Section 3.2, on the other hand, is devoted to defining a procedure for abstracting $unify$ to arbitrary depth, denoted depth-∞.

3.1 Abstracting substitutions to depth-∞

An abstract substitution is structured as a set of sharing groups where a sharing group is a (possibly empty) set of program variable and path pairs.

Definition 3 (Occ_{Svar}) *The set of sharing groups, Occ_{Svar} is defined by:* $Occ_{Svar} = \wp(Svar \times Path)$.

$Svar$ is a finite set of program variables. The intuition is that a sharing group records which program variables are bound to terms that share a variable. Additionally, a sharing group expresses the positions of the shared variable, that is, where the shared variable occurs in the terms to which the program variables are bound. $Svar$ usually corresponds to $Pvar$. It is necessary to parameterise Occ, however, so that abstract substitutions are well-defined under renaming by Υ. The precise notion of abstraction is first defined for a substitution via *type* and then lifted to sets of substitutions.

Definition 4 (*occ* and *type*) *The mappings* $occ : Uvar \times Subst \rightarrow Occ_{Svar}$ *and type* $: Subst/\approx \rightarrow \wp(Occ_{Svar})$ *are defined by:* $occ(u, \phi) = \{\langle v, p \rangle \mid u = term_p(\phi(v)) \wedge v \in Svar\}$ *and* $type([\phi]_\approx) = \{occ(u, \phi) \mid u \in Uvar\}$.

The mapping *type* is well-defined since $type([\phi]_\approx) = type([\varphi]_\approx)$ if $\phi \approx \varphi$. The mapping *occ* is defined in terms of $Svar$ because, for the purposes of analysis, the only significant bindings are those which relate to the program variables (and renamed program variables).

Example 1 *Suppose* $Svar = \{v, w, x, y, z\}$ *and* $\phi = \{v \mapsto f, \ w \mapsto u, \ x \mapsto u, \ y \mapsto u', \ z \mapsto g(u, u', u')\}$. *The variables that occur through* $Svar$ *are* u *and* u'. *The variable* u *occurs in* w, x *and* z: *in* w *at position* λ; *in* x *at position* λ; *and in* z *at position* $1 \cdot \lambda$. *Thus* u *defines the sharing group* $occ(u, \phi) = \{\langle w, \lambda \rangle, \langle x, \lambda \rangle, \langle z, 1 \cdot \lambda \rangle\}$. *Similarly, the variable* u' *yields the sharing group* $occ(u', \phi) = \{\langle y, \lambda \rangle, \langle z, 2 \cdot \lambda \rangle, \langle z, 3 \cdot \lambda \rangle\}$. *Note that* $occ(v, \phi) = \ldots = occ(z, \phi) = \emptyset$, *and more generally,* $\emptyset \in type([\phi]_\approx)$ *for arbitrary* ϕ *since the codomain of a substitution is always finite. Thus the abstraction for* ϕ *is given by* $type([\phi]_\approx) = \{occ(u, \phi), \ occ(u', \phi), \ \emptyset\}$.

The abstraction *type* is analogous to the abstraction $\mathcal{A}$ used in [13] and implicit in [9]. Both abstractions are formulated in terms of sharing groups. The crucial difference is that *type*, as well as expressing the presence of a shared variable, additionally represents the position of the shared variable in the terms to which the program variables are bound.

The abstract domain, the set of abstract substitutions, is defined below using the convention that the abstraction of a concrete object or operation is distinguished with a * from the corresponding concrete object or operation.

Definition 5 ($Subst^{\bullet}_{Svar}$) *The set of abstract substitutions,* $Subst^{\bullet}_{Svar}$, *is defined by:* $Subst^{\bullet}_{Svar} = \wp(Occ_{Svar})$.

As before [9, 13], $Subst^{\bullet}_{Svar} (\subseteq)$ is a complete lattice with set union as the lub. Unlike before, however, the finiteness of $Svar$ is not enough to ensure the finiteness of $Subst^{\bullet}_{Svar}$. The *type* abstraction extends to sets of substitutions as follows.

Definition 6 (α_{type} and γ_{type}) *The abstraction and concretisation mappings* $\alpha_{type} : \wp(Subst/\approx) \rightarrow Subst^{\bullet}_{Svar}$ *and* $\gamma_{type} : Subst^{\bullet}_{Svar} \rightarrow \wp(Subst/\approx)$ *are defined by:* $\alpha_{type}(\Phi) = \cup_{[\phi]_\approx \in \Phi} type([\phi]_\approx)$ *and* $\gamma_{type}(\phi^{\bullet}) = \{[\phi]_\approx \in Subst/\approx \mid type([\phi]_\approx) \subseteq \phi^{\bullet}\}$.

The abstraction of a set of substitutions Φ merely combines all the sharing information from all the substitutions in Φ. The mappings α_{type} and γ_{type}

are monotonic. Note that $\alpha_{type}(\emptyset) = \emptyset$ whereas $\alpha_{type}(\Phi) = \{\emptyset\}$ if Φ is a set of substitutions which all ground $Svar$. The bottom element of $Subst^{\bullet}_{Svar}$ $(\subseteq)$ is meaningful and, in fact, represents failure.

Abstract substitutions inherit their simple lub and their ability to propagate groundness because, like in [9, 13], the domain is formulated in terms of sharing groups. Examples 2 and 3 illustrate the lub and the expressiveness which comes from encoding structural properties of substitutions.

Example 2 *Suppose* $\mu = \{u \mapsto f(x, g(x))\}$, $\nu = \{u \mapsto f(x, g(x)), v \mapsto f(w, y)\}$ *and* $Svar = \{u, v, w, x, y\}$. *Then* $type([\mu]_{\approx}) = \mu^{\bullet}$ *and* $type([\nu]_{\approx}) = \nu^{\bullet}$ *where* $\mu^{\bullet} = \{\{\langle v, \lambda \rangle\}, \{\langle w, \lambda \rangle\}, \{\langle u, 1 \cdot \lambda \rangle, \langle u, 2 \cdot 1 \cdot \lambda \rangle, \langle x, \lambda \rangle\}, \{\langle y, \lambda \rangle\}, \emptyset\}$ *and* $\nu^{\bullet} = \{\{\langle v, 1 \cdot \lambda \rangle, \langle w, \lambda \rangle\}, \{\langle u, 1 \cdot \lambda \rangle, \langle u, 2 \cdot 1 \cdot \lambda \rangle, \langle x, \lambda \rangle\}, \{\langle v, 2 \cdot \lambda \rangle, \langle y, \lambda \rangle\}, \emptyset\}$. *Observe that* $[\mu]_{\approx}, [\nu]_{\approx} \in \gamma_{type}(\mu^{\bullet} \cup \nu^{\bullet})$.

Example 3 *Returning to* ϕ *of example 1, let* $\phi^{\bullet} = type([\phi]_{\approx}) = \{\{\langle w, \lambda \rangle, \langle x, \lambda \rangle, \langle z, 1 \cdot \lambda \rangle\}, \{\langle y, \lambda \rangle, \langle z, 2 \cdot \lambda \rangle, \langle z, 3 \cdot \lambda \rangle\}, \emptyset\}$. $\phi^{\bullet}$ *can be interpreted as follows. The variables of* $Svar$ *which* ϕ *grounds, do not appear in* $\phi^{\bullet}$; *and the variables of* $Svar$ *which are independent (unaliased), never occur in the same sharing group of* $\phi^{\bullet}$. *Thus* $\phi^{\bullet}$ *represents that* v *is ground and that* x *and* y *are independent. Additionally,* $\phi^{\bullet}$ *captures the fact that grounding either* x *or* w *grounds the other. Also* $\phi^{\bullet}$ *indicates that* w, x *and* y *are possibly free whereas* z *is non-free [12]. It also shows that grounding* w, x *or the variable at the first argument of the term* $\phi(z)$, *grounds the others.*

3.2 Abstracting unification to depth-∞

The abstract $unify$ operator, $unify^{\bullet}$, is defined by mimicking the unification algorithm, and just as $unify$ is defined in terms of mgu, $unify^{\bullet}$ is formulated in terms of an abstraction of mgu, mge. The unification algorithm takes as input, E, a set of unification equations. E is recursively transformed to a set of simplified equations which assume the form $v = t$. These simplified equations are then solved. The abstract equation solver mge adopts a similar strategy, but relegates the solution of the simplified equations to $solve$. (To be precise, mge abstracts a slight generalisation of mgu. Specifically, if $\varphi \in mgu(\phi(E))$ and $mge(E, type([\phi]_{\approx}), \psi^{\bullet})$ then $[\varphi \circ \phi]_{\approx} \in \gamma_{type}(\psi^{\bullet})$. The generalisation is convenient because it spares the need to define an extra (composition) operator for abstract substitutions.)

Definition 7 (mge) *The relation* $mge : Eqn \times Subst^{\bullet}_{Svar} \times Subst^{\bullet}_{Svar}$ *is defined by:*

$$mge(\emptyset, \phi^{\bullet}, \phi^{\bullet})$$
$$mge(v = v : E, \phi^{\bullet}, \psi^{\bullet}) \, if \, mge(E, \phi^{\bullet}, \psi^{\bullet})$$
$$mge(v = t : E, \phi^{\bullet}, \psi^{\bullet}) \, if \, mge(E, solve(v, t, \phi^{\bullet}), \psi^{\bullet}) \wedge$$
$$v \notin var(t)$$
$$mge(t = v : E, \phi^{\bullet}, \psi^{\bullet}) \, if \, mge(v = t : E, \phi^{\bullet}, \psi^{\bullet})$$
$$mge(f(t_1 \ldots t_n) = f(t'_1 \ldots t'_n) : E, \phi^{\bullet}, \psi^{\bullet}) \, if \, mge(\{t_i = t'_i\}^n_{i=1} : E, \phi^{\bullet}, \psi^{\bullet})$$

To define *solve*, and thereby *mge*, two auxiliary operators are required. The first, denoted $rel(t, \phi^{\cdot})$, calculates the sharing groups of $\phi^{\cdot}$ which are relevant to the term t, that is, those sharing groups of $\phi^{\cdot}$ which share variables with t. This is analogous to the *rel* operator of [9]. The second operator, $scale(o, P)$, denotes the sharing group formed by binding a variable to a non-ground term. The intuition behind *scale* is that if o ($\in Occ_{Svar}$) is the sharing group for a certain shared variable, and the variable is subsequently bound to a non-ground term containing a variable at p, then the sharing group for the new variable includes the sharing group $scale(o, \{p\})$. Definition 8 formally defines *rel* and *scale* and examples 4 and 5 demonstrate their use.

Definition 8 (*rel* and *scale*) *The mappings rel* $: Term \times Subst^{\cdot}_{Svar} \rightarrow Subst^{\cdot}_{Svar}$ *and scale* $: Occ_{Svar} \times \wp(Path) \rightarrow Occ_{Svar}$ *are defined by:* $rel(t, \phi^{\cdot}) = \{o \in \phi^{\cdot} \mid var(o) \cap var(t) \neq \emptyset\}$ *and* $scale(o, P) = \{\langle u, p_u \cdot p_P \rangle \mid \langle u, p_u \rangle \in o \wedge p_P \in P\}.$

Example 4 *Adopting $\mu^{\cdot}$ and $\nu^{\cdot}$ from example 2 and denoting $\phi^{\cdot} = \mu^{\cdot} \cup \nu^{\cdot}$,* $rel(u, \phi^{\cdot}) = \{\{\langle u, 1 \cdot \lambda \rangle, \langle u, 2 \cdot 1 \cdot \lambda \rangle, \langle x, \lambda \rangle\}\}$ *and* $rel(v, \phi^{\cdot}) = \{\{\langle v, \lambda \rangle\}, \{\langle v, 1 \cdot \lambda \rangle, \langle w, \lambda \rangle\}, \{\langle v, 2 \cdot \lambda \rangle, \langle y, \lambda \rangle\}\}.$

Example 5 *Using ϕ of example 1, if $\varphi = \{u \mapsto h(u')\}$ then $\varphi \circ \phi = \{v \mapsto f, w \mapsto h(u'), x \mapsto h(u'), y \mapsto u', z \mapsto g(h(u'), u', u')\}$ and therefore $type([\varphi \circ \phi]_{\approx}) = \{occ(u', \varphi \circ \phi), \emptyset\} = \{\{\langle w, 1 \cdot \lambda \rangle, \langle x, 1 \cdot \lambda \rangle, \langle y, \lambda \rangle, \langle z, 1 \cdot 1 \cdot \lambda \rangle, \langle z, 2 \cdot \lambda \rangle, \langle z, 3 \cdot \lambda \rangle\}, \emptyset\}$. Note that $scale(occ(u, \phi), \{1 \cdot \lambda\}) = \{\langle w, 1 \cdot \lambda \rangle, \langle x, 1 \cdot \lambda \rangle, \langle z, 1 \cdot 1 \cdot \lambda \rangle\}$ which corresponds to the subset of $occ(u', \varphi \circ \phi)$ induced by φ binding u to $h(u')$.*

The nub of the equation solver is *solve*. In essence, $solve(v, t, \phi^{\cdot})$ solves the syntactic equation $v = t$ in the presence of the abstract substitution $\phi^{\cdot}$, returning the composition of the unifier with $\phi^{\cdot}$. *solve* is formulated in terms of the fixed-point of *close*. The recursive definition of *close* generalises to the closure under union operation of [9, 13] and models the propagation of the aliases which arise during the solution of $v = t$. The full definition of *solve* is given below in definition 9. In definition 9, the notation $S \triangle S'$ denotes $(S \setminus S') \cup (S' \setminus S)$, the symmetric set difference of two sets S and S'.

Definition 9 (*solve*, *close* and *extend*) *The mappings solve* $: Svar \times Term \times Subst^{\cdot}_{Svar} \rightarrow Subst^{\cdot}_{Svar}$, *close* $: Svar \times Term \times Subst^{\cdot}_{Svar} \rightarrow Subst^{\cdot}_{Svar}$, *extend* $: Svar \times Term \times Occ_{Svar} \times Occ_{Svar} \rightarrow Subst^{\cdot}_{Svar}$ *are defined by:*

$$solve(v, t, \phi^{\cdot}) = lfp(close(v, t, \phi^{\cdot})) \setminus (rel(v, \phi^{\cdot}) \triangle rel(t, \phi^{\cdot}))$$

$$close^0(v, t, \phi^{\cdot}) = \phi^{\cdot}$$

$$close^{i+1}(v, t, \phi^{\cdot}) = \varphi^{\cdot} \cup \left\{ o_{vt} \left| \begin{array}{c} \varphi \in Subst \wedge o_v, o_t \in type([\varphi]_{\approx}) \cap \varphi^{\cdot} \wedge \\ o_{vt} \in extend(v, t, o_v, o_t) \end{array} \right. \right\}$$

$$where \; \varphi^{\cdot} = close^i(v, t, \phi^{\cdot})$$

$$extend(v, t, o_v, o_t) =$$

$$\left\{ scale(o_v, S) \cup o_t \;\middle|\; \begin{array}{c} \langle v, p_v \rangle \in o_v \,\wedge\, s \in S \,\Leftrightarrow\, \langle v_t, p_t \rangle \in o_t \,\wedge \\ v_t = term_r(t) \,\wedge\, p_v \cdot s = r \cdot p_t \end{array} \right\} \cup$$

$$\left\{ o_v \cup scale(o_t, S) \;\middle|\; \begin{array}{c} \langle v_t, p_t \rangle \in o_t \,\wedge\, v_t = term_r(t) \,\wedge \\ s \in S \,\Leftrightarrow\, \langle v, p_v \rangle \in o_v \,\wedge\, p_v = r \cdot p_t \cdot s \end{array} \right\}$$

Example 6 *Consider again* $\phi^\bullet = \mu^\bullet \cup \nu^\bullet$ *of example 4 and specifically the abstract substitution produced by solving the equation* $v = u$ *in the context of* $\phi^\bullet$. *For brevity let* $\phi^\bullet = \{o_1, \ldots, o_6, \emptyset\}$ *where* $o_1 = \{\langle v, \lambda \rangle\}$; $o_2 = \{\langle w, \lambda \rangle\}$; $o_3 = \{\langle u, 1 \cdot \lambda \rangle, \langle u, 2 \cdot 1 \cdot \lambda \rangle, \langle x, \lambda \rangle\}$; $o_4 = \{\langle y, \lambda \rangle\}$; $o_5 = \{\langle v, 1 \cdot \lambda \rangle, \langle w, \lambda \rangle\}$; *and* $o_6 = \{\langle v, 2 \cdot \lambda \rangle, \langle y, \lambda \rangle\}$. *The close operator tracks the substitutions that can arise during the computation of a unifier in the unification algorithm. Sharing groups are iteratively combined until no more sharing groups can be generated and the fixed-point is reached.*

$$close(v, u, \phi^\bullet) = \phi^\bullet \cup \{o_7, o_8, o_9\} \text{ where}$$
$$o_7 = scale(o_1, \{1 \cdot \lambda, 2 \cdot 1 \cdot \lambda\}) \cup o_3$$
$$= \{\langle u, 1 \cdot \lambda \rangle, \langle u, 2 \cdot 1 \cdot \lambda \rangle, \langle v, 1 \cdot \lambda \rangle, \langle v, 2 \cdot 1 \cdot \lambda \rangle, \langle x, \lambda \rangle\}$$
$$o_8 = o_3 \cup o_5$$
$$= \{\langle u, 1 \cdot \lambda \rangle, \langle u, 2 \cdot 1 \cdot \lambda \rangle, \langle v, 1 \cdot \lambda \rangle, \langle w, \lambda \rangle, \langle x, \lambda \rangle\}$$
$$o_9 = scale(o_6, \{1 \cdot \lambda\}) \cup o_3$$
$$= \{\langle u, 1 \cdot \lambda \rangle, \langle u, 2 \cdot 1 \cdot \lambda \rangle, \langle v, 2 \cdot 1 \cdot \lambda \rangle, \langle y, 1 \cdot \lambda \rangle, \langle x, \lambda \rangle\}$$

$$close(v, u, \phi^\bullet \cup \{o_7, o_8, o_9\}) = \phi^\bullet \cup \{o_7, o_8, o_9, o_{10}\} \text{ where}$$
$$o_{10} = scale(o_6, \{1 \cdot \lambda\}) \cup o_8 = o_5 \cup o_9$$
$$= \{\langle u, 1 \cdot \lambda \rangle, \langle u, 2 \cdot 1 \cdot \lambda \rangle, \langle v, 1 \cdot \lambda \rangle, \langle v, 2 \cdot 1 \cdot \lambda \rangle, \langle w, \lambda \rangle, \langle x, \lambda \rangle, \langle y, 1 \cdot \lambda \rangle\}$$

$$close(v, u, \phi^\bullet \cup \{o_7, o_8, o_9, o_{10}\}) = \phi^\bullet \cup \{o_7, o_8, o_9, o_{10}\}$$

Each iteration of close combines a sharing group for a variable through v *with a sharing group for a variable through* u. *In the case of* o_7, *for instance, the sharing groups* o_1 *and* o_3 *dictate the inclusion of the sharing group* $o_7 = \{\langle u, 1 \cdot \lambda \rangle, \langle u, 2 \cdot 1 \cdot \lambda \rangle, \langle v, 1 \cdot \lambda \rangle, \langle v, 2 \cdot 1 \cdot \lambda \rangle, \langle x, \lambda \rangle\}$. *This is because on unification of* v *and* u, x *will occur through* v *at positions* $1 \cdot \lambda$ *and* $2 \cdot 1 \cdot \lambda$.

Note that sharing group o_{10} can be formed from either o_5 and o_9 or o_6 and o_8; and o_8 and o_9, in turn, are respectively derived from o_3 and o_5, and o_3 and o_6. The fact that o_{10} can be derived in two ways from o_3, o_5 and o_6 is a consequence of the non-determinism implicit in the unification algorithm. Note also that o_1 (and o_3) are barred from being combined with o_7 by virtue of the type check incorporated in close. In general, this check improves both the precision and analysis time by reducing the number of sharing groups that have to be combined. The underlying observation is that only consistent sharing groups need to be considered, that is, sharing groups that can share a common substitution. In the case of o_1 and o_7, for instance, no substitution can leave v free and bind v to a non-variable term. Thus o_1 and o_7 must *characterise different substitutions. In fact, in this case, o_1 and o_7 correspond to substitutions which arise at different stages of the unification algorithm. Hence o_1 and o_7 never need to be combined.*

From example 4, $rel(v, \phi^\bullet) \triangle rel(u, \phi^\bullet) = \{o_1, o_3, o_5, o_6\}$, and therefore it finally follows that $solve(v, u, \phi^\bullet) = \{o_2, o_4, o_7, o_8, o_9, o_{10}, \emptyset\}$. The intuition behind $rel(v, \phi^\bullet) \triangle rel(u, \phi^\bullet)$ is that it represents those sharing groups for shared variables which pass through either v or u, but not both. After unification, any variable which passes through v must also pass through u and vice versa. Sharing groups which do not possess this property are redundant, and in fact represent grounded variables, and hence can be removed.

Theorem 3.1

$$[\phi]_\approx \in \gamma_{type}(\phi^\bullet) \wedge \varphi \in mgu(\phi(E)) \wedge$$
$$var(E) \subseteq Svar \wedge mge(E, \phi^\bullet, \psi^\bullet) \Rightarrow [\varphi \circ \phi]_\approx \in \gamma_{type}(\psi^\bullet)$$

It is convenient a shorthand to regard mge as a mapping, that is, $mge(E, \phi^\bullet) = \psi^\bullet$ if $mge(E, \phi^\bullet, \psi^\bullet)$. Strictly, it is necessary to show that $mge(E, \phi^\bullet, \psi^\bullet)$ is deterministic for $mge(E, \phi^\bullet)$ to be well-defined. Like in [5], the conjecture is that mge yields a unique abstract substitution $\psi^\bullet$ for $\phi^\bullet$ regardless of the order in which E is solved (though, in practice, any $\psi^\bullet$ is safe).

To approximate the *unify* operation it is convenient to introduce a collecting semantics, concerned with sets of substitutions - the collecting domain, to record the substitutions that occur at various program points. In the collecting semantics interpretation, *unify* is extended to $unify^c$, which manipulates (possibly infinite) sets of substitutions.

Definition 10 ($unify^c$) *The mapping $unify^c$: $Atom \times \wp(Subst/\approx) \times Atom \times \wp(Subst/\approx) \rightarrow \wp(Subst/\approx)$ is defined by: $unify^c(a, \Phi, b, \Psi) = \{[\theta]_\approx \mid [\phi]_\approx \in \Phi \wedge [\psi]_\approx \in \Psi \wedge [\theta]_\approx = unify(a, [\phi]_\approx, b, [\psi]_\approx)\}$.*

The usefulness of the collecting semantics as a form of program analysis is negated by the fact that it can lead to non-terminating computations. The collecting semantics, however, is a useful tool for reasoning about the correctness of *unify*. To define *unify* and prove safety it is necessary to introduce an abstract restriction operator, $\cdot \upharpoonright^\bullet \cdot$, defined by: $\mu^\bullet \upharpoonright^\bullet U = \{o \upharpoonright^\bullet U \mid o \in \mu^\bullet\}$ and $o \upharpoonright^\bullet U = \{\langle u, p \rangle \in o \mid u \in U\}$. The definition of *unify* is given below and theorem 3.2 assumes $var(a) \cup var(b) \subseteq Pvar$.

Definition 11 ($unify^\bullet$) *The mapping $unify^\bullet$: $Atom \times Subst^\bullet_{Pvar} \times Atom \times Subst^\bullet_{Pvar} \rightarrow Subst^\bullet_{Pvar}$ is defined by: $unify^\bullet(a, \phi^\bullet, b, \psi^\bullet) = mge(\{a = \Upsilon(b)\}, \phi^\bullet \cup \Upsilon(\psi^\bullet)) \upharpoonright^\bullet Pvar$.*

Theorem 3.2 (local safety of $unify^\bullet$)

$$\Phi \subseteq \gamma_{type}(\phi^\bullet) \wedge \Psi \subseteq \gamma_{type}(\psi^\bullet) \Rightarrow$$
$$unify^c(a, \Phi, b, \Psi) \subseteq \gamma_{type}(unify^\bullet(a, \phi^\bullet, b, \psi^\bullet))$$

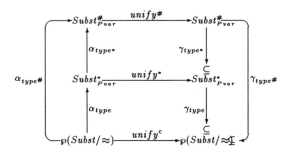

Figure 1: The relationship between depth-∞ and depth-k abstractions.

4 Depth-k analysis for sharing

The usefulness of the depth-∞ framework is compromised by its infiniteness. Since $Path$ is not finite, $Subst^{\bullet}_{Svar}(\subseteq)$ is not a finite lattice, and therefore a fixed-point computation, of the sort employed in [1, 13] does not automatically terminate. Section 4.1 explains how convergence of the iterates can be enforced by replacing $Subst^{\bullet}_{Svar}$ ($\subseteq$) with $Subst^{\#}_{Svar}$ ($\subseteq$) and throttling paths to length k. The mappings $\alpha_{type\bullet}$ and $\gamma_{type\bullet}$ formalise this depth-k abstraction. Section 4.1 describes an abstract analog of $unify^{\bullet}$, $unify^{\#}$, which safely operates on truncated paths. Figure 1 illustrates that by cascading the depth-∞ and depth-k approximations end-to-end, $unify^{\#}$ can be regarded an abstraction of $unify^c$ via the abstraction and concretisation mappings $\alpha_{type\#}$ and $\gamma_{type\#}$. These two mappings are respectively defined by composing $\alpha_{type\bullet}$ with α_{type} and γ_{type} with $\gamma_{type\bullet}$. (The $\#$ notation is used to distinguish depth-k objects from their depth-∞ counterparts.)

4.1 Abstracting depth-∞ abstract substitutions to depth-k

Depth-k abstractions [14, 17] normally represent the principal functor of a term complete with descriptors for its sub-terms. Sub-term descriptions are given to the depth of a predetermined constant bound k. (Depth-k analyses are conventionally good at representing structure but are often weak at tracing groundness and aliasing information.) In the spirit of the depth-k approach, the arbitrary length paths of the depth-∞ framework can be truncated to length k. (By discarding paths all together, the sharing analysis of [9] is obtained [10]!) Truncating at k induces an approximation and the notion of an abstract path $Path^{\#}_{\infty}$. $Path^{\#}_{\infty}$ thus includes a symbol nf to denote approximation and is formally defined to be the least set such that: $\lambda \in Path^{\#}_{\infty}$, $nf \in Path^{\#}_{\infty}$ and $n \cdot p^{\#} \in Path^{\#}_{\infty}$ if $p^{\#} \in Path^{\#}_{\infty}$ and $n \in \mathcal{N}$ (for n less or equal to the maximum arity of $Func$). The nf terminator can be interpreted as representing a set of paths. For example, $1 \cdot 2 \cdot nf$, finitely represents the infinite set $\{(1 \cdot 2 \cdot \lambda) \cdot p \mid p \in Path\}$. Note that $Path \subseteq Path^{\#}_{\infty}$.

Like before, $\cdot$ is interpreted as concatenation so that $(1\cdot2\cdot\lambda)\cdot(3\cdot nf) = 1\cdot2\cdot3\cdot nf$. It is also convenient (to simplify $\propto_{path}$ and $diff_\infty$) to let $(1\cdot nf)\cdot(2\cdot3\cdot\lambda) = 1\cdot2\cdot3\cdot\lambda$ and $(1\cdot2\cdot nf)\cdot(3\cdot nf) = 1\cdot2\cdot3\cdot nf$. Finiteness is introduced by the mapping $depth_k$.

Definition 12 *The mapping* $depth_k : Path_\infty^\# \to Path_\infty^\#$ *is defined by:*

$$depth_k(n_1\cdot\ldots\cdot n_l\cdot n) = \begin{cases} n_1\cdot\ldots\cdot n_l\cdot n & \text{if } l \le k \\ n_1\cdot\ldots\cdot n_k\cdot nf & \text{if } l > k \end{cases} \text{ where } n_i \in \mathcal{N}, n \in \{\lambda, nf\}$$

The codomain of $depth_k$ defines a finite set of truncated paths: $Path_k^\# = \{depth_k(p^\#) \mid p^\# \in Path_\infty^\#\}$. $Path_k^\#$ is finite because, for a given program, $Func$ is finite. The notion of approximation implicit in the set of abstract paths is encapsulated by the poset $Path_\infty^\#$ $(\propto_{path})$ defined as the least reflexive relation such that: $p\cdot nf \propto_{path} p\cdot p^\#$ if $p \in Path$ and $p^\# \in Path_\infty^\#$. Thus, for example, $1\cdot nf \propto_{path} 1\cdot2\cdot\lambda$, $1\cdot nf \propto_{path} 1\cdot2\cdot nf$, $\lambda \propto_{path} \lambda$ and $nf \propto_{path} nf$.

It is convenient to use abstract paths from both $Path_k^\#$ and $Path_\infty^\#$ in the analysis. For precision, the intermediate calculations of the abstract unification algorithm use $Path_\infty^\#$. For termination, the abstract unifiers are approximated (widened) by collapsing paths into $Path_k^\#$. $Path_k^\#$ and $Path_\infty^\#$ induce two notions of abstract sharing group: $Occ_{Svar,k}$ and $Occ_{Svar,\infty}$. $Occ_{Svar,k}$ is finite whereas $Occ_{Svar,\infty}$ is infinite. The abstract domain $Subst_{Svar}^\#$ is formulated in terms of $Occ_{Svar,\infty}$.

Definition 13 $(Occ_{Svar,k}^\#$ **and** $Occ_{Svar,\infty}^\#)$ *The sets of (abstracted) sharing groups are defined by:* $Occ_{Svar,k}^\# = \wp(Svar \times Path_k^\#)$ *and* $Occ_{Svar,\infty}^\# = \wp(Svar \times Path_\infty^\#)$.

Definition 14 $(Subst_{Svar}^\#)$ *The set of (abstracted) abstract substitutions,* $Subst_{Svar}^\#$, *is defined by:* $Subst_{Svar}^\# = \wp(Occ_{Svar,\infty}^\#)$.

$Subst_{Svar}^\#$ has $\cup$ as its lub. The poset $\propto_{path}$ induces the preorders $Occ_{Svar,k}^\#$ $(\propto_{share})$ and $Occ_{Svar,\infty}^\#$ $(\propto_{share})$ which formalise approximation among abstract sharing groups. The preorders are defined by: $o^\# \propto_{share} o'^\#$ if and only if $var(o^\#) = var(o'^\#)$ and for all $\langle u, p'^\#\rangle \in o'^\#$ there exists $\langle u, p^\#\rangle \in o^\#$ such that $p^\# \propto_{path} p'^\#$. Note that $\propto_{share}$ formalises approximation but does not specify how to threshold a sharing group. The operator $share_k$ is thus introduced to perform thresholding.

Definition 15 $(share_k)$ *The mappings* $share_k : Occ_{Svar,\infty}^\# \to Occ_{Svar,k}^\#$ *is defined by:* $share_k(o) = \{\langle u, depth_k(p)\rangle \mid \langle u, p\rangle \in o\}$.

Since $Occ_{Svar} \subseteq Occ_{Svar,\infty}^\#$, $share_k$ can threshold sharing groups as well as abstract sharing groups. Thus $\alpha_{type\bullet}$ can be defined in terms of $share_k$ whereas the concretisation $\gamma_{type\bullet}$ can be formulated in terms of $\propto_{share}$.

Definition 16 ($\alpha_{type\bullet}$ and $\gamma_{type\bullet}$) *The mappings* $\alpha_{type\bullet}$: $\wp(Subst^\bullet_{Svar})$ → $Subst^\#_{Svar}$ *and* $\gamma_{type\bullet}$: $Subst^\#_{Svar}$ → $\wp(Subst^\bullet_{Svar})$ *are defined by:* $\alpha_{type\bullet}(\Phi^\bullet)$ = $\cup_{\phi^\bullet \in \Phi^\bullet} \{share_k(o) \mid o \in \phi^\bullet\}$ *and* $\gamma_{type\bullet}(\phi^\#) = \{\phi^\bullet \in Subst^\bullet_{Svar} \mid \forall o \in \phi^\bullet. \exists o^\# \in \phi^\#. o^\# \propto_{share} o\}$.

Finally, the link between the collecting domain $\wp(Subst/\approx)$ and $Subst^\#_{Svar}$ can be made explicit by cascading $\alpha_{type\bullet}$ with α_{type} and γ_{type} with $\gamma_{type\bullet}$.

Definition 17 ($\alpha_{type\#}$ and $\gamma_{type\#}$) *The mappings* $\alpha_{type\#}$: $\wp(Subst/\approx)$ → $Subst^\#_{Svar}$ *and* $\gamma_{type\#}$: $Subst^\#_{Svar}$ → $\wp(Subst/\approx)$ *are defined by:* $\alpha_{type\#}(\Phi)$ = $\alpha_{type\bullet}(\{\alpha_{type}(\Phi)\})$ *and* $\gamma_{type\#}(\Phi^\#) = \cup_{\phi^\bullet \in \gamma_{type\bullet}(\Phi^\#)} \gamma_{type}(\phi^\bullet)$.

To strike an analogy with conventional sharing groups [9], it is insightful to introduce depth-k versions of occ and $type$, namely $occ_k^\#$ and $type_k^\#$.

Definition 18 ($occ_k^\#$ and $type_k^\#$) *The mappings* $occ_k^\#$: $Uvar \times Subst$ → $Occ^\#_{Svar,k}$ *and* $type_k^\#$: $Subst/\approx$ → $\wp(Occ^\#_{Svar,k})$ *are defined by:* $occ_k^\#(u, \phi) = \{\langle v, depth_k(p)\rangle \mid u = term_p(\phi(v)) \wedge v \in Svar\}$ *and* $type_k^\#([\phi]_\approx) = \{occ_k^\#(u, \phi) \mid u \in Uvar\}$.

If $depth_\infty$ is regarded as the identity mapping on $Path_\infty^\#$, then $occ_\infty^\# = occ$ and $type_\infty^\# = type$, and lemma 4.1 immediately follows. Lemma 4.1 succinctly expresses $\alpha_{type\#}$ and $\gamma_{type\#}$ in a familiar format.

Lemma 4.1 $\alpha_{type\#}(\Phi) = \cup_{[\phi]_\approx \in \Phi} type_\infty^\#([\phi]_\approx)$ *and* $\gamma_{type\#}(\phi^\#) = \{[\phi]_\approx \in Subst/\approx \mid \forall o^\# \in type_\infty^\#([\phi]_\approx). \exists o'^\# \in \phi^\#. o'^\# \propto_{share} o^\#\}$.

4.2 Abstracting depth-∞ abstract unification to depth-k

A truncated path version of $unify^\bullet$, $unify^\#$, is constructed by defining a depth-k analog of mge. The analog, denoted $mge_\infty^\# \subseteq Eqn \times Subst^\#_{Svar} \times Subst^\#_{Svar}$, simplifies and solves syntactic equations in the style of mge in the obvious way with the exception that $solve$ is replaced with $solve_\infty^\#$. The operator $solve_\infty^\#$ solves a syntactic equation of the form $v = t$ in the presence of the abstract substitution $\phi^\#$, returning the abstract unifier composed with $\phi^\#$. Thus $solve_\infty^\#$ abstracts $solve$ and, like before, is the key element of $mge_\infty^\#$.

Concatenation implicitly defines a notion of difference and to flesh out $solve_\infty^\#$, it is necessary to introduce an abstract difference operator, $diff_\infty$.

Definition 19 ($diff_\infty$) *The partial mapping* $diff_\infty$: $Path_\infty^\# \times Path_\infty^\#$ → $Path_\infty^\#$ *is defined by:*

$$diff_\infty(p^\#, r^\#) = \begin{cases} q & if \ p^\# \in Path \ \wedge \ r^\# \in Path \ \wedge \quad p^\# \cdot q = r^\# \\ nf & if \ p^\# \notin Path \ \wedge \ r^\# \in Path \ \wedge \quad p^\# \cdot s = r^\# \\ nf & if \ p^\# \in Path \ \wedge \ r^\# \notin Path \ \wedge \qquad p^\# = r^\# \cdot s \\ q^\# & if \ p^\# \in Path \ \wedge \ r^\# \notin Path \ \wedge \ p^\# \cdot q = r^\# \\ nf & if \ p^\# \notin Path \ \wedge \ r^\# \notin Path \end{cases}$$

Lemma 4.2 states precisely how $diff_\infty$ relates to $\cdot$.

Lemma 4.2 $p^* \propto_{path} p \wedge r^* \propto_{path} r \wedge p \cdot q = r \Rightarrow diff_\infty(p^*, r^*) \propto_{path} q$

Additionally, an auxiliary operator $scale^\#_\infty$ is required to abstract $scale$.

Definition 20 $(scale^\#_\infty)$ *The mapping* $scale : Occ^{\backprime}_{Svar,\infty} \times \wp(Path^\#_\infty) \to Occ_{Svar,\infty}$ *is defined by:*

$$scale^\#_\infty(o^*, S^*) =$$
$$\left\{ \langle u, p^* \cdot s^* \rangle \ \middle| \ \begin{array}{c} \langle u, p^* \rangle \in o^* \wedge \\ p^* \in Path \wedge s^* \in S^* \end{array} \right\} \cup \left\{ \langle u, p^* \rangle \ \middle| \ \begin{array}{c} \langle u, p^* \rangle \in o^* \wedge \\ p^* \notin Path \end{array} \right\}$$

With rel^*, the analog of rel for $Subst^\#_{Svar}$, $solve^\#_\infty$ and $close^\#_\infty$ can be constructed by plugging the appropriate depth-k operators into $solve$ and $close$.

Definition 21 $(solve^\#_\infty, close^\#_\infty \text{ and } extend^\#_\infty)$ *The mappings* $solve^\#_\infty :$ $Svar \times Term \times Subst^\#_{Svar} \to Subst^\#_{Svar}$, $close^\#_\infty : Svar \times Term \times Subst^\#_{Svar}$ $\to Subst^\#_{Svar}$, $extend^\#_\infty : Svar \times Term \times Occ_{Svar,\infty} \times Occ_{Svar,\infty} \to Subst^\#_{Svar}$ *are defined by:*

$$solve^\#_\infty(v, t, \phi^*) = lfp(close^\#_\infty(v, t, \phi^*)) \setminus (rel^*(v, \phi^*) \triangle rel^*(t, \phi^*))$$

$$close^{\#\,0}_\infty(v, t, \phi^\cdot) = \phi^*$$
$$close^{\#\,i+1}_\infty(v, t, \phi^\cdot) = \varphi^* \cup \left\{ o^\#_{vt} \ \middle| \ o^\#_v, o^\#_t \in \varphi^* \wedge o^\#_{vt} \in extend^\#_\infty(v, t, o^\#_v, o^\#_t) \right\}$$
$$where \ \varphi^* = close^{\#\,i}_\infty(v, t, \phi^*)$$

$$extend^\#_\infty(v, t, o^\#_v, o^\#_t) =$$
$$\left\{ scale^\#_\infty(o^\#_v, S^*) \cup o^\#_t \ \middle| \ \begin{array}{c} \langle v, p^\#_v \rangle \in o^\#_v \wedge s^* \in S^* \Leftrightarrow \langle v_t, p^\#_t \rangle \in o^\#_t \wedge \\ v_t = term_r(t) \wedge diff_\infty(p^\#_v, r \cdot p^\#_t) = s^* \end{array} \right\} \cup$$
$$\left\{ o^\#_v \cup scale^\#_\infty(o^\#_t, S^*) \ \middle| \ \begin{array}{c} \langle v_t, p^\#_t \rangle \in o^\#_t \wedge v_t = term_r(t) \wedge s^* \in S^* \Leftrightarrow \\ \langle v, p^\#_v \rangle \in o^\#_v \wedge diff_\infty(r \cdot p^\#_t, p^\#_v) = s^* \end{array} \right\}$$

Note that $solve^\#_\infty$ and each of its constituent parts are independent of k. Thus $solve^\#_\infty$ is an abstract equation solver for depth-k abstractions of arbitrary k. Precision is throttled (without touching the core components of the analysis) at the level of $mge^\#_\infty$. Specifically, an intermediate construction, $mge^\#_k$, is employed to threshold the abstract unifier to depth-k.

Definition 22 $(mge^\#_k)$ *The relation* $mge^\#_k : Eqn \times Subst^\#_{Svar} \times Subst^\#_{Svar}$ *is defined by:* $mge^\#_k(E, \phi^*, \varphi^*)$ *if* $mge^\#_\infty(E, \phi^*, \psi^*)$ *where* $\varphi^* = \{share_k(o^*) \ | \ o^* \in \psi^*\}$.

Like before, it is convenient to regard $mge^\#_k$ as a mapping. Then, with the addition of some renaming machinery, $mge^\#_k$ defines a depth-k version of $unify^\cdot$, $unify^\#_k$. Safety is stated as theorem 4.3 and is couched in terms of $unify^c$. Like theorem 3.2, theorem 4.3 assumes $var(a) \cup var(b) \subseteq Pvar$. Also $\upharpoonright^\#$ is the obvious depth-k analog of restriction.

Definition 23 ($unify^{\#}$) *The mapping* $unify^{\#} : Atom \times Subst^{\#}_{Pvar} \times Atom \times Subst^{\#}_{Pvar} \to Subst^{\#}_{Pvar}$ *is defined by:* $unify^{\#}(a, \phi^{\#}, b, \psi^{\#}) = mge^{\#}_k(\{a = \Upsilon(b)\}, \phi^{\#} \cup \Upsilon(\psi^{\#})) \upharpoonright^{\#} Pvar.$

Theorem 4.3 (local safety of $unify^{\#}$)

$$\Phi \subseteq \gamma_{type^{\#}}(\phi^{\#}) \wedge \Psi \subseteq \gamma_{type^{\#}}(\psi^{\#}) \Rightarrow$$
$$unify^c(a, \Phi, b, \Psi) \subseteq \gamma_{type^{\#}}(unify^{\#}(a, \phi^{\#}, b, \psi^{\#}))$$

5   Depth-∞ and depth-k freeness

The applications domain of the analysis can be enriched by augmenting the domains $Subst^{\bullet}_{Svar}$ and $Subst^{\#}_{Svar}$ with a definite freeness component. Although $Subst^{\bullet}_{Svar}$ and $Subst^{\#}_{Svar}$ succinctly express possible freeness and definite groundness, they cannot adequately record definite freeness. For instance, if $\Phi = \{\{u \mapsto f\}, \{u \mapsto v\}\}$ and $Svar = \{u, v\}$ then $\alpha_{type}(\Phi) = \{\{\langle u, \lambda\rangle, \langle v, \lambda\rangle\}, \emptyset\}$, and information about the non-freeness of u is lost. By additionally recording possible groundness, however, definite freeness can be inferred. For example, by adopting a domain $Subst^{\bullet}_{Svar} \times Grnd^{\bullet}_{Svar}$ in which $Grnd^{\bullet}_{Svar} = \wp(Svar \times Path)$, then Φ could be represented as $\langle \{\{\langle u, \lambda\rangle, \langle v, \lambda\rangle\}, \emptyset\}, \{\langle u, \lambda\rangle\}\rangle$ indicating that a sub-term $term_\lambda(\phi(u))$ is ground for some $\phi \in \Phi$. Conversely, without a pair $\langle u, p\rangle$, $term_\lambda(\phi(u))$ must definitely be free. Extending the depth-∞ and depth-k analyses in this way is straightforward (though technical) and reuses a lot of the (possible) freeness abstract interpretation machinery. For brevity, example 7 illustrates the basic idea behind the tracking of (possible and definite) freeness in sub-terms with an example adapted from a benchmark program.

Example 7 *Consider the head unification* $unify^{\#}_1(a, \phi^{\#}, b, \psi^{\#})$ *where* $a = dfri(tree(L, R), -(LFriHead, RFriTail))$, $b = dfri(Tree, DFri)$, $\phi^{\#} = \{\{\langle L, \lambda\rangle\}, \{\langle LFriHead, \lambda\rangle\}, \{\langle R, \lambda\rangle\}, \{\langle RFriHead, \lambda\rangle\}, \{\langle RFriTail, \lambda\rangle\}, \emptyset\}$ *and* $\psi^{\#} = \{\{\langle DFri, 1 \cdot \lambda\rangle\}, \emptyset\}$. *Supposing* $\Upsilon(Tree) = Tree'$ *and* $\Upsilon(DFri) = DFri'$, *then* $unify^{\#}_1(a, \phi^{\#}, b, \psi^{\#}) = mge^{\#}_1(E, \phi^{\#} \cup \Upsilon(\psi^{\#})) \upharpoonright^{\#} Pvar$ *where* $E = \{Tree' = tree(L, R), DFri' = -(LFriHead, RFriTail)\}$ *and* $\phi^{\#} \cup \Upsilon(\psi^{\#}) = \{\{\langle L, \lambda\rangle\}, \{\langle LFriHead, \lambda\rangle\}, \{\langle R, \lambda\rangle\}, \{\langle RFriHead, \lambda\rangle\}, \{\langle RFriTail, \lambda\rangle\}, \{\langle DFri', 1\cdot\lambda\rangle\}, \emptyset\}$. *But* $mge^{\#}_\infty(E, \phi^{\#} \cup \Upsilon(\psi^{\#})) = \{\{\langle DFri', 1\cdot\lambda\rangle, \langle LFriHead, \lambda\rangle\}, \{\langle RFriHead, \lambda\rangle\}, \emptyset\}$ *and thus* $unify^{\#}_1(a, \phi^{\#}, b, \psi^{\#}) = \{\{\langle LFriHead, \lambda\rangle\}, \{\langle RFriHead, \lambda\rangle\}, \emptyset\}$. *Hence, L and R are grounded by head unification whereas LFriHead and RFriHead remain (possibly) free and unaliased. If, in addition, the possible grounding analysis does not include any pairs* $\langle LFriHead, p\rangle$ *and* $\langle RFriHead, p\rangle$, *then the definite freeness of LFriHead and RFriHead immediately follows. Here, depth-1 analysis is vital for the required precision.*

6   Related and future work

Recently, three relevant proposals for computing sharing have been put forward in the literature. In the first proposal [7], multiple analyses are run in lock step. This paper likewise follows the trend for simultaneously tracing different properties (namely groundness, sharing and freeness), but instead explains how the restructuring of domains can yield a depth-k analysis which cannot be synthesised in terms of the combined domain approach.

In the second proposal [6], the correctness of sharing and definite freeness analyses are considered. An abstract unification algorithm is proposed as a basis for constructing accurate freeness analyses with a domain formulated in terms of a system of abstract equations. Safety follows because the abstract algorithm mimics the unification algorithm in an intuitive way. Correctness is argued likewise here. One essential distinction between the two works is that the approach proposed in this paper uses paths to encode more accurate sharing information than the abstract equations of [6].

Very recently, in the third proposal [2], an analysis for sharing, groundness, linearity and definite freeness is formalised as a transition system which reduces a set of abstract equations to an abstract solved form. Sharing is represented in a sharing group fashion with variables enriched with linearity and freeness information by an annotation mapping. The domain, however, essentially glues the Jacobs and Langen [9] structure with a conventional notion of freeness. Freeness is not generalised to depth-k and is not embedded into sharing groups in the way that is described in this paper.

Future work will focus on incorporating linearity into sharing groups embellished with depth-k freeness. Benchmarking will quantitatively assess the usefulness and efficiency of this refinement, and suggest also suitable k.

7   Conclusions

A powerful and formally justified analysis has been presented for inferring groundness, freeness, and sharing between the variables of a logic program. The analysis elegantly represents freeness information in a sharing group format. By revising sharing groups to capture freeness, aliasing behaviour can be precisely captured; groundness information can be accurately propagated; and in addition, the freeness of sub-terms can be tracked.

References

[1] M. Bruynooghe. A practical framework for the abstract interpretation of logic programs. *J. of Logic Programming*, 10:91–124, 1991.

[2] M. Bruynooghe and M. Codish. Freeness, sharing, linearity and correctness – all at once. In *WSA '93*, pages 153–164, September 1993.

[3] A. Cortesi and G. Filé. Abstract interpretation of logic programs: an abstract domain for groundness, sharing, freeness and compoundness analysis. In *PEPM'91*, pages 52–61, 1991.

[4] J. Lassez *et al. Foundations of Deductive Databases and Logic Programming*, chapter Unification Revisited. Morgan Kaufmann, 1987.

[5] M. Codish *et al.* Derivation and safety of an abstract unification algorithm for groundness and aliasing analysis. In *ICLP'91*, pages 79–93, Paris, 1991. MIT Press.

[6] M. Codish *et al.* Freeness analysis for logic programs - and correctness? In *ICLP'93*, pages 116–131. MIT Press, June 1993.

[7] M. Codish *et al.* Improving abstract interpretation by combining domains. In *PEPM'93*. ACM Press, 1993.

[8] M. Hermenegildo and F. Rossi. Non-strict independent and-parallelism. In *ICLP'90*, pages 237–252, Jerusalem, 1990. MIT Press.

[9] D. Jacobs and A. Langen. Static Analysis of Logic Programs. *J. of Logic Programming*, pages 154–314, 1992.

[10] A. King. Depth-k sharing and freeness. Technical Report CSTR 93-14, Southampton University, S09 5NH, UK, 1993.

[11] J. W. Lloyd. *Foundations of Logic Programming*. Springer Verlag, 1987.

[12] K. Muthukumar and M. Hermenegildo. Combined determination of sharing and freeness of program variables through abstract interpretation. In *ICLP'91*, pages 49–63, Paris, 1991. The MIT Press.

[13] K. Muthukumar and M. Hermenegildo. Compile-time derivation of variable dependency through abstract interpretation. *J. of Logic Programming*, pages 315–437, 1992.

[14] T. Sato and H. Tamaki. Enumeration of success patterns in logic programs. *Theoretical Computer Science*, 34:227–240, 1984.

[15] H. Søndergaard. An application of the abstract interpretation of logic programs: occur-check reduction. In *ESOP'86*, pages 327–338, 1986.

[16] R. Sundararajan and J. Conery. An abstract interpretation scheme for groundness, freeness, and sharing analysis of logic programs. In *12th FST and TCS Conference*, New Delhi, December 1992.

[17] A. Taylor. *High Performance Prolog Implementation*. PhD thesis, Basser Department of Computer Science, July 1991.

Towards a Practical Full Mode Inference System for CLP(H,N)

Veroniek Dumortier, Gerda Janssens
K.U. Leuven, Department of Computer Science
Celestijnenlaan 200A, B-3001 Heverlee, Belgium
phone : +32 16 20 10 15; fax : +32 16 20 53 08;
email : {veroniek,gerda}@cs.kuleuven.ac.be

Abstract

A full mode analysis system for CLP(H,N) could result from a straightforward combination of the definiteness analysis (developed at U.P.M.) and the freeness analysis (developed at K.U.Leuven). However, the computational complexity of the freeness abstraction, which is due to an exhaustive enumeration of possible dependencies between variables, impedes its use. This paper proposes two orthogonal approaches to reduce the size of the freeness abstraction. Using the definiteness information the first approach splits off the definite variables and their dependencies without any loss of precision. The second approach retains only basic freeness information – the *minimal* information – from which a safe approximation of the rest can be reconstructed. The combination of both approaches results in a practical full mode analysis system; to our knowledge this is the first full mode analysis system for CLP. The optimisations are implemented and timings of the resulting systems show their effectiveness for a set of benchmark programs.
Keywords : Abstract Interpretation, Constraint Logic Programming

1 Introduction

Recently, two applications of abstract interpretation have been developed in the context of Constraint Logic Programming (CLP) : inference of definiteness information [7] and of freeness information [8]. These top-down analyses currently focus on CLP(H,N) programs, in which constraint systems may contain unifications over the Herbrand domain (H) and numerical constraints over an infinite domain of numbers (N). The definiteness analysis infers whether variables are *definite*, i.e. constrained to a unique value. Put in terms of modes, it derives modes **d** (definite) and **a** (any). The analysis takes into account *definite* dependencies between variables in order to perform accurate definiteness propagation. The freeness analysis derives whether variables are *free*, i.e. whether they can still take any possible value (at least according to their type, e.g. a variable that is constrained to be numerical but still ranges over the complete domain of numbers is considered as free). In terms of modes, the analysis infers modes **f** (free) and **a** (any). It keeps track of *possible* dependencies between variables to take care of non-freeness propagation. The dependency information is also useful to perform constraint shifting (cf. [8]). It should be noted that the freeness analysis must be extended in order to be useful for constraint specialisation. More precisely, mode f must be refined into f_u and f_n. If a variable X has mode f_u it means that X is free and X is either unconstrained or occurs only in constraints of the form $X = Y$ where Y is of mode f_u; X having mode f_n means that X is free but possibly appears in a numerical constraint. Only variables with mode f_u are useful for specialising constraints to assignments. Refining the analysis can be done in a straightforward way; the possible dependency information is again essential to propagate the f_n mode. In the sequel we concentrate on the original freeness abstraction and its optimisations; the refinement of mode f to f_u and f_n is orthogonal to it.

Example 1.1
Consider the constraint system $C = \{X = 3, X - T = 2, Y = Z\}$. The definiteness analysis infers that C gives rise to the modes $X : d$, $T : d$, $Y : a$, $Z : a$. The freeness analysis yields $X : a$, $T : a$, $Y : f$, $Z : f$ (after refinement: $Y : f_u$, $Z : f_u$).

Several issues arise when developing a practical mode inference system. First of all, the freeness analysis by itself as described in [8] leads to computational problems, both with respect to space and time. The abstract constraint systems tend to become quite large due to an exhaustive enumeration of all possible variable dependencies that are used for non-freeness propagation. In this paper, two ways to compress the abstract constraint system are proposed. A first approach extracts the dependency information that involves definite variables from the abstraction and compresses it to the set of definite variables, without loss of precision. An abstract constraint system is thus split in two parts: one part containing the definite variables and another part containing information on the non-definite variables and their dependencies. A second approach to get a more compact freeness abstraction is to keep track of only a minimum of information, rather than representing all information exhaustively. In this case, the compressed abstract constraint system is a safe approximation of the original abstract system. It allows to reconstruct a superset of the original set of variable dependencies. Both approaches are orthogonal, so they can be combined.

Another practical issue is that applying only the freeness or the definiteness analysis does not yield enough information for compiler optimisations (such as transforming constraints into assignments, constraint reordering, etc.). Combining the two analyses does not only allow to compress the freeness abstraction (cf. first approach mentioned above), but also results in a sufficiently powerful mode inference system.

The paper is structured as follows. Section 2 introduces the notations and recalls the basic notions of the freeness abstraction from [8]. Section 3 describes the first approach to compress the freeness abstraction, making use of definiteness information. In section 4, the second approach to minimise the freeness abstraction is presented. Section 5 shows how both approaches can be combined, yielding a practical mode inference system. The proofs of propositions are omitted due to space limitations. Each approach is implemented within the abstract interpretation system PLAI [14, 15]. A set of benchmarks is analysed with each of the systems; the results are evaluated in section 6. Section 7 concludes and discusses related work.

2 Preliminaries

In the following we assume familiarity with the standard definitions and notation for constraint logic programs [3, 4, 10] and abstract interpretation [6]. We assume a set of variables Var and a set of function symbols $\Sigma = \Sigma_N \cup \Sigma_A$ (Σ_N and Σ_A overlap). Function symbols are classified as *numerical* or *alphabetical*, i.e. in Σ_N or Σ_A respectively. The numerical function symbols will typically include: *numerical constants* such as real, integer or rational numbers — depending on the specific domain; and *numerical functors* such as $+, -, \times$ and $/$. The alphabetical function symbols include the constants (including numbers) and non-numerical function symbols. The corresponding term algebras are denoted respectively $T(\Sigma_N, Var)$ and $T(\Sigma_A, Var)$.

A *numerical constraint* is an equation, disequation or inequality between $T(\Sigma_N, Var)$ terms. A *unification constraint* is an equation between $T(\Sigma_A, Var)$ terms. A *constraint system* is a finite conjunction of numerical and unification constraints, written as a set. Note that while an equation of the form $X = f(Y + 1, 2 * Z - 3, T)$ is neither a numerical nor a unification constraint, it can be *normalised* into the system $\{X = f(A, B, T), A - Y = 1, B - 2Z = -3\}$ consisting of a unification and two numerical constraints.

An important notion is *entailment*. The definiteness as well as the freeness analysis keeps track of variable dependencies. These are used to infer how a change in the mode of some variables affects the mode of others. They are established via the constraints in the program, either directly or through entailment. E.g. the constraint system $\{X = f(Y), Y + Z = 3\}$ directly establishes a dependency between X and Y and between Y and Z; it also entails a dependency between X and Z. Given a constraint system C, $unif^*(C)$ and $num^*(C)$ respectively denote the conjunctions of all unification and all numerical constraints entailed by C. Both $unif^*(C)$ and $num^*(C)$ have a finite solved form (for the former, it corresponds to the *mgu* of the unifications [12]; for the latter, a solved form is described in [13]).

For simplicity, we assume the standard framework of abstract interpretation as defined in [6]. Abstraction is formalised in terms of a Galois connection, which involves the definition of a concrete domain $(Dom_c, \leq_c)$, an abstract domain $(Dom_a, \leq_a)$ and an abstraction function α (the concretisation function γ is uniquely determined by α as described in [6]).

The concrete domain for each of the considered analyses is $(Con_C, \subseteq)$ and consists of *sets of satisfiable constraint systems*. In the sequel, an element of Con_C is denoted by CS (with or without subscript). For each of the abstract domains, an element of the domain is called an *abstract constraint system*.

We let $(Con_D, \leq_D)$ and α_D denote the abstract domain and abstraction function for the definiteness analysis; their definition can be found in [7]. For the sequel, the only relevant point about the definiteness abstraction is that it infers a.o. a safe (lower) approximation of the variables that are definite (denoted $defvars(\alpha_D(\{C\}))$).

For the freeness analysis, we recall some definitions of [8] that form the basis for the adaptations to the analysis proposed in the following sections (more details on the domain can be found in [8]). The abstract domain and abstraction function are denoted $(Con_F, \leq_F)$ and α_F. The abstract constraint systems in Con_F are sets of sets of variables. Each set of variables describes a possible dependency between those variables. In the remainder we use $\wp_\emptyset(S)$ to denote $\wp(S) \setminus \{\emptyset\}$, where $\wp(S)$ is the powerset of a set S.

Definition 2.1 (Abstracting a single constraint system)
Let C be a satisfiable constraint system, let $\theta = unif^*(C)^1$ and let

$$W = \begin{cases} \{X\} \mid X\theta \text{ is a non-variable } \} \cup \\ \{X, Y\} \mid X \not\equiv Y, \ vars(X\theta) \cap vars(Y\theta) \neq \emptyset \} \cup \\ \{X_1, \ldots, X_n\} \left| \begin{array}{l} (a_1 X_1 + \ldots + a_n X_n \ OP \ b)^2 \in num^*(C), \\ OP \in \{=, \neq, <, \leq\}, \ a_i \neq 0 \ (i = 1..n) \end{array} \right\} \cup \\ \{Y_1, \ldots, Y_q, X_1, \ldots, X_n\} \left| \begin{array}{l} Y_k\theta \text{ is a compound term,} \\ Z_i \in vars(Y_k\theta), \text{ all } Z_i \text{ are distinct variables,} \\ (b_1 Z_1 + \ldots + b_m Z_m + a_1 X_1 + \ldots + a_n X_n = b) \in num^*(C), \\ b_i \neq 0, \ a_j \neq 0 \ (i = 1..m, \ j = 1..n, \ k = 1..q, \ q \leq m) \end{array} \right\} \end{cases}$$

Then $\alpha_F(\{C\}) = close(W)$ (close(W) is the closure under union of W).

The first set in the definition of W yields information on the non-freeness of variables (variables bound to a ground or compound term). The second and third set describe variable dependencies that are established through all possible entailed unification constraints, resp. through entailed numerical constraints. The last set indicates dependencies between non-numerical and numerical variables, established through a combination of unification constraints and numerical constraints.

Example 2.1
Let $C = \{X = f(A, B), A + B + T = 3\}$. Then,

$$unif^*(C) = \{X = f(A, B)\},$$
$$num^*(C) = \{A + B + T = 3, 2A + 2B + 2T = 6, \ldots\},$$
$$W = \left\{ \begin{array}{l} \{X\}, \{X, A\}, \{X, B\}, \{A, B, T\}, \{X, B, T\}, \\ \{X, A, T\}, \{X, T\} \end{array} \right\},$$
$$\alpha_F(C) = \left\{ \begin{array}{l} \{X\}, \{X, A\}, \{X, B\}, \{A, B, T\}, \{X, B, T\}, \\ \{X, A, T\}, \{X, T\}, \{X, A, B\}, \{X, A, B, T\} \end{array} \right\}.$$

---

[1] θ is the solved form of $unif^*(C)$, i.e. the *mgu* of the unifications entailed by C.

[2] This form includes only *linear* constraints. A non-linear constraint c is currently approximated in a very naive way, i.e. its abstraction is $\wp_\emptyset(vars(c))$.

Definition 2.2 (Abstracting a set of constraint systems)
Let $CS \in Con_C$. Then $\alpha_{\mathcal{F}}(CS) = \bigcup_{C_i \in CS} \alpha_{\mathcal{F}}(\{C_i\})$.

Definition 2.3 (Abstract domain)
The abstract domain $Con_{\mathcal{F}}$ is defined as $Con_{\mathcal{F}} = \{F \mid F \in \wp(\wp_{\emptyset}(Var))\}$.

Definition 2.4 (Abstract order relation and least upper bound)
Let $AC_1, AC_2 \in Con_{\mathcal{F}}$. Then
- *$AC_1 \leq_{\mathcal{F}} AC_2$ iff $AC_1 \subseteq AC_2$;*
- *$lub_{\mathcal{F}}(AC_1, AC_2) = AC_1 \cup AC_2$.*

Proposition 2.1 (Mode inference)
Let $AC \in Con_{\mathcal{F}}$ and $CS \in Con_C$ such that $\alpha_{\mathcal{F}}(CS) \leq_{\mathcal{F}} AC$. If $\{X\} \notin AC$ then X is free in CS (mode $\mathbf{f}$); otherwise, X is possibly non-free (mode $\mathbf{a}$).

Taking the closure under union in Definition 2.1 implies that all variable dependencies are explicitly represented. Also note that not all abstract constraint systems are closed under union. E.g. $AC = \alpha_{\mathcal{F}}(\{\{X + Y = 3\}, \{X + Z = 5\}\}) = \{\{X, Y\}, \{X, Z\}\}$. AC indicates a dependency between X and Y and between X and Z; since $\{Y, Z\}$ does not belong to AC, Y and Z do not depend on each other.

To define the computation on the abstract domain, the abstract interpretation of CLP requires the introduction of two basic abstract operations:
- abstract conjunction: to enable the addition of an abstract constraint system to an accumulated abstract constraint system (corresponds to abstract unification in the context of LP);
- abstract projection: to enable the projection of an abstract constraint system onto a given set of variables.

Definition 2.5 (Abstract conjunction)
The abstract conjunction of $AC_1, AC_2 \in Con_{\mathcal{F}}$ is defined as
$$AC_1 \wedge_{\mathcal{F}} AC_2 = AC_1 \cup AC_2 \cup ((AC_1 \oplus AC_2) \setminus \{\emptyset\}) \quad \text{where}$$
$$AC_1 \oplus AC_2 = \left\{ (A_1 \cup A_2) \setminus D \;\middle|\; A_1 \in AC_1, A_2 \in AC_2, D \subseteq A_1 \cap A_2 \right\}.$$

Definition 2.6 (Abstract projection)
Given an abstract constraint system AC, the abstract projection of AC on $V \subseteq Var$ is defined as $AC \mid_V = \{S \in AC \mid S \subseteq V\}$.

Other operations, such as *procedure-entry* and *procedure-exit* as required in the framework of [1], are easily expressed in terms of the above operations. As an example, we show the results of the freeness analysis for the sumlist/2 program with initial call pattern *sumlist*($\mathbf{a}, \mathbf{f}$). The abstract constraint system is written out at each program point.

Example 2.2

$$
\begin{array}{ll}
\textit{sumlist(L, S)} \ :- & \%\ \{\ \{L\}\ \} \\
\quad \{L = [\ ], & \%\ \{\ \{L\}\ \} \\
\quad S = 0\}. & \%\ \{\ \{L\}, \{S\}, \{L, S\}\ \} \\
\textit{sumlist(L, S)} \ :- & \%\ \{\ \{L\}\ \} \\
\quad \{L = [H \mid T], & \%\ \{\ \{L\}, \{L, H\}, \{L, T\}, \{L, H, T\}, \{H\}, \{T\}, \{H, T\}\ \} \\
\quad S = H + S'\}, & \%\ \{\ \{L\}, \{L, H\}, \{L, T\}, \{L, H, T\}, \{H\}, \{T\}, \{H, T\}, \\
& \%\quad \{S, S', H\}, \{S, S', H, L\}, \{S, S', L\}, \{S, S', H, L, T\}, \\
& \%\quad \{S, S', L, T\}, \{S, S'\}, \{S, S', H, T\}, \{S, S', T\}\ \} \\
\quad \textit{sumlist(T,S')}. & \%\ \wp_\emptyset(\{L, S, H, T, S'\})
\end{array}
$$

The analysis indicates that at the end of each clause, L and S are possibly non-free. In the second clause, S and S' are free before the recursive call.

3 Approach 1 : the $\mathcal{DF}$ abstraction

Definite variables contribute in a specific way to the set of possible dependencies of a freeness abstraction, such that the corresponding part can easily be split off. Given the set of definite variables D, $\alpha_{\mathcal{F}}(CS)$ can be split into a set of sets containing no definite variables – $compl(D, \alpha_{\mathcal{F}}(CS))$ – and a set of sets that do contain definite variables – $defrelated(D, \alpha_{\mathcal{F}}(CS))$:
$\alpha_{\mathcal{F}}(CS) = compl(D, \alpha_{\mathcal{F}}(CS)) \cup defrelated(D, \alpha_{\mathcal{F}}(CS))$ where

- $compl(D, \alpha_{\mathcal{F}}(CS)) = \{S \in \alpha_{\mathcal{F}}(CS) \mid S \cap D = \emptyset\}$ and
- $defrelated(D, \alpha_{\mathcal{F}}(CS)) = \wp_\emptyset(D) \cup \{S_1 \cup S_2 \mid S_1 \in \wp_\emptyset(D), S_2 \in compl(D, \alpha_{\mathcal{F}}(CS))\}$.

The $\mathcal{DF}$ abstraction is based on the observation that the freeness abstraction can be expressed in terms of $compl(D, \alpha_{\mathcal{F}}(CS))$ and D. A safe approximation of D is computed by $\alpha_{\mathcal{D}}$ [7].

Definition 3.1 ($\mathcal{DF}$ abstraction)
Let $CS \in Con_C$. Then $\alpha_{\mathcal{DF}}(CS) = (D, F^*)$ where $D = defvars(\alpha_{\mathcal{D}}(CS))$ and $F^* = compl(D, \alpha_{\mathcal{F}}(CS))$.

Definition 3.2 ($\mathcal{DF}$ abstract domain)
$Con_{\mathcal{DF}} = \{(D, F^*) \mid D \in \wp(Var), F^* \in \wp(\wp_\emptyset(Var \setminus D))\}$.

$\alpha_{\mathcal{F}}(CS)$ (and $\alpha_{\mathcal{D}}(CS)$) are used to compute $\alpha_{\mathcal{DF}}(CS)$; vice versa, $\alpha_{\mathcal{F}}(CS)$ can be reconstructed from $\alpha_{\mathcal{DF}}(CS)$ without loss of precision, via the *extend* operation defined below. This is illustrated in Figure 1.

Definition 3.3 (extend)
Let $(D, F^*) \in Con_{\mathcal{DF}}$. Then $extend(D, F^*) = F^* \cup \wp_\emptyset(D) \cup \{S_1 \cup S_2 \mid S_1 \in \wp_\emptyset(D), S_2 \in F^*\}$.

Definition 3.4 (Order relation and least upper bound)
Let $(D_1, F_1^*), (D_2, F_2^*) \in Con_{\mathcal{DF}}$. Then

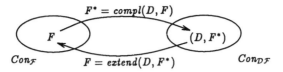

$$F^* = compl(D, F)$$

$F \quad\quad (D, F^*)$

$Con_{\mathcal{F}} \quad\quad F = extend(D, F^*) \quad\quad Con_{\mathcal{DF}}$

Figure 1: Relation between $\mathcal{F}$ and $\mathcal{DF}$ abstraction (for a given D)

- $(D_1, F_1^*) \leq_{\mathcal{DF}} (D_2, F_2^*)$ iff $D_1 \supseteq D_2$ and $extend(D_1 \setminus D_2, F_1^*) \subseteq F_2^*$;
- $lub_{\mathcal{DF}}((D_1, F_1^*),(D_2, F_2^*)) = (D, F^*)$ with $D = D_1 \cap D_2$ and
  $F^* = extend(D_1 \setminus (D_1 \cap D_2), F_1^*) \cup extend(D_2 \setminus (D_1 \cap D_2), F_2^*))$.

Proposition 3.1 (Mode inference)
Let $CS \in Con_{\mathcal{C}}$ and $(D, F^*) \in Con_{\mathcal{DF}}$ such that $\alpha_{\mathcal{DF}}(CS) \leq_{\mathcal{DF}} (D, F^*)$. If $X \in D$, then X is a definite variable in CS (mode d), else if $\{X\} \notin F^*$ then X is free in CS (mode f). Otherwise nothing can be said about X (mode a).

A $\mathcal{DF}$ abstraction is more compact than the corresponding $\mathcal{F}$ abstraction. The abstract operations are more efficient, both with respect to space and time. However, some care is needed when defining abstract conjunction.

Definition 3.5 (Abstract conjunction w.r.t. D)
Let $F_1^*, F_2^* \in \wp(\wp_0(Var))$ and $D \in \wp(Var)$. The abstract conjunction of F_1^* and F_2^* with respect to D, denoted $F_1^* \mathbin{\triangle} F_2^*$, is defined as
$$F_1^* \mathbin{\triangle} F_2^* = reduce(D, F_1^*) \;\Lambda_{\mathcal{F}}\; reduce(D, F_2^*)$$
where $reduce(D, F^*) = \{S \setminus D \mid S \in F^*\} \setminus \{\emptyset\}$.

Definition 3.6 (Abstract conjunction)
Let $(D_1, F_1^*),(D_2, F_2^*) \in Con_{\mathcal{DF}}$. Then $(D_1, F_1^*) \;\Lambda_{\mathcal{DF}}\; (D_2, F_2^*) = (D, F^*)$ where D is obtained using the abstract conjunction operation on Con_D [7] and $F^* = F_1^* \mathbin{\triangle} F_2^*$.

Note that F^* could also be computed as $F^* = compl(D, extend(D_1, F_1^*) \;\Lambda_{\mathcal{F}}\; extend(D_2, F_2^*))$. However, computing F^* via $F_1^* \mathbin{\triangle} F_2^*$ is more efficient, since the conjunction is performed on smaller abstract constraint systems. The idea is to join the definiteness parts first and then to propagate the obtained definiteness information (via *reduce*) onto the freeness parts F_1^* and F_2^* before joining them.

Definition 3.7 (Abstract projection)
Let $(D, F^*) \in Con_{\mathcal{DF}}$ and $V \subseteq Var$. Then $(D, F^*)\mid_V = (D_p, F_p^*)$ with $D_p = D \cap V$ and $F_p^* = \{S \in F^* \mid S \subseteq V\}$.

4 Approach 2 : the $\mathcal{F}^m$ abstraction

The freeness abstraction explicitly enumerates all possible dependencies between variables, even dependencies that can be obtained by combination (union) of others. The latter are called *non-minimal* dependencies. The abstract conjunction benefits from the explicit enumeration because it must consider all possible combinations. Also note that, although $\alpha_{\mathcal{F}}(\{C\})$ is closed under union, an abstract constraint system is not necessarily closed in general, e.g. the least upper bound operation can compute non-closed abstract systems. Having non-closed (exhaustive) abstract systems therefore contributes to the expressive power and precision of the analysis. However, the abstraction is quite space and time consuming. A way to reduce its size is to retain only minimal sets in the abstraction. If all abstract systems were closed under union, this could be done without loss of precision/expressivity.

Definition 4.1 (Minimal set)
Let $SS \in \wp(\wp_{\emptyset}(Var))$. Then $S \in SS$ is minimal in SS iff $\nexists S_1, \ldots, S_m \in SS \setminus \{S\}$ ($m \geq 2$) such that $S = S_1 \cup \ldots \cup S_m$.

Definition 4.2 (Minimal abstract constraint system)
Let $AC \in Con_{\mathcal{F}}$. Then AC is minimal iff $\forall S \in AC : S$ is minimal in AC.

Definition 4.3 ($\mathcal{F}^m$ abstraction)
Let $CS \in Con_{\mathcal{C}}$. Then $\alpha_{\mathcal{F}^m}(CS) = min(\alpha_{\mathcal{F}}(CS))$ with $min(SS) = \{S \in SS |$ S is a minimal set in $SS\}$.

Definition 4.4 ($\mathcal{F}^m$ abstract domain)
The abstract domain is $Con_{\mathcal{F}^m} = \{AC \in Con_{\mathcal{F}} \mid AC$ is minimal $\}$.

Given a constraint system C, it is not easy to compute minimal abstractions directly (without first computing $\alpha_{\mathcal{F}}(\{C\})$). However, in Definition 2.1 we have $\alpha_{\mathcal{F}}(\{C\}) = close(W)$; so only W has to be computed, i.e. $\alpha_{\mathcal{F}^m}(\{C\}) = min(W)$ (note: W is not necessarily minimal !). For a constraint system C consisting of only *one* constraint, $\alpha_{\mathcal{F}^m}(\{C\})$ can be computed directly as follows [3]:

1. $X = Y$ with X and Y being variables $\Rightarrow \alpha_{\mathcal{F}^m}(\{\{X = Y\}\}) = \{\{X, Y\}\}$;
2. $X = t$ with t a Herbrand term that is not a variable
   $\Rightarrow \alpha_{\mathcal{F}^m}(\{\{X = t\}\}) = \{\{X\}\} \cup \{\{X, Y\} \mid Y \in vars(t)\}$;
3. $a_1 X_1 + \ldots + a_n X_n\ OP\ b$ with $OP \in \{=, \neq, <, \leq\}$, $a_1, \ldots, a_n, b$ being numbers ($a_i \neq 0$ for i in $1..n$) and $X_1, \ldots, X_n$ variables
   $\Rightarrow \alpha_{\mathcal{F}^m}(\{\{a_1 X_1 + \ldots + a_n X_n\ OP\ b\}\}) = \{\{X_1, \ldots, X_n\}\}$.

Figure 2 illustrates the relation between the $\mathcal{F}$ and the $\mathcal{F}^m$ abstraction. Let $F \in Con_{\mathcal{F}}$, $F^m \in Con_{\mathcal{F}^m}$ and $F^m = min(F)$. Closing the $\mathcal{F}^m$ abstraction yields an upper approximation of the $\mathcal{F}$ abstraction, i.e. $F \leq_{\mathcal{F}} close(F^m)$.

The order relation $\leq_{\mathcal{F}^m}$ is defined in the same way as $\leq_{\mathcal{F}}$ (Definition 2.4). The least upper bound is defined as follows :

---

[3]Programs are assumed to be normalised, i.e. all constraints are of the form $X = Y$ or $X = t$ with $t \in T(\Sigma_A, Var)$ and t is not a variable (for unifications) or $a_1 X_1 + \ldots + a_n X_n\ OP\ b$ with $OP \in \{=, \neq, <, \leq\}$ (for numerical constraints).

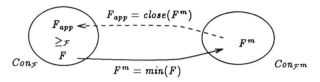

Figure 2: Relation between $\mathcal{F}$ and $\mathcal{F}^m$ abstraction

Definition 4.5 (Least upper bound)
Let $AC_1, AC_2 \in Con_{\mathcal{F}^m}$. $lub_{\mathcal{F}^m}(AC_1, AC_2) = min(lub_{\mathcal{F}}(AC_1, AC_2))$.

Proposition 4.1 (Mode inference)
Let $AC \in Con_{\mathcal{F}^m}$ and $CS \in Con_C$ such that $\alpha_{\mathcal{F}^m}(CS) \leq_{\mathcal{F}^m} AC$. Then $\{X\} \notin AC$ implies that X is free in CS (mode **f**); otherwise X is possibly non-free (mode **a**).

Definition 4.6 (Abstract conjunction)
Let $AC_1, AC_2 \in Con_{\mathcal{F}^m}$. The abstract conjunction $AC_1 \wedge_{\mathcal{F}^m} AC_2$ is defined as $AC_1 \wedge_{\mathcal{F}^m} AC_2 = min(close(AC_1) \wedge_{\mathcal{F}} close(AC_2))$.

This is a straightforward definition. An equivalent and efficient algorithm is obtained by closing only the necessary parts of AC_1 and AC_2 (i.e. those parts containing common variables) and by taking care of not generating non-minimal sets when combining the two.

The abstract projection is defined as in Definition 2.6.

5 Combination: the $\mathcal{DF}^m$ abstraction

The approaches 1 and 2 are orthogonal, so they can be combined. Starting from the original freeness abstraction, the minimal $\mathcal{F}^m$ abstraction is computed in the direct way mentioned in the previous section. Then the definite part (at that point a set of singletons of definite variables due to minimisation) is split off. Note that the first step may cause some loss of precision but this does not affect the definite part.

Definition 5.1 ($\mathcal{DF}^m$ abstraction)
Let $CS \in Con_C$. Then $\alpha_{\mathcal{DF}^m}(CS) = (D, F^{*m})$ where $D = defvars(\alpha_D(CS))$ and $F^{*m} = compl(D, \alpha_{\mathcal{F}^m}(CS))$.

Definition 5.2 ($\mathcal{DF}^m$ abstract domain)
The abstract domain is $Con_{\mathcal{DF}^m} = \{(D, F^{*m}) \mid D \in \wp(Var),\ F^{*m} \in \wp(\wp_\emptyset(Var \setminus D)),\ F^{*m}\ is\ minimal\}$.

The $\mathcal{DF}^m$ abstraction is more compact than the $\mathcal{DF}$ or $\mathcal{F}^m$ abstraction. Figure 3 illustrates the relations between the different abstractions. The $extend_m$ operation is used to go from a $\mathcal{DF}^m$ abstraction to a $\mathcal{F}^m$ abstraction.

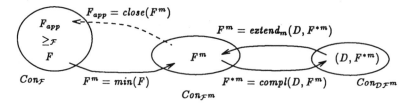

Figure 3: Relation between $\mathcal{F}$, $\mathcal{F}^m$ and $\mathcal{DF}^m$ abstraction

Definition 5.3 (extend$_m$)
Let $(D, F^{*m}) \in Con_{\mathcal{DF}^m}$. Then $extend_m(D, F^{*m}) = F^{*m} \cup \{\{X\} \mid X \in D\}$.

Definition 5.4 (Order relation and least upper bound)
Let $(D_1, F_1^{*m}), (D_2, F_2^{*m}) \in Con_{\mathcal{DF}^m}$. Then
- $(D_1, F_1^{*m}) \leq_{\mathcal{DF}^m} (D_2, F_2^{*m})$ iff $D_1 \supseteq D_2$ and $extend_m(D_1 \setminus D_2, F_1^{*m}) \subseteq F_2^{*m}$;
- $lub_{\mathcal{DF}^m}((D_1, F_1^{*m}), (D_2, F_2^{*m})) = (D, F^{*m})$ with $D = D_1 \cap D_2$ and $F^{*m} = min(extend_m(D_1 \setminus (D_1 \cap D_2), F_1^{*m}) \cup extend_m(D_2 \setminus (D_1 \cap D_2), F_2^{*m}))) = min(F_1^{*m} \cup F_2^{*m} \cup \{\{X\} \mid X \in (D_1 \cup D_2) \setminus (D_1 \cap D_2)\})$.

Proposition 5.1 (Mode inference)
Let $CS \in Con_{\mathcal{C}}$ and $(D, F^{*m}) \in Con_{\mathcal{DF}^m}$ with $\alpha_{\mathcal{DF}^m}(CS) \leq_{\mathcal{DF}^m} (D, F^{*m})$. If $X \in D$, then X is a definite variable in CS (mode **d**), else if $\{X\} \notin F^{*m}$ then X is a free variable in CS (mode **f**). Otherwise nothing can be said about X (mode **a**).

The operations on the $\mathcal{DF}^m$ abstractions are defined in terms of the operations on its D and F^{*m} components.

Definition 5.5 (Minimal abstract conjunction w.r.t. D)
Let $F_1^{*m}, F_2^{*m} \in \wp(\wp(Var) \setminus \{\emptyset\})$ and $D \in \wp(Var)$. The minimal abstract conjunction of F_1^{*m} and F_2^{*m} with respect to D, denoted $F_1^{*m} \mathbb{\Lambda}_m F_2^{*m}$, is defined as $F_1^{*m} \mathbb{\Lambda}_m F_2^{*m} = reduce_m(D, F_1^{*m}) \Lambda_{\mathcal{F}^m} reduce_m(D, F_2^{*m})$ where $reduce_m(D, F^{*m}) = min(\{S \setminus D \mid S \in F^{*m}\}) \setminus \{\emptyset\}$.

Definition 5.6 (Abstract conjunction)
Let $(D_1, F_1^{*m}), (D_2, F_2^{*m}) \in Con_{\mathcal{DF}^m}$. Then $(D_1, F_1^{*m}) \Lambda_{\mathcal{DF}^m} (D_2, F_2^{*m}) = (D, F^{*m})$ where D is obtained using the abstract conjunction on $Con_{\mathcal{D}}$ [7] and $F^* = F_1^{*m} \mathbb{\Lambda}_m F_2^{*m}$.

The abstract projection operation is defined as in Definition 3.7.

Example 5.1
We show the results of the $\mathcal{DF}^m$ analysis for the sumlist program. The initial call pattern is sumlist($\mathbf{d}, \mathbf{f}$), which is also the call pattern of the recursive call. The definiteness information is as in [7]; we obtain the same freeness information as in Example 2.2 but in a much more compact form.

$sumlist(L,S)$:-   % $(\{L\}, \emptyset)$
  { $L = [\,]$,   % $(\{L\}, \emptyset)$
    $S = 0$ }.   % $(\{L, S\}, \emptyset)$
$sumlist(L,S)$:-   % $(\{L\}, \emptyset)$
  { $L = [H \mid T]$,   % $(\{L, H, T\}, \emptyset)$
    $S = H + S'$ },   % $(\{L, H, T\}, \{\{S, S'\}\})$
    $sumlist(T, S')$.   % $(\{L, S, H, T, S'\}, \emptyset)$

6 Implementation results

The definiteness as well as the original freeness analysis and the different optimisations are implemented within the abstract interpretation system PLAI of Muthukumar and Hermenegildo [14, 15] (which is based on the abstract interpretation framework of Bruynooghe [1]). The system is written in SICStus Prolog. For the $\mathcal{DF}$ and $\mathcal{DF}^m$ abstractions, the definiteness analyser and the optimised freeness analyser run interleaved : the definiteness analysis is performed first at each program point, yielding the set of definite variables needed by the optimised freeness analysis.

Program	Cls	Var	Description
sumlist	2	7	computes the sum of a list of numbers
listlength	2	7	computes the length of a list
mortgage	2	12	well-known mortgage
laplace	4	36	solves Dirichlet problem for Laplace's equation [10]
runkut	5	45	differential equation solver (runge-kutta method)
trapezoid	5	50	differential equation solver (trapezoid method)
sendmm	8	26	send+more=money puzzle
rectangle	10	55	filling a rectangle with squares [4]
meal	11	26	meal program [4]
vec-mat	15	77	vector and matrix addition and multiplication
dnf	32	133	puts propositional formula in disjunctive normal form
power	43	204	minimises the production cost of power stations
mining	52	241	optimises the revenue of a mine
num	97	382	number to letters-phonems translation

Table 1: Benchmark programs

The different analysers have been run on a set of benchmarks listed in Table 1, which indicates also the number of clauses and the total number of variables (sum of the number of variables in the clauses). Table 2 shows the timings obtained on a SUN Sparc 2 (SICStus 2.1, fastcode) for the different abstractions; "OOM" stands for "Out Of Memory".

The speed of the analysers is compared in Table 3. Each figure gives the percentage of time taken by an optimised analysis with respect to the weaker analysis it is compared to; "Inf" indicates that the optimised analysis is definitely better than the weaker one, since the latter did not give a result. Columns 1 and 2 consider the improvement of the $\mathcal{DF}$ abstraction (i.e. split-

Program	Analysis times (seconds)				
	$\mathcal{F}$	$\mathcal{D}$	$\mathcal{DF}$	$\mathcal{F}^m$	$\mathcal{DF}^m$
sumlist	0.070	0.030	0.040	0.040	0.039
listlength	0.060	0.030	0.039	0.040	0.039
mortgage	13.559	0.040	0.109	0.070	0.070
laplace	OOM	0.090	0.120	205.418	0.120
runkut	OOM	0.120	0.969	0.400	0.210
trapezoid	OOM	5.608	OOM	0.530	6.089
sendmm	71.759	28.909	98.798	10.759	37.978
rectangle	343.529	9.569	594.028	1.449	10.409
meal	0.219	0.100	0.150	0.130	0.130
vec-mat	405.569	0.260	0.420	0.620	0.380
dnf	126.439	0.480	1.159	2.209	1.110
power	OOM	2.238	OOM	18.529	5.739
mining	OOM	2.298	OOM	78.859	140.389
num	51.789	10.289	15.119	11.189	11.329

Table 2: Timings of the $\mathcal{F}$, $\mathcal{D}$, $\mathcal{DF}$, $\mathcal{F}^m$ and $\mathcal{DF}^m$ analysers

ting off the definite part from the original freeness abstraction), first with respect to the freeness part only and secondly with respect to the total mode analysis. Column 3 indicates the effect of minimisation on the freeness analysis. Columns 4 and 5 resp. show the extra improvement of splitting off the definite part with respect to the minimised freeness part, and of minimising the freeness part after splitting off the definite part. Columns 6 and 7 indicate the total improvement obtained by the $\mathcal{DF}^m$ abstraction (which combines the optimisations) over the freeness part only and over the total mode analysis.

The figures show that the presented optimisations yield a substantial speed-up and result in a practical mode analysis system. A more careful look allows to distinguish different classes of inputs (i.e. programs and associated call patterns). For inputs that from the start give rise to a lot of definite variables and related dependencies (e.g. sumlist, laplace, vec-mat, dnf), especially the first approach pays off, i.e. splitting off the definite part and thereby almost completely reducing the freeness part. Other inputs (e.g. trapezoid, sendmm, rectangle, power, mining) do not allow to infer much definite information or infer it only towards the end of the program; they establish large sets of possible dependencies. In that case, the minimising approach ($\mathcal{F}^m$) is the effective one. For any input, combining the optimisations results in an efficient analysis compared to separately running the definiteness and freeness analyser (cf. Column 7) : the speed-up is at least 57 %. Only the result for mining in Column 4 (concerning the $\mathcal{DF}^m$ abstraction) and the results for rectangle in Columns 1 and 2 (concerning the $\mathcal{DF}$ abstraction) need some further explanation. In those cases, the definiteness analysis performs more iterations before reaching its fixpoint than the freeness analysis. When combining the two, the $\mathcal{DF}$ or $\mathcal{DF}^m$ analysis

Program	Speed ratios						
	$\frac{D\mathcal{F}-D}{\mathcal{F}}$	$\frac{D\mathcal{F}}{\mathcal{F}+D}$	$\frac{\mathcal{F}^m}{\mathcal{F}}$	$\frac{D\mathcal{F}^m-D}{\mathcal{F}^m}$	$\frac{D\mathcal{F}^m}{D\mathcal{F}}$	$\frac{D\mathcal{F}^m-D}{\mathcal{F}}$	$\frac{D\mathcal{F}^m}{\mathcal{F}+D}$
sumlist	0.1429	0.4000	0.5714	0.2250	0.9750	0.1286	0.3900
listlength	0.1500	0.4333	0.6667	0.2250	1.0000	0.1500	0.4333
mortgage	0.0052	0.0081	0.0052	0.4286	0.6422	0.0022	0.0052
laplace	Inf	Inf	Inf	0.0001	1.0000	Inf	Inf
runkut	Inf	Inf	Inf	0.2250	0.2167	Inf	Inf
trapezoid	1.0000	1.0000	Inf	0.9075	Inf	Inf	Inf
sendmm	0.9739	0.9814	0.1499	0.8429	0.3844	0.1264	0.3773
rectangle	1.7013	1.6823	0.0042	0.5797	0.0175	0.0024	0.0295
meal	0.2238	0.4702	0.5936	0.2308	0.8667	0.1370	0.4075
vec-mat	0.0004	0.0010	0.0015	0.1935	0.9048	0.0003	0.0009
dnf	0.0054	0.0091	0.0175	0.2852	0.9577	0.0050	0.0087
power	1.0000	1.0000	Inf	0.1889	Inf	Inf	Inf
mining	1.0000	1.0000	Inf	1.7511	Inf	Inf	Inf
num	0.0933	0.2435	0.2160	0.0929	0.7493	0.0201	0.1825

Table 3: Comparison of the speed of the analysers

has to perform at least as many iterations as the definiteness analysis, however now not only computing the definite part but also taking into account the (reduced) freeness part. If the latter is still quite large after splitting off the definite information, the overhead of the extra iterations outweighs the effect of reducing the freeness part.

For most inputs, the analysers derive precise information. For the given benchmarks, the $\mathcal{F}^m$ and $D\mathcal{F}^m$ abstractions derive the same freeness information as the $\mathcal{F}$ and $D\mathcal{F}$ abstractions (it is only represented in a more compact form); so no information is lost there by minimising the abstract constraint systems. The reason is that in these programs (in fact, this can be generalised to most "real" programs) the same dependencies are created in all clauses defining a predicate. However, precision can still be improved with respect to the treatment of non-linear numerical constraints (now abstracted by taking the powerset of the variables occurring in the constraint).

7 Conclusion and related work

Starting from an existing freeness abstraction for CLP programs [8], we have presented two orthogonal approaches for space/time optimisation. The first one uses definiteness information [7] to obtain more compact abstract constraint systems, while maintaining the precision of the original freeness abstraction. Moreover, it leads to a *full* mode inference system (deriving modes **d**, **f** and **a**); to our knowledge, this is the first full mode system for CLP. The second approach allows to compress the abstract system by keeping track only of the minimal information, from which the rest can be reconstructed. This compaction may cause some loss of precision (although this is not the case for all of the benchmarks that have been considered so far). Combining the two approaches results in an efficient and practical mode inference system, as shown by the benchmark timings. The obtained information is precise for most programs occurring in practice.

The paper [5] describes an approach for combining domains (applied in [2]) that does not change the abstractions and keeps the original components of the basic operations. During analysis, interactions occur to refine the abstractions. This results in a precise combined analysis, in particular when the analyses being composed contain a sufficient degree of "overlapping" information. Our approach is different in the sense that the freeness abstraction is redefined in terms of the D and F^* components, yielding a more efficient but equivalent freeness abstraction. The D component is an integral part of the $\mathcal{DF}$ abstraction. For the $\mathcal{DF}$ abstraction, new definitions have to be given in terms of the D and F^* components. However, it is possible to retain important basic operations such as $\Lambda_{\mathcal{F}}$.

Further work consists of improving the abstraction of disequations and inequalities and of non-linear constraints. One issue is to deal with the delay of non-linear constraints in practical CLP systems. In [9], a method is described to detect whether non-linear constraints *eventually* become linear, based on definiteness information (closely related to the definiteness analysis of [7]). For our freeness analysis, dealing with *possible* dependencies, it is necessary to detect when exactly non-linear constraints may *possibly* wake up, based on possible non-freeness information. Once a non-linear constraint may have become linear, it has to be abstracted in the appropriate way. The following example shows that this is not an easy problem. Consider the non-linear constraint $X - X * Y + T = 0$. If Y obtains a value, the non-linear constraint is reduced to a linear one. However, depending on the value of Y, different cases may occur: $X + T = 0$ if $Y = 0$, $T = 0$ if $Y = 1$ or $X - c * X + T = 0$ if $Y = c$ (with $c \neq (0 \text{ or } 1)$). The abstraction should cover each of these cases. Having more precise information on the set of possible values of variables, which could e.g. be derived by the abstraction proposed in [11], could lead to the elimination of some cases.

Acknowledgements

The authors are greatly indebted to M. García de la Banda and the other members of the PLAI team (U.P.Madrid) for providing a generic version of the PLAI system and the definiteness analyser in PLAI, and for the collaboration in integrating the definiteness and freeness analyser. They would also like to thank W. Simoens (K.U.Leuven) who implemented most of the $\mathcal{DF}$ and $\mathcal{DF}^m$ abstractions. This work was supported by the ESPRIT project 5246 PRINCE and also by the Belgian National Fund for Scientific Research of which the second author is a post-doctoral researcher.

References

[1] M. Bruynooghe. A practical framework for the abstract interpretation of logic programs. *Journal of Logic Programming*, 10(2):91–124, Feb. 1991.

[2] M. Codish, A. Mulkers, M. Bruynooghe, M. García de la Banda, and M. Hermenegildo. Improving abstract interpretations by combining domains. In *Proceedings of the ACM Symposium on Partial Evaluation and Semantics-Based Program Manipulation*, pages 194–205, Copenhagen, June 1993.

[3] J. Cohen. Constraint logic programming languages. *Communications of the ACM*, 30(7):52–68, 1990.

[4] A. Colmerauer. An introduction to PROLOGIII. *Communications of the ACM*, 30(7):69–96, 1990.

[5] P. Cousot and R. Cousot. Systematic design of program analysis frameworks. In *Proceedings 6th ACM Symposium on Principles of Programming Languages*, pages 269–282, San Antonio, Texas, 1979.

[6] P. Cousot and R. Cousot. Abstract interpretation and application to logic programs. *Journal of Logic Programming*, 13(2&3):103–179, 1992.

[7] M. G. de la Banda and M. Hermenegildo. A Practical Approach to the Global Analysis of CLP Programs. In D. Miller, editor, *Proceedings of the 1993 International Logic Programming Symposium*, pages 437–455. MIT Press, October 1993.

[8] V. Dumortier, G. Janssens, M. Bruynooghe, and M. Codish. Freeness analysis in the presence of numerical constraints. In D. S. Warren, editor, *Proceedings of the Tenth International Conference on Logic Programming*, pages 100–115. MIT Press, June 1993.

[9] M. Hanus. Analysis of nonlinear constraints in CLP(R). In D. S. Warren, editor, *Proceedings of the Tenth International Conference on Logic Programming*, pages 83–99. MIT Press, June 1993.

[10] J. Jaffar and J.-L. Lassez. Constraint logic programming. In *Proceedings of the Fourteenth ACM symposium of the principles of programming languages*, pages 111–119, Munich, 1987.

[11] G. Janssens, M. Bruynooghe, and V. Englebert. Abstracting numerical values in CLP(H,N). Technical Report CW189, Department of Computer Science, Katholieke Universiteit Leuven, Mar. 1994.

[12] J.-L. Lassez, M. Maher, and K. Marriott. Unification revisited. In J. Minker, editor, *Foundations of Deductive Databases and Logic Programming*, pages 587–625. Morgan Kaufmann, Los Altos, Ca., 1988.

[13] J.-L. Lassez and K. McAloon. A canonical form for generalised linear constraints. *Journal of Symbolic Computation*, 13(1):1–24, Jan. 1992.

[14] K. Muthukumar and M. Hermenegildo. Deriving A Fixpoint Computation Algorithm for Top-down Abstract Interpretation of Logic Programs. Technical Report ACT-DC-153-90, Microelectronics and Computer Technology Corporation (MCC), Austin, TX 78759, Apr. 1990.

[15] K. Muthukumar and M. Hermenegildo. Compile-time Derivation of Variable Dependency Using Abstract Interpretation. *Journal of Logic Programming*, 13(2&3):315–347, July 1992.

A proof method for run–time properties of Prolog programs

Dino Pedreschi
Dipartimento di Informatica
Università di Pisa
Corso Italia 40
56125 Pisa, Italy
pedre@di.unipi.it

Abstract

We propose a notion of correctness with respect to types for pure Prolog programs, which naturally combines types and directionalities. On this basis, we develop a simple method for proving various run–time properties of pure Prolog programs. These include analysis of generalized directionalities, verification of absence of errors in programs extended with arithmetic built–in's, and absence of floundering in programs with negation. The method is illustrated on a number of realistic programs, including some operating on incomplete data structures. An adaptation of the method to logic programming is also provided.

1 Motivations

Types and type systems were introduced in programming languages with the aim of statically checking some relevant run–time properties of programs. From one side, well–typed programs do not incur, at run–time, errors of a certain class: quoting [18], such programs "do not go wrong." Absence of type errors at run–time offers both a computational advantage (there is no need to check for those errors during execution), and a programming advantage (the developer can concentrate on the other errors.) On the other side, types are used to describe the input/output behavior of a program, i.e., the shape of admissible inputs, and that of possible outputs. Input/output type information is essential in large–scale programming, as it supports all stages of program development.

A crucial issue in designing a type system is to identify the class of intended types and type errors. Of course, a whole spectrum of possibilities exists, ranging from poor to highly expressive type systems, as well as a trade–off between expressiveness and the possibility of designing fully automated type–checkers. In the case of imperative and functional programming paradigms, however, a certain consensus was achieved, and a mature type–checking technology is now available.

The situation is more controversial in the case of the logic programming paradigm. Logic and Prolog programs operate on *incomplete* (or *partial*) data structures, due to the presence of logic variables, whereas imperative and functional programs operate on *ground* data structures. For this reason, a new form of errors may occur, due to the fact that data values are not sufficiently instantiated when certain control points are reached. Examples of sources of this phenomenon are the arithmetic built–in's of Prolog (which end in an error if some of their arguments are not ground expressions), and the use of negation–as–failure (a floundering error occurs if a negative non–ground literal is selected.) From the point of view of input/output behavior, the phenomenon of *non–ground output* arises: logic programs may deliver incomplete data structures as a result. Several realistic programs fall in this class, including most of programs studied in this paper, and many of the programs advertised as logic programming jewels.

Several proposals of type systems for logic programs are based on systems developed for imperative or functional programs, and share with the latter the view that types are sets of *ground* terms. Proposals in this class are in the chapters by Hill and Topor, Yardeni et al., and Hanus in [19]. The logic language Gödel is equipped with a type–checker of this kind [14]. A problem then arises. In an imperative or functional well–typed program, any call to a procedure with well–typed input does not incur run–time type errors. By adopting such a type system for logic programs, we can only conclude that the *ground* well–typed derivations are free of type errors, whereas the queries of interest are generally non–ground. For the same reason, we cannot appropriately describe non–ground output.

Starting from the above observations, a large body of research focused on issues like *directionalities* (or *modes*), and several methods and tools were proposed to check various run–time properties [16, 12, 4, 11]. Often, the technique of abstract interpretation was adopted [9, 17]. Until recently, though, the cited research provided ad–hoc solutions to separate problems, and no serious attempt was made to identify the unifying principles of a comprehensive type system, capable of addressing the various relevant run–time properties. Notable exceptions are the proposal in [8], which combines types and directionalities, and its generalization reported, for instance, in [3]. Other methods are based on *assertions* instead of types, such as [7]. An account of the cited methods based on modes, types and assertions is [4].

This paper tries to make another step forward in this direction, by proposing a simple proof method for reasoning about run–time properties, capable of addressing "conventional" types, incomplete data structures, and directionality. We build over the approach in [3, 4], where types are sets of terms closed under substitution. A problem with this approach is that incomplete data structures are not closed under arbitrary substitution (see, e.g., partial lists, or difference lists.) In this paper, we propose, in a more liberal way, that types are sets of *atoms*, with a weak form of closure under substitution. On the basis of this principle, we build a notion of *directional types* and *well–typed queries and programs* which reveals useful in proving absence of run–time errors, and reasoning about a general form of input/output directionalities. Some classical programs from Sterling and Shapiro's book [20] are properly dealt with, from both points of view. Some applications cannot be handled using the other proposals, such as the dictionary look–up program, or the Curry program. In all cases, we provide types which accurately describe the shape of queries and their computed instances.

Similarly to [3, 4], we do not fix a specific type definition language. We rather try to put on the introduced notions the least burden of requirements needed to achieve the desired result, namely that types *persist* during the evaluation process. From the persistence property we are then able to derive a method for proving the desired run–time properties. Although the method is developed for pure Prolog and its extensions with arithmetic and negation, it is immediate to modify it into a method for logic programming (and its extensions with arithmetic and negation.)

Compared to the assertional methods surveyed in [4], ours is halfway between the methods adopting *monotonic* assertions (i.e., those invariant under substitution), such as [7], and those adopting *non monotonic* assertions, such as [13] and [10]. In fact, the types adopted here are more general than monotonic assertions, and more specific than non monotonic assertions (e.g., the built–in var/1 of Prolog cannot be handled.) Our method is an attempt at combining, as far as possible, the simplicity of monotonic assertions with the expressiveness of non monotonic assertions.

1.1 Preliminaries

We adopt here *queries*, i.e. sequences of atoms, instead of goals. We call an atom a *p-atom* if its relation symbol is p. Next, we denote by $rel(A)$ the relation symbol occurring in atom A. So an atom A is a $rel(A)$-atom. Given two atoms A and B which unify with m.g.u. ϑ, the *most general instance* of A and B, denoted $mgi(A, B)$ is $A\vartheta$ (or, equivalently, $B\vartheta$.) Given a substitution ϑ and a sequence of atoms $\mathbf{A}$, $(\vartheta \mid \mathbf{A})$ denotes the restriction of ϑ to the variables of $\mathbf{A}$. We refer to SLD–resolution with the leftmost selection rule of Prolog as LD–resolution. Two extensions of pure Prolog are considered: arithmetic, and negation. In the latter case, LD–resolution is extended with the negation–as–failure rule, denoted LDNF–resolution. Apart from this, we use the standard notation of [15] and [1].

2 Types

To the purpose of this paper, a type is a set of atoms.

Definition 2.1 A *type* for a relation symbol p is a set of p-atoms. A *type* is a type for some relation symbol. □

The following limited forms of closure under substitution will be useful.

Definition 2.2

- We say that a type T is *weakly closed w.r.t. a type* S if, for any atoms A, B such that $B \in T$, and for any substitution ϑ, if $A\vartheta \in S$ then $B(\vartheta \mid A) \in T$.

- We say that a type T is *unification closed w.r.t. an atom* H if, for every $A \in T$, if C is an mgi of A and H, then $C \in T$. □

In what follows we do *not* assume that types for relation symbols are closed under substitution. However, we shall need to make the following:

Assumption. *All considered types are pairwise weakly closed.*

Informally, this assumption reflects the natural requirement that, if the variables of an atom A can be instantiated in such a way to bring A into a type, then the same variables can be consistently instantiated in the same way wherever they occur, preserving types. In other words, the property of weak closure models abstractly the fact that variables are *typed*: as in a conventional typed language, variables are bound to compatible terms. The role of the notion of being unification closed will be clarified later.

In most applications, types for relations are constructed by suitably combining sets of terms. Therefore, we overload the term *type* to denote either a set of atoms or a set of terms, the actual meaning being clear from the context. Although we do not commit ourselves to any specific type definition language, certain types will be of special interest in the applications presented in this paper. The following types of lists and partial (or incomplete) lists are often used.

Given a set of terms E, the type $List(E)$ of *lists* of elements from E can be inductively defined as follows:

$$[\,] \in List(E), \quad \text{and} \quad [x \mid xs] \in List(E) \; \Leftarrow \; x \in E \; \wedge \; xs \in List(E).$$

For instance, define: $T = \{\ app(xs, ys, zs) \mid xs, ys, zs \in List(E)\ \}$. Then T is a type for *app* and, for instance, $app([\ ], [\ ], [\ ]) \in T$. Also, we have that T is unification closed w.r.t. $app([\ ], Xs, Xs)$, although $app([\ ], Xs, Xs) \notin T$.

The type $PList(E)$ of *partial* lists of elements from E can be inductively defined as follows, with reference to a specific set V of variables:

$$[\ ] \in PList(E)$$
$$X \in PList(E) \qquad \text{where } X \text{ is a variable from } V$$
$$[x \mid xs] \in PList(E) \quad \Leftarrow \quad x \in E \ \wedge \ xs \in PList(E)$$

To comply with the requirement of weak closure, we assume that any variable from V occurs only at the end of a partial list in all (the atoms of) the types used in this paper. For instance, define: $T' = \{\ app(xs, ys, zs) \mid xs, ys, zs \in PList(E)\ \}$. Then T' is also a type for *app*. Also, we have $app([\ ], Xs, Xs) \in T'$.

Observe that the type $PList(E)$ is not closed under arbitrary substitution. Other examples of this kind include the difference lists (see Example 4.3), the data structure representing polymorphic types for functional programs (see Example 5.4).

We now introduce the other basic notion of our method.

Definition 2.3 Given atoms $A_1, \ldots, A_n, A_{n+1}$ and types $T_1, \ldots, T_n, T_{n+1}$, where $n \geq 0$, we write

$$\models A_1 \in T_1, \ldots, A_n \in T_n \ \Rightarrow \ A_{n+1} \in T_{n+1}$$

to denote the fact that for all substitutions ϑ:

$$\text{if } A_1\vartheta \in T_1, \ldots, A_n\vartheta \in T_n, \quad \text{then } A_{n+1}(\vartheta \mid A_1, \ldots, A_n) \in T_{n+1}. \qquad \square$$

A construct of the form $A_1 \in T_1, \ldots, A_n \in T_n \ \Rightarrow \ A_{n+1} \in T_{n+1}$ is called a *type judgement* in [4]. Type judgements represent conditional type membership. Observe that the premise of a type judgement plays the role of an *environment* in the type systems for λ–calculus or functional languages. The above definition generalizes the concept of a type judgement in [4], as we consider only substitutions that bind no variables in the conclusion, which do not occur in the premise. Differently from [4], in our framework a type judgement with an empty premise coincides with type membership, that is: $\models true \Rightarrow A \in T$ iff $A \in T$. The following Lemma points out the transitivity property of type judgements, which will play an important role later. Observe that such property is not trivial, as types are not closed under arbitrary substitution.

Lemma 2.4 (Transitivity) *Assume, for $n \geq m \geq 0$:*

$$\models B_1 \in T_1, \ldots, B_m \in T_m \ \Rightarrow \ A \in T, \tag{i}$$

$$\models A \in T, B_{m+1} \in T_{m+1}, \ldots, B_n \in T_n \ \Rightarrow \ C \in T'. \tag{ii}$$

Then

$$\models B_1 \in T_1, \ldots, B_n \in T_n \ \Rightarrow \ C \in T'.$$

Proof. Let ϑ be a substitution, and assume:

$$B_1\vartheta \in T_1, \ldots, B_n\vartheta \in T_n. \tag{a}$$

By (i) and Definition 2.3 we obtain:

$$A(\vartheta \mid B_1, \ldots, B_m) \in T. \tag{b}$$

By the weak closure property and the fact (b), we have, for $j \in [m+1, n]$:

$$B_j \vartheta \in T_j \;\Rightarrow\; A(\vartheta \mid B_1, \ldots, B_m)(\vartheta \mid B_j) \in T$$

which implies:

$$A(\vartheta \mid B_1, \ldots, B_n) \in T. \qquad\qquad (c)$$

Finally, we obtain:

$$C(\vartheta \mid B_1, \ldots, B_n) \in T$$

from (ii), (a) and (c), since $((\vartheta \mid B_1, \ldots, B_n) \mid A, B_1, \ldots, B_n) = (\vartheta \mid B_1, \ldots, B_n)$. $\square$

In this paper, we deliberately abstract from any specific language for defining types, as well as from a proof theory for type judgements, as these issues are immaterial to the purpose of this presentation. However, in order to achieve a fully automated implementation of the method presented in this paper, it is needed that the problem of proving the truth of a type judgement is decidable. In fact, this is also a sufficient condition for automating the method, as all the other notions presented in the paper are derived from type judgements in a constructive way.

3 Directional types and Prolog

In conventional languages, procedures are assigned a single (perhaps polymorphic) type. Associating a single type to the relations of a logic program is not sufficient for dealing with a large class of run–time properties. This is due to the fact that a single type cannot take into account how the query variables become more instantiated in the computed instances.

Therefore, we associate with relations *directional types*.

Definition 3.1 A *directional type* for a relation symbol p is a pair pre_p, $post_p$ of types for p. We call pre_p (resp. $post_p$) a *pre-type* (resp. a *post-type*) associated with p. $\qquad\qquad \square$

In this section we introduce a notion of well–typed queries and program, with reference to directional types. In designing this notion, we were driven by the following intuition. Assume that, with reference to specified directional types, the program P and (for simplicity) the atomic query A are well–typed. Then A belongs to $pre_{rel(A)}$, and all computed instances of A belong to $post_{rel(A)}$. We refer here to pure Prolog queries and programs, although later an adaptation to logic programs will be discussed.

We now abbreviate $A \in pre_{rel(A)}$ to $\models pre(A)$ and analogously for *post*. We say that an atom A *has its pre-type* if $\models pre(A)$, and analogously for *post*. Observe that, according to this notation, we have: $\models pre(A)$ iff $\models true \Rightarrow pre(A)$.

Definition 3.2

- A query $A_1, \ldots, A_n$ is called *well–typed* if for $j \in [1, n]$

$$\models post(A_1), \ldots, post(A_{j-1}) \;\Rightarrow\; pre(A_j).$$

- A clause $H \leftarrow B_1, \ldots, B_n$ is called *well–typed* if

  $-\ pre_{rel(H)}$ is unification closed w.r.t. H,

– for $j \in [1, n+1]$

$$\models pre(H), post(B_1), \ldots, post(B_{j-1}) \Rightarrow pre(B_j),$$

where $pre(B_{n+1}) := post(H)$.

- A program is called *well–typed* if every clause of it is. □

The above definition generalizes that of a well–typed query and clause in [3], that of a well–moded query and clause in [8], and that of well–asserted query and clause in [7]. Observe that an atomic query A is well–typed iff $\models pre(A)$.

The following result motivates the introduction of the previous notions. It shows that being well–typed is a property that persists during the process of LD–resolution. The method presented in this paper was developed on the basis of this result.

Lemma 3.3 (Persistence) *An LD-resolvent of a well–typed query and a well–typed clause that is variable disjoint with it, is well–typed.*

Proof. Let $A, \mathbf{B}$ be a well–typed query, $H \leftarrow \mathbf{C}$ be a well–typed, and $\vartheta = mgu(A, H)$. We now prove that $(\mathbf{C}, \mathbf{B})\vartheta$ is well–typed.

Let $\mathbf{C} = C_1, \ldots, C_m$. A is the leftmost atom af a well–typed query, so it satisfies

$$\models pre(A)$$

which implies

$$\models pre(H\vartheta) \qquad\qquad (i)$$

as $pre_{rel(H)}$ is unification closed w.r.t. H, and $A\vartheta = H\vartheta$. $H \leftarrow \mathbf{C}$ is well–typed, so

$$\models pre(H), post(C_1), \ldots, post(C_m) \Rightarrow post(H)$$

and, for $j \in [1, m]$:

$$\models pre(H), post(C_1), \ldots, post(C_{j-1}) \Rightarrow pre(C_j).$$

Since ϑ is an mgu of A and H, we have $dom(\vartheta) \subseteq vars(A) \cup vars(H)$; therefore, by Definition 2.3, we obtain:

$$\models pre(H\vartheta), post(C_1\vartheta), \ldots, post(C_m\vartheta) \Rightarrow post(H\vartheta)$$

and, for $j \in [1, m]$:

$$\models pre(H\vartheta), post(C_1\vartheta), \ldots, post(C_{j-1}\vartheta) \Rightarrow pre(C_j\vartheta).$$

By (i) and Transitivity Lemma 2.4, we obtain

$$\models post(C_1\vartheta), \ldots, post(C_m\vartheta) \Rightarrow post(H\vartheta) \qquad\qquad (ii)$$

and, for $j \in [1, m]$:

$$\models post(C_1\vartheta), \ldots, post(C_{j-1}\vartheta) \Rightarrow pre(C_j\vartheta). \qquad\qquad (iii)$$

Now, let $\mathbf{B} = C_{m+1}, \ldots, C_n$. $A, \mathbf{B}$ is well–typed, so, for $j \in [m+1, n]$:

$$\models post(A), post(C_{m+1}), \ldots, post(C_{j-1}) \Rightarrow pre(C_j).$$

Again, $dom(\vartheta) \subseteq vars(A) \cup vars(H)$, so, by Definition 2.3, we obtain:

$$\models post(A\vartheta), post(C_{m+1}\vartheta), \ldots, post(C_{j-1}\vartheta) \Rightarrow pre(C_j\vartheta)$$

which, together with (ii), implies by the Transitivity Lemma 2.4 that, for $j \in [m+1, n]$:

$$\models post(C_1\vartheta), \ldots, post(C_{j-1}\vartheta) \Rightarrow pre(C_j\vartheta)$$

as $A\vartheta = H\vartheta$. This and (iii) imply the thesis. □

As a direct consequence of Lemma 3.3 we obtain that, in any LD-derivation from a well–typed query, all selected atoms have their pre–types. This is stated by the following corollary, which will provide the basis for proving absence of run–time errors.

Corollary 3.4 (Pre–type) *Let P and Q be well–typed, and let ξ be an LD-derivation of $P \cup \{Q\}$. Then $\models pre(A)$ for every atom A selected in ξ.* □

As another consequence of Lemma 3.3 we obtain that the computed instances of well–typed queries are are formed by atoms which have their post–types. This is stated by the following corollary, which is the main tool for reasoning about input/output directionalities.

Corollary 3.5 (Post–type) *Let P and Q be well–typed, and let Q' be a computed instance of Q. Then $\models post(A)$ for every atom A in Q'.*

Proof. Let $Q = p_1(\mathbf{t}_1), \ldots, p_k(\mathbf{t}_k)$. Let p be a new relation of arity equal to the sum of the arities of $p_1, \ldots, p_k$, and define pre_p, $post_p$ as follows, for any $\mathbf{s}_1, \ldots, \mathbf{s}_k$:

$$pre(p(\mathbf{s}_1, \ldots, \mathbf{s}_k)) \text{ iff } post(p(\mathbf{s}_1, \ldots, \mathbf{s}_k)) \text{ iff } post(p_1(\mathbf{s}_1)) \wedge \ldots \wedge post(p_k(\mathbf{s}_k)).$$

With the above assumptions, $(Q, p(\mathbf{t}_1, \ldots, \mathbf{t}_k))$ is a well–typed query. Now, $Q\vartheta$ is a computed instance of Q in P iff $p(\mathbf{t}_1, \ldots, \mathbf{t}_k)\vartheta$ is a selected atom in an LD–derivation of $(Q, p(\mathbf{t}_1, \ldots, \mathbf{t}_k))$ in P. The conclusion now follows by the Persistence Lemma 3.3 and the fact that types are weakly closed. □

We essentially achieved the key property of type persistence with more liberal notions of a type and a type judgement.

3.1 Logic programming

The proposed notion of well–typed programs was designed with reference to Prolog and LD–resolution. However, it can be readily modified into a notion of well–typed *logic* programs, capable of dealing with *any* selection rule. To this purpose, we amend the definition of a well–typed query and clause as follows.

Definition 3.6

- A query $A_1, \ldots, A_n$ is called *strongly well-typed* if $\models pre(A_j)$, for $j \in [1, n]$.

- A clause $H \leftarrow B_1, \ldots, B_n$ is called *strongly well-typed* if

    - $pre_{rel(H)}$ is unification closed w.r.t. H,
    - $\models pre(H) \Rightarrow pre(B_j)$, for $j \in [1, n]$, and
    - $\models pre(H), post(B_1), \ldots, post(B_n) \Rightarrow post(H)$.

- A program is called *strongly well–typed* if every clause of it is. □

Observe that, in a strongly well–typed query, any atom has its pre–type: this justifies the fact any such atom can be selected in an SLD-resolution step. Also, observe that a strongly well–typed query (or clause) is well–typed, as a consequence of the assumption that types are weakly closed. According to this modified notion, the following analogous of the Persistence Lemma 3.3 holds, in the case of SLD–resolution.

Lemma 3.7 *An SLD-resolvent of a strongly well–typed query and a strongly well–typed clause that is variable disjoint with it, is strongly well–typed.* □

3.2 Applications

In the examples, we use a compact notation for defining types. We specify a directional type for a relation p as follows:

$$p : S \rightarrow T$$

as an abbreviation of: $pre_p = \{p(\mathbf{s}) \mid \mathbf{s} \in S\}$ and $post_p = \{p(\mathbf{t}) \mid \mathbf{t} \in T\}$.

Our first example shows how directional types model multiple directionalities in a compact way.

Example 3.8 Consider the Append program:

```
app([X | Xs], Ys, [X | Zs]) ← app(Xs, Ys, Zs).
app([], Ys, Ys).
```

It is readily checked that Append is a *strongly* well-typed program w.r.t. the following directional type:

app : $(List(E) \times List(E) \times PList(E)) \cup (PList(E) \times PList(E) \times List(E)) \rightarrow$
$\qquad (List(E) \times List(E) \times List(E))$

where E is any type. This type for relation app specifies its two possible modes in a compact way. The pre–type specifies that, in a well–typed query, either the first two arguments or the third one are lists, whereas the other arguments are partial lists (e.g., variables.) By the Post–type Corollary 3.5, any computed instance of a well–typed query has lists on all three argument positions. The following is another, less informative, type for **app**:

app : $(PList(E) \times PList(E) \times PList(E)) \rightarrow (PList(E) \times PList(E) \times PList(E))$.

Notice that, using this typing, we conclude by the Post–type Corollary 3.5 that, in all computed instances of the query app([1, 2, 3], X, Y), variable Y is bound to a partial list. This kind of reasoning cannot be conducted using types (or assertions) closed under arbitrary substitution, as in [4, 7]. In these methods, partial lists collapse to $\mathcal{T}$, i.e., the set of all term, as a variable is partial list, and the above type for app boils down to $\mathcal{T} \times \mathcal{T} \times \mathcal{T} \rightarrow \mathcal{T} \times \mathcal{T} \times \mathcal{T}$. This applies to all programs which may deliver non–ground terms, such as partial lists, as an output. □

The next application to the classical map–coloring program shows how a generalized form of directionality is expressible with directional types, which cannot be modeled using input/output modes associated with argument positions.

Example 3.9 Consider the `MapColor` program:

```
color_map([Region | Regions], Colors) ←
    color_region(Region, Colors), color_map(Regions, Colors).
color_map([], Colors).

color_region(region(Name, Color, Neighbors), Colors) ←
    select(Color, Colors, Colors1), subset(Neighbors, Colors1).

select(X, [X | Xs], Xs).
select(X, [Y | Xs], [Y | Zs]) ← select(X, Xs, Zs).

subset([X | Xs], Ys) ← member(X, Ys), subset(Xs, Ys).
subset([], Ys).

member(X, [Y | Xs]) ← member(X, Xs).
member(X, [X | Xs]).
```

It is readily checked that `MapColor` is a (*strongly*) well–typed program by defining the following types. Here, $ColorVar$ is a set of distinguished fresh variables. Also, given a type T and a function symbol f, we write $f(T)$ for the type $\{ f(\mathbf{t}) \mid \mathbf{t} \in T \}$.

$$
\begin{aligned}
Color &= \{blue, \ldots\} & PreColor &= Color \cup ColorVar \\
Region &= \{italy, \ldots\} & & \\
Coloring &= \mathbf{region}(Region \times Color \times List(Color)) & & \\
PreColoring &= \mathbf{region}(Region \times PreColor \times List(PreColor)) & & \\
Map = List(Coloring) & & PreMap &= List(PreColoring)
\end{aligned}
$$

$$
\begin{aligned}
\texttt{color\_map} &: (PreMap \times List(Color)) \to (Map \times List(Color)) \\
\texttt{color\_region} &: (PreColoring \times List(Color)) \to (Coloring \times List(Color)) \\
\texttt{select} &: (PreColor \times List(Color) \times PList(Color)) \to \\
& \quad (Color \times List(Color) \times List(Color)) \\
\texttt{subset} &: (List(PreColor) \times List(Color)) \to (List(Color) \times List(Color)) \\
\texttt{member} &: (PreColor \times List(Color)) \to (Color \times List(Color)).
\end{aligned}
$$

Observe that the program `MapColor` cannot be analyzed using ordinary input/output modes. In the example, the first argument of `color_map` serves both as an input and an output position. Indeed, program `MapColor` computes by progressively instantiating the initial incomplete map. By the Post–type Corollary 3.5, we have that any computed instance of a well–typed query to the `color_map` relation yields a completely colored map. □

4 Pure Prolog with arithmetic

We now address the extension of pure Prolog with arithmetic built–in's, i.e., the comparisons relations $>, \geq$, etc., and the relation `is`. The effect of such built–in's is that LD-derivations may *end in an error*: the evaluation of a query (s > t) ends in an error iff either t or s is not a *ground arithmetic expression* of Prolog, or a *gae*, using the terminology of [5]. Similarly, the query (s is t) ends in an error iff t is not a *gae*.

It is therefore relevant to prove absence of errors, namely the fact that, for a given program in this class and a set of queries of interest, all LD–derivations do not end in an error. How can we adapt the method of well–typed programs to prove absence of errors?

In the case of Prolog programs with arithmetic, we assume that pre–types satisfy the following constraints:

$$\models pre(\mathtt{s\ op\ t}) \quad \text{implies} \quad \mathtt{s,t} \in gae$$

for any comparison relation op, and

$$\models pre(\mathtt{s\ is\ t}) \quad \text{implies} \quad \mathtt{t} \in gae.$$

Clearly, with the above requirement, the evaluation of any well–typed, atomic built–in query A does not end in an error, i.e., it either succeeds or fails. We can now apply the Pre–type Corollary 3.4, which ensures that $\models A : T$, for any selected literal A in any LD–derivation, and conclude the following:

Theorem 4.1 *Consider a well–typed program with arithmetic P and a well–typed query Q. Then any LD-derivation in P from Q does not end in an error.* □

Moreover, an analogous of the Post–type Corollary 3.5 also holds for Prolog programs with arithmetic.

Also, observe that the proof method for absence of errors can be literally rephrased in the context of *logic programming* extended with arithmetic, by using Lemma 3.7. We thus obtain an analogous of Theorem 4.1 for SLD–resolution.

4.1 Applications

Example 4.2 Consider the following version of the Length program:

```
len([X|Xs],N1)  ←  len(Xs,N), N1 is N+1.
len([ ], 0).
```

It is readily checked that Length is a well–typed program by defining:

$$
\begin{aligned}
\mathtt{len} \quad &: \quad (List(E) \times PreGae) \to (List(E) \times Num), \\
\mathtt{is} \quad &: \quad (PreGae \times Gae) \to (Num \times Gae).
\end{aligned}
$$

Here, Gae is the type of ground arithmetic expressions of Prolog, Num is the type of numbers, and $PreGae = Gae \cup GaeVar$, where $GaeVar$ is a set of fresh variables. By Theorem 4.1, we obtain a proof of the fact that program Length is error–free w.r.t. the built–in is, since an atom x is y is selected only if y is a Gae. □

We now show how to prove absence of errors for a program which makes use of difference lists, namely a version of the Quicksort program.

Example 4.3 Consider the Quicksort_DL program:

```
qs(Xs,Ys)  ←  qs_dl(Xs,Ys,[ ]).

qs_dl([X | Xs], Ys, Zs) ←
    part(X, Xs, Littles, Bigs),
    qs_dl(Littles, Ys, [X|Y1s]),
    qs_dl(Bigs, Y1s, Zs).
qs_dl([], Xs, Xs).

part(X, [Y | Xs], [Y | Ls], Bs)  ←  X > Y, part(X, Xs, Ls, Bs).
part(X, [Y | Xs], Ls, [Y | Bs])  ←  X ≤ Y, part(X, Xs, Ls, Bs).
part(X, [], [], []).
```

It is readily checked that `Quicksort_DL` is a well–typed program by defining:

$$
\begin{aligned}
\texttt{qs} \;:\;& (List(Gae) \times PList(Gae)) \rightarrow (List(Gae) \times PList(Gae)), \\
\texttt{qs\_dl} \;:\;& (List(Gae) \times PList(Gae) \times PList(Gae)) \rightarrow \\
& (List(Gae) \times PList(Gae) \times PList(Gae)), \\
\texttt{part} \;:\;& (Gae \times List(Gae) \times PList(Gae) \times PList(Gae)) \rightarrow \\
& (Gae \times List(Gae) \times List(Gae) \times List(Gae)), \\
>, \leq \;:\;& (Gae \times Gae) \rightarrow (Gae \times Gae).
\end{aligned}
$$

By Theorem 4.1, we obtain a proof of the fact that program `Quicksort_DL` is error–free w.r.t. the built–in's $>$ and $\leq$. The above directional type, although sufficient to prove absence of errors, does not satisfactorily describe computed instances. A more accurate directional type for this program was suggested by Sandro Etalle, which allows us to properly describe the input/output behavior of relation `qs_dl`.

$$
\begin{aligned}
\texttt{qs} \;:\;& (List(Gae) \times PList(Gae)) \rightarrow (List(Gae) \times List(Gae)), \\
\texttt{qs\_dl} \;:\;& (List(Gae) \times PList(Gae) \times PList(Gae)) \rightarrow \\
& \{(t,u,v) \mid t \in List(Gae),\ u,v \in PList(Gae),\ \text{and } end(u) = end(v)\}
\end{aligned}
$$

where, for a partial list t, $end(t) = [\ ]$ iff t is a list, and $end(t) = V$ iff t is ended by the variable V. Observe that the post–type of `qs_dl` is not closed under arbitrary substitution.

By exchanging the recursive `qs_dl` atoms, we obtain a version of `Quicksort` with accumulators, as follows:

```
qs_acc([X | Xs], Ys, Zs) ←
    part(X, Xs, Littles, Bigs),
    qs_acc(Bigs, Y1s, Zs),
    qs_acc(Littles, Ys, [X|Y1s]).
qs_acc([], Xs, Xs).
```

In this case, a simpler directional type can be achieved, which precisely characterizes the input/output behavior of relation `qs_acc`:

$$
\begin{aligned}
\texttt{qs} \;:\;& (List(Gae) \times PList(Gae)) \rightarrow (List(Gae) \times List(Gae)), \\
\texttt{qs\_acc} \;:\;& (List(Gae) \times PList(Gae) \times List(Gae)) \rightarrow \\
& (List(Gae) \times List(Gae) \times List(Gae)).
\end{aligned}
$$

$\square$

The next example points out how some meta–logical builtin's of Prolog, such as `nonvar`, can be readily accommodated in our method. Notice, however, that non–monotonic builtin's, such as `var`, cannot be treated, due to the assumption that types are weakly closed.

Example 4.4 Consider the following program `Dictionary`, which is a version of the dictionary look–up program in [20]:

```
lookup([(K,V) | D], K, V).
lookup(D, K, V) ←
    nonvar(D), D = [(K1,V1) | D1], K =/= K1, lookup(D1, K, V).

X = X.
```

Here, we use the extra–logical (monotonic) builtin `nonvar/1` of Prolog, which checks for non–variable terms, and the arithmetic inequality builtin `=/=`. A dictionary is represented as a partial list of pairs $(key, value)$, where key is a gae. The program `Dictionary` can be used either for searching a pair with a designated key, or for inserting a pair with a unique key at the end of the dictionary. It is readily checked that `Dictionary` is a well–typed program by defining the following types. Here, $nonvar$ is the set of non–variable terms, $Dict = PList(Gae \times T)$ is the type of dictionaries, and $Dict'$ is the type of non–variable dictionaries.

$$
\begin{array}{rcl}
\texttt{lookup} & : & Dict \times Gae \times T \rightarrow Dict \times Gae \times T, \\
\texttt{nonvar} & : & T \rightarrow nonvar, \\
\texttt{=} & : & Dict' \times [(T \times T)|Dict] \rightarrow Dict' \times Dict', \\
\texttt{=/=} & : & Gae \times Gae \rightarrow Gae \times Gae.
\end{array}
$$

By Theorem 4.1, we obtain a proof of the fact that program `Dictionary` is error–free w.r.t. the built–in `=/=`. Observe that the original program in [20], p. 250, which omits the `nonvar` check, is *not* error–free, and trades error for failure. Also, we precisely characterize the (*non–ground*) output of the program. □

5 Pure Prolog with Negation

We now address the extension of pure Prolog with negation, by adopting the syntax of *general* programs, which allow negated atoms in clause bodies, and the proof procedure of LDNF–resolution, based on the negation–as–failure rule. The effect of negation–as–failure is the introduction of another form of error in LDNF–derivations, called *floundering*: the evaluation of a query $\neg A$ ends in a floundering if A is not ground. It is therefore relevant to prove absence of floundering, namely the fact that, for a given general program and a set of queries of interest, all LDNF–derivations do not flounder. How can we adapt the method of correctly typed programs to prove absence of floundering?

In the case of Prolog programs with negation, we make the extra assumption that types are extended to sets of *literals*, and that any directional type satisfies the following constraints:

$$
\begin{array}{lll}
\models pre(\neg A) & \text{implies} & A \in ground(A') \text{ for some } A' \text{ such that } \models pre(A'), \quad (1) \\
\models pre(\neg A) & \text{implies} & post(\neg A). \quad (2)
\end{array}
$$

Basically, we require that negated atom in the pre–type are ground instances of (positive) atoms in the pre–type, and that pre– and post–types agree on negated atoms. We have the following simple result, which points out the persistence property of types also in the case of negation–as–failure steps, viewed as an atomic step in the evaluation process.

Lemma 5.1 *Let* $\neg A, \mathbf{B}$ *be a well–typed query. Then* $\mathbf{B}$ *is a well–typed query.*

Proof. Let $\mathbf{B} = B_1, \ldots, B_n$. By Definition 3.2, we have $\models pre(A)$ and, for $j \in [1, n]$:

$$
\models post(A), post(B_1), \ldots, post(B_{j-1}) \Rightarrow pre(B_j). \quad (i)
$$

By (2) we obtain $\models post(A)$ which, together with (i), implies the conclusion by the Transitivity Lemma 2.4. □

Next, we obtain the persistence of types in a single LDNF–derivation step.

Lemma 5.2 *Consider a well–typed general program P, and a well–typed general query Q. Let Q' be an LDNF–resolvent of Q from P. Then Q' is well–typed.*

Proof. If the leftmost literal of Q is positive, then the Persistence Lemma 3.3 applies. If the leftmost literal of Q is negative, then Lemma 5.1 applies. □

The following result about Prolog programs with negation holds.

Theorem 5.3 *Consider a well–typed general program P and a well–typed general query Q. Then any LDNF–derivation in P from Q does not flounder.*

Proof. As a consequence of the Lemma 5.2, we obtain the property of type persistence in all LDNF–derivations in the *main* LDNF–tree for Q in P, in the sense of [2]. Hence, $\models pre(L)$ holds for any selected literals L in any such derivation: by (1), if L is negative then it is ground, and therefore no floundering can arise. To conclude the proof, we have to show that no LDNF–derivation in a *subsidiary* LDNF–tree flounders. Observe that all such derivations start with a ground atomic query, which, by (1), is an instance of a well–typed query. The thesis then follows from the observation that, if all LDNF–derivations of a query R do not flounder, then all LDNF–derivations of a query R' do not flounder, provided that R' is an instance of R. □

Moreover, an analogous of the Post–type Corollary 3.5 also holds for Prolog programs with negation.

Also, observe that the proof method for absence of floundering can be literally rephrased in the context of *logic programming* extended with negation, by using Lemma 3.7. We thus obtain an analogous of Theorem 5.3 for SLDNF–resolution.

5.1 Applications

Example 5.4 Consider the following general program `Curry` for type assignment in the λ–calculus:

```
type(E,var(X),T)  ←  in(E,X,T).
type(E,apply(M,N),T)  ←  type(E,M,arrow(S,T)), type(E,N,S).
type(E,lambda(X,M),arrow(S,T))  ←  type([(X,S)|E],M,T).

in([(X,T)|E],X,T) .
in([(Y,S)|E],X,T)  ←¬(X = Y), in(E,X,T).

X = X.
```

It is readily checked that `Curry` is a (*strongly*) well–typed program by defining the following types. *TypeVar* is a set of distinguished fresh variables. *BasicType* and *LambdaVar* are disjoint sets of constants. A *TypeTerm* is either a *BasicType*, or a *TypeVar*, or a term $\texttt{arrow}(t, u)$ where t and u are *TypeTerm*'s. A *LambdaTerm* is either a term $\texttt{var}(x)$ where x is a *LambdaVar*, or a term $\texttt{apply}(m, n)$ where m and n are *LambdaTerm*'s, or a term $\texttt{lambda}(x, m)$ where x is a *LambdaVar* and m is a *LambdaTerm*. Finally, $Env = List(LambdaVar \times TypeTerm)$.

$$\texttt{type} \; : \; Env \times LambdaTerm \times TypeTerm \rightarrow Env \times LambdaTerm \times TypeTerm$$
$$\texttt{in} \; : \; Env \times LambdaVar \times TypeTerm \rightarrow Env \times LambdaVar \times TypeTerm$$
$$=, \neg = \; : \; LambdaVar \times LambdaVar \rightarrow LambdaVar \times LambdaVar.$$

Notice that type–terms are partial data structures, in that type–variables are represented as logic variables. By Theorem 5.3, program `Curry` does not flounder on well–typed queries. In fact, in any derivation starting from a well–typed query, a selected atom $\neg(x = y)$ is such that $x, y \in LambdaVar$, hence it is ground. $\qquad\square$

6 Final remarks

Two natural directions for future work originate from the proposal of this paper.

One is *type–checking*: it is natural to ask ourselves if it is possible to devise a type definition language and an automated tool able to check the correctness w.r.t. types, in the sense explained in this paper. From this perspective, some extension of the language adopted in [8, 6] to incomplete data structures appears as a promising candidate. We anticipate that the use of typed variables directly enforces the conditions of weak and unification closure. A more ambitious goal is the construction of an inferential type–checker.

The other direction is *verification*: from preliminary investigations, it appears that some form of dependency between pre– and post–types would greatly increase the expressivity of the proposed method as a tool for the verification of (partial) correctness. More generally, it would be interesting to investigate whether the proposed method can facilitate the proofs of total correctness, in the sense of [5].

Acknowledgements

I am particularly grateful to Krzysztof Apt, who contributed to improve this paper in many ways. Also, thanks are owing to A. Bossi, S. Etalle, P. Mancarella, P. Mascellani, S. Ruggieri and F. Turini. This work was partly done during the author's stay at CWI, Amsterdam, and was partly supported the ESPRIT B.R.A. 6810 — Compulog 2.

References

[1] K. R. Apt. Logic programming. In J. van Leeuwen, editor, *Handbook of Theoretical Computer Science*, pages 493–574. Elsevier, 1990. Vol. B.

[2] K. R. Apt and K. Doets. A new definition of SLDNF–resolution. ILLC Precpublication Series CT–92–03, Dept. of Methematics and Computer Science, University of Amsterdam, 1992. Accepted for publication in *Journal of Logic Programming*.

[3] K. R. Apt and S. Etalle. On the unification free Prolog programs. In S. Sokolowski, editor, *Proc. of the Conference on Mathematyical Foundations of Computer Science (MFCS 93)*, LNCS, Berlin, 1993. To appear.

[4] K. R. Apt and E. Marchiori. Reasoning about Prolog programs: from Modes through types to assertions. Technical Report CS-R9358, Centre for Mathematics and Computer Science, Amsterdam, 1993.

[5] K. R. Apt. Program Verification and Prolog. In E. Börger, editor, *Specification and Validation methods for Programming languages and systems*, Oxford University Press, 1994. To appear.

[6] A. Aiken and T. K. Lakshman. Automatic mode checking for logic programs. Technical Report, Dept. of Computer Science, University of Illinois at Urbana–Champaign, 1993.

[7] A. Bossi and N. Cocco. Verifying correctness of logic programs. In *Proceedings of Tapsoft '89*, Lecture Notes in Computer Science, pages 96–110. Springer-Verlag, 1989.

[8] F. Bronsard and T. K. Lakshman and U. S. Reddy. A framework of directionalities for proving termination of logic programs. In K. R. Apt, editor, *Proc. of the Joint International Conference and Symposium on Logic Programming*, pages 321–335. The MIT Press, 1992.

[9] M. Bruynooghe. A Practical Framework for the Abstract Interpretations of Logic Programs. *Journal of Logic Programming*, 10:91–124, 1991.

[10] L. Colussi and E. Marchiori. Proving correctness of logic programs using axiomatic semantics. In *Proceedings of the Eight International Conference on Logic Programming*, pages 629-644-38. The MIT Press, 1991.

[11] S. K. Debray and D. S. Warren. Automatic Mode Iinference for Logic Programs. *Journal of Logic Programming*, 5:207–230, 1988.

[12] P. Dembinski and J. Maluszynski. AND-parallelism with intelligent backtracking for annotated logic programs. In *Proceedings of the International Symposium on Logic Programming*, pages 29–38, Boston, 1985.

[13] W. Drabent and J. Maluszynski. Inductive assertion method for logic programs. *Theoretical Computer Science*, 59(1):133-155, 1988.

[14] P.M. Hill and J.W. Lloyd. The logic programming language Gödel. Technical report, University of Bristol, 1991.

[15] J. W. Lloyd. *Foundations of Logic Programming*. Springer-Verlag, Berlin, second edition, 1987.

[16] C. S. Mellish. The automatic generation of mode declaration for Prolog programs. In *Proceedings of the Workshop on Logic Programming for Intelligent Systems*, 1981.

[17] C. S. Mellish. Abstract interpretation of Prolog programs. In S. Abramski and C. Hankin, editors, *Abstract interpretation of declarative languages*, pages 191–198. Ellis Horwood Ltd, 1987.

[18] R. Milner. A theory of type polymorphism in programming. *Journal of Computer and System Sciences*, 17(3):348–375, 1978.

[19] F. Pfenning, editor. *Types in Logic Programming*, Logic Programming Series, The MIT Press, 1992.

[20] L. Sterling and E. Shapiro. *The Art of Prolog*. The MIT Press, Cambridge, MA, 1986.

Fast and Precise Regular Approximations of Logic Programs

J.P. Gallagher   **D.A. de Waal**

Department of Computer Science, University of Bristol
Queen's Building, University Walk, Bristol BS8 1TR, U.K.

john@compsci.bristol.ac.uk, andre@compsci.bristol.ac.uk

Abstract

A practical procedure for computing a regular approximation of a logic program is given. Regular approximations are useful in a variety of tasks in debugging, program specialisation and compile-time optimisation. The algorithm shown here incorporates optimisations taken from deductive database fixpoint algorithms and efficient bottom-up abstract interpretation techniques. Frameworks for defining regular approximations have been put forward in the past, but the emphasis has usually been on theoretical aspects. Our results contribute mainly to the development of effective analysis tools that can be applied to large programs. Precision of the approximation can be greatly improved by applying query-answer transformations to a program and a goal, thus capturing some argument dependency information. A novel technique is to use transformations based on computation rules other than left-to-right to improve precision further. We give performance results for our procedure on a range of programs.

1   Introduction

Given a definite logic program P, the problem we address is how to compute a regular approximation of P. An approximation is a program whose least Herbrand model contains the least Herbrand model of P. Regular approximations provide a way of deciding certain properties of a program, since regular programs have a number of decidable properties and associated computable operations [1].

The question of how to define regular safe approximations of a program has been discussed before [25], [35], [18], [13], [20]. Most of this work considered the definition and precision of various different approximations. Little work emphasising efficient, practical implementation has been presented. In this paper we present an algorithm for computing a regular approximation of a logic program, discuss its performance, with possible trade-offs of precision and efficiency. We then show how to increase precision greatly by the use of query-answer transformations, and present results for a range of programs.

Our method of approximation is based on the framework of *bottom-up abstract interpretation* of logic programs [23]. Like [35] and [18], we define an abstraction of the well-known T_P function, say $\mathcal{T}_P$. We define an abstract function $\mathcal{T}_P$ that maps one regular program to another. The least fixed point (*lfp*) of T_P is the least Herbrand model of a program P. By computing $lfp(\mathcal{T}_P)$ we obtain a description of some superset of $lfp(T_P)$.

The important practical questions in such an abstract interpretation are, firstly, whether the least fixed point is computed in a finite number of iterations, and secondly, to compute successive elements of the sequence as efficiently as possible. We use the strongly connected components of the predicate dependency graph to decompose the fixed-point computation into a sequence of smaller computations.

In the next section we define RUL programs, and the abstract semantic function T_P. An important concept here is the *shortening* of an RUL program, which ensures termination of the abstract interpretation. Shortening is an approximation step that introduces recursive definitions. Its properties influence the algorithm greatly, since it is mainly responsible for the rate of convergence of the fixpoint computation. In Section 5 we give the bottom-up algorithm. It is interesting that good results can be achieved using such standard techniques drawn mainly from deductive database methods. In Section 6 the analysis of a program with a goal is discussed. The key idea is the combination of different computation rules (left-to-right and right-to-left) to increase precision. A discussion of related work is in Section 7.

2   Regular Approximations

Definition 2.1 *canonical regular unary clause*
A **canonical regular unary clause** *is a clause of the form*

$$t_0(f(x_1, \ldots, x_n)) \leftarrow t_1(x_1), \ldots, t_n(x_n) \quad n \geq 0$$

where $x_1, \ldots, x_n$ are distinct variables.

Definition 2.2 *canonical RUL program*
A **canonical regular unary logic (RUL) program** *is a finite set of regular unary clauses, in which no two different clause heads have a common instance.*

The class of canonical RUL programs was defined by Yardeni and Shapiro [35]. More expressive classes of regular program can be defined, but this one allows convenient and efficient manipulation of programs. 'RUL program' from now on in this paper will mean 'canonical RUL program'.

Definition 2.3 *regular definition of predicates*
Let $\{p^1/n^1, \ldots, p^m/n^m\}$ *be a finite set of predicates. A* **regular definition** *of the predicates is a set of clauses $Q \cup R$, where*

- Q *is a set of clauses of form $p^i(x_1, \ldots, x_{n^i}) \leftarrow t_1(x_1), \ldots, t_{n^i}(x_{n^i})$ ($1 \leq i \leq m$), and R is an RUL program defining $t_1, \ldots, t_{n^i}$; and*

- *no two heads of clauses in $Q \cup R$ have a common instance.*

Definition 2.4 *regular approximation*
Let P be a definite program and P' a regular definition of predicates in P. Then P' *is a* **regular approximation** *of P if the least Herbrand model of P is contained in the least Herbrand model of P'.*

For convenience, abusing notation, an RUL program can be obtained from a regular definition of predicates by replacing each clause $p^i(x_1, \ldots, x_{n^i}) \leftarrow B$ by a clause

$$approx(p^i(x_1, \ldots, x_{n^i})) \leftarrow B$$

where *approx* is a distinguished unary predicate not used elsewhere. Strictly, each predicate p^i/n^i should be replaced by a corresponding function symbol. This transformed program will also be referred to as a regular definition (or approximation), though strictly the original form without the *approx* predicate is meant. This allows us for the remainder of the paper to restrict attention to RUL programs.

3 Operations on RUL Programs

A number of operations and relations on RUL programs are next defined.

Definition 3.1 $success_R(t)$
 Let R be an RUL program and let U_R be its Herbrand universe. Let t be a unary predicate. Then $success_R(t) = \{s \in U_R \mid R \cup \{\leftarrow t(s)\}$ has a refutation$\}$

Definition 3.2 *inclusion*
 Let R be an RUL program, and let t_1 and t_2 be unary predicates. Then we write $t_1 \subseteq t_2$ if $success_R(t_1) \subseteq success_R(t_2)$.

Definition 3.3 *intersection and upper bound of unary predicates*
 Let t_1 and t_2 be unary predicates, defined in an RUL program R. Then the **intersection** $t_1 \cap t_2$ is defined as a predicate t_3, such that $success(t_3) = success_R(t_1) \cap success_R(t_2)$. An **upper bound** $t_1 \sqcup t_2$ is defined as a predicate t_3, such that $success_R(t_1) \cup success_R(t_2) \subseteq success(t_3)$.

Note that the upper bound as defined in general includes the union of t_1 and t_2. Our algorithm computed a tuple-distributive upper bound.

Procedures for checking inclusion, and computing intersection and a suitable upper bound of predicates in RUL programs can easily be defined. The algorithms correspond to well-known algorithms in finite automata theory. If $size(p)$ is number of predicates on which predicate p depends, then the complexity of inclusion, intersection and tuple-distributive upper bound operations on predicates s and t are all $O(size(s) * size(t))$.

Definition 3.4 *upper bound of RUL programs*
 Let R and S be RUL programs. Their upper bound $R \sqcup S$ is obtained by the following steps:

1. *For any predicate t that occurs in both R and S (possibly with different definitions), rename t by predicates t^R in R and by t^S in S (where t^R and t^S are new predicates not occurring in R or S). Compute their upper bound $t^R \sqcup t^S$, and call it t.*

2. *Obtain $R \sqcup S$ from $R \cup S$ by replacing the old clauses for t by the newly computed definition (including subsidiary predicates) of t.*

3.1 Shortening of RUL programs

Definition 3.5 *calls, call-chain, depends on*
 Let R be a program containing predicates t and s $(t \neq s)$. Then t *calls* s if s occurs in the body of clause whose head contains t. A sequence of predicates $t_1, t_2, \ldots, t_i, \ldots$ where t_i calls t_{i+1} $(i \geq 1)$ is a *call-chain*. We say t *depends on* s if there is a call-chain from t to s.

Definition 3.6 $D(t, s)$

Let R be an RUL program containing predicates t and s $(t \neq s)$. Then the relation $D(t, s)$ is true if t depends on s and the set of function symbols appearing in the heads of clauses in the procedure for t is the same as the set of function symbols appearing in the heads of clauses in the procedure for s.

Definition 3.7 *shortening*

Let R be an RUL program, and let t and s be unary predicates defined in R such that $D(t, s)$ holds. Then a program $Sh(R)$ is obtained from R as follows:

- If $s \subseteq t$ and $t \subseteq s$ then $Sh(R)$ is obtained by replacing all occurrences of s in clause bodies in R by t.

- Otherwise, if $s \subseteq t$ then obtain $Sh(R)$ by replacing by t all occurrences of s in clause bodies in R, where that occurrence depends on t and does not depend on s. (I.e. one changes the definition of t, not that of s).

- If $s \not\subseteq t$ then compute $r = s \sqcup t$, with definition R_r. Replace all occurrences of t in clause bodies in R by r, giving R'. Then $Sh(R) = R' \cup R_r$. (Thus all calls to t are replaced by calls to r).

Example 1 Let $R =$

$$\{t(a) \leftarrow true, t(f(x)) \leftarrow r(x), r(a) \leftarrow true,$$
$$r(f(x)) \leftarrow s(x), s(b) \leftarrow true\}$$

$D(t, r)$ holds, and $r \not\subseteq t$, so the upper bound $t \sqcup r$ is computed, called q below. So $Sh(R) =$

$$\{t(a) \leftarrow true, t(f(x)) \leftarrow q(x), q(a) \leftarrow true, q(f(x)) \leftarrow q_1(x), q_1(a) \leftarrow true,$$
$$q_1(b) \leftarrow true, q_1(f(x)) \leftarrow s(x), s(b) \leftarrow true, r(a) \leftarrow true, r(f(x)) \leftarrow s(x)\}$$

Definition 3.8 *shortened RUL program*

A **shortened** program R is one in which there are no two predicates t and s such that $D(t, s)$ holds.

A shortened program can be obtained from R by performing a finite number of applications of Sh to R, i.e. computing $Sh^n(R)$ for some finite n. This is proved in [16].

Definition 3.9 Let R be an RUL program. Then **short**$(R) = Sh^n(R)$ such that $Sh^n(R)$ is shortened.

The main justification for shortening is to limit the number of RUL programs (see Lemma 3.2), and thus ensure termination of our approximation procedure. We have seldom found a serious lack of expressiveness imposed by shortening, though nested occurrences of the same function symbol are (sometimes) merged. In terms of finite automata, a shortened RUL program corresponds to an automaton in which no two connected states have the same set of labels on transitions leading from them. Shortening also puts RUL definitions into a minimal form and this leads to more efficient processing.

Shortening can introduce recursive definitions. For example, the set of atoms

$$\{p(a), p(f(a)), p(f(f(a)))\}$$

can be described by the RUL program

$$\{p(a) \leftarrow true, p(f(x)) \leftarrow t_1(x), t_1(a) \leftarrow true, t_1(f(x)) \leftarrow t_2(x), t_2(a) \leftarrow true\}$$

In this program, $D(p, t_1)$ holds, and $t_1 \subseteq p$. Its shortened form is thus

$$\{p(a) \leftarrow true, p(f(x)) \leftarrow p(x), t_1(a) \leftarrow true, t_1(f(x)) \leftarrow t_2(x), t_2(a) \leftarrow true\}$$

Other kinds of shortening are possible. In [5] an operation on "type graphs" is used, that has some relation to our operation. Other possible shortenings are discussed in Section 7. Study of suitable shortenings remains a key issue, since it is here that tradeoffs of precision and complexity are focussed.

The next lemma (proved in [16]) states that shortening increases the size of the success set of any predicate that occurs in both R and $Sh(R)$.

Lemma 3.1 *Let R be an RUL program containing a predicate t such that t occurs both in R and $Sh(R)$. Then $success_R(t) \subseteq success_{Sh(R)}(t)$.*

Let U_F be some Herbrand universe, constructed from a finite set of constants and function symbols $F = \{f_1/n_1, \ldots, f_m/n_m\}$. Let R be any program whose Herbrand universe is a subset of U_F. Then clearly $success_R(t) \subseteq U_F$, for each unary predicate t in R. A special predicate called *any* is such that $success_R(any) = U_F$.

The next lemma shows that where R is a shortened RUL program with some fixed Herbrand universe, there is only a finite set of possible sets $success_R(t)$. This property is later used to show the termination of the algorithm for deriving a regular approximation of a program.

Lemma 3.2 *Let $F = \{f_1/n_1, \ldots, f_m/n_m\}$ be a finite set of constant and function symbols. Then there is a finite number of different sets of the form $success_R(t)$, where R is any RUL program containing constants and functions from F (and no others), and t is a unary predicate in R.*

PROOF. (sketch)

A deterministic finite automaton corresponding to a program can be constructed. It can be seen that only a finite number of distinct automata can be constructed from RUL programs with an upper bound on the length of acyclic call-chains. The maximum length of acyclic call-chains in a shortened RUL program with m function symbols of non-zero arity is $2^m - 1$. The result follows. □

4 Computing a Regular Approximation of a Program

In this section the abstract semantic function T_P is defined. First the *regular solution of a definite clause* is defined, by means of the following operator **solve**. For reasons of space we give only a sketch. The full definition is in [15]. A related procedure was used by Frühwirth [12].

The procedure **solve**(C, R) takes a clause C and a regular definition of predicates, R. The procedure returns a regular definition of the predicate in the head of C. The body of C is "solved" in R. This involves unfolding the body until it consists of unary atoms with variable arguments, followed by intersection of predicates with the same argument. The terms in the head of the clause are then given definitions in terms of the unary body predicates.

If the procedure returns $\emptyset$ this is interpreted as failure. This can happen either because unfolding fails, or because some intersection is empty. If it does not fail, the procedure yields a unique result which is an RUL program.

Example 2 *Let the clause C be*

$$append([x|xs], ys, [x|zs]) \leftarrow append(xs, ys, zs)$$

and let $R = \{approx(append(x, y, z)) \leftarrow t_1(x), any(y), any(z), \quad t_1([]) \leftarrow true\}$.
$\mathbf{solve}(C, R)$ yields the following program.

$$\{approx(append(x, y, z)) \leftarrow t_2(x), any(y), t_3(z),$$
$$t_1([]) \leftarrow true,$$
$$t_2([x|xs]) \leftarrow any(x), t_1(xs),$$
$$t_3([z|zs]) \leftarrow any(z), any(zs)\}$$

Definition 4.1 *the function T_P*
Let P be a definite program. Let D be an RUL program (a regular definition of predicates in P). A function $T_P(D)$ is defined as follows:

$$T_P(D) = \mathbf{short}(\bigsqcup \{\, \mathbf{solve}(C, D) \,|\, C \in P \,\} \bigsqcup D)$$

That is, $\mathbf{solve}$ is applied to each clause, their upperbound with D is computed and the whole result shortened.

Definition 4.2 $\gamma(R)$
Let R be an RUL program. The set $success_R(approx)$ is called the concretisation of R, and is referred to as $\gamma(R)$.

Let P be a program with Herbrand base B_P and let R be a regular definition of predicates in P. Then $\gamma(R)$ can be identified with some subset of B_P (allowing for the shortcut in notation mentioned earlier that confuses predicate and function symbols). An RUL program (containing a predicate $approx$) can be thought of as describing some Herbrand interpretation.

Our next problem is to establish that T_P has the required properties, namely,

- that its least fixed point exists and is computable, and

- that it is a safe abstraction of T_P.

Space does not allow the details, which are based on well-known methods from abstract interpretation (e.g. [9], [4], [24]). The following is the required safety result.

Lemma 4.1 *Let P be a definite program. Then $\forall n(T_P^n(\emptyset) \subseteq \gamma(T_P^n(\emptyset)))$.*

The fixed point of T_P is found in a finite number of iterations, because of Lemma 3.2. From this it follows that $lfp(T_P) \subseteq \gamma(lfp(T_P))$.

Prolog built-ins are handled either by defining some basic regular types (such as integer expressions) or simply by using the trivial approximation *any* for each built-in argument.

5 Efficient Implementation

5.1 Naive and Semi-Naive Evaluation

In the field of deductive databases, considerable investigation has been made of the efficient evaluation of least fixed points for recursive query answering [34]. Also, in abstract interpretation, generic fixed-point-finding algorithms have been defined which use related techniques [22].

We cannot give a detailed description here, but simply point to the main techniques we have used. Some similar optimisation methods were used in another fast bottom-up abstract interpretation [8]. The key is to use the ideas of *semi-naive* evaluation [34] to exploit the new information Δ_i derived on the ith iteration, to limit the work in the $i + 1$th iteration. The exploitation of the Δ_i part can be effected in various ways.

In our algorithm we do not use any dynamic dependency information (as is used in other abstract interpretation frameworks [22], [27] and [4]). We apply the idea of semi-naive evaluation in a simple but effective way. When computing $T_P(D)$ on some iteration, we identify the predicates whose approximation are changed by that application. On the subsequent iteration, we only look at clauses whose bodies contain one of the changed predicates. All other clauses can be ignored since they will obviously return exactly the same as on the previous iteration.

In effect, the definition of T_P is modified to include a set of "changed predicates" S as an argument, and to return another set of changed predicates in its result. Let C_S stand for any clause whose body contains a predicate from the set S. The definition is then as follows:

$$T_P(D, S) = (D_1, S_1) \text{ where}$$
$$D_1 = \mathbf{short}(\bigsqcup \{ \mathbf{solve}(C_S, D) \mid C_S \in P \} \bigsqcup D)$$
$$S_1 = \{ p \mid \text{definition of } p \text{ changed from } D_1 \text{ to } D_2 \}$$

A further optimisation in our algorithm is to apply **short** only to the predicates in S_1. These are major optimisations for most programs. Furthermore, a sufficient condition for termination is that S_1 is empty on some iteration.

The question of how to access efficiently all clauses whose bodies contain a given predicate can be solved in different ways, perhaps using an index from predicates to clause bodies. However, using the optimisation discussed in the next section based on strongly connected components, the number of clauses that need to be examined on each iteration is cut down, so indexing is not a great advantage.

5.2 Use of Strongly Connected Components

An optimisation that has appeared in the literature in various settings, but seems not so well-known as the semi-naive algorithm, is the use of strongly connected components (SCCs) [26], [31]. Given the predicate-dependency graph of a program, an SCC is a set of predicates all of which depend on each other. A linear algorithm to decompose a graph into its SCCs was discovered by R. Tarjan [33]. The set of SCCs of a graph themselves form an acyclic graph, and this set can then be topologically sorted to give a sequence of SCCs.

The fixed-point-finding algorithm can then be decomposed into a sequence of fixpoint computations, starting from the bottom of the SCC graph and working upwards. In each SCC, only the clauses for the predicates in that SCC are considered, and a fixed point for the meaning of the SCC predicates is computed. By working through the sorted sequence of SCCs, it is assured that predicates lower in the dependency graph are computed before the predicates that depend on them.

In typical user programs, the number of mutually recursive predicates in an SCC is rarely more than two. So this means that relatively few clauses need to be examined on each iteration of the algorithm, with consequent speed-up. (In programs that are generated automatically, such as the query-answer transforms discussed in Section 6 we have found that SCCs are often much larger).

The SCCs can also be used to identify which predicates are recursive and which are not. When computing the meaning of a non-recursive predicate (whose SCC is obviously a singleton) no fixpoint computation and no shortening are needed.

Note that the SCC optimisation involves some trade-off. Firstly, the SCCs have to be computed (a linear computation, as observed already). Secondly, although each iteration is simpler, there may be more iterations in total over the whole algorithm, since some SCCs are independent and their results would be computed simultaneously without use of SCCs. This suggests experimenting with merging SCCs that are independent (such as $\{r\}$ and $\{s\}$ in the example above).

Other dependency graphs could be used apart from the predicate dependencies. For example, a clause dependency graph can be defined, and its SCCs exploited in a similar way. However, although this gives finer grain dependency information, the optimisations obtainable here would appear to be similar to those obtained by the semi-naive algorithm.

5.3   The Effect of Shortening

Shortening determines the number of iterations that are required to reach a fixed point, since recursive approximations are introduced only by shortening. One could gain precision at the expense of complexity and vice versa, by employing different shortenings. One could force recursive approximations to be generated from weaker conditions on the RUL clauses and hence accelerate termination of the approximation. This is further discussed in Section 7. Secondly, shortening has the effect of minimising the size of the RUL definitions, and so the cost of basic operations such as intersection, which depends on the size of definitions, is minimised.

5.4   Factors Influencing Performance

Complexity analysis of this method can establish worst cases. Shortening places a worst-case upper bound on the size of RUL definitions. The depth of call-chains in a language with m function symbols of non-zero arity is at most $2^m - 1$, as noted in Lemma 3.2. This implies exponential upper-bounds on the cost of operations such as intersection, and on the number of iterations required to reach a fixed point.

Average complexity is influenced by a number of factors. In practice average cases are quite tractable, since the number of function symbols of non-zero arity that can appear in a given argument position of a predicate is the relevant value of m, and this tends to be small.

Our experiments indicate that the performance of the algorithm is affected roughly linearly by the number of SCCs, the average size of clauses and the average size of SCCs. The average number of times that predicates within an SCC occur in each other's clauses would appear to be another important factor, since the effectiveness of our semi-naive algorithm depends on this.

6   Experimental Results

In this section we demonstrate how the accuracy of the regular approximations can be improved by using of a class of program transformations that includes the "magic set" and "Alexander" transformations. We call these "query-answer" transformations. These transformations were introduced as recursive query evaluation techniques [2], [30], but have since been adapted for use in program analysis [6], [11], [21], [32], [16]. They allow top-down computation to be performed in a bottom-up manner.

Bottom-up analysis does not take into account possible queries to a program. By analysing the computation of a general call to a predicate $p(x_1, \ldots, x_n)$ we may get a more precise result for that predicate than by analysing the program bottom-up. This was pointed out in [16] and discussed in detail in [7]. Examples of query-answer transformations can be found in in [16] and [14].

Consider the following permutation program that computes permutations of lists of integers. ($integer(X)$ is a built-in predicate for which a predefined approximation $numeric(X)$ is derived).

$perm(X, Y) : -intlist(X), permutation(X, Y).$
$permutation([], []).$
$permutation(X, [U|V]) : -delete(U, X, Z), permutation(Z, V).$
$delete(X, [X|Y], Y).$
$delete(X, [Y|Z], [Y|W]) : -delete(X, Z, W).$
$intlist([]).$
$intlist([X|Xs]) : -integer(X), intlist(Xs).$

The following program is the regular approximation produced by our analysis (showing the result for *perm* and *permutation* only). The *t*-predicates, *any* and *numeric* are generated by the approximation procedure.

$perm(A1, A2) : -t42(A1), t28(A2).$
$permutation(A1, A2) : -t21(A1), t28(A2).$
$t28([]) : -true.$
$t28([A1|A2]) : -any(A1), t28(A2).$
$t42([]) : -true.$
$t42([A1|A2]) : -numeric(A1), t42(A2).$
$t21([]) : -true.$
$t21([A1|A2]) : -any(A1), any(A2).$

Although the second argument of *perm* is shown to be a list, it cannot be inferred to be a list of integers. The results for the first argument of *permutation* are very imprecise. Note that no other method of regular approximation in the literature based on bottom-up approximation, with no argument dependency information, would give better results than this.

6.1   Increasing Precision with Query-Answer Transformation

Assuming a left-to-right computation rule, a "magic" style transformation of the program with respect to the goal $\leftarrow perm(x, y)$ is generated and analysed. In the transformed program, the predicate *perm_ans* gives the answers for *perm*. A regular approximation of the "magic" transformed program, showing this predicate is:

$perm\_ans(A1, A2) : -t23(A1), t23(A2).$
$t23([]) : -true.$
$t23([A1|A2]) : -numeric(A1), t23(A2).$

It is now much more precise than the original result. The second argument of *perm* is shown to be a list of numeric values. Effectively, variable sharing information in the original program has been made explicit, detecting that the *perm* predicate returns a list of integers when given a list of integers.

For some programs the regular approximation procedure might still not be unable to infer optimal information even with a "magic" transformed version of a program. An example of such a program is a similar *perm* program, but with the second argument known to be a list of integers but not the first argument. In this case the transformation above would not detect that the first argument must also be a list of integers. We now describe an improvement over the "magic set" transformation used so far to enable us to infer even more detailed information.

6.2 Further Precision by Adding Right-to-Left Computation

As we are only interested in the success set of a program, not its computation tree, the left-to-right computation rule we assumed is not a prerequisite. An analysis assuming a right-to-left computation rule (or any other computation rule) is just as valid. The improved ''magic" transformation generates two "answer" and "query" predicates for each predicate, one for the left-right rule and one for the right-left. The final answers are obtained by intersecting the left and right answers. For each predicate a clause is added to the query-answer transformed program to compute this. For example for the *perm* predicate the following clause is added

$$perm\_ans(X, Y) : -perm\_left\_ans(X, Y), perm\_right\_ans(X, Y).$$

The intersection of regular approximations using different computation rules might give even more precise regular approximations, as information from the "right" of a clause may now be propagated to the literals to its left. The use of additional right-to-left analysis has some relation to "reexecution" to gain precision in other abstract interpretation frameworks.

Analysing computations using two computation rules might seem like an unacceptable overhead. However near-optimal or optimal information (within the limits of RUL programs) can often be computed by this means. Furthermore the two approximations using the two computation rules can be done independently (this is detected by the decomposition into SCCs, Section 5) and are intersected only at the final step. The approximation time will therefore approximately double, but it might be an acceptable price to pay for the increase in precision.

A regular approximation of the permutation program with second argument known to be a list of integers using the improved magic set transformation enables us to infer the most precise RUL approximation possible for this program. Different intermediate levels of precision are also possible by using simplified versions of the improved "magic" transformation presented here with a corresponding decrease in execution times.

6.3 Benchmarks

We now give some performance results for some typical examples used in the abstract interpretation literature. The query-answer transformations were performed with respect to a "top" goal for each program. A Sun Sparc-10 running Sicstus Prolog was used in all the experiments and all timings are in seconds. The number of clauses in brackets is the number of clauses in the left-transformed program. (The number of query clauses generated is equal to the number of body literals in the original program). The number of predicates in the left and left+right programs are respectively 2 and 5 times the number of predicates in the original. The number of clauses in the left+right program is $2k + p$ where k is the number of clauses in the left-transformed version and p is the number of predicates in the original program.

Benchmarks					
Program	Number of Clauses	Number of Predicates	Bottom-Up	Left	Left+ Right
Board Cutting	110 (238)	37	1.08	7.22	13.88
Scheduling	64 (137)	34	0.61	4.66	8.56
Gabriel Benchmark	46 (84)	20	0.33	1.22	3.30
Peephole Optimiser	228 (319)	22	3.63	7.63	19.88
Press	156 (282)	50	1.33	8.34	19.65
Quicksort	8 (15)	4	0.06	0.13	0.43
N-Queens	10 (19)	5	0.07	0.14	0.52
Prolog Tokeniser	169 (358)	43	1.04	7.99	21.44

Table 1: Approximation Times for Benchmark Programs

The increase in complexity due to the "query-answer" transformation is significant but not prohibitive, and is 3 to 7 times more expensive than the bottom-up analysis for these benchmarks. This represents the overhead for top-down over bottom-up. The increase for additional right-to-left analysis is roughly a further factor of 2 to 3. We have not yet made detailed analysis of the precision gains from the left+right transformation.

7 Discussion

7.1 Other Approaches to Regular Approximation

Mishra [25] suggested using regular structures to approximate the success set of a program, and called these approximations "types". The approximation was obtained by solving a set of recursive equations derived from the program. This general approach was continued by Heintze and Jaffar [18] and by Frühwirth et al. [13]. Both of these papers shed much light on the general problem of defining regular approximations, and the precision of different classes of approximation.

The approach to regular approximation based on abstract interpretation of the T_P function was initiated by Yardeni and Shapiro [35], but theirs was a theoretical construct that did not yield an explicit form. Jones [20] also gave an algorithm to compute a regular tree-grammar which approximated a set of rewrite rules. This is a fixpoint algorithm with a strong connection to abstract interpretation. Frühwirth et al. showed the relation (for logic programs) between the approaches based on set equations and on abstract interpretation.

The approaches based on set equations seem at first sight to be more direct, but in practice the difficult part is putting the equations into some usable solved form. Heintze [17] outlines an implementation of such an algorithm, and gives experimental evidence that it is efficient for fairly small programs. He also employs a construction for simulating the top-down left-to-right computation rule, which appears to be identical to well-known "magic set" methods used in this paper. Algorithms for getting solved form have similarities to the fixpoint computations of abstract interpretation methods. There may be deeper connections between these streams yet to be investigated. Very recently, some other work in the abstract interpretation framework shows that fast and precise results can be obtained [19]. This work uses a generic top-down abstract interpretation framework, and is a useful contrast to our approach using the bottom-up framework with query-answer transformations. Their approach uses a "widening" operator to ensure termination.

The phrase "type inference" was used (in a non-standard way) by several authors when speaking of regular approximations. Zobel [36], Frühwirth [12] and Reddy [29] defined algorithms that infer descriptions of success "types". Comparison of their results with ours is difficult, but for small examples is similar.

Domains for abstract interpretation of logic programs have been defined that include type-like structures by Kanamori [21] and Bruynooghe and Janssens [5]. The former is not comparable to ours, since it relies on a given set of basic types whose properties are built in to the abstract interpretation. The latter also uses given basic types in the domain, as well as sharing information, but it seems that one could remove these from their abstract domains and extract regular types similar to ours.

7.2 Precision

In bottom-up regular approximation the main loss in precision is due to loss of information about dependencies between arguments. Other aspects of precision, such as those discussed by [18] and [13] are comparatively insignificant. In view of this it is worthwhile to sacrifice a little precision (due to our shortening operation) in return for speed. In particular, derivation of non-deterministic regular programs (in which one dropped the condition that clause heads have no common instances) would greatly increase the cost of basic operations on RUL programs.

A far more important aspect of precision is to capture argument dependencies. Our approach to this is to analyse with respect to a given goal, by performing a query-answer transformation. We have shown that argument dependencies can be captured, and precision is thus greatly increased. Optimal results are often obtained. The alternative is to develop richer abstract domains incorporating sharing information (as in [5]) and it is not clear yet whether one approach is better than the other.

Other shortenings on RUL programs are possible that could increase precision. We have experimented with a shortening that introduces recursive approximations directly from the recursive structure of the program being analysed (this was suggested by the method in [13]). Another possibility is to look ahead further than the set of functions symbols occurring in clause heads when shortening. Similar ideas occur in machine learning, and in fact our shortening was originally inspired by a procedure for inferring automata in [3]. An operation on type graphs is defined in [5]. Repetitions of function symbols on a branch of a type graph are merged into a loop. Our shortening is similar in spirit but is usually more precise.

7.3 Applications

The main purpose of this paper is not to describe applications of regular approximations, of which there are many. Type inference and related debugging applications are discussed in [25], [35], and elsewhere. These applications are well presented by Naish [28]. Regular approximation can be combined with the declaration of intended types (stated as regular programs) and program errors detected. Compile-time optimisation using information about argument structure is another important application.

The combination of regular approximation with partial evaluation was developed by us in [14]. Deletion of *useless clauses*, detected by a regular approximation, can greatly improve the results of partial evaluation. This was applied with good results in specialising theorem provers [10].

Acknowledgements

This work is supported by ESPRIT Project PRINCE (5246). We thank the ICLP referees for their suggestions and corrections.

References

[1] A.V. Aho, J.E. Hopcroft, and J.D. Ullman. *The Design and Analysis of Computer Algorithms*. Adddison-Wesley, 1974.

[2] F. Bancilhon, D. Maier, Y. Sagiv, and J. Ullman. Magic sets and other strange ways to implement logic programs. In *Proceedings of the 5th ACM SIGMOD-SIGACT Symposium on Principles of Database Systems*, 1986.

[3] A. Biermann. Fundamental mechanisms in machine learning and inductive inference. In W. Bibel and Ph. Jorrand, editors, *Fundamentals of Artificial Intelligence: An Advanced Course*, Springer-Verlag, 1987.

[4] M. Bruynooghe. A practical framework for abstract interpretation of logic programs. *Journal of Logic Programming*, 10(2):91–124, 1991.

[5] M. Bruynooghe and G. Janssens. Deriving descriptions of possible values of program variables by means of abstract interpretation. *Journal of Logic Programming*, 13(2&3):205–258, 1992.

[6] M. Codish. *Abstract Interpretation of Sequential and Concurrent Logic Programs*. PhD thesis, The Weizmann Institute of Science, 1991.

[7] M. Codish, M. García de la Banda, M. Bruynooghe, and M. Hermenegildo. *Top-Down vs Bottom-Up Analysis of Logic Programs – Closing the Circle*. Technical Report Report CW 177, Department of Computer Science, K.U. Leuven, 1993.

[8] M. Codish and B. Demoen. Analysing logic programs using "Prop"-ositional logic programs and a magic wand. In D. Miller, editor, *Proceedings of the 1993 International Symposium on Logic Programming, Vancouver*, MIT Press, 1993.

[9] P. Cousot and R. Cousot. Abstract interpretation: a unified lattice model for static analysis of programs by construction or approximation of fixpoints. In *Proceedings of the 4th ACM Symposium on Principles of Programming Languages, Los Angeles*, pages 238–252, 1977.

[10] D.A. de Waal and J. Gallagher. Logic program specialisation with deletion of useless clause (poster abstract). In D. Miller, editor, *Proceedings of the 1993 Logic programming Symposium, Vancouver*, page 632, MIT Press, (full version appears as CSTR-92-33, Dept. Computer Science, University of Bristol), 1993.

[11] S. Debray and R. Ramakrishnan. *Canonical computations of logic programs.* Technical Report, University of Arizona-Tucson, July 1990.

[12] T. Frühwirth. Type inference by program transformation and partial evaluation. In H. Abramson and M.H. Rogers, editors, *Meta-Programming in Logic Programming*, MIT Press, 1989.

[13] T. Frühwirth, E. Shapiro, M.Y. Vardi, and E. Yardeni. Logic programs as types for logic programs. In *Proceedings of the IEEE Symposium on Logic in Computer Science, Amsterdam*, July 1991.

[14] J. Gallagher and D.A. de Waal. Deletion of redundant unary type predicates from logic programs. In K.K. Lau and T. Clement, editors, *Logic Program Synthesis and Transformation*, pages 151–167, Springer-Verlag, 1993.

[15] J. Gallagher and D.A. de Waal. *Fast and Precise Regular Approximation of Logic Programs.* Technical Report TR-93-19, Dept. of Computer Science, University of Bristol, 1993.

[16] J. Gallagher and D.A. de Waal. *Regular Approximations of Logic Programs and Their Uses.* Technical Report CSTR-92-06, University of Bristol, March 1992.

[17] N. Heintze. Practical aspects of set based analysis. In K. Apt, editor, *Proceedings of the Joint International Symposium and Conference on Logic Programming*, pages 765–769, MIT Press, 1992.

[18] N. Heintze and J. Jaffar. A Finite Presentation Theorem for Approximating Logic Programs. In *Proceedings of the 17th Annual ACM Symposium on Principles of Programming Languages, San Francisco*, pages 197–209, ACM Press, 1990.

[19] P. Van Hentenryck, A. Cortesi, and B. Le Charlier. *Type Analysis of Prolog Using Type Graphs.* Technical Report, Brown University, Department of Computer Science, December 1993.

[20] N. Jones. Flow analysis of lazy higher order functional programs. In S. Abramsky and C. Hankin, editors, *Abstract Interpretation of Declarative Languages*, Ellis-Horwood, 1987.

[21] T. Kanamori. *Abstract interpretation based on Alexander templates.* Technical Report TR-549, ICOT, March 1990.

[22] B. le Charlier, K. Musumbu, and P. van Hentenryck. A generic abstract interpretation algorithm and its complexity analysis. In K. Furukawa, editor, *Proceedings of the 8th International Conference on Logic Programming*, pages 64–78, MIT Press, 1991.

[23] K. Marriott and H. Søndergaard. Bottom-up abstract interpretation of logic programs. In *Proceedings of the Fifth International Conference and Symposium on Logic Programming, Washington*, August 1988.

[24] K. Marriott, H. Søndergaard, and N.D. Jones. Denotational abstract interpretation logic programs. *ACM Transactions on Programming Languages and Systems*, to appear, (also appears as Technical Report 92/20, Dept. of Computer Science, University of Melbourne).

[25] P. Mishra. Towards a theory of types in prolog. In *Proceedings of the IEEE International Symposium on Logic Programming*, 1984.

[26] K. Morris, J.D. Ullman, and A. Van Gelder. Design overview of the NAIL! system. In E. Shapiro, editor, *Proceedings of the 3rd International Conference on Logic Programming*, pages 554–568, Springer-verlag Lecture Notes in Computer Science, 1986.

[27] K. Muthukumar and M. Hermenegildo. Determination of Variable Dependence Information at Compile-Time Through Abstract Interpretation. In *1989 North American Conference on Logic Programming*, pages 166–189, MIT Press, October 1989.

[28] L. Naish. *Types and the intended meanings of logic programs*. Technical Report, University of Melbourne, Department of Computer Science, 1990.

[29] U. Reddy. Notions of polymorphism for predicate logic programming. In R.A. Kowalski and K. Bowen, editors, *Proceedings of the 5th International Conference on Logic Programming*, MIT Press, 1988.

[30] J. Rohmer, R. Lescœr, and J.-M. Kerisit. The Alexander method, a technique for the processing of recursive axioms in deductive databases. *New Generation Computing*, 4, 1986.

[31] D. Sahlin and T. Sjoland. Towards an Analysis for the AKL Language. In *1993 ICLP Workshop on Concurrent Constraint Programming*, SICS, June 1993.

[32] H. Seki. On the power of Alexander templates. In *Proceedings of the 8th ACM SIGACT-SIGMOD-SIGART Symposium on Principles of Database Systems, Philadelphia, Pennsylvania*, 1989.

[33] R. Tarjan. Depth-first search and linear graph algorithms. *SIAM Journal of Computing*, 1(2):146–160, 1972.

[34] J.D. Ullman. *Principles of Knowledge and Database Systems; Volume 1*. Computer Science Press, 1988.

[35] E. Yardeni and E.Y. Shapiro. A type system for logic programs. *Journal of Logic Programming*, 10(2):125–154, 1990.

[36] J. Zobel. Derivation of polymorphic types for Prolog programs. In R.A. Kowalski and K. Bowen, editors, *Proceedings of the 5th International Conference and Symposium on Logic Programming*, MIT Press, 1988.

Constraints II

Constraint Solving by Narrowing in Combined Algebraic Domains

Hélène Kirchner & Christophe Ringeissen *
CRIN-CNRS & INRIA-Lorraine
BP 239, 54506 Vandœuvre-lès-Nancy Cedex, France
{Helene.Kirchner,Christophe.Ringeissen}@loria.fr

Abstract

Narrowing is a way to integrate function evaluation and equality definition into logic programming. Here we show how this can be combined with the constraint paradigm. We propose a solver for goals with constraints in theories defined by unconstrained equalities and rewrite rules with constraints expressed in an algebraic built-in structure. The narrowing method reduces the goal solving problem in the whole theory to rewriting and constraint solving in an adequate combined theory. The combined solver is obtained through the combination of a solver in the built-in structure and a solver for the unconstrained equalities. Sufficient syntactic conditions are proposed to get a process that enumerates a complete set of solutions.

1 Introduction

Narrowing provides integration of function evaluation and equality definition into logic programming [6, 12, 8, 18, 10]. In this work, we show how this can be connected with the constraint paradigm to get a constraint solver on combined algebraic domains and to incorporate built-in structures like integers, booleans, finite fields, Post algebras, matrix rings over finite fields .... But in this context, it is needed to combine constraint solving in specific theories with other function symbols that may be free or may have properties like commutativity and associativity. In [17, 20], we show how to combine a constraint solver in finite algebras with another unification algorithm by extending the techniques used to combine unification algorithms. Combination of matching algorithms can be derived in a similar way [21]. Matching and unification algorithms in the combination of built-in structures with abstract symbols satisfying equational properties are used to perform rewriting and narrowing with constrained rules, thus leading to a constraint solver in the theory associated to the rewrite system with constraints.

In order to illustrate the kind of theories we want to deal with, let us consider an elementary example. Assume given a built-in algebra $\mathcal{A}$ of domain A with sort Nat, built-in functions $\mathcal{F}_0 = \{0, +\}$ and predicates $\mathcal{P}_0 = \{=, >\}$. Declarations of functions are $0 :\mapsto Nat$, $+ : Nat, Nat \mapsto Nat$. Declarations of predicates are $> : Nat, Nat$ and $= : Nat, Nat$. This signature is then enriched by adding function symbols $\mathcal{F}_1 = \{g\}$ where g a binary operation ($g : Nat, Nat \mapsto Nat$) is commutative i.e. satisfies the set C of equalities $\{g(x, y) = g(y, x)\}$. In a model that combines these two signatures, the fonction g is axiomatized by a recursive definition given

---

*This work is partially supported by the Esprit Basic Research working group 6028, CCL.

by a set R of two rewrite rules with constraints

$$g(x : Nat, 0) \quad\rightarrow\quad x : Nat$$
$$g(x : Nat \,+\, y : Nat, \, y : Nat) \quad\rightarrow\quad g(x : Nat, y : Nat) \quad\|\quad y : Nat > 0$$

This example illustrates the different problems to be solved. To compute with these rules, we need to combine constraint solving in the algebra $\mathcal{A}$ with unification or matching modulo a theory C axiomatically defined. Here we build a congruence $\sim_C$ that takes into account equality in $\mathcal{A}$ like $1 = 0 + 1$ and commutativity of g. Then for instance, the value of g for arguments $(1, 1)$ is computed as follows:

$$g(1, 1)(\sim_C g(0 + 1, 1)) \rightarrow_{R,C} g(0, 1) \rightarrow_{R,C} 1.$$

Note that the system does not terminate if the constraint is dropped. Indeed, since any natural x is equal to the natural $x + 0$, we would have the loop:

$$g(x, 0) \sim_C g(x + 0, 0) \rightarrow g(x, 0).$$

Then narrowing using R modulo $\sim_C$ provides an abstract solver for this theory. But to be complete, termination and confluence in equivalence classes of the rewrite system with constraints must be checked. To achieve confluence, we require the constraints in the rules to be in the built-in language. This is naturally expressed within an order-sorted framework [7, 23] as in [1], where the built-in domain is a subsort of the whole domain of interest. Checking confluence modulo a congruence relation $\sim_C$ requires $\sim_C$ to be sort-preserving and $\rightarrow_R$ sort-decreasing. Although these assumptions could be dropped as in [11, 4], they make proofs easier and are often satisfied in programming in a rewrite rule-based language like OBJ [9, 13].

To achieve termination, the argument is to find a well-founded ordering compatible with $\sim_C$, but such an ordering does not always exist. In particular axiomatizations of integers or booleans involve collapse and non-regular axioms that prevent termination of rewriting in equivalence classes modulo $\sim_C$. To avoid any hypothesis on the axiomatisation of the built-in structure, the termination argument in our order-sorted context is based on the fact that a term is structured in levels with either built-in symbols or other function symbols. The number of levels must be preserved by $\sim_C$ and must not increase by rewriting. The congruence $\sim_C$ is closed under admissible substitutions that do not change the number of levels of a term and solutions for constraint are required to be admissible.

So the paper is built as follows.
- Section 2 state the definition of constraint languages and introduces the three constraint solvers considered in this paper.
- In Sections 3 and 4, an algebraic structure is defined for making precise the domain in which constraint solving is performed. The proposed structure is a quotient algebra using a congruence relation generated by $\mathcal{A}$-equality and equality modulo C. A constraint solver in this structure is built by adapting tools for combining unification algorithms.
- Thanks to the restricted form of constraints in the original set of rules, the local confluence and coherence of the rewrite relation with constraints can be checked on critical pairs with constraints in Section 5.
- Given a confluent and terminating rewrite relation in congruence classes, narrowing with constraints can be proved correct and complete for solving goals in the theory defined by the constrained rewrite rules. We thus get another constraint solver based on narrowing which uses both rewrite rules and the previous combined solver. This is developed in Section 6.

All proofs omitted in this paper can be found in [16].

2   Constraint languages

We first adopt a general definition of a symbolic constraint language and its solver, and then introduce the different constraint languages used in this paper.

Let $(\mathcal{S}, \prec)$ be an ordered set of sort symbols, $\mathcal{F}$ be a set of function symbols, $\mathcal{P}$ a set of predicate symbols, $\mathcal{D}$ be a set of subsort declarations ($\mathcal{D}_{\mathcal{S}} = \{s \prec s' \mid s, s' \in \mathcal{S}\}$), function declarations ($\mathcal{D}_{\mathcal{F}} = \{f : s_1 \ldots s_n \mapsto s' \mid s_1 \ldots s_n, s' \in \mathcal{S}, \ f \in \mathcal{F}\}$), and predicate declarations ($\mathcal{D}_{\mathcal{P}} = \{p : s_1 \ldots s_n \mid s_1 \ldots s_n \in \mathcal{S}, \ p \in \mathcal{P}\}$). $\mathcal{X}$ denotes a set of sorted variables denoted $(x : s)$. An order-sorted signature Σ is given by an ordered set of sorts $\mathcal{S}$, a set of function symbols $\mathcal{F}$, a set of predicate symbols $\mathcal{P}$, and a set of subsort, function and predicate declarations $\mathcal{D}$.

Let $\mathcal{A}$ be an $(\mathcal{S}, \mathcal{F}, \mathcal{D}_{\mathcal{S}} \cup \mathcal{D}_{\mathcal{F}})$-algebra, whose carrier is denoted by A. $\mathcal{T}(\Sigma, \mathcal{X})$ is the free $(\mathcal{S}, \mathcal{F}, \mathcal{D}_{\mathcal{S}} \cup \mathcal{D}_{\mathcal{F}})$-algebra over $\mathcal{X}$, whose carrier is the set of terms. The set of variables occurring in a term t is denoted by $\mathcal{V}(t)$.

An order-sorted equational theory (Σ, E) is given by an order-sorted signature Σ and a set of universally quantified equalities E. Σ is a *lowest-sorted signature* if every Σ-term t has a lowest sort $ls(t)$. (Σ, E) is *sort-preserving* if $\forall t, t' \in \mathcal{T}(\Sigma, \mathcal{X})$, $t =_E t' \Longrightarrow ls(t) = ls(t')$. An order-sorted rewrite system (Σ, R) is given by an order-sorted signature Σ and a set of universally quantified rewrite rules R. (Σ, R) is *sort-decreasing* if $\forall t, t' \in \mathcal{T}(\Sigma, \mathcal{X})$, $t \to_R t' \Longrightarrow ls(t) \succeq ls(t')$.

These properties are easily decidable and sufficient syntactic conditions on the signature are given for instance in [7].

A first-order algebraic Σ-structure $\mathcal{A}$ is given by
- a carrier A which is a collection of non-empty sets $(A_s)_{s \in \mathcal{S}}$, such that $A_s \subseteq A_{s'}$ when $(s \prec s') \in \mathcal{S}$,
- for each function symbol in $\mathcal{F}$ with a rank $f : s_1, \ldots, s_n \mapsto s$, a function $f_{\mathcal{A}}$ from $A_{s_1} \times \ldots \times A_{s_n}$ to A_s,
- for each predicate symbol except $=$ in $\mathcal{P}$ with a rank $p : s_1, \ldots, s_n$, a relation $p_{\mathcal{A}}$ on $A_{s_1} \times \ldots \times A_{s_n}$. Whenever Σ contains the predicate symbol $=$, it will be interpreted as the equality relation in $\mathcal{A}$.

An assignment α is a mapping from $\mathcal{X}$ to A that assigns to a sorted variable $(x : s)$ an element of A_s; it uniquely extends to an order-sorted homomorphism $\underline{\alpha}$ from $\mathcal{T}(\Sigma, \mathcal{X})$ to $\mathcal{A}$. The restriction of an assignment α to a set of variables $V \subseteq \mathcal{X}$ is denoted by $\alpha_{|V}$. This notation is extended to sets of assignments. The set of all assignments is denoted by $ASS_{\mathcal{A}}^{\mathcal{X}}$ or $ASS_{\mathcal{A}}$, when $\mathcal{X}$ is clear from the context.

A Σ-*substitution* σ is an endomorphism of $\mathcal{T}(\Sigma, \mathcal{X})$ from a finite set of variables $\mathcal{D}om(\sigma) = \{(x : s) \mid (x : s) \in \mathcal{X} \text{ and } \sigma(x : s) \neq (x : s)\}$ that are not mapped to themselves, such that $\forall (x : s) \in \mathcal{D}om(\sigma), ls(\sigma(x : s)) \preceq s$. From now on, we assume that all substitutions are Σ-substitutions. We use letters $\sigma, \mu, \gamma, \phi, \ldots$ to denote substitutions. We call *range* of σ the set of terms $\mathcal{R}an(\sigma) = \cup_{(x:s) \in \mathcal{D}om(\sigma)} \sigma(x : s)$ and *variable range* of σ the set of variables $\mathcal{V}\mathcal{R}an(\sigma) = \cup_{(x:s) \in \mathcal{D}om(\sigma)} \mathcal{V}(\sigma(x : s))$. A substitution σ is *idempotent* if $\sigma \circ \sigma = \sigma$.

The definition of constraint languages adopted in this paper is similar to those given in [22, 15].

Definition 1 Let $\Sigma = (\mathcal{S}, \mathcal{F}, \mathcal{P}, \mathcal{D})$ be an order-sorted signature, $\mathcal{X}$ a set of variables, a *constraint language* $L_{\mathcal{K}}[\Sigma, \mathcal{X}]$ (or $L_{\mathcal{K}}$ for short) is given by:
• a set of *constraints* which are first-order formulae built over Σ and variables $\mathcal{X}$. The empty conjunction $\top$ is also a constraint. Constraints are syntactically distinguished by a question mark exponent on predicates. The set of free variables of the constraint c is denoted $\mathcal{V}(c)$.

• An interpretation $\mathcal{K}$ is an order-sorted Σ-structure given by a domain K and a solution mapping that associates to each constraint the set of assignments $Sol_{\mathcal{K}}(c)$ defined as follows:

- $Sol_{\mathcal{K}}(\top) = \{\alpha \in ASS_K^{\mathcal{X}}\}$
- $Sol_{\mathcal{K}}(t_1 =^? t_2) = \{\alpha \in ASS_K^{\mathcal{X}} \mid \underline{\alpha}(t_1) = \underline{\alpha}(t_2)\}$
- $Sol_{\mathcal{K}}(p^?(t_1, \ldots, t_m)) = \{\alpha \in ASS_K^{\mathcal{X}} \mid (\underline{\alpha}(t_1), \ldots, \underline{\alpha}(t_m)) \in p_{\mathcal{K}}\}$
- $Sol_{\mathcal{K}}(c \wedge c') = Sol_{\mathcal{K}}(c) \cap Sol_{\mathcal{K}}(c')$
- $Sol_{\mathcal{K}}(\neg c) = ASS_K^{\mathcal{X}} \backslash Sol_{\mathcal{K}}(c)$
- $Sol_{\mathcal{K}}(\exists x : c) = \{\alpha \in ASS_K^{\mathcal{X}} \mid \exists \beta \in ASS_K^{\mathcal{X}}, \ \alpha_{|\mathcal{X} \backslash \{x\}} = \beta_{|\mathcal{X} \backslash \{x\}} \text{ and } \beta \in Sol_{\mathcal{K}}(c)\}$.

An assignment in $Sol_{\mathcal{K}}(c)$ is a *solution* of c in $L_{\mathcal{K}}$. A constraint c is *valid* in $L_{\mathcal{K}}$, written $L_{\mathcal{K}} \models c$, if any assignment is a solution of c in $L_{\mathcal{K}}$. As usual, we can also define abbreviations to write more complex constraints like: $c \vee c' = \neg(\neg c \wedge \neg c')$, $\forall x : c = \neg(\exists x : \neg c)$ and $\bot = \neg(\top)$. Two constraints c and c' are *equivalent* if $Sol_{\mathcal{K}}(c) = Sol_{\mathcal{K}}(c')$.

We also make precise the notions of symbolic solutions and complete sets of symbolic solutions for a given constraint. A *symbolic solution* of a $L_{\mathcal{K}}[\Sigma, \mathcal{X}]$-constraint c is a substitution σ such that $L_{\mathcal{K}} \models \sigma(c)$. The set of all symbolic solutions of c is denoted $SS_{\mathcal{K}}(c)$. A substitution ϕ is an *instance* on $V \subseteq \mathcal{X}$ of a substitution σ, written $\sigma \leq_{\mathcal{K}}^V \phi$, if there exists some substitution μ such that $\forall x : s \in V, \ L_{\mathcal{K}} \models \phi(x : s) = \mu(\sigma(x : s))$.

Definition 2 A set of substitutions is a *complete set of symbolic solutions* of the $L_{\mathcal{K}}[\Sigma, \mathcal{X}]$-constraint c, denoted by $CSS_{\mathcal{K}}(c)$, if
(1) $\forall \sigma \in CSS_{\mathcal{K}}(c), \ \mathcal{D}om(\sigma) \cap \mathcal{V}\mathcal{R}an(\sigma) = \emptyset$ (idempotency).
(2) $CSS_{\mathcal{K}}(c) \subseteq SS_{\mathcal{K}}(c)$ (correctness).
(3) $\forall \phi \in SS_{\mathcal{K}}(c), \ \exists \sigma \in CSS_{\mathcal{K}}(c), \ \sigma \leq_{\mathcal{K}}^{\mathcal{V}(c)} \phi$ (completeness).

In this paper, three different constraint languages will be considered:
(1) $L_{\mathcal{A}}$ denotes the built-in language, whose syntax is given by an order-sorted signature Σ_0 and a set of variables $\mathcal{X}_0$. The interpretation is the Σ_0-structure $\mathcal{A}$. A built-in constraint solver is assumed given for $L_{\mathcal{A}}$.
(2) A combined language $L_{\mathcal{C}}$ is an enrichment of $L_{\mathcal{A}}$ based on a signature $\Sigma \supseteq \Sigma_0$ and a set of variables $\mathcal{X}$. Equalities C define properties, such as associativity and commutativity, satisfied by newly introduced symbols. The interpretation is a Σ-algebra which is a consistent enrichment of $\mathcal{A}$. It is built as a quotient of the set of Σ-terms by a congruence generated from C and theorems valid in $\mathcal{A}$. Constraints in $L_{\mathcal{C}}$ involve constraints c in $L_{\mathcal{A}}$ and equations to solve modulo C, but more generally they are conjunctions of constraints built with the same predicates as in $L_{\mathcal{A}}$ and terms in the whole enriched signature Σ and variables in $\mathcal{X}$. A constraint solver for $L_{\mathcal{C}}$ is built from the constraint solver in $L_{\mathcal{A}}$ and from a unification algorithm for C by adapting the combination techniques for unification algorithms.
(3) A constrained rule language $L_{R,\mathcal{C}}$ is based on the same signature $\Sigma \supseteq \Sigma_0$ and variables $\mathcal{X}$. Additional properties of symbols from $\Sigma \backslash \Sigma_0$ are defined using a set R of constrained rewrite rules. These rules are assumed to have constraints expressed only in $L_{\mathcal{A}}$. This restriction allows building the interpretation as a Σ-algebra which is again a consistent enrichment of $\mathcal{A}$. Constraints in $L_{R,\mathcal{C}}$ are goals with constraints of the form $(p^?(t_1, \ldots, t_n) \parallel S)$ where $p \in \Sigma_0$, $t_1, \ldots, t_n$ are Σ-terms and S is a conjunction of $L_{\mathcal{C}}$-constraints. A constraint solver for $L_{R,\mathcal{C}}$ is based on constrained narrowing that reduces the constraint solving problem in $L_{R,\mathcal{C}}$ to rule application and constraint solving in $L_{\mathcal{C}}$.

3 The built-in language

In order to stay as general as possible, we consider built-in structures with several sorts and possible inclusions.

Definition 3 Let $\Sigma_0 = (\mathcal{S}_0, \mathcal{F}_0, \mathcal{P}_0, \mathcal{D}_0)$ be an order-sorted signature, $\mathcal{X}_0$ a set of sorted variables and $\mathcal{A}$ a Σ_0-structure. $\mathcal{A}$ is said *built-in* if $\mathcal{A}$ is term-generated and there exists a biggest sort s_* which coincides with the carrier A.

Built-in constraints will be built from this signature.

Definition 4 The *built-in language* denoted by $L_{\mathcal{A}}$ is defined by the order-sorted signature $\Sigma_0 = (\mathcal{S}_0, \mathcal{F}_0, \mathcal{P}_0, \mathcal{D}_0)$, the set of sorted variables $\mathcal{X}_0$, and the built-in Σ_0-structure $\mathcal{A}$.

The set of all equalities that holds in $\mathcal{A}$ is denoted $Th(\mathcal{A})$.
Notation: Sort, function and predicate symbols from Σ_0 are said built-in. Terms and constraints built on $L_{\mathcal{A}}$ are called *built-in terms* and *built-in constraints*. Variables of $\mathcal{X}_0$ are called *built-in variables*.

Typically useful built-in structures are integers, booleans and Post algebras.

4 The combined language

The signature Σ_0 is now enriched by new sort and function symbols into a signature $\Sigma = (\mathcal{S}, \mathcal{F}, \mathcal{P}, \mathcal{D})$ such that $\mathcal{S} \supseteq \mathcal{S}_0$, $\mathcal{F} \supseteq \mathcal{F}_0$ and $\mathcal{P} = \mathcal{P}_0$. Let us define $\mathcal{F}_1 = \mathcal{F} \backslash \mathcal{F}_0$, $\mathcal{S}_1$ as the set of sorts in the rank of function symbols of $\mathcal{F}_1$, $\mathcal{D}_1 = \mathcal{D} \backslash \mathcal{D}_0$, and $\Sigma_1 = (\mathcal{S}_1, \mathcal{F}_1, \{=\}, \mathcal{D}_1)$. Note that the signatures Σ_0 and Σ_1 have by construction disjoint function symbol sets but possibly non-disjoint sort symbol sets, and only share the equality predicate. The set of built-in variables $\mathcal{X}_0$ is also extended to a set of variables $\mathcal{X}$ thanks to a set of variables $\mathcal{X}_1$ of sorts $\mathcal{S}_1 \backslash \mathcal{S}_0$ such that $\mathcal{X} = \mathcal{X}_0 \cup \mathcal{X}_1$.

Definition 5 A term t of $\mathcal{T}(\Sigma, \mathcal{X})$ is *i-pure* (for $i = 0, 1$) if t contains only function symbols from $\mathcal{F}_i$ and possibly variables of $\mathcal{X}$. An equation $(s =^? t)$ is *i-pure* if s and t are. An atomic constraint $p(t_1, \ldots, t_n)$ is *i-pure* (for $i = 0, 1$) if $p \in \mathcal{P}_i$ and $t_1, \ldots, t_n$ are *i-pure*. A term with its top symbol in $\mathcal{F}_i$ is called *i-term*. *Alien* subterms of a *i*-term are *j*-(sub)terms $(i \neq j)$ such that each prefix symbol is in $\mathcal{F}_i$. The set of alien subterms of t is denoted $AST(t)$.

Definition 6 The number of 1-levels in a term t, denoted by $nc_1(t)$ is inductively defined by: $nc_1(x) = 0$ if $x \in \mathcal{X}$, $nc_1(t) = 1 + \sum_{s \in AST(t)} nc_1(s)$ if $t(\epsilon) \in \mathcal{F}_1$ else $nc_1(t) = \sum_{s \in AST(t)} nc_1(s)$.

4.1 Hypotheses

We assume that function symbols from $\mathcal{F}_1$ have properties expressed by a set of Σ_1-equalities C, such as commutativity and (or) associativity. We now have to consider the combination of two order-sorted equational theories (Σ_0, E_0) and (Σ_1, E_1), where E_0 is the set of equalities $Th(\mathcal{A})$ valid in $\mathcal{A}$, and E_1 is a set of Σ_1-axioms. Both are assumed consistent. Beyond the hypothesis of disjoint function symbols, we also need the hypothesis that new sorts of $\mathcal{S}_1$ are not lower than s_* and $\mathcal{S}_0 \cap \mathcal{S}_1 \subseteq \{s_*\}$. This is required to build a conservative extension. With respect to axioms $(g = d)$ in E_1, we also require several properties, namely to be regular

$(\mathcal{V}(g) = \mathcal{V}(d))$, collapse-free $(g, d \notin \mathcal{X})$ and sort-preserving. These hypotheses are needed to work with order-sorted rewriting modulo a congruence relation on terms built on the union of both signatures $\Sigma_0 \cup \Sigma_1$.

In order to define an interpretation for the combined language, we need to build a congruence relation on $\mathcal{T}(\Sigma, \mathcal{X})$ and to define the interpretation of predicates.

4.2 Congruence on combined terms

The problem is due to the fact that we do not want to put any syntactic hypothesis like regularity or non-collapsing on axioms in $Th(\mathcal{A})$ since the built-in theory must be any theory. But in order to rewrite and perform narrowing modulo this congruence, we need to avoid cycles on equivalence classes. They could appear for instance by application of non-regular or collapse axioms in $Th(\mathcal{A})$ to a term of basic sort but involving symbols from $\mathcal{F}_1$.

Example 1 In the example of the introduction, $Th(\mathcal{A})$ contains the equality on natural numbers $x * 0 = 0$ (non-regular), or $x + 0 = x$ (collapse).

The proposed solution is to restrict $=_{E_0 \cup E_1}$ so that the top symbol theory and number of 1-levels are preserved in two equivalent terms.

Definition 7 The relation $\sim_C$ is defined by: $t \sim_C t'$ if $t =_{E_0 \cup E_1} t'$, $t(\epsilon), t'(\epsilon) \in \mathcal{F}_i \cup \mathcal{X}$ and $nc_1(t) = nc_1(t')$.

It is worth emphasizing that with this definition no 1-term can be equivalent with $\sim_C$ to a 0-term.

Example 2 (Example 1 continued). We have $g(x, y) + g(y, z) \sim_C g(y, z) + g(x, y)$, $g(x + y, z) \sim_C g(y + x, z)$ but $g(x, y) + 0 \not\sim_C g(x, y)$, $g(x, y) * 0 \not\sim_C 0$.

4.3 Abstraction

Interpretation of predicates needs the notion of variable abstraction which consists of replacing alien subterms by new variables such that equivalent terms are replaced by the same variable. For this purpose, we introduce a convergent rewrite relation $\rightarrow_{R_c}$ with the same expressivity as the union of both theories $(\Sigma_0 \cup \Sigma_1, E_0 \cup E_1)$. Let $\Sigma = \Sigma_0 \cup \Sigma_1$ and $>$ be a simplification ordering total on $\mathcal{T}(\Sigma \cup \mathcal{X})$, such that variables are minimal. Let $E_i^>$ be the set of orientable instances, $l = \sigma(g) \rightarrow \sigma(d) = r$, where $g, d \in \mathcal{T}(\Sigma_i, \mathcal{X})$ and $g =_{E_i} d$. These rules are used to define a combined rewrite relation $\rightarrow_{R_c} = \rightarrow_{E_0^>} \cup \rightarrow_{E_1^>}$ which is convergent and simulates $=_{E_0 \cup E_1}$ i.e. $t =_{E_0 \cup E_1} t' \iff t \downarrow_{R_c} = t' \downarrow_{R_c}$ [16].

Definition 8 A *variable abstraction* is a one-to-one mapping π from the set of non-variable terms in R_c-normal forms $T \downarrow_{R_c} = \{u \downarrow_{R_c} | u \in \mathcal{T}(\Sigma \cup \mathcal{X})$ and $u \downarrow_{R_c} \in \mathcal{T}(\Sigma \cup \mathcal{X}) \backslash \mathcal{X}\}$ to a subset of variables of $\mathcal{X}$ such that $\pi(u \downarrow_{R_c}) = x : s_*$.

π^{-1} denotes the substitution with a possibly infinite domain which corresponds to the inverse of π. Given a term t, the i-abstraction t^{π_i} of a term t is a well-formed term, inductively defined as follows:

- if $t = x : s \in \mathcal{X}$ then $t^{\pi_i} = x : s$,
- if $t = f(s_1, \ldots, s_p)$ and $f \in \mathcal{F}_i$ then $t^{\pi_i} = f(s_1^{\pi_i}, \ldots, s_p^{\pi_i})$,
- else if $t \downarrow_{R_c} \notin \mathcal{X}$ then $t^{\pi_i} = \pi(t \downarrow_{R_c})$ else $t^{\pi_i} = t \downarrow_{R_c}$.

Given a substitution σ, σ^{π_i} denotes its i-abstraction defined by $\sigma^{\pi_i}(x) = (\sigma(x))^{\pi_i}$ for any variable $x \in \mathcal{D}om(\sigma)$.

Example 3 In the example of the introduction, $g(x+1,y)^{\pi_1} = g(v_0,y)$ if $\pi(x+1 \downarrow_{R_c}) = v_0$ and $(g(x,y)+g(y,x)+1)^{\pi_0} = v_1+v_1+1$ if $\pi(g(x,y) \downarrow_{R_c}) = \pi(g(y,x) \downarrow_{R_c}) = v_1$.

4.4 Extension of the built-in language

Definition 9 The *combined language* denoted L_C is defined by the order-sorted signature $\Sigma = \Sigma_0 \cup \Sigma_1$, the set of sorted variables $\mathcal{X}$, and the Σ-structure $\mathcal{C} = \mathcal{T}(\Sigma,\mathcal{X})/\sim_C$. If $p \in \mathcal{P}_0$ then the interpretation of p in $\mathcal{C}$ is the relation p_C defined by $p_C(t_1,\ldots,t_n)$ if $L_A \models p(t_1^{\pi_0},\ldots,t_n^{\pi_0})$.

This definition is compatible with equality in $\mathcal{C}$: indeed if $t_k =_{E_0 \cup E_1} s_k$, their abstractions verify $t_k^{\pi_0} =_A s_k^{\pi_0}$. According to the chosen interpretation of predicates, validity of 0-pure atomic constraints is preserved in the interpretation.

Proposition 1 [16] L_C is a conservative extension of L_A i.e. $L_A \models c_0 \Leftrightarrow L_C \models c_0$ if c_0 is 0-pure.

The congruence $\sim_C$ is not preserved under substitutions in general, but it is if we restrict to substitutions that do not change the number of 1-levels, which is achieved when terms in their range always have at most one 1-level. In particular built-in variables are instantiated by built-in terms.

Definition 10 The set of *admissible Σ-substitutions* is $SUBST_0 = \{\mu = \mu_1\mu_0 \mid \mathcal{D}om(\mu_1) \subseteq \mathcal{X}_1, \mathcal{R}an(\mu_1) \subseteq \mathcal{T}(\Sigma_1,\mathcal{X}), \ \mathcal{D}om(\mu_0) \subseteq \mathcal{X}_0, \mathcal{R}an(\mu_0) \subseteq \mathcal{T}(\Sigma_0,\mathcal{X}_0)\}$.

Since E_1 does not contain collapse axioms, two admissible substitutions are equivalent modulo $\sim_C$ iff they are equivalent modulo $=_{E_0 \cup E_1}$. For a given constraint c, we restrict our attention to the set of its *admissible solutions* $SS_C^*(c) = SS_C(c) \cap SUBST_0$. A complete set of admissible solutions of a L_C-constraint c is denoted $CSS_C^*(c)$.

Our goal now is to build a constraint solver for L_C from the built-in solver available for L_A and from a unification algorithm for E_1. We first transform a problem in L_C into another one expressed with $=_{E_0 \cup E_1}$, and then extract admissible solutions.

From the definition of the congruence $\sim_C$, it is easy to check the following facts for two terms t, t' and an admissible substitution σ:
(1) If $t(\epsilon), t'(\epsilon) \in \mathcal{F}_i$ and $nc_1(t) = nc_1(t')$, then $\sigma(t) \sim_C \sigma(t')$ iff $\sigma(t) =_{E_0 \cup E_1} \sigma(t')$.
(2) If $t \in \mathcal{X}$ and $nc_1(t') \leq 1$, then $\sigma(t) \sim_C \sigma(t')$ iff $\sigma(t) =_{E_0 \cup E_1} \sigma(t')$.
(3) In all other (non-symmetric) cases, there is no admissible σ s.t. $\sigma(t) \sim_C \sigma(t')$.

We are now left to solve constraints with respect to the equational theory $=_{E_0 \cup E_1}$.

4.5 Combination principles

We recall here what are the main steps for combining two unification algorithms or procedures, which requires more than a blind use of each algorithm. The technique [2] is based on the next built-in steps:
(1) Abstraction produces pure constraints in each language by introducing new variables to split terms. These new variables are shared by the two theories and may further be instantiated in both of them. To avoid this problem, all possible choices for instantiating a variable in a theory have to be considered. When a

variable is instantiated in E_i, it is considered as a constant in E_j, $j \neq i$. The second problem due to abstraction is that two distinct variables may be introduced that actually denote two equal or equivalent terms. This needs to perform all possible variable identifications after the abstraction step. A variable identification is just a substitution whose range is a set of variables.

Definition 11 An identification on a set of variables V is an idempotent substitution σ such that $\mathcal{D}om(\sigma) \subseteq V$ and $\mathcal{R}an(\sigma) \subseteq V$. The set of all identifications on V is denoted by ID_V.

(2) Solving pure constraints in the related language is obviously correct. For the completeness part, we need the following result proved in [16].

Proposition 2 Let $p(t_1, \ldots, t_n)$ be a 0-pure atomic constraint and σ a R_c-normalized substitution. Then $L_C \models p(\sigma(t_1), \ldots, \sigma(t_n)) \Leftrightarrow L_A \models p(\sigma^{\pi_0}(t_1), \ldots, \sigma^{\pi_0}(t_n))$.

As a consequence, we yet have that $CSS_A(c_0)$ is a $CSS_C(c_0)$ if c_0 is a 0-pure constraint.

(3) Recombining the solutions obtained in each component is performed by propagation of the values. But cycling equations between two theories may appear and must be solved. For instance, if $x_1 =^? t_1[x_2]$ is solved in the first theory (where x_2 is considered as a free constant symbol) and $x_2 =^? t_2[x_1]$ is solved in the second (where x_1 is considered as a free constant symbol), their propagation yields a cycle. The problem is avoided by a priori choosing a linear ordering $<$ on the set $V \cup C$ of all variables and constants occurring in the constraint. Then to each constant a is associated a set of variables $V_a = \{x \mid x \in V \text{ and } x < a\}$. Solving a constraint w.r.t. a linear restriction $<$ is finding symbolic solutions σ s.t. $\forall x, a$ with $x \in V_a$, then a does not occur in $\sigma(x)$ and $\sigma(a) = a$. The set of symbolic solutions of a i-pure constraint c_i w.r.t. a linear restriction $<$ on $V_1 \cup V_2$ is denoted $SS^<_{E_i}(c_i, V_j)$ if V_j denotes the set of variables instantiated in E_j, $j \neq i$, and considered as constants in E_i.

It is worth emphasizing that if nothing is known about the axiomatisation of the built-in structure $\mathcal{A}$, the given built-in solver must be able to deal with linear restrictions.

So the combined constraint solver works as follows: A L_C-constraint c is first transformed into a conjunction of pure constraints $c_0 \wedge c_1$. A combined solution is then obtained from two pure partial solutions by transforming a dag solved form (the union of the two parts) into a tree solved form where replacement has been performed.

Definition 12 The *combined solution* $\sigma_0 \odot \sigma_1$ of $c_0 \wedge c_1$ obtained from $\sigma_0 \in SS^<_{E_0}(c_0, V_1)$ and $\sigma_1 \in SS^<_{E_1}(c_1, V_0)$ is defined as follows: let x be a variable in V_i and $\{y_1, \ldots, y_n\}$ be the set of (smaller) variables in V_j, $j \neq i$, occurring in $\sigma_i(x)$. Then $\sigma(x) = \sigma_i(x)[y_k \hookleftarrow \sigma(y_k)]_{k=1,\ldots,n}$.

Example 4 $(\sigma_0 = \{x_0 \mapsto 1, y_0 \mapsto 0\}) \odot (\sigma_1 = \{v_1 \mapsto g(g(x_0, y_0), x_0)\}) = \{x_0 \mapsto 1, y_0 \mapsto 0, v_1 \mapsto g(g(1, 0), 1)\}$.

In order to be complete, all linear restrictions should be considered. However, thanks to the restriction to admissible substitutions, a part of nondeterminism in the combination of solutions may be eliminated:

- Built-in variables in $\mathcal{V}(c)$ of sorts in $\mathcal{X}_0$ are included in V_0 and are minimal for $<$.
- Variables from $V_0 \cap \mathcal{V}(c)$ and from $V_1 \cap \mathcal{V}(c)$ do not interleave.

Theorem 1 *[16] Constraint solving in L_C is decidable (resp. finitary) if constraint solving in L_A and unification in C with linear restriction are decidable (resp. finitary).*

In this combined language L_C, we are now able to solve constraints, in particular equational constraints. Matching and word problem are special instances of equation solving, so they are also available in the combined model we have built. It is now possible to define rewriting and narrowing relations.

5 The constrained rewrite language

An equational specification with built-in constraints contains equalities that are constrained in a built-in language.

Definition 13 A *specification with a built-in structure A* is given by (Σ, E, C, L_A) such that:
- L_A is a constraint language whose interpretation is the built-in Σ_0-structure A,
- Σ is an enrichment of the order-sorted signature Σ_0,
- C is a set of equalities on $\mathcal{T}(\Sigma, \mathcal{X})$,
- E is a set of constrained equalities $(l = r \| c)$, where $l, r \in \mathcal{T}(\Sigma, \mathcal{X})$ and c is a constraint in L_A.

We indeed assume the same hypotheses on Σ, C and L_A as in the previous section.

5.1 Construction of the interpretation

The Σ-structure associated to a specification (Σ, E, C, L_A) is an order-sorted term algebra quotiented by a congruence relation that takes into account A-equality, C-equality and the schematization of constrained equalities E.

Following [15], the set of equalities schematized by a constrained equality $(l = r \| c)$ is: $S_A(l = r \| c) = \{\sigma(l) = \sigma(r) \mid \sigma \in SUBST_0,\ \sigma_{|\mathcal{X}_0} \in SS_A(c)\}$. The set of rewrite rules schematized by a constrained rewrite rule $(l \to r \| c)$ is defined in the same way. The set of equalities schematized by a set E of constrained equalities is $S_A(E) = \bigcup_{(l=r\|c)\in E} S_A(l = r \| c)$. The interpretation associated to a specification (Σ, E, C, L_A) is now obtained as follows:

Definition 14 The *interpretation $\mathcal{M}$* of the specification (Σ, E, C, L_A) is the quotient algebra $\mathcal{T}(\Sigma, \mathcal{X})/\sim_{\mathcal{M}}$ where $\sim_{\mathcal{M}}$ is the transitive closure $(\sim_C \cup \sim_{S_A(E)})^*$ and $\sim_{S_A(E)}$ is the smallest congruence relation on $\mathcal{T}(\Sigma, \mathcal{X})$ including $S_A(E)$.

5.2 Constrained rewriting

Assume now that E is oriented into a set R of rewrite rules with constraints.

Definition 15 The relation $\to_{R,C}$ is defined on $\mathcal{T}(\Sigma, \mathcal{X})$ by: $t \to_{R,C} t'$ if $\exists (l \to r \| c) \in R,\ \exists \sigma$ s.t. $t_{|\omega} \sim_C \sigma(l),\ \sigma \in SS_C^*(c),\ t' = t[\sigma(r)]_\omega$.

Note that the matching problem is solved in the combined language L_C. Then σ is a solution modulo $\sim_C$ of the matching problem that instantiates variables in l by Σ-terms.

In order to check validity of the constraint, we have to check that $\sigma \in SS_C^*(c)$. Note that if we assume that all the constraints c in the rules are built-in, then

$SS_{\mathcal{C}}^*(c) = SS_{\mathcal{A}}(c)$. Therefore, the relation $\sim_{R,\mathcal{C}} = (\sim_{\mathcal{C}} \cup \longleftrightarrow_{R,\mathcal{C}})^*$ coincides with $\sim_{\mathcal{M}}$ if constraints in R are built-in.

Definition 16 A set R of *rewrite rules with built-in constraints* satisfies the following conditions $\forall (l \to r \| c) \in R$: $\mathcal{V}(l) \supseteq \mathcal{V}(r)$, $ls(\sigma(l)) \geq ls(\sigma(r))$ for any $\sigma \in SS_{\mathcal{C}}^*(c)$, $l(\epsilon) \in \Sigma_1$, and variables in $\mathcal{V}(c)$ are built-in.

Proposition 3 If $t \to_{R,\mathcal{C}} t'$ then $ls(t) \geq ls(t')$.

Proof: Consider $t_{|\omega} \sim_{\mathcal{C}} \sigma(l)$. Since C is sort-preserving, $ls(t_{|\omega}) = ls(\sigma(l))$, and $ls(\sigma(l)) \geq ls(\sigma(r))$ because R is sort-decreasing. Hence $ls(t) \geq ls(t')$ if $t' = t[\omega \longleftrightarrow \sigma(r)]$. □

Proposition 4 A built-in term is irreducible with $\to_{R,\mathcal{C}}$.

Proof: Assume that t is a reducible built-in term. So $t_{|\omega} \sim_{\mathcal{C}} \sigma(l)$. Since C is collapse-free, $(t_{|\omega})^{\pi_0} =_{E_0} (\sigma(l))^{\pi_0}$. The term l has a top-symbol in Σ_1, thus $(\sigma(l))^{\pi_0}$ is a variable which does not occur in the built-in term $(t_{|\omega})^{\pi_0} = t_{|\omega}$. Then E_0 would be inconsistent. □

Definition 17 The relation $\to_{R,\mathcal{C}}$ is convergent modulo $\sim_{\mathcal{C}}$ if the relation $\to_{R/\mathcal{C}}$ defined as $\sim_{\mathcal{C}} \circ \to_{R,\mathcal{C}} \circ \sim_{\mathcal{C}}$ is terminating and $\overset{*}{\longleftrightarrow}_{R,\mathcal{C}} \subseteq \overset{*}{\longrightarrow}_{R/\mathcal{C}} \circ \sim_{\mathcal{C}} \circ \overset{*}{\longleftarrow}_{R/\mathcal{C}}$.

For this rewrite relation just defined, the definitions of confluence, coherence, local confluence and coherence are defined as usual (see [14]).

5.3 Confluence

Confluence and coherence can be checked thanks to the computation of adequate constrained critical pairs and extensions.

Definition 18 A *constrained critical pair* of $(g \to d \| c')$ and $(l \to r \| c)$, at a non-variable position ω of g, is the constrained equality $(g[r]_\omega = d \| c \wedge c' \wedge (g_{|\omega} =_{\mathcal{C}}^? l))$ if $c \wedge c' \wedge g_{|\omega} =_{\mathcal{C}}^? l$ is satisfiable.
A *constrained extension* of $(l \to r \| c)$ w.r.t. $(g = d) \in C$, at a non-variable position ω of g, is $(g[l]_\omega = g[r]_\omega \| c \wedge (g_{|\omega} =_{\mathcal{C}}^? l))$ if $c \wedge (g_{|\omega} =_{\mathcal{C}}^? l)$ is satisfiable.

The sets of constrained critical pairs and extensions of a set of rules R will be denoted respectively by $CCP(R)$ and $CCE(R)$.

Since we assume that any left-hand side of rules in R cannot have a symbol of Σ_0 as top symbol, local coherence with E_0 is always satisfied. For instance in our example, $+$ is an associative commutative symbol in $\mathcal{C}$ but there is no need to add associative commutative extensions because no rule in R begins with a $+$ symbol. In the same way, if $f \in \Sigma_1$ is associative and commutative, we do not need extensions of rules in $E_0^>$, thanks to the disjointness assumption of function symbols in Σ_0 and Σ_1.

Example 5 In the example of the introduction, there is no constrained extension w.r.t. commutativity of g, and there is no constrained critical pair. The only possibility would be: $g(x,y) = x' \| y > 0 \wedge g(x',0) =_{\mathcal{C}}^? g(x+y,y)$. Solving the system $y > 0 \wedge g(x',0) =_{\mathcal{C}}^? g(x+y,y)$ in the combination of commutativity of g and constraint solving in $\mathcal{A}$ leads to two systems: $x' =^? x + y \wedge y =^? 0 \wedge y > 0$ which has no solution, and $x' =^? y \wedge x + y =^? 0 \wedge y > 0$ which has no solution either.

Transition rules for checking local confluence and coherence modulo $\sim_{\mathcal{C}}$ are given below.

Deduce
$CE, CR \cup \{(g \to d \parallel c'), (l \to r \parallel c)\}$

$\longmapsto$

$CE \cup \{g[r]_\omega = d \parallel c \wedge c' \wedge (g_{|\omega} =^?_{\mathcal{C}} l)\},$
$CR \cup \{(g \to d \parallel c'), (l \to r \parallel c)\}$
if $c \wedge c' \wedge (g_{|\omega} =^?_{\mathcal{C}} l)$ satisfiable

Extend
$CE, CR \cup \{(l \to r \parallel c)\}$

$\longmapsto$

$CE \cup \{g[l]_\omega = g[r] \parallel c \wedge (g_{|\omega} =^?_{\mathcal{C}} l)\},$
$CR \cup \{(l \to r \parallel c)\}$
if $(g = d) \in C$ and $c \wedge (g_{|\omega} =^?_{\mathcal{C}} l)$ satisfiable

Simplify
$CE \cup \{(g = d \parallel S)\}, CR$

$\longmapsto$

$CE \cup \{(g' = d \parallel S)\}, CR$
if $g \to_{R,C} g'$

Delete
$CE \cup \{(p = q \parallel S)\}, CR$

$\longmapsto$

CE, CR
if $p \sim_{\mathcal{C}} q$ or S unsatisfiable

Propagate
$CE \cup \{(p = q \parallel S)\}, CR$

$\longmapsto$

$CE \cup \{(\theta(p) = \theta(q) \parallel c)\}, CR$
if $S \equiv_{\mathcal{C}} c \wedge \hat{\theta}$ and $c \in L_{\mathcal{C}}$

The correctness of these rules is stated in the next theorem proved in [16].

Theorem 2 *If there exists a finite derivation* $(\emptyset, R) \longmapsto (CE_1, R) \longmapsto \ldots \longmapsto (CE_i, R)$ *such that* $CE_i = \emptyset$ *and* $CCP(R) \cup CCE(R) \subseteq \bigcup_{0 \le j \le i} CE_j$, *then* R *is locally confluent and coherent modulo* $\sim_{\mathcal{C}}$.

Theorem 3 *Assume that* R *is a set of rewrite rules with built-in constraints. If the relation* $\to_{R,C}$ *is convergent modulo* $\sim_{\mathcal{C}}$, $\mathcal{M}$ *is a consistent enrichment of* $\mathcal{A}$.

Proof: Consider two elements a, a' of $\mathcal{A}$ equal modulo $\sim_{R,C}$. Then $a \xrightarrow{*}_{R,C} w \sim_{\mathcal{C}} w' \xleftarrow{*}_{R,C} a'$. But no rule in R and no equality in C can apply on a neither on a', so $a \sim_{\mathcal{A}} a'$. $\square$

5.4 Interpretation of predicates

From now on, we assume that R is convergent modulo $\sim_{\mathcal{C}}$. Validity modulo $\xleftrightarrow{*}_{R/C}$ then corresponds to validity modulo $\sim_{\mathcal{C}}$ after normalization w.r.t. $\to_{R,C}$. This allows interpreting predicates of $\mathcal{P}_0$ in $\mathcal{M}$.

Definition 19 The constraint language $L_{R,C}$ associated to the specification $(\Sigma, R, C, L_{\mathcal{A}})$ is defined by the signature Σ, the interpretation $\mathcal{M}$ and the set of variables $\mathcal{X}$. If $p \in \mathcal{P}_0$ then the interpretation of p in $\mathcal{M}$ is the relation $p_{\mathcal{M}}$ defined by $p_{\mathcal{M}}(t_1, \ldots, t_n)$ if $L_{\mathcal{C}} \models p(t_1 \downarrow_{R,C}, \ldots, t_n \downarrow_{R,C})$.

This definition of predicates is obviously compatible with $\sim_{R,C}$ since $\to_{R,C}$ is convergent modulo $\sim_{\mathcal{C}}$. The following result states that a constraint valid in $L_{\mathcal{C}}$ is still valid in $L_{R,C}$.

Proposition 5 [16] If $L_{\mathcal{C}} \models p(t_1, \ldots, t_n)$ then $L_{R,C} \models p(t_1, \ldots, t_n)$.

Proof: (Sketch) If $L_{\mathcal{C}} \models p(t_1, \ldots, t_n)$ then $L_{\mathcal{A}} \models p(t_1^{\pi_0}, \ldots, t_n^{\pi_0})$. According to our assumptions on R, we can prove that $p((t_1 \downarrow_{R,C})^{\pi_0}, \ldots, (t_n \downarrow_{R,C})^{\pi_0})$ is an $\mathcal{A}$-instance of $p(t_1^{\pi_0}, \ldots, t_n^{\pi_0})$. So, $L_{\mathcal{A}} \models p((t_1 \downarrow_{R,C})^{\pi_0}, \ldots, (t_n \downarrow_{R,C})^{\pi_0})$, $L_{\mathcal{C}} \models p(t_1 \downarrow_{R,C}, \ldots, t_n \downarrow_{R,C})$ and $L_{R,C} \models p(t_1, \ldots, t_n)$. $\square$

6 Constrained narrowing

We now consider the constraint solving problem in the language $L_{R,C}$. The idea is to define a process of constrained narrowing to enumerate solutions of goals expressed in this language. This provides an incremental way to build constraint solvers, since the method allows building a constraint solver in $L_{R,C}$ from a constraint solver in L_C. Similar definitions of constrained narrowing have been introduced in different contexts by [5, 3].

Constrained narrowing is defined on formulas called goals with constraints and of the form $(\exists X, p^?(t_1, \ldots, t_n) \, \| \, S)$ where X denotes a set of existentially quantified variables, $p^?(t_1, \ldots, t_n)$ is an atomic constraint such that $p \in \mathcal{P}_0$ to solve in $L_{R,C}$, and S is a constraint to solve in L_C. $\mathcal{V}(G)$ denotes the set of all variables occurring in a goal G.

Definition 20 The set of solutions modulo $\sim_{R,C}$ of a goal $G = (\exists X, p^?(t_1, \ldots, t_n) \| S)$ is defined by $SOL_{R,C}(G) = \{\sigma_{|\mathcal{V}(G)\backslash X} \mid \sigma \in SS_C^*(S) \text{ and } L_{R,C} \models p(\sigma(t_1), \ldots, \sigma(t_n))\}$. The set of solutions modulo $\sim_C$ of a goal $G = (\exists X, p^?(t_1, \ldots, t_n) \| S)$ is defined by $SOL_C(G) = \{\sigma_{|\mathcal{V}(G)\backslash X} \mid \sigma \in SS_C^*(S \wedge p(t_1, \ldots, t_n))\}$.

6.1 Correctness

From now on, for a better readability, we restrict to atomic constraints with a binary predicate like for example $=, \neq, <$.

Definition 21 The goal $(\exists X, p^?(g, d) \| S)$ is *narrowed* with $(l \to r \| c)$ to: $(\exists X \cup \mathcal{V}(l \to r \| c), \quad p^?(g[r]_\omega, d) \| S \wedge c \wedge (g_{|\omega} =_C^? l))$ if $S \wedge c \wedge (g_{|\omega} =_C^? l)$ is satisfiable.

Proposition 6 Let $G = (\exists X, p^?(g, d) \| S)$ and $G' = (\exists X', p^?(g', d') \| S')$ s.t. G is narrowed with $(l \to r \| c)$ to G'. Then $SOL_{R,C}(G') \subseteq SOL_{R,C}(G)$.

As a consequence of Propositions 5 and 6, the next proposition proves the correctness of narrowing:

Proposition 7 If there exists a narrowing derivation:

$$G_0 = (\exists \emptyset, \, p^?(g_0, d_0) \| \top) \leadsto G_1 \leadsto \ldots \leadsto G_n = (\exists X_n, p^?(g_n, d_n) \| S_n),$$

then $SOL_C(G_n) \subseteq SOL_{R,C}(G_0)$.

6.2 Completeness

The aim is now to prove that given a goal $G_0 = (\exists \emptyset, p^?(g_0, d_0) \| \top)$, for any solution $\sigma \in SOL_{R,C}(G_0)$, there exists a narrowing derivation

$$G_0 = (\exists \emptyset, \, p^?(g_0, d_0) \| \top) \leadsto G_1 \leadsto \ldots \leadsto G_n = (\exists X_n, p^?(g_n, d_n) \| S_n)$$

such that $\sigma \in SOL_C(G_n)$.

Lemma 1 Let $G_i = (\exists X_i, p^?(g_i, d_i) \| S_i)$ a goal and μ_i a substitution defined and normalized for $\to_{R,C}$ on $\mathcal{V}(G_i)$. If $\mu_i \in SS_C^*(S_i)$ and $\mu_i(p^?(g_i, d_i))$ is reducible with $\to_{R,C}$, then there exist a reduction $\mu_i(p^?(g_i, d_i)) \to_{R,C} p^?(u, v)$, a narrowing step

$$G_i = (\exists X_i, p^?(g_i, d_i) \| S_i) \leadsto G_{i+1} = (\exists X_{i+1}, p^?(g_{i+1}, d_{i+1}) \| S_{i+1})$$

and a substitution μ_{i+1} defined and normalized for $\to_{R,C}$ on $\mathcal{V}(G_{i+1})$, such that $\mu_{i+1} \in SS_C^*(S_{i+1})$, $\mu_{i+1}(p^?(g_{i+1}, d_{i+1})) \sim_C p^?(u, v)$ and $\mu_{i+1} =^{\mathcal{V}(G_i) \backslash X_i} \mu_i$

Proof: If $\mu_i(p^?(g_i, d_i)) \to_{R,\mathcal{C}} p^?(u,v)$, there exists a position ω say in $\mu_i(g_i)$ (or $\mu_i(d_i)$), a rule $(l \to r\|c) \in R$, and a substitution α such that $\mu_i(g_i)_{|\omega} \sim_{\mathcal{C}} \alpha(l)$, $\alpha \in SS^*_{\mathcal{C}}(c)$, $u = \mu_i(g_i)[\alpha(r)]_\omega$. Since μ_i is normalized for $\to_{R,\mathcal{C}}$, we have $\mu_i(g_i)_{|\omega} = \mu_i(g_{i|\omega})$. So $g_{i|\omega}$ and l are unifiable modulo $\sim_{\mathcal{C}}$ and $c \wedge g_{i|\omega} =^?_{\mathcal{C}} l$ is satisfiable modulo $\sim_{\mathcal{C}}$. Since there exists an innermost normalizing reduction strategy, we can assume w.l.o.g. that α is defined and normalized for $\to_{R,\mathcal{C}}$ on $\mathcal{V}(l \to r\|c)$, with $(\mathcal{V}(G_i) \cup \mathcal{VR}an(\mu_i)) \cap \mathcal{V}(l \to r\|c) = \emptyset$. The substitution μ_{i+1} defined on $\mathcal{V}(G_{i+1})$ by $\mu_{i+1} =^{\mathcal{V}(G_i)} \mu_i$, $\mu_{i+1} =^{\mathcal{V}(l=r\|c)} \alpha$ is normalized for $\to_{R,\mathcal{C}}$. Moreover $\mu_{i+1} = \mu_i\alpha \in SS^*_{\mathcal{C}}(S_{i+1})$, $\mu_{i+1}(p^?(g_{i+1}, d_{i+1})) = \mu_{i+1}(p^?(g_i[r]_\omega, d_i)) \sim_{\mathcal{C}} p^?(u,v)$ and $\mu_{i+1} =^{\mathcal{V}(G_i)\backslash X_i} \mu_i$. $\square$

Lemma 2 Let $G_i = (\exists X_i, p^?(g_i, d_i)\|S_i)$ a goal and μ_i a substitution defined and normalized for $\to_{R,\mathcal{C}}$ on $\mathcal{V}(G_i)$. If $\mu_i \in SS^*_{\mathcal{C}}(S_i)$ and $\mu_i(p^?(g_i, d_i))$ is reducible for $\to_{R/\mathcal{C}}$, then there exist a reduction $\mu_i(p^?(g_i, d_i)) \xrightarrow{+}_{R/\mathcal{C}} p^?(s,t)$ where s, t are irreducible with $\to_{R/\mathcal{C}}$, a narrowing derivation

$$G_i = (\exists X_i, p^?(g_i, d_i)\|S_i) \rightsquigarrow G_{i+1} \rightsquigarrow \ldots \rightsquigarrow G_k = (\exists X_k, p^?(g_k, d_k)\|S_k)$$

and a substitution μ_k defined and normalized for $\to_{R,\mathcal{C}}$ on $\mathcal{V}(G_k)$, such that $\mu_k \in SS^*_{\mathcal{C}}(S_k)$, $\mu_k(p^?(g_k, d_k)) \sim_{\mathcal{C}} p^?(s,t)$ and $\mu_k =^{\mathcal{V}(G_i)\backslash X_i} \mu_i$.

Proof: By nœtherian induction on $\to_{R/\mathcal{C}}$. If $\mu_i(p^?(g_i, d_i))$ is reducible with $\to_{R/\mathcal{C}}$ then it is also reducible with $\to_{R,\mathcal{C}}$ since $\to_{R,\mathcal{C}}$ is coherent with $\sim_{\mathcal{C}}$ and $\to_{R/\mathcal{C}}$ terminates. So $\mu_i(p^?(g_i, d_i))$ is reducible with $\to_{R,\mathcal{C}}$ and according to Lemma 1, there exists a reduction $\mu_i(p^?(g_i, d_i)) \to_{R,\mathcal{C}} p^?(u,v)$, a narrowing step $G_i \rightsquigarrow G_{i+1}$ and a substitution μ_{i+1} defined and normalized for $\to_{R,\mathcal{C}}$ on $\mathcal{V}(G_{i+1})$ such that $\mu_{i+1} \in SS^*_{\mathcal{C}}(S_{i+1})$, $\mu_{i+1}(p^?(g_{i+1}, d_{i+1})) \sim_{\mathcal{C}} p^?(u,v)$ and $\mu_{i+1} =^{\mathcal{V}(G_i)\backslash X_i} \mu_i$.

If $p^?(u,v)$ is irreducible with $\to_{R/\mathcal{C}}$ then we take $k=i+1$. Otherwise $\mu_{i+1}(p^?(g_{i+1}, d_{i+1}))$ is reducible with $\to_{R/\mathcal{C}}$ and by induction hypothesis, there exists a reduction $\mu_{i+1}(p^?(g_{i+1}, d_{i+1})) \xrightarrow{+}_{R/\mathcal{C}} p^?(s',t')$ where s', t' are irreducible with $\to_{R/\mathcal{C}}$, a narrowing derivation $G_{i+1} \rightsquigarrow \ldots \rightsquigarrow G_k = (\exists X_k, p^?(g_k, d_k)\|S_k)$, and a substitution μ_k defined and normalized for $\to_{R,\mathcal{C}}$ on $\mathcal{V}(G_k)$ such that $\mu_k \in SS^*_{\mathcal{C}}(S_k)$, $\mu_k(p^?(g_k, d_k)) \sim_{\mathcal{C}} p^?(s,t)$ and $\mu_k =^{\mathcal{V}(G_{i+1})\backslash X_{i+1}} \mu_{i+1}$. Since $\mathcal{V}(G_{i+1})\backslash X_{i+1} = \mathcal{V}(G_i)\backslash X_i$ and $\mu_{i+1} =^{\mathcal{V}(G_i)\backslash X_i} \mu_i$, we have $\mu_k =^{\mathcal{V}(G_i)\backslash X_i} \mu_i$. $\square$

Theorem 4 Let $G_0 = (\exists\emptyset, p^?(g_0, d_0), \top)$ be a goal and μ_0 be a substitution defined and normalized for $\to_{R,\mathcal{C}}$ on $\mathcal{V}(G_0)$. If $\mu_0 \in SOL_{R,\mathcal{C}}(G_0)$ then there exists a narrowing derivation $G_0 = (\exists\emptyset, p^?(g_0, d_0)\|\top) \rightsquigarrow G_1 \rightsquigarrow \ldots \rightsquigarrow G_n = (\exists X_n, p^?(g_n, d_n)\|S_n)$ such that $\mu_0 \in SOL_{\mathcal{C}}(G_n)$.

Proof: If $\mu_0(p^?(g_0, d_0))$ is irreducible with $\to_{R,\mathcal{C}}$ then $L_{R,\mathcal{C}} \models \mu_0(p(g_0, d_0))$ implies $L_{\mathcal{C}} \models \mu_0(p(g_0, d_0))$ by definition of $L_{R,\mathcal{C}}$. If $\mu_0(p^?(g_0, d_0))$ is reducible with $\to_{R,\mathcal{C}}$ then it is also reducible with $\to_{R/\mathcal{C}}$. According to Lemma 2, there exist a reduction $\mu_0(p^?(g_0, d_0)) \xrightarrow{+}_{R/\mathcal{C}} p^?(s,t)$ where s, t are irreducible with $\to_{R/\mathcal{C}}$, a narrowing derivation $G_0 = (\exists\emptyset, p^?(g_0, d_0)\|\top) \rightsquigarrow G_1 \rightsquigarrow \ldots \rightsquigarrow G_n = (\exists X_n, p^?(g_n, d_n)\|S_n)$ and a normalized substitution μ_n such that $\mu_n \in SS^*_{\mathcal{C}}(S_n)$, $\mu_n(p^?(g_n, d_n)) \sim_{\mathcal{C}} p^?(s,t)$ and $\mu_n =^{\mathcal{V}(G_0)} \mu_0$. The terms s and t are normalized for $\to_{R,\mathcal{C}}$ and $L_{R,\mathcal{C}} \models p(s,t)$ by hypothesis on μ_0. Consequently, $L_{\mathcal{C}} \models p(s,t) \sim_{\mathcal{C}} \mu_n(p(g_n, d_n))$, $\mu_0 = \mu_{n|\mathcal{V}(G_n)\backslash X_n} \in SOL_{\mathcal{C}}(G_n)$. $\square$

Example 6 Consider the constraint language $L_{\mathcal{B}}$ with the Σ_0-structure $\mathcal{B}$ of booleans with $\Sigma_0 = (\{Bool\}, \{\wedge, \vee : Bool, Bool \to Bool, ^- : Bool \to Bool, 0, 1 :\to$

$Bool\}, \{=, \neq, <\})$ and the set $\mathcal{X}_0$ of built-in variables $\{x, y, z, v : Bool, \ldots\}$. Given the incomplete specification $(\Sigma, R \cup AC(xor), L_\mathcal{B})$: $R = \{xor(x, x) \rightarrow 0, xor(x, 1) \rightarrow \bar{x}\}$, one want to solve the goal $G_0 = (\exists \emptyset, \ xor(xor(s, t), 0) \neq^? xor(1, v) \| \top)$ where s, t are built-in terms. By narrowing G_0, one get

$$
\begin{aligned}
G_0 \ \leadsto \ & G_1 = (\exists x, \ xor(0, 0) \neq^? xor(1, v) \| xor(s, t) =^? xor(x, x)) \\
\leadsto \ & G_2 = (\exists x, y, \ 0 \neq^? xor(1, v) \| xor(s, t) =^? xor(x, x) \wedge xor(0, 0) =^? xor(y, y)) \\
\leadsto \ & G_3 = (\exists x, y, z, \ 0 \neq^? \bar{z} \| xor(s, t) =^? xor(x, x) \wedge xor(0, 0) =^? xor(y, y) \\
& \wedge xor(1, v) =^? xor(z, 1)) \quad \text{such that} \\
SOL_\mathcal{C}(G_3) \ = \ & SS_\mathcal{C}^\bullet(\exists x, y, z, \ 0 \neq^? \bar{z} \wedge xor(s, t) =^? xor(x, x) \wedge xor(0, 0) =^? xor(y, y) \\
& \wedge xor(1, v) =^? xor(z, 1)) \\
= \ & SS_\mathcal{C}^\bullet(\exists x, y, z, \ 0 \neq^? \bar{z} \wedge x =^? s =^? t \wedge y =^? 0 \wedge v =^? z) \\
= \ & SS_\mathcal{C}^\bullet(0 \neq^? \bar{v} \wedge s =^? t) = SS_\mathcal{B}(0 \neq^? \bar{v} \wedge s =^? t)
\end{aligned}
$$

7 Conclusion

We have presented a stratified approach of constraint solving in presence of built-in structures thanks to narrowing and combination techniques. As a particular case we get constrained narrowing modulo an equational theory if the built-in structure is empty. The difficulty was to find the adequate combined constraint solver able to integrate a built-in structure without any assumption on it. The proposed solution is to restrict the form of solutions, which may appear as a limitation, but actually simplifies the complexity of the solver.

Constrained narrowing already incorporates a part of strategy in its definition, since it is essentially another formulation of basic narrowing [19]. How to combine it with various strategies, like innermost or lazy ones, and with normalization is certainly possible and useful in practice. This is an interesting topic for future work.

References

[1] J. Avenhaus and K. Becker. Operational specifications with built-ins. In P. Enjalbert, E.W. Mayr, and K.W. Wagner, editors, *Proceedings of STACS-94*, volume 775 of *LNCS*, pages 263–274, Caen, (France), February 1994. Springer-Verlag.

[2] Franz Baader and Klaus Schulz. Unification in the union of disjoint equational theories: Combining decision procedures. In *Proc. 11th CADE Conf., Saratoga Springs (N.Y., USA)*, pages 50–65, 1992.

[3] Jacques Chabin. *Unification Générale par Surréduction Ordonnée Contrainte et Surréduction Dirigée*. Th. univ., Université d'Orléans, January 1994.

[4] H. Comon. Completion of rewrite systems with membership constraints. In W. Kuich, editor, *Proceedings of ICALP 92*, volume 623 of *LNCS*. Springer-Verlag, 1992.

[5] M. Fernández. Narrowing based procedures for equational disunification. *Applicable Algebra in Engineering, Communication and Computation*, 3:1–26, 1992.

[6] L. Fribourg. SLOG: A logic programming language intepreter based on clausal superposition and rewriting. In *Proceedings of the IEEE Symposium on Logic Programming*, pages 172–184, Boston, MA, July 1985.

[7] I. Gnaedig, Claude Kirchner, and Hélène Kirchner. Equational completion in order-sorted algebras. *TCS*, 72:169–202, 1990.

[8] J. A. Goguen and J. Meseguer. EQLOG: Equality, types, and generic modules for logic programming. In Douglas De Groot and Gary Lindstrom, editors, *Functional and Logic Programming*, pages 295–363. Prentice-Hall, 1986. An earlier version appears in *Journal of Logic Programming*, Volume 1, Number 2, pages 179–210, September 1984.

[9] J. A. Goguen and T. Winkler. Introducing OBJ3. Technical Report SRI-CSL-88-9, SRI International, 333, Ravenswood Ave., Menlo Park, CA 94025, August 1988.

[10] M. Hanus. Incremental rewriting in narrowing derivations. In H. Kirchner and G. Levi, editors, *Proceedings 3rd International Conference on Algebraic and Logic Programming, Volterra (Italy)*, volume 632 of *LNCS*, pages 228–243. Springer-Verlag, September 1992.

[11] C. Hintermeier, C. Kirchner, and H. Kirchner. Dynamically-typed computations for order-sorted equational presentations. research report, INRIA, Inria Lorraine & Crin, November 1993.

[12] S. Hölldobler. *Foundations of Equational Logic Programming*, volume 353 of *LNAI*. Springer-Verlag, 1989.

[13] J.-P. Jouannaud, Claude Kirchner, Hélène Kirchner, and A. Mégrelis. Programming with equalities, subsorts, overloading and parameterization in OBJ. *JLP*, 12(3):257–280, February 1992.

[14] J.-P. Jouannaud and Hélène Kirchner. Completion of a set of rules modulo a set of equations. *SIAM J. of Computing*, 15(4):1155–1194, 1986. Preliminary version in Proceedings 11th ACM Symposium on Principles of Programming Languages, Salt Lake City (USA), 1984.

[15] Claude Kirchner, Hélène Kirchner, and M. Rusinowitch. Deduction with symbolic constraints. *Revue d'Intelligence Artificielle*, 4(3):9–52, 1990. Special issue on Automatic Deduction.

[16] H. Kirchner and Ch. Ringeissen. Constraint solving by narrowing in combined algebraic domains (extended version). research report, CRIN-CNRS and INRIA-Lorraine, 1993.

[17] Hélène Kirchner and Ch. Ringeissen. A constraint solver in finite algebras and its combination with unification algorithms. In K. Apt, editor, *Proc. Joint International Conference and Symposium on Logic Programming*, pages 225–239. MIT Press, 1992.

[18] J. Moreno-Navarro and M. Rodriguez-Artalejo. Logic programming with functions and predicates: the language BABEL. *JLP*, 12(3):191–223, February 1992.

[19] W. Nutt, P. Réty, and G. Smolka. Basic narrowing revisited. *JSC*, 7(3 & 4):295–318, 1989. Special issue on unification. Part one.

[20] Ch. Ringeissen. Unification in a combination of equational theories with shared constants and its application to primal algebras. In *Proc. 1st LPAR Conf., St. Petersburg (Russia)*, volume 624 of *LNAI*, pages 261–272. Springer-Verlag, 1992.

[21] Ch. Ringeissen. Combination of matching algorithms. In P. Enjalbert, E.W. Mayr, and K.W. Wagner, editors, *Proceedings of STACS-94*, volume 775 of *LNCS*, pages 187–198, Caen, (France), February 1994. Springer-Verlag.

[22] G. Smolka. *Logic Programming over Polymorphically Order-Sorted Types*. PhD thesis, FB Informatik, Universität Kaiserslautern, Germany, 1989.

[23] G. Smolka, W. Nutt, J. A. Goguen, and J. Meseguer. Order-sorted equational computation. In H. Aït-Kaci and M. Nivat, editors, *Resolution of Equations in Algebraic Structures, Volume 2: Rewriting Techniques*, pages 297–367. Academic Press, 1989.

A Grammatical Approach to DCG Parsing

François Barthélemy

Departamento de Informática,
Universidade Nova de Lisboa,
2825 Monte de Caparica – Portugal
frb@fct.unl.pt

INRIA Rocquencourt
BP 105, 78153 Le Chesnay
France
Francois.Barthelemy@inria.fr

Abstract

Definite Clause Grammars can be implemented in many different ways, using
alternative parsing algorithms such as SLD-resolution, chart parsing either
top-down or bottom-up, and so on. We present here a formal framework in
which most of these techniques can be expressed. The two issues of building a parse-tree and handling non-determinism are considered separately.
A grammar is first compiled into an intermediate form that encodes the
construction of the corresponding language's parse-trees. This intermediate
form is a machine that belongs to a class of extended push-down automata
(X-automata). The extension takes into account the unifications occurring at
each node of the tree. The X-automata execution, when non-deterministic,
can make use of either a backtracking or a tabulation device.

X-automata provide a single formalism to encode alternative implementations of the same grammar, and in so doing, offer a way to compare parser
performance. Furthermore, static analysis of X-automata can be designed
independently of the implementation the automata encode. We give some
experimental results comparing the efficiency of the X-automaton implementation of the most common parsing techniques.

1 Introduction

The class of Definite Clause Grammars (DCGs) was originally conceived by
Pereira and Warren in [8]. It has found at least two kind of applications: the
definition of object languages within Prolog and the description of natural
language (more or less independently of Prolog).

Although a direct translation into Prolog code is the most common implementation of DCGs, several other implementations exist. For example,
[10] describes top-down and bottom-up tabular parsers and [7] is devoted to
an LR implementation with backtracking. These are just a few examples of
parsing algorithms for DCGs. All the alternatives are correct and complete
with respect to DCG logical semantics, but they differ in their operational
behavior, i.e., termination and efficiency.

The aim of this paper is to provide a framework to express most of the
usual parsing algorithms in common terms in order to make them compara-

ble.

Parsing with respect to a DCG involves two interrelated tasks: building a tree by combining elementary trees (the clauses), just as for a context-free grammar, and performing a unification for each node of the tree. A new equation appears at the moment when a clause instance is grafted to a tree. The graft may be invalid if unification fails.

The context-free part of DCG parsing, namely parsing according to the context-free backbone of the DCG, can be expressed using a Push-Down Automaton (PDA). Well-known techniques allow the automatic compilation of any context-free grammar into a non-deterministic PDA.

We propose to extend both these techniques and the PDA formalism itself to take into account the equation solving process. We call the new formalism *X-automaton* (XA, for eXtended Push-Down Automaton). A grammar is a purely declarative description of a language. An X-automaton is an intermediate level that retains the grammar information and part of the operational semantics chosen to parse it. The operational supplement is the tree building method. We may also view this part as "everything but the treatment of non-determinism."

We may automatically compile arbitrary DCGs into XAs using algorithms adapted from context-free parsing.

Like PDAs, XAs may be non-deterministic, i.e., different evolutions are possible from a given state. As with PDAs, two kinds of execution are possible: backtracking execution, or tabular execution. These techniques can apply to an automaton independently of the parsing technique it implements. In our framework, how we parse and how we handle non-determinism are orthogonal issues.

The appeal of unifying the description of alternative implementations is threefold.

First of all, X-automata are convenient for static analysis. Properties such as termination, groundness, and variable sharing are highly dependent on the chosen strategy. Note that these are properties of parsers, not grammars, which are purely declarative. Our approach lets us study the operational properties of parsers independently of the grammar they represent. Many of these properties are naturally studied at the automaton level. This allows us to build strategy-independent procedures that work for top-down, bottom-up, LL, LR, or any other strategy that may be encoded by X-automata.

Other properties must be studied at the parser level (X-automaton + control strategy), most notably termination. Tabular and backtracking executions behave quite differently with respect to termination.

The second benefit of our approach is that it makes the different implementations comparable. Comparing parsing techniques is a difficult task. Benchmarks of actual implementations reveal little because they depend of the quality of these implementations. SLD-resolution with backtrack freely exploits the very efficient compilation techniques of Prolog. Although many of these efficient techniques could apply to other strategies, it would require time and effort to adapt them, so alternative implementations are often meta-interpreters that we cannot compare fairly with the built-in implementation given by Prolog.

Our framework gives a more abstract basis to comparison. Efficiency can be measured in terms of X-automata basic computation steps. Comparison remains a difficult task, however. We readdress this topic later in this paper as an example of the use of XAs.

The third advantage of our approach is that we have a strategy-independent definition of a parser: it is an X-automaton plus an execution technique. A system that takes an X-automaton (plus an execution technique) as a parser can use transparently any number of implementations of a grammar. This is interesting because there is no such thing such as the overall best parsing method. It depends on the grammar. Imagine a system that, for a given grammar, tries and evaluates alternative compilations with respect to general automata static analyses. It would select the most efficient automaton and tell the user whether there is a risk of non-termination. Although this system does not yet exist, we hope that this paper contributes to this vision.

The next section is devoted to the presentation of the parsing of languages defined by DCGs. Section 3 contains the definition of X-automata. Section 4 describes algorithms that compile any DCG into an X-automaton. The fifth section touches on the execution of X-automata. The sixth section is devoted to some experimental results obtained by a prototype implementation of XAs. The last section is a short comparison with related work.

2 DCGs, syntax trees, and parsing

Definite clause grammars are now well known, so the following reminders are quite brief. More details can be found in the original paper [8].

DCGs are an extension of context-free grammars but differ in that non-terminals are first-order terms instead of simple symbols. The use of logic variables allows one to express equality of otherwise unknown parts of terms.

We don't mention the *procedure calls* introduced by Pereira and Warren (literals appearing in the right-hand sides of rules and defined by logic programs) as a special feature of DCGs: as long as we limit ourselves to pure DCGs (i.e., without negation, built-ins, or control predicates), procedure calls can be conveniently seen as ordinary non-terminals and their definition as ordinary rules deriving the empty string.

The grammar obtained by removing all the arguments of every non-terminal occurring in a DCG is called the *underlying context-free grammar* of the DCG, or its *context-free skeleton*.

The usual way of defining the semantics of DCGs is a translation into definite clause programs. A DCG rule looks very much like a clause. There is only one implicit piece of information, namely the sequentiality of the symbols. This information is easily made explicit with additional arguments added to the symbols, defining the part of the string that the symbol derives.

Another way of defining a semantics for DCGs is more grammatical. It consists in defining the notion of syntax tree.

Definition 2.1 *DCG Syntax tree*
A syntax tree of a DCG G is a labeled tree such that:
- *every leaf node is labeled either by a terminal or by a pair (c, σ) where c is a unit clause of G (rule whose right-end side is empty) and σ is a substitution.*
- *every internal node is labeled by a pair (c, σ) where c is a rule of G and σ is a substitution.*
- *every leaf node labeled by a terminal t is the ith child of a node labeled by a pair (c, σ) where c is a clause $c_0 :- c_1, \ldots, c_n$, $n \geq i$, and $t = c_i \sigma$.*
- *every other node except the root is such that:*
  - *it is labeled by a pair (c, σ), where c is the clause $c_0 :- c_1, \ldots, c_n$.*
  - *it is the ith child of its parent*
  - *the parent is labeled by (k, θ), where k is the clause $k_0 :- k_1, \ldots, k_m$. and $i \leq m$.*
  - *$k_i \theta = c_0 \sigma$*

The string associated with a syntax tree is the sequence of terminals formed by following the leaves of the tree in a preorder traversal. The language defined by a DCG G is the set of terminal strings associated with at least one syntax tree from G.

To parse is to try to find a syntax tree (or all the syntax trees) associated with a given string.

A pre-order can easily be defined by extending the usual instance relation in a straightforward way. This allows to work modulo subsumption. Only equivalence classes are considered, thus reducing the search space for parsing. In particular, systematically renaming clauses is sound because the trees obtained cover all the equivalence classes.

Following definition 2.1, an equation $k_i \theta = c_0 \sigma$ appears for each node of the tree (except the root), identifying the head of the clause labeling this node with the relevant atom of the body of the clause labeling its parent. The minimal requirement for this equation to be satisfied is obtained by unifying the two atoms (after renaming). A global substitution for the whole tree is the result of the resolution of all the equations of the tree.

One point we wish to emphasize is that unifications can be delayed. An interesting property of unification is that it depends only on the equations being considered, not on the order in which they are taken into account. The unifier may be computed incrementally, as the tree grows and the equations appear. But it can also be computed afterwards.

As shown by Deransart and Maluszynski in [3], a tree can be built considering only the context-free constraints of the grammar, that is, matching only predicate symbols instead of unifying the complete terms. This gives a structure for a candidate syntax tree. Of course, to transform it in an actual parse tree, all the unifications must be performed, and the result must be applied on the tree. But this can be done afterwards, once the whole tree has been built.

Between the two extremes – unifying as soon as possible (at the moment a new clause instance is grafted to a partial syntax-tree) or delaying until a whole tree is constructed – many intermediate steps are available. Notice that no unification is performed before the corresponding part of the tree has been built.

Parsing with DCGs may be divided in two distinct parts:

– Constructing the tree *skeleton*, that is the tree labeled by clauses and renamings. This part is similar to a context-free parsing with the underlying context-free grammar of the DCG.
– Solving the equations of this skeleton.

The two parts of parsing may be mixed in many different ways. A sound and complete parsing method blends a sound and complete context-free parsing method with the consideration of all the tree equations.

3   X-automata

We now define a new kind of automata, especially designed to perform DCG parsing following the principles exposed in the previous section. They are an extension of push-down automata classically used for context-free parsing. The aim of the extension is to handle the contextual constraints of the DCGs (the equations).

Informally, an X-automaton is a stack automaton where each level of the stack stores four pieces of information:

– an atom
– a substitution
– an equation set that contains delayed unifications
– the end of the string (the part that has to be recognized)

Following Bernard Lang [6], we consider a machine whose only storage is a lone stack. There is no state indicator and no string beside the stack. This implies that all relevant information must be encoded in the stack. For instance, the state of an automaton, if necessary, has to be stacked in such a way that the current state appears in the top element.

A configuration of the automaton reduces to a stack. There are three stack operations:

– PUSH pushes a tuple on top of the stack
– HOR changes the top of the stack for another tuple
– POP replaces the top two tuples by only one, possibly different from these two

Any usual stack transition can be translated into one or several operations PUSH, HOR, and POP. For instance, state changes with no change in the stack are achieved by the HOR. The equivalence between the usual PDA definition and ours is given in [2].

Definition 3.1 *X-automaton*
An X-automaton is a 5-tuple $(\Sigma, V, init, F, T)$ *where*
- Σ *is a graded alphabet*
- V *is a denumerable set of variables*
- *init is a nullary initial predicate*
- F *is a set of final predicates*
- T *is a finite set of transition functions, respecting the requirements described below*

Requirements for the transition functions (abbreviated as "transitions"):
- they are partial functions from stacks to stacks
- each transition applied on any stack in its domain performs one of the three basic operations PUSH, HOR, and POP. We call PUSH-transition (respectively, HOR-transition, POP-transition) a transition that performs a PUSH (respectively, a HOR, a POP).
- whether a stack belongs to the domain of a transition only depends on the top of the stack, namely the top tuple for PUSH and HOR-transitions and the two top tuples for a POP-transition.

In other words, a transition is any function that locally applies one of the three basic operations (PUSH, HOR, or POP) to the top of the stack.

In the rest of this paper, we will indicate a stack using the Prolog list notation, the top being on the left-hand side. We will use $< a, b, c, d >$ as a notation for the 4-tuples in the stack.

Definition 3.2 *Configuration*
Let $A = (\Sigma, V, init, F, T)$, *an X-automaton.*
- *the stack* $[< init, id, \emptyset, s >]$ *where init is the initial predicate, id is the identity substitution, $\emptyset$ the empty set, and s a string of terminals, is a configuration of A called* initial configuration.
- *The stack obtained by the application of a transition t of T to a configuration c (c belonging to the domain of t) is a configuration of A.*

Definition 3.3 *Computation*
Let $A = (\Sigma, V, init, F, T)$ *be an X-automaton. A computation of A is any sequence* $c_0, c_1, \ldots, c_n$, $n \geq 0$, *of configurations of A such that:*
- c_o *is the initial configuration* $[< init, id, \emptyset, s >]$ *where s is the input string.*
- $\forall i,\ 0 < i \leq n,\ \exists t \in T$ *such that* $t(c_{i-1}) = c_i$.

Definition 3.4 *Success*
Let $A = (\Sigma, V, init, F, T)$, *an X-automaton. A configuration of A is said to be a success if it contains only two tuples: the top tuple must have its first*

component (the atom) belong to F and its last component must be the empty string; the second tuple of the stack must be the initial one.

We need a language to write the transitions. We will use a functional language inspired by ML (and especially the CAML dialect [13]), in which functions can be described by pattern matching. We change the syntax slightly in order to use Prolog notation for lists, and the previously defined syntax for tuples. To distinguish between logical variables (for instance those appearing in the grammar) and the transition language variables, each of the latter will be prefixed by a $. The most useful operations such as unification, substitution, and renaming, are predefined in the language. Unification failure raises an exception. Substitution application and substitution composition are denoted by an infix dot. We also use the dot for the string constructor, for the last component of tuples.

4 Compiling grammars into X-automata

This section is devoted to the ways of compiling grammars into automata with respect to a parsing strategy. We first give two algorithms, each of which, when applied to any pure DCG, produces an X-automaton. The first one produces a top-down parser and the second a bottom-up parser. Then we discuss other methods.

We introduce new predicates *ci-k-i* (for *clause instance*), where k is anything uniquely identifying a clause and i is an integer. This integer denotes a position in the body of the clause k, that separates the already recognized part of this body from the part that is still to be processed. The integer is the number of atoms in the body that have been recognized so far. A *ci-k-i* predicate contains exactly the same information as the *dotted rules* used by Earley and LR parsing algorithms. For instance, let $1 : noun\text{-}phrase :\text{-} article, noun.$ be a rule. *ci-1-1* is equivalent to the dotted rule $noun\text{-}phrase :\text{-} article, \bullet, noun.$ and means that the parser tries to use the 1st clause, has already recognized an *article*, but has still to parse a *noun*.

4.1 Top-down parsing

For each clause $k :\ k_0 :\text{-} k_1, \ldots, k_n.$ such that k_0 is unifiable with the goal g by a unifier σ_k, create the following transition:

1. $function\ [< init, id, \emptyset, \$I >] \ \rightarrow$
   $\qquad let\ theta\ =\ renaming(k)\ in$
   $\qquad\quad let\ sigma = unify(k_0.theta, g)\ in$
   $\qquad\qquad [< ci\text{-}k\text{-}0, theta.sigma, \emptyset, \$I >, < init, id, \emptyset, \$I >]$

Furthermore, for each such transition, *ci-k-n* is a final predicate of the automaton.

For each clause $c : c_0 \text{ :- } c_1, \ldots, c_n.$, for all i, $0 \leq i < n$, such that c_{i+1} is a non-terminal, and for each clause $d : d_0 \text{ :- } d_1, \ldots, d_m.$ such that c_{i+1} and d_0 are unifiable, create the two transitions:

2. $function\ [< ci\text{-}c\text{-}i, \$S, \emptyset, \$I > |\$End] \rightarrow$
$\quad$ $let\ theta = renaming(d)\ in$
$\quad\quad$ $let\ sigma = unify(c_{i+1}.\$S, d_0.theta)\ in$
$\quad\quad\quad$ $[< ci\text{-}d\text{-}0, theta.sigma, \emptyset, \$I >,$
$\quad\quad\quad$ $< ci\text{-}c\text{-}i, \$S, \emptyset, \$I > |\$End]$

3. $function\ [< ci\text{-}d\text{-}m, \$S1, \emptyset, \$I >, < ci\text{-}c\text{-}i, \$S2, \emptyset, \$J > |\$End] \rightarrow$
$\quad$ $[< ci\text{-}c\text{-}i+1, \$S2.\$S1.sigma, \emptyset, \$I > |\$End]$

For each clause $c : c_0 \text{ :- } c_1, \ldots, c_n.$, for all i, $0 \leq i < n$, such that c_{i+1} is a terminal, create the transition:

4. $function\ [< ci\text{-}c\text{-}i, \$S, \emptyset, \$A.\$I > |\$End] \rightarrow$
$\quad$ $let\ sigma = unify(c_{i+1}.\$S, \$A)\ in$
$\quad\quad$ $[< ci\text{-}c\text{-}i+1, \$S.sigma, \emptyset, \$I > |\$End]$

The work of top-down X-automata should seem quite obvious to people familiar with SLD-resolution with the standard strategy. Transitions of type 1 and 2 correspond to the non-deterministic choice of a clause to reduce a (sub-)goal. The chosen clause must be renamed with fresh variables.

In usual SLD-resolution, the result of unifications is immediately applied to the remaining subgoals. Here, we do it lazily, when popping. The current computed substitution is stored only in the top tuple. Type 3 transitions consist in propagating this substitution one level down into the stack.

The type 4 transition reads a terminal. There is a unification in these transitions because variables may stand for a terminal in some rules. The stored substitution is applied in order to rename them according to the renaming of the rule.

At each level of the stack, the substitution contains the composition of the renaming of the corresponding node and the answer substitution. This substitution is used mainly for the renaming (cf., $\$S2$ in transition 3).

4.2 Bottom-up parsing

Among the many ways of expressing a bottom-up method, we choose those that seems the most understandable, not necessarily the most efficient.

1. Create the transition :
$\quad$ $function\ [< \$1, \$2, \emptyset, \$A.\$I > |\$End] \rightarrow$
$\quad\quad$ $[< \$A, id, \emptyset, \$I >, < \$1, \$2, \emptyset, \$A.\$I > |\$End]$

2. For each clause $k : k_0 \text{ :- } k_1, \ldots, k_n.$ create the following transition:
$\quad$ $function\ [< \$1, \$2, \emptyset, \$I > |\$End] \rightarrow$
$\quad\quad$ $let\ theta = renaming(k)\ in$
$\quad\quad\quad$ $[< ci\text{-}k\text{-}0, theta, \emptyset, \$X >, < \$1, \$2, \emptyset, \$I > |\$End]$

3. For each clause $k : k_0 \text{ :- } k_1, \ldots, k_n.$ create the following transition:
$\quad$ $function\ [< ci\text{-}k\text{-}n, \$S, \emptyset, \$I > |\$End] \rightarrow$
$\quad\quad$ $[< k_0.\$S, id, \emptyset, \$I > \$End]$

4. For each clause $k : k_0 :\text{-} k_1, \ldots, k_n.$ and each position i in its body ($0 \leq i < n$), create the transition:

$function \; [< \$A, \$S1, \emptyset, \$I >, < ci\text{-}k\text{-}i, \$S2, \emptyset, \$J > | \$End] \; \rightarrow$
$\qquad let \; sigma = unify(k_{i+1}.\$S2, \$A) \; in$
$\qquad\qquad [< ci\text{-}k\text{-}i+1, \$S2.\$S1.sigma, \emptyset, \$I > | \$End]$

5. Add a final transition to filter the success. Let g be the goal.

$function \; [< \$A, \$S, \emptyset, \epsilon >, < i, id, \emptyset, \$I >] \; \rightarrow$
$\qquad let \; sigma = unify(\$A, g) \; in$
$\qquad\qquad [< success, \$S.sigma, \emptyset, \epsilon >, < i, id, \emptyset, \$I >]$

Intuitively, the transitions have the following meanings:
1. You can always push a terminal on the stack and advance one step in the string.
2. You can always try to reduce any rule.
3. If you have recognized the entire body of a rule and synthesized the substitution that instantiates that rule, then you may reduce and obtain the head of the clause, on which this substitution applies.
4. If you have already recognized the ith first symbols of the body of a rule, and the $i + 1^{th}$, is on the top of the stack, then you have recognized the $i + 1$ first atom of the rule. Unification must be performed, with the proper renaming, and the answer substitution must be passed along.

This kind of automaton is highly non-deterministic.

4.3 Other parsing techniques

Many other parsing methods can be implemented by algorithms analogous to our two examples. The author has already written LR(0), left-corner bottom-up, Earley, and Earley with restriction compilers. Notice that using the LR(0) technique in no way restricts the class of grammars considered. If the grammar is not LR(0), then the LR(0) parser will be non-deterministic, but it is correct and complete. Similarly, Prolog does not restrict us to LL(0) grammars, since it supports non-determinism with backtracking.

Many of the parsing algorithms developed for DCGs can be encoded into X-automata plus an execution scheme, and many of the context-free parsing methods can be extended in order to cope with arguments of non-terminals.

At the moment, XA are meant for left-to-right parsing. Non left-to-right parsing requires more information about the string and the already parsed part of it than a simple suffix. Adapting the formalism with a more complex representation of the string should be easy.

The main limitation of our framework is that it implies a completely static compilation of the grammar. It expresses more easily those algorithms that in some way have a *context-free behavior*, i.e., the search strategy depends only on the label of the search tree node considered, not on the shape of the context of this node. We have only considered these kinds of algorithms because they are the most common.

4.4 Look-ahead and unification delay

We now present two special devices encodable into X-automata: look-ahead and unification delay.

Look-ahead involves examining tokens of the string before considering the corresponding nodes of the parse tree in order to eliminate parsing choices certain to fail.

We may simply compute look-ahead sets using context-free techniques on the context-free backbone of the grammar. More precise results may be obtained by extending these techniques to take into account part of the non-terminals' arguments.

To add a one symbol look-ahead to a transition:

$$function[< \$S, \ldots, \$I > \ldots \ldots] \rightarrow \ldots text\text{-}of\text{-}the\text{-}function \ldots;;$$

just write:

$$function[< \$S, \ldots, \$A.\$I > \ldots \ldots] \rightarrow$$
$$if\ member(\$A, lookahead\text{-}set(\$S))\ then$$
$$\ldots text\text{-}of\text{-}the\text{-}function \ldots else\ raise\ undefined$$

Where *lookahead-set* retrieves the statically computed set of terminals that can follow $\$S$. Look-ahead of arbitrary length may be added not only to LR automata, but also to top-down and bottom-up automata.

Another possibility to vary parsing strategies is to delay contextual checking, namely unifications. This makes use of the third component of stack tuples.

Delaying unification may be a way of simulating attribute-grammar-like multi-pass evaluation of DCGs, where a context-free technique parses the whole string, just collecting the equations that are eventually reduced in a special order.

This is of course the most simple means to use the delay mechanism. It can be used more locally, as is done with the classical freeze predicate. The delayed unification may also be kept in a more complex structure than a simple equation set.

Another important point we can only address briefly in this paper concerns the integration of extra-logic devices to perform side-effects. The methods we present here apply to pure DCGs. Unfortunately, pure DCGs often lack practical expressive power. To overcome this limitation, adding some imperative features seems necessary.

To preserve the versatility of X-automata, additional devices must remain independent of the parsing strategy. If built-ins or imperative constructs rely on an evaluation order, the grammars can't be parsed using another order. For instance, the behavior of some Prolog built-ins depends on the groundness of their arguments. This groundness is highly dependent on the evaluation strategy. The programmer uses his knowledge about it when writing a program/grammar.

5 Executing X-automata

Expressing different kinds of parsers in the same formalism is interesting from a declarative point of view. It allows comparison between alternative methods expressed in the same words. In addition to this advantage, X-automata can be executed.

The two usual ways of executing non-deterministic push-down automata – backtracking and tabulation – may be extended to X-automata.

First, automata can be extended by stacking choice points and backtracking on failures. This poses no particular difficulty. This may be used with the Prolog goal-directed strategy, but it is not restricted to it. It has also been successfully used (among others) by Nilsson [7] with an LR method.

The second alternative is to use tabular techniques. These techniques break down computations into elementary steps whose partial results are cached in tables (or other data structures). Some examples (non exhaustive list) of tabular techniques: for logic programming, OLDT by Sato and Tamaki [12], Earley Deduction by Pereira and Warren [9]; for parsing, Earley [4].

Lang in [5] gives a tabular procedure to execute any Push-Down automaton. The idea is to compute the complete set of stack tops that may appear in any calculation of the PDA. The reachable stacks, and especially success ones, can be extracted from this set of tops.

This approach was later extended to more complex stack automata. [1] proposes a sufficient condition on a stack machine for dynamic programming with subsumption to be sound and complete. X-automata do not generally satisfy this condition, but the author shows in [2] that the X-automata generated by the algorithms given above, and some others (LR, Earley) do.

6 Experimental Results

This section presents an example of work for which our unified approach of DCG parsing has been fruitful.

We used a prototype implementation in ML of a sub-class of X-automata to generate alternative parsers for some little grammars. We measured the executions in terms of a basic operation, i.e., we counted the number of transition applications.

Comparing parsing algorithms is a difficult task. Complexity measurements are interesting, but they don't reflect the algorithm's behavior on the class of grammars we are practically interested in, because we can't formally define this class.

Comparisons based on experimental results also pose problems. First, how do we define a significant criterion with respect to a given property? It must be implementation-independent. Second, how do we select a representative sample of grammars and strings? Our framework gives a single form to alternative parsing algorithms –an X-automaton + an interpreter.

This allows us to use basic X-automata computation steps as a unit for experimental measurements. We think it is significant, although it is not perfect.

Our approach does not allow a comparison between backtracking and tabular parsers. Both executions apply transitions, but the costs of these applications are incomparable: tabular execution costs more because of table management overhead.

We have written several pure DCGs, having from 2 to 50 rules. For each of them, we generated alternative X-automata, for a variety of parsing strategies. Then we executed these automata on several strings, with both backtracking and tabulation. With backtracking, we sought only one solution. With tabulation, we sought all solutions. In both cases, we counted the number of transitions applied.

For lack of space, we can't elaborate on the pertinence of the grammars or strings we chose. We limited ourselves to pure definite clause grammars because it was not obvious how we might integrate side-effects fairly.

We implemented six parsing methods, namely ll, lr, earley (noted e+), earley with the maximal restriction (noted e-), left-corner bottom-up (lc) and a pure bottom-up without any kind of top-down filtering. The latter is so costly that we withdrew it from the following tables. The length of the look-ahead (here 0 or 1) is given as an argument of the method being used.

The first grammar is a very ambiguous one for the regular language $a+$, which allows any binary tree having the proper number of leaves as a correct structure for a string.

backtracking execution for $a+$ ambiguous				
string	ll(0), ll(1), e+(0), e+(1), e-(0), e-(1)	lr(0)	lc(0)	lc(1)
a^5	44	48	31	26
a^{10}	144	93	61	51
a^{20}	329	183	121	101

In the following table, the first integer is the number of transitions applied and the second is the number of table entries at the end of the process. When these two integers are the same, we just write it once.

Tabular execution for $a+$ ambiguous				
str	ll(0), e+(0) e-(0)	ll(1), e+(1) e-(1)	lr(0)	lc(0)	lc(1)
a^5	176-94	152-90	122-97	84-61	76-59
a^{10}	741-279	697-275	652-342	464-216	446-214
a^{20}	4071-949	3987-945	4412-1282	3124-826	3086-824

The second grammar is a non-ambiguous definition of the same language.

backtracking execution for $a+$ non-ambiguous				
string	ll(0), ll(1), e+(0), e+(1), e-(0), e-(1)	lr(0)	lc(0)	lc(1)
a^5	36	72	31	22
a^{10}	96	237	86	42
a^{20}	291	867	271	82

Tabular execution for $a+$ non-ambiguous					
string	ll(0), e+(0), e-(0)	ll(1), e+(1), e-(1)	lr(0)	lc(0)	lc(1)
a^5	42	40	74	35	25
a^{10}	102	100	239	90	45
a^{20}	297	295	869	275	85

The third grammar describes the correct bracketing using several kind of opening and closing symbols (parentheses, square brackets, curly braces). This grammar is non-ambiguous and the type argument can be used to disambiguate the parses.

backtracking execution for brackets					
string	ll(0), e+(0)	e-(0)	ll(1), e+(1), e-(1)	lr(0)	lc(0), lc(1)
	41	45	28	55	25
	54	57	39	69	35
	144	153	105	195	95
	549	585	402	777	365

Tabular execution for brackets					
string	ll(0), e+(0)	e-(0)	ll(1), e+(1), e-(1)	lr(0)	lc(0), lc(1)
	48	52	35	56-55	32
	67	77	47	71	45
	181	213	126	196-195	123
	699	835	484	771-763	479

Our testing explored more than these three grammars. The preliminary results must be cautiously interpreted, but we can observe some trends.

The left-corner bottom-up wins: in almost every case, it obtains the best results. LR seems to be an efficient technique for use with backtracking when the grammar is locally ambiguous. In this case, LR's complex prediction mechanism (top-down filtering) avoids backtracking. With a tabular execution, LR is not competitive. Look-ahead gives slightly better results. Of course, this depends to a great extent on the grammar being studied.

7 Related work

We don't know of any other attempts to design a multi-strategy parsing machine for DCGs. Most papers describe a specific algorithm either including control or letting Prolog take care of it. They usually can be expressed by an X-automata compiler plus a control technique.

The closest work is in the area of logic programming: Lang ([6]) designed a machine called a *logical push-down automaton (LPDA)* that allows the encoding of the evaluation of a definite clause program using one of several resolutions methods. Top-down, bottom-up, and Earley are considered. This is a generalization of the techniques developed for context-free parsing [5].

This is the principal source of inspiration behind the present work. X-automata are an extension of LPDA, that overcome some of their limitations. Whereas an XA transition may be any arbitrary function respecting the stack mechanism, LPDA's have a fixed and rigid form, consisting in
- a systematic renaming
- a unification with a fixed pattern
- the application of the unifier to a fixed pattern to be stacked

LPDA are therefore more static than XA. They can't generally encode devices such as look-ahead, delayed unification, and restriction [11]. They can describe only one way of renaming.

The drawback of this extended expressive power is that XA's lose the property of soundness of dynamic programming with subsumption. It must be proved separately for subclasses of XAs.

8 Conclusion

We presented a general framework for DCG parsing. This consists in a clear distinction between the parsing method (how a syntax-tree is build) and the control mechanism (how to cope with choices). The paper mainly addresses the first point. A formalism, the X-automaton, is proposed to express parsers. Examples of its use are given for two parsing techniques: bottom-up, top-down. These methods may be enriched by adding look-ahead or delay of unifications.

X-automata are tools to express and study most aspects of DCG parsing. They are also machines that can be executed by the same interpreter (or compiler), whatever parsing method is employed.

Acknowledgements

The author is grateful to Ian B. Jacobs and Gabriel Pereira Lopes for their help.

References

[1] F. P. Barthélemy and E. Villemonte de la Clergerie. Subsumption-oriented push–down automata. In *Proc. of PLILP'92*, pages 100–114, 1992.

[2] François Barthélemy. Outils pour l'analyse syntaxique contextuelle. Thèse de doctorat, Université d'Orléans, february 1993.

[3] Pierre Deransart and Jan Maluszynski. *A grammatical view of logic programming*. MIT Press, 1993.

[4] J. Earley. An efficient context-free parsing algorithm. *Communications of the ACM*, 13(2):94–102, 1970.

[5] Bernard Lang. Deterministic techniques for efficient non-deterministic parsers. In *Proc. of the 2nd Colloquium on automata, languages and Programming*, pages 255–269, Saarbrücken (Germany), 1974. Springer-Verlag (LNCS 14).

[6] Bernard Lang. Complete evaluation of Horn clauses: an automata theoretic approach. Technical Report 913, INRIA, Rocquencourt, France, nov 1988.

[7] Ulf Nilsson. Aid: An alternative implementation of DCGs. *New Generation Computing*, 4:383–399, 1986.

[8] F. C. N. Pereira and D. H. D. Warren. Definite clause grammars for language analysis - a survey of the formalism and a comparison with augmented transition networks. *Artificial Intelligence*, 13:231–278, 1980.

[9] F. C. N. Pereira and D. H. D. Warren. Parsing as deduction. In *Proc. of the 21st Annual Meeting of the Association for Computationnal Linguistic*, pages 137–144, Cambridge (Massachussetts), 1983.

[10] Fernando C. N. Pereira and Stuart M. Shieber. *PROLOG and natural-language analysis*. CSLI (Center for the study of language and information), 1987.

[11] Stuart M. Shieber. Using restriction to extend parsing algorithms for complex–feature–based formalisms. In *Proceedings of the 23rd Annual Meeting of the Association for Computational Linguistics*, pages 145–152, Chicago (Illinois), 1985.

[12] H. Tamaki and T. Sato. OLD resolution with tabulation. In E. Shapiro, editor, *Proc. of Third Int. Conf. on Logic Programming*, pages 84–98, London, 1986. Springer–Verlag.

[13] P. Weis, M.V. Aponte, A. Laville, M. Mauny, and A. Suárez. *The CAML Reference Manual*. INRIA-ENS, 1989.

Compiling Intensional Sets in CLP

Paola Bruscoli
Università di Ancona, Ist. di Ingegneria Informatica
ANCONA (Italy)
e-mail: `paola@di.unipi.it`

Agostino Dovier
Università di Pisa, Dip. di Informatica
PISA (Italy)
e-mail: `dovier@di.unipi.it`

Enrico Pontelli
New Mexico State University, Dept. of Computer Science
LAS CRUCES (USA)
e-mail: `epontell@cs.nmsu.edu`

Gianfranco Rossi
Università di Parma, Dip. di Matematica
PARMA (Italy)
e-mail: `gianfr@prmat.math.unipr.it`

Abstract

Constructive negation has been proved to be a valid alternative to negation as failure, especially when negation is required to have, in a sense, an 'active' role. In this paper we analyze an extension of the original *constructive negation* in order to gracefully integrate with the management of set-constraints in the context of a Constraint Logic Programming Language dealing with finite sets. We show that the marriage between *CLP* with sets and constructive negation gives us the possibility of representing a general class of *intensionally defined sets* without any further extension to the operational semantics of the language. The presence of intensional sets allows a definite increase in the expressive power and abstraction level offered by the host logic language.

1 Introduction

In [7] we have shown that an increase in expressivity and abstraction capability can be obtained by embedding the basic notion of *set* in a logic programming language. By adding simple set constructors ({} and `with`) and a limited collection of predicates ($\in$, $=$, $\neq$, and $\notin$) we get a language (called {log}–read 'setlog') able to express rather complex set expressions, allowing to sensibly narrow the gap between problem specification and program development. While the construction of a declarative semantics for a logic programming language extended with these new features is quite natural (thanks also to the many works devoted to set theory axiomatization) the design of a sound and complete operational semantics presents challenging problems. In previous works [5, 6, 7] we have developed a suitable operational framework based on an extended unification procedure (able to deal with unification between sets) and a constraint manager (used to deal with the negative distinguished predicates $\neq$- and $\notin$). These results have been successively refined and integrated in the context of Constraint Logic Programming [9], where all the new four set-predicates are uniformly manipulated as constraints. Unfortunately the expressive power of {log} is still not satisfactory, especially when applied to many real-life problems. This is due to the lack of a real *set grouping capability*, i.e. the capability of defining *intensional* set expressions of the form $\{X : p(X)\}$, where p is an arbitrary property. Simply put, {log} lacks a setof facility, like the one used in Prolog.

The purpose of this work is to show how intensional sets can be added to a *CLP* language dealing with sets, maintaining soundness and completeness (which are lost in the setof of Prolog), without imposing too severe restrictions on the admissible programs/queries (like in LDL [1], for instance). The basic idea of our approach is the reduction of the set grouping problem to the problem of dealing with *normal logic programs*, i.e. programs containing negation in the body of the clauses. This creates an interesting line of contact between negation and intensional sets (which was, by the way, already implicitly exploited by the various works on circumscription and similar forms of non-monotonic reasoning techniques).

The work is organized in three parts. The first part is dedicated to a review of the general ideas about logic programming with sets with an emphasis on the definitions related to the {log} language. The second part analyzes the core relationship between intensional sets and negation, showing a detailed algorithm which allows to convert programs containing set grouping operations into equivalent programs without set grouping (containing negative literals). The third part analyzes an extended *CLP*-like operational semantics endowing the management of negative literals. This extension has been inspired by the various works on *constructive negation* [3, 4, 12, 14], which appears to be the most suitable form of negation to be integrated in the {log} framework.

2   The {log} language

We will first recall the basic *CLP* concepts as defined in [10]. The *CLP* framework is defined using a many-sorted first order language, where $SORT=\bigcup SORT_i$ denotes a finite set of sorts. One sort is sufficient for our purposes.

By Σ and Π we denote possibly denumerable collections of function symbols and predicate symbols with their signatures. We assume there is a denumerable set of variables V. Moreover, $\Pi = \Pi_C \cup \Pi_B$ and $\Pi_C \cap \Pi_B = \emptyset$, where Π_C and Π_B are the sets of constraint predicate symbols and programer defined predicate symbols, respectively. $\tau(\Sigma \cup V)$ and $\tau(\Sigma)$ denote the set of terms and ground terms built on $\Sigma \cup V$ and Σ (ground terms), respectively. A (Π, Σ)-*atom* is an element $p(t_1, \ldots, t_n)$ where $p \in \Pi$ is n-ary and $t_i \in \tau(\Sigma \cup V)$, $i = 1, \ldots, n$. A (Π, Σ)-*literal* is a (Π, Σ)-atom or its negation. An *atomic constraint* is a (Π_C, Σ)-atom. A (Π_C, Σ)-*constraint* is a first order formula of atomic constraints (for a more detailed description of the form of constraints used see section 5). The empty constraint will be denoted by *true*. A (Π, Σ)-*normal program* is a finite set of clauses of the form $H \leftarrow c \square B_1, \cdots, B_n$ where c is a finite (Π_C, Σ)-constraint, H (the head) is a (Π_B, Σ)-atom and $B_1, \ldots, B_n$ (the body) are (Π_B, Σ)-literals (n $\geq$ 0). A *normal goal* is a program clause with no head and with a non-empty body. In the following (Π, Σ)-normal programs and (Π_C, Σ)-constraints will be called normal programs and constraints, respectively.

As a further notation, the symbol $^-$ will denote a finite sequence of symbols. If t is a syntactic object, $FV(t)$ is the set of variables which are not explicitly quantified in t and by $t[x]$ we mean a term in which x occurs, except x itself. A sentence is a well formed formula with no free variables.

We can now define the basic {log} syntactic entities. The set of constraint predicates Π_C is fixed in {log} to be equal to $\{\in, \notin, =, \neq\}$. As shown in [9] this set of primitive set-theoretic operations suffices to define other usual set operations (such as union, intersection, ...).

Definition 2.1 *A* {log}-term *is either an* extensional *or an* intensional *term.*

- *An* extensional term *is an element of* $\tau(\Sigma \cup V)$, *i.e.*
  1. X, *for each* $X \in V$;
  2. $f(t_1, \ldots, t_n)$ *s.t.* $\forall i \in \{1, \ldots, n\}$, t_i *is an extensional term and* $f \in \Sigma$;
- *an* intensional term *is*
  1. $\{X : c \square B_1, \ldots, B_n\}$ *s.t.* $X \in FV(c \square B_1, \ldots, B_n)$, *where* c *is a conjunction of* (Π_C, Σ)-*atoms and* $B_1, \ldots, B_n$ *are* (Π_B, Σ)-*literals;*
  2. $f(t_1, \ldots, t_n)$ *s.t.* $\exists i, 1 \leq i \leq n$, t_i *is an intensional term,* $f \in \Sigma$.

Definition 2.2 *A* {log}-extended literal *is either*

- *a* {log}-literal $p(t_1, \ldots, t_n)$ *or* $\neg p(t_1, \ldots, t_n)$ *(resp. positive, negative), where* $t_1, \ldots, t_n$ *are* {log}-terms;
- *a* RUQ-literal[1] $(\forall X_1 \in t_1) \ldots (\forall X_n \in t_n)(c \square \bar{B})$ *where* c *is a conjunction of* (Π_C, Σ)-*atoms,* $\bar{B}$ *is a finite sequence of* (Π_B, Σ)-*literals,* $X_j s$ *are pairwise distinct variables, and* $t_i s$ *are extensional terms s.t.* $X_j \cap FV(t_i) = \emptyset$ *for* $i \leq j$.

A few words about *RUQ*-literals are in order. First, recall that $(\forall x \in t)\varphi$, φ any first order formula, is a shorthand for $\forall x \, (x \in t \rightarrow \varphi)$. Moreover, observe that the condition $X_j \cap FV(t_i) = \emptyset$ prevents us from writing formulas such as $(\forall v \in x)(\forall x \in y)\varphi$, where the two occurrences of x would refer to

---

[1] *RUQ* stands for Restricted Universal Quantifier.

two distinguished variables. In [6] we have proved the equivalence between {log} programs containing restricted universal quantifications and {log} programs which are *RUQ*-free. Each occurrence of a *RUQ* may be removed by performing a simple syntactic translation. Thanks to this we can assume from now on that the program on which we are working does not contain any *RUQ*.

Definition 2.3 *A* {log}-*clause is a normal clause* $A \leftarrow c \square B_1, \ldots, B_n$ *where A is a positive literal, c is a conjunction of* (Π_C, Σ)-*atoms and* $B_1, \ldots, B_n$ *are* {log}-*extended literals. A* {log}-*goal is a* {log}-*clause with empty head. A* {log}-*program is a finite set of* {log}-*clauses.*

As a notational convenience we will write $\{X : B_1, \ldots, B_n\}$ and $A \leftarrow B_1, \ldots, B_n$ whenever c is *'true'* (the empty constraint).

In order to be able to deal with extensional sets, as well as standard Herbrand terms, the following two functional symbols are assumed to be always present in Σ [5]:

- $\emptyset$, nullary, to be interpreted as the empty set;
- a binary function symbol, with (used as an infix left associative operator), to be interpreted as follows: s with t stands for the set that results from adding t as a new element to the set s.

In view of the intended interpretation, an extensional term of any of the forms, $\emptyset$ or X with t_n with $\cdots$ with t_1 or k with t_n with $\cdots$ with t_0, $n \leq 0$, X variable, and k a non variable extensional term with main functor different from with/2, is called a *set term*. The term k is the *kernel* of the set and a set term where k is not $\emptyset$ is intended to designate a *colored set* based on the kernel k^2. For the sake of simplicity special syntactic forms are introduced to designate set terms: $\{t_1, \ldots, t_n | s\}$ stands for s with t_n with $\cdots$ with t_1 and $\{t_1, \ldots, t_n\}$ stands for $\emptyset$ with t_n with $\cdots$ with t_1 where $n \geq 1$ and $s, t_1, \ldots, t_n$ are terms. {} is a syntactic sugar for $\emptyset$. For example:

- {}, {1,X,Y,2}, {1,1,{2,{}},f(a,{b})}, and any term {t$_1$, . . . ,t$_n$|R} with a 'tail' variable R, are set terms;
- f(a,{5}), i.e. f(a,{} with 5), is an extensional term, but not a set term;
- {a | f({b})} is a colored set term based on the kernel f({b});
- {X : X ≠ 1 □ p(X)}, f(Y,{Z : Z ∈ Y □ p(Z,W)}) are intensional set terms.

Here are a few sample {log} programs (the precise meaning of these programs will be clarified in the next section).

- Checking membership of an element to the set Set1 \ Set2:
  in_difference(X, Set1, Set2) ← X ∈ Set1 ∧ X ∉ Set2 □.
- Sorting a set into an ordered list:
  quicksort({ }, []).
  quicksort(S, L) ← X ∈ S □

---

[2]Colored set terms do not designate sets of any conventional kind. Nevertheless, we deem it convenient to always regard such terms as legal set terms when $t_1, \ldots, t_n, k$ are legal, to make the language structure absolutely uniform and the inference mechanisms (e.g. unification) more straightforward.

$$\text{quicksort}(\{Y \ : \ Y \in S \ \Box \ \text{less}(X, Y)\}, L1),$$
$$\text{quicksort}(\{Y \ : \ Y \in S \ \Box \ \text{less}(Y, X)\}, L2),$$
$$\text{append}(L1, [X|L2], L).$$

- Computing the set of prime numbers less than a given limit N:

$$\text{primes}(N, S) \leftarrow S = \{X : \text{between}(1, N, X), \text{prime}(X)\}.$$
$$\text{prime}(X) \leftarrow S = \{Y : \text{between}(1, X, Y)\} \Box (\forall Z \in S)(\text{non\_div}(Z, X)).$$
$$\text{between}(A, B, C) \leftarrow \text{less}(A, C) \ , \ \text{less}(C, B).$$

3 Compiling intensional sets

In [5] we argued that intensional sets can be programmed in a logic language with sets like {log}, provided the language supplies either a set grouping mechanism or some form of negation in goals and clause bodies. This allows us, on one hand, to consider intensional sets as a syntactic extension to be dealt with a simple preprocessing phase, and, on the other hand, not to be concerned with intensional sets when defining the semantics of our language.

Let us try, first of all, to understand why the negative information representable in {log} by the use of $\neq$ and $\notin$ is not sufficient for a satisfactory definition of a set grouping mechanism, and full negation is required instead. An intensional set S can be defined in the following equivalent ways:

$$\{X : p(X)\} \ = \ S \leftrightarrow \forall X(X \in S \leftrightarrow p(X))$$
$$\{X : p(X)\} \ = \ S \leftrightarrow \forall X(X \in S \to p(X)) \land \forall X(p(X) \to X \in S).$$

As we can see, a set grouping feature requires the ability to perform *restricted universal quantification* as well as universal quantification of the solutions of an arbitrary predicate.

Though {log} supports restricted universal quantification [6], it is unable to express the other form of quantification. However, one can observe that:

$$\forall X(p(X) \to X \in S) \leftrightarrow \forall X(\neg p(X) \lor X \in S) \leftrightarrow \neg \exists X(X \notin S \land p(X)).$$

The outcome shows that what we need is just a form of negation (notice that the negated formula can be easily expressed by using a new clause with a local variable).

The correlation between set grouping and negation can be further shown by the following example. Suppose that given a natural number N we want to define a predicate returning the greatest prime number X in its decomposition in prime factors. We use an intensional construct to collect the prime divisors of N as follows:

$$\text{max}_{\text{pdiv}}(N, X) \quad \leftarrow \quad \text{max}(\{Y \ : \ \text{pdiv}(N, Y)\}, X).$$
$$\text{max}(S, M) \qquad \leftarrow \quad M \in S \ \Box \ (\forall Z \in S)(\text{geq}(M, Z)).$$

where pdiv and geq define the divisibility relation and the greatest or equal relation, respectively.

In order to compute max_{pdiv} we should be able to collect the set of prime divisors computed by the predicate pdiv and, at the same time, to reject any partial solution, namely any element in the powerset of the set of all possible solutions. This could be implemented as follows:

$$\mathsf{setof}_{\mathsf{pdiv}}(\mathsf{S},\mathsf{N}) \quad\leftarrow\quad (\forall \mathsf{Y} \in \mathsf{S})(\mathsf{pdiv}(\mathsf{N},\mathsf{Y})), \neg\mathsf{partial}_{\mathsf{pdiv}}(\mathsf{S},\mathsf{N}).$$
$$\mathsf{partial}_{\mathsf{pdiv}}(\mathsf{S},\mathsf{N}) \quad\leftarrow\quad \mathsf{Z} \notin \mathsf{S} \ \square \ \mathsf{pdiv}(\mathsf{N},\mathsf{Z}).$$

with the call to max in the clause defining $\mathsf{max}_{\mathsf{pdiv}}$ replaced by $\mathsf{setof}_{\mathsf{pdiv}}(\mathsf{S},\mathsf{N})$, $\mathsf{max}(\mathsf{S},\mathsf{X})$.

Replacement of intensional set terms by the setof predicates which allow the corresponding extensional sets to be constructed is performed by a two steps program transformation. This process will transform a given $(\Pi_C \cup \Pi_B, \Sigma)$-program into the equivalent $(\Pi_C \cup \Pi'_B, \Sigma)$-program where Π'_B contains Π_B and all the new predicate symbols which are required to express both the *discriminant* part of intensional sets and set grouping (along with the new predicate symbols generated by RUQ's translation).

The first step leads the source code to a *normal form* where all variable instantiations in clauses and goals are expressed as constraints and each *discriminant* $(c\square\bar{B})$ of intensional terms is expressed by a unique predicate symbol. Such a predicate symbol has arity equal to $|FV(c\square\bar{B})|$, and it is defined by a unique clause having the corresponding discriminant as its body.

Step 1 - Program normalization

Let C be the {log}-clause
$$p(s_1,\ldots,s_m) \leftarrow c\square A_1(t_1^1,\ldots,t_{n_1}^1),\ldots,A_r(t_1^r,\ldots,t_{n_r}^r)$$
where s_i's and t_j^i's are terms, and $A_i(t_1^i,\ldots,t_{n_i}^i)$ are {log}-literals (as it ensues from the discussion following def. 2.2, there is no need here to consider RUQ-literals).

Repeatedly perform the following actions until none applies.

- Replace C by the equivalent clause

$$p(X_1,\ldots,X_m) \leftarrow c \wedge \bigwedge_{i=1,\ldots,m} (X_i = s_i) \wedge \bigwedge_{\substack{i=1,\ldots,r \\ j=1,\ldots,n_i}} (X_j^i = t_j^i)\square$$
$$A_1(X_1^1,\ldots,X_{n_1}^1),\ldots,A_r(X_1^r,\ldots,X_{n_r}^r)$$

  where X_i's, X_j^i's and Y_j^i's are new distinct variables.

- Replace each atomic constraint $s \ \pi \ t$, where $\pi \in \Pi_C$ and s and/or t are intensional terms, by the constraint

$$s' \ \pi \ t' \wedge \bigwedge_{i=1}^m (S_i = s_i) \wedge \bigwedge_{j=1}^n (T_j = t_j),$$

  where s_i's and t_j's are all the basic intensional terms occurring in s and t respectively, s' and t' are the extensional terms obtained by replacing the intensional terms s_i's and t_j's in s and t with the new variables S_i's and T_j's respectively.

- Replace each atomic constraint of the form $X = \{Y : c\square\bar{B}\}$ by the constraint
$$X = \{Y : \delta(Y, Z_1,\ldots,Z_m)\},$$

  where $\{Y, Z_1,\ldots,Z_m\} = FV(c\square\bar{B})$, and δ is a newly generated predicate symbol, and add to the program the new clause

$$\delta(Y, Z_1,\ldots,Z_m) \leftarrow c\square\bar{B}.$$

Step 2 - Eliminating intensional set terms

The second step is intended to remove intensional set terms from a normalized program according to the general idea for implementing set grouping sketched at the beginning of this section. For each predicate symbol δ generated by the normalization step to represent discriminants in intensional set terms, two new predicate symbols $setof_\delta$ and $partial_\delta$ are introduced, and their corresponding {log} definitions added to the generated program, according to the following transformation rule:

- Replace each normalized clause of the form

$$h(\bar{Y}) \leftarrow c \wedge X_1 = \{X : \delta(X, \bar{Z})\} \square \bar{B}$$

by the set of clauses

$$
\begin{aligned}
h(\bar{Y}) &\leftarrow c\square setof_\delta(X_1, \bar{Z}), \bar{B}. \\
setof_\delta(X_1, \bar{Z}) &\leftarrow (\forall X \in X_1)\delta(X, \bar{Z}), \neg partial_\delta(X_1, \bar{Z}). \\
partial_\delta(X_1, \bar{Z}) &\leftarrow V \notin X_1 \square \delta(V, \bar{Z}).
\end{aligned}
$$

For example, the definition of the predicate $\mathsf{max_{pdiv}}$ shown above is first replaced by the following clauses:

$$
\begin{aligned}
\mathsf{max_{pdiv}}(\mathsf{N}, \mathsf{X}) &\leftarrow \mathsf{Z} = \{\mathsf{Y} : \delta(\mathsf{Y}, \mathsf{N})\} \square \mathsf{max}(\mathsf{Z}, \mathsf{X}). \\
\delta(\mathsf{Y}, \mathsf{N}) &\leftarrow \mathsf{pdiv}(\mathsf{N}, \mathsf{Y}).
\end{aligned}
$$

Then (second step), the normalized definition of the predicate $\mathsf{max_{pdiv}}$ is replaced by:

$$\mathsf{max_{pdiv}}(\mathsf{N}, \mathsf{X}) \leftarrow setof_\delta(\mathsf{Z}, \mathsf{N}), \mathsf{max}(\mathsf{Z}, \mathsf{X}).$$

adding the clauses defining $setof_\delta(\mathsf{Z}, \mathsf{N})$ to the transformed program.

4 Negation

Different forms of negation can be introduced in logic programming, most of them based on the notion of *Completed Program* [13]. In particular, the well-known *negation as failure* technique could be used to handle negation in {log} programs. Negation as failure has various advantages, related in particular to its simplicity: it is quite easy to come up with a reasonable and fairly efficient implementation. On the other hand, negation as failure has various drawbacks, mostly related to the strict requirements necessary in order to maintain soundness and completeness results. Just to point out one of such restrictions: soundness of the SLD + negation as failure resolution rule is guaranteed only if the program and the goal are *allowed*. Allowedness requires that every variable occurring in a clause occurs in a positive literal in the body of the clause. While this restriction may be acceptable in many contexts (e.g. deductive databases), in our framework it may create some serious complications. Just to mention one, the algorithm which translates Restricted Universal Quantifiers to pure {log} programs [5, 6] generates clauses which do not satisfy the allowedness restriction.

Various proposals have been made in the last few years to get around the inability of providing computed answers to non-ground negative literals in negation as failure. The approach that we are following here is the one called *constructive negation* [3, 4]. As we will see later on, this approach gracefully integrates with {log}. The basic idea behind constructive negation is the following. Given a program P the set of all the solutions to a goal ($\leftarrow G$), $\sigma_1, \ldots, \sigma_n$, is such that $Comp(P) \models G \leftrightarrow \sigma_1 \vee \cdots \vee \sigma_n$ where $Comp(P)$ is the completed version of the program P. Taking the negation of the formula, $Comp(P) \models \neg G \leftrightarrow \neg(\sigma_1 \vee \cdots \vee \sigma_n)$, gives an idea of how to obtain a solution to a negative literal. The key point is the development of an effective procedure to extract actual solutions from the negation $\neg(\sigma_1 \vee \cdots \vee \sigma_n)$. The description given by Chan [3, 4] is specialized for the case of pure logic programming (each σ_i is a substitution). The relations between constructive negation and *CLP* have been studied in [14].

5   Constraints

In [9] we have shown that {log} can be conveniently viewed as an instance of the general *CLP* scheme [10]. To this purpose first we have fixed Σ and Π_C to be equal to $\{\emptyset, \text{with}, \ldots\}$ and $\{=, \neq, \in, \notin\}$, respectively, and then we have defined a suitable algebraic structure $\mathcal{S}$, whose domain S is defined as the quotient set of the Herbrand universe w.r.t. a suitable congruence over $\tau(\Sigma)$ to abstract from the ordering of the elements of with-based terms [9].

Also we have characterized the kind of sets to be handled via axioms of a suitable set theory *Set* [6, 9], from which it is easy to derive, among others, the two fundamental properties of the set construct with, namely *Right permutativity* (i.e. $(X \text{ with } Y) \text{ with } Z = (X \text{ with } Z) \text{ with } Y$) and *Right absorption* (i.e. $(X \text{ with } Y) \text{ with } Y = X \text{ with } Y$).

It has been proved that the structure $\mathcal{S}$ is *solution compact*. Moreover, it has been proved that the satisfaction complete theory *Set* and the structure $\mathcal{S}$ correspond. Thus, having developed also a suitable constraint satisfaction procedure (cf. [9]), we have been in the position of using the ordinary machinery of the general *CLP* scheme to implement both the algebraic and the logical derivation (actually, the implementation of {log} described in [8] is a specialized version of the *CLP* logical derivation for {log} programs).

In this section we show how the {log} constraint satisfiability procedure and the general *CLP* operational semantics need to be modified in order to accommodate for constructive negation. More precisely, the resolution procedure needs to deal with positive atoms as well as with the negative ones (i.e. literals of the form $\neg p(\bar{t})$, where p is a user-defined predicate), whereas the constraint solver needs to deal with positive atomic constraints of the form $t_1 \in t_2$ or $t_1 = t_2$, as well as with negative constraints of the form $\forall \bar{X} (t_1 \notin t_2)$ or $\forall \bar{X} (t_1 \neq t_2)$ where $\bar{X}$ represents some (eventually none) of the variables in t_1, t_2.

Indeed the latter kind of constraints, though not present in the program generated by the transformation process described in the previous section, may be generated during the computation due to the presence of negation (i.e. dealing with negation leads to explicit universal quantifications).

We first examine the constraint satisfaction procedure and then the extended resolution procedure, devoting special care to the way constructive negation is dealt with.

The key notion of the constraint satisfiability procedure developed for {log} [9] is represented by the concept of *normal form* (or, following the nomenclature used in [6, 7, 9], *canonical form*) for a constraint.

Definition 5.1 *Given a constraint C, an atomic constraint c in C is in* normal form *whenever it satisfies one of the following conditions:*
a. $c \equiv X = t$ and X is a variable which does not occur elsewhere in C;
b. $c \equiv t \notin X$ and X is a variable which does not occur in t;
c. $c \equiv X \neq t$ and X is a variable which does not occur in t.[3]

A constraint C is in normal form *if either it is 'false' or all the atomic constraints in it are in normal form.*

It can be proved that if C is in normal form and other than *'false'* then C is satisfiable in the theory *Set* (or, equivalently, solvable in the structure $\mathcal{S}$).

The approach used in {log} to detect satisfiability of a generic constraint C, therefore, is based on the use of a procedure, called $\mathcal{SAT}$, which tries to transform C into an equisatisfiable disjunction of constraints in normal form (whose satisfiability is guaranteed). The transformation of C to a normal form is performed by using the following non-deterministic function

$$\mathsf{step}(C) \quad = \quad \textbf{if} \; \textit{'false'} \; \textbf{in} \; C \; \textbf{then} \; \textit{'false'}$$
$$\textbf{else} \; \mathsf{notequal}(\mathsf{notmember}(\mathsf{unify}(\mathsf{member}(C)))).$$

Each of the functions **unify**, **notmember**, and **notequal** (see [9]) reduces =-constraints, $\notin$-constraints, and $\neq$-constraints to their normal forms, respectively, whereas $\in$-constraints are completely eliminated by **member** by replacing them with suitable =-constraints. Since each of these functions may produce constraints of a different form (for example *notequal* may produce $\in$-constraints), then **step** needs to be iterated as long as a fixpoint is reached:

$$\mathcal{SAT}(C) \quad = \quad \textbf{while} \; \mathsf{step}(C) \neq C \; \textbf{do}$$
$$C = \mathsf{step}(C);$$
$$\textbf{return} \; C.$$

It has been proved [9] that this fixpoint is always reached in a finite number of steps and that each constraint that $\mathcal{SAT}$ non-deterministically computes is in normal form.

The key result proved in [9] is that given a constraint C, then

$$Set \vdash C \leftrightarrow \exists(C_1 \vee \cdots \vee C_n),$$

where $C_1, \cdots, C_n$ is the collection of constraints in normal form computed by $\mathcal{SAT}$. Therefore, C is satisfiable if and only if there exists a non-deterministic choice such that $\mathcal{SAT}(C) \neq$ *'false'*.

---

[3]For the sake of simplicity, hereafter, we will not consider set terms based on a kernel other than $\emptyset$. Actually, the results proved here are still valid when considering colored sets, too, provided the constraint satisfiability procedure is suitably extended to accommodate for this more general case as shown in [9].

When dealing with negation we need to update these definitions, due to the possibility, as announced before, of generating explicit universal quantification over negative constraints.

First of all, a constraint C may contain not only (Π_C, Σ)-atoms but also universally quantified formulae of the of the form $\forall \bar{Z}(X \neq t)$ or $\forall \bar{Z}(t \notin X)$. Thus the previous definition of normal form (def. 5.1) must be updated by replacing cases *(b)* and *(c)* with the following new ones:

b'. $c \equiv \forall \bar{Z}(t \notin X)$, X *does not occur in* t *nor in* $\bar{Z}$ *and, if* $t \equiv Y$, Y *variable, then* Y *should not occur in* $\bar{Z}$;

c'. $c \equiv \forall \bar{Z}(X \neq t)$, X *and* t *as above.*

Dealing with constraints of the form $\forall \bar{Z}(X \neq t)$ requires the ability to manage disjunctions of constraints as well as conjunctions. Indeed, to solve a constraint of the form $\forall \bar{Z}\left(f(t_0, \ldots, t_n) \neq f(s_0, \ldots, s_n)\right)$, where f is different from `with` and $\{\bar{Z}\} \subseteq FV(t_0, \ldots, t_n, s_0, \ldots, s_n)$, one needs to solve the disjunction $\forall \bar{Z}(t_0 \neq s_0 \vee \cdots \vee t_n \neq s_n)$.

Unfortunately, the following general result, used for instance by Chan [3], does not hold in our theory *Set*.

> Let t be a term such that $FV(t) = \{x_1, \ldots, x_n\}(= \{\bar{x}\})$, and D
> be a f.o.f. such that $\{y_1, \ldots, y_m\} = FV(D) \backslash \{x_1, \ldots, x_n, u\}$, then
> $\vdash_{EQ} \forall u \left(\forall \bar{x}\bar{y}\, (u \neq t \vee D) \leftrightarrow \forall \bar{x}\, (u \neq t) \vee \exists \bar{x}\, (u = t \wedge \forall \bar{y}\, D)\right).$ (1)

In particular, the $\leftarrow$ part of (1) is not true in our theory[4]. As an example, the formula $\forall xyvw\, (\{\emptyset, \{\emptyset\}\} \neq \{x, y\} \vee x \neq \{w|v\})$ (equivalent to $\forall xy\, (\{\emptyset, \{\emptyset\}\} \neq \{x, y\} \vee \forall vw(x \neq \{w|v\})))$ is not true in *Set* (e.g., by taking $x = \{\emptyset\}, y = \emptyset$), while $\forall xy\, (\{\emptyset, \{\emptyset\}\} \neq \{x, y\}) \vee \exists xy\, (\{\emptyset, \{\emptyset\}\} \neq \{x, y\} \wedge \forall vw(x \neq \{w|v\}))$ is true in *Set* (e.g., by taking $x = \emptyset, y = \{\emptyset\}$).

The problem here originates from the fact that the *uniqueness* property of the mgu which holds in the standard theory EQ and is exploited to prove (1), does not hold in our theory *Set*. The following lemma that can be proved to hold in *Set* will provide us an alternative to (1).

Lemma 5.2 *Let* t *be a term such that* $FV(t) = \{x_1, \ldots, x_n\}(= \{\bar{x}\})$, *and* D *be a f.o.f. such that* $\{y_1, \ldots, y_m\} = FV(D) \setminus \{x_1, \ldots, x_n, u\}$, *then*
$$\vdash_{Set} \forall u \left(\forall \bar{x}\bar{y}(u \neq t \vee D) \leftrightarrow \forall \bar{x}(u \neq t) \vee \exists \theta_1 \cdots \theta_k \bigwedge_{1 \leq i \leq k}(u = t^{\theta_i} \wedge \forall \bar{y}\, D^{\theta_i})\right)$$
where $\theta_1 \cdots \theta_k$ *are independent substitutions and* $\{\bar{x}\} \subseteq \mathrm{dom}(\theta_i)$.

As an effective application of this lemma, one can prove, for instance, that the following equivalence holds:
$$\forall u \left(\begin{array}{l} \forall xy(u \neq \{x, y\} \vee \varphi) \leftrightarrow \\ \forall xy(u \neq \{x, y\}) \vee \exists xy \left(u = \{x, y\} \wedge \varphi \wedge \varphi^{\{x \mapsto y, y \mapsto x\}}\right) \end{array} \right)$$

This result will be exploited in the constraint satisfiability procedure, in particular in that part of the procedure aimed at simplifying $\neq$-constraints (function `notequal`), and in the extended resolution procedure. The function

---

[4] For the other direction, notice that $\forall x, y\, (\varphi(x) \vee \psi(x, y)) \rightarrow \forall x\, \varphi(x) \vee \exists x\, (\neg\varphi(x) \wedge \forall y\, \psi(x, y))$ is a theorem of predicate calculus.

notequal is shown in detail in the following (notice that $C_{\neq}$ is used in the function to denote the part of the given constraint C containing $\neq$-constraints only). $\not\in$-constraints can be dealt with in a similar, though simpler way, so the pertaining function notmember is not shown here. Nothing needs to be changed w.r.t. [9] in the treatment of $=$ and $\in$ constraints.

function notequal(C);

if $C_{\neq}$ is in canonical form **then return** C

else choose any c not in canonical form in $C_{\neq}$; let $C = C' \wedge c$;

    case c **of**

1. $\forall Z_1 \ldots Z_n \, (s \neq t)$, and $Z_1, \ldots, Z_k$ do not belong to $FV(s \neq t)$, $k > 0$:
   return notequal($C' \wedge \forall Z_{k+1} \ldots Z_n(s \neq t)$);

2. $\forall \bar{Z} \, (f(t_1, \ldots, t_n) \neq g(s_1, \ldots, s_m))$, f and g are different function symbols: **return** notequal(C');

3. $\forall \bar{Z} \, (f(t_0, \ldots, t_n) \neq f(s_0, \ldots, s_n))$, f is different from with, and $\{\bar{Z}\} \subseteq FV(t_0, \ldots, t_n, s_0, \ldots, s_n)$:
   return notequal($C' \wedge \forall \bar{Z}(t_0 \neq s_0 \vee \cdots \vee t_n \neq s_n)$);

4. $\forall \bar{Z} \, (s \neq t \vee D)$, and $\{\bar{Z}\} \subseteq FV(s \neq t \vee D)$, $\{\bar{Z}\} = \{\bar{Z}_D\} \cup \{\bar{Z}_C\}$, $\{\bar{Z}_D\} = \{\bar{Z}\} \cap FV(D)$, $\{\bar{Z}_C\} \cap \{\bar{Z}_D\} = \emptyset$:
   if unify(s, t) fails **then return** C'
   else let θ_i, $i = 1, \ldots, k$ be the mgu's of s and t such that
       $\{\bar{Z}_C\} \subseteq dom(\theta_i)$ and $Z_i = FV(s^{\theta_i} \neq t^{\theta_i}) \setminus \{\bar{Z}_C\}$:
           return notequal($C' \wedge \bigwedge_{i=1}^{k} \forall \bar{Z}_i \bar{Z}_D D^{\theta_i}$);

5. $f \neq f$, f is a constant: **return** *false*;

6. $X \neq X$ or $\forall X(X \neq X)$, X is a variable: **return** *false*;

7. $\forall \bar{Z} \, (t \neq X)$ and t is not a variable: **return** notequal($C' \wedge \forall \bar{Z}(X \neq t)$);

8. $\forall \bar{Z}_1 X \bar{Z}_2 (X \neq t)$ and t is not a variable, or $\forall XY \, (X \neq Y)$ or $\forall XY \, (Y \neq X)$: **return** *false*;

9. $\forall \bar{Z}(X \neq f(t_1, \ldots, t_n))$, f is different from with and $X \in FV(f(t_1, \ldots, t_n))$, or $\forall \bar{Z} \, (X \neq h \text{ with } s_m \ldots \text{ with } s_0)$, h is a variable or $\emptyset$ and $X \in FV(s_0) \cup \ldots \cup FV(s_m)$: **return** notequal($C'$);

10. $\forall \bar{Z} \, (X \neq X \text{ with } t_n \ldots \text{ with } t_0)$:
    return notequal($C' \wedge \forall \bar{Z}(t_0 \not\in X \vee \cdots \vee t_n \not\in X)$);

11. $\forall \bar{Z} \, (r \neq s)$, where $s \equiv h \text{ with } t_n \ldots \text{ with } t_0$ and $s \equiv k \text{ with } t'_m \text{ with } \cdots \text{ with } t'_0$, h, k terms with main functor different from with:
    select non-deterministically one of the following actions (let X and N denote new variables):
    - i. take a solution θ for the constraint $X \in r$; **case** θ **of**
      - a. $\{X \mapsto t_i\}$, $i = 0, \ldots, n$: **return** notequal($C' \wedge \forall \bar{Z} \, (X^{\theta} \not\in s)$)
      - b. $\{h \mapsto N \text{ with } X\}$, h variable <u>not</u> in $\bar{Z}$:
        return notequal($C' \wedge (h = N \text{ with } X) \wedge \forall \bar{Z} \, (X \not\in s)$)
      - c. $\{h \mapsto N \text{ with } X\}$, h variable in $\bar{Z}$:
        return notequal($C' \wedge \forall \bar{Z}' N \, (X \not\in s^{\{h \mapsto N \text{ with } X\}})$)
        where $\bar{Z}'$ is the list of variables obtained by eliminating h from $\bar{Z}$.
    - ii. take a solution θ for $X \in s$; symmetrical to the previous case.

A remark on action 4 of the function notequal. If the unification between

s and t fails then $\forall \bar{Z}_C(s \neq t)$ is always true and the selected constraint c can be deleted. If, on the contrary, the unification between s and t terminates successfully, yielding the complete set of unifiers $\{\theta_1, \ldots, \theta_k\}$, then lemma 5.2 is applied to simplify the selected constraint c. Actually, notice that a weaker form of this lemma is used here where the variable u is instantiated to the specific term s and the equation $(s = t)^{\theta_i}$ has been deleted being necessarily true (the full power of lemma 5.2 will be exploited, instead, in the extended resolution procedure to be discussed in the next section).

6   Resolution Procedure

The resolution procedure adopted represents an extension of the classical *CLP* operational semantics. The main difference is related to the explicit management of negative atoms. We express the resolution procedure following the rewriting model proposed for AKL [11]. A resolvent at each step is represented by a *goal*, defined as follows.

$$
\begin{array}{lcl}
< goal > & ::= & < and - box > | < or - box > \\
< and - box > & ::= & \textbf{and}(< literals > \Box < constraint >) \\
< or - box > & ::= & \textbf{or}(< sequence\ of\ goals >).
\end{array}
$$

The resolution procedure assumes that the constraints to be dealt with are always transformed into a *simplified normal form* which is obtained by removing from a constraint C in normal form all the redundant variables and equalities and all the irrelevant negative constraints which can possibly occur in it, as described by the following procedure.

function nored($C, vars$);
select a constraint c in C enabling one of the following actions;
if no such c exists **then return** C; **let** $C = C' \wedge c$;
1. (remove redundant variables and equalities)
   if $c \equiv X = Z$ and $X \in vars$ and $Z \notin vars$ **then return** nored($C'^{\{Z \mapsto X\}}, vars$);
   if $c \equiv Z = t$ and $Z \notin vars$ **then return** nored($C', vars$);
2. (remove irrelevant inequalities)
   if $c \equiv \forall Y_1 \cdots Y_h(s \neq t)$ and $FV(\forall Y_1 \cdots Y_h(s \neq t)) \setminus (vars \cup FV(C_=)) \neq \emptyset$
   then return nored($C', vars$);
3. (remove irrelevant non-memberships)
   if $c \equiv \forall Y_1 \cdots Y_h(s \notin t)$ and $FV(\forall Y_1 \cdots Y_h(s \notin t)) \setminus (vars \cup FV(C_=)) \neq \emptyset$
   then return nored($C', vars$).

Lemma 6.1 *If $D_i = $ nored($C_i, FV(C)$), and C_i is one of the constraints returned by $\mathcal{SAT}(C)$, then C_i and D_i are equi–satisfiable.*

Function nored is used in the definition of the *normalization procedure* $\mathcal{N}$, which takes a constraint C and performs the following two actions:
- call $\mathcal{SAT}(C)$ to obtain a disjunction of normal form constraints $C_1, \ldots, C_k$.
- if $k > 0$ (i.e. C is satisfiable), then for each $i = 1, \ldots, k$ call the procedure nored($C_i, FV(C)$) to obtain the constraint C_i' in simplified normal form.

Thus $\mathcal{N}(\mathcal{C})$ non-deterministically returns the constraints $C_1', \ldots, C_k'$.

The resolution procedure is essentially based on two *rewriting* rules, called **Fork** and **Negate** rule, used to deal respectively with positive and negative atoms.

Rule 1. (**Fork**) if $\mathsf{p}(s_1^i, \ldots, s_n^i) \leftarrow C_i \Box \bar{B}_i$, for $i = 1, \ldots, m$, are the clauses defining a given predicate p, then

$$\mathbf{and}(A_1, \ldots, A_{i-1}, \mathsf{p}(t_1, \ldots, t_n), A_{i+1}, \ldots, A_n \Box C) \mapsto$$
$$\mathbf{or}(\mathbf{and}(A_1, \ldots, A_{i-1}, \bar{B}_1, A_{i+1}, \ldots, A_n \Box \mathcal{N}(C \wedge C_1 \wedge \bigwedge_{j=1}^{n}(t_j = s_j^1))), \cdots,$$
$$\mathbf{and}(A_1, \ldots, A_{i-1}, \bar{B}_m, A_{i+1}, \ldots, A_n \Box \mathcal{N}(C \wedge C_m \wedge \bigwedge_{j=1}^{n}(t_j = s_j^m))))$$

For the sake of simplicity we have indicated a unique and-box for each of the possible resolvents. In the actual system the procedure $\mathcal{N}$ is non-deterministic and may lead to multiplication of the relative and-boxes. Analogously, we have not indicated the cases in which the procedure $\mathcal{N}$ fails to report a normalized form (due to unsatisfiability of the original constraint). In this case the corresponding and-box is removed.

Rule 2. (**Negate**) if a negative literal $\neg A$ occurs in an and-box $\mathbf{and}(A_1, \ldots,$ $A_{i-1}, \neg A, A_{i+1}, \ldots, A_n \Box C)$, a subcomputation is started, by applying the derivation rules to the goal $\mathbf{and}(A \Box C)$ and producing a resulting or-box $\mathbf{or}(C_1, \ldots, C_m)$. If $\{C_1', \ldots, C_r'\}$ is the solution returned by the procedure $\mathsf{NegateSolution}(C_1 \vee \cdots \vee C_m)$ (defined below), then the Negate rule acts in the following way:

$$\mathbf{and}(A_1, \ldots, A_{i-1}, \neg A, A_{i+1}, \ldots, A_n \Box C) \mapsto$$
$$\mathbf{or}(\mathbf{and}(A_1, \ldots, A_{i-1}, A_{i+1}, \ldots, A_n \Box C \wedge C_1'), \cdots,$$
$$\mathbf{and}(A_1, \ldots, A_{i-1}, A_{i+1}, \ldots, A_n \Box C \wedge C_r')).$$

The rewriting system is composed by these two basic rules together with some auxiliary rules used to simplify goals such as[5],

Alternatives – Promotion :	$\mathbf{or}(\bar{A}_1, \mathbf{or}(\bar{B}), \bar{A}_2)$	$\mapsto$ $\mathbf{or}(\bar{A}_1, \bar{B}, \bar{A}_2)$
Fail – Propagation	$\mathbf{and}(\bar{A}_1, \mathbf{fail}, \bar{A}_2 \Box C)$	$\mapsto$ **fail**
Choice – Elimination :	$\mathbf{or}(\bar{A}_1, \mathbf{fail}, \bar{A}_2)$	$\mapsto$ $\mathbf{or}(\bar{A}_1, \bar{A}_2)$.

The $\mathsf{NegateSolution}$ procedure represents the key of the implementation of constructive negation. Let us see, briefly, how it works.

By the assumption that *the resolution tree for the goal* $\mathbf{and}(G)$ *in* P *is finite* the resolution procedure will return a number k of computed answers $C_1, \ldots, C_k$, such that $Comp(P) \vdash_{Set} \forall(G \leftrightarrow \exists C_1 \vee \cdots \vee \exists C_k)$. Now let us consider each of the C_is. Firstly we may simplify it by using the procedure nored, i.e. by calling $\mathsf{nored}(C_i, FV(G))$. As corollary of lemma 6.1, we have that $Comp(P) \vdash_{Set} \forall(G \leftrightarrow \exists \bar{w}_1 D_1 \vee \cdots \vee \exists \bar{w}_k D_k)$, hence $Comp(P) \vdash_{Set} \forall(\neg G \leftrightarrow \forall \bar{w}_1 \neg D_1 \wedge \cdots \wedge \forall \bar{w}_k \neg D_k)$.

$\mathsf{NegateSolution}$ then proceeds as follows:

1. simplify each $\forall \bar{w}_i \neg D_i$ using the transformation defined in lemma 5.2 so as to obtain a disjunction of normal form constraints E_i;

---

[5] the symbol **fail** is used to denote an empty or-box.

2. perform all the boolean operations over the $E_i s$ so as to obtain a constraint in disjunctive normal form $F_1 \vee \cdots \vee F_p$;

3. apply the satisfiability algorithm $\mathcal{SAT}$ to each F_i, obtaining the disjunction $F_1^i \vee \cdots \vee F_{k_i}^i$;

4. finally, let $C_1', \ldots, C_r'$ (output of the function) be the non-'false' constraints in $F_1^1, \ldots, F_{k_1}^1, \ldots, F_1^p, \ldots, F_{k_p}^p$.

Consider the following example (read w for *wife*, h for *husband*):

$$\text{proper\_pair(U)} \leftarrow \qquad\qquad \text{proper\_pair(U)} \leftarrow$$
$$U = \{X, Y\} \wedge X = w(Y)\square. \qquad U = \{X, Y\} \wedge X = h(Y)\square.$$

Suppose to call the goal **and**$(\neg\text{proper\_pair}(U), \varepsilon)$: from *Comp(P)* we get:

$$\forall U \left(\begin{array}{ll} \neg\text{proper\_pair(U)} & \leftrightarrow \quad \forall X_1 Y_1 (U \neq \{X_1, Y_1\} \vee X_1 \neq w(Y_1)) \wedge \\ & \qquad \forall X_2 Y_2 (U \neq \{X_2, Y_2\} \vee X_2 \neq h(Y_2))) \end{array} \right)$$

By applying step 1 the r.h.s. is equivalent to:

$\forall X_1 Y_1 (U \neq \{X_1, Y_1\}) \vee \exists X_1 Y_1 (U = \{X_1, Y_1\} \wedge X_1 \neq w(Y_1) \wedge Y_1 \neq w(X_1)) \wedge$
$\forall X_2 Y_2 (U \neq \{X_2, Y_2\}) \vee \exists X_2 Y_2 (U = \{X_2, Y_2\} \wedge X_2 \neq h(Y_2) \wedge Y_2 \neq h(X_2))$

After performing steps 2–4, we have:

$C_1' \equiv \forall X_1 Y_1 (U \neq \{X_1, Y_1\}) \wedge \forall X_2 Y_2 (U \neq \{X_2, Y_2\})$, and
$C_2' \equiv U = \{X_1, Y_1\} \wedge X_1 \neq h(Y_1) \wedge Y_1 \neq h(X_1) \wedge X_1 \neq w(Y_1) \wedge Y_1 \neq w(X_1)$.

7 Conclusions and Future Works

This work represents the natural continuation of our previous studies on embedding sets in logic programming. In fact it supplies a sound and complete technique to deal with both extensional and intensional sets. This has been obtained by slightly modifying the standard *CLP* operational semantics (through the use of a negation rule) and by supplying a new constraint manager capable of dealing with constraints containing explicit universal quantifications. As a side-effect of this study, we have shown how the problem of performing set grouping operations can be reduced to the problem of dealing with negation.

Various issues are still open. First of all, the relations between set grouping and negation need to be studied in more depth. We are currently investigating also the inverse reduction, i.e. reducing the management of negative literals to set grouping operations. Moreover, we are planning to consider forms of negation different from the constructive one (like the *intensional negation* proposed in [2]), comparing the kind of requirements that they impose on the admissible programs in order to obtain soundness and completeness results. Finally, the marriage of negation and *CLP* seems to provide a very promising framework to support some more general forms of sets (like hypersets or other forms of infinite sets).

Acknowledgements

The research presented in this paper has benefited from discussions with D. Aliffi, M. Carro, G. Gupta, G. Levi, E. G. Omodeo, and A. Policriti all of whom we would like to thank. E. Pontelli is partially supported by NSF Grant CCR92-11732 and by a fellowship from Phillips Petroleum.

References

[1] C. Beeri, S. Naqvi, O. Shmueli, and S. Tsur. Set Constructors in a Logic Database Language. *Journal of Logic Programming*, 10:181–232, 1991.

[2] P. Bruscoli, F. Levi, G. Levi, and M. C. Meo. Compilative Constructive Negation in Constraint Logic Programs. In *Proc. 1994 Coll. on Trees in Algebra and Programming*. To appear in *LNCS*, Springer-Verlag, Berlin, 1994.

[3] D. Chan. Constructive Negation Based on the Completed Database. In R. A. Kowalski and K. A. Bowen, eds., *Proc. Fifth Int'l Conf. on Logic Programming*, pp. 111–125. MIT Press, 1988.

[4] D. Chan. An Extension of Constructive Negation and its Application in Coroutining. In E. Lusk and R. Overbeek, eds., *Proc. North American Conf. on Logic Programming'89*, pp. 477–493. MIT Press, 1989.

[5] A. Dovier, E. G. Omodeo, E. Pontelli and G. Rossi. {log}: A Logic Programming Language with Finite Sets. In K. Furukawa, ed., *Proc. of the Eighth Int'l Conf. on Logic Programming*. MIT Press, 1991.

[6] A. Dovier, E. G. Omodeo, E. Pontelli and G. Rossi. Embedding Finite Sets in a Logic Programming Language. In E. Lamma and P. Mello, eds., *ELP92*, volume 660 of *LNAI*. Springer-Verlag, Berlin, 1993.

[7] A. Dovier, E. G. Omodeo, E. Pontelli and G. Rossi. Embedding Finite Sets in a Logic Programming Language. RAP.04.93, Università di Roma: "La Sapienza", May 1993.

[8] A. Dovier, E. Pontelli. A WAM-based Implementation of a Logic Language with Sets. In M. Bruynooghe and J. Penjam, eds., *PLILP'93*, volume 714 of *LNCS*, Springer-Verlag, Berlin, 1993.

[9] A. Dovier, G. Rossi. Embedding extensional finite sets in *CLP*. In *Proceedings of 1993 Int. Logic Programming Symp.*, (D. Miller ed.), MIT Press, 1993.

[10] J. Jaffar and J.-L. Lassez. Constraint Logic Programming. Technical report, Dept. of Computer Science, Monash University, June 1986.

[11] S. Janson, S. Haridi. Programming Paradigms of the Andorra Kernel Language. In *Proc. 1991 Int. Logic Programming Symp.*, MIT Press, 1991.

[12] T. Przymusinski. On Constructive Negation in Logic Programming. In *Proc. North American Conf. on Logic Programming'89*, Addendum to the volume, MIT Press, 1989.

[13] J. C. Shepherdson. Language and equality theory in logic programming. Technical Report PM-91-02, School of Mathematics, University of Bristol, 1991.

[14] P. J. Stuckey. Constructive Negation for Constraint Logic Programming. In *Proc. Sixth IEEE Symp. on Logic In Computer Science*, pp. 328–339. IEEE Computer Society Press, 1991.

Transformation and Synthesis

The Halting Problem for Deductive Synthesis of Logic Programs

Kung-Kiu Lau
Department of Computer Science, University of Manchester
Oxford Road, Manchester M13 9PL, United Kingdom
kung-kiu@cs.man.ac.uk

Mario Ornaghi
Dipartimento di Scienze dell'Informazione
Universita' degli studi di Milano
Via Comelico 39/41, Milano, Italy
ornaghi@imiucca.csi.unimi.it

Sten-Åke Tärnlund
Computing Science Department, Uppsala University
P.O. Box 520, S-751 20 Uppsala, Sweden
stenake@csd.uu.se

Abstract

Deductive synthesis methods derive programs in an incremental manner, and therefore pose a halting problem – when can synthesis stop with a correct program? We give a characterisation of this problem and state a halting principle as a solution. Another characteristic of deductive synthesis is that it may derive several correct programs, giving rise to another question – which correct programs are desirable? We show that the answer is related to the halting problem, via the notion of steadfast, or reusable, programs as desirable programs. Our work also reveals that Clark's idea of the completion of a program is central to deductive synthesis, since it is the basis of our halting principle and our notion of steadfast programs.

1 Introduction

Writing a correct program is a major problem in programming. It is theoretically interesting and practically significant. Incorrect programs may have dire consequences, and are unfortunately related to the software crisis in practice. Methods have been proposed and tried out for solving this problem, for almost half a century. Although some progress has been made, an adequate solution has yet to be found.

Historically, significant progress towards potential solutions of this problem has often followed from theoretical advancements in programming methodology. This experience suggests that further developments of programming methodology are not only sufficient but also necessary for continued progress towards the eventual solution of the correctness problem, as well as the software crisis hopefully.

A classic proposition for writing a correct program is to write a specification S and deduce a program P such that P is correct with respect to S. This is a good idea in its simplest form, but already in logic, difficulties can arise when the axioms in S are too numerous or too complex. This is certainly true for the applied sciences, mathematics, and programming. A natural development of this idea for programming is to develop a more interactive method between a specification S and a program P. Such a deductive synthesis method starts with a specification and derives a program P_1, and then $P_2 \supseteq P_1$, and so on until P_n, such that $P_n \supseteq \cdots \supseteq P_2 \supseteq P_1$, is the entire program P.

There are some important problems that can arise in deductive synthesis, that we shall address in this paper. Firstly, it is possible to derive several different programs which all are correct, but some of which are not necessarily desirable. We shall introduce the concept of a *steadfast program* and show that steadfast programs are desirable.

The deductive synthesis method also leads to a halting problem for program synthesis: when can we stop the synthesis with a correct program P? We shall give a characterisation of and a solution to this halting problem for logic program synthesis.

Before introducing our main ideas, we should first comment on the deductive method in general. The basic idea of the deductive method is neither new nor specific to computing since it was already to be found in Euclides' work 300 B.C. An important development took place around the turn of the century when the Italian mathematician Peano formalised arithmetic, $\mathcal{PA}$ for short, as a model for the deductive method. We shall often use $\mathcal{PA}$ in our framework below.

Several developments of program synthesis have taken advantage of the deductive method, for example Manna and Waldinger [13]. For logic programming, Hogger [8], Hansson and Tärnlund [7], and Lau and Prestwich [10] derived correct logic programs, while Clark and Tärnlund [5] developed a Peano-like theory for logic programs. More recently, Lau and Ornaghi [11] formalised deductive synthesis of logic programs and gave an incompleteness result.

Clark's idea of the completion of a program [3] was originally conceived to justify semantically the inference rule 'negation as failure' in logic programming. As we shall see, the notion of completion turns out to be a profound concept in deductive synthesis. It is the basis for a halting principle for deductive synthesis, and for the notion of steadfast programs.

In Section 2 we describe the basic notation that we shall employ, and define a general specification framework and the notion of synthesising correct, total, and terminating programs. Section 3 takes up Clark's completion of a program. We shall split the completion into two sub-parts, the *if*-part and the *only-if*-part. We use the former to establish correctness criteria, and the latter for a halting criterion for deductive synthesis. In Section 4, we define the halting problem and show a *halting principle* for deductive synthesis. In Section 5, we define steadfast programs, and show that they are desirable programs of a deductive synthesis. We also state a halting principle for the synthesis of steadfast programs.

2 Basic Notation and Terminology

In this section, we describe the basic notation and terminology that we shall use in this paper.

We will use *first-order classical logic with identity* (i.e. the identity axioms will be assumed), interpreted according to the usual model theoretic semantics (see e.g. [2]).

We shall use H, K, R to denote formulas. $H(x)$ will indicate that the *free variables* of H are x. We use x, y, z, w to stand for (tuples of) variables; p, q, r for *predicate symbols*; f, g, h for *function symbols*; t for (tuples of) *terms*; $\forall(H)$ and $\exists(H)$ for the universal and existential closure of H.

$\mathcal{A}, \mathcal{B}, \ldots$, will denote axiomatisations, i.e. sets of closed formulas, and we will use '$\vdash$' to mean provability in classical logic, while $\mathcal{F} \models H$ will indicate that H is a logical consequence of $\mathcal{F}$.

For logic programs, we adopt the definitions and the formalism of standard works such as [4, 9, 12]. Atoms will be denoted by $A, A_1, \ldots$, clauses by $C, C_1, \ldots$, and substitutions by $\sigma, \theta, \ldots$ Programs will be denoted by $P, Q, P_1, \ldots$ For every computed answer substitution θ, we also consider as computed answers the more instantiated substitutions $\theta\gamma$ (by the Lifting Lemma).

2.1 Specifications

In our approach, a specification is given in a general formal framework which axiomatises the problem domain in question, thereby allowing us to specify and synthesise programs for computational problems in that domain. We have already mentioned Peano Arithmetic, which we will denote by $\mathcal{PA}$, as a good example of such a framework for natural numbers. Its language contains identity '$=$', successor 's', sum '$+$' and product '$\cdot$'. In $\mathcal{PA}$ every natural number $\mathbf{n}$ is represented by a *numeral* $s^n(0)$, and every computable function $f(x)$ can be expressed by a formula $F(x, z)$ such that, for every pair of natural numbers $\mathbf{m}$ and $\mathbf{n}$, $\mathbf{m} = f(\mathbf{n})$ iff $F(m, n)$, where m and n are the numerals corresponding to $\mathbf{m}$ and $\mathbf{n}$ respectively, is provable in $\mathcal{PA}$. Thus, in $\mathcal{PA}$ we can specify any computable function by a formula. Other examples of first-order theories interesting for Computer Science are presented in [14].

Thus we define a specification in a general framework as follows:

Definition 2.1 A *specification framework* is a first-order theory with identity, and we shall assume that it is consistent. We will denote specification frameworks by $\mathcal{F}, \mathcal{G}, \ldots$.

In a framework $\mathcal{F}$ with language $\mathcal{L}_{\mathcal{F}}$, a *specification* consists of:

- a *definition axiom* D_r:
$$\forall (r(x) \leftrightarrow R(x))$$
  where r is a new predicate symbol[1] and R is a formula in $\mathcal{L}_{\mathcal{F}}$. That is D_r defines r, the relation to be computed.

- a set G of *goals* of the form $\exists r(t_0), \exists r(t_1), \ldots$

An *answer* of $\exists r(t) \in G$ in $\mathcal{F}$ is any $r(t\sigma)$ such that $\mathcal{F} \cup D_r \models r(t\sigma)$, where σ is a substitution. $\odot$

Example 2.1 In the framework $\mathcal{PA}$, we can specify the problem of finding the square root, if it exists, of a given numeral as follows:

- $D_{sqrt} = \forall (sqrt(x, y) \leftrightarrow y \cdot y = x)$

- $G = \{\exists z\, sqrt(n, z) \mid n \text{ is a numeral}\}$

The goal $\exists z\, sqrt(s(0), z)$ has the unique answer $sqrt(s(0), s(0))$, for example, but the goal $\exists z\, sqrt(s(s(0)), z)$ has no answer, and so on. $\diamond$

---

[1] This preserves consistency. We will also use symbols in $\mathcal{L}_{\mathcal{F}}$, without introducing definition axioms for them.

2.2 Logic Program Synthesis

Given the specification of a problem in a framework $\mathcal{F}$, the goal of logic program synthesis is to find a program P which is *correct, total,* and *terminating* for every goal $\exists r(t) \in G$, according to the following definition:

Definition 2.2 A program P is *(partially) correct* for a goal $\exists r(t)$ if for every computed answer substitution σ, $\mathcal{F} \cup D_r \models r(t\sigma)$.

P is *total* for a goal $\exists r(t)$ if for every ground substitution σ, $\mathcal{F} \cup D_r \models r(t\sigma)$ entails that σ is a computed answer substitution of P for $\exists r(t)$.[2]

P *terminates* for a goal $\exists r(t)$ iff the *SLD*-tree[3] of P with root $\leftarrow r(t)$ is finitely failed, or it contains at least one success node. ⊙

For convenience, we shall say P is *totally correct* if it is partially correct and total for each goal in G.

Example 2.2 Consider **Example 2.1** and the following trivial program P

$$sqrt(0,0) \leftarrow$$
$$sqrt(s(0), s(0)) \leftarrow$$

P is correct and terminates for every goal, but it is not total. Indeed, for the goal

$$\exists z \, sqrt(s(s(s(s(0)))), z)$$

the answer in $\mathcal{PA}$ is $sqrt(s(s(s(s(0)))), s(s(0)))$, but P has a finitely failed *SLD*-tree and hence no answer substitution. ◇

Synthesis aims to build a program P which is totally correct and which also terminates for any goal $\exists r(t)$. In this paper, we shall consider totality but not termination. Termination of P is clearly desirable if P is to be of practical use. However, we shall not address the important and non-trivial issue of how to synthesise programs that are guaranteed to terminate. Instead, we shall assume that synthesis gives rise to P that terminates for any goal $\exists r(t)$. This implies the decidability of '$\forall(P) \vdash \exists r(t)$': indeed, '$\forall(P) \vdash \exists r(t)$' is either true or 'finitely' false (see **Proposition 3.1** later). Otherwise, if P does not terminate, then '$\forall(P) \vdash \exists r(t)$' is 'infinitely' false.

If synthesis is done in an iterative manner, i.e. we derive $P_1 \subseteq P_2 \subseteq \cdots$, as in deductive synthesis (see Section 4), then it is natural (and usual) to ensure that partial correctness of each P_i are guaranteed by the synthesis steps. However, totality of P_i cannot be attained until the final step (which yields P_n say). Thus the problem of ensuring that P_n is total is equivalent to the problem of determining when a synthesis can halt. This halting problem is our main concern in this paper.

Definition 2.3 We say that synthesis *successfully halts* if it stops when a total program (P_n) has been synthesised. ⊙

Thus it is of vital importance to have a suitable criterion for successfully halting synthesis. We will propose one such criterion in Section 3.1.

---

[2]We use *total* instead of the commonly used *complete.*

[3]We assume a complete search strategy.

3   Correctness Criteria for Deductive Synthesis

In this section, we propose a halting criterion based on Clark's completion $Comp(P)$ of a program P [3]. We normally assume that every predicate symbol $r(x)$ of the current program P is introduced in the framework $\mathcal{F}$ by a definition axiom

$$\forall\, (r(x) \leftrightarrow R(x))$$

We will use D_P to denote the set of such definition axioms for P.

In case some predicate r in P cannot be defined by a definition axiom, then our framework $\mathcal{F}$ is too weak to characterise the relation we want to compute. We will briefly address this and other issues related to weak frameworks in Section 5.1.

3.1   A Halting Criterion based on Clark's Completion

For a program P, we shall decompose its completion $Comp(P)$ into two parts $Comp^+(P)$ and $Comp^-(P)$. First, we define $free(P)$ to be the freeness axioms for the constant and function symbols of P [15]. Informally, these axioms ensure the unique meanings of these symbols. Now we define $Comp^+(P)$ and $Comp^-(P)$ as follows:

- $Comp^+(P) = free(P) \cup Ax(P)$, where $Ax(P)$ is the set $\{Ax(C)\,|\,C$ is a clause of $P\}$ defined as follows:

$$
\begin{aligned}
Ax(A \leftarrow) &\quad \text{is} \quad \forall(A) \\
Ax(A \leftarrow A_1, \ldots, A_k) &\quad \text{is} \quad \forall(A \leftarrow A_1 \wedge \cdots \wedge A_k)\,.
\end{aligned}
$$

  $Ax(P)$ is logically equivalent to the *if*-part of the completion, and the successful computations of P can be interpreted as proofs in classical logic with identity, using axioms from $Ax(P)$.[4]

- $Comp^-(P)$ is the *only-if*-part of $Comp(P)$, together with $free(P)$. It contains, apart from $free(P)$, for every predicate symbol r in P,

$$\forall\, (r(x) \rightarrow E_1 \vee \cdots \vee E_k) \tag{1}$$

  which is the *only-if*-part of the completed definition of r. Note that if $k = 0$, i.e. if there is no clause in P with r in its head, then (1) is $\forall\,\neg r(x)$.

  For convenience, we shall denote (1) by $Comp^-(P,r)$, to be read as 'the *only-if*-part of r in P'. We shall also write $Comp^-(P, r_1, \ldots, r_n)$ for multiple predicate symbols.

  $Comp^-(P)$ is needed to interpret any finitely failed computation of P as a proof in classical logic with identity, of the negation of the goal.[5]

Note that $Comp^+(P)$ is *monotonic*, i.e. $P \subseteq Q$ implies $Comp^+(P) \subseteq Comp^+(Q)$, whereas $Comp^-(P)$ is *non-monotonic*, i.e. there are $P \subseteq Q$ such that $Comp^-(P) \not\subseteq Comp^-(Q)$.

---

[4] We call $Ax(P)$ *success axioms* in [11].

[5] We call $Comp^-(p)$ *failure axioms* in [11], where we use the *contrapositive* form $\forall(\neg p(x) \leftarrow \neg E_1 \wedge \cdots \wedge \neg E_k)$.

Example 3.1 Consider the program P:

$$sum(x, 0, x) \leftarrow$$
$$sum(X, s(y), s(z)) \leftarrow sum(x, y, z)$$

$free(P)$ contains the freeness axioms for the constant symbol '0' and the function symbol 's':

$$\forall \neg(0 = s(x))$$
$$\forall (s(x) = s(y) \rightarrow x = y)$$

These axioms guarantee the unique meanings of '0' and 's'.

- $Comp^+(P) = free(P) \cup Ax(P)$ where $Ax(P)$ contains:

$$\forall sum(x, 0, x)$$
$$\forall (sum(x, s(y), s(z)) \leftarrow sum(x, y, z))$$

These axioms characterise the computations of P that will (successfully) solve $\exists sum(t_1, t_2, t_3)$.

- $Comp^-(P)$ contains $free(P)$ as well as:

$$\forall (sum(a, b, c) \rightarrow \exists x\, (a = x \wedge b = 0 \wedge c = x) \vee$$
$$\exists x, y, z\, (a = x \wedge b = s(y) \wedge c = s(z) \wedge sum(x, y, z))$$

Computations of P that will finitely fail to solve $sum(t_1, t_2, t_3)$ can be interpreted as proofs of $\neg \exists sum(t_1, t_2, t_3)$ using this axiom and $free(P)$.

$\diamond$

Now, before we give the halting criterion, we note the following proposition on termination, and state a theorem on partial correctness:

Proposition 3.1 If a program P terminates for $\exists r(t)$, then either $Comp(P) \vdash \exists r(t)$ or $Comp(P) \vdash \neg \exists r(t)$.

Proof. This follows readily from the definition of termination and the soundness of completion. $\square$

Theorem 1 *If*

$$\mathcal{F} \cup D_P \models Comp^+(P)$$

then P is partially correct for every goal $\exists r(t)$ for any term t.

Proof.

$$\sigma \text{ is a computed answer substitution of } \leftarrow r(t)$$
$$\Rightarrow \quad Comp^+(P) \models r(t\sigma) \quad \text{(by soundness)}$$
$$\Rightarrow \quad \mathcal{F} \cup D_P \models r(t\sigma) \quad \text{(by cut)}$$
$$\Rightarrow \quad \mathcal{F} \cup D_r \models r(t\sigma) \quad (\mathcal{F} \cup D_P \text{ is a conservative extension of } \mathcal{F} \cup D_r)$$

$\square$

Now we can state our halting criterion:

Theorem 2 *For a program P, if $\mathcal{F} \cup D_P \models Comp(P)$, and P terminates for a goal $\exists r(t)$, then P is total for $\exists r(t)$.*

Proof. Since P terminates for the goal $\exists r(t)$, we have either

(a) that there is a finitely failed *SLD*-tree, or

(b) that the *SLD*-tree contains at least one success node.

In the case of (a), $Comp(P) \models \neg \exists r(t)$ holds; since $\mathcal{F} \cup D_P \models Comp(P)$, we have:

$$\mathcal{F} \cup D_P \models \neg \exists r(t)$$

and there is no answer and we are all right.

In the case of (b), assume, by *absurdum*, that

$\mathcal{F} \cup D_P \models r(t\sigma)$, for some ground σ, but σ is not a computed answer substitution of P.

This means that no success node with computed answer substitution σ exists in the *SLD*-tree. However, this contradicts the completeness of *SLD*-resolution, since $r(t\sigma)$ is a logical consequence of $Comp^+(P)$. The fact that it is a logical consequence of $Comp^+(P)$ can be proved by absurdum as follows.

Assume by absurdum that $Comp^+(P) \not\vdash r(t\sigma)$. Since P terminates and $r(t\sigma)$ is ground, by **Proposition 3.1** $Comp(P) \vdash r(t\sigma)$ or $Comp(P) \vdash \neg r(t\sigma)$, and hence:

$$Comp(P) \vdash \neg r(t\sigma)$$

Since $\mathcal{F} \cup D_P \vdash Comp(P)$ we obtain $\mathcal{F} \cup D_P \vdash \neg r(t\sigma)$, and hence absurdum due to the consistency of $\mathcal{F} \cup D_P$ (indeed a framework $\mathcal{F}$ is consistent by definition and definition axioms give rise to conservative extensions). $\square$

Intuitively, we can explain **Theorem 2** as follows: a partially correct (and terminating) P is not total unless all its failed computations $(Comp^-(P))$ are also logical consequences of $\mathcal{F} \cup D_P$. In other words, if P is partially correct and only fails when it is supposed to, then it is total.

4   The Halting Problem for Deductive Synthesis

In this section, we shall use the halting criterion to state a halting principle which tells us precisely when we can stop synthesis knowing that we have synthesised a total program.

Let $\mathcal{F}$ be a framework and consider a specification consisting of a definition axiom D_0

$$\forall \, (r(x) \leftrightarrow R(x)) \tag{2}$$

and a set G of goals.

A *deductive synthesis* process (for this specification) generates a possibly infinite sequence of programs

$$P_1 \subseteq P_2 \subseteq \cdots \subseteq P_k \subseteq \cdots \tag{3}$$

where, for every P_j, there is a corresponding set D_j of definition axioms, introducing the new predicate symbols of P_j .

Now, for partial correctness, we require that, for every P_j:[6]

$$\mathcal{F} \cup D_j \vdash Comp^+(P_j) \tag{4}$$

---

[6]Thanks to completeness, we can use provability and hence do synthesis in the theory.

By **Theorem 1**, (4) implies partial correctness. $\mathcal{F} \cup D_j \vdash Ax(P_j)$ alone would be sufficient to ensure partial correctness. However, we require (4) to hold since *free(P)* is monotonic (if (4) does not hold in a step, then it will never hold in the subsequent steps, in particular the final step).

Example 4.1 Let $\mathcal{F}$ be $\mathcal{PA}$ and consider the specification

$$
\begin{array}{ll}
D_{prod} & : \quad \forall \, (prod(x, y, z) \leftrightarrow x \cdot y = z) \\
G_{prod} & : \quad \{\exists z \, prod(n, m, z) \, | \, n, m \text{ ground}\}
\end{array}
$$

A partial deductive synthesis process would be the following:

1. Synthesise a clause for the goal $prod(x, 0, z)$. In $\mathcal{PA} \cup D_{prod}$ we can prove:

$$prod(x, 0, z) \leftrightarrow x \cdot 0 = z \leftrightarrow z = 0$$

Thus $\mathcal{PA} \cup D_{prod} \vdash Comp^+(prod(x, 0, z) \leftarrow z = 0)$ and we get the program P_1:

$$prod(x, 0, z) \leftarrow z = 0$$

2. Next synthesise a clause for $prod(x, s(y), z)$. In $\mathcal{PA} \cup D_{prod}$ we can prove:

$$prod(x, s(y), z) \leftrightarrow x \cdot s(y) = z \leftrightarrow x \cdot y + x = z \leftrightarrow \exists w \, (prod(x, y, w) \wedge w + x = z)$$

From this we could synthesise the clause $prod(x, s(y), z) \leftarrow prod(x, y, w), w + x = z$. However, '+' cannot be used in a program, since it does not satisfy the freeness axioms. Therefore we have to introduce a new relation *sum* defined by D_{sum}:

$$\forall (sum(x, y, z) \leftrightarrow x + y = z)$$

and we get $D_2 = \{D_{prod}, D_{sum}\}$ and we have

$$\mathcal{PA} \cup D_2 \vdash Comp^+(prod(x, s(y), z) \leftarrow prod(x, y, w), sum(w, x, z))$$

That is our new program P_2 is:

$$
\begin{array}{rcl}
prod(x, 0, z) & \leftarrow & z = 0 \\
prod(x, s(y), z) & \leftarrow & prod(x, y, w), sum(w, x, z)
\end{array}
$$

$\diamond$

Now the problem with the program P_2 is that although it is partially correct, it is not total. So we need further synthesis steps. To recognise halting, we use **Theorem 2**, and the halting criterion is the following:

If $\mathcal{F} \cup D_n \vdash Comp^-(P_n, p)$ for every predicate p of P_n, then the synthesis can successfully halt.[7]

Looking at **Example 4.1**, we see that

$$\mathcal{PA} \cup D_2 \vdash Comp^-(P_2, prod)$$

but

$$\mathcal{PA} \cup D_2 \vdash \neg Comp^-(P_2, sum)$$

(indeed $Comp^-(P_2, sum)$ is $\forall \, \neg sum(x, y, z)$).

Thus we have to go on with the synthesis, searching for clauses for *sum*.

This example shows that the halting criterion can be used in a subtle way. This leads to the following principle:

---

[7]This is sufficient to obtain $Comp(P_n)$, since $Comp^+(P_n)$ has already been proved.

The Halting Principle
If $\mathcal{F} \cup D_n \vdash Comp^-(P_n, p)$ for a predicate p, do not search for any more clauses for p. Furthermore, if this holds for every predicate p of P_n, then synthesis can successfully halt.

It follows directly from **Theorem 2** that this principle holds.

For instance, for **Example 4.1** we can stop synthesis for *prod*, but not for *sum*, and synthesis for *sum* can be summarised as follows:

1. $\mathcal{PA} \cup D_2 \vdash Comp^+(sum(x, 0, x))$, then synthesise P_3 containing this new clause; continue synthesis because $\mathcal{PA} \cup D_2 \vdash \neg Comp^-(P_3, sum)$.

2. $\mathcal{PA} \cup D_2 \vdash Comp^+(sum(x, s(y), s(w)) \leftarrow sum(x, y, w))$, then synthesise P_4 containing this new clause; now synthesis successfully halts because $\mathcal{PA} \cup D_2 \vdash Comp^-(P_4, sum)$.

Our synthesis method has several desirable modularity properties that can be used in practice, for example in an implementation of a synthesis system. $Comp^+(P)$ and $Comp^-(P)$ can be divided into sub-parts, viz. $free(P)$, $Ax(C)$ for every clause C and $Comp^-(P, p)$ for each predicate p in P.

5 Steadfast Programs

Theorem 2 says that the provability of $Comp^-(P_n)$ is a *sufficient* condition for halting synthesis with a totally correct P_n. A natural question then arises as to whether or not it is also a *necessary* condition. In this section, we shall show that the answer is negative for the entire class of synthesised programs. However, if we consider the synthesis of what we shall call *steadfast programs*, which are the programs we consider to be desirable, then the provability of completion is a sufficient and necessary condition for halting synthesis.

The notion of the steadfastness of a program arises in the context of an *open* specification framework, namely one which does not completely specify the program. We shall first informally introduce and discuss the concepts of *open frameworks* and *steadfast programs*, and show by examples that, if in our synthesis we search for steadfast programs, then the provability of completion also becomes a *necessary* condition for successfully halting synthesis. This enables us to state a halting principle for the synthesis of steadfast programs. Then we give a formal treatment of steadfastness in open frameworks, which enables us to establish formally that the provability of completion is indeed a *necessary* condition for successfully halting the synthesis of steadfast programs.

5.1 Open Frameworks and Steadfast Programs

Informally speaking, an *open* (or *loose*) framework leaves open the possibility of different interpretations of the symbols of its language, corresponding to different intended models, while a *closed* framework has a unique intended model, determining a unique interpretation.

In an open framework, it is convenient to distinguish between the *defined* and *defining* predicate symbols of a program P in the following manner. We will say that P is of type $r_1, \ldots, r_k \Leftarrow q_1, \ldots, q_m$, written $P : r_1, \ldots, r_k \Leftarrow q_1, \ldots, q_m$, to indicate that $r_1, \ldots, r_k$ are the *defined* predicates of P, namely the ones occurring in the head of at least one clause, and $q_1, \ldots, q_m$ are *defining* predicates, namely the ones occurring only in the bodies.

In such a framework, it is meaningful and interesting to study the possibility of synthesising a program $P : r_1, \ldots, r_k \Leftarrow q_1, \ldots, q_m$ that contains *all* the clauses needed to compute $r_1, \ldots, r_k$, but not necessarily any clauses to compute $q_1, \ldots, q_m$. That is, such a P will use the same set of clauses to compute $r_1, \ldots, r_k$ in a different way for every model of the framework, depending on the interpretation of $q_1, \ldots, q_m$. Such programs will be called *steadfast* in that framework.[8]

We use 'steadfast' in the ordinary sense of being unchanging, because a steadfast program P has the following important characteristic: for every model of our framework, if we have a program Q that correctly computes the predicates not defined by P, then $P \cup Q$ is also a correct program in that model. We note that for different models we have different Q's,[9] whilst P is always the same. Thus $P \cup Q$ represents a *class* of correct programs. Hence a steadfast program has the desirable property of *reusability*.

Now we will show in **Example 5.1** that completion enables us to identify steadfast programs. In other words, completion can be used to state both a *sufficient* and a *necessary* halting condition if our aim is to synthesise steadfast, and hence reusable, programs.

Example 5.1 Consider the (open) framework $\mathcal{F}$:[10]

$$\{q(a) \vee q(b), \forall (p(x) \leftrightarrow x = c), \neg a = b, \neg b = c\}$$

and the specification:

$$
\begin{aligned}
D_r &: \quad \forall (r(x) \leftrightarrow p(x) \vee q(x)) \\
G &: \quad \{\exists x \, r(x)\}
\end{aligned}
$$

We can easily see that the only answer of $\exists x \, r(x)$ that is correct in $\mathcal{F}$ is $r(c)$. Therefore, the program P_1:

$$r(c) \leftarrow$$

is totally correct and terminating for the goal considered and we should halt synthesis immediately. However, $Comp^-(P_1, r)$ is

$$\forall (r(x) \rightarrow x = c)$$

and we can easily see that

$$\mathcal{F} \cup D_r \models \neg Comp^-(P_1, r)$$

Thus, the provability of $Comp^-(P_1, r)$ is not a necessary condition for synthesising the totally correct program P_1. This is due to the following.

Our framework $\mathcal{F}$ is *open* wrt the predicate q occurring in the definition axiom of r. Therefore there are many models of $\mathcal{F}$, interpreting q in different ways, and, for every model M, D_r defines an expansion N of M by a new relation r. For

---

[8]Note that a steadfast program may or may not be total.

[9]For example, Q may be a set of facts in a database.

[10]This example shows that our notion of specification frameworks is very general. In particular, we allow the use of examples as (incomplete) specifications.

example, M_1, M_2, M_3 as defined below are Herbrand models of $\mathcal{F}$ with expansions (by r) N_1, N_2, N_3 respectively:[11]

$$
\begin{aligned}
M_1 &= \{p(c), q(a)\} & N_1 &= \{p(c), q(a), r(a), r(c)\} \\
M_2 &= \{p(c), q(b)\} & N_2 &= \{p(c), q(b), r(b), r(c)\} \\
M_3 &= \{p(c), q(a), q(f(f(a)))\} & N_3 &= \{p(c), q(a), q(f(f(a))), r(c), r(a), r(f(f(a)))\}
\end{aligned}
$$
(5)

This illustrates that $\mathcal{F} \cup D_r$ is open wrt r, and r depends on q. In contrast, the completion of P_1 is closed wrt r and gives rise to the interpretation $r(c)$, which is at variance with the possible interpretations stated by the definition axiom D_r.

Another correct program, in which r depends on q, as stated by D_r, is the following program P_2:

$$
\begin{aligned}
r(x) &\leftarrow p(x) \\
r(x) &\leftarrow q(x) \\
p(c) &\leftarrow
\end{aligned}
$$

We consider P_2 to be a better program than P_1 because P_2 is steadfast, which means that P_2 has the following reusability property: P_2 can be extended to a program in each of the expansions N_1, N_2, N_3 in (5) (or more generally, in each model of $\mathcal{F} \cup D_r$), without changing the clauses for computing r and p, but by simply adding the right clauses for q, such that each extended version of P_2 is totally correct and terminating.

Steadfastness of P_2 is guaranteed by the fact the completion axioms of its defined predicates, namely $Comp^-(P_2, r)$ and $Comp^-(P_2, p)$, are provable. (Indeed, they are $\forall (r(x) \rightarrow p(x) \vee q(x))$ and $\forall (p(x) \rightarrow x = c)$, and are both immediate.) On the other hand, we cannot prove the whole of $Comp^-(P_2)$, since it contains $\forall x \neg q(x)$ and $\mathcal{F} \vdash \exists x\, q(x)$. This corresponds to the fact that $\mathcal{F}$ is open wrt q and therefore we must consider only the part $Comp^-(P_2, r, p)$ which is open wrt q. Therefore, to halt the synthesis of a steadfast program, we have to prove the completion of its defined predicates. ◇

This example shows that in synthesis we can go beyond correctness, i.e. we should and can synthesise the steadfast programs, for which the completion is provable for the symbols defined by them. In the next subsection we shall demonstrate that the converse holds equally, namely that steadfastness implies the provability of the completion of the defined symbols.

Now we can state the following halting principle for the synthesis of steadfast programs:

The Halting Principle (for steadfast programs)
For every predicate p defined by the current program P_n:

  (i) if $\mathcal{F} \cup D_n \vdash \neg Comp^-(P_n, p)$, search for other clauses with p in their head;

  (ii) if $\mathcal{F} \cup D_n \vdash Comp^-(P_n, p)$, do not search for any more clauses defining p.

If (ii) holds for every defined predicate p of P_n, then synthesis successfully halts.

(If neither (i) nor (ii) holds, then no steadfast program exists for this specification. This can arise in weak frameworks (see below).)

----
[11] L_{M_3} contains a new function symbol f, i.e. we consider models M of $\mathcal{F}$ with language $L_M \supseteq L_{\mathcal{F}}$.

It is worth pointing out that the Halting Principle applies equally to the synthesis of steadfast programs in both open and closed frameworks. For example, in **Example 4.1**, where we use the closed framework $\mathcal{PA}$, the Halting Principle says that we could successfully halt synthesis wrt *prod*, without synthesising any clause for *sum*. This means that the part synthesised for *prod* works as a steadfast program, never changed by subsequent synthesis steps.

In general, in a closed framework, we try to continue synthesis until we have reached the final totally correct program. By **Theorem 2** this happens when P_n is of type $r_1, \ldots, r_k \Leftarrow$, i.e. when it does not contain defining predicates.

On the other hand, as we saw in **Example 5.1**, in an open framework the Halting Principle tells us to halt synthesis when P_n involves only defining predicates $q_1, \ldots, q_m$ which belong to the language of the framework, and are open in it. The result of the synthesis is a steadfast program $P_n : r_1, \ldots, r_k \Leftarrow q_1, \ldots, q_m$. If $q_1, \ldots, q_m$ have no provable instances in the framework, then P_n is a total program.

In Section 5.2, we will give a formal treatment of the halting problem for synthesis in open frameworks. To conclude this section, it is worthwhile to briefly comment on frameworks which are too weak with respect to a specification. This may happen when the framework is too weak to prove the completion of a program, or when the relation to be computed cannot be specified in the framework by a definition axiom.

In the first case, we reach a program P_n where $\neg Comp^-(P_n, r)$ (for some defined r) is no longer provable. So we try to prove $Comp^-(P_n, r)$, but we discover that $Comp^-(P_n, r)$ too cannot be proved. In this case we can consistently add $Comp^-(P_n, r)$ to the axioms of our framework. By adding it, we eliminate some models of the framework. If the eliminated models are undesirable ones, we are happy to discard them and thereby improve our formalisation of the problem domain. Otherwise we have to reconsider our formalisation of the problem. That is, if and when we discover that no steadfast program exists for this specification, we have to determine whether we have discovered an improvement to the framework or there is some drawback in our formalisation.

In the second case, we cannot define the relation r to be computed by a definition axiom D_r. For example, if our framework is Presburger Arithmetic (where we have successor and sum, but not product), we cannot define product. In this case we have to enrich our framework, adding a 'fresh' symbol '·' and new axioms, which codify the usual recursive definition of product. Once we have '·', we obtain $\mathcal{PA}$. Note that in $\mathcal{PA}$ this kind of problems no longer occur, since every partial recursive function can be defined in it by a definition axiom.

These two points show that in deductive synthesis there is a feedback mechanism, where synthesis can also help us to understand better, improve and enrich a specification framework. With each loop, hopefully such feedback will become more rare, i.e. step by step, we obtain axiomatisations sufficiently strong for handling larger and larger classes of problems.

5.2 Completion is Necessary for Halting Synthesis

Now we give a formal characterisation of steadfastness, and show formally the link between steadfastness and reusability. Then we discuss the Halting Principle for steadfast programs, and establish formally that the provability of the completion of the defined symbols is a *necessary* condition for halting the synthesis of steadfast programs.

For the sake of simplicity we will consider only *free frameworks*, namely frameworks that satisfy the freeness axioms of the symbols of their language; and *free models*, namely models satisfying the freeness axioms of the symbols of their language.[12]

The notion of steadfast programs is related to a class of models, according to the following definition:

Definition 5.1 A program P is *steadfast* in a class $\mathcal{M}$ of models iff every model $M \in \mathcal{M}$ is a steadfast model (as defined below) of P.   ⊙

Now, we define the steadfast models of P. Intuitively, a steadfast model of P : $r_1, \ldots, r_k \Leftarrow q_1, \ldots, q_m$ is a model which interprets the defined predicates according to P, depending on the interpretation of the defining predicates. To give a precise definition, we use *diagrams* as follows.

Let L_M be a first-order language and M a model for L_M (i.e. a first-order structure interpreting L_M). We say that M is *reachable* (in L_M) if every element of the domain of M is denoted by a ground term of L_M. Henceforth we will deal with reachable models only. This is not restrictive, since we allow 'ideal' L_M's of arbitrary cardinality.

Let r be a relation symbol of L_M. The *positive diagram, negative diagram*, and *diagram* of r in M are respectively defined by:

$$diag^+(M, r) = \{r(t) \mid t \text{ are ground terms and } M \models r(t)\}$$

$$diag^-(M, r) = \{\neg r(t) \mid t \text{ are ground terms and } M \models \neg r(t)\}$$

$$diag(M, r) = diag^+(M, r) \cup diag^-(M, r)$$

For many relations, $diag^+(M, r_1, \ldots, r_k)$, $diag^-(M, r_1, \ldots, r_k)$, $diag(M, r_1, \ldots, r_k)$ are defined in the obvious way. For convenience we shall call $diag^+(M)$, $diag^-(M)$, $diag(M)$ collectively *diagrams* of M, i.e. the diagrams of all the relation symbols of L_M.

Since we are only dealing with reachable, free models, $diag^+(M)$ is the Herbrand model corresponding to M, and we define a steadfast model as follows:

Definition 5.2 M is a *steadfast model* of P : $r_1, \ldots, r_k \Leftarrow q_1, \ldots, q_m$ iff the diagram $diag^+(M, r_1, \ldots, r_k, q_1, \ldots, q_m)$ is the minimum Herbrand model of $Comp^+(P)$ $\cup diag^+(M, q_1, \ldots, q_m)$.   ⊙

Example 5.2 Consider the programs P_1 and P_2 of **Example 5.1**. Their types are $P_1 : r \Leftarrow$ and $P_2 : p, r \Leftarrow q$ respectively. The model $N_1 = \{p(c), q(a), r(a), r(c)\}$ is a steadfast model of P_2; indeed, $diag^+(N_1, q) = \{q(a)\}$ and N_1 is the minimum model of $P_2 \cup \{q(a)\}$. A model that is not a steadfast model of P_2 is, for example, $\{p(c), q(a), r(a), r(b), r(c)\}$, since it properly contains N_1 and q has the same diagram in the two models.

P_2 is steadfast in N_1, N_2, N_3, whilst P_1 is not steadfast in any of them (i.e. none of them is a steadfast model of P_1).   ◇

Now, steadfastness in a class of models implies reusability. A program Q 'reusing' a steadfast $P : r_1, \ldots, r_k \Leftarrow q_1, \ldots, q_m$ must correctly compute $q_1, \ldots, q_m$, but in general it may contain other predicates. To discuss Q's total correctness, it will be more appropriate to talk about total correctness in a model, as opposed to total correctness in a framework as defined in **Definition 2.2** (in Section 2.2),

---

[12]This restriction can be avoided by using isoinitial models (see [1]) instead of canonical Herbrand models that we will consider here.

by substituting truth in a model for validity in a framework. Thus, we will say that Q is *totally correct wrt* $q_1, \ldots, q_m$ *in a model* M if $q_1, \ldots, q_m$ are the predicate symbols of Q belonging to L_M, and Q is totally correct in M wrt $q_1, \ldots, q_m$, namely $diag^+(M, q_1, \ldots, q_m)$ coincides with the success set of Q restricted to $q_1, \ldots, q_m$.

Then we have the property:

Property 5.1 Let a program $P : r_1, \ldots, r_k \Leftarrow q_1, \ldots, q_m$ be steadfast in a class $\mathcal{M}$ of models and let M be any model belonging to $\mathcal{M}$. For every program Q_M totally correct wrt $q_1, \ldots, q_m$ in M, if $P \cup Q_M$ terminates, then $P \cup Q_M$ is totally correct in M wrt $r_1, \ldots, r_k, q_1, \ldots, q_m$.

In other words, if a program $P : r_1, \ldots, r_k \Leftarrow q_1, \ldots, q_m$ is steadfast in a class of models, then it can be correctly *re-used* in different larger programs Q_M, which also compute $q_1, \ldots, q_m$ according to a chosen model M. Thus steadfastness of P works as a kind of 'parametric correctness' in a class of models, where P assumes in each model M the appropriate behaviour that depends on Q_M.

It is interesting to observe that Deville [6] defined a similar notion of correctness for a logic procedure $LP(p)$ that defines a predicate p. His criterion preserves what he calls the monotonicity of correctness of $LP(p)$, which corresponds to our notion of steadfastness of $LP(p)$.

Now we return to the Halting Principle for steadfast programs. Our aim is to show that the provability of the completion of the defined symbols works as a necessary and sufficient condition for halting with steadfast programs.

First of all, we need a precise definition of closed and open (free) frameworks.

Definition 5.3 A (free) framework $\mathcal{F}$ is *atomically complete* iff $\mathcal{F} \models A$ or $\mathcal{F} \models \neg A$, for every ground atom A.

$\mathcal{F}$ is *closed* if it is atomically complete and has at least one model that is reachable in the language $L_{\mathcal{F}}$. $\odot$

If $\mathcal{F}$ is closed and M is a model of $\mathcal{F}$ that is reachable in $L_{\mathcal{F}}$, then $diag^+(M)$ is the *unique* Herbrand model of $\mathcal{F}$,[13] which we call the *canonical model*.

Moreover, every ground atomic formula $r(t)$ is true in the canonical model iff $\mathcal{F} \models r(t)$; hence the definition of total correctness in $\mathcal{F}$ given in **Definition 2.2** means total correctness in the canonical model of $\mathcal{F} \cup D_r$.[14]

A (free) framework $\mathcal{F}$ is *open* if it is consistent and is not closed. An open framework thus formalises a class of canonical models. Indeed, for every closed (free) framework $\mathcal{F}^* \supseteq \mathcal{F}$ (with $L_{\mathcal{F}^*} \supseteq L_{\mathcal{F}}$), we can consider the canonical model of $\mathcal{F}^*$ as a canonical model of the class axiomatised by $\mathcal{F}$.

Now for classes of models, we have to parameterise the notion of total correctness. From the previous discussion, the 'correct', i.e. desirable, programs are the programs which are *steadfast* in the class of models of the framework (or in a significant subclass).

To state a sufficient condition for halting the synthesis of steadfast programs, we consider the subclass of $(q_1, \ldots, q_m)$-*models*, namely the models M such that there is at least a finite program Q totally correct wrt $q_1, \ldots, q_m$ in M. This restriction is sensible, since it corresponds to the models where the program P can be used in a finite, totally correct, and terminating program Q. Note that if $diag^+(M, q_1, \ldots, q_m)$ is finite (e.g. if it is the set of facts in a data base), then $diag^+(M, q_1, \ldots, q_m)$ itself is the finite program Q.

---

[13] We can prove that any two models of a closed framework $\mathcal{F}$ reachable in $L_{\mathcal{F}}$ are isomorphic.

[14] We assume that D_r preserves the canonical model. See also the discussion on closed frameworks at the end of this section.

Furthermore, we shall also need a notion of *parametric termination*.

Definition 5.4 We say a program $P : r_1, \ldots, r_k \Leftarrow q_1, \ldots, q_m$ *parametrically terminates* if, for every program Q which does not contain $r_1, \ldots, r_k$ and terminates for the goals in $q_1, \ldots, q_m$, $P \cup Q$ terminates for the goals in $r_1, \ldots, r_k$. $\odot$

Using this, we can now state the following theorem:

Theorem 3 *Let $P_n : r_1, \ldots, r_k \Leftarrow q_1, \ldots, q_m$ be a synthesised program (in a framework $\mathcal{F}$) and D_n the corresponding definition axioms. If $\mathcal{F} \cup D_n \vdash \mathrm{Comp}^-(P_n, r_1, \ldots, r_k)$, and P_n parametrically terminates, then P_n is steadfast in the class of the $(q_1, \ldots, q_m)$-models of $\mathcal{F} \cup D_n$.*

Proof. Let M be a $(q_1, \ldots, q_m)$-model of $\mathcal{F} \cup D_n$ and Q a program correct wrt $q_1, \ldots, q_m$ in M. We have to prove that M is a steadfast model of P_n. Indeed:

Let $p_1, \ldots, p_h$ be the predicate symbols of Q not in L_M. Let M^* be the expansion of M by $p_1, \ldots, p_h$, interpreting the new symbols as the minimum Herbrand model of Q. M^* is a model of $\mathcal{F} \cup D_n \cup \mathrm{Comp}(Q)$ and hence of $\mathrm{Comp}(P_n \cup Q)$ (since $\mathcal{F} \cup D_n \vdash \mathrm{Comp}^+(P_n)$, $\mathcal{F} \cup D_n \vdash \mathrm{Comp}^-(P_n, r_1, \ldots, r_k)$, and $q_1, \ldots, q_m$ are defining symbols in P_n)

Now $diag^+(M^*, r_1, \ldots, r_k, q_1, \ldots, q_m, p_1, \ldots, p_h)$ is the minimum Herbrand model of $P_n \cup Q$, since $P_n \cup Q$ terminates and M^* is a reachable model of $\mathrm{Comp}(P_n \cup Q)$. Using this fact, we can prove that $diag^+(M, r_1, \ldots, r_k, q_1, \ldots, q_m)$ is the minimum Herbrand model of $P_n \cup diag^+(M, q_1, \ldots, q_m)$, i.e. it is a steadfast model of P_n. $\square$

This theorem works from the point of view of synthesis. Indeed, if we are synthesising a program $P : r_1, \ldots, r_k \Leftarrow q_1, \ldots, q_m$ in an open framework $\mathcal{F}$, then we are interested in the closed frameworks $\mathcal{F}^* \supseteq \mathcal{F}$ where a program Q for $q_1, \ldots, q_m$ can be found. Thus **Theorem 3** guarantees that the Halting Principle for steadfast programs is a *sufficient condition* for the synthesis of programs that are steadfast at least in the class of the models where correct programs exist that use them.

Our aim now is to prove that our Halting Principle also works as a necessary condition, namely that if a program P steadfast in the class of all the models of the framework exists, then there is a synthesis process that halts with P as the resulting program.

To prove this, let M be a model and let $P : r_1, \ldots, r_k \Leftarrow q_1, \ldots, q_m$ be a program. Consider the (possibly infinite) program $P \cup diag^+(M, q_1, \ldots, q_m)$. To avoid infinitary formulas we use the weak completion $Wcomp$ defined by:

$$Wcomp(P, M) = Comp^+(P) \cup Comp^-(P, r_1, \ldots, r_k) \cup diag(M, q_1, \ldots, q_m)$$

Then the following property can be proved:

Property 5.2 A steadfast model M of P is also a model of $Wcomp(P, M)$.

We can obtain:

Property 5.3 Let P_n be a synthesised program (in a framework $\mathcal{F}$) and D_n the corresponding definition axioms. If $P_n : r_1, \ldots, r_k \Leftarrow q_1, \ldots, q_m$ is steadfast in a non-empty class of models of $\mathcal{F} \cup D_n$, then $Comp^-(P_n, r_1, \ldots, r_k)$ is consistent with $\mathcal{F} \cup D_n$.

Proof. Assume, by *absurdum*, that $Comp^-(P_n, r_1, \ldots, r_k)$ is inconsistent with $\mathcal{F} \cup D_n$. Then every model M of $\mathcal{F} \cup D_n$ is also a model of $\neg Comp^-(P_n, r_1, \ldots, r_k)$.

Since the class of the steadfast models is non-empty, we can choose M in this class. We get absurdum as follows.

M is a model of $Wcomp(P, M)$, since it is a steadfast model of P, by **Property 5.2**, hence absurdum because $Wcomp(P, M)$ contains $Comp^-(P_n, r_1, \ldots, r_k)$ and M is a model of $\neg Comp^-(P_n, r_1, \ldots, r_k)$. □

This property justifies point (ii) of our Halting Principle. However, it guarantees only the consistency of $Comp^-(P_n, r_1, \ldots, r_k)$, not its provability. It could happen that we reach a steadfast P_n but we cannot prove its completion. This will not be the case, however, if we require steadfastness wrt the entire class of models. Indeed, we can prove the following theorem:

Theorem 4 *Let $P_n : r_1, \ldots, r_k \Leftarrow q_1, \ldots, q_m$ be a synthesised program and D_n the corresponding definition axioms. If P_n is steadfast in the class of the models of $\mathcal{F} \cup D_n$, then $\mathcal{F} \cup D_n \vdash Comp^-(P_n, r_1, \ldots, r_k)$.*

Proof. Assume, by *absurdum*, that $\mathcal{F} \cup D_n \nvdash Comp^-(P_n, r_1, \ldots, r_k)$. Then there is a model M of $\mathcal{F} \cup D_n \cup \{\neg Comp^-(P_n, r_1, \ldots, r_k)\}$. Since P_n is steadfast on the class of *all* the models of $\mathcal{F} \cup D_n$, M is a steadfast model of P_n, and we get absurdum like in **Property 5.3** □

Theorem 3 and **Theorem 4** explain the rôle of the provability of completion (for the defined symbols) in the Halting Principle for steadfast programs, namely:

- **Theorem 4** shows that it is a *necessary* condition for successfully halting synthesis of programs that are steadfast in the class of models of the framework.

- **Theorem 3** shows that it is also a *sufficient* condition for synthesis of parametrically terminating programs that are steadfast at least in the class of models which are of interest for synthesis.

We conjecture that **Theorem 3** can also be proved for the class of all models, by extending the notion of parametric termination in a suitable way.

Finally, we point out that the provability of the completion of the defined predicate symbols is not sufficient to guarantee that the synthesised programs are total. As we do not have space for an in-depth discussion here, we shall only briefly and informally touch on this issue.

We say that a predicate symbol q is *completely open* in a framework $\mathcal{F}$ if there is no instance $q(t)$ provable (hence valid) in $\mathcal{F}$. To synthesise steadfast programs that are total, the halting principle becomes:

The Halting Principle (for steadfast and total programs)
For every predicate p defined by the current program P_n:

(i) if $\mathcal{F} \cup D_n \vdash \neg Comp^-(P_n, p)$, search for other clauses with p in their head;

(ii) if $\mathcal{F} \cup D_n \vdash Comp^-(P_n, p)$, do not search for any more clauses defining p.

If (ii) holds for every defined predicate p of P_n and all the defining predicates are completely open in the framework, then synthesis successfully halts.

The case of closed frameworks, where no open predicate exists, works as a limiting case, where synthesis goes on until all the symbols that have been introduced become defined symbols of the program.

The Halting Principle for steadfast and total programs works in a very wide class of cases. However there are open frameworks where steadfast programs exist, but no steadfast program is total. Clearly, in this case, if we search for steadfast programs, we will not end up with total programs.

In a closed framework, where a canonical model exists, the situation is more fortunate. It can be proved that, if a total program exists, then the canonical model of the framework and the minimum Herbrand model of the program coincide on the common symbols. Therefore, either the completion of the program is provable, or it is consistent and can be added, enriching the framework in a consistent way that also preserves its semantics (i.e. its canonical model). Thus, if in some step, for some defined symbol p, neither (i) nor (ii) can be proved, we simply add $Comp^-(P_n, p)$ to the axioms of the framework and go on with our synthesis process. We will reach a total program P_n, if it exists.

6 Conclusion

In this paper, we have characterised the halting problem for deductive synthesis of logic programs, and stated a halting principle. We have done so for the synthesis of not only correct programs, but also steadfast, or reusable, program modules. Thus we have contributed to the theoretical foundations of deductive synthesis, as well as to practical synthesis of modular programs.

Our halting criteria are for the synthesis of *totally correct* programs. They thus enable us to determine when to stop our iterative synthesis process with a totally correct program. This is an important step forward for deductive synthesis. Hitherto, synthesis could only guarantee partial correctness, and there are no criteria for halting synthesis; total correctness has to be proved after synthesis has been stopped by some arbitrary rules.

The completion of a program plays a central rôle in the halting problem. A program P is totally correct in a framework $\mathcal{F}$ if the answers computable by P coincide with the answers that are valid (and hence provable) in $\mathcal{F}$. The provability of the completion is a sufficient but not a necessary condition for correctness. However, as we have shown in Section 5, total correctness in $\mathcal{F}$ is not adequate to express correctness wrt the models of $\mathcal{F}$. Indeed, different models may require different behaviours of the program. We have shown that here the provability of the completion (of the defined symbols only) becomes a sufficient *and necessary* condition for successfully halting synthesis with steadfast programs.

Steadfastness of programs is related to their reusability. Thus we have shown that in deductive synthesis we can go beyond correctness, and we have provided theoretical results that should enable us to study *object-oriented* synthesis of steadfast logic program modules. Moreover, the precise relationships between steadfastness and correctness are more intricate and complex than we can explain in this paper. In future work, we also intend to address this issue more fully.

The completion of a program also points a way to incrementally improving our starting specification framework as a result of the actual synthesis process itself. This suggests that deductive synthesis is a promising approach to real-world program synthesis or software engineering, where the entire process is typically: unsatisfactory or incorrect specification $\overset{\text{synthesis}}{\longrightarrow}$ unsatisfactory program $\rightarrow$ better specification $\overset{\text{synthesis}}{\longrightarrow}$ better program ... until the specification and the program are both satisfactory. Beyond this 'software cycle', our approach suggests that the more significant specification frameworks should survive any individual program synthesis process, and accumulate the knowledge provided interactively during synthesis processes, thereby becoming more and more complete.

Acknowledgements

We thank the referees for their helpful comments and for their constructive suggestions for future work.

References

[1] A. Bertoni, G. Mauri, and P. Miglioli. On the power of model theory in specifying abstract data types and in capturing their recursiveness. *Fundamenta Informaticae* **VI**(2):127–170, 1983.

[2] C.C. Chang and H.J. Keisler. *Model Theory*. North-Holland, 1973.

[3] K.L. Clark. Negation as failure. In H. Gallaire and J. Minker, editors, *Logic and Data Bases*, pages 293-322. Plenum Press, 1978.

[4] K.L. Clark. Predicate Logic as a Computational Formalism. Research Report 79/59, Dept of Computing, Imperial College, 1979.

[5] K.L. Clark and S.-Å. Tärnlund. A first order theory of data and programs. In *Proc. IFIP 77*, pages 939–944. North-Holland, 1977.

[6] Y. Deville. *Logic Programming: Systematic Program Development*. Addison-Wesley, 1990.

[7] Å. Hansson and S.-Å. Tärnlund. A natural programming calculus. In *Proc. IJCAI-79*, pages 348–355, 1979.

[8] C.J. Hogger. Derivation of logic programs. *Journal of the ACM*, **28**:372–392, 1981.

[9] R. Kowalski. Predicate Logic as Programming Language. In *Proc. IFIP 74*, pages 569–574. North-Holland, 1974.

[10] K.K. Lau and S.D. Prestwich. Top-down synthesis of recursive logic procedures from first-order logic specifications. In D.H.D. Warren and P. Szeredi, editors, *Proc. 7th Int. Conf. on Logic Programming*, pages 667–684. MIT Press, 1990.

[11] K.K. Lau and M. Ornaghi. An incompleteness result for deductive synthesis of logic programs. In D.S. Warren, editor, *Proc. 10th Int. Conf. on Logic Programming*, pages 456–477, MIT Press, 1993.

[12] J.W. Lloyd. *Foundations of Logic Programming*. Springer-Verlag, 2nd edition, 1987.

[13] Z. Manna and R. Waldinger. A deductive approach to program synthesis. *ACM TOPLAS*, **2**(1):90–121, Jan 1980.

[14] Z. Manna and R. Waldinger. *The Deductive Foundations of Computer Programming*. Addison-Wesley, 1993.

[15] J.C. Shepherdson. Negation in logic programming. In J. Minker, editor, *Foundations of Deductive Databases and Logic Programming*, pages 19-88. Morgan Kaufmann, 1988.

A New Transformation based on Process-Message Duality for Concurrent Logic Languages

Kouichi Kumon
Institute for New Generation Computer Technology
Mita-Kokusai Bldg 21F, Mita 1-4-28, Minato-ku, Tokyo 108, Japan
kumon@icot.or.jp

Keiji Hirata
NTT Basic Research Laboratories
3-1, Morinosato Wakamiya, Atsugi-shi, Kanagawa 243-01, Japan
hirata@nefertiti.ntt.jp

Abstract

In a concurrent logic language, mapping from the objects in a programmer's mind to actual processes and messages often results in less-than-optimum performance. One reason for this is that an incorrect prediction of the dynamic behavior and the resulting irrelevant mapping make the execution threads short and thus result in frequent suspensions. Also, good performance may be less important than the ease of writing and reading programs. Although in typical language processing systems for a concurrent logic language, shorter execution threads are likely to cause inefficiency, only few attempts extend the thread length by improving the scheduling policy of processing systems.

We are proposing a new technique for extending thread length, by exchanging the roles of the processes and messages of a source program; we call this technique a *duality transformation*. This technique improves program performance without the need for modifying the language processing systems. Processes and messages in a concurrent logic language can perform the same roles, making it is possible to transform processes to messages, and vice versa. Furthermore, the notion of process-message duality not only improves efficiency, but also gives rise to new programming methodologies, which allow meta-level programming without meta-language facilities. In this paper, we discuss the concept of duality of processes and messages, details of the transformation to a dual program, and some actual applications of this transformation.

1 Introduction

When a programmer writes a program in a concurrent logic language, he/she is faced with making the important choice of which of the objects in his/her mind are to be mapped to processes and which should be mapped to messages. Thus, user programs often employ an object-oriented programming style, where a series of messages are sent to a perpetual process [8, 9]. We call this the message-oriented programming style.

However, a programmer's choice may result in poor performance, the reasons perhaps being that the mapping of objects to processes and messages is poorly suited to the execution environment, that is, the programmer's prediction of the dynamic behavior of his/her program is wrong, or achieving ease of writing and reading programs degrades efficiency. In general, since language processing systems for concurrent logic languages (the Monaco system[10], the PIM system[7] and the KLIC system[1] and others [12, 2, 5]) assume that, during execution many shorter threads, resulting from suspension, are the most likely cause of inefficiency. Therefore, the above systems have attempted to reduce the switching overhead incurred by suspension and resumption. On the other hand, only few attempts extend the thread length for message-oriented programs by improving the scheduling policy of processing systems[11].

We are proposing a new method where, in the rewriting of a source program, the roles of processes and messages are exchanged to improve the efficiency. As a result, despite no modifications being made at the language processing system level, our method can yield the same effect as improving the scheduling policy. Since processes and messages in a concurrent logic language work in the same way as a data container, it is possible to transform processes to messages, and vice versa. Hence, we can say that processes and messages are dual to each other. Furthermore, the notion of process-message duality provides us not only with efficiency improvement, but also enables new programming methodologies, that allow meta-programming without the need for meta-language facilities.

Section 2 of this paper discusses the notion of duality of processes and messages in the concurrent logic language, FGHC. Section 3 presents the procedure of transformation to a dual program. Section 4 shows some actual applications of the transformation to efficiency improvement and new programming methodologies. Section 5 concludes this paper.

2 Duality in a Concurrent Logic Language

2.1 Message-Oriented Programs and Process-Oriented Programs

When a programmer writes a program in a concurrent logic language, he/she has to use the notion of messages and processes. To discuss the meanings and roles of messages and processes, we first define a message-oriented program and a process-oriented program. These two types of programs are distinguished by the way in which they initiate their execution: message sending or predicate invocation.

Message-Oriented Program: A sequence of messages is sent to a perpetual process. Upon receiving it, the process is activated and updates its internal state, and may send newly created messages to other perpetual processes. After that, the process returns to the suspended state [8, 9]. Figure 1 is a schematic diagram illustrating the behavior of a simple message-oriented program. In this figure, the shaded ovals represent suspended processes,

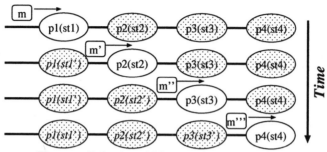

Figure 1: Behavior of Message-Oriented Program

while the white ovals represent active processes. Before message m arrives, all perpetual processes are suspended. Then, m activates process p1, which sends the new message m' to successive process p2. After that, p1 is suspended again. As a result, many suspensions and resumptions occur during the execution of this type of program.

Process-Oriented Program: A predicate is invoked to process the bulk of the data. As the predicate is being executed, it may invoke other predicates to process data, and may create new data. If the previous example is rewritten in a process-oriented manner (Figure 2), predicates may be suspended less frequently, because enough data may already exist to execute process m. In this figure, the rounded rectangles represent the data lists to

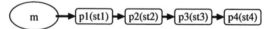

Figure 2: Behavior of Process-Oriented Program

be input to process m.

In message-oriented programs, we can think of messages as being active entities, with the processes waiting to be fed the messages. On the other hand, in process-oriented programs, the processes are active entities, that take in and process the data.

2.2 Duality of Messages and Processes

Before discussing the duality of processes and messages, we will first describe the execution of predicates by examining a sample program (Figure 3). We use FGHC, a concurrent logic language, in the following discussion.

At first, we look into how execution proceeds until predicate p commits. During the execution of the body of top, the message [m|n] is generated by active unification with variable Mi (%a), and predicate p is called (%b).

```
top:- true |
        Mi=[m|n],                        %a
        p(Mi,st,Mo).                     %b
p(Mi,ST,Mo):-                            %1
    Mi=[M|Mis],                          %2
    ST=st, M=m |                         %3
        Mn=m', STn=st',                  %4
        Mo=[Mn|Mos], r(Mis,STn,Mos).     %5
```

Figure 3: Sample Program for Illustrating Duality

This predicate invocation passes the argument values to the variables occurring at the head of the definition (%1). Then, the passive unification at %2 decomposes a message packet, for which the message container is a list cell ([|]). Finally, it is checked whether the process state ST and the received message M for committing (%3). Here, we regard %1 and %2 as being the basic contribution to clause selection and %3 as being an additional selection. The information required for the body execution of predicate p is:

- The data ST, which is carried as a process state of p (extracted at %1 in Figure 3).
- The data M, which is carried by a message container [|] (extracted at %2 in Figure 3).

At this point, we may exchange the carriers of the information (ST and M), thus obtaining the program shown in Figure 4. In this transformation, data structure [|] is read as cons(,). The commented numbers in this

```
top:- true |
        cons(Mi,m,n),                    %a'
        Mi=p(st,Mo).                     %b'
cons(Mi,M,Mis):-                         %2'
    Mi=p(ST,Mo),                         %1'
    ST=st, M=m |                         %3
        Mn=m', STn=st',                  %4
        Mo=[Mn|Mos], r(Mis,STn,Mos).     %5
```

Figure 4: Transformed Program

program indicate the correspondence with the lines in the original program shown in Figure 3. In Figure 4, cons initiates the calculation and carries m as its process state (%a'), while p acts as a message container and brings st as the message contents (%b'). Correspondingly, the predicate callee and the message decomposer should be transformed (%1', %2'). Note that it makes no difference whether the body execution of predicate p is initiated by a message or by a predicate call, but the body execution could possibly be transformed in a similar way (%4, %5).

We have already seen that the original program treats cons (*i.e.*[|]) as a message carrier and m as its contents. In the transformed program, they are treated as the process and process states, respectively. The original program in this example and the transformed program behave in much the same way, because the transformation changes the execution behavior of the program without changing of the meaning of the program. We define this relation as *dual*, and summarize this observation in the following table:

Process Invocation	Caller	Callee
	Predicate Call in Body	Head in Definition
	$\updownarrow$ *dual*	$\updownarrow$ *dual*
Message Sending	Sender	Receiver
	Active Unification	Passive Unification

The next section discusses the details of these transformation rules.

3 Transformation to Dual Programs

3.1 Streams

A stream is the basic and useful data structure used by a concurrent logic language. We define a stream in an FGHC program as follows:

- A stream has a tree structure (no loops and no node sharing).

- Each node may have a distinct label (functor symbol).

- All nodes are single-referenced by their parent nodes. This means that there are no external references to the intermediate nodes of a tree.

We then have two kinds of streams; one where all nodes consist of messages and another where all nodes are processes. In a message stream (a stream consisting of messages), a predecessor directly references its successors. In a process stream, each reference is represented by a variable, shared by a predecessor and its successor.

The following two program examples show a message stream (ms) and a process stream (ps), respectively. Note that these two streams have an identical structure.

```
ms(S) :- true | S=a(1,R1), R1=b(R2,N), N=nil, R2=b(2,3).
ps(S) :- true | a(S,1,R1), b(R1,R2,N), nil(N), b(R2,2,3).
```

In the definition of ms, variables R1, R2 and N refer to the successor nodes. On the other hand, in the definition of ps, each stream node, which is realized by a process, shares variables R1, R2 and N with the successor nodes; there are always two references to the shared variables.

3.2 Restricted FGHC Program

To mechanically transform FGHC programs to dual ones, first, the programs must be translated into a *normal form*. Here, *normal form* means that the following restrictions are applied:

(1) There are no nested structures; that is, the entire data structure is expressed in a flat form by using '='. Consequently, at the top level of arguments of literals and function symbols, only variables and atoms occur.

(2) Passive unification for one level of a structure is performed in a clause.

(3) A predicate which is target of the transformation has, at most, one stream input.

(4) Variables, which are bound to the stream structure, are treated in a one-writer, one-reader manner.

(5) A reader process must read every created stream structure.

Here, *stream* refers not only the message stream but also the process stream.

Restrictions (1) $\sim$ (2) can be textually (statically) checked but, in general, the precise checking of restrictions (3) $\sim$ (5) is difficult to realize textually. The aliasing, modes, types, size and cost analyses enabled by abstract interpretation can be used for the checking [3]. We intend to pursue this in the future. Restriction (5) is necessary to avoid deadlock of the transformed program. An example concerning the duality between unread data and deadlock processes will be presented in Section 4.2. The following is an example of a restricted FGHC program.

```
p(S,T) :- S=cons(X,Ss), X > 1 | T=cons(X,Ts), p(Ss,Ts).
p(S,T) :- S=nil | T=nil.
```

Also, the program segments for the stream representation (ms, ps) in the previous section are written in restricted FGHC.

Many practical FGHC programs can be translated into restricted ones. Even if a predicate has more than one input stream, it is not necessary to transform all of these. Instead, you can select only the most appropriate stream for transformation. We shall use this method in Section 4.1.2. But, once an input stream has been selected, all the possible generators and consumers of the stream must be transformed. As a result, it may become necessary to transform more than one input stream simultaneously. In other cases, an input stream variable may be used for more than one level of passive unification.

In both cases, to realize (2) and (3), fresh intermediate predicates can be introduced, after which an original predicate takes the form of a one stream-input and a one-level decomposition of the stream. Consider the following sample program:

```
add(X,Y,Z):- X=i(A,Xs),Y=i(B,Ys) |
    S := A+B, Z=i(S,Zs), add(Xs,Ys,Zs).
```

By introducing a new predicate add2, this definition is translated into a restricted FGHC program:

```
add(X,Y,Z) :- X=i(A,Xs) | add2(Y,A,Xs,Z).
add2(Y,A,Xs,Z) :- Y=i(B,Ys) |
    S := A+B, Z=i(S,Zs), add(Xs,Ys,Zs).
```

To achieve (4), we may duplicate an active unification, provided the meaning does not change. Suppose that the following program is given:

```
h :- true | X=p, q(X), r(X).
```

Variable X has multiple references: one writer and two readers. Then, we can rewrite this without changing its meaning:

```
h :- true | X=p, Y=p, q(X), r(Y).
```

Moreover, we may introduce some syntactic support to encourage a one-writer one-reader manner [4, 5]. However, the duplication and syntactic support do not cover all the cases needed to satisfy restriction (4) (Section 4.2).

You will notice that there are some kinds of programs which cannot be translated into restricted FGHC. Such programs include non-deterministic predicates, such as merger. Therefore, dual merger does not exist in our current framework. We will discuss this facet in a forthcoming paper.

3.3 The Transformation Procedure

This section presents the procedure for transforming a restricted FGHC program to a dual one, using the sample programs shown in Figure 5. In the

```
top :-sg(17,S),sc(S,0). %a1          top :-sg(17,S),S=sc(0). %b1


sg(N,So) :- N > 0 |                  sg(N,So) :- N  > 0 |
      So=c(N,Sos),     %a2                 c(So,N,Sos),      %b2
      N1 := N-1,                           N1 := N-1,
      sg(N1,Sos).                          sg(N1,Sos).
sg(N,So) :- N =< 0 |                 sg(N,So) :- N =< 0 |
      So=nil.          %a3                 nil(So).          %b3


sc(Si,T) :-            %a4           c(Si,X,Sis) :-          %b4
      Si=c(X,Sis) |    %a5                 Si=sc(T) |        %b5
      Tn:=T+X,                             Tn:=T+X,
      sc(Sis,Tn).      %a6                 Sis=sc(Tn).       %b6
sc(Si,T) :-            %a7           nil(Si) :-              %b7
      Si=nil      |    %a8                 Si=sc(T) |        %b8
      print(T).                            print(T).
```

    (a) Message Stream   (b) Process Stream

Figure 5: Transformation to Dual Program

figure, sg represents a stream generator, while sc represents a stream consumer. Program (a) in the left-hand column generates and consumes a message stream, while (b) does the same for a process stream. Both streams form a list of integer elements in descending order. In this example, the stream generators have their single internal states, N, and also the consumers have T as their internal states.

The first step of transformation is to determine the stream variable at the top level that connects a stream generator and a stream consumer. In this case, the variable is S at %a1 or %b1.

The second step is to determine the variable used for stream generation within a stream generator. Here, this is the second argument of the stream generator, So. Next, if So is bound to a message stream (%a2, %a3), these active unifications are transformed to process invocations (%b2, %b3). Otherwise, the inverse transformation (from process invocation to active unification) is performed. Here, it is sufficient to take only the body part into account.

The third step is to correspondingly transform the consumer program. In the guard part, the left- and right-hand sides of the neck operator (':-') are exchanged with respect to the variable for stream input (Si). Thus, the correspondence of the lines in Figure 5 is: %a4↔%b5, %a5↔%b4, %a7↔%b8, %a8↔%b7. At the same time, the form of message decomposition is rewritten into the form of the process callee (e.g. %a5→%b4) and vice versa. Finally, in the body part, the invocation of a stream consumer is transformed: %a1↔%b1, %a6↔%b6.

Note that, since a restricted FGHC program after transformation still belongs to restricted FGHC, the transformed program can also be transformed to a dual program. By applying the above transformation procedure, a *dual dual* program, which is identical to the original, is produced.

4 Applications

4.1 Performance Improvement Obtained By Applying Duality

This section highlights the efficiency improvement gained by the transformation to a dual program, taking two programs as examples: a binary tree search program and (the kernel part of) a life-game program. All timings are measured using one processing element of the PIM/p system[7, 6] and the KLIC system[1] (Version 1.010, running on a SparcStation 10/30). The PIM/p system is a parallel inference machine developed by ICOT. It employs tagged architecture and shared memories. User programs in KL1 are compiled into its RISC-like native instruction set. The KLIC system is a KL1 implementation for UNIX systems, which has already been ported onto several commercial UNIX systems. First, the KLIC system compiles user programs written in KL1 into C programs. Next, the system compiles the C code and links the object code with the KLIC runtime libraries.

We recognized from our experiments that certain types of programs run faster if they are first transformed. Currently, the transformation is done by hand. We think that it will be practical to formalize and automate the transformation procedure that is informally presented in Section 3.3. However, while we also consider it also feasible to determine all the stream variables (i.e. all the points that can be rewritten), it may prove difficult to determine to which stream variables the duality transformation should be applied to improve the program performance. At present, we believe that using a user's preferences will provide a practical solution to this problem.

4.1.1 Binary Tree Search

Program Description: A binary tree search program[11] represents tree nodes by using the 5-ary predicate which receives the search and update messages for searching for a specified key, and for updating the value for a specified key (Figure 6). We say that the tree is represented by *process tree*,

```
nt([],                    _, _, L,R) :- true | L=[], R=[].       %1
nt([search(K,V)|Cs], K, V1,L,R) :- true |                        %2
            V=V1, nt(Cs, K, V1, L, R).
nt([search(K,V)|Cs],K1,V1,L,R) :- K<K1 |                         %3
            L=[search(K,V)|L1], nt(Cs,K1,V1,L1,R).
nt([search(K,V)|Cs],K1,V1,L,R) :- K>K1 |                         %4
            R=[search(K,V)|R1], nt(Cs,K1,V1,L,R1).
nt([update(K,V)|Cs],K,_,L,R) :- true  | nt(Cs,K,V,L,R).          %5
nt([update(K,V)|Cs],K1,V1,L,R) :- K<K1 |                         %6
            L=[update(K,V)|L1], nt(Cs,K1,V1,L1,R).
nt([update(K,V)|Cs],K1,V1,L,R) :- K>K1 |                         %7
            R=[update(K,V)|R1], nt(Cs,K1,V1,L,R1).

t([]              ) :- true | true.                              %8
t([search(_,V)|Cs]) :- true | V=undefined,t(Cs).                 %9
t([update(K,V)|Cs]) :- true | nt(Cs,K,V,L,R),t(L),t(R).          %10
```

Figure 6: Ueda's Binary Tree Search Program (Original)
(process tree, list stream notation)

and that the search and update messages are carried by a *list stream* (the stream whose constructors are list cells, i.e. [search(K,V)|Cs]). In general, the stream carrier, 2-ary cons, is used only for pointing to the subsequent message carrier. If the message itself can point to the next message, such as search(K,V,Cs), the stream carrier, 2-ary cons, can be omitted. We call this representation of a stream the *functor stream*. The functor stream is more efficient than the list stream, since the functor stream requires fewer unification operations. We measured the performance of dual programs in terms of both streams.

In this example, we prepare two types of message generators. When the first sends a message, it does not check whether the previous message has already been processed. Therefore, we call this the *no-wait* generator. The second defers the sending of a new message until all previously sent search messages have been processed. The second message generator is called the *acknowledge-wait* generator.

Duality Transformation: Prior to being transformed to its dual program, first, the source program is translated into restricted FGHC. Thus, all list cells are explicitly treated as the 2-ary cons functor, after which we obtain the 3-argument cons predicate. Figure 7 shows the transformed program. Each clause in Figure 6 is numbered by comments %1~%10, the same-numbered comments in Figure 7 indicating the corresponding clauses. The transformed program uses the 4-ary functor symbol, nt, to represent a tree node (*functor tree*), the 2 arguments of nt being used to hold the key and the value. The remaining 2 arguments are used to point to the left and right branches of the tree node. This dual representation of the binary tree is also straightforward and easy to understand.

```
nil(C) :- C=nt(_ ,_ ,L,R) | nil(L),nil(R).                    %1
nil(C) :- C=t                | true.                          %8

cons(C,search(K,V),Cs) :- C=nt(K ,V1,L,R)      . |            %2
              V=V1, Cs=nt(K,V1,L,R).
cons(C,search(K,V),Cs) :- C=nt(K1,V1,L,R), K<K1 |            %3
              cons(L,search(K,V),L1), Cs=nt(K1,V1,L1,R).
cons(C,search(K,V),Cs) :- C=nt(K1,V1,L,R), K>K1 |            %4
              cons(R,search(K,V),R1), Cs=nt(K1,V1,L,R1).
cons(C,update(K,V),Cs) :- C=nt(K ,_ ,L,R)      |            %5
              Cs=nt(K,V,L,R).
cons(C,update(K,V),Cs) :- C=nt(K1,V1,L,R), K<K1 |            %6
              cons(L,update(K,V),L1), Cs=nt(K1,V1,L1,R).
cons(C,update(K,V),Cs) :- C=nt(K1,V1,L,R), K>K1 |            %7
              cons(R,update(K,V),R1), Cs=nt(K1,V1,L,R1).
cons(C,search(_,V),Cs) :- C=t                   |            %9
              V=undefined,Cs=t.
cons(C,update(K,V),Cs) :- C=t                   |            %10
              Cs=nt(K,V,L,R),L=t,R=t.
```

Figure 7: Binary Tree Search Program (Transformed)
(functor tree, list stream notation)

Measured Results: All update and search messages are generated by the message generator. It sends, to the binary tree, 5000 update messages with randomly generated keys. It then sends 5000 search messages, having the same key sequence as the update messages.

Table 1 shows the measured timings and suspension counts. The parenthesized number is the number of suspensions and their ratios, as measured for the KLIC system. In this case, a programmer would probably assume

| Input Stream | KLIC system (Ver.1.010) | | | PIM/p system | | |
Type	Original	Dual Prog.	Speedup	Original	Dual Prog.	Speedup
	No-wait generator					
List stream	299 ms	421 ms	0.71	1834 ms	1823 ms	1.01
	(0)	(0)	–			
Functor stream	267 ms	306 ms	0.87	1623 ms	1511 ms	1.07
	(0)	(0)	–			
	Acknowledge-wait generator					
List stream	957 ms	421 ms	2.25	2930 ms	1802 ms	1.63
	(103986)	(0)	–			
Functor stream	965 ms	309 ms	3.12	2826 ms	1489 ms	1.90
	(103986)	(0)	–			

Table 1: Performance of Binary Tree Search Program

that the generator and binary-tree processes operate like coroutines; each message is generated, then consumed, one after the other. But, since the no-wait generator generates all the messages before the binary-tree processes accept the first message, no suspension occurs. Therefore, the performance of both programs deviates only slightly (for the PIM/p system) or degraded about 30 % (for the KLIC system). The main reason of this performance degradation in the KLIC system is the execution overhead of functor processing in the KLIC system. Without suitable process-priority control, many generators in actual programs may run as no-wait generators. If the list stream of the original program is converted to a functor stream, the performance of the both systems improves.

For the acknowledge-wait generator, the performance of the original program is degraded significantly, since every search message incurs a suspension/resumption overhead. However, the transformed program is never suspended at all. As a result, the performance is up to 3.1 times faster on the KLIC system, and twice as fast on the PIM/p system.

4.1.2 Life-Game Program

Program Description: Figure 8 shows the kernel part of a life-game simulation program. In this program, the processes construct a mesh network where each node process is connected to its upper, lower, left- and right-hand neighbors. Each node process awaits messages from its neighbors. Once a node receives four messages, i.e. one from each neighbor, the node sends a new message back to those neighbors, then enters a new generation. Therefore, no node process can continuously run for two reductions without suspension. In an actual life-game program, each node is connected to eight neighbors and also computes the next state, but this example omits the state calculation for simplification. Figure 8 shows the kernel part of the life-game program. The transformed program is shown in Figure 9.

```
node(Li,Lo,Ri,Ro,Ui,Uo,Di,Do) :- Li=cons(T,Lis),
                  Ri=[T|Ris],Ui=[T|Uis],Di=[T|Dis],T>0,T1:=T-1 |
        Lo=[T1|Los], Ro=cons(T1,Ros), Uo=[T1|Uos], Do=[T1|Dos],
        node(Lis,Los,Ris,Ros,Uis,Uos,Dis,Dos).
node(Li,Lo,Ri,Ro,Ui,Uo,Di,Do) :- Li=cons(T,Lis),
                  Ri=[T|Ris],Ui=[T|Uis],Di=[T|Dis],T=:=0          |
        Lo=[], Ro=nil, Uo=[],Do=[],
        node(Lis,Ris,Uis,Dis).
node(Li,Ri,Ui,Di) :- Li=nil, Ri=[],Ui=[],Di=[]                    | true.
```

Figure 8: Kernel Part of the Life-Game Program (Original)

```
cons(Li,T,Lis) :- Li=node(Lo,Ri,Ro,Ui,Uo,Di,Do),
                  Ri=[T|Ris],Ui=[T|Uis],Di=[T|Dis],T>0,T1:=T-1 |
        Lo=[T1|Los], cons(Ro,T1,Ros), Uo=[T1|Uos],Do=[T1|Dos],
        Lis=node(Los,Ris,Ros,Uis,Uos,Dis,Dos).
cons(Li,T,Lis) :- Li=node(Lo,Ri,Ro,Ui,Uo,Di,Do),
                  Ri=[T|Ris],Ui=[T|Uis],Di=[T|Dis],T=:=0         |
        Lo=[], nil(Ro), Uo=[], Do=[],
        Lis=node(Ris,Uis,Dis).
nil(Li) :- Li=node(Ri,Ui,Di), Ri=[],Ui=[],Di=[]                  | true.
```

Figure 9: Kernel Part of the Life-Game Program (Transformed)

Duality Transformation: Compared to the previous example, a dual program is hard to conceive and write from scratch. To transform it into a dual program, although each node actually has four input streams, here,

we treat only Li (the input from the left neighbor) as the input stream.
Therefore, Ro (the output to the right neighbor) should be treated as the
output stream and the rest of the arguments as a process state as a whole.
Since this transformation does not change the substantial algorithm, the
transformed program does not deadlock, in the same way as the original.

Measured Results: We created a small mesh network (10×10) and a
large mesh network (20×20), and executed 1000 generations. The measured
results (Table 2) show that, in both systems, the transformed programs are
always faster than the originals. As in the previous table, the figures within
parentheses are those for suspension. As we mentioned before, each node
predicate in the original program is suspended at least every reduction and,
worse still, two or more suspensions may occur during one reduction. The
behavior of a transformed program may be difficult to understand, but it
can continue to run for a certain number of reductions without suspension.
Consequently, the thread is prolonged 2.9 to 5.2 times of the original one,
and the performance is improved $1.3 \sim 1.9$ times.

Mesh Size	KLIC system (Ver.1.010)			PIM/p system		
	Original	Dual Prog.	Speedup	Original	Dual Prog.	Speedup
10×10	1040 ms	600 ms	1.73	3009 ms	2334 ms	1.30
	(220858)	(76982)	(2.87)			
20×20	4580 ms	2390 ms	1.92	13843 ms	9415 ms	1.47
	(845516)	(162452)	(5.20)			

Table 2: Performance of Life-Game Program (1000 Generations)

4.2   New Programming Methodologies Based on Duality

We have seen how processes in a source program correspond to messages in
its dual program. And, processes in a source program are treated as first-
class objects in its dual program. Therefore, our transformation may provide
a means for meta-control in concurrent logic languages. This section presents
how to describe continuation based on duality in FGHC, as an example of
meta-control. Further, we have prototyped the migration of FGHC processes
based on the notion of the process-message duality. However, because of
space limitations, we must skip the subject of migration.

Continuation: Consider the sample program shown in Figure 10. This
program searches for a given value in a binary tree in a depth-first manner.
The result from the left tree is provided to the right tree via the third
argument of search and the first argument of search1 (CPs). search1
relays the message found or not_found. The result determines whether the
program has located the right tree. Note that the data structure bound
to CPs is a process stream whose length is equal to the depth of the tree.
Since this program is a restricted FGHC program, we can transform the
program with respect to the variables CP and CPs (Figure 11). Then, after the

```
?- search(Key,Tree,Res), cont(Res,Args).

search(K,T,CP):- T=leaf(Ts), K = Ts  | CP = found.
search(K,T,CP):- T=leaf(Ts), K \= Ts | CP = not_found.
search(K,T,CP):- T=node(T0,T1)        |
        search(K,T0,CPs), search1(CPs,K,T1,CP).

search1(CP,K,T1,CPs):- CP = found     | CPs = found.
search1(CP,K,T1,CPs):- CP = not_found | search(K,T1,CPs).

cont(CP,Args):- CP=found     | found_proc(Args).
cont(CP,Args):- CP=not_found | not_found_proc(Args).
```

Figure 10: Tree Search in FGHC

```
?-search(Key,T,Res), Res=cont(Args).

search(K,T,CP):- T=leaf(Ts), Ts = K  | found(CP).
search(K,T,CP):- T=leaf(Ts), Ts \= K | not_found(CP).
search(K,T,CP):- T=node(T0,T1)        |
        search(K,T0,CPs), CPs=search1(K,T1,CP).

found(CP):- CP=search1(K,T1,CPs) | found(CPs).
found(CP):- CP=cont(Args)        | found_proc(Args).

not_found(CP):- CP=search1(K,T1,CPs) | search(K,T1,CPs).
not_found(CP):- CP=cont(Args)        | not_found_proc(Args).
```

Figure 11: Dual Tree Search Program

transformation, each clause has a maximum of one body predicate. Hence, we may say that the transformed program presents its intrinsic sequentiality more explicitly, and runs efficiently from an implementation point of view. In Figure 11, the data structure occurring at the third argument of search has the following form (called search1-chain):

```
CP=search1(K,T1,CP'),CP'=search1(K,T1',CP''),...,CP'''=cont(Args)
```

The function symbol search1 can be regarded as being the future execution after searching the left tree, and the chain of the terms, search1-chain, in a heap explicitly designates the possible execution order. Here, we say that the transformed program is of the continuation-passing style (CPS).

When a leaf whose value is equal to a given key is found, the predicate found is invoked, and traverses the search1-chain. Finally, the traverse reaches cont, after which control is passed to the next computation found_proc. However, considering the behavior of this program, it is not efficient to traverse every search1 of the chain once the target leaf has been found. Thus, more efficient execution can be realized by invoking the found_proc predicate directly (Figure 12). In the program shown in Figure 12, the number of arguments of search is increased from three to four; the extra argument holds the continuation to be executed immediately upon found is being invoked. By performing a transformation with respect to the

```
?-search(Key,T,Res,Res), Res=cont(Args).

search(K,T,CP,FC):- T=leaf(Ts), Ts = K | found(FC).
search(K,T,CP,FC):- T=leaf(Ts), Ts \= K | not_found(CP,FC).
search(K,T,CP,FC):- T=node(T0,T1)        |
            search(K,T0,CPs,FC), CPs=search1(K,T1,CP).

found(FC):- FC=cont(Args) | found_proc(Args).

not_found(CP,FC):- CP=search1(K,T1,CPs) | search(K,T1,CPs,FC).
not_found(CP,FC):- CP=cont(Args)         | not_found_proc(Args).
```

Figure 12: More Efficient Dual Tree Search

variables to derive a computation result, we obtain a program where the execution is represented by first-class objects.

Consider the program obtained by the duality-transformation of the program in Figure 12. Prior to the transformation, the goal in the figure must be normalized by the duplication method, as follows:

```
?-search(Key,T,Res1,Res2),Res1=cont(Args),Res2=cont(Args).
```

Subsequently the transformation with respect to Res1 and Res2 seems applicable. However, as you have probably noticed, the normalized program does not satisfy restriction (5) in Section 3.2, since the normalized program discards the search1-chain without reading it. If we ignore restriction (5), unprocessed data (garbage data) in the program will be transformed to unexecuted processes (deadlock processes) from the duality point of view.

5   Conclusion

We have proposed a new transformation method for concurrent logic languages. The method enables transformation between message-oriented programs and process-oriented programs. By examining predicate invocation and message sending/receiving processes in a concurrent logic language, we have clarified the notion of the duality of processes and messages. Our method does not change the algorithm of a program, instead changing the data carriers (process to message and vice versa). With our method, a programmer can write programs as he or she desires, then transform them to more efficient (dual) ones. That is, to some extent, our method can free programmers from considering their programs' dynamic behavior and performance. We have evaluated the performance improvement gained by the use of our method on two systems, the KLIC system and the PIM/p system, both of which were developed at ICOT. For the benchmark programs referenced in this paper, the duality transformation achieves a threefold maximum speedup.

Furthermore, our method not only increases the choices available during programming and improves performance, but also enables us to express control as a first-class object. Hence, meta-programming based on duality is becomes possible. As an example, continuation can be described in FGHC without meta-language facilities.

Consequently, the duality of messages and processes in concurrent logic languages enriches our programming techniques and methodologies, and also contributes to performance improvement.

Acknowledgments

The authors thank Kazunori Ueda for his valuable advice. The authors are also grateful to the anonymous referees of a previously submitted version of this paper for their useful suggestions. Mention is also due to our ICOT researchers, and the stimulating research environment they generate.

References

[1] T. Chikayama et al. A Portable and Reasonably Efficient Implementation of KL1. In *Proc. of the Tenth International Conference on Logic Programming*, page 833. The MIT Press, 1993.

[2] J. Crammond. The Abstract Machine and Implementation of Parallel Parlog. *New Generation Computing*, 10(4):385–422, 1992.

[3] S. K. Debray. Static Analysis of Logic Programs. In *An Advanced Tutorial of the ILPS'93*, 1993.

[4] I. Foster and S. Taylor. *Strand: New Concepts in Parallel Programming*. Prentice-Hall, Englewood Cliffs, 1989.

[5] D. Gudeman, K. De Bosschere, and S. K. Debray. jc: An Efficient and Portable Sequential Implementation of Janus. In *Proc. of ICLP'92*, 1992.

[6] K. Hirata et al. Parallel and Distributed Implementation of Concurrent Logic Programming Language KL1. In *Proc. of International Conference on Fifth Generation Computer Systems*, pages 436–459. ICOT, 1992.

[7] K. Kumon et al. Architecture and Implementation of PIM/p. In *Proc. of International Conference on Fifth Generation Computer Systems*, pages 414–424. ICOT, 1992.

[8] E. Shapiro and A. Takeuchi. Object-oriented programming in Concurrent Prolog. *New Generation Computing*, 1(1):25–49, 1983.

[9] A. Takeuchi. *Parallel Logic Programming*. John Wiley & Sons, Inc., 1992.

[10] E. Tick and C. Banerjee. Performance Evaluation of Monaco Compiler and Runtime Kernel. In *Proc. of ICLP'93*, 1993.

[11] K. Ueda and M. Morita. Message-Oriented Parallel Implementation of Moded Flat GHC. In *Proc. of International Conference on Fifth Generation Computer Systems*, pages 799–807. ICOT, 1992.

[12] R. Yang et al. Performance of the Compiler-based Andorra-I System. In *Proc. of ICLP'93*, 1993.

Compiling Control Revisited: A New Approach based upon Abstract Interpretation

Dmitri Boulanger
Danny De Schreye
Department of Computer Science
Katholieke Universiteit Leuven
Celestijnenlaan 200 A, B-3001, Heverlee, Belgium
{dmitri,dannyd}@cs.kuleuven.ac.be

Abstract

A new approach for source level logic program transformations is presented. The framework is based on an abstract interpretation scheme in which the source program is formulated in a constraint form. Abstract interpretation is guided by the specified computation rule. The result of the abstract interpretation is used for controlling the transformation of the source program.

1 Introduction

Sometimes it is worthwhile to consider nonstandard computation rules. For example, coroutining in the following generate-and-test type program

$solutions(N, Q) \leftarrow init(N, L), perm(L, Q), safe(Q).$ % N queens

$init(0, [\,])$.   % Initial positions of N queens (list of integers)
$init(N, L) \leftarrow N > 0, N1 = N - 1, L = [N|L1], init(N1, L1)$.

$perm([\,], [\,])$.   % Generator of possible positions of N queens
$perm([X|Y], [U|V]) \leftarrow delete(U, [X|Y], W), perm(W, V)$.
$delete(X, [X|L], L)$.
$delete(X, [Y|L], [Y|W]) \leftarrow delete(X, L, W)$.

$safe([\,])$. % Main Engine to test that queens do not attack each other
$safe([U])$.
$safe([X, U|V]) \leftarrow non\_diag(X, 1, [U|V]), safe([U|V])$.
$non\_diag(X, I, [\,])$.
$non\_diag(X, I, [Y|Z]) \leftarrow test(X, I, Y), J = I + 1, non\_diag(X, J, Z)$.
$test(X, D, Y) \leftarrow Y \neq X, Y \neq X + D, Y \neq X - D$.

runs the tester ($safe$-atom) as soon as the generator ($perm$-atom) has generated enough instantiation to test. Hence, some atoms, called "G-atoms", are only partly solved before the control is passed to others. Other atoms, called "c-atoms", are completely solved once the control is passed to them. To achieve the same effect under the standard computation rule **S**, the initial program P need to be transformed by T into another program P^{new} by integrating the control of the non-standard computation rule into the derived program (*compiling control transformation* [1]). The paper is concerned with transforming programs with *deterministic instantiation-based computation rules*, which includes the computation rule for coroutining mentioned above. In this paper, the purpose is achieved through a detour. First the given program P with non-standard computation rule **R** is converted into a constraint program P_C with constraint computation rule $\mathbf{R}_C$, then it is transformed by T_C into another constraint program P_C^{new} with the standard computation rule **S**, and lastly it is converted into a program P^{new} with **S**.

$$P \text{ with } \mathbf{R} \quad \xrightarrow{\ T\ } \quad P^{new} \text{ with } \mathbf{S}$$

$$
\begin{array}{ccc}
P \text{ with } \mathbf{R} & & P^{new} \text{ with } \mathbf{S} \\
\downarrow & & \uparrow \\
P_C \text{ with } \mathbf{R}_C & \xrightarrow{\ T_C\ } & P_C^{new} \text{ with } \mathbf{S}
\end{array}
$$

One reason of detouring is the necessity of good definitions of new predicates to derive new programs by transformation. In the unfold/fold transformation, the definitions of new predicates are usually suggested by *generalisation* of the atoms appearing in the transformation process. If c-atoms are treated in the same way as G-atoms, there sometimes occur infinite growths of the number of c-atoms in the unfolded definite clauses, which prevent the generalisation for good definitions. In this paper, c-atoms are treated as constraints.

The other reason is the necessity of a formal way to express computation rules. In this paper, whether an argument is instantiated to a term of specific form is expressed using constraints.

Now, the problem is how to transform "P_C with $\mathbf{R}_C$" to "P_C^{new} with **S**". The framework of unfold/fold transformation can be adapted for constraint programs. However, though the infinite growth of the number of c-atoms is inhibited by treating c-atoms as constraints, obtaining good definitions of new predicates by *generalisation of constraints* still remains a difficult problem.

A tabled interpreter of constraint logic programs, which memos in a table the solutions of each new call of the goals and utilise them to solve the later calls of the same form, is used to analyse the run-time properties of logic programs. The graph obtained by running it on an abstract domain shows an approximated behaviour of the execution of the logic programs, hence suggests a run-time property. Similarly, the graph obtained by running a tabled interpreter tuned for constraint form on an appropriately constructed abstract domain according to $\mathbf{R}_C$ shows an approximated behaviour of the execution of "P_C^{new} with $\mathbf{R}_C$", hence suggests the candidates for generalisation. The program analysis proposed in this paper, thereby, guides the transformation of "P_C with $\mathbf{R}_C$" to "P_C^{new} with $\mathbf{S}$".

The rest of the paper is arranged as a "running example" around the $NQueens$ program above. Sections 2 and 3 introduce all the basic notions for concrete and abstract interpretation. In the section 4 we present the tabulation based technique to prove correctness of *deterministic instantiation-based* computation rules. In section 5 we present an example, which illustrates the code generation technique for the compiling control transformation.

The paper assumes background in logic programming [11] and familiarity with abstract interpretation for (constraint) logic programming [3].

2 Abstract and Concrete Constraint Systems

This section introduces the notion of constraint systems which is an adapted version (to allow a special abstract domain generation technique) of a generic constraint system elaborated in [5, 8, 9]. An important feature of the constraint system is that *exactly* the same semantics can be used for abstract and concrete computations.

Let P be a finite set of predicate symbols containing a binary predicate symbol "=" and predicate constants **true** and **false**. The set of well-formed first order formulas based on P and on a countable set of variables $\mathcal{V}$ is denoted by $\mathcal{L}_P$, which is a "flat" language (it *does not* contain terms). A (concrete) interpretation I of formulas from $\mathcal{L}_P$ has the domain of interpretation which is the Herbrand universe HU_F based on a finite set of function symbols F. The predicates "=", **true** and **false** are always interpreted as identity, true and false respectively.

A set of *flat constraints*, noted $\mathcal{C} \subseteq \mathcal{L}_P$, is such that only the logical operations $\wedge$, $\vee$, $\exists_\Delta$, $\Delta \subseteq \mathcal{V}$ are used for formula construction. The formulas $\mathbf{c} \in \mathcal{C}$ are used to express constraints and arbitrary formulas $\mathbf{f} \in \mathcal{L}_P$ will be used to express *properties* of the constraints. For example, the formula $\mathbf{c} \rightarrow \mathbf{c}' \in \mathcal{L}_P$ ("$\rightarrow$" denotes implication) is *not* a constraint, but can be used to express that the constraint $\mathbf{c}'$ is weaker than the constraint $\mathbf{c}$.

A preorder $(\mathcal{L}_P, \trianglelefteq)$ is defined as follows: given two formulas $\mathbf{f}_1, \mathbf{f}_2 \in \mathcal{L}_P$, $\mathbf{f}_2$ is said to be *weaker* than $\mathbf{f}_1$, noted $\mathbf{f}_1 \trianglelefteq \mathbf{f}_2$, iff $I \models \mathbf{f}_1 \rightarrow \mathbf{f}_2$. The formulas $\mathbf{f}_1, \mathbf{f}_2$ are equivalent, noted $\mathbf{f}_1 \equiv \mathbf{f}_2$, iff $\mathbf{f}_1 \trianglelefteq \mathbf{f}_2$ and $\mathbf{f}_2 \trianglelefteq \mathbf{f}_1$.

A (concrete) *flat constraint system* is a pair $\mathcal{S} = <\mathcal{C}, I>$. In the sequel we will deal with constraint systems $\mathcal{S}$ *generated* by a definite logic program (see below). A definite logic program P is a collection of definite clauses $H \leftarrow A_1, \ldots, A_n$, $n \geq 0$. A program is said to be *flat* if it is composed of *flat range-restricted* clauses, i.e. neither constant symbols nor function symbols occurs in *any* clause and any variable occurring in the head of a clause occurs in its body. Also, a program constructed using disjoint sets of predicates $A \cap B = \emptyset$ is said to be in *flat stratified form* iff the collection of clauses having a predicate symbol from A in the head is a flat definite logic program, noted P_A, and any clause having a predicate symbol from B in the head is a unit clause (facts possibly containing terms, noted P_B). Any definite logic program P can be transformed into equivalent program P_{AB} having a flat stratified form.

"Flattening" has been considered before elsewhere, and it is a rather trivial transformation (see example 2.1 below). Let $(P_{AB})^u$ denote the program obtained from P_{AB} by unfolding of *all* occurrences of the B-atoms in the bodies of the clauses of P_A by applying the algorithm of Tamaki and Sato [13] (it preserves a least Herbrand model of a definite logic program, noted $\mathcal{M}$ below). Also, $\mathcal{M}\mid_A$ denotes a subset of $\mathcal{M}$ restricted to the set of predicates A. Then the program P_{AB} is a flat stratified form of a program P iff $(P_{AB})^u\mid_A = P$ and P_B is a set of facts such that for any function symbol f/n of arity $n \geq 0$ occurring in P there exists $p(\overline{X}, f(\overline{X})) \in P_B$, where $p \in B$ has arity $n + 1$ and $\overline{X}$ is a vector of n distinct variables. Obviously, if the program P_{AB} has a model $\mathcal{M}(P_{AB})$, then $\mathcal{M}(P_{AB})\mid_A$ is a model for P.

Example 2.1 The flat stratified form $NQueens_{AB}$ for the $NQueens$ program of section 1 is as follows (from here on the predicate names are abbreviated, e.g. *perm – p, safe – s*, etc.):

A − part :
$solutions(N, Q) \leftarrow init(N, L), p(L, Q), s(Q).$
$init(N, L) \leftarrow zero(N), el(N).$
$init(N, L) \leftarrow sum(N1, X, N), one(X), greater\_than(N, Y), zero(Y),$
$\qquad\qquad l(N1, L1, L), init(N1, L1).$
$p(L, Q) \leftarrow el(L), el(Q).$
$p(L, Q) \leftarrow l(X, Y, L), l(U, V, Q), d(U, L, W), p(W, V).$
$d(X, Q, R) \leftarrow l(X, R, Q).$
$d(X, Q, R) \leftarrow l(Y, L, Q), l(Y, W, R), d(X, L, W).$
$s(Q) \leftarrow el(Q).$
$s(Q) \leftarrow el(T), l(U, T, Q).$
$s(Q) \leftarrow l(X, W, Q), l(U, V, W), one(I), nd(X, I, W), s(W).$
$nd(X, I, L) \leftarrow el(L), any(X), any(I).$
$nd(X, I, Q) \leftarrow l(Y, Z, Q), test(X, I, Y), sum(I, N, J), one(N), nd(X, J, Z).$
$test(X, D, Y) \leftarrow not\_equal(Y, X), sum(X, D, W), not\_equal(W, Y),$
$\qquad\qquad sum(U, D, X), not\_equal(U, Y).$

B − part :
$any(X).$ $\qquad$ $not\_equal(?, ?).$ $\qquad$ $one(1).$ $\qquad$ $el([\,]).$
$sum(?, ?, ?).$ $\qquad$ $greater\_than(?, ?).$ $\qquad$ $zero(0).$ $\qquad$ $l(H, T, [H|T]).$

All function symbols have been packed into *new* facts. The built-in predicates *greater_than/2* $(X > Y)$, *sum/3* $(Z\ is\ X + Y)$, *not_equal/2* $(X \neq Y)$ are assumed to have a natural interpretation implied by their names over the set of integers (the infinite set of facts defining the built-ins are abbreviated as e.g. $sum(?,?,?)$). The fact $any(X) \in NQueens_{\mathsf{B}}$ is introduced to have only flat range-restricted clauses in $NQueens_{\mathsf{A}}$. □

Given a definite logic program P and its flat stratified form P_{AB}, the flat constraint system $\mathcal{S} = <\mathcal{C}, I>$ based on $\mathsf{P} = \mathsf{A} \cup \mathsf{B} \cup \{=, \mathbf{true}, \mathbf{false}\}$, is called a *computation space generated* by P iff $I = \mathcal{M}(P_{\mathsf{AB}})$. This means that the domain of I is the Herbrand universe HU_{F}, where the set of function symbols F is implied by P. A computation space generated by a program is a flat constraint system. This enables us to construct its abstractions only by changing the interpretation. However, we are interested in the abstractions, which preserve particular properties of the concrete system. Therefore, we use a *precision theory* $\mathcal{T} \subseteq \mathcal{L}_{\mathsf{P}}$, which is a set of flat first order formulas such that $\mathcal{T} = \mathcal{T}_{\mathsf{B}} \cup P_{\mathsf{A}} \cup \Psi$, where $\mathcal{T}_{\mathsf{B}} = \{\exists_{\mathcal{V}}\mathbf{g} \mid \mathcal{M}(P_{\mathsf{B}}) \models \mathbf{g}\}$, $\mathbf{g}$ denotes a flat conjunction of B-atoms and $\Psi \subseteq \mathcal{L}_{\mathsf{P}}$ is a *finite* set of *extra* properties of $\mathcal{M}(P_{\mathsf{AB}})$, i.e. $\mathcal{M}(P_{\mathsf{AB}}) \models \Psi$. The latter insures that the precision theory $\mathcal{T}$ is *consistent* with the program, i.e. $\mathcal{M}(P_{\mathsf{AB}}) \models \mathcal{T}$.

The precision theory $\mathcal{T}$ contains a possibly *infinite* subset $\mathcal{T}_{\mathsf{B}}$. The theory $\mathcal{T}_{\mathsf{B}}$ includes representations of *all* possible unifiable sets of terms, which can be constructed from terms occurring in the program P. The set of extra properties Ψ is a *parameter*, which should be chosen to fit the problem in hand. Below we show how the compiling control problem of [1] can be solved using a special set of extra properties, which are derived from the corresponding computation rule (see def.4.2 in section 4).

Example 2.2 The precision theory consistent with $NQueens$ program can be constructed using the set of extra properties Ψ, which is the set of flat "integrity constraints" $\{\mathbf{f_i(L)} \wedge \mathbf{f_j(L)} \rightarrow \mathbf{false} \mid i, j = 0, 1, 2, i < j\}$, where

$\mathbf{f_0(L)}$: $el(L)$ % Empty list L
$\mathbf{f_1(L)}$: $\exists_{\{H,T\}}(\, el(T) \wedge l(H,T,L)\,)$ % Singleton list L
$\mathbf{f_2(L)}$: $\exists_{\{H,T,H',T'\}}(\, l(H',T',T) \wedge l(H,T,L)\,)$% L has at least two elements

The formulas above are simply intended to fix that an empty list, a singleton list and a list having at least two elements are distinguishable (not unifiable) in the computation space $\mathcal{S}$ (the reason to fix these extra properties will be explained later, section 4). It is clear that $\mathcal{M}(NQueens_{\mathsf{AB}}) \models \Psi$. □

Now we can introduce a notion of *abstraction*. Let F^{α} be a finite set of (abstract) constants (no function symbols). Consider a constraint system $\mathcal{S} = <\mathcal{C}, I>$ and the precision $\mathcal{T}$ such that $I \models \mathcal{T}$. The constraint system $\mathcal{S}^{\alpha} = <\mathcal{C}, I^{\alpha}>$ is said to be an *abstraction of $\mathcal{S}$ with precision $\mathcal{T}$* iff the domain of I^{α} is the set F^{α} and $I^{\alpha} \models \mathcal{T}$. It is crucial that the abstraction of constraint system preserves the precision theory $\mathcal{T}$. The example below shows the influence of $\mathcal{T}$ when constructing an abstract computation space.

Example 2.3 The abstraction of the $NQueens$ computation space with the precision of example 2.2 is defined by the following *finite* interpretation I^{α}:

- A set of the abstract constants is $F^\alpha = \{0, 1, 2\}$ (below we use "$*$" to denote an arbitrary constant from F^α). Then a possible interpretation of the B-predicates $I_B{}^\alpha$ is the following:

$$el(0) \quad l(*, 0, 1) \quad any(*) \quad greater\_than(*, *)$$
$$l(*, 1, 2) \quad zero(*) \quad sum(*, *, *)$$
$$l(*, 2, 2) \quad one(*) \quad not\_equal(*, *)$$

- The interpretation of the A-predicates is obtained by bottom-up execution of the program $NQueens_A$ using $I_B{}^\alpha$ as an initial set of facts:

$$init(*, *) \quad d(*, 1, 0) \quad p(0, 0) \quad s(*)$$
$$d(*, 2, 1) \quad p(1, 1) \quad nd(*, *, *)$$
$$d(*, 2, 2) \quad p(2, 2) \quad test(*, *, *)$$

The interpretation I^α is a model for the theory $\mathcal{T}$ (see example 2.2). The interpretation I^α implies the following intuition: 0 represents terms which are either empty lists or different from lists; 1 represents lists having exactly one element (it can be any term); 2 represents lists having at least two elements. If the set of extra properties is empty, then the simplest model for the theory is $p(\overline{*})$ for all predicates symbols p. The latter corresponds to "total" abstraction (all information concerning unification is lost). □

Proposition 2.4 *Given a concrete computation space* $\mathcal{S} = <\mathcal{C}, I>$ *with consistent precision theory* $\mathcal{T}$ *and its abstraction* $\mathcal{S}^\alpha = <\mathcal{C}, I^\alpha>$ *wrt* $\mathcal{T}$*, for any constraint* $c \in \mathcal{C}$ *holds:* $I \models c$ *implies* $I^\alpha \models c$. □

The above proposition is not true for arbitrary formulas of $\mathcal{L}_P$. For example, in the context of examples 2.2 and 2.3 we have that $I \models d(U, L, L) \to false$ but $I^\alpha \not\models d(U, L, L) \to false$. However, the most important consequence of the proposition is that any abstraction preserves the satisfiability of constraints. The latter is sufficient to have safe abstract constraint computations (see section 4).

The discussion above can be summarised into the Abstract Space Generation algorithm as follows. Given a program P, construct its flat stratified form P_{AB}; construct the precision theory $\mathcal{T}$ using some set of extra properties Ψ (derived from the computation rule, see def.4.2 in section 4) and generate a finite model I^α for $\mathcal{T}$, obtaining an abstract computation space $\mathcal{S}^\alpha = <\mathcal{C}, I^\alpha>$. It is crucial to generate a finite interpretation I^α with minimal number of abstract constants F^α for a given set of extra properties Ψ. If Ψ can contain arbitrary formulas, then, in general, a finite interpretation does not exist. The reason is that $\mathcal{T}$ includes representations of all unifiable sets of terms which, if they are combined with non-empty set Ψ, can produce too precise description of the original infinite model.

However, the current paper aims only at providing analysis of the behaviour of a program under a rather restricted class of computation rules (see section 3). Therefore, we use a simple set of extra properties Ψ — a finite set of flat "integrity constraints" of the form $\mathbf{c} \to \mathbf{false}$, where the constraint $\mathbf{c} \in \mathcal{C}$ is only composed from the B-atoms. This restriction simplifies the problem: the set Ψ can only be used to express some properties of unifiable sets of terms which are implied by $\mathcal{M}(P_\mathbf{B})$, i.e. $\mathcal{M}(P_\mathbf{B}) \models \Psi$. Therefore, the problem is reduced to the generation of a finite interpretation $I_\mathbf{B}{}^\alpha$ which is only a model for $\mathcal{T}_\mathbf{B} \cup \Psi$ ($\mathcal{T}_\mathbf{B}$ includes representation of all unifiable sets of terms). The finite "complete" interpretation $I^\alpha \models \mathcal{T}$, $\mathcal{T} = P_\mathbf{A} \cup \mathcal{T}_\mathbf{B} \cup \Psi$ can be obtained as a result of the bottom-up execution of the flat program $P_\mathbf{A}$ starting from the finite set of "facts" $I_\mathbf{B}{}^\alpha$.

The model generation algorithms similar of [4] can be applied to generate a finite model $I_\Psi{}^\alpha$ for a set of properties Ψ. The finite model having a minimal number of constants F^α can be generated. The model $I_\mathbf{B}{}^\alpha$ for $\mathcal{T}_\mathbf{B} \cup \Psi$ can be obtained from $I_\Psi{}^\alpha$ as follows. Recall that if $p \in \mathbf{B}$ then the corresponding predicate has the form $p(\overline{X}, Y)$, where the variables $\overline{X} = X_1, \cdots, X_n$, $n \geq 0$ correspond to the arguments of a term and Y to its functor. $\mathcal{T}_\mathbf{B}$ enforces $\exists_{V - \{X_i\}} \mathbf{p}(\mathbf{X_1}, \cdots, \mathbf{X_n}, \mathbf{Y}) \equiv \mathbf{true}$ for all X_i. Thus, all missing abstract constants have to be added in a consistent way as possible values for each X_i. For example, in the context of examples 2.2 and 2.3 the model $I_\Psi{}^\alpha$ for predicate l is $\{l(*, 0, 1), l(*, 1, 2)\}$ and it should be transformed into $\{l(*, 0, 1), l(*, 1, 2), l(*, 2, 2)\}$, i.e. the missing abstract constant 2 has been added to the set of values of the second argument; and there exists only one consistent value 2 for the "functor" argument.

3   Computations Guided by a Computation Rule

A computation is performed wrt a computation space and it is a sequence of constraint goals starting from the initial goal. A computation step consists of resolving an atom of the current goal by a constraint clause of the program. The selection of the atom is controlled by the given computation rule.

A *constraint program* $P_\mathcal{C}$ over a computation space is a collection of definite clauses of the form $h(\bar{\mathbf{t}}_0) \leftarrow a_1(\bar{\mathbf{t}}_1), \cdots, a_n(\bar{\mathbf{t}}_n) \diamond \{\mathbf{c}\}$, $n \geq 0$, $\mathbf{c} \in \mathcal{C}$, where $\bar{t}_0, \bar{t}_1, \cdots, \bar{t}_n$ are vectors of terms and $h, a_1, \cdots, a_n$ are predicate symbols of corresponding arity.

Example 3.1 The $NQueens_C$ program below is one of the possible constrained forms of the $NQueens$ program.

c_0 : $solutions(N, Q) \leftarrow p(L, Q), s(Q) \diamond \{\mathbf{init(N, L)}\}.$
c_1 : $p([\,], [\,]) \leftarrow \diamond \{\mathbf{true}\}.$
c_2 : $p([X|Y], [U|V]) \leftarrow p(W, V) \diamond \{\mathbf{l(X, Y, L)} \wedge \mathbf{d(U, L, W)}\}.$
c_3 : $s([\,]) \leftarrow \diamond \{\mathbf{true}\}.$
c_4 : $s([U]) \leftarrow \diamond \{\mathbf{true}\}.$
c_5 : $s([X, U|V]) \leftarrow s([U|V]) \diamond \{\mathbf{one(I)} \wedge \mathbf{l(U, V, Q)} \wedge \mathbf{nd(X, I, Q)}\}.$

The $NQueens$ program (see examples 2.1 and 2.2) has been used to generate the computation space. The particular constraint form of the program is chosen to fit the problem. Below we show that the program above can be chosen as the result of an analysis of the computation rule of [1]. □

Constraint programs can contain terms. However, we use only flat constraint systems. So, we need a *flattening* operation: $\flat(\bar{t} = \bar{t}')$ denotes a flat constraint which is composed only from B-predicates and equivalent with the unification $\bar{t} = \bar{t}'$. This operation is always correct if the computation space is generated by the program itself (see section 2).

We only consider instantiation-based computation rules – an atom can be selected only if it is sufficiently instantiated:

Definition 3.2 *Instantiation-based Computation Rule*
An instantiation-based computation rule $\mathbf{R} = < r_1, \cdots, r_n >$ is a finite *ordered* sequence of *selectors* r_i having the form $< p(\overline{X}) \diamond \{c^P\} \Rightarrow Op > \in \mathbf{R}$ (*p*-selector), where $p \in \mathsf{A}$, $\overline{X}$ is a vector of distinct variables, $Op \in \{\mathrm{resolve}, \mathrm{refute}\}$ and the constraint c^P is only composed from B-predicates such that $free\_var(c^P) \subseteq \overline{X}$ and the formula $\exists_{\mathcal{V}}(p(\overline{X}) \wedge c^P)$ is satisfiable. For any $p \in \mathsf{A}$ there exists at least one *p*-selector. □

To have an automatic analysis of the program behaviour under the given computation rule we impose restrictions on the structure of the computation rule. Firstly, the computation rule $\mathbf{R}$ has to be *deterministic*, i.e. for any pair of *p*-selectors $r, r' \in \mathbf{R}$ of the forms $< p(\overline{X}) \diamond \{c\} \Rightarrow Op >$ and $< p(\overline{X}) \diamond \{c'\} \Rightarrow Op' >$ respectively, holds $c \wedge c' \to \mathbf{false}$. Secondly, the computation rule is assumed to be *complete*, i.e. for any A-predicate p holds: $p(\overline{X}) \trianglelefteq c_1^P \vee \cdots \vee c_k^P$, where $< p(\overline{X}) \diamond \{c_i^P\} \Rightarrow Op_i >$, $i = 1, \ldots, k$ are *all* *p*-selectors of $\mathbf{R}$. The completeness means that the collection of *p*-selectors is an approximation of a success set of the predicate p. It is "disjoint" due to the determinism. These restrictions ensure correctness of *atom selection* by an instantiation-based deterministic complete computation rule $\mathbf{R}$. A constraint atom $p(\bar{t}) \diamond \{c\}$, $p \in \mathsf{A}$, $c \in \mathcal{C}$ is said to be *acceptable* with the operation Op by the *p*-selector $r \in \mathbf{R}$ of the form $< p(\overline{X}) \diamond \{c^P\} \Rightarrow Op >$ if $\exists_{\mathcal{V}\_\overline{X}}(c \wedge \flat(\overline{X} = \bar{t}_s) \wedge p(\overline{X})) \trianglelefteq c^P$. The atom $p(\bar{t}) \diamond \{c\}$ is said to be *non-selectable* if there exist at least two different *p*-selectors $r_i, r_j \in \mathbf{R}$, $i \neq j$ such that the atoms $p(\bar{t}) \diamond \{c \wedge c_i^P\}$, $p(\bar{t}) \diamond \{c \wedge c_j^P\}$ are acceptable by the *p*-selectors $r_i, r_j \in \mathbf{R}$ respectively. The atom is *selectable* with the operation Op if it is acceptable with the operation Op by the *p*-selector $r \in \mathbf{R}$ and it cannot be classified as non-selectable.

Given a goal $G = \leftarrow A_1, \cdots, A_m \diamond \{c\}$, $m > 0$, a computation rule $\mathbf{R} = < r_1, \cdots, r_n >$ has to be applied *correctly* as follows. For each selector $r_i \in R$, $i = 1, \cdots, n$ construct the sequence S_i of atoms selectable by r_i (a sequence S_i is generated by parsing the atoms $A_1, \cdots, A_m$ from left to right). If $S_i = \emptyset$ for all $i = 1, \cdots, n$ report error; otherwise the first atom of the first non empty S_i is selected by the computation rule $\mathbf{R}$. The order of selectors defines priority between them. The correct application of the computation rule implies that *each* atom in the current goal is classified as selectable or non-selectable.

Example 3.3 The computation rule of [1] can be represented as follows:

1. r_- : $_- \lozenge \{ \mathbf{true} \}$ $\Longrightarrow$ refute

2. $r_{solutions}$: $solutions(Q) \lozenge \{ \mathbf{true} \}$ $\Longrightarrow$ resolve

3. r_{s_1} : $s(Q) \lozenge \{ \mathbf{el(Q)} \}$ $\Longrightarrow$ resolve

4. r_{s_2} : $s(Q) \lozenge \{ \exists_T (\mathbf{el(T)} \wedge \mathbf{l(_-, T, Q)}) \}$ $\Longrightarrow$ resolve

5. r_{s_3} : $s(Q) \lozenge \{ \exists_{T,T'} (\mathbf{l(_-, T', T)} \wedge \mathbf{l(_-, T, Q)}) \}$ $\Longrightarrow$ resolve

6. r_p : $p(V, W) \lozenge \{ \mathbf{true} \}$ $\Longrightarrow$ resolve

where "$_-$" denotes any atom not mentioned in the selectors 2-6 above. Notice that the computation rule is deterministic and complete wrt the computation space of example 2.2. The predicates which are not important for the coroutining between p and s atoms are always selected first and are refuted completely, i.e. they are moved to the constraint store of the current goal. Therefore, the $NQueens_C$ program (see example 3.1) can be considered as a "partial evaluation" of the "static" part (selector 1 above) of the computation rule because the predicates used to construct constraint stores of the clauses of $NQueens_C$ occur in the constraint store of a current goal. Thus, by taking the $NQueens_C$ program instead of the $NQueens$ program we concentrate on the "dynamic" part of the computation rule (the selectors 2-6 above) which is controlling the coroutining between $\{solutions, p, s\}$-atoms (they have to be resolved step by step). $\qquad \square$

In the sequel we follow the above example to simplify the presentation by considering a restricted notion of the computation, where an atom can be only selected with the operation **resolve** (following [9] one can include the selection of an atom with operation **refute**). Consider a program P_C over a computation space and a deterministic complete computation rule $\mathbf{R}$. A constraint computation of $P_C \cup G_0$ is a sequence of goals $G_0 \xrightarrow{c_1} G_1 \cdots \xrightarrow{c_n} G_n \cdots$, $c_1, \cdots, c_n \cdots \in P_C$ such that for any transition $G_i \xrightarrow{c_{i+1}} G_{i+1}$, $i \geq 0$, with a standardised apart clause c_{i+1} of the form $a(\bar{t}) \leftarrow Body \lozenge \{c\}$, hold:

- $G_i = \leftarrow A_1, \cdots, A_{k-1}, \underline{A_k}, A_{k+1}, \cdots, A_m \lozenge \{c_i\}$, $m > 0$, where A_k is an atom of the form $a(\bar{s})$, which is selected with operation **resolve** by the correct application of $\mathbf{R}$ to the goal G_i;
- $G_{i+1} = \leftarrow (A_1, \cdots, A_{k-1}, Body, A_{k+1}, \cdots, A_m)\theta \lozenge \{c_{i+1}\}$, where $c_{i+1} = c_i \wedge \flat(\bar{s} = \bar{t}) \wedge c$ is a satisfiable constraint and $\theta = mgu(\bar{s} = \bar{t})$

The constraint c_{i+1} associated to the goal G_{i+1} is called the *accumulated* constraint of the goal G_{i+1}. The constraint $\flat(\bar{s}_s = \bar{t}_0) \wedge c$ is called the *incremental* constraint of the goal G_{i+1}. A computation is *complete* if it is finite and if it cannot be continued in any way.

Example 3.4 The program $NQueens_C \cup \{ \leftarrow solutions(N, Q) \lozenge \{\mathbf{true}\}\}$ has the computation tree shown in fig.1. The constraints associated to the nodes of the tree are *incremental* constraints. The tree is constructed over the computation space of example 2.2 by applying the computation rule

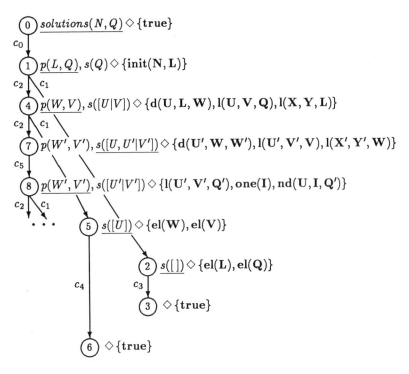

Figure 1 *Constraint Computation Tree for the $NQueens_C$ Program*

of example 3.3. To avoid unnecessary variables, we standardise clauses (if possible) in such a way that clause heads are exactly equal to the selected atoms. Also, in the constraint stores the symbol "$\wedge$" is replaced by ",".

The tree is error-free (this will be proved in a formal way in section 4 below): any atom occurring in the tree is selectable or non-selectable. If the error-condition is discovered then it is no longer possible to synchronise the coroutining of the atoms. The shape of the tree has the following property: any s-atom, which is not selected at some goal (the p-atoms are always selectable), reappears later as selectable by *different* selectors. For example, the s-atom of G_4 reappears in G_5 and G_7 where it is more instantiated and, therefore, it is selected by r_{s_2} and r_{s_3} respectively.   □

4   Proving Correctness of Computation Rules

This section introduces a static analysis algorithm which can prove that a given program has an error-free computation tree under the given computation rule. The analysis derives a graph which is subsequently used for the compiling control transformation of the original program (see section 5).

The main idea is to perform constraint *tabled* computations over an abstract computation space. The idea of tabulation is very simple: collect in a table all the call patterns of the goals found so far in the computation tree, and whenever a new goal G is produced, check whether the table already contains a call pattern equivalent to the call pattern of G and, in this case, use for resolving G the solutions of this already found call pattern (introduced in [14] for OLD resolution). The definition below formulates the basic notions, which are adaptations of those in [5].

Definition 4.1 *Call Pattern and Equivalence of Call Patterns*
Given a constraint goal $G = \leftarrow Atoms \diamond \{\mathbf{c}\}$, the call pattern of the goal G, noted $call_G$, is defined as $call_G = Atoms \diamond \{\exists_{V-var(Atoms)}\mathbf{c}\}$, where $\mathbf{c} \in \mathcal{C}$ is the accumulated constraint of the goal G. The call patterns $call_G = Atoms \diamond \{\exists_{V-var(Atoms)}\mathbf{c}\}$, $call_{G'} = Atoms' \diamond \{\exists_{V-var(Atoms')}\mathbf{c}'\}$ are said to be equivalent (or variants of each other), noted $call_G \simeq call_{G'}$ iff
$$\overline{var}(Atoms) = \overline{var}(Atoms') \wedge \exists_{V-var(Atoms)}\mathbf{c}$$
$$\equiv \overline{var}(Atoms) = \overline{var}(Atoms') \wedge \exists_{V-var(Atoms')}\mathbf{c}'$$
and the equation $\overline{var}(Atoms) = \overline{var}(Atoms')$ is a bijection, which renames each atom $A \in Atoms$ into the atom $A' \in Atoms'$ and vice versa. □

We use a restricted variant of tabulation — the table only has entries of the form $< call_G, \{call_G\} >$, i.e. not more than one answer is allowed for each entry of the table. The answers are generalised by taking their upper bound which is the call pattern itself. The latter is always a safe approximation (see [3] although in SLD setting). Therefore, in order to apply tabulation, the abstract tabled interpreter only checks that the call pattern of the current goal has already been recorded in the table and that it has an answer, and, in this case, the goal is refuted completely.

Our version of tabled constraint computations is a "constraint" generalisation of Extended OLDT resolution [2]. The extension is that tabulation is applied to a collection of atoms (blocks) rather than to the leftmost atom of the current goal as in [14, 5]. Also, our treatment of the constraint system and its abstraction satisfies the generic conditions of [8, 5] (follows from proposition 2.4). Therefore, our tabulation technique allows us to construct a safe *finite* approximation of the call patterns of a normal concrete computation. Indeed, given a constraint logic program $P_{\mathcal{C}} \cup \{G_0\}$ over the computation space $\mathcal{S}$, any abstract tabled computation for $P_{\mathcal{C}} \cup \{G_0\}$ with $\mathbf{R}$ over $\mathcal{S}^\alpha$ is finite if the maximal depth of the terms and the number of atoms occurring in the goals of the abstract computation are bounded from above. However, a safe approximation of the *behaviour* of a program under a computation rule requires extra conditions.

Definition 4.2 *Precision Induced by Computation Rule*
The precision theory $\mathcal{T}$ consistent with computation space $\mathcal{S} = < \mathcal{C}, I >$ fits the deterministic complete computation rule $\mathbf{R}$ if $\mathcal{T}$ includes a set of extra properties Ψ, which implies the determinism and completeness of $\mathbf{R}$. □

Proposition 4.3 *Let $P_C \cup G_0$ be a program over the computation space S and $\mathbf{R}$ be a deterministic complete computation rule. Suppose that S^α is an abstraction of S with precision T satisfying def.4.2. Then the normal computation tree for $P_C \cup G_0$ with $\mathbf{R}$ over S is error-free (the computation rule is well-defined) if there exists a finite complete error-free computation graph (the abstract tabled computation tree) for $P_C \cup G_0$ with $\mathbf{R}$ over S^α.* □

Example 4.4 The upper portion of the computation tree shown in fig.1 is a finite complete computation graph over the abstract computation space of example 2.3. Indeed, the theory T of the computation space of example 2.2 satisfies def.4.2 and there exists only one pair of equivalent call patterns: $call_4 \simeq call_8$. Tabulation is applied correctly to *refute* the goal G_8 because there exists an answer for $call_4$ (the path $4 \to 5 \to 6$). The graph is *complete* because none of the nodes can be extended in any way (G_8 is assumed to be refuted completely by the answer from the table entry of $call_4$). According to proposition 4.3, the computation rule is well-defined. □

If abstract interpretation discovers the error-condition for some goal (all atoms are non-selectable wrt abstract space) then an extra analysis is required. If the error-condition also occurs in the concrete space, then the computation rule is not well-defined. Otherwise the abstract space is not precise enough to derive the conclusion concerning the correctness of the computation rule. Therefore, the constraints which are not satisfiable in the concrete space but satisfiable in the abstract space should be added to the parameter Ψ of the precision theory and the new more precise finite interpretation $I^{\alpha'}$ should be generated ($\Psi' = \Psi +$ new not satisfiable constraints). The tabled abstract computation under the given computation rule should be started from "scratch" using the interpretation $I^{\alpha'}$.

Thus, the analysis is sound. However, we cannot ensure that a proof can be generated for *any* well-defined computation rule.

5 Compiling Control Transformation

This section illustrates by an example the use of the control flow graph to derive the compiling control transformation which is performed for constraint clauses. The transformation is guided by the computation graph and includes three successive steps which are applied to the clauses of the original *constraint* (source) program.

First, the new definitions are derived from the call patterns of the computation states of *special* nodes of the abstract computation tree. The special nodes are: the root node and the nodes referred in the tabulation extensions occurring in the tree (the *lookup* pairs of nodes of the form $< Call, Lookup >$). In this way we avoid introducing the so-called *Eureka*-predicates of [12] — the new definitions are suggested as a result of the analysis of the behaviour of the source program under the given computation rule. *Second*, the bodies of the new definitions introduced by **step 1** are unfolded following the corresponding *maximal continuous* paths of the computation tree, which are maximal directed paths not passing a *lookup* node (more details can be found in [2] although in SLD setting). This step is rather close to the specialisation of [7]. The difference is that we unfold the new constraint definitions rather than the ordinary clauses of the source program. *Third*, all the constraint bodies of the clauses obtained by step 2 are be folded using the definitions introduced by step 1 (similar as in [2]).

The "skeleton" of the new constraint program $NQueens_C^{new}$ has the form:

$$c_{0\to 1\to 2\to 3} : \quad solutions(N,Q) \leftarrow \Diamond\{k_1\}.$$
$$c_{0\to 1\to 4} : \quad solutions(N,Q) \leftarrow \pi(U,V,W,\Delta)\Diamond\{k_2\}.$$
$$c_{4\to 5\to 6} : \quad \pi(U,V,W,\Delta) \leftarrow \Diamond\{k_3\}.$$
$$c_{4\to 7\to 8} : \quad \pi(U,V,W,\Delta) \leftarrow \pi(U',V',W',\Delta')\Diamond\{k_4\}.$$

where π is a predicate symbol of the new definition suggested by the *lookup* pair $< 4,8 >$, Δ and Δ' are special *meta variables* having bindings which are *sets of pairs* of the form $< \mathcal{U},\mathcal{I} >$ and the "coefficients" k_1, k_2, k_3 and k_4 denote constraints. The new definitions

$$\mathcal{D}_{<root>} : \quad solutions(N,Q) \leftarrow solutions(N,Q)\Diamond\{\mathbf{true}\}.$$
$$\mathcal{D}_{<4,8>} : \quad \pi(U,V,W,\Delta) \leftarrow p(W,V), s([U|V])\Diamond\{\eta(\mathbf{U},\mathbf{V},\boldsymbol{\Delta})\}.$$

are suggested by the root node and by lookup node pair $< 4,8 >$, respectively, where $\eta(\mathbf{U},\mathbf{V},\boldsymbol{\Delta})$ denotes the constraint

$$\exists_{\{\mathbf{Q}\}}(\,\mathbf{l}(\mathbf{U},\mathbf{V},\mathbf{Q})\bigwedge\nolimits_{<\mathcal{U},\mathcal{I}>\in\boldsymbol{\Delta}}(\exists_{\{\mathfrak{u},\mathcal{I}\}}\mathbf{nd}(\mathcal{U},\mathcal{I},\mathbf{Q})))$$

consisting of the *nd*-constraints, one for each pair $< \mathcal{U},\mathcal{I} >$ in Δ.

The calls $call_4$ and $call_8$ are proved to be variants of each other in the abstract space. Therefore, the problem is to find a *syntactical* generalisation of the calls in the concrete computation space. The form of the new definition $\mathcal{D}_{<4,8>}$ is the solution because the syntactical values of $call_4$ and $call_8$ can be obtained from $\eta(\mathbf{U},\mathbf{V},\boldsymbol{\Delta})$ by instantiating $\Delta = \emptyset$ and $\Delta = \{< U,I >|\ \mathbf{one}(\mathbf{I})\}$ respectively. The unfolding/folding of $\mathcal{D}_{<root>}$ and $\mathcal{D}_{<4,8>}$ produces the following values for the coefficients:

$$
\begin{array}{ll}
k_1 : & \exists_{\mathcal{V}-\{\mathbf{N},\mathbf{Q}\}}\mathbf{c_3} \\
k_2 : \mathbf{empty}(\boldsymbol{\Delta}) & \wedge \ \exists_{\mathcal{V}-\{\mathbf{N},\mathbf{Q},\mathbf{U},\mathbf{V},\mathbf{W}\}}\mathbf{c_4} \\
k_3 : \tau(\mathbf{U},\boldsymbol{\Delta}) & \wedge \ \exists_{\mathcal{V}-\{\mathbf{U},\mathbf{V},\mathbf{W}\}}(\mathbf{c_6}-\mathbf{c_4}) \\
k_4 : \tau(\mathbf{U},\boldsymbol{\Delta})\wedge\delta(\mathbf{U},\boldsymbol{\Delta},\boldsymbol{\Delta'}) & \wedge \ \exists_{\mathcal{V}-\{\mathbf{U},\mathbf{V},\mathbf{W},\mathbf{U'},\mathbf{V'},\mathbf{W'}\}}(\mathbf{c_7}-\mathbf{c_4})
\end{array}
$$

where $\tau(\mathbf{U},\boldsymbol{\Delta})$ denotes the constraint $\bigwedge_{<\mathcal{U},\mathcal{I}>\in\boldsymbol{\Delta}}(\exists_{\{\mathfrak{u},\mathcal{I}\}}\mathbf{test}(\mathcal{U},\mathcal{I},\mathbf{U}))$ and $\delta(\mathbf{U},\boldsymbol{\Delta},\boldsymbol{\Delta'})$ denotes the constraint defined as

$$\boldsymbol{\Delta'} = \{<\mathbf{U},\mathbf{I}>|\mathbf{one}(\mathbf{I})\} \cup \{<\mathcal{U},\mathcal{I'}> \mid <\mathcal{U},\mathcal{I}>\in \boldsymbol{\Delta}, \mathbf{one}(\mathbf{I}), \mathbf{sum}(\mathcal{I},\mathbf{I},\mathcal{I'})\}$$

Also, c_i, $i = 3,4,6,7$ are the accumulated constraints of the goals G_i, respectively (see fig.1) and $c_i - c_j$ denotes "syntactical" difference of the accumulated constraints. The operations above were obtained exploiting the following properties of the *concrete* constraint system:

$$\text{el}(\mathbf{V}) \wedge \qquad \text{l}(\mathbf{U}, \mathbf{V}, \mathbf{Q}) \wedge \text{nd}(\mathbf{X}, \mathbf{I}, \mathbf{Q}) \equiv \text{test}(\mathbf{X}, \mathbf{I}, \mathbf{U})$$
$$\text{l}(\mathbf{U}', \mathbf{Q}', \mathbf{V}) \wedge \text{l}(\mathbf{U}, \mathbf{V}, \mathbf{Q}) \wedge \text{nd}(\mathbf{X}, \mathbf{I}, \mathbf{Q}) \equiv \text{test}(\mathbf{X}, \mathbf{I}, \mathbf{U}) \wedge$$
$$\text{one}(\mathbf{K}) \wedge \text{sum}(\mathbf{I}, \mathbf{K}, \mathbf{J}) \wedge \text{nd}(\mathbf{X}, \mathbf{J}, \mathbf{Q}')$$

The new logic program $NQueens^{new}$ below is obtained by implementing Δ-variables as ordinary lists (one could use difference lists) and by replacing constraints by the corresponding predicates:

$c_{0 \to 1 \to 2 \to 3}$: $solutions(0, [\,])$.

$c_{0 \to 1 \to 4}$: $solutions(N, [U|V]) \leftarrow init(N, [X|Y]), delete(U, [X|Y], W),$
$$\pi(U, V, W, [\,]).$$

$c_{4 \to 5 \to 6}$: $\pi(U, [\,], [\,], \Delta) \leftarrow \tau(U, \Delta)$.

$c_{4 \to 7 \to 8}$: $\pi(U, [U'|V'], [X'|Y'], \Delta) \leftarrow delete(U', [X'|Y'], W'),$
$$\hat{\tau}(U, \Delta, \Delta'), \pi(U', V', W', [<U, 1>|\Delta']).$$
$$\tau(U, [\,]).$$
$$\tau(U, [<\mathcal{U}, \mathcal{I}>|T]) \leftarrow test(\mathcal{U}, \mathcal{I}, U), \tau(U, T).$$
$$\hat{\tau}(U, [\,], [\,]).$$
$$\hat{\tau}(U, [<\mathcal{U}, \mathcal{I}>|T], [<\mathcal{U}, \mathcal{I}'>|T']) \leftarrow test(\mathcal{U}, \mathcal{I}, U),$$
$$\mathcal{I}' = \mathcal{I} + 1, \hat{\tau}(U, T, T').$$

where the predicate $\tau(U, \Delta)$ is an implementation of the constraint $\tau(\mathbf{U}, \mathbf{\Delta})$ and the predicate $\hat{\tau}(U, \Delta, \Delta')$ is a "joint" implementation of the constraints $\tau(\mathbf{U}, \mathbf{\Delta})$ and $\delta(\mathbf{U}, \mathbf{\Delta}, \mathbf{\Delta}')$. This is a solution of the compiling control problem of [1] which has not been known so far. It should be considered as a better solution than that [1]. Indeed, the code is more compact due to the more efficient and precise analysis of the computation tree (a much smaller upper portion of the tree has been considered and the *append* predicate is avoided due to the optimisation of the coefficients). The solution of [1] can be obtained from $NQueens^{new}$ by unfolding of the π-atoms, i.e. the solution of [1] contains some unnecessary code.

6   Conclusion

We have presented a framework which can be the basis of an automatic technique for performing a class of compiling control transformations. The example arranged around the N-Queens problem demonstrates that a lot of applications are feasible. The framework can be used to "explain" well-known transformation techniques of [13, 7, 6, 10, 12] due to the flexibility of the constraint fold/unfold algorithms combined with a "constraint" generalisation. However, we still have no complete automation for the transformation phase. The most interesting improvement can be obtained by elaborating the abstract domain construction technique. More complex formulas could be allowed to express the desired granularity of the abstract domain and, in this way, to use a much more general concept of computation rule.

Acknowledgements

We are grateful to Maurice Bruynooghe for discussions and careful reading of drafts. Also, we would like to express gratitude to Marc Denecker, Roberto Giacobazzi, Philippe Codognet and to the referees for their accurate remarks and suggestions.

References

[1] Bruynooghe,M., De Schreye,D., Krekels,B. Compiling Control, *Proc. 3rd Int. Symp. on Logic Programming*, 1986, 70-78, *see also: J. Logic Programming*, 1989, Vol.6, Nos.1-2, 135-162.

[2] Boulanger,D., Bruynooghe,M. Deriving Fold/Unfold Transformations of Logic Programs Using Extended OLDT-based Abstract Interpretation, *J. Symbolic Computation*, 1993, Vol.15, 495-521.

[3] Bruynooghe,M., Boulanger,D. Abstract Interpretation for (Constraint) Logic Programming, *in: Constraint Programming*, NATO Advanced Science Series, Computers and System Sci., Springer, 1993 (to appear).

[4] Bry,F., Decker,H., Mathey,R. A Uniform Approach to Constraint Satisfaction and Constraint Satisfiability in Deductive Databases, *Proc. Extended Database Technology 1988*, LNCS, Springer, 1988.

[5] Codognet,P., File, G. Computations, Abstractions and Constraints in Logic Programs, *Proc. 4th Int. Conf. Prog. Languages,*Oakland, 1992.

[6] Gallagher,J., Bruynooghe,M. The Derivation of an Algorithm for Program Specialisation, *New Generation Computing*, 1991, Vol.9, 305-333.

[7] Gallagher,J., Codish M., Shapiro E. Specialisation of Prolog and FCP Programs Using Abstract Interpretation, *New Generation Computing*, 1988, Vol.6, Nos.2-3, 159-186.

[8] Giacobazzi,R., Debray,S., Levi,G. Generalised Semantics and Abstract Interpretation for Constraint Logic Programs, *Proc. 5th Int. Conf. FGCS*, Tokyo, 1992.

[9] Jaffar,J., Maher, M. Constraint Logic Programming, *J. Logic Programming*, 1994 (to appear).

[10] Kawamura, T. Derivation of Efficient Logic Programs by Synthesising New Predicates, *Proc. Int. Symp. Logic Programming*, 1991, 611-625.

[11] Lloyd,L. Foundations of Logic Programming, Springer, Berlin, 1987.

[12] Proietti,M., Pettorossi,A. The Loop Absorption and the Generalisation Strategies for the Development of Logic Programs and Partial Deduction, *J. Logic Programming*, 1993, Vol.16, No.1-2, 123-161.

[13] Tamaki,H., Sato,T. Unfold/Fold Transformation of Logic Programs, *Proc. 2nd Int. Conf. Logic Programming*, 1984, 127-138.

[14] Tamaki,H., Sato,T. OLD Resolution with Tabulation, *Proc. 3rd Int. Conf. Logic Programming*, 1986, 84-98.

Completeness of Some Transformation Strategies for Avoiding Unnecessary Logical Variables

Maurizio Proietti
IASI-CNR
Viale Manzoni 30, 00185 Roma, Italy
proietti@iasi.rm.cnr.it

Alberto Pettorossi
Electronics Department
University of Rome II
00133 Roma, Italy
adp@iasi.rm.cnr.it

Abstract

An unnecessary variable of a logic clause is a variable which either occurs more than once in the body or it does not occur in the head. Unnecessary variables often cause inefficiency, because during program execution they generate redundant computations and create useless intermediate structures.

In order to eliminate the unnecessary variables from a given program, we may apply transformation strategies based on the application of the unfold/fold rules. Some of these strategies have been presented in a previous paper of ours [17].

Here we prove some completeness results about those strategies. Our notion of completeness can be formulated as follows: given a set R of transformation rules, we say that a strategy S is complete w.r.t. R iff for any given program P, if P can be transformed into an equivalent program Q without unnecessary variables by an arbitrary use of the rules in R, then P can be transformed into an equivalent program (possibly different from Q) without unnecessary variables by using the strategy S.

1 Introduction

A variable X of a clause C in a logic program is said to be *unnecessary* if at least one of the following conditions is true: 1) X occurs more than once in the body of C (in which case we say that X is a *shared* variable), 2) X does not occur in the head of C (in which case we say that X is an *existential* variable).

The multiplicity of occurrences of variables in the body of clauses and the values of the existential variables are usually not needed for describing the semantics of a logic program as a relation between queries and answers. In this sense shared and existential variables are called unnecessary.

Unnecessary variables are often used in logic programs for allowing a compositional style of programming. This style may be described as follows: a clause, say C, is introduced so that a given task, corresponding to the head of C, is decomposed into small and easy subtasks, corresponding to the atoms of the body of C, and then programs which solve these subtasks are constructed. The variables shared among the atoms of the body of C transfer the relevant information among the various subtasks.

Programs written using the compositional style of programming can easily be understood and proved correct w.r.t. their semantics. However, this style may produce inefficient programs, if the evaluator does not take advantage of the interactions among the subtasks.

Various transformation techniques have been proposed in the literature to improve programs written according to the compositional style. Among these techniques, we recall: *finite differencing* [14], *composition* or *deforestation strategy* [12, 22], *tupling strategy* [15], *promotion strategy* [2], *compiling control* [5], and *unnecessary variable elimination* [17]. Many of them are based on the *unfold/fold* rules introduced by Burstall and Darlington [6]. Unfolding and folding are elementary, semantics preserving transformations which can be combined together to obtain more complex transformations, called *strategies*, which improve efficiency.

Different sets of unfold/fold transformation rules have been introduced for the case of logic programming and they have been shown to preserve different semantics (see, for instance, [3, 13, 19, 20]). Here we consider the simple case of definite programs with the least Herbrand model semantics, and we use a slight variant of the transformation rules introduced by Tamaki and Sato, which can be shown to preserve that semantics.

Unfold/fold rules are not semantically complete, in the sense that one can find two programs which have the same semantics, and neither of them can be transformed into the other by using the unfold/fold rules only [23]. However, in order to study the power of some given transformation strategies, it is useful to introduce suitably weaker definitions of completeness. In particular, for the problem of eliminating unnecessary variables, we introduce the following notion.

DEFINITION 1. (*Complete strategies*) Given a set R of transformation rules, a strategy S is *complete* w.r.t. R iff for any given program P, if P can be transformed into an equivalent program, say Q, without unnecessary variables by an arbitrary use of the rules in R, then P can be transformed into an equivalent program (possibly different from Q) without unnecessary variables by using the strategy S.   ∎

In Section 2 we describe our set of transformation rules which are: unfolding, folding, definition, goal replacement, and clause deletion.

In Section 3 we consider a strategy for eliminating unnecessary variables, called Elimination Strategy, which is an enhancement of the one presented in [17], and we will prove its completeness w.r.t. the set of rules considered in Section 2.

In Section 4 we present a more deterministic version of the Elimination Strategy by introducing a more powerful variant of the clause deletion rule.

2 Preliminaries

We consider definite programs with the least Herbrand model semantics. We assume that variables of clauses can be renamed, so that two distinct clauses can always be assumed to share no variables, and all operations on sets of clauses, such as union and difference, are defined modulo renaming of variables.

We also assume that bodies of clauses are *multisets* of atoms and, when dealing with bodies of clauses, we will use the notions of inclusion, union, difference, etc. in the multiset sense. (In what follows we will present an example which motivates this choice.) Thus, the deletion of a duplicate atom in the body of a clause (which obviously preserves the least Herbrand model semantics) has to be performed by an application of a transformation rule (see the goal replacement rule below).

Given a term t, we denote by vars(t) the set of variables occurring in t. Similar notation will be used for variables occurring in atoms, goals, and clauses.

Given a clause C, we denote its head by hd(C) and its body by bd(C). Given any syntactic expression E, we denote by preds(E) the set of predicate symbols occurring in E. In particular, given the program P, preds(P) denotes the set of predicate symbols occurring in P.

2.1 The Transformation Rules

We now describe the set of rules [20] which we use for transforming programs. We assume that when the transformation rules are applied, two distinct clauses do *not* have variables in common.

Definition Rule. Let P be a program. By *definition* we derive from P a clause D of the form $newp(X_1,...,X_m) \leftarrow A_1,...,A_n$, such that: 1) newp does not occur in P, 2) $X_1,...,X_m$ are distinct variables occurring in $A_1,...,A_n$, and 3) preds(bd(D)) $\subseteq$ preds(P). We say that newp is the *predicate defined by* D.

Unfolding Rule. Let C and D be two clauses and A be an atom in bd(C) unifiable with hd(D), with most general unifier θ. By *unfolding* C *w.r.t.* A *using* D we derive the clause $(hd(C) \leftarrow (bd(C) - \{A\}) \cup bd(D))\theta$.

Folding Rule. Let C and D be two clauses and let B be a multiset of atoms contained in bd(C). Suppose that there exists a substitution θ for the variables of bd(D) such that B = bd(D)θ, and consider the substitutions η and v which are the restrictions of θ to the existential and non-existential variables of bd(D), respectively. Suppose also that η is a variable renaming whose image does not share any variable with either hd(C), or bd(C) – B, or the image of v. By *folding* C *w.r.t.* B *using* D we derive a clause hd(C) $\leftarrow$ (bd(C) – B) $\cup$ hd(D)θ.

Goal Replacement Rule. We assume that we are given a finite set L = $\{G_i \Rightarrow H_i \mid i = 1,...,n\}$ of ordered pairs, called *replacement laws*, of (finite) multisets of atoms. We assume that variables of replacement laws can be renamed. Thus, any replacement law can be assumed to share no variables with any other replacement law or program clause.

Let C be a clause, B a multiset of atoms contained in bd(C), G $\Rightarrow$ H a replacement law in L, and θ a substitution for the variables of G such that B = Gθ. Let us consider the substitutions η and v which are the restrictions of θ to the variables of G in occurring in H and not-occurring in H, respectively. Suppose that η is a variable renaming whose image does not share any variable with either hd(C), or bd(C) – B, or the image of v. By *replacement* of B in C using G $\Rightarrow$ H we derive the clause hd(C) $\leftarrow$ (bd(C) – B) $\cup$ Hθ.

Notice that we use G $\Rightarrow$ H for replacing Gθ by Hθ, and not viceversa. Notice also that the folding rule can be viewed as an instance of the goal replacement rule.

We say that a multiset of atoms is *failing* in a program P iff it contains an atom which is not unifiable with the head of any clause in P.

Clause Deletion Rule. Let P be a program and C a clause in P. If bd(C) is failing in

P, then by *clause deletion* from C we derive the *true clause* **T**.

The clause **T** can be deleted from any program P because for any program P we have that P ∧ **T** is semantically equivalent to P.

We would like now to motivate our choice of considering bodies of clauses as multisets of atoms and not simply sets of atoms. The following two derivations show that unfolding and folding steps cannot be interchanged if bodies of clauses are sets of atoms, and the interchange of those steps is useful for proving Lemma 6 below. Consider the clauses:

     1. h ← a, b   2. n ← a   3. b ← a

If we first fold clause 1 using clause 2 we get the clause h ← n, b. If we then unfold this clause using clause 3 we get h ← n, a. On the other hand, if we first unfold clause 1 using clause 3 we get h ← a. If we then fold this clause using clause 2 we get h ← n, which is different from h ← n, b.

2.2 The Transformation Process

In order to preserve the semantics of our programs, the above transformation rules should be applied according to some metarules. For the description of those metarules and the transformation strategies of the next section, we represent the transformation process as a *set of trees of clauses*, called *transformation forest*, where a clause D is son of a clause C if D can be derived from C by applying a transformation rule.

Suppose that we are given an initial program P and a set L of replacement laws such that preds(L) ⊆ preds(P).

A transformation forest TF for P and L is a set of directed trees whose nodes are labeled by clauses and whose arcs are labeled by transformation rules. By Roots(TF) we denote the sets of all clauses which label the roots of the trees in TF. By Leaves(TF) we denote the set of all clauses different from **T** which label the leaves of the trees in TF. By Defs(TF) we denote the set Roots(TF) − P of clauses which are introduced by Definition steps (see below).

A transformation forest TF is constructed from P and L in a non-deterministic way as follows. We start with the empty forest for which the set Defs is empty. Given a transformation forest E, either we stop or we modify E (and Defs(E)) according to one of the following metarules:

1) If C is a clause of P which does not label any root node of E, then we add to E a new tree with one node only, labeled by C.

2) (*Definition Step*) If a clause D can be derived by definition from P and the predicate defined by D does not occur in any root of the trees of E, then we add to E a new tree with one node only labeled by D. (As a consequence, clause D is added to Defs(E).)

3) (*Unfolding Step*) Let N be a node of a tree in E labeled by a clause C and let A be an atom in bd(C) which is unifiable with the head of at least one clause in P. If $\{U_1,...,U_k\}$ is the set of *all* clauses which can be derived by unfolding C w.r.t. A using clauses in P, then we construct the sons $N_1,...,N_k$ of N. For i=1,...,k, node N_i is labeled by U_i and the arc from N to N_i is labeled by 'unfolding'.

4) (*Folding Step*) Let N be a node of a tree T in E labeled by a clause C and let D be

a clause in Defs(E). Suppose that either the root of T belongs to P or on the path from the root of T to N there exists at least one arc labeled by 'unfolding'. If clause F can be derived by folding C using D, then we construct a son N_1 of N. Node N_1 is labeled by F and the arc from N to N_1 is labeled by 'folding'.

5) *(Goal Replacement Step)* Let N be a node of a tree in E labeled by a clause C. If by replacement of a goal in the body of C using a replacement law in L we derive a clause D, then we construct a son N_1 of N. Node N_1 is labeled by D and the arc from N to N_1 is labeled by 'goal replacement'.

6) *(Clause Deletion Step)* Let N be a node of a tree in E labeled by a clause C. If in P $\cup$ Defs(E) we have that bd(C) is failing, then we construct a son N_1 of N. Node N_1 is labeled by T, that is, the true clause, and the arc from N to N_1 is labeled by 'clause deletion'.

From the transformation forest TF for P and L constructed as described above, we derive a new program TransfP = (P − Roots(TF)) $\cup$ Leaves(TF). TF will also be called a *transformation forest from* P *to* TransfP.

One can show that the semantic equivalence of P and TransfP is guaranteed by the transformation rules we use, if we choose the set L of replacement laws which satisfy suitable conditions. Among these conditions, we have that the two sides of a replacement law should be equivalent goals w.r.t. the given semantics.

We do not discuss here the problem related to the choice of the set L, and we refer the reader to [20]. The main difference between our approach and the one in [20] is that for an unfolding step we always use the clauses of the initial program P, not those of the current one.

2.3 Eliminating Unnecessary Variables by Transformation: An Example

Let us consider the following program P which computes the length of a given list and checks that the elements of this list are all positive integers:

1. length_pos([], 0)
2. length_pos([A| B], C) ← nat(A), pred(A, D), length_pos(B, E), pred(C, E)
3. nat(0)
4. nat(s(A)) ← nat(A)
5. pred(s(0), 0)
6. pred(s(A), s(B)) ← pred(A, B)
7. eq(A, A)

and the following replacement law:

length_pos(A, B), pred(C, B) $\Rightarrow$ length_pos(A, B), eq(C, s(B)).

In P clause 2 contains the unnecessary (shared or existential) variables A, D, and E. A transformation forest from P to a program without unnecessary variables is depicted in Fig. 1. Obviously, many other transformation forests could have been generated from P because at each step of the construction of the forest many transformation rules are applicable.

The final program can be obtained from the initial one by replacing clause 2 by the clauses different from T which are the leaves of the transformation forest of Fig. 1. This final program does not contain unnecessary variables and it is made out of the following clauses:

> length_pos([], 0)
> length_pos([A| B], s(C)) ← new(A), length_pos(B, C)
> new(s(0)) ← nat(0)
> new(s(A)) ← new(A)

together with clauses 3, 4, 5, 6, and 7.

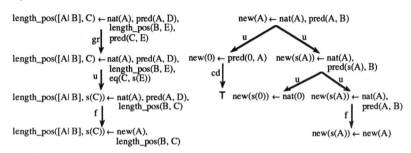

Figure 1. A transformation forest. The labels u, f, gr, and cd stand for unfolding, folding, goal replacement, and clause deletion, respectively.

3 A Complete Elimination Strategy

In this section we consider the set of transformation rules R = {unfolding, folding, definition, goal replacement, clause deletion} and we introduce a strategy for eliminating unnecessary variables using the rules in R. We then prove the completeness of this strategy w.r.t. R. Throughout the section we denote by Prog the initial program and we denote by L the set of replacement laws to be used when applying the goal replacement rule.

In our strategy we use the notion of *blocks of a clause* and an instance of the folding rule, called *block-folding* (see [17, 4] where similar notions were considered).

DEFINITION 2. (*Blocks of a clause*) Consider a multiset A of atoms. We define a binary relation ↓ over A as follows. Given two atoms A_1 and A_2 (not necessarily distinct) in A, we have that:
  $A_1 ↓ A_2$ iff vars(A_1) ∩ vars(A_2) ≠ ∅.
We denote by Part(A) the partition of A into *blocks* w.r.t. the equivalence relation which is the reflexive and transitive closure of the relation ↓ over A. ∎

Notice that each block in Part(A) is a *multiset* of atoms and Part(A) is a *multiset* of blocks.

Example 1. Let C be the clause:
  p(X) ← q(u(X)), q(u(X)), r(t(u(X),a),Y), s(a), s(a), q(Z).
Part(bd(C)) is the multiset of the following four blocks:
  {q(u(X)), q(u(X)), r(t(u(X),a),Y)}, {s(a)}, {s(a)}, and {q(Z)}. ∎

DEFINITION 3. (*Block-folding*) Let C and D be two clauses and let B be a multiset of atoms contained in bd(C). Suppose that there exists a substitution θ for the variables of bd(D) such that B = bd(D)θ and C can be folded using D. Suppose also that:

1) B is the (multiset) union of one or more blocks in Part(bd(C)),
2) Xθ is an existential variable of C iff X is an existential variable of D, and
3) any variable occurs at most once in the multiset of terms which are the image of θ.
We say that the folding step of C w.r.t. B using D is a *block-folding* step of C w.r.t. B using D. We also say that clause D is a *block-generalization* of C w.r.t. B. ∎

An arc of a transformation forest corresponding to a block-folding step will be labeled by 'block-folding', instead of 'folding'.

Notice that: i) by the metarule for folding steps, a clause which is a block-generalization must have been introduced by a definition step, and ii) there exists a finite number of block-generalizations of a given clause C w.r.t. a (multiset) union B of blocks of C. Each of these block-generalizations is a clause D such that bd(D) is obtained by generalizing B with the following constraints:
– each generalization is performed by using a fresh variable,
– terms with occurrences of existential variables cannot be generalized,
– terms without unnecessary variables may be generalized, and
– all occurrences $t_1, ..., t_n$ in B of a single term t may be generalized to the *same variable* if vars(t) is made out of shared (non-existential) variables of B and no variable of vars(t) occurs in B outside the occurrences $t_1, ..., t_n$.
The arguments of the predicate of hd(D) are the following distinct variables: i) the variables introduced by generalization, and ii) the non-existential variables of B which occur in terms which have not been generalized.

Example 2. Let us consider again clause C of Example 1. The following clause D:

new1(U,A) ← q(U), q(U), r(t(U,A),Y)

is a block-generalization of C w.r.t. {q(u(X)), q(u(X)), r(t(u(X),a),Y)}. ∎

LEMMA 4. Suppose that we have derived a clause F by performing a block-folding step on a clause C w.r.t. a multiset B of atoms using a clause D. Let θ be the substitution such that B = bd(D)θ. In this block-folding step, B has been replaced by hd(D)θ, and in F the atom hd(D)θ does not have unnecessary variables.
PROOF. Immediate consequence of Definition 3. ∎

Thus, from any clause we can derive a new clause without unnecessary variables by performing definition and block-folding steps only (see the Elimination Strategy below).

Example 3. The unnecessary variables of clause C of Example 1 can be eliminated by using the definition rule and introducing the following block-generalizations of C w.r.t. {q(u(X)), q(u(X)), r(t(u(X),a),Y)} and {q(Z)}, respectively:

new1(U,A) ← q(U), q(U), r(t(U,A),Y)
new2 ← q(Z).

Indeed, by block-folding we get: p(X) ← new1(u(X),a), s(a), s(a), new2. ∎

The following strategy eliminates (if it terminates) all unnecessary variables of the given program Prog.

THE ELIMINATION STRATEGY
Input. A program Prog and a set L of replacement laws.
Output. A program TransfProg with the same least Herbrand model of Prog such that no unnecessary variable occurs in TransfProg.

UVclauses := {C | C is a clause in Prog with unnecessary variables};
Defs := ∅;
TransfProg := Prog − UVclauses;
while there exists a clause C ∈ UVclauses *do*

    (*Goal Replacement*) Derive a clause D from C by zero or more applications of the goal replacement rule using replacement laws in L.

    if D does not contain unnecessary variables *then* add D to TransfProg *else*

    if bd(D) is failing in Prog

    then (*Clause Deletion*) do not add D to TransfProg

    else (*Definition*) Let bd(D) be of the form $M_1 \cup \ldots \cup M_n \cup \ldots$ with $n \geq 1$, where
        $M_1, \ldots, M_n$ are multisets of atoms such that:
        − each M_i is the multiset union of one or more blocks of bd(D),
        − each unnecessary variable of D occurs in (precisely) one M_i, and
        − each M_i contains at least one unnecessary variable of D.
        For i=1,…,n, let us consider a clause $NewM_i$ such that:
        − hd($NewM_i$) has a fresh predicate symbol, and
        − $NewM_i$ is a block-generalization of D w.r.t. M_i.
        For i=1,…,n add the clause $NewM_i$ to Defs, unless in Defs there exists already a block-generalization of D w.r.t. M_i.

        (*Block-folding*) Perform n block-folding steps on clause D w.r.t. the multisets $M_1, \ldots, M_n$ of atoms, using clauses in Defs which are block-generalizations of D w.r.t. $M_1, \ldots, M_n$, respectively. Add to TransfProg the resulting clause.

        (*Unfolding*) For i=1…,n, select an atom A_i in bd($NewM_i$) and add to UVclauses all clauses which can be derived by unfolding $NewM_i$ w.r.t. A_i using clauses of Prog.

    UVclauses := UVclauses − {C}. ■

The Elimination Strategy is a nondeterministic procedure because it leaves undetermined the particular choices of the replacement laws, the block-generalizations, and the unfolding steps. We will not address here the problem of controlling this nondeterminism for which one can apply the techniques presented in [18].

Every execution of the Elimination Strategy can be viewed as the construction of a transformation forest according to the metarules of Section 2.2. Let us consider one such forest, say TF. It can be shown that: 1) Roots(TF) is a set of clauses with unnecessary variables, 2) for every path in a tree of TF from the root to a leaf the corresponding sequence of labels is a regular expression of the form:

    unfolding (goal replacement)* (clause deletion + block-folding*)

if the root of the path is a clause in Defs(TF), and

    (goal replacement)* (clause deletion + block-folding*)

if the root of the path is a clause in Prog.

An application of the Elimination Strategy to the program of Section 2.3 generates the transformation forest depicted in Fig. 2 below. The final program has no unnecessary variables and can be obtained from the initial program P by replacing clause 2 in P by the clauses different from T which are the leaves of the transformation forest of Fig. 2. The final program is made out of the following clauses:

    length_pos([], 0)
    length_pos([A| B], C) ← new1(A), new2(B, C)
    new1(s(A)) ← new3(A)

new2(A, s(B)) ← length_pos(A, B)
new3(0) ← nat(0)
new3(A) ← new1(A)

together with clauses 3, 4, 5, 6, and 7. The program derived in Section 2.3 can be obtained (apart from the names of the predicates) from the above one by unfolding the predicates new2 and new3.

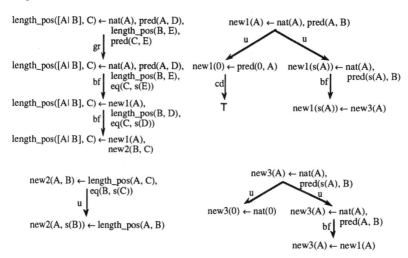

Figure 2. An execution of the Elimination Strategy. bf stands for block-folding.

THEOREM 5. (*Partial Correctness*) The Elimination Strategy is *partially correct*, in the sense that, for any program Prog and set L of replacement laws, if the Elimination Strategy terminates then the derived program TransfProg has the same least Herbrand model of Prog and TransfProg does not contain unnecessary variables.
PROOF. By the correctness of the transformation rules, we have that TransfProg is equivalent to Prog. Indeed, when a transformation forest is constructed using the Elimination Strategy all conditions indicated in the metarules 1,..., 6 of Section 2.2 are true. In particular, the applicability condition for the unfolding rule (see metarule 3) is true because at least one atom in the body of the clause to be unfolded is unifiable with the head of a clause in Prog. (Indeed, only a clause with non-failing body can be considered for unfolding.) The applicability condition for the folding rule (see metarule 4) follows from the fact that each clause which is the result of a folding step, is either a descendant of a clause of Prog or it is a descendant of a clause which is the result of an unfolding step.

The absence of unnecessary variables in the clauses of TransfProg follows from the fact that every clause added to TransfProg during the Elimination Strategy does not contain unnecessary variables. In particular, by Lemma 4 the clause resulting after each application of the n block-folding steps in the Block-folding phase, does not contain unnecessary variables, because:
i) each unnecessary variable occurs in an M_i for some i=1,...,n, and
ii) we perform a block-folding step w.r.t. M_i for i=1,...,n. ∎

The halting problem of the Elimination Strategy is partially solvable and it is not solvable (see [17] for a similar result).

Given a transformation forest we say that a step, say S2, *follows* another step, say S1, iff the node labeled by the clause where S2 is applied is a descendant of the node labeled by the clause where S1 is applied.

In order to show the completeness of the Elimination Strategy we need the following lemma.

LEMMA 6. Suppose that there exists a finite transformation forest from Prog to a program without unnecessary variables. Then there exists a finite transformation forest from Prog to a program without unnecessary variables where: 1) no unfolding, or goal replacement, or clause deletion step follows a folding step, 2) no unfolding step follows a goal replacement or unfolding step, and 3) each folding step is a block-folding step.

PROOF. Omitted due to lack of space. It is based on the possibility of suitably re-arranging the various steps in a transformation forest. ∎

We are now in the position of presenting the following completeness result.

THEOREM 7. (*Completeness of the Elimination Strategy*) The Elimination Strategy is complete w.r.t. the set of rules {unfolding, folding, definition, goal replacement, clause deletion}.

PROOF. By the Partial Correctness Theorem, it is enough to prove that if there exists a finite transformation forest TF from Prog to a program without unnecessary variables, then there exists a terminating execution of the Elimination Strategy.

By Lemma 6 we may assume that in TF: 1) no unfolding, or goal replacement, or clause deletion step follows a folding step, 2) no unfolding step follows a goal replacement or unfolding step, and 3) each folding step is a block-folding step.

Without loss of generality we may also assume that each root-clause in TF contains at least one unnecessary variable. Moreover, we have that in any transformation forest no step follows a clause deletion step.

From these facts we have that for every path in a tree of TF from the root to a leaf the corresponding sequence of labels is a regular expression of the form:

unfolding^{0,1} (goal replacement)* (clause deletion + block-folding*).

In particular, we have that the sequence of labels is of the form:

unfolding (goal replacement)* (clause deletion + block-folding*)   (†)

if the root of the path is a clause in Defs(TF), and

(goal replacement)* (clause deletion + block-folding*)   (††)

if the root of the path is a clause in Prog. Indeed, if the root is a clause in Prog, we can transform every tree T into the trees T1 and T2 as shown in Fig. 3.

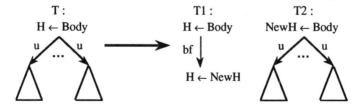

Figure 3. Avoiding an initial unfolding step when the root-clause is in Prog.

We will now prove that there exists a terminating execution of the Elimination

Strategy by showing that any finite transformation forest whose paths can be described by regular expressions of the forms (†) or (††) can be mimicked by the Elimination Strategy as we now describe.

(Case 1) Let C be a clause of Prog which is a root-clause in TF. While constructing TF, we perform on C the transformation steps indicated by (††), that is, zero or more goal replacement steps, followed by either a clause deletion step or a sequence of block-folding steps using clauses which occur in Defs(TF).

Initially, C belongs to UVclauses, thus the same goal replacement steps occurring in TF can be performed using the Elimination Strategy. Similarly, if the subsequent transformation in TF is a clause deletion step, the Elimination Strategy can perform that step.

Let us now consider the case where in TF the goal replacement steps are followed by a sequence of block-folding steps. Let D be the clause to which that sequence is applied. Each unnecessary variable of bd(D) occurs in the instance of the body of at least one clause used for folding, because otherwise the clause on the leaf of the path corresponding to the sequence of block-folding steps would contain an unnecessary variable.

Let us consider the following execution of the Elimination Strategy. Suppose that in TF we perform a block-folding step on D w.r.t. a multiset M of atoms using a clause NewM. The Elimination Strategy is now able to perform this same step unless: i) M does not contain any unnecessary variable, or ii) a block-generalization of D w.r.t. M already occurs in Defs.

In case i) the Elimination Strategy does not introduce any new definition and does not perform any block-folding step. Obviously, this does not introduce non-termination and does not affect subsequent folding steps.

In case ii) in order to perform that folding step the Elimination Strategy uses a clause already existing in Defs and by doing so it eliminates the unnecessary variables which were eliminated by the folding performed in TF. As in case i), the fact that no new clause is introduced in Defs affects neither termination nor subsequent folding steps.

(Case 2) Let us consider the case where C is a root of TF which belongs to Defs(TF) and C has been introduced by a previous step during the Elimination Strategy. The sequence of transformation steps which are applied to C is of the form indicated by (†). Thus, C is first unfolded and then each resulting clause is transformed by performing a sequence of steps of the form (††). In this case the Elimination Strategy performs the same unfolding step and it continues the mimicking process as described in Case 1.

Notice that the Elimination Strategy while mimicking a given transformation forest, may ignore some transformation steps which are performed on clauses without unnecessary variables. ■

4   An Improved Strategy Using Semantic Clause Deletion

In this section we introduce a more specific definition step which allows us to significantly cut down the amount of nondeterminism in the execution of the Elimination Strategy.

When applying the definition rule in the strategy described in Section 3, we have to make the nondeterministic choice of a *multiset* of atoms which is the union of one or more blocks and constitutes the body of the new clauses to be introduced. This choice may lead to an exponential number of alternatives.

We would like to modify our Elimination Strategy so that each new clause is defined by restricting the choice to a multiset of atoms constituting exactly one block. By doing so, we will avoid an exponential number of possible new definitions. This saving motivates the introduction of the following *single-block* folding rule.

DEFINITION 8. (*Single-block Folding*) Suppose that F has been derived by block-folding a clause C w.r.t. a multiset B of atoms using a clause D. We say that F has been derived by *single-block folding* iff B ∈ Part(bd(C)). We also say that D is a *single-block generalization* of C w.r.t. B. ∎

Let us consider the strategy, which we call *Naive Single-block Elimination Strategy*, obtained by replacing the *Definition* phase of the Elimination Strategy by the following one:

(*Single-block Definition*) Let bd(D) be of the form $M_1 \cup \ldots \cup M_n \cup \ldots$ with $n \geq 1$, where $M_1, \ldots, M_n$ are *blocks* such that:
– each unnecessary variable of D occurs in (precisely) one M_i, and
– each M_i contains at least one unnecessary variable of D.
For i=1,…,n, let us consider a clause $NewM_i$ such that:
– $hd(NewM_i)$ has a fresh predicate symbol, and
– $NewM_i$ is a block-generalization of D w.r.t. M_i.
For i=1,…,n add the clause $NewM_i$ to Defs, unless in Defs there exists already a block-generalization of D w.r.t. M_i.

As a consequence, in the Naive Single-block Elimination Strategy every folding step is a single-block folding step. Unfortunately, the Naive Single-block Elimination Strategy is *not* complete, as the following example shows.

Example 4. Let us consider the following program:

C_0:   p ← q, r(X)
        q ← fail
        r(X) ← r(f(X))

together with the empty set of replacement laws. We can obtain a program without unnecessary variables by unfolding C_0 w.r.t. q and then by applying the clause deletion rule. On the other hand, the only possible execution of the Naive Single-block Elimination Strategy is the following one.
We start off with UVclauses = $\{C_0\}$.
(*Goal Replacement*) We have nothing to do because no replacement law is available.
(*Single-block Definition*) Part(bd(C_0)) is $\{\{q\},\{r(X)\}\}$ and the only block with unnecessary variables is $\{r(X)\}$. Thus we introduce the clause:

N_1:   new1 ← r(X).

(*Single-block Folding*) By folding C_0 using N_1 we get the clause p ← q, new1, which is added to TransfProg and never considered again during the transformation process.
(*Unfolding*) By unfolding N_1 we get the clause:

C_1:   new1 ← r(f(X))

which replaces C_0 in UVclauses.

The second iteration of the while loop of the Naive Single-block Elimination Strategy is as follows. No goal replacement step is performed.

(*Single-block Definition*) In the body of C_1 the atom $r(f(X))$ has the unnecessary variable X. Thus we introduce the clause:

$$N_2: \quad new2 \leftarrow r(f(X))$$

Notice that N_1 is not a block-generalization of C_1 w.r.t. the block $\{r(f(X))\}$, because C_1 cannot be folded using N_1.

(*Single-block Folding*) By folding C_1 using N_2 we get the clause: $new1 \leftarrow new2$.

(*Unfolding*) By unfolding N_2 we get the clause: $new2 \leftarrow r(f(f(X)))$, which replaces C_1 in UVclauses.

At the k-th iteration we will define the new clause: $newk \leftarrow r(f^k(X))$ and the strategy will not terminate. ∎

As shown by the above example, the incompleteness of the Naive Single-block Elimination Strategy may be due to the fact that in the body of a clause C there is a block, say B, with unnecessary variables and there is an atom (not in B) which will become failing because of subsequent transformations. In this case the Naive Single-block Elimination Strategy tries to eliminate the unnecessary variables of C occurring in B. This task, which is not needed because clause C can be deleted, may be impossible to accomplish and thus the strategy does not terminate.

Example 4 suggests the introduction of the following more powerful rule for deleting clauses. This rule will allows us to achieve completeness.

(*Semantic Clause Deletion Rule*) Let P be a program and C be a clause in P. We say that bd(C) is *false* in the least Herbrand model of P iff for each ground instance G of bd(C) there exists an atom in G which does not belong to the least Herbrand model of P. If bd(C) is false in the least Herbrand model of P then by *semantic clause deletion* from C we derive the true clause **T**.

For the construction of a transformation forest, instead of the Clause Deletion Step metarule of Section 2.2, we will apply the following metarule.

(*Semantic Clause Deletion Step*) Let N be a node of a transformation forest E. Let N be labeled by a clause C. If bd(C) is false in the least Herbrand model of P $\cup$ Defs(E), then we construct a son N_1 of N. Node N_1 is labeled by **T** and the arc from N to N_1 is labeled by 'semantic clause deletion'.

Let us now consider a new transformation strategy, called *Single-block Elimination Strategy*, which is obtained from the Elimination Strategy of Section 3 by: 1) replacing the Definition phase of the Elimination Procedure by the above mentioned Single-block Definition phase, and 2) replacing the condition 'bd(D) is failing in Prog' before the Clause Deletion phase by 'bd(C) is false in the least Herbrand model of Prog $\cup$ Defs'.

Unfortunately, also the Single-block Elimination Strategy is *not* complete w.r.t. {unfolding, folding, definition, goal replacement, semantic clause deletion} as shown by the following example.

Example 5. Let us consider the following program:

C: $p \leftarrow q, r(X)$ $r(X) \leftarrow$

        $q \leftarrow$ $r(X) \leftarrow r(f(X))$.

Suppose that the set of replacement laws is the singleton $\{q, r(f(X)) \Rightarrow q, r(X)\}$. A transformation forest from the above program to a program without unnecessary variables is depicted in Fig. 4 below. On the other hand, the Single-block Elimination Strategy is unable to eliminate the unnecessary variables of the above program. Indeed, the following new clause, say N, is introduced during the Single-block Definition phase: new ← r(X).

It is impossible to apply the goal replacement rule to any clause derived from N and thus, the Single-block Elimination Strategy does not terminate. ∎

It can be shown that the Single-block Elimination Strategy is complete if we consider the following weaker version of the goal replacement rule.

(Block-Replacement Rule) Let C be a clause, B a multiset of atoms contained in bd(C), G ⇒ H a replacement law, and θ a substitution such that the conditions for the applicability of the goal replacement rule are satisfied (see Section 2.1). Suppose also that B (= Gθ) is contained in a block of bd(C). By *block-replacement* of B in C using G ⇒ H we derive a clause D such that: 1) hd(D) = hd(C) and 2) bd(D) = (bd(C) – B) ∪ Hθ.

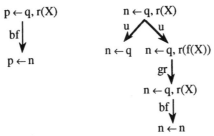

Figure 4. A transformation forest for eliminating
the unnecessary variable X in p ← q, r(X)

Example 6. Let us consider the following clause:
   C: remove(X,L,R) ← append(B,[X],M), append(M,A,L), append(B,A,R)
and the following replacement law, expressing the associativity of append:
   append(T, U, V), append(V, W, Y) ⇒ append(T, Z, Y), append(U, W, Z).
The replacement of append(B,[X],M), append(M,A,L) in C using the above law is a block-replacement, because {append(B,[X],M), append(M,A,L)} is contained in the unique block constituting bd(C). ∎

We have the following result.

THEOREM 9. *(Completeness of the Single-block Elimination Strategy)* The Single-block Elimination Strategy is complete w.r.t. the set of rules {unfolding, folding, definition, block-replacement, semantic clause deletion}. ∎

The proof of Theorem 9 is analogous to the one of Theorem 7.

Notice that the applicability condition for the semantic clause deletion rule is not decidable (not even semidecidable, in general). This means that the Single-block Elimination Strategy cannot be implemented in practice.

In order to overcome this difficulty one may pursue two alternative approaches. On one hand one may apply the strategy to a proper subclass of programs where the condition is decidable (as in the case of programs with no function symbols, apart from constants). On the other hand, one may consider a partially correct algorithm (which sometimes may fail to terminate) for checking the above mentioned applicability condition. By following the latter approach, one looses completeness, but a considerable power may still be retained depending on the cleverness of the algorithm itself.

Conclusions

We have presented two strategies for transforming logic programs and eliminating their unnecessary variables, and we have shown their completeness w.r.t. some given sets of transformation rules.

We have considered definite programs with the least Herbrand model semantics. However, since slight variants of the transformation rules we have adopted here, have also been proved to preserve other semantics of logic programs (see [16] for a survey), our completeness results can easily be extended to the case where one considers those semantics.

Although we have not proved any formal result which relates the efficiency of the initial program to that of the transformed one, our experience shows that by eliminating unnecessary variables, many redundant computations can be avoided, and the program performances are often improved. The improvement which can be realized depends also on the set of replacement laws one considers.

Completeness results have already been presented in the literature [7, 17, 22], but they refer to particular classes of programs for which the proposed strategies are always terminating. Our strategies do apply to all programs and they are not guaranteed to terminate only when no transformation exists which eliminates all unnecessary variables (using the given rules).

The interest of the results presented here also derives from the fact that many transformation strategies described in the literature may be rephrased in terms of the strategies for eliminating unnecessary variables. In particular, this is the case for the compiling control technique [5], the techniques for getting tail-recursive programs [1,8], and those for improving the recursive structure of the programs [9].

The elimination of unnecessary variables may also be applied as a useful transformation method for producing efficient object code. Examples of this use are: i) the Bin-Prolog compiler [21] with the continuation passing style, and ii) the compilers supporting AND-parallelism [10].

Bin-Prolog compiles Prolog programs by first transforming them into programs with at most one call in the body of every clause, and then using a simplified set of WAM instructions. In [11] it is shown that the Bin-Prolog compiler produces very efficient code if the programs derived during the initial phase of compilation do not contain unnecessary variables.

The AND-parallel execution of logic programs is particularly simple when at runtime no two calls share unbound variables. The strength of our transformation strategies for parallel programs derives from the fact that the evaluation of a query without shared variables produces goals without shared variables if we use a program without shared variables.

Acknowledgements

This work has been partially supported by "Progetto Finalizzato Sistemi Informatici e Calcolo Parallelo" of CNR under grant n. 89.00026.69, and by Esprit Project, Computational Logic (Compulog II).

Our gratitude goes to our colleagues of the Compulog II project for helpful comments and discussions.

References

[1]   N. Azibi, "TREQUASI: Un système pour la transformation automatique de programmes PROLOG récursifs en quasi-itératifs", PhD thesis, Université de Paris-Sud, Centre D'Orsay, France, 1987.

[2]   R.S. Bird, "The Promotion and Accumulation Strategies in Transformational Programming", ACM TOPLAS, vol. 6, no. 4, pp. 487-504, October 1984.

[3]   A. Bossi and N. Cocco, "Basic Transformation Operations which Preserve Computed Answer Substitutions of Logic Programs" J. Logic Programming, vol 16, pp. 47-87, 1993.

[4]   D. Boulanger and M. Bruynooghe, "Deriving Unfold/Fold Transformations of Logic Programs Using Extended OLDT-based Abstract Interpretation" J. Symbolic Computation, vol. 15, pp. 495–521, 1993.

[5]   M. Bruynooghe, D. De Schreye, and B. Krekels, "Compiling Control", J. Logic Programming, vol. 6, no. 1&2, pp. 135-162, 1989.

[6]   R.M. Burstall and J. Darlington, "A Transformation System for Developing Recursive Programs", JACM, vol. 24, no. 1, pp. 44-67, January 1977.

[7]   W.N. Chin, "Automatic Methods for Program Transformation", PhD Thesis, Univ. of London, Imperial College, Department of Computing, 1990.

[8]   S.K. Debray, "Optimizing Almost-Tail-Recursive Prolog Programs", In: Proc. IFIP Int. Conf. Functional Programming Languages and Computer Architecture, Nancy, France, LNCS 201, pp. 204-219, 1985.

[9]   S.K. Debray, "Unfold/Fold Transformations and Loop Optimization of Logic Programs", In: Proceedings SIGPLAN '88, Atlanta, Georgia, 1988.

[10] D. DeGroot, "Restricted AND-Parallelism", In: Proc. Int. Conference on Fifth Generation Computer Systems 1984, North, Holland, pp. 471-478, 1984.

[11] B. Demoen, "On the Transformation of a Prolog Program to a More Efficient Binary Program", In Proc. Lopstr '92, Workshops in Computing, Springer-Verlag, 1993.

[12] M.S. Feather, "A System for Assisting Program Transformation", ACM TOPLAS, vol. 4, no. 1, pp.1-20, January 1982.

[13] T. Kawamura and T. Kanamori, "Preservation of Stronger Equivalence in Unfold/Fold Logic Program Transformation", Theoretical Computer Science vol. 75, pp. 139-156, 1990.

[14] R. Paige and S. Koenig, "Finite Differencing of Computable Expressions", ACM TOPLAS, vol. 4, no. 1, pp. 402-454, July 1982.

[15] A. Pettorossi, "Transformation of Programs and Use of Tupling Strategy", In: Proc. Informatica '77, Bled, Yugoslavia, pp. 1-6, 1977.

[16] A. Pettorossi and M. Proietti, "Transformation of Logic Programs: Foundations and Techniques" R. 369, IASI-CNR, Roma (Italy), 1993.

[17] M. Proietti and A. Pettorossi, "Unfolding-Definition-Folding, in This Order, for Avoiding Unnecessary Variables in Logic Programs", In Proc. PLILP '91, Passau, Germany, Lecture Notes in Computer Science 528, pp. 347-358, 1991.

[18] M. Proietti and A. Pettorossi, "Best-first Strategies for Incremental Transformations of Logic Programs", In Proc. Lopstr '92, Workshops in Computing, Springer-Verlag, pp. 82-98, 1993.

[19] H. Seki, "Unfold/Fold Transformation of General Logic Programs for the Well-founded Semantics" J. Logic Programming, Vol. 16, 1&2, 1993, pp. 5–23.

[20] H. Tamaki and T. Sato, "Unfold/Fold Transformation of Logic Programs", In Proc. 2nd Int. Conf. Logic Programming, Uppsala, Sweden, pp. 243-251, 1984.

[21] P. Tarau and M. Boyer, "Elementary Logic Programs", In: Proc. PLILP '90, P. Deransart and J. Maluszynski (eds.), Springer Verlag, pp. 159-173, 1990.

[22] P. Wadler, "Deforestation: Transforming Programs to Eliminate Trees", In: Proc. ESOP '88, Lecture Notes in Computer Science 300, pp. 344-358, 1988.

[23] H. Zhu, "How Powerful are Folding/Unfolding Transformations?", Techn. Report CSTR-91-2, Brunel University, U.K., 1991.

Poster Abstracts

Conjunto: Constraint propagation over set constraints with finite set domain variables

Carmen Gervet

ECRC, Arabellastrasse 17, D-81669 Munich, Germany

(E-mail: carmen@ecrc.de)

Abstract

The most common representation of sets is as lists of atomic variables ranging over (different) domains of computation. This representation brings expressive power at the cost of exponential satisfaction procedures (taking into account duplication and permutation of elements). We propose a new approach in Conjunto[1] to define set terms and solve set constraints. A set variable S is constrained to range over a *finite set domain* specified by its lower and upper bounds for set inclusion, respectively $glb(S)$ and $lub(S)$. We provide Conjunto with set operators (union, intersection, difference, cardinality) and set constraints (membership, nonmembership, inclusion, disjunction). The operational semantics is based on new consistency algorithms for enforcing local consistency of set constraints over set variables. The underlying motivations behind this new computation domain are (i) to state in a more natural way partitioning or covering Operations Research problems usually stated as boolean integer problems, (ii) to maintain efficiency when extending a language with sets constraints, (iii) to apply the simple notion of set domain for the definitions of relations and graphs as constrained objects.

Various CLP languages based on computations over finite (integer) domains have proved their efficiency in the CLP framework by a powerful use of consistency checking techniques. In Conjunto we define new consistency algorithms as well as partial lookahead search procedures for set constraints handling. Unlike for arithmetic constraints over finite domains, consistency checking is not seen as a single test (possible element or not) but as two tests (possible set of values or not, definite set of values or not). These definite values are the ones from the upper bound which *must* belong to the lower bound. For example $S :: \{f(a)\}..\{1, 2, f(a), 3\}$, $S_1 :: \{\}..\{1, f(a)\}$, $S \subseteq S_1$ is consistent iff $glb(S) \subseteq glb(S_1)$ is true (*i.e.*, $glb(S)$ becomes $\{f(a)\}$) and $lub(S) \subseteq lub(S_1)$ holds (*i.e.* $lub(S)$ becomes $\{1, f(a)\}$. $f(a)$ has become a definite element of S_1. The description of the algorithms as well as a Conjunto program for a bin-packing problem are described in a technical report in preparation [gerv94].

Acknowledgements: This work was supported in part by the ESPRIT Project 5291 CHIC.

References

[gerv94] Gervet, C., *Conjunto: Constraint Logic Programming with Finite Set Domains*, technical report 94/, Germany, 1994.

---

[1]Conjunto: [konrʊnto], Spanish for set.

Logic Programs with Refutation Rules

Marion Mircheva
Institute of Mathematics & Computer Science
Bulgarian Academy of Sciences
"Acad. G.Bonchev" str. bl 8, Sofia 1113 , Bulgaria
e-mail: marion@bgearn.bitnet

Abstract

We extend logic programming to deal with theories that include both ordinary clauses and new *refutation rules*. While the ordinary rules are supposed to add knowledge, when they are activated, the refutation rules are supposed to remove knowledge. Such kind of rules are important in the areas where reasoning with mixed rules is advocated: decision support systems, normative domains governed by implicit or explicit regulations, case based reasoning and problem solving methods for assessment tasks.

For example default logic can be considered as a system that operates with rules of the form: if δ_i are accepted and σ_j are not accepted ($\neg \sigma_j$ are consistent with the current state) then l is accepted. Loosely this is also the meaning of a clause $l \leftarrow \delta_i, \sim \|\sigma_j$ according to stable model semantics. In fact any maximal consistent set of such rules from a given default system or a normal logic program define an *extension* in default logic or *stable model* in Stable Model Semantics correspondingly. We propose to extend logic programming to reason with *refutation rules* that explicitly states which sentences to be removed if some others are accepted. Loosely *refutation rules* have the form: if δ_i are accepted and σ_j are not accepted then l should be rejected. We also insist that after removing of certain sentences, the reasons for these changes should remain unchanged.

To adapt logic programming to manage with such kind of mixed reasoning two alternative decisions are proposed - to modify Two Valued and Three Valued Stable Model Semantics by giving a higher priority to refutation rules.

We also propose a transformation which eliminates refutation rules by using negation by failure over the initial language augmented with a new *test operator*. To proof that the proposed transformation preserves the original meaning of the program and the refutation rules we prolong Stable Model Semantics and Three Valued Stable Model Semantics to programs that include *test sentences*.

We extend our results to include disjunctive logic programs. The transformed programs can be implemented by logic programming methods that implement stable models semantics.

Efficient and complete demo predicates for definite clause languages

Henning Christiansen

Roskilde University P.O. Box 260, DK-4000 Roskilde, Denmark
E-mail: henning@dat.ruc.dk

Abstract

We present an implementation method for the binary demo predicate which is logically complete. A call

$$\text{demo}(\textit{prog-repr}, \textit{query-repr})$$

is true whenever its arguments represent (ground names of) a program and query, respectively, such that the query is provable from the program. Completeness implies that the predicate is equally well suited for executing programs as well as for generating them. A variable in the first argument represents, thus, an unknown program fragment and, if possible, the complete demo predicate produces an answer for it which makes the query provable. Tasks such as abduction and diagnosis can be expressed by putting additional conditions into the query as follows.

$$\text{condition}(A), \text{demo}(\cdots A \cdots, \cdots)$$

The use of coroutine control (e.g., *freeze*) provides acceptable execution characteristics with an interleaved or "lazy" execution of these conditions. The principle has also been used in order to synthesize grammar rules and context descriptions in natural language processing. — In the mentioned examples, the additional conditions need only be of a simple syntactic nature; for more complicated problems they may also involve other calls of demo.

Demo was introduced by Kowalski in 1979, but logically complete implementations seem to have been lacking until simultaneous results by Sato and the present author in 1992. While these works are mostly of a theoretical interest, the aim of the present is to produce an implementation of practical relevance. We use a straightforward definition of demo enhanced with constraint techniques to handle uninstantiated variables, which stand for program text taking part in the actual computation. For such variables, unevaluated (but satisfiable) constraints are accumulated and reflected back into a (partial) construction of the program whenever enough information is present. The implementation of the constraints employs a reflection of object language variables and unification by the variables and unification of Prolog. Thus an inefficient and high-level simulation of these critical notions is avoided.

In this way, we obtain an implementation of the logically complete demo which, with respect to efficiency, is comparable with the vanilla interpreter, i.e., only a constant factor slower than the Prolog system, which executes it. For details and references, see [Christiansen94].

References

[Christiansen94] Christiansen, H., Efficient and complete demo predicates for definite clause languages, *Datalogiske skrifter*, (tech. report), Department of Computer Science, Roskilde University, 1994.

Towards a verified OR-Parallel WAM

Stephan Diehl

FB 14 - Informatik , Universität des Saarlandes
Postfach 15 11 50 , 66041 Saarbrücken , GERMANY
Phone: ++49-681-3023915 , Email: diehl@cs.uni-sb.de

Abstract

First we sketch, what, given a verified compiler for a sequential machine, has to be done to get a verified compiler for a parallel machine. We present formal descriptions of three different abstract machines. The first is Russinoff's description of a sequential WAM, then we extend this machine, such that it can create an unbounded number of processors without any need of further synchronization. For this model we prove, that for every terminating sequential WAM execution there is an equivalent unsynchronized one. Next we present an abstract machine, which has only a fixed number of processors. For this machine synchronization and communication are essential. Finally we explain some changes to this machine, which improve scheduling and reduce the copying overhead.

Approach The sequential model is basically extended by changing the definitions of some of the notations introduced by Russinoff. As a result most of his specifications of the WAM instructions don't have to be modified. In other words we use his meta-language, but change its interpretation. In our new definitions we model concurrency by continuations and synchronization by shared locks. In the sequential model, given a program and a query, there is only one possible computation. In the parallel model there can be different computations and we would actually have to prove, that all of these yield the same sequence of answer substitutions.

Conclusion We developed a parallel WAM and described it using and extending Russinoff's formal framework. Furthermore we proved the equivalence of a simplified version of the parallel WAM and the sequential WAM. We feel, that the formal description of the final version of the parallel WAM is an important step towards a verified parallel WAM.

Because of all the details which we added to the framework to model parallel execution, the proof of the equivalence of the parallel WAM and the sequential WAM has become very difficult. We expect that the use of an automated theorem prover will help to keep track of the details and thus enable us to find a reliable proof.

References

[1] hayri A.M. Ali and Roland Karlsson Scheduling OR-Parallelism in MUSE. In *Proc. of the 1990 North American Conference on Logic Programming*, pages 807–821. MIT Press, 1990.

[p2] Stephan Diehl, Prolog and Typed Feature Structures: A Compiler for Parallel Computers. Master's thesis, Worcester Polytechnic Institute, Worcester, Massachusetts, 1993.

[p3] J.W. Lloyd *Foundations of Logic Programming*. Springer Verlag, second extended edition, 1987.

[p4] David M. Russinoff A verified Prolog Compiler for the Warren Abstract Machine. *Journal of Logic Programming*, 13:367–412, 1992.

Recomputation-Free Lemmatization by Program Transformation

P.J. Azevedo and M.J. Sergot
Department of Computing,
Imperial College
SW7 2BZ London,
U.K.
email: {pja2,mjs}@doc.ic.ac.uk

Abstract

Elimination of redundant computation is a subject that has been studied by several authors [Bird80, Cohen83]. The redundancy arises due to the multiplication of the same call to a procedure in a program. Recursive programs are a common example where the phenomenon appears. In the special case of logic programming, several proposals exist in the literature to overcome the situation, e.g. [Tamaki&Sato86, Vieille89, Dietrich87]. These are known as tabulation techniques. The basic idea common to all these proposals is to eliminate subquery redundancy by storing intermediate results that further are shared between identical queries. One can see this technique as a form of bottom-up programming [Warren92, Tamaki&Sato86]. However, due to their non-deterministic behaviour, a problem emerges when one applies the tabulation technique to logic programs. If an identical query requires more solutions than the stored ones, recomputation will occur since evaluation will continue by restarting the computation from the program, obtaining once again the solutions previously stored. Hence, paradoxically, we have a technique to avoid redundant computation that itself gives rise to recomputation.

This is known as *the lemma generation problem*.

A lengthly discussion can be conducted to justify avoidance of recomputation but other reasons are also concerned with undiserable side-effects. Such situations arise, for instance, when programs have user-interface facilities [Sergot83], leading to a confusing interface that asks the user repeatedly for the same information.

In [Azevedo&Sergot94], we have proposed a general solution to this problem by taking into consideration the consumed part of the search space associated to a performed query. The use of the *consumption* term refers to the traversing process that occurs during a computation. We have proposed a computation-driven process that avoids the described phenomenon of recomputation. The search space is represented through consumed paths. The initial programs are rewritten to yield, jointly with an answer, the used path. We have introduced a family of algorithms to infer the unvisited part of the search space using the paths attached to the already computed solutions. These algorithms work by constructing the search space of the most general query associated to the lemmatized predicate. Afterwards, the inferred search space is explored by computing the new query with the unvisited paths blended in. In this way, computation is diverted from earlier visited paths. In this paper we introduce a set of program transformations that emulate the paths inference algorithms. Each original clause has correspondingly several clauses in the transformed program. The transformed clauses mimic the various situations where a clause would be used under the diversion mechanism.

Acknowledgements: Paulo Azevedo is supported by Junta Nacional de Investigação Científica e Tecnológica - Programa Ciência grant number BD/1297/91-IA.

References

[Azevedo&Sergot94] Azevedo P.J., Sergot M.J.,
A Proof Procedure based on Recomputation-Free Lemmatization
in Journal of Computers and A.I., Vol 13 No 2, 1994.

[Bird80] Bird R. S.,
Tabulation Techniques for Recursive Programs
in Computing Surveys, Vol 12, No 4, ACM December 1980, pp 403-417.

[Cohen83] Cohen N. H.,
Eliminating Redundant Recursive Calls
in ACM Transactions on Programming Languages and Systems,
vol 5, No 3, July 1983, pp 265-299.

[Dietrich87] Dietrich S.,
Extension Tables: Memo relations in logic programming
in Proceedings of the 1987 Symposium of Logic Programming, San Francisco, CA (1987), pp 264-273.

[Sergot83] Sergot M. J.,
A Query-The-User facility of logic programming
in P. Degano & E. Sandewall, Editors, Integrated Interactive Computer Systems,
North Holland 1983, pp 27-41.

[Tamaki&Sato86] Tamaki H., Sato T.,
OLD Resolution with Tabulation
in Proceedings of the 3rd International Conference of Logic Programming
London U.K. 1986, pp 84-98.

[Warren92] Warren D. S.,
Memoing for Logic Programs
in Communications of the ACM Vol 35, No 3, March 1992, pp 93-111.

[Vieille89] Vieille L.,
Recursive Query Processing: The Power of Logic
in Theoretical Computer Science, vol 69,
Elsevier Science Publishing 1989, pp 1-53.

IsaWhelk: Whelk Interpreted in Isabelle[1]

David A. Basin
Max-Planck-Institut für Informatik
Im Stadtwald, D-66123, Saarbrücken, Germany
Email: basin@mpi-sb.mpg.de

Abstract

In [1], Geraint Wiggins presents Whelk, an adaptation of the proofs-as-programs idea to logic program synthesis. Whelk is proposed as a new kind of logic and synthesis methodology where specifications are manipulated in a kind of "tagged" formal system where tags provide information on how to construct programs. I use Isabelle, a logical framework supporting proof construction by higher-order resolution, as a tool to reconstruct, simplify, implement, and use Whelk.

In my interpretation, I formulate tagged formulas directly as equivalences between specifications and program schemas; hence the Whelk rules constitute a simple calculus for manipulating equivalences. I use Isabelle to formally derive these rules in the appropriate first-order theory, or, in several cases, to uncover flaws in the proposed rules. I show how application of these proof rules by higher-order resolution permits program synthesis from specification in the manner of Whelk. I call the resulting Isabelle theory *IsaWhelk*; it has functionality similar to Whelk but is formally verified and very simple to understand.

Conceptually, the interpretation simplifies and clarifies. By stripping Whelk of its notational baggage and bringing us back to the familiar mathematical setting of first-order logic, I can use conventional means to address questions of derivability and correctness. The interpretation quickly exposes that some of the Whelk rules are invalid. Of course, these defects are present in the original Whelk theory, but their presence there is perhaps harder to ascertain.

Pragmatically, IsaWhelk illustrates how proofs based on higher-order resolution can construct programs during proofs and the practical benefits of using Isabelle. For example, I directly employ standard tactics distributed with the Isabelle system. Using these, derivation of the Whelk rules is mostly automatic. I give an example of program synthesis carrying out the same example as Wiggins (synthesizing the subset program) but my proof requires only 15 simple steps as opposed to 105 in Whelk where program development tactics are only now being developed.

References

[1] Geraint A. Wiggins. Synthesis and transformation of logic programs in the Whelk proof development system. In K. R. Apt, editor, *Proceedings of JICSLP-92*, 1992.

---

[1] The full paper is available via anonymous ftp to "mpi-sb.mpg.de". The compressed dvi file is found in "pub/papers/conferences/Basin-ICLP94.dvi.Z".

Reflection through Constraint Satisfaction

Jonas Barklund and Pierangelo Dell'Acqua[1]
Uppsala University
E-mail: jonas@csd.uu.se, costanti@imiucca.csi.unimi.it,

Stefania Costantini and Gaetano A. Lanzarone
Università degli Studi di Milano
pier@csd.uu.se, lanzarone@hermes.mc.dsi.unimi.it

Abstract

The need for expressing and using meta-level knowledge has been widely recognized in the AI literature. Meta-knowledge and meta-level reasoning are suitable, for example, for devising proof strategies in automated deduction systems, for controlling the inference in problem solving, and for increasing the expressive power of knowledge representation languages.

In order to carry out meta-level reasoning there must be a stated relationship between expressions at different levels, i.e., a reflection principle and a naming relation.

We present a new mechanism [1] that allows us to model reflection principles in meta-level architectures. Such a mechanism is based on the integration of constraint satisfaction techniques into the inference process of such systems. We employ an abstract language and introduce the concept of a name theory for such a language. The semantics of a name theory is a name interpretation, which generalizes the name relation of other reflective formalisms. We present a reflective inference system that is parameterized with a name theory and whose semantics is expressed in terms of a name interpretation. This mechanism is completely general and can be easily concretized for a family of metalogic languages.

Relevant applications of the proposed formalization have been investigated in legal reasoning [2], in the context of communication-based reasoning, where the interaction among agents is based on communication acts, and in the context of analogical reasoning [3].

References

[1] Barklund, J., Costantini S., Dell'Acqua P., Lanzarone, G.A., *Reflection through Constraint Satisfaction*, Unpublished paper, Department of Computing Science, Uppsala University, 1994.

[2] Barklund, J., Hamfelt, A. *Hierarchical Representation of Legal Knowledge with Metaprogramming in Logic*, J. Logic Programming, 18:55–80, 1994.

[3] Costantini, S., Lanzarone, G.A., Sbarbaro, L., *A Formal Definition and a Sound Implementation of Analogical Reasoning in Logic Programming*, To appear in the Annals of Mathematics and Artificial Intelligence.

PP-clauses: a Means for Handling Resources

J.-M. Jacquet

Dpt. Computer Science, Univ. of Namur, 5000 Namur, Belgium

E-mail: jmj@info.fundp.ac.be

Luis Monteiro

Dpt. Computer Science, Univ. of Lisbon, 2825 Caparica, Portugal

E-mail: lm@fct.unl.pt

Abstract

A new framework is proposed for handling resources while separating their treatment from logical derivations both at the conceptual and programming levels. In its basic form, it rests on clauses of the form $H \leftarrow G \quad < C : D >$ where H is a (usual) atom, G is a goal, formed of (usual) atoms combined with sequential and parallel composition operators, C and D are lists of (resource-oriented) atoms. Such clauses are called *pp-clauses*. They thus consist essentially of Horn clauses decorated by a pair of conditions $< C : D >$. This slight extension induces the following modificiation to the usual SLD-derivation. Condition C lists the atoms (possibly duplicated) that should be present in the considered world of resources at the time of the reduction of a considered goal wrt the clause. If so, these atoms are removed from the current world of resources and the (induced instance) of the body of the clause is evaluated. Then, the atoms of D are added as new resources. Conditions C and D thus act as pre- and post-conditions, respectively.

The framework is simple yet expressive enough to code a wide variety of applications involving objects, databases, actions, and changes. It has the merit of staying in the tradition of classical logic programming. Operational and declarative semantics have been developed in this line. The former semantics rests on an extension of the usual derivation relation for Horn clauses. The latter semantics adapts the classical model and fixed-point theories to account for the evaluation of pre- and post-conditions, and, in particular, for the non-monotonic behavior in the general case of the world of resources they induce.

The reader is referred to [JaMo94] for further details including a comparison with related work.

Acknowledgements: The authors like to thank the Belgian National Fund for Scientific Research and Junta Nacional de Investigação Científica e Tecnológica for support.

References

[JaMo94] Jacquet, J.-M. and Monteiro, L., *Towards Resource Handling in Logic Programming: the* PPL *Framework and its Semantics*, Technical Report, Universities of Namur and Lisbon, 1994.

Logic, Algebra and Static Analysis in DM Systems, the IE Way

Esther D. Shilcrat
Department of Mathematics and Computer Science
Dowling College
Oakdale, NY 11964
esther@sbcs.sunysb.edu

Abstract

We have introduced the Interactive Declarative Environments (ID EST - IE) framework for Direct Manipulation systems based on *logic* and *logic programming*. In this object based approach, logic database represents the model world of interest to the user. Four independent declarative modules are used to manage each distinct kind of task required in a DM system. An IE system is a proper composition of four modules.

This modular approach provides look and feel independence and supports easy code re-use. For example, the code for generating a given type of menu can easily be used in multiple systems. More interestingly, however, an entire IE system may be used as a single component of a more complex system. For example, a molecule is a kind of graph. An IE graph editor can be used as a component in an IE molecule editor, thus raising the level of the latter designer's task, who can now translates from molecule objects (ex. atom, bond, insert-bond) to graph objects (ex. node, edge, insert-edge) vs. to graphic objects (ex. circle, line, right-down), thereby taking advantage of prior resolution of myriad low level details. We call this transforming the level of the O-GRAM.

Logic permits us to provide a formal basis to each type of module, based on the semantics of Horn clauses. This leads to an *algebra* for system design, with precise definitions of module combining operations, that is, IE system building. We prove that composition of deductive schemas is interference-free; that is, the meaning of the composition of deductive schemas equals the composition of the meanings of the schemas. This establishes that transformed O-GRAMs may be treated as black-boxes in creating other IE systems.

Our declarative logic approach is also the basis for a new and unique solution to incremental screen update, via static analysis. Via a form of symbolic execution, semantic connections between object are discovered across module boundaries, thus supporting code encapsulation and obviating the need for explicit pointers. The algorithm has these properties: 1. No new "re-draw" code required; 2. Pre-compute *affected* picture set at compile time; 3. Provably correct; 4. Implemented, in Prolog; 5. Supports code encapsulation, including multiple independent picture versions of a single data object; 6. Sound: No illegal action will be allowed; 7. Complete: Always performs legal user actions.

Proving Hardware Designs

Peter T. Breuer and Luis Sánchez and Carlos Delgado Kloos
Departamento de Ingeniería de Sistemas Telemáticos,
Universidad Politécnica de Madrid, ETSI Telecomunicación,
Ciudad Universitaria, E–28040 Madrid, Spain
<{ptb,lsanchez,cdk}@dit.upm.es>

Abstract

VHDL is a standardized hardware description language with almost universal market penetration. Originally developed in the 1980s with the support of the US DoD, several formalizations of its hardware simulation semantics have appeared in the last few years, including operational semantics in higher order logic and translations to Petri Nets and finite state machines. But in recent work [1] we have set out the first simple, formal compositional denotational semantics for VHDL. It generates an axiomatic pre-/post-condition semantics and, in classic style, when read as a PROLOG program, the logical rules run as a *validation condition* generator, automating the derivation of correctness proofs.

The semantics is based on the idea that VHDL statements are pure side effects on a pair consisting of

- a bi-infinite sequence of historic and planned program states $\mathcal{W}$, one for each moment of time;

- a pointer $\mathcal{T}$ to the current time.

This design makes Hoare-style programming logic applicable. Importantly for safety-critical requirements on reliability, the rules code up directly in PROLOG:

$\{H1 \vdash Pre, T1\}$wait on x$\{H2 \vdash Post, T2\}$
$:-\ \ldots$

where H1, H2 gather lemmas to be proved. Giving Post generates Pre.

References

[1] P.T. Breuer, L. Sanchez, and C. Delgado Kloos. A clean formal semantics for VHDL. In *European Design and Automation Conference, Paris '94*, 1994. IEEE CS Press.

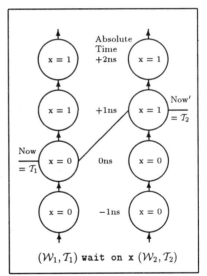

$(\mathcal{W}_1, \mathcal{T}_1)$ wait on x $(\mathcal{W}_2, \mathcal{T}_2)$

Figure 1: The semantics of the **wait on x** statement. No change in historic or planned states, but a forward shift in the current time pointer.

A Dataflow Analysis Method for Ground Prolog

Andreas Kågedal
Dept. of Computer and Information Science
Linköping University
S-581 83 Linköping, Sweden
E-mail: andka@ida.liu.se

Abstract

Ground Prolog (as described by Kluźniak [2, 3]) is a restriction of Prolog that enables a very good data flow analysis, and thereby compilation to efficient object code. Two important restrictions are: (1) *Directionality (mode) declarations* for every predicate must be provided by the programmer, i.e. all argument positions for all predicates must be defined as either "in" or "out" arguments. (2) The *groundness restriction*: whenever a call is executed, all its parameters at "in" argument positions must be ground, and when it succeeds all "out" parameters must be ground.

These restrictions exclude some common programming techniques used in (standard) Prolog programs, such as open-ended lists. To compensate for this a high quality dataflow analysis is *essential*. Kluźniak defined a method for data flow analysis of Ground Prolog programs and described how the result can be used for *type synthesis* and *compile time garbage collection*.

Kluźniak constructed a graph with the program variables as nodes and with edges between variables occurring in corresponding formal and actual argument positions. In principle, the transitive closure of the graph then represents the result of the dataflow analysis. This produces an over approximation of the dataflow in that there might be edges between variables that will not pass data between them. The approach is however unnecessarily imprecise.

We improve the approach by putting "constraints" on the edges. These can prevent some pairs of edges from producing new transitive edges that are obviously wrong. This is an extension of [1], and shows more clearly the problems with Kluźniak's method, and in a more formal way describes how it can be considerably improved.

References

[1] A. Kågedal. Improvements in compile-time analysis for Ground Prolog. In M. Bruynooghe and J. Penjam, editors, *PLILP'91*, LNCS 714, pages 92–107, Tallinn, 1993. Springer-Verlag.

[2] F. Kluźniak. Type synthesis for Ground Prolog. In J.-L. Lassez, editor, *Proc. of ICLP'87*, pages 788–816, Melbourne, 1987. The MIT Press.

[3] F. Kluźniak. Compile time garbage collection for Ground Prolog. In R. A. Kowalski and K. A. Bowen, editors, *Proc. of ICSLP'88*, pages 1490–1505, Seatle, 1988. The MIT Press.

Logic programming as quantum measurement

R.R.Zapatrin
Department of Mathematics,
SPb UEF, Griboyedova 30/32,
191023, St.-Peterburg, Russia
E-mail: rrz@finec.spb.su, vad@pavlov.spb.su

Abstract

The emphasis is made on the juxtaposition of (quantum theorem) proving versus quantum (theorem proving). The logical contents of verification of the statements concerning quantum systems is outlined. The Zittereingang (trembling input) principle is introduced to enhance the resolution of predicate satisfiability problem provided the processor is in a position to perform operations with continuous input. A realization of Zittereingang machine by a quantum system is suggested.

What is the desirable way to broaden the facilities of processors in order to have progress in solving NP-hard problems? The principle of trembling input I am going to put forth in this paper will require a flexibility of processor. That means that it will be assumed that the processor is able to deal with "intermediate outputs", or, in other words, that it will be possible to pass continuously from one input to another. We shall also assume that all possible inputs form a linear space, and that the result depends continuously on input preserving linear combinations.

I endeavored to show how quantum effects such as superposition of states and wave properties of the particles can be used for calculation purposes. The proposed Quantum Theorem Prover (QTP) is merely an imaginary machine. However, suppose it may exist, it can drastically influence many principles of programming. For example, such problem as SAT. Accepting QTPs requires new options in programming languages: the assignment of value should be replaced by the preparation of the input register.

Acknowledgements: I would like to thank the Referees for many helpful comments. The financial support from ISF (George Soros Emergency Grant) is aknowledged.

References

[1]   Deutsch, D. (1989), *Quantum Computational Networks*, Proceedings of the Royal Society, **A425**, 73

[2]   Grib A.A., Zapatrin R.R.(1990), *Automata Simulating Quantum Logics*, International Journal of Theoretical Physics, **29**, 113

[3]   Deutsch D., Jozsa R.(1992), *Rapid solution of problems by quantum computation*, Proceedings of the Royal Society of London, ser. A, **439**, 553

[4]   Bennett, C.H.(1993), *Quantum Computers: Certainty from Uncertainty*, Nature, **362**, 694

Author Index

Logic Programming

Ehud Shapiro, editor
Koichi Furukawa, Jean-Louis Lassez, Fernando Pereira, and David H. D. Warren, associate editors

The Art of Prolog: Advanced Programming Techniques, Leon Sterling and Ehud Shapiro, 1986

Logic Programming: Proceedings of the Fourth International Conference (volumes 1 and 2), edited by Jean-Louis Lassez, 1987

Concurrent Prolog: Collected Papers (volumes 1 and 2), edited by Ehud Shapiro, 1987

Logic Programming: Proceedings of the Fifth International Conference and Symposium (volumes 1 and 2), edited by Robert A. Kowalski and Kenneth A. Bowen, 1988

Constraint Satisfaction in Logic Programming, Pascal Van Hentenryck, 1989

Logic-Based Knowledge Representation, edited by Peter Jackson, Han Reichgelt, and Frank van Harmelen, 1989

Logic Programming: Proceedings of the Sixth International Conference, edited by Giorgio Levi and Maurizio Martelli, 1989

Meta-Programming in Logic Programming, edited by Harvey Abramson and M. H. Rogers, 1989

Logic Programming: Proceedings of the North American Conference 1989 (volumes 1 and 2), edited by Ewing L. Lusk and Ross A. Overbeek, 1989

Logic Programming: Proceedings of the 1990 North American Conference, edited by Saumya Debray and Manuel Hermenegildo, 1990

Logic Programming: Proceedings of the Seventh International Conference, edited by David H. D. Warren and Peter Szeredi, 1990

The Craft of Prolog, Richard A. O'Keefe, 1990

The Practice of Prolog, edited by Leon S. Sterling, 1990

Eco-Logic: Logic-Based Approaches to Ecological Modelling, David Robertson, Alan Bundy, Robert Muetzelfeldt, Mandy Haggith, and Michael Uschold, 1991

Warren's Abstract Machine: A Tutorial Reconstruction, Hassan Aït-Kaci, 1991

Parallel Logic Programming, Evan Tick, 1991

Logic Programming: Proceedings of the Eighth International Conference, edited by Koichi Furukawa, 1991

Logic Programming: Proceedings of the 1991 International Symposium, edited by Vijay Saraswat and Kazunori Ueda, 1991

Foundations of Disjunctive Logic Programming, Jorge Lobo, Jack Minker, and Arcot Rajasekar, 1992

Types in Logic Programming, edited by Frank Pfenning, 1992

Logic Programming: Proceedings of the Joint International Conference and Symposium on Logic Programming, edited by Krzysztof Apt, 1992

Constraint Logic Programming: Selected Research, edited by Frédéric Benhamou and Alain Colmerauer, 1993

Concurrent Constraint Programming, Vijay A. Saraswat, 1993

Logic Programming Languages: Constraints, Functions, and Objects, edited by K. R. Apt, J. W. de Bakker, and J. J. M. M. Rutten, 1993

Logic Programming: Proceedings of the Tenth International Conference on Logic Programming, edited by David S. Warren, 1993

Constraint Logic Programming: Selected Research, edited by Frédéric Benhamou and Alain Colmerauer, 1993

A Grammatical View of Logic Programming, Pierre Deransart and Jan Maluszynski, 1993

Logic Programming: Proceedings of the 1993 International Symposium, edited by Dale Miller, 1993

The Gödel Programming Language, Patricia Hill and John Lloyd, 1994

The Art of Prolog: Advanced Programming Techniques, second edition, Leon Sterling and Ehud Shapiro, 1994

Logic Programming: Proceedings of the Eleventh International Conference on Logic Programming, edited by Pascal Van Hentenryck, 1994